RENOVATION
A Complete Guide

RENOVATION
A Complete Guide

Second Edition

MICHAEL W. LITCHFIELD

ROSMARIE HAUSHERR, photographer
TERRY MURPHY, technical editor

PRENTICE HALL, Englewood Cliffs, New Jersey 07632

Library of Congress-in-Publication Data

Litchfield, Michael W.
  Renovation, a complete guide / Michael W. Litchfield. — 2nd ed.
    p. cm.
  Includes bibliographical references (p.).
  ISBN 0-13-159336-6
  1. Dwellings—Remodeling. I. Title.
TH4816.L57 1990
643.7—dc20   90-35411
                                     CIP

Editorial/production supervision:
  Eileen M. O'Sullivan
Cover design: Bruce Kenselaar
Cover photo: Douglas Keister
Manufacturing buyer: Lori Bulwin
Page layout: Diane Koromhas

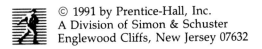

Printed in the United States of America

10 9 8 7 6 5 4 3 2

ISBN 0-13-159336-6

PRENTICE-HALL INTERNATIONAL (UK) LIMITED, *London*
PRENTICE-HALL OF AUSTRALIA PTY. LIMITED, *Sydney*
PRENTICE-HALL CANADA INC., *Toronto*
PRENTICE-HALL HISPANOAMERICANA, S.A., *Mexico*
PRENTICE-HALL OF INDIA PRIVATE LIMITED, *New Delhi*
PRENTICE-HALL OF JAPAN, INC., *Tokyo*
SIMON & SCHUSTER ASIA PTE. LTD., *Singapore*
EDITORA PRENTICE-HALL DO BRASIL, LTDA., *Rio de Janeiro*

CONTENTS

APPENDICES

PREFACE

This second edition of *Renovation* has been in the works for eight years, and may well be the most comprehensive single volume on residential renovation ever attempted.

It represents, all told, thousands of conversations with carpenters, electricians, plumbers, masons, engineers, painters, architects, energy consultants and the like. Many I met while launching *Fine Homebuilding* magazine, and many more offered tips and techniques on job sites across the country.

When you're ready to renovate, you'll find this first-hand information invaluable because, above all, it's specific. You'll know which blade to use, what size nails spaced how closely, when to tear out and when to make do, how to lay out and prepare a job so it goes smoothly. Armed with lifetimes of practical advice, you can proceed confidently.

This book is as much concerned with *what* and *why* as it is with *how to*. Thus, for every topic from seismic retrofits to wallpapering, you'll find a thorough discussion of the problems you might encounter and several workable solutions to each. Moreover, the text follows the sequence of an actual renovation, so you're rarely in doubt what to do next.

The artwork also rings true. Several drawings began life as pencil sketches on plywood scraps or leftover drywall, and many of the photos were unexpected—you never know what you'll find on a job. When my colleagues and I found a thorny problem or a particularly ingenious solution, we recorded it.

Finally, this second edition of *Renovation: A Complete Guide* is itself a major renovation. We added new chapters on tiling, foundations, doors, windows and skylights; updated charts and technical tables; reworked or replaced five or six hundred illustrations; and extensively rewrote the text of the first edition—did everything we could think of, in short, to make this new *Renovation* clear, concise and complete. Whether you're a seasoned professional or a serious amateur, we hope it works hard for you.

HOW TO USE
THIS BOOK

To get the most out of this book, *please heed all safety warnings*. They are there for your protection. We have made every attempt to describe construction procedures in this book in a clear and straightforward manner. But because of the differences in skill and experience of each reader and because of variations in materials and workmanship, neither the author nor the publisher can assume responsibility for the proper application or suitability of these techniques to a particular project.

Read the opening remarks of each chapter before you start: they delineate the information that follows and suggest where to find more about related topics. Terms specific to the subject at hand are usually introduced in the chapter opening, too; if you're not sure about more commonly used words, consult the Glossary.

You'll find that techniques are presented more or less chronologically, in the manner you'd need them in an actual renovation. Therefore, the information tends to be somewhat cumulative. Once a topic is discussed in depth, it's assumed in subsequent chapters that you're familiar with it. Thus the Index is crucially important to you. If any task seems insufficiently explained, chances are that it has been covered earlier: browse through the Contents or preceding chapters—or consult the Index.

If you need yet more information about tools, materials or techniques, see the Bibliography; a lot of research went into it. Speaking of tools and materials, please don't construe our use of any trade name as an endorsement. We do try to be specific throughout this book, but in the case of product names, we mention them to suggest a type of or possible source for such materials.

Lastly, when you've read up, go talk to people. Experience is the best teacher—even if it's someone else's experience. A friend or neighbor who's been through a renovation is an invaluable guide to reliable contractors and suppliers, and a wise, calm voice when you most need it. So, go to it. As some venerable wag once said, ''Courage is first among human virtues, for without it we're unlikely to practice many of the others.''

ACKNOWLEDGMENTS

As much work as it's been, revising *Renovation* has been fun. The information in the first edition weathered pretty well, but it was deeply satisfying to cull those things that weren't clear, didn't fit or became dated. In that respect, writing books is a lot like gardening or renovating. It's also grand to renew old friendships and make new ones out on the job site. I have yet to meet a pro who didn't love to tell how he or she would do it.

To the mainstays of the first edition, thanks again: reviewers Dan Browne, Chuck Mitchell, John Scobie, Alan Keiser, John Kruse, Joseph Kitchel, Bill Whitney; Paul Roman and Roger Barnes of *Fine Homebuilding* magazine; Alan Lesure, Walter Brownfield and Susan Weiss; Richard Lear and Leonard Davis.

Once again it was a delight working with photographer Rosmarie Hausherr—may future editions of *Renovation* find us dottering around on some roof, looking for a shot we don't have yet. And a million thanks—one for each question asked—to Terry Murphy, who joined us as a technical editor and made this a far better book. Much love to his wife, Elle Hoffnagel, for her patience and chocolate chip cookies through it all.

I'm also indebted to neighbor Ron Kyle for his generosity at every turn; Leigh Marymor of Marymor Plumbing; Ed Bussa for his help on the electrical chapter; Lev Liberman for crucial support as deadlines loomed; Sally and George Kiskaddon of Builders Booksource in Berkeley; Dave Smith, Andrea Lappen, Gary Parsons, John Coveney, Blake Gilmore, Tom MacNair and all the rest of the crew; Patti Breitman for being so wise; Kitty Monahan and everyone else at Prentice Hall—but most especially Eileen O'Sullivan, without whom there would be no second edition.

Finally, thanks to all the people listed below, and to the countless workers whose names I never knew—the good Joes, Janes and Sams who smiled at my interruptions, answered my questions and then got on with the job. "Many hands make work light" goes an old saw, and to those many hands that helped mine, I dedicate this book.

Mike Litchfield
Berkeley, California

And thanks to:

Dennis Abbas
Al Abrams
Tim Andersen
Donald Anderson
Gary Anderson
Bruce Andrews
Hoover Austin
Jim Banfield
Dimas Barragan
William Barthelmess
Paul Belienberg
Kim Berreckman
David Bolton
Carl Burchfiel
Jeff Bryson
Pat Burrell
Christie & Bruce Campbell
Dale Carstensen
John Casner
Al Cetta
Sam Clark
Hubbard Cobb
Gail Coney
Michael Conley
Henry Cortes
Peter Dechar
John de Keany
Nate Dembowitz
Dave Dickson
Michael Dowling
Mike Duvall
Les Elliott
Dan Emmet
George Eriksen
Judy Ettlinger
Kristina Filipovich
David Fitch
Bob Flaner
Alan Fleming
Jeff Fox
Craig Frost
Jeff Gaines
Paul Gamez

Abe Gershbein
Tony Gibson
Ken Gillespie
Richard Golden
Christine Grinnell
David Harper
Ted Hilles
Victor Hines
Chris & Steve Hochschild
Dennis Hourany
Kurt Housch
Bud Hubbell
Larry Hunt
Samuel Johnson
Douglas Jones
Eric Jones
Matthew Kaplan
Nat Kaplan
Larry Kasser
Bill Keany
Doug Keister
Susan & Charles Kittredge
Dick Kreh
Jim Lachner
Martin Lee
Nicholas Lembo
Alan Lowry
Ian MacLeod
Frank Manno
Joe Marchesi
Sandy McKinney
Larry Mead
Bill Meredith
Michael Mitschang
Paul Mrozinski
John Muir
Dick Nagler
Frank Newbold
Rick Oriel
Val Ory
Thomas Paine
Frank Petrone
Don Pearman

Steve Peck
Karen & Tenold Peterson
Rip Phipps
Michael Pieters
Paul Pugliese
Michael Reitman
Ed Rivers
Andrew Rudin
Bill Russel
Rick Rutherford
Michael Ruttenberg
Carolynne & Rusty Schipa
Alan Schoenfeld
Harold Schoenfeld
Jack Shepherd
Louis Singer
Roger Smith
Skip & Sally Sowko
Gene Spagnoli
Sid Spanier
Gary Striker
Chip Stone
Steven Strong
Phil & Jody Sunshine
J. F. Sweeney
Neil Taylor
Reed Thomas
Chris Thomson
Rick Troy
Ghel Tucker
Glenn Tucker
George Tway
Jack Ullrich
Anthony Vigilante
William Walther
Rip Webster
Gale Westcott
Joshua White
Ken Woznack
Paul Yacknick
Roberto Zamora

RENOVATION
A Complete Guide

·1·

ASSESSMENT

A house, whatever its age, reveals much to those willing to look closely. Even if you have never owned a home before, you can make an intelligent assessment whether to buy if you take the time to train your eye, learn the language of building, and proceed systematically.

The old beauty shown on the facing page, for example, tells much to a passerby. Nicely crafted though it is, there are some troubling signs. For starters, it has not been painted in 20 or 30 years, so the part of the house that you cannot see probably wasn't maintained either. The shutters are in shambles. The porch roof, with its fascia trim falling off in slivers, is ruined and would have to be gutted.

On the positive side, it looks well constructed, the siding is largely intact, the ridge does not sag, and the roofing is in good shape—particularly important, because a roof is the first line of defense against water and rot.

From what we can see from the street, though, the front of the house could have major structural problems. The gutters and eave trim are shot. And if the flashing where the porch joins the house has also gone bad, chances are that the framing has started to rot. If that is case, this house may be one to pass up. But before making any decision of this magnitude, there's more to look at.

A personal aside. The hardest thing about buying a house is being unemotional. When we look for a home, after all, we are building a nest; we envision friends and family and all the warm feelings they engender—not the best way to make the biggest business decision of your life. By all means, listen to your feelings; just don't lead with them.

Get some experience first. Read this chapter to get an overview, look at the glossary to learn the jargon, then go inspect some houses that you have no intention of buying. Be cold-eyed. Investigate each house, top to bottom, outside to in. Soon you'll be able to spot certain patterns of weathering and deterioration if they are present. Then, when you find that certain place that wins your heart, you won't lose your head.

One other nontechnical tip. If you like a house, check out the neighborhood. Talk to neighbors. Ask them about traffic, stores, the other neighbors. In short, imagine what it would be like to live there.

Getting started. This chapter is a pared-down assessment list that focuses on *major* failings of house systems. Minor repairs and maintenance are discussed elsewhere in the book. Here, we're concerned with conditions bad enough to dissuade you from buying at all or, if you decide to go ahead, important enough to give you real leverage when you negotiate the price with the seller. In short, this chapter can help you determine the true cost of the house: what it will cost you up front, and what you can expect to pay shortly to make major repairs.

When you first meet with the realtor or owner, ask for a recent termite report and a disclosure statement, and read them. Most states now require such disclosures, and if you are working with a realtor, they are mandatory almost

3

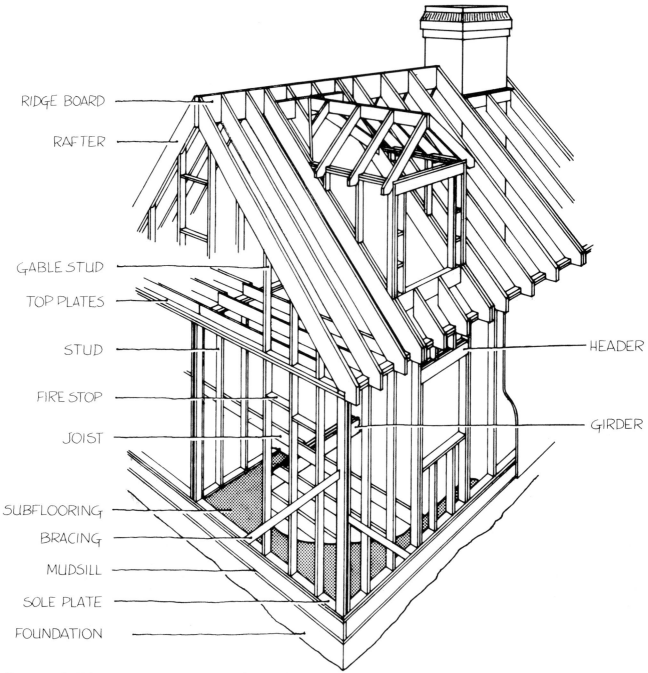

RIDGE BOARD

RAFTER

GABLE STUD

TOP PLATES

STUD

FIRE STOP

JOIST

SUBFLOORING

BRACING

MUDSILL

SOLE PLATE

FOUNDATION

HEADER

GIRDER

Figure 1.1 Building terms. These drawings contain most of the building terms used in this chapter. For additional terms, consult the index, the glossary (Appendix A), or pertinent chapters.

everywhere. The disclosure statement should describe (1) things not originally built with a permit, or not built according to code; (2) code violations presently observed by an inspector; and (3) other conditions that the homeowner knows need fixing.

Armed with this information, you are ready to look for the additional, unreported problems which always exist. To make your inspection, dress the part; wear sneakers or crepe-soled shoes that won't slip, and old clothes. Take along a pad and pencil, a flashlight, a pocketknife, a marble, and a pair of binoculars. As you see flaws or suspect areas, note them on a sketch of the building. Finally, *get a tetanus shot.*

Ask the homeowner/realtor to provide an extension ladder so that you can observe the roof up close; otherwise,

bring your own. *Note:* You are after facts, not opinions, so it's best to make the inspection without the distraction of someone anxious to sell. You'll need to concentrate.

For a thorough inspection, scrutinize the house top to bottom on the outside, then go inside and repeat the process, as described below.

THE ROOF

Time spent looking at the roof is well spent, because it is the front line of defense against a house's principal enemy: water. Start on the ground, getting an overview of the roof through your binoculars.

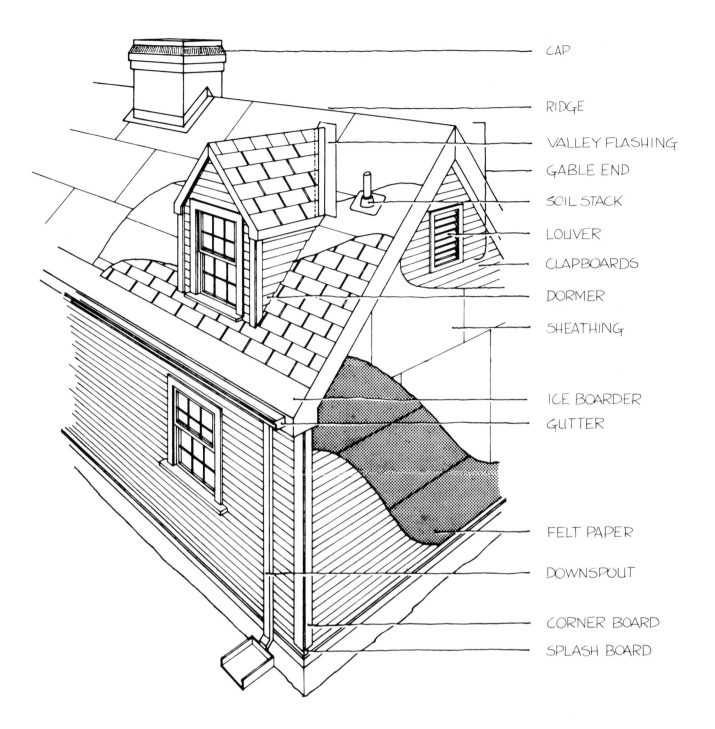

CAP

RIDGE

VALLEY FLASHING

GABLE END

SOIL STACK

LOUVER

CLAPBOARDS

DORMER

SHEATHING

ICE BOARDER

GUTTER

FELT PAPER

DOWNSPOUT

CORNER BOARD

SPLASH BOARD

Then, after carefully footing the extension ladder (p. 40), get a closer look. You can learn a lot without actually getting on the roof, by peering through your field glasses. Stay off if heights bother you, if it's wet or cold out, if the pitch is steep, or if the roofing material is slippery to walk on, such as tile or slate.

Roofs in General

1. Sight along the ridge to see if it's straight. If it is, you have a first clue that the house was well constructed, important because a well-made house simply lasts longer. If the ridge sags in the middle, suspect too many layers of roofing (needs a new roof), or rafters that were too small from the start (*very* costly to remedy).

2. Next look at the flashing, especially in valleys or around soil stacks. Is it in good condition? Flashing with some surface rust can be painted, but extensive patching or pitting indicates replacement, which means a new roof. It should also alert you to water damage beneath.

3. Especially important flashings are metal drip edges (p. 76), which should protrude just beneath the lowest courses of shingles. They allow water to drip clear of the roof. In older homes that lack drip edges, overhanging shingles were expected to clear the water, but frequently it will seep behind trim and cause damage behind. If you don't see metal drip edges, be alert to water damage at the tops of walls when you continue your inspection inside.

4. Along the gable ends of a house, look for thin strips of rake flashing along the edge of the roofing. If it's absent, water may have blown up under the roof during storms.

Asphalt Shingles

1. Is the surface flat? If not, chances are there are two or more layers of roofing. (Count the layers along the eaves to see just how many, keeping in mind that courses along the eaves are customarily doubled.) Many layers of roofing will make strip-off and reroofing somewhat more expensive. But the real question is: If the original roof was leaky enough to roof over, did rot occur?

2. Are shingle rows evenly spaced? If not, wonder how good a job was done.

3. Are existing shingles dog-eared? Are they faded and abraded? If so, a new roof is imminent. The ridge, which gets a lot of exposure, is a good indicator.

4. Are there odd-colored shingles? They are probably patches over earlier leaks.

Wood Shingles and Shakes

1. What is the general appearance of the roof? If the rows are regular and orderly, it is a reasonable assumption that a craftsman—who cared about things like flashing—did the job. If the roof has closed valleys (p. 78), this is particularly important.

2. Are the shingles appreciably checked or split? Another sure sign of age is mossy areas: water is being absorbed by the shingles. This will definitely require reroofing.

3. Do the shingles seem springy or spongy to the touch? Suspect nails that are not nailed solidly into the sheathing because there are too many layers of roofing.

4. Are there patches from earlier problems?

Slate

1. Do not get up on slate roofs. Even when dry, they're slippery.

2. Are there off-color areas? There may have been damage from a tree branch years ago. When you are in the attic, check for water stains on the rafters.

3. Are there rust-colored streaks or general rusty discoloring? Are any slates cockeyed? These symptoms may indicate a builder who used nails that were not galvanized, which are now rusted through. **Do not get up on such a roof,** for slates so nailed could easily slough off. Should the slate be removed and renailed? *Very* expensive.

Tile

1. Stay off tile roofs. Even when the roof slope is not steep, you can do a lot of damage walking on tiles. Atop an extension ladder, scan the roof through binoculars instead.

2. Look for odd-colored tiles from earlier repairs, and check for water stains when you are in the attic.

3. Are any tiles obviously cracked or broken? Tile replacement is specialized and expensive.

4. Spend a lot of time looking at the ridge. Major cracks along the ridge indicate a building that's shifting, or too great a load for the roof framing. If the latter, the ridge will probably sag, as well. Given the cost of removing the tile, bolstering or replacing the sagging rafters, and sheathing and replacing the roof, this may not be a house to buy.

Metal

1. Very slick, be careful.

2. In general, metal roofs do a good job of clearing precipitation, but their seams can be problematic. An attic inspection is very important.

3. Does the ridge have a standing seam (correct) or merely metal flashing folded lengthwise (leaky)?

4. Is there rust? Isolated stains will be caused by a few nails that aren't galvanized, larger areas by roof panels that are worn out. It is possible to paint a rusty roof inexpensively, but concomitant water stains beneath the roof mean replacement.

5. Any signs of corrosion? If so, it was probably caused by galvanic action; corrosion of dissimilar metals is taking place. If the problem is at all widespread, say, along the ridge or in the valleys, replacement is the only remedy.

6. Look at the nails. If there are a few popped up, seasonal maintenance is all that's needed. But note also *where* they are nailed: they should be nailed at the high spots of the metal folds. If nailing in low spots—where the water runs—is pervasive, you are looking at the work of an inept roofer, and the expense of a new one.

Flat (Hot Mop)

1. Are there blisters in the roofing? They usually indicate water trapped beneath the membrane. Although they can be successfully repaired, you should reroof if there are more than three or four blisters.

2. Are there signs of foot traffic, lawn chairs, and the like? People partying on a hot-tar roof shorten its life. Note areas particularly where stones are missing or the membrane is abraded.

3. What is the condition of the turn-ups, where the flat roof joins walls, parapets, and other vertical surfaces? This is where most leaks occur. If the surfaces are cracked, split, sagging, or unpainted, water may have gotten in and done some damage. If they are well coated with reflective paint, those junctures have probably kept cool and dry.

4. Check the condition of all downspout outlets. Where there are internal drains, proper maintenance is imperative to the health of the structure. Cracking and blistering here are very bad signs. So are overhanging trees that might clog the drains. Are there wire baskets in the openings? Are they free of debris? If you have doubts, ask to flush the outlets with a hose to see how well they drain.

5. Is there enough rock on the roof to reflect sunlight?

6. Is the flashing around soil stacks sound? This is not a major repair, but it can indicate general neglect.

Flat (Rubber)

See the comments above for hot-mop roofs.

1. Are edges and seams well sealed? Rubber roofing is increasingly popular because it is durable, but the seams are the vulnerable points of this system.

2. Are turn-ups and parapets painted to reflect sunlight?

3. Are downspout outlets clear?

4. Is there enough rock ballast to hold the sheets down or, if attaching mechanisms were used, is the rubber intact around them?

5. Is flashing sound around soil stacks and the like?

The Chimney

To inspect the chimney thoroughly, you need to get up on the roof. You don't need to do this during a first inspection; if you are interested in the house, make any purchase agreement contingent upon a later chimney examination. If you're unsteady on roofs, have a professional do it. What to look for:

1. Is the mortar between the bricks solid or crumbly? Are there any holes that go all the way through? Repointing mortar courses is not a big job unless they have eroded more than half a brick width, in which case, the chimney may be structurally unsound and need to be torn down.

2. Is the chimney cap sound? Again, this repair is not a big thing in itself, but it suggests a lack of general maintenance and, possibly, water damage to the surrounding structure. Look closely around the chimney when you are in the attic.

3. Is the flashing around the chimney intact? Flashing is critically important and where water damage indicates its failure, sufficient cause to replace the roof.

4. With a flashlight, look down into the chimney.

    a. If you see only unlined brick on the inside of the chimney, it has no flue tile and is unsafe. Some codes allow such chimneys to vent furnaces, but *in no case* should such a chimney be used with a fireplace or a wood stove—it's a fire hazard.

    b. If there is flue tile within, it should be a relatively smooth surface. If it is scaly with soot, it just needs to be cleaned, but if any tile kicks into the opening, that tile has probably collapsed. This, too, is a major problem because it can allow superheated air to leak from the chimney and set fire to the structure around it. Such fires are particularly insidious because they start in the attic, where they can't be seen.

THE EXTERIOR

After you have examined the roof and are still on the ladder, take a look at the gutters and eaves. The eaves are technically the lowest part of the roof but are actually a complex transition of building materials from roof to walls.

Figure 1.2 The flue tile at left has probably cracked because it was poorly made. But whatever the cause, it is unsafe: superheated gases could escape and set fire to wood framing.

Figure 1.3 Cracks over windows usually indicate shifting headers and probable foundation failure.

Figure 1.4. Cracking through the corners of a building suggests serious foundation failings, here compounded by faulty drainage.

Gutters and Eaves

1. Eyeball the eaves. For starters, are they straight? Any signs of blistering or splitting that might indicate water behind? If there are dark stains on the underside of the eave, that discoloration is probably caused by a roof leak through asphalt which ran down the rafters.

2. Prod the eaves with a penknife. They should be solid. If they are soft, suspect even more rot behind them, in the rafter "tails" and wall plates.

3. Are the gutters clear, or clogged with debris? Water damage will be apparent if they have been stopped up for a long time.

4. If the gutters are wood, they were probably nailed directly to the fascia trim. Prod behind them with your penknife to see if there is rot. Wood gutters are expensive to replace; metal, less so.

Siding

1. *Wood clapboards or shingles.* Patches or repairs? Splits or checking? If shingles, are the butt ends feathering and curling? The south-facing wall, which gets the most sun, will tell the most. Is there flashing over doors and windows? Any water stains? If they are dark, they have run over the felt paper beneath the siding. A generally dog-eared appearance means new siding.

2. *Brick.* Sight down the walls: Are they plumb? Is the mortar sound, or can it be dislodged with your penknife? Especially prod the mortar if the house looks recently painted. Repointing a house is costly. If painted, is it in good shape? Blistering may be efflorescence or moisture from within.

3. *Stucco.* Stucco is very rigid, so if it is cracking, something is wrong. Look closely around corners, along eaves, and above doors and windows for extensive patching or open cracks. They are a near-sure sign that the structure is shifting. Heed them.

Note: Whatever the siding material, cracks above windows and doors are probably telling you that the header—a load-bearing member over the opening—is not sitting on a firm footing. That is, the foundation or the structure on it is shifting. Major trouble.

Windows and Doors

1. If you see a lot of cracked glass, it is caused by a lack of maintenance or a structure that is shifting. The same is true for doors and windows that do not fit properly—that stick or jam.

2. Examine windows and doors very carefully. Are the frames solid? If wooden windows are cracked and swollen at corners, where the rails and stiles meet, they should be replaced. This is a major expense if all windows are so afflicted.

3. Examine door and window sills, where water can collect. (Sills in brick houses will often stay moist and wick moisture to the wood sills they encase.) They will need to be replaced if they're punky.

4. Is there flashing over doors and windows? If not, suspect water damage behind.

5. Windows and doors in stucco houses are particularly good indicators of shifting structure, look for cracks over both types of openings.

Around the Base

Walk the perimeter of the house:

1. Are there at least splash blocks beneath downspouts? If not, water may be causing the foundation to settle and the structure to shift.

2. Is the ground sloped away from the base of the house to aid runoff?

3. Are bushes or dirt in contact with the siding? If so, prod the siding and splashboard with your penknife. That area is getting—and retaining—a lot of moisture and is probably sodden or rotten.

4. The dirt can also be an avenue for termites. Prod the underside of all splashboards to dislodge punky wood, and look for the telltale dirt tubes (p. 171) that termites construct. This is especially a problem if dirt is piled up against stucco posts or siding.

The Foundation

1. Look for cracks in the foundation, or new mortar patches that might be hiding something. This is a very important step in the inspection, so take your time.

2. A serious crack is anything $\frac{1}{8}$ in. or bigger, for as you've learned above, it indicates that something is moving. Try to find out the cause, because it will tell you if the building has finished settling. Cracks might be caused by:

    a. An absence of reinforcing bar (rebar) in the foundation.

    b. Excessive water around the foundation because of absent or undirected downspouts, ground sloped toward the foundation, runoff from a hill above, subterranean springs, and so on.

   c. Some change in the structure, such as a second-story addition that is too heavy for the original foundation.

3. Given the magnitude of the problem and the expense of the remedy, you might want to walk away from a house with a cracked foundation. If not, have a structural engineer look at it.

THE INTERIOR

Armed with your notes from the outside, now walk inside to examine living spaces, bedrooms, bathrooms, kitchen, closets, hallways, and stairs. Here, you are looking for information that reinforces what you've seen outside. If, for example, the eave was splitting on the southeast corner of the roof, look for water damage on the corresponding corner inside the house.

In General

1. Be methodical. In every room, look at walls, ceilings, and floors. Note corners, where surfaces meet, for they often show stress when something is amiss.

2. Where walls intersect ceilings are particularly telling. There you will first see water damage from above, if it exists; and cracks, if the wall is dropping.

3. Closets are important points on your itinerary because they are frequently ignored when the rest of the house has been gussied up for sale. Look over the door trim for cracking.

4. These interior exams are especially important if the exterior is wood; wood is forgiving and usually disguises structural shifting. Because interior surfaces are drywall or plaster—both rigid materials—they tell more to the observant eye.

5. Use your ears, too. Squeaky floors or stairs may not be major problems, but may indicate rotted or inadequate joists below. This is also true if there are dips and bows in the floor; use your marble to locate them. Make floor maps, too. If something is shifting, there has to be a reason why.

Windows and Doors

1. Because the headers over windows and doors transfer heavy loads, cracking or bulging above such openings may indicate structural failing—take note! In a new house, small cracks are common enough because of lumber shrinkage, but papered or plastered-over bulges in an old house suggest chronic problems.

2. Scrutinize the lower rails of windows and the sills they rest on. If there is splitting or rot, you will most likely find it here.

3. Within reason, open all the windows in the house. Granted, some may just be painted shut and others, lacking sash weights, may be too heavy to budge. But others clearly will be swollen shut because they have absorbed water over the years. Replacing one window is a modest expense, but a half-dozen can cost real money.

4. Poke door sills for rot, particularly if carpet abuts an exterior doorsill.

Bathrooms

1. Look around the base of the toilet for water damage. If you see dips, springiness, or obvious staining around the base of the toilet, there is probably damage to the subfloor and, not uncommonly, rot in the joists below. The cause of such leakage is usually simple—a worn-out wax flange at the base of the toilet—but subfloor repairs can be complicated and expensive.

2. Look under the tub, sink, cabinets, and shower stalls for similar signs. Prod with your penknife. Shower stalls that fail usually do so because the pan underneath is faulty or nonexistent; the only way to fix this is to rip out the whole unit.

3. Another critical area is the grout line where tiles meet sinks or tubs. Ideally, the seam should be caulked, but sometimes it's not done. In such circumstances, you'll see moldy or missing grout, springy or missing tile, and other signs of pervasive damage.

4. Inspect tile generally by pushing with the heel of your hand. If you find areas that are springy but the tile is intact, the drywall behind it has probably lost some of its firmness because it has absorbed water. In the worst case, the wood framing behind it has deteriorated and you'll have to replace it. But in either case, you'll have to rip out tiles and drywall to set things right.

5. Missing or discolored grout by itself isn't a major problem: it can be removed and regrouted. But its absence may presage more serious water problems.

6. If the floor is linoleum, is it well adhered? Are there dips, soft spots, or blisters?

7. Look carefully around sinks, poking gently around the lip and inspecting carefully under the sink cabinet with your flashlight. If the sink is inset below the surface of the counter, was it properly grouted, and is the grout intact? If set atop the counter (lip-set), was it caulked all around? Where the counter meets the wall behind is also problematic, because water collects there.

8. While inspecting the cabinets under sinks, also look at the pipes. Check the traps and supply valves of all sinks and appliances for signs of blistering and rotting. If they are chrome, you are seeing rot from the inside out. They'll have to be replaced shortly. Look for staining, rot, or any signs of standing water in the base of the cabinet or where pipes exit into the wall.

9. If the supply pipes are galvanized steel, their useful life is about 25 years. After that, there's usually so much mineral buildup inside that the pressure at the tap is greatly reduced. To test the pressure, turn on the cold-water faucet in the highest bathroom and flush the toilet simultaneously. If the faucet flow is cut to a trickle, the piping is undersized or corroded. If the pipes are lead, they must be replaced at once.

A.

B.

Figure 1.5 Before rebuilding a house it's often necessary to unbuild it first, as shown in Figures 1.5 to 1.8. This house is further chronicled at the end of Chapter 2. (A) The east wall, atop a new foundation. (B) Stripping the roof.

Kitchens

1. Many of the tests you made in the bathroom are appropriate here, too. Pay close attention to the areas around and under sinks, where water might stand.

2. Check also beneath refrigerators, water heaters, and dishwashers for signs of leakage and damage to the floor and subfloor. Look for stain and springiness.

3. Roll your marble across countertops. As cabinets are frequently installed along an exterior wall, badly slanting tops can be caused by a gamut of defects: from rotted subflooring to a cracked foundation.

Stairs

As you head up to the attic for the next stage of your inspection, pay attention to the stairs. They are meant to be sound.

1. If there's a lot of creaking, you will at least have to shim beneath the treads; if they're decrepit, you may have to remove all treads and risers and reglue them.

2. Use your marble to see if the stairs slope to one side. If the slope is pronounced, the supports on one side may need to be jacked and resecured, a complicated task in most cases.

3. The handrails and newel posts should be solid. A little drift is common over the years, but movement much more than an inch needs to be corrected. If the underside of a post is exposed in the floor below, the remedy can be simple; if not, flooring will have to be ripped up. Really shaky setups, with missing balusters, should be replaced, which is a major expense.

UPSTAIRS, DOWNSTAIRS

Now it's time to make some deductions from the many clues that you've gathered, by looking closely in the attic and the basement. Here, where its structure is exposed, the house really gives up its secrets. You're going to get dirty crawling around, so dress the part.

Stay on ceiling joists or walkways in the attic. It's unsafe to walk anywhere else. Watch out for roofing nails from above, especially as you investigate the tight spaces where rafters meet walls. (This is perhaps the primary reason for having gotten that tetanus shot.)

In the Attic

1. Review your notes about the roof, the eaves, and the chimney. Look for patterns of water damage.

2. Look for water staining around the chimney. If stains are dark brown and smell of creosote, suspect wash down the inside of the lining (i.e., a cracked tile). If the wood is discolored by water alone, it is probably the flashing that is to blame. Note the general condition of the mortar. Protected by the roof, the mortar will not be weathered, but it may be cracked by an undersized or shifting chimney footing—the major cause of flue cracking.

3. Leaks will reveal themselves by long streaks down rafters. Follow those tracks down to the top plates of the walls and prod them with your penknife to see if the wood's solid.

4. Insulation will also show leaks clearly. Pull up affected sections and see if water has collected and damaged joists or the ceiling. Insulation should be at least R-30 in the attic; you will want to upgrade if it's not. Insulation should stop 2 in. short of chimneys and electrical junctions, to prevent fire.

5. Sight down the rafters: if the framing is undersized for the weight of the roof, they'll sag.

6. Note any insect infestation to rafters or roof sheathing. Certain wood-boring beetles enter ventilators and live undetected in the attic for a long time.

7. If leaking is widespread, tour the perimeter of the attic to determine the condition of the top plates. Probe them with your penknife and note any badly deteriorated areas. Replacing top plates is a major expense.

8. Turn off your flashlight. Can you see daylight through the roof? You'd be surprised how often you can. Where you see light, look for leaks.

A.

B.

Figure 1.6 (A) The east wall in shambles. (B) The new wall going up.

In the Basement

1. Take the time to examine the entire perimeter of the cellar, including crawl spaces.

2. Any crack greater than $\frac{1}{8}$ in. should be considered major, especially if the house is on a sloped lot where the soil may be shifting.

3. Muddy areas indicate drainage that is inadequate. The solution may be as simple as new downspouts and splash blocks or as complex as new perimeter drains. The cause may also be plumbing leaks.

4. Excessive efflorescence on foundation walls also suggests too much water around the house; again, the cure may be extensive perimeter drains.

5. Following the mud sill, check all jack studs, joist ends, and wall plates for insect damage or rot. Prod posts and beams for deterioration. This inspection will take time, but it's critically important.

6. Any agreement to buy should be contingent upon a thorough report by a *licensed* pest control inspector. If you see any insects around, check Figure 8.27 to identify them. You may find only traces of them:

    a. Subterranean termites need access to the moisture of the soil, so they build distinct tubes up along the surface of the foundation; when they burrow, they go with the wood grain.

    b. Nonsubterranean termites don't need tubes, burrow any which way, and frequently leave pellets outside their holes.

    c. Powder-post beetle holes look like BB-gun holes; their borings, like flour.

    d. Carpenter ants are ill-tempered little creatures with red forebodies and borings that resemble coarse sawdust.

7. Foundation walls and pads under posts must be at least 8 in. above the ground to forestall termite infestation and water damage.

8. Are posts plumb? If not, there's been uneven settlement, which should be corrected.

Plumbing

1. Where pipes enter the basement from floors above, prod adjacent joists and subfloor for signs of water damage. Pervasive rot beneath toilets and tubs is not uncommon.

2. Scrutinize waste pipes. Deteriorating waste pipes will often show a powdery green or white deposit along their horizontal runs, where wastes accumulate. Although they look sound, some sections are, in fact, so frail that they can be dented by rapping them with the handle of a screwdriver. Obviously, such pipes need to be replaced. If the house has only a crawl space for plumbers to get around in, the job will take longer and cost more.

3. Because waste-pipe fittings are heavier, they will last longer than the pipe itself, but they do leak. Note staining or septic smells.

4. If clean-out traps show fresh wrench marks, suspect recent clogging. If the house has a septic tank, ask when it was last emptied. Have the owner tell you the *exact* location of the septic tank clean-out and then walk that area. If the ground is at all damp or smelly, the tank or the drainage field may be undersized or incorrectly installed.

5. If the house has its own well, make a water test by the health department part of the sales agreement.

6. What type of water supply pipe is there? If it's galvanized and the house is at least 20 years old, the pipes need to be replaced with copper. Ditto if the pipes are brass—because brass hasn't been used for 50 years. If it's a dull, silvery metal that's soft enough to scrape with a knife, you're looking at lead. Replace it immediately.

7. Copper pipe is good almost indefinitely if properly installed. Its only weak points, if any, will be pinhole leaks around the fittings, where corrosion eats through or where they're joined to disparate metals. Unless such corrosion is common, this is not a major expense.

8. Examine the water heater for rust or staining around its burner. Can you hear any drips? If it is 12 or 15 years old (a manufacturer's plate will tell its age and capacity), it is nearing the end of its useful life. Newer models will also be more energy efficient; a 40-gallon heater is now considered optimal.

Gas lines. If there is any smell of gas or if lines look old or abused, have the gas company or an experienced plumber investigate further. Most utilities will do it for free. Although you can detect gas leaks by daubing pipes with soapy water, only a professional should replace or repair them. Gas pipes are commonly joined by threading together sections of "black iron," or by flare-fitting copper. Gas lines should *never* be PVC plastic, sweated (soldered) copper, or compression fittings such as those used for water supply. Such gas-line connections are relatively inexpensive to replace, but manifestly unsafe to use.

Electrical

Turn the electricity off and make sure it's off, with a voltage tester (p. 235), before handling any electrical component.

1. In older homes, electrical systems are often undersized. Renovating those systems becomes a trade-off between leaving existing circuits and running new ones. How much you can expand your present system depends on the number of main wires running from the utility pole to the house and the size of the main panel. If your house is served by only two main wires, you'll need the service upgraded to three wires, which gives you 240-volt service.

2. Now look at the existing entrance panel. These days, a 100-ampere main is minimal. If you find a fuse panel, it will typically be 60 amperes or less, with six or fewer individual fuses. If the panel and its wires are in good condition, you can continue to use them, but they should be supplemented with another subpanel to reduce the load on the existing system.

3. The easiest way to judge the condition of the wires is to examine them as they run along the joists in the basement. Any wire whose casing is cracked or frayed should be replaced. *Note:* If you find old-fashioned knob-and-tube

A.

B.

Figure 1.7 (A) The east wall and the second-story addition largely framed. (B) The new roof up, sheathing nearly complete.

wiring, pay close attention to the fiber bushings where wires enter boxes, cracked insulation on individual wires, and wire splices—which should be properly soldered and taped. Knob-and-tube wiring may still be serviceable, but it must be properly installed to be safe.

4. Next, with the power off, randomly remove a few switch and receptacle plates and examine the condition of those boxes, looking for fraying, corrosion, rust, and the like.

5. Electrical code requires ground-fault circuit interrupters (p. 253) wherever water might be present: in bathrooms, near kitchen sinks, on the outside of the house, and so on. You'll need to install them to meet the building code.

6. By now, you should have a pretty good idea of the electrical system. If it's in bad shape, rewiring it will be expensive.

Heating

If the heating system is a fairly old one, bring in an expert to assess it, for there are a number of problems beyond the ken of an amateur inspector:

1. How energy efficient is it?

2. How many years of useful life has it, and what are the chances that it may fail altogether?

3. Are there any problems that might endanger your family? A porous heat exchanger, for example, might leak carbon monoxide into living spaces.

4. Protect yourself by making a professional inspection part of the contract for purchase. In this way you won't risk losing a house to other prospective buyers, and you'll be spared any unforeseen expense.

Fireplace

Compare earlier observations from the roof or the exterior with what you now find in the basement and living areas.

1. The fireplace must sit on a foundation more or less independent of that supporting the walls, because of the great weight of the masonry. Are there any signs of shifting? Examine the juncture of brick to wall. Be suspicious of any cracks that have been filled in or repainted. Also examine the pad on which the fireplace rests: it should be free of cracks and spalling.

2. Inside the living area, is the hearth level? Has it separated from the firebox? This may be a relatively minor repair, say, replacing the hearth and its support beneath, but it may also indicate widespread structural failings that converge at the hearth.

3. Look at the firebox: it must be intact to confine flames and superheated fumes.

4. Look up the chimney to see if there's a fire shelf and a damper. If not, you can lose a lot of heat. Then, with the damper open, look up the chimney for any signs of cracked or kicked-in flue tiles.

5. As noted earlier, these concerns are preeminently important to your safety, for when chimney fires occur, they often do so behind the walls or in the attic, where they can rage undetected.

Figure 1.8 Finishing stages.

HOW MUCH WORK WILL IT BE?

Having got some sense of how much repairs may cost, you may now wonder how much work is involved. It is tough to generalize when individual skills vary greatly, but in the following list we have attempted to grade jobs by difficulty.

Beginner to intermediate.

Demolition. Always cut power to the area, and make sure that you're not disturbing the structure. Always take your time, removing debris as you work and being careful to lift only loads you can handle.

Interior painting. Preparation of the walls and patience are the keys to success.

Exterior painting. More difficult than interior painting because of safety factors. Again, surface preparation is crucial. Rented scaffolding is a good investment.

Stripping paint, inside or out. Not difficult, just messy. To avoid gouging the surface underneath, allow your chemicals (or heat) time to work, and get adequate ventilation. Avoid open-flame paint stripping; the fire hazard is too great.

Wallpapering. Can be tricky; always start with a small area that is out of the way. Wall preparation is crucial.

Hanging drywall. Not difficult once you get the hang of it. Getting the edges of the first sheets plumb (or level) is the key to success.

Panelling. Hanging sheet panels is not difficult, provided that there is a good flat surface beneath to nail into, and that you take care to plumb the edges of the sheets.

Patch-repairing walls. Generally, quite easy. Sand or cut back the damaged parts to ensure a good surface for the fix.

Insulating. Not difficult, but if you want to keep out drafts, you must be fastidious about securing insulation. Always wear gloves, a long-sleeved shirt, a hat, and a respirator mask.

Weatherstripping. Easy, but be sure the stripping fits snugly against the surface. You'll be surprised how long this takes.

Hanging storm windows, awnings, and shutters. Not difficult, but accuracy in leveling and measuring is crucial. For a pleasing visual effect, any exterior appurtenances must be aligned. For example, windows of the same size on the same floor should be the same height.

Mixing a small masonry slab. Not tough at all, but be sure to level your forms before you start.

Intermediate to difficult.

Framing and sheathing. Not too tough; in fact, it's fun, especially if you can nail accurately and are working with someone who is experienced, so that you keep moving. Measure accurately and cut pieces of the same size at the same time, so you can work faster. Framing and sheathing upper stories and roofs requires a lot of experience and is probably not for the beginner. Fabricating first-story decks is easy.

Hanging windows and doors. Tricky, even with precased units. Some professionals can't, and some greenhorns can.

Subflooring. In new work, just a question of correct nailing; in old work, it may take a lot of work to shim up low spots.

Flooring. To ge a good job, you must (a) make sure that the subflooring is level and solid, and (b) lay out the material very carefully.

Plastering. Difficult for the novice. Plaster consistency, technique, and room temperature are all crucial. The skill of plastering takes time to master.

Refinishing floors. Take your time, especially with power sanders; be picky about vacuuming and sanding lightly between finish coats.

Installing prebuilt cabinets. A job of fine-tuning parts, not overwhelming if you are good at measuring and leveling. Base cabinets must be shimmed beneath and wall units behind.

Interior trim work. Requires patience, a good eye for close measuring, and an accurate miter box or miter trimmer.

Exterior trim and siding. Layout and leveling are important, as is caulking all seams.

Roofing and reroofing. Not difficult, but you must understand flashing and be able to lay out roofing courses evenly; roof jacks and safety apparatus are important.

Setting up a wood stove. Not tough, just heavy. You must make sure that the floor will support the weight, that you are not too close to combustible surfaces, and that all junctions between walls (or roofs) and chimney pipe are correctly mounted and flashed before you cover them with finish surfaces. First, check with your insurance company and local code authorities.

Furnace ductwork. Not difficult, but can be aggravating when the pieces don't fit together as they should (which can often happen). Cursing and yelling may help.

Plumbing and electrical wiring. Skills that can be acquired by working with a licensed tradesman for a day or two, but local codes may prohibit you from doing your own work. The work is enjoyable, steady, and logical but requires close attention to detail. Don't do it if you are not fastidious; connections indifferently made are hazardous. You'll need special tools for either wiring or plumbing.

Just plain tough.

Framing stairs and dormers. Many angles must be reckoned with.

Masonry. Each masonry unit—whether brick or block—must be placed exactly. The work requires deft hands and an experienced eye.

Changing bearing walls. Get an engineer's help if you have any doubts.

Furnace adjustments. Other than basic maintenance tasks, tinkering with furnace settings is not recommended for the ill at ease or the inexperienced.

Tiling in fresh mortar. A new mortar bed is sometimes the only way to level and plumb an area so that you can tile it. It takes a lot of experience to prepare the surface correctly, to mix mud to the right consistency, and to trowel it on and screed it off. Hire someone to do the bed for you so that you can concentrate on tiling.

Building your own cabinets from scratch. Measurements must be extremely exact. This task requires good tools and incredible patience, but it is a job that experienced wood-workers, whether amateur or professional, may enjoy the most.

A BRIEF RECAP

Don't be intimidated by the inspection list above: it's just common sense applied over and over. Reduced to a few suggestions, it says:

1. Try to find patterns in what you observe.
2. Water is the big bugaboo.
3. The roof and the foundation are the most important parts of the house.
4. Maintenance is the only way to thwart time and water. If a house has been maintained, it's probably a good one to buy.
5. Believe in yourself. Look at a few houses, learn the lingo, and stand your ground when it's time to make a deal. Remember, *everything* is negotiable.

You'll do fine.

Figure 1.9 When you assess, look for patterns. Here you can see the descent of water and rot: a worn-out roof, clogged gutters, eaves in disrepair, blistering paint, and likely structural problems behind.

·2·

PLANNING, DRAWING, AND DOING

Planning is one of the most satisfying aspects of renovation. On paper, you can live imperially, with fruit trees beneath every window and Italian marble in every bathroom; when you're tired of those accommodations, you can level walls with an eraser. What you finally build is, of course, a trade-off between what you want and what you can afford. But let your imagination run free initially. Envisioning what you want is an important step: before you can build it, you've got to imagine it.

PLANNING

Who Are You?

Your house should fit you comfortably, should be an expression of who you are, your lifestyle, your loved ones, your dreams. So start planning by getting in touch with who you are—which is not so easy. Because few homeowners think spatially and fewer still can draw, one particularly good architect has his clients write up a scenario of a happy day in a perfect house. It's surprising how quickly people get beyond fancy trappings and on with what makes them happy: it may be waking up slowly over coffee, out in the garden; reading in bed; getting work out of your soul by puttering in the garden; playing with your kids; having dinner with neighbors you never see; having a heart-to-heart talk. Does your present home help you do these things?

Another good planning tool is a family notebook. Much as you'd add to a shopping list, jot down housing thoughts as they happen. It is also a convenient place to store nice details you clip from housing magazines. Encourage your kids to scribble in their thoughts, too. The random questions below should generate some answers; there are additional ones about kitchen and baths later in the chapter.

Cooking and Eating. In your present home, is there room to set down groceries? Are counters at the right height? Can you reach all the shelves? Is there enough storage space? Do dishes seem to pile up, or is it an easy kitchen to keep clean? Can people hang out while you cook? Do you talk on the phone or watch TV while you cook? Is there room to roll out dough? If you recycle cans and bottles, is there room to store them? Is it easy to get food to and from the table? Is there a safe place to store your best dishes? Is your refrigerator big enough?

Being Sociable. If you had a party, what kind would it be—dancing, cards, noisy, dinner, talking? Is there room if it's your turn to host the club? Is the living room cozy? If you have visitors from out of town who stay over, do they have privacy, room to unpack, places to hang their clothes? When the kids have friends over, can they entertain without driving you crazy? (This may have nothing to do with houses.)

Family Doings. If you have small children, are finish surfaces easy to keep clean? Is there a place to store toys easily? Can you secure kitchen and bathroom cabinets from youthful explorers? Is there an enclosed area outside so that you don't have to watch over them? Is there a place where they can play on a rainy day? If you want your kids to read more and watch TV less, is their room conducive to that? What do your kids fight about most? Does it have anything to do with privacy, personal possessions? Will the rooms meet their needs in five years?

Bathrooms. Is there a jam-up during rush hours? Enough cabinet space for sundries? Can you relax and soak in peace? Do you read in the tub? Is the tub long enough to stretch? Big enough for two? Can you shower without making a mess? Is there a half-bath close to the kitchen?

Outer Spaces. Is there room to store tools? Do you love fresh herbs and tomatoes that taste like something? Does the yard get enough sun for a garden? Dream about shady trellis seats on muggy summer days? Is there room to work on the car? Do you cook out often? Want a deck? Is the backyard fence about to fall over? Wish you could see less of your neighbors? Is there room for your hobby?

Working at Home. A lot of us are bringing work home these days. Is there place to spread out your papers? Is there room for a computer? Filing cabinets? Bookshelves? Are walls insulated so that you can work late without disturbing others? Are there enough outlets? Is the lighting adequate? Can you shut a door on it all when you call it a day? Is it safe from dogs that chew and children with crayons? Do you think about working at home full-time?

Are You Comfortable? Can you shut out street noise? Is the house drafty? Cold? Can you shut off sections so that you're not heating what you're not using? Are utility bills costing an arm and a leg? Is there sun with breakfast? Does

Figure 2.1 Place a tissue overlay on a basic floor plan to make a quick, accurate sketch.

everything mean a trip upstairs? Do you feel secure? If not, what parts of the house do you worry about? Can you see who's on the porch without opening the door? Are you out of the rain when looking for your keys or shaking your umbrella? Is the house easy to keep clean? Is there room to do aerobics? Is there enough storage space?

Seeing Changes

The easiest way to see change is to draw it. Start with a basic plan of each floor. Using a 25-ft retractable tape measure, record the overall dimensions of each room, noting the position of existing doors, windows, closets, fireplaces—anything that affects space. To make the first set of floor plans accurate, transfer measurements to graph paper. Graph paper is handy because it enables you to draw square corners and maintain scale without a lot of fancy drafting equipment. Use a scale that is comfortable: most people find that $\frac{1}{4}$ in.:1 ft is large enough for detail without being overwhelming.

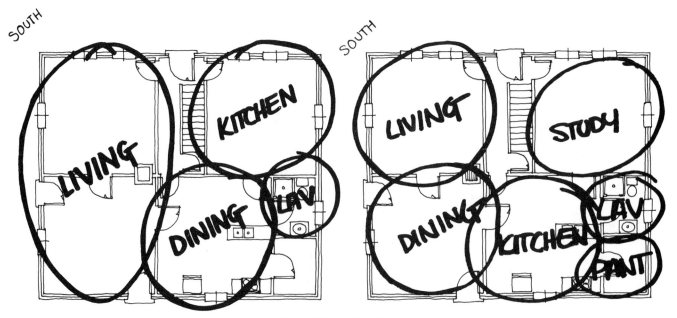

Figure 2.2 Bubble diagrams.

With the measurements of the house depicted on graph paper, you can now make quick, reasonably accurate sketches by taping tracing paper over the graph paper. Don't be shy about using tracing paper: it is available in rolls and it is the cheapest building material that you'll ever encounter. Whether you draw ''bubble diagrams'' to indicate room usage, as in Figure 2.2, or flow sketches to show how people move between areas, draw a lot of arrangements, including some you know you won't like. They may have possibilities that you wouldn't have noticed otherwise.

Some layouts—dining rooms next to kitchens, lavatory nearby—are obvious, but most are fluid and all should be based on common sense. Put bedrooms away from noisy rooms and busy streets if possible. When going to the bathroom in the middle of the night, you shouldn't have to go through another bedroom or a public room. Don't forget closets in or near each bedroom, and by the front door.

Give nature a hand in the design, too. If your kitchen is toward the east, you'll have morning sun with your tea; a living room on the west gives a view of the sunset. Glazing along the south wall gives you a lot of free heat, and rooms facing north are best reserved for sleeping. This is a layout for the North, of course; people in the Sun Belt should be concerned more with the overall orientation of the house to prevailing breezes and with proper overhangs on the southern wall. If you live in Florida, where the afternoon sun can be a blast furnace, you'll want only a few windows facing west.

There are other ways of envisioning layout. If your task is dividing a large space, mock up walls by hanging sheets from the ceiling. If floors are slated to be refinished or replaced, snap chalk lines to indicate walls and to give you a sense of how big the new rooms will really be. If you're at all dexterous, make a model out of cardboard; most artist supply stores will have the materials you need. Using a scale of $\frac{1}{2}$ in.:1 ft, draw floor plans and an elevation for each face onto the cardboard, cut them out with a utility knife and tape them together, and raise a roof after the fact.

Recording What's There

Design is a constant revision that doesn't stop until the thing is built, if then. The closer you get to a design that works, the more information you need.

Respecting what's there. Having given some thought to who you are, now take a close look at your house. There are admonitions throughout this book to save time and money by renovating no more than you must. The same is true for aesthetic reasons. Design is tricky stuff to articulate, but a building's integrity comes from the proportion of its windows, the width and contour of its trim, the slope of its roof—from its parts, in short—just as we humans are distinctive by the color of our hair, the set of our eyes, the shape of our noses. Each historical period has its own architectural elements, and you're better off not mixing them. When you must change something, be guided by what is already there.

It may be, of course, that your house has already been renovated. If that is the case, walk around the neighborhood with your camera, for your house probably has relatives nearby. Polaroid photos are also useful, by the way, when you are thinking about buying a house or are not living in one that you're fixing up. Photos provide an unromanticized vision of what you saw, and if there is some mysterious crack, shape, or detail that you want to investigate later, circle it on the picture.

Mapping mechanical systems. At some point you'll need to know what's behind the walls: not every last wire and pipe, but where things are generally so that you can avoid the larger and more problematic ducts, pipes, and wires. You won't know exactly where everything is until you open up walls, but you will save a lot of time by not proceeding full-bore on an obviously flawed layout.

If your plans entail upgrading mechanical systems or rerouting them, map them first. Although they may be largely hidden behind walls and in floors, start with what is visible—fixtures, receptacles, registers, stacks—and extrapolate from that. To minimize confusion, draw a separate tissue overlay for each system.

1. Map the electrical system by having a helper stand at the entrance panel and turn the circuit breakers off and on, or unscrew fuses as you plug a voltage tester into each receptacle. (A lamp will also do.) By standing in the basement and noting where wires exit into the floors above, and by extrapolating from the circuit maps that you've made, you can usually guess accurately where most wires are hidden. Be sure to heed the safety rules listed on page 235.

Figure 2.3 A cardboard model of the Smith house.

2. Plumbing fixtures are usually grouped around a 3-in. soil stack, which enables materials and space to be used economically. The soil stack is often hidden in a wall near the toilet, and drainage pipes are often routed between floor joists. Supply pipes, being smaller, can be tricky to locate exactly, although, again, you can get a pretty good idea of their location by noting where pipes ascend from the basement.

3. The heating system can be traced back from registers to the furnace. In most cases, ductwork and piping will be visible in the basement. Where there are upper-story heat outlets, delivery ducts and pipes generally travel straight up between studs.

Exploratories. Occasionally, a builder needs to know more than the covered walls will tell. The builder might want to know, for instance, whether a proposed cut will hit a girder, whether wires running inside a wall must be removed, whether pipes inside a floor are active. Such "exploratories" are much more common in urban situations, where there are shared walls and many previous renovations. Here are a few tips for making searches:

1. Turn off electricity and gas to (or through) the area affected.

2. Have materials handy to patch holes made.

3. Make the smallest hole possible. A handy tool is an exploratory bit, usually 18 in. long (see Chapter 3). Flat bars are popular tools for breaking through finished walls and ceilings, as are reciprocating saws.

4. Explore in the least conspicuous place. Wall exploratories are handily made at the base of the wall after carefully removing any baseboard trim. If you aren't sure about joist direction, you might pull up subflooring in a closet.

Design Constraints

Now we'll look at the implications of what you have just unearthed. The primary design constraints are imposed by structure, plumbing, heating and cooling ductwork, and wiring. Consider safety and energy conservation, too.

Structure. If you don't intend to remove existing walls, the structure will probably not affect your renovation. If your plans do require moving walls, you must explore the building's framing to determine whether or not the walls in question are load bearing.

In most wood-frame houses, bearing walls run perpendicular to the joists they are supporting; in effect, shortening the distance those joists must span. Bearing walls will

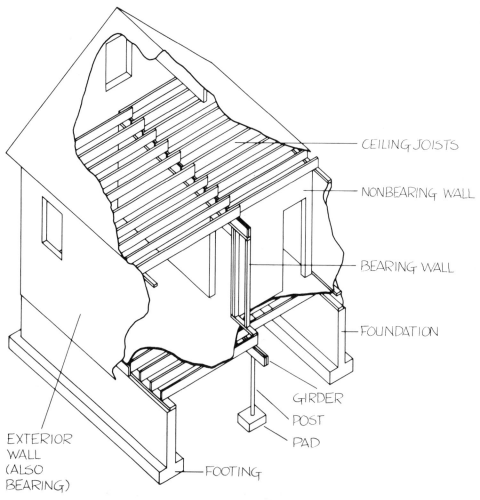

Figure 2.4 Bearing and nonbearing walls.

probably be supported by bearing walls below, on down to the basement, where they will be supported by a girder and posts. There are framing eccentricities, however, especially with additions.

In apartments and row houses, interior walls are usually not bearing. Most apartments are framed out with steel girders; floors are reinforced concrete slabs. In row houses, joists and rafters customarily run the width of the house, between exterior walls. Thus interior walls running parallel to joists or rafters are almost never bearing. Partitions running perpendicular to framing members are *probably* not bearing walls either, but they may be if joists were undersized to begin with, or if their effective spans were reduced by "remuddlers" cutting into them. In such instances partitions become bearing walls, and floors may tilt markedly toward them.

If a wall is nonbearing, removing it will not cause problems, but if it is bearing, you must transfer the loads it presently bears before you can alter it. Similarly, structural buttresses such as braces and collar ties cannot be removed with impunity: unsupported, the structure can deform and over the long run, collapse. Have a structural engineer help size and position replacement walls or new braces. See Chapter 8 for more on shoring, framing partitions, and the like.

Plumbing. Plumbing has many constraints, but it is still flexible to a degree. The flexible tubing of gas lines is, of course, the easiest to position and the least intrusive upon design.

Supply pipe can be run most anywhere. Because water is under pressure, pipes don't need to be pitched. This is not true in the case of waste and vent pipes, however. Waste pipes must maintain a downward pitch of at least $\frac{1}{4}$ in. per ft; venting, when not plumb, should run upward, toward the soil stack, at a similar rate. The real bugbears of plumbing are the 3- or 4-in. vent or soil stacks (which direct gases up and out of the house) and which continue downward as the main waste (which carries waste out). Because of their size it is common to group fixtures as near the stack as possible. In apartments, that is usually done using a discrete, centrally located mechanical shaft. In most separate residences, pipes are concealed in "wet walls," which are customarily framed out with 2×6s so that there is plenty of room for even the biggest pipe. For vertical runs, vent and waste pipes run in these walls; for horizontal runs, pipes are routed between and parallel to the joists.

Pipes can also run *across* joists, but that requires cutting holes through the joists, which can weaken them. To meet this problem, *truss joists* have become popular in renovation. Because they are not solid expanses of wood, mechan-

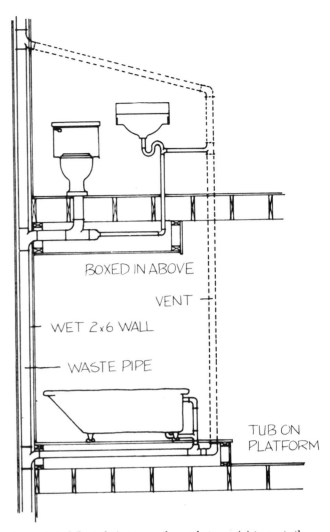

Figure 2.6 Where drains cannot be run between joists, route them through lowered ceilings or raised platforms.

ical systems can be channeled through them. Such joists are strong and relatively light and are usually cheaper than wood joists of comparable load-bearing capacity.

Where your plans don't allow you to route pipes in existing walls, floors, or ceilings, renovation costs rise significantly. If the present joists don't provide the depth necessary to pitch waste pipes, you can build up a platform over the existing floor. This is also a common strategy where existing floors are masonry and just not worth the bother of cutting into. False walls or ceilings, as shown in Figure 2.6, are another possibility. When things get this complicated, however, it's probably a good time to consider a simpler design solution.

Heating and cooling systems. Heating, cooling, and ventilation systems can also affect design plans, depending on the type of system. Electric heat is the easiest to install, but it is also the most expensive to operate. The constraints of hot-water systems are similar to those for supply plumbing described above.

Hot-air heat requiring ducts is by far the most difficult to situate, mainly because it is so bulky. False walls, floors, and ceilings are commonly employed where space is tight. Unlike waste plumbing, however, forced hot air is under

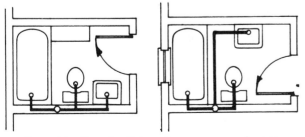

Figure 2.5 Grouping fixtures to save space and money.

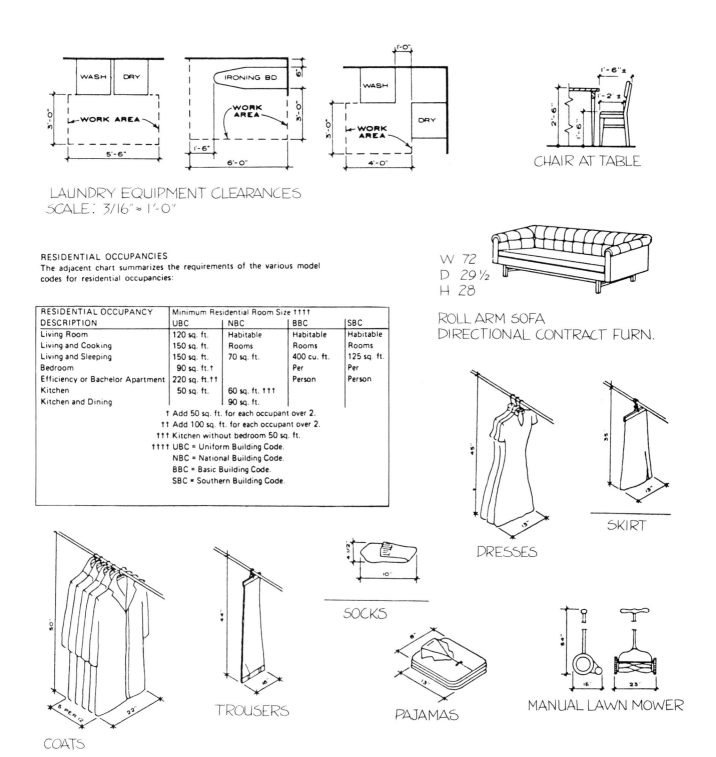

LAUNDRY EQUIPMENT CLEARANCES
SCALE: 3/16" ≈ 1'-0"

CHAIR AT TABLE

RESIDENTIAL OCCUPANCIES
The adjacent chart summarizes the requirements of the various model codes for residential occupancies:

RESIDENTIAL OCCUPANCY DESCRIPTION	Minimum Residential Room Size ††††			
	UBC	NBC	BBC	SBC
Living Room	120 sq. ft.	Habitable	Habitable	Habitable
Living and Cooking	150 sq. ft.	Rooms	Rooms	Rooms
Living and Sleeping	150 sq. ft.	70 sq. ft.	400 cu. ft.	125 sq. ft.
Bedroom	90 sq. ft.†		Per	Per
Efficiency or Bachelor Apartment	220 sq. ft.††		Person	Person
Kitchen	50 sq. ft.	60 sq. ft. †††		
Kitchen and Dining		90 sq. ft.		

† Add 50 sq. ft. for each occupant over 2.
†† Add 100 sq. ft. for each occupant over 2.
††† Kitchen without bedroom 50 sq. ft.
†††† UBC = Uniform Building Code.
NBC = National Building Code.
BBC = Basic Building Code.
SBC = Southern Building Code.

W 72
D 29½
H 28

ROLL ARM SOFA
DIRECTIONAL CONTRACT FURN.

DRESSES

SKIRT

SOCKS

COATS

TROUSERS

PAJAMAS

MANUAL LAWN MOWER

Figure 2.7 These excerpts from *Architectural Graphic Standards* can help you refine your floor plans. In all your sketches, allow room for people to move. (Courtesy of the American Institute of Architects and John Wiley & Sons, Inc.)

pressure from the system's fan. Thus air ducts need not be sloped upward (although this is desirable); in fact, they can even pitch slightly downward. Where renovations involve gutting wall surfaces, vertical duct runs are easily fitted between standard 2 × 4 studs. Further, flexible insulated duct greatly expands the renovator's options.

Ventilators for bathrooms and appliances are rarely problematic, since exhaust fans draw air from relatively small, isolated areas. Hence, cumbersome, centralized hookups aren't a problem. By placing ovens, cooktops, or stoves near exterior walls or beneath a venting bonnet, you can easily route cooking exhaust to the outside.

The renovator's primary concern in placing heating and cooling systems is to make sure that pipes and ductwork do not encounter joists, fire stops, bridging, or other impediments.

Wiring. Electrical wiring is rarely a serious constraint, except when you must move a service panel. Small and flexible, electrical cable is easily routed through walls, floors,

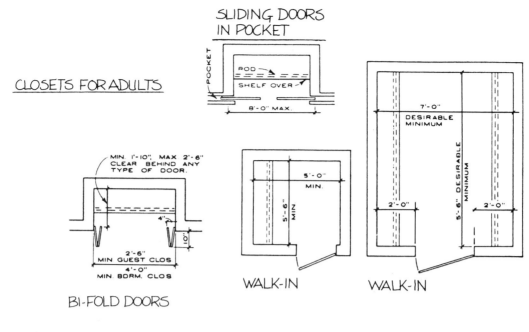

CLOSETS FOR ADULTS

SLIDING DOORS IN POCKET

BI-FOLD DOORS

WALK-IN

WALK-IN

WALL SPACE REQUIREMENTS FOR BED & NIGHT TABLE ARRANGEMENTS

The average person requires 8 linear feet of drawer space for clothing. Clearances required for the pulling out of drawers and for access and entry into room must be taken into consideration. The bedroom clearances shown are recommended for passage and are desirable for bedmaking. The diagrams below show a relationship of square foot areas required when planning bedrooms with clothes storage. Sitting, writing, and makeup areas are not included. These must be included if required.

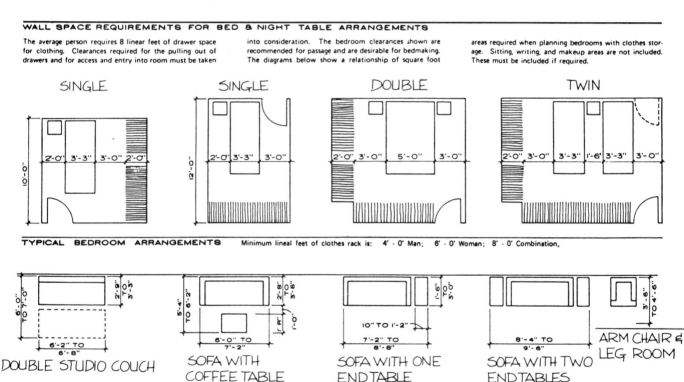

SINGLE   SINGLE   DOUBLE   TWIN

DOUBLE STUDIO COUCH   SOFA WITH COFFEE TABLE   SOFA WITH ONE END TABLE   SOFA WITH TWO END TABLES   ARM CHAIR & LEG ROOM

TYPICAL BEDROOM ARRANGEMENTS   Minimum lineal feet of clothes rack is: 4'-0' Man;   6'-0' Woman;   8'-0' Combination.

Figure 2.7 (Continued)

---

and ceilings. Where you don't want to cut into existing surfaces, or can't—as with masonry floors—run rigid conduit or track wiring along the surface.

Conservation and safety. These two concerns are not exactly constraints, but both affect design to a degree and are important to your comfort and well-being. Conserving energy by insulating, upgrading windows, and possibly replacing a furnace is as important as any task you undertake when renovating. An uninsulated house presents a cost

that you'll pay as long as you own the house. If there is presently no insulation, it may pay to gut the walls to do the job properly (see Chapter 13 for more). Accordingly, layout affects conservation: bathrooms are often situated in the middle of a house, away from windows, for warmth. Any bathroom on an exterior wall should be insulated, as should floors (if over an unheated area) and walls. You may also want to insulate interior bathroom walls to muffle sound. It goes without saying that water heaters and pipes should be insulated, and heating ducts as well.

Because a high percentage of household accidents take place in bathrooms and kitchens, give a thought to preventing falls, for they are not limited to older people. Anyone rising from a long, hot soak can get lightheaded, so tubs and showers should have integral grab rails—not flimsy towel racks or soap indents—mounted to framing behind the finish walls.

Adequate lighting and shock protection are also crucial to safety. When upgrading wiring, allow 3 to 4 watts of incandescent light per square foot of a bathroom, or 1 to 2 watts of fluorescent light. Kitchens require 2 to 3 watts of incandescent light per square foot and 1 to 2 watts of fluorescent light; work areas near sinks should have 150 to 200 watts of concentrated light. Receptacles in kitchens, bathrooms, and other high-moisture areas must have a ground-fault circuit interrupter (GFCI), which cuts off power within $\frac{1}{40}$ second if even a slight leak (4 to 6 milliamperes) is detected. For more about GFCI receptacles and circuits, see Chapter 11.

Final Drawings

Once you've reconsidered your layouts in light of the constraints noted above, proceed to final drawings, which should include accurately drawn floor plans and eleva-

tions. How detailed these drawings must be depends on several variables, the most important being how big the job is and who's doing the work. A conscientious, experienced builder knows more or less intuitively what is sound construction, what will satisfy codes, and how to solve the unanticipated problems that always surface.

But you need final plans because (1) you are more likely to get what you pay for if you're clear about what you want; (2) plans are a necessary part of the construction document, from which the contractor makes his or her estimate; (3) your contractor can anticipate problems and suggest changes while they are still easy to make (i.e., before the subcontractors have been scheduled); (4) you'll have a final price much closer to what it will eventually be; and (5) many municipalities require plans before issuing work permits. You will also be a lot less anxious and better informed about why it's costing so much.

There is no simple answer about how detailed the drawings must be. If the job is at all extensive—a major kitchen remodel or more than one common room—I'd suggest having them drawn up by a professional because a lot of money will be involved. Because construction documents are usually 40 to 50 percent of an architect's total fee, and that fee is customarily 10 to 15 percent of total costs, figure that working drawings with floor plans, elevations,

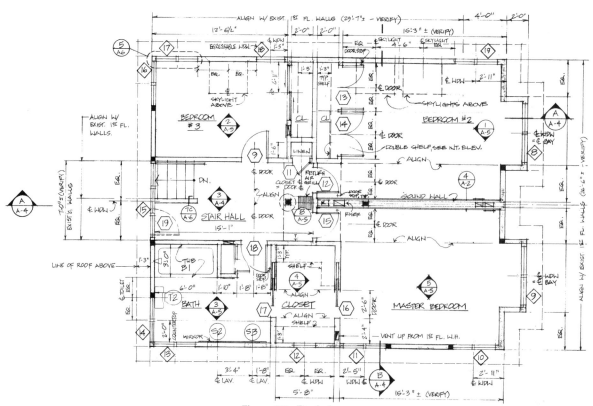

Figure 2.8 Final plans.

and cross sections will be roughly 5 percent of your total budget. Municipalities may require a cross section from foundation to roof to see how the building's framed, insulated, sheathed, and finished. From a small sample of builders around the country, I hear that roughly 80 percent of renovation jobs have working drawings; of those, about 50 percent are drawn by architects, 50 percent by contractors, and 10 percent by homeowners. Yes, that does add up to 110 percent—infer what you will.

KITCHEN AND BATHROOM TIPS

Kitchens and bathrooms are very private places. For that reason, they are the rooms most often renovated. When tailored to previous inhabitants, these rooms never quite fit us: they are always short in the arms and big in the seat.

Kitchens

There are no set rules for kitchen planning, because uses vary so greatly from family to family. For that matter, kitchen use varies greatly within a family as its members grow and their interests change. The best kitchens are those that use space economically regardless of the overall dimensions of the room. Obviously, a lot of equipment must be fit in a kitchen; but the cook actually moves in a small space bounded by the refrigerator, stove, and sink—the so-called *work triangle*. All plans for kitchens that claim to be efficient should give top priority to kitchen users; the placement of appliances, counters, and cabinets will follow.

Kitchen use. How do *you* use your kitchen—for cooking, dining, family, other?

Cooking. Do you cook a lot, or a little? Are you a fastidious cook who cleans up as preparation of the meal progresses, or are you "creative," using all the pots in the house and then cleaning up? Do you have enough counter space for preparing several dishes at the same time? Do you entertain often? Are meals large or small? Do you have special cooking interests? Are foodstuffs and utensils placed conven-

iently? Jot down your thoughts about a new kitchen while continuing to work in the old one.

Dining. Do you eat in the kitchen? If so, is there enough room for eating, for serving and clearing with ease? Does the table interfere with meal preparation? If you linger or socialize at meals, is the view from the table pleasant? Do you like company while you cook?

Family. Does the family hang out in the kitchen? If the children do their homework or play in the kitchen, can this center be cleared or cleaned up easily at mealtime? Are cabinets sufficiently childproof; that is, are their contents relatively inaccessible? If your family reads or watches TV there, is the lighting adequate?

Other. Often the kitchen doubles as a laundry or sewing area. Is there sufficient room around the washer and dryer to move freely? Is there sufficient counter or closet space for storing supplies or folding clothes? Are such appliances disguised unobtrusively beneath counters or behind doors? If the kitchen doubles as an office or homework area, are countertops at a comfortable height for writing?

Finally, are kitchen uses compatible? If they aren't, either move some to other areas or consider enlarging the kitchen to accommodate them.

The work triangle. The three most important appliances in a kitchen are the sink, the stove, and the refrigerator. The cook spends most of his or her time at or moving between these three points. Over years of kitchen use, and through many kinds of layouts, designers have theorized that a kitchen is used most effectively if these three items are arranged in a triangle of sorts and if the distance traveled between them is 12 to 22 ft.

Of the basic kitchen plans shown in Figure 2.9, three have just such a work triangle; yet in the fourth, the single-line kitchen, the distance from stove to refrigerator and back is still optimally between 12 and 22 ft.

U-Shaped Kitchen. The U-shaped kitchen is thought by many to be the best design, for it effectively isolates the

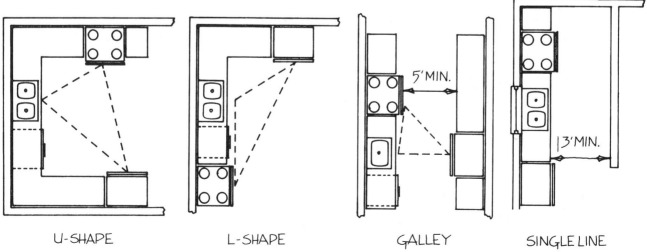

| U-SHAPE | L-SHAPE | GALLEY | SINGLE LINE |

Figure 2.9 Typical kitchen layouts.

work area from the flow of family traffic. Since the most time is spent at the sink, the sink is the apex of the work triangle; that is, it is the bottom of the U. The sink should be placed beneath a window whenever possible.

L-Shaped Kitchen. The L-shaped kitchen might be the most popular because of its flexibility, which makes it possible to fit a dining table in the imaginary fourth corner. It is a less efficient setup, however, and the distance between fridge and stove can become excessive.

Galley Kitchen. The galley kitchen usually has a lot of counter space, and it forms an effective triangle; but this design has some drawbacks. First, it can become too highly trafficked if a door is at one end. Second, storage can be a problem. Third, to allow doors on both sides of the galley to be opened simultaneously, or to allow the cook to get by when one door is open, there must be at least 5 ft between the two sides.

Single-Line Kitchen. The single-line kitchen, common to apartments, is workable, though somewhat spread out. Allow a minimum of 3 ft to the opposite wall for getting by an opened door.

Island Kitchen. An island kitchen is not shown here because of the nearly infinite varity of appliance arrangement in such a design. Islands are great if yours is a multiple-use kitchen, providing a buffer for the cooking tasks. Make sure that the island does not interfere with the work triangle, and observe the minimum aisle dimensions where appliance doors open toward the island.

Counter and cabinet space. Meal preparation consists of at least three functions: preparing the food, cooking it, and cleaning up. There should be counter space for each function. Because cooking involves hot pots and pans coming and going, cooking space must be discrete, separate from food preparation in particular. There should be at least 2 ft of clear counter space to one side of the stove cooktop (which should be of heat-resistant material). Although the stove should be near an outside wall, to minimize the length of ventilation ductwork, it should not be beneath a window; drafts could blow out a burner and grease buildup could be unsightly. Locate washable surfaces behind stove and counter areas.

The sink should have counters on both sides—3 ft at one side, to receive dirty dishes, and 2 to 3 ft on the other side, where dishes can drain. Because dishwashers are 24 in. wide, they are often placed beneath the smaller counter. Definitely have a splash panel behind your sink.

The food-preparation area, while more flexible, is best positioned near the refrigerator and sink, so foodstuffs can be handled, washed, and prepared faster. Small appliances are best stored near here; thus you should have a 3- to 4-ft section of counter with at least two receptacles. A built-in chopping block is also desirable.

There are few set rules for the cabinets you need; a better indication is the number of appliances, bowls, and assorted paraphernalia that you have. Most codes that say anything about cabinet space specify 18 sq ft of basic storage plus 6 sq ft for each person in the household.

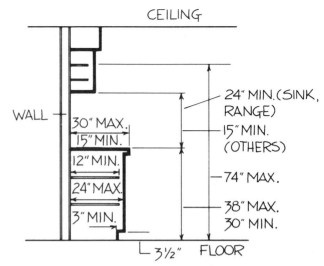

Figure 2.10 Kitchen cabinet dimensions.

Figure 2.10 shows maximum and minimum cabinet dimensions. Countertops are routinely 33 in. above the finish floor, and upper cabinets at least 16 to 18 in. above that to allow you to operate appliances freely. Standard depths are 24 in. for the base cabinet and 12 in. for the top cabinet.

If you are having cabinets custom-made, cabinet height is optimally 3 in. below the elbow of the primary user. If that person is unusually tall or unusually short, though, a single counter of that height may suffice. Counters where mixing will be done should also be somewhat lower, so a bowl's contents can be mixed comfortably with a long-handled spoon.

Note: If you are unusually tall or short, cabinets closely tailored to your own dimensions could discourage future buyers, should you want to sell the house.

Bathrooms

If your renovation is extensive, locate bathrooms early. Those people with sizable budgets may prefer a bath for each bedroom, while many others will be content with a centrally located room accessible to all rooms. Where the bathroom is well trafficked, a half-bath off the master bedroom, with a lav and a toilet (or a bidet), might serve adults well. There should also be at least one half-bath downstairs, for guests, the cook, the weekend gardener, and so on.

Once you have an idea of the fixtures you'd like, list the activities that are secondary but related to normal bathroom use. Note the fixtures and spatial requirements of each. Some activities are reading, exercising, tub sharing, tanning, tending plants, laundering, and watching TV.

How much space do you need? Most distances cited in illustrations are minimal; if you have more space, by all means, use it. The minimum distance to an adjacent fixture is the "fixture line" indicated in Figure 12.21.

In addition to raw floor space, the number of wet walls in a bathroom is an important consideration. Keep in mind that where branch vents rise from individual fixtures, vent pipes (usually 2 in.) must rise in the walls behind, often joining with a soil stack in the horizontal spaces between

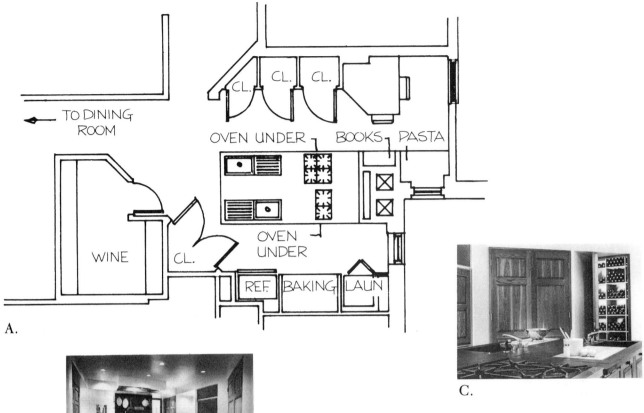

A.

B.

C.

D.

E.

Figure 2.11 A *kitchen portfolio*. (A) Floor plan of a kitchen for two people who are both gourmet cooks: an island allows both to work at the same time without being in each other's way. (B) A 2-in.-thick cleft slate is the island's top, as well as the wall covering behind the array of copper pots. (C) Each side of the island has its own sink, cutting board, and commercial cooktop. Just off the kitchen is a wine vault. (D) The kitchen is compact because the space beneath the counter is used so well: the solid cherry cabinets house, among other things, an electric oven on each side and many drawers. (E) Pull-out storage.

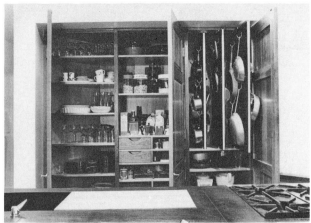

F.

F.

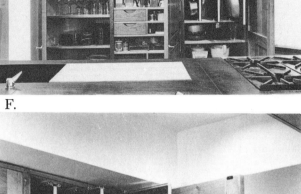

F.

G.

Figure 2.11 (Continued) (F) The generous storage areas are the cabinetmaker's tour de force. Closed, the cabinet doors form a warm red wall of wood with Mediterranean details. (G) Off to the sides are baking and pasta alcoves with marble counters. (Matthew Kaplan, architect; Peter Dechar, cabinetmaker; Clayton Wilson Construction, contractors; all of Brooklyn, New York.)

ceiling joists. Whenever possible, position the fixtures so vent and waste pipes run between joists. Otherwise, you'll have to cut holes in each joist a pipe crosses.

Two-wall setups seem to be a reasonable balance between economical fixture placing and layout flexibility. The five-fixture layout allows bathroom use from two directions without sacrificing essential privacy.

The vertical dimensions of fixtures and accessories should reflect your height. Shower heads set 80 in. high will satisfy even very tall people; the tops of shower curtains and other enclosures should be 10 to 12 in. above the shower head. The *tops* of mirrors should be about 6 ft above the floor; shorter users may be accommodated by long vertical mirrors. Again, counter heights are variable; although 30 in. is standard, 36 in. is comfortable for most people. For children, build a sturdy step-up platform to the lav, one that can easily be pushed underneath the lav.

Note: When you plan your bathroom, consider its maintenance as well. Waste pipes and water-supply pipes for lav and toilet are usually accessible, but those for a tub often are not. A removable panel in the tub's head wall is a wise idea.

Figure 2.12 A futuristic group from the Hastings II Bagno collection.

A.

B.

Figure 2.13 A nondescript attic in a California country house transformed into an airy bathroom off a master bedroom. (Paul Mrozinski, architect, Salinas, California. Photos by Philip Mrozinski.)

Figure 2.14 Barn timbers and boards, Mexican terra-cotta tiles, and a salvaged tub in Connecticut. (Mike Greenberg, designer.)

TWO HOUSES

In this last section, we'll look at two renovations which end well—they don't always. Even the happy endings can take more time, money, and stamina than you ever dreamed possible; that, you hear over and over again. But if you want it badly enough, somehow it happens. To better understand the daily drama, frustrations, and compromises of building, read Tracy Kidder's excellent *House*.

To understand some of the conflicts in our case histories, here's a skeletal outline of what happens—or should happen—during a renovation. As you peruse it, keep in mind that many steps are concomitant and not a few are ongoing.

A Sequence of Renovation

1. Planning. Make wish lists, rough sketches, and exploratories; hold initial discussions with contractors and architects; obtain preliminary financing; get ballpark estimates.

2. Obtain permits. If you will be living in the house while working on it, obtain the necessary permits, including a temporary certificate of occupancy (C.O.).

3. Plan. Make preliminary lists of materials, meet with architects, contractors, and other specialists.

4. Clean up. Clean out debris and add rough weatherproofing to gaping holes.

5. Secure the building, which will allow you to store materials and, if necessary, live there.

6. Install temporary amenities such as electrical field receptacles, chemical toilets; hook up temporary utilities.

7. Do major structural work in the basement.

   a. Masonry. Repair major damage and flaws that can cause the building to shift or move. Eliminate water problems that might threaten the structure.

   b. Wooden underpinning. Replace or reset posts, columns, girders, and joists that have deteriorated.

8. Demolish walls, ceilings, and floors; remove debris as it accumulates.

9. Frame structural carpentry: alter load-bearing walls, joists, collar ties, and similar items.

10. Attend to the roof as soon as possible. (This step is placed here only because changes in the structure can affect a finished roof.)

11. Do weatherproofing and exterior work. Like roofing, this task can be delayed if it is minor; otherwise, do it now.

12. Erect interior partitions and curtain walls not framed earlier. Prepare openings for the next step.

13. Rough out heating, plumbing, gas, and electrical systems (no fixtures yet).

14. Hang wall and ceiling surfaces, for example, drywall.

15. Install underlayment for finish floors; apply tile floors now.

16. Set plumbing fixtures and radiators for baseboard heat; wire electrical receptacles, and so on.

17. Finish taping drywall.

18. Install cabinetwork.

19. Paint and wallpaper (some renovators prefer to do this after the trim is in place).

20. Replace and repair trim around windows, doors.

21. Finish floors. Remove marks from traffic earlier in the renovation sequence, as well as splattered paint and debris.

22. Complete miscellaneous carpentry, such as installing baseboard trim, hanging interior doors, and installing outlet plates, hardware, and floor registers.

The order in which you complete tasks also depends on the coordination of subcontractors. In many renovations, the roof needs replacement, hence its early position in the list; only a small percentage of houses require major structural work.

The Cookes

Elizabeth and James Cooke found an early nineteenth-century farmhouse; they liked the house and bought it. It was extremely large for a north-country house of its era, having nearly 3600 sq ft on three floors. The house had an excellent southern exposure, nice views, several outbuildings, and a reasonable price. Much of the original trim and most of the original doors and windows remained, so that, although the Cookes weren't interested in a period restoration, they could achieve a renovation compatible with the early spirit of the house. During their first two years in the house, they renovated the first floor, removing a wall to make a large living-dining room; put in a new kitchen; refinished the floors and replaced walls and ceilings; and repaired the hundred and one little things that are wrong with old houses.

They gave too little thought to the structure. To be sure, they knew the floors slanted toward the center of the building; but that was part of its charm. Charm begat horror, however, when they realized that the foundation was shifting, with a concomitant cracking of new finish surfaces. Their next task—which should have been the first—was to bolster the old foundation by pouring new walls within the old and, in spots, replacing entire sections. They considered jacking up the house to make all the floors level, but that would have destroyed the work they had already done on the first floor.

Figure 2.15 A north-country farmhouse.

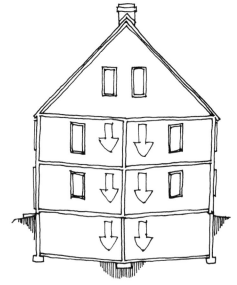

Figure 2.16 A faulty foundation and structural settling.

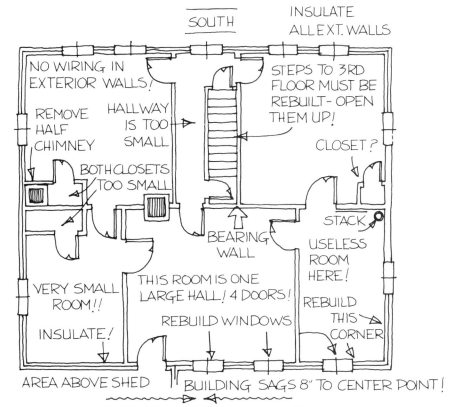

Figure 2.17 Initial reactions to the old layout.

At the point where we join the Cookes, the new foundation is in place and, because they are expecting a new baby, they have hired a local contractor to renovate the second floor and the attic.

Planning the changes. Having lived in the house for two years, the Cookes had definite opinions about what worked and what didn't. They began their renovation of the upper floors with a list:

1. Insulate all exterior walls and cut drafts, particulary around the windows. The upstairs is too hot in the summer.

2. Investigate skylights in the front rooms, because they face south.

3. Put in a new furnace and heating system, probably hot-water baseboard. Add a bathroom. Extend the electrical systems beyond the few outlets that presently exist.

4. The space upstairs doesn't work; rearrange it somehow. The rooms are too small. There are too many doors; you have to go through rooms to get to the hall. Let's shoot for a master bedroom suite and move the boys upstairs to the attic.

4. There are almost no closets!

6. Rework the floors; repair or replace the stairs to the

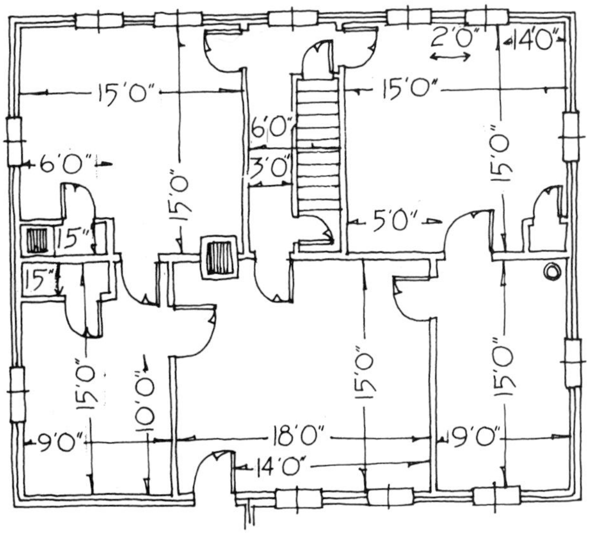

Figure 2.18. Rough measurements of the second floor.

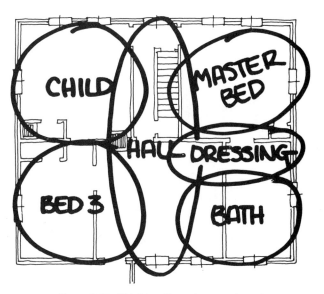

Figure 2.19 Thinking through a new layout.

A.

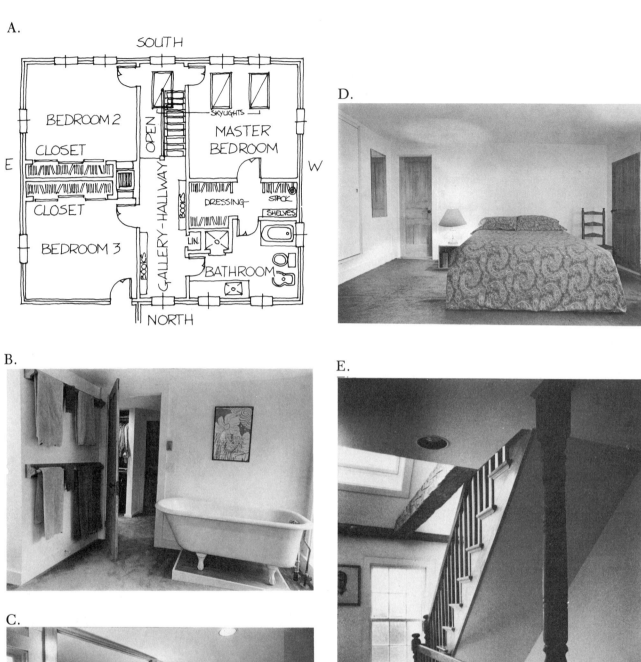

D.

B.

C.

E.

Figure 2.20 The *Cooke house*. (A) The final sketch, second floor. (B) Looking from the bathroom into the walk-in closets between bath and master bedroom. Despite the distortion of the wide-angle camera lens, the room slopes downward from right to left; the shower stall is just out of sight on the left. (C) Looking from the tub toward the hallway. (D) In another bedroom, where the slope of the floors was most pronounced. (E) In the hallway, the builder replaced a bearing wall with a salvaged porch post, thus allowing an open flight of stairs to the attic.

F.

G.

H.

Figure 2.20 (Continued) (F) Across the hall from the master bedroom, the baby's room. (G) Diagram of the finished job; side view. (H) Master bedroom, looking south. (R. Lear Design)

third floor; paint and patch all over. Is there something we can do about the windows? They're beauties but in bad shape.

7. Schedule this work while the kids are at camp, and see if we can grab a few weeks' vacation ourselves. Tell the contractor that the work *must* be done by mid-May, because Liz's mother is coming to stay then.

Enter the contractor. It was the first time that Rich Lear, the designer-contractor, had been in the house. As Elizabeth and James walked through the second-floor rooms pointing out items on their list, full of enthusiasm for the changes to come, Lear was in a funk about the settlement of the house. The floors didn't merely tilt; in the back bedroom they dropped 8 in. from the outside wall to the hall doorway. Lear considered leveling the floors, but that would mean losing 8 in. of room height. The ceiling was 6 ft 9 in., James 6 ft 3 in.; no good. Other solutions were even more farfetched. To still his panic of the moment, Lear took out a mechanical pencil and started sketching, noting the trouble areas and, on a separate sheet, the dimensions of the existing rooms.

Through several subsequent meetings, the Cookes and Lear refined plans for the work to come. A master bedroom-bathroom suite would dominate the second floor, running the entire western length of the house. Across the hall from the master bedroom would be the new baby's room, that room would be the least affected by the proposed changes. In the back, opposite the bathroom, the room with the 6-ft-9-in. ceiling became an enlarged third bedroom, with easy access to the bath. Some walls would have to go. Fortunately, 8 × 8 hand-hewn beams spanned the building; therefore, only the walls that ran perpendicularly to the beams would be load-bearing walls. The only load-bearing point to be disturbed would be the wall in the hallway; there, the new stairs would have an open railing. To improve the flow of traffic and provide space for books and paintings, the hall would run the width of the house.

Except for the waste pipes in the bathroom, the mechanical systems were unlikely to be a problem. The old oil-fired boiler in the basement would be replaced and an extension of the hot-water radiation system to the upper floors could be hooked up when the new furnace arrived. Electrical wires could easily be hidden behind baseboard molding. The waste pipes in the bathroom promised to be a problem, however; those serving fixtures in the middle of the room would have to cross through 8 × 8 beams in the floor to get to the existing soil stack. (Since there was a bathroom immediately below the proposed new one, it made little sense to relocate the stack itself.) Unsure what he would find when he exposed the carrying beams, Rich Lear sketched several bathroom layouts.

It all worked out. Other than the uncertainty about the plumbing, which was resolved by putting the toilet on the same wall as the existing stack, things went smoothly. Most of the supplies were milled new, although the stairway had several recycled elements: 30 ft of hardwood railing and three nicely turned newel posts came from an elegant old home ''down country.'' They were also able to strip all the existing doors. The renovation took a four-man crew about 4 weeks to complete.

The Smiths

The second story takes place a continent away and a decade later in the San Francisco Bay area. Dave and Andrea Smith

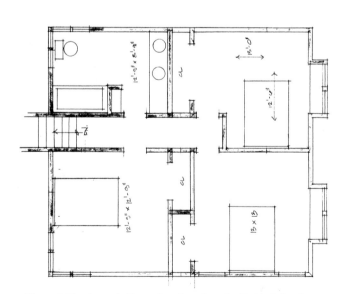

Figure 2.21 An early floor plan, based on the Smiths' sketch: narrow hallway, bedrooms largely the same size.

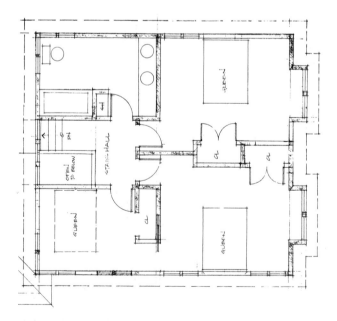

Figure 2.22 A second scheme: a hallway with light and sense of entry, rooms with more character, closets between the two largest bedrooms.

had been looking for a house for more than a year in a white-hot market, with prices escalating 20 to 25 percent annually. Finally, after looking at scores of houses they didn't bother to bid on, they found one with real promise. It was high anxiety from the start: within the next 24 hours there were four more competing offers and the house hadn't even been listed. But somehow they got it.

If it had taken a long time to find a house, it wasn't because the Smiths were indecisive, not at all. They had very definite opinions about what they wanted, and about what they liked in this house. For starters, it had an old-world charm that was tough to pigeonhole into an architectural style. Built in the 1920s, it had the casement windows of a French country house, the overhangs of the Prairie School, the hip roofs of a Viennese town house—yet it all worked together. The interior space flowed well from room to room. Living areas had mostly southern exposure, so there was lots of natural light. And across the street was a pocket park with redwoods, live oak, and bay laurel that you could smell in the morning.

They were equally decisive about what to change. Knowing that they'd have to move out in 6 months when

construction began in earnest, they nevertheless moved in so that they could get to know the house. The bedrooms, it was clear from the start, were an architectural afterthought: too few, too small, and too dark. (Had the bedrooms been bigger, they would not have undertaken a major renovation.) Where they would put additional bedrooms was a problem, but it was soon apparent that they would have to build up: nice as the yard was, there would be little left if they extended out. They also wanted a study isolated from the rest of the house, a bigger family room, and a stairway that looked as if it had always been there. Above all, they wanted an addition that didn't look like one.

Thus when their architect, Gary Parsons, asked them to sketch the space they envisioned in the addition, Dave and Andrea had already given it a lot of thought. He also asked them to measure the storage space they had in their previous quarters so that closets, drawers, and counters to come would be adequate. The more they talked and doodled, their wants became clearer and the rooms took shape (see Figures 2.21 to 2.23).

At the second-floor landing, the architect suggested a

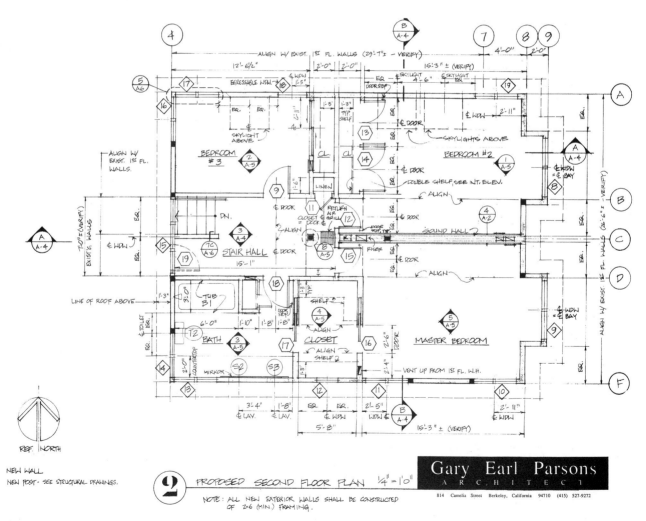

Figure 2.23 The final plan. The east wall moved out 4 ft, the bathroom now next to the conjugal bedroom, the closets moved so that the long wall could be further insulated to deaden sound.

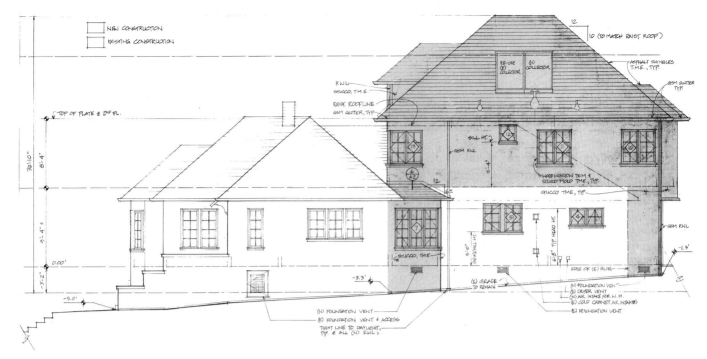

Figure 2.24 Elevation, south face. Shaded areas are new construction.

dormer with clerestory windows so that there would be more light and a sense of arrival. The bedrooms, all the same size initially, developed some personality. The closets moved onto the long wall between the big bedrooms—and moved off again when the Smiths worried about noise (which led, indirectly, to replacing some ABS drains with cast iron, so they'd be quieter). The bath and a southerly bedroom swapped places so that the bath was now next to the master bedroom. To make it more cheerful, the largest bedroom on the north got a skylight. The back end of the house moved out 4 feet. Downstairs, changes percolated too. A lightwell disappeared. Pocket doors with glass lights now graced the sunroom. And the kitchen sprouted a breakfast nook. For all of the spirited disagreements, it was a good match between clients who got involved and an architect who listened. The design phase went smoothly, then came construction.

Whoever said ''building is just like life, only more so'' must have renovated a house. The inherent conflict between designing a house and building it affordably is continually exacerbated by the unexpected revelations of renovation: the asbestos the inspector doesn't see, the dry rot in the deck, the foundation that costs twice what you expected, the retaining wall that has to come out so that the crane can get up the driveway, the 3-month delay which looms large in the middle of the building season unless you can placate a neighbor unhappy about the height of the addition. Happily, the Smiths had a general contractor who knew his subs and a project superintendent who was a wizard at solving problems. Once a week the client, the architect, and the project super sat down to make decisions.

Admittedly, the Smith's budget got trashed. ''If there's one piece of advice I'd give,'' Dave said much later,

A.

B.

Figure 2.25 *The Smith house.* (A) Parallel roof slopes of the original house and the addition, west face. (B) Southeast corner, addition in foreground.

C.

D.

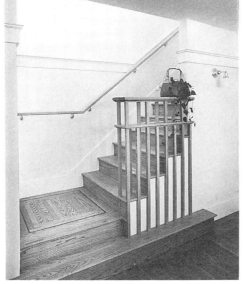

E.

F.

Figure 2.25 (Continued) (C) Master bedroom under construction. (D) Master bathroom, second floor. (E) Landing, first floor. (F) Dining room. Gary Parsons, architect; Blake Gilmore, general contractor; John Coveney, job supervisor; Thomas MacNair, senior carpenter, Martine Zabaleta, stairs.

''it's get numbers from a contractor as early as possible. Get the whole thing drawn up completely and send it out to bid. If you have been living in a dream world, you need a dose of reality. Fast.''

But it's a great house. Hidden from view, the massive hip rafters fit so perfectly that you couldn't slip a match-book into their joints. The stairs are masterful. The second floor landing never fails to delight you. The afternoon sun in the bedrooms is limpid and restful. If there's any poetry in your soul, you'd feel it here. Early in the new year, not long after moving in, Andrea gave birth to their first child, a healthy girl.

·3·

TOOLS

Assembling a complete list of renovation tools is a daunting—if not impossible—task, because jobs are always unpredictable. And even if experts could divine every last detail, they'd disagree on how to execute them. The following list, then, contains most of the tools you'd need for an extensive renovation. For those of us who are tool-crazy, it is broken down further into tools to buy and tools to rent. If you don't see a tool pictured here, look for it in a pertinent chapter.

TOOL SAFETY

Few things will halt the progress of a job more than an injury, to say nothing of pain and expense. While tools should not be feared, they must be respected: all the cutting, drilling, and bashing they can do on building materials, they can do much easier on human tissue. The following suggestions were gathered from people who use tools for a living; please read and follow them.

Essential Safety Rules

1. **Keep the work area clean.** It's a nicer place to work and much more productive.

    a. Clean up as you go. This is especially true during demolition.

    b. Pull nails from boards at once. It is the odd piece

of material or the unexpected descent from a ladder that causes most minor injuries.

    c. Clean up at the end of every day. It doesn't take long, you'll lose fewer tools, you can start right to work the following morning, and it's safer.

2. **Wear safety gear:**

    a. Hearing protection when you work with power tools: you'll be less fatigued and will avoid permanent ear damage.

    b. Safety glasses are a must for most tasks, especially those involving power tools or hammering anything.

    c. A hard hat whenever you are working above shoulder height or when someone is working above you.

    d. A mask where it's dusty, around airborne fibers, or around noxious fumes; use a respirator mask with changeable filters.

3. **Always cut the power**—and check electrical outlets with a voltage tester—to areas that you may cut into or otherwise disturb. Keep in mind that there may be wires and pipes behind those finish surfaces.

4. **Take time** to think things through. With the tools and materials you'll need at hand, the job will be smoother and safer. Regular breaks are a good idea.

5. **Never work when you are excessively tired,** preoccupied, or taking any substance that might impair your judgment.

Figure 3.1 Safety aids. *Clockwise, from upper left:* sound protectors, knee pads, work gloves, face shield, goggles and tempered safety glasses, respirator with replaceable filters.

6. Never remove safety devices from a tool; they are there for a reason. Never use a tool whose electrical wires are frayed, cut, or otherwise exposed. And *never* use power tools in wet conditions.

7. Never work alone on a steep roof or a tall ladder without having someone close by. They don't have to be working with you, just within earshot if you need help.

8. Always read instructions before using tools.

9. Never force a tool. Chisels can slip and cut you; saws can burn out or kick back; drills with a lot of torque can sprain your wrist. If you've got to force them to make them cut, they probably need sharpening. For this reason, carbide-tipped blades or bits are well worth the money.

10. See what you're doing. If you must cut power to a room, run an extension cord and a drop light.

11. Stretch before you start. Take 5 minutes to warm up and you may miss a lot of aches and strains—especially important if you don't physically labor for a living.

12. Miscellany. As you work, you'll notice other things that require care. If you've got kids, lock up power tools, dangerous solvents, and the like. Avoid baggy clothes or dangling jewelry when using power tools. Never hand-hold small pieces you are trying to cut.

In short, safety rules are just a keen eye and common sense.

LADDERS AND SCAFFOLDING

We'll consider scaffolding and ladders first because both are important to the safety and productivity of most jobs. Whether for drywall, plaster, painting, siding, or starting the important first rows of roofing—the pros rent scaffolding.

Ladders

Don't scrimp when you buy a ladder. Although most professionals prefer wood, the occasional builder will be well served by heavy-duty aluminum ladders—they're lighter.

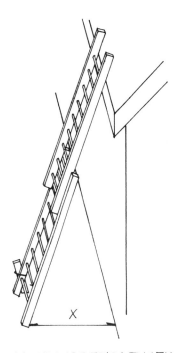

X = ¼ OF LADDER'S LENGTH

Figure 3.2 Safe placement of a ladder.

If you choose wood, avoid "household" grades; for a little extra you can own a construction grade rated for 225 lb working weight or greater. Buy a 6- or 8-ft stepladder and a 20-ft extension ladder.

Any ladder must be solidly footed to be safe; this is especially true of extension ladders. After setting up the ladder so that its sides are as plumb as possible, stand on the bottom rungs to seat the feet. Extendable feet are available for leveling ladders on slight slopes. You can also buy ladder stand-offs, which hold the upper end of the ladder away from the first course of roofing or from eave trim.

Any ladder leaning against a building should be set away from it one-quarter of the ladder's extended length. That length, by the way, is something less than the length of both sections: they should overlap about a quarter. If you're at all unsure about the ladder's footing, stake its bottom to forestall "creeping." As you work, always keep your hips within the ladder sides.

Scaffolding

In its most basic form, scaffolding is a couple of 2-in. planks spanning the distance between two sawhorses. Even the simplest setup, however, takes some thought:

1. All supports must be solidly footed; to make sure they are, check them every morning before you start.

2. Planks should be without twists or major cracks; typically, they are cleated together so that they flex in unison.

3. Plank-ends must not overhang more than 1 ft beyond supports, lest a worker step beyond those supports and fall.

4. Ideally, planks should be level.

5. Per OSHA, all platforms 10 ft or higher must have guardrails, midrails, and toeboards.

Pipe-frame scaffolding. Pipe scaffolding is far too expensive for most of us to buy, but considering the increased productivity of working from a safe, freestanding platform, it is a bargain to rent. Rent scaffold planks, too: typically, 2×3s on-edge, strapped together in sections 2-ft wide.

Where resting on a level surface such as a subfloor, pipe-frame scaffolding can easily be assembled by one person. Each stage consists of two rectangular end frames and diagonal braces secured with wing nuts or self-locking cleats. Once the first stage is assembled, adjust the self-leveling feet until the platform is level. To raise successive stages, simply stack end frames over coupling sleeves and lock the pieces in place with uplift and cotter pins. Additional lock arms may join the bracing. Platforms should be planked their entire width, either with 2× lumber or with metal planks provided by the rental company. Before you mount the platform, always lock the roller locks; it's dangerous to try to move an unlocked scaffold while atop it. Always use the guardrails. If your platform is 10 ft or higher, most codes also require midrails and toeboards as well.

If you are working outside, have the rental company put up the scaffolding and take it down when you're done—it's the first-class way to go. Exterior scaffolding is harder to set up because footing on uneven ground is problematic and units must be attached to the building every 20 ft or so. Installation won't add much to the cost of the rental, you'll be sure of a safe setup, and because scaffolding companies have their own insurance, you reduce your liability.

Figure 3.4 Pump jack.

Pump jacks. Pump jacks are perhaps the most widely used scaffolding for exterior work. New, they can be adjusted easily and require a minimum of rigging. But for the reasons cited below, we cannot recommend their use for inexperienced builders or for people working alone. The heart of the jack is a pair of spring-loaded clamps that work in tandem, alternately binding or sliding as a user raises or lowers scaffolding along a post. As the user raises the platform by stepping down on the upper clamp, the lower clamp digs into the post. To lower the rig, the user releases pressure on the lower clamp with his heel, while easing down the upper clamp with a crank on the backside of the jack.

The operation begins by sliding the jack onto a post, which is then plumbed and secured to the building. For the uninitiated or the single-handed, that's the beginning of the fun. The post, a 4×4 or two 2×4s nailed together, is unwieldy, as it must be as long as the job is high. Raising it is an onerous task, as is footing it so that it won't sink into your lawn, as is plumbing it, as is nailing or bolting it to the otherwise unpunctured siding or trim of your house.

The jack mechanism is designed successfully to raise one's ire. These gizmos probably work fine when new, but once they have seen a few seasons of rain and rust, they invariably bind, which can produce eye-popping freefalls of a foot or more or blind rage when, 20 ft in the air, the

Figure 3.3 Scaffolding with diagonal bracing and safety railings.

jack refuses to go up or down. Consequently, most rental pump jacks have been hammered silly for their failings.

Out in the field, not one pump jack setup in 10 is safe. To forestall sway, the posts should be diagonally braced, which usually interferes with the movement of the jacks. And as critically important as guardrails are, they are rarely used and frequently unavailable. Granted, these problems are not the manufacturer's fault; but where the issue is your safety, we'll pass on pump jacks.

Brackets and ladder jacks. Brackets can be used successfully on sides of houses gutted for renovation, preferably stripped to sheathing and studs. Otherwise, you'd damage siding to attach them. To support wall brackets safely, through-bolt them to 2×4s spanning the interior edges of studs. Somewhat less strong is lagbolting them to studs or other structural members; nailing alone is insufficient to withstand lateral strains.

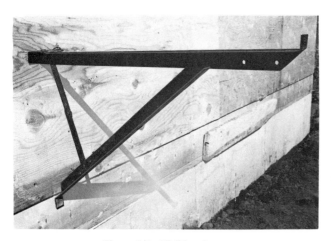

Figure 3.5 Wall bracket.

Ladder-jacks are a relatively inexpensive, quickly adjustable setup which can be safe if both ladders are well footed. Jacks brackets pivot so that you can hang the scaffolding over or under the ladder. Avoid platform heights higher than 6 or 8 ft, however.

TOOLS TO OWN

In addition to the ladders mentioned earlier, you should buy:

Safety Equipment. Safety equipment includes a face shield, goggles, or safety-tempered glasses, hearing protectors, a respirator mask with replaceable filters, heavy gloves, and a hard hat. Combination face shield and hearing protectors are also available.

First-Aid Kit. Keep one on the job site.

Tool Bags or Boxes. These are necessary to keep you organized, keep tools from getting underfoot, and aid transport from job to job. Bags should be heavy canvas with leather handles; Goldblatt makes nice ones.

Clean-Up Tools. These tools include a household broom, a push broom, a dustpan, a heavy-duty rubber garbage can, and a flat shovel for scooping debris. A large-capacity Sears wet-dry vacuum is a boon to cleanup: excellent product, good service. A wheelbarrow is very handy but not imperative.

Tarps. Tarps are absolutely necessary: at least one 9 ft × 12 ft tarp and one 45 in. × 12 ft runner. Buy good-quality, heavy canvas duck; cheap tarps will let paint soak through

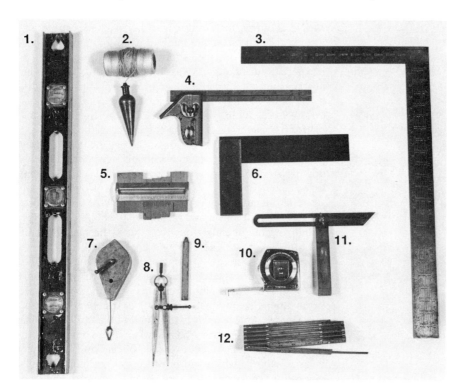

Figure 3.6 Layout tools. 1, Level; 2, plumb bob and string; 3, framing square; 4, combination square; 5, profile gauge; 6, try square; 7, chalk line; 8, divider; 9, lumber pencil; 10, retractable tape measure; 11, adjustable bevel gauge; 12, folding rule.

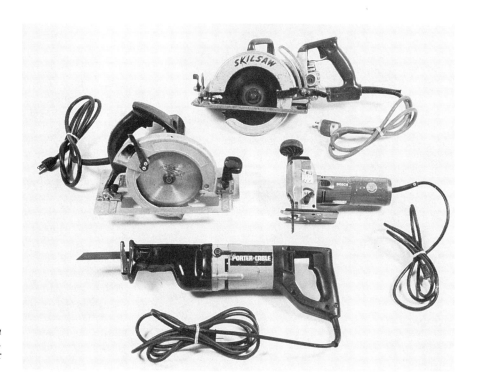

Figure 3.7 Power saws. *Clockwise, from top:* worm-drive circular saw, saber saw, reciprocal saw, "sidewinder" circular saw.

and won't contain dust as well. If you are working on finish floors, however, tarps won't protect them from dropped tools and the like. In that event, cover floors with cheap 5/16-in. particleboard.

Sawhorses. Sawhorses are indispensable to working at a comfortable height. The metal-leg variety—which nail to lengths of 2 × 4—are sturdy and easy to collapse and store. They now come with brackets that transform 2 × 4s and plywood into a first-rate worktable. Also worth mention is Black & Decker's Workmate, a folding, clamping bench that goes just about anywhere.

Measuring and Layout Tools. These tools include a 25-ft tape measure, which can span 7 ft without collapsing so that you can read across an opening; a folding rule with a sliding insert, which doubles as a depth gauge; a framing square; a combination square; and an adjustable bevel for transferring the odd angles of old houses. Levels come from 6 in. to 8 ft: a 2- or 4-ft level will be most versatile. To fit trim to irregular surfaces, a profile gauge or a scribe is needed. Also buy a plumb bob, a chalk line, and carpenter's pencils.

Power Saws. Among professional builders, worm-drive circular saws are the favorites. Unlike the more common sidewinder types, worm-drive saws spin slower and thus burn out blades less often; if you're right-handed, it is also easier to see the line you're cutting. When it comes to blades, carbide-tipped is the only way to go: they stay sharp far longer and will give you much cleaner cuts.

Reciprocating saws, indispensable to cutting in tight spaces, come in a number of designs. Milwaukee, a well-regarded brand, offers variable and two-speed models. Porter-Cable offers a choice of speeds and stroke adjustment for metal or wood cutting.

A saber saw is a handy tool for fine cuts in delicate materials; Bosch makes a great one.

A power-miter saw is a good investment if you've got a lot of finish work to do; otherwise, the cost is probably not warranted. A 10-in. power miter is best for all-round use, light enough to move easily, and very accurate. (On occasion, power miters are mistakenly called chop saws, which look similar but are limited to 90-degree cuts.)

A 10-in. table saw is a big-ticket item, nice to have but probably not justified unless you've got a lot of work, money, or room.

Figure 3.8 Power miter.

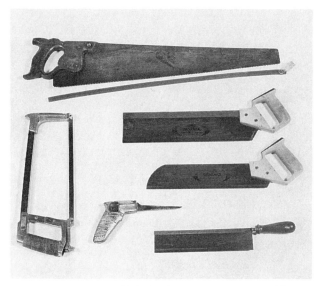

Figure 3.9 Handsaws. *Clockwise, from top:* crosscut saw with sawtooth protector, backsaw, flooring saw, dovetail saw, keyhole saw, hacksaw.

Handsaws. A number of inexpensive handsaws are nice to have on hand: a keyhole saw for starting electrical boxes in existing surfaces; an 8-pt crosscut saw; a hacksaw; a flooring saw for various tight spaces; a backsaw or dovetail saw for fine work.

Drills. For general use, a $\frac{3}{8}$- or $\frac{1}{2}$-in. reversible power drill will provide the muscle you need for most tasks. Get the standard nest of $\frac{1}{16}$- to $\frac{1}{4}$-in. drill bits, plus a 12-in. exploratory bit and a small hole-cutting set.

The *must-buy tool* for renovators is a rechargeable drill or screw gun, with Phillips-head bits to drive drywall screws. The fir or hemlock framing in old houses bends nails like crazy, and you are more likely to miss old nails if you use drywall screws. Also, drywall screws hold better than nails, by far. (Makita makes some beautiful screw guns: reversible, two-speed, quick recharge, adjustable torque, and no cord to tangle with in tight spaces.) After you've bent a few dozen nails in the hardened lumber of

old houses, you develop a new appreciation for Sheetrock screws.

Bars, Knives, and Nail Pullers (Figure 8.4). If there are a lot of nails to pull, use a cat's paw. If you're tearing out walls, use a 36-in. wrecking bar and a sledge; if reclaiming old lumber, use a sliding-handle nail puller. If you'll be disturbing siding or roofing, a shingle hook is handy. To remove trim with a minimum of damage, ease it off with putty knives, painter's pry bars, and flat bars (also called Wonder Bars or handy bars). If you're refinishing, get several sizes of scrapers. Utility knives seem part of every job. Because patching walls is so frequent, get your own taping knives, plastering trowels, and hawk.

Hammers. Get a 16- or 18-oz framing hammer that feels comfortable, a finish hammer for fine work, and a hand sledge if you'll be doing a lot of demolition or stake pounding. *Note:* Claw hammers are made to pound nails—not other hammers, wrecking bars, or cold chisels; also, their claws may be too weak for protracted nail pulling. If you're roofing, get a shingling hatchet. A hammer-tacker is a quick way to staple felt paper, insulation, sheet plastic, and the like.

Electrical and Plumbing. These specialized tools are discussed in greater length in their respective chapters, but they see a lot of general use. *Electrical* (see p. 241): a voltage tester, to make sure the power's off; slot and Phillips-head screwdrivers with insulated handles; needle-nosed and lineman's pliers, both with insulated handles; Romex cable ripper; combo wire stripper and crimper; adapter plugs; 50-ft extension cord with No. 12 wire; flashlight; electrical tape. *Plumbing* (see p. 273): a pipe cutter; large and small crescent wrenches; slip-nut pliers; a pair of pipe wrenches.

Miscellany. Miscellaneous tools include a block sander, nail sets, a center punch, Vise-Grips, a set of wood chisels in a case, a block plane, a nest of Allen wrenches, a cold chisel, a four-in-hand file (file with four textures), tin snips, a round-point shovel, an ax, and a pickax, as needed.

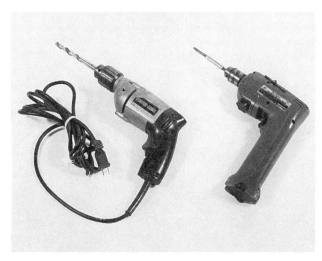

Figure 3.10 Power drill, rechargeable drill.

Figure 3.11 Hammers, from left: Asphalt-shingle hatchet, wood-shingle hatchet, finish hammer, framing hammer, hammer tacker (stapler).

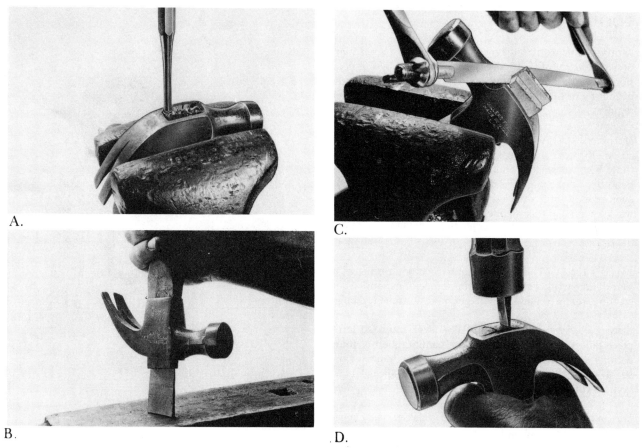

Figure 3.12 Replacing a hammer head. (A) Secure the hammer head in a vise and drive out the remnants of the old handle. (B) Add new wooden wedges as shown. (C) Use a hacksaw to cut off the excess handle and wedge. Do not use a wood saw or you'll ruin the blade. (D) Drive the metal wedges flush to finish the job. (Work courtesy of John Kruse.)

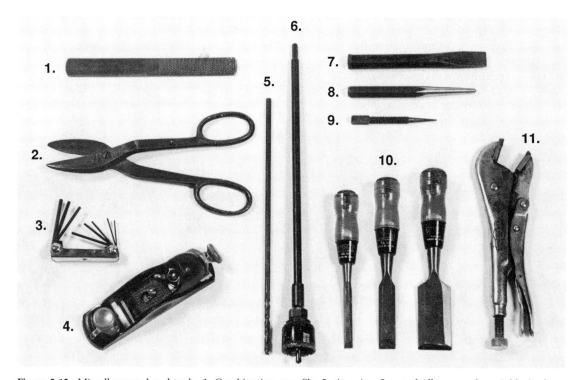

Figure 3.13 Miscellaneous hand tools. 1, Combination rasp-file; 2, tin snips; 3, set of Allen wrenches; 4, block plane; 5, exploratory bit; 6, long bit with hole saw; 7, cold chisel, 8, center punch; 9, nail set; 10, wood chisels; 11 Vise Grips.

TOOLS TO RENT

A professional contractor may want to own the tools mentioned below, but their cost is not warranted by the occasional user. In addition to the scaffolding mentioned at the beginning of this section, rent the following items as need requires.

Dumpster. Always get the largest size available, usually 20 cu yd. If, however, you're demolishing masonry, order a "low boy," a smaller unit specially built for the load. A good tip: Be set to go the day the dumpster arrives. Don't even order it until you're well into the tear-out, say, a half-week's work. In this manner you won't keep it any longer than you need it, and it'll less likely be filled by neighbors' debris.

Builder's Level. When you've got to level long runs, as in foundation work, additions, dropped ceilings, and wainscotting, rent a 6-ft level. You'll get more accurate readings.

Cement Breaker and Compressor. Whenever you need to replace defective cement, change the configuration of foundations, get down to soil level to put in new drainage, and so on—rent this tool. Note that it takes a special high-volume compressor to run it.

Pneumatic Nailers and Staplers. These tools can really speed up the job when nailing framing, sheathing, roofing, shingling, and so on. Guns are powered by air hoses running to a compressor, and calibrated by a pressure adjustment on the gun. If nails aren't going deep enough, increase the pressure. Have the rental company explain their safe use. In general, don't use pneumatic tools for finish carpentry or hanging drywall, where you often need a light touch.

Impact Drill. Also known as a Rotohammer, this tool can drill holes in concrete. When you're installing anchor bolts in foundations or threading rod to tie sections together, use a $\frac{5}{8}$-in. carbide-tipped bit. For smaller holes, say for anchoring strapping over masonry, try $\frac{1}{4}$- or $\frac{5}{16}$-in. bits.

Figure 3.15 Router.

Radial Arm Saw. These saws are very handy for framing, especially rafter framing, but they are generally not accurate enough for finish work; for that, use a power miter or a table saw. Contractors will want a 12-in. carbide crosscut blade; for owner-builders, a 10-in. model should do.

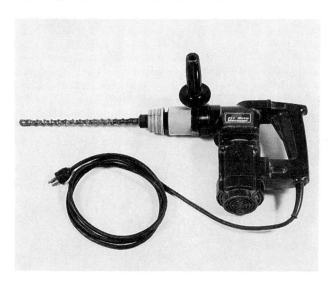

Figure 3.14 Roto-hammer or impact drill.

Figure 3.16 Right-angle drill.

Router. Routers are not that expensive, but they are very dangerous: because this high-rpm tool is typically used at eye level, **safety glasses or goggles are imperative.** Routers are indispensable when trimming laminate on a counter; use a carbide-tipped laminate-trimmer bit. Otherwise, the normal renovator doesn't need a router much; hence, rent.

Right-Angle Drill. This heavy drill with a right-angle attachment is very useful when roughing out plumbing and electrical lines. When drilling through framing, use a double-spiral bit, which clears wood better; or a hole-cutting bit, where bigger holes are required. This tool will save you from burning out your regular drill, which just doesn't have the power required. Whenever you use this tool, wear goggles and watch out for nails. A variation of the right-angle drive, the Milwaukee Hole Hawg, has even slower speeds, lower torque, and more power. Because the space between framing members is always tight, these tools are godsends, but you rarely need them for more than a half-day at a time.

Soil Tamper. Use it before you pour a concrete slab, lay a brick walk, and so on.

Powder-Actuated Tools. **Potentially very dangerous** but useful when setting plates to concrete. Always ask for specific instructions and follow them closely; ask for a demonstration as well. Some local governments prohibit renting these tools to nonprofessionals. Wear safety glasses and ear plugs.

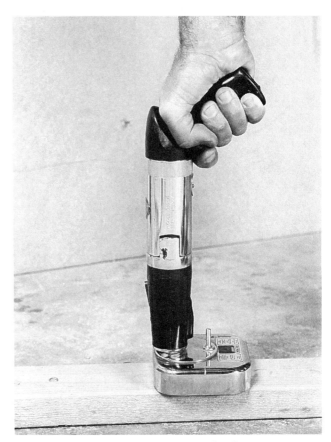

Figure 3.17 Powder-actuated nail gun.

·4·

BUILDING MATERIALS

Of the many building materials available, wood is by far the most commonly used for residential construction; it is strong, economical, and easily worked. Since wood construction is most often a lumber frame sheathed with sheet materials, this chapter's major headings are Lumber, Sheet Materials, and Connectors; the use of these materials is also the subject of Chapter 8. Probably the best advice we can give about building supplies is to get down to a lumberyard and see what's available.

LUMBER

Wood is a superb building material, both strong and elastic. Whether as a tree or as lumber, it is able to withstand great loads and resilient enough to regain its shape when pressures are removed. Because wood is so useful, it has many names according to its sources, sizes, uses, and so on. The general term *stock* will apply to any building material in its unworked form, as it comes from the lumberyard or mill.

Lumber, Boards, and Timber

Almost all construction lumber is softwood, from conifers, which don't drop their leaves in the fall. Hardwoods are largely deciduous trees (which do drop their leaves) such as maple, oak, and walnut; other hardwoods come from tropical varieties. The distinction between hardwood and softwood is usually helpful, but it is occasionally confusing because some hardwoods, such as basswood, are much softer than such hardwoods as southern yellow pine.

Lumber, *boards*, and *timber* are terms for softwood and are often used indiscriminately. If you want to be understood in the lumberyard, note the following distinctions:

Boards. 1 to $1\frac{1}{2}$ in. thick (nominal size), used as trim, sheathing, and subflooring. (*Strapping*, or *furring strips*, are usually boards less than 2 in. wide.) Generally, boards are graded by appearance.

Lumber. 2 to 4 in. thick (nominal size) and wider than 2 in. Also called *dimension lumber*. In this group is most of the construction lumber used for framing. In most cases, lumber is graded by its strength.

Timber. Minimum dimension is 5 in., graded according to strength.

If you need a catch-all term for the three above, *lumber* is probably the most serviceable, for it encompasses the largest group. *Yard lumber* is a classification used to describe most residential lumber; *factory and shop lumber* is lumber that is milled into window casings, trim, and so on.

Units of Measure: Lineal Feet, Square Feet, and Board Feet

The price of long thin pieces of wood such as molding or furring strips is determined solely by their length, or *lineal feet*. Sheet materials such as plywood and composite board

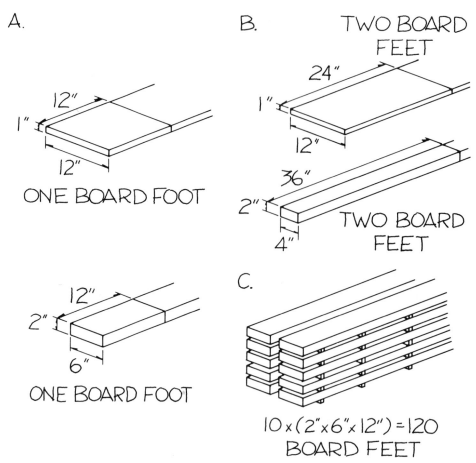

Figure 4.1 Measuring board feet.

are sold by *square feet*, which is length times width; thickness affects price, but it is not computed directly. Roofing and siding materials are often sold in *squares* of 100 sq ft. Most yard lumber is sold by *board feet*, according to the formula

$$\frac{\text{width (in.)} \times \text{thickness (in.)} \times \text{length (ft)}}{12}$$

Calculating Board Feet

In the two examples below, each board contains 1 bd ft:

$$\frac{12 \text{ in.} \times 1 \text{ in.} \times 1 \text{ ft}}{12} = 1 \text{ bd ft}$$

$$\frac{6 \text{ in.} \times 2 \text{ in.} \times 1 \text{ ft}}{12} = 1 \text{ bd ft}$$

In each of the following two examples, the dimensions given yield 2 bd ft:

$$\frac{12 \text{ in.} \times 1 \text{ in.} \times 2 \text{ ft}}{12} = 2 \text{ bd ft}$$

$$\frac{2 \text{ in.} \times 4 \text{ in.} \times 3 \text{ ft}}{12} = 2 \text{ bd ft}$$

When calculating the total board feet of a number of pieces, that number becomes a multiplier in the numerator of your

fraction. Thus, for 10 pieces 2 in. × 6 in. × 12 ft, we get

$$\frac{2 \text{ in.} \times 6 \text{ in.} \times 12 \text{ ft} \times 10}{12} = 120 \text{ bd ft}$$

Lumber Sizes

The manner in which logs are transformed into lumber determines the final size and moisture content of the wood. In a simple mill, lumber is rough cut and allowed to air dry for a period of 4 to 6 months. Because rough-cut lumber is not milled further, its surface is somewhat rough. Depending on the accuracy of the sawyer, rough-cut size may vary slightly: the *nominal size* of, say, a 2 × 4 is a full 2 in. by 4 in.

Most lumber available today, however, is rough cut, then run through a thickness planer (for uniform thickness, called *dressing*) and then kiln dried. At each stage, lumber size decreases. Thus, when you order a 2 × 4 (nominal size), you receive a $1\frac{1}{2} \times 3\frac{1}{2}$ (*actual size*); you pay for the nominal size. There is an intermediate green size between dressing and drying, which is larger than the actual size to allow for shrinkage. Table 4.1 gives nominal and actual sizes for commonly used yard lumber.

Kiln drying is important. When logs arrive at the mill, they have a moisture content of 30 to 55 percent and are thus quite green. If lumber were used green, it would shrink as it dried, which would wreak havoc with finish

TABLE 4.1

Nominal and actual sizes of softwoods (in.)

Nominal	Actual
1 × 2	$\frac{3}{4} \times 1\frac{1}{2}$
1 × 4	$\frac{3}{4} \times 3\frac{1}{2}$
1 × 6	$\frac{3}{4} \times 5\frac{1}{2}$
1 × 8	$\frac{3}{4} \times 7\frac{1}{4}$
1 × 10	$\frac{3}{4} \times 9\frac{1}{4}$
1 × 12	$\frac{3}{4} \times 11\frac{1}{4}$
2 × 4	$1\frac{1}{2} \times 3\frac{1}{2}$
2 × 6	$1\frac{1}{2} \times 5\frac{1}{2}$
2 × 8	$1\frac{1}{2} \times 7\frac{1}{2}$
2 × 10	$1\frac{1}{2} \times 9\frac{1}{2}$
2 × 12	$1\frac{1}{2} \times 11\frac{1}{2}$

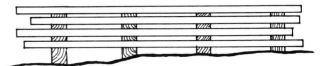

Figure 4.2 "Sticker" lumber to prevent warpage while drying.

surfaces and create great gaps around window and door casings. The ideal moisture content for construction lumber is 19 percent (15 to 19 percent is acceptable); wood much drier than that will absorb moisture and swell. Kiln drying is the most common method of reducing moisture, although air drying is effective and uses less energy. Air drying takes time, however, 4 to 6 months under optimum conditions. Also, air-dried wood must be evenly "stickered" or it will warp. (By the way, you should never assume that lumber is straight or cut square across the end. Always check by eyeballing the length of the board and by holding a framing square against both ends.)

Another way to size wood, especially hardwood and select finished woods, is by the quarter inch: $\frac{2}{4}, \frac{3}{4}, \frac{4}{4}, \frac{4}{5}, \frac{6}{4},$ and so on. The nominal–actual difference is present here, too: if you need an actual size of $\frac{5}{4}$ select fir for stair treads, you had better specify that to the supplier—you will probably pay for $\frac{6}{4}$ (nominal size) fir.

Dressed and Treated Lumber

Some of the notations used to describe the dressing of wood may baffle new builders. D2S means "dressed two sides"; D4S means "dressed four sides." Also common on lumberyard price lists are RW (random width) and RL (random length).

The *length* of lumber, by the way, is little affected by the dressing and seasoning of the wood, since nominal length and actual length are virtually the same. Lumber is sold in lengths up to 24 ft—in increments of 2 ft (8 ft, 10 ft, 12 ft, and so on)—although pieces longer than 16 ft are expensive and may have to be specially ordered. (It's cheaper to shorten the spans of your design.)

Wood may also be marked "pressure treated." Such wood, after treatment, may be left exposed to weather, used near the foundation, or otherwise subjected to moisture, insects, or extremes of climate. Pressure treating is the most effective way to preserve wood: the lumber is placed in a closed container, and a preservative or fire-retardant is forced into it. Nonpressure treating involves dipping or immersing; absorption is sometimes aided by the alternate heating and cooling of the mixture. This method, however, is not as effective as pressure treating.

Lumber Categorized According to Use

Some vertical structural elements are *columns, posts,* and *studs.* Studs are usually 2 × 4s (or 2 × 6s) placed 16 in. or 24 in. on-center; they are the primary vertical elements in frame construction. Posts are the major vertical elements in a post-and-beam house; *post* is a catch-all term for vertical pieces with square cross-sections such as 4 × 4s or 6 × 6s. Columns and posts transfer weight to the foundation or to separate pads in the basement.

Girders (or *carrying timbers*), *beams,* and *joists* are primarily horizontal structural elements. Joists are dimension lumber set on edge to support flooring or ceilings. Like studs, they are regularly spaced at 16 in. or 24 in. on-center. Beams are the horizontal supports in a post-and-beam house; they are usually bigger than joists, though not necessarily longer, and are laid on edge for maximum load-bearing depth. Girders, the major horizontal elements of a house, often support walls and floors above. Like columns, they rest on part of the foundation.

Planks and *decking* are lumber at least 2 in. thick, used as flooring or roof sheathing. In post-and-beam construction, decking is often tongue-in-groove for greater rigidity; resting right on beams, such decking is both exposed ceiling and flooring above.

Rafters, bridging, and *bracing* are members placed diagonally. Rafters support the roofing and are dimension lumber. Bridging and bracing are often low-grade lumber used to keep structural elements from twisting and turning; bracing is usually associated with studs, and bridging with joists and rafters.

Grading Lumber

Wood is graded according to type (fir, hemlock, and so on), strength, imperfections, and sometimes usage. The categories of grading are quite complex; but since your lumberyard is likely to carry only a mixed stock of sizes and grades, your choice will be limited to what the yard has on hand. The span chart given in Table 4.2 will enable you to compare your needs to the supplier's stock.

The charts in Table 4.2 are reprinted courtesy of the Canadian Wood Council, whose data is approved by the American Labor Standards Committee "on the advice of the U.S. Forest Products Laboratory." Their categories of select structural, No. 1, No. 2, and No. 3 appear below. Not listed in the table are construction, standard, and utility grades; these grades are reserved mostly for the evaluation of 2 × 4 stock. I mention this because some U.S. lumberyards use the terms *construction, standard-better,* and *utility* to grade framing lumber of all sizes—construction being roughly the same grade as the Canadians' No. 1, and so on. In both grading systems, *economy* lumber is wood of poor quality for nonstructural use.

Building specialists in your area should have the final say on sizing wood for span, for they may have lumber such as southern yellow pine, which does not appear on the charts that follow. Where required by building code, hire a structural engineer to make such load–span calculations. The information that follows is quite reliable, but, by all means, supplement it with further inquiry about materials available in your region.

TABLE 4.2

The tables which follow (pages 52–57) are reprinted courtesy of the Canadian Wood Council; spans have been determined according to stress data approved by the American Lumber Standards Committee. Similar species combinations from the United States and Canada may have, in certain instances, slightly different stress values. See also the comments in "Grading Lumber," at the bottom of page 51.

Floor Joists (30 psf Live Load) (10 psf Dead Load) – Sleeping Rooms and Attic Floors
Maximum Allowable Span (ft.-in.)

Species	Grade	2 × 6		2 × 8		2 × 10		2 × 12	
		Joist spacing (inches)							
		12	16	12	16	12	16	12	16
Douglas fir-larch (North)	Select structural	12-3	11-2	16-2	14-8	20-8	18-9	25-1	22-10
	No. 1/appearance	12-3	11-2	16-2	14-8	20-8	18-9	25-1	22-10
	No. 2	12-0	10-11	15-10	14-5	20-3	18-5	24-8	22-5
	No. 3	10-4	9-0	13-8	11-10	17-5	15-1	21-2	18-4
Hem-fir (North)	Select structural	11-7	10-6	15-3	13-10	19-5	17-8	23-7	21-6
	No. 1/appearance	11-7	10-6	15-3	13-10	19-5	17-8	23-7	21-6
	No. 2	11-3	10-2	14-11	13-5	19-0	17-2	23-1	20-10
	No. 3	9-1	7-10	11-11	10-4	15-3	13-2	18-6	16-0
Eastern hemlock-tamarack (North)	Select structural	11-0	10-0	14-6	13-2	18-6	16-10	22-6	20-6
	No. 1/appearance	11-0	10-0	14-6	13-2	18-6	16-10	22-6	20-6
	No. 2	10-5	9-6	13-9	12-6	17-6	15-11	21-4	19-4
	No. 3	9-7	8-3	12-7	10-11	16-1	13-11	19-7	16-11
Spruce-pine-fir	Select structural	11-7	10-6	15-3	13-10	19-5	17-8	23-7	21-6
	No. 1/appearance	11-7	10-6	15-3	13-10	19-5	17-8	23-7	21-6
	No. 2	11-0	9-9	14-6	12-10	18-6	16-4	22-6	19-11
	No. 3	8-6	7-4	11-3	9-9	14-4	12-5	17-5	15-1
Western hemlock (North)	Select structural	11-10	10-9	15-7	14-2	19-10	18-0	24-2	21-11
	No. 1/appearance	11-10	10-9	15-7	14-2	19-10	18-0	24-2	21-11
	No. 2	11-3	10-3	14-11	13-6	19-0	17-3	23-1	21-0
	No. 3	9-9	8-5	12-10	11-1	16-4	14-2	19-11	17-3
Coast sitka spruce	Select structural	12-0	10-11	15-10	14-5	20-3	18-5	24-8	22-5
	No. 1/appearance	12-0	10-10	15-10	14-4	20-3	18-3	24-8	22-3
	No. 2	11-6	10-0	15-2	13-2	19-4	16-9	23-6	20-5
	No. 3	8-8	7-6	11-6	9-11	14-8	12-8	17-9	15-5
Ponderosa pine	Select structural	10-9	9-9	14-2	12-10	18-0	16-5	21-11	19-11
	No. 1/appearance	10-9	9-9	14-2	12-10	18-0	16-5	21-11	19-11
	No. 2	10-5	9-6	13-9	12-6	17-6	15-11	21-4	19-4
	No. 3	8-6	7-4	11-3	9-9	14-4	12-5	17-5	15-1
Western cedars (North)	Select structural	10-5	9-6	13-9	12-6	17-6	15-11	21-4	19-4
	No. 1/appearance	10-5	9-6	13-9	12-6	17-6	15-11	21-4	19-4
	No. 2	10-1	9-2	13-4	12-1	17-0	15-5	20-8	18-9
	No. 3	8-8	7-6	11-6	9-11	14-8	12-8	17-9	15-5
Western white pine	Select structural	11-3	10-3	14-11	13-6	19-0	17-3	23-1	21-0
	No. 1/appearance	11-3	10-3	14-11	13-6	19-0	17-3	23-1	21-0
	No. 2	10-10	9-4	14-3	12-4	18-2	15-9	22-1	19-2
	No. 3	8-4	7-3	11-0	9-6	14-0	12-2	17-0	14-9
Red pine (North)	Select structural	11-0	10-0	14-6	13-2	18-6	16-10	22-6	20-6
	No. 1/appearance	11-0	10-0	14-6	13-2	18-6	16-10	22-6	20-6
	No. 2	10-9	9-6	14-2	12-6	18-0	15-11	21-11	19-5
	No. 3	8-4	7-3	11-0	9-6	14-0	12-2	17-0	14-9
Eastern white pine (North)	Select structural	10-9	9-9	14-2	12-10	18-0	16-5	21-11	19-11
	No. 1/appearance	10-9	9-9	14-2	12-10	18-0	16-5	21-11	19-11
	No. 2	10-5	9-6	13-9	12-6	17-6	15-11	21-4	19-4
	No. 3	8-4	7-3	11-0	9-6	14-0	12-2	17-0	14-9

Source: Adapted from *Canadian Dimension Lumber Data Book*, 4th ed., Canadian Wood Council, Ottawa, 1979.

[a]Spans have been determined according to stress data approved by the American Lumber Standards Committee. Similar species combinations from the United States and Canada may have, in certain instances, slightly different stress values.

TABLE 4.2 (Continued)

Floor Joists (40 psf Live Load) (10 psf Dead Load) – All Rooms Except Sleeping Rooms and Attic Floors
Maximum Allowable Span (ft.-in.)

Species	Grade	2 × 6		2 × 8		2 × 10		2 × 12	
		Joist spacing (inches)							
		12	16	12	16	12	16	12	16
Douglas fir-larch (North)	Select structural	11-2	10-2	14-8	13-4	18-9	17-0	22-10	20-9
	No. 1/appearance	11-2	10-2	14-8	13-4	18-9	17-0	22-10	20-9
	No. 2	10-11	9-11	14-5	13-1	18-5	16-9	22-5	20-4
	No. 3	9-3	8-0	12-2	10-7	15-7	13-6	18-11	16-5
Hem-fir (North)	Select structural	10-6	9-6	13-10	12-7	17-8	16-0	21-6	19-6
	No. 1/appearance	10-6	9-6	13-10	12-7	17-8	16-0	21-6	19-6
	No. 2	10-3	9-1	13-6	12-0	17-3	15-4	21-0	18-8
	No. 3	8-1	7-0	10-8	9-3	13-7	11-9	16-7	14-4
Eastern hemlock-tamarack (North)	Select structural	10-0	9-1	13-2	12-0	16-10	15-3	20-6	18-7
	No. 1/appearance	10-0	9-1	13-2	12-0	16-10	15-3	20-6	18-7
	No. 2	9-6	8-7	12-6	11-4	15-11	14-6	19-4	17-7
	No. 3	8-7	7-5	11-3	9-9	14-5	12-5	17-6	15-2
Spruce-pine-fir	Select structural	10-6	9-6	13-10	12-7	17-8	16-0	21-6	19-6
	No. 1/appearance	10-6	9-6	13-10	12-7	17-8	16-0	21-6	19-6
	No. 2	10-0	8-8	13-2	11-6	16-10	14-8	20-6	17-9
	No. 3	7-7	6-7	10-0	8-8	12-10	11-1	15-7	13-6
Western hemlock (North)	Select structural	10-9	9-9	14-2	12-10	18-0	16-5	21-11	19-11
	No. 1/appearance	10-9	9-9	14-2	12-10	18-0	16-5	21-11	19-11
	No. 2	10-3	9-4	13-6	12-3	17-3	15-8	21-0	19-1
	No. 3	8-8	7-6	11-6	9-11	14-8	12-8	17-9	15-5
Coast sitka spruce	Select structural	10-11	9-11	14-5	13-1	18-5	16-9	22-5	20-4
	No. 1/appearance	10-11	9-9	14-5	12-10	18-5	16-4	22-5	19-11
	No. 2	10-3	8-11	13-7	11-9	17-4	15-0	21-1	18-3
	No. 3	7-9	6-9	10-3	8-11	13-1	11-4	15-11	13-9
Ponderosa pine	Select structural	9-9	8-10	12-10	11-8	16-5	14-11	19-11	18-1
	No. 1/appearance	9-9	8-10	12-10	11-8	16-5	14-11	19-11	18-1
	No. 2	9-6	8-7	12-6	11-4	15-11	14-5	19-4	17-7
	No. 3	7-7	6-7	10-0	8-8	12-10	11-1	15-7	13-6
Western cedars (North)	Select structural	9-6	8-7	12-6	11-4	15-11	14-6	19-4	17-7
	No. 1/appearance	9-6	8-7	12-6	11-4	15-11	14-6	19-4	17-7
	No. 2	9-2	8-4	12-1	11-0	15-5	14-0	18-9	17-0
	No. 3	7-9	6-9	10-3	8-11	13-1	11-4	15-11	13-9
Western white pine	Select structural	10-3	9-4	13-6	12-3	17-3	15-8	21-0	19-1
	No. 1/appearance	10-3	9-4	13-6	12-3	17-3	15-8	21-0	19-1
	No. 2	9-8	8-4	12-9	11-0	16-3	14-1	19-9	17-1
	No. 3	7-5	6-5	9-10	8-6	12-6	10-10	15-3	13-2
Red pine (North)	Select structural	10-0	9-1	13-2	12-0	16-10	15-3	20-6	18-7
	No. 1/appearance	10-0	9-1	13-2	12-0	16-10	15-3	20-6	18-7
	No. 2	9-9	8-6	12-10	11-2	16-5	14-3	19-11	17-4
	No. 3	7-5	6-5	9-10	8-6	12-6	10-10	15-3	13-2
Eastern white pine (North)	Select structural	9-9	8-10	12-10	11-8	16-5	14-11	19-11	18-1
	No. 1/appearance	9-9	8-10	12-10	11-8	16-5	14-11	19-11	18-1
	No. 2	9-6	8-6	12-6	11-2	15-11	14-3	19-4	17-4
	No. 3	7-5	6-5	9-10	8-6	12-6	10-10	15-3	13-2

Source: Adapted from *Canadian Dimension Lumber Data Book*, 4th ed., Canadian Wood Council, Ottawa, 1979.

TABLE 4.2 (Continued)

Ceiling Joists – Drywall Ceiling (20 psf Live Load) (10 psf Dead Load) – No Future Sleeping Rooms but Limited Storage Available Maximum Allowable Span (ft.-in.)

Species	Grade	2 × 4		2 × 6		2 × 8		2 × 10	
		Joist spacing (inches)							
		12	16	12	16	12	16	12	16
Douglas fir-larch (North)	Select structural	10-3	9-4	16-1	14-7	21-2	19-3	27-1	24-7
	No. 1/appearance	10-3	9-4	16-1	14-7	21-2	19-3	27-1	24-7
	No. 2	10-0	9-1	15-7	13-6	20-7	17-10	26-3	22-9
	No. 3	7-11	6-10	11-11	10-4	15-9	13-8	20-1	17-5
Hem-fir (North)	Select structural	9-8	8-9	15-2	13-9	19-11	18-1	25-5	23-1
	No. 1/appearance	9-8	8-9	15-1	13-1	19-10	17-2	25-4	21-11
	No. 2	9-5	8-2	13-7	11-9	17-11	15-6	22-10	19-10
	No. 3	6-11	6-0	10-5	9-1	13-9	11-11	17-7	15-3
Eastern hemlock-tamarack (North)	Select structural	9-2	8-4	14-5	13-1	19-0	17-3	24-3	22-1
	No. 1/appearance	9-2	8-4	14-5	13-1	19-0	17-3	24-3	22-1
	No. 2	8-8	7-11	13-8	12-4	18-0	16-3	22-11	20-8
	No. 3	7-5	6-5	11-0	9-7	14-7	12-7	18-7	16-1
Spruce-pine-fir	Select structural	9-8	8-9	15-2	13-6	19-11	17-10	25-5	22-9
	No. 1/appearance	9-8	8-5	14-2	12-4	18-9	16-3	23-11	20-8
	No. 2	8-10	7-8	13-0	11-3	17-1	14-10	21-10	18-11
	No. 3	6-8	5-9	9-10	8-6	12-11	11-3	16-6	14-4
Western hemlock (North)	Select structural	9-10	8-11	15-6	14-1	20-5	18-6	26-0	23-8
	No. 1/appearance	9-10	8-11	15-6	14-0	20-5	18-5	26-0	23-6
	No. 2	9-5	8-7	14-6	12-7	19-1	16-7	24-5	21-1
	No. 3	7-5	6-5	11-3	9-9	14-10	12-10	18-11	16-4
Coast sitka spruce	Select structural	10-0	9-1	15-9	13-9	20-10	18-2	26-6	23-2
	No. 1/appearance	9-11	8-7	14-6	12-7	19-1	16-7	24-5	21-1
	No. 2	9-0	7-10	13-3	11-6	17-6	15-2	22-4	19-4
	No. 3	6-9	5-10	10-0	8-8	13-3	11-6	16-11	14-8
Ponderosa pine	Select structural	8-11	8-1	14-1	12-9	18-6	16-10	23-8	21-6
	No. 1/appearance	8-11	8-1	14-1	12-4	18-6	16-3	23-8	20-8
	No. 2	8-8	7-8	12-10	11-1	16-10	14-7	21-6	18-8
	No. 3	6-6	5-8	9-10	8-6	12-11	11-3	16-6	14-4
Western white pine	Select structural	9-5	8-7	14-9	12-10	19-6	16-10	24-10	21-6
	No. 1/appearance	9-5	8-2	13-11	12-0	18-4	15-10	23-5	20-3
	No. 2	8-5	7-4	12-6	10-10	16-5	14-3	21-0	18-2
	No. 3	6-5	5-6	9-7	8-4	12-8	11-0	16-2	14-0
Western cedars (North)	Select structural	8-8	7-11	13-8	12-5	18-0	16-4	22-11	20-10
	No. 1/appearance	8-8	7-11	13-8	12-5	18-0	16-4	22-11	20-10
	No. 2	8-5	7-8	13-0	11-3	17-1	14-10	21-10	18-11
	No. 3	6-8	5-9	10-0	8-8	13-3	11-6	16-11	14-8
Red pine (North)	Select structural	9-2	8-4	14-5	13-1	19-0	17-2	24-3	21-11
	No. 1/appearance	9-2	8-4	13-11	12-0	18-4	15-10	23-5	20-3
	No. 2	8-8	7-6	12-8	10-11	16-8	14-5	21-3	18-5
	No. 3	6-6	5-8	9-7	8-4	12-8	11-0	16-2	14-0
Eastern white pine (North)	Select structural	8-11	8-1	14-1	12-9	18-6	16-10	23-8	21-6
	No. 1/appearance	8-11	8-1	13-11	12-0	18-4	15-10	23-5	20-3
	No. 2	8-8	7-6	12-8	10-11	16-8	14-5	21-3	18-5
	No. 3	6-5	5-6	9-7	8-4	12-8	11-0	16-2	14-0

Source: Adapted from *Canadian Dimension Lumber Data Book*, 4th ed., Canadian Wood Council, Ottawa, 1979.

TABLE 4.2 (Continued)

Rafters – Any Slope with Drywall Ceiling (30 psf Live Load) (15 psf Dead Load)
Maximum Allowable Span (ft.-in.)

Species	Grade	2 × 6		2 × 8		2 × 10		2 × 12	
		Joist spacing (inches)							
		12	16	12	16	12	16	12	16
Douglas fir-larch (North)	Select structural	14-1	12-9	18-6	16-10	23-8	21-6	28-9	26-1
	No. 1/appearance	14-1	12-9	18-6	16-10	23-8	21-6	28-9	26-1
	No. 2	13-8	11-10	18-0	15-7	23-0	19-11	27-11	24-3
	No. 3	10-6	9-1	13-10	11-11	17-7	15-3	21-5	18-6
Hem-fir (North)	Select structural	13-3	12-0	17-5	15-10	22-3	20-2	27-1	24-7
	No. 1/appearance	13-2	11-5	17-5	15-1	22-2	19-3	27-0	23-4
	No. 2	11-11	10-4	15-8	13-7	20-0	17-4	24-4	21-1
	No. 3	9-2	7-11	12-1	10-5	15-5	13-4	18-9	16-3
Eastern hemlock-tamarack (North)	Select structural	12-7	11-5	16-7	15-1	21-2	19-3	25-9	23-5
	No. 1/appearance	12-7	11-5	16-7	15-1	21-2	19-3	25-9	23-5
	No. 2	11-11	10-9	15-9	14-2	20-1	18-1	24-5	22-0
	No. 3	9-8	8-4	12-9	11-0	16-3	14-1	19-9	17-1
Spruce-pine-fir	Select structural	13-3	11-10	17-5	15-7	22-3	19-11	27-1	24-3
	No. 1/appearance	12-5	10-9	16-5	14-2	20-11	18-1	25-5	22-0
	No. 2	11-4	9-10	15-0	12-11	19-1	16-6	23-3	20-1
	No. 3	8-7	7-5	11-4	9-10	14-6	12-6	17-7	15-3
Western hemlock (North)	Select structural	13-6	12-3	17-10	16-2	22-9	20-8	27-8	25-1
	No. 1/appearance	13-6	12-3	17-10	16-2	22-9	20-7	27-8	25-0
	No. 2	12-8	11-0	16-9	14-6	21-4	18-6	25-11	22-6
	No. 3	9-10	8-6	12-11	11-3	16-6	14-4	20-1	17-5
Coast sitka spruce	Select structural	13-9	12-0	18-2	15-10	23-2	20-3	28-2	24-8
	No. 1/appearance	12-8	11-0	16-9	14-6	21-4	18-6	25-11	22-6
	No. 2	11-8	10-1	15-4	13-3	19-7	16-11	23-9	20-7
	No. 3	8-10	7-7	11-7	10-0	14-9	12-10	18-0	15-7
Ponderosa pine	Select structural	12-3	11-2	16-2	14-8	20-8	18-9	25-1	22-10
	No. 1/appearance	12-3	10-9	16-2	14-2	20-8	18-1	25-1	22-0
	No. 2	11-2	9-8	14-9	12-10	18-10	16-4	22-11	19-10
	No. 3	8-7	7-5	11-4	9-10	14-6	12-6	17-7	15-3
Western cedars (North)	Select structural	11-11	10-10	15-9	14-3	20-1	18-3	24-5	22-2
	No. 1/appearance	11-11	10-10	15-9	14-3	20-1	18-3	24-5	22-2
	No. 2	11-4	9-10	15-0	12-11	19-1	16-6	23-3	20-1
	No. 3	8-10	7-7	11-7	10-0	14-9	12-10	18-0	15-7
Western white pine	Select structural	12-11	11-2	17-0	14-9	21-9	18-10	26-5	22-11
	No. 1/appearance	12-2	10-7	16-1	13-11	20-6	17-9	24-11	21-7
	No. 2	10-11	9-5	14-5	12-6	18-4	15-11	22-4	19-4
	No. 3	8-5	7-3	11-1	9-7	14-2	12-3	17-3	14-11
Red pine (North)	Select structural	12-7	11-5	16-7	15-1	21-2	19-3	25-9	23-4
	No. 1/appearance	12-2	10-7	16-1	13-11	20-6	17-9	24-11	21-7
	No. 2	11-1	9-7	14-7	12-8	18-7	16-1	22-8	19-7
	No. 3	8-5	7-3	11-1	9-7	14-2	12-3	17-3	14-11
Eastern white pine (North)	Select structural	12-3	11-2	16-2	14-8	20-8	18-9	25-1	22-10
	No. 1/appearance	12-2	10-7	16-1	13-11	20-6	17-9	24-11	21-7
	No. 2	11-1	9-7	14-7	12-8	18-7	16-1	22-8	19-7
	No. 3	8-5	7-3	11-1	9-7	14-2	12-3	17-3	14-11

Source: Adapted from *Canadian Dimension Lumber Data Book*, 4th ed., Canadian Wood Council, Ottawa, 1979.

TABLE 4.2 (Continued)

Rafters – Low Slope (3 in 12 or less) with No Finished Ceiling (30 psf Live Load) (10 psf Dead Load)
Maximum Allowable Span (ft.-in.)

Species	Grade	2 × 6		2 × 8		2 × 10		2 × 12	
		Joist spacing (inches)							
		12	16	12	16	12	16	12	16
Douglas fir-larch (North)	Select structural	14-1	12-9	18-6	16-10	23-8	21-6	28-9	26-1
	No. 1/appearance	14-1	12-9	18-6	16-10	23-8	21-6	28-9	26-1
	No. 2	13-9	12-6	18-2	16-6	23-2	21-1	28-2	25-7
	No. 3	11-1	9-7	14-8	12-8	18-8	16-2	22-8	19-8
Hem-fir (North)	Select structural	13-3	12-0	17-5	15-10	22-3	20-2	27-1	24-7
	No. 1/appearance	13-3	12-0	17-5	15-10	22-3	20-2	27-1	24-7
	No. 2	12-8	10-11	16-8	14-5	21-3	18-5	25-10	22-4
	No. 3	9-8	8-5	12-10	11-1	16-4	14-2	19-10	17-2
Eastern hemlock-tamarack (North)	Select structural	12-7	11-5	16-7	15-1	21-2	19-3	25-9	23-5
	No. 1/appearance	12-7	11-5	16-7	15-1	21-2	19-3	25-9	23-5
	No. 2	11-11	10-10	15-9	14-3	20-1	18-3	24-5	22-2
	No. 3	10-3	8-11	13-6	11-8	17-3	14-11	21-0	18-2
Spruce-pine-fir	Select structural	13-3	12-0	17-5	15-10	22-3	20-2	27-1	24-7
	No. 1/appearance	13-2	11-5	17-5	15-1	22-2	19-3	27-0	23-4
	No. 2	12-0	10-5	15-10	13-9	20-3	17-6	24-8	21-4
	No. 3	9-2	7-11	12-0	10-5	15-4	13-4	18-8	16-2
Western hemlock (North)	Select structural	13-6	12-3	17-10	16-2	22-9	20-8	27-8	25-1
	No. 1/appearance	13-6	12-3	17-10	16-2	22-9	20-8	27-8	25-1
	No. 2	12-11	11-8	17-0	15-4	21-9	19-7	26-5	23-10
	No. 3	10-5	9-0	13-9	11-11	17-6	15-2	21-4	18-6
Coast sitka spruce	Select structural	13-9	12-6	18-2	16-6	23-2	21-1	28-2	25-7
	No. 1/appearance	13-6	11-8	17-9	15-4	22-8	19-7	27-6	23-10
	No. 2	12-4	10-8	16-3	14-1	20-9	18-0	25-3	21-10
	No. 3	9-4	8-1	12-4	10-8	15-8	13-7	19-1	16-6
Ponderosa pine	Select structural	12-3	11-2	16-2	14-8	20-8	18-9	25-1	22-10
	No. 1/appearance	12-3	11-2	16-2	14-8	20-8	18-9	25-1	22-10
	No. 2	11-11	10-4	15-8	13-7	20-0	17-4	24-4	21-1
	No. 3	9-2	7-11	12-0	10-5	15-4	13-4	18-8	16-2
Western cedars (North)	Select structural	11-11	10-10	15-9	14-3	20-1	18-3	24-5	22-2
	No. 1/appearance	11-11	10-10	15-9	14-3	20-1	18-3	24-5	22-2
	No. 2	11-7	10-5	15-3	13-9	19-5	17-6	23-7	21-4
	No. 3	9-4	8-1	12-4	10-8	15-8	13-7	19-1	16-6
Western white pine	Select structural	12-11	11-9	17-0	15-6	21-9	19-9	26-5	24-0
	No. 1/appearance	12-11	11-2	17-0	14-9	21-9	18-10	26-5	22-10
	No. 2	11-7	10-0	15-3	13-3	19-6	16-10	23-8	20-6
	No. 3	8-11	7-9	11-9	10-2	15-0	13-0	18-3	15-10
Red pine (North)	Select structural	12-7	11-5	16-7	15-1	21-2	19-3	25-9	23-5
	No. 1/appearance	12-7	11-2	16-7	14-9	21-2	18-10	25-9	22-10
	No. 2	11-9	10-2	15-6	13-5	19-9	17-1	24-0	20-9
	No. 3	8-11	7-9	11-9	10-2	15-0	13-0	18-3	15-10
Eastern white pine (North)	Select structural	12-3	11-2	16-2	14-8	20-8	18-9	25-1	22-10
	No. 1/appearance	12-3	11-2	16-2	14-8	20-8	18-9	25-1	22-10
	No. 2	11-9	10-2	15-6	13-5	19-9	17-1	24-0	20-9
	No. 3	8-11	7-9	11-9	10-2	15-0	13-0	18-3	15-10

Source: Adapted from *Canadian Dimension Lumber Data Book*, 4th ed., Canadian Wood Council, Ottawa, 1979.

TABLE 4.2 (Continued)

Rafters – High Slope (over 3 in 12) with No Finished Ceiling (30 psf Live Load) (7 psf Dead Load – Light Roofing)
Maximum Allowable Span (ft.-in.)

Species	Grade	2 × 4		2 × 6		2 × 8		2 × 10	
		Joist spacing (inches)							
		12	16	12	16	12	16	12	16
Douglas fir-larch (North)	Select structural	9-10	8-11	15-6	14-1	20-5	18-6	26-0	23-8
	No. 1/appearance	9-10	8-11	15-6	14-1	20-5	18-6	26-0	23-8
	No. 2	9-8	8-9	15-1	13-1	19-10	17-2	25-4	21-11
	No. 3	7-8	6-8	11-6	10-0	15-3	13-2	19-5	16-10
Hem-fir (North)	Select structural	9-3	8-5	14-7	13-3	19-2	17-5	24-6	22-3
	No. 1/appearance	9-3	8-5	14-7	12-7	19-2	16-7	24-6	21-2
	No. 2	9-1	7-10	13-2	11-4	17-4	15-0	22-1	19-1
	No. 3	6-8	5-9	10-1	8-9	13-4	11-6	17-0	14-8
	Construction	7-8	6-8						
Eastern hemlock-tamarack (North)	Select structural	8-10	8-0	13-10	12-7	18-3	16-7	23-4	21-2
	No. 1/appearance	8-10	8-0	13-10	12-7	18-3	16-7	23-4	21-2
	No. 2	8-4	7-7	13-1	11-11	17-4	15-8	22-1	20-0
	No. 3	7-2	6-2	10-8	9-3	14-1	12-2	17-11	15-6
Spruce-pine-fir	Select structural	9-3	8-5	14-7	13-1	19-2	17-2	24-6	21-11
	No. 1/appearance	9-3	8-2	13-9	11-11	18-1	15-8	23-1	20-0
	No. 2	8-7	7-5	12-6	10-10	16-6	14-3	21-1	18-3
	No. 3	6-5	5-7	9-6	8-3	12-6	10-10	16-0	13-10
Western hemlock (North)	Select structural	9-6	8-7	14-10	13-6	19-7	17-10	25-0	22-9
	No. 1/appearance	9-6	8-7	14-10	13-6	19-7	17-9	25-0	22-8
	No. 2	9-1	8-3	14-0	12-1	18-5	16-0	23-6	20-5
	No. 3	7-2	6-2	10-10	9-5	14-3	12-5	18-3	15-9
Coast sitka spruce	Select structural	9-8	8-9	15-2	13-3	20-0	17-6	25-6	22-4
	No. 1/appearance	9-7	8-4	14-0	12-1	18-5	16-0	23-6	20-5
	No. 2	8-9	7-7	12-10	11-1	16-11	14-8	21-7	18-8
	No. 3	6-7	5-8	9-8	8-5	12-9	11-1	16-4	14-1
Ponderosa pine	Select structural	8-7	7-10	13-6	12-3	17-10	16-2	22-9	20-8
	No. 1/appearance	8-7	7-10	13-6	11-11	17-10	15-8	22-9	20-0
	No. 2	8-4	7-5	12-4	10-8	16-4	14-1	20-9	18-0
	No. 3	6-4	5-5	9-6	8-3	12-6	10-10	16-0	13-10
Western cedars (North)	Select structural	8-4	7-7	13-1	11-11	17-4	15-9	22-1	20-1
	No. 1/appearance	8-4	7-7	13-1	11-11	17-4	15-9	22-1	20-1
	No. 2	8-1	7-4	12-6	10-10	16-6	14-3	21-1	18-3
	No. 3	6-5	5-7	9-8	8-5	12-9	11-1	16-4	14-1
Western white pine	Select structural	9-1	8-3	14-3	12-4	18-9	16-4	23-11	20-9
	No. 1/appearance	9-1	7-10	13-5	11-8	17-8	15-4	22-7	19-7
	No. 2	8-2	7-1	12-0	10-5	15-10	13-9	20-3	17-6
Red pine (North)	Select structural	8-10	8-0	13-10	12-7	18-3	16-7	23-4	21-2
	No. 1/appearance	8-10	8-0	13-5	11-8	17-8	15-4	22-7	19-7
	No. 2	8-4	7-3	12-2	10-7	16-1	13-11	20-6	17-9
	No. 3	6-4	5-5	9-3	8-0	12-3	10-7	15-7	13-6
Eastern white pine (North)	Select structural	8-7	7-10	13-6	12-3	17-10	16-2	22-9	20-8
	No. 1/appearance	8-7	7-10	13-5	11-8	17-8	15-4	22-7	19-7
	No. 2	8-4	7-3	12-2	10-7	16-1	13-11	20-6	17-9
	No. 3	6-2	5-4	9-3	8-0	12-3	10-7	15-7	13-6

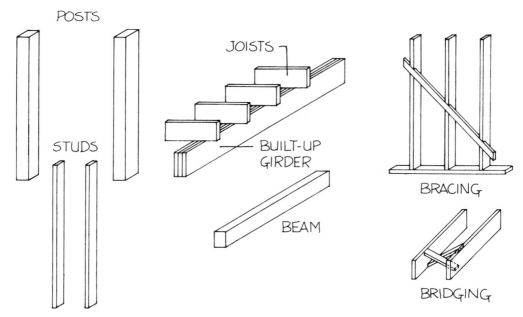

Figure 4.3 Lumber named according to use.

OTHER STRUCTURAL CHOICES

Lumber is probably the easiest of any building material to work with, and it is readily available; but codes or other factors may limit its use. Here are some other materials to consider:

Light steel framing. Light steel framing consists primarily of metal studs set into runner channels, elements of the system being joined by sheet-metal screws. It is the material recommended where fire codes are stringent. Though light-weight, the system is quite strong; it can bear approximately twice the load borne by wood-stud walls. The structural integrity of metal-stud walls, however, depends in large part on all the elements of the system being tied together by sheet materials. That is, metal studs seem almost flimsy, and migration or distortion are possible, until exterior sheathing or interior drywall, or both, are screwed on.

You may encounter some difficulty in using metal-stud walls in renovation work. First of all, they are expensive. Second, they may be incompatible with existing wood framing. Third, because of the way they gain rigidity, they may be impractical where floors are not level; metal is neither as resilient as wood nor as easily cut to make it fit to irregular surfaces. Fourth, metal can corrode in high-moisture areas. Fifth, unless a layer of rigid insulation is used on at least one side of a wall, a thermal bridge will form across the metal studs, with resultant cold spots.

Joists and beams. As spans increase, solid-wood joists and beams become considerably more expensive and, proportionate to their size, capable of bearing less. The following items are generally cost-effective for spans 14 ft or longer.

Trusses. Trusses can be fabricated from metal or wood. In addition to being strong and relatively lightweight, trusses allow the builder to channel ducts, pipes, and wiring through the open spaces, a great advantage in renovation work. In most large cities, open-web metal joists and wood trusses can be ordered through lumberyards. Using truss-plate connectors, the owner-builder can fashion wood trusses out of 2×4s; size and configuration, however, should be determined by a structural engineer. Trusses are also suitable as oversized headers over doors and windows.

Box Beams and Trus-Joists. Box beams and Trus-Joists should also be engineered, for configuration is crucial to their strength. Fabricated from junk wood, these beams are lightweight, quite strong, and cost-competitive with solid-wood lumber. There are limitations to their use, though. Cutting into them to run pipes can be a problem, and nails not centered precisely in the solid-wood flanges can cause splitting. Blocking or bridging between such joists is particularly important.

Laminated Beams. Long available for commercial use, glue-laminated beams are found increasingly in residences. "Glu-lams," as they are called, are fabricated from relatively short pieces, overlapped or finger-jointed in an appropriate manner, glued, and pressure-clamped. Glu-lams are expensive, but their stability and strength makes them better suited than solid wood in high-loading situations such as headers and clear-span beams. They are far less likely to warp, cup, or check.

Flitch Plates. Flitch plates are steel plates sandwiched between, or attached to, existing beams. Because plates are quite hard, they should be predrilled with bolt holes ($\frac{1}{4}$ in. to $\frac{1}{2}$ in. should be sufficient). Most flitch plates are $\frac{1}{8}$ in. thick. With their ability to bolster existing members, flitch plates are effective in renovation: sagging beams can be jacked up and a flitch plate bolted on. A homemade flitch of 18-gauge sheet metal adds rigidity when laminated between two joists.

Salvage Lumber. Salvage materials have striking advantages and disadvantages, the major trade-offs being time and labor versus money. Salvaging molding, flooring, and other materials from your own home is the best way to match existing materials; but used materials from other sources should be closely scrutinized. (My second book, *Salvaged Treasures*, may interest readers; see Appendix G.)

Salvaging materials from other buildings can also be worthwhile if you need materials of unusual size or appearance, such as an 8×8 hand-hewn beam or oak flooring of a particular hue. All materials should be structurally sound, however. Be sure to test with a penknife any lumber for rot or insects. Any lumber that will be used as sills or that will be exposed to moisture should be treated with a wood preservative.

Salvage materials usually aren't worth the effort if they are in small quantities or if, after removing them, you find that they will be too short. Used 2×4s, for example, usually aren't worth the trouble; by the time you yank them free from plates, remove nails, and cut off frayed ends, you have studs that are only 7 ft long. Some materials just aren't worth removing. Siding and other exterior trim is rarely worth saving, for it's probably old and weather-beaten. Barn board, in vogue years ago, is hardly charming when it is half-rotted, warped, and crawling with carpenter ants. If there is any danger of your destroying a piece of salvage by removing it, leave it alone. Parts of many beautiful old places that were restorable have been destroyed by people who didn't know what they were doing.

If you have any qualms about the structural strength of a building, stay out of it. Dismantling a building is a special skill, and inexperienced people who undertake the task can get hurt or even killed. Perhaps the best advice for would-be users of salvage is for them to buy the object from a salvage yard, where somebody has already done the dirty and dangerous work of removing the piece. If you are determined to go ahead with on-site salvage, here are a few suggestions:

1. Get a tetanus shot; wear a long-sleeved shirt and heavy pants, thick-soled shoes, goggles, gloves, and a hard hat.

2. Always cut power to affected areas. Then test outlets to make sure they're off.

3. Don't hurry. Look at the joints involved and remove pieces slowly, bit by bit.

4. As you free pieces, *remove nails immediately.* Footing on construction sites is chancey at best, and you don't want to land in a bed of nails when descending from a ladder in a hurry.

5. If the piece is at all complex, such as a mantel, photograph it and then label elements while carefully removing them.

6. Most salvage is old, dry, and highly vulnerable to rot. Get it under cover at once. Because it is so dry, it will absorb moisture and rot before you know it.

7. Before reusing wood, always check it by using a magnet to look for nails and by inserting an ice pick in suspect holes. Use a carbide-tipped blade to cut wood and *always* wear goggles when cutting salvage lumber.

SHEET MATERIALS

Plywood is a laminate of thin veneers, or plies, sliced or rotary-cut from logs. Although plies are sometimes thin, the wood fibers run continuously along their length and when cross-stacked in pressure-glued sheets, those fibers impart great structural strength. In *compositeboard,* a category that includes *particleboard* and *hardboard,* wood fiber is shredded, pulped, and pressure-molded in sheet form.

Plywood

The strength of plywood is achieved by alternating the grain of adjacent plies. The racking strength of a sheet is not perfectly uniform (it's easier to bend the sheet in the direction of its face ply grain), but almost uniform. For this reason, plywood is the favored sheet material for sheathing, subflooring, and other structural uses. Alternating the grain also avoids the problem of splitting common to solid wood as it expands and contracts. Thus interior-grade plywood is a staple in cabinetmaking. Plywood has some limitations—it will, for example, split if you try to nail or screw into its edges—but there are so many varieties to choose from that you can probably find a type to suit your purposes exactly.

Plywood customarily comes in sheets 4 ft by 8 ft; it's also available in oversized sheets of 4×9, 4×10, 5×8, 5×9, and 5×10 if you can wait a week or two for your lumber yard to special-order it. The extra foot or two allows you to sheath across the framing of two stories for *shear wall* strength, and thereby tie the framing of an addition to that of the main house. All plywood is graded according to the quality of its faces (face plies), the poorer one being considered the back face. The core of the plywood may be particleboard, solid lumber, crossbands of veneer, or some other material. Plywood also comes in sheets with solid-lumber edging, which provides an attractive edge that can take screws or be used as a finish edge. Plywood ranges in thickness from $\frac{1}{16}$ in. to more than 1 in. The more plies, the greater the strength.

Plywood is divided broadly into hardwood and softwood varieties. Hardwood is used for cabinets, furniture, and paneling, and softwood for the underlying structure. As has been noted, plywood is graded according to appearance and strength; it is also graded according to its weathering capacities—exterior or interior—with the differences depending largely on the glues used.

Softwood plywood. The two major groups of softwood plywood are interior (the glues are water resistant) and exterior (glues are waterproof). Don't use interior plywood for exterior purposes such as sheathing, for it can delaminate. Softwood plywood is further graded according to strength ("engineered" grades) and appearance ("appearance" grades).

Appearance Grades. Grade N (usually hardwood) is the best, but it must often be specially ordered. A and B grades are good (B is the inferior of the two), and both can be painted or stained to good effect. In grade C, the lowest grade that should be exposed to weather, the imperfections are plugged up, hence the designation PTS, for "plugged and touch-sanded.'' Thus when you buy CDX (C/D exterior-grade), place the C side toward the weather—or up, if you are using it as underlayment. Grade D is the lowest grade of interior plywood sheets. Appearance grades affect cost greatly.

Engineered Grades. Plywood's strength is indicated by two marks. One is a species group number (1–5). The lower the number, the stiffer and stronger the sheet. The other, which may not be present on all sheets, is a fraction indicating the maximum distance the sheet should span rafters and joists. A mark of 32/16 indicates that the sheet can be used over rafters spaced 32 in. on-center and over joists spaced 16 in. on-center.

Uses. The numbers given in Table 4.3 for subflooring and roof sheathing are variable, depending on the loads present. If you have any doubts about the maximum span, get advice for your region (e.g., the snow load); otherwise, going up $\frac{1}{8}$ in. to the next thickness is probably best.

Nailing schedules for different uses of plywood are the same: nail every 6 in. around the perimeter, not closer than $\frac{3}{8}$ in. to the edge; elsewhere, nail every 12 in. For subflooring, annular ring or spiral nails hold best; use hot-dipped galvanized nails for all exterior purposes. An 8d nail is sufficient for $\frac{1}{2}$ in. to $\frac{3}{4}$ in. plywood. For subflooring, annular ring or spiral shank nails hold best; on exteriors, 8d hot-dipped galvanized nails should be sufficient for $\frac{1}{2}$- to $\frac{3}{4}$-in. plywood.

Pneumatic nail guns are widely used to nail down plywood and they save a lot of time, but one thing a nail gun won't do is ''suck up'' a piece of plywood to framing. This is worth noting because almost all plywood is warped to a degree. So after you nail down plywood with pneumatic tools, go back over the surface and give each nail an additional shot with a 20-oz framing hammer. The hammer head, being larger than the striker of the gun, will drive the plywood down as well.

Leave a gap of $\frac{1}{16}$ in. between sheets, for expansion, more where humidity is high. For greatest strength, always run the longer length of a 4×8 sheet perpendicular to the structural members you are nailing to, and always stagger the butt ends of sheets. In the intervals between framing, support plywood edges with *blocking clips,* also called *plyclips* or *H-clips.*

If you have a special building need, describe it to your supplier. There may be a special type of plywood for your purpose. Plywood facings, in particular, are variable, ranging from textured plywood siding to sheets bonded with a hardboard finish. Marine plywood is a high-quality exterior type that has A-A to B-B faces, the best waterproof glue, and no voids in the core layers.

Hardwood plywood. Hardwood plywood comes in a great variety, classified according to species, face plies, core material, and glues. The range of uses is suggested by the many variations in thickness—from $\frac{1}{16}$-in. aircraft plywood to 2-in. door stock.

Since most hardwood plywood is used in interior settings, appearance grading is of paramount importance. Be sure to specify the grade of both faces, and check the stock carefully when it arrives to make sure it has been handled properly. Because this type of plywood is extremely expensive, sheets are often used right up to the edges; they should not be damaged or frayed in any manner. A list of hardwood grades follows.

Specialty. Specially ordered by the customer, often involving closely matched flitches, striking repetitions of grain for visual effect, and so on.

Premium (A). Grain patterns and colors are matched precisely.

Good (No. 1). Colors of matched veneers on a face do not vary greatly, but patterns are less closely matched than for premium grade.

Sound (No. 2). Although colors and patterns are not matched, there are no open flaws.

Utility (No. 3). Some small flaws, tight knotholes, discoloring, splits that can be filled; but no rot.

Backing (No. 4). Defects are allowed as long as they don't detract from the strength or use of the sheet; often the concealed face of hardwood plywood, the backing side may be a different species tree than that of the exposed face.

Compositeboard

Compositeboard products are made from wood, but the strength and form of the materials is engineered not by nature but by man. This is the fastest-growing group of building materials and is likely to become even more important, with some predicting that compositeboard will overtake solid-wood lumber. There is also some controversy about the glues used to create particleboard, particularly urea-formaldehyde, suspected of being a carcinogen. Now that it's possible to make an older house relatively airtight, you might want to know what gases you are trapping in.

There are basically two groups of compositeboard, *particleboard* and *fiberboard:* the groups are differentiated largely

TABLE 4.3

Acceptable plywood spans

Uses	Min. thickness (in.)
Subflooring[a]	
Joists 16 in. O.C.	$\frac{1}{2}$
18–20 in. O.C.	$\frac{5}{8}$
24 in. O.C.	$\frac{3}{4}$
48 in. O.C.	$1\frac{1}{8}$
Roof sheathing	
Rafters 12 in. O.C.	$\frac{5}{16}$
16 in. O.C.	$\frac{3}{8}$
24 in. O.C.	$\frac{3}{8}-\frac{1}{2}$
32 in. O.C.	$1\frac{1}{2}-\frac{5}{8}$
Wall sheathing	
Studs 16 in.	$\frac{5}{16}$ or $\frac{3}{8}$
24 in.	$\frac{1}{2}$

[a]It's opportune here to distinguish among *sheathing, subflooring,* and *underlayment.* Sheathing is the covering of the exterior of a building's frame, whether plywood or diagonally run boards. Subflooring, again either plywood or boards, goes over the joists and provides a working deck. Underlayment goes over the subflooring, making it more level for the finished floor that follows. If the subflooring is sufficiently level and strong, underlayment may not be necessary.

by the manufacturing process involved. Particleboard is manufactured by chipping or flaking wood, adding glue, and pressing the mixture into sheets. Fiberboard products are similar to those of particleboard, with the wood being pulped into a soupy texture before the glues are added and the pressure stamping done.

Although compositeboard products have been marketed successfully, their use is still controversial, largely because of inferior quality when compositeboard was introduced in the 1950s. Since then, the technology has improved greatly, and with it, product reliability. Further, because the raw materials for compositeboard are often inferior-grade wood or lumber mill wastes, their manufacture constitutes an ecologically sound use of forest resources. Still, the controversy persists. Because compositeboard isn't cross-laminated, as plywood is, it isn't as strong and hence not as appropriate for structural sheathing.

Particleboard. Particleboard is classified by size of particle and by type, strength, and density of glue used. Type I particleboard is intended for interior use, whereas type II has waterproof glue and is intended for exterior use. The two types are further divided into two classifications based on density, with class II being the stronger.

Because particleboard is of uniform consistency, it is well suited to interior uses, especially cabinet construction. It is particularly good as a base for laminates and veneers, as in cabinet doors and countertops. Because particleboard lacks the tensile strength of plywood, however, shelves made of it should be supported at closer intervals than plywood of comparable thickness. Screws hold well in particleboard faces but not well in edges. Glue solid-wood strips to edges, as you would with plywood.

Particleboard is also used structurally. It works well as an underlayment on floors. Subflooring of $\frac{5}{8}$-in. plywood with an underlayment of $\frac{5}{8}$-in. particleboard is a solid base for flooring in high-use areas. Because it decomposes when wet and lacks the strength of plywood, however, do not use particleboard as subflooring. In bathrooms, you may use type II particleboard. Type II particleboard is also touted for exterior sheathing, but that claim has not been substantiated: under sustained moisture and loading, it deteriorates and distorts somewhat.

Medium-density fiberboard. Medium-density fiberboard (MDF) is similar to particleboard in its classification and range of uses. Because MDF has no particles that can fragment during cutting, it is even more uniform, making it a favorite material for preshaped countertops and the like. Its screw-holding characteristics are about the same as those for particleboard.

Although exterior-grade MDF products are also proferred as exterior sheathing, building experts have reservations. Such MDF products as Celotex and Homosote have performed reasonably well, but questions about their racking strength are unanswered. If you decide to use these economical materials, *sheath the corners of the building with $\frac{1}{2}$-in. plywood* for greater rigidity. Of course, the butt edges of all sheet materials should be staggered and all joints backed with studs or blocking. To attach fiberboard sheathing that is $\frac{1}{2}$-in.-thick, use $1\frac{1}{2}$-in. galvanized roofing nails (large head).

Hardboard. Hardboard is a high-density fiberboard, Masonite is a familiar brand. This fiberboard, ranging in thickness from $\frac{1}{12}$ in. to $\frac{3}{8}$ in., has numerous applications—underlayment, drawer bottoms, furniture backing, and so on. Exposure to wetness causes it to deteriorate, but tempering and plastic coating extends its use; there is even hardboard siding, for example, but that product must be carefully sealed and is best not used near the ocean, for salt air seems to degrade it. In short, it is questionable for exterior use.

CONNECTORS

If wood is the universal building stock, metal is the universal connector. Nails of many types, screws, and bolts are discussed in this section, as well as specialty plates that reinforce structural members. Closing the chapter is a review of construction adhesives which, some say, are destined to supplant metal connectors.

Nails

Nails vary according to length, size of head, shape of shank, point, and composition.

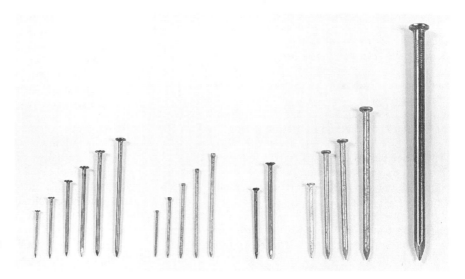

Figure 4.4 Nail types, from left: Box nails, finish, rosin-coated (hold better), common, spike.

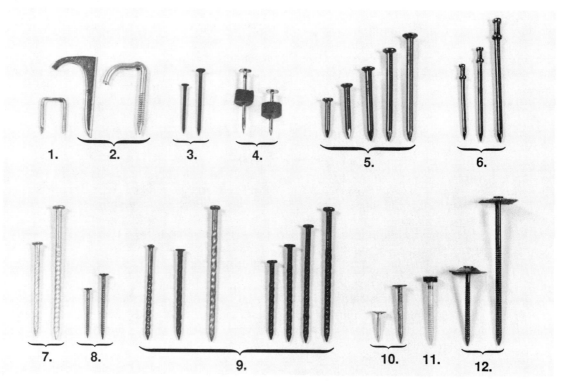

Figure 4.5 Specialty nails. 1, Romex staple; 2, pipe/conduit hold-downs; 3, drywall nails; 4, furring nails; 5, hanger nails; 6, duplex nails; 7, galvanized subflooring nails; 8, underlayment nails; 9, subflooring nails; 10, big-head roofing nails; 11, glass panel nail with rubber gasket; 12, tabbed nails to hold down felt paper.

Length. Nail length is reckoned in "d" (penny) sizes; the larger the nail, the greater the penny rating. Nails 20d or longer are called "spikes."

				Penny size (d)						
2	4	6	8	10	12	16	20	30	40	60

				Length (in.)						
1	$1\frac{1}{2}$	2	$2\frac{1}{2}$	3	$3\frac{1}{4}$	$3\frac{1}{2}$	4	$4\frac{1}{2}$	5	6

Heads. The shape of a nail's head depends on whether that nail is to be left exposed or is to be concealed. Smaller heads—such as those on casing, finish, or some kinds of flooring nails—can easily be sunk.

Shank Shapes. Nail shanks usually have straight shafts; variations impart greater holding strength. Spiral flooring nails resist popping, as do annular ring nails. Nails of shorter shank are favored for hardwoods.

Points. Nail points usually taper to a four-sided point, but there are a few variations. Blunt-point nails are less likely to split wood; you can make your own by hammering down a nail point.

Composition. Most nails are fashioned from medium-grade steel (often called "mild steel"). Nail composition will vary, however, as follows:

Material being nailed into. Masonry nails are case-hardened; so are the special nails supplied with joist hangers and other metal connectors—do not use regular nails to attach them.

Presence of other metals. Because some metals corrode when mixed, you should match nail composition to metals present. The choice of nails includes aluminum, stainless steel, brass, copper, Monel metal, and galvanized (zinc-coated).

Exposure to weather, corrosion. Neither stainless steel nor aluminum nails will stain, but the former is very expensive and the latter is brittle and somewhat tricky to nail. Galvanized nails, which are reasonably priced, will stain only a modest amount where the hammer chips the coating off the heat; hence, seal galvanized nails as soon as possible with primer. Galvanized nails are also specified when framing with redwood or treated lumber, which will corrode common nails.

Holding power. Nails that are rosin-coated, cement-coated, or hot-dipped galvanized hold better. Hot dips are particularly good for attaching exterior sheathing.

Sizing nails. Common sense dictates the size of most nails—about three times as long as the thickness of the piece being nailed down. Because most sheathing is $\frac{1}{2}$ in. thick, it should be attached with 8d nails, 6d if the sheathing is $\frac{3}{8}$ in. thick or less. The workhorse of framing is the 16d common, although 12d and even 10d nails are good bets where you have to "toenail" one member to another. Also, 10d or 12d nails should be used to nail laminate lumber: top plates, double joists, and headers (see Table 4.4). Nail points should not protrude through the second piece.

TABLE 4.4

Recommended nailing schedule (quantity and size), using common nails

Joist to sill or girder, toe nail	3–8d
Bridging to joist, toe nail each end	2–8d
Ledger strip	3–16d
	at each joist
1 in. × 6 in. subfloor or less to each joist, face nail	2–8d
Over 1 in. × 6 in. subfloor to each joist, face nail	3–8d
2 in. subfloor to joist or girder, blind and face nail	2–16d
Sole plate to joist or blocking, face nail	16d @ 16 in. O.C.
Top plate to stud, end nail	2–16d
Stud to sole plate, toe nail	4–8d
Doubled studs, face nail	16d @ 24 in. O.C.
Doubled top plates, face nail	16d @ 16 in. O.C.
Top plates, laps and intersections, face nail	2–16d
Continuous header, two pieces	16d @ 16 in. O.C.
	along each edge
Ceiling joists to plate, toe nail	3–8d
Continuous header to stud, toe nail	4–8d
Ceiling joists, laps over partitions, face nail	3–16d
Ceiling joists to parallel rafters, face nail	3–16d
Rafter to plate, toe nail	3–8d
1-in. brace to each stud and plate, face nail	2–8d
1 in. × 8 in. sheathing or less to each bearing, face nail	2–8d
Over 1 in. × 8 in. sheathing to each bearing, face nail	3–8d
Built-up corner studs	16d @ 24 in. O.C.
Built-up girders and beams	20d @ 32 in. O.C.
	along each edge

Source: J. H. Callender, ed., *Time-Saver Standards for Architectural Design Data*, 5th ed., McGraw-Hill, New York, 1974.

When nailing near the edge or the end of a piece, be cautious: splits occur. Minimize splits by staggering nails, not nailing too closely to the edge, properly sizing nails, and blunting nailheads where splits persist. Note that box nails have a slightly thinner shank than do common nails; coated box nails have great holding power. If you sprinkle soap flakes in your nail apron, you'll find that nails will go in much more easily, particularly in harder softwoods.

Staples

Use these staple sizes for these tasks:

Attaching vapor barrier, insulation—$\frac{5}{16}$ in.
Attaching screens to frames—$\frac{5}{16}$ to $\frac{3}{8}$ in.
Attaching felt paper—$\frac{1}{2}$ in. (large-head roofing nails are preferable to staples)
Attaching ceiling tiles to wooden runner—$\frac{9}{16}$ in.
Metal plaster lath—$1\frac{1}{2}$ in.

Screws and Bolts

Screws and bolts have greater holding power than nails, yet they are easily removed and reused. There is some overlap of the two groups, but screws are generally smaller and require a screwdriver for tightening. In Chapter 9 there is also an extensive section on mechanical and chemical connectors commonly used in masonry.

Screws. The materials being attached influence the choice of the screw, its composition and shape. Softwood screws are of relatively soft metal and are coarse-threaded: hardwood screws have much finer threads. Since metal is usually thinner than wood, sheet-metal screws are smaller and are self-tapping. Screw heads vary too, some matching special screwdrivers—flat, round, oval, slot, Phillips, Allen, and square finish.

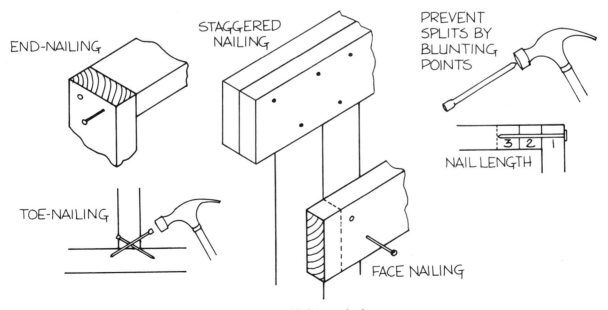

Figure 4.6 Nailing methods.

Because screws are of soft metal, it is easy to strip their slots or twist off the heads. Predrill pilot holes, particularly when screwing into hardwood, using a drill bit slightly smaller than the shank of the threaded end. (A nail whose head has been snipped off makes a passable bit.) The countersink bit shown in Figure 4.7 is useful; it allows you to drill the pilot hole and countersink the head in one operation. For optimal gripping, half to two-thirds of a screw should lodge in the base material. A little soap can be used to lubricate screw threads.

One of the most useful materials for renovators is the drywall wood screw, also called the Sheetrock screw. Because these screws are made of steel that is much stronger than that of ordinary wood screws, drywall screws are a favorite among experienced cabinetmakers and professional woodworkers. They are perfect for urban renovators, in that they eliminate hammering, a task that can be the bane of neighbors. Also, where hammering might jar existing wall membranes, drywall screws join materials gently but firmly. With a magnetic bit in your drill or screw gun, you will have one hand free to align the sheet as you attach it.

Bolts. Bolts are used to join major building elements—for example, sill plates to foundations, beams to steel plates, and studs to masonry. Their length varies greatly. Some are gargantuan bolts more than an inch in diameter and longer than two feet. Machine bolts and carriage bolts have nontapering, threaded shanks. The carriage bolt has a brief section of square shank just below its head. Lag bolts have a hex head, but the lower half of the shank tapers like a wood screw.

There are several types of specialty bolt: molly, toggle, spring, and gravity. For all types, a pilot hole must be drilled in the receiving surface. The molly bolt allows at-

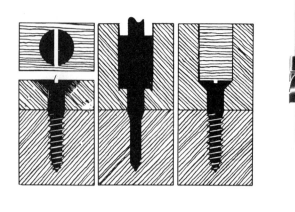

Figure 4.7 Countersink bit. (Stanley Tools)

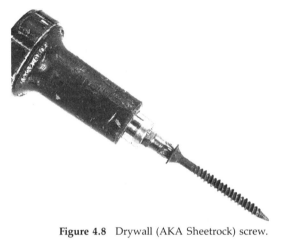

Figure 4.8 Drywall (AKA Sheetrock) screw.

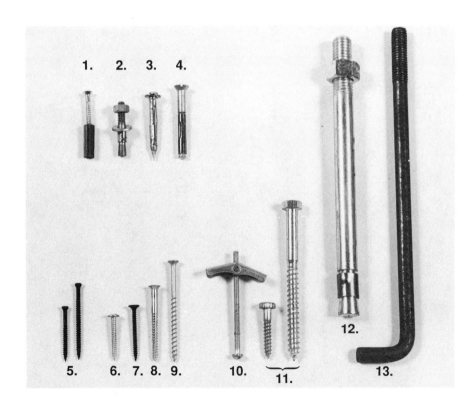

Figure 4.9 Screws and bolts. 1, Wood screw with plastic anchor; 2, wedge anchor; 3, drive anchor; 4, sleeve anchor; 5, square-drive trim screws; 6, sheet-metal screw; 7, drywall screw; 8, wood screw; 9, aluminum-coated drywall screw (can be used for exterior trim); 10, spring-loaded toggle bolt; 11, lag bolts; 12, wedge anchor; 13, anchor bolt.

tachment to thin surfaces such as drywall; the molly stays in place even when the bolt is withdrawn. Toggle bolts, both spring and gravity, allow the attachment of a great load to a hollow wall; toggles are commonly used to attach elements to cement block walls. Drill the pilot hole with a carbide-tipped masonry bit. To attach elements to solid masonry such as a concrete foundation, first drill with a carbide-tipped bit, then insert a lead shield (also called a ''sleeve''); don't overtighten the bolt, or you'll shear off its head. A similar application is a wood screw (with washer) turned into a predrilled dowel.

Metal Connectors

Metal connectors are among the most exciting, innovative building materials to be developed in the last decade:

1. They offer wood-to-wood connections superior to most traditional construction methods. Unlike toe-nailed joints, for example, metal connectors are unlikely to split lumber ends or loosen under stress. Because connectors are galvanized steel, they're strong and durable.

2. They greatly strengthen joints against earthquakes, wind, and other racking forces. They can tie rafters to walls, walls to floor platforms, and the substructure to its foundation.

3. Most can be installed on existing structures, a great boon to renovators, and in many cases metal connectors are the only way to bolster the existing structure and tie additions to the original structure in a cost-effective manner.

Note: When attaching metal connectors, use the special *case-hardened nails* supplied by manufacturers—and wear goggles when hammering them in. These nails are harder and squatter than regular nails and are less likely to shear under pressure. Regular nails may also be too long for the metal device.

Hangers. Joist hangers are familiar to most builders and are especially important when you want to add joists but aren't able to end-nail. There are hanger configurations for single joists, doubled joists, and beams.

Two tips for using joist hangers. First, cut joists full length (no more than $\frac{1}{4}$ in. shy) and install hangers once joists are in place; that is, don't nail on hangers beforehand. Too short a joist puts too much stress on the metal connectors and is likely to be springy. Second, let hangers into the underside of ceiling joists so that you don't have a raised welt in finish surfaces. Chisel joist ends before you hang them. (See page 165.)

Straps. Straps also come in myriad shapes—tees, right angles, twists, perforated plates—but they function primarily to keep joints from pulling apart. Perforated *nailing plates*, or *gang plates*, join the top plates of intersecting walls, as do *tee plates*. There are straps intended to straddle the ridge board and tie opposing rafter pairs together; and strap connectors that keep floor platforms from separating, much as shear-walling does. *Twist straps,* or *hurricane ties,* have a 90-degree twist to join rafters to top plates and thereby fight the tendency of roofs to lift during a strong cross-wind.

Hold-downs. Hold-downs are massive steel brackets that hold framing to foundations, and when used with long threaded rods, link framing on different floors. When retrofitting to a foundation, use epoxy to attach hold-down bolts to concrete, as described in Chapter 9.

Post anchors and caps. It is common practice to toe-nail deck posts to the small blocks of wood inset in the tops of pier blocks. This works well enough, but is only as strong as the block. Posts will last longer and be more securely positioned if you first nail on a *post anchor*, which is then cast in concrete. A *post cap* resembles a pair of U-brackets set at right angles to each other: one U, upside down, straddles the top of the cap, while the other, right side up, receives the beam on which the joists will sit.

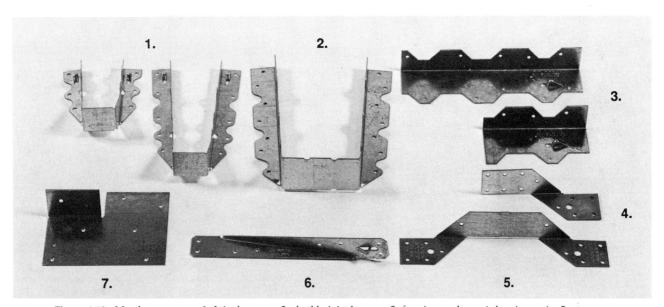

Figure 4.10 Metal connectors. 1, Joist hangers; 2, double-joist hanger; 3, framing anchors; 4 hurricane tie; 5, strap connector; 6, twist strap; 7, multiplate.

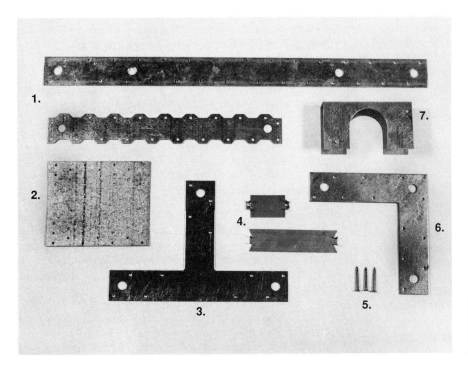

Figure 4.11 Metal connectors. 1, strap ties; 2, tie plate/gang-nail plate; 3, tee plate; 4, nail plates/nail guards; 5, hanger nails; 6, L-plate; 7, reinforcing shoe.

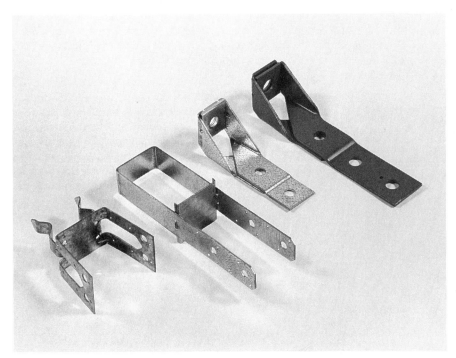

Figure 4.12 *From left:* post base, column base, hold-down, large hold-down to anchor house to foundation.

Reinforcers. In this group, we have *wall bracing*, which has all but replaced let-in 1 × 4 diagonal bracing in new construction, and for good reason. Steel bracing is far faster, requiring only a snapped chalkline and a single saw cut across the edges of the studs; and far stronger, for the steel fills the saw kerf so completely that the stud suffers no loss in compressive strength. Metal *bridging* stiffens joists nicely. And where it's unavoidable to notch stud edges to accommodate plumbing, a metal *shoe plate* reinforces the stud and protects the pipe from errant nails. Speaking of protection, this discussion would be incomplete without mentioning *nail plates*, which protect wires and pipes from stray nails when finish walls go up.

Clips. Clips are a mixed bag, functionally. *H-clips* join plywood edges to minimize flexion and obviate the need for blocking; H-clips also act as $\frac{1}{16}$-in. spacers so that roof sheathing has space to expand when it's hot. Otherwise, it would buckle. *Drywall clips* allow you to forgo some blocking behind drywall corners; it's best to use them sparingly, however. *Deck clips* are nailed to deck joists, whereupon 2 × decking is driven onto the sharpened point of the clip. In this manner, you can lay down decking without having to face-nail it; the clip also acts as a spacer so that water can run down between decking.

ADHESIVES

To choose an adhesive from the great range available, consider the materials involved and the expected demands on the adhesive chosen. Ask such questions as the following:

How strong and elastic is the adhesive?
How long will it last?
Does it resist water?
Will it degrade under sunlight?
Is it easy to apply?
How long will it take to cure, and under what temperatures?

The adhesives listed below are loosely grouped; some materials could be in several categories. The names in parentheses are representative brands.

Cabinet-maker's

Aliphatic. Aliphatic glues dry quickly and are useful when positioning parts temporarily before clamping. Under sustained directional loads, however, glued parts can shift slightly. This glue is not water resistant; it is cleaned up with warm water. (Titebond)

Epoxy. Epoxies are available in many forms, usually two-part mixtures of resins and hardeners. Because setting time is brief, press the parts together for best results. In most cases, epoxies are waterproof. Acetone is preferred as a solvent; but, in fact, epoxies are very difficult to clean up once they have hardened. (Weldwood Epoxy)

Hide. Hide glues, both liquid and flake, are organic glues that can be cleaned up with warm water. Their water resistance is low. These glues are long-time favorites of cabinetmakers. Although they must be clamped, there is no movement of parts once the glue has dried. (Franklin Hide Glue)

Hot-melt. Hot-melt glues are applied with an electric glue gun and are excellent for tacking surfaces quickly, where clamping isn't necessary. Strength and water resistance are not great, because hot glues are only applied as spots.

Polyvinyl acetate (PVA) and polyvinyl chloride (PVC). PVA and PVC are chemical cousins with different properties. PVA, a good all-purpose glue, dries and cures slowly and has poor water resistance. PVC adhesive is of the same family as PVC water pipes, but it dries quickly and is waterproof. Thin PVC adhesive with acetone.

Urea-formaldehyde. A strong glue with high moisture resistance. It is good for veneer work but requires a long clamping time. (Elmer's Plastic Resin)

Construction-grade.

Acrylic. A good glue for outdoor use, it is quick-drying, extremely strong, and completely waterproof. Work with small amounts for best results; clean up with acetone. (F-88)

Construction adhesives. A large group of adhesives used to bond sheathing to framing members. These adhesives come in caulking tubes; cut the nozzle in a V and apply beads $\frac{3}{16}$ to $\frac{1}{4}$ in. wide. Because most construction adhesives (such as latex-based or butyl rubber) are elastomeric, they bridge minor irregularities, reduce squeaks, and so on. They also grip well to clean and dry surfaces (their use is limited below about 20°F, however). The resultant, strong wood-to-wood bond allows the builder to use far fewer nails. Construction adhesives vary greatly; some are intended for drywall, some for fiberboard, and so on. [Durabond Multipurpose (U.S. Gypsum) and PL-400 (Goodrich)]

Contact cement. Commonly used to bond veneers and laminates to a base material, often particleboard. Both surfaces to be attached are covered with a thin brushing of contact cement, allowed to dry, and then pressed firmly together. Once the sheets come in contact with each other, separation or realignment is all but impossible. (Alignment tips are given in Chapter 17.)

Epoxy resins. For exterior use. There are many brands, such as Waterplug and Thoroseal, that solidify on contact with water. Famous for their strength, epoxies can bond different materials where almost nothing else will—that is, where the surface areas to be bonded are small or where dampness is extreme. For more, see Chapter 9.

Mastics. A broad family of adhesives which can bond to large surface areas, such as tiles and paneling. Generous application of the mastic fills minor irregularities in the subsurface. Mastic paste is spread with a notched trowel, other types with caulking guns. Because mastic paste is highly water resistant, it is often used to "bed" bathroom tile; nevertheless, spaces between tiles must be grouted.

Resorcinol. A strong, waterproof glue used by boat builders, among others. Like epoxy, it is a two-part glue that is very difficult to remove once it has set. Wood parts fastened with resorcinol will probably shear before the glue itself does. It is excellent under stress. (U.S. Plywood Waterproof Glue; Elmer's)

Styrene-butadene. A good all-purpose exterior and interior glue suitable for joining materials of low porosity such as tile and masonry. Although waterproof, it can be dissolved by petroleum products.

·5·

ROOFS

The most important nonstructural part of a building is its roof, a first line of defense against water, wind, and sun. When the roof is properly constructed and maintained, water runs down and is routed away from the surfaces of the house.

A variety of roofing materials—from straw to slate—can be used as primary membranes to deflect water. Were roofs simply sloped planes, life would be simple. But today's roofs are complicated affairs, with vent pipes, chimneys, skylights, dormers, and the like sticking up—each,

potentially, a dam for water. So each must be *flashed* to direct water downward around it. As water approaches the lower reaches of the roof, it is further directed away from the faces of the building by overhangs, drip edges, and finally, gutters, which are discussed in Chapter 7.

In this chapter we are concerned mainly with the roof membrane; skylights are discussed in Chapter 6. We'll assume that the foundation and superstructure of the house are stable, for it makes little sense to repair or replace a roof if its integrity can be disturbed later by structural shifting or settling. Structure is discussed in Chapter 8. Whatever the scope of your project, please review the safety pointers in Chapter 3 and read the section below.

ROOF SAFETY

Among professional building trades, roofing is considered the most dangerous—not because its tasks are inherently hazardous, but because they take place so high above the ground. If you are uneasy with heights or not particularly agile, please stay off the roof and have someone else do what needs doing. Heed these rules:

1. Always have a second person within earshot, in case something happens.

2. Don't go up when the weather is near freezing, extremely warm, or wet. Cold asphalt shingles are brittle,

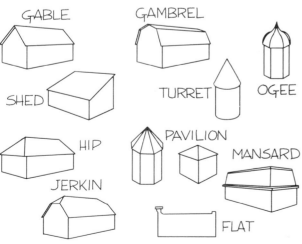

Figure 5.1 Roof types.

warm asphalt can stretch and tear, and any material is slippery when wet.

3. Wear sneakers or crepe-soled shoes. Avoid tight clothes which restrict movement.

4. Foot all ladders securely, setting them away from the building one-quarter of the ladder's extended length. Don't lean—if you can't reach without moving your hips from within the ladder's sides, move the ladder.

5. Use scaffolding with a safety rail when reroofing or applying new. The most dangerous part of a roofing job—apart from tearing off—is applying the first few rows along the eaves.

6. When you walk on a roof, try to walk along rafters. When inspecting or working on the ridge, straddle it.

7. Stay off tile roofs. Tiles can shift, and just by walking on such roofs, you can do extensive damage.

8. Leave hot-tar roofs to professionals: tar is molten at 400°F.

REPAIRS

The best way to avoid repairs is to maintain your roof: keep trees and overhanging bushes cut back so that your roof can dry thoroughly after storms, clean out gutters at least once a year, and stay off the roof so that it doesn't get abraded. That's about all there is to it. Repairs, after all, are little more than stopgap measures to get you to the next roofing season. The only way to cure extensive water damage is with a new roof.

It does sometimes happen, however, that an otherwise sound roof will leak. Finding that leak is your first task, which can be tricky if your roof is pitched, for wet spots are seldom right under the leak itself.

Note the general area of leakage while you are inside, then go to the roof to look for obvious sources of trouble. They might include broken, torn, or missing shingles; a puncture from a fallen tree limb; shingles blown up by the wind; roofing abraded by someone's walking on it; a flat roof that has blistered because it was incorrectly applied; flashing that has been damaged. A worn shingle might also be the cause but, again, any roof that old would probably leak all over.

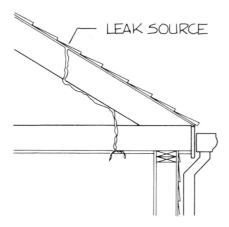

Figure 5.2 The source of a leak is often uphill.

TABLE 5.1

Roof longevity (years)

Slate	80–100
Cedar shingles or shakes	30–40
Metal	50–60 (more if maintained)
Asphalt shingles	20
Rolled roofing	20
Built-up roll roofing (flat roof)	10–15
EPDM rubber (flat roof)	20–25

Should the underside of your roof be exposed and you can see daylight, simply drive a small nail up to pinpoint that leak on the outside. If your roof is relatively new (see Table 5.1), yet you have widespread leaks, suspect the flashing. It doesn't happen as often as it once did, but the roofer may have left the tired old flashing in place. The remedy for that, unfortunately, is stripping away the existing roofing to get at the faulty flashing—a new roof, in other words.

Repairing Asphalt Shingles

Asphalt shingles are the most commonly used roofing surface in North America and, happily, easy to repair. Made of heavy felt saturated with asphalt and covered with mineral grit, they wear well. Shingle damage is most often caused by winter storms, when asphalt is brittle from the cold. Accordingly, it is best to repair during the warm months, when shingles are pliable.

For the best-looking repair, use shingles identical to those already in place. Buy an extra bundle when you reroof and you'll have future repairs covered. Cutting shingles is easy: simply score the back with a utility knife and fold along the cut.

Perhaps the most common repair is a shingle blown up by a storm, which requires a little roofing cement applied to the underside of each corner, and light pressure to spread the cement. Cement comes in caulking tubes and cans. As the sun shines on the shingles, the cement will soften and adhere; you can also buy self-adhering shingles manufactured with dabs of cement on their underside.

Where a shingle has a slight tear, gently lift it and use a putty knife to spread roofing cement under the rip, along its length. Press the area down to help it adhere and nail down each side with one nail.

When replacing a shingle, be gentle with those around it: break their seal by sliding a putty knife beneath, then use a flat utility bar to remove the nails holding the damaged shingle. Keep in mind that those nails are actually holding down two courses of shingles—the one you're trying to remove and the top of the course below. If you extricate the shingle and the nails don't come up with a reasonable amount of trying, just knock them down with your hammer and a utility bar, as shown in Figure 5.3.

Cover all nail holes with roofing cement and slide the new shingle into place. Gently lift the course above and position nails so they'll be overlapped by that course. When nailing, start at one side and nail across: nailing edges first may yield a bulge in the middle.

When a ridge shingle seems the source of a leak (water

Figure 5.3 Replacing a single defective shingle. (A) Lift the undamaged shingle above to locate and pull the damaged shingle's nails. (B) Align the bottom of the replacement shingle and nail it down. To minimize damage to shingles above, hammer the nail indirectly, using the utility bar as shown. (C) Dab roofing cement under all affected edges.

Figure 5.4 Replacing a damaged shingle on the ridge. (A) If the flaw is minor, leave the shingle in place and cover the hole with roofing cement. (B) Press a shingle patch over the flaw and nail down all four corners. (C) Because the patch's nails will be exposed, dab cement or silicone caulk beneath before nailing down.

damage will appear on both sides of the ridge), apply a generous layer of roofing cement to the bad spot and place a new shingle over it. Put a dab of cement or silicone caulking beneath all nail heads before nailing them down; use $2\frac{1}{2}$-in. barbed roofing nails to hold shingles down.

Replacing Wood Shingles

To remove split or broken wood shingles, use scrap blocks to elevate the butt ends of the course above. (You can also just slide a piece of metal flashing up under the defective shingle and tack it in place, but the metal will be glaringly obvious.) Work the point of a chisel into the butt end of the defective shingle, and with twists of your wrist, split the shingle into slivers.

Before fitting in a new shingle, remove the nails that held the old one. Slide a hacksaw blade or, better, a shingle bar (also known as a slate hook) up under the course above and cut through the nail shanks as far down as possible. If you use a hacksaw blade, wear a heavy glove to protect your hand.

Wood shingles should have a $\frac{1}{4}$-in. gap on both sides, so size the replacement shingle $\frac{1}{2}$ in. narrower than the width of the opening. Tap in the replacement with a wood block. Nail down that shingle with only two 4d galvanized shingle nails, each set in from the edge 1 in. If the replacement shingle won't slide in all the way, pull it out and whittle down its tapered end, using a utility knife. Use only No. 1 shingles on roof work; lesser grades won't do.

Fixing Slate

Have a pro repair your roof if it's slate. Slate roofs are slippery even when dry, and a heavy-footed amateur can do considerable damage—both to the slate and to himself. If at any point, you find roofing nails rusted through, **get off the roof at once.** Chances are that the original roofer did not use galvanized nails, so most of the nails are almost rusted through by now.

Those alarums aside, slate is pretty remarkable stuff: life spans of 80 or 90 years are not uncommon, and some roofs have lasted centuries with nary a leak. Leaks are rarely caused by the slate's failing; more often the culprit is a shifting structure, falling limbs, or as noted above, rusted nails.

If you will be doing the repairs, buy a *slate hook* to remove damaged pieces. Work the head of the tool up under the damaged piece until its hook catches a nail shank. Then, striking the handle of the tool with a hammer, cut through the shank. When both shanks are severed, slide out the damaged slate, being careful not to disturb adjacent pieces.

Once on the ground, transfer the dimensions of the old piece onto a replacement slate. Ideally, the new piece should be the same size as the one it's replacing, but that is usually not possible because of protruding nail shanks or variances in slate thickness. Test-fit and trim the replacement until it fits.

Wear goggles when cutting slate. The easiest way to cut slate is with a *tile-cutting saw;* rent one if you have a lot of cutting to do. A good second choice is a carborundum blade in a power saw. A distant third is a ruined screwdriver or an old chisel drawn along a straightedge: score both sides of the slate repeatedly. Then, centering the scored line over a table edge, snap the waste portion abruptly, as you would snap scored glass. Using tile nippers or gentle hammer blows, you can clean up ragged cuts, but keep in mind that slate shatters easily.

Return to the roof for a final test-fit. If you don't need to trim further, align the bottom edge of the piece to those of its neighbors and drill two nail holes, each one 1 in. from the edge and about 1 in. below the course above. (A re-

Figure 5.5 Shingle bar or slate hook. (Brookstone Company)

chargeable drill is ideal for this task.) Size the drill bit just slightly larger than the thickness of the nail shank.

Because this pair of nails won't be covered by the course of slate above, use roofing nails with a neoprene gasket. Or you can put a dab of clear silicone under each nail head before hammering it down. It's also prudent to caulk a bead of clear silicone around the perimeter of the replacement piece. Drive nails down just snug and no more; too heavy a hand will split slate.

Metal Roofs

There's not a lot that can damage metal roofs, so repairs are infrequent. Maintenance is still important, however, for most leaks occur when wind and ice lift the sheets and pop up nails. Once a year, scrutinize the roof with a pair of binoculars, and nail down any pop-ups you see. For extra security, put a dab of clear silicone caulk beneath nail heads.

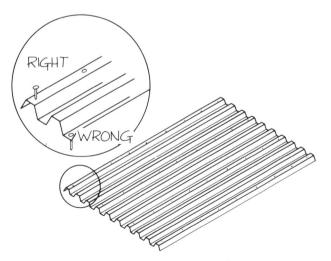

Figure 5.6 Nailing metal roofing.

If leaking is persistent, chances are that the roofer drove nails into the valleys of the corrugated roof, where water runs; always nail metal roofs at high spots. If that is the case and silicone caulking doesn't do the trick, you probably need a new roof. Although some manufacturers tout thick, aluminized roofing paint as a cure-all for such problems, paint membranes rarely hold more than a year.

Flat-Roof Repairs

Most flat roofs are comprised of alternating layers of heavy felt paper and hot tar or asphalt. After the paper is rolled out with a good overlap, the entire surface is saturated with hot tar, creating a continuous, water-resistant membrane. Carefully applied, the four or five layers are effective, but relatively fragile. The surface is short-lived because it is easily abraded when cold and stretched when warm. If your present flat roof is more than 10 years old or has more than a handful of blisters, get a bid on a new EPDM sheet rubber roof; they're good for 20 to 30 years and they're tight.

On flat roofs, the primary causes of membrane damage are:

1. Water trapped between layers, because of improper installation (e.g., putting down roofing too soon after rain). Or by seasonal contraction and expansion of the seams, which first shrink to admit water and then expand to trap it.

2. Inadequate flashing around pipes, skylights, and adjoining walls.

3. Drying out and cracking from ultraviolet rays.

4. People walking on the roof.

Locating the causes of leaks on flat roofs is relatively easy, as they will be directly above wet spots inside. The cardinal rule of flat-roof repair is: *Disturb extant membranes as little as possible.* Leave as many layers as possible, and never cut down through the lowest layer. An expert resurfacing a flat roof may cut down to the sheathing, but an amateur shouldn't. Make all repairs on a warm, dry day.

To identify a water blister, prick it with the point of a utility knife and prod it with your foot: water should ooze out. (An air blister probably isn't the source of a leak.) If there is water, extend the cut through the middle of the blister.

Prop up the edges of the cut so the blister can dry out. Then trowel roofing cement such as Hydroseal under both sides of the cut and press down to seat the adhesive. Next smear cement over the cut and nail down both sides. Cover this "suture" with a thick layer of roofing cement, followed by a patch of 30-lb felt paper or an asphalt shingle. Nail carefully around the edges of the patch with $1\frac{3}{4}$-in. barbed roofing nails, then apply a generous layer of cement.

Repairing an abraded spot is similar, except that you first cut out a square of roofing around the flaw. Ease out

A.

B.

C.

D.

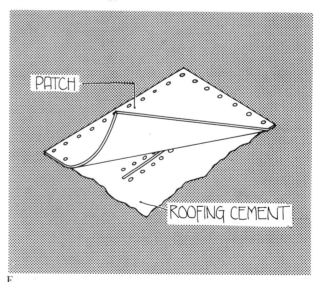
E.

Figure 5.7 Repairing a flat-roof blister. (A) Cut the blister with a utility knife; don't cut too deeply. (B) After allowing moisture within the blister to evaporate, apply roofing cement under both sides of the cut. (C) Nail down both sides of the cut with roofing nails. (D) Cover the entire area with roofing cement. (E) Nail a repair patch or 90-lb roll roofing over the area and cover it with cement.

A.

B.

C.

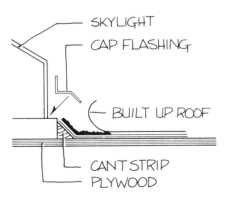

D.

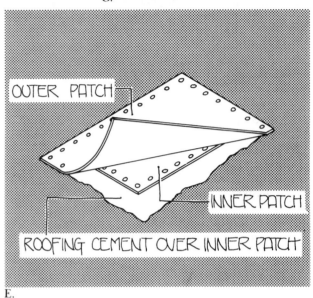

OUTER PATCH

INNER PATCH

ROOFING CEMENT OVER INNER PATCH

E.

Figure 5.8 Patching a flat-roof hole. (A) After scoring around the flawed section, gently pry it up. (B) Spread roofing cement over the exposed area. (C) Trace the flawed piece of felt paper onto replacement stock, cut it out and press the new piece into place. (D) After nailing around the perimeter of the replacement patch, cover it with roofing cement. (E) Cover the first patch with a second, larger one; nail and cement it as well.

the cut piece and trace its replacement on heavy felt paper (45 lb or more). Spread roofing cement in the cutout area before placing the new paper, then nail down the patch with roofing nails spaced 2 to 3 in. apart. Cover the patch with roofing cement and a second patch 6 in. longer and wider than the first. Apply the second patch, nail it down, and cover it with roofing cement as well.

To repair built-up flashing, you won't need nails; roofing cement will adhere layers. To seal the base of stacks, shape roofing cement with a flat knife. Allow each layer to dry before applying the next. At the base of parapet walls and the like, slope alternating layers of 30-lb felt paper (cut it in 8-in.-wide strips) and roofing cement. The trick is to avoid low spots where water might collect. You can nail a

cant strip along the base of the wall to shed water. Then flash the strip with alternating layers of felt paper and roofing cement, as above. While you're going to all this trouble, rip the cant strip out of a 4×4 so that it's a formidable barrier to water.

Again, you'll get best results if you cut no deeper than you must, and avoid roof work when temperatures are extreme.

Decks on Flat Roofs

If your flat roof presently has no deck, do without; or if you must, have a professional install one the next time you strip the roof. Decks atop flat roofs present these problems:

1. Most rafters are inadequately sized for the concentrated weight of a deck—and the people on it. Have an engineer make such calculations; it may be necessary to bolster the rafters from below.

2. Decking directly atop a hot tar roof is a disaster in the making. An EPDM rubber roof can stand the weight, but hot tar roofs are relatively fragile and you'll have extensive leaks before you know it.

3. The correct way to support a deck, roofside, is to rest it on "floating posts" bolted through the sheathing into the rafters. Obviously, to get to the sheathing, you've got to pierce the roof membrane. Add such posts only when you are stripping down to the sheathing to reroof. That's the only way to flash posts properly.

SKYLIGHT

CAP FLASHING

BUILT UP ROOF

CANT STRIP

PLYWOOD

Figure 5.9 Flat-roof flashing.

PREPARING FOR A NEW ROOF

Roofs are expensive. If you can save some money by installing a new roof over an old one, by all means do so. But you should strip existing roofing when:

1. There are at least two layers already. This is true for flat roofs, wood shingles, and asphalt shingles; if you have a shake roof, you'll have to strip even one layer, because its surface is simply too irregular to roof over.

2. There is extensive water damage. Where it's difficult to know exactly what's causing leaks, it is safer to strip. In many cases the flashing will have failed and must be replaced; replace rotted sheathing at the same time.

3. Rafters are undersized. If your present roof is causing the rafters to deform, best not add any more weight. If your rafters are only 2×4s and already sagging, strip the roof, sheath with $\frac{1}{2}$-in. plywood to stiffen things up and put down a new roof.

4. An adjacent roof section must be replaced. When a house has additions roofed at different times, their replacement rarely coincides—one section's always got a few good years left. The real issue is the flashing they share: if it's at all questionable, replace both sections and install new flashing.

At the end of this section, you'll find how-to tips for roofing over.

Stripping the Old Roof

Stripping an old roof is one of the nastiest, dirtiest, most backbreaking jobs in renovation, and because it takes place high above the ground, one of the most dangerous. Have someone else do it for you. In many communities, there is a service that will take care of all permits, rip off the old roof, and cart away all the debris; or you can subcontract the job through a roofer. The stripping will take at most a couple of days, and it is money well spent to get a job under way.

If you must strip it yourself, minimize the mess by buying a heavy (6-mil) plastic tarp to catch shingles as you tear them off. Wrap one end of that tarp several times around a 10-ft or 12-ft 2×4 and tack-nail the board to the top of the wall, just under the eaves. So you won't be picking shingle shards from the lawn for years to come, lay tarps from the house to the dumpster. It's also a good idea to lean sheets of plywood in front of windows so they don't get KO'd by falling objects.

Other than that, stripping is mostly grunt work. Most strippers just go at it with a flat shovel, starting at the top and working down, scooping shingles as they go. Of course, the shovel rams into thousands of nail shanks, which must be pulled up with a claw hammer or, that failing, driven down. And old tar paper should also be pulled up.

Scaffolding with a safety rail, and another person nearby will make the job safer, but almost nothing can reduce the sheer tedium of it all.

Sheathing

Once your roof is stripped of roofing and roofing nails, survey the sheathing for water damage, being careful to walk over rafters. Poke suspect areas with a pen knife and replace any sheathing that's soft, cutting bad sections back to the centers of the nearest rafters. Wear safety glasses and use an old saw blade for this operation, because you'll probably hit old nails. Replacement pieces should be roughly the same thickness as the original.

If the old roof was shingled, chances are that its sheathing is 1×4s spaced 5 in. on-center. This is a good way of circulating air under the roof in hot, humid areas. If the boards are in good shape, you can nail new shingles directly to them, but many contractors prefer to sheath over the 1×4s with $\frac{3}{8}$- or $\frac{1}{2}$-in. CDX plywood because it makes a safer surface to work on. Run plywood perpendicular to the rafters, nailing it every 6 in. with 8d galvanized nails. Center plywood edges over rafter centers; elsewhere, use *H-clips* to stiffen joints and create $\frac{1}{16}$-in. expansion gaps so

Figure 5.10 When stripping a roof, try to contain the mess. By working a flat-nose shovel under a roof's original layer of felt paper, this worker is able to roll up paper and old shingles in one bundle.

that sheets won't buckle. Give the roof a final once-over for splinters, stray nails, and the like, and you're ready to roll on felt paper.

Roofing Paper

Technically, roofing paper is a kind of flashing, because it directs water away from building surfaces. Use 15-lb felt paper to cover sheathing generally, and 30-lb felt paper in valleys, as described below. Work from the bottom up. The first course of felt paper overlaps a metal drip edge nailed to the eave. Align the felt's lower edge to the metal and unroll the paper, stapling it as you go. This will prevent bunching, but staples are only a temporary aid; go back later and nail the felt paper with the tabbed nails shown in

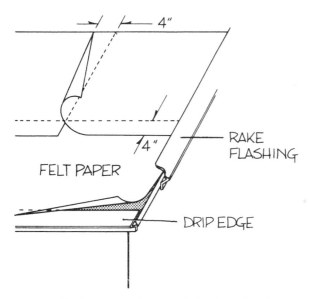

Figure 5.11 Flashing particulars. Attach the drip edge along the eave first, then cover it with the first course of felt paper. The rake flashing goes over the felt paper—and over the drip edge where they intersect.

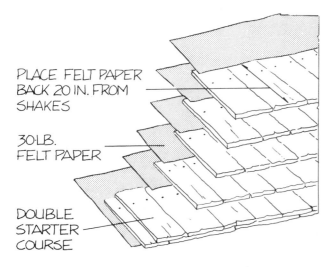

Figure 5.12 To flash a shake roof, alternate courses of shakes with 30-lb felt paper. For shakes exposed 10 in., set back the paper 20 in. from shingle butts.

Figure 4.5. The steeper the roof, the more nails should be used to keep paper from slipping.

Overlap subsequent courses of felt paper at least 4 in.—paper above *always* overlapping that below. Overlap vertical seams at least 4 in. Roll out only as much felt paper as you will cover in a day—left uncovered overnight, it will pucker.

If you're installing wood shakes, use *shake liner:* 18-in.-wide rolls of 30-lb felt paper, alternated between shake courses as shown in Figure 5.12.

Flashing

Flashing is critically important along building seams, where dissimilar materials meet, or wherever vertical surfaces or objects interrupt the downward run of water. Spot-repairing flashing just doesn't make much sense: you can buy a little time by covering a leak with epoxy paste, fiberglass, or bituthene sealing tape, but it's a false economy. Replace all flashing when you reroof.

The only exception to the rule above is cap flashing on the chimney, which, being mortared into the chimney, is a fright to remove and replace. Chances are the cap flashing will be sound because, constantly exposed to air, it stays dry and degrades slowly.

Materials. A number of sheet materials are suitable for flashing. Unformed, they come in sheets 10 ft long or in rolls of varying lengths, widths, and gauges. Copper is longest lasting and most expensive. Lead is most malleable, but also easiest to tear or puncture. Galvanized steel is next in longevity, but its rigidity requires that you buy it pre-shaped or rent a metal-bending brake to use on site. Lightweight aluminum (26 gauge) is probably the most common flashing shaped on site, because it is a good trade-off of expense and durability. As shown in Figure 7.2, aluminum can be worked with relatively simple tools. The heavier grade of roofing felt (90 lb) is sometimes used as valley flashing, but it is the least durable of materials mentioned and so is not recommended.

Important: Nail as far as possible from the center of a flashing channel, using as few nails as possible. Otherwise, you'll be routing water over nail heads. Position nails so they can be overlapped by roofing above, never where heads will be exposed.

The electrolytic sequence. A number of metals, if paired, will corrode. This action is called galvanic action. Because water is an electrolyte, any moisture present will increase that corrosion. The following metals comprise a group known as the electrolytic sequence:

1. Aluminum
2. Zinc
3. Steel
4. Iron
5. Nickel
6. Tin
7. Lead
8. Copper
9. Stainless steel

Of each pair, the metal with the lower number will corrode most. If you must pair any two metals, galvanic action can be retarded by insulating between the metals with a layer of heavy (30-lb) felt paper or (less good) a thick coat of asphalt-based paint. Do not, however, coat a tin roof with hot tar, which will eat away the zinc coating on the tin.

Note: The nails you use to attach flashing must be compatible with it, or galvanic corrosion can occur. To be safe, use nails or clips that are the same material as the flashing. Your lumber yard can counsel you further.

Drip edges. The first flashing to install is the drip edge along the eaves. Drip edges come with a precrimped edge,

which should extend $\frac{1}{2}$ in. beyond the sheathing, so that water can drip free. Nail along the *upper* edge of the drip edge only, spacing 4d big-head roofing nails every 18 in. The drip edge is thus overlapped by the first course of felt paper, itself covered by the first rows of shingles. Those shingles, being doubled, will hold the drip edge down and prevent blow-back.

Ice borders. Where winters are severe and ice buildup along the eaves is common, install an ice border, a specialized drip edge 18 in. wide. Commonly, 12 in. of the ice border are left exposed so that snow will slide off, the remainder being overlapped by courses of roofing above. To prevent the border's being lifted by storms, bed the ice bor-

A.

B.

C.

D.

E.

Figure 5.13 A roofing sequence in Vermont. (A) After stripping the old roof, nail down the drip edge. (B) Cover the drip edge with felt paper. (C) Because of the region's long winters and the roof's slight pitch (3 in 12), the roofer spread roofing cement over the lowest course of felt paper. (D) Double the starter courses along the eaves, putting the first course of shingles upside-down—with tabs up. (E) All subsequent courses have tabs down.

Figure 5.14 A closed valley. To create a closed valley, first line with 3-ft-wide, 30-lb felt paper; some roofers use metal. Then alternate incoming courses from side to side.

der in roofing cement applied directly to the sheathing. Once you have nailed the border along its upper edge, seal that juncture with roofing cement as well, then overlap it with the first course of felt paper and, eventually, shingles. If you are plagued by ice buildup and concomitant water damage inside, you need to add *eave vents* (p. 346) and *gable-end vents* (p. 348) so that heated air can exit higher up.

Valley flashing.   There are two kinds of valley flashing: *open*, where the flashing is visible, and *closed*, where it isn't. Most people should go with open flashing: it's easier to get a good watertight job, and much easier to shingle up to. The only time a closed valley isn't difficult is with asphalt shingles, because they just overlap. Closed valleys of wood shingles and shakes take a lot of cutting and fitting.

Prepare for open or closed valleys by first running 30-lb felt paper the length of the valley. Ideally, the paper should be 3 ft wide, minimally, 18 in.—but in any case, wider than any metal flashing you install over it. If you can't run one continuous piece of paper down the valley, overlap pieces below by at least 6 in. Nail down the tar paper—but not in the center of the valley—and snap a chalk line down its center to help align the roofing materials that follow. The 15-lb felt paper rolled across the rest of the roof will overlap the outer edges of this heavier ''valley felt.''

Closed Valleys.   In closed valleys, shingles from adjoining roof sections converge and overlap each other to provide a double layer of shingles over the valley felt. More fastidious builders put down a valley of 18-in. metal flashing (folded lengthwise) over the felt paper first: it's overkill, but it makes a stronger valley.

Open Valleys.   Where there's ice and snow and lots of wet, go with an open valley. Code requires metal 18 in. wide for asphalt and wood shingles, 24 in. wide for wood shakes, but better roofers use 24-in.-wide metal for all open valley installation. The heavier the metal, the more durable the valley: 18- or 20-gauge metal is standard, 16-gauge is heavy but harder to work. Fold metal lengthwise and overlap sections at least 6 in.

When the shingles are in place, about 6 in. of the valley width will be visible. For this reason, nail well outside the channel in which water will run, say, 8 in. from the center of the valley. Nails are thus covered well by overlapping shingles. There are also compatible-metal clips which obviate nailing through the metal at all.

If you live in a high-wind area, have a shake roof, or just want a deluxe job, have a metal shop fabricate valley flashing with a *standing seam* and turned-back edges, as shown in Figure 5.16C. Tell them the slope of the roof and the type of roofing and they'll do the rest. A shake valley, by the way, is open 8 in. on either side of the standing seam.

Figure 5.15 Flashing an open valley. After lining an open valley with 3-ft-wide, 30-lb felt paper, cover the paper with metal flashing—here, flashing with a standing seam up the middle. Note that felt paper from the field runs into the valley and overlaps the edges of the metal flashing. Figure 5.31 shows the next step.

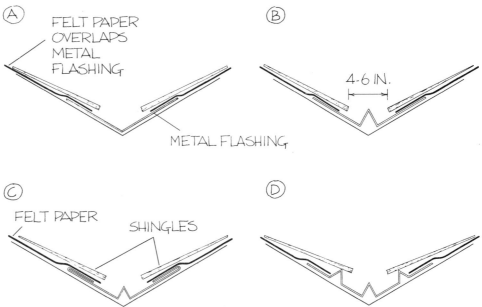

Figure 5.16 Metal-flashing details. (A) Simple fold; (B) standing seam; (C) standing seam with crimped edges; (D) three-seam, often specified for shake-roof valleys.

Rake flashing. Rake flashing is a right-angle cap over the gable ends of a roof, usually nailed down after the sheathing is covered with 15-lb felt. Where rake flashing intersects the drip edges along the eaves, therefore, it overlaps. Rake flashing is not generally used with wood shingles, however, because they are usually doubled and extended beyond the sheathing to form a drip edge of their own. Rake flashing also seals the ends of sheathing from rot.

Stack flashing. In new construction, stack flashing is a single-piece unit with a neoprene collar and a metal flange. Some roofers swear by all-metal units, though, arguing that metal is less likely to be degraded by sunlight. So if you find all-metal stack flashing in good shape, reuse it.

Questions of longevity aside, the primary difference between the two types is ease of installation. In either case you'll shingle up to the base of the stack, slide the stack flashing down, nail the upper part of the base, and overlap

Figure 5.17 The stack-flashing flange overlaps shingles below and is itself covered by courses above.

that with shingles. But whereas the neoprene collar just slides over the stack, the metal collar must be cut with snips and then caulked with silicone or butyl rubber.

Chimney flashing. Chimneys are counterflashed, upper cap flashing extending down to cover pieces of base flashing attached to the roof itself. These two components can thus settle independently, yet still maintain a watertight seal.

As mentioned earlier, it is unlikely that you'll have to replace the cap flashing mortared into the chimney. If it needs replacing, cut it out with a cold chisel and repack it with fresh mortar or lead wool to lodge the new flashing securely. But considering the complexity of the operation and the exposure of the chimney, it would be wise to have a mason do it for you.

Base flashing is another matter, and should be replaced when you reroof. Pry up old base flashing with a utility bar, and pull up or hammer down old nails. The most important piece of base flashing is the cricket along the upper (back) face of the chimney, for it's there that leaks occur most often. Have a metal shop fabricate one out of 20-gauge metal, which will be stiff enough to require no additional support beneath.

You may have to predrill the three nail holes needed to secure the cricket along its upper edge. Those nails will be overlapped by shingles above, but you can add an ounce of prevention by using neoprene-gasketed roofing nails. The upper leg of the cricket will be overlapped by cap flashing on the back of the chimney.

Along the sides of the chimney, alternate pieces of step flashing with shingle courses, as shown in Figure 5.19. Here, too, keep nails as far back from the flashing crease as possible. Use a single nail to nail down both flashing and the shingle covering it. If you have any apprehensions that shingle ends may lift, put a dab of roofing cement under each corner.

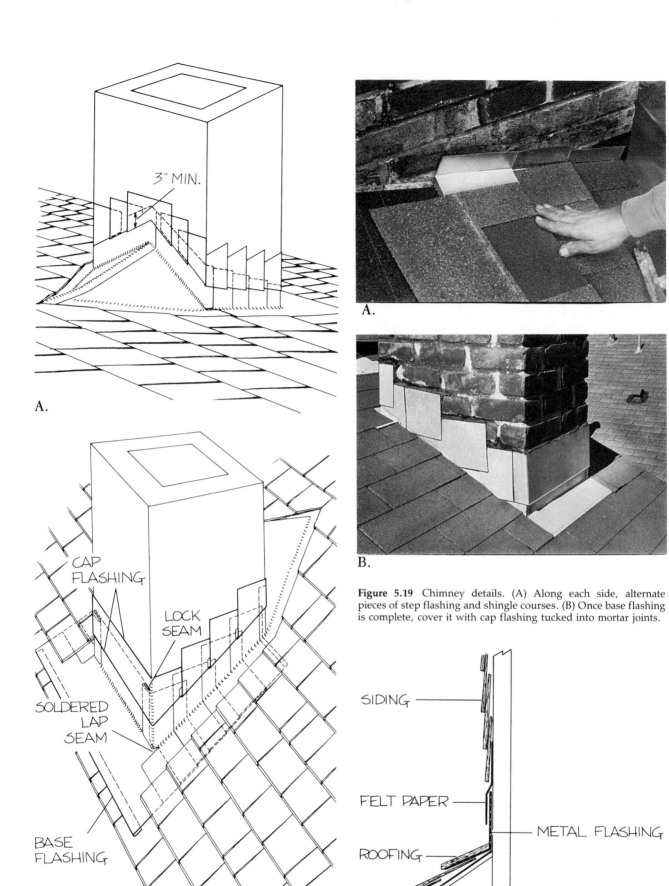

A.

B.

Figure 5.18 Have two pieces of chimney flashing fabricated by a metal shop: (A) the cricket above the chimney and (B) the base flashing along its lower face.

A.

B.

Figure 5.19 Chimney details. (A) Along each side, alternate pieces of step flashing and shingle courses. (B) Once base flashing is complete, cover it with cap flashing tucked into mortar joints.

Figure 5.20 Where a shed roof abuts a wall, run flashing up at least 4 in. under the siding.

The base shoe along the lower face of the chimney can be of lighter metal, but because it's complex, have it fabricated too. The bottom of that base shoe overlaps the tops of shingles below.

Note: Attaching large aerials to chimneys can strain mortar joints, which can lead to leaks. A chimney is a freestanding unit that safely carries hot gases out of the house; don't ask it to be more than that.

Flashing adjoining structures. Where roofs abut other roofs or walls, there are a number of ways to flash, but one underlying principle: always allow water to run downhill freely.

Where a shed roof abuts a wall, as in Figure 5.20, the metal flashing goes over the last course of shingles on the shed roof, and under the felt paper and siding on the wall. You'll probably have to pull siding nails to insert flashing.

Where a gable-end addition abuts a side wall, step-flash the siding. Begin by backing the junction with 30-lb

A.

B.

Figure 5.21 A gabled porch meets a wall. (A) Use a separate piece of step flashing for each course of shingles. (B) Where many planes converge, flashing can be complex. At the ridge of the porch roof, oncoming pieces of step flashing simply overlap, to be covered shortly by a third piece of metal and the course of felt paper above. *Note:* Siding should not rest on the asphalt shingles, but stop about $\frac{1}{2}$ in. above them—so that the junction can dry out. (In this photo, the small wooden strip beneath the clapboards is only a spacer, to be removed later.)

felt paper about 1 ft wide, folded lengthwise. The lower leg of that felt paper should go *over* the felt paper on the addition. The metal flashing, 5 in. × 10 in. ells folded in half, then alternate with rows of shingles as they abut the side wall. Slide the upper legs of those ells up under the siding on the wall—under the wall's felt paper, if possible. And again, place nails as far as possible from the flashing creases: nail only the upper corners of each ell; the weight of the shingles will hold down the rest. Here the doing is much easier than the telling: just imagine water running downhill and you'll know what goes under what.

The last examples, where shed roofs slope downward to a wall, are just plain messy. (Maybe that's why they're called "hog troughs.") Line the intersection with a 30-lb felt paper 36 in. wide, folded lengthwise and running continuously beneath the metal flashing. The leg of flashing that runs up behind the wall siding should be at least 8 in. high; and its other leg—that runs beneath the shingles on the shed roof—must extend out far enough so that its eventual rise is also 8 in. (Figure 5.22). Counterflashing is another approach. Finally, where a downsloping shed roof feeds into a blind corner (water can exit at only one end), there is such potential for leakage that a sheet-metal specialist should fabricate a tapered pan for you.

Ridge flashing. There are conflicting opinions about flashing ridges of peaked roofs at all, for what little water accumulates dries quickly. But they are subject to water blown in by storms. In any event, metal ridge flashing seems excessive: a continuous piece of 30-lb felt paper, folded lengthwise and placed over the ridge, should do the trick. That paper should be about 12 in. wide, so that the 6-in. leg will be covered by the ridge shingles.

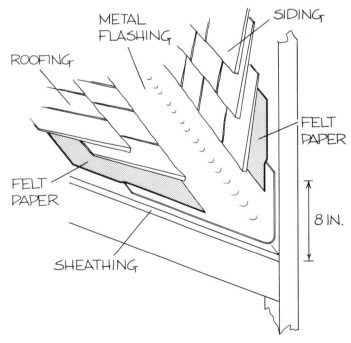

Figure 5.22 A shed roof sloping down to a wall is difficult to flash well; continuous metal flashing should rise at least 8 in. on both sides of the valley.

Figure 5.23 Where a nearly flat roof abuts a wall, one builder chooses to counterflash as shown, then seal the joint with hot-mopped tar before putting down roofing.

The ridge of a shed roof is another situation, because it overhangs a wall. There, the metal flashing will resemble a reverse drip edge, running at least 4 in. over the top row of shingles and extending $\frac{1}{2}$ in. beyond the wall so that water can drip free. To dress it up a bit, nail a beveled redwood or cedar 1×6 cap over the 4-in. leg of the flashing, using gasketed nails.

Ridge vents (p. 347) are a final ridge treatment, with the additional benefit of improving the flow of air beneath the roof. They can also leak like crazy during storms, so talk to a local contractor about their suitability in your area.

INSTALLING A NEW ROOF

If you haven't done so already, read the preceding sections on safety, sheathing, and flashing.

Tools

Scaffolding can make the most dangerous part of roofing, applying the first few courses along the eaves, safe. After the lower courses are done, the scaffolding serves as a waystation for materials and tools to come.

Wall brackets are frequently used during new construction, where nailing through the sheathing into the studs isn't a problem. Ladder brackets are more appropriate if you don't want to disturb existing siding, although, again, neither of these brackets is as safe as scaffolding. As a platform for either, use two 2×10s cleated together to prevent shifting. If the cleats are on the outside of the brackets, your planks will be less likely to "walk" off the brackets.

Roofing jacks enable you to work safely on the roof; install them after you've put on the first five or six courses of shingles and you can no longer work comfortably from the scaffolding. Using two 8d galvanized common nails per jack, nail jacks into rafters; nails should be galvanized because they'll stay in place after the jacks are removed.

As you work up the roof, install additional roofing jacks every eight to 10 courses (i.e., when you have to stretch to nail the next course). Each pair of jacks should be

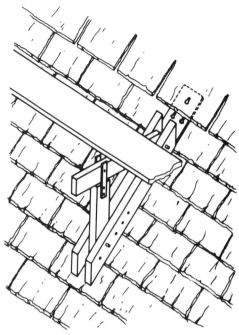

Figure 5.24 To be safe, scaffold planks should overhang jacks at least 1 ft and jacks should be soundly nailed to rafters. Because you'll nail shingles over jack tabs, leave enough room below single butts to drive the jacks free when you're done.

spaced about 8 ft apart, so you can use 10-ft-long 2×10s as platforms. Measure up from the eaves when setting jacks so that each set is more or less level. Nail 1×2 cleats to the underside of planks to keep them from "walking" off the jacks.

Leave all sets of jacks in place until the job is done, at which point you can remove them by hammering jacks upward to free their nailing tabs from the 8d nails. For this reason, be sure to leave enough space between shingle butts and the top of the jacks when you set the jacks initially.

Sturdy *kneepads* with integral plastic cups are a must for roof work. They were originally designed for floorlayers, but they spare roofers a lot of pain.

Rent a *pneumatic nail gun* to speed the job along; have the supplier explain loading and using it. *Important:* Many roofers don't use a nail gun for the first half-dozen courses; they hand-nail instead. The danger is the gun's hose: inadvertently step on it and you'll roll right off the edge.

Other than that, you won't need a lot of specialized tools. Get a utility knife with a lot of spare blades. A shingling hatchet and a nail apron are also very handy; as you'll note in Figure 3.11, there are different hatchets for asphalt and wood shingles. Wear sneakers on the roof.

Wood Shingles

Use only No. 1 grade shingles for roofing, which are free of troublesome sapwood and knots. Lesser grades are fine for side walls and shims, but they'll leak on a roof.

The *pitch*, or slope, of the roof determines how much shingles are exposed and, accordingly, how many bundles of shingles you'll need to do the job. (Pitch is the ratio of a roof's rise to its corresponding horizontal run. A 5-in-12 pitch denotes a roof that rises 5 ft for every 12 ft it runs.) Don't use wood shingles on any roof with a pitch of less than 3 in 12.

Calculating materials. See Table 5.2 to determine the shingle exposure that's right for your roof pitch. Assuming that your shingles will have a maximum exposure, four bundles will cover a *square*—100 sq ft of roof. To calculate the number of squares you'll need, multiply the length of your roof by its width and divide by 100. Because shingles are doubled along eaves, add an extra bundle for each 60 lineal feet of eave. For valleys, ridges, and hips, add an extra bundle for each 30 lineal feet.

You'll need 2 lb of galvanized shingle nails per square of shingles. For 16-in. shingles on roofs with pitches of 5 in 12 or greater, use 3d nails; otherwise, 4d. For shingle caps along ridges and hips, use 6d shingle nails to accommodate the greater thickness of materials.

Have your supplier deliver the materials in a lift-bed truck, so that you can unload squares right onto the roof. It'll save a lot of sweat.

Starter courses. Start by measuring up to the ridge from both ends of the eave to see how true your roof is. By knowing of discrepancies in advance, you can fudge each shingle course a little to correct things.

Double the first courses of shingles—the starter courses—along the eave, extending them beyond the fascia board by 1 in., and overhanging the rake trim by an equal amount. To establish the overhang along the rake boards, tack a 1-in. guide strip; to establish the 1-in. overhang along the eave, tack on a guide strip or stretch a taut string. Once you've aligned and nailed the first starter course of shingles, remove the string.

Speaking of nailing, never use more (or less) than two nails per shingle, no matter how wide the shingle. Nails should be placed as shown in Figure 5.25: in 1 in. from the edge of the shingle and up far enough from the butt so that they will be overlapped at least 1 in. by the course above. The only variation of this rule is the first starter course, which is nailed about 1 in. up from the butts, into the edge of the fascia board. But here there's no problem with overlap, because the second starter course goes directly over the first.

When nailing the second starter course, position these nails high enough so they are covered by the course above. As before, place nails in 1 in. from the edges. Another important point: always offset shingle gaps at least $1\frac{1}{2}$ in. from course to course; allow gaps to vertically line up only every

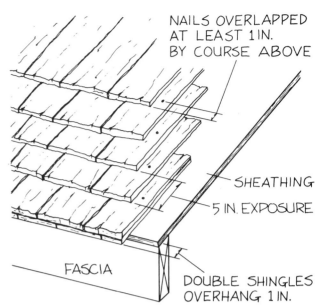

Figure 5.25 For a wood shingle roof that wears well, double the first course of shingles, use only two nails per shingle, and offset gaps for at least three courses. For clarity, felt paper not shown.

fourth course. Gaps between shingles should be $\frac{1}{8}$ to $\frac{1}{4}$ in. to allow expansion; if the bundle is wet, however, you can butt shingles right next to each other—they'll shrink.

The doubled starter courses in place, continue shingling up the roof, snapping a chalk line to align the butts of each new course. As noted in the section above, roof jacks will allow you to proceed safely and effectively. If the roof is not square, say, it's 2 in. longer up one side, fudge one end of the chalk line up 1 in. when you're about one-third up the roof, the remaining 1 in. when you're two-thirds up the roof. By doing that, shingle exposures will be uniform along the ridge.

A few more tips. Don't drive nails flush—the nail head should just rest on the surface. Otherwise, you'll encourage splits. If the shingle is cupped, put the cup down to aid runoff. If a shingle is exceptionally wide, save it for use along a valley; but no matter how wide, it gets only two nails. If you think a shingle may split, flex it to be sure it's sound.

Valleys: Read valley flashing (p. 78) before you start. For most situations, an open valley is the way to go: it clears water better, is less likely to clog with debris and dam up water, and requires much less fitting and cutting.

Shingling an Open Valley. Start by snapping parallel chalk lines down both sides of the metal flashing, each line 2 in. from the center fold of the flashing. As the starter course approaches the valley, don't nail the last four or five shingles initially, just lay them out. Where the last shingle in the course crosses a chalk line, mark the shingle with a utility knife and trim it to that angle of the intersection. It may take several cuts to get the angle exact, and several shingles. But once you've established the angle, use that shingle as a template for several courses above and build up the valley, as shown in Figure 5.26. Then shingle out from the valley into the general field of the roof. Wide shingles are

TABLE 5.2
Shingle exposure

Shingle Length (in.)	Amount of Shingle Exposed		
	Roof Slope 5 in 12 or More	Roof Slope 4 in 12	Roof Slope 3 in 12
24	$7\frac{1}{2}$	$6\frac{3}{4}$	$5\frac{3}{4}$
18	$5\frac{1}{2}$	5	$4\frac{1}{4}$
16	5	$4\frac{1}{2}$	$3\frac{1}{2}$

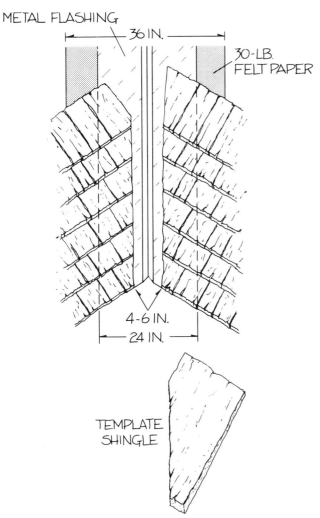

METAL FLASHING

36 IN.

30-LB. FELT PAPER

4-6 IN.

24 IN.

TEMPLATE SHINGLE

Figure 5.26 Because closed valleys require a lot of hand-fitting and don't clear water as readily as open valleys, most people choose open valleys. In either case, line both valleys with (at least) 30-lb felt paper.

particularly useful in the valley. Keep nails as far as possible from the center of the valley.

Shingling a Closed Valley. Closed valley shingles are fit in like manner, except that shingles go all the way into the valley until they meet shingles approaching from the adjacent roof plane. At that juncture, rough-cut each shingle to the correct angle, then back bevel its leading edge with a block plane. By cutting and planing, you create a compound angle so that shingles fit tightly; this can only be done on the roof, shingle by shingle. For best weathering, alternate miters right and left, from course to course. Again, build up several courses in the valley and shingle out to the rest of the field.

Ridges. Use either ridge boards or shingles to cap the ridge. When you're within 5 or 6 ft of the ridge, measure up on each end of the roof to see if your courses are equally spaced—now is your last time to adjust exposures if you must.

When the uppermost course of shingles is in place, trim their tapered ends cut back with a utility knife and

snap chalk lines along each side of the ridge to position of ridge boards or cap shingles to follow. (Actually, snap these lines just a big shy so that they'll be covered by the cap.) Then fold 30-lb felt paper lengthwise, and staple it along the ridge.

Ridge Boards. Ridge boards butt to each other; for a weathertight fit, they should be mitered. To establish the miter angle, lap two pieces of scrap at the peak and, using an adjustable bevel, transfer this angle to your table saw. Test-cut several pieces of scrap; when they join tightly along the ridge, rip down the ridge boards on the table saw. Because ridge boards should be as long as possible, get help nailing them down. If it takes several boards to achieve the length of the ridge, bevel joints 60 degrees and caulk each with silicone caulk. Using 8d galvanized barbed roofing nails, nail ridge boards to rafters; use two nails per rafter. Then go back and draw the beveled joint together by nailing it with 6d galvanized box nails spaced every 12 in. As you work, push down on ridge boards to force them together. Be careful not to split the boards, predrilling them if necessary.

Shingle Caps. You can also butt and bevel individual shingles to form a cap. There are preformed shingle caps, but because ridges vary, a standardized angle won't fit as well as one you cut yourself. Lay up pairs of shingles with their lengths parallel to the ridge, so that they straddle the roof as in Figure 5.27B. Nail down a first shingle so that it over-

A.

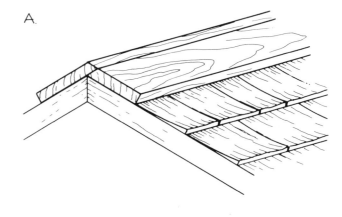

B

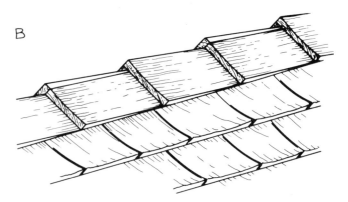

Figure 5.27 Two options for finishing a ridge: ridge boards and Boston shingle caps which alternate overlaps from side to side.

shoots the peak a little, butt a second shingle to its underside, then trim the first with a block plane. You may want to bevel both shingles for a tighter fit, but plane at least one so that the joint is neat looking. You can also bevel a pair of shingles at a time on your table saw, if you alternate butt and tapered ends. As you nail up shingles, alternate their laps from one side of the ridge to the other. As you install these cap shingles, maintain the same exposure you did elsewhere on the roof to overlap nail heads. If you shingle in from both ends, trim the last shingle pair to 8 in., alternate their butt and tapered ends, and nail them down with 6d galvanized shingle nails.

Asphalt Shingles

Asphalt shingles are manufactured as 1 ft × 3 ft strips, called three-tab shingles. They're also available as individual shingles, but strips are overwhelmingly more popular because they are easier to align and faster to install. If you live in a high-wind area, buy shingles with roofing cement dabs already applied to the underside, to hold shingles down. When the sun warms such shingles, the cement melts and adheres.

Ordering materials. Unlike wood shingles, whose exposure varies according to the pitch of the roof, most asphalt shingles have a standard 5-in. exposure. Roofing products with metric specifications favor an exposure or approximately $5\frac{5}{8}$ in., so read product literature to be sure.

Asphalt shingles also come 4 bundles to the square (100 sq ft), so multiply the length of your roof times the widths to get the area, then divide that to determine the number of squares you need. For future repairs, get an extra bundle or two. When you rent a pneumatic nail gun, tell suppliers the square footage of your roof—and the thickness of the sheathing—and they'll recommend the number of nail cartridges to do the job.

Roofing nails are generally sized not by *penny*, but by gauge and length. For best holding power use *barbed, big-head roofing nails*. The length depends on the thickness of

Figure 5.28 Stack your shingles along the ridge (if the roof is not too steep) and you'll have more room to work. If your supplier has trucks with lift beds, you can unload shingles directly onto the roof. (Thanks to Elliott & Elliott Roofing, Oakland, CA, for the sequence.)

Figure 5.29 Many professionals think it's safer to hand-nail the first five or six courses along the eaves. Here's how to hold roofing nails.

the sheathing. For $\frac{5}{8}$-in. plywood, use $\frac{3}{4}$-in nails so they won't be visible from the underside of the overhangs; $\frac{7}{8}$-in. nails if the sheathing is $\frac{3}{4}$ in. or thicker. Those lengths are also appropriate elsewhere in the nailing field, but if you rent a pneumatic nail gun, it will probably come with $1\frac{1}{4}$-in. nails.

Working with asphalt shingles. To cut an asphalt shingle, simply score its back side with a utility knife and fold the shingle along the crease. Change blades often; they gum up quickly. Even handier is an asphalt-shingle hatchet, which has a replaceable blade in the fore end of the head. As shown in Figure 5.30, the tool also has a depth gauge which enables you quickly to set exposure and *set-back* (the distance shingles are staggered, left to right).

On the subject of set-back, manufacturers and roofers sometimes disagree. Makers of three-tab strips suggest that you cut the shingles at mid-tab. Several roofers we talked to scorned that notion, saying that such a layout aligns tabs with cut shingle ends, thereby hastening wear. But if you use the 5-in. exposure setting on the hatchet as the set-back distance, tabs and shingle ends won't line up. (Actually, when using the hatchet as a set-back gauge, you fudge a little to $5\frac{1}{7}$ in., so that 7 set-backs equal the length of the shingle strip, 36 in.)

When nailing, start at one end and nail across: nailing ends first may pucker the middle. Full-length strips get four nails: one at each end, in about 1 in. from the edge, the other two approximately over each tab. All nails must be high enough on the shingle so that they are overlapped at least 1 in. by the course above—it's obvious on the shingle where to nail. Every shingle should have at least two nails. Because asphalt is more susceptible to tears and abrasion when it's warm, don't work in the heat of the day. It's more productive—and safer—to start early in the morning and knock off by early afternoon.

Starter courses. Start by assessing the roof for square, as described for wood shingles; if you must vary exposures at some point, it's best to know early.

Double the first course of shingles, the starter course, after drip edges and 15-lb felt paper are in place. The first layer of the starter course can be regular three-tab shingles

A.

B.

C.

Figure 5.30 Using a shingle hatchet. (A) Hatchets have a replaceable razor in their blade, here used to score a shingle. Whenever possible, score shingles on the back side so your blade will last longer. (B) You can quickly align successive courses by butting them to the head of the hatchet. The blade of the hatchet has an adjustable exposure gauge, more clearly seen in (A). (C) The gauge can also be used to offset shingle joints.

laid upside down (with tabs up), or it can be heavy-weight *starter roll*. This first starter course overhangs the drip edge about $\frac{1}{4}$ in. The second starter course, right side up, is nailed directly over the first.

Note: Some builders prefer to stiffen asphalt-shingle edges along eaves and rakes, with a course of wood shingles beneath. If you adopt this method, you needn't double

Figure 5.31 Instead of doubling up starter courses (Figure 5.31D), you can also use a starter roll, applied after the drip edge is covered by felt paper.

the starter course: one thickness of asphalt shingles will suffice.

Shingling the field. Thereafter, space shingle courses according to the standard exposure, 5 in. Start nailing from one end of the roof and work to the other. If you're right-handed, start left and work right; otherwise, you'll be reaching across yourself continually. Left-handers start right and work left.

To establish the shingle pattern (i.e., how often shingle gaps repeat), set up several courses along one end of the roof before shingling across. Lay a first shingle strip uncut, aligning one end to the edge of the roof. Above it, lay the first shingle of the second course, cut down one-third. Above that, lay the first shingle of the third course, cut down two-thirds. To continue the pattern, simply butt subsequent shingles to those stepped at the end.

As you lay each strip, use your hatchet gauge to set the correct exposure. Periodically, say every six courses, measure up from the eaves to make sure that your courses are evenly spaced and, as noted earlier, compensate for irregularities in the roof so that a full course coincides with the ridge.

Figure 5.32 A pneumatic nailer.

Valleys. Open valleys should be papered and flashed, as described above. To lay out open valleys, snap parallel chalk lines down each side of the valley, each line 2 in. from the center fold of the flashing. Where the leading shingle of each course enters the valley and crosses a chalk line, notch the shingle top and bottom with a knife. Then flip the shingle over and, using another shingle as a straight-edge, score the back of the shingle from notch to notch. In that manner, work your way up the valley.

On an open valley, you can speed the job considerably by just running shingle ends into the valley, then, when the roof section is done, snapping a chalkline diagonally across the shingles, to indicate a cut line. Cut along that line with snips rather than a utility knife, which could

Figure 5.33 Shingling the field goes faster if you step shingle joints first—here, using the hatchet gauge to step up along a valley.

Figure 5.34 Trimming the valley. After running shingles into the open valley, come back and trim them with a straightedge. Here, the roofer uses a shingle as a straightedge to guide the razor point.

puncture the flashing beneath. Because the center of the flashing will be obscured by shingles, the cut lines may not be exactly 2 in. from the center fold; but the line will be close and, as important, it will be straight.

On a closed valley of asphalt shingles, it is not imperative that you line the valley with metal flashing. But at the very least, flash it with 30-lb felt paper. In closed valleys, shingle both sides of the valley simultaneously so that you can weave oncoming shingles together, alternating the overlap from one side to the other.

Whether your valley is open or closed, nail as far from the center fold as possible, in no case closer than 5 in.

Ridges. To finish the ridge, trim the uppermost course of shingles so that they don't extend beyond the ridge, and snap chalk lines on both sides, down about 4 in. from the top. Cover the ridge with 30-lb felt paper folded lengthwise. Then cap that with regular shingles cut at each tab (i.e., 12 in. long) and folded over the ridge. Nail down each shingle with two 2-in. barbed roofing nails, observing the exposure you used (e.g., 5 in.) elsewhere on the field. The last shingle on the ridge, not being overlapped by any subsequent shingles, gets four nails—one in each corner.

New Roofing over Old

Applying a new layer of roofing over an old one is much the same as starting from scratch, except that you must level out the existing roofing as best you can. Here are two tips:

1. To offset the butt ends of wood shingles, rip down beveled siding and place it flush against the shingle butts; nail down the strips with 5d galvanized shingle nails. Nail the new roofing down with 6d (2 in.) galvanized nails, to compensate for the thickness of two roofs. Do not, however, double the first course of shingles along the eaves. It's acceptable to put asphalt shingles over wood ones, but the latter must be completely dry to forestall rot. Check with local codes before you begin.

Figure 5.35 Cover seams along ridges and hips with shingle ''saddles.''

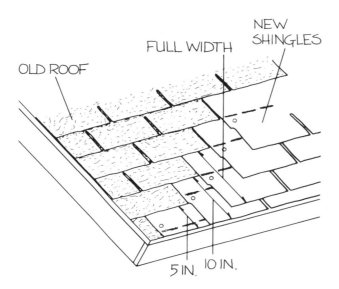

Figure 5.36 When putting a new roof over an old one, avoid a wavy-looking job by trimming the first two courses to establish a flat surface.

2. To level out an existing asphalt roof, rip down (reduce the height of) two courses of shingle strips, as shown in Figure 5.36. Because asphalt shingles are routinely exposed 5 in., rip down the first strip so that it is 5 in. high. Lay it over the original starter course so that the strip is flush against the butts of the original second course above. Next rip down a second strip 10 in. high and put it flush against the butts of the original third course. You now have a flat surface along the eaves. The third shingle strip—and all subsequent strips—need not be cut down at all, just butted to an original course above and nailed down. Use 4d big-head barbed roofing nails to reach the sheathing.

·6·

DOORS, WINDOWS, AND SKYLIGHTS

We ask a great deal of doors, windows, and skylights: they must be solidly attached, yet movable; they must let light in while keeping rain out; they must admit guests, but deny drafts. Called upon to do so much, it's surprising that they operate so well.

OVERVIEW

Let's start with a brief review of structure as it pertains to doors, windows, and skylights; for additional information, see Chapter 8. Because of quirks in framing or irregularities in lumber itself, rough openings are rarely perfectly square—*never* would be closer to the truth. Therefore, it is necessary to fit finished door or window *frames* to the rough opening with thin *shims* (tapered pieces between frame and opening). Once the unit is installed in the rough opening, cover gaps with *casing,* or finish trim, described in Chapter 17.

To save time and get professional results:

1. Buy *prehung* units whenever possible. Hanging interior doors yourself is fine, but exterior doors framed and weatherstripped at a mill cut drafts, save energy, and prevent water damage to the house. Prehungs are also easier to install. Avoid *precased* units (prehungs with trim already attached) for exterior installations, however: they are difficult to shim adequately.

2. Flash doors, windows, and skylights so that water will flow around them, not behind them. Felt paper, fiberglass-reinforced strip flashing, and flashing are discussed at length in Chapter 7; flashing skylights is discussed further in Chapter 5.

3. Shim frames squarely and nail them securely to rough openings. Shimming enables doors, windows, and skylights to operate freely, without binding; solid nailing ensures that they'll continue to work properly. Done well, shimming takes time, as you'll see below.

DOORS

Door frames consist of several pieces: two side pieces, or *jambs;* a *head* (or frame head) across the top; and on exterior doors, a *sill* spanning the bottom. (The sill may also have a *threshold,* but more about that later.) The term ''jamb'' is sometimes used for all pieces of the frame—that is, ''side jambs'' and ''head jamb''—but this use is confusing; in this book, ''jambs'' refer only to side pieces. The side on which the door is hung is thus the *hinge jamb;* the side that receives the latch is the *latch jamb* or *strike jamb.*

Most prehung units arrive with the door hinged to the hinge jamb, the frame head cut to the correct width, and all other parts milled with correct clearances around the door—but the parts are unassembled. This allows you to trim the jambs down so that they are the right length for

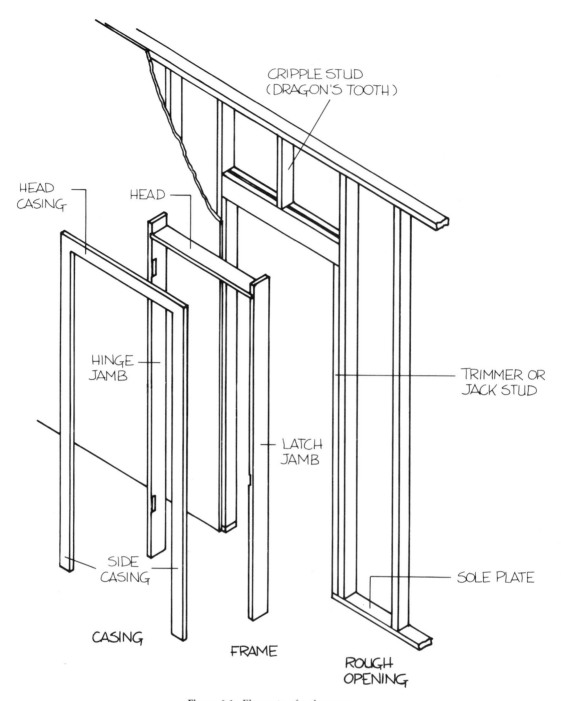

CRIPPLE STUD
(DRAGON'S TOOTH)

HEAD
CASING

HEAD

HINGE
JAMB

TRIMMER OR
JACK STUD

LATCH
JAMB

SIDE
CASING

SOLE PLATE

CASING

FRAME

ROUGH
OPENING

Figure 6.1 Elements of a doorway.

your flooring and/or threshold heights. Suppliers will cut exterior sills to fit if you ask them to, but many contractors prefer to buy sills separately and fit them on-site. Finally, doors come predrilled for the hardware you choose, but the hardware is generally unattached so that it doesn't get marred in transit.

Because the section below presents the basics of door hanging, it is germane to both exterior and interior installation. Readers installing exterior doors should also note the comments on sills, weatherstripping, and flashing in the major section immediately following, ''Upgrading a Double-Door Entry.''

Finally, a reminder: There is no one way to hang a door. Four or five approaches are given in the sections that follow, and there are scores more in the field. Use what works.

Installing a Prehung Interior Door

Prehung doors come in a wide range of standard sizes, but it's wise to measure your rough opening beforehand. Should your walls be unusually thick, for example, you can specify extra-wide frame stock and save yourself a lot of work during installation.

Assessing the opening. Let's assume that your doors are on hand and you are ready to begin installation.

1. Start by checking the height and width of the opening: the rough opening (R.O.) should be 2 in. taller than the height of the door and $2\frac{1}{2}$ in. wider.

2. Measure the thickness of the wall, from finish surface to finish surface. Standard 2×4 walls covered with drywall are $4\frac{1}{2}$ in. thick, so typical frame stock is $4\frac{5}{8}$ in. wide: frame edges thus stick out $\frac{1}{16}$ in. beyond finish surfaces to accommodate irregular wall surfaces. If your walls are not standard construction, size frame-stock $\frac{1}{8}$ in. wider than they are thick.

3. If the finish floor is not yet installed, determine its thickness so that you'll know how much to cut down the jambs. Jambs must sit directly on the subflooring (or flooring) because the hinge jamb will be the only thing holding up the door. Jambs are, of course, nailed to the rough opening, but they must also be solidly footed so that they can't drift downward later.

Whatever the thickness of the finish floor allow $\frac{1}{4}$ in. clearance above it so the door can swing freely. If, for example, you're installing a 6 ft 8 in. door and $\frac{5}{16}$-in. oak flooring, make jambs 80 in. $+ \frac{5}{16}$ in. $+ \frac{1}{4}$ in., or $80 \frac{9}{16}$ in. long. If you'll be laying heavy carpet and a thick pad, allow $1\frac{1}{4}$ in. $+ \frac{1}{4}$ in. clearance.

4. Use a level to see if the floor in the doorway slopes; if it does, add the amount below level to the jamb on that side. By doing this, you ensure that the frame head will be more or less level when jambs rest on the floor (or subfloor).

Assembling and locating the frame. Pull the hinge pins if the door was shipped attached to the hinge jamb.

5. Using a circular saw, cut the jambs to length, as described above. Cut from the back side so that you get a nice clean line on the front, and cut through stop pieces, if any.

6. Assemble the jambs to the head, using white or aliphatic glue and three or four 6d to 8d finish nails per side. Blunt nail heads will be less likely to split the stock. (If it's an exterior door, you can attach the sill now or wait until the jambs are plumbed and secured to the rough opening.)

7. Locate the frame in the rough opening. If stray drywall or too-long sole plates sticking into the opening might interfere with the frame, cut them off. If screws from hinge plates protrude through the jamb stock—as they frequently do—remove them so you can slide shims easily.

8. "Margin" the frame in the opening (i.e., center the frame in relation to the wall's thickness). For most 2×4 construction covered with drywall, the edges of a standard-width ($4\frac{5}{8}$ in.) jamb will extend $\frac{1}{16}$ in. beyond finish walls on both sides.

9. Check the frame head to make sure that it's more or less level.

10. With the frame "margined" in the opening, tack it in place with 10d finish nails to keep it from flopping while you shim the hinge jamb. Start by throwing shims behind the top corners of the frame and nailing an inch or so below the shims. By nailing below the shims, you can still adjust

Figure 6.2 When installing a prehung door, first clear the doorway of obstructions sticking into the opening, then margin (center) the frame to the thickness of the wall. (Photo sequence courtesy of Carl Burchfiel Construction, Berkeley, CA.)

them. *Note:* Center these tack-nails in the middle of the frame so that they'll be covered later by the stop pieces.

Shimming the frame. Plumb the hinge jamb first, using a 6-ft level for accuracy. You can also hang a plumb bob from a nail in the top of the jamb, as shown in Figure 6.4, and measure from that plumb line. When the jamb is plumbed, all measurements from that line will be equal.

11. Start by shimming behind the lower hinge, pairing shims so that their tapers alternate, thus creating a flat surface behind the jamb. Work up the jamb, adjusting shims in and out and checking for plumb. Where the jamb bows into the opening, you may need additional nails to draw it to the rough opening.

Doors are commonly shimmed with three pairs of shims along each jamb. Interior doors need at least three shim points: behind the two hinges, and halfway between them. Exterior doors, which have three pairs of hinges, require at least five pairs of shims to secure the hinge jamb.

Once the hinge jamb is plumb, nail through each shim point with two 10d finish nails; if you split shims, don't worry about it. Place these nails outside the stop-piece area, to keep the frame from rocking. Leave nail heads above the

Figure 6.3 Tack-nail the hinge jamb first, using at least three pairs of shims. Adjust the shims in and out until the frame is plumb.

Figure 6.5 This carpenter prefers to level and tack the frame head next, shimming the latch jamb last.

Figure 6.4 Use a 6-ft level or a plumb bob to plumb the jamb. Hang the bob from a nail near the top of the frame: when the jamb is plumb, readings to the string will be equal along its length.

surface of the jamb, however, in case you need to fine-tune later. After nailing, check plumb and margin again. Use galvanized nails for both interior and exterior door frames.

12. Now secure the latch jamb. Margin that jamb and tack it to hold its position. Reinstall the hinge butts (if you removed them) and hang the door.

Close the door into the opening and note its clearance all around. Mill specs will vary, but there's usually a $\frac{1}{8}$-in. gap along the hinge jamb, and $\frac{1}{16}$ in. of clearance from head and latch jamb. If the latch jamb bows into the opening, use nails to draw it back toward the rough opening. Check margins again, then shim up from the bottom of the latch jamb so that there is uniform clearance along the length of the door. Make sure that there is a pair of shims directly behind the strike location.

13. Shim the frame head, inserting a pair of shims at either corner. Don't drive shims in too far or you'll bind the top of the door.

14. This is the last chance to check margins and adjust shims if necessary. Make sure that all clearance around the door are uniform. Does the door open and close freely? If the door hits along the latch jamb, the frame head was cut a little short, in which case you need to rip down the door's latch stile slightly. Before resorting to that, however, try planing a 7-degree bevel on the latch stile to see if the door will clear the jamb upon closing. (These days, the mill will preplane the leading edge if you ask.)

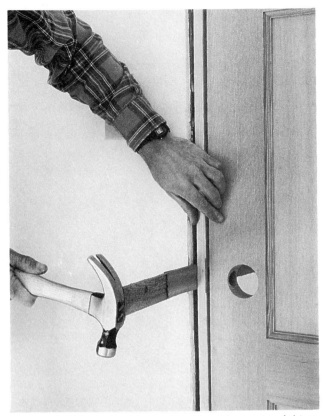

Figure 6.6 Shim the latch jamb with at least three pairs of shims, including one pair near the strike plate.

Figure 6.7 When all shims are tentatively positioned, go back and check the door's fit to the frame. The slight gap between the door and the frame should be equal all the way around.

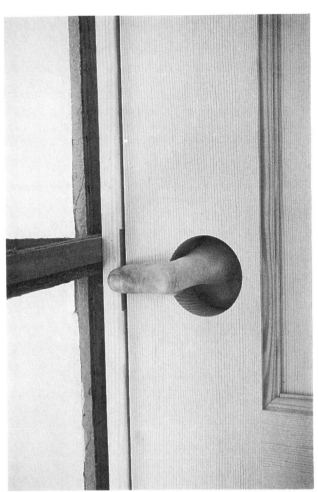

Figure 6.8 When installing stop pieces, be sure the face of the door is flush to the edge of the frame. A finger through a latch hole is a good test for flush.

Final touches. Now you're in the home stretch.

15. Install the door stop. To see where the door edge will stop when closed, hold the door flush by tacking a scrap of $1\times$ to the edge of the latch jamb—or snake a finger through the door as shown in Figure 6.8. That inner edge established, place the stop back $\frac{1}{16}$ to $\frac{3}{32}$ in. The door and its stop should not make contact now, for they've yet to be painted.

16. Set all nails with a nail set, and fill holes. If you'll be painting, fill the holes with spackling compound; if using a clear finish, fill with a wood dough or a stick-type filler.

17. Using a sharp mat knife, score the shims along the wall, tight to the frame. Score as deeply as you can (shingle butts may take several passes), then snap off the waste. Don't try to snap shingles that are too thick, or you may torque the jamb out from the opening.

18. Now install the lock set in the door and mortise the strike plate into the latch jamb. Make sure that the alignment is good, as shown in Figure 6.27.

19. When your door swings open, it should not "pattern" your carpet or abrade the finish floor; if it does, trim the bottom rail of the door. To register the height of the carpet on the base of the door, slide a flat builder's pencil across the carpet. The pencil, being fat, won't sink into the carpet as much. Add $\frac{1}{8}$ in. of clearance to that rough line and *score* the final cutoff line onto the door, using a matt knife drawn along a straightedge. Scoring the door is important, for it prevents vertical grain from splitting and veneer from lifting and splintering. This cleaner cut is especially important if you'll be staining the door.

For best results, use a circular saw with a sharp mastercut blade, which has a close configuration of at least four fine teeth and a raker to clear chips. Use a straightedge clamped to the door to guide the blade. Clean the saw sole (base plate) well: de-gum it with turpentine (or paint thinner) and steel wool, rub it with metal-polishing cloth or paraffin to help it glide across the wood. Smooth the cut with 220-gauge sandpaper, sanding with the grain.

20. Installing interior casing (trim) is discussed on pages 407–410; exterior casing, on pages 128–131. A few nail specifics: use only galvanized finish nails, inside or out. To attach exterior casing to sheathing, 8d nails; to attach interior casing to walls, 6d nails; to draw either casing to jamb edges, 4d nails.

Upgrading a Double-Door Entry

This section, which builds on the preceding section, shows how to upgrade an exterior double-door entry. If any step is insufficiently explained, reread "Installing a Prehung Interior Door." This seems an appropriate time to reiterate the benefits of buying a unit prehung to a frame, rather than just replacing doors.

First, exterior doors see a lot of weather, and there may well be rot behind an old frame, which bodes poorly for doors attached to it. Second, the existing frame may be out of square, which can be nightmarish to hang doors to—especially double doors. Finally, the manufacturer can mill precise kerfs, rabbets, and the like into doors and frames so that weatherstripping fits tightly.

Assessment and tear-out. Begin by scrutinizing what's there and proceed carefully, saving finish surfaces whenever possible.

1. Measure the existing frame before you order the new unit. Take readings from the outer edges so that you know how big the rough opening is. Note, too, whether the frame is plumb, level, and square. You can shim a square frame to an out-of-square opening, but remember that you'll need about 2 in. of space above the door, and $2\frac{1}{2}$ in. of extra width.

2. In your measurements, note the thickness of the walls from interior finish surface to exterior sheathing, and size the frame-stock accordingly (i.e., $\frac{1}{8}$ in. strong, as in step 2, p. 93). Next determine the height of the finish floor if it's being upgraded, for the installed sill should be the same height as the finish floor. (The threshold sits atop both.)

The new finish floor height and the thickness of the sill may also determine the jamb length, as noted in the preceding section.

3. Note the existing sill, for it's generally easier to install a replacement that's similar. If the original R.O. was prepped for an oak sill, replace it with oak. If the old sill is a *combo* (a sill–threshold combination), order a new combo of the same dimensions.

4. Protect interior floors with particleboard or heavy cardboard, and tarp off the work area to contain the mess.

A.

B.

Figure 6.9 Upgrading a double-door entry. (A) Before: These doors were badly weathered and, with the hinges on the outside, not very secure. (B) After: New doors, frame, casing, and brightwork. (For the installation sequence below, and that shown in Figure 6.27, many thanks to Harold Schoenfeld, Schoenfeld Construction, San Leandro, CA, and San Leandro Doors.)

Figure 6.10 When replacing an old entryway with new, prehung doors, first remove the old frame. To minimize damage to stucco keyed to the old casing, cut the nails holding the casing to the frame—it's less concussive than hammering.

5. Before removing trim, use a utility knife to cut along the seams where it meets finished walls. This is especially important if the casing is caulked.

6. Remove interior and exterior trim. If trim would be difficult to replace, use the gentle methods shown on page 153. Once you've pried the molding up a bit, you can cut through nails with a metal blade in a reciprocating saw. Cutting nails is far less destructive to surrounding surfaces than is hammering and prying. However, some trim can't be removed without destroying it. Stucco molding, for example, is often keyed on its backside and locked in place with stucco screeded right up to it.

7. Remove the existing frame, preferably by cutting nails from the back side so that you can pull out the frame in one piece. Should something go wrong—say, the new frame won't fit—you can nail back the old frame and rehang the doors so that you won't be without a front door while you correct the problem.

Prepping the opening. Once the old frame is removed, prepare the opening for the new one.

8. Check to see if the bottom of the R.O. is level. If it's not, shim it up so that it is; otherwise, the doors will be uneven at the top.

9. Do you need to build up the base of the opening to make the new sill the same height as the finish floor? To answer that question, the contractor in Figure 6.12 subtracted the thickness of the existing linoleum ($\frac{1}{8}$ in.) from that of the new tile to come ($\frac{1}{2}$ in.) and found that his new floor would be $\frac{3}{8}$ in. higher than the old one.

This is an important step, for the area around an entryway is visually conspicuous and subject to a lot of wear. If floor and sill are the same height, that joint can be covered by a threshold; if not, the joint can look awful and wear worse. In the example just cited, merely butting tiles to the back side of a sill—with no thought to its height—would leave a weak mortar joint totally exposed to foot traffic.

Figure 6.11 It's preferable to remove a frame in one piece so that you can nail it back up and rehang the old doors if something goes awry. Here, the frame was double-rabbeted, so it had to be cut into pieces to be removed.

A.

B.

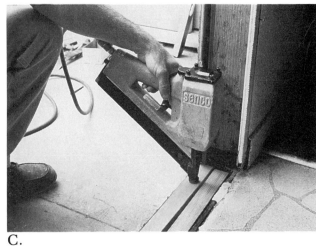

C.

Figure 6.12 Building up the sill. (A) After removing the old frame, check the opening for level and (B) check the height to the finish floor. When the new frame is installed, the replacement sill should be the same height as the finish floor so that the threshold can cap both. (C) As necessary, treat with a preservative to forestall rot, cover old wood with felt paper or metal flashing, and build up the bottom of the opening.

10. If doors arrive hinged to jambs, pull the pins and cut the jambs to length. If the frame is unassembled, glue and nail it together now.

(The sill may or may not be attached at this point; some professionals prefer to install it separately, after the jambs are plumbed, shimmed, and secured. Since our photo sequence features the sill preassembled, that's the approach we'll stick with.)

11. Test-fit the frame in the opening, roughly centering and "margining" it. Are the sill and the frame head more or less level? Are the edges of the frame more or less flush with interior walls and exterior sheathing? How much space is there between the jambs and the sides of the R.O.?

if there's much more than $\frac{1}{2}$ in. on either side, you should furr out the opening; otherwise, just shim the frame.

12. Remove the frame and alter the opening so that the frame fits well; trim drywall that might impede shims, furr out the opening, hammer in nail shanks that are protruding into the opening, and so on.

13. Test-fit the frame until you're satisfied that it's seating correctly, then apply sill flashing. Flashing varies according to the type of siding, the sill detail, whether the unit is precased, how much weather the opening will see, and so on. Where a big overhang protects the entry, some builders won't flash the sill at all.

Figure 6.13 Test-fit the new frame in the opening.

To prevent wood-on-wood contact, builders in wet areas often staple felt paper around the inside of the rough opening. Where the sill you removed was rotted or in high-wind areas, flash with 16-gauge metal along the base of the opening, keying it into a kerf cut into the sill for the tightest seal (see Figure 7.4B).

Install cap flashing later unless you bought precased units, in which case you should cut back the siding above the opening now so that you can slip cap flashing under the siding and the felt paper beneath, as shown in Figure 7.1. Then cover the upper leg of metal with 6-in.-wide fiberglass-reinforced flashing and new siding. To insert a precased unit into a rough opening, you'll have to tilt the frame up under the flashing, taking care not to bend it. This process is rather cumbersome, and it's impossible to caulk the seam properly—one of the reasons why we earlier recommended against precased units.

Shimming the frame. Having discussed shimming at great lengths in the section "Interior Door," we'll condense it somewhat here.

14. You will eventually shim each jamb at five points: top corner, bottom corner, and behind each hinge. To shim behind each hinge you'll probably have to remove the middle two screws, which protrude through the back side of the jambs.

A.

B.

Figure 6.14 To support the considerable weight of exterior doors, use at least five pairs of shims along each jamb, including a pair behind each hinge. (A) Remove the center screws in each leaf so that you can slide shims behind. (B) Check and recheck for plumb as you set and adjust shims.

Start by shimming each jamb behind its hinges. Shim the upper and lower hinges, then, using a level to plumb the jamb, shim behind the middle hinge. Margin the frame, then tack the frame to the R.O., nailing below the shims so that they can be adjusted. Use as few nails as possible; a pro can get by with just four 8d nails, two to a jamb.

15. The frame tacked up, temporarily hang the doors, leaving hinge pins loose so that you can remove them easily. Now "read" the doors to see what needs doing: reading doors is mostly close observation and common sense. In Figure 6.15, the installer noticed uneven door heights, binding in the lowest corner, an astronomical gap in the center, and doors not flush along the *astragal* (the half-round molding where the doors meet).

16. According to what you've read, tweak the frame (this is called "working the frame" by professionals). Here are a few things you might see, and what to do about each:

a. Doors hitting in the center. Ease off the shims behind the jambs; if the problem is a bowed jamb, use additional nails to pull it back toward the rough opening. Even better than nails are screws: professionals sometimes remove one of the short hinge-plate screws and replace it with a $2\frac{1}{2}$- to 3-in. brass-plated drywall screw, which really sucks the frame to the R.O.

Figure 6.15 With the hinges shimmed on both sides, temporarily hang the doors to test their fit. Here, a gap along the astragal indicates a frame that's racked.

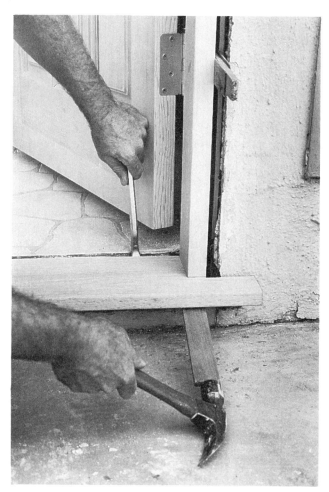

Figure 6.16 To correct doors of uneven heights, shim under the low corner of the frame.

b. Doors too far apart in the center. Shim out from the rough opening more. If that doesn't work, or if you must shim so much that the center of the jamb is bowed, the head was probably milled too long; either you or your supplier will have to cut it down. Ideally, the gap between double doors should be about $\frac{3}{16}$ in.
c. Uneven door heights, binding in a corner. One corner is lower than the other; hammer a shim in under the low spot.
d. Doors not flush along the astragal. The frame is twisted: "eyeball" the frame edges, noting where they're higher (or lower) than the surrounding finish surface. Push high edges in, low edges out.
e. The door won't stay shut, or one hinge binds while the others work fine. The hinge is irregular. This surprisingly common failing can be rectified by bending the gnurls on one of the hinge leafs, as in Figure 6.17. Bend the leaf on the door, though, because you'll probably split the jamb if you try to bend the leaf attached to it.

17. Working the door takes a lot of time, shim adjustments, level and plumb readings, and patience. If you haven't yet shimmed upper and lower corners, and the frame head, do so now. When the doors fit reasonably well, drive nails below shim points, using 16d galvanized nails

Figure 6.17 If a door won't stay shut or it binds at one point, a hinge may be irregular: bend a leaf on the door. Do this as a last resort.

Figure 6.18 When the doors are installed correctly, nail the frame to the rough opening. Those nails in the center of the frame will be covered later by stop pieces; others must be sunk and filled. For extra purchase, replace center leaf screws with screws long enough to sink into the framing behind.

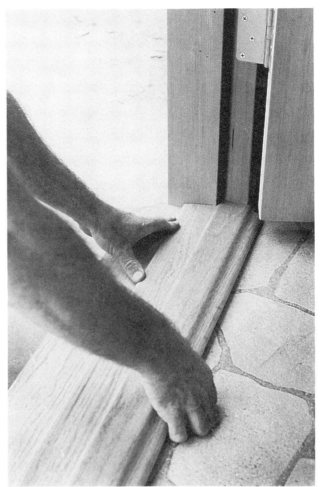

Figure 6.19 The threshold should straddle the gap between the sill and the finish floor: caulk its underside and screw it down securely.

to anchor the frame solidly to the opening. Leave nail heads sticking up until you're all done, however.

Now put the weatherstripping in—which you'll remove before finishing the door—and test the fit again.

18. Once you're happy with the way the doors operate and fit, replace any hinge-leaf screws that you may have removed earlier. These screws will probably split the shims, which is OK; but if you find that they change the inclination of the hinge leafs, bend the gnurls a tad until things are right.

19. Test for plumb, level, and fit one last time. Finally, nail the frame on both sides of the integral stop so that jambs can't twist when the doors swing.

Final touches and tips. Don't tear your hair out if the installation seems to take forever: double doors are notorious for migrating just when you're sure they're finally right.

20. Nail down the sill; an exterior trim skirtboard nailed beneath it will prevent it from further twisting.

21. Cut the threshold—if the threshold is a separate piece—to the full width of jamb rabbets, then notch it to fit around the integral stops milled into jambs. Do not cut the threshold too strong, however, or you'll push out the frame. The astragal, by the way, should clear the threshold by $\frac{1}{16}$ to $\frac{1}{8}$ in. If you need to strip the existing floor before applying a new one, don't attach the threshold now; do it when the new floor and the sill are finished.

22. Cut off shims so that you can attach casing. Stuff insulation between the frame and the rough opening.

23. Attach the hardware as described in Figure 6.27.

24. When you're done, remove the doors and to their bottoms screw rubber-gasketed *door wipes*, which seal tightly to the threshold.

25. Miscellany:
    a. If your double doors swing toward the outside, specify nonremovable hinges. Otherwise, someone can break into your house just by pulling hinge pins.
    b. If your doors require $4\frac{1}{2}$-in.-wide hinges (Table 6.1), whose screws are quite long, you may have to cut down screws in the jamb leaf so that you can shim behind. (Use a metal-cutting blade in a reciprocating saw.)

TABLE 6.1

Sizing hinges[a]

Hinge Size (in.)	Door Thickness (in.)	Door Width (in.)
$3\frac{1}{2}$	$1\frac{1}{8}$–$1\frac{3}{8}$	Up to 32
4	$1\frac{1}{8}$–$1\frac{3}{8}$	32–37
$4\frac{1}{2}$	$1\frac{3}{8}$–$1\frac{7}{8}$	Up to 32
5	$1\frac{3}{8}$–$1\frac{7}{8}$	32–37
5, extra heavy	$1\frac{7}{8}$ and up	37–43
6, extra heavy	$1\frac{7}{8}$ and up	43 and up

[a]Information adapted from U.S. Navy Bureau of Naval Personnel, *Basic Construction Techniques for Houses and Small Buildings* (reprinted by Dover Publications, New York, 1972).

c. Don't think that you can correct racked doors with the edge bolts—the sliding bolts that secure the second door at the top and bottom. This is a common mistake; instead, you must unrack the frame.

d. A venerable how-to tip debunked! Correcting binding hinges by shimming up hinge leads is a waste of time; bend the leaf gnurls instead (Figure 16.17).

e. To help support the considerable weight of oak doors, remove one standard screw in each jamb hinge leaf and replace it with an extra-long ($2\frac{1}{2}$ to 3 in.) brass-plated screw.

f. Kerfed weatherstripping is really the wave of the future: good-looking, available in a range of colors, effective, durable, and easily replaced.

g. Some carpenters don't bother shimming the frame head because, they reason, it will be held in place by the head casing. Shim it anyhow: you'll know it's level, and it will jump less when you nail casing to it.

h. *Very important:* Prime and paint all six sides of exterior doors—especially top and bottom edges—before putting on weatherstripping. On bare wood, that means at least one coat of primer and two coats of a good-quality oil-based paint (not latex). The bottom of the door is particularly vulnerable.

Hanging a Door

Since the preceding sections featured prehungs, now we'll see how to hang a door from scratch. Having thoroughly described shimming in earlier sections, let's focus here on hanging a door to a frame that's already in place—a common enough task in older houses.

Before we proceed, a few terms: the vertical elements of a door are called *stiles*, the horizontal parts, *rails*. The *hinge stile* is the stile into which hinges are set; the opposite stile, into which the latch is set, is the *latch stile* or *lock stile*. Cutting hinges into doors or frames is called *mortising the hinge*; the cutout areas, *mortises* or *gains*.

Preparation. Because it's not always feasible to set a new door in an existing frame, don't buy the door until you've had a close look at the frame.

1. Assess the doorway. Ideally, the hinge jamb of the frame will be plumb and its corners square. More likely, it will have become a parallelogram. It's possible to hang a door to a hinge jamb that is not plumb, but the more out

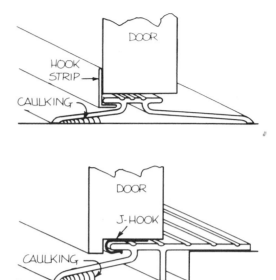

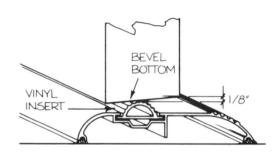

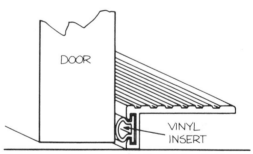

Figure 6.20 Exterior sills and thresholds.

of whack the frame is, the more you'll have to cut down the door to make it fit. At very least, the hinge jamb must be straight: if it's bowed and you can't draw the bow back with screws, either rip out the old frame or forget the new door.

2. Size the hinges. If the frame already has gains from an earlier set of hinges—and they're not too crusted with paint, measure them to size the hinge. Otherwise, consult Table 6.1. Loose-pin hinges are by far the easiest to install, because you can pull the pin and set the hinges separately. Most interior doors require two hinges, unless the door is heavy (e.g., oak); exterior doors, three hinges.

3. Transfer frame measurements to the door. Note not only the height and width of the frame—take several readings—but also the precise angles of the corners, using an adjustable bevel to transfer them to the door. When cutting

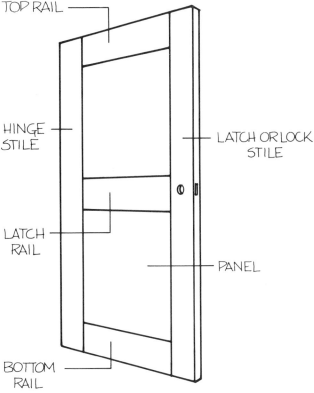

Figure 6.21 Door parts.

down or building up the door, keep in mind that it must have these minimal clearances when hung: a $\frac{1}{8}$-in. gap along the hinge jamb, $\frac{1}{16}$ in. along the strike jamb, $\frac{1}{16}$ in. above the door, $\frac{1}{4}$ in. clearance above the finished floor.

If you have $\frac{1}{4}$ in. or more to remove from a door edge, use a circular saw guided by a straightedge clamped to the stock. If you have only a small amount to remove, use a jack plane or a joiner plane; to avoid splitting stiles, plane from the outside edge in. To free both hands for the planing, build a jig from two pieces of 2×10 nailed on-edge to a 2×4 base; the 2×10s should be set apart $\frac{1}{4}$ in. plus the thickness of the door. To secure the door in the jig, slip in shims or (if it's a finish-grade door) carpet scraps.

4. Decide which way the door should swing. Make sure that there is an electric light switch on the latch side, just inside the room, so that you can turn lights on easily upon entering the room.

5. Nail temporary stop pieces to the inside of the jambs, setting the pieces as far back from the edge of the frame as the doors are thick. Stated another way, when you push the still-unhinged door into the door frame, these makeshift stops will keep the face of the door flush with the edges of the frame.

6. After checking the frame measurements one last time, bevel the latch stile of the door before installation. This bevel, which should be slight (about 7 degrees), ensures that the door will swing freely and not bind against the latch-side jamb. The bevel may also save you the annoying task of planing down a door swollen shut by humid

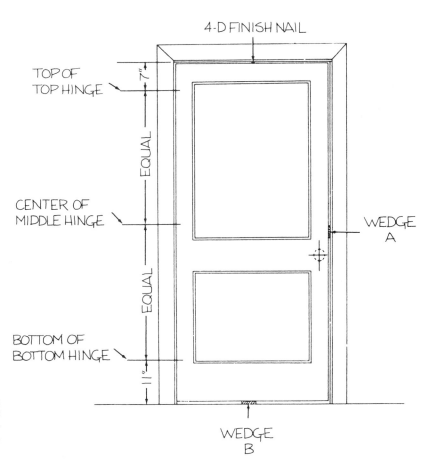

Figure 6.22 Fitting the door to the frame: locating hinges. (From U.S. Navy Bureau of Naval Personnel, Navy *Basic Construction Techniques for Houses and Small Buildings*, reprinted by Dover Publications, New York, 1972.)

weather. Although beveling enlarges the space between the door edge and jamb, the gap will be hidden by the stop pieces.

7. Fit the door into the frame thus: insert a cedar shim between the lock stile and the lock jamb, halfway up, so that the hinge stile is forced against the hinge jamb. Don't overdo it. Lay a 4d finish nail on top of the door in the middle, between the top rail and the header jamb; then wedge a shim under the door, between the bottom rail of the door and the floor. This second shim pushes the door up, lodging the 4d nail firmly and forming a perfect gap—$\frac{1}{16}$ in.—between the door and the head jamb above.

8. Holding a hinge leaf in place and using a sharp knife, simultaneously mark the hinge locations on both the hinge jamb and the hinge stile of the door. If the frame hinge gains are usable, transfer them to the door. Otherwise, set the top of the top hinge 7 in. from the top of the door; the bottom of the bottom hinge, 11 in. from the bottom of the door. If there's a third hinge, place the middle hinge equidistant from the other two.

9. Pull out the temporary shims and remove the door; secure the door on-edge and mortise-in the hinge leaves.

Setting hinges. Use a utility knife to trace the hinges and outline cuts; where you're worried about splitting wood, use a utility knife instead of a chisel.

10. Pull the pins from the hinges; that way, you can work with one hinge leaf at a time. If a door is to work properly, the edge of each leaf must be perfectly parallel with the edge of the door. Place the leaf between the hinge marks already scribed and trace around the leaf.

Note: Set the hinge leaf slightly back from the edge of the door, usually $\frac{1}{4}$ in., but at least in $\frac{1}{8}$ in. As an example, for a door $1\frac{3}{8}$ in. thick, use hinges $3\frac{1}{2}$ in. by $3\frac{1}{2}$ in., and set each leaf of the hinge back from the door edge about $\frac{1}{4}$ in. Thus, the mortise you cut in the door (the cut is also called a ''gain'') will be $1\frac{1}{8}$ in. wide by $3\frac{1}{2}$ in. long. The cut is $1\frac{1}{8}$ in. wide, it should be apparent, because a hinge edge is *set back* $\frac{1}{4}$ in. from the edge of the $1\frac{3}{8}$ in.-thick door.

11. Set the hinge leaves into the hinge jamb in the same way, including the setback shown in Figure 6.23. When you apply the permanent stop piece, it will also be at a setback distance from the hinge; otherwise, the door would bind on the stop.

12. Mortise hinge leaves so they are precisely flush with the edge of the door and the face of the hinge jamb. Gains can be cut out in one of several ways; perhaps the easiest way is to use a *butt marker* or a butt gauge. The butt marker, which comes in varying sizes, stamps the outline of the hinge leaf into the wood; then all the renovator has to do is chisel out the area inside to the correct depth.

Another time-honored technique is to gently score along the outline of the hinge with a straight chisel, being careful when the chisel edge is parallel to the grain, so that you don't split the wood. Chisel out the hinge gain, as shown in Figure 6.24 B and C. Chisel no deeper than is necessary; if the hinges are too deep, the door won't shut fully, and in time the hinges will pull free.

Carpenters with many hinges to mortise often use a router in a template. Hinges for these special mortises have corners that are slightly rounded. When mortising hinges by hand, however, use standard hinges, which have square corners; mortising a round corner with a chisel would be very difficult.

13. Screw the hinges into the gains cut, using only one screw per hinge leaf until you've assessed your progress. As you attach the leaves to door and frame, make sure the loose hinge-pins will be up when it's time to insert them.

14. Fit the door into the frame again, this time without the wedges and 4d nail of step 7. Gently lift the door so that the hinge leaves on the door mesh with those on the stile jamb. If the clearance along the hinge stile is too great, and the clearance along the lock stile too scant, set the hinges a little deeper.

15. If the gaps seem right but the door sticks slightly as it nears the lock jamb, take the door down and bevel the leading edge further.

16. When all is well and all hinge leaves are securely screwed down, place the permanent stop pieces as neces-

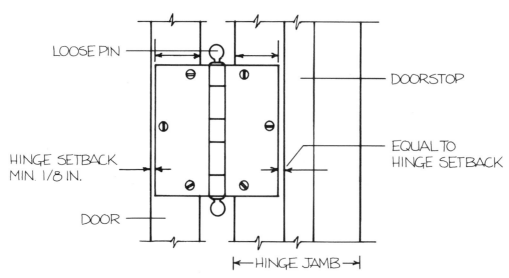

Figure 6.23 Setting back the hinges.

A.

B.

C.

D

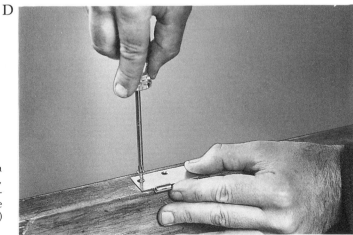

Figure 6.24 Mortising hinges. (A) Trace the hinge leaf with a very sharp pencil or a utility knife. (B) With a straight chisel, trace the outline of the leaf; then cut a series of parallel, shallow cuts to produce a mortise of even depth. (C) Keeping the beveled face of the chisel down, pare out the hinge gain. (D) Refit the hinge leaf until it is flush to the edge of the door.

sary. For the best-looking results, miter the corners of the stop joints. Tack the stops into place with 4d finish nails every 10 in. or so, but don't drive the nails down all the way until you have set locks, latches, handles, and so on. Be sure the stop on the lock jamb is tight against the door; it receives most of the impact. Then apply the finish trim.

17. Some final thoughts:

a. Hinges are manufactured with provision for a $\frac{1}{16}$-in. gap along the hinge jamb when the hinge leaves are mortised flush to the jamb and the door. In other words, when the door is shut, hinge leaves do not quite touch.

b. A marking gauge is sometimes used to mark the set-back lines on doors and jambs.

c. When you are about to screw hinge leaves down, start screw holes with an awl or a fine-pointed nail set; this will prevent screws from going in at an angle. Even better is predrilling all screw holes with a self-centering bit (Vix bit), which prevents screw points from migrating along the wood grain.

Door Frames

As noted earlier, interior door frames consist of two jambs (sides), a head (top), and stop pieces usually added later. Most often, the tops of the jambs are dadoed or rabbeted to receive the head, which is glued and end-nailed through the jambs. The frame stock is usually 1-in. pine or fir.

Three variables determine the dimensions of the frame:

1. The thickness of the walls. The frame stock should be $\frac{1}{8}$ in. wider than the thickness of the walls, measured finish surface to finish surface. "Margined" in the rough opening, frame edges will thus stick out $\frac{1}{16}$ in. beyond the finish surfaces on both sides of the wall, facilitating trim work.

2. The width of the door. The inside width of the frame should be the width of the door plus $\frac{3}{16}$ in.: $\frac{1}{8}$ in. clearance from the hinge jamb, and $\frac{1}{16}$ in. from the latch jamb. Thus if the dadoes into the jambs are $\frac{3}{8}$ in. deep, the length of the head will be: the width of the door + $\frac{3}{16}$ in. + $\frac{3}{4}$ in.

3. The length (height) of the door plus the height of the finish floor. If the finish floor is already installed, the jambs will sit directly on it, but if it is yet to be installed, sit the jambs directly on the subfloor. In that case, the length of the jamb will be: the thickness of the finish floor + $\frac{1}{4}$ in. clearance above the floor + the height of the door + $\frac{1}{16}$ in. clearance above the door + 1 in. above the dado/rabbet joint.

One final variable will affect the length of the jambs: any slope in the doorway—but that can be corrected when installing the frame, as described on page 93. For that reason and the varying thickness of flooring, commercially milled jambs are usually left 2 to 3 in. long.

Constructing the frame is straightforward if all cuts are square to the stock and uniformly deep. Cut dadoes with a dado blade in a table saw, or with double-fluted straight bits in a router.

Door Hardware

In this section, you'll find the three most common locksets: cylinder locks, mortise locks, and interconnected locksets. To keep hardware from being marred, don't install it until finish work is done.

Door knobs are usually centered 36 in. above the finish floor, although it is common practice to set new hardware at the same height as existing knobs and handles elsewhere in the house. Because it's imperative that the door be steady as you cut and drill into it, pull the hinge pins, remove the door, and support it in a door buck. It is possible to work on a hanging door, but it's not very productive.

Specifics vary, but most locksets come with paper templates that position three sets of holes: one set drilled in the face(s) of the door, for handle spindles or cylinders; another in the edge of the door for latching assemblies; and a third in the latch jamb (or second door, if there are double doors) to receive latch and dead bolts. *Important:* Measure the thickness of the door before you buy a lockset or key cylinder; some mechanisms are adjustable, but others are matched to door dimensions.

Installing a cylinder lock. Cylinders, probably the least secure of the three locks we'll consider, are popular because they have a key cylinder in the handle and a small spring-loaded *dead latch* (or plunger) which, when properly installed, prevents the latch bolt's being jimmied open with, say, a credit card. Cylinder locks can, however, be snapped with a pry bar or a swift kick; to be secure, install a dead bolt, too.

1. Remove existing hardware (if any) and mark off new holes to be drilled according to the template provided by the lock manufacturer.

2. Drill cylinder holes into the face of the door stile, using an expandable auger bit—or, better, a $2\frac{1}{8}$-in. hole-cutting drill bit. After drilling almost all the way through the stile, back the bit out and finish the hole by drilling from the other face; this prevents splitting.

3. Drill the latch-bolt hole into the edge of the door, using a $\frac{7}{8}$-in. spade bit; it will intersect with the cylinder hole.

4. Insert the latch-bolt assembly into its hole and use a utility knife to trace around the latch plate. Mortise the inscribed area so that the plate is flush to the edge of the door.

5. Screw down the plate and insert the lock chassis as instructed by the manufacturer. Try the handle; it should turn freely.

6. Position the strike plate on the jamb. You can put lipstick on the end of the latch bolt, shut the door, and release the bolt against the jamb. Or use the *center marker* shown in Figure 6.27.

7. Using a $\frac{7}{8}$-in. spade bit, drill into the jamb $\frac{1}{2}$ in. deep. Center the strike plate over the hole and trace around it with a utility knife. Mortise the area so that the plate is flush. An important detail to note: When the door is shut, the latch bolt should descend into the strike plate hole; the small plunger next to the bolt should not. Rather, that

A.

B.

C.

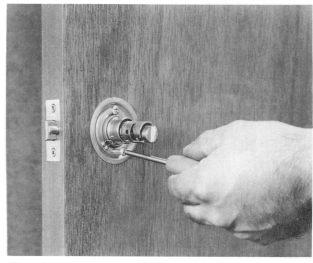

D.

Figure 6.25 Installing a tubular lock. (A) It's easiest to put the replacement lock at the same height as the old one. Keeping the bit perpendicular, bore the cylinder hole with a hole-cutting saw in your drill. (B) Mortise the gain for the latch-bolt assembly and screw it down. (C,D) Insert the lock spindle to fit around the lock mechanism, screw on the plate, which draws the lock spindle tightly to the door, and attach the handle.

spring-loaded plunger should be stopped short by a lip on the strike plate.

8. Note the strike-plate reinforcer in Figure C.1A.

Installing a mortise lock. Mortise locks have been around for a long time because they're convenient and effective. As the latch and dead bolts are housed in a single casing, they can be opened with a single key-turn. It's a bit of work to set the lock case into the edge of the door—but so housed, the unit is very secure. The stile of the door must be solid or it cannot support such a lock.

1. Using a template, mark spindle holes onto the face of the stile. These spindles, to which handles attach, run through the mortise case.

2. Holding a $\frac{5}{8}$-in. drill bit perpendicular to the stile, drill until the point of the bit just starts through the other side. Back the drill out and finish drilling from the other side.

3. Again using the template, mark the edge of the door. Using a square, mark across the edge to indicate the upper and lower limits of the lock case; then mark a line running between them, exactly in the center of the edge.

4. Along this centered line, drill holes with a $\frac{5}{8}$-in. bit held perpendicular to the edge—overlapping the holes slightly.

5. Holding the bevel of a chisel toward the inside of the hole, square up the edges. As you chisel, test-fit the lock case periodically to avoid chiseling away any more than is necessary.

6. When the lock case fits all the way into the hole, trace around the edge of the latch plate with a utility knife. Chisel out that small area until the plate is flush to the edge of the door.

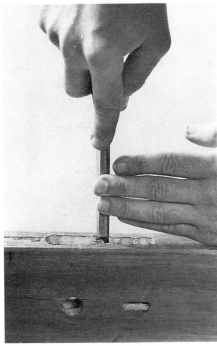

A.

B.

C.

D.

E.

Figure 6.26 Installing a mortise lock. (A) Using the paper template provided by the supplier, mark holes to be drilled into the door face and edge. Drill and pare out the mortise in the edge of the door. (B) Periodically test-fit the lock mechanism so that you chisel out no more than necessary. (C) When the fit is good, trace and let in the lock's face plate so that it is flush to the edge of the door. (D) Use a try square to make sure that the escutcheon is parallel to the edge of the door, then center-punch holes for the screws which follow. (E) Slide the spindle through the escutcheon, and screw the knobs to the spindle.

7. Insert the spindle handles and make sure that they turn freely. Screw the case to the edge; slide escutcheons over the spindles and screw down; screw the handles or knobs to the spindles.

8. Mark strike jambs and set strike plates as mentioned above. When the door is shut, the bolts should not rattle in their strike plates.

Interconnected locksets. To illustrate this type of lock, we'll conclude the installation begun in ''Upgrading a Double-Door Entry.''

1. Although they arrived without hardware attached, the door frames had been partially predrilled; both doors, face-drilled for cylinders, but only the first door was edge-

A.

Figure 6.27 Installing an interconnected lockset on double doors. (A–C) Most prehung doors come predrilled but without hardware attached. To align the deadbolt from one door to the strike area of the other, use a *center marker.* Use a screwdriver to push its point against the edge of the second door; then drill that spot with a spade bit, going no deeper than the length of the bolt. Attach the strike plate (Figure C.1A). (D,E) Install the dead- and latch-bolt assemblies in the first door and feed in spindles from handles or lock cylinders. The second door (Figure 6.9B) has dummy hardware; to secure it, mark off and drill edge-bolt holes (F) in the frame head and the sill.

B.

D.

E.

F.

drilled for bolt assemblies. Temporarily insert latch-bolt assemblies into such edge holes to be sure that they're deep enough; drill deeper if necessary.

2. Position strike marks on the edge of the second door. The easiest way to do this is with the *center marker* shown in Figure 6.27A and B. Insert the tool into the edge holes of the first door and press its point against the second door.

Using those points to center your bit, drill about 1 in. deep into the second door.

3. Mortise the dead and latch bolts into the edge of the first door and screw them down.

4. Insert the handle spindle into the latch bolt shank, and the key cylinder into the dead bolt shank; secure.

5. Mortise the strike plates in the second door, shut the door, and test the bolts for fit in the plates. As noted earlier, the latch-bolt plunger should not descend into the strike-plate hole. You will greatly strengthen the strike plate area with the reinforcer shown in Figure C.1A, whose extra-long screws solidly anchor elements to the framing behind.

6. Attach the dummy hardware on the second door.

7. With both doors shut, extend edge bolts, trace around them, and mortise holes into the head frame above, and into the threshold and sill below. Screw down bolt plates to keep the bolts from migrating.

Common Repairs

Most problems involving a door or a doorway can be easily deduced using common sense and close observation. Are frame jambs plumb? heads level? parts square to each other? Quite often, the hinge jamb will sag from the weight of the door. When the door is closed, are the gaps around it uniform? Look closely at the edges of the frame and at the surfaces of the door. Scuffing, scraping, or splintering indicates binding and abrasion, in which case you must plane the door or, in the case of gliding doors, pare the sides of the pocket opening.

Hinged doors. By far the most common ailment of old hinged doors is top hinge-leaves pulling loose because of the door's weight, with the top of the lock stile striking the lock jamb. Try the simplest remedy first: rescrew the hinge leaves to door and jamb. Chances are, the screw holes are stripped; build up the hole with round toothpicks snapped in two and stuffed butt-end-first into the hole. If that doesn't do it, try slightly longer screws.

If the wood is too tired to accommodate longer screws, fill the spots with wood filler—or better yet, wood patches—and reset the hinges nearby but higher. Don't try to set hinge leaves in wood filler; they won't hold. If your wood patch is $\frac{1}{2}$ in. or more thick and is well glued, it may hold a reset hinge.

A less likely cause of a sticking door is insufficient nailing of the hinge jamb to the rough opening behind. If that's the case, the jamb will be springy to the touch; renail with 16d casing nails. Another possibility is that the door's rails and stiles have separated; you'll see gaps if that has happened. If the door has settled, pull the hinge pins, glue the gaps between rails and stiles, and clamp the parts together with bar clamps. (My second book, *Salvaged Treasures*, has a chapter on overhauling old doors; see Appendix G.)

Finally, the problem may simply be that the house has shifted, the frame is out of square, and the door is bumping on the frame. That's easily remedied; take down the door and plane the offending corner or edge until it fits. As you plane stile ends, work from the outside edge of the door inward; you are planing end grain, and splits can develop if you plane in the opposite direction.

It is rarely worth the trouble to tear apart and square up a door frame; each frame is too interconnected with baseboard trim, finish wall surfaces, and so forth. Also, it's doubtful that you could reassemble the pieces to fit well.

Gliding doors. Gliding doors, also called pocket doors, open by sliding into wall cavities, allowing a large passage-way between rooms and maximum usable space, primarily because there are no door arcs to contend with. This type of door is a nuisance to repair, however; the mechanisms involved often are hidden in a wall or behind trim. The hardware for a gliding door varies, making it somewhat difficult to generalize about their assembly. The main problems encountered, though, are: (1) rollers that need adjusting, (2) binding because a track's bent or a door's jumped the track, and (3) binding because a stud has warped into the opening.

Try an easy remedy first. Thoroughly vacuum along the bottom track of a door, if it has one. Dust, scrub, or scrape off grease, built-up wax, or varnish. If yours is a two-door setup, there is probably a stop in the middle of the top track; unscrew the stop so you can slide each door, one at a time, all the way out of its wall cavity. Do so. Then, with a long-nosed vacuum attachment, clean out the accumulated grime within the walls. These remedies should

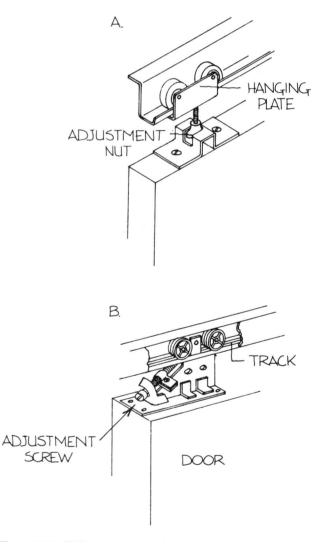

Figure 6.28 Gliding-door mechanisms. If a gliding door scrapes along the floor, you may need to tighten its adjustment screws. If the mechanism is overhead, as in these examples, drive shims under the door to take the weight off the wheels; then tighten the screw (or nut) with a screwdriver. If the door face is abraded, chances are that it's off its track or the track is bent: you'll have to remove casings to get at mechanisms.

make the doors slide freely. Lightly grease metal tracks and oil wheels that are accessible.

Another easy remedy that is frequently overlooked: if the doors pull out only with the greatest of effort, squealing, and resistance, they may simply be off their tracks. If the wheels are located underneath, lift the doors and, with a friend sighting at floor level, set them aright. Doors without floor channels probably are hung from above; lift the doors to reposition the wheels in the metal channels. If the doors glide but not easily, the rollers may need adjustment (Figure 6.28). You may also have to remove trim to get at the mechanisms.

If a door has fallen off its track into the open side of the cavity, its face may be abraded on that side. If, however, the door is abraded on its opposite face, it's likely that a stud has warped into the opening. Start by pulling the door out of the pocket; if necessary, remove wood trim so that you can get a better grip on the door. Protect the floor, too: insert a shim or a piece of wax paper under the leading edge of the door so that it won't scrape. Once the door is clear of the cavity, lift it off its track and scrutinize the track. If the track is bent, either hammer it straight or replace it.

To replace the track, you'll have to remove the finish wall on one side. New tracks are readily available, with matching hardware for the top of the door. The size of the assemblies depends on the weight of the door: medium, heavy, and extra heavy. With one finish wall removed, you're also in a position to correct warped studs—usually the first stud, going into the pocket. Cut halfway through the outside of the stud (the side away from the pocket) and drive a wedge into that cut. The wedge will force the edges of the cut apart and straighten the stud. Smear the wedge with glue before hammering it in.

WINDOWS

Many of the terms used to describe doors and door frames are common to windows: frames are made of *jambs, head,* and *sill,* with *stops* to guide the window. Looking at the window sashes, we see horizontal *rails* and vertical *stiles.* With double-hung windows, the top rail of the lower sash and the bottom rail of the upper sash are also called *meeting rails.*

Windows arrive installed in a preassembled frame, complete with hardware necessary to operate them. Unlike door installation, there is no need to trim window jambs, so the sill is always preattached. If the unit is large, the frame may also be braced diagonally to keep it square. In most cases, the stops will be tacked to the frame so that

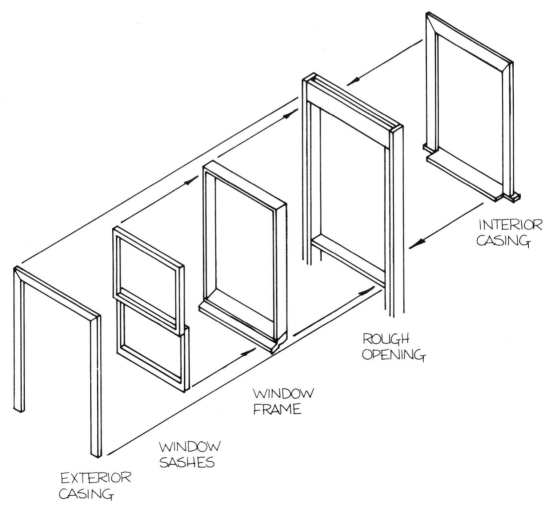

INTERIOR CASING

ROUGH OPENING

WINDOW FRAME

WINDOW SASHES

EXTERIOR CASING

Figure 6.29 Elements of a window. Sashes are almost always prehung in frames and installed as a unit.

you can remove sashes to prime and paint them. You can also get windows precased (trim already attached), but as is the case with precased doors, you can't shim them properly and they can be tricky to flash. If possible, get the casing precut but not attached.

A few words about materials. Wood windows are the first choices of most professionals: they're reasonable to work with and they look good. Vinyl-clad wood units, which cost more, are virtually a maintenance-free alternative—an especially good choice in very wet climates. Metal windows generally don't look good as retrofits in older houses; and because of problems with condensation and heat loss, they're poor choices in cold climates.

Installing a Double-Hung Window

Double-hung units are by far the most common type of openable window, comprising almost 95 percent of the category.

Preparation. Assess the rough opening well in advance of installing the window; if your unit requires a special order, it could hold up your job.

1. Size the rough opening. The dimensions of the R.O. are usually the same as the *call-out size* for the window. A 4030 window, for example, requires a 4 ft×3 ft rough opening; the frame itself being about $\frac{1}{2}$ in. smaller than those dimensions so that there is room to shim. *Note:* Check manufacturer's specs for each window; some specify a bigger opening.

2. Measure the thickness of walls, from interior finish surface to exterior sheathing. As with door frames (p. 93), the width of a window frame should be the thickness of the wall + $\frac{1}{8}$ in.

3. It is possible to extend window frames after the fact, by ripping down $\frac{3}{4}$-in. stock, then gluing and nailing it to the existing edges of the frame. Use 4d finish nails if the stock is $\frac{3}{4}$ in. or less; 6d nails if it's greater. Be forewarned, however, that some manufacturers bevel frame edges slightly; if that's the case, set your table saw blade at a complementary angle when ripping the stock.

4. Check for level. When hanging doors, the jambs ultimately carry the weight; with windows, it's the sill. It is possible to shim an existing opening to make it level, but if you are framing out a R.O., take pains to make the sill level. Although it's not necessary structurally, doubling the sill gives you more to nail to. If the sill is level, the rest of the installation is child's play.

5. Wrap the opening in felt paper. Ideally, extend the felt paper covering the sheathing into the rough opening, wrapping it into the R.O. and stapling it down. The frame thus sits surrounded by felt paper. Later, slit the paper along the head of the frame so that you can slip cap flashing up underneath it. Around the exterior of the opening, better builders also add a layer of 6-in.-wide fiberglass-reinforced strip flashing, which further cuts infiltration along the seams where siding abuts the exterior casing.

Positioning the frame. Because window frames are also, in part, channels in which sashes glide, manufacturers gen-

erally construct them well, of kiln-dried stock not likely to warp. Thus it's rarely necessary to correct for bowed stock when shimming and nailing.

6. Approximately center the window frame in the opening, left to right, top to bottom. If the window is considerably smaller than the opening, use blocks—rather than shims—to build up beneath the sill.

7. Margin the frame so that the frame is centered in relation to the thickness of the wall.

8. Check the top of the sill for level; shim as necessary.

9. Shim the bottom corners of each jamb, inserting a pair of shims between the frame and the R.O. on each side. Shim the frame just snug, keeping it roughly centered in the opening.

10. Using a tape measure, measure "diagonals" (i.e., opposite corners of the frame). If these diagonal measurements are exactly equal, the jambs are plumb. If jambs are not plumb, gently push the top of the frame over until they are. If, for example, the diagonal from upper left to lower right is longer, push the top of the frame to the right. Check the diagonals again; when they are equal, shim the top corners of the frame.

11. See that the sashes slide freely with the frame so shimmed.

12. Install a third set of shims on each side, midway between the other two. Place these shims gently so that you don't bind the sashes. Check the level, margins, and diagonals again, then nail the shims: one 10d (minimum) galvanized finish nail through each shimming point—just three nails per side. That's enough to hold the window.

13. Slide the sashes again to ensure that they're still operating freely, then shim the head at each corner, again using just one nail through shim points. If you haven't done so already, nail through the blocks (or shims) beneath the frame sill.

If the window unit is large, add additional shims to prevent it from sagging or flopping in the opening. If, for example, the unit is a picture window with openable casements on either side, be sure to shim beneath the mullions on either side of the fixed window, in addition to the other shim points around the windows that open. In brief, shim or block beneath the sill at least every 18 in. on a really large unit.

14. Go outside and look at the unit; from the inside, parting strips may prevent you from seeing the whole picture. Is the frame centered well in the rough opening? Are there gaps between the sash and the frame?

Finishing touches, parting thoughts. If the unit looks good both outside and in, and the sashes slide freely, you're almost done.

15. Set the nails holding the frame to the opening. Score and cut off the shims flush to the finish surfaces. Pack fiberglass insulation between the frame and the R.O., using a putty knife. Fiberglass is good because it's unaffected by moisture.

16. Install casing inside (p. 410) and out (p. 129). Nail casing to the exterior sheathing with 8d galvanized finish

A.

B.

C.

D.

Figure 6.30 Installing a pre-hung window. (A) After assessing the rough opening and wrapping its sides in felt paper, insert the window, centering it in opening. (B) Drive a pair of shims at each corner to hold it in place, then go back and check for plumb and level, adjusting the shims as you go. (C) Margin the frame as well so that its inside edge is flush to finish surfaces—or will be when they are installed. (D) After adding a third set of shims on each side, final-check for plumb and nail off the frames.

nails; to interior surfaces with 6d finish; to the edges of the frame with 4d finish.

17. Do *not* set the nails holding the stops to the frame until you have painted the sashes! You'll need to give sashes—including edges—at least one coat of primer and one coat of an oil-based exterior paint to seal out moisture.

18. Using silicone or butyl rubber, caulk: where the exterior casing meets the frame, where the exterior casing meets the finish wall surface, and beneath the apron under the sill. Most manufactured sills have a *drip kerf* cut into the underside of the sill to prevent water from wicking up under the siding, but a caulk bead beneath the apron is a bit

of insurance; it also prevents blow-back during a heavy storm.

Repairs and Replacements

Ailing windows are common to old houses. Their maladies usually fall into two groups: (1) those which have been insufficiently maintained and thus have swollen, shrunk, or rotted; (2) those which have been buried in paint and no longer open. Many windows will suffer from both ills. (Since double-hung windows are the most common, they are featured in the examples that follow.)

If possible, pick a dry spell for window work; have a roll of sheet plastic (polyethylene) handy to tack over openings should a storm arise. When working with old windows, be patient and use force very sparingly.

Glazing. Because so much heat is lost through windows, it is imperative that glazing be in good shape. Cracked or loose glass should be removed and reset in fresh putty. Where putty is missing, patch-repair it so that water does not collect and rot the wood of the sash.

A word about glazing and glass: *glazing* refers to the transparent medium in a window or door. Glazing is usually glass, but it may also be plastic. The term also refers to the act of setting glass or plastic in its frame, hence the

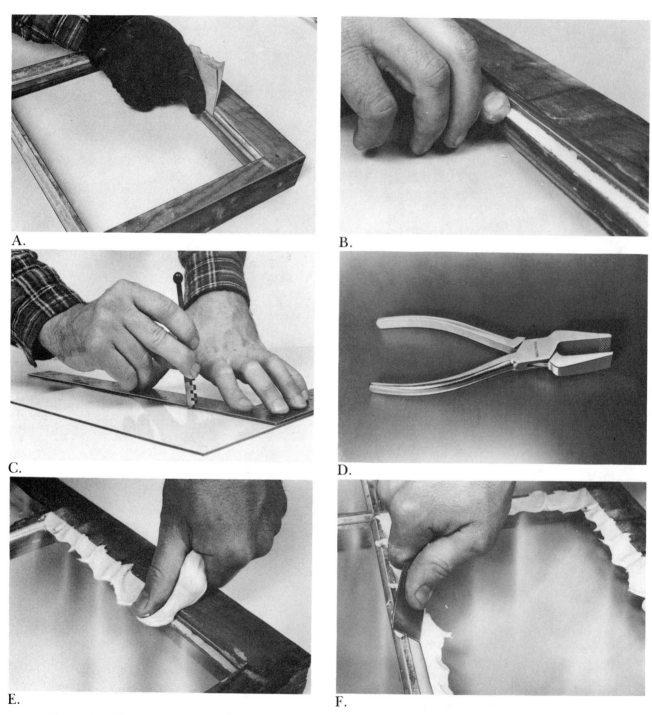

A.

B.

C.

D.

E.

F.

Figure 6.31 Glazing a window. (A) After removing glass shards, old putty and glazier's points, sand the frame lightly. (B) Seal or lightly oil the frame and spread a bed of putty. (C) Using a straightedge to guide your cut, pull the glass cutter with even pressure; one pass should do it. (D) Glass pliers are necessary to snap waste pieces less than 1 in. wide. (Brookstone Co.) (E) Once the glass is pressed into the putty, push in glazier's points and apply putty generously, pressing it into place. (F) Holding the putty knife at an angle, pull with a steady motion to cut free excess putty.

replacement of glass and the puttying that follows is also called "glazing." Putty, by the way, is also known as "glazing compound."

A glazier's chisel is best for scraping away putty, although any stiff putty knife will do. Even with the gentlest treatment, though, glass sometimes breaks; so gloves are a must and goggles are advisable. Always take your time in this work, so that you save as much old glass as you can and avoid gouging sashes.

Although most putty comes out easily, some is difficult. There are a number of ways to dislodge tough stuff. If you are stripping paint from the sash as well, the stripper usually softens putty at the same time. Heat is also effective, whether it is an electric putty softener or a propane torch with a small point. Because direct heat can cause glass to break, though, cover individual lights (panes) with a piece of hardboard wrapped in aluminum foil. When you clean out old putty and remove glazier's points, sand the frame very lightly. (Do not use chemical stripper *and* heat at the same time.)

Brush onto the exposed wood a sealant or a half-and-half mixture of alcohol (or turpentine) and linseed oil. This will prevent the dry wood from sucking the oil out of fresh putty. When this treatment is dry, spread a thin bed of putty along the lip that receives the glass. This bed of putty will prevent rattling and seal air leaks.

The replacement pane should be $\frac{1}{8}$ in. less than the width and length of the frame opening, to allow for variations in temperature and for shifting of the house. Glass must be clean; kerosene is an effective lubricant suitable for the cutting that follows.

Using a straightedge to guide your cut, pull the glass cutter, with even pressure, toward you. One pass of the cutter should do it. After scribing the cut, gently rap the ball end of the cutter along the underside of the cut—up and down its length—until a clear line develops. Then, with the cut directly over a table edge, quickly snap the waste portion free. If the waste piece is too small to grip, use glass pliers.

Note: Old glass is imperfect and often hard to cut. If you're using old glass as replacement stock, plan on breaking at least a third; get extras.

As you place the glass in the frame, press around the edges so that the putty will seat evenly beneath the pane. With a putty knife held almost flat against the glass, push in new glazier's points until they are half-buried. (Never hammer the points in or you'll break the glass.) Sink a point every 6 in., or at least one for each side of the glass. Be particularly careful when pushing points into *muntins* (the wooden strips between panes); if you push a point in too far, you could crack the pane adjacent. Glass in metal-frame windows is usually held in place by metal spring clips, which can be reused.

Once the replacement pane is held fast by glazier's points, apply putty generously. Scoop out a palmful of putty and knead it in one hand until it is soft and pliable. Press the putty in place as shown, continuously kneading it and feeding it out to your index finger and thumb. You'll recover any excess when you trim, so use a lot of putty now; it will give you a good seal.

To trim off the excess, hold the knife blade at an angle of about 45 degrees to the glass, with a corner of the blade touching the glass and the middle of the blade resting on the frame. Pull the knife evenly toward you, plowing a steady furrow through the putty. Go back and clean up the corners after removing most of the excess. You shouldn't be able to see putty from the inside of the window once the unit has been reinstalled.

If the putty does not stick, either you're holding the knife handle too high or there is dust on the frame or the glass. If the problem is just the drag of the knife blade across the putty, a bit of saliva on the blade will do the trick. When the putty has cured for a week, overpaint it slightly (i.e., paint onto the glass) to seal the putty from weather.

Simple repairs to frame and sash. Your window may merely be painted shut. Rap around the perimeter of the sashes with a hammer, using a wooden block to prevent marring; then run a scraper or a putty knife along the edges of the sashes.

If the lower sash still won't slide smoothly, remove the inside stop, a thin piece of wood which guides the lower sash. These stops usually are easily replaced. Many stops are held to the jamb with screws—if you can find the screws under all that paint. If you can't, pry up the stop with a chisel, utility bar, and so on. If you must, it's better to destroy the stop than to damage the jamb.

Before removing the sash, you may have to disconnect the sash weights: pull the window out and tie the sash cord in a knot, as shown. Pry the cord free from the sash and lift the sash free.

Clean up the channels in which the sash moves, with a putty knife, and then sand. Try the sash to see if it now slides more smoothly. If so, wax the channels and the sides of the sash, replace the sash, and reattach the inside stop.

If a sash weight has come loose from its cord or chain, reattach it while the sash is out. Access to these weights varies, but there is often a removable panel toward the bottom of each jamb. If there is no such panel, pry the jamb trim off.

If the sash still does not slide easily after these ministrations, the stiles (the vertical pieces) of the sash are probably too encrusted with paint. Remove the paint from the stiles with paint remover, a sander, or both. It's not wise to remove this paint with a plane or a chisel because there may be nails that could damage a cutting tool's edge; also, it's easy to gouge the wood.

After removing the paint, try the sash again. The fit should be close, with just a bit of lateral movement possible. Seal the edges of the sash with a coat of primer-sealer or with a penetrating oil such as tung oil. When the sealer or oil is dry, wax both sash and channel and refit the parts.

Freeing a bound upper sash is more difficult, because it is held in place by an outer stop, accessible only from outside the house—an obvious problem for those windows on upper stories. Further, exterior window trim often partially obscures the outside stop. The only alterntive is to remove the lower sash and then remove the parting (middle) stop to get at the upper sash from the inside. Since the parting stop is usually dadoed into the jamb, that stop is usually destroyed when it is pried out.

A.

B.

C.

D.

Figure 6.32 Simple repairs. (A) If a sash is impossible to free by scoring around it with a putty knife, remove the trim. (B) To remove the lower sash without losing the sash weight, tie off the sash cord. (C) The cord removed, you can now lift out the sash, remove excess paint, wax both sash and channels, and if necessary, plane down the sash to make it slide freely. (D) When the lower sash is removed, the access panel is accessible: replace cords or refasten sash weights now.

Old frames, new sashes. Some repairs are possible if windows have deteriorated. Let's start by looking at those situations where repair is *not* advisable. Gut the existing unit and install a new one when:

1. Sashes or frames are so soft that you can impress the point of a screwdriver into the wood, with slight pressure.

2. There is a gap where rails and stiles meet; such sashes are probably not operable and are likely to deteriorate quickly.

3. Frame jambs are out-of-parallel by more than $\frac{1}{8}$ in. Although it is possible to cut down sash rails to accommodate out-of-level sills or heads, jambs that are not parallel will

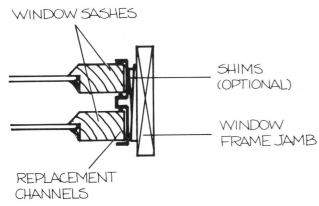

WINDOW SASHES

SHIMS
(OPTIONAL)

WINDOW
FRAME JAMB

REPLACEMENT
CHANNELS

Figure 6.33 To insert replacement channels you must remove the parting strip between the upper and lower sashes.

either bind sashes or require them to fit so loosely that energy losses will be astronomical.

4. It's obvious that the window area is badly leaking. Here, the culprit is probably the flashing around the unit. In this instance, gut the exterior casing, too: if a window is dead, chances are that the old tar paper flashing (if any) gave up the ghost years before. Strip and replace flashing and casing, as described in Chapter 7.

So, assuming that the frame is largely parallel and solid, consider:

Replacement Units. These preframed, preassembled units are sort of a frame within a frame. Remove the existing sashes and pull out all parting stops, especially the middle one, so that existing jambs are flat. The unit is then placed into the old frame, shimmed minimally, and screwed or nailed down. This is not the greatest approach aesthetically, because you'll have to build up the casing to cover the seam between the old frame and the new. But you won't have to disturb finish surfaces, and the new sashes fit tightly and slide well.

Replacement Channels. These products try to improve the operation and weathertightness of sashes by replacing old wooden stops with plastic channels set into the old frame. They try, but they don't succeed very well. For starters, you must remove sashes, rip out old stops, and sand down jambs so that they are as flat as possible. Then, after fitting sashes into channels, insert the whole configuration into the old frame and secure. Trouble is, the channels are generally so light that they can't be shimmed effectively, and many sashes fit poorly in the channels, being either too loose or too big.

INSTALLING A SKYLIGHT

By letting in light, skylights can transform a room—making a bathroom seem larger, a kitchen warm and cheery, a bedroom a place to watch the stars. And because of marked improvements in flashing and quality control, skylights can now be installed without fear of leaks from outside or excessive heat loss from within.

Selecting, Situating, and Sizing

There are a range of options to consider when buying a skylight, not least of which is the manufacturer. Although sizes have become pretty much standardized, quality varies greatly—so ask local contractors or lumber suppliers which makers they prefer. Decide the following:

1. Should it open or not? Operable skylights vent excess heat and some models spin 360 degrees for easier cleaning.

2. Is it energy-efficient? Most units come with doubled thermal-pane glass, but does the unit also have a thermal break to minimize loss by conduction? A frame with metal continuous from inside to out will wick off a lot of heat. A better bet is sealed wood.

3. Does it have step flashing along its sides (desirable), or strip flashing which must be caulked to keep water out? Does the maker supply a cricket to flash the upper edge of the skylight, or must you have one fabricated? Crickets held shed water and debris—particularly important for wider units.

4. Does the unit have tempered glass? That's an important consideration if a tree overhangs your roof. Your building code may require such glass.

5. Does it have a screen, and if so, how easy is it to remove? If the unit will be installed beyond reach, how easy is it to open and close?

6. What other options does it offer, such as blinds or polarizing tints?

Where you put the skylight is largely an aesthetic matter. If it's a kitchen unit, catch the morning sun by facing east. If placed in a hallway, even a small unit provides enough light to do without artificial light. In a bathroom, privacy is the main consideration. In general, avoid skylights in south-facing roofs unless you are designing for passive solar gain; such a skylight will let in a lot of heat. Similarly, skylights in west-facing roofs may provide too much heat in parts of the southern and southwestern United States, where the afternoon sun is strong. Finally, avoid skylights straddling the ridge of the house unless you have a lot of money; they are inclined to leak and can be a horror, structurally.

Sizing. Sizing a skylight is manifestly a structural concern, which we'll get to next, but first a few other things to think about. Oversizing skylights is a common mistake: even the smallest unit brightens a room greatly. Moreover, much of the light is reflected off the sides of the skylight *well*—that's why wells are usually painted white. (Skylight "wells" are also called "shafts," "light shafts," "light wells," and so on.) You can increase the amount of light markedly just by flaring out the sides of the well. Finally, the size of your skylight decides how many rafters and ceiling joists (if any) you must cut into—a big decision. In general, a long, skinny skylight disturbs the structure less and hence will be less expensive to install.

Structural Considerations

When you cut rafters or ceiling joists to install a skylight, you weaken the structure at several points, which creates

A.

B.

C.

D.

Figure 6.34 Installing a skylight: an overview. (A) Expose existing framing; (B) frame rough opening in roof (frame lightwell or new ceiling, as necessary); (C) insulate; (D) install and flash skylight, install finish surfaces. (Murphy Construction, Orinda, California)

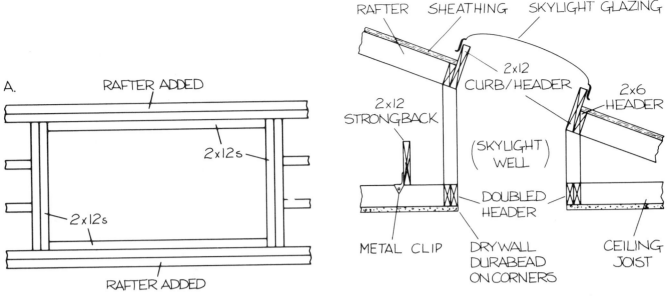

Figure 6.35 Framing for a skylight. (A) If you cut into only one rafter, it may not be necesary to add trimmer rafters. (B) Note that the 2 × 12s create a curb which raises the skylight well above the roof plane.

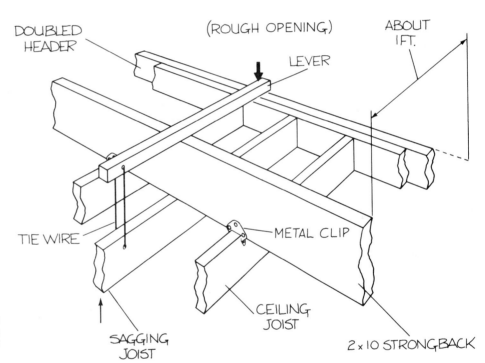

Figure 6.36 Using a strongback as a fulcrum to raise sagging joists. Once the joist is raised, nail it to the strongback with the hurricane clip shown.

point-loading. If you can move the opening slightly to avoid cutting a rafter or a ceiling joist, you're already ahead of the game. If your ceiling joists are also your rafters, your task is much simpler: you don't have to build a skylight well. Otherwise, altering the structure is primarily a matter of redistributing point loads to other members.

You can also downsize the skylight to save cutting: many modern skylights are sized incrementally to fit between rafters on standard spacings. Choose a skylight that is narrow enough, say, 26 in. wide*, and you won't have

*In standard construction, rafters are nominal 2-in. lumber, set 16 in. on-center. Remove one rafter and there is an opening 30½ in. wide between rafter faces. From this width subtract 3 in. for the sides of the skylight curb, allow ½ in. of clearance, and you have 26 in. for the width of the skylight.

to disturb more than one rafter. In that case you may not need to double up rafters along both sides of the opening, either. However, you should always double up rafters if the roof is heavy (clay tile, slate, wood shakes), or if rafters are undersized or spaced too far apart. And in all cases, double the headers at both ends of the opening. If, on the other hand, you cut two rafters, you *must* bolster each side of the opening by adding a rafter. Rafters added must run the full distance from ridge to top plate if they are to be effective.

The ceiling is another structural consideration: support ceiling joists with a *strongback* (Figure 6.36), before cutting into them. A strongback is a piece of dimension lumber that supports from above: it's set on-edge above ceiling joists to keep them from sagging. To be effective, it should (1) run perpendicular to the joist grid, (2) be set as close as possible to the cut ends of the joists, (3) distribute the load across several joists, by resting on continuous members well beyond the opening, and (4) be attached to joists below with *hurricane ties*, or a similar metal framing connector.

If the width of your skylight suggests cutting out three or more rafters, call in a structural engineer. You are radically altering the frame and may need *purlins*, posts and the like, to take up the load.

Cutting and Framing the Openings

Go up into the attic or crawl space above to locate wires, pipes or anything else that might be hazardous if you cut through it. If that's not possible, cut off all electricity and punch up through the ceiling to see what's there. Remove ceiling insulation, if any; then disconnect and cap any wires and/or pipes so you can reroute them around the opening later. (Chapters 11 and 12 show how to do this safely.) Where possible, work from a step ladder rather than atop the joists; you're less likely to crack the finish ceiling.

One final aside: Get a tetanus shot before you go into the attic. It's easy to bump into a roofing nail protruding from the underside of a roof.

Exploratories and layout. Using a reciprocating saw with a plaster-cutting blade, cut a hole into the ceiling; wear goggles and a mask. Don't cut this opening to its final width just yet, however, because you may need to move it slightly to accommodate changes in the light well. Make the opening wide enough for the top of a stepladder, because it's easier to work atop a ladder than crouching beneath a roof.

Now lay out the rough openings. To get some sense of where the corners of the skylight and the light well will go, tack four plumbed strings from the underside of the roof. Move the strings until you're pleased with the approximate position of the unit, then use your tape measure to mark off more exact dimensions.

Figure 6.37 Before cutting into a finish ceiling, reconnoiter the area above: remove wires and push back insulation so that it won't rain down. Initially, cut no deeper than you must to remove the finish ceiling—note the shallow angle of the reciprocating saw. (Thanks to Strong Construction, San Leandro, CA for the skylight installation through the end of the chapter.)

Cutting into the ceiling. Cut out ceiling joists within the opening, after first tacking them to a strongback so they can't sag. Use a framing square to make sure cuts are square. Cut ceiling joists so their ends will be set back 3 in. from the final opening in the ceiling. This *setback*, shown in Figure 6.38A, ensures that the doubled headers at both ends will be flush with the edges of the finish ceiling. Use three 16d common nails to nail the first board of each doubled header to the joist ends; nail the second header of each pair to the face of the first. Once the headers are in place, nail into their ends, through the contiguous joists. Use double-joist hangers for greater strength.

Opening up the roof. Now cut the opening in the roof. Although skylight configurations vary, the rough opening required is typically: the length and width of the skylight frame, plus 3 in., for the two $1\frac{1}{2}$ in.-thick sides (and ends) of the 2× curb that raises the skylight above the roof, plus $\frac{1}{4}$ in. on all sides, for clearance.

After you put on your goggles, drill up through one of the corners you established on the underside of the roof. Use at least a $\frac{3}{4}$-in. bit, which is large enough to accommodate your saw blade. Then, using a combination blade in a reciprocating saw, cut around the rough opening. You needn't cut out the full opening on the first pass. To get started you may want to cut along existing rafters, using them as a guide for your blade. Don't cut through the rafters yet, however.

If you cut out sections of roofing that straddle at least one rafter, you needn't fear a cut-out section's falling on you. After you cut around the section, rock it until the nails holding it to the rafter pull free. If that doesn't work, insert a wrecking bar between the sheathing and the rafter and pry it loose. This method—pulling out intact sections of sheathing and shingles—saves a lot of mess. Working from underneath is also safer, and it's easier than going aloft and trying to figure out where the cutout should go. Trim the rough opening until it's exact.

Framing the skylight opening. Once you've cut out the section of sheathing/roofing, double up existing rafters, if that's necessary. As noted earlier, rafters should run from top plate to ridge and should be nailed to existing rafters with 16d nails staggered every 18 in. or so. Space will likely be tight under the roof, so you may need to drive in new rafters with a light sledge or a framing hammer.

At this point, if there is only one existing rafter within the rough opening, go ahead and cut it out; use a framing square to mark cuts. You don't need to support its severed ends. But if your opening is wide or your roofing is heavy, support above and below the cuts with 2×4 tees running down to the floor.

Cut rafter ends back $1\frac{1}{2}$ in. from the edge of the sheathing so that the first header will be flush to the edge of the sheathing. Header off the cut rafters: Use three 16d common nails to face-nail the first board of each double header to each rafter end, then end-nail each header, through adjacent rafters.

The second boards of both headers create the ends of a curb on which the skylight sits. (This is true for most but not all makes of skylight.) This curb raises the skylight well above the roof, thus making it less likely to leak in a heavy

A.

B.

C.

Figure 6.38 Framing the lightwell. (A) After removing the finish ceiling, use a power saw to cut out the ceiling joists. Take care to cut the joist ends square. Note too that the ends are cut back 3 in. from the edge of the drywall so that (B) doubled headers will be flush with the edge of the drywall. (C) Cut into the roof and frame out the curb for the skylight, then toe-nail the short studs of the lightwell.

rain. For this reason, the second headers are typically 2×12s. The sides of the box may also be 2×12s, and can be face-nailed with 16d commons to the rafters on either side. Always build this curb between the existing rafters if you can; it's stronger that way.

But sometimes it happens that there's not room for a 2×12 curb within the opening—if you have to double up rafters on the inside of the opening, for example. In that event, build the curb *atop* the sheathing and toe-nail it down into the rough opening, as shown in Figure 6.39. In this case, use 2×4s or 2×6s for curb sides.

Once the skylight curb is complete, cut the short studs that frame the skylight well. These studs, which run from the rough opening in the roof to the one in the ceiling, should be spaced 16 in. on-center and toe-nailed with 10d common or box nails. To minimize splits, predrill the nail holes. Because you'll want a flat surface for the drywall to follow, align studs with a taut string or a straight board. Add nailing blocks in all corners for the drywall to come.

A.

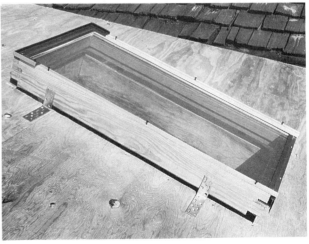

B.

Figure 6.39 The skylight curb from above. (A) The curb amid a section of roofing to be replaced. (B) A prefabricated curb, held above the roof sheathing with L-angles.

Installing and Flashing the Skylight

This section began with some of the criteria for choosing a skylight. If you chose well and bought a unit with well-made flashing, including step flashing along the sides, the best advice is to follow the manufacturer's instructions carefully so your warranty will be honored should the unit leak.

Start by centering the unit in the 2 × 12 curb. Check it for square and make sure that it can open and close without binding. That done, attach it securely.

How you attach flashing will be affected by whether you are stripping the roof for reroofing or just intending to patch-repair the existing roof, around your new skylight. If you're patching, you may be able to salvage enough shingles from the section of roofing you cut out. Otherwise, buy a new bundle of shingles that will match the old ones as closely as possible.

Installing the base shoe. Center the *base shoe* along the bottom end of the skylight box so that its "ears" stick out an equal amount.

If you are applying a new roof, stop shingling one course short of the lower edge of the skylight. The bottom flange of the base shoe will overlap the upper edge of those shingles, and will itself be overlapped by a successive course of shingles along the sides, as in Figure 6.40B. If working with an existing roof, just place the shoe over the shingles below and nail it down with three gasketed aluminum nails along its bottom edge. Fold each ear flat against the side of the skylight curb, then attach each with one nail driven into an upper corner.

Step-flashing the sides. The lower corners of the curb are perhaps the most problematic part of the skylight to weatherproof, because of the gap in the flashing necessary to fold the metal ears around the corners. You can mitigate the

A.

B.

C.

D.

Figure 6.40 Flashing a skylight. (A) This skylight, here shown before flashing, has an extended perimeter lip which acts as a cap flashing for the base flashing shown in steps B and C. (B) The base shoe along the lower side of the skylight goes *over* the roofing below (here, shakes). Have this piece fabricated. (C) The first piece of step flashing along the side overlaps the corner of the base shoe in step B. Thereafter, alternate step flashing, shakes, and felt paper as shown. (D) The head flashing that runs along the upper edge of the skylight overlaps the last pieces of step flashing along the sides. Note that the felt paper above overlaps the head flashing. Because of the possibility of leaks above a skylight, have this piece fabricated by a metal shop, too. (Skylight made by Skylight and Sun, Berkeley, CA.)

problem by caulking those ears with silicone and overlapping them with the step flashing shown in Figure 6.40C.

As you proceed up the side of the unit, alternate L-shaped pieces of step flashing and courses of shingles, as described on page 80. If you are installing a new roof, stop shingle courses $\frac{1}{2}$ in. shy of the curb. If working with an existing roof, pry up the edges of adjacent shingles carefully with a flat bar, and slip flashing between courses. (It may be easier to slip in this step flashing before you build the curb in the rough opening.)

The vertical leg of each piece of step flashing should extend up to the top edge of the curb, there to be overlapped by the counter flashing built into the unit. The lower leg of the ell should extend under the shingles at least 4 in. If you are having your flashing fabricated, tell the sheet-metal maker the height of the curb above the roof so he will make the upper leg tall enough. Trim as necessary.

As with all flashing, avoid nailing in the channel where the water will run; nail each ell as high up, and as far from the curb as possible. Two nails will suffice for each piece of step flashing. If there's any question that a shingle edge might blow up, put a dab of roofing cement under its corners. The last pieces of step flashing stop at the uppermost edge of the curb, there to be overlapped by the head flashing.

Installing the head flashing. The head flashing can be a flat ell-shaped flashing with ears soldered at the corners, or it may be a *cricket* fabricated with a peak in the middle to divert water away from the head. (Crickets are highly recommended.) In either case, the top of this flashing slips under the last course of shingles above. The head flashing (or cricket) should rest directly on the sheathing. If working with existing roofing, you may need to pry up a few nails to fit the flashing under; caulk any resultant holes with silicone. As necessary, fold the ears of the head flashing around the skylight curb, nail each with one nail high up, and caulk the seams with silicone.

One final note: A 20-gauge metal cricket is stiff enough to stand without any additional support beneath; nailed to the skylight box, it becomes even more formidable.

Counter flashing. Counter flashing is usually an integral part of the skylight cover. It caps the skylight curb and, extending over the sides, should overlap the base flashing by at least 2 in. Installation will vary from maker to maker.

Finishing off inside. To reflect the most light, the skylight well should be drywalled and painted white. Because of the point-loading around skylight wells, drywall panels become shear walls of sorts, so use $\frac{1}{2}$- or $\frac{5}{8}$-in. water-resistant drywall. Such drywall is commonly known as "greenboard" and is recommended for kitchen, bathroom, and other humid areas. Further stiffen outer corners with metal *cornerbeads* (page 373).

·7·

EXTERIORS

The exterior of a house is a membrane much like a roof. It intercepts water and directs it downward, protects the structure underneath, and allows people to moderate the climate within. If the exterior of a house is in reasonable condition, you can put off repairs until later; but if there are water stains on walls and floors inside, or rotted siding and trim outside, it's time to act. Only leaking roofs or shifting foundations are more pressing concerns.

The best way to prevent rot and infestation is to keep water from wood—in short, maintenance. By keeping your roof in good repair and your gutters cleaned, water will have a tough time getting behind siding. The edges of materials are particularly susceptible to rot, so caulk gaps wherever board ends abut, clapboards join corner trim, stucco meets door casings, and so on. Replace broken glass or missing putty. Cut back bushes that are too close to the house, for shrubbery retains moisture. Ventilate attics and crawlspaces so that moist air can't linger. If you can feel wind whistling around a door or window, water can probably get through, too; put in new weatherstripping.

Finally, and perhaps most important, maintain painted surfaces; a paint membrane must be continuous to be effective. The same is true for stains: being thinner, they should be reapplied more often. To protect wood in high-moisture areas, there are also preservatives which, when dry, can be painted over (p. 445).

So maintain, maintain. Don't wait until things deteriorate: shabby exteriors may lead to serious structural damage within.

FLASHING

Flashing, which directs a flow of water, is critically important along the seams of a building, where disparate materials meet, or wherever something protrudes that could dam up water. Flashing is discussed at great length in Chapter 5, so if you have questions about some material or method not discussed here, look there.

Water runs downhill. If you keep that in mind, installing flashing should be no mystery: pieces uphill always overlap those downhill, so that water never meets an impediment.

Walls and Corners

Exterior sheathing should be covered with at least 15-lb felt paper, to prevent direct contact with wood siding, which could lead to rot. (We'll use felt paper as the generic wall covering in this section; there are many more, Dupont's Tyvek being very popular these days.) Felt paper also cuts air infiltration to a degree, which saves energy and makes a home more comfortable. Finally, felt paper is a barrier to any moisture that gets behind the siding, and so acts as a flashing of sorts. Accordingly, when you apply felt paper to sheathing, start at the bottom of the wall and work up, the pieces above overlapping those below by 6 in.

Many builders continue felt paper into the rough opening and staple it to the framing lumber, thus putting a layer of paper between the opening and the frame. As an extra bit of protection against blow-in under a window sill, fold over the edge of the felt paper so that it forms a dam of sorts.

Give a building's corners some extra attention, too. After covering them with 15-lb felt paper rolled across the sheathing, further clad those corners with vertical strips of 30-lb felt paper cut 2 ft wide and folded lengthwise. Some builders also recommend covering corners—especially interior corners that see a lot of water—with lightweight sheet metal, but that seems excessive. If you go to the trouble of using metal, however, cut it 1 ft wide, fold it lengthwise, and nail only along its outer edges, using big-head roofing nails.

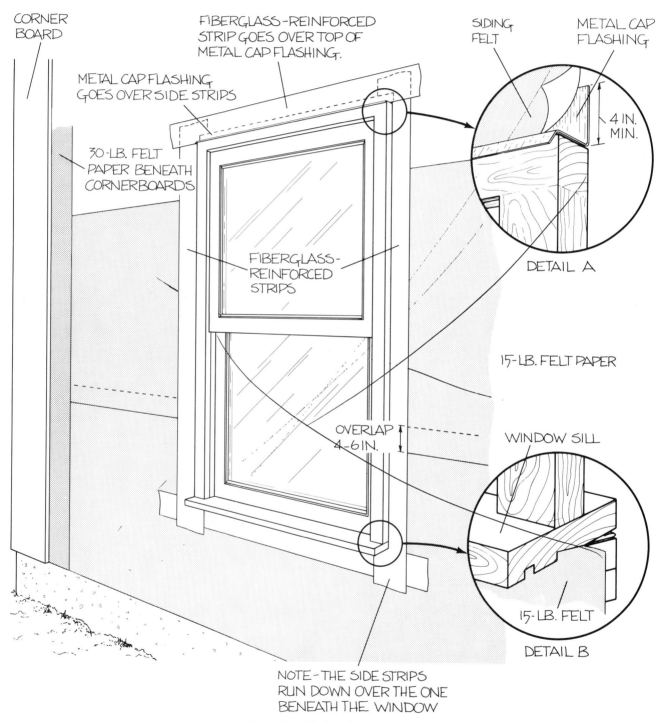

Figure 7.1 Window flashing details.

A.

B.

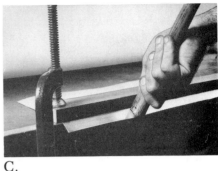
C.

Figure 7.2 Working with sheet metal. (A) Reduce the binding on tin snips by gently pulling upward on one side of the cut. (B) Shape the metal by bending it along a straightedge—the edge of a table as shown here, a 2×4, or a window's head casing. (C) Smooth the fold by running a hard object along it.

Windows and Doors

Mildew on interior walls, blistered paint, swollen sashes, and water stains around doors and windows are in many instances caused by improper or absent flashing. When you upgrade such units, it's imperative that you strip back exterior siding far enough to add strip flashing and cap flashing.

Strip flashing. Strip flashing is available in several forms, the most convenient being fiberglass-reinforced rolls 6 and 9 in. wide. These strips are reinforced to withstand the considerable racking around rough openings. Strips cut from regular roll roofing are not quite as durable, but they'll cut infiltration a lot; use at least 30-lb felt paper.

Apply the strip below the window sill first, tucking its top edge into the rabbet cut into the underside of the sill; extend the strip at least 9 in. beyond the jambs on each side. The three other pieces of strip flashing around the opening should run from the inside edge(s) of the frame out to the sheathing, thus sealing the gaps between the window frame and the rough opening. Cut the flashing strips running along the jambs long, so that they overlap the ends of the piece running under the sill. Last, cut the strip over the head of the frame 9 in. long on each side, so that it can overlap jamb strips. You then apply the window casing over this strip flashing, trimming off excess along the inside of the casing.

There arises the question whether this strip flashing goes over or under the felt paper covering the sheathing. It doesn't really matter: the strip flashing is extra protection. The only detail worth fussing about is the area over the opening, as shown in Figure 7.1, which brings us to cap flashing.

Cap flashing. Cap flashing is probably the most important single flashing element on an exterior wall, for it diverts water around openings. Without cap flashing, head casings are dams that impede water flow and increase the chances that it will run behind trim.

Because of its importance, cap flashing is usually metal: copper, aluminum, or more likely, galvanized. You can make it yourself, using methods shown in Figure 7.2, but if you're flashing any number of openings, have it bent by a sheet-metal shop. The top leg of the flashing should extend up under the siding (and paper flashing) above at least 4 in., its top bend should be slightly more than 90 degrees, and its lowest leg should extend beyond the head casing at least $\frac{3}{8}$ in. to prevent water from blowing in under the flashing.

In new construction, you would install the window, the window casing, the cap flashing, and then the siding. In renovation, you must slide the cap up under existing siding, which complicates things somewhat. If you're also installing new window casing, you have several options. You can fabricate the cap flashing in place, prefolding the metal into an ell, inserting the head casing, then using a 2×4 to shape the protruding metal down over the casing.

Figure 7.3 Flashing over head casing.

Perhaps a better way to go is to loosely install the preformed flashing over the opening, tack up the head casing, then pull down the cap flashing so it fits snugly against the casing. Then nail off the flashing. In either case, nail the cap flashing within 1 in. of its top edge; the siding will hold down the lower edge of the flashing. The cap flashing should extend slightly beyond the head casing on either end—say, $\frac{1}{16}$ in. Or extend it $\frac{1}{8}$ in. and crimp it to the ends of the casing so that the metal won't interfere with the siding.

Sill flashing. Having touched on window-sill flashing, we'll look at door sills here. It's an important area, subject to a lot of weather and wear, so it's wise to use metal flashing beneath a door. A simple and effective way to prevent water's being blown under the door frame is to insert a piece of sheet metal into a rabbet cut into the underside of the sill, as in Figure 7.4A.

A somewhat more exacting sill flashing is shown in Figure 7.4B, in which the metal has two folds, its top leg fitting into a kerf cut into the middle of the sill. Caulk the underside of that sill with silicone caulking as well. This brings to mind the importance of the door's threshold (p. 101) in keeping water outside and protecting not only the finish floor inside but also the subflooring and joists beneath.

Figure 7.5 Precased units are attached to the house through a nailing flange: nail it directly to the sheathing and run strip flashing over it.

Flashing precased doors. Precased doors like those shown in Figure 7.5 have a metal flange through which you nail. Put the metal right onto the plywood sheathing, without an intervening layer of felt paper. Flash the sill as described above; then, once you've nailed the unit to the sheathing, staple up fiberglass strip flashing along each jamb casing, running it 6 to 9 in. above the head casing. Cover the end of these strips with a strip running over the head. Cap-flash (some units have an integral cap flashing), then run regular felt paper to the door, overlapping strip flashing along the jambs and above the head.

EXTERIOR TRIM

Like most things exterior, trim not only covers building seams and makes the building look good but is an important defense against weather. It covers critical seams: where the roof meets the walls, at exterior corners, where siding abuts doors and windows, and so on. To get the most out of your trim, attach it securely and caulk it periodically.

General Preparation

Apply trim to sheathing before putting up siding. Where trim will be exposed to weather, as at corners and around doors and windows, flash it as described above; but where it's protected by an overhang, a strip of felt paper between the trim and the sheathing is sufficient.

Nailing. As a rule, nail through the sheathing into the framing for the best attachment. In those rare instances where you have only sheathing to nail to, angle the nail so that it will be less likely to pull out. When a run requires several trim boards, though, it is imperative that you center all butt joints over stud centers so that both board ends can be nailed down well.

Pick a nail meant for exteriors. If you'll be sealing the exterior with a clear finish and nail heads will be visible, stainless steel nails absolutely won't rust; but be advised that they are expensive and frequently hard to find. Aluminum nails are increasingly popular because they also won't stain, but they're brittle. Most people will be well served by galvanized nails, which stain minimally and hold well. For stained exteriors, where nails are somewhat visible,

A

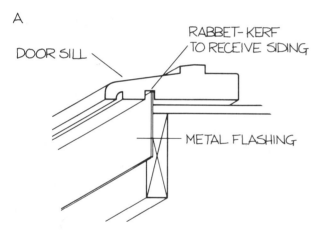

B

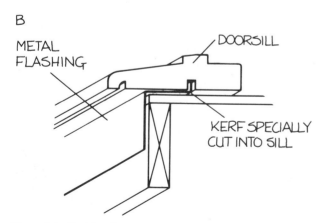

Figure 7.4 Flashing door sills. (A) To prevent water's being blown under a door sill, slide a piece of sheet metal into the kerf cut into its underside. (B) This detail, which requires a kerf specially cut in the middle of the sill and flashing folded twice, is effective even in high-wind areas and provides a metal barrier between the bottom of the sill and the subflooring. Caulk under the metal.

some contractors prefer galvanized finish or *casing* nails. But headed nails always hold better, so if you're staining or painting, we'd recommend galvanized *box* nails to attach trim: they have smaller shanks than common nails and so are less likely to split wood; being headed, they hold better than finish nails.

Nailing schedules. The nail sizes below assume 1-in. trim (actual thickness, $\frac{3}{4}$ in.) and sheathing $\frac{1}{2}$ to 1 in. thick. Where there's a question, go with a somewhat smaller size so that you don't split trim. Nail trim every 16 in., roughly each time it crosses a stud, nailing both edges of the trim so that it won't cup. To prevent splits, place nails no closer than $\frac{1}{2}$ in. to the edge.

For friezeboards and other flat cornice trim, use 8d nails. When siding butts to cornerboards, nail ends down with 6d to 8d nails; when cornerboards go over siding (rare), use 8d to 10d nails. To draw cornerboard edges to each other, use 6d nails spaced every 12 in. and driven in an angle; if you'll be painting trim, also caulk this butt joint. To attach exterior window and door casing, attach that trim to sheathing with 6d to 8d nails; use 4d nails, however, to draw casing to the edges of window or door frames.

A final word about nailing: Take the time to align nail heads, it looks much better. When nailing up jamb casing, for example, use a combination square to ensure that nail pairs are the same height. When nailing a larger area such as siding, snap chalk lines onto felt paper so that you'll know where to nail.

Miscellany. Do all shaping—such as the rabbet cut in Figure 7.9A or the beveled splashboard in Figure 7.8D—before you put up the trim; cutting already nailed pieces is arduous, and the results are usually disappointing. Avoid exposing end grain at corners—it's very susceptible to rot; do so only if you're going to paint it. Finally, if the trim is dry, prime both sides before you put it up, to prevent its absorbing water and cupping; if the wood is damp, however, nail it up, allow it to dry, and paint it in place.

Door and Window Casing

Once the frame is nailed in, pack the gap between the rough opening and the frame with fiberglass insulation to cut infiltration, and staple on the strip flashing described above. Then attach the exterior casing. Review Chapter 17 for the correct way to install casing, for it should be cut and recut to get a proper fit. Accordingly, our treatment here is cursory, and we'll assume that the casing has square-cut corners.

If you're recasing an old unit that looks to be askew, check the sill for level. If one side is lower, install the jamb casing on that side first, for it may be longer. Start by cutting a bevel in the bottom of the casing, equal to the downward pitch of the sill; use an adjustable bevel to record the angle. That done, mark the top cut: hold the casing against the edge of the frame and note where it crosses the underside of the frame head—then mark back $\frac{1}{4}$ in.

The "reveal" revealed. The $\frac{1}{4}$-in. setback from the edge of the frame is called a *reveal*. All door and window casing— interior or exterior—should have this $\frac{1}{4}$ in. reveal. Were boards perfectly straight, it would be easier just to set casing flush to the frame edge, but they're not straight. By "revealing" edges, you save yourself a lot of frustration and fool the eye.

You can use a marking gauge to scribe a faint line $\frac{1}{4}$ in. from the edges of frames or, more easily, align boards with a combination square set to $\frac{1}{4}$ in. and held flush against the face of the frame. Cut the first piece of jamb casing square across the top and tack it into place, its inner edge "revealed" $\frac{1}{4}$ in. from the face of the frame jamb. Next bevel, "reveal," and tack up the second piece of jamb casing. To make its top cut, run a level from the top of the first piece, or if the

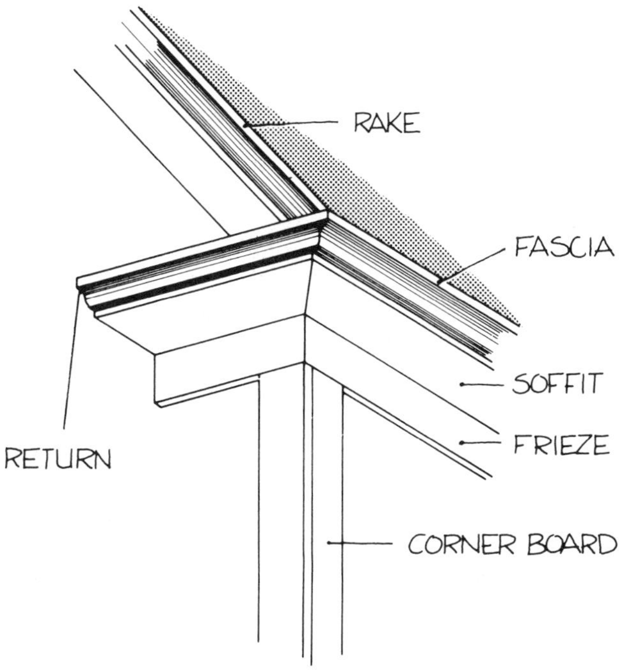

Figure 7.6 Cornice details.

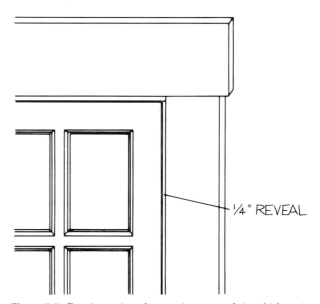

Figure 7.7 Exterior casing also requires a *reveal*, in which casing is set back $\frac{1}{4}$ in. from the edges of the window frame. Head casing should overhang slightly, to protect the end grain of the side casing.

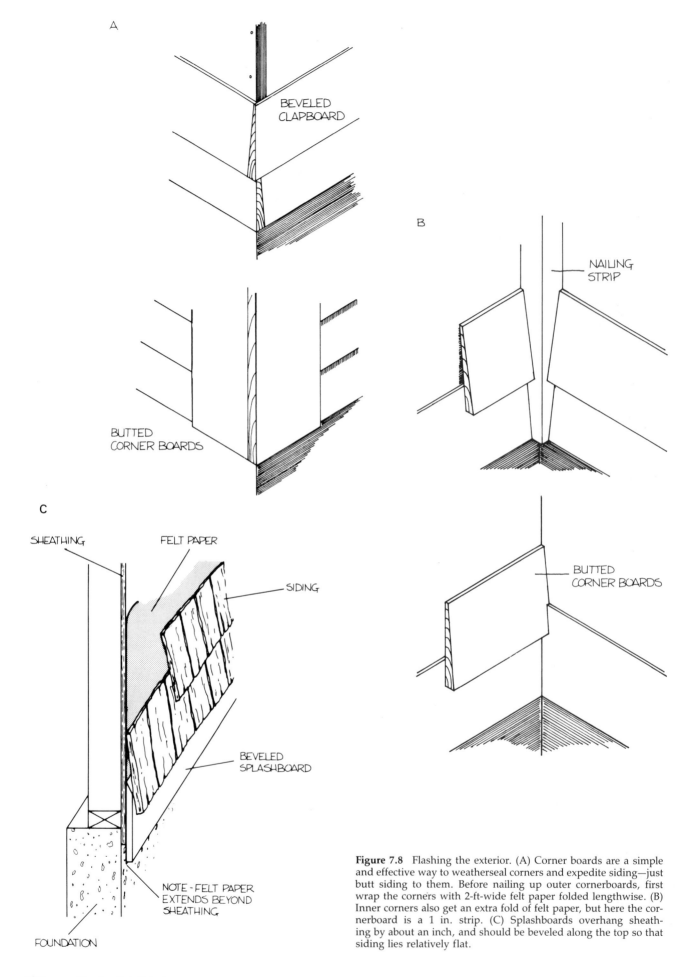

A

BEVELED
CLAPBOARD

BUTTED
CORNER BOARDS

B

NAILING
STRIP

BUTTED
CORNER BOARDS

C

SHEATHING

FELT PAPER

SIDING

BEVELED
SPLASHBOARD

NOTE - FELT PAPER
EXTENDS BEYOND
SHEATHING

FOUNDATION

Figure 7.8 Flashing the exterior. (A) Corner boards are a simple and effective way to weatherseal corners and expedite siding—just butt siding to them. Before nailing up outer cornerboards, first wrap the corners with 2-ft-wide felt paper folded lengthwise. (B) Inner corners also get an extra fold of felt paper, but here the cornerboard is a 1 in. strip. (C) Splashboards overhang sheathing by about an inch, and should be beveled along the top so that siding lies relatively flat.

window is badly out of square, use a straightedge to extend the reveal line across the frame head onto the side casing.

To determine the length of the head casing, simply measure from the outer edges of the side casings, and add $\frac{1}{2}$ in. so that the head casing overhangs $\frac{1}{4}$ in. on each end. This overhang protects the end grain of the side casings. When you are happy with the casing, set nails, caulk seams where casings meet sheathing, and get ready to nail up the siding. To prevent shrinking putty, spackle nail holes *after* priming the casing; when the spackle is dry, paint.

The ''ears'' of the sill, which stick out slightly beyond the side casing, should be cut off before installing the frame. If you install *apron* trim beneath a window sill, caulk first so that the joint will be as watertight as possible.

Corners and Splashboards

There is nothing fancy about this trim. As described in ''Walls and Corners'' above, corner boards are basically flat boards (1×4, 1×6, etc.) nailed up after first flashing well. Siding then butts right to the boards, making an attractive and weathertight corner. Simply align the edge of the first corner board flush to the corner, nail it up, then overlap that edge with the second board. For the tightest fit, caulk after boards are nailed together. If one board won't run the height of the corner, join two with 60-degree bevel cuts overlapped so that water can't run into the joint.

Occasionally, corner boards are nailed *over* siding run all the way to the corner. This is problematic, because the nails securing the trim are likely to split the thinner siding beneath—and, nailed over an irregular surface, corner boards can't seal well.

The corner boards described above cover *outer* exterior corners; in inner corners, nail up 1 in. $\times$ 1 in. strips to butt siding to. Inner corners get less weather, so it's not necessary to use wider boards. Without these little strips, you'd have to join siding with compound miter and lap cuts.

One final tip: Because the first course of siding usually overhangs the bottom of the sheathing, install corner boards 3 to 4 in. long. Once you determine the height of that first course, trim the corner board ends level to the bottom of the siding.

Splashboards, which run along the lower edges of walls, are not used universally; many builders just begin with a doubled first course of siding. To level splashboards, use a water level, as described under ''Siding'' below. Bevel the upper edge of the splashboard so that it won't kick out the first course of siding, which overlaps about 1 in.

Cornice and Rake Trim

Many terms are used to describe trim that finishes off the intersection of roof and walls. *Eave* and *cornice* are used more or less interchangeably to describe the lower part of the roof which overhangs the walls. The term *cornice* is more correctly applied to the trim that adorns the eave; when the roof is flat, however, the term denotes the entire eave trim. *Gable-end* and *rake* trim mean roughly the same thing, denoting the trim running along the sloping ends of gable roofs.

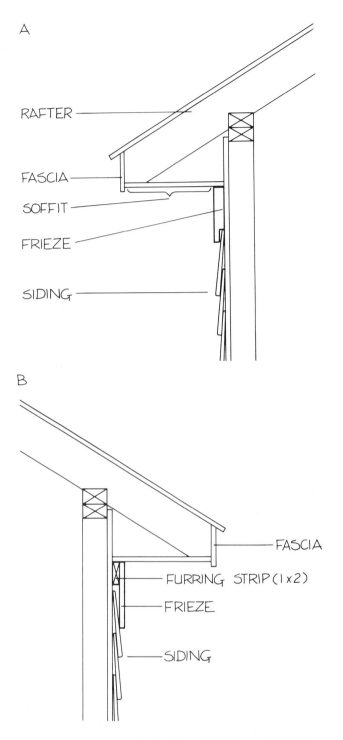

Figure 7.9 Two ways to detail a frieze. (A) Rabbet out the bottom of the frieze to receive the top of siding. The rabbet is somewhat fragile, inclined to split or curl (B) Build out the frieze with furring strips: not quite as elegant, but sturdier.

These various trim pieces seal off the critical structural junctures of rafters, top plates and studs, thus keeping moisture and pests out. Like the courses of roofing above, trim should always overlap materials below so that water will course downward without obstruction. Metal drip edges (p. 76) overhang *fascia* boards, which, in turn, should be beveled to fit tightly under the sheathing. The underside of *frieze* boards should be rabbeted $\frac{3}{8}$ in. $\times \frac{3}{8}$ in. to receive (and protect) the uppermost edges of siding. Another approach, shown in Figure 7.9B, builds out frieze and rake boards so that you can slip clapboards or shingles up under.

If your eave has missing brackets, create a template for replacements by tracing an existing bracket onto a piece of hardboard. Cut replacements from 2×12 Douglas fir stock, prime and paint all surfaces well, and predrill nail holes to prevent splitting. To adhere brackets, give their top and back edges a bead of construction adhesive; then toe-nail the bracket, using 16d galvanized box nails.

Repairing Exterior Trim

If the trim is shot, tear it off and replace it; it's not protecting anything. If you're not sure what to do, carefully remove a small representative section and take it to a mill to see what new molding would cost. (Old trim is notoriously difficult to remove without destroying it. Pry it up slightly and cut nails with a metal-cutting blade in a reciprocating saw; or try prying up part of the eave *return*, which is relatively inconspicuous.)

If, on the other hand, rot is localized, you can repair trim or ornamental woodwork without removing it, by using epoxy compounds. Two products well regarded by restorationists are LiquidWood and WoodEpox (available from Abatron, Inc., Gilberts, IL), the former a viscous liquid brushed onto porous surfaces, the latter an epoxy putty that can be built up or shaped to replace rotted areas. Because the epoxy will be far stronger than the original material, this is a good fix for millwork that would be prohibitively expensive to fabricate. But keep in mind that you're curing only a symptom: correct the cause of the rot and probe surrounding areas—especially structural areas—to be sure you're not masking far more serious conditions.

SIDING

In this section we discuss the sidings most favored for older homes: wood shingles, clapboards, and stucco. But first, a quick overview.

1. Siding must be secured to a sound, dry surface. If you're repairing a section that's rotted, cure the cause of the leak and replace rotted sheathing before proceeding.

2. To forestall rot, put a layer of felt paper between sheathing and siding, and metal flashing where appropriate.

3. Put up trim before siding, nailing trim to framing whenever possible.

4. Caulk all seams: around window and door casings, where siding butts trim, wherever gaps might admit water. Use a durable caulk such as silicone or, if you're painting, butyl rubber. Table 13.4 has more.

5. Use nails that won't rust and stain.

6. A word about putting new siding over old: don't. It won't be weathertight, may trap rot, is difficult to secure, and—because the buildup will dwarf the trim—will look terrible.

Layout

For clapboards and shingles, the two most important parts of layout are setting the first course, and varying subsequent courses so that they align with horizontal sections of trim.

Setting the first course. Start by stapling up felt paper, letting it overhang the bottom of the foundation by several inches; you can cut off the excess later. Then level the first course of siding all around the house.

The bottom of the first course of siding—or splashboard—should overhang the sheathing by about 1 in. Were the sheathing perfectly level, you could just measure down from it—but because it usually isn't, use a *water level* instead. (A water level is a long length of clear plastic tubing filled with water; keep it capped when transporting it so that you don't have to refill it continually.) You'll need a helper to use the level.

Lay out the front of the building first. Uncap the ends of the level and hold them against the corner boards. When the water has stopped moving, pencil its position—about 1 in. below the bottom of the sheathing—onto each corner board. Cap the tubing. Then, while your helper holds his or her end of the level in position, walk the other end around to the next face of the building; uncap the tubing and let the water stabilize. Raise or lower your end of the tubing until the water in your helper's end of the level aligns to the original pencil mark; then mark the new corner. In this manner, mark all the corner boards.

When you're done, use a combination square to draw light lines through your pencil marks, across the faces of the corner boards. These lines indicate the bottom of the first course of siding; stretch a chalkline between corner boards and snap it right onto the felt paper that overhangs the sheathing. You'll align the bottoms of splashboards, starter strips, and shingle butts to this chalk line. When the siding is installed, the squared lines across the corner boards become your cutoff lines.

Varying subsequent courses. By aligning siding courses to the bottom of window sills, the tops of header casing and the underside of frieze boards, you can save yourself some cutting and get a better-looking job. Achieve these alignments by increasing or decreasing the *exposure* (the amount exposed to the weather) of individual courses. There are limits—clapboards must overlap at least 1 in.—but the process is otherwise straightforward. As long as exposure adjustments are slight, say $\frac{1}{4}$ in or so, courses will look evenly spaced.

Start by measuring the full height of a wall, from a cutoff line at the base of a corner board to the underside of the frieze trim. Let's say that we want to shingle a wall whose window casing measures 63 in., top to bottom. Shingles are customarily exposed 5 in., so we have about 12 courses, with 3 in. left over. Because we want courses to align exactly to the top and bottom of the window casing, we'll have to spread that 3 in. over 12 courses, which we can do easily by increasing the exposure to $5\frac{1}{4}$ in. Calculate the exposures over the head casing (to the underside of the frieze) and under the sill (to the bottom of the wall) in the same manner. Then do likewise for the other walls.

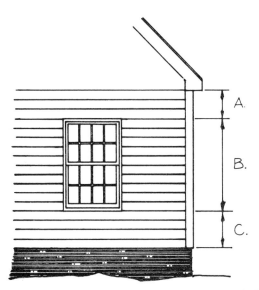

Figure 7.10 For the best visual effect, align courses with the top and bottom of windows and doors. This will require three separate calculations for the exposure, as represented by A, B, and C.

Your ultimate goal is one set of course marks with which to lay out all walls so that each course will be roughly the same height all the way around the house. Obviously, you'll have to fudge some numbers. If it's too difficult to reconcile calculations for different walls, just give precedence to the front wall of the house, and transfer its course marks to all others. Anyhow, when you have one set of course marks, pencil them onto a *story pole*, a long straight board that aids layout. Align the bottom line of the story pole to that of each corner board and, working your way around the house, pencil course marks for all the siding. To align each course of siding, simply snap a chalk line through each set of pencil marks. By measuring up from that first chalk line, you can also use the story pole to mark courses onto window and door casings.

About power nailers. A lot of people are using air-powered nail guns these days; they really speed things up. But there are trade-offs. Whatever their use, whether on subflooring or siding, power nailers just don't "suck up" the wood to whatever you're nailing to. For this reason, it's a good idea to go back and hammer (or set) each nail after you shoot it in. Headed nails shot into siding do pretty well, but power-stapling shingles and shakes seems insufficient. Staple shanks are too thin to grip well, and their two points are more likely to split wood than is a single nail.

Wood Shingles

Take the time to install shingles correctly and you'll have an exterior surface that will last a lifetime.

Materials. For shingling exterior walls, specify No. 1 cedar *sidewall* shingles; they don't have visible knots, and their butt ends seem to be cut squarer. Shingles, generally 16 in. long and of varying widths, come in bundles called *squares*. The exposure determines how many squares you need: for a 5-in. exposure, figure four squares per 100 sq ft of wall (after subtracting for windows and doors). Because you start with a doubled course, use a lesser grade for the

A.

B.

Figure 7.11 Nailing aids. (A) Pneumatic nailer; the arrow indicates the exposure gauge on the underside of the shoe. (B) A nail stripper allows you to summon one nail at a time, without getting nail points under your fingernails.

Figure 7.12 Align shingle courses to exposure marks on cornerboards. To save motion, "step up" several courses at once and work across the face of the building.

starter course underneath: order one bundle of No. 2 shingles per 50 lineal feet of wall.

When your shingles are delivered, note two things. First, is there a good assortment of widths? Because you must stagger shingle joints, you need a variety of widths. If bundles contain only narrow shingles, send them back. Second, are the shingles dry or wet? You'll know by picking up a bundle. Either are fine, but wet shingles will shrink. Accordingly, if the shingles are dry, leave a $\frac{1}{4}$-in. gap between them as you nail them up; with wet shingles, don't leave a gap, just butt edges together. To attach shingles, use 5d galvanized shingle nails, figuring 2 lb per square.

While on the subject of nailing: Use only two nails per shingle, whatever its width. Because nails must be covered by the course above, place shingle nails in 1 in. from each edge and 1 in. above the butt line of the course above.

Installation. Staple felt paper over the sheathing, use a story pole to lay out the courses, and snap chalk lines for each new course—as described above.

Double the first course, which overhangs the sheathing about an inch. Align the butt ends of starter-course shingles (No. 2 grade) to the first chalk line you snapped, then nail the first course of No. 1 shingles directly over them, remembering to offset joint lines at least 1 in. Snap another chalk line for the second course, and so on.

If there are two people working, it's easiest for each to work from a corner in toward the middle; only the last shingle will need to be fitted. If it needs trimming, score both sides with a utility knife drawn along a straightedge. Snap it and nail it up. When overlapping shingles at a corner—instead of butting them to corner boards—first nail up one that extends beyond the corner, then butt a shingle on the adjacent wall to it. Trim the first shingle in place with a plane, as shown in Figure 7.13. Alternate overlaps from course to course, and draw shingles together with a single 4d galvanized finish nail through each overlapping edge.

There are as many techniques as there are shinglers. Some pros think that it's faster to align shingle courses by setting them atop a 1×2 tacked to the wall; it's a good

Figure 7.13 At corners, overlap shingles and trim the excess with a block plane.

method, but you still have to snap a chalkline to locate the 1×2, and you're putting extra holes (which won't be covered) into shingles below.

Take pains to fit shingles closely to window and door casings. The last course of shingles running under a sill should butt squarely to the rabbet cut in the underside;

caulk the seam well. If there is not an *apron* under the sill to cover the tops of shingles, their nails will show; set their heads slightly so they'll be inconspicuous. Along jamb casing, use shingles 6 in. wide or narrower; they're less likely to split. And again, caulk those seams well with silicone or butyl rubber.

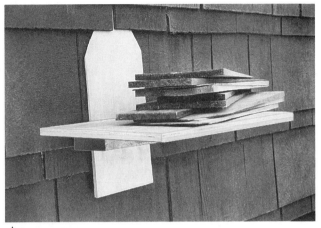

A.

B.

Figure 7.14 Two shingling aids. (A) A homemade shingle tray can be fashioned from a plywood platform, a 2 × 4 support, and a shingle upright which friction-fits under courses as shown. (B) A shingle hook is indispensable when replacing weathered sections.

The other critical area is at the top of the wall. Rabbet or build out trim as shown in Figure 7.9B, to protect the top edges of shingles. Along gable-end walls and dormers, you'll have to cut tops or bottoms at an angle; save wide shingles for these areas. Use an adjustable bevel gauge to copy angles and transfer them to shingles. If there are many such cuts, have a helper on the ground with a table saw.

If you split a shingle, tear it out, beat the nails in, and replace it. To remove a few damaged shingles on an otherwise good wall, a *shingle hook* (Figure 7.14B) makes the task almost easy. To avoid damaging replacement shingles as you drive them into place, cushion hammer blows with a scrap block.

Clapboards

Before putting up clapboards, please review preceding sections which discuss flashing, nail choices, trim details (especially inner and outer corners), and layout.

Materials. Clapboards are a beveled siding milled from redwood, cedar, or pine. They come in varying widths and thicknesses, but all are nominally 1-in. boards. Thus a 1×6 is actually $\frac{1}{2}$ in. × $5\frac{1}{2}$ in., a 1×8 is actually $\frac{5}{8}$ in. × $7\frac{1}{2}$ in., and so on. By varying clapboard exposures slightly you can align courses to casing and frieze trim, as described under "Layout" above. (*Note:* The clapboard overlap should be no less than 1 in., except for 1×4s, where a $\frac{1}{2}$-in. overlap is permissible.)

Clapboards come in varying lengths and are sold by the lineal foot. To estimate the amount you need, calculate the square footage of your walls, less window and door openings. Then use Table 7.1, which assumes $\frac{1}{2}$ in. of overlap for 1×4 clapboards, and 1 in. of overlap for all other sizes. Figures also include a 5 percent waste factor.

Use 5d galvanized box nails to attach clapboards if you're painting them; otherwise, use one of the nonstaining nails discussed on page 62. For every 1000 lineal feet of siding, buy 5 lb of 5d nails. Nail clapboards each time they cross a stud, placing nails $\frac{1}{2}$ to $\frac{3}{4}$ in. up from butt edges. This nailing distance is critical: closer than $\frac{1}{2}$ in., you risk splitting the board; farther than $\frac{3}{4}$ in., and the nail will be too high to secure the top edge of the clapboard beneath. (The clapboard below will also lessen the springiness when you set nail heads later.)

If you preprime or prestain siding before you install it, you'll save a lot of time later, and seal the wood better. Have your lumber supplier arrange it. Experts disagree about what to prime, some arguing that priming front but not back surfaces will cause cupping, others that it's unnecessary. Both camps agree, however, that the siding must be dry or you'll be sealing in moisture.

TABLE 7.1

Clapboard needed to cover 100 sq ft

Clapboard Size	Lineal Feet
1×4	440
1×6	280
1×8	200
1×10	160

A.

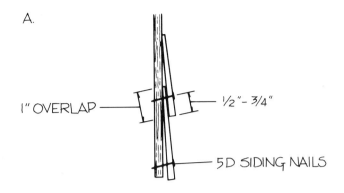

1" OVERLAP

1/2" - 3/4"

5D SIDING NAILS

B.

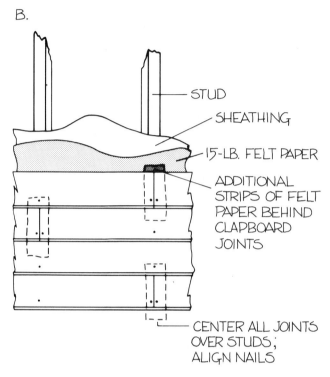

STUD

SHEATHING

15-LB. FELT PAPER

ADDITIONAL
STRIPS OF FELT
PAPER BEHIND
CLAPBOARD
JOINTS

CENTER ALL JOINTS
OVER STUDS;
ALIGN NAILS

C.

MARK CUTLINE ALONG
EDGE OF GAUGE

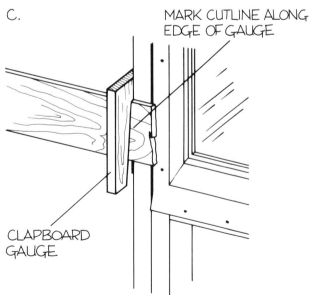

CLAPBOARD
GAUGE

Figure 7.15 Clapboard details. (A) Clapboard nails should just catch the top of the course beneath, yet not be so close to the edge that you split the shingle butt. (B) Center all clapboard joints over studs, and back joints with an extra piece of felt-paper flashing. (C) A scribing jig enables you to fit clapboards tightly to trim.

Installation. Before nailing up clapboards, attach trim, cover sheathing with felt paper, determine course heights and mark them on corner boards, as described above. Also, to align clapboard nails, chalk-line stud centers onto felt paper as you work up the wall.

The first course of clapboards goes over a beveled splashboard or, more commonly, a beveled *starter strip*, which is often a strip ripped from the top 2 in. of a clapboard. Using the chalk line snapped along the bottom of the felt paper (p. 132) as a guide, nail up the starter strip so that it overhangs the sheathing by $\frac{1}{2}$ to 1 in. Line up the butt of the first clapboard to the butt of the starter strip.

Start at one corner board and work all the way across the wall, nailing clapboards to each stud center they cross. All butt joints should be cut squarely and centered over a stud so that both boards can be securely nailed. Stagger joints so that no two successive courses have a butt joint over the same stud. To weatherproof clapboard joints further, back them with strips of felt paper, as shown in Figure 7.15B.

Cutting squarely. Cutting squarely is the key to a professional job, and here are several tips to help you do it.

Rent or buy a *chop saw* to make cuts on-site. For best results, buy a carbide-tipped blade: an 80- or 100-tooth blade for 10-in. saws, a 200-tooth blade for 14-in. saws.

Don't be afraid to recut a joint. When fitting the second board of a butt joint, leave it long until you've made a cut you're satisfied with; if the joint isn't perfectly square on the first try, you'll have excess to work with.

When butting clapboards to corner boards and casings, use the homemade gauge shown in Figure 7.15C. Using the gauge to hold the clapboard tight to the trim, scribe the cutoff line with a utility knife. Take care not to fit clapboards so tightly that you have to force them into place: you may push the trim away from courses already installed. It's better to shave the back corner of the siding slightly so that it won't catch; use a block plane.

Finishing touches. Where clapboards run to the underside of sills, frieze trim, and rake boards, fit them tightly into the rabbets or build-outs provided (Figure 7.9) and caulk those joints well, using a good-quality caulk. Where nail heads will be unprotected by trim, set and fill them.

In fact, set all nail heads if you'll be painting your new clapboard walls; this draws clapboards to framing, especially if you've used a power nailer. After setting, prime nail holes and spackle. Allow the spackle to dry, sand as needed, and paint.

Stucco

This section concerns itself solely with stucco repair. Coating a whole house from scratch (no pun intended) is almost all technique, and it takes years to learn. Stucco repairs are well within the ken of a diligent novice, but even so, you might want to find a stucco job that's going on somewhere in the neighborhood and watch the crew for a couple of hours.

About stucco. Stucco is a cementitious mix applied in several layers to a wire-lath base (over wood-frame construction) or to a masonry surface such as brick, block, or struc-

Figure 7.16 Replacing a damaged clapboard. (A,B) Remove the clapboard in one piece if you can. To raise nails, pry up the clapboard with a flat bar and then smack the clapboard back down. This is a useful technique for removing old trim too. (C) Use a shingle hook or chisel to cut through the shanks of any nails you can't pull up. (D) If all else fails, break the old clapboard in slivers. (E) Trace the old clapboard onto replacement stock. (F) Level the new clapboard as you tap it into place. For best results, stain or paint the wood before installing it.

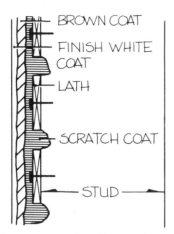

Figure 7.17 Plaster cross–section. The scratch coat oozes through the lath and hardens to form *keys*, the mechanical connections of plaster to wood.

tural tile. Like plaster, stucco is usually applied in three coats: a *scratch coat* approximately $\frac{1}{2}$ in. thick, scored horizontally to help the next coat adhere better; a *brown coat* about $\frac{3}{8}$ in. thick; and a *finish coat* (called a *dash coat* by old-timers) $\frac{1}{8}$ to $\frac{1}{4}$ in. thick. For repair work and masonry-substrate work, two-coat stucco is common.

The Mix. The mix always contains portland cement and sand, but it varies according to the amount of lime, pigment, bonders, and other agents, which are described below. Standard stucco mix is as follows (in parts):

Portland Cement	Masonry Cement	Lime	Sand
1	—	$\frac{1}{4}$–1	$3\frac{1}{4}$–4
1	1	—	$3\frac{1}{4}$–4

The consistency of a mix is easy to recognize, hard to describe. It should be stiff enough that when you cut it with a shovel or a trowel it retains the edge, yet loose enough that when dropped from a height of 1 ft it slumps into a loose patty. It should not be runny.

Metal Lath. Cover sheathing with 30-lb felt paper before attaching metal lath. When nailing up lath, use galvanized *furring nails* (p. 62) with a furring "button" that goes under the lath. When you drive these nails in, you thus pinch the lath between the nail head and the button. Avoid using aluminum nails; they react adversely to cement. You'll use about 20 nails (or staples) per square yard of lath, spacing nails at least every 6 in. Overlap mesh at least 2 in. on vertical joints, and extend lath around corners at least 6 in.

Application. Applying the base, or scratch coat, goes like this:

1. Cover sheathing with felt paper and nail up wire lath.
2. Establish screed strips, which can be window edges, corner boards, or strips specially manufactured for the purpose. [Screed strips are also used in tiling (Figure 16.25).]

3. Mix and trowel on the first coat, pressing it to the wire lath; put it on thick.
4. When the "mud" has set somewhat, screed it (i.e., get it a more or less uniform thickness), using the screed strips as depth guides.
5. Float the stucco with a wood float to even out the surface further.
6. Press your fingertips lightly against the surface; when it is dry enough that your fingers no longer sink in, steel trowel the surface. Steel troweling compacts the material, setting it well in the lath and driving out air pockets.
7. Scratch the surface horizontally.

To apply the brown coat, paint on bonder to the scratch coat; trowel on the stucco; float; steel-trowel to make the surface uniform; then rough up the surface slightly with a wood float. Do the same for the finish coat, but stop after steel troweling. If you intend to texture the patch (p. 141), it is still necessary to steel-trowel the surface first to make it uniform.

For two-coat jobs, put a finish coat directly over a scratch coat. In general, wait a day between coats. After applying the finish coat, keep the stucco damp for 3 days; stucco allowed to cure slowly is far stronger.

Stucco Trim. If doors or windows in a stucco wall are cased with wood trim, flash them with cap flashing as you would for wood siding. The weight of the stucco will press down on the cap flashing, creating a good seal. Metal windows set in stucco usually have no casing to dam up water and so need no cap flashing; in fact, such windows are actually set below the surface of the stucco. If it's necessary to cut back stucco siding, say, to repair rot or to install a new window, install fiberglass-reinforced strip flashing (p. 127) to cut infiltration.

When installing trim over stucco, as when upgrading an entryway, for example, caulk well. Tack the casing to the edge of the frame, then nail to the stucco, using 8d galvanized finish nails. If the stucco is too hard, you may have to predrill. Because a stucco surface is irregular, caulk with silicone (or butyl rubber if you'll be painting) where the casing meets the stucco. *Note:* If you'll be sealing or staining the casing, caulk *after* you finish the wood.

Helpful materials. These materials are particularly useful for repair work and can be purchased from any masonry supplier.

Paperbacked Mesh. This material, which typically comes in 3 ft × 50 ft rolls, has metal lath and felt paper combined to hasten application. Tack-staple the upper edge of the paper up, noting the built-in overlap so that the membrane will be continuous once installed. Then come back and insert furring nails to secure the lath.

Weep Screed. Weep screed is a metal strip nailed to the base of exterior walls, providing a straight edge to which you can screed stucco. Because it is perforated, it allows moisture to "weep" or migrate free from the masonry surface, thus allowing it to dry thoroughly after a rain.

A.

B.

C.

D.

Figure 7.18 A stucco sequence. (A) After troweling the first coat of stucco onto the lath and floating it smooth, scratch it so that the next coat will adhere well. (B) Apply the brown coat over the scratch coat, and (C) screed it level. When the brown coat has been steel-troweled smooth and has set somewhat, (D) float it to roughen the surface slightly so that the finish coat will adhere well. (Thanks to Rick Rutherford Plastering, Berkeley, CA, for the sequence.)

Weep screeds are an easy way to make a job look crisp and clean and, because the weight of the stucco flattens the screed down against the top of a foundation, it provides a positive seal against termites and other pests. (Stucco's tendency to retain moisture makes termites a particular problem.) Weep screed is also a good solution for the frequently rotted intersection of stucco walls and porch floors.

Weep screed is not difficult to retrofit, but you will have to cut back the base of walls 6 to 9 in. high so that you can properly flash the upper edge of the strip, as shown in Figure 7.19. Cut it with metal snips and nail it up with large-head 8d galvanized nails.

Bonders. Latex bonders—which look a lot like white wood glue—are mixed into each batch of stucco and painted directly onto walls. To be sure the admixture is distributed uniformly, first stir the bonder into water, then mix the liquid with dry ingredients. Reduce the amount of water accordingly, as recommended by the manufacturer. Add bonder to each stucco coat.

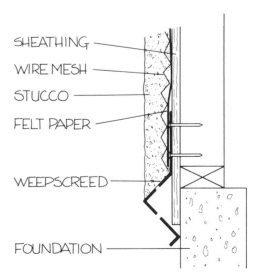

SHEATHING

WIRE MESH

STUCCO

FELT PAPER

WEEPSCREED

FOUNDATION

Figure 7.19 Weep screed.

To make sure that a patch adheres well, also brush bonder full strength all around the edges of a hole or crack to be filled with new stucco. Merely applying new stucco to old without bonder creates a "cold joint" likely to fracture. In most cases, you must apply new stucco before the bonder dries or the joint will not be as strong, although products such as Thorobond and Weldcrete reemulsify when moistened by the next stucco coat.

Speaking of ThoroSystem products (Miami, FLA), they also have a two-coat application which adheres well to concrete block or brick: fill mortar joints flush to the rest of the wall with Thorite mix, brush on a coat of sealer-bonder, and trowel on a finish coat of Thoroseal Stucco Mix.

Prepackaged Stucco Mix. This dry mixture is helpful because it eliminates worry about correct proportions between sand, cement, and plasticizing agents. You will, however, need to add bonder to it.

Color-Coat Pigments. Also known as "Lahabra colors" or "permanent color top coat," this pigmented finish coat is available in a limited range of colors. Its principal advantage is ease of mixing (just add liquid) and depth of color, which is as deep as the finish layer; but it won't be of much use to renovators because its colors are unlikely to match what's already on a house. If a house is already painted white, though, white pigmented stucco will require fewer coats of paint to blend in.

Masonry Paint and Primer. Use this alkali-resistant paint to coat any new masonry surface. You should still wait 2 or 3 weeks for the stucco to cool off, but that's far shorter than the 6 to 8 months' wait required for standard paint over masonry. Use two coats of primer and two coats of finish paint.

Repairing damaged areas. Start by figuring out what caused the failing and attend to that. Cracks around headers (Figure 1.3) and through corners (Figure 1.4) indicate a shifting foundation; get professional help. Crumbling material near the base of a wall suggests standing water; cut

back the damaged area and install a weep screed so that water can exit; stucco should not run all the way to the ground, nor should it be in contact with shrubbery. Large patches falling off suggest faulty flashing, rotted sheathing, or lath insufficiently attached. If a patch falls off and you see a shiny surface beneath, chances are that an earlier renovator waited too long to trowel on stucco and the bonder dried; rough it up with a chisel and apply new bonder.

To repair, first determine the extent of the damage by pressing your palms firmly on both sides of the hole or crack. Springy areas should be removed. Press on till you find stucco that's solidly attached. Do not cut out any more than you must.

Wear goggles, a mask, and a pair of heavy leather gloves when cutting away old materials. To cut away springy sections, put a carborundum blade in your circular saw and set it just to the depth of the stucco. You don't want to cut into the sheathing. Cut around the area to isolate it, then remove it with a 3-lb hand sledge and a brick chisel. You can also outline the hole with a brick chisel, but a carborundum blade is quicker. Always rough up the edges of a cutout area before patching: straight-cut lines are hard to disguise. Once you've removed the old stucco, snip the old metal lath with a sturdy pair of diagonal cutters or tin snips; use a 2-ft crowbar to remove old nails. Wire-brush the area to remove debris. When you're done, there should be 2 to 3 in. of the old metal lath sticking into the hole, to tie old to new.

Staple up new felt paper, making sure to slip it under paper above and over that below. Tack up new lath and you're ready to apply new stucco, as described under "Application" above.

Repairing cracks is much the same, except that it's more important to *undercut* cracks (i.e., chisel back under the surface so that the crack is wider toward the bottom). This helps key in new stucco. Brush the crack well with bonder.

Remember: Cut away no more than you must to get a good mechanical attachment. If only the finish coat is defective (lower coats are in good shape), rough the brown coat, apply fresh bonder, and trowel in a new finish coat. Which brings to mind the question "Can you fill in low spots that

Figure 7.20 Applying a stippled texture to disguise plaster patches.

have been painted over?'' Usually not, but the answer is equivocal: if the wall does not see a lot of weather and the paint is in good condition, it's worth brushing on some Thorobond and applying a finish-coat patch.

Texturing and finishing. To disguise new stucco patches, it's often necessary to match the texture of the surrounding wall. Before texturing the finish coat, steel-trowel it smooth and allow it to set a bit; the waiting time depends on temperature and humidity, but $\frac{1}{2}$ hour should be about right. For best results, keep patches damp for 3 days.

Here are the three most common textures, and how to achieve them.

Stippled Texture. For this effect you'll need rubber gloves, an *open-cell sponge float* such as that used to spread grout in tiling, a 5-gallon bucket (a clean joint-compound container is perfect), and lots of clean water.

Dampen the sponge float and press it against the partially set finish coat, then pull it straight back toward you. As you pull the float away from the wall, it lifts a bit of the stucco material and so creates a stippled texture (somewhere between pebbly and pointy). Repeat this process over the entire surface of the patch, feathering it onto surrounding (old) areas as well, to blend the patch in. A feathered patch is also less likely to crack once it dries.

It's important to rinse the float often; otherwise, its cells get packed with stucco and it no longer creates little points when you lift the float. It's equally important that the sponge be damp and not wet, to get the desired effect. If you want a grosser texture than the float provides, use a large open-celled sponge—a natural sponge is good.

If the new finish is somewhat more pointy than the surrounding stucco, that's probably because the old finish has been softened by many layers of paint. You can knock down the new texture a little by *lightly* skimming it with a steel trowel.

Swirl Texture. Screed the finish coat of the patch to the top of the hole and feather it onto surrounding areas. Get it fairly flat, then texture it with a wet brush (a wallpaper paste brush works really well). For best results, keep a light touch and rinse well; otherwise you'll drag globs of stucco out of the hole. By varying the pressure on the brush, you change the texture: do whatever's necessary to match the pattern of the original.

A.

B.

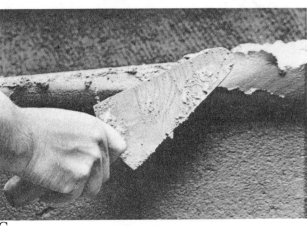

C.

Figure 7.21 Restoring a brownstone facade. (A) In these steps note the several stages of brownstone restoration, the lower steps chiseled free of loose material, and the upper steps shaped and scratched, awaiting a smooth finish coat. (B) Chisel back to solid material, subsequent coats won't adhere if the base is unstable. Here, the mason uses a hand chisel, a slow but sure method. (C) After sweeping free any debris from the chiseling, dampen the surface and build up its contours with successive layers of brownstone stucco. This is a tricky stage of the process, the approximation of the shape being governed by the mason's sense of proportion.

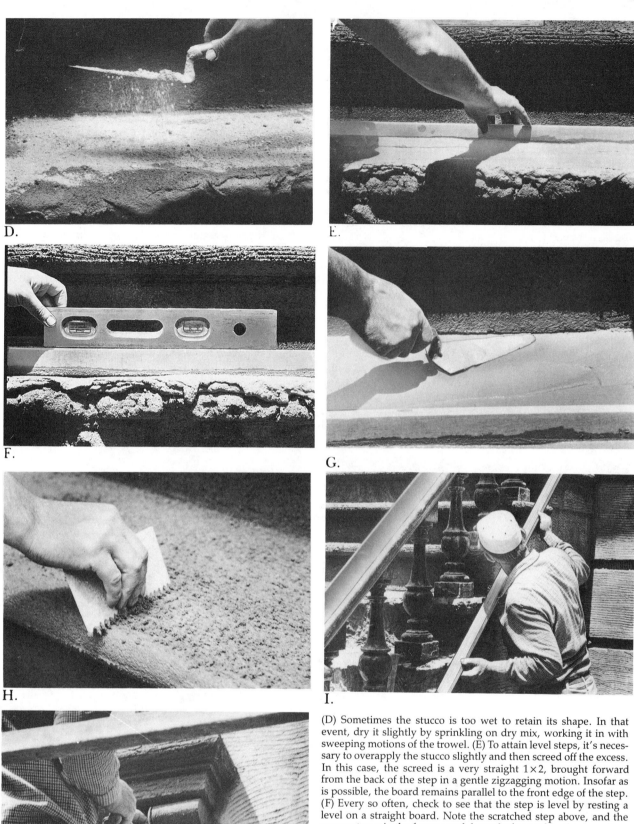

D.

E.

F.

G.

H.

I.

J.

(D) Sometimes the stucco is too wet to retain its shape. In that event, dry it slightly by sprinkling on dry mix, working it in with sweeping motions of the trowel. (E) To attain level steps, it's necessary to overapply the stucco slightly and then screed off the excess. In this case, the screed is a very straight 1×2, brought forward from the back of the step in a gentle zigzagging motion. Insofar as is possible, the board remains parallel to the front edge of the step. (F) Every so often, check to see that the step is level by resting a level on a straight board. Note the scratched step above, and the excess stucco in the foreground, brought forward by the screeding. (G) Once level has been attained, trowel the step quickly and allow it to dry. (H) When the entire step has been shaped and the stucco has set, scratch its surface for the subsequent coat. On this job, all surfaces got three coats. (I) Whenever possible, reconcile individual elements to the whole. Here, a mason sights along a straightedge to see how much individual step ends need to be built up. (J) Where certain forms recur, fashion a template from a stiff piece of cardboard or metal. Here, the area beneath all the windowsills has curved brackets, a design repeated on three of the building's four floors. (Work by Brooklyn Stone Co.)

Spanish Stucco Texture. Visually, this texture looks rather like flocks of amoebas or clouds, and is the favored finish for entire communities in California. To achieve this look, screed off the patch so that it is just below the level of surrounding areas. Then, using a steel trowel, scoop small amounts of stucco off a mortar board and, with a flick of the wrist, throw it at the wall. Then skim the stucco flecks with a *swimming pool trowel,* flattening the stucco slightly. You will thus have an irregular pattern of miniature mesas, hopefully matching the original surface.

A few tips. Use a swimming pool trowel because its rounded edges are less likely to gouge the stucco as you flatten it. Coat the hole well with bonder beforehand so that new material adheres well. Getting the right texture takes some experimenting: vary the pressure of the trowel, the stiffness of the mix, the amount you flick, the technique you employ.

GUTTERS

Gutters direct water away from a house. To work effectively, they should be used in tandem with metal drip edges (p. 76) installed along the lower edge of the roof. Drip edges prevent blow-back in storms and so keep fascia boards from rotting out, while directing water from the roof into the gutters.

Gutters must be properly sized and maintained twice a year—in spring and in fall. Size them based on the rainfall in your area and the square footage of the roof; your local lumberyard can advise you. Your biannual gutter cleaning will help you spot problems before they become serious: clogged outlets, metal separation caused by snow loads, nail holes starting to rot.

Gutter Maintenance

Begin by flushing the entire system with a hose. Use a plumber's snake if clogging persists. After cleaning the gutters of debris, see if any parts need replacing. Sagging or broken straps are the most common cause of gutter droop; renail those that need it. Ideally, gutters should be nailed to every other rafter tail (i.e., every 32 in.); in snow belts, to every rafter. Always try to nail into rafter ends rather than into fascia boards alone, which can pull loose.

Treat gutters gingerly when working with them. Where you must replace a hanger, use locking pliers to pull the nail out; don't collapse the gutter by pulling nails with a hammer. If a nail doesn't feel solid in a hole, use a longer nail; if that doesn't work, pull the nail, fill the hole with silicone caulk, and place a new hole nearby. For that matter, caulk all nail holes to prevent rot.

The outside edge of the gutter should be below the plane of the roof so that melting or sliding snow won't carry away the gutter or rain runoff overshoot it. For a roof with a 12 in 12 pitch, the outside edge of the gutter should be $\frac{1}{4}$ in. below the projected roof plane (hold a wood shingle at the edge of the roof to see); for a 6 in 12 roof, $\frac{1}{2}$ in. below the plane; and for a nearly flat roof (1 in 12), 1 in. below the roof plane. Note that the front edge of wood gutters should be lower than the edge nailed against the

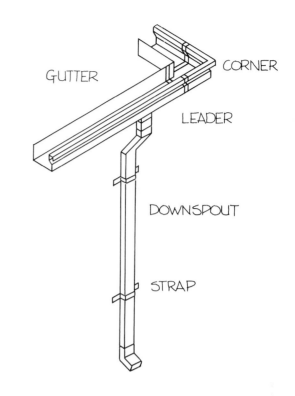

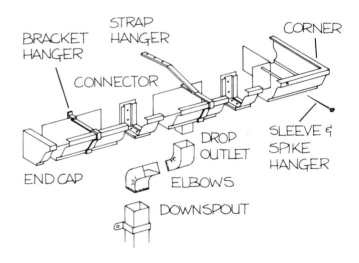

Figure 7.22 Gutter components. Several hanging devices are shown here, but you'd probably use only one type on an installation.

house; should the gutter clog, water will thus spill over the front edge rather than soaking the fascia board.

Spot Repairs

Clean and dry gutters before repairing. If gutters are scaly with old paint, wirebrush them clean before spot-priming them. Cover small cracks or gaps inside the gutter with asphalt roofing paint; use exterior enamel on the outside.

To patch holes in metal gutters, scrape and use a wire brush; then cut a new piece of compatible metal several inches larger than the flaw. Clean away any grit and, using epoxy, position the patch. Paint with a metal primer or

Gutters **143**

cover the patch with roofing cement. Fiberglass intended for auto-body repair also works well; for larger holes, build up layers of fiberglass compound and cloth.

Where gutters seams part, secure metal joints with self-tapping sheet-metal screws, working from the inside so that screw points don't stick into the gutter channel. Cover the screw heads with roofing cement or silicone caulk. Pop rivets also work well for such repairs.

Wooden gutters must be very dry before painting: otherwise, a thick coat of paint will seal in moisture and promote rot. Paint gutters during a dry spell; allow morning dew to evaporate before beginning. Sand the wood well, and use a rag damp with turpentine or thinner to remove grit. Apply a water-repellant preservative first, prime, then apply two finish coats of paint. Consult a paint supplier about paints that can withstand prolonged contact

A.

B.

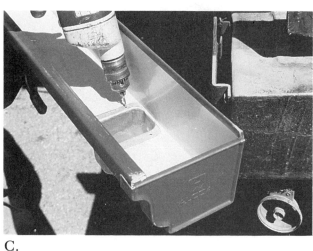

C.

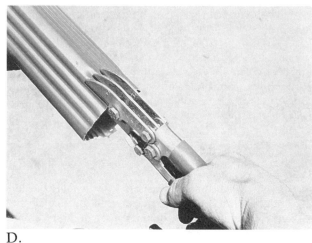

D.

Figure 7.23 Gutter installation. For best results, caulk all joints well with a durable caulk. (A) Cut most metal stock easily with a hacksaw. (B) Attach a corner connector with pop rivets. (C) Drill a drop outlet so that it can be pop-riveted. (D) Use a crimping tool to reduce one section of downspout so that it can fit inside another. (E) Have a helper hang gutters—it's much easier with two people.

E.

with water (one old-timer in New York swears by aluminum roofing paint). Sand between coats. Wooden gutters need painting (or touch-up painting) every 2 to 3 years. Each year, check around the gutters for signs of rot.

New Gutters

New gutters may be fabricated on-site from rolled metal (usually aluminum) by a specialist, or they can be assembled from prefabricated parts. The materials available are:

1. *Aluminum.* Resists corrosion, is easily worked; reasonably priced; minimum thickness, $\frac{1}{40}$ in.

2. *Galvanized iron.* Somewhat cheaper than aluminum but will rust if not maintained; minimum, 26-gauge

3. *Copper.* Very handsome; weathers well; expensive; minimum, 16 oz

4. *Stainless steel.* Requires almost no maintenance but is almost as costly as copper; minimum, 28-gauge

5. *Plastic.* Easy to install; needs little maintenance; can shatter

6. *Wood.* Romantic holdout in an age of ersatz; expensive, requires scrupulous maintenance

Ideally, gutters should slope down toward downspouts at a $\frac{1}{16}$ pitch (1 in. per 16 ft), but this is not always possible; and next to a level fascia board, not always desirable. As long as there is a slight pitch, with no low spots en route to the downspout, a gutter will drain. Don't forget splash blocks under the downspouts.

Being light, gutter sections are easy to hang. Before you go aloft, preassemble the parts that you can, for example, end caps, connectors, and corners. The easiest way to lay out the gutter is to put a level against existing fascia trim. If the trim is level, you need only tack a nail to one end and stretch a string to another nail, one that is lower by the requisite amount.

To position the gutter sections temporarily, fashion makeshift hangers from wire; tack the wire loops to nails placed on the fascia boards; and slide the gutter sections into the wire loops. Tinker with the gutters until they are approximately right, then attach a permanent hanger to one end in the manner prescribed by the manufacturer. Because gutter sections are usually 10 ft long, put a hanger every 10 ft at first, just enough to prevent sections from sagging. Then go back and add hangers until they are spaced to accommodate the expected snow load in your area—that is, a hanger every 32 in. or every 16 in., whichever is appropriate. When the gutters are attached, remove that guide string you tacked up at first. If you are using sleeve-and-spike hangers, be sure to nail them into something substantial (such as a rafter end) behind the fascia trim. Connect and attach leader sections after the gutters are in place.

Where a section has rotted out, it may be difficult to match the section with new stock. Take an old section to your building supplier and see if you can find a compatible replacement piece.

·8·

STRUCTURAL CARPENTRY

Wood, strong and pliable, is the king of building materials. The earliest wood houses, built amid virgin forests, were fashioned from massive timbers that took half a neighborhood to raise. Because nails were scarce, those great *post-and-beam* frames were joined without metal, fitted tightly with little more than a settler's ax and a knife with which to whittle pegs. The technology was crude but the houses survived, in large part because of the mass and strength of wood.

Early in the nineteenth century came plentiful metal nails and circular-sawn lumber of uniform, if smaller, dimensions. Although these lighter components had to be spaced closer than rough-hewn timbers, their reduced weight made it possible for only two people to raise a wall. And here boards sheathing the frame become structurally important because they keep lumber from racking under pressure, thereby ensuring that each "stick" shares the load equally. *Balloon framing* was the earliest of the stick-built type, with studs running from one story to the next. It is little used today. Since the beginning of the twentieth century, *platform framing* (also called western framing) has been the most widely used method. In this type of framing, each story is capped with a floor platform. Because the studs of a platform-framed house run only one story, they are more easily managed.

UNDERSTANDING STRUCTURE

A house must withstand a variety of forces or loads: the *dead load* of the building materials; the *live loads* of the people in the house and their possessions; and *shear loads,* the effects of earthquakes, soil movement, wind, and the like, which try to twist or rack a building. There are other, finer distinctions that we might make, including *point loads,* where concentrated weights dictate beefing up the structure, and *spread loads,* in which a roof, say, tries to push out or spread walls—but this quick look gets us started.

Ideally, loads are transferred downward, more or less equally, by the framing members. This is accomplished primarily by the exterior walls resting on a perimeter foundation; and by interior *bearing walls,* often supported by a secondary foundation of a girder, posts, and pads. *Nonbearing walls,* as their name denotes, are not intended to bear anything but their own weight. *Headers* (or lintels) are bearing beams that carry loads across openings in walls. A *partition* is any interior dividing wall, bearing or not.

Before you decide to demolish old walls or frame up new ones, determine what is a bearing wall and what's not. This will influence how you frame up: the size of headers; whether you need shoring; whether you need additional support below—if, indeed, you should disturb the structure

147

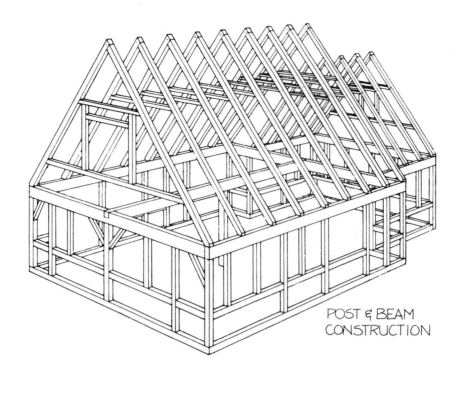

POST & BEAM
CONSTRUCTION

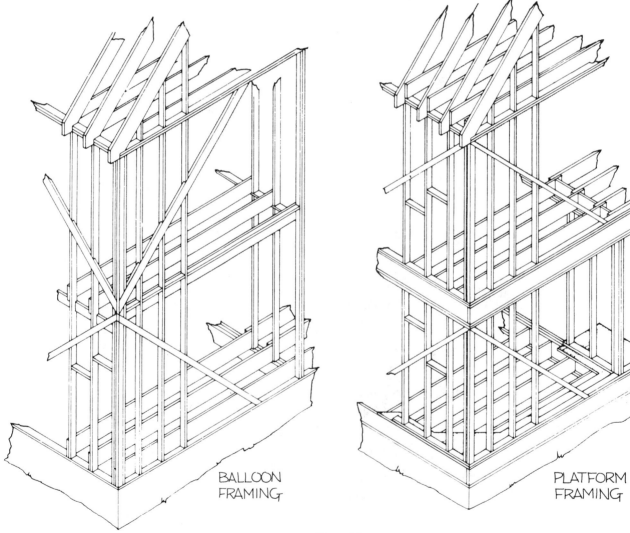

BALLOON
FRAMING

PLATFORM
FRAMING

Figure 8.1

at all. Get as much information as you can before you commit to a plan, because there are always surprises once you start.

Behind the Walls

To assess the framing hidden behind finish surfaces, go where it's exposed: in the basement and the attic. Joists often run in the same direction from floor to floor.

Generally, a girder (also called a carrying timber or beam) runs the length of the house, with joists perpendicular to it. Main bearing walls often run directly above the girder, but any wall that runs parallel to, and within 5 ft of, the girder is probably bearing weight and should be treated accordingly.

Bearing walls down the middle of the house are also likely to be supporting pairs of joists for the floors above. That is, most joists are not continuous from exterior wall to exterior wall—they end over bearing walls and are nailed to companion joists running from the opposite direction. This allows the builder to use smaller lumber to run a shorter span. Cut into such a bearing wall without adding a header and the joists above will sag.

Another thing to look for in the basement is the emergence of mechanical systems—plumbing, heating, and electrical—from the floor above. Pipes, ducts, and wires are frequently routed in walls, which may be an important nonstructural reason to leave a wall alone. Wiring can be removed safely and run elsewhere, but a 3- or 4-in. soil stack should give you pause.

Finally, don't overlook the obvious. Walls running beneath wood stoves, tubs, pianos, water beds, and the like are being point-loaded by those heavy objects. Either move the weight or leave the walls.

How Big a Job Is It?

Your local building authorities have the final say about altering the structure of your house. Hence you should have a structural engineer review your working drawings. But be forewarned: no matter how carefully you plan, you're not going to know exactly what you can—or must—do until you've ripped out finish surfaces and exposed the structure.

That caveat noted, here are some general observations that hold true for renovating most single-family, wood-frame houses:

1. Removing or cutting an opening into a nonbearing partition shouldn't be too difficult because it doesn't require

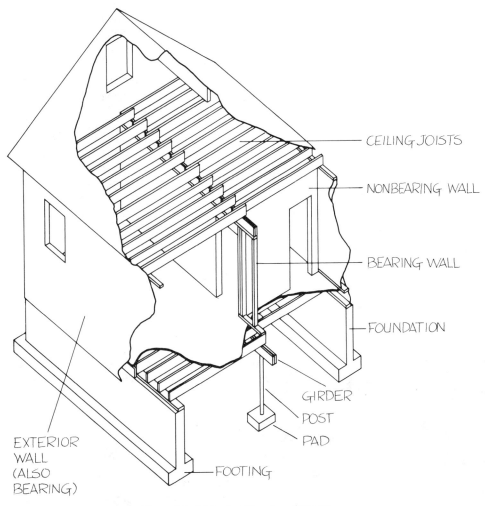

Figure 8.2 Major load-bearing elements.

shoring to do the job safely. Similarly, you can add an opening without shoring up *exterior* walls if that opening is 8 ft wide or less. True, exterior walls are load bearing, but the weight above can be borne *temporarily* by the top plates and floor platforms in place. Once you cut into framing, however, put the new header in at once.

2. Openings in load-bearing partitions will be more difficult. If they're carrying joists above, you'll have to support those joists with shoring and ultimately add a new header to pick up the load—a considerable task. The same is true of adding openings wider than 8 ft in an exterior wall. You can probably put in a sliding door without adding shoring, but you're pushing it for widths greater than that. Also moderately difficult are partitions containing 2-in. waste pipes; to reroute that pipe, you may have to move a fixture or two.

3. *Not advisable* are do-it-yourself changes: in structures three stories or more; to multiple-family dwellings; or where there's extreme point loading above. Also, think long and hard about removing walls that have 3- or 4-in. waste pipe running inside. If it's the house's main soil stack, moving it means moving all the fixtures and waste pipes connecting to it. It's possible, but that means gutting an existing system.

Whatever the scope of your structural changes, you'll need to disturb some finish surfaces. This may be as modest as cutting back trim to accommodate a new partition—or as radical as a total gut. In either case, conserve as much of the existing finishes and structure as you can to preserve the character of the house. The next section will help you do that methodically and safely.

GETTING READY FOR TEAR-OUT

Whatever the scope of your job, please read this section. It has some useful tips to minimize mess and keep you safe.

Living in a house that's being torn apart and put back together isn't fun, and it can be murder on marriages—but you can minimize the strain caused by the noise, confusion, and dirt. If you don't have to be around the house during demolition, don't be; it's a good time to take a vacation. If you just bought the house and can afford the expense of

Figure 8.3 A living room during renovation.

keeping your old apartment until the demolition is over, do so. But if you're there for the duration, set aside a clean zone in which you do no work at all.

In the clean room, keep clothes, stereo equipment, art—anything that could get ruined by the omnipresent dirt of demolition. At the end of the day, go there and relax. Isolate the zone by covering the doorway with sheet plastic held up by duct tape, which adheres better than anything else.

Situate your shangri-la upstairs if you can, because dust filters down. If you are beneath a room being renovated, particularly one in bad repair, tape plastic to the ceiling.

Last-Minute Preliminaries

Take care of these items before you start:

1. Notify gas, water, and electric companies if you haven't done so already. Utility representatives can tell you what temporary hookups are safe and who must do them.

2. If you've newly purchased the building and have not yet moved in, call in an exterminator to fumigate the building at some point. (Roach-Prufe, a nontoxic powder that kills insects through dehydration, is an excellent product.)

3. Make sure that your contractor is properly covered by insurance (p. 504) or, if you're doing the work yourself, check with your insurance company to make sure that you—and any helpers—are covered.

4. Get help. If you have inexperienced workers (e.g., high school kids) helping you, they're *your* responsibility; supervise them. The job will go smoother and you won't have to undo their mistakes later.

5. Have a telephone hooked up or locate one you can use in an emergency. Have a first-aid kit on the site.

6. Get everyone in the family a tetanus shot.

Useful Tools and Equipment

Pages 39–47 have more information about the tools listed below.

For Safety. Voltage tester, hard hat, goggles or safety glasses, a respirator mask with changeable filters, drop light, shoes with thick soles, heavy clothing (but not so heavy as to impair movement), a tetanus shot.

Dismantling. Wrecking bars of various sizes, depending on your job, smaller utility bar (also called a Wonder Bar), cat's paw, 3-lb hand sledge, heavy scrapers. A 22-oz framing hammer also comes in handy, but make sure that its head is smooth-faced; hammering bars with a milled-face head will destroy it. If you're also tearing out masonry, rent an impact hammer with carbide-tipped bits.

Work Aids. Rent scaffolding if you're doing a lot of tear-out over your head. Rolls of sheet plastic, heavy tarps, particleboard to protect finish floors, heavy rubber trash cans (they work better than metal ones), small boxes for incidental rubble, wheelbarrows, push brooms, dustpans, square-

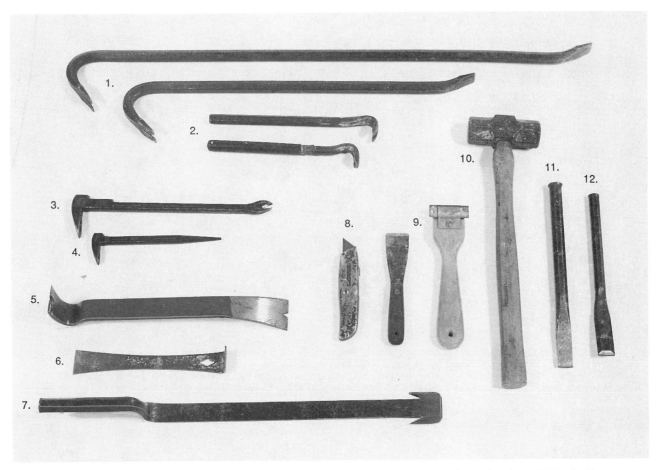

Figure 8.4 Demolition tools. 1, Wrecking bars; 2, cat's paws; 3, nail puller; 4, nail puller with nail set; 5, Wonder Bar; 6, painter's pry bar; 7, shingle hook; 8, utility knife; 9, scrapers; 10, hand sledge; 11, cold chisel; 12, rough wood chisel.

nosed shovels for scooping debris, stepladders, planks, a dumpster for big jobs.

Cutting. A circular saw with carbide-tipped blades. A heavy-duty reciprocating saw with a variety of blades, including one that's broken. A wood-cutting blade broken so that it shows only $\frac{5}{8}$ in. on the downstroke of the saw is one of the most useful items in tear-out. Because it can cut no deeper than $\frac{5}{8}$ in., it cuts just through finish surfaces, all but eliminating accidental cuts through wires or pipes. Nevertheless, heed the safe practices below.

Electrical Safety

Before you cut into finish surfaces, always shut off electrical, water, or gas service to that area. Start slowly and proceed carefully. Before you start, read ''Safety First! Use a Voltage Tester'' on page 235.

Circuits. Identify the circuit breakers or fuses controlling electricity to construction areas. This will require one person at the panel and another testing the various outlets with a voltage tester, as shown in Figure 8.5. To identify individual outlets, the person at the panel flips circuits or unscrews fuses until the tester light goes out. Test every outlet in the area.

Junction boxes. As you break open walls or pull up floors, you may find junction boxes. To get at wires, remove the junction box cover. The wires inside will either be spliced together with *wire nuts* or they will be taped. Using pliers with insulated handles, carefully pull wire groups out of the box and remove wire nuts or tape to expose wire ends. (If you are at all uneasy about handling the wires, turn off all the electricity in the house and remove the wire nuts—then proceed.) Test as you did for receptacles, touching your voltage tester to black and white wires simultaneously.

Hidden wires. If you unexpectedly discover cables hidden in a wall you are demolishing, stop and turn off all power in the house. Then snip the cable in two with a pair of insulated wire cutters—*never* do this when the power is on. After testing both ends of the snipped cable with your voltage tester to make sure that there is no live current, wrap cable ends with electrical tape or cap them with wire nuts. While the power is off, also pull any staples holding the cable to the studs so that you can remove the studs without damaging the cable.

With the cable thus severed and protected, you may proceed with the demolition. If the cable is to be discarded, disconnect it from the entrance panel. If the panel is to be reconnected, reroute it after structural work is complete:

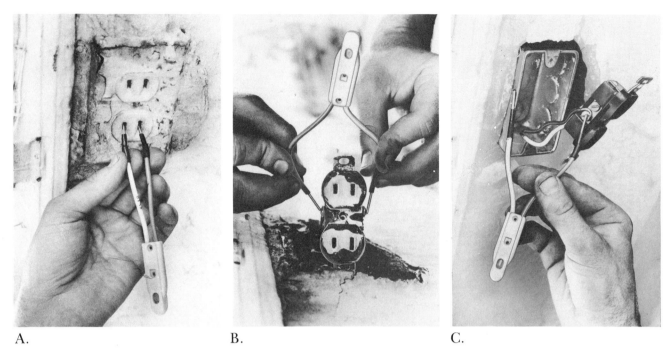

A.   B.   C.

Figure 8.5 Making sure that the electricity is off. (A) After turning off the electricity, insert the voltage tester into the receptacle as shown, being careful not to touch bare tester prongs. If the tester lights, the outlet is still live. (B) To double-check the receptacle, remove the cover plate and, being careful not to touch the sides of the device, apply tester prongs to screws on opposite sides and finally, (C) apply prongs to black wire ends and to the side of the metal box.

house that new connection in a junction box. In either case, consult Chapter 11 for correct procedures.

Containing the Mess

One of the keys to a successful renovation is managing the mess. Torn-out plaster and drywall are nasty stuff to handle and worse to breathe. The dust gets everywhere, and the volume of debris is prodigious. If you're sloppy as you renovate, you'll pay later: finish floors are particularly vulnerable to grit that isn't swept up and to nails that go astray. Lathe with nails sticking out creates as hazardous a workplace as there is. Heed these tips and your life will be a lot easier:

1. Cover the floors with heavy plastic, at the very least. If you have hardwood floors—even if you plan to refinish them—cover them with cheap particleboard duct-taped together.

2. Isolate the demolition area. Drape clear plastic (6 mil) over every door and window opening to contain the dust. Clear plastic is nice because it lets in light.

3. Clean up as you tear out. Insulation, drywall, lath, and plaster are unhealthful.

4. When demolishing outside, drape heavy tarps all around. You'll protect your plants and forgo a lot of raking later on. After throwing away large pieces of debris, two people can lift the tarp and shake remnants directly into the dumpster.

5. When working under the house, space is always limited, so:

   a. Clean out the crawl space or basement before you start. If it's a dirt floor, rake it.

Figure 8.6 To work safely and contain the mess, tape up sheet plastic and set up sturdy scaffolding.

b. Cut lumber, bend steel, and mix concrete outside the house and carry your materials inside. These heavy tasks require good light and room to pick and move. Concrete for pads can be carried in a 5-gallon plastic pail half-full, but if you're pouring a retaining wall or a floor, order concrete premixed and have it pumped into your basement by a pumper truck.

c. Carry out rotted beams, plaster lath, and other debris as you remove them.

TEARING OUT AND BEEFING UP

Before you build anything in renovation, it's usually necessary to tear out part of what's there and beef up what remains. No sooner have you torn out plaster than you're nailing up blocking for partitions to come. This natural flow from demolition to construction is a little frustrating for how-to writers who like to pigeonhole everything, but it's a fact of life if you're renovating. Frequently you're doing both at the same time. Thus the sections below present tear-out and build-up cheek by jowl.

Whatever the scope of your job, conserve existing surfaces whenever possible. Remove any nice details that might get damaged, and cut no wider or deeper than you absolutely must: you'll have less to repair later and fewer inadvertent cuts into wires, pipes, or the framing itself. Finally, where the text says ''plaster,'' remarks also hold true for drywall.

Removing Trim

Doors, hardware, and trim make a house distinctive. Remove and store them until you are done with tear-out and rough framing. Remove all doors and hardware you want to save. Most doors have removable hinge pins that can be popped out with a nail or another hinge pin. Remove the top pin last so that the door won't topple over. Since old hardware is often encrusted with paint, use an old screwdriver good for little else to chip away from screw heads.

If you want to save the trim (which is often expensive to mill specially), remove it carefully. How you remove it depends on the condition of surrounding walls. In the first method, the finish walls are worth saving. Run a joint knife between the wall and the trim to break any paint seal. Gently tap a flat bar behind the trim, preferably near the nails holding it down. Pry up along the entire length of the trim, raising it little by little. Be patient. As you remove it, number the trim so that it can be replaced as a unit; embossed plastic tapes stapled to the back of the wood can withstand almost any abuse. Remove finish nails immediately, pulling them through the back of the wood so that you won't splinter the face. Stack the trim in a dry, out-of-the-way place so that it won't get damaged.

Use the second method when you're gutting plaster walls. With a utility bar, rap holes around the trim, about 3 to 4 in. out from the edges. This will expose the lath so that you can cut around the perimeter of the trim with a reciprocating saw. If the trim is nailed over lath, insert a flat

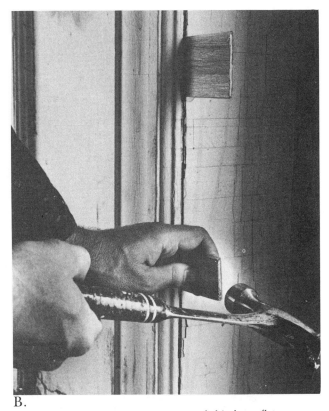

A.

C.   B.

Figure 8.7 Removing trim. (A) To pry up trim, first score its paint seal with a knife, then insert a wood chisel or a flat bar behind. (B) Once the trim starts to lift, work its length with a flat bar so that the entire piece comes up evenly. (C) A gentler way to raise the trim is to drive shims along its length; conversely, if the trim is hardy and you don't care about finish surfaces, break through the plaster to insert tools more easily.

bar between the lath and the framing of the rough opening, and pry up slightly. This will give you enough room to insert the blade of the reciprocating saw and cut through the nail shanks holding the trim. Use a metal-cutting blade.

Cutting into the Ceiling

Demolition. If you're cutting a big hole—say, for a skylight—or just gutting the ceiling, try to remove it in manageable sections. If the joists are exposed above, reconnoiter first. If it's insulated above your cutout, move insulation over to the next joists; use a dustpan to shovel it if it's loose insulation. This will save you a lot of mess later.

You can usually work safely from planks resting on two stepladders, but very high ceilings require movable scaffolding. Using a reciprocating saw, cut out sections 2 ft square. Because they're nailed (or screwed) to joists, these sections won't fall—nor do you want them to. The mess of demolition is greatly removed if you can remove plaster still keyed to its lath. Work the square against the joist so that the nails pull through, then hand the section to a helper to throw away. Before you put up the new ceiling, pull all old nails.

Again, tear out no more than you must. Gutting a ceiling presupposes that the old ceiling is not worth reattaching with long drywall screws, or covering over with $\frac{1}{4}$ in. drywall, as described in Chapter 15.

Blocking for a top plate. To solidly attach the top plate of a new partition to the ceiling, you must first cut back the finish surfaces so that the ceiling joists are exposed. Snap two parallel chalk lines to indicate the width of the plate.

At the very least, you will have to cut out a slot of ceiling, but if, when you expose the first section of joists, you find that the joists are not running perpendicular to the new wall, you will have to rip out a greater area so you can add blocking between the joists.

If you cannot get at the ceiling joists from above, this complicates things considerably, because you'll then have to open the ceiling to the nearest joist-center on either side so that you will have room to nail the blocking.

So, after making your cuts in the finish material, pry or pull out sections, and push back insulation (if any) into the adjacent joist bays. If joists are in fact perpendicular to the new wall, pull out any nails sticking out of the joists, clean up ragged ceiling edges (use a utility knife), and you're ready to nail up the new plate. At every point the plate crosses a joist, use two 16d common nails.

If you must add blocking between the joists, use at least 2×6s spaced on-edge every 24 in. on-center (O.C.). Be sure to cut those blocks squarely so that they'll fit tightly; knock them into place, and make sure that their lower edges are flush to the underside of the joists. Ideally, blocks should be end-nailed with three 16d nails, through adjacent joists; if you must toe-nail them, use four 12d nails on each end of the blocking—predrilling nail holes may make this task easier.

Finally, you'll have to add backing for the finish surfaces to follow, as in Figure 8.9A; set it flush to the underside of joists. You may also use metal drywall-clips (Figure 15.9), which nail to the top edge of the top plate and prevent the ceiling drywall from flexing when you butt wall sheets up to it.

Figure 8.8 Clean up as you tear out. These workers are nearly finished demolishing a plaster wall, yet there is little clutter afoot.

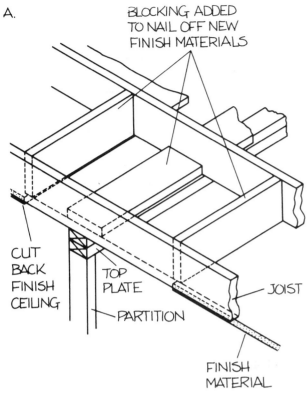

A.

BLOCKING ADDED TO NAIL OFF NEW FINISH MATERIALS

CUT BACK FINISH CEILING

TOP PLATE

PARTITION

JOIST

FINISH MATERIAL

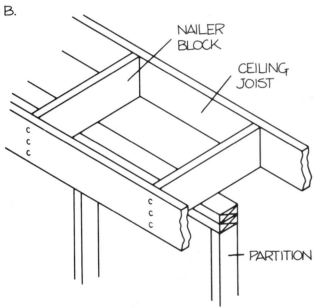

B.

NAILER BLOCK

CEILING JOIST

PARTITION

Figure 8.9 Securing partitions: top plates. (A) A wall perpendicular to joists. You don't have to double the top plate if the partition is nonbearing, but remember to add blocking so that you can nail off finish patches. (B) Add blocking if a wall runs parallel to ceiling joists.

Floors

Old floors are generally left intact, to be refinished later or floored over. If the old floor is sound and room height is not a problem, it's not worth the trouble to tear it out. It sometimes happens, though, that you need to pull up indi-

vidual boards: to run wires, to install joists, or to add blocking so that you can nail off a new partition above.

Prying up. Always start to pry up boards in the least conspicuous spot, especially if you're refinishing them later. Along the base of an existing wall is usually a good bet. Remove the baseboard trim and insert your flat bar there. You may have to destroy the first row of boards to get them out if they're face-nailed; successive rows will likely be toenailed.

If you'll be demolishing walls, the space between studs is a good place to fit the curved head of a wrecking bar, when prying up the first row of floor boards. The best way to remove flooring, however, is to knock it up from underneath, working up and down the length of each board to minimize splitting.

Blocking for a sole plate. To firmly anchor a new partition, it must be nailed to the framing below, not merely to flooring or subflooring. If the partition is perpendicular to joists 16 in. O.C., this means nailing with two 16d nails at each point where the sole plate crosses a joist. If joists are spaced wider—say, there's 2-in. tongue and groove (T&G) over 3-ft-O.C. beams—drive two 16d commons at each beam and some 10d commons intermediately. (If the T&G

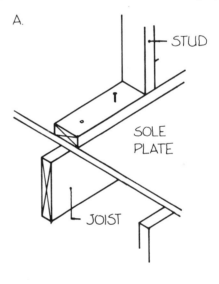

A.

STUD

SOLE PLATE

JOIST

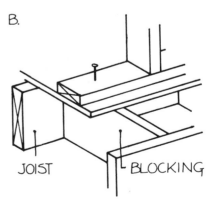

B.

JOIST

BLOCKING

Figure 8.10 Securing partitions: sole plates. (A) Where a wall runs parallel to joists, the easiest way to secure its sole plate is to locate it over a joist. (B) Where that's not practicable, add blocking.

is exposed in the floor below, make sure that nails don't protrude below.)

If, however, the wall is parallel to the joist grid, you must beef up the framing beneath. When that wall is non-bearing, block between existing joists, using at least 2×6s, and preferably 2×8s, spaced on-edge every 24 in. O.C. As noted above, this blocking must be cut carefully, square, so that it will fit tightly. Knock it into place and end-nail it through adjacent joists, with three or four 16d common nails each end. It's also important that the top of this blocking be flush to the underside of the subflooring.

When the new wall is bearing, it should be supported by two full-length joists, on-edge, running directly under the sole plate. Those joists should be blocked to keep them from twisting, and secured at either end with a double-joist hanger. Because these doubled joists are, in effect, a girder, they'll probably need post support beneath, to shorten their span. Table 10.1 recommends girder sizes, but because your local codes will supersede all others, talk to a structural engineer in your area.

Walls

If you're gutting a wall, start at the top and work down, removing sections methodically.

Tearing out old surfaces. As is recommended for ceilings, cut out manageable sections 2 ft square and remove them with the plaster still keyed to the lath. Remove all the nails sticking out of studs if you'll be putting up new drywall or plaster. Now is also the time to remove wires or pipes within, if that's part of your plan. To do so safely, see pages 151 and 152.

If the wall is nonbearing, proceed. Cut through the middle of each stud, using a wood-cutting blade in a reciprocating saw—it's less likely to bind than a circular saw is in this instance. Once cut, the studs can be pulled away from their plates. As necessary, beat them out with a hammer. Removing the plates will be a bit more work: use a hand sledge and a wrecking bar, and be sure to wear goggles and a hard hat.

If the wall is bearing, the operation is similar except that you must add shoring first, as described in the following section.

Adding blocking. To effectively nail off a new wall where it abuts an old one, first cut into the existing wall to expose the framing. Start with a small exploratory hole to determine exactly where the studs are, then cut back finish surfaces to the nearest stud-center on either side. Even if your new wall runs directly to a stud in place, you'll have to add blocking to reattach finish surfaces.

If, as is more likely the case, there are no studs in the spot where you need a nail-off, add them, as shown in Figure 8.11. These nailers will be stronger if you preassemble them and then beat them into place. Face-nail them together with 16d nails every 16 in. or so. Nailers should run the full distance from top to bottom plates, and should be toe-nailed with three to four 10d common nails top and bottom, driven in at a 45- to 60-degree angle. Metal angles prenailed to the studs will also give you a solid connection. Make sure that there is sufficient backing for the new finish walls to come.

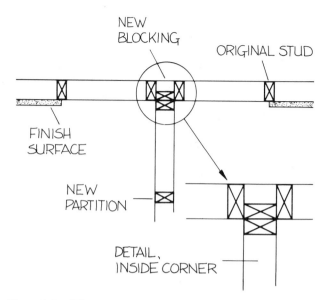

Figure 8.11 Where a partition abuts an existing wall, cut back finish surfaces to the nearest stud-centers and add studs to nail the partition to.

SHORING

Shoring is a temporary partition that supports loads while you cut into bearing walls. If your wall is bearing twinned joists above, for example, shoring will keep the ceiling from sagging while you alter or replace that wall. It's also useful when there are live loads or point loading above a nominally nonbearing wall. Having said what shoring is, let's clarify what it is *not*. First and foremost, it is not a jacking device, not intended to raise much of anything, and is not permanent. Shoring merely keeps things from coming down. Jacking is discussed on page 216.

Shoring is routinely fabricated from 2×4 stock, with single bottom and top plates, although plates are occasionally 4×4s to better distribute loads. Place shoring roughly 2 ft from, and parallel to, the bearing wall being altered. Because shoring is so close to the girder which presumably supports the bearing wall, you generally needn't concern yourself with supports under the shoring. Shoring on both sides of a bearing wall thus gives you a corridor 4 ft wide in which to work safely.

While the exact position of shoring is not critical, you should give some thought to how it will rest on your floors. If your floors are hardwood, cover them with particleboard before erecting shoring; at the very least, lay down sheet plastic. Carpet remnants also work well. If your floor is tile, protect it with rubberized carpet padding—scraps are fine—and a 2×6 sole plate to spread the load.

It's possible to build shoring on the floor and tilt it up, but that means shimming beneath each ceiling joist to pick up the loads evenly. Further, there may not be room to tilt up shoring as high as your ceiling. Thus it's easier to build shoring in place.

First cut the plates and *tack* the top one to existing joists. Three or four 16d common nails should suffice to hold the top plate up. Leave the nail heads sticking up for easy removal when you're through with the shoring. And

Figure 8.12 To the left, shoring added to support ceiling joists after a wall was removed (Figure 8.8); eventually this shoring was replaced with a header beam. To the right, new balloon framing which became one wall of a stairwell.

don't bother to cut back finish surfaces, you'd just have to repair them later.

Plumb down to locate the sole plate. One 10d nail at each end of a 2 × 4 sole plate is all that's needed to keep the plate from drifting; to prevent splits in a hardwood floor, predrill the two holes first. If your floor is tile, obviously you can't nail the plate, but the carpet backing will resist drifting. Next, measure down from top plate to bottom and cut a stud for each end, $\frac{1}{8}$ to $\frac{1}{4}$ in. long. Tilt these studs up, check for plumb, then tack them (toe-nailed) top and bottom with 10d nails. Tacking everything in place allows you to remove it easily when the job is done.

Now measure off 16-in.-O.C. intervals and cut the remaining studs as you did the end studs, making each a little long. As you force the studs into place, you thus unload the existing wall. Make sure that all studs are plumb before nailing them off. Once shoring is in place, you may now repair the original wall, move rough openings, add headers, add studs or posts, extend plates, install beams to open up the space—whatever needs doing.

FRAMING A PARTITION

As we've noted throughout this book, things never are as they seem in renovation. The building methods that follow are standard, but they're not carved in stone. If you tear out plaster and find a window frame supported only by nails in the sheathing, with nary a stud to be found; or structural shifts that have changed a nonbearing wall into a bearing one—be inventive.

In the discussion that follows, we'll assume that you've read the preceding sections which explain the need for shoring, why it's preferable to nail a new partition to framing, and so on. One thing we won't get to, because of spatial constraints, is light-gauge steel framing, which has become increasingly popular for partitions because it's noncombustible. For those who'd like to know more, see ''Light-Gauge Steel Framing,'' in issue 32 of *Fine Homebuilding* magazine, cited in Appendix G.

Measuring

When constructing a new wall, start by surveying what's there: use a long level to see if ceilings or floors slope, because that can affect your measurements. Once you have cut back the ceiling to expose joists, take several measurements down from those joists to the floor, holding your tape measure as plumb as possible. Several measurements are necessary because stud lengths often vary in renovation framing.

In any event, the length of studs will be the height of your plumbed measurement(s), less the thickness of a doubled top plate and a single sole plate. The length of the new partition should be measured from the *framing* of intervening walls, not from finish surfaces. If you're replacing a bearing wall with a beam spanning the room, calculate its

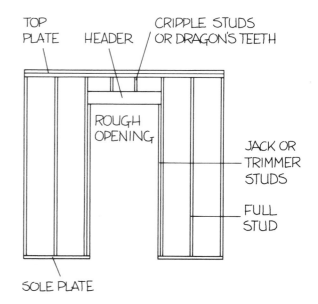

Figure 8.13 Wall components. When a 4 × 12 is used as a header, there are no cripple studs. Nonbearing partitions may have a single top plate.

length from the outside of the posts that support it; frequently, such posts are hidden in intervening walls.

One final word about top plates. They're doubled to give you a continuous plate, because individual top plates are usually not as long as a wall. Doubled top plates also allow you to overlap plates at corners, thus tying them together. Hence a doubled top plate is not necessary for relatively short, nonbearing partitions.

Layout

The easiest way to frame a wall is to construct it on the ground and tilt it up into place. It's also stronger, because you can end-nail the studs to the plates. This method is not always possible in renovation, but we'll consider it first and then look at alternative ways to frame later. Here, we're assuming 2×4 construction, although you may want to consider 2×6s if you'd like to hide 3- or 4-in. waste pipes in the walls.

Start by laying sole plate and top plate side by side, with edges butting and ends aligned, as in Figure 8.14A. The top plate is often doubled, but you need mark only one.

Using a tape measure, mark off full-sized studs 16 in. O.C. on one plate; then, using a square, extend those marks to both plates. *Note:* You're actually measuring from

A.

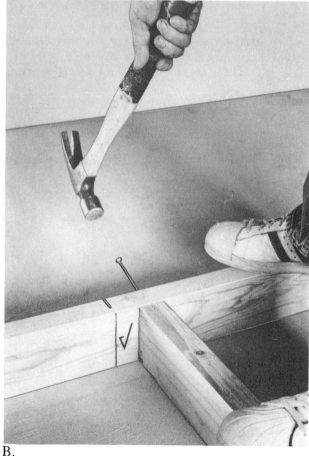

B.

C.

Figure 8.14 Erecting a partition. (A) Mark stud locations on top and bottom plates at the same time, marking "regular studs" with an "X" and jack studs with a "J." (B) Cut halfway through the bottom plate next to jack studs—you can finish the cut once the wall is up. One way to make sure that studs and plates are flush is to stand on both while you're nailing them. End-nail with two 16d common nails per stud. (C) Once you have end-nailed all the regular studs through the plates, walk the wall up into place. Plumb it, shim it as necessary, and nail it off with 16d nails.

the *outside* of the first stud, and 16 in. O.C. thereafter. This adjustment for the first stud allows you to butt a sheet of 48-in.-wide drywall into the corner and still have its opposite edge occur over a stud center, as shown in Figure 8.15A. All subsequent sheet edges, however, are on-center (i.e., over the center of the stud).

With studs located on plates, now lay out any rough openings. R.O.s are so named because they are about 1 in. wider and 1 in. higher than *cased* doors or windows—to allow room for shimming. If you are casing the door yourself, make the rough opening $2\frac{1}{2}$ in. wider than the width of the uncased door and 2 in. higher than the door is high, unless there will be a threshold—in which case, make the rough opening 3 in. higher.

Mark the width of the rough opening on the plates, keeping in mind that there must be a full stud and a shortened "trimmer" stud (also called a "jack stud") to support the header on each side of the opening. If you can move the rough opening so that a full stud coincides with an O.C. mark, do so. It may save you a 2×4.

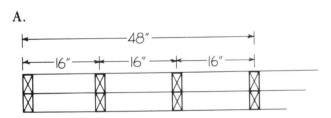

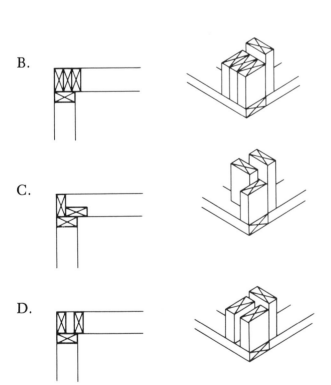

Figure 8.15 Framing details. (A) When marking off plates 16 in. on-center, start from the *outside* of the first stud; all subsequent marks indicate stud centers. (B–D) Corners require at least three studs to provide adequate backing for finish materials. In B, the middle stud need not be continuous (i.e., you can use pieces).

Headers

Wherever there's an opening in a wall, there must be a header over it. Headers must be able to carry a cumulative load and transfer it downward without warping, flexing, or pulling away from the sides of the opening. Thus headers must be sized according to the loads they carry and the distances they span.

Table 8.1 sizes headers (called *lintels*) in a variety of situations; it is fairly conservative because of the considerable weight of snow loads in Canada; your local building code will likely cite other figures. Many builders in America use this rule of thumb:

> 4×6 spans 6 ft
> 4×8 spans 8 ft
> 4×10 spans 10 ft
> 4×12 spans 12 ft

These figures assumed that the builder is using No. 1 grade Douglas fir, on-edge. This rule is overly simplistic, but it generally holds for one- or two-story single-family residences.

In the field, however, experienced builders routinely oversize all headers—using 4×12s to span *all* openings, interior and exterior. This is a considerable overkill for, say, a 4-ft-wide window, but it has several advantages:

1. The additional cost of using too big a beam is more than offset by the peace of mind it brings; there won't be any cracks in finish surfaces.

2. Same-size headers ensure that the tops of most exterior openings will be at the same height, which is aesthetically pleasant.

3. It saves time to use one size of stock for all headers; one cut and your header is done.

4. The reasons for using a 4×10 or 4×12 for a partition are equally compelling: should a nonbearing partition become point-loaded at a future time, it has the heft to bear the load.

5. Even in nonbearing walls, the header is the weakest point, structurally. Every time you shut a door, you compress the air in the room and cause the wall to flex. The more solid wood you've got to nail to, the stronger the connection. Thus it is that a production carpenter might use a 4×12 over a standard 6 ft 8 in. door, or a 4×10 if he needs extra room for a threshold.

But perhaps the most compelling reason to use an oversized header from solid stock is time: there's much less cutting and assembling. The common alternative is a header of two pieces of 2× laminated to a core of $\frac{1}{2}$-in. plywood. (The $\frac{1}{2}$-in. plywood makes the whole package exactly $3\frac{1}{2}$-in. thick, the width of a nominal 2×4.) A laminated header is strong, but there's simply less solid wood to nail into—and code requires at least five 16d nails through-nailed into each end of a header. Finally, you save time with an oversized header because you don't have to cut "dragon's teeth" (also called "cripple studs"), the small pieces that fill the space between a header and the top plate.

TABLE 8.1

Spans for various depths of lintels made from nominal 4-in.-thick lumber or two thicknesses of nominal 2-in. lumber installed on edge

Location of Lintels	Supported Loads Including Dead Loads and Ceiling	Nominal Depth of Lintels (in.)	Maximum Allowable Spans (ft.–in.)
Interior partitions or walls	Limited attic storage	4	4–0
		6	6–0
		8	8–0
		10	10–0
		12	12–6
	Full attic storage, or roof load, or limited attic storage plus one floor	4	2–0
		6	3–0
		8	4–0
		10	5–0
		12	6–0
	Full attic storage plus one floor, or roof load plus one floor, or limited attic storage plus two floors	4	—
		6	2–6
		8	3–0
		10	4–0
		12	5–0
	Full attic storage plus two floors, or roof load plus two floors	4	—
		6	2–0
		8	3–0
		10	3–6
		12	4–0
Exterior walls	Roof, with or without attic storage	4	4–0
		6	6–0
		8	8–0
		10	10–0
		12	12–0
	Roof, with or without attic storage plus one floor	4	2–0
		6	5–0
		8	7–0
		10	8–0
		12	9–0
	Roof, with or without attic storage plus two floors	4	2–0
		6	4–0
		8	6–0
		10	7–0
		12	8–0

Source: Canadian Mortgage and Housing Corporation, *Canadian Wood-Frame House Construction*, Ottawa, Canada, CMHC, 1979 (reprint of U.S. Agriculture Handbook No. 73).

Assembly

With the plates marked, now cut the full-length studs; you'll cut trimmer studs later. Make sure that all cuts are square. Position studs along the plates and end-nail them through the plates, using two 16d common nails at each end. *Important:* If your sole plate will sit on concrete, all nails must be *galvanized;* all nails set into redwood or pressure-treated plates must also be galvanized, whether they're end-nailed, toe-nailed, or face-nailed.

Now cut the header, which runs the full width of the rough opening and is supported underneath by trimmer studs. Each end of the header must also be nailed through the full stud on either side, using a minimum of five 16d nails per side. Once the header is so nailed, measure down from the bottom of the header to the sole plate to determine

the length of trimmer studs. Cut and nail a trimmer to the full stud on either side of the opening, staggering nails every foot or so; use 10d nails, or 16d driven at an angle.

If you're framing a window opening instead, cut and attach the sill *before* the trimmer studs. (When framing out window openings, the trimmer stud on each side is actually two pieces, as in Figure 8.16B.) Measure down from the header to determine the height of the sill. Square and end-nail the sill through the full studs on either side, using three 16d nails per end. Then cut and nail the trimmer studs *beneath* each end of the sill, and all other jack studs 16 in. O.C.; end-nail all studs with two 16d nails per end. Last, add the trimmer-stud sections that run from the top of the sill to the header, face-nailing those trimmers to the full studs.

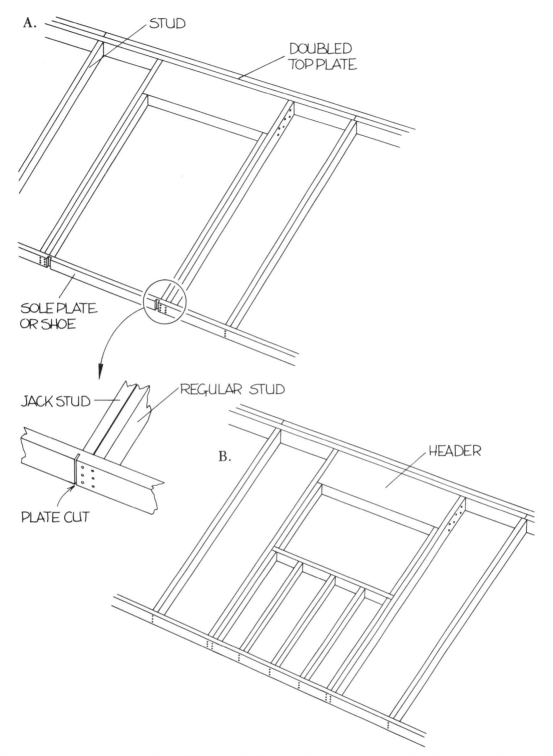

Figure 8.16 Rough openings with 4 × 12 headers. (A) Face-nail trimmer (jack) studs to the full studs on either side of the opening, using 16d nails staggered every 12 in. or so; end-nail trimmers through the sole plate. (B) To construct a window opening, cut and nail the header, then the jack studs under the sill, then the sill. Last, nail in the trimmer studs running between the sill and the header.

You're now ready to tilt up the wall and nail it securely to the framing. Note, however, that we have not yet cut out the sole plate within the rough opening, and for good reason: it's much easier to raise a wall if its bottom plate is continuous. A nice compromise is cutting halfway through the sole plate, as shown in Figure 8.14B, then finishing the cut once the wall is up and nailed down.

Before you raise the preassembled wall, however, nail the top 2 × 4 of the doubled top plate to the exposed ceiling joists above. The top plates are not doubled on the ground because you might have difficulty tilting up a full-height wall. Hence, nail the ''top'' top plate to the joists, using two 16d nails per joist; then raise the preassembled wall, *slide it over* beneath the top plate, and plumb the wall.

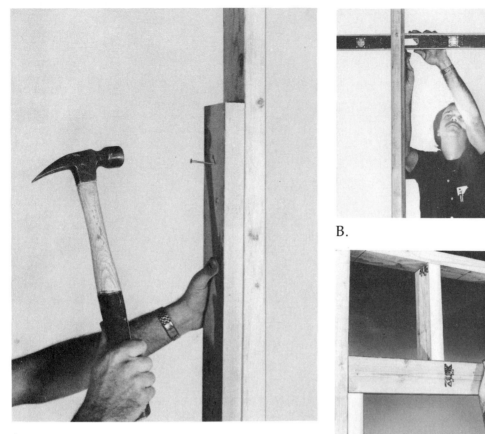

A.

B.

C.

Figure 8.17 You can also compensate for a sloping floor by measuring and cutting the doorway elements once the rest of the wall is up. (A) First nail up the trimmer (jack) stud on the low side of opening, then (B) level across the opening and mark the stud the other side. Cut and nail up that second trimmer; (C) then measure, cut, and nail up the header and any dragon's teeth above.

If you measured carefully, you shouldn't have to do much shimming; any shims you do drive go between the two top plates. (Don't shim under the sole plate. To distribute loads evenly, the sole plate must be in continuous contact with the floor.) Check for plumb one last time, then nail the two top plates together with two 16d nails between each stud. Nail off the sole plate to the blocking or joists below (p. 155), using two 16d nails at each point the sole plate crosses. Nail the end studs of the new wall where it butts existing walls.

Alternative Framing Methods

Another way to measure and attach the header and trimmer studs is shown in Figure 8.17, which allows you to compensate for a sloping floor by leveling and nailing the header in place after the rest of the wall has been erected. Once you've nailed off the header, face-nail trimmers to the full studs.

Building a partition in place. At the beginning of this section, we noted that preassembling a wall and tilting it up into place is the easiest way to go. Where that's not possible—say, shoring is in the way or you don't have enough people to tilt the partition up—build it in place, piece by piece.

Conceptually, a wall built in place is not all that different. Expose framing and add blocking, as described under "Tearing Out"; erect shoring, as needed; measure the dimensions of the new partition accurately; lay out the top and sole plates, placing studs 16 in. O.C.

Start construction by nailing the top top-plate to the ceiling joists above, using two 16d nails at each joist the top plate crosses. Then nail the second top plate to the first, being careful to align the two boards. (Have someone help hold the plates.) Plumb down to establish the sole plate, and nail it down in the same manner.

For the most accurate readings, measure studs after the plates are nailed; then cut studs just slightly long so that they fit tightly. Toe-nail each end of the studs with three 10d nails or four 8d nails; 45 to 60 percent is the optimal angle for toe-nailing. To further minimize stud migration, prenail each end so that the first hammer blows will quickly anchor the studs to the plates. Holding your foot against the bottom of the stud also helps. Admittedly, toe-nailing is not as strong as end-nailing, but sometimes there's no choice.

Take pains to make sure that studs are plumb before nailing them off. Level the header in place and end-nail it through the full studs on either side, then face-nail trimmer studs. The little tip of sawing halfway through the bottom plate will also be helpful here to keep studs in line until the framing is done; then cut through.

Framing beneath slopes. Framing beneath stair stringers, rafters, and such isn't difficult if you measure carefully and

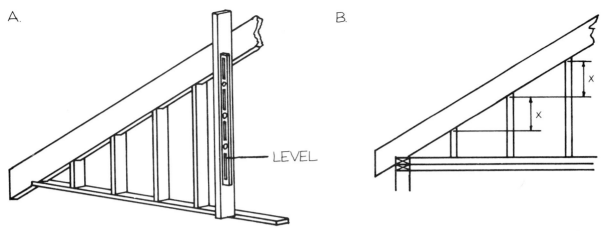

Figure 8.18 Studs beneath rafters (or any sloping member) should still be spaced 16 in. on-center. (A) Mark off the sole plate with that interval, then plumb up to the rafter above. (B) Once you have cut two consecutive studs you will have established the bevel on top and you'll know the difference in length between adjacent studs, indicated by "X." Such walls may not need a top plate, but should have adequate blocking for finish materials.

use an adjustable bevel. First nail up the top plate—you'll need only a single top plate—to the underside of the rafter or stringer. Ideally, the inner edge of the plate (the side toward the living space) should be flush with the inner face of the structural member, so that there is a flat surface for finish materials. If there is not $3\frac{1}{2}$ in. to accommodate the width of that plate, build out the rafter or stringer so that there is. Plumb down to establish the sole plate, nailing both plates with 16d nails at least every 16 in. Mark off 16-in.-O.C. intervals on the sole plate, for the studs.

To establish the angle at which you'll cut the top of the studs, plumb a piece of 2×4 stock to the top plate and use an adjustable bevel to duplicate the acute angle at which they intersect. Set your circular saw to the bevel. Holding

2×4 stock against the 16-in.-O.C. marks on the sole plate, plumb and mark the tops of two adjacent studs. The difference in their lengths, represented by X in Figure 8.18B, will be constant for all successive pairs. Toe-nail studs with four 8d nails on each end.

Knee walls. Knee walls are short partitions, about knee-high, which isolate the largely unusable space where rafters approach the top plates of exterior walls. Usually running perpendicular to the rafters, knee walls are relatively easy to construct—consisting of single top and sole plate, with studs 16 in. O.C. The only tricky part of this construction is the top plate, which is face-nailed to the underside of rafters, but whose inner edge must be flush with the plane

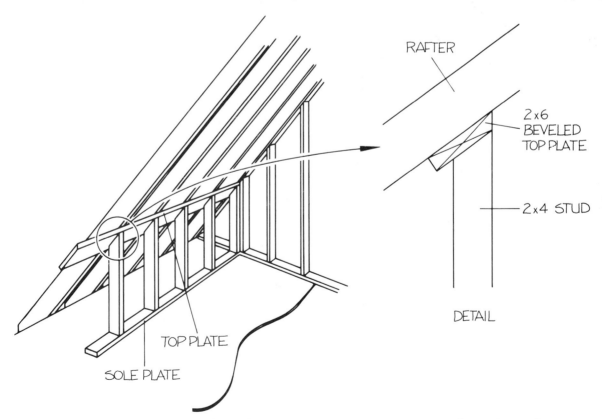

Figure 8.19 Knee-wall construction. Although they nail to the underside of rafters, knee walls must be plumb: rip a 2×6 as shown so that the edge of the top plate will be flush to the plane of the studs.

created by the edges of the sole plate and studs. In short, the inner edge of the knee wall's top plate must be ripped, with a bevel cut.

To establish the angle of the bevel cut, tack a piece of scrap to the side of a rafter, plumb that scrap with a level, and adjust a bevel gauge to the acute angle created. Discard the scrap, and adjust your saw to that gauge. When the 2×6 top plate is rip-beveled and nailed to the rafters, the beveled edge will be vertical (i.e., plumb to the rest of the knee wall). So run a chalk line perpendicular to the rafters to locate the top plate, and nail it off with two 16d nails per rafter. Plumb down from the beveled edge to locate the sole plate, also nailed with 16d nails. Next adjust your saw blade back to 90 degrees and cut across the faces of the studs in the angle established by the bevel gauge. (*Note:* This is not a bevel cut, but a square cut at an angle.) To attach studs to plates, toe-nail each end with four 8d nails. All of this is easier to construct than explain; see Figure 8.19 for details.

Odd walls. As you renovate, you'll encounter all sorts of anomalies that test your ingenuity. In Figure 8.20 a carpenter had to build a wall within a wall so that he had a flat surface to which to nail finish materials. The area inside the

Figure 8.20 This wall within a wall creates a flat nailing surface for finish surfaces.

window opening is tied in with plywood gussets, shimmed for position, then anchored with case-hardened nails driven into mortar joints. To secure the top of such a stud wall to ceiling joists, use metal "hurricane ties." Wherever wood meets masonry, caulk liberally with silicone. To forestall heat loss and condensation on the back of drywall, staple insulation to the wood frame and cover it with a plastic vapor barrier.

REMODELING

Having discussed the rudiments of tearing out safely, shoring, sizing the header, and framing up a partition, we will assume that the reader is now conversant with them. In this section we build on that knowledge with several less common, more complicated constructions.

Openings in Load-Bearing Partitions

Here, we'll look at two methods for removing all or part of a bearing wall and replacing it with posts and a beam to header off the load. In the first method, the beam will be visible; in the second, it will be hidden in the ceiling above.

If you're remodeling only part of the bearing wall, remove finish surfaces judiciously, opening up only one side of the wall initially. Open up one stud beyond the width of the proposed opening to give you enough room to add a header, posts, and additional studs, as necessary. Once you've framed up that new rough opening, you can drill through its corners to locate it exactly on the side of the wall you didn't disturb, thereby saving you some finish work. But we've gotten ahead of ourselves.

Bolster the structure for the changes to come, particularly beneath the proposed posts. The bearing wall is probably supported by a girder (or another bearing wall) below, but you may need to add doubled blocking over the girder, as shown in Figure 8.21B so that the floor doesn't deflect beneath the point loading of the posts. It may also be wise to put posts and pads beneath the girder, as described in Chapter 10: in brief, a post every 6 ft beneath a girder.

Once you've erected shoring, safely rerouted wires and pipes, removed all or part of the bearing wall—and so exposed joists above and studs in intervening walls—you're ready to install the header. At this point, the two methods diverge.

Method one: the exposed beam. In this construction, a 4× beam is placed on-edge, flush against the underside of the ceiling joists, and is itself supported by a post at either end.

Where there are intervening walls, the posts are hidden within those walls; therefore, you must notch the ends of the beam to receive the top plates of intervening walls. Measure from the outer edges of the top plates to determine the length of the beam, and down from the top of the doubled plates to determine the height of the cutout. The posts, which sit atop the wall's sole plate, should be cut just slightly long—say, $\frac{1}{8}$ in.—to be sure that the beam picks up the ceiling joists.

A.

4x BEAM

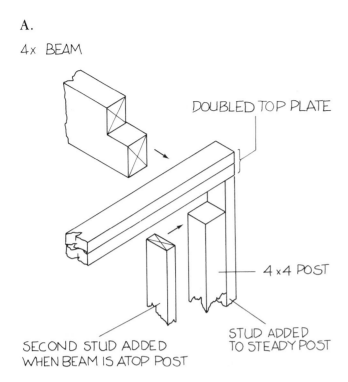

DOUBLED TOP PLATE

4 x 4 POST

SECOND STUD ADDED
WHEN BEAM IS ATOP POST

STUD ADDED
TO STEADY POST

B.

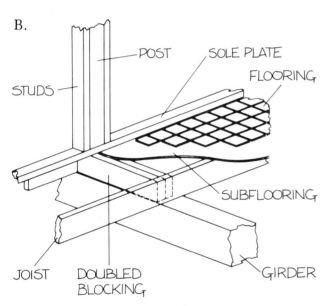

POST   SOLE PLATE

FLOORING

STUDS

SUBFLOORING

JOIST   DOUBLED
          BLOCKING

GIRDER

Figure 8.21 Supporting an exposed beam. (A) To keep the post from migrating when you beat in the beam, toe-nail the post to a contiguous stud. Once the beam is in place atop the post, "capture" it with a second stud, nailed to the other side. (B) Posts must be adequately supported, either by a joist beneath or by blocking running between joists. Hang blocking with joist hangers.

Before notching the beam, however, eyeball it for crown. If its arc seems excessive, snap a chalk line and power-plane down the crown so you don't have ceilings that bow up.

It's easier to raise the beam with a helper, but you can do it single-handedly with a few jigs. First, add a full-length stud to the intervening wall, right next to the proposed location of the post: this will keep the beam from

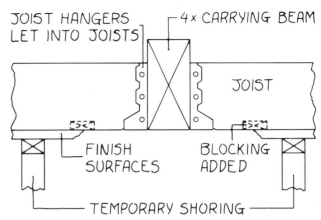

JOIST HANGERS   4x CARRYING BEAM
LET INTO JOISTS

JOIST

FINISH   BLOCKING
SURFACES   ADDED

TEMPORARY SHORING

Figure 8.22 The carrying beam shown will rest atop a wall plate and/or a post at either end. Cut ceiling joists as square and as tight as possible to the beam, to minimize flexion later.

moving side to side. (Do the same to the intervening wall on the other end, if there is one; otherwise, you'll need two 2×4 braces to safely support the free end of the beam.) Then, using 16d duplex nails, tack a long 2×4 "leg" to the side of the beam, to hold one end up while you raise the other. It's possible to raise a beam with adjustable jacks, but they are often in the way when it's time to place the posts.

To fit the posts, beat them in place with a hand sledge; if the post will be exposed, use a hardwood block to cushion the blows. Snug the post against the stud you added earlier. Then nail a second full-length stud to the other side of the post, thus locking it—and the beam above—firmly in place. Secure the other end of the beam in the same manner. Toe-nail both ends of the post with at least two 16d nails per side; where it meets the notched-out beam, use 10d nails to forestall splitting. Metal connectors such as an HD-9 are also appropriate.

Method two: the hidden beam. This method takes a bit more work but yields a much more finished result. Here, joists will hang from the beam rather than sitting atop it. The beam thus sits atop the top plates of intervening walls, so it needn't be notched, and can even extend beyond those walls, as space permits. Posts are still plumbed beneath beams, of course, but in this instance they can be installed before the beams, to bolster the top plates on which the beam sits. Here, metal connectors are an excellent idea to keep the posts in place, because you can't add studs to lock the beam in place. Some builders add blocking to adjacent studs, though, to keep the posts plumb.

Before raising the beam, however, you must cut back the finish ceiling about a foot on either side of the old bearing wall, giving you a 2-ft-wide channel in which to cut joists and attach joist hangers. Snap a chalk line to make patching the ceiling easier. As noted earlier, a broken ($\frac{5}{8}$ in. long) blade in a reciprocating saw enables you to cut finish surfaces alone, without disturbing wires or weakening structure above. Remove any nails sticking out of the joists.

Now the most exacting part of the job: cutting through the joists (usually twinned) that were supported by the bearing wall. Snap two chalk lines across the undersides of joists, to indicate the width of the beam. A $4 \times$ beam is actually $3\frac{5}{8}$ in. thick, but leave a little space for variations in cutting. Next, using a combination square, extend those marks from the undersides to the faces of the joists. Then, wearing goggles and a mask, cut along those lines squarely with a circular saw.

If your cuts and your beam are straight, you should be able to slide the beam between the severed joists and up onto the top plate of an intervening wall. Raise the second end and pull the beam toward you so that its second end also sits atop a wall. Use a ''hurricane tie'' or an angle brace to tie the beam to the top plates.

Before nailing up the joist hangers, however, trace the underside of a hanger across the bottom edge of each joist and chisel out to the thickness of the metal. This operation, called ''letting in'' the hanger, assures that the hanger will be flush to the bottom of the joist. Otherwise, there'd be a bulge in the finish ceiling when it came time to patch-repair.

Using the case-hardened nails provided by the manufacturer of the joist hangers, hang the joists from the beam. That done, you've transferred the loads to the posts and beam, and you may remove the shoring. Above the edges of the channel you cut, center and end-nail 2×4 backing between joists, for the finish surfaces to come.

Openings in Exterior Walls

Adding or enlarging an opening in an exterior wall is dramatic visually, but structurally it's often easier than opening up a load-bearing partition.

A.

B.

C.

D.

Figure 8.23 Enlarging an existing opening. (A) To minimize repairs later, remove interior finishes first, cutting back to the nearest stud center on either side of the opening. Remove the finish surfaces from floor to ceiling. (B) Next cut back the siding and sheathing to the dimensions of the new rough opening. Use a reciprocal saw or a circular saw run atop a flat board. (C) Cut out the header, here a boxed 6×8 because of the thickness of the old walls. (D) Frame out the rough opening as described in Figure 8.16.

Adding an opening. As noted in the sections "How Big a Job Is It" (p. 149) and "Headers" (p. 159), you probably don't need shoring if the opening is less than 8 ft wide. Shoring usually is not necessary in most platform-framed houses because doubled top plates and floor platforms can temporarily carry loads above while you add a header. But if you are adding an opening to the side wall of a balloon-framed structure (p. 148), get a structural engineer's advice. Similarly, talk to a professional if your house is post-and-beam and you'd have to cut a major post to fit your header.

Otherwise, layout is primarily a matter of adding 1 in. to the dimensions of the cased window (or door) unit—to allow for shimming—and aligning the top of your new window to the tops of other windows along the wall. This will not always be possible for you to do, but the results will look much better if you can. If you use the 4 × 12 header recommended on page 159, chances are that the top of the opening will align perfectly to the tops of existing doors—and you won't have to cut "dragon's teeth" over the header.

To minimize repairs later, tear out interior wall surfaces before disturbing the exterior siding. If you're enlarging an opening, start by removing the window (or door), trim, and casing; see pages 153–154 if the elements are worth saving. Having removed the casing, now expose the wall framing from floor to ceiling so that you can frame out the new rough opening. Again, to minimize finish repairs yet give you room to work, cut back to the nearest stud center on either side of the new opening. Safely remove (p. 151) and reroute wires or pipes in the wall.

With the framing thus exposed, lay out your rough opening by snapping its dimensions across the edges of existing studs. If there's an existing rough opening, it will probably need to be torn out, but if any of its elements can be incorporated into the new opening, do so. Before framing up the new R.O., however, make sure that no sheathing nails will interfere with its placement.

Once the rough opening is nailed off, drill through corners to locate its perimeter on the exterior siding. Outside, stretch chalk lines between those holes, then cut along them, keeping your blade on the inside of the perimeter. A reciprocating saw with a metal-cutting blade should handle any nails you encounter. A carbide-tipped blade in a circular saw will give a good straight cut if you first tack a board over the siding so the saw has a flat surface to ride on. In either case, cut back the sheathing flush to the edge of the R.O.

That done, temporarily shim the precased window (or door) in the rough opening and, outside, trace around the perimeter of its trim, onto the siding. Remove the unit and cut back the siding so that the window's exterior trim, when reinstalled, will rest solidly on the sheathing. (Before final-nailing the window unit, however, nail the sheathing to the R.O. with 8d galvanized nails.) To effectively weatherproof the unit, follow the recommendations in Chapter 7—flashing, caulking, and the like.

Closing an opening. First remove whatever's in the opening—window or door unit, casing, trim—all the way down to the floor. If it was a door, you'll have to add a new section of sole plate, face-nailing it into floor joists with 16d nails, and toe-nailing it into adjacent studs with 10d nails.

Again using 16d commons, add a stud to either side of the opening so that you'll have nail-off for finish surfaces inside and sheathing outside. Add whatever studs are necessary within the opening to establish intervals 16 in. O.C. If the old studs are full 2×4s, you may have to build up the edges of new studs with plywood strips. You may also have to build up your sheathing to match the full 1-in. sheathing of years past.

Insulate and apply a vapor barrier before closing up the wall. On the outside, blend in the new siding to disguise the old opening. If the wall is stucco, this means cutting back wire mesh irregularly so you don't butt a new patch to a straight seam. If the wall is sided with clapboards, strip back so that board joints are staggered. Once painted, these patches will be virtually undetectable.

Tying to Additions

Where the old structure meets new, we've really reached the outer limits of this discussion. Framing an addition is properly the purview of new construction—another book altogether! So, for the little good a cursory treatment affords, these brief remarks.

Floor tie-ins. In general, continue the lines of the old building, whenever possible. Start by noting the height of the existing first floor: this determines the height you must come up above the new foundation—hence the combined height of pony walls, joists, and subflooring.

The physical tie-in typically begins by bolting (not nailing) a rim joist to the existing floor platform, again taking into account the thickness of the new subflooring to come. After you've framed the new floor joists out from that point comes the fine work of leveling new to old, shimming beneath, or planing down, as in Figure 8.24. Increasingly, such tie-ins favor metal connectors.

To nail down $\frac{5}{8}$- or $\frac{3}{4}$-in. plywood subflooring, use $2\frac{1}{4}$-in. annular ring shank or spiral shank nails spaced every 8 in. O.C.; for $1\frac{1}{8}$-in. plywood or 2× run diagonally, use $3\frac{1}{2}$-in. nails.

Wall tie-ins. Continue the lines of the existing building whenever possible. If you are extending out from an existing corner, take pains to brace the old wall so that it is not pulled out of plumb by your labors on the new. That aside, there should be sufficient nail-off for the new wall extension, because built-up corners have been standard for years. Between each stud, drive two 16d nails into sole plates so that the new wall will be anchored into joists, rim joists, and/or blocking.

When laying out the plates for your new end wall, begin by measuring from the *outside* corner of the side plate so the edges of 4 × 8 sheathing will be centered over studs. Laying out from the exterior of the building may mean wasting a little drywall inside, but it's far less expensive than, say, $\frac{5}{8}$-in. exterior plywood. For good shear strength, nail off sheathing every 3 in. along edges, and every 4 to 6 in. in the field, over stud centers; use 6d to 8d galvanized nails.

To further bolster stud walls against racking, "let in" diagonal steel cross-bracing—a great improvement over

A.

B.

C.

Figure 8.24 Extending a floor platform. (A) Once the mud sill is bolted to the foundation, establish the height of the new rim joist by leveling out from the existing floor platform. Set the tops of the new joists to the height of the old subfloor, then cover both with plywood. (B,C) Because of milling irregularities, this operation is one of continual planing and checking for level.

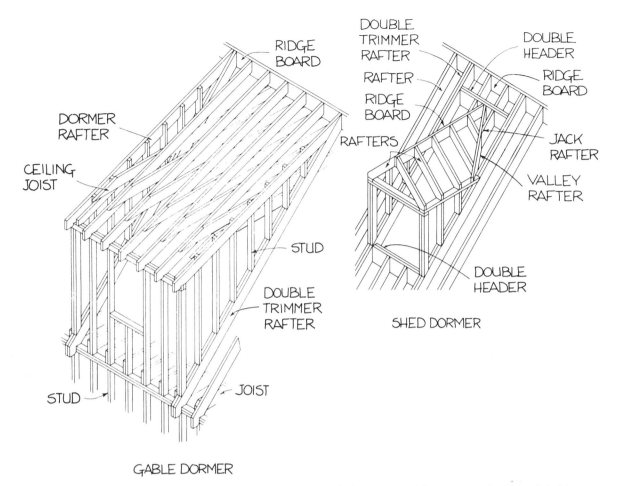

Figure 8.25 Dormer framing. (From *Architectural Graphic Standards,* courtesy of the American Institute of Architects and John Wiley & sons, Inc.)

old-fashioned 1 × 4 cross-bracing, which had to be chiseled in. Because this 90-degree galvanized steel bracing fits into the kerf of a single saw cut, it's much quicker to install, and studs suffer virtually no loss of compressive strength. Use case-hardened nails to attach the steel bracing.

Roof tie-ins. The best-looking roof on an addition is one that continues the slope(s) of the original roof, even though their planes may not be continuous. If possible, make one plane of the new roof continuous to the old—it will shed water better.

Whenever the roof of an addition abuts a wall of the main house, you see, that's problematic: water from the new roof will be partially directed against the siding of the old structure, which greatly increases the chance of seepage, rot, and the like. The fewer such junctures, the better.

To make a new roof plane continuous, lay out its framing so that its ridge board runs (perpendicular) into the outermost rafter of the main roof. To get at that rafter, you'll probably have to remove the rake trim along the eaves; and cut back roofing, sheathing, and overhang, flush to the face of the rafter. When setting that ridge and all subsequent rafters of the addition, keep in mind that sheathing of the new (continuous) roof must be the same height as that of the old.

For strength, use a joist hanger to attach the new ridge board to the outermost rafter. The first pair of rafters in the addition thus nail off to the ridge board at the top and to the main structure in the following manner. Bolt the first rafter of the addition to the outermost rafter of the main house, staggering $\frac{5}{16}$-in. bolts every 18 in. or so. To forestall rot, put a piece of felt paper between the two boards.

The second rafter of the pair bolts to the studs in the gable end of the house, after you have cut back some siding. Set your saw blade just to the depth of the siding, so that the sheathing remains intact. When laying out the cut, measure up from the top of the rafter $\frac{5}{8}$ in., to allow for the thickness of the new roof's sheathing. To provide a flat plane for your circular saw, tack a straight board atop the siding, at the angle of the new rafter.

Cut and remove the siding, but before attaching the rafter, run 90-degree flashing up under the old felt paper and the remaining siding. That flashing, 16- to 18-gauge galvanized, will be held in place when you nail down the ends of the siding you just cut. Flashing should extend up under the siding at least 4 in. and out onto the new sheathing 4 to 6 in. Using at least two bolts per stud, attach the rafter. When you put on the new roofing, put felt paper and shingles over the flashing—but avoid nailing into it, because it must carry water out to the gutters on the new exterior overhang.

A.

B.

C.

Figure 8.26 Removing a roof section. (A) The easiest way to remove an old roof is to cut out squares of roofing and sheathing, using a carborundum blade set to their combined thickness. This is a slow process—don't force the blade—which requires safety glasses and sound protection. (B) After using a wrecking bar to pry squares up, lift them free from the rafters and pitch them onto a debris pile below. Once the roofing and sheathing was removed in this manner, the crew gradually removed rafters until the ridge was supported by only two hip rafters on its free end. (C) Before removing rafters, however, carpenters shored up the section of roof that remained, to prevent its sagging.

STRUCTURAL REPAIRS

To repair a failed structural element successfully, you must figure out why it failed in the first place (i.e., whether it was deficient or deteriorated). Deficiency generally denotes a failure of design or execution, such as joists inadequately spaced, rafters sized too small for a roof load, stair carriages insufficiently attached to their rough opening, and so on. In these instances, materials are essentially sound, but installed incorrectly. Deficiency may also be caused by some radical change, such as point-loading, which overwhelms the structural member. Most of the repairs in this chapter deal with deficiencies in joists, stairs, rafters, or walls.

Deterioration, on the other hand, suggests outside agents—water and infestation—weakening the structure. Therefore, diagnosing and treating the *cause* of the deterioration is imperative if the repair is to be effective.

Dealing with Deterioration

Start by surveying the damage thoroughly, as described in Chapter 1—just how widespread is it?

Insect infestation. Where infestation is extensive, it should be identified and remedied by a professional exterminator, if for no other reason than the toxicity of the chemicals required. Further, the amateur, being unfamiliar with the habits of these creatures, may not destroy all their nesting sites.

Termites, the most famous of these pests, are both terranean and subterranean. Because subterranean termites need access to the moisture of the soil, they build distinctive dirt tubes up along the surface of foundations; when they burrow, they go with the wood grain; they swarm in spring and fall. The other type burrows almost anywhere, frequently across the grain, and leaves pellets outside its holes; terranean termites, which swarm year-round, do not create earth tunnels. Fumigation is the most common remedy for either type. You'll discourage the return of subterranean termites by lowering the soil grade around your foundation or, inside, raising pads and pier blocks at least 8 in. above grade (preferably more). Most pests won't crawl over 8 in. of exposed concrete to get to wood. Treating the bottoms of posts with preservatives (see below) is also wise.

Carpenter ants are red or black, $\frac{1}{4}$ to $\frac{1}{2}$ in. long; sometimes confused with termites, these ants have constricted waists and, when winged, wings of different sizes. While they do burrow in wet or rotting wood, they do not eat it as food and are therefore less destructive than termites. To locate their nests, look for borings rather like coarse sawdust. To destroy these nests, drill into them and spray with some insecticide safe enough for inside use; dusting with boric acid is another common treatment. Finally, if any of your house's underpinnings are moist to the touch—which may have attracted the pests—your basement may need ventilation.

Powder-post beetles' holes look like BB-gun holes; their borings resemble flour. Because these insects favor the sapwood of the tree, their borings may be only superficial: prod with your penknife to find out. After sweeping up any borings present, spray the infested area with a contact insecticide and monitor periodically; if borings recur or appear elsewhere, call a professional.

Water damage. If wood is spongy, shows a lot of wispy fibers that look like cotton, and disintegrates without reference to the grain, it has dry rot. (The white strands are spores.) ''Dry rot'' is actually a misnomer, because it too is caused by high moisture; here, though, the wood is intermittently dry. If, on the other hand, the wood looks dark or charred and disintegrates along the grain, it has wet rot because it's probably wet all the time.

If your basement walls or floors are damp or wet, consider the waterproofing methods discussed in Chapter 9. If the rot is most pronounced along the perimeter of the building, particularly the sills, start by cutting back all shrubs at least 1 ft from the building, and grading the soil so that the top of the foundation is at least 8 in. above grade. It's also likely that your downspouts are discharging water next to the foundation; at the very least, add splash blocks. If the rot is more widespread, the problem may be inadequate ventilation: 1 sq ft of vent per 100 sq ft of floor space is recommended. If you've got a crawl space with a dirt floor, try covering the earth with plastic.

If, however, the rot is limited to a few spots, suspect leakage and look for other clues above. It may be entering from inadequate roof flashing, blocked gutters, or—quite common in older houses—windows or doors that lack flashing altogether, in which case there will probably be water damage to walls and ceilings inside. Finally, look for structural rot beneath tubs, sinks, and water heaters; if you find it, you must also replace subflooring.

Treating damaged areas. Once you've eliminated the source of the deterioration by exterminating insects or repairing leaks, make sure that it doesn't recur by controlling moisture and by inspecting for insects periodically.

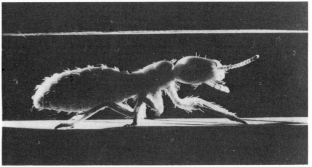

A.

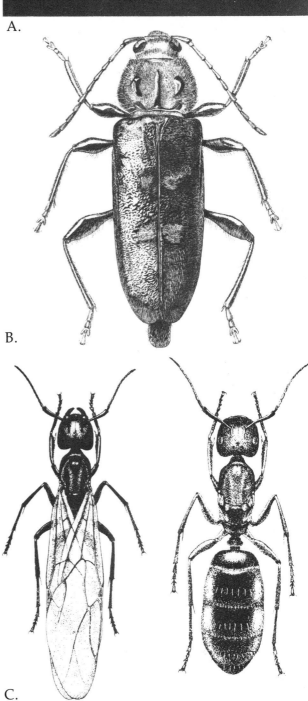

B.

C.

Figure 8.27 Wood-destroying insects. (A) Adult termite; (B) powder-post beetle; (C) carpenter ants. (Courtesy of *Pest Control* magazine.)

Rotted wood, unsightly as it is, poses no threat to healthy wood as long as you control moisture. Remove badly deteriorated sections, but it's not necessary to remove the entire member; in fact, it's preferable to leave it in place if there's flooring nailed to it. If you want to bolster weakened wood with new, that's discussed in a following section. Before doing so, however, heed these suggestions:

1. Allow old members to dry thoroughly before laminating on new wood.

2. Put a layer of felt paper (which is impregnated with tar) between new wood and old to forestall rot; in a pinch, aluminum flashing also works.

3. Spray the old wood with a preservative. *Note the safety tips below.*

4. Use only galvanized nails when nailing into wood treated with preservatives, or into redwood.

Using preservatives safely. *Preservatives are hazardous to your health.* Read directions carefully and follow them religiously.

1. Use only in situations indicated. Penta and creosote, where permitted at all, are restricted to outdoor use. As of this writing, copper green is still allowed on substructure inside—but check with your local authorities before buying anything.

2. Heed ventilation requirements and drying times rigorously.

3. Wear rubber gloves, goggles, a respirator mask with changeable filters, a hat, and long-sleeved clothing. Protect exposed skin with a layer of Vaseline.

4. Handle preservatives and treated wood as little as possible.

5. To reduce splatter, don't overpump the spray can.

Renovating Stairs

Squeaks are caused by wood rubbing against wood or nail shanks, as stair parts have shrunk or worked loose over the years. If the underside of the staircase is exposed, you can easily fix even widespread squeaking. But concomitant cracking, gapping, or tilting along the stairwell means serious structural failings.

(Before we proceed, let's clear up a confusion that has more to do with construction than with function, for both *stringers* and *carriages* support steps. Carriages *carry;* hence a piece of lumber cut out in a sawtooth pattern is a carriage. Where the ends of treads and risers rest in a piece of lumber grooved or routed out to receive them, that is a stringer—as in the *housed stringer* shown in Figure D.10. Occasionally, stringers and carriages are laminated together. In this book the terms are used more or less interchangeably.)

Squeaky steps. If the underside of your staircase is covered and you have only a few squeaks, try fixing them without tearing out finish materials. The most common fix is nailing down offending treads with finish nails—except that it doesn't work. The nails may split the nosing and they'll almost certainly pull loose. It's far better to predrill and screw down the tread, driving finishing screws into a riser or center carriage beneath.

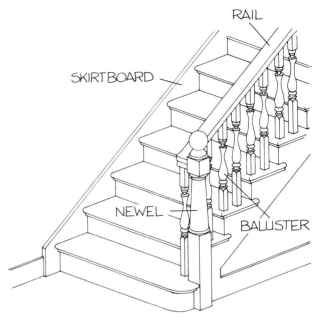

Figure 8.28 Stair superstructure.

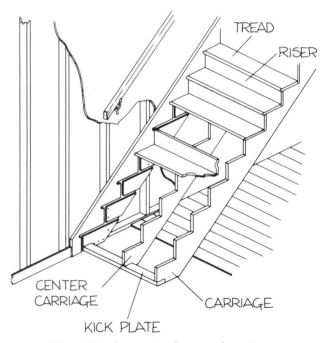

Figure 8.29 Supporting elements of a staircase.

If the stairs can be painted or carpeted over, caulk the squeaky joint with subflooring adhesive. This doesn't bind the pieces together as screws do, but the butyl in the adhesive cushions them, in effect. Keep people off the stairs until the compound has cured. If that doesn't do it, expose the underside of the staircase to get at its underpinnings.

What you do next depends on the construction of the stairs. If there are blocks glued along the riser–tread joint, chances are that the glue has failed. First, alleviate tread movement by nailing through the back side of risers into treads: predrill, and use two or three 6d finish nails per tread. Then reglue errant blocks with white glue or, better yet, with construction adhesive.

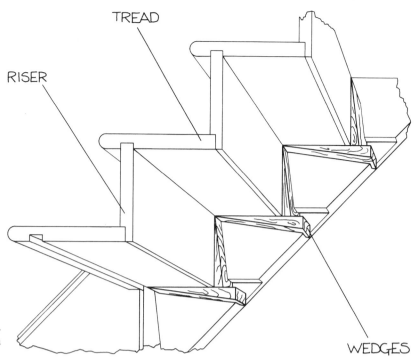

Figure 8.30 If your stair has housed-stringer construction, drive wedges in to eliminate squeaking steps.

If your stairs are wedged, they may squeak because the wedges have worked loose and the trend is not supported equally. To fix this, drive in wedges equally—it may be necessary to cut new wedges if old ones are too slender to fit tightly. Drive in wedges behind risers first, then treads. A spot of white glue on each wedge should hold it in place.

If there is squeaking and a lot of flex in the middle of the treads, they may be insufficiently supported down the middle. Adding or bolstering a center carriage is discussed below, under "Sagging Stairs."

Balusters. If you have one or two broken balusters, it's possible to dowel and glue them together, but repaired balusters always look a little cockeyed. It makes more sense to have a wood-turner fabricate new ones from the existing pattern. If a lot of balusters are damaged or missing, replace

A.

B.

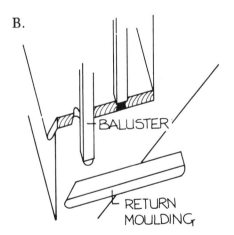

Figure 8.31 Attaching balusters. (A) The tops of balusters are usually toe-nailed to the underside of a railing; plumb the baluster to determine the angle of the cut. (B) The bottom of the baluster is either doweled to a hole in the tread or dovetailed and held in place with a piece of return molding.

them all with stock balusters; repairing large numbers is a waste of time and will look piecemeal.

If balusters are intact but shaky, remove and reglue them; simply nailing them won't do much good. To get at balusters, pry free the return molding at the end of the tread by inserting a putty knife or small chisel into the nosing seam. Once you start prying, you'll see small finish nails holding the nosing in place; remove these nails, then gently knock out the bottom of the baluster, which is usually joined to the tread by a dovetail joint. If that dowel breaks, it's easy to drill out. The top of the baluster is sometimes nailed to the underside of the railing, so take it easy.

To fit the baluster back in place tightly, dip both ends in white glue and replace the tenoned or doweled end first. Replace the return molding and wipe off the excess glue. To prevent marring during this operation, use a rubber mallet or a scrap of wood to cushion hammer blows.

Newel posts. If many of the balusters are loose, check the railing and the newel post: they may not be firmly attached. Typically, the upper end of the railing turns and continues on to the floor above or it runs into a wall where it is anchored with a bracket beneath. Make sure that this bracket is tight.

If the newel post is shaky, try shimming underneath its base, or screwing the post down with 3-in. type W drywall screws; predrill and sink the screws. If this easy repair doesn't suffice, determine what internal hardware needs tightening. Quite often newel posts are hollow, with a long, threaded rod down the inside. The upper end of this rod, concealed by the post cap, is tightened by turning a nut against a restraining plate, as in Figure 8.32. Because it may be difficult to find the cap joint through many years of polish and grime, rap the side of the cap with a rubber mallet to loosen it. The other end of the threaded rod often emerges on the underside of the subflooring—if it's exposed, have a look.

On occasion, newel posts also connect to another plate-and-rod assembly on the inside of the nearest stair carriage. About the only way to get at that assembly (if it exists at all) is to pull up the first tread. Where the railing meets the newel, the railing is held tight by wood joinery or by a double-ended hanger bolt accessible through a plug on the underside of the railing.

Replacing stair treads. Treads crack because they aren't supported correctly, or they weren't made from good stock in the first place. To replace them, you'll have to pry or cut them out; the former method is preferable but rarely possible, especially if the treads are rabbeted to risers or housed in stringers.

To cut them out, first remove the balusters from the step's open end, saving that end as a template for the new tread. Drill into the middle of the tread and, driving a chisel with the wood grain, split out the old tread. Clean up any old glue or wood fragments. After fabricating the new tread and testing its fit, apply glue to its edges and to the tops of the carriages on which it will sit. To each carriage, screw down the tread with two or three finish screws, predrilled to prevent splitting. Reinsert and glue balusters and nosing.

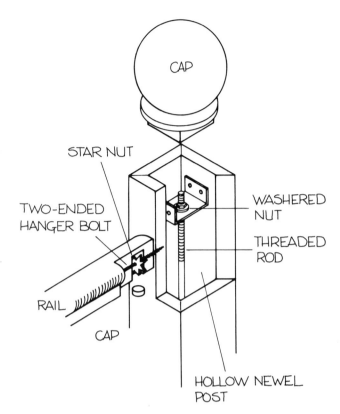

Figure 8.32 The railing may attach to the newel post in a number of ways, one of the more common being a star nut centered in the end of a railing. The bottom of the post may be screwed to a stringer or held fast by a rod-and-plate assembly running down the middle of the post.

Sagging stairs. If the staircase has several of the ailments just described, it may also have major troubles underneath. Investigate further. If the stairs tilt to one side, the carriage on the low side is having difficulty: nails or screws holding it to the wall may be pulling out, the wood may be rotting or splitting, or the carriage may be pulling free from the stringer. Sagging on the open side of a stairway is common, for there's no wall to which to bolt a carriage. If there are large cracks or gaps at the top and bottom of the stairs, you're seeing symptoms of a falling carriage.

To get more information, you will have to remove the finish surfaces from the underside of the staircase. Before cutting into anything, however, rent a dumpster for the rubble and confine the mess by sealing off the stairwell with sheet plastic. When you cut, set your circular saw just to the depth of the finish materials so that you don't cut into carriages; using a carborundum blade, cut out the surface in 2-ft squares. Wear goggles.

You can probably save any decorative plaster molding along the staircase by cutting parallel to it—about 1 in. from its edge, thus isolating the section of lath nailed to the underside of the outer carriage. Leaving a 1-in. strip will also make it easier to disguise the seam when you reattach the ornamental border after the job is done.

With the underside of the stairs exposed, you can see exactly what the problem is. If the carriages have pulled loose from adjacent walls, you'll see a definite gap. Replace wood that is rotted or badly cracked, especially wood cracked across the grain. If the wood sags or is otherwise distorted, bolster it with additional lumber; it may also need to be reattached. All of these repairs are big ones; to do them right, you'll need complete access to the substructure, from one end of the carriages to the other.

Starting at the top, remove all nosing, balusters, treads, and risers. You could theoretically bolster undersized carriages without removing all the treads, risers, and balusters, but it's better to remove them: otherwise, misaligned or distorted carriages will be held askew by all the pieces nailed to them. So remove the treads and risers and jack up the distorted carriages to realign them—you may want to stretch taut strings as an alignment aid.

Number all parts as you remove them, grouping pieces according to the step number. Embossed plastic tape tacked to stair pieces is much more durable than chalk or pencil marks.

Play it safe. If you are stripping stairs over an open well (i.e., there is another flight of stairs below), first secure your footing. Cover the stairwell with $\frac{5}{8}$-in. plywood tacknailed around its perimeter; this platform should be thick enough to support your weight. Work from a sturdy stepladder. If you will be jacking up the structure above, you'll need to support the jack on a 4×6 or 4×8 on-edge, which spans the opening.

Realigning and Reinforcing Carriages

To realign the substructure, you'll have to jack. If the outside carriage has bowed outward, force it back into place with a 2×4 jammed against a near wall or, if the carriage resists your efforts, use an adjustable screw column lying on its side. (Nail column plates to hold the jack horizontal between stringer and wall.)

Where a carriage has separated from its stringer, renail existing nails and add $2\frac{1}{4}$-in. lag bolts, staggering bolts every 18 in. along the length of the boards. If a carriage has pulled free from a stud wall, reattach it with washered lag bolts. Where a carriage is attached to a masonry wall, drill through the carriage into the masonry, using a carbide-tipped masonry bit. Slip a lead sleeve into the hole and expand the sleeve by tightening a washered $\frac{3}{8}$-in. lag bolt into it. To forestall rot, slip a piece of 30-lb felt paper behind the carriage before bolting it down.

Occasionally, stringers or carriages come loose at the top and bottom. In a well-built staircase, the upper ends of carriages are nailed to the inside of the header above; the lower ends of those carriages sit *on,* and are nailed to, the doubled joists of the rough opening below.

It sometimes happens, however, that the lower ends of center carriages are ill-advisedly nailed to the *inside* of a rough opening: in time the nails pull free and the carriages slip down. To remedy this defect, jack up the fallen carriages, using a plumbed, adjustable screw column securely footed on the floor or atop a 4×8 beam on-edge. To create a flat jacking surface for the top of the column, screw a triangular piece (with the same slope as the stairs) to the underside of the carriage. Should old nails resist your effort, cut through them with a metal-cutting blade in a reciprocating saw. Goggles, please.

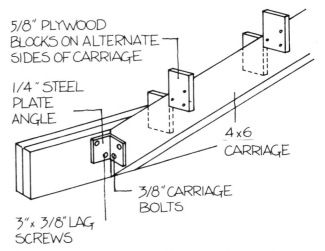

Figure 8.33 Inadequate support for the middle of a staircase can lead to tread splits or major failures. Where the center carriage has been attached to the *inside* of the stairwell header, reinforce that attachment (which has probably slipped) with a $\frac{1}{4}$-in. steel mending plate. Not infrequently, the center carriage is an unnotched 2×8 or 2×10 running down the middle; it will carry better if you screw plywood tread supports to alternate sides of the carriage.

Jack up the center carriage and join its lower end to the header with metal connectors or $\frac{1}{4}$-in. right-angle mending plates. Secure the plates to the header with $\frac{3}{8}$-in. lag bolts, and *through* the bottom of the carriage with $\frac{1}{4}$-in. carriage bolts. It is usually not necessary to use mending plates on the upper end of the carriage, since the lower end is bearing most of the weight.

Where a center carriage is not sawtoothed to receive treads, add plywood supports beneath each step. Cut supports from scrap plywood $\frac{1}{2}$ in. thick, then glue the screw supports to alternate sides of the carriage—one per tread. If the stair is sagging and has no center carriage, add one.

When carriages are bolstered and reattached, and stairs and balusters reinstalled, replace finish surfaces. Be sure that the nailing plane on the underside of the carriages is flat, shimming as needed. To reattach plaster lath or drywall, use type W drywall screws: hammering in nails often cracks surrounding materials.

Bolstering Joists

Joist failures will usually show up as a sag or bow in the floors above; use your level to determine low spots. Squeaks are other good indicators. Localized joist failure is usually caused by insects or water damage, point loading, and earlier renovations that weakened the member. Widespread sagging or excessive springiness in a floor is more likely to be caused by joists too small for the span; or by post, pad, and foundation failure. The methods used to bolster tired joists—adding "sisters"—will also be useful to remodelers adding rough openings to floors.

Adding joists. As noted above, under "Treating Damaged Areas," deal with the cause of the infestation or rot; treat the damaged area with preservative; and leave as much of the original joist(s) as possible.

The most common way to reinforce a weakened joist

is to nail a new one to it, of the same dimension and length. The new "sister joist" needn't be the exact length as the original, but should be long enough to be supported by the foundation on either end. (The foundation includes not just the concrete perimeter walls, but also girders, posts, pads, and the like.) For this reason, short sections scabbed on just don't work, and are usually proscribed by local codes.

To position the new joist, first remove blocking or bridging between the joists affected. Bend over any flooring nails protruding from the underside of the floor. Before raising the new joist, eyeball it and note its crown. If its arc is excessive, power-plane it down so that you don't bow up the floor with it. Which of the following methods you use depends on the space you've got to work with and how the joists are supported.

Notch-and-Shim Method. Where both ends of a joist are captured (i.e., they sit *on* sills or girders), the easiest way to get a joist up into the limited space is to notch the lower edge of each end. Using a $1\frac{1}{2}$-in. chisel, make the notch about 18 in. long and $\frac{1}{2}$ in. deep. Slide the joist up on its side, then stand it up on-edge. You may have to rap the side of the joist with a hand sledge to get it fully on-edge.

Once the notched joist is in place next to the old one, raise them both slightly to take up the sag. You can wedge 2×4 tees beneath, or raise them with foundation jacks plumbed at either end—but don't overdo it! Raise the joists just until they are both flush to the underside of the sub-flooring and no more. That accomplished, drive two tapered hardwood shims under each notch, as shown in Figure 8.34A. Lower and remove the tees (or posts), then nail the joists together using 16d nails staggered every 12 in. (If the joists clatter when you start nailing, C-clamp them together.) Replace the blocking between the joists.

The notch-and-shim method is good because it allows you to use joists as near full length as practicable. Where you're picking up a bearing partition or compensating for point loading above, it also allows you to position doubled joists beneath the load, or to laminate a girder in place, as in Figure 8.34B.

Angled-End Method. Where joists hang from a girder (rather than sitting on it), the notch-and-shim method isn't appropriate. In that case, cut one end of the sister joist square, to butt to the girder, and cut the top of the other end at an angle (Figure 8.34C) so that you can easily place it on-edge over the sill and then lift the square end up to the girder.

Joists raised in this manner must be about 1 in. shorter than the original because it is necessary to slide the joist all the way in—enabling the square corner to clear the girder—and then back it out so that the joist end is flush to the girder.

Once the free end of the joist is within a foot or two of the subflooring, you may need a 2×4 tee or an adjustable column to raise it the rest of the way, until it is flush to the underside of the subflooring. At that point, attach it to the girder with a double-joist hanger, remove the tee, then join the two joists, with 16d nails staggered every 12 in. (Should one flange of the double-joist hanger overlap a hanger al-

A.

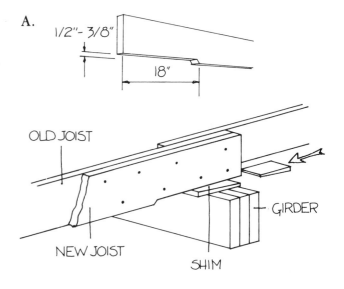

B.

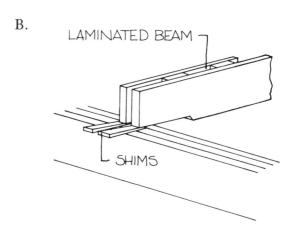

C.

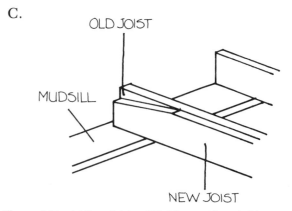

Figure 8.34 Adding joists. (A) The notch-and-shim method makes it easier to get the joist into the limited space between the subflooring and the top of a sill or girder. Jack the new joist slightly so that its top edge is flush to the underside of the subflooring— or as flush as you can get it—then shim it and laminate the new joist to the old. (B) Because of its bulk, a laminated beam is best assembled in place. (C) When one end of a joist will hang from a girder rather than sitting atop it, bevel the joist end that will rest on the mudsill.

ready there, predrill the metal so that you can nail through both with case-hardened hanger nails.)

An aside. In many cities, fire codes require that joist ends resting in masonry pockets be cut at an angle. This cut, called a *fire cut*, runs upward at about a 60-degree angle from the lower corner of the joist. Should joists burn and collapse in the middle, their angled ends can thus fall free from the pocket, without dislodging bricks.

Adding metal, plywood. It is sometimes necessary to ad-lib when reinforcing joists, too; Figure 8.35 shows a few improvisations in the field. Where joist ends have weakened by cracking, their underside can be raised and supported by $\frac{1}{4}$-in. angle iron bolted on, useful when odd-sized joists preclude using joist hangers. In like manner, angle-iron run along the length of a joist imparts strength; use a minimal number of bolt holes, however, for they weaken the wood.

Plywood is also used to stiffen joists, either sandwiched to the outside of the weakened joist or as a core between two joists. Such plywood should be $\frac{1}{2}$-in. five-ply at least, and all plywood joints should occur over support points.

Adding a strongback. A strongback (Figure 6.36) is a carrying timber that carries from above and is used primarily to keep ceiling joists from sagging when a rough opening is added, or to raise joists once they have sagged. Because strongbacks spread loads across many joists, they **mitigate point-loading around rough openings in the ceiling.**

Typically, a strongback is a very straight, very dry 2×10 or 2×12 set on-edge, big enough to have almost no flex and long enough to run from the top plate of one wall to that of another. Although it is not imperative that strongbacks sit on top plates, it's highly desirable: the less weight on ceiling joists, the better.

Eyeball the lumber and install it crown up; so that you don't have a ceiling that bows up, reject any stock with an excessive arc. Since a board this long may prove difficult to get up into an attic, consider taking out an existing attic vent—or adding one—and pulling in the strongback through its opening.

Once the strongback is in place, tack either end with side-flanged hurricane ties to keep it on-edge. Using hurricane ties also minimizes concussions and thereby spares finished ceilings. Speaking of which, if ceiling joists presently sag, you can raise them by levering a piece of scrap against the strongback, as shown in Figure 6.36.

Adding a girder. If your joists are excessively springy and/or sagging down toward the middle of the floor, chances are that they're undersized (i.e., too small for the distance they span). The easiest way to solve this problem is to shorten the span by adding a girder beneath—a straightforward operation described in a following chapter. Where girders sag, add posts to support them where they're point-loaded. Where joists slope downward from the girder, you may have a failed perimeter foundation—a major undertaking (see Chapter 10).

Rafter Repair

As with other structural elements, first determine why rafters have failed: if the reason is insects or water damage, attend to that first. Happily, the most common rafter ailment, sagging, is not caused by deterioration and can be easily cured within the attic.

Collar ties. Rafters most often sag because they're undersized to start with. In temperate parts of the country where there are no snow loads, in fact, 2×4 rafters were commonly used. With the additional loads of reroofing, rafters sagged and plaster ceilings below cracked and crazed. Yet puny as those rafters were, they might have been strong enough had they been bolstered with collar ties.

Collar ties are horizontal members that run between rafter pairs, thereby creating a triangular brace that stiffens and positions rafters. Adding collar ties is essentially a threefold task: marking collar ties, raising sagged rafters, and attaching collar ties.

Layout. Start at gable ends, where rafter pairs, supported by gable-end studs, haven't sagged. You will use those rafter pairs, at each end of the house, to align all rafters in between. Measure down from the ridge approximately one-

A.

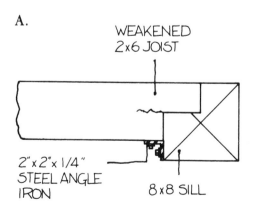

WEAKENED
2x6 JOIST

2" x 2" x 1/4"
STEEL ANGLE
IRON

8 x 8 SILL

B.

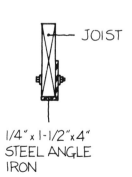

JOIST

1/4" x 1-1/2" x 4"
STEEL ANGLE
IRON

Figure 8.35 (A) When rot is localized, as at the end of a beam, soak the end of the wood with preservative and bolt on a section of angle iron. Joist hangers are also effective, but many old beams have odd dimensions. (B) Where there's not enough space to add a new joist, a length of angle iron will bolster an old one.

third the rafter length and tack a nail; using a level atop a perfectly straight board (or a line level), measure over and drive a nail at the same height into the other rafter of the pair. Then mark the pair of rafters at the other gable end, in like manner.

To mark the positions of collar ties on the underside of sagging rafters, stretch and snap chalk lines from the nails you drove. Mark from one gable end to the other, one side at a time.

Now cut a collar tie template, using at least 2×6 stock. Again, use a pair of rafters at a gable end as your model, because they haven't sagged. Hold the board at the nail points you leveled earlier and mark the angles where it intersects the *underside* of the rafters. (*Note:* Collar ties are sometimes nailed to the face of rafters, which just isn't as strong.) Cut that template, test-fit it at both gable ends to be sure, then cut all the collar ties. At both ends of each tie, tack on a *gang-nail plate* (Figure 4.11) so that you can attach collar ties quickly when you're ready.

Raising Sagged Rafters. Raise rafters a pair at a time. In most cases, a 2×4 tee wedged beneath will give you more than enough purchase to raise up a sagging rafter; ''fine-tune'' the collar ties with a hammer until they're aligned to the chalk lines you snapped. If you are concerned that the pressure from the 2×4 might crack finish ceilings below, lay a heavy plank or a strongback atop the attic joists and push up from that.

Attachment. The rest is easy; having prenailed one gang-nail plate to each end of the collar tie, nail them off when the tie is in position. Once all the ties are up, go back and add second plates to the other side of each collar tie. To prevent loosening what you've already nailed, have a helper brace the back side of the tie as you hammer from the other side. Use only the case-hardened nails provided by the maker of the gang-nail plates.

Purlins. Where rafters are so undersized that you cannot drive them up and brace them with collar ties, you have three alternatives, all expensive. The first two require adding rafters: jacking and ''sistering'' larger rafters to existing ones; or ripping off the entire roof and framing anew. The third alternative, perhaps the least offensive, is adding purlins.

Purlins are carrying timbers beneath rafters. In effect, they reduce the load along the entire rafter by supporting it partway, much as a girder shortens the free span of joists. But structurally, purlins are very complex and it is imperative that you have an engineer (not an architect) design your purlin system.

This caution is necessary because the considerable loads that purlins pick up must be supported below, all the way down to the foundation. Whether your purlin braces (also called ''knees'') come straight down or at an angle, they rest atop an oversized sole plate, which is in turn supported by a bearing wall. Typically, that wall is a shear wall, sheathed on one side with 5-ply $\frac{1}{2}$-in. plywood and shear-nailed with 10d nails spaced 4 in. O.C. That shear wall, in turn, must be supported by an array of girders, posts, and piers beneath—in short, a lot of work.

Spreading walls. It sometimes happens that rafter sag is accompanied by walls kicking out at the top. Although not exactly a common problem, I've seen it in several nineteenth-century houses, including the first one I ever owned. Whether post-and-beam or stick-framed, the attic joists of such unlucky houses usually run parallel to the ridge, providing little incentive for side walls to remain upright. That, coupled with an absence of collar ties, a newer, heavier roof and perhaps a dash of foundation failure, is all the fun you'll ever want.

The standard advice—just pull the walls together with a *comealong*—is correct as far as it goes, but the comealong, only slightly less capricious than a rusted pump jack (p. 41), must pull a $\frac{5}{8}$-in. steel cable as taut as a banjo string, while the house shudders and creaks like the Voice of Doom. And there's still the roof to raise, collar ties or purlins to add, bearing walls to build, and probably a foundation to replace. By all means, call a contractor experienced with old houses.

Rot at the top. We'll close this chapter with another situation requiring professional help: rot at the top plates. Although water stains are common enough on old roof sheathing, water damage to rafters is relatively rare, usually occurring at the rafter–top plate intersection. It couldn't happen at a worse place—for if it's extensive, you'll have to rebuild part of the wall and most of the roof to fix it. Probably the walls will also have started to spread. If you're thinking about buying such a house, it better be cheap.

If the rot is limited to a rafter or two and a small section of top plate, repair is possible. The most thorough repair—advisable if you need a new roof anyhow—is to cut back sheathing to expose the damaged rafter, remove it by cutting it into pieces, and replace it with a full rafter running from ridge to top plate. To stabilize the rest of the roof while making these repairs, leave the rest of the rafters sheathed. *Important:* Do as much work as possible from scaffolding erected on the attic floor; *avoid* getting on the roof above damaged areas.

The alternative method is cutting out blighted areas, adding new wood and tying it all together with metal connectors, while leaving roofing pretty much intact. To jack

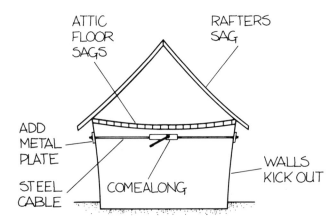

Figure 8.36 When the walls of a building kick out at the top, pull them back with a comealong.

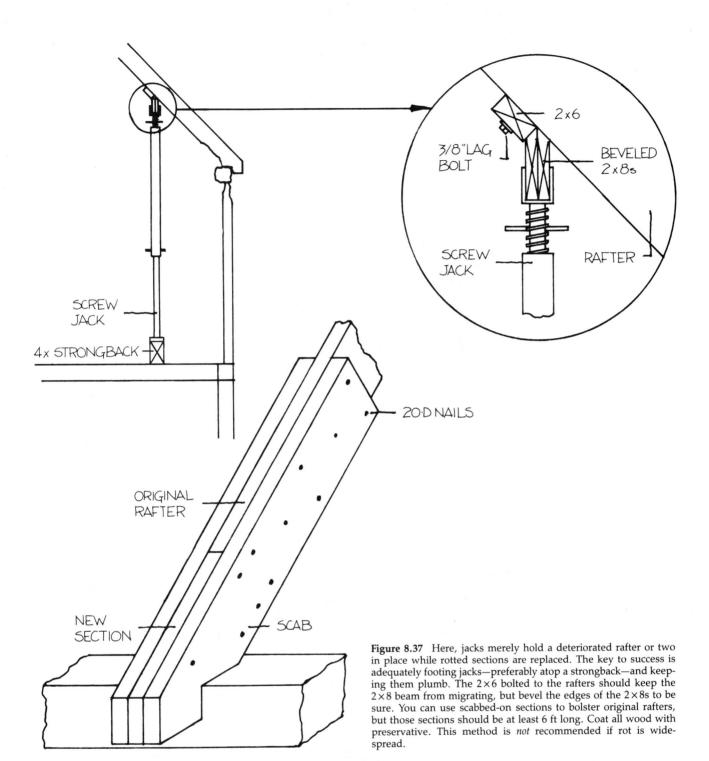

SCREW
JACK

4x STRONGBACK

2×6

3/8"LAG
BOLT

BEVELED
2×8s

SCREW
JACK

RAFTER

20·D NAILS

ORIGINAL
RAFTER

NEW
SECTION

SCAB

Figure 8.37 Here, jacks merely hold a deteriorated rafter or two in place while rotted sections are replaced. The key to success is adequately footing jacks—preferably atop a strongback—and keeping them plumb. The 2×6 bolted to the rafters should keep the 2×8 beam from migrating, but bevel the edges of the 2×8s to be sure. You can use scabbed-on sections to bolster original rafters, but those sections should be at least 6 ft long. Coat all wood with preservative. This method is *not* recommended if rot is widespread.

up damaged rafters without destroying the ceiling below, jack up from a strongback. To keep the top of the jack from migrating, bolt a cross brace to the underside of rafters, as shown in Figure 8.37; that brace should extend at least one rafter beyond the rot, on each end. Once you've jacked, cut out bad sections, making sure all cuts are square across the face of the lumber. Pry loose severed sections from the sheathing nailed to them, and cut roofing nail shanks flush to the underside of the sheathing. Treat remaining rafter ends with preservative. Replacement stock should be of the same dimensions as the original rafter, and supporting ''scabs'' should extend beyond joints at least 3 ft; bolt the entire assembly together with $\frac{1}{4}$-in. lag bolts, slightly predrilled so that you don't split the wood. Overlap replacement top-plate sections; if pony-wall studs are defective, however, replace them down to the floor platform. Use metal straps across top-plate junctures, and hurricane ties to hold rafters to top plates.

·9·

MASONRY

asonry encompasses stone, brick, tile, concrete, and other minerals which, when used in combination, become strong and durable. It's an ancient craft. The oldest surviving buildings are stone, of course; but stone, common as it is, is heavy and difficult to work. Brick, on the other hand, is less durable but is eminently better suited to common dwellings. Clay, the basic component of brick, is found almost everywhere, and being lighter, it requires fewer workers to lay up a wall. Brick masonry was a great conceptual leap, on two counts. First, the builder began with a plastic form (mud and straw); then he shaped it, ending with something hard and durable as a building material. Second, the manufacture of brick is one of the earliest examples of mass production, of making units of uniform size and standardizing their assembly. The idea was so right, in fact, that the basic tools and, probably, the techniques of brick masons have changed little over several millennia.

This chapter concerns itself with repairing, altering, and attaching to masonry walls and floors. Stucco is discussed in Chapter 7; plaster, in Chapter 15; tiling, in Chapter 16; and upgrading foundations in Chapter 10.

TERMS, TOOLS, AND TECHNIQUES

This section offers an overview of the types of masonry. Unless otherwise specified, mixes and methods are appropriate for brick, block, and other units set in courses.

Materials

In masonry work, the materials most frequently used are portland cement, masonry cement, aggregate, mortar, grout, concrete, reinforcing bars, admixtures, and masonry units.

Portland cement. The basic component of all modern masonry mixtures. It consists of finely ground mineral compounds, including lime (60 to 66 percent), silica (19 to 25 percent), alumina (3 to 8 percent), iron (1 to 5 percent), and gypsum. When water is added to cement, it reacts chemically with the cement, giving off heat and causing the mix to harden, thus bonding together materials in contact with it. By varying the proportions of the basic ingredients of cement, the renovator can alter its setting time, strength, resistance to certain chemicals, and so on. It is available in 94-lb bags.

Masonry cement. Also called *mortar cement*, masonry cement is a mix of portland cement and lime, although its exact proportions vary. The lime plasticizes the mix and makes it workable for a longer period. Once dry, the mix is also durable.

Aggregate. Fine aggregate is sand, whereas course aggregate is gravel.

Mortar. The mixture used to lay brick, concrete block, stone, and similar materials. As indicated in Table 9.1, it is a mixture of masonry cement and sand, or of portland cement, lime, and sand.

Grout. A mix of portland cement and sand, or masonry

TABLE 9.1

Mortar types (ASTM C 270-68)

		Parts by Volume			
Type	Portland Cement	Masonry Cement	Hydrated Lime or Lime Putty	Aggregate Measured in a Damp, Loose Condition	
M	1	1	—		Not less than $2\frac{1}{4}$ and not more than 3 times the sum of the combined volumes of cement and lime used
	1	—	$\frac{1}{4}$		
S	$\frac{1}{2}$	1	—		
	1	—	Over $\frac{1}{4}$ to $\frac{1}{2}$		
N	—	1	—		
	1	—	Over $\frac{1}{2}$ to $1\frac{1}{4}$		
O	—	1	—		
	1	—	Over $1\frac{1}{4}$ to $2\frac{1}{2}$		
K	1	—	Over $2\frac{1}{2}$ to 4		

Source: Adapted from publications of the American Society for Testing and Materials, as are the compression figures given in the text.

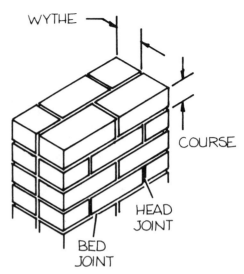

Figure 9.1 Masonry terms.

cement and sand. Mixed with enough water so that it flows easily, it is used to fill cracks and similar defects. (In tiling, grout is the cementitious mixture used to seal tile joints.)

Concrete. A mixture of portland cement, sand, and gravel. Supported by forms until it hardens, it is afterward a durable, monolithic mass.

Reinforcing bars. Also called *rebar* and *reinforcing mesh,* reinforcing bars are steel elements embedded in masonry materials to increase resistance to tensile, shear, and other loads.

Admixtures. Mixtures added to vary the character of masonry mixtures. They can add color, increase plasticity, resist chemical action, extend curing time, and allow work in adverse situations. Particularly important are recent advances in *binders,* which greatly aid adhesion, and *sealants,* which seal masonry against moisture. These are discussed further toward the end of the chapter.

Masonry unit. Individual brick, block, stone, or tile.

Tools

There are many more masonry tools than those shown here, but these will see you through the tasks described in this chapter. (Most items mentioned but not depicted are shown in Chapter 3.) Wear goggles when using any striking tool.

Trowel. The one indispensable masonry tool. If you have no others, a trowel can cut brick, scoop and throw mortar, tap masonry units in place, and shape mortar joints. A good-quality trowel has a blade welded to the shank. Cheap trowels are just spot-welded. An 8-in. trowel is a good size for beginners.

Mason's hammer. Used to score and cut brick with the sharp end and to strike hand chisels with the other.

Brick set. Also used to score and cut masonry. It is best for making precise cuts and for dislodging deteriorated brick.

Line block (or pin). Used to secure a taut line to which the mason aligns a masonry course.

Mason's level. Should be 4 ft long, have an all-metal casing and replaceable vials. Indispensable for correct masonry work.

Jointer. Compresses and shapes mortar joints. The tool shown in Figure 9.2D produces concave joints. Figure 9.12 shows some other joints.

Tuck-pointing chisel. The chisel to use if you are cleaning out old joints before repointing them.

Power grinder. With an abrasive wheel, can be used to clean out old mortar; but it is hard on brick, even when used by an experienced worker. For the best results, use a tuck-pointing chisel.

Cold chisel. When used with a hand sledge, cuts back spalled or otherwise loose masonry so that repair materials will adhere.

Flat bar. Not really a masonry tool, but handy for prying out old bricks from loose mortar.

Half-inch drill with carbide-tipped masonry bit. Can drill into most masonry materials—for example, when setting a bolt. If you are drilling into concrete, however, an impact hammer (also called a *hammer drill*) is best. Impact hammers have either rotary- or straight-drilling actions, or both. Impact hammers are extremely powerful and should not be used on brick or block. The model shown in Figure 3.14 comes equipped with a depth gauge and can deliver 46,000 blows per minute.

Homemade items. Two useful homemade items are a mortar board, which holds a supply of mortar near your work (use $\frac{3}{8}$-in. or $\frac{1}{2}$-in. exterior-grade plywood), and a story pole, which has brick course heights evenly spaced (a useful tool but not crucial to renovation work).

Concrete finishing tools. Shown in Figure 9.2I, such tools are: floats (long tools with closed handles, used to level concrete); finishing trowels (long steel tools with open handles, for smoothing surfaces); and edgers (short tools to contour edges). Not shown is a strike-off (usually a straight 2×4 board), for drawing across the tops of forms and leveling freshly laid concrete.

Useful miscellany. Sturdy scaffolding, cement mixer, sheet plastic, wheelbarrow, buckets, rubber boots, square-nosed shovel, garden hose, and pickup truck.

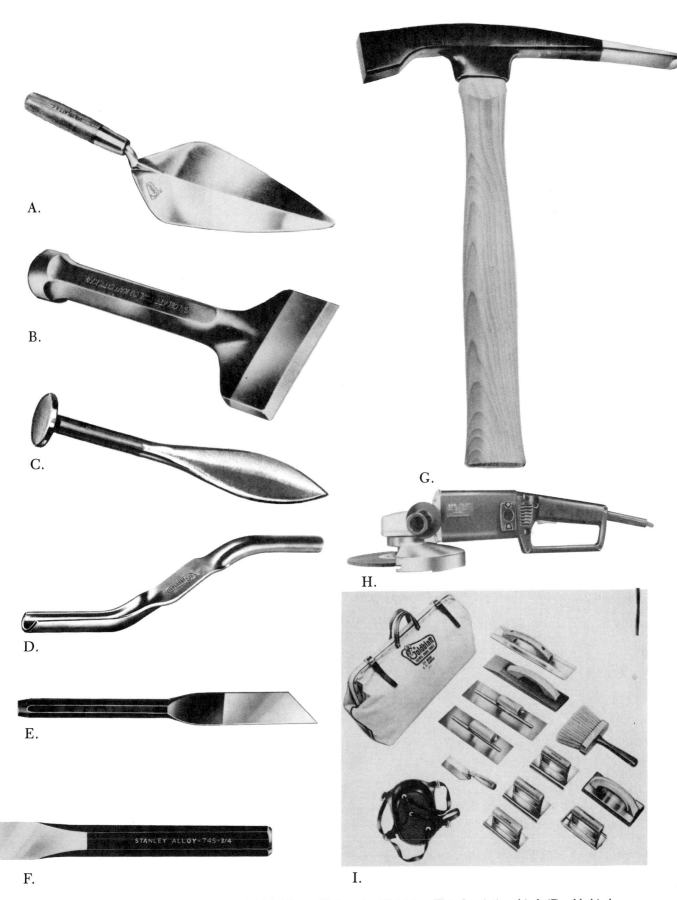

A.

B.

C.

D.

E.

F.

G.

H.

I.

Figure 9.2 Masonry tools. (A) Trowel; (B) brick set; (C) line pin; (D) jointer; (E) tuck-pointing chisel; (F) cold chisel; (G) mason's hammer; (H) power grinder; (I) concrete-finishing tools. (Courtesy of Goldblatt Tool Co.)

Setting Up the Job

Following is a suggested checklist:

1. Check your local building codes before beginning.

2. Anticipate the arrival of materials, and get them under cover as soon as possible. Because water causes cement to set, sacks of portland or mortar cement left on the ground—or even on a seemingly dry concrete floor—will harden and become useless to you. Place sacks on a pallet or a piece of plastic; cover the pile with sheet plastic and weigh down the edges with rocks. (Cement sometimes gets a "factory pack," in which it seems set but isn't. Lift the sack 2 or 3 ft above a clean, dry floor and drop it squarely on its face. If that shock doesn't loosen up the sack, it has taken on moisture and should be discarded.)

Although bricks are wetted as they are being used, they should not be left uncovered in a downpour. If they are, they will absorb too much water—which will dilute the cement after the bricks are set, and weaken the bond. Cover concrete blocks and keep them dry; unlike bricks, concrete blocks are laid up dry. Never wet them.

Although sand and gravel are little affected by water, their dampness will affect the amount of water you add to the mix. Damp sand, which won't ball up when you squeeze a fistful, contains about 1 qt of water per cubic foot; wet sand, which will ball up, about 2 qt; and dripping wet sand, about 3 qt per cubic foot.

Of greater concern is the *purity* of these aggregates; keep them from mixing with soil or other organic matter by unloading them onto an old sheet of plywood, a tarp, or heavy (6-mil) plastic. To determine whether the aggregate is clean, put about 2 in. of it in a jar and nearly fill the jar with clean water. Then shake. If you end up with a layer of fine silt $\frac{1}{8}$ in. or more, wash the aggregate carefully or get a new lot. Because seashore sand is coated with salt and its particles are dulled, it shouldn't be used as an aggregate.

3. To save time and labor, have materials delivered conveniently close to whatever you're working on, so that you can concentrate on laying level, evenly spaced courses and keeping the wall plumb. Although blocks and bricks can be stacked within 4 or 5 ft of the work area, the mortar should be close—say, within 2 ft, and about waist high. For this reason, scaffolding is a sensible investment if you will be working higher than shoulder height. Hire a "go-fer" to carry supplies as needed.

4. Carry masonry materials correctly. Pick loads you can handle without straining, and use ramps and wheelbarrows whenever you can. As you lift, get close to the object and pick with your knees, not your back. And when cutting brick or mortar, always wear safety glasses.

5. Before mixing mortar, be sure that the preparatory work, such as chiseling out old joints and removing old brick, is complete and that the receiving surface is clean. This is critically important during adhesion; say, if you're setting anchor bolts in epoxy.

6. The bond will be weakened if mortar or concrete freezes before it has fully set. Although there are admixtures that effectively extend the temperature range in which you can work, it's easier to do masonry work outside in the spring or fall, when the 24-hour temperature range is 40 to 80°F.

On hot summer days, start early, preferably on a shady side of the house; follow the shade around as the day progresses. The longer masonry stays moist, the stronger it cures. Cover fresh work with burlap sacks dampened periodically, or with sheet plastic.

7. Masonry work can be messy, so spread tarps below the work area to catch mortar drippings. At the end of the day, clean tools well. Scrub hardened spots with a wire brush. If you are using a cement mixer, run a few shovelfuls of gravel and a load of water in the mixer, to clean it out. If you are working high up and you are not sure-handed, tack plywood over the windows to save the glass from breakage.

Note: Although the section that follows is largely about brickwork, it contains information about types of mortar and the techniques for using it, which are also pertinent to working with concrete block, structural tile, and stone.

BRICKWORK

Renovating brickwork is mostly reclaiming what's there or disguising new bricks among the old. Because techniques haven't changed much, the next few pages should give you all you need to get started. If the mortar joints between your bricks are tired, see the section "Repointing" below.

Types and Terms

Of the many types of brick available, we are concerned most with building brick, which is also called *common brick*. Building brick is classified according to its weathering grade: SW (severe weathering), MW (moderate weathering), and NW (nonweathering). SW grade should be used where brickwork will be below grade, that is, in contact with the soil and hence subject to freezing in cold climates. Use it on all floors, whether indoor or outdoor. MW grade is used indoors or on exteriors above grade. NW is used only indoors, though not as flooring.

Standard-sized brick is nominally 8 in. × 4 in. × $2\frac{2}{3}$ in.; but it is actually smaller than that, as noted in Figure 9.3, to accommodate mortar joints $\frac{3}{8}$ in. thick. Thus three courses of brick (and mortar) will be 8 in. high.

Brick is named according to its positioning, whether it is laid on its face, end, or side (Figure 9.4). *Stretcher* and *header* are the most common placements, with *rowlock* pat-

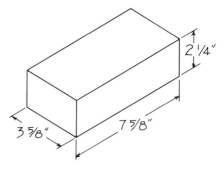

Figure 9.3 Standard brick dimensions.

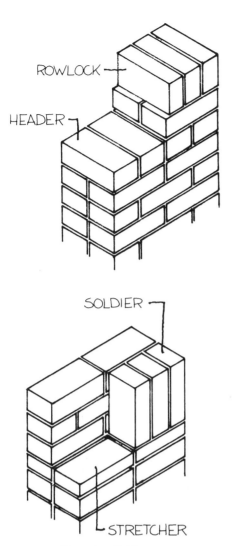

Figure 9.4 Brick positions.

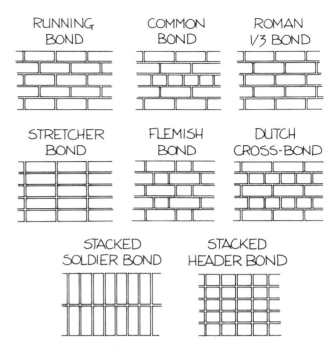

Figure 9.5 Pattern bonds. *Running, common, Roman 1/3, Flemish,* and *Dutch cross-bond* are the strongest bonds because their head joints are staggered. The other bonds, being weaker, are used primarily in veneer applications.

terns often being used to finish courses beneath window sills or to cap the tops of walls where coping isn't used.

The word *bond* is used in several ways. *Mortar* bond denotes the adhesion of brick (or block) to mortar. *Structural* bond refers to the joining or interlocking of individual units to form a structural whole. If there are two wythes of brick, the wythes may be bonded structurally by metal ties, by header bricks mortared into both wythes, or by grout poured into the cavity between the two wythes. Finally, *pattern* bond indicates patterns of brick placement, as shown in Figure 9.5.

If you're laying up a typical brick pattern—say, running bond—you will need about $6\frac{3}{4}$ bricks per square foot of wall; figure 7 bricks per square foot and have enough extra for waste. As you handle bricks, inspect each for soundness; all should be free of major cracks and crumbling, and when struck with a trowel should ring sharp and true.

Layout and Preparation

Layout is less important to renovation brickwork, primarily because you are limited by, and must conform to, the existing structure. In new work, one proceeds from a sound footing, snapping a chalk line (to indicate the baseline of the wall), using a story pole (to make sure that each course is evenly spaced), and building from the corners (or ends) of the wall inward. This is not true of old work.

An obvious example of accommodating new bricks to old is closing off an existing doorway. First, lift the door from its hinges; then, using a flat bar, pry off the interior and exterior trim. Next, remove the door frame by working a utility bar or a wrecking bar between the frame and the rough opening in the brick. If you want to save the trim, and the nails or screws holding it are tenacious, cut through their shanks with a hacksaw or a metal-cutting blade in a reciprocating saw. Leave existing lintels (if any) in place over the opening.

To blend new brick into the opening, tooth out the sides of the rough opening; that is, remove any half-bricks on either side of the opening (Figure 9.6). Toothing out the opening forms a staggered rather than a straight line—which helps disguise the opening when it's filled in with brick. First try to pry out the half-bricks around the perimeter by driving a utility bar into mortar joints. Wear goggles and be careful not to damage whole bricks nearby. (For that reason, do *not* use power grinders or circular saws with carborundum blades to cut out mortar.) If the mortar is strong and resists your efforts, use a brick set or an all-purpose mason's chisel to cut out the half-bricks. With a tuck-pointing chisel, cut back the mortar around the old half-bricks.

Once the rubble has been brushed free, you're ready to start laying new brick. If the opening is wider than 4 ft (the length of your level), use a mason's line to align courses to what's there.

Before mixing mortar, set in a first course of bricks dry (without mortar). Then place a finger between each pair of bricks, to approximate the spacing of a $\frac{3}{8}$-in. head joint. By doing this first, you'll know whether you must cut the

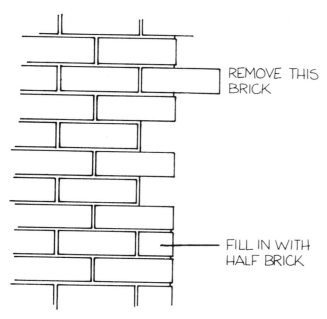

Figure 9.6 "Toothing out" the edge of an opening.

REMOVE THIS BRICK

FILL IN WITH HALF BRICK

weak. Otherwise, lay up bricks according to the standard practice described below, checking for plumb and level as you progress.

Basic Brickworking Techniques

Wet the bricks before using them; that way, they won't absorb moisture from the mortar mix. Hose down the brick pile once a day (more often in hot, dry weather), but don't overdo it. If the bricks become too wet, they will slide around on the mortar bed.

Cutting bricks: It's easiest to cut bricks when they're supported by a bed of sand; the brick is less likely to jump when you strike it. An experienced mason can score and cut bricks with only a trowel, but most of us will find a brick chisel (brick set) handy. After marking the line to be cut on the face of the brick, hold the chisel perpendicular to the brick and strike with a 4-lb hammer. Because the edge of the chisel is beveled, keep the bevel on the waste side of the line.

You can also use a mason's hammer to cut brick, controlling the cut by first scoring entirely around the brick, using the hammer point. Then rap the scored line sharply to break the brick.

Working with mortar: Mortar is usually *typed* according to its strength and weatherability:

bricks to make them fit. If, at the end of your dry run, you have less than half a brick's length, you can probably move bricks, slightly increasing the width of the head joints between them. Avoid using brick pieces less than half a brick long; they look terrible, and the resultant bond will be

A.

B.

C.

D.

Figure 9.7 Cutting brick. (A) Use a straightedge to mark cutting lines on all sides. (B) Score along those lines with a brick set or the chisel end of a mason's hammer. (C) Scoring first also helps lengthwise cuts. (D) It's possible to score and split brick with a trowel, but more difficult.

Type M. The most durable; has the highest compressive strength. It is recommended for masonry below grade and for masonry that is not reinforced. The minimum average compressive strength (MACS) is 2500 pounds per square inch (psi).

Type S. Has good compressive strength and the best tensile strength of any mortar listed here. Good for reinforced mortar as well as for attaching ceramic veneers where flexion is possible. MACS, 1800 psi.

Type N. Medium strength, suitable for all above-grade uses. MACS, 800 psi.

Type O. Generally should not be exposed to freezing but is suitable for most interior uses, including moderate load-bearing partitions. MACS, 325 psi.

Type K. Low strength. Should not be subjected to load-bearing. MACS, 100 psi.

Of the types of mortar listed above, type N is adequate for most purposes. A simplified version of the proportions given in Table 9.1 for type N would be: 1 part portland cement, 1 part lime, 6 parts sand (*or* 1 part masonry cement, 3 parts sand). Before portland cement became widely used in the nineteenth century, however, mortar was strictly a mixture of lime and sand (and maybe animal hair). If the building you are renovating is 100 years old or older and its mortar needs repointing, use the mortar proportions given for type O above or for the mixture presented under the topic "Repointing".

Dry mixing. When mixing mortar, mix the ingredients dry first to ensure a uniform mixture. Keep the proportions the same regardless of whether you mix by the shovelful or by larger units. After mixing the ingredients dry, scoop a pocket in the middle and add water *slowly*. As you add water, be fastidious about turning out the material in the corner of the mixing pan, so that there will be no dry spots. A right batch of mortar will be moist, yet stiff. A mistake that beginners often make is to let the batch get too wet. This is a mistake because excess water weakens the mix, hence the bond. Add water slowly; once the mix is nearly right, its texture will change radically if you add even small amounts of water.

Mortar will remain usable for about 2 hours; mix approximately two buckets at a time. If the batch seems to be drying out, "temper" it by sprinkling a little water on the batch and turning it over a few times with a trowel. As you scrape excess mortar from the joints, gently (so it doesn't splash in your eyes) throw the excess back into the pan or onto the mortar board and trowel it into the batch from time to time. Don't reuse any mortar that drops on the ground, however.

Troweling. The right way to hold a trowel is with the thumb on top of the handle—*not* on the shank or the blade. This position keeps your thumb out of the mortar, while at the same time giving you the control you need. The other fingers should wrap around the handle in a relaxed manner.

There are two basic ways to load a trowel with mortar. The first is to make two passes: Imagine that your mortar pan is the face of a clock. With the right-hand edge of the trowel raised slightly, take a pass through the mortar "from 6:30 to 12:00." Make the second pass with the left-hand side of the blade tipped up slightly, traveling from 5:30 to 12:00. According to Dick Kreh, the owner of the hands in Figure 9.8A, the trowelful of mortar should resemble "a long church steeple, not a wide wedge of pie."

The second method is to hold the trowel blade at an angle of about 80 degrees to the mortar board. Separate a portion of mortar from the main pile and, with the underside of the trowel blade, compress the portion slightly, making a long, tapered shape. To lift the mortar from the board, put the trowel (blade face up) next to the mortar, with the blade edge farthest away slightly off the board. With a quick twist of the wrist, scoop up the mortar. This motion is a bit tricky; if the mortar is too wet, it will slide off.

To unload the mortar, twist your wrist 90° as you pull the trowel toward you. This motion spreads, or strings, the mortar in a straight line. It is a quick motion, at once dumping and stringing the mortar, and it will take practice to

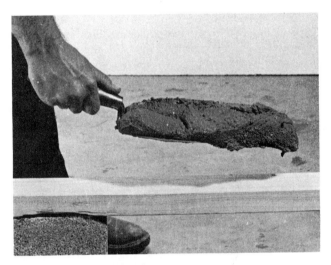

A.

B.

Figure 9.8 Throwing mortar. (A) A correctly loaded trowel has a long, tapered mound of mortar. (B) To get the technique, practice throwing mortar along a 2 × 4, which is about as wide as a common brick. As you turn the trowel to unload the mortar, pull it toward you quickly, thus stringing the mortar in a line. (Photos by Richard T. Kreh, Sr., from his book *Masonry Skills*, highly regarded by those teaching the trade.)

master. If you are laying brick, practice throwing mortar along the face of a 2×4, about the same width as a wythe of brick. Both bricks and blocks get a full bed of mortar beneath the first course; thereafter, concrete blocks are mortared only along their webs and ends, but *every* course of brick gets a full bed of mortar as wide as the wythe.

After you've strung out the mortar, furrow it lightly with the point of the trowel so that the bed will spread evenly (Figure 9.8B). Too deep a furrow means insufficient mortar for a good bond. Trim off the excess mortar that hangs out beyond the wythe, and begin laying brick or block.

Laying. If the first course is at floor level (rather than in the middle of a wall), snap a chalk line to establish a base line for that course. Set up the course dry, as described above. As you apply mortar, remove only two or three bricks at a time, leaving the others until it is their turn to be mortared. In this way, you keep bricks properly spaced.

Throw and furrow a bed of mortar for the first two or three bricks. If you're filling in an opening, ''butter'' the end of the first brick, as shown in Figure 9.9B, thus forming a head joining between the first new brick and the first brick in the existing wall. Press the brick in position and trim away the excess mortar that squeezes out as you press. As you'll note in Figure 9.9C, both the bed and the head joints are $\frac{1}{2}$ to $\frac{5}{8}$ in. thick until the brick is pressed into place, and about $\frac{3}{8}$ in. thick when the brick is in final position. (Any trademark stamped in the brick is laid face down in the mortar.)

The position of the mason's hands is all-important, and is learned only through practice. Use *both* hands when you work; one hand handles the bricks while the other works the trowel, scooping and applying mortar and tapping bricks in place with the handle of the trowel. Note that the man in Figure 9.9 wears a glove on his left hand (to protect against cement burn) but not on his right. If you use a line to align your bricks it is important to get your thumb out of the way of the string just as you put the brick into the mortar bed. As you place a brick next to one already in place, let your hand rest on both bricks; this gives a quick indication of level.

When you have laid about six bricks in a course, it's time to fine tune their placement. Lay a level atop the bricks

A.

B.

C.

D.

Figure 9.9 Laying bricks. (A) For stability and ease in alignment, lay up bricks from the corners in, moving string guides up as you complete each course. (B) After throwing and furrowing bed joints, butter one end of the brick to create a head joint. (C) Holding the brick with your fingers and thumb straddling it, release your thumb at the same time that you place the brick in the mortar bed. This is a quick motion, as you can see by the blur of mason's thumb; done correctly, you should not touch the string guide. Note, too, the thickness of the uncompressed mortar—about $\frac{1}{2}$ to $\frac{5}{8}$ in. thick. (D) To compress the mortar and create a good bond to the brick, tap the brick down with the handle of the trowel. Clean off excess mortar.

to see whether they're level. If they aren't, tap the high ones down with the edge of the trowel blade; tap as near the center of the bricks as the level will allow. All the bricks should be as near perfect level as possible. If a brick is too high, it can be tapped down; but if you have scrimped on mortar, and a brick is too low, better remove it and remortar. (Tap the bricks, *not* the level.)

Now plumb the bricks, as shown in Figure 9.10B, beginning with those at the ends of the course already laid. Hold the level vertical against the edge of the brick. Using the handle of your trowel, tap the brick until its edge is plumb. (Hold the level lightly against the brick; you should not push against the face of the brick with the level.) Do the same for the brick at the other end. To align the brick faces between the two plumbed end bricks, hold the level flush as in Figure 9.10C, tapping bricks toward or away from the level, again with the handle of the trowel.

The last brick in a course is called the closure brick. Butter both ends of that brick liberally and slide it in place. The bed of mortar should also be generous. As you tap the brick in place with the handle of your trowel, some excess mortar will need to be scraped off; but you're ensuring a tight fit. If you scrimped and didn't apply enough mortar, you may have to pull the brick out and remortar it, thus, perhaps, disturbing bricks nearby.

Pointing. When mortar joints have dried—but before they have hardened—point the joints. The ideal time to point comes when you can press your finger in the mortar and the indentation stays. (If you do this too early, the wet mortar will cling to your finger and not stay indented.) Using an appropriate pointing tool, first point the head joints in a given section, then the bed joints. Pointing compresses the mortar and makes it more weathertight. The shape of the pointed joint also affects its weatherworthiness: concave (the most common), V-joint, and weathered joints shed water well; flush joints are fair; struck, raked, and extruded joints are poor exterior joints because they provide horizontal shelves where water will collect.

Laying brick to a mason's line. When the width of an opening exceeds 4 ft—the length of most levels—masons align brick courses with a string. On larger jobs of new work, more experienced masons lay the corners, which require more skill; journeymen then lay bricks between the corners. Line blocks are commonly used to hold a string taut to the corners; where this is not possible, use line pins.

Drive the pins into head joints rather than bed joints. Because the tension of the string is perpendicular to head joints, pins secured in these joints are less likely to pull out. When you have driven the pin in with a masonry hammer,

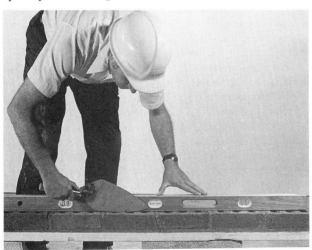

A.

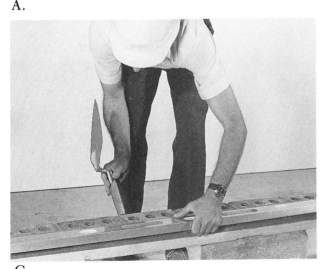

C.

B.

Figure 9.10 Leveling and plumbing the courses. (A) For every six bricks that you lay up, level and plumb them as a course. Using a mason's level, first level the tops of the bricks, gently tapping down high spots with the edge of the trowel. (B) Next, holding the level vertical, plumb the end bricks. (C) Finally, hold the level across the face of the course and tap bricks forward or back so that their faces are flush. (Photos by Richard T. Kreh, Sr., in *Masonry Skills.*)

A.

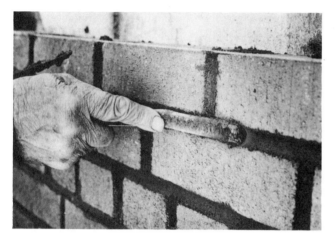

B.

C.

Figure 9.11 Finishing off. (A) As you work from both corners toward the center of the wall, butter the closure brick (the last brick in the course) on both ends and place it in a generous bed of mortar. (B) After the mortar has set enough to retain a thumbprint, *point* mortar joints to compress them and improve weatherability. Work head joints first, then bed joints. (C) If the weather is hot and dry, dampen the wall periodically for 2 or 3 days.

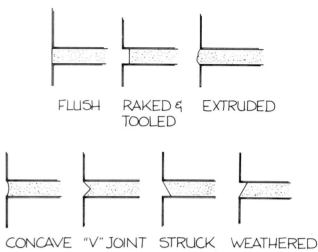

FLUSH   RAKED &   EXTRUDED
         TOOLED

CONCAVE "V" JOINT STRUCK WEATHERED

Figure 9.12 Mortar joints.

pull on the attached line, to make sure the pin is in to stay. As each course is finished, remove the pins and fill the holes; holes filled later may show a different color. The line should be about $\frac{1}{8}$ in. from the face of the brick courses; bricks should *not* touch the line.

Topping off a wall. The standard way to top off a parapet or any other wall top exposed to the elements is to use precast concrete or terra-cotta *coping*. The coping is mortared with the same mortar mix used elsewhere on the wall. A rowlock of bricks is sometimes used, and it looks good; but so many joints on top will cause the rowlock to deteriorate faster than coping pieces. If a rowlock is used to cap a parapet wall, however, the rowlock course should be pitched about $\frac{1}{4}$ in., so rain will run off. (If your house has a flat roof with drains in the middle, the rowlock should tilt $\frac{1}{4}$ in. toward the roof, so water will run toward the drains and not down the outside of the wall.) To increase the life of coping mortar joints, treat them with a silicone one-part sealant or a liquid polymer polysulfide rubber sealant (suggested by Orin M. Bullock, in *The Restoration Manual*). These treatments are usually brushed on over the mortar.

Repointing

Even materials as durable as brick and mortar break down in time, most commonly near the top of a wall or chimney, where the masonry is most exposed to the elements. Commonly, eroded mortar joints are caused by improper coping at the top of the wall, by a lack of flashing to direct water elsewhere, or simply by old age. Tired mortar joints can be reworked and upgraded by *repointing* (also called *tuck pointing*).

If the wall is painted, and you intend to repoint all its mortar joints, it makes sense to strip the paint first. That is no small undertaking, however. Although sandblasting has for years been a common method for removing paint, preservationists have pointed out, correctly, that it is an extremely destructive process, often abrading much of the brick. It is preferable to use such water-based methods as methylene chloride and steam. Whatever method is used, first spread tarps below the area affected. The volume of paint globs is prodigious even on a small stripping job.

Tarps are also advisable even if there is no paint to be stripped, for repointing, itself, is very messy.

Removing old mortar. If the work is above comfortable reach, rent scaffolding. There are two methods of cleaning out old joints: (1) a power grinder with an abrasive wheel (Figure 9.2G) and (2) a tuck-pointing chisel (Figure 9.2F) used with a hammer. The power grinder gets the job done much faster (the job will seem interminable anyway), but the process is very hard on the brick. Sometimes mortar is as hard as the brick, and even an experienced operator has difficulty keeping the wheel in the mortar joint. The hand-powered tuck-pointing chisel is favored by those who want to do the job right.

The blade of the chisel is set diagonally and is rather thin, which enables the user to get deep into a joint. Most other chisel blades are too blunt. Cut into the joint $\frac{3}{4}$ to 1 in. deep, checking the depth of the cuts as you work and doing your best to cut a square trough (not a V groove) in the old mortar.

Note: Whether you use a power grinder or a tuck-pointing chisel, wear goggles to protect your eyes. Using the grinder, you should also wear a respirator mask.

Once you've cut joints to the correct depth, clean them out well. An air hose is effective, so is a heavy-duty vacuum. A wallpaper's brush is better; it will clean out the joints, and later, when it's time to add new mortar, it can be used to wet down the joints.

The mortar mix. It is important to match the old mortar as closely as possible when repointing. (You can get the name or names of a mortar analyst from a preservation agency.) In the days before portland cement was available, mortar was largely a resilient mix of lime and sand. The danger of most modern mixes is that they will be too hard for the old brick. New mortar (one rich with portland cement) expands at a different rate than old material, and could cause the surface of the brick to spall and fall off.

Although mortar analysis is the best way to match old mixes, type O mortar (discussed above, under ''Working with Mortar'') is a close match for most old mortars. Use hydrated lime, and mix 1 part portland cement, 2 parts lime, and 7 or 8 parts fine sand. The mix should be fairly stiff as mortar mixes go; it should, however, keep its shape when squeezed in a ball. The mix is rich in lime; to rejuvenate it, keep adding water.

A.

B.

C.

D.

Figure 9.13 Repointing. (A) Clean out old mortar to a depth of 1 in. or so, using a tuck-pointing chisel and a hand sledge. Wear goggles! (B) A faster but more destructive way to clean out old mortar is to use a carborundum blade in a circular saw or an abrasive wheel in a power grinder. Head joints still have to be chiseled out by hand, however. (C) After sweeping out debris and dampening the joint, apply new mortar with a striking tool, or slick; it may take two passes. (D) When mortar has set slightly, point joints.

Repointing techniques. Work the new mortar into the newly cleaned out (and dampened) joints with a *joint filler* (also called a *striking slick*; Figure 9.13C. Press the mortar into the joint firmly, so that it will stick.

Point the mortar (in this case, repoint the joint) when the mortar has dried enough to retain the imprint of a thumb. Match the existing joint type (if any remains), but remember that a concave shape weathers best. Point the head joints first, then the bed joints.

Wait a few days before wire-brushing or scraping any spots of mortar that may have adhered to the bricks. If stains persist, wash down the wall with a mild solution (1 part acid, 20 parts water) of muriatic acid. Wear rubber gloves, a long-sleeved shirt, and goggles, and rinse down the surface well with water afterward.

If any of the old bricks have spoiled, cut them out with a brick set and replace them with a new ''old brick'' (SW or MW grade) that looks right. Reusing old bricks is chancy; you can't tell how long they'll last. If they ring true when struck with a trowel, however, they're probably OK. Cut out all the mortar around the old brick with a tuck-pointing chisel, and butter every side of the replacement brick except the one that faces out. Place that brick and trim off the excess mortar. When the mortar is dry, point.

Cleaning and sealing exteriors. When deciding what agent to use to clean off stains, choose the mildest possible agent; then try progressively stronger ones. Always wear safety glasses, protective clothing, and rubber gloves. If you rent equipment, get detailed instructions and follow them to the letter. Whatever cleaning agent you choose, try it on a small area first and observe the result for a week.

Efflorescence (a powdery white crust caused by salts in masonry mixtures) can often be removed by scrubbing the masonry exterior with soap and water and rinsing well. If that doesn't work, try a mild mixture of muriatic acid (1 part acid, 20 parts water), again scrubbing it with a stiff-bristle brush and rinsing well with water. A weak (5 percent) solution of muriatic acid is also recommended for removing mortar or grout stains. Another agent frequently preferred for reducing efflorescence is dilute hydrochloric acid; again, rinse with water afterward. Hydrochloric acid is not recommended for light-colored bricks or for bricks that have a sandy texture. Ask the supplier to recommend solution strength and safety precautions.

Organic stains are commonly removed with a dilute bleach solution or with a mild oxalic acid solution mixed according to the manufacturer's recommendations. In addition to straight cold-water pressure systems and steam applications, methylene chloride used with steam has received attention lately. Effective, relatively nontoxic, and gentle to most surfaces, methylene chloride is the preferred method for removing paint from masonry buildings.

When brickwork has been painted over with masonry paint, it is often because the owner didn't feel like repointing tired mortar joints. Thus most stripping of paint on brick walls usually involves extensive repointing work. Today, renovators who want to seal brick, yet retain its original look, spray on clear weatherproofing. On brick, a 4 percent naphtha-based silicone solution is appropriate; for stone and stucco, a 4 percent water-soluble silicone should be used. If your building is brick with stucco or stone trim,

avoid overlapping the two solutions; brush them on carefully where disparate materials meet.

Several other sealants get good press, although we haven't personally tried them: clear silicone acrylics, silicone alkyd solutions, and acrylic emulsions.

Blending interior patches. Newly patched brick may be discernible even if you color the mortar and use old bricks. To blend a new section to an old one, rub over the area of the patch and 2 ft beyond with an old brick fragment. Sponge off the dust, then wash the entire wall with a *dilute* mixture of wood stain (1 part stain to 10 parts turpentine or solvent). A quart of medium brown exterior-wood stain will suffice for most walls. This mixture yields a warm, faintly amber wash. Leave the windows open until the smell of solvent has dissipated.

Chimneys

The masonry chimney is a freestanding unit that carries exhaust gases out of the house. Inside and out, it should be in good repair and its mortar and bricks in good shape so that gases will be safely directed from living areas. Readers thinking of supplementing their current heating systems with a coal- or wood-burning stove should have their chimney inspected and cleaned first. Also check with the fire department and your insurance company before hooking up any stove or furnace. Although safe distances from combustible surfaces have been established (see Figure 14.23), some authorities prohibit wood and coal stoves—period.

Cleaning a chimney. *Note:* Before going up on the roof for any reason, see ''Roof Safety,'' Chapter 5.

Clean your chimney at least once a year, preferably in the fall. Most communities have chimney sweeps; but if you want to do it yourself, first shut off the power to the furnace and disconnect its exhaust pipe, as well as pipes from other appliances that vent to the chimney. Tape plastic over the thimbles that open into the living space, to prevent soot entering as it is dislodged. If there is a fireplace on one of the flues, open the damper (remove it if you can) and tape sheet plastic around the fireplace opening.

The time-honored method of cleaning a chimney is to use a stout sack filled with old chains and/or brickbats—heavy, but small enough so that you can raise and lower it in a flue without getting it stuck. Tie a sturdy rope to the top of the sack, and lower and raise the sack until all the soot has been knocked off the sides of the flue. Another method is to use a chimney sweep's wire brush, which has a handle with detachable sections. This tool, although expensive, is more effective at removing creosote buildup.

After the dust and debris have settled, carefully remove the plastic from the openings, and clean up. Be sure to sweep out any soot that may be resting in thimbles or lurking on the smoke shelf of the fireplace.

While looking down your chimney or into its thimbles, you may find that there is no flue lining within. Such a unit is manifestly unsafe to vent the high temperatures of wood or coal stoves. You may also find creosote leaking through the roof, in which case there are likely other gaps in the brick—hidden by walls—through which superheated gases could leak and set your house ablaze.

If your chimney has no flue lining, these are your choices:

1. Insert a metal liner in the existing chimney, if it is straight enough. You'll have to cut thimble openings to tie into the liner, but otherwise you won't have to break into existing brickwork.

2. Rip out the face of the brickwork in each room through which it passes, and insert a masonry flue tile; rebrick.

3. Ask a supplier of wood stoves for information about the European method—in which a heavy rubber tube is inflated inside an existing chimney, and then a groutlike substance is poured around it, which hardens and becomes a flue.

4. Add a new, properly lined chimney elsewhere; tear out or simply don't use the unlined chimney.

Repairing the chimney cap. Chimney mortar gets a lot of weather and so will deteriorate over the years if it's not maintained. But repair is straightforward: at worst, tearing down and resetting a few courses of brick. The key to making such repairs safely and successfully is preparation.

At the very least, you'll need a sturdy ladder, a bucket tied to a long rope, and someone within earshot should need arise. If several courses of brick are loose, a small roof platform (Figure 9.15) is very handy.

To protect the roof from mortar stains, spread sheet plastic immediately beneath the chimney mass. Finally, to protect the inside of the chimney from errant globs of mortar, overstuff a plastic trash bag with bunched-up newspaper and gently lodge it in the chimney.

If the brickwork merely needs repointing, proceed as described above. More likely, you will have to remove a few courses of brick, then clean and remortar them. Never tear down a chimney any farther than you must; once you

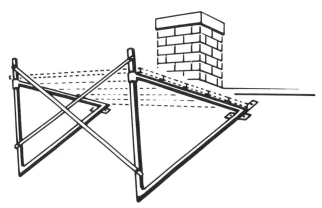

Figure 9.15 Rooftop platform for holding masonry materials. (Goldblatt Tool Co.)

reach sound mortar, stop. (If you must replace any bricks, use only SW grade, which can withstand severe weathering.) Lower the bricks thus removed for cleaning; raise and lower materials with a bucket and rope. A helper on the ground should strike free any old mortar with a chisel, wash the bricks in a 1:10 muriatic acid solution, rinse them well with water, and allow them to dry somewhat (about an hour) before sending them back up to you.

Don't mess with the chimney flashing unless it is rusted through, riddled with holes, or the obvious cause of leaks around the chimney. If it is, have a sheet metal shop fabricate new cap flashing and install it as in Figure 5.18. Cap flashing should seat at least 1 in. into mortar joints.

Top off the top course of brick with a cap of mortar, sloping it so that water runs down the outside of the chimney. The cap should be rich in portland cement, so that it will weather well. Regardless of the mortar mixture used elsewhere on the chimney, use type M mortar for the cap.

Adding an opening to a chimney. Before adding an outlet to an existing chimney, check the local fire code. In many large urban areas, only one heating appliance per flue is allowed; but codes in suburban and rural areas are considerably more lenient. If adding another opening to the flue does not violate local ordinances, ascertain whether the total area of the openings exceeds the area of the flue itself; it shouldn't. (For example, an 8×13 tile is 104 sq in. and can theoretically handle three 6-in. thimbles; each thimble opening has an area of about 28 sq in.) If the total area of the outlets exceeds that of the flue, poor draft can result.

Exactly where on the chimney you locate the new opening depends in part on the position of the heat source. Center the thimble on a chimney face so that you cut into as few courses of brick or block as possible.

Trace the circumference of the thimble with a piece of chalk, making the circle slightly larger than the thimble. It's easy to fill in a hole that's a bit too large, but tedious to drill or chisel small amounts off. Put on goggles before proceeding.

Drilling the opening is a two-step operation. Drill through the block or brick, then the flue tile. Using a carbide-tipped masonry bit in a heavy-duty drill, drill around the chalk circle; drill holes as close to each other as possible, to minimize the chiseling out to follow. As you drill, frequently back the bit out so that the ground masonry mate-

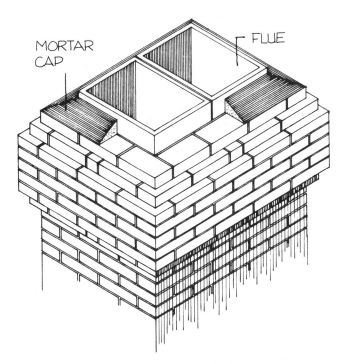

MORTAR CAP

FLUE

Figure 9.14 To hasten water runoff, pitch the mortar cap away from flue tiles.

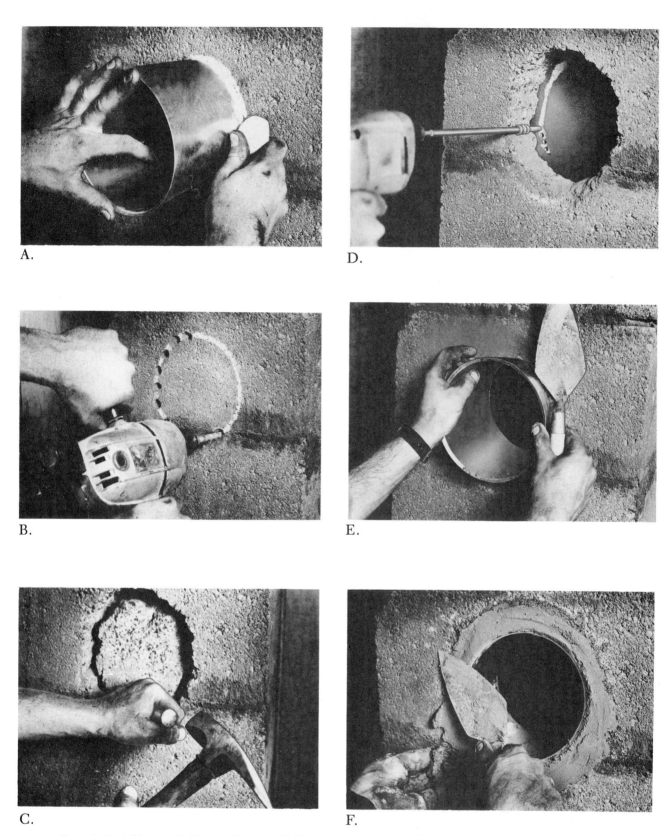

A.

D.

B.

E.

C.

F.

Figure 9.16 Adding a thimble to a chimney. (A) After positioning the thimble so that it crosses the fewest masonry joints, trace its shape with chalk. (B) Keeping the bit perpendicular to the face of the chimney, drill around the chalk circle. (C) When you've drilled completely around the circle—through the concrete block but not the tile liner—chisel out the ringed area with a cold chisel. (D) Next drill through the tile liner. Go slowly and avoid punching the tile with the drill bit, for tiles are easily cracked. (E) As you near the end of the drilling, test the fit of the thimble against the hole, cutting back no farther than you must. (F) Clean away debris and smooth the ragged opening with mortar. The thimble should fit very tightly; shave away excess mortar as you insert the thimble.

rial will fall out. When the bit clears the brick or block, it will encounter tile and go much more slowly, for the tile is harder. Finish the circle in the brick before drilling through the tile.

Once you've completed this stage of drilling, keep your goggles on and chisel out the area you circled, using a masonry chisel and a mason's hammer (or a hand sledge). Chipping out is slow, tedious work, so rest often. Once you have chiseled out a reasonably smooth circle in the block or brick, drill a ring of holes into the tile. Again, the work will be tedious, but you must take your time or you will crack the tile. Use a chisel with a small point for chiseling out flue tile.

After cutting through the tile, test the thimble for closeness of fit. You will need at least $\frac{1}{4}$ in. space for the mortar to come. Brush out the debris, dampen the brick slightly, and lay in a thick layer of refractory cement. Insert the thimble with the lip toward the living space, and trowel mortar up to the thimble's edge. Smooth the mortar and wait several days for it to cure. Although regular mortar mixes are serviceable, they are not as durable as refractory cement.

Fireplaces. If your fireplace is smoky, you can improve its draft by rebuilding the firebox according to principles laid down by Count Rumford, a contemporary of Ben Franklin (see the book by Vrest Orton cited in Appendix G).

Adding Openings in Brick Walls

Most residences with brick exteriors are either one wythe of brick tied to a stud wall behind or two wythes of brick interlocked, forming a cavity wall. (There are other variations, such as brick facing over concrete block, but we must limit our discussion here.) Cutting out a section of brick usually is not complicated, although it can be arduous. Sizing windows and doors, and casing them, is fairly standard, but it's important to consult a building-materials supplier during the layout stage. Describe the construction and thickness of your walls and ask for suggestions about

the best type of window or door unit, as well as how to size, fit, and trim it in a rough masonry opening.

An hour with an engineer is also a good idea, even if the brick's just a veneer wall. He or she may be able to see concentrated loads you aren't aware of, size the steel lintel across the top of the of the opening and, in general, put your mind at ease.

Safety. Rent a stage of scaffolding for any work that will be above your shoulders; you will do a better, faster job if you work at a comfortable height. Wear a hard hat at all times, and goggles and a respirator when cutting, grinding, or drilling. Because the openings we will be discussing are less than 4 ft wide, shoring can be simple. Those builders still earning their calluses should read the sections in Chapter 7 on flashing, as well as the sections in Chapter 8 on structure.

Laying out the opening. The most sensible way to lay out an opening is to minimize the number of bricks you have to cut. Whenever practicable, vary the size of the opening slightly so that your cuts will coincide with mortar joints; mortar is easier to dislodge and dress than brick. It's easy to build up and shim the extra space around the door or window frame. Thus, if the wall has common building brick laid up in a plain running-bond pattern, size the width of the opening in increments of 4 in., which is half the length of the masonry unit (a brick $7\frac{5}{8}$ in. long, plus a head joint $\frac{3}{8}$ in. wide).

In sizing the rough opening, first determine whether the window or door unit is preframed. If it is not encased in a frame, you must add the thickness of the frame to the width and length of the unit. Windows are nearly always preframed, and doors are usually so. To shim either framed unit in place, you will need a minimum of $\frac{1}{2}$ in. on each side. The extent to which you must build up or shim the unit is a function of the unit's width.

Sizing the width of the opening. Calculating width for preframed doors and windows is essentially the same, so we'll use doors as our example. Since door sizes vary in increments of 2 in., the Masonry Industrial Advancement Committee suggests dividing doors into two groups when sizing openings. Group 1 includes doors 2 ft 0 in., 2 ft 4 in., 2 ft 8 in., 3 ft 0 in., and 3 ft 4 in.; group 2 includes doors 2 ft 2 in., 2 ft 6 in., 2 ft 10 in., 3 ft 2 in., and 3 ft 6 in. Let's look at a door in each group, to see what differences there are in building it up and shimming it in a rough masonry opening.

Group 1. A door whose width is 28 in. (2 ft 4 in.) falls in the 4-in. interval suggested above. To accommodate the thickness of a $\frac{3}{4}$-in. frame, however, and still leave some room for shimming, jump up one increment to an opening 32 in. wide. Because that opening is a bit roomy, we must build it up with 1- or $1\frac{1}{4}$-in. stock (the *subjamb* in Figure 9.18A) on either jamb. Note that when you cut into masonry joints, you don't cut down the middle of the joint, but rather to the edge of the brick adjacent. Thus you remove four masonry units ($7\frac{5}{8}$-in. brick plus $\frac{3}{8}$ in. of mortar) *plus* an "extra" head joint $\frac{3}{8}$ in. wide—yielding a true rough opening of $32\frac{3}{8}$ in. All doors in group 1 can be built up in a similar manner.

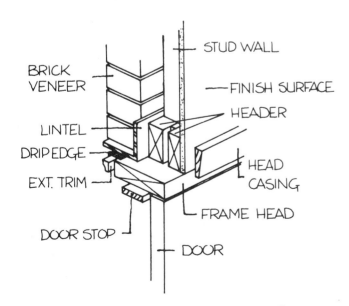

Figure 9.17 Head detail of a brick-veneer wall.

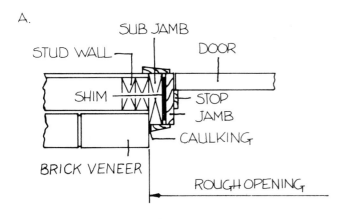

A.

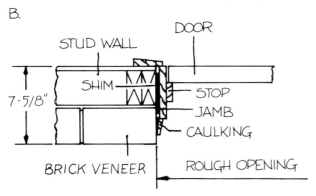

B.

Figure 9.18 Jamb details described in text. (A) Group 1; (B) group 2.

Group 2. A door whose width is 26 in. (2 ft 2 in.) misses the 4-in. interval by about 2 in. Because 2 in. to spare allows the builder enough room to frame and shim, there's no need to step up to the next 4-in. interval, as we did in the example above. (No subjamb is necessary, either.) In fact, if the door is precased with $\frac{3}{4}$-in. stock, we need only shim it to make it fit tightly in the opening. Here, the dimensions of door, frame, and shims add up to $28\frac{3}{8}$ in., roughly $3\frac{1}{2}$ masonry units plus the extra $\frac{3}{8}$-in. head joint. All doors in group 2 can be built up in a similar manner.

Sizing the height of the opening. In determining the height of the rough opening, several factors are involved; thus calculations for doors and windows vary slightly.

Note: Whatever the size of the window's opening, try to align its top to the tops of other windows or doors on the same wall.

Doors: To determine the height of a door opening, measure up from the subfloor: the height of the door and the thickness of the sill/threshold assembly, plus $\frac{1}{2}$ in. to shim beneath the sill if the subfloor isn't level, plus the thickness of the head frame above the door, plus $\frac{1}{2}$ in. for adjustments.

Less important is room to shim above the head casing: the real job of aligning and securing the frame to the opening takes place along the side jambs. Shimming the head merely tweaks it up or down so that there a uniform gap above the door.

Once you've tallied the height of the door and its frame, you must reconcile it to the height of the nearest

mortar joint. (The steel lintel above the opening rests in the joint between brick courses.) This reconciliation shouldn't be too hard. If you need to go up to the next mortar joint above, gain 1 to 2 in. of space between the head frame and the lintel, which you can later pack with insulation and cover with trim. To go down to the mortar joint below, trim a small amount off the door and its jambs.

Windows. Rough openings for windows are somewhat more complex, mainly because they occur in the middle of a wall. Establish the height of the lintel and measure (down) the height of the window unit. Then measure down an additional two courses, to accommodate the thickness and pitch of the window sill and that of the masonry sill underneath (Figure 9.19). Sills in masonry openings are commonly a rowlock course of brick or precast concrete.

The lintel. To place the lintel across the top of the opening, you will need to disturb at least two, and possibly three, courses of brick above. Thus, when you cut the sides of the opening, extend jamb cuts at least a course above the intended top of the opening. Theoretically, it's possible to place the lintel by disturbing only one course; but you can better integrate the steel—and the new bricks placed atop it—if you give yourself room to work. (You may also want to vary the thickness of the mortar over several courses, to accommodate the thickness of the lintel.)

For openings up to 4 ft wide, $3 \times 3\frac{1}{2} \times \frac{1}{4}$ steel angle iron is adequate—the $3\frac{1}{2}$-in. leg resting beneath the 4-in. width of brick. (Some sources specify $\frac{5}{16}$-in.-thick steel if the angle will be exposed to the weather.) Support the lintel at least 4 in. on each side of the opening, roughly the length of a half-brick. If the wall is two wythes thick, use two lintels in a T-configuration, putting the vertical legs of each back to back. Precast concrete lintels are also available for use in brick walls; they vary in width from one to three wythes. Don't use wood lintels; they rot out. If they burn through in a fire, a wall can collapse.

When you are certain of the dimensions of the cuts to be made, carefully mark the brick exterior. To make sure that the cuts will be level and plumb, use a level. Snap a chalk line through marks so that you can clearly see the cuts to be made.

Figure 9.19 A prehung window in a brick wall usually rests on a rowlock course. The downward tilt of the bricks is accomplished by building up their back corners with a slope of mortar.

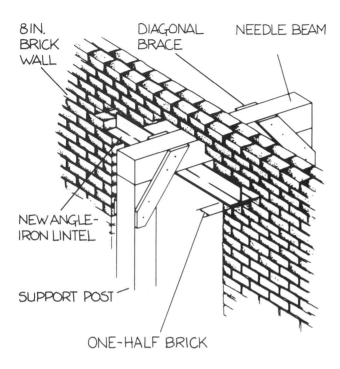

8 IN.
BRICK
WALL

DIAGONAL
BRACE

NEEDLE BEAM

NEW ANGLE-
IRON LINTEL

SUPPORT POST

ONE-HALF BRICK

Figure 9.20 A needle brace. Note that lintels must protrude at least one-half brick into the wall on each side.

Supports. At this point it's pertinent to discuss two types of shoring. The first, discussed at length in Chapter 8, is a temporary stud wall. In brief, this type of shoring runs parallel to the load-bearing wall and picks up the load so that you can cut into the original wall without ill effect.

The second type of shoring runs perpendicular to the masonry wall—through it, in fact—and supports the bricks or blocks over the new opening. This support is sometimes called *needle bracing*. Typically, the needle is $\frac{1}{4}$-in. steel angle iron, or a 4×8 on-edge, supported by 4×4 posts. The 4×8 wood beam is probably the better bet because you can nail into it and so add diagonal braces to the posts. In either case, be sure to plumb the posts and foot them securely atop concrete pads or piers. The needle slides into place once you've punched a starter hole above the rough opening in the brick. For more about footings, see Chapter 10.

For openings less than 4 ft wide, braces will be somewhat superfluous in nonbearing walls. Even if the mortar is weak and some bricks fall, the remaining bricks will likely corbel along mortar joints—thus forming a stepped triangle no more than 2 ft high above the opening—and there stabilize.

Cutting and finishing the opening. Use goggles, masks, and a hard hat, of course. Start by cutting a hole about three bricks high, above the rough opening to follow. The hole needn't be much wider than the needle brace you'll slide into it. Use a 4-lb hand sledge and a cold chisel to cut this hole, and take care not to damage any more bricks than necessary; replacing them later is time-consuming.

Once the needle brace is in place, cut around the perimeter of the rough opening with an abrasive wheel in a power grinder. A carborundum blade in a power saw will do in a pinch, but a grinder is stronger and better suited to the task. In either case you'll go through several wheels or blades. Because common brick is nearly 4 in. across, make several passes to cut through, lowering the blade $\frac{1}{2}$ in. for each pass.

The shortcoming of either tool is that its blade (or wheel) will not cut through an entire wythe of brick, which forces you to finish the cut in another, separate operation. In addition, after scoring the opening around its perimeter, you must still punch through the opening. Start in the middle of the proposed opening and work out. If the mortar is weak, you can dislodge bricks by hammering in a flat bar and prying them out; otherwise, start the operation with an impact hammer and finish it with a chisel. Do not use an impact hammer along the perimeter, however; it obliterates brick.

As you approach the sides of the opening, your job becomes easier, for the brick is scored almost all the way through (the cuts will be $2\frac{1}{2}$ to 3 in. deep). With some careful chisel work, you should be able to remove brick halves protruding into the opening without having to tooth out. Clean any ragged cuts with a joint chisel or the grinder wheel, and/or cover them with the jamb trim. If the cuts are extremely ragged, chisel out remnants and mortar in half-bricks.

Setting the lintel. Paint the lintel with at least two coats of rust-preventive paint before installing it. In the course above the final height of the opening, cut back a half-brick deep on either side, into which space you'll set the lintel. There is some disagreement about setting a lintel. Some experts maintain that the lintel should be mortared above and below—above so that the first course of brick over the opening will have a bed of mortar to lie on, and below, where the lintel rests on supporting bricks. This technique yields a joint almost $\frac{3}{4}$ in. thick: $\frac{3}{8}$-in. of mortar above the lintel, $\frac{1}{4}$ in. for the thickness of the lintel, and at least $\frac{1}{4}$ in. for the mortar under the ends of the lintel. So thick a joint demands that three or four courses of brick above the opening must be removed, so that this first, especially fat joint can be accommodated. Because mortar does not stick to steel, moreover, putting mortar below a lintel seems superfluous to us.

Instead, set the lintel in the following manner. Again, remove a half-brick's length from the course above the opening. Smooth the pockets, removing any old mortar and making a flat shelf for the lintel. Set the lintel directly on the brick below, with the inside of the lintel's vertical leg flush with the back of the courses above. Dampen the surrounding bricks. Without putting any mortar on top of the lintel, butter the ends of the bricks with mortar and place them on the lintel. Fit bricks together end to end, trim the head joints between these bricks, apply a full bed of mortar over them, and lay up successive courses until you reach the needle brace. Slide it out and fill in the hole, finishing with a closure brick. In this method, the course of brick resting on the lintel is held in place by head joints and by the mortar bond to the course above. That's sufficient. In neither application is the lintel connected mechanically to the brick beneath; it just sits there.

Flash the lintel before placing the first course of brick over it, however. Bend a 2-in.-wide piece of 26-gauge metal lengthwise so that $\frac{1}{2}$ in. of the metal projects beyond the

A.

B.

C.

D.

Figure 9.21 Replacing a wooden lintel with a steel one. (A) Where wood meets masonry, rot is common. Cut out deteriorated wood with a chisel. (B) After removing the old lintel, replace it with a steel one. (C) If the section is to be stuccoed and blended into the adjoining surfaces, it must be flush. (D) As subsequent courses go up, check them against a straightedge. (The mason's hat, incidentally, is a paper bag: light, inexpensive, and disposable.)

edge of the lintel along its length. Hold the piece to the lintel with a thin bead of silicone. The brick will firmly anchor the flashing afterward.

Finishing. Hanging doors and windows, discussed in detail in Chapter 6, is trickier in masonry walls because you can't easily drive nails to adjust shims. Many units precased for masonry walls come with integral shimming mechanisms that press against the opening. More commonly, carpenters first build up the rough opening with 2×4 or 2×6 *sleepers* nailed with case-hardened nails into the masonry joints. They then shim between sleepers and the frame. This creates a rather wide joint to be cased, but oversized molding will cover it.

In brick-over-frame or cavity-wall brick construction, where there is actually a wall within a wall, set the edges of window and door frames flush to the finish surfaces of the innermost wall, as shown in Figure 9.18. Gaps or cavities between wall layers are straddled by the unit's frame; cavities around the frames can be covered with casing trim. Trim details will vary due to differences in manufacturing and quirks in the house's construction, but these rules are constant:

1. All frames must be shimmed and attached securely to the masonry opening. For a choice of masonry fasteners, see the end of this chapter.

2. Prime and seal all frames and casings, whether wood or metal.

3. There should be a water-resistant layer between wood and masonry, whether this layer is construction adhesive, silicone caulking, sheet plastic, and so on. Otherwise, moisture will wick from the masonry to the wood.

4. Pack any gaps around the frame with insulation (small cans of spray-foam insulation are good), and caulk behind each piece of casing before attaching it.

Replacing wood lintels. Wood is poorly suited as a material for exterior lintels, since most varieties will rot. When replacing a wood lintel, you'll probably have to disturb a course or two of brick above, to get at the old wood. Use shoring or braces, as the situation requires. After chopping free the old wood and removing any fragments, dress the shelves on which the lintel rests. If necessary, level the shelves with mortar.

As you lay courses of brick above the lintel, use a

straightedge to align each course flush to the face of the building. Although the first course often sits right on the lintel (for reasons cited above), spread full mortar beds for all subsequent courses. Remember to dampen surroundings courses so they don't draw moisture from new ones.

Closing up an opening. Close off an opening by removing window sashes or doors, pulling off the trim, then prying out and removing the frame. Cut it out with a reciprocating saw if you must. Prepare the opening by toothing it out, that is, removing any half-bricks along the sides so that you can disguise the seams where new bricks join old. Lay up brick as described in the beginning of this section, setting two 6-in. corrugated ties in the mortar every fourth or fifth course, to tie to the wood-frame wall behind. Set in ties 1 in. from the face of the brick; nail their other ends to sheathing.

CONCRETE BLOCK

Because block work is rare in renovation, this section will be brief. Read the preceding sections if you need to bone up on masonry basics.

Materials

The dimensions of a standard stretcher block are nominally 16 in. (L) by 8 in. (W) by 8 in. (H); but each dimension actually is $\frac{3}{8}$ in. less, to allow for mortar joints. Shapes vary according to use, as shown in Figure 9.22. A number of special precast concrete units, such as lintels, are also available, designed to bear the weight of blocks over openings.

The mortar mixture is the same as for brick, except that block mortar is slightly stiffer, drier. The mixture, however, should be sticky enough to cling to the edge of the block. Type N mix (see Table 9.1) is suitable for most uses; use

type M where high winds or heavy soil loads are anticipated. Don't dampen block before using it; cover it during inclement weather.

Working with Concrete Block

Your materials should be close at hand so that you don't waste energy lugging them around. Put your mortar pan within 2 ft of the section you're working on. Level the footing on which you'll lay block, and sweep it free of debris. Remember, this is hard hat and goggles work.

Closing an opening. To close an opening in a block wall, begin by removing the old casings, cutting them free with a reciprocating saw if they don't pry out easily. At this point you've got two choices: (1) tooth out half-blocks around the opening, the better to disguise the new blocks you are filling in with; or (2) leave the existing blocks as they are and cut new blocks as necessary to fill the opening.

The second choice makes the most sense, because concrete block is pretty unsightly to begin with. It's work to cut away block, and removing a cast concrete lintel is a real chore. It's far easier just to block up the opening, and if appearances are important, plaster or panel over it.

To remove sections of block, first score them with a brick set or the sharp end of a mason's hammer; then rap along the scored line until the block cracks. You can also cut the block, using a carborundum blade in a power saw. Chip out all the old mortar with a chisel, being careful not to damage the edges of adjacent blocks.

Lay up the block dry within the opening first, to determine whether you can move blocks and thus vary the thickness of the head joints slightly, or whether you must cut blocks to fit in the opening.

Beneath the first course, spread and furrow a full bed of mortar. Carefully bed each block, trimming off the excess mortar squeezed out as the blocks are positioned. As you

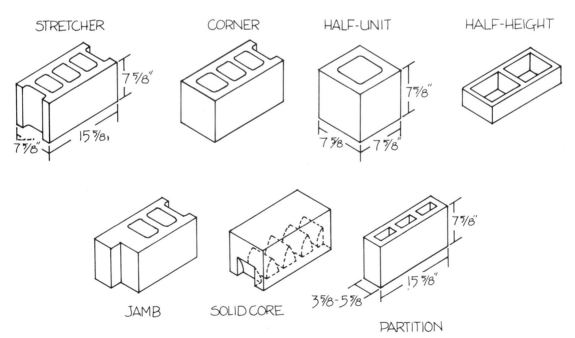

Figure 9.22 Types of concrete block.

A.

B.

C.

D.

E.

F.

Figure 9.23 Laying concrete blocks. (A) Temporarily set the first course of block dry, without mortar, to forsee any problems. (B) Spread and furrow a full bed of mortar for the first course, to securely bond it to the footing. (C) Set corner blocks first and work back toward the center of the wall or walls. Set blocks with their thicker faces up, thus providing a broad area for bed joints. When setting individual blocks, butter the ends of several blocks at a time. (D) Set each block into its mortar bed, and abut the buttered ends to preceding blocks, thus compressing head joints. (E) After setting every three or four blocks, check their alignment against the straight edge of the level as shown; see that they are level across their top faces; and plumb the outside faces with the level held vertically. To make small adjustments in the blocks' alignment, tap them with the handle of a trowel. (F) To ensure the wall's stability as it is going up, build from the corners in. As you fill in each new course, set a string level to align the next course.

G.

H.

I.

J.

K.

(G) Closure blocks, the last in a course, require buttering on both ends. (H) When mortar has set enough to retain a thumbprint, point joints—head joints first, and then bed joints. The vertical joint being pointed here is a control joint. (I) Intersecting block walls do not tie together with overlapping blocks as brick walls do. Instead, tie-bars are placed every 4 ft, vertically. (J) Concrete lintels are precast in a single piece, with offsets that the builder specifies for window or door units. (K) Capping the top course of blocks by filling them with mortar helps them bear loads more uniformly. To keep the mortar from settling into the hollow cells of courses below, place a strip of screen or metal lath in the top bed joint. (Photo series from "Recommended Practices for Laying Concrete Blocks," published by the Portland Cement Association.)

progress, check each group of three blocks to be sure the tops are level and the faces plumb. Use a straightedge to align new courses with the surrounding walls.

In the second course, and all successive courses, you don't need a full bed of mortar. Butter the mortar to the edges and to the ends of the blocks. Actually, you need mortar only on one end of most blocks; butter both ends only on the closure block (the last one in a course). When

a thumbprint will remain in the mortar, that mortar is dry enough to point; in most cases, a concave pointing is suitable.

Finish the top of the last course so that it matches the other sections of the wall. If a lintel is in place over an old opening that you are blocking up, leave the lintel there and cut the top course as necessary, so the course will fit beneath the lintel, allowing $\frac{3}{8}$ in. for mortar joints.

If the top of the wall is exposed, cap it with solid-core blocks. Or you can fill the top course after bedding a piece of screen or wire mesh in the last bed joint; fill the cells of the top course with mortar.

Creating an Opening

Review ''Sizing the Opening'' in the preceding section on brick; the process is similar. First determine how big the opening in the block wall should be. To the dimensions of the door or window, add the thickness of the casings on each side, the thickness of the cast-concrete lintel above (usually 8 in.), the precast sill below, and about $\frac{1}{2}$ in. for shimming on each side.

Don't try to cut openings wider than 4 ft in block. Not bonded by full beds of mortar like bricks, blocks are more likely to cave in. To support the blocks above an opening temporarily, insert a needle brace (Figure 9.20) centered above it; use a mason's hammer to chop the hole. Disturb as few blocks as possible with this hole, but do give yourself room to maneuver the lintel into place.

Chalk-line the dimensions of the opening on the face of the wall and cut along the lines with a carborundum blade in a power saw. Wear goggles, of course. The face of the block is less than 1 in. thick, so the blade should cut all the way through in one pass. With an impact hammer, knock out the center of the opening. When you get close to the scored line, work slowly with a mason's hammer and a chisel. If you can get at the back side of the wall, also cut through the backs of blocks with a carborundum blade.

The edges of blocks around the opening should be smooth. If any blocks have cracked or crumbled, cut them (and the surrounding mortar) free with a chisel; set in half-blocks. For greater load-bearing, fill with mortar the blocks on which the lintel ends will rest. To keep the mortar from running down into the cells of blocks below, fit a piece of screen in the bed joint below the supporting blocks. The lintel should be supported at least 8 in. on each end.

Spread mortar on the faces of the receiving blocks around the opening, as well as on the top and the ends of the lintel, for a $\frac{3}{8}$-in. mortar joint all around. Be generous

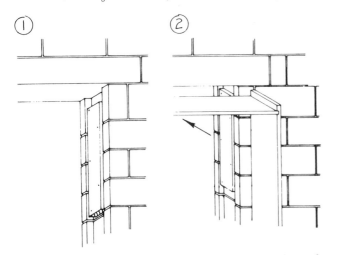

Figure 9.24 To build up low spots in a block opening and provide a nailing surface for wooden frames to come, epoxy nailing–blocks to the exposed block cells.

with the mortar; you can easily trim off the excess. When the lintel is in place, remove the needle brace; replace the blocks you cut out above.

Where cuts in the side of the opening expose block cells, build them up with nailing blocks to which you can nail subjambs and/or frames. These blocks should be sealed to prevent rot; paint them with creosote, primer-sealer, or something similar. Attach the nailing blocks with one of the masonry fasteners shown at the end of this chapter.

Seal all wood against moisture, which can migrate through masonry. In fitting a window or door into an opening, finish details will vary, but keep in mind that building suppliers have precast units or trim kits to aid you.

CONCRETE

Concrete, a mixture of portland cement, sand, and gravel, hardens and assumes the shape of the form into which it is poured. Its strength and resistance to abrasion depend on the proportions of the mixture and the care taken in mixing, finishing, and curing it.

The Mixture

Generally, the greater the proportion of cement, the greater the mixture's bearing capacity and the greater its resistance to abrasion. Conversely, too little cement and/or too much water will produce a weaker concrete, more likely to spall or crack.

A good all-purpose mix is 1:2:4, the first number denoting the amount of cement; the second, sand, also called small aggregate; the third, gravel, or large aggregate. The 1:2:4 mix, rated at 2000 psi, is fine for floors, load-bearing pads, and most other uses. However, if you need much more than 1 cu yd of concrete—about six wheel-barrows full—have it delivered ready-mixed. That's also about the smallest amount a truck will deliver. If your pour is far from the road or in a basement, you'll also need a pumper truck.

Concrete suppliers describe strength by the number of sacks of cement per cubic yard of concrete. For foundations and walls a five-sack mix is standard—a six-sack mix if you're pumping the concrete, which requires smaller aggregate.

If, however, you elect to mix it yourself, keep in mind that the final amount of concrete you mix will be somewhat less than the volume of the components unmixed. This is so because the smaller particles fill in the spaces between larger ones. Using the 1:2:4 mix above, 1 cu yd (27 cu ft) of concrete would require 6 sacks of cement, 12 cu ft of sand, and 24 cu ft of gravel. A 94 lb sack of cement is about 1 cu ft.

Have your materials delivered to save time. As noted at the beginning of the chapter, dump sand and gravel on plastic so that they don't get fouled with dirt, and swaddle sacks of cement in plastic so that they don't pick up moisture. It doesn't matter if the aggregate gets wet—but the wetter the sand, the less water you have to add to the mix. (One cubic foot of damp sand contains about 1 qt of water.) Finally, when you mix, use only clean water.

Mixing. Whatever your means of mixing, mix close to your materials. Because this is hot, heavy work, pick a shady area; there, your concrete will set up less quickly. If you are mixing the batch by hand, first combine dry components: mix sand and cement well, then work in the gravel with a mixing hoe or a square-nosed shovel. When the dry ingredients are uniformly mixed, scoop out a pocket (as you would in a dollop of mashed potatoes) and add water sparingly.

To test the mixture's consistency, tamp down the fresh concrete with a shovel, then cut grooves in the smooth surface, as in Figure 9.25B. If the surface is slick and the grooves stay sharply defined, the mix is correct. If there isn't enough water, the surface will look rough and lumpy; if there is too much water, the grooves will last only a moment. To stiffen a batch, add dry elements in the same proportions as before.

Rent an electric mixer if you have a lot to mix; consider buying one if you'll be at it more than 2 or 3 weeks. If

A.

B.

Figure 9.25 Mixing concrete. To mix concrete without a mixer, you need a clean, flat, dry surface; for smaller amounts, use a mixing pan or a wheelbarrow. Mix the dry ingredients first: sand and cement, then gravel. (A) After materials are well mixed, scoop a pocket in the middle and add water gradually. As you mix, pull the dry ingredients into the pocket. (B) To test the concrete, tamp it flat with the back of a shovel and then jab grooves into the smooth surface. If the grooves stay crisp, the mix is right.

you've got power at the job site, electric mixers are less trouble than gas-powered ones.

Shovel gravel into the turning mixer first, keeping in mind the proportions of the other materials to come. Then add a couple of gallons of water initially—you'll learn the right amount after a few batches. Then shovel in the sand and cement and add water slowly, watching the consistency of the mixture closely. Stop adding water as soon as the mix first *slides* off the blades of the mixer. After 2 or 3 minutes, the concrete will be uniformly mixed.

Whenever you quit for lunch or at the end of the day, scour the inside of the mixer drum with several shovelfuls of gravel and a lot of water. Then empty the drum and rinse it with water.

Finishing. Because concrete is composed of such disparate materials, once it is mixed it should be placed and not moved any more than is necessary. For this reason, the long hose of a pumper truck saves you work and yields a superior final product. When moving the concrete, use a square-nosed shovel, not a rake (which separates the gravel).

"Striking off" the surface makes it roughly level. This is usually done by drawing a straight *screed board* across the top of the form—in a sawing motion, back and forth. Once you've screeded, *float* the surface. Floating brings the cream (heavy cement and sand) up to the surface and presses aggregate down.

Let the concrete sit until the surface water is reabsorbed or evaporated (usually in an hour or two), then work the surface with a steel trowel. Even if the surface will eventually be rough, you must first steel-trowel it to make it uniform. Add texture later with a stiff push broom. To do steel troweling, many masons kneel on plywood blocks, which they move as they work across the concrete. At this point, edge driveways and sidewalks. Or if you've poured a footing, now's the time to insert anchor bolts.

Allow the concrete to cure for a week. Keep moisture from evaporating too fast by covering the concrete with plastic or with old sacks dampened once a day.

Two final thoughts: (1) If you have concrete delivered, tell the driver where the septic system is, so that he won't drive over the tank and crush it. (2) Have the delivery driver rinse and empty the remainder of the load somewhere other than on your site, even if it's torn up and unsightly; you may want to plant a lawn there some day.

Forms for pads. A form must be strong enough to contain the concrete until it hardens. The easiest way to make sure that footings are level is to level the tops of forms and fill them flush with concrete.

Forms for footings are merely boxes with no tops or bottoms, whose sides are usually staked into place. Scrap boards 1 in. thick are commonly used for forms, although scrap plywood is adequate if it is thicker than $\frac{3}{8}$ in. To keep the sides of a form from bulging, nail spreaders across the tops of the forms, as shown in Figure 9.27B. Further, dirt banked against the outside of the forms will strengthen them and prevent loss of mortar.

The size of footings will vary, but they should be at least 1 ft below the frost line in your area. Exterior footings for deck posts and the like should be at least 12 in. on a

Figure 9.26 A small concrete grade slab. (A) A rebar bender. (B) A pumper truck saves a lot of shoveling. (C) Screed the surface flat, pulling the screed back and forth in a sawing motion. (D) Bull floating. (E) Edging. (F) Setting anchor bolts. (Thanks to Bolton Construction.)

A.

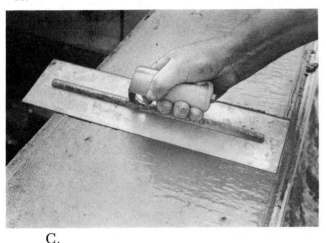

C.

B.

Figure 9.27 Two details seen on-site. (A) This 4×4 hoisting rig brought concrete up four stories. Because the house was gutted, workers chopped through the old roofing so that they could bolt the two back legs of the rig directly to rafters. (B) Capping a parapet wall with concrete. The sides of the forms were scrap $\frac{1}{2}$ in. plywood, the spreaders 1×2s. (C) After the concrete was screeded, it was steel-troweled to bring up the cement "cream," which becomes hard and smooth when dry.

side. Concrete poured directly into a fence posthole, at least $2\frac{1}{2}$ ft deep. Footings for exterior walls should be engineered as necessary, depending on the load they bear and the soil they sit on.

Inside the house, footings for bearing posts are optimally 24 in. square and 1 ft deep, reinforced at least with WWS mesh 6 × 6 in. 10/10. That mesh, as with all reinforcement, should be held up off the bottom of the pad with *dobie blocks.* Such post supports should rest directly on the earth, not on an existing basement floor. If the existing floor is not reinforced with steel, the new pad may punch right through when loaded. To be safe, jackhammer a hole in the floor and pour a pad that sits on the ground. Chimney pads should be specified by an engineer, but as a rule of thumb they should be at least 18 in. deep, extend 18 in. beyond each side of the chimney mass, and be bolstered by rebar spaced every 6 in.

Waterproofing Basements

The remedies offered in this section presuppose a stable foundation, one not presently shifting. If that is not the case—as described in Chapter 1—you'll have to stabilize your foundation before any waterproofing method can be effective.

The primary cause of a wet basement is excess surface water around the house. Start by checking the downspouts: Do they direct water away from the house, or do they concentrate water around the foundation?

The least expensive remedy is a splash block beneath the downspout, or a perforated plastic hose attached to the end of the downspout. In the latter device, as water pressure builds, the hose uncoils and distributes water away from the house. If it's moist around basement windows, it could be that water is draining down around the window well. Fix this flaw by excavating around the window well, filling a trough with crushed gravel, and laying perforated plastic pipe leading away from the house. Grading the ground to slope away from the building will also help runoff.

If you don't mind water in your basement, a sump pump at a low point is a reasonable solution. Where a high water table is the cause, a sump pump is about all you can do.

If these modest remedies don't work, you're in for a bit of work: waterproofing the basement walls from within, or exposing the foundation and coating the foundation on the outside.

Because exterior waterproofing is far more complicated and expensive than interior methods, choose it only if you have running or standing water (i.e., a flooding condition); or if spalling is widespread throughout the foundation, which indicates low-quality concrete. If your basement is merely damp or musty, try sealing the inside of the walls first.

Waterproofing from the outside. The standard method of waterproofing a building from the outside is to excavate to the base of the foundation and install, in a trench a foot wide and a foot deep, a 4-in. perforated plastic drainage pipe with 4 in. of rock on all sides. Next, wash down the foundation so that it is free of soil or loose debris that might interfere with the adhesion of the waterproofing. If your foundation is fairly smooth, you can apply the waterproofing agent directly to it.

Otherwise, you should *parge* the foundation walls to even out the surface for the waterproofing membrane. Parging is usually a $\frac{1}{2}$-in.-thick cement plaster trowelled on in two layers. For best adhesion, wet the walls with a masonry binder before applying the plaster; otherwise, use the binder as an admixture. Mix the cement plaster in a ratio of $1:2\frac{1}{2}$ (cement to sand) and apply the mix in two coats, allowing the first to set 24 hours before applying the second. When the first coat has set for an hour or two, scratch it horizontally as you would a rough coat of plaster; the second coat will adhere better. Keep both coats moist as they set.

Parging is not, however, a waterproofing in itself—it is too permeable to withstand hydrostatic pressure. Therefore, consider one of the materials below, to be applied over a clean, dry surface. Each material, being relatively thin, must be protected—say, with sheets of Styrofoam insulation—during backfill.

Figure 9.28 Parging the outside of a foundation with two coats of cement plaster makes the surface more water–resistant. Roughen the first coat so that the second will adhere better.

Asphalt emulsion is rolled or brushed on. Very cost-effective and perhaps the least expensive exterior option, probably the thinnest as well.

Hot-mop, hot tar and overlapped felt paper, should be handled by a subcontractor because it must be applied at 400 to 425°F. A somewhat thicker membrane than asphalt.

Bituthene is a self-sealing sheet material whose sticky adhesive seals firmly when pressed by hand. For two people, an easy application.

EPDM rubber is essentially the same material as that used for flat roofs, although its adhesive is slightly different for below-grade installation. This is the thickest, most durable, and most expensive of the methods discussed here. Corners are reinforced with special boots.

Epoxy paints and gel coats are excellent, easy to roll or brush on (wear a respirator mask), and very hard. But being so hard, they are susceptible to breaks in their membrane if point-loaded.

Bentonite, a volcanic clay sheathed in cardboard panels, was developed initially for underground housing. When wet, the clay swells to 10 times its original volume. Vol-Clay is one manufacturer. Because this is a relatively specialized material, distribution may be a problem.

Watersealing admixtures to concrete have the same failing as parging: by themselves, they just are not impervious to water. Don't rely on them alone.

Waterproofing from the inside: A damp basement may be caused by inadequate ventilation, by leaking pipes, or by condensation on cold-water pipes. Try to solve this problem by adding basement windows or installing a dehumidifier before considering the methods described below.

If you have widespread efflorescence or spalling, your first task is brushing down the walls—and the floor, if it's also concrete—with a stiff brush and a weak solution of muriatic acid (1 part acid to 20 parts water). Wear goggles, protective clothing, and rubber gloves. Ventilation is important, as is rinsing the walls well afterward.

As was the case with exterior waterproofing, you should correct interior holes and spalling before sealing walls. Similarly, surface remedies will not be effective if the foundation is unstable.

Hydraulic cement can fill cracks and holes, even when water is trickling through. One such product is Waterplug from Thorosystems. For best adhesion, undercut the hole with a masonry chisel, clean it well, and jam in a wad of the material; within seconds it'll start setting.

Bulk-loading caulk can be used if the crack is long and narrow. A flexible sealant such as silicone is fine, but check its compatibility with the paint you'll be using on the walls.

Gel coats, such as those made by SIKA, do an excellent job over the pitted areas caused by spalling, and are compatible with epoxy paints from the same maker.

Whole-wall treatments. If the water is entering the basement by permeating walls or floors, there are a number of treatments that you can use to waterproof masonry surfaces. With all of these products, however, it is assumed that the foundation is stable and that the products are applied carefully over the entire surface.

Important: Once you've treated holes and rough areas,

waterproof the entire wall surface above grade, *and* waterproof cement floors 6 to 12 in. from the base of the walls so that water can't seep in along the base of the foundation. If water still percolates up through the floor, get a sump pump.

Cement-based waterproofing texture coatings such as Thoroseal adhere well to masonry surfaces and are often used in swimming pools and other areas that are wet continually. The surface should be moist when you apply cement-based paint. Keep it damp for 2 to 3 days to allow thorough curing. Cement-waterproofing paints resist alkali and thus are not affected by it when it is present in fresh masonry.

Epoxy-based coatings are usually two-part compounds that are mixed just before application. They are strong and versatile. Because they are expensive, however, they are often reserved for wall-floor joints and other areas where maximal adhesion is needed. Roll or brush on these solid-filled paints; they'll even bond to damp concrete. But do follow directions closely: if they say they'll set in 30 minutes, they will do so precisely. These paints will bond well to the substrate and form a good membrane.

Rubber-based paints are thick, covering irregularities in the masonry. They are applied with a roller or a brush. The surface may be dry or moist. Rubber-based paints are not suitable where active cracks appear in foundation walls, for the paint's membrane will start to lift along the line of the crack. These paints offer good resistance to alkali but are far less durable than epoxy-based paints.

Latex paints adhere well to masonry, resist alkali, and can be applied to damp or dry surfaces. They cost somewhat more than average masonry paints, but this group is durable and, in most cases, is the most versatile paint for use in basements. You can also obtain clear latex coatings. They are not, however, true membranes.

Oil-based paints can be applied safely only to dry surfaces whose alkalinity has already been treated. Limited use.

Surface-bonding compounds such as Surewall contain fibers that impart great lateral strength. A $\frac{1}{8}$-in. layer of this compound, when spread over the face of a dry-stacked block wall (a wall with no mortar) will hold the blocks in place. Surewall also claims to be waterproof. It is, however, trowelled on, and is more a parge than a paint.

Resurfacing Concrete Floors

Assess the current problem and try to determine what caused it. If the floor is merely flaked or spalled, it was probably troweled improperly (a minor problem). A surface that is also cracked is usually the result of an improper mix (too much sand, too little cement, etc.) or of pouring the concrete when the temperature was too low. Where the floor or concrete driveway is sound but weathered, resurface it with new concrete after preparing the original surface properly. If the floor is badly cracked, however, with buckling and heaving, do not resurface; instead, rip it out, as described later.

Resurfacing. It's possible to resurface concrete driveways and floors by troweling on a thin 1:1:3 mixture of portland cement, lime, and fine sand, but this won't last very long.

It makes more sense to roughen and resurface with a concrete overlay at least $\frac{3}{4}$ in. thick.

To get a good bond, first roughen the old concrete and remove all loose materials. Where the surface is large, you can rent a scarifying machine to roughen; otherwise, use a jack hammer or an impact drill. Wear goggles, of course. It isn't necessary to go deep when scarifying—just deep enough to roughen the surface and expose the coarse aggregate underneath. If the concrete has become stained with oil, scrub spots well with a commercial detergent such as sodium metasilicate (which contains rosin soap). Rinse the surface well with water. Stiff push brooms are suitable for the scrubbing.

Ideally, while the concrete is still damp from washing, you should now etch the surface with acid to aid bonding. *Note:* This operation is dangerous and *safety is imperative:* open all basement windows (for ventilation), and wear a respirator, rubber boots and gloves, and goggles. Cover any exposed skin with petroleum jelly. Use a stiff push broom to spread the acid solution, brushing only away from yourself. The solution, to quote a Portland Cement Association publication, should be ''commercial hydrochloric acid (20 deg. baumé scale) . . . applied at a rate of 1 gal per 100 sq ft.'' After the acid has stopped foaming, hose down the entire surface with water and scrub it well. Keep rinsing until all acid residue and loose sand have been removed.

Forms. Forms aren't usually necessary for resurfacing work. Where the reworked surface is not the entire floor, scarify it up to the nearest expansion joint. You can also attach 1×2 screed strips to the floor with spots of mastic paste. Level the new surface to the top of the strips. Where the new floor surface abuts a basement wall, place isolation cushions along the base of the wall, to allow expansion of the floor slab. Use redwood expansion strips and you can leave them in place.

Bonding and placing the new concrete. Immediately before placing the new concrete, brush on a thin layer of bonding grout mixed 1 part cement to 1 part sand, with enough water to make it creamy. Spread the grout to a

Figure 9.29 After scarifying and etching an old concrete floor, spread a thin layer of bonding grout with a stiff broom so that the new concrete will bond well.

thickness of $\frac{1}{16}$ to $\frac{1}{8}$ in. and pour the new concrete at once, before the grout sets and turns white.

The new concrete should be 1:2:2 (cement:sand:gravel) and about $\frac{2}{3}$ part water by volume. This is a fairly stiff (dry) mixture, but it must be so for strength and resistance to cracking. There are also plasticizing admixtures to make working easier; your supplier can advise you. The size of the gravel is also important: $\frac{3}{8}$ in. diameter per piece is the maximum size; or, in resurfacing, you may want to forgo gravel altogether. Because the new concrete is thin, you can easily mix a section 5 × 10 ft by hand. If the area is much larger than that, rent a portable mixer. And if you're thinking of having a truck deliver it premixed, 1 cu yd is equivalent to a slab 15 ft by 10 ft by 2 in.

If your new slab is 2 in. or thicker, lay the concrete to a depth of 1 in. before placing the wire-mesh reinforcement (6 × 6 in. 10/10). Precut the wire mesh so that it can be placed quickly.

In either case, once you've finished laying the concrete, screed it so that the top is level (or pitched toward a drain). Power-float and trowel it once the surface water, if any, has evaporated. As is mentioned above, don't overtrowel the concrete, or you'll bring the lighter cement solution to the surface, which eventually will flake.

Allow the new concrete to cure for at least 3 days, keeping it moist by covering it with damp sacks or plastic.

You can also rehabilitate concrete with epoxy adhesives such as the Sikadur line. Developed for heavy industrial uses, these 100 percent-solid coatings are remarkably durable, water resistant, nonshrinking, and so on. But they must be prepared and applied *exactly* as specified by the manufacturer, with the safety precautions noted.

Replacing an Existing Floor

Floors that buckle or heave exhibit one or more of several problems, including tree roots, hydrostatic pressure, faulty or absent reinforcement in the slab, and improper compaction of the soil underneath. The only sensible thing to do is rip out the old concrete with a jackhammer and re-do the job right. If part of the problem is tree roots beneath the

Figure 9.30 A basement floor ready for concrete. The dirt floor is covered with plastic to prevent moisture's seeping through later. Elevate the wire mesh slightly so that it will reinforce the middle of the slab.

slab, chop them out and discourage their return by sprinkling copper sulfate on the soil inside the foundation.

The ground should be graded and compacted and then covered with 1 in. of gravel, also compacted. If your site has shown itself to be damp, set perforated ABS drain pipe in troughs in the gravel, sloping it down to a low point where a drain to the outside is located. (A sump pump may also be placed at a low spot in lieu of a drain emptying outside the building.) After covering the drain with gravel, spread a layer of sheet plastic, being careful to overlap the pieces by at least 6 in., to prevent moisture from wicking up through the concrete from the soil. For a standard 4-in.-thick floor, use mesh 6 in. by 6 in. 10/10 WWS for reinforcement.

ATTACHMENTS TO CONCRETE AND MASONRY

There is an enormous range of fasteners for concrete and masonry. Some will support a painting, others will hold down a house during an earthquake. Don't buy larger fasteners than you need, however: they are more work to install, and the final result is only as good as the material you're attaching to. Brick, for example, can be soft and crumbly. And as has been stated many times in this chapter, if the masonry is unstable and wetness is present, remedy those problems before attaching anything.

Choosing a Fastener

Whenever a fastener requires a predrilled hole, that means using an impact drill (Figure 3.14) or a heavy drill with a carbide-tipped bit. Buy commercial-quality bits, which are usually black; cheap, shiny fast-spiral bits will get you nowhere. Fast-spirals are particularly useless on wood, as when you're drilling through a 2 × 4 plate to position holes on a slab. Note, too, that bits are specialized. Standard rotary drill bits will break down if used in an impact drill; use percussion bits instead.

Speaking of impact drills, they're worth buying if you've a lot of holes to drill; they are the *only* drill to use in concrete. Impact drills can punch through aggregate that leaves rotary drills spinning in place. A $\frac{3}{8}$-in. impact drill with a side handle will suffice for most nonprofessionals. *Wear goggles.*

Hammered fasteners. Masonry nails are still around because they're cheap and relatively simple to install. Spiral masonry and cut nails require no predrilling, just a heavy (28 oz at least) hammer and strong wrists. For best results, drive them into the mortar joints of brick or block, and any way you can into concrete.

The problem with nails is that they don't forgive a glancing blow or one that's too deep. In the former case they bend or go shooting off; too deep and they shatter concrete, which means that you've got to start all over.

An improvement over plain nails are *pins* or *threaded studs* inserted into an installation tool, which is then struck with a hammer. The rubber grip of this tool protects your fingers and keeps the fasteners from veering off, but there is still the problem of driving them too deep.

More effective are hammered fasteners that are pre-drilled. This is a bit more work, but types such as the crooked RawlSpike have great holding ability, equal to that of some sleeve devices. Other predrilled nail-in devices, not unlike rivets, have an interior pin which, when struck, expands a sleeve inside the hole. They come in a variety of materials from aluminum to zinc alloy, hold very well, and are moderately priced.

Powder-actuated tools (Figure 3.17). These tools use a .22-caliber charge to drive in pins; they should be used only on dry concrete—not on brick or block. **This is a very dangerous tool and should be used exactly as specified by the manufacturer.** Wear hearing protection *and* safety goggles.

Powder-actuated tools are most commonly used to attach sole plates to concrete slabs. Start with the recommended load and observe the first pin you shoot: the head should be slightly buried in the 2×4 plate. The hardness of concrete can vary, so you may have to try a different charge—loads are color coded—to increase or decrease the height of the pin. Like hammered nails, these pins can fragment concrete if they hit a weak spot or are driven in too deep.

Toggle bolts (Figure 4.9). Toggle bolts are specialized to attach to concrete block or other hollow spaces. To predrill here, use a regular drill; an impact hammer will shatter unfilled block. The most common variety is spring-loaded: once inserted into a predrilled hole, it opens up and is tightened against the block. Two problems: you must drill a hole much bigger than the bolt shaft, and if you remove the bolt, you lose the toggle. The gravity toggle obviates the first problem; the second is solved by plastic toggles, which stay in place when the bolt's removed.

Chemical fasteners. Chemical fasteners disperse into the surrounding masonry and form a bond as strong as the material to which you're anchoring. Typically, you drill a hole to a specified depth, inject (or pour) the chemical agents in the hole, and twist the rebar or threaded rod into place.

The chemicals vary, as do the methods of getting them into the hole. Some you mix by hand and pour in, others combine at the tip of a plunger; Ackerman-Johnson's Poly-All system features a pneumatic caulking gun. Other types are sealed in a glass capsule that shatters when a steel rod is shoved into the hole after it.

Whatever your choice, clean the hole well (with forced air or a vacuum) before putting in the chemicals; twist the rebar or rod to mix the agents and seat the steel; and allow the reaction to cure completely before putting any stress on the materials.

Shields, sleeves and anchors (Figure 4.9). These fasteners have a tremendous range of sizes and strengths. Traditional anchors—from plastic to lead—fit into a hole drilled in solid masonry and expand to hold fast the screw or bolt that follows. Plastic sleeves are probably adequate if, say, you're hanging cabinets on a brick wall. But sleeves and shields have several drawbacks—and lead ones, a fatal failing.

Imagine, if you will, bolting a 2×4 to a slab. First, you've got to drill two different holes: one, the thickness of the bolt shank, through the 2×4; the other, the width of the shield, into the concrete. Second, those holes often don't align because drill bits often skitter on concrete before digging in. Third, lead shields, being soft, can vibrate loose.

Wedge and sleeve anchors, happily, are a great improvement. Made of steel, they're much stronger than lead, and they require only one size hole. Both types of anchors feature an integral bolt and gain their strength by expanding in the bottom of the hole. As a sleeve anchor is tightened, its tip flares out and grips the hole, making it an especially good bet for attaching to brick. Wedge sleeves are the strongest mechanical connectors discussed here and are favored for seismic retrofits and the like.

Attaching to Walls and Floors

If the basement is dry, these tasks are straightforward—largely a matter of measuring carefully and using one of the fasteners described above.

Putting up furring. One of the most common renovations in the basement is putting up paneling or drywall over masonry foundations. The key to a successful installation is

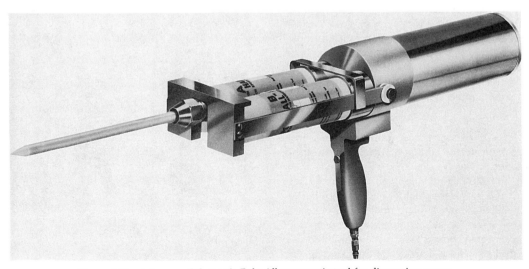

Figure 9.31 Ackerman Johnson's Poly-All pneumatic tool for dispensing epoxy.

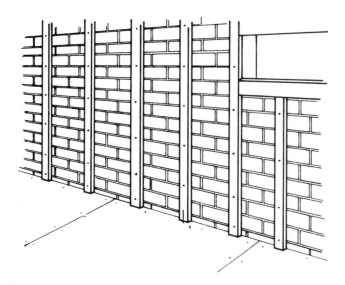

Figure 9.32 Covering a masonry wall. Place furring strips 16 or 24 in. on-center, attaching them with epoxy or by nailing into mortar joints with case-hardened nails. Wear goggles. To forestall rot, put a sheet of plastic between the wood and the masonry.

correctly laying out intervals for the furring, so that the edges of paneling or dry wall always occur over furring. Since most sheet materials are 4 ft wide, snap your chalk lines every 16 in. and center your furring strips over those lines.

The job will be faster if you predrill furring strips and then merely pencil those marks onto the masonry. Also check your walls for plumb. If there is more than 1 in. of variation from top to bottom, you may want to shim up furring strips to create a flat plane, as in Figure 9.32.

Plastic anchors or wood plugs spaced every 16 in. will be plenty of support for the light weight of furring strips. If, however, you'll be hanging things from these new walls, use 2×4s on-face instead of furring, and attach them with lead anchors or expansion anchors every 2 ft.

An alternative. It may happen that even after you have sealed the water, the basement still seems damp or there is condensation on the foundation walls. In that instance, forgo attaching furring strips and instead, build freestanding 2×4 stud walls 1 ft in from the foundation (i.e., toward the living space). First improve ventilation by knocking out blocking between the two joists nearest the foundation and putting in foundation vents. You will thus have air circulating at each end of the air space behind the new partitions. Then isolate any future dampness by wrapping with plastic the foundation side of each stud wall. To forestall moisture's wicking up through the floor, put a good heavy bead of silicone caulking on the underside of the sole plate and use redwood or treated lumber for that plate. *Note:* Whenever you use treated lumber or redwood, always use galvanized nails.

Setting sole plates. To locate a new wall, snap chalk lines on the floor to indicate the sole plate, then plumb up to ceiling joists to locate the top plate.

Attaching the sole plate depends on the attacher you choose. If you use powder-actuated pins, remember to caulk the underside of the sole plate first; once it's down, it's down to stay. Wear goggles and hearing protection.

If you choose expansion anchors, drill through the sole plate using a drill bit whose diameter is the same size as

the anchor bolt shank. Insert a pencil into those holes and mark anchor positions onto the concrete. Then, setting the plate aside, drill into the concrete with a carbide-tipped bit. Clean out the holes (plastic tubing duct-taped to a shop vacuum works well), insert the expansion anchors, caulk the underside of the plate, align the holes in the plate to those in the floors, insert the bolts, and tighten away.

If you're inserting threaded rod (always galvanized) into epoxy or some other adhesive, remember to drill holes into the slab at least $\frac{1}{8}$ in. larger than the diameter of the rod and at least 4 in. deep. Try to keep the drill plumb so that the bolts will be straight. With a hacksaw, or a reciprocating saw with a metal-cutting blade, cut the rod into $6\frac{1}{2}$-in.

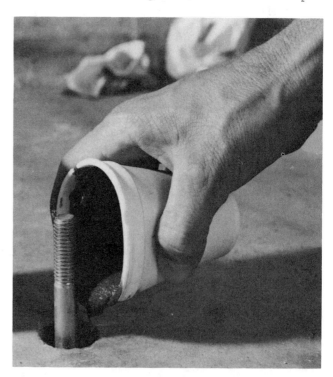

Figure 9.33 To set bolts into concrete slabs, drill with a carbide-tipped masonry bit, clean out debris with a shop vac and set the bolt with anchoring cement.

lengths. Clean the holes, then fill them with the adhesive to within 1 in. of the top. As you insert the threaded rod, do so with a twisting motion to avoid trapping air. Let the adhesive fully set; then, so that the plates will sit flat, strike off the excess adhesive with a cold chisel. Now set the plate atop the rods and align it to the chalk line you snapped earlier; tap down on the plate to mark off the locations of the bolt holes. Drill the holes, caulk the plate, check the fit, and tighten the whole assemblage down, using nuts and washers.

·10·

FOUNDATIONS

This chapter has no pretenses of being more than a gloss of the subject; Appendix G lists other titles for those who want more. We'll limit our inquiries to an overview of foundation failure, a survey of foundation types, and a few remedial tasks that most people can safely effect. We'll assume that the house is wood frame; because masonry buildings are heavier and more likely to crack if incorrectly supported, call a professional if their foundations need fixing.

Before you lift a tool, however, have an engineer assess what's there and prescribe what's needed. Qualified soil or civil engineers can identify conditions not readily apparent to novices, such as the load-bearing capacity of the soil, seasonal shifting, seismic activity, and so on. Their solutions will be conservative and overdesigned, but that's a virtue when your house is riding on it.

THE BASICS

Before renovating foundations, let's look at how they work, why they fail, and what choices you have to set things right. By the way, when we speak of foundations, we include not only the perimeter foundation, but also interior systems such as girders, posts, and pads.

A foundation is an intermediary of sorts between the loads of the house and the soil on which it rests. A critical design consideration is *area:* how big the footprint of the foundation is, and hence how much of the soil is used to support the weight of the house. Equally important is the *depth* of the foundation. Where there are extremes of temperature, as in the Northeast, footings must be below the frost line so that the foundation remains stable while the soil around expands and contracts. Everywhere, footings must be below excessive moisture levels (i.e., surface run-off). This is particularly true in the West, where adobe soil becomes saturated and unstable during rainy months.

Steel reinforcing bar (rebar) basically carries and distributes loads within the foundation, transferring loads from high-pressure areas to others less loaded. It thereby lessens the likelihood of *point failure*, either from point loading above or soil pressures laterally. Whenever joining sections of concrete, extend rebar to bridge that *cold joint. Anchor bolts* or threaded rods, tied to rebar, mechanically fasten the structure above to the foundation. For good compression over a large area, always use washers when bolting down sills. *Steel dowels* are usually short pieces of rebar that pin together foundation walls to footings, additions to main house, new caps to old substructure, and so on. Bolts and dowels are optimally $\frac{5}{8}$-in. steel; minimally, $\frac{1}{2}$-in.

The quality of the concrete is critically important, in both composition and placement. Water, sand, and aggregate must be clean and well mixed with the cement. Foundation concrete should contain 5 sacks of cement per cubic yard, minimum; if you use smaller aggregate (say, $\frac{3}{8}$ in.) to aid pumping the mixture, use at least 6 sacks of cement per cubic yard. When placing concrete, vibrate all forms as soon as possible to drive out air pockets. For smaller jobs,

A.

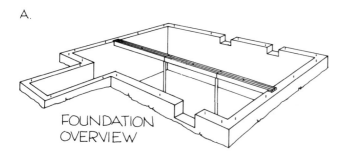

FOUNDATION
OVERVIEW

B.

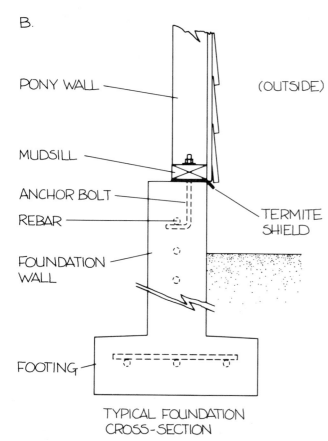

PONY WALL

MUDSILL

ANCHOR BOLT

REBAR

FOUNDATION
WALL

FOOTING

(OUTSIDE)

TERMITE
SHIELD

TYPICAL FOUNDATION
CROSS-SECTION

Figure 10.1 Foundation details. (A) Overview; (B) cross section, with spread footing.

hammer on form sides or vibrate them with a reciprocating saw without a blade. For larger pourings, rent a concrete vibrator. Under normal temperatures, allow minimally 3 days to cure before putting weight on it; optimally, a week.

For other specifics about concrete, see Chapter 9.

Common Foundation Failings

Most foundations that fail do so because they were poorly designed in the first place, poorly executed, or subjected to some change that exceeded their load-bearing capacity. To decipher the problem, look closely—in what direction are things moving, and why? Here are some common symptoms and likely causes.

1. Localized springiness, low spot in flooring. Probably caused by a failed or absent post beneath a girder. Look for

signs of rot around the post base: if none, suspect the pad. If the post or pad is canted, the pad is probably not big enough.

If you do find wet rot or insect damage at the base of the post, first correct those situations, then put in a new pad which is minimally 8 in. above grade to forestall future failure. If for any reason you are unsure about the size or condition of pads, replace them.

2. Widespread springiness in floors, joists sag in mid-span. Failed or absent girder. If an existing girder seems sound, adding posts and/or new pads may do it. Otherwise, add a girder.

3. Widespread crowning in flooring above the girder, downward sloping toward the outside of the house; windows and doors difficult to open; gapping in the frames; cracking at corners of openings. This condition is caused by a failure of all or part of the perimeter foundation.

4. Cracks in the foundation are but symptoms; they are caused by soil shifting or subsiding, and design insufficient to deal with it.

a. Wide cracks in the foundation, as in Figure 10.2, indicate little or no steel reinforcement, a common failing of older homes in temperate climates.

b. Cracks wider at the top mean that one end of the foundation is sinking; typically, a corner with poor drainage.

c. Deflection toward the inside (i.e., a crack wider on the inside of the foundation) suggests excessive ground pressure pushing things in.

d. Cracks wider at the base of the foundation are caused by footings that are too small. Verify this movement by putting a level on nearby joists; they'll probably tilt down toward the crack.

e. Gaps between chimney and house are usually caused by an undersized chimney pad.

5. When second-story additions are accompanied by widespread cracking and binding around doors and windows, you're seeing central downward failure. In other words, the old foundation was too small for the additional load.

Figure 10.2 Foundation failure. This crack through a corner is serious, probably caused by shifting soil, poor drainage, insufficient rebar in the foundation, and a footing too small for the house.

Foundation Types

To remedy a failed foundation, you'll have to increase its footprint so that it can bear more, and/or sink it farther down so that it can withstand soil or water pressures. It may be possible to bolster the present foundation, or it may be necessary to rip it out and replace it with something beefier—engineers should have the final say. In brief, their recommendations will incorporate one or more of the following foundation types, depending on the source of the original problem, access for different kinds of equipment, and how much you have to spend.

Drilled concrete piers. Concrete piers used in tandem with grade beams are *the* premier foundation for most situations. Called ''drilled'' because pier holes are typically drilled down to bearing strata, this type is unsurpassed for lateral stability, as replacement foundations for old work, or for new construction.

Piers have a greater cross section than driven steel and hence greater skin friction against the soil; they are much less likely to migrate. The stability of these piers is further enhanced by grade beams (concrete beams placed at or below grade), for such beams typically run as deep as the footings of a tee foundation.

The primary disadvantages of drilled concrete piers are cost and access, particularly if your design requires drilling straight down. In new construction, holes require 10 or 12 ft of vertical clearance to operate an auger on the power takeoff of a backhoe.

Driven steel piles. Where you don't have the access to drill concrete piers, or bearing strata are so deep that piers would be too costly, you can drive piles. Driven to bedrock and capped with pile caps, steel piles can support considerable vertical loads; as retrofits they can stabilize a wide range of problem foundations.

Actually, there are many types of pilings, from wood to precast concrete; our example on pages 225–228 features steel piles or *jacked pipe*, which, being hollow, can be reinforced with rebar and filled with concrete or epoxy. Because their points rest directly on rock and can bear almost as much as concrete, steel piles need no footings.

Like concrete piers, steel pile setups are expensive, and it's important that your engineer do a test boring to ascertain that the bedrock is thick enough to support the total load.

Tee, or spread foundation. Where there are no great loads, no severe water problems, no radical movement of the soils—in short, where you don't have the room or the money to drive steel piles or drill concrete piers—put in a tee foundation.

So named because its cross section looks like an inverted tee, this foundation was long the mainstay of builders and is probably the configuration beneath your house. Where such foundations fail they probably do so because they lack enough steel or have too small a footprint; they must be torn out and replaced with something bigger and stronger.

In addition to being less expensive, tee foundations are markedly quicker to install: you can form and pour one in the time it takes just to drive steel pilings.

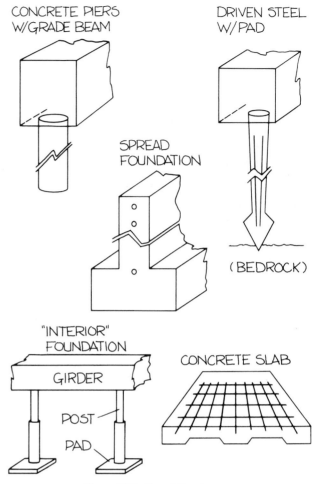

Figure 10.3 Foundation types.

Interior foundations. Keep in mind that there can be foundations within foundations: girders, posts, and the pads that support them. Such systems pick up the loads of joists and interior walls, true, but in so doing they reduce the total load on the perimeter foundation. Where the exterior foundation is marginally sized, adding or upgrading the interior foundation may be all that you need. This approach is very cost-effective and feasible wherever there is enough space under the house to accommodate the height of girders, posts, and pads at least 8 in. above grade.

Slabs. Reinforced concrete slabs are rare in renovation because there's already a house in place above them. Although shallower than the foundations described above, the immense footprint of a slab sometimes makes it the only workable foundation on weak bearing materials.

JACKING AND SHORING

After identifying the cause of foundation failure, do what you can to prevent its recurrence. If there was an insect infestation, for example, treat it as described in Chapter 8; if excessive surface water, put in downspouts, drainage, and so on. Then, working from the design your engineer provides, repair failed sections. But first you'll have to support the structure above, which requires shoring or jacking.

Although they employ many of the same principles and materials—notably, big timber—shoring and jacking have different purposes. Shoring timbers temporarily support the structure as it is, or prevent sagging when the structure is altered. Jacking, on the other hand, lifts the structure to its original position or temporarily raises a section to make some task easier—say, raising a girder just a bit so that you can fit a full-sized post beneath without having to beat it into place.

Thus you might need only shoring to add a girder beneath a floor that is merely springy; but you should jack that floor to level if it has sagged appreciably, say $\frac{1}{2}$ in. Use shoring to support joists while you create a rough opening in a floor or add a doorway to a bearing wall. But you'll have to jack when a pad or post has failed, when the perimeter foundation has sunk, when earlier plumbers or electricians cut so much of a joist that it split, and so on.

Materials and Tools

When used as a temporary partition (p. 156), shoring can be fabricated from 2×4s; in foundation work, 4×4s are more commonly used for shoring studs and plates, with 4×8s or 4×10s on-edge used as carrying beams. To fully support loads above, studs are cut nearly to length, plumbed, and fit tightly to plates by driving cedar shims in with a hand sledge. Jacking also uses 4×4s or 6×6s as posts, and as *cribbing* beneath the jack, which provides a level platform from which to jack and distributes loads over a broader area.

There are a variety of jack types to choose from. *Screw jacks*, perhaps the oldest type, vary from 12 to 20 in. high in repose and extend another 9 to 15 in. Never raise the threaded shaft more than three-fourths its total length; it will be unstable beyond that. *Hydraulic jacks* are the workhorses of foundation work and are rated according to the loads they bear: 16 to 20 tons is typical. In general, hydraulics are easier to operate and fit in tighter spaces than screw jacks; but because they lower by releasing hydraulic pressure, you can't lower them as slowly as screw types. *Adjustable columns* feature a screw mechanism atop a sleeved column, and a plate or bracket atop which attaches to the wooden member being raised. These lightweight columns, which bolster girders or joists, are intended to be permanent posts and are not rated as jacking devices. Lumber can also be used as a jack of sorts if your jacking is minimal, say, $\frac{1}{8}$ in.; cut posts oversized by that amount and beat them into place.

Jacking Safely

Jacking houses is scary and should be: there are tremendous loads involved. But it can be done safely if you proceed slowly and observe the following precautions:

1. Wear a hard hat. Get a tetanus shot. Set up adequate light. **Always have help within shouting distance.**
2. Have a professional engineer assess the foundation's failing, design an appropriate remedy, and recommend jack sizes and placement.
3. Supplement that advice with a thorough inspection of

Figure 10.4 Left, a hydraulic jack atop cribbing; right, a screw jack atop a concrete pier block.

your own. Know what's above: where bearing walls are, what heavy items put additional stress on joists, what pipes or ductwork might interfere with shoring or jacks, and so on.

4. Think things through. How much digging is there, who's going to do it, where are you going to put the dirt? What machines can you rent? If you need more than 1 cu yd of concrete and will have it delivered, do you need a pumper truck? Where will you store materials? What happens if it rains?

5. **Important:** Never jack more than you must, and raise all jacks in equal increments—say, $\frac{1}{8}$ in. at a time.

6. If repairs are extensive, raise an entire wall at a time; repairing shorter sections wastes too much time setting and moving jacks.

7. **Jacks and posts must be footed adequately:**

a. Pads or cribbing must be wide enough to bear the load. Putting posts or jacks directly on earth is a waste of time, and precast concrete pier blocks right on the ground aren't much better. Instead, put 8-in. pier blocks atop 2 ft × 2 ft concrete pads at least 6 in. thick. Or avoid the hassle of concrete altogether and use cribbing.

Cribbing must also be substantial—ideally, 4×4s or 6×6s stacked so that they taper up from a base of 3 or 4 ft square to a top about 1 ft square, as in Figure 10.5A. Some

A.

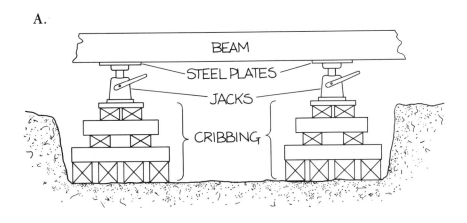

B.

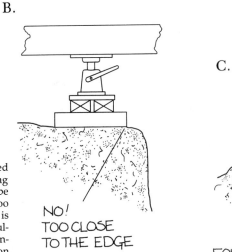

NO!
TOO CLOSE
TO THE EDGE

C.

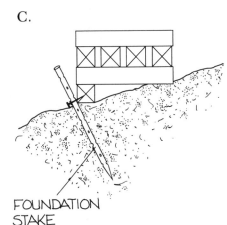

FOUNDATION
STAKE

Figure 10.5 Jacks and posts must be footed adequately. (A) A safe setup for the cribbing cannot be undermined and will not have to be moved later. (B) Unsafe! Here the jack is too close to the edge of a hole. When the jack is loaded, it could easily collapse the dirt shoulder. (C) Where you must jack on a slight incline, hold cribbing in place with foundation stakes—or dig into the ground to create a level shelf from which to jack.

builders also place a piece of $1\frac{1}{8}$-in. plywood atop the cribbing, for an even more stable platform from which to jack. (*Aside:* When using screw or hydraulic jacks, whose heads are relatively small, place $\frac{1}{8}$-in. steel plate atop those heads so that they don't sink into the wood being jacked.)

b. Never jack a post that is not plumb, and never jack from a base that is not level. The logic of this should be self-evident: When loads are transmitted straight down, there is less danger of jacks or posts kicking out and injuring someone.

Accordingly, cut the ends of all posts perfectly square, plumb posts when you set them, and check them for plumb periodically as the job progresses. If jacking posts are longer than 5 or 6 ft, brace their tops with 1-in. boards run diagonally.

Where it's necessary to build a platform of cribbing on sloping ground, add an extra crib on the low side, as shown in Figure 10.5C. To hold cribbing on a slope, nail the crib to foundation stakes, using duplex nails for easy removal.

c. Don't put jacking platforms too close to the edge of an excavation, for the soil could cave in when the jack is loaded. The rule of thumb is to go back 1 ft for each 1 ft you dig down. Also, don't put jacks where they'll be undermined later: if, for example, you need a needle beam to

support joists parallel to the foundation, excavate on either side of the foundation and place the jacking platforms in those holes. In that manner, you can remove the foundation without undercutting the jacking platform.

Placing the Jacks

Ideally, place jacks directly under the area to be jacked. This is usually possible when raising a sagged girder or when adding a new one. If you're putting in new posts, jack up in the intervening spaces between old posts. Jacks every 8 ft should be sufficient under joints of a laminated girder and under girder ends not supported by the foundation wall.

Frequently, though, it's not possible to place jacks directly underneath (e.g., when replacing a foundation). In that event you'll need to pick up the load above with a beam. Where joists run perpendicular to the foundation, place a 4×8 or 4×10 beam on-edge under the house, within 2 ft of the foundation. This distance should be close enough to the end of the joists so that they won't deflect, yet far enough back to give you room to work. A jack every 6 ft under the beam should suffice.

When replacing a foundation whose joists run parallel to the foundation, rip off siding up to the underside of the

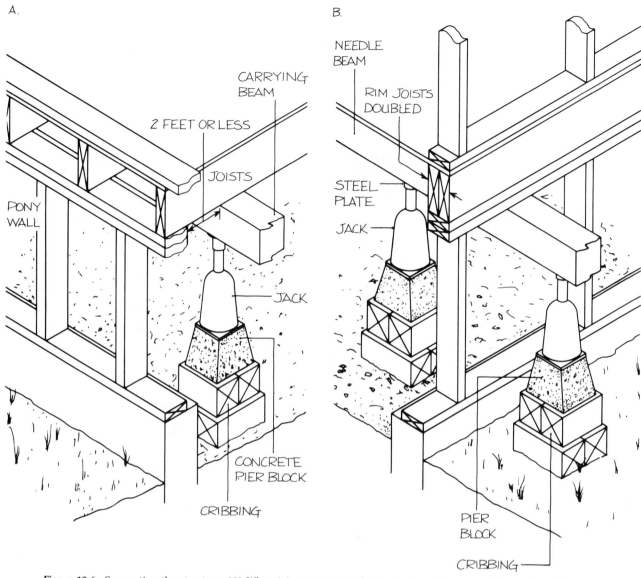

A.

CARRYING
BEAM

2 FEET OR LESS

JOISTS

PONY
WALL

JACK

CONCRETE
PIER BLOCK

CRIBBING

B.

NEEDLE
BEAM

RIM JOISTS
DOUBLED

STEEL
PLATE

JACK

PIER
BLOCK

CRIBBING

Figure 10.6 Supporting the structure. (A) When joists run perpendicular to the wall you want to work on, support their load with a beam parallel to the wall. Allowing yourself room to work, put this beam as close to the wall as possible; it should be no further than 2 ft. Place jacks at least every 6 ft beneath the beam. (B) Where joists run parallel to the wall, run your beam (here called a ''needle beam'') perpendicular to the wall as shown. To prevent its deflection under pressure, double the outer joist and run blocking to the next joist in. Again, place jacks as close to the wall as possible, and no further than 2 ft.

joist platform—and insert needle beams every 6 ft, running perpendicular to the wall, as in Figure 10.6B. Thus you'll need two stands of jacks to support the needle beams: one stand under the house, as above, and a second stand, roughly 2 ft from the foundation, outside. To keep the rim (outer) joist from deflecting under the load, nail a second rim joist to it, and add blocking from those doubled joists to the first adjacent joist. Use 16d nails to end-nail blocking, and 10d nails to face-nail rim joists.

PUTTING IN A GIRDER

As noted above, adding a girder stiffens a springy floor and, in so doing, reduces some of the loading on perimeter foundation walls. Although the surest test of that springiness is daily use, you probably need a girder if your joists

exceed these spans, especially if joists lack blocking or bridging:

Joist Size	Typical Span, (ft)
2 × 6	8
2 × 8	10
2 × 10	12
2 × 12	14

Your engineer will recommend a girder size; Table 10.1 shows maximum spans for built-up beams in two-story houses.

In the sequence immediately following, we'll assume that joists are not sagging badly and so do not need to be jacked. The steps additionally required for jacking are summarized at the end of the section.

TABLE 10.1

Maximum spans for built-up wood beams in basements, cellars, and crawl spaces, two-story houses[2][5]

Species	Grade [1]	Supported Joist Length ft [3][4]	Size of built-up beam, inches [6][7][8]											
			3-2×8		4-2×8		3-2×10		4-2×10		3-2×12		4-2×12	
			ft.	in.	ft.	in.	ft.	in.	ft.	in.	ft.	in.	ft.	in.
Douglas Fir Western Larch	No. 1	8	8	10	10	5	11	4	13	4	13	9	16	3
		10	7	4	9	4	9	4	11	11	11	5	14	6
		12	6	4	8	0	8	0	10	3	9	9	12	5
		14	5	7	7	0	7	1	9	0	8	8	10	11
		16	5	0	6	4	6	5	8	0	7	10	9	9
	No. 2	8	8	2	9	5	10	5	12	0	12	8	14	8
		10	7	3	8	5	9	4	10	9	11	4	13	1
		12	6	4	7	8	8	0	9	10	9	9	11	11
		14	5	7	7	0	7	1	9	0	8	8	10	11
		16	5	0	6	4	6	5	8	0	7	10	9	9
Pacific Coast Hemlock Amabilis Fir Grand Fir	No. 1	8	7	7	9	1	9	8	11	7	11	9	14	1
		10	6	4	8	0	8	0	10	3	9	9	12	5
		12	5	5	6	10	6	11	8	9	8	6	10	8
		14	4	10	6	1	6	2	7	9	7	6	9	5
		16	4	4	5	5	5	7	6	11	6	10	8	6
	No. 2	8	7	0	8	1	8	11	10	3	10	10	12	6
		10	6	3	7	2	7	11	9	2	9	8	11	2
		12	5	5	6	7	6	11	8	5	8	6	10	2
		14	4	10	6	1	6	2	7	9	7	6	9	5
		16	4	4	5	5	5	7	6	11	6	10	8	6
Pacific Coast Yellow Cedar Tamarack Jack Pine Eastern Hemlock	No. 1	8	8	5	9	9	10	9	12	6	13	1	15	2
		10	7	0	8	9	8	11	11	2	10	10	13	7
		12	6	0	7	7	7	8	9	9	9	4	11	10
		14	5	4	6	8	6	10	8	7	8	3	10	5
		16	4	10	6	0	6	2	7	8	7	6	9	4
	No. 2	8	7	8	8	10	9	9	11	4	11	11	13	9
		10	6	10	7	11	8	9	10	1	10	8	12	4
		12	6	0	7	3	7	8	9	3	9	4	11	3
		14	5	4	6	8	6	10	8	6	8	3	10	5
		16	4	10	6	0	6	2	7	8	7	6	9	4
Balsam Fir Lodgepole Pine Ponderosa Pine Spruces (all species) Alpine Fir Aspen Poplar Large-toothed Aspen Poplar Balsam Poplar	No. 1	8	6	4	8	0	8	0	10	3	9	9	12	5
		10	5	3	6	8	6	9	8	6	8	2	10	4
		12	4	7	5	9	5	10	7	4	7	2	8	11
		14	4	1	5	1	5	3	6	6	6	5	7	11
		16	3	9	4	7	4	9	5	10	5	10	7	2
	No. 2	8	6	4	7	10	8	0	10	0	9	9	12	2
		10	5	3	6	8	6	9	8	6	8	2	10	4
		12	4	7	5	9	5	10	7	4	7	2	8	11
		14	4	1	5	1	5	3	6	6	6	5	7	11
		16	3	9	4	7	4	9	5	10	5	10	7	2
Western Red Cedar Red Pine Western White Pine White Pine	No. 1	8	6	9	8	6	8	7	10	10	10	5	13	2
		10	5	7	7	1	7	2	9	1	8	9	11	0
		12	4	10	6	1	6	3	7	10	7	7	9	6
		14	4	4	5	5	5	7	6	11	6	9	8	5
		16	3	11	4	10	5	1	6	3	6	2	7	7
	No. 2	8	6	7	7	7	8	5	9	9	10	3	11	10
		10	5	7	6	10	7	2	8	8	8	9	10	7
		12	4	10	6	1	6	3	7	10	7	7	9	6
		14	4	4	5	5	5	7	6	11	6	9	8	5
		16	3	11	4	10	5	1	6	3	6	2	7	7

Source: Adapted from *Canadian Wood-Frame Construction*, with permission of the National Research Council, Ottawa, Canada.

NOTES

[1] Graded in conformance with 1971 "NLGA Standard Grading Rules for Canadian Lumber" published by the National Lumber Grades Authority, Vancouver.

[2] These tables provide maximum allowable spans for main beams or girders which are built up from nominal 2 in. members in the species, sizes, and grades indicated. Allowable spans for solid wood beams, glued-laminated wood beams, or built-up beams in sizes or grades other than shown shall be determined from standard engineering formulas.

[3] Supported joist length means $\frac{1}{2}$ the sum of the joist spans on both sides of the beam.

[4] For supported joist lengths intermediate between those shown in the tables, straight-line interpolation may be used in determining the maximum beam span.

[5] Beams for $1\frac{1}{2}$-story houses shall be taken from the table for 2-story houses.

[6] The 2-in. members shall be laid on edge and fastened together with a double row of common nails not less than $3\frac{1}{2}$ in. in length. Nails shall be spaced not more than 18 in. apart in each row with the end nails placed 4 in. to 6 in. from the end of each piece.

[7] Where built-up wood beams are employed over a single span, the length of each individual piece used to fabricate the beam shall equal the length of the beam.

[8] Where built-up wood beams are continued over more than one span and where lengths of individual pieces are less than the total length of the complete beam, the location of butt joints shall conform to Articles 23H(3) and 23H(4) of this Code.

Preparation

Locate the new girder in the middle of the joist span. Plumb down to locate pads and posts, which should be placed every 8 ft, and beneath girder joints, should any exist. There should also be posts at each end of the girder or, failing that, pockets in the foundation wall to receive those ends.

Pads are typically 2 ft square and 6 in. deep, with a single layer of $\frac{1}{2}$ in. steel rebar tied together: one bar running around the perimeter, 3 in. from the edge; and within the pad, rebar every 6 in.

Line the forms with sheet plastic so that the water in the concrete won't wick into the soil and weaken the pad. To make sure that the pad is level, level the form boards carefully and simply screed off the concrete to them. As the pad starts to set, set the pier block in and rock it gently so that it settles down in about 1 in. Check its top for level. Allow concrete to set before putting weight on it: 3 days minimum, 7 days optimum.

Raising the Girder

When the concrete has cured, bring in the girder. Whether it is solid or is to be laminated from two pieces of 2-in. stock and a $\frac{1}{2}$-in. plywood core, note its crown and install it crown up. (Plywood joints should occur over posts.)

Precut posts now, measuring down from the bottoms of joists to the tops of the pads, subtracting the height of the new girder. Raising a girder is much easier with many helpers, but you can raise a small one solo if you lift one end at a time and nail it to joists, using a metal connector (e.g., a hurricane tie) nailed to each side. Nailed with just one nail the tie acts as a kind of hinge, allowing the girder

A.

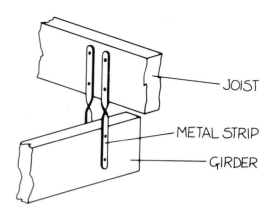

B.

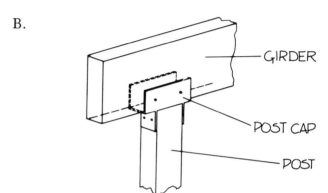

Figure 10.7 Raising a girder. (A) By raising one end of the girder as high as possible and then tacking it up with metal straps, you'll find that the other end will be easier to raise. Note, however, that this is only a temporary setup so you can get the two end posts in quickly. (B) A metal cap will prevent posts from drifting. Plumb all posts.

TABLE 10.2

Maximum spans for steel beams in basements, cellars, and crawl spaces[1][3][4]

No. of Storeys	Minimum Depth (in.)	Minimum Weight/Foot (lb.)	Width (2) of Floor to be Supported				
			8 ft.	10 ft.	12 ft	14 ft.	16 ft
1	4	7.7	10	9	8.5	8	7.5
	5	10.0	12.5	11.5	11	10.5	10
	6	12.5	15	14	13	12.5	12
	7	15.3	18	17	16	15	14.5
	8	18.4	21	19.5	18.5	17.5	16.5
1½ or 2	4	7.7	8	7.5	7	6.5	6
	5	10.0	10.5	9.5	8.5	8	7.5
	6	12.5	12.5	11.5	10.5	9.5	9
	7	15.3	15	14	13	12	11
	8	18.4	17.5	16	15	14	13

Source: Adapted from Canadian Wood-Frame Construction, with permission of the National Research Council, Ottawa, Canada.

NOTES

[1] A beam may be considered to be laterally supported if wood joists bear on its top flange at intervals of 24 in. or less over its entire length and if all the load being applied to this beam is transmitted through the joists and if 1-in. by 2-in. wood strips in contact with the top flange are nailed on both sides of the beam to the bottom of the joists supported. Other additional methods of positive lateral support are acceptable.

[2] Supported joist lengths means $\frac{1}{2}$ the sum of the joist spans on both sides of the beam.

[3] For supported joist lengths intermediate between those shown in the tables, straight-line interpolation may be used in determining the maximum beam span.

[4] This table provides maximum spans for main steel beams or girders, of the sizes and weights indicated. Allowable spans for steel beam in sizes, weights, or shapes other than shown, shall be determined from standard engineering formulas.

to swing freely. Raise the other end of the girder and nail it up temporarily with metal connectors, too.

With the ends of the girder hanging a few inches from the underside of the joists, installing posts is straightforward. Place the two end posts first, beating them into place with a 3-lb hand sledge. To be a little gentler on finish surfaces above, you can also cut posts $\frac{1}{4}$ in. short and drive in shims. Plumb end posts and nail them off, then raise others in between.

To prevent migration, prenail post caps to the tops of posts before raising them. Once all the posts are plumbed, pull the few nails holding the hurricane ties and re-nail the connectors properly. Simply toe-nailing the girder to joists is also adequate. Finally, toe-nail the bottom of posts to the wood blocks inset in the top of the concrete piers. If your crawl space has had moisture problems, treat posts to forestall rot, as described on page 172.

Steel Beams

If headroom or clearance under your house is limited, steel beams provide a lot of strength for not much depth. They are, however, very expensive, and cumbersome to work with; hire a specialist to install them. Not only are they heavy, they're problematic to attach to wooden members, requiring holes drilled in or connectors spot-welded to steel. Although your engineer will furnish exact specifications, Table 10.2 gives a rough idea of the size beam you'll need.

CAPPING OR REPLACING A FOUNDATION

When a house's framing is too close to the ground, surface water will splash up and/or wick up through the foundation, often rotting the mudsill. To correct this condition, you'll have to raise the top of the foundation at least 8 in. above grade: by shoring (or jacking up) the house, removing the sill and shortening the pony wall, then capping the foundation—or replacing it altogether.

(The procedures that follow assume that your house has *pony walls*, short walls running from the foundation to the first-floor platform. If it lacks pony walls, and if joists rest directly on the foundation, you have two options: cutting back the grade on the outside of the house to gain the necessary height, which may not be possible if the foundation is shallow; or jacking up the house at least 8 in., which is complicated and extremely expensive.)

Capping the foundation means pouring a new foundation atop or around the old foundation, after first adding rebar dowels to tie old concrete to new. It also assumes that the old concrete foundation is sound enough to tie into; if it's cockeyed or cracking, it makes more sense to tear it out and replace it with a new foundation. In most cases, this is a job for a specialist.

Supporting the Wall

Please read the sections on shoring and jacking thoroughly before proceeding. Then survey the underside of the house and the area around the foundation for sewer lines, water pipes, wiring, and the like—move jacks or support beams to avoid crushing them. A few points to keep in mind:

Jack up no more than you must: $\frac{1}{8}$ in. should be enough to get the weight off pony walls. All jacks must be firmly footed, and all posts, plumbed. Repair no more than you must. If the entire foundation needs capping or replacing, raise only one wall at a time.

Place jacks and support beams close enough to the foundation to pick up loads, but back enough to give you room to work: 2 ft is optimal in most cases. The direction of floor joists dictates the placement of support beams. Remember to double up rim joists and add blocking if joists are parallel to the foundation wall you're replacing.

It's possible to support the house with temporary wooden posts, but it makes more sense to rent a few extra jacks and leave them in place beneath support beams until

Figure 10.8 A needle beam supporting a wall while its pony wall is being replaced.

you're done with your repairs. Should the house settle, as houses frequently do, you'll have jacks in place to set things right.

Replacing the Sill

Once support beams are in place and you've jacked up low spots, as necessary, lay out the height of the new sill by snapping chalk lines across pony wall studs. If the top of the old foundation is level, measure up the requisite amount you must raise the sill; otherwise, measure down from the top plate of the pony wall to mark your cuts.

At this point, it's convenient to rip off siding up to the top of the pony wall, but prudent to rip off no more than you must to allow the saw to pass unobstructed. Siding can serve as one side of your cap forms and, in any event, will need to be replaced when the job is done. (Of course, if you needed needle braces to support joists, you will have already punched through the siding.)

The siding off, use a square to extend cutoff marks across the face of the studs. It's important that these cuts be square so that studs sit fully on the new sill. For this reason, use a circular saw rather than a reciprocal saw. If the first stud "chatters" as you cut through it, you may want to tie together successive studs with strapping tacked just above the cut line.

The replacement sill should be redwood, or pressure-treated with a preservative such as Copper Green, to resist bugs or moisture; and end-nailed to each stud with two or three 16d *galvanized* nails. *But* before nailing up the new mudsill, drill dowel holes in your foundation and rough out rebar—much easier without the sill in the way.

Tying Old Concrete to New

Dowels are steel pins grouted or epoxied in the original foundation. They are particularly important because they provide positive mechanical attachments between sections and transfer loads to the larger footprint of the new foundation. In short, they tie old to new.

Figure 10.9 Drilling the foundation with an impact drill. Because it's helpful to lean into this task, drill before framing out the pony wall.

Dowel types. Several materials are appropriate. One is threaded rod (*all-thread bar*), which can be cut long enough to run continuously from old foundation through new sill, thus acting as both dowel and anchor bolt. If you can drill

A.

B.

Figure 10.10 Capping a foundation. (A) Pony wall studs in midair. Drill and clean out holes in the foundation before adding the mudsill—it's much easier. (B) A corner section almost ready for the concrete pour. The formboards, lying in the foreground, are ready to be tilted up and tied off. (Photos by Donald V. Pearman, from his excellent book, *The Termite Book*, see Appendix G.)

straight down into the foundation, it's easy to align threaded rods to holes predrilled in the sill.

More likely, you'll have to drill at an angle because the house is in the way. For this reason, it's often easier to install rebar dowels at a slight angle in the foundation, as a separate operation from setting anchor bolts. Dowels set at an angle are also less likely to pull out should shifting occur.

Placing steel. Because tie-ins are only as strong as the material around them, you should center dowel holes in the top of the old foundation and drill them 6 to 8 in. deep. If you're drilling into concrete, use an impact drill; into brick, use a heavy-duty power drill with a carbide bit. Holes should be $\frac{1}{4}$ in. larger than the diameter of the dowel so that there is room for epoxy: for $\frac{3}{4}$-in. all-thread, drill 1-in. holes; for $\frac{1}{2}$-in. rebar, $\frac{3}{4}$-in. holes will suffice.

Anchor bolts are routinely placed every 6 ft, and not more than 1 ft from corners or board joints, so if you alternate all-thread with anchor bolts, drill holes for the all-thread accordingly. In earthquake country, space the bolts every 4 ft. When using rebar dowels, some contractors prefer to space them every 3 ft, with anchor bolts in intervening spaces so there is steel of some sort every 18 in. or so.

The steel reinforcement running with the length of the foundation is thus tied to the rebar and the anchor bolts at each point they cross. If you are capping a brick foundation, the cap must straddle the old foundation with a minimum of 3 in. concrete on each side, and should be further reinforced with rebar running along each leg, and with saddle ties spaced every 4 ft to tie together the three lengths of steel.

If you pour your cap (or new foundation) a wall at a time, always extend rebar through the ends of the forms so that it continues at least 2 ft into the next section you pour.

Concrete "cold joints" are inherently weak, but steel running continuous across those joints will keep them from separating. When drilling into the ends of such sections, angle the drill bit slightly downward, so the adhesive added later will not run out.

Setting dowels. When you're done with drilling and have cut the rebar to length, clean out holes and set dowels. Because clean-out is critical to sound attachment, one builder duct-tapes a length of $\frac{1}{2}$-in. flexible tubing to the hose of his shop vacuum and inserts that tubing in holes. That rig has enough suction to raise the dead and is as effective with the vac on a blow mode.

There are a number of masonry adhesives suitable for attaching dowels; epoxy compounds are among the strongest. To avoid air pockets, fill holes from the bottom, using a funnel and a tube, or a special epoxy injector. The epoxy should flow in easily. As you insert the rebar (or all-thread) dowels, twist them to distribute the adhesive evenly. If epoxy runs out of holes drilled in the ends of foundations, insert dowels and pack the holes with clay until the epoxy has cured.

Securing the Sill

Before hanging rebar off the dowels, predrill for anchor bolts in the new sill. (You have not yet attached the sill plate to cutoff studs.) Space the bolts as noted above, making sure that no bolt occurs under a stud. When the new cap is installed, your foundation will rise well above grade, but if local codes still require termite shields, add them now. You need only tack each shield to the underside of the sill, but predrill anchor bolt holes through it, too. All that attended to, nail up the sill to the studs. A nail gun can be helpful here.

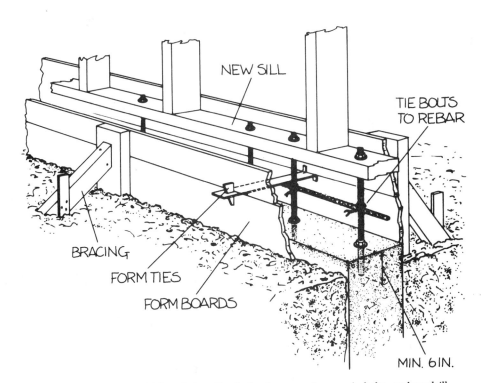

Figure 10.11 Capping an old foundation. Ready for the pour: formwork, bolts, and mudsill.

The sill finally in place, insert anchor bolts, screw on washers and nuts, and tie the free ends of the bolts to the rebar. At this point, nuts should be just snug; you can really tighten them down after the concrete has cured.

The Forms

Because a cap contains a modest amount of concrete, forms can be simple. If you stripped the siding earlier to facilitate cuts or to position beams, nail boards to the outside of the pony wall to create the outer wall of the form. Two-inch-thick boards are customarily used for forms, but in this instance you can use 1-in. boards if you take care that all joints are centered over stud edges and are braced with stakes running diagonally to the ground. For ease in removing forms, use duplex nails throughout.

On the inside, you'll need at least 3 in. of clearance between the inside of the form board and the inside edge of the new sill, to fit the nozzle of the grout pump. If the old foundation is too narrow or the sill too wide, notch the forms to accommodate that nozzle. The inner form board should also be staked for strength and backed by 2×4 *walers* every 4 ft, and at board joints. The top of the form should be slightly higher than the bottom of the sill.

These forms should be sturdy enough without spreaders, especially if your forms are 2-in. planks, but for a really first-class job, use foundation stakes and spreaders. These stakes, which are perforated, can be driven solidly into the ground and then tacked to the form boards. After leveling

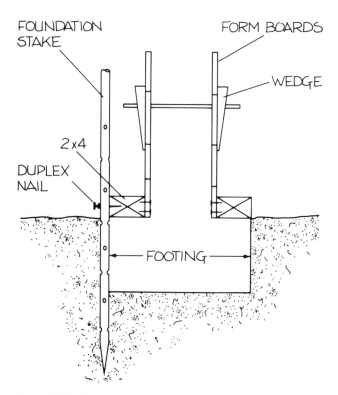

Figure 10.12 Formwork for a spread footing. By nailing a 2×4 on-edge to the foundation stakes, you easily create the 4-in. footing on both sides of the form walls (i.e., you can pour footing and walls in one operation). Take pains to make sure that concrete fills the footings.

the bottom form board, you can use spreaders and wedges to hold subsequent form boards perfectly in place.

Stakes, spreaders, and wedges are imperative, in fact, if your cap overlaps the old foundation, as it must when capping brick. To hold forms out from the foundation the minimal amount, just place a few standard bricks ($3\frac{5}{8}$ in. wide) in the bottom of each form. And because the exterior face of this cap will extend beyond the present foundation (and siding), taper its edge 45 degrees to shed water. You can shape this edge with a trowel after the concrete has started to set up a bit.

Pouring the Concrete

As concrete sets up, it shrinks a small amount. To compensate for this shrinkage, crank your jacks about $\frac{1}{8}$ in. high. Thus when you fill up concrete to the edge of the forms—slightly above the bottom of the new sill—and the concrete shrinks, there will be a slight pocket beneath the sill. When the concrete has cured and you lower the house, it will be true level; and the sill, now resting in that pocket, will be quite unlikely to migrate thereafter.

But the key to a strong cap is the care with which you place the new concrete and drive out air from the forms. If your job is more than 1 cu yd, have it delivered premixed, in tandem with a grout pumper. As pumping requires smaller aggregate ($\frac{3}{8}$ in.), specify a six-sack mix from the concrete supplier.

Vibrate the forms to drive out air: hammering the side of the forms works well, a reciprocating saw with no blade vibrates superbly. As the concrete approaches the tops of forms, signal the pump to shut off so that it doesn't slop over the side. When the forms are full and you've poked and vibrated to exorcise air pockets, float the top and sponge off any globs on stakes or forms.

As noted earlier in the chapter, allow concrete to cure 3 days minimum, 7 days optimum before removing the forms, setting down the house, replacing the siding, and tightening down the washered anchor bolts. For further protection against moisture, seal the outside of the foundation with asphalt emulsion.

Replacing a Foundation

Supporting, removing and replacing a failed foundation section can be substantially the same as capping a foundation. It depends on the size of the old foundation; in most cases it's advisable to have a professional replace it. The major difference is the amount of excavation necessary to expose the foundation and provide room to install a new footing. Supporting the house correctly (p. 216) becomes correspondingly more difficult as excavations get bigger—have an engineer recommend jacking platforms and support-beam sizes when designing the replacement foundation. That person can also pinpoint the cause of the failure, but it will probably be an absence of reinforcing steel or an insufficient footprint (i.e., no footing).

To tear out the old foundation, you've got two choices. Both require safety glasses, sound protection, heavy gloves, a mask, patience, and a strong back. Rent a gas-powered saw with a 10-in. blade, which cuts 4 to 5 in. deep,

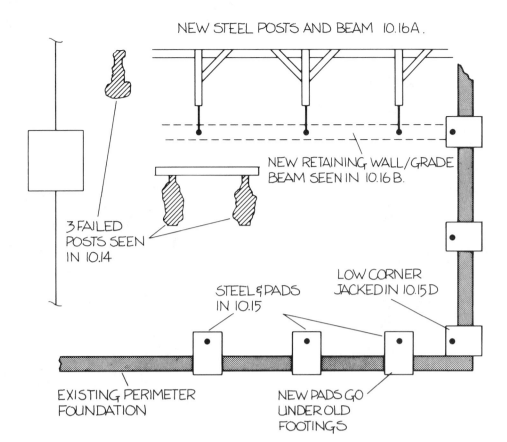

NEW STEEL POSTS AND BEAM 10.16A.

NEW RETAINING WALL/GRADE BEAM SEEN IN 10.16 B.

3 FAILED POSTS SEEN IN 10.14

STEEL & PADS IN 10.15

LOW CORNER JACKED IN 10.15 D

EXISTING PERIMETER FOUNDATION

NEW PADS GO UNDER OLD FOOTINGS

Figure 10.13 A floor plan of our case history. To the left center of the drawing, the three failed concrete columns seen in Figure 10.14. Down the middle, the new steel posts and beam seen in Figure 10.16A and embedded in concrete in Figure 10.16B. The driven steel and pads shown lower right appear in Figure 10.15A–D. (Thanks to Ken Woznak, Woznak Construction, Orinda, CA, for the following sequence.)

to cut the concrete into manageable chunks. An alternative is Rotohammering a line of $\frac{5}{8}$-in. holes across the foundation and then smacking them with a hand sledge and a large mason's chisel. Should you encounter rebar after all, have someone with a torch cut through it. This is monstrously hard work.

Once that's out of the way, locate the new foundation by plumbing down from the outside edge of the sill. (If the sill needs replacing or the pony wall shortening to get it above grade, do that now.) Foundations are typically 8 in. wide and their footings 16 in. wide, so lay out forms accordingly.

Foundation stakes are a great boon here. Keeping them as plumb as possible, drive stakes solidly into the ground and tack through them into 2×4 spacers, as shown in Figure 10.12. These 2×4s, themselves tacked to the first course of form boards, establish the width of the footing beyond the foundation wall proper. To level the form boards, and all boards atop them, tap down the foundation stakes. Place metal spreaders across the tops of these first boards. Spreaders vary, but in our example, wedges on the outside of the form draw boards tight. These wedges, in turn, restrain the bottoms of the boards above.

The deeper the footings, the taller the forms and hence the more important that bolstering devices such as walers and diagonal braces become. Overjack the house as described above to compensate for concrete shrinkage, set anchor bolts in sills, and tie them to the rebar grid within the forms.

Figure 10.14 Because the soil is excavated in the foreground, one can see how small earlier footings were.

A.

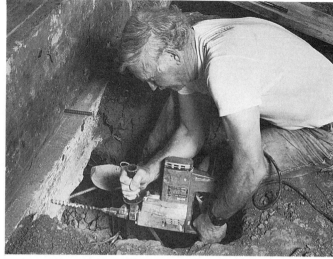

B.

C.

D.

Figure 10.15 Adding driven steel. (A) Drive in the steel until it hits bedrock. (B) Once the steel pipe hits bedrock, cut it off below grade. Then drill the old foundation with an impact hammer. After cleaning out the holes, pour in epoxy and insert rebar. (C) Tie the rebar in the foundation to that sticking out of the steel pipe. (D) Here, the lowest corner of the foundation is raised by a hydraulic jack capable of lifting 15 tons.

A CASE HISTORY

Out on the job site, you have to go with whatever works, which usually means several types of foundation, to solve a problem. In this case history, veteran builder Ken Woznak found a pretty little house in Orinda, California, that had been well built for its day, and whose foundation had been bolstered several times, yet was still sliding downhill.

The Problem. The problem was the downward drift of being built on a hill, several small springs seeping down toward one corner, largely impermeable clay soil which held water close to the building, and an inadequate foundation. The most telling symptom was a crack in the middle of the lower perimeter wall: a crack $\frac{1}{8}$ in. wide at the top, tapering down to a hairline at the bottom. To an inexperienced eye, it didn't look like much, but that $\frac{1}{8}$-in. gap told

Ken that the corner of the foundation, 16 ft away, had fallen 2 in. and was likely to fall more.

The foundation was basically a stepped perimeter foundation with a doubled 2×10 girder running the length of the house. Several decades earlier, a secondary girder and several posts had been added, as shown in Figure 10.14, but both girders were in the process of migrating downhill.

While the owners thought about turning the basement into a master bedroom, Ken's first task was to stabilize the building, which he did by jacking up the main girder and supporting its posts on driven steel pilings, later to be incorporated in a retaining wall.

The technology. Ken has found steel pilings to hold well in the adobe soil of Northern California. These 3-in. (I.D.) pipes of No. 80 steel are driven down and sleeved every 5 ft (rather like oil-drilling pipe) until they hit bedrock. Fre-

quently, pipes and sleeves fuse under the pressure. After hitting rock, the steel is hammered another minute or so, until it's clear that it won't go any deeper. As the point of the piling is hammered against the rock, it sculpts a cup which minimizes drift later. At the end of the driving there is a surge of a few inches which indicates the point of the pipe collapsing. At that point you stop. Each piling can take a vertical load of 30,000 lb.

The pipe's point keeps the interior of the pipe clear, so that you can pour in adhesive and insert rebar; Ken favors epoxy filler and No. 3 rebar to tie his pilings to the concrete caps he adds later. Sometimes in soft soil it's appropriate to drive in pipe without a point, later pumping in concrete under pressure so that it displaces the dirt and mushrooms out of the bottom in a footing of sorts.

The solution. To pick up the main girder and incorporate it in the back wall of the new bedroom to be created, Ken

A.

B.

Figure 10.16 (A) A new beam, temporarily supported by braces atop steel pipes. (B) The same beam, with new posts and the steel pipes embedded in a concrete grade beam/retaining wall.

decided to cast a grade beam/retaining wall. After excavating a trench and building forms for that beam, he temporarily shored up the posts supporting the girder, added concrete and rebar to that line of pilings, then poured the grade beam. After the beam cured, the posts would rest directly atop it.

Bolstering the perimeter foundation was similarly inventive. Because the weakest point was the northwest corner where springs converged, Ken decided to jack up that corner and reinforce its two contiguous walls by tying them into several steel pilings capped with concrete cubes 2 ft on a side. Thus each piling, driven to bedrock, sported a cluster of rebar as in Figure 10.15C, further tied to rebar epoxied into the perimeter foundation. At some points it was necessary to drill up into the *underside* of the foundation to add the necessary rebar. In those cases the excavation holes themselves served as forms for the concrete that followed.

SEISMIC RETROFITS

In the last few years, seismic retrofits on the West Coast have boomed as the Big One, long overdue according to most geologists, draws near. (The quake of 1989 was just a preliminary.) Happily, these retrofits—anchor bolts, shear walls, and metal connectors—are relatively easy to install in wood-frame houses, requiring little tear-out and, hopefully, providing the additional strength a house would need during a major earthquake. Retrofits primarily improve the connection of housing materials at various points: holding the sill fast to the foundation so that the structure doesn't walk off, and keeping the multitude of nailed-together joints from pulling apart during a good shaking. Chapters 4 and 9 contain additional information about these materials.

Anchor Bolts

Many older houses simply sit atop a foundation, without benefit of anchor bolts. There, you need to retrofit expansion bolts dropped into holes drilled through the sill and into the foundation; such bolts expand against the sides of the hole to hold the sill fast. Typically, retrofit bolts are $\frac{5}{8}$ in. × $8\frac{1}{2}$ in. long, spaced 4 ft O.C., and within 6 in. of board ends; any short sections of sill get at least two bolts. Center bolts in the middle of sills.

Bolt holes should be at least 4 in. deep, and preferably deep enough so that the washered bolt sticks above the sill about 1 in. Thus a $8\frac{1}{2}$-in. bolt holding down a nominal 2×6 requires a hole about 6 in. deep in the foundation. Drill the hole through the sill and into the foundation in one operation, using a rotary hammer with a depth gauge; the hole should be the same diameter as that of the bolt. For this reason, it's imperative that you clean the hole well, as described under ''Setting Dowels'' on page 223. A piece of coat hanger used as a depth gauge is also very useful to make sure that your hole is deep enough: as anchor bolts have to be pounded in with a hand sledge, it's a nuisance to find that a hole isn't deep enough after the bolt has been inserted.

Try to drill holes as vertical as possible, given the space constraints under your house. If the floor platform rests directly on the foundation—without a pony wall—you'll have to bolt predrilled $\frac{3}{8}$-in. steel plate to the side of the foundation, again using a rotary hammer. Tie the plate to concrete with $\frac{1}{2}$-in. anchor bolts, and to sills with $\frac{1}{2}$-in. lag bolts, As the plates should be spaced every 4 to 5 ft, this will be an arduous job.

With the power of a rotary hammer, drilling is pretty straightforward, except when you hit rebar or bind the bit. If the bit stops digging about 4 in. down, you've probably hit rebar: try another spot close by. If you consistently encounter rebar at that depth, insert 7-in. bolts (which require holes only 4 in. deep) spaced 32 in. O.C. (i.e., a bolt between every other 16 in. O.C. stud). Drill bits also bind, in which case you must release them from the hammer and turn them out by hand, using a large pair of Vise-Grips.

Not all foundations are strong enough to receive anchor bolts. Should your concrete be poor, you'll discover that when you tighten down the first few anchor bolts: the bolts will turn freely in the hole or start to rise out. In that event, redrill $\frac{5}{8}$-in. holes and set $\frac{1}{2}$-in. threaded rods in Pourstone. In fact, rods set in Pourstone are a good alternative to expansion bolts, and much cheaper.

Shear Walls

Shear walls are sheets of plywood nailed to a pony wall, from the top of the top plate to the bottom of the sill, primarily intended to stiffen the wall and keep it from racking

Figure 10.17 A hold-down.

during a quake. Install shear walls after you've retrofitted anchor bolts.

Measure the height of the walls carefully and cut plywood accordingly, favoring lengthwise cuts if they don't waste too much wood. Every plywood joint must occur over a stud edge. Although $\frac{1}{2}$-in. 5-ply plywood is sufficient for most shear walls, some builders favor $\frac{5}{8}$-in. on side walls, where loads are greater. What makes a shear wall a shear wall is the nailing pattern. After snapping chalk lines to indicate studs and plates, nail up the sheets with galvanized *10d nails every 4 in.*

When the shear wall is nailed off to studs and sills, drill two $\frac{1}{2}$-in. vent holes per bay, to relieve moisture that might be present. Speaking of which, it's advisable to treat the members of the pony wall with preservative before nailing up the plywood, to forestall rot and infestation. Because these chemicals are toxic and space is limited under the house, use a sprayer for installation, and get out of the area as soon as the task has been completed. Don't return to install the shear walls until the fumes have abated. *Important:* See page 172 about applying preservatives safely. Use a fan to increase ventilation under the house, and get the best ventilator mask you can get, one with an ammonia-type filter capable of screening vapors. Check to make sure that the filter can handle the preservative you're using.

As a final aside, make sure that the outermost joists in your floor platform have blocking to the adjacent joists. If not, add blocking to forestall their collapse during a shake-down. After the 1989 quake, some contractors advocated further buttressing shear walls with 2×6 braces run at a 45-degree angle from the bottom edges of joists to the mudsill, spacing such braces every 6 to 8 ft.

Metal Connectors

See pages 61–65 for an overview of metal connectors. Many metal connectors can be attached to framing members without disturbing exterior siding.

Hurricane ties from rafters to top plates are imperative in cyclone country, where wind moving over a roof tends to lift it like an airplane wing. Such ties are desirable but not imperative in seismically active areas. Under the house, add steel tees or straps to join girders atop posts, or posts atop pier blocks. Galvanized steel plumber's tape wrapped around the hot-water tank and nailed to framing will keep it from walking and possibly snapping a gas line.

Where you're gutting finish surfaces in an extensive renovation, add metal hold-downs in addition to the other methods mentioned above. Ideally, these connectors run between floors. After predrilling for the threaded rod that joins hold-down brackets, lag- or through-bolt these brackets to studs. Attach washered nuts to threaded rods and insert them down through the two brackets; adjust and tighten the washered nuts on the floor below. Use hold-downs at all corners and around any particularly large openings for doors or windows.

·11·

ELECTRICITY

Electrical work is among the most predictable, pleasant aspects of construction. There is no heavy lumber to be wrestled around, no large sheets that would fit if only your fingers weren't in the way, no quick-drying compounds driving you into a frenzy. Installing electrical parts is methodical work; it requires attention to detail and some dexterity. Nor are you ever long in doubt about whether you've done the work correctly. If you goof, a fuse pops or a breaker trips harmlessly; if you do it right, bulbs shine and radios play.

Misconceptions abound about electricity—that it is a capricious, malevolent genie waiting to zap the unwary. That's nonsense. Electricity should be respected, and it must be taken seriously; but it is a natural phenomenon and subject to the laws of physics. If you observe the safety tips given in this chapter—those about shutting off power and testing with a voltage tester, to make sure the power is off—it's virtually impossible to get hurt. Otherwise, successful electrical work is simply a matter of making correct, solid mechanical connections.

Whether you're gutting an entire electrical system or merely adding a receptacle, read this chapter in its entirety. As it presents important information on a given topic, that information may be presented in one place, often for the only time.

It's also important—in fact, imperative—that you check with local code authorities even before purchasing supplies. Although most building authorities do not forbid an owner-builder doing his or her own work, most do require inspections when the system is "roughed out," that is, before wires are connected to switches, receptacles and so on. Besides, building-codes people are usually quite knowledgeable, and they can offer useful tips about buying and installing parts. Where there is no local code, follow the *National Electrical Code®*, hereafter referred to as "Code."

For the most part, the discussion in this chapter stops short of the subject of connections above the main entrance panel. With the electrical meter removed from its base, you can work in the entrance panel with complete safety. If you are at all apprehensive about working around the panel, however, or you want to upgrade the entire service, hire a licensed electrician. You'll pick up a lot by watching one work. Finally, Appendix G lists several good titles covering advanced work.

UNDERSTANDING ELECTRICITY

Although we know what electricity does, what work it performs, describing it is more difficult. We might say that it's the movement of electrons, that it has mass, and so on: but because such descriptions are abstract, we offer analogies to other natural forces, such as water. But two concepts are useful to those working with electricity: (1) it flows in a circle, or makes a circuit; and (2) it follows the path of least resistance.

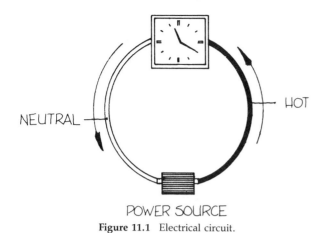

Figure 11.1 Electrical circuit.

The Circuit

Electrical circuits are so named because electricity moves in a circle from power source back to power source, whether that electricity is traveling across the country in great transmission lines or coursing through the cables in your walls.

At a power plant or a substation, electricity is multiplied (charged) and given pressure (*voltage*); in that form, electricity is unstable: it seeks to discharge its load, to return to a zero, or neutral, voltage. When electricity is put to work at an outlet, electrons flow through wires, and voltage is discharged as heat or light. *Amperes*, or *amps*, are the measure of this flow. The amount of energy consumed at a given point—say, at a toaster or a light bulb—is measured in *watts*.

Volts, amperes, and watts are thus interrelated:

volts—the potential to do work (pressure)
amperes—the measure of electricity as it flows (flow)
watts—the measure of energy consumed (work done)

Thus we might say, "work done = pressure × flow," or "watts = volts × amperes." Or we might say, "flow = work done ÷ pressure," or "amperes = watts ÷ volts."

To reiterate briefly, electricity, impelled by voltage, flows from the power source. Along the way, at outlets, it encounters resistance and does work. It then flows on, its voltage reduced or spent.

The Path of Least Resistance

The fact that electricity flows along the path of least resistance is the governing law of an electrical safety system. In its journey, electricity runs through copper wires (low resistance) insulated with rubber or plastic (very high resistance). However, whenever electricity encounters an easier way to discharge its load, it does so. If the insulation breaks at some point, electricity flows along the short circuit created. A short circuit is dangerous because it can overheat wires and set the house on fire. And it can kill people. Human bodies are composed largely of water, making them potentially better conductors of electricity than copper. In the unhappy circumstance that a person comes in contact with an ungrounded circuit that has shorted, electricity will discharge its voltage through the body as it *grounds* (returns

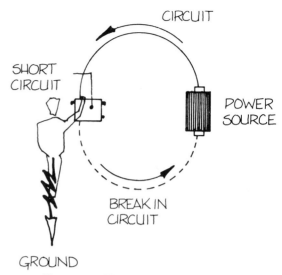

Figure 11.2 How an electrical shock occurs.

to zero voltage). Happily, these threats to property and personal safety have been all but eliminated in present-day houses wired according to Code.

Electricity in the House

A modern electrical system consists of three large cables, or conductors, which run from utility distribution lines to a *service head* or *weather head* atop a length of rigid conduit. Two of the cables are *hot*; that is, they have voltage. The third is *neutral*; it has zero voltage. This type of service delivers 240 volts. A service with only two wires—one hot and one neutral—delivers only 120 volts, which is inadequate for modern household demand, and should be upgraded.

The three cables run down inside the conduit and attach to the *meter base*. From the meter base runs another length of rigid conduit, containing cables to the service panel. Straddling the two sets of lugs on its base, the meter measures the wattage of electricity as it is consumed.

At the *service panel*, or *entrance panel*, the two hot cables attach to the terminals of the main breaker, and the neutral cable attaches to the main lug of the ground/neutral bar. (In some panels there are separate ground and neutral bars; in others, one bar suffices for both ground and neutral cables.) In a fuse box the hot wires attach to the main power lugs and the neutral cable to the main neutral lug. Whether the panel has breakers or fuses, metal *bus bars* issue from the bottom of the main breaker/main fuse. Running down the middle of the panel, these bars distribute power to the various branch circuits.

Branch circuits are individual cables or conduits that run from the entrance panel to various outlets around the house. Inside each cable are several wires color-coded for safety. In most 120-volt circuits, there is one *hot* wire (coded black), one *neutral* wire (coded white), and one bare copper (or green) *ground* wire. (Metallic cable and conduit carry no grounding wires within, because their casings act as grounds.) **Important: Hot and neutral wires must never be attached.**

Think of hot and neutral wires as parallel wires which are never joined. Ground wires, discussed below, must

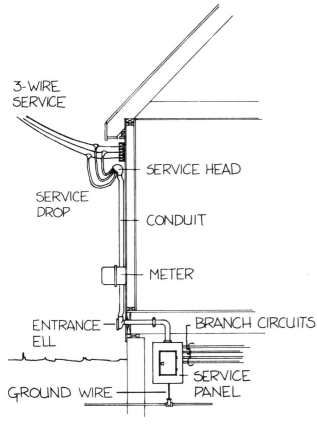

Figure 11.3 A service entrance.

also be kept separate from hot and neutral wires when you run branch circuits. (Ground and neutral wires may share a bus bar in the service panel, but that's another issue.) In 240-volt circuits, such as those "dedicated" to a heavy user like a stove, there are typically two hot wires, coded black and red.

Each branch circuit serves one or more *outlets.* At outlets, individual wires connect to various *devices* such as receptacles, light fixtures, and so on. To ensure a safe hookup, connecting screws or terminals of devices are color-coded or otherwise clearly designated: hot wires attach to brass- or gold-colored screws, neutral wires to silver screws, and ground wires to green screws (when present).

Switches cut or vary the flow of power by interrupting hot lines. Neutral wires are always uninterrupted; so are ground wires. *Wire nuts* are insulated caps that screw onto the bare ends of wire clusters, thereby joining them mechanically and preventing those bared ends from coming in contact with other wires, devices, or the outlet box itself.

The Safety System

In one sense, the electrical safety system of your house begins at the meter, for when the meter is removed, there can be no power to the panel. At the meter base, the two hot incoming cables are stripped and attached to two lug terminals at the top of the meter base. Whereupon, two outgoing hot cables issue from two similar lugs at the bottom of the meter base. The two sets of lugs, however, are physically separated until the meter is inserted to bridge the gap. The neutral cable, on the other hand, is *continuous*, secured by

a single lug that tightens down on bare wire. (The neutral cable may be bare or white.)

At the panel, the hot lines attach to a main disconnect while the neutral cable is secured to the ground/neutral bar. Because the hot wires of all branch circuits issue from the main disconnect, once the main breaker is shut off (or the main fuse removed), power is present in the panel only in the small area above the main breaker terminals. (Often, these terminals are located within the body of the breaker and are not even visible from the front.) Thus, with the main breaker off, you can work safely on the panel. To cut *all* power to the panel, you must yank the meter out of the meter base.

To the ground/neutral bar (in some panels, two distinct bars) connect the ground and neutral wires from all branch circuits. Hot, or load-carrying, wires from branch circuits are attached to hot bus bars.

The first line of safety is the fuses or breakers to which hot wires connect. Since amperage is a measure of electricity as it flows, each fuse or breaker is rated at so many amps. When a circuit becomes overloaded, its amperage (flow) is excessively high, and the breaker flips off; or a strip in the fuse melts, cutting voltage to the hot wire or wires. If there were no breakers or fuses, the electricity would continue flowing until the wire overheated and a fire started. For this reason, the amperage ratings of breakers and fuses are closely related to the size (diameter) of wire (Table 11.3).

Fuses were among the earliest safety devices, and they greatly reduced the likelihood of electrical fires. Still, something additional was needed—a path with less resistance, one that could discharge errant voltage faster than it took a wire to overheat or a fuse to melt. Thus the grounding system was developed. A grounding system, which usually carries no electical current, is an emergency express line for the discharge of voltage gone astray. Because of this function, *ground and neutral wires are always continuous; they are never interrupted, never fused, never attached to switches.*

In a grounding system, metal wires (usually bare or green) run to every outlet, and from there back to the ground bar in the panel. To this bar is also secured a large, bare, copper cable (No. 6 wire for a 200-ampere system), which runs out of the panel and clamps to a copper-coated grounding rod or to the house's cold-water pipe. Where a water meter is connected to the pipe, there should be a *bonding wire* to ensure continuity of grounding (even when the water meter is removed), by jumping the meter (Figure 11.4). Because the grounding wire and the rod or pipe are so large, they offer little resistance to electrical flow. Again, the large grounding cable does not normally carry electrical charge; nor do the smaller ground wires that attach to individual outlets around the house. Individual ground wires connect to every part of the electrical system that could be short-circuited—metal boxes, receptacles, fixtures, and through a three-pronged plug, the metallic covers of tools and appliances.

Despite the presence of grounding sytems, however, people were still being killed by electrical shock, particularly when moisture was present. To remedy this problem, the industry developed *ground-fault circuit interrupters* (GFCIs), highly sensitive devices that can detect minuscle

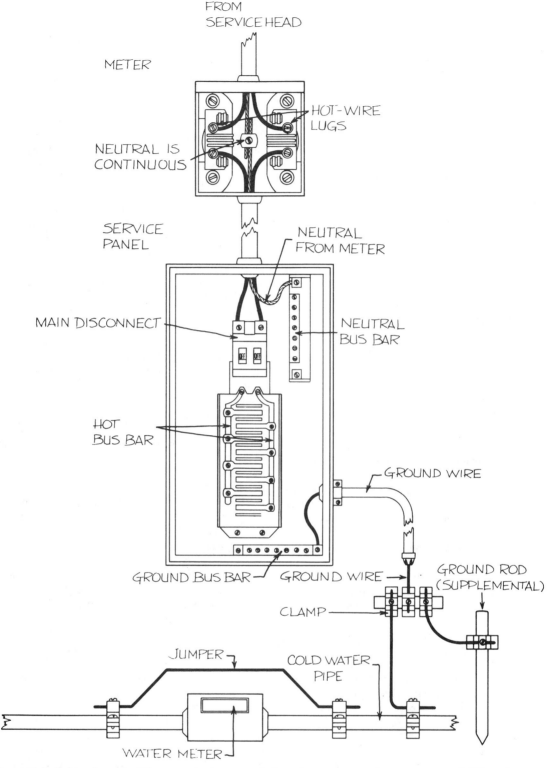

Figure 11.4 Safety elements. When a meter is removed, there is *no* power to the entrance panel. When the main disconnect in an entrance panel is switched off, there is no power below the main lugs—*but always test to be sure*. The ground wire runs from a ground/neutral bar in the panel to a grounding clamp on a cold-water pipe *or* to a copper-coated ground rod driven into the earth. *Note:* Dielectric unions (p. 298) on water pipes also require jumpers.

current leaks and shut off power almost instantaneously. A *ground fault* is any failure of the electrical system that leaks current from a hot wire. Normally, the current in hot and neutral wires is identical. But when there is as small a variance as 0.005 ampere between hot and neutral wires, a

GFCI will shut off all power within 1/40 of a second. A GFCI circuit breaker will thus cut all power to a circuit; a GFCI receptacle will cut all power downstream from that receptacle. Installing GFCI receptacles is described on page 253; GFCI breakers, on page 267.

Safety Tips

1. Check your local code before starting. If there is no code, use the *National Electrical Code®*. Have a licensed electrician make all connections from the service head to the service panel.

2. All tools should have insulated handles.

3. Before doing any work in the vicinity of an existing circuit, disconnect the circuit. Flip off the governing breaker or remove the fuse. (Don't merely loosen fuses; remove them.)

4. Before beginning work, use a *voltage tester* to make sure that the circuit is dead. See below.

5. Leave a note on your service panel announcing work in progress, so that others in the house won't inadvertently turn on the electricity.

6. Never stand on a damp or wet surface while doing electrical work (including removing fuses). Rubber gloves and rubber-soled shoes provide good insulation, and a simple wooden platform will keep you off a damp floor.

7. Unplug tools and appliances before adjusting them or tinkering with them.

Safety first! Use a voltage tester. Before working on any electrical equipment—or before cutting into finish surfaces—turn off the power to that area and test with a voltage tester to make sure that it is off.

A voltage tester is an inexpensive device that detects electric current in wires, receptacles, switches, and the like: when the power's on, the tester lights. To make sure that your tester is working properly, test it first in an outlet you know to be live.

Using a Tester. To test an outlet, grasp the insulated part of the tester and simply insert its prongs into the receptacle. *Do not touch the bare wire tips of the prongs.* If the tester lights, return to the service panel until you disconnect the circuit that controls it and the light goes out.

Receptacles. If you doubt your test of a receptacle, unscrew its cover plate and then the two screws holding the receptacle to the box. Being careful not to touch the sides of the receptacle or any wires, gently pull the receptacle out from the wall. (To be doubly safe, use insulated pliers.) Touch the tester to screws on opposite sides of the receptacle (brass-colored on one side, silver on the other). Then touch the tester prongs to the bared wire ends on the opposite sides (black wires will connect to brass screws, white wires to silver ones). As a final test, touch the tester to the black wire ends and to the metal box. Any light in the tester, however faint, means that the power is on. (Any unsheathed wire in the box is a ground wire.)

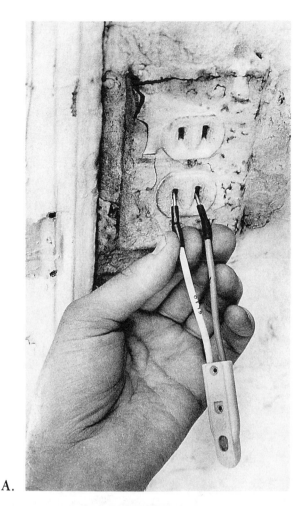

A.

B.

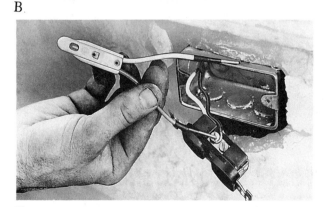

C.

Figure 11.5 Making sure that the power is off. (A) To make sure that a receptacle is not live, insert the voltage tester as shown, being careful not to touch the bare tester prongs. If the tester lights, the power is still on. (B) To double-check a receptacle, remove the cover plate and, being careful not touch the sides of the receptacle, hold the tester prongs to screws on opposite sides. (C) Also hold tester prongs to black-wire ends and to the metal box.

Fixtures. Remove fixtures by unscrewing the long machine screws holding them to outlet boxes. Carefully pull the fixture out from the box. Test the screw terminals on the underside of the fixture as described for receptacles above. If a switch controls the fixture, test it as described below.

Switches. To identify the circuit that serves a particular switch, turn on the fixture it controls and have a helper at the service panel flip breakers until the light goes out. If

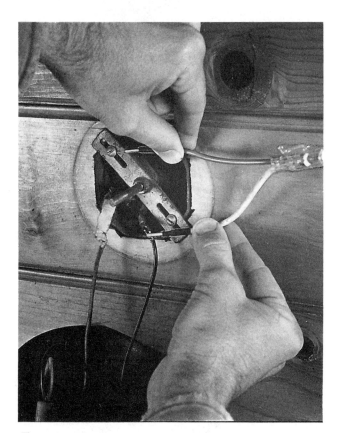

D.

E.

Figure 11.5 (Continued) (D) Test switches as well, testing screw terminals with the toggle both up and down; then hold one tester prong to a screw terminal and one prong to the side of the box. (E) To make sure that power is off at a fixture, apply tester prongs to incoming wires, and to the metal box as shown.

that test is inconclusive or you aren't sure the switch is operable, remove the cover plate and the two screws holding the switch to the box. Test the wires leading to the switch, again being careful not to touch the screws on the side of the switch or the wires leading to them. Switches interrupt hot wires, so apply tester prongs to each screw on the switch as well as to any group of wires spliced together.

PLANNING AND ESTIMATING

The changes you make in your electrical system will invariably be a trade-off between all that you'd like and what you can reasonably afford. Upgrading the electrical system is one time when you should spend for the future, however. Assess what's there now, see what Code requires, calculate your future needs, and then plan the changes you'd make.

Assessing the Present System

The two most important questions to ask of your current electrical system: Is it adequate? Is it safe?

Is it adequate? If you've lived in the house for a while, you'll have a fair idea of whether the system is big enough. Are there enough outlets, or do you have to piggyback receptacles with multiplugs and extension wires? Do you blow fuses often, especially when starting up a small appliance or power tool? Does your TV screen shrink momentarily when the water pump kicks in? These and similar symptoms indicate a system that's close to its present limits, to say nothing of future needs.

How much you can extend your system depends in large part on the size of the electrical *service*. There will be either two or three large cables running from the utility pole to the meter on your house. Two cables (one *hot* and one *neutral*) indicate a house wired for 120 volts only; this system is probably not big enough for most people, especially those with a number of small appliances. Three incoming service cables (two hot, one neutral) deliver 120- and 240-volt service, adequate for even heavy users like dryers and electric stoves, and sufficiently large for you to upgrade the service panel or add circuits.

The next place to look is the service panel. If you've got only two-wire service, chances are that the panel is rated 60 amperes or less: look at the nameplate of the panel. You can get by with a 60-ampere panel if your lifestyle is modest and you have mostly gas appliances, but it won't allow many (if any) additional circuits. These days, a 100-ampere entrance panel is considered *minimal* for future needs, and many thoughtful professionals will urge you to get a large panel, (e.g., 200 amperes), so that you'll never have to upgrade your panel again, come what may.

To get three-cable service, contact your utility; they're responsible for supplying cables to the service head (Figure 11.3) and for the meter. You are responsible for everything beyond that, including meter base and entrance panel. In Appendix G we offer titles for those who want to install their own panel; most people will be well served by having an electrician do it.

Is it safe? No system is adequate if it's unsafe. If you suspect that your system is unsafe, have an electrician make a formal assessment and advise you what to do. But these simple observations will tell you much:

1. Is the entrance panel grounded? There should be a large grounding wire running from the panel and clamped to a cold-water pipe and/or a grounding rod.

2. Is the *system* grounded? Grounding the panel is not enough. For the entire electrical system to be grounded, there must be continuous ground wires running to every device in the house. If there is only two-cable service to the house and/or receptacles are only the two-prong variety, the system is probably not grounded.

3. Are there GFCI devices (p. 253) in high-risk areas, as prescribed by Code?

4. Is the electrical equipment in good shape? Rusty entrance panels, receptacles encrusted with paint, and wires whose insulation is cracked and frayed may be as unsafe as they are unsightly.

5. Electrical equipment near any damp or wet surface is *extremely unsafe.*

6. Any corroded equipment—whether boxes, wiring, or devices—is unacceptable. Before examining individual outlet boxes for signs of corrosion, turn off power to them and test with a voltage tester (p. 235).

Figure 11.7 Type S fuses are matched to adapter bases, so it's impossible to insert too large a fuse for a circuit. (Leviton)

7. Is current usage safe? Installing fuses too big for a circuit—to prevent blown fuses—is a fool's bargain, as are overloaded receptacles, extension cords under carpets, and the like.

Code Requirements

Local electrical codes have the final say, but standard usage dictates:

1. Lighting circuits and appliance circuits should be distinct. The lighting load is calculated at 3 watts per square foot, or roughly one 15-ampere circuit for every 500 to 600 sq ft. of floor space. When laying out the lighting circuits, do not put all the lights on a floor on one circuit. Should there be a blowout, a floor entirely on one circuit would be without power.

2. General-use circuits are intended primarily for lighting, but small users such as televisions, record players, vacuum cleaners, and the like are allowable as long they don't exceed the current-carrying capacity of the circuit. Although No. 14 wire is sufficient for lighting alone and for switch runs, run No. 12 wire for general-use circuits and you'll be covered for future uses.

3. Many local codes require a receptacle every 8 ft of wall space. The NEC states that no space along a wall should be more than 6 ft from a receptacle, which translates into at least one receptacle for every 12 ft of *usable* wall space. Any small sections of wall at least 2 ft wide should have a receptacle, and there should be at least one receptacle for outdoor use.

4. The electrical inspector in your area has the final say on the number of outlets per circuit. Assuming 180 volt-amperes per circuit, NEC 220-2(C) recommends nine outlets per 15-ampere circuit, and 12 outlets per 20-ampere circuit.

5. There must be at least one wall switch for controlling lighting in each room, including the garage, storage areas (including the attic and the basement), and outdoor entrances. There should be three-way switches at each end of corridors and at the top and bottom of stairs.

6. There should be at least two 20-ampere small-appliance circuits in the kitchen, served with No. 12 wire. You should

Figure 11.6 An outmoded knob-and-tube fuse panel.

install outlets along any counter 12 in. wide or wider. Do not hook any *permanent* appliances such as disposals to these small-appliance lines, however.

7. All critical-use stationary appliances must have their own *dedicated* (separate) circuits: water pump, freezer, refrigerator, oven, cooktop, microwave, furnace and/or whole-house air-conditioning unit, disposal, window air conditioners, water heater. Heavy-duty exhaust fans (e.g., $\frac{1}{3}$ to $\frac{3}{4}$ hp) may also require dedicated circuits.

8. If cable does not attach to an appliance directly, its receptacle should be within 6 ft of the appliance.

9. Code also requires that there be GFCI receptacles in bathrooms, on kitchen counters within 6 ft of the sink, in accessible garage outlets, outdoors, and in other locations where the risk of shock is great. There must also be at least one GFCI receptacle in the basement.

Calculating the Total Electrical Load

The next stage in planning the changes to come is to figure out how much electricity you need, including any future additions or purchases of major appliances. Look closely, for energy conservation in the home is becoming an economic necessity. First, ask yourself what gadgets you might be able to do without. Air-dried dishes and laundry use no energy, nor does ventilating and heating your home with wind and sun. Set furnaces and water heaters lower, and air conditioners higher. Replace seals around appliances, keep them well maintained and if you shop for new ones, ask about their energy consumption. Many manufacturers have energy-efficient models. Chapters 13 and 14 give more suggestions for saving on heating and cooling costs.

To determine the total capacity you need, add up the wattage of (1) general-use circuits, (2) small-appliance circuits (include a workshop even if it's still a dream), (3) laundry circuit, and (4) dedicated circuits.

Calculate the wattage of general-use circuits first, by determining the square footage of the house; measure the outside dimensions and include all areas to be finished living space (if you intend to add space, include that square footage, too). Then multiply the area in square feet to obtain the general-use wattage. Assign small-appliance and laundry circuits 1500 watts each. The watt values of major appliances are listed on the nameplate of each, as are the values for air conditioners and furnaces. (If the value is given in amps, multiply that number by the voltage rating to obtain the wattage.)

The chart and calculations in Table 11.1 are adapted from the *National Electrical Code*®, and represent usage for a typical single-family dwelling. To plug a hypothetical house into the chart, let's assume that the living space is 2000 sq ft, that there are three small-appliance circuits (two in the kitchen and one in the workshop), that there is a laundry circuit, and that you have a hot-water heater (4000 W), dryer (5000 W), wall oven (6000 W), dishwasher (1200 W), refrigerator (1000 W), and central air conditioner (5000 W). Multiply 2000 sq ft by 3 watts per square foot to get 6000 watts for the general-use circuits. Three small-appliance circuits add up to 4500 watts, and the laundry circuit adds another 1500 watts. The major appliances (excluding the air conditioner in this calculation) add up to 17,000 watts. The

TABLE 11.1

Total electrical usage[a]

General-use circuits	
_____ sq ft × 3 watts per sq ft	_____ watts*
Small-appliance circuits	
_____ 20-ampere circuits × 1500 watts	_____*
Laundry circuit	
(1500 watts each)	_____*
Major appliances/Dedicated circuits	
Water heater	_____
Cooktop/oven or range	_____
Garbage disposal	_____
Dishwasher	_____
Microwave	_____
Other	_____
Subtotal for all major appliances	_____*
Add the starred subtotals of each circuit group above and multiply any wattage *over* 10,000 watts by 0.40:	
Total wattage − 10,000 watts × 0.40 =	_____ watts A
Add subtotal A to 10,000 watts +	10,000 B
	_____ C
To this new subtotal C, add the wattage D of the heating system *or* the air conditioner, which is greater:	_____ D
TOTAL WATTAGE	_____ watts
To convert this total wattage to amperes, divide by volts:	
_____ watts ÷ 240 volts = _____ amperes	

[a]Asterisks indicate subtotals for distinct groups.

four circuit groups (the starred subtotals in the table) add up to 29,000 watts.

Next, multiply the amount over 10,000 watts by 0.40: $29,000 - 10,000 = 19,000$; 19,000 watts × 0.40 = 7,600 watts (subtotal A in the table). Adding this amount to 10,000 watts, we get 17,600 watts (subtotal C in the table). The wattage rating of the central air conditioner is higher than that of the gas furnace; therefore, we add the wattage of the air conditioner (5000) to the above total, to get 17,600 watts + 5000 watts = 22,600 watts (final total).

To convert the total wattage to amps, divide by 240 volts: 22,600 watts ÷ 240 volts = 94.16 amperes. A 100-ampere service panel for such a house is adequate, although an addition of any size—for example, appliances that use greater amounts of energy—could exceed a 100-ampere capacity.

It's best to spend a bit more now, if you're close to the limits of the system: buy a 200-ampere panel and you'll have plenty of capacity to expand in the future. Considering the total expense of rewiring a house, the additional cost of a bigger panel is negligible.

A few words about the calculations above: the NEC multiplies the amount over 10,000 watts by 0.40 because not all outlets are drawing energy at the same time. The dweller chooses between the rating of the air conditioner and that of the heating system because it is most unlikely that both systems would be running at the same time.

Having calculated the total load you anticipate, you can now plan the work. Electrical service to the house is your first concern; if it's adequately sized, attend to the safety of the system; then decide whether to extend existing circuits and add new ones.

Upgrading Service

If you decide to upgrade the service panel by replacing it with one having greater capacity, or if the utility must upgrade its service lines from two cables to three, you will need a licensed electrician to do the work. Following is a quick overview of what to expect.

The power company is responsible only to the service head mounted on the outside of the house. It will also supply the meter, but you must hire an electrician to install a meter base and all rigid conduit (including the service head itself) from the head to the service panel. Cables from the meter that breach the wall and head for the panel are usually housed in conduit.

If there is now three-wire, 240-volt service, upgrading the service becomes a matter of upgrading the stretch of cable from the meter to the panel and replacing the existing panel with a larger one. Entrance-cable size and panel capacity must be matched (Table 11.2). You may be able to upgrade your present service simply by running a subpanel off the main panel. Have your electrician explain this option. If there is enough play in the existing branch-circuit cables, the wires can be attached directly to the breakers in the new box; otherwise, they will first have to be spliced (in junction boxes) to new leads.

Improving Safety

To be completely safe, a house should be wired according to Code; if yours is not, plan to upgrade it as soon as possible. But you can make your system safer in the interim by following these suggestions:

1. Replace any equipment (panels, boxes, etc.) that is corroded and any wiring that has deteriorated. If this means rewiring the entire house, do it. It's not safe otherwise.
2. Relocate any indoor electrical equipment mounted near damp or wet surfaces—which is extremely hazardous. (Here, we are not talking about equipment intended for outside use.)

3. Add GFCI receptacles (p. 253) or GFCI breakers (p. 267) to areas specified by Code. Note, however, that every outlet served by such devices must be grounded to be protected, which may mean adding ground wires to the nearest cold-water pipe or running a new, grounded cable back to the entrance panel.
4. If your entrance panel is ungrounded, ground it, as shown in Figure 11.4.

Adding or Extending Circuits

If there's room in the service panel for additional breakers or fuses, adding circuits is straightforward: just run cable and make good mechanical connections along the way, as described in the sections that follow.

Extending circuits is slightly more complicated, as you must disconnect an existing outlet and *fish* new cable from it, as described in pages 260–261. But first you must determine the load-bearing capacity of the circuit you want to extend.

Begin by identifying the circuit breaker (or fuse) controlling the circuit: flip off breakers until a lamp on that circuit goes out. Note the rating of the breaker: if it's a general-purpose circuit, the breaker will probably be 15 or 20 amperes. A circuit controlled by a 15-ampere breaker has a capacity of 1800 watts (15 amperes × 120 volts); a 20-ampere breaker, 2400 watts. The total wattage of all energy users on the newly extended circuit must not exceed these capacities, or you risk overheating the cable.

Figuring out the capacity of a circuit should be that easy. Unfortunately, people sometimes use fuses (or breakers) that are too big for the circuit wires. If the fuse controlling the line is 20 amperes or more, play it safe and ascertain the size of the incoming wire. To do this, turn off the main disconnect for the panel, unscrew the panel cover to expose the wiring within, and test with a voltage tester (p. 235) to be sure that the power to individual branch wires is off. If the size of the wire is not written on its insulation, use a *wire-thickness gauge* to determine it. That done, put the panel cover back on and restore power. As noted in Table 11.3, No. 14 wire should be protected by a 15-ampere breaker (fuse); No. 12 wire, by a 20-ampere breaker.

Once you've ascertained the true capacity of the cir-

TABLE 11.2

Matching panel ampacity to cable size[a]

Service Panel	Copper Cable	Aluminum Cable
100	No. 4	No. 2
125	No. 2	No. 1/0
150	No. 1	No. 2/0
175	No. 1/0	No. 3/0
200	No. 2/0	No. 4/0

Source: Reprinted by permission from NFPA 70, 1987, *National Electrical Code®*. Copyright © 1987, National Fire Protection Association, Quincy, MA 02269. This reprinted material is not the complete and official position of the NFPA on the referenced subject which is represented only by the standard in its entirety.

[a]These sizes given for type R and type T cable, as specified in NEC 70-167. Aluminum cable must attach to connectors marked "AL" or "AL/CU"; coat aluminum cable with anticorrosive paste before connecting the cable.

TABLE 11.3

Circuit load requirements (copper wire)

Amperage	Wire Size	Typical Load[a]
15	No. 14	Lighting circuit
20	No. 12	Small-appliance circuit
30	No. 10	Most large 120-volt appliances
40	No. 8	Dryer; oven
50	No. 6	Stove
70	No. 4	Other large appliances

Source: Reprinted by permission from NFPA 70, 1987, *National Electrical Code®*. Copyright © 1987, National Fire Protection Association, Quincy, MA 02269. This reprinted material is not the complete and official position of the NFPA on the referenced subject which is represented only by the standard in its entirety.

[a]Check the nameplate for the exact rating of the appliance. If the appliance has a motor, the ampacity of the circuit should be 125% of the amperage given on the motor's nameplate.

ELECTRICAL SYMBOLS

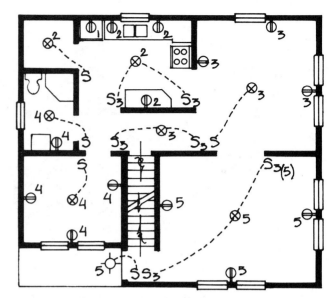

Figure 11.9 Circuit map. Numbers indicate separate circuits, except for the notation "S3," which indicates a three-way switch. Dashed lines link switches and the fixtures (or receptacles) they control.

⊖ DUPLEX RECEPTACLE

⊖ₛ SWITCH & RECEPTACLE

⊖ᵣ RANGE OUTLET

⊖_WP WEATHERPROOF OUTLET

Ⓙ JUNCTION BOX

Ⓕ FAN OUTLET

Ⓒ CLOCK OUTLET

⊕ CEILING OUTLET

⊢O WALL OUTLET

S₃ THREE-WAY SWITCH

S SINGLE-POLE SWITCH

◀ TELEPHONE OUTLET

⊖_GFI GROUND FAULT INTERRUPTER

Figure 11.8 Electrical symbols.

cuit, add the total wattage of energy users present and future to be served by that circuit. As a general rule of thumb, 12 outlets for a general-purpose or lighting circuit is the maximum.

Mapping the System

Whatever the extent of your electrical renovation, "draw before you do." At the entrance panel, assign a number to each circuit. Then, with the help of a friend who flips breakers or removes fuses, map the outlets controlled by each circuit. To save some shouting between floors, borrow a walkie-talkie from a neighborhood kid. Use the electrical symbols listed in Figure 11.8 for various devices, drawing dashed lines between switches and the receptacles or fixtures they control.

TOOLS AND MATERIALS

All materials should bear the Underwriters' Laboratory (UL) stamp, which indicates that a component meets the safety standards of the electrical industry.

Tools

Few tools are needed to wire your house successfully. Purchase the ones discussed below. All tools should have insu-

lated handles. Avoid touching the uninsulated parts of tools, such as bare leads of voltage testers.

Voltage tester. A voltage tester, such as the ones shown in Figure 11.10, is indispensable for safety. Use it to determine whether a circuit is live or not. Because this inexpensive tool contains resistors, it can be used with equal success on 240-volt, 120-volt, or low-voltage lines. A length of half-inch pipe taped at the ends makes a good crush-proof case for this tool, enabling you to carry it in a toolbox.

Continuity tester. With batteries in its case, a continuity tester is used on wires that are not carrying power. This device tests switches, sockets, wiring runs, and the like for short circuits and other wiring flaws. Be sure to read the instructions for use.

Insulated screwdriver. Insulated screwdrivers can save you, should an outlet unexpectedly be live.

Lineman's pliers. Lineman's pliers are the workhorse of your tool collection. In addition to holding wire fast while you work on it, the pliers twist free knockouts and cut wire.

Needle-nosed pliers. Used for fine work, especially in the limited space within a box. Avoid putting too much lateral (twisting) pressure on plier jaws, for they can misalign.

Multipurpose tool. A multipurpose tool is used to strip individual wires of insulation, as well as cut wire and crimp connections.

Cable splitter. A cable splitter strips the plastic sheathing from Romex electrical cable (RX) without harming the insulation on individual wires inside.

Fish tape. Fish tapes are used to run cable behind finish surfaces.

Electrician's tape. Plastic electrician's tape adheres far better than the fabric variety. Keep a roll in your tool box.

Heavy-duty $\frac{1}{2}$-in. drill. Commonly used with a right-angle drill, this tool easily drills through studs and joists, thus enabling you to run cable. A reversible drill is particularly useful if your bit becomes jammed or lodged against a nail shank. Although spade bits are often used, a $\frac{3}{4}$- or $\frac{7}{8}$-

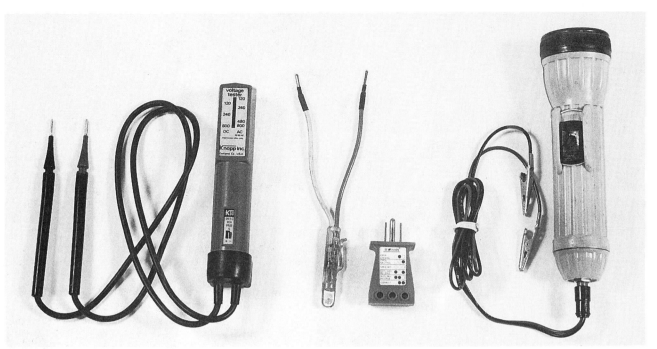

Figure 11.10 Three voltage testers and (at right) a flashlight with a continuity tester.

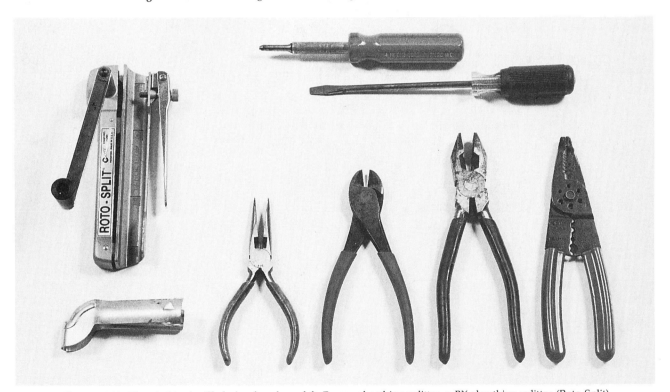

Figure 11.11 Electrical tools. *Clockwise, from lower left:* Romex sheathing splitter, a BX sheathing splitter (Roto-Split), four-way screwdriver, screwdriver with insulated handle, wire stripper and crimper (also called a multipurpose tool), lineman's pliers, diagonal cutters, needle-nosed pliers.

in. spiral bit is far sturdier. To determine what obstacles might be hidden behind finish surfaces, use an exploratory bit (p. 45).

Rechargeable drill/screwdriver. Frequently, you must shut down all or part of the electrical system so that you can work on it safely. A rechargeable drill is perfect for such situations, for it has its own power. Screwing in new boxes can also be a lot kinder to finish surfaces than hammering, say, when you're adding an outlet box to a plaster ceiling.

If you work with BX cable, you will also need a hacksaw and diagonal-nosed pliers to cut the metallic sheathing of the cable. Better yet, get a *Roto-Split BX cutter* (Seatek Co., Stamford, Connecticut), which cuts quickly and cleanly. It's shown in the composite Figure 11.11. For work on rigid conduit, an EMT cutter with a deburring attachment and a conduit bender are necessary.

Materials

Individual wires, or *conductors*, vary in thickness according to the amperage of electricity that flows through them (Table 11.3). Wires are enclosed in cable—flexible metallic (armored), or plastic-sheathed—or in conduit—rigid metal EMT or PVC plastic. Individual branch circuits, whether enclosed in cable or conduit, run from the entrance panel to individual outlets. The outlet devices are attached to boxes firmly secured to the structure or to a finish surface.

Electrical parts—receptacles, switches, fixtures, and boxes—are standardized, so there is (or should be) little variation. Most variations have to do with how the cable (or conduit) is attached to a box, the number of wires in the box (Table 11.4), how much wall space is available, and whether the work is new work (no finish walls in place) or old work (finish walls in place).

Types of wiring. Individual wire conductors are sheathed in insulation, usually thermoplastic. Type T wire is used mostly for residences; type TW wire, with its greater weathering capacity, is used where there is dampness, such as at outside hookups. Individual wires within a cable or conduit are color coded. White wires are neutral conductors; green wires are grounds; and any other colors—black, red, and so on—designate hot, or load-carrying conductors.

Any bare (uninsulated) wires are also ground wires, which must be continuous throughout an electrical system. Because most of the wiring in a residence is 120-volt service, most cable (or conduit) will contain two wires (one black and one white), plus a ground wire. Other colors are employed when a hookup calls for more than two wires, for example, 240-volt circuits, and three- or four-way switches.

Copper is the preferred material for residential-circuit wiring. Aluminum wire is frequently used to serve an entrance panel (to AL to AL/CU lugs), but its use in branch circuits isn't recommended. Aluminum is not as good a conductor as copper; it requires special split-bolt clamps to fasten it down adequately; and residences wired with it have an inordinate number of electrical fires. If your house presently has aluminum branch circuits, and you want to extend or replace them, hire a licensed electrician.

Note: Never connect copper *and* aluminum wires together in house circuits.

Whether you use conduit or cable depends on (1) code requirements, (2) where you use it, and (3) whether finish surfaces are in place. Plastic-sheathed cable is by far the most commonly used wiring in houses. It's often called Romex (RX) because of a particular brand's predominance. The three principal grades of RX cable are NM, used for most indoor installations; NMC, indoor wiring used where moisture exists; and UF, used underground. The size and type of Romex is printed on the cable sheathing: 12/2 *w grd.*, for example, contains two insulated 12-gauge wires plus a ground wire.

TABLE 11.4

Maximum number of conductors per box

Type of Box	Size (in.)	Number of Conductors[a]/Wire Gauge			
		No. 14	No. 12	No. 10	No. 8
Octagonal	$4 \times 1\frac{1}{4}$	6	5	5	4
	$4 \times 1\frac{1}{2}$	7	6	6	5
	$4 \times 2\frac{1}{8}$	10	9	8	7
Square	$4 \times 1\frac{1}{4}$	9	8	7	6
	$4 \times 1\frac{1}{2}$	10	9	8	7
	$4 \times 2\frac{1}{8}$	15	13	12	10
	$4\frac{11}{16} \times 1\frac{1}{4}$	12	11	10	8
	$4\frac{11}{16} \times 1\frac{1}{2}$	14	13	11	9
	$4\frac{11}{16} \times 2\frac{1}{8}$	21	18	16	14
Switch	$3 \times 2 \times 1\frac{1}{2}$	3	3	3	2
	$3 \times 2 \times 2$	5	4	4	3
	$3 \times 2 \times 2\frac{1}{4}$	5	4	4	3
	$3 \times 2 \times 2\frac{1}{2}$	6	5	5	4
	$3 \times 2 \times 2\frac{3}{4}$	7	6	5	4
	$3 \times 2 \times 3\frac{1}{2}$	9	8	7	6

Source: Adapted from NEC Table 370-6(a). Reprinted by permission from NFPA 70, 1987, *National Electrical Code*®. Copyright © 1987, National Fire Protection Association, Quincy, MA 02269. This reprinted material is not the complete and official position of the NFPA on the referenced subject which is represented only by the standard in its entirety.

[a]*Conductors* refers to the individual wires of a cable (or conduit), including ground wires but not including the short "pigtails" that ground to the box. For each of the following, subtract one conductor from the box's capacity: mounting device, fixture stud, receptacle, switch, or any conductor running through the box. Do not subtract wire nuts; subtract only conductors. The capacity of a box can be extended slightly by plaster rings, as marked on the ring face.

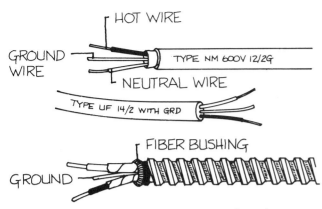

Figure 11.12 Electrical cable contains several conductors, or wires. It is specified according to the type, size, and number of wires it carries: "12/2 w/grd," for example, contains two No. 12 wires and a bare ground wire.

By the way, Romex 12/2 *w grd.*, is the workhorse of wiring today. Although No. 14 wire is acceptable for lighting circuits or runs to switches, No. 12 wire is specified for all light-appliance circuits. To give the homeowner the widest range of future uses, many electricians wire all general-use circuits with No. 12.

BX, or metal-armored cable, is not rated for use in damp or wet areas; use it only in dry conditions. There is a variation of BX with lead sheathing under the armor, but it's expensive and hard to find. All types of BX cable require plastic bushings at boxes, to keep metal sheathing from galling the insulation of individual wires within.

Both thin-walled (EMT) and thick-walled (IMC) conduit are suitable for indoor and outdoor use, since both are made of galvanized steel. You should use type TW wire within conduit for outdoor work, however. Underground or outdoor conduit is usually coated with a tar- or rubber-based waterproofer, and there must be waterproof gaskets for all junction boxes, receptacles, switches, and so on.

Plastic conduit (PVC) also has good weathering properties. If you use type TW wire, $\frac{1}{2}$-in. conduit will hold up to six strands of No. 12 wire and five strands of No. 10 wire. Beyond that, go to $\frac{3}{4}$-in. conduit. All types of conduit are merely rigid coverings, initially without wire inside. The worker feeds in wires during installation.

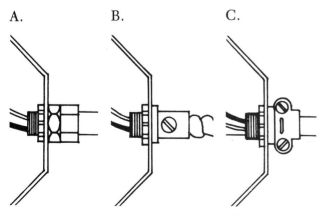

Figure 11.13 Connectors: (A) Metal conduit, (B) armored cable; (C) nonmetallic cable (Romex).

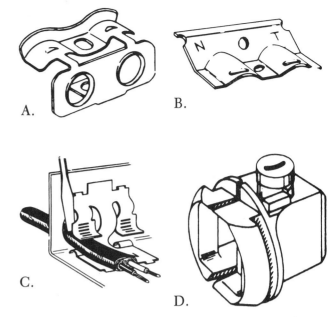

Figure 11.14 More connectors: A, B, and C usually come installed in boxes. (A) X clamp holds BX cable and conduit; (B) BN clamp for nonmetallic cable; (C) Q clamp for nonmetallic cable; (D) RACO plastic clamp for nonmetallic cable. (RACO, Inc.)

Knob-and-Tube Wiring. Knob-and-tube wiring (Figure 11.6) is no longer installed, but there's plenty of it still around in older houses. If its sheathing is intact and not cracked, it may still be serviceable. In exceptional situations, you may even be able to extend from it. But don't do the work yourself. Knob-and-tube is rather eccentric, requiring soldering, air gaps, and clamping. Have a licensed electrician make any modifications to it.

Boxes. The three basic types of electrical box are *octagonal, square,* and *switch.* By far the most common boxes, routinely used to enclose receptacles and switches, are switch boxes—also known as 2×4s, device boxes, work boxes, or wall boxes. Switch boxes can also be "ganged up" to create square boxes, as in Figure 11.24.

Octagonal boxes are used primarily for fixtures and, covered, as junction boxes. Square boxes, also known as 4×4s, frequently house two receptacles or switches and, with a cover, serve as junction boxes. A variety of accessories greatly extends the use of all boxes, however, and some renovators simplify matters by ordering mostly 4×4s and then using plaster rings to accommodate receptacles, switches, and the like.

The type of mounting bracket, bar, or tab you use depends on what you're mounting to: finish surfaces or structural members. Most mounting devices are available for all box types. Particularly useful are *remodel boxes* such as those shown in Figure 11.56, which allow you to mount boxes directly to finish surfaces; these are very handy when you're not tearing out walls or ceilings and so cannot nail off boxes to studs.

The size of the box is important, as well: too many wires in a box are unwieldy and unsafe and may occasionally cause short circuits. Table 11.4 shows acceptable numbers of conductors in differing box sizes.

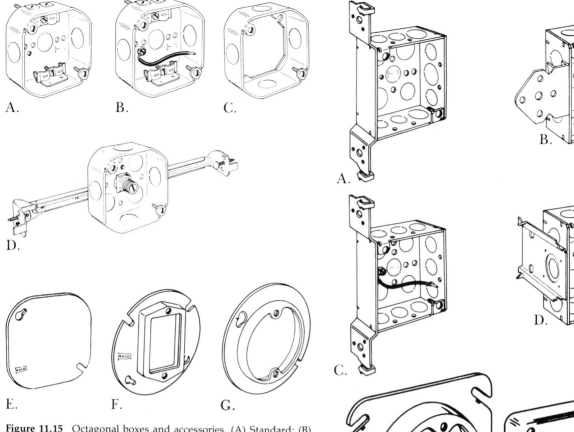

Figure 11.15 Octagonal boxes and accessories. (A) Standard; (B) standard with grounding pigtail; (C) extension ring; (D) setup box with adjustable bar hanger and fixture stud; (E) 4-in. round cover; (F) plaster ring for single device; (G) plaster ring, open. (RACO, Inc.)

Every wiring system—whether RX, BX, or conduit—has connectors specific to that system; use appropriate ones. These connectors do two things. They provide a mechanical connection of the cable to the box, so there will be no strain on electrical connections within the box. And, as important, connectors protect wires from burrs that may be present when a metal box's knockouts are removed.

A last and very important consideration when buying boxes is composition. In the last 10 years, plastic boxes have virtually supplanted metal ones in new construction. About one-third the cost of metal, plastic boxes are somewhat

Figure 11.16 Square boxes (4-in.) and accessories. (A) With FH-bracket (exceptionally sturdy); (B) with B-bracket (mounts on face of stud); (C) with FH-bracket and grounded pigtail; (D) with J-bracket; (E) plaster-ring cover, open; (F) raised cover for duplex receptacle and switch. (RACO, Inc.)

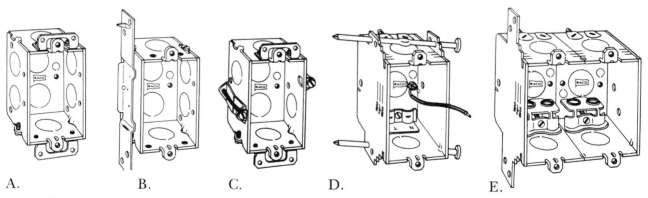

Figure 11.17 Switch boxes (3 in. × 2 in.). (A) Standard; (B) with FA-bracket; (C) Griptite box for old work; (D) with S-bracket and grounding pigtail; (E) ganged boxes with D-bracket.

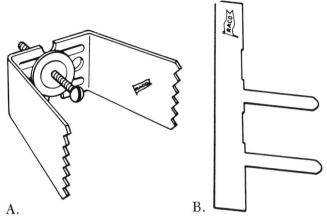

A.

B.

Figure 11.18 Old work accessories. (A) Switch-box support, also seen in Figure 11.56; (B) mounting tab (see Figure 11.57).

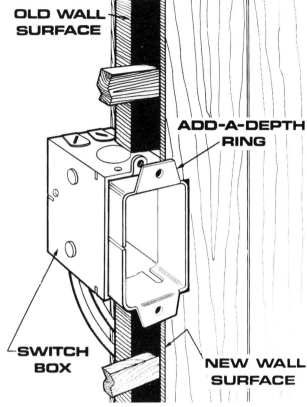

Figure 11.19 Add-a-depth ring for old work. (RACO, Inc.)

quicker to install because, being nonconductive, most of them needn't be grounded (although all *devices* must be grounded). Although most codes don't require attaching the wires mechanically to plastic boxes, there are bushings and integral hold-downs to minimize abrasion.

Plastic has some limitations, though: you can't use it to extend existing EMT or BX wiring, because plastic lacks the knockouts (and connectors) necessary to attach those systems. You can't gang plastic boxes either.

Fixtures, switches, receptacles, combinations. This section merely hints at the wide range of electrical components that are available; the essential ones, however, are covered.

Fixtures vary greatly, but most attach to an outlet box with two machine screws. Branch-circuit wires, in turn, attach to two screws (white wire to silver screw, black to brass screw) or to two color-coded lead wires from the fixture. The basic porcelain light fixture shown in Figure 11.29 is very versatile. The choice of bulbs and shades further extends decorating options.

A range of switches is available, including three-way, which control lights from two locations: four-way, which

control lights from three locations; and single-pole, with which most of us are familiar. A passing glance at even one group, single-pole switches, shows how varied its members are.

A simple toggle switch may vary according to the position or type of terminal. Or there may be no toggle switch at all; instead, touch pads turn the lights off and on. Rheostats allow you to dim lights gradually; they should be used, however, only for lights (appliances must have full

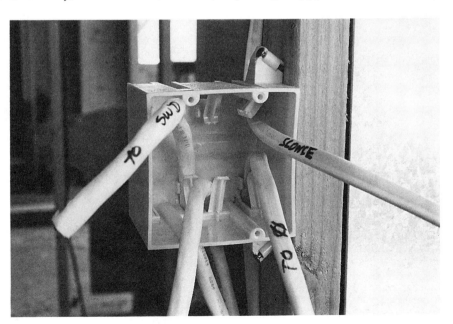

Figure 11.20 Double plastic box. Mark wires when you rough them in and you'll avoid confusion later.

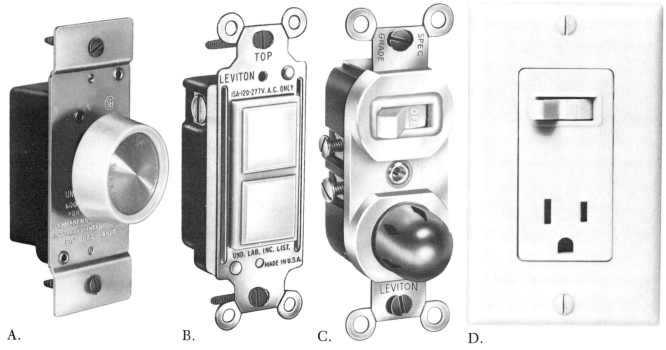

A.   B.   C.   D.

Figure 11.21 Specialty switches. (A) Rheostat; (B) touch pad; (C) pilot light; (D) receptacle combination. (Leviton)

power coming in, or they are likely to burn out). Among rheostats are ones for incandescent and fluorescent bulbs, three-way rheostats, and rheostats that change lighting intensity by finger pressure alone. To remind you to turn off basement or outside lights, there is a pilot-light-and-switch combination.

Some switches are linked to receptacles and fixtures, whereas others are designed to be space savers, fitting, for example, two switches in the space of one standard-size box. Before hooking up any exotic varieties, though, check the amperage rating of the switch and recalculate circuit loads; then add outlets.

Note, too, that many programmable switches take up more space in a workbox than does a standard duplex receptacle: place them in extra-deep switch boxes or in a 4 × 4 box with a 2 × 4 plaster ring.

Receptacles come in a similar diversity. Among the more useful ones are childproof models that require an adult's grip to uncover them; field receptacles, which combine cover and receptacle in one integral unit; recessed receptacles in which the wire from a clock can be hidden; and ground-fault circuit interrupters (GFCIs), demanded by Code where high humidity increases the chance of shock.

Figure 11.22 Waterproof boxes feature gaskets and snap covers; mounting tabs slide out from the back of the box. (RACO, Inc.)

Figure 11.23 A nice detail. The contractor built up a base from a piece of treated 2 × 6 and sank his weatherproof box in it. In so doing he raised the metal box above the runoff and created a surface to which he could butt siding. (Hoover Austin)

WIRING BASICS

Important: In the field, electricians refer to "new work" and "old work." "New work" refers not so much to new construction as to job sites where the framing is exposed and running wire is relatively easy. Thus, wiring a renovation with gutted walls is new work. "Old work" refers to situations where cables must be fished behind walls, and switch boxes mounted to finish surfaces. We note this distinction because in new work, cable is routinely run and connected to outlet boxes and devices—before being hooked up to the service panel. Thus there is no need to test wires to see if power's on, nor any danger of being shocked.

All basic wiring which follows assumes that cables are not hooked up. To work safely on existing circuits, disconnect power at the service panel, and verify with a voltage tester (p. 235).

Although Romex, BX, and EMT systems are physically different, their wiring configuration *within* outlets is essentially the same. Below, we refer to the most popular of these types, Romex, although the principles hold for all types. Specifics of BX and EMT are discussed toward the end of the section. Simplified, wiring goes like this:

1. Locate and mount boxes.
2. Drill holes, run cable, and staple it.
3. Strip cable sheathing, secure cables to boxes, and strip the insulation off individual wires.
4. Attach wires to receptacles, fixtures, switches, and the like. All connections must be housed in a box.

Boxes

Locating boxes. There are few set rules about locating boxes. In renovation, conform to what's already there. Wall receptacles are usually centered 12 in. above the finished floor, measuring from their midpoint, and spaced so that no point along a wall is more than 6 ft from a receptacle.

A.

B.

Figure 11.24 Alter boxes before mounting them. (A) Decide which knockouts to remove and pry them out with a screwdriver. (B) To gang boxes, simply remove one side from each box and use the screws provided to join sections.

A.

B.

Figure 11.25 Boxes in place. (A) Mount boxes to adjustable bars or blocking before nailing those mounting devices to studs. Nailing a box to an already placed block could loosen it. (B) To tighten connectors, turn their locknuts with the point of an old screwdriver; strike the handle of the screwdriver with the heel of your hand or with lineman's pliers.

Any wall section wider than 2 ft must have at least one receptacle.

Work counters wider than 12 in. should have receptacles set 2 to 5 in. above the surface, so that working on or cleaning up the counter won't affect electrical service. As prescribed by Code, receptacles near sinks or lavatories must be ground-fault circuit interrupters (GFCIs).

Wall switches are customarily centered 4 ft above the floor, on the lock side of the door (the side opposite the hinges). Wall boxes holding lighting fixtures are usually 6 ft above the floor, although this is a matter of personal taste rather than Code. Whatever height you choose, be consistent with outlets already there. Ceiling fixtures are roughly centered in a room, or over the area they illuminate.

Mounting boxes. Mount boxes before you run wiring. Boxes with integral mounting plates can be nailed up with 8d nails, or screwed up with $1\frac{5}{8}$-in. Type W drywall screws (if you're using a screw gun).

As you mount boxes, keep in mind the thickness of the finish material to follow. Ideally, hold a scrap of that material next to the front edge of the box, as a depth gauge. In drywall, boxes should be just slightly—no more than $\frac{1}{4}$ in.—below the surface; in wood paneling and other combustible surfaces, flush.

To attach fixture boxes in ceilings, you have three choices: (1) nailing the box directly to the side of a joist, (2) end-nailing a piece of blocking between joists and nailing the box to that, or (3) using an adjustable metal hanger bar between joists, to which the box is mounted. Whatever the method you choose, ceiling boxes must be secured to the structure, not merely to the finish ceiling, so that even a heavy fixture will be adequately supported. Mounting boxes is discussed further on page 261.

Working with Cable

Running cable. With the boxes in place, drill holes through studs or joists, to get the cable from one point to the next. Always try to connect two points with a continuous length of cable, for each time you join wires there's the chance they could come unjoined and short-circuit. Besides, joining wire takes time. Remember: *All* wire connections must be housed within a covered box.

Pulling wire through will be much easier if you measure and drill holes in a straight line (e.g., 6 in. down from top plates). Using a drill with a right-angle drive is also helpful, for it allows you to drill straight through the stud (or joist) without having to tilt the drill bit. Finally, have a helper pull cable as you feed it into holes.

A professional's tip for running RX: run it loosely, with a generous loop here and there. If you must move a box at some time, or you make a slight miscalculation when making connections, you can summon some of the extra wire to bail you out. Adding about 4 ft of cable to the measured distance between boxes usually allows enough extra. The section of cable that runs between the first outlet and the service panel should be especially generous, long enough to run to the opposite side of the panel from the knockout where the cable enters.

When running and securing Romex, however, be careful not to pinch it: NEC 336-10 advises that no bends in the cable have "a radius less than five times the diameter of the cable." Because RX is flexible, it must be supported along its run by stapling it to the sides of joists or studs, or, where it traverses open space wider than 24 in., it must be backed with a board.

When running Romex through holes in studs, the installer should take care that the edge of any hole be not less than $1\frac{1}{4}$ in. from the edge of the stud. If it is, the nearest edge of the stud should be reinforced with a steel nail-plate $\frac{1}{16}$ in. thick, to prevent finish-wall nails from puncturing the cable. Cables notched into studs must have similar protection.

Staple Romex every 4 ft or so, within 12 in. of a metal-box connection and within 8 in. of a plastic box. When stapling, hammer in the staples securely. Don't gouge the plastic sheathing, though.

Stripping and securing the cable. Cutting and connecting Romex is quite simple. Using a cable splitter, puncture the sheathing with the splitter's single tooth and pull the stripper down to the end of the cable. The tooth punctures the sheath but does not harm individual wires inside. Cut free the ripped section of sheathing with the cutting edge of pliers or with a pocketknife. Also cut free any kraft paper covering the wires inside. If you strip back the cable's sheathing at least 8 in., you will have exposed enough wire to proceed.

When it is apparent where wires will converge upon a box, knock out the exact number of openings in the box, one for each cable. (Some electricians prefer to do this before attaching the box to the stud.) Use a screwdriver point or a punch to start the knockout and a lineman's pliers to twist it free. If you remove too many knockouts, there are seals with which to plug the hole or holes.

Many boxes have connectors built in. There, merely pull out the knockout, slide the wires in, and tighten down the connector screw. Where no such clamps are provided, buy Romex connectors with threaded ends tightened with a locknut, as shown in Figure 11.25. Feed the stripped cable into the box so the still-intact sheathing just passes under the clamp of the Romex connector—the connector should not tighten down on individual, unsheathed wires.

With the wires thus secured to the box, you're ready to strip the insulation off individual wires and attach them to receptacles, fixtures, switches, and so on. Stripping the ends of the wires is easy with a multipurpose tool. Feed the wire into the appropriate jaw of the wire gauge; then squeeze the handles and rock the tool so it severs the wire's insulation. How much you strip depends on the attachment you are marking. If you are joining wires with wire nuts, strip each wire back about 1 in.; if attaching to receptacle or fixture screws, strip back $\frac{1}{2}$ to $\frac{3}{4}$ in. Back-wired receptacles have stripping gauges on the back, to show how much insulation to remove.

When the wire has been roughed-in to various outlets—but before being connected—call for an inspection, to be sure that it's safe to close up the walls. The next inspection comes after all devices have been wired.

Joining wires. All electrical connections must be housed in covered boxes. Where circuit cables diverge to receptacles, switches, and the like, they first join in junction boxes, perhaps the simplest connection on a circuit. But before looking at one, let's first clarify a few terms.

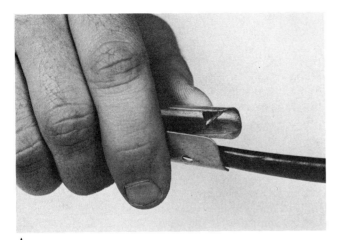

A.

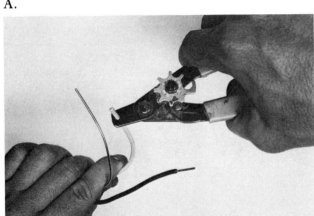

B.

C.

Figure 11.26 Stripping wire. (A) To sever the sheathing of nonmetallic cable, use a cable splitter; its tooth will not disturb the insulation of the individual wires within. (B) To strip individual wires, use a multipurpose tool or the small stripper shown, which employs a notched wheel to calibrate the opening of the cutting jaws. (C) Leave 6 to 8 in. of wire sticking out of the box so that you can make connections comfortably. The cable connector in the box, however, must clamp down a still-sheathed section of cable.

Cables running from the service panel to an outlet are called *source, from source,* or *upstream,* and they attach to GFCI leader wires marked "line." Cables running on to the next outlet (away from the power source) are denoted *next outlet* or *downstream,* and they attach to GFCI leaders marked "load."

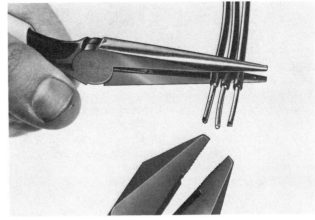

A.

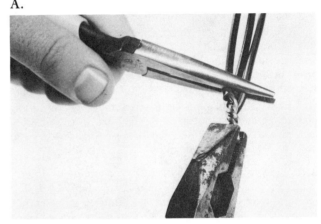

B.

C.

Figure 11.27 Joining wires with wire nuts. (A) Join only like wires: hot wires to hot wires, neutral to neutral, ground to ground. Strip insulation back $\frac{3}{4}$ to 1 in. and simply screw wire nuts on the grouped wires. (B) Or you can hold wires fast with needle-nosed pliers and twist them clockwise with lineman's pliers. (C) In either case, screw on the wire nuts and gently push each group into the box. Be sure that each wire nut completely covers all stripped wire ends before covering the junction box.

A splice in a junction box. We'll assume that three cables converge at a junction box, with one cable running toward the service panel. The other two cables are a single branch circuit that divides and serves parts of two floors. The cable, Romex 12/2 with ground, has been run and stapled to within 1 ft of the box.

Remove three knockouts from the box and add RX connectors. Where each cable will enter the box, strip back the cable's sheathing so about $\frac{1}{2}$ in. of it protrudes from beneath a Romex connector in the box. Tighten the connector until it grips the sheathed cable tightly; you should not be able to pull a clamped-down cable out of its box.

Next, group the three colors of wire—black to black, white to white, bared copper to bared copper—with a minimum tangling of colors. Give each group a gentle twist so each group stays together. Then snip individual wires so that wires, when bunched, are about the same length—4 to 6 in.

Strip about 1 in. of insulation off the end of each wire. Holding each group of wires together with a pair of pliers, twist on a wire nut until the nut is snug. Wire nuts are color-coded to indicate the number of wires they can join; but colors vary from one manufacturer to another. If you want to be especially careful, or if codes require it, wrap each group of insulated wires with electrical tape after the wire nut is on. Tape should not be used in place of wire nuts, however.

Wires can also be joined with a compression ring. Twist the wires together as described above; then crimp them together (using a crimping tool), with a compression ring around the wire group. Finally, place an insulating cap over the joined wires.

Grouping ground wires. To ensure a continuous ground, wire-nut or crimp together bared copper wires and then ground them to the metal box. (Ground-wire clusters are grounded to all metal boxes, regardless of the device they house.) To ground the cluster to the box, add a short *pigtail* of wire to the ground-wire group. This pigtail can be a piece of regular wire that you snip off for the purpose, or you can purchase precut grounding wire. Some boxes come with a pigtail already attached, as shown in the materials section. Join the pigtail to the box with a screw (there is a threaded hole beside the UL stamp in boxes) or with a grounding clip. Another method of grounding the cluster is the "Canadian method," in which one ground wire is left longer than the others; the wires are twisted, and the longest wire is screwed directly to the box, without the aid of a wire nut or a pigtail.

When all three wire groups have been secured, look closely to make sure that no bunch of insulated wires has any bare wire visible. Nest each group of wires in the box and screw on a metal cover plate, to protect the splices.

Testing for short circuits. If you are careful about clamping down incoming cables on the section still sheathed, and you take pains to prevent any insulated wires from touching the metal box, shorts are unlikely. Occasionally, a short occurs, however, and here's how you locate it.

Figure 11.28 Grounding accessories. *From left to right,* screw, pigtail with screw, grounding clip (attaches to side of box). (RACO, Inc.)

Before hooking up receptacles, go around to all boxes and temporarily connect all wires that would be linked at switches or at receptacles (e.g., black to black, white to white); but do *not* connect wires that would meet at a power user (i.e., do not connect hot to neutral). Just connect wires gently with tape or wire nuts; these are only temporary connections. Keep all wires except ground wires from touching the boxes.

Using a *continuity tester,* touch one probe to a box or to a ground wire and one to the exposed end of a white wire; then do the same with a ground wire and a black wire. If the tester (which has its own batteries) lights up, you have a short circuit. By moving along the circuit and disengaging some of the temporary connections as you go, you can isolate the trouble spot. Often, the short will be caused by a wire being nicked where it enters a box.

Note: This testing is done *before* the circuit cable has been attached to the service panel. Once the circuit has been connected at the service panel, you can also ascertain that it is correctly wired; use a *plug-in tester* (p. 241). Everyone should own this handy little device: simply plug it into a three-prong receptacle and it tells you instantly—red or green bulbs light—exactly what's right or wrong with your circuit.

Attaching Fixtures

Attaching a single incoming cable to the terminals of a fixture is quite simple and it provides a good opportunity to look at attaching wire to screw terminals. As before, secure the box to a joist or a stud; run, staple, and strip cable and clamp it with Romex connectors to the box. Strip the insulation off individual wires to about $\frac{3}{4}$ in. Ground the bared wire to the box with a pigtail, while also running a pigtail to a grounding screw on the fixture, if there is one.

Figure 11.29 On the underside of many fixtures are two screws: a brass one to which a hot wire connects, and a silver one to which a neutral wire connects. There may be insulated wire leads instead of screw terminals, coded black (hot) and white (neutral). (Leviton)

With needle-nosed pliers, twist the exposed ends of the white and the black wires in a semicircle. Attach the black wire to the brass-colored screw on the fixture, and the white wire to the silver screw. Feed a twisted wire end onto a screw so the *clockwise* tightening of the screw will grab the wire. Pinch each wire once it is around the screw, and the screw will tighten down without the wire slipping off. Then screw the base of the fixture to the outlet box with the two machine screws provided.

Where a light fixture comes with two stranded leader wires rather than screw terminals, use wire nuts to join the leaders to incoming wires. Because leader wires are finer than incoming wires, you should strip leader ends a little longer so that both will seat correctly when the nuts are applied.

Fixture wiring that is more complex is shown in the switch-wiring schematics that follow. If you intend to have fixtures in walls not yet framed out, allow a long lead of cable to feed the outlet when roughing in the wiring.

Attaching Receptacles

Here, we'll discuss 120-volt receptacles: 240-volt receptacles are covered in the last section of this chapter. There are two kinds of mechanical connections to receptacles, screws and back-wiring holes. Receptacles with screw terminals require that individual wires be stripped of insulation $\frac{3}{4}$ in. from the end of the wire and looped with needle-nosed pliers, as described above.

The second type of attachment, back-wiring, requires stripping the ends of individual wires to the length specified on the back of the device. The stripped wire ends are then fed into holes in the back of the receptacle, where they are held by springlike clamps. To release wires thus secured, insert a screwdriver point in the slot provided. Check the wire rating of such devices: because some back-holes are sized for No. 12 wire, they may not grip No. 14 tightly enough. Another variation has both back holes and screw terminals. Be sure that screws are turned down before placing the receptacle in the outlet box—even if you insert wires in the back holes.

As described above, black wires connect to brass-colored screws and white wires to silver-colored screws. All modern types of receptacles should also have green grounding screws, and they should receive three-pronged plugs. Many older receptacles lack such features.

Receptacles in midcircuit. A receptacle in midcircuit has at least two cables which enter its box, one from the power source and one that runs to the next outlet. With a cable stripper, strip the sheathing from each cable, then secure cables to the box, using Romex connectors. Strip the insulation from individual wires.

There are two methods for wiring receptacles in midcircuit. In both, you group, strip, and wire-nut wires of the same color; then ground boxes and devices with short pigtails running from the ground-wire group.

In the first method, as depicted in Figures 11.31A, 11.33A, 11.34A, you also run pigtails from hot and neutral groups to receptacle terminals. In this manner, you attach only one wire to each side of the device—which is adequate; *and* (this is the point that appeals to purists) you ensure the continuity of power to outlets downstream no matter what. This is the method approved by Code.

The second method, as depicted in Figures 11.31B, 11.33B, and 11.34B, is probably the more widespread of the two—in part because it's quicker, requires fewer wire nuts, and takes up less room in the box. Here, power is through-wired through the device: incoming wires from the source attach to one pair of terminals on the receptacle, outgoing wires to the other pair. This method's detractors point out that should wires work loose or the device fail, power would be interrupted to outlets downstream.

Whichever method you choose, the receptacle is generally set with its green ground screw up. Finally, to belabor the point somewhat, it doesn't matter whether the source wire is attached to the bottom or the top set of screws; just don't mix colors.

When all wires are connected, gently shove the entire complex in the box, so the wires "crumple" like an accordion. Take care that no bare wires or screw terminals touch the sides of the box. (The ground wire, of course, may

A.

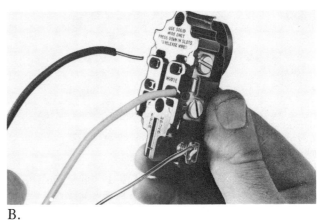

B.

Figure 11.30 Wiring receptacles. (A) When a box is crowded and the screw terminals of a receptacle might short against the sides of a box, wrap electrician's tape around the side of the device. Although rarely required by Code, this is a preventive measure. (B) Wires fed into back-wired devices should be stripped according to the strip gauge on the back. Give each wire a gentle tug to make sure that it's clamped tightly.

Figures 11.31–11.47 WIRING SCHEMATICS. The following section contains wiring schematics for receptacles, switches, and fixtures. "Source" refers to the cable running from the power source (e.g., from the entrance panel); "next outlet" refers to cable continuing to the next outlet downstream (i.e., away from the source).

In these figures, neutral wires are coded white, and ground wires are represented as single lines. Hot wires are coded black, striped (for red), and crosshatched (for a third hot wire) in the rare instance where you'd use four-wire cable. White wires whose ends are painted black are being used as hot wires, as explained in the text.

Although ground-wire leads to fixtures and switches are not indicated in the figures below, make such connections if the devices have grounding terminals.

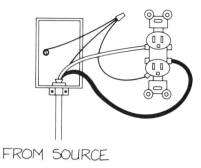

FROM SOURCE

Figure 11.32 Receptacle at the end of a circuit.

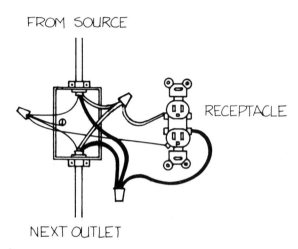

A.

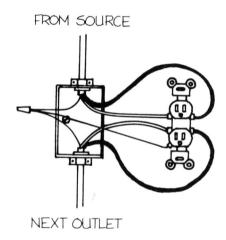

B.

Figure 11.31 Receptacles in the middle of a circuit: The first method (A) is preferred by Code. The second example (B) requires fewer wire nuts, but should one of the wires slip off a terminal, you'd lose power downstream.

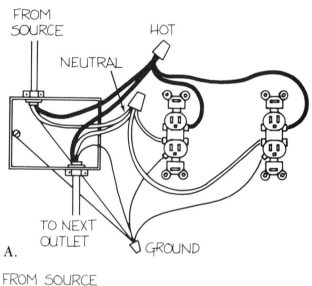

A.

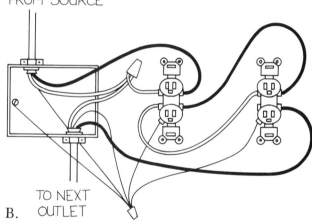

B.

Figure 11.33 Double receptacles in the middle of a circuit: The first method (A) is preferred by Code. As with Figure 11.31A, part A has additional wire nuts to ensure continuity of power downstream. Always wire-nut neutral and ground wires to ensure their continuity. House such configurations in ganged switch boxes or 4-in. square boxes. Check Table 11.4 to be sure that the box is big enough.

touch the box, since it's grounded to the box.) Push the receptacle in by hand; if you use the screws to pull the receptacle into place, there is a good chance of stripping the threads on the screw or the box. When the finish wall surface is in place, attach a cover plate over the receptacle.

If the cable is BX, hooking up receptacles is slightly different, because the metal cable may serve as the continu-

ous ground. (Figure 11.52). In that case, a single pigtail grounds the receptacle to the box. BX cables that contain a distinct ground wire within connect as described above, clustering ground wires with wire nuts.

Receptacles at the ends of circuits. A receptacle at the end of a circuit has only one cable entering the box; there are no outlets beyond that point. Where only two wires attach to a receptacle, it is common practice to stagger the wires as shown rather than, say, to attach them to the top set of screws (although either way is acceptable).

Doubling up receptacles. Where fixtures or appliances are clustered, it's sometimes convenient to double up receptacles—house two of them in a single 4 × 4 box or in two switch boxes ganged together. Consult Table 11.4 to make sure that the box is big enough. Applying the table's formula to the *conductors* in Figure 11.33, there would be seven: two hot wires, two neutral wires, two receptacles, and the cluster of ground wires counting as one conductor. Jumper wires between receptacles and pigtails are not counted because they begin and end inside the box.

Because of the number of conductors in a tight space, use insulated wires as grounding pigtails, to prevent a ground wire's accidentally touching a terminal when the receptacles are pushed into the box.

A.

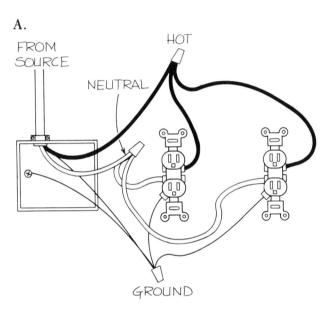

B.

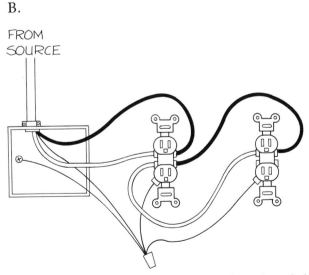

Figure 11.34 Two ways to wire double receptacles at the end of a circuit. Again, the first method (A) is preferred by Code.

GFCI Receptacles

Ground-fault circuit interrupters (GFCIs), first discussed on page 234, are required in bathroom circuits, above kitchen counters within 6 ft of the sink, outdoors, in accessible garage locations, in the basement (at least one), and in other high-risk areas. GFCIs are available as portable plug-in units, circuit breakers, and receptacles. We are concerned here with receptacles; for wiring GFCI circuit breakers, see p. 267.

GFCI receptacles are a wonderfully cost-effective way to make your electrical system safer. For starters, they cost $10 to 15, compared to $70 to 80 for a GFCI circuit breaker. Because hot and neutral wires are routed through the GFCI, the device protects not only the outlet in which it's installed, but all other outlets downstream.

GFCI receptacles are particularly well suited to renovation, for they upgrade a previously unprotected circuit from the point of installation. In short, you don't have to run a new cable back to the panel. Speaking of which, if your entrance panel has fuses rather than breakers, GFCI receptacles are literally the only way to go. Finally, if a cold-water pipe is close enough to run a ground wire to, you can add GFCI protection even to circuits that presently lack ground wires. More about that in a bit.

Hooking up GFCI receptacles. Read the manufacturer's instructions very carefully: your warranty—and your safety—depend on proper installation. Note too that GFCIs are amperage rated, so that they should match the capacity of the fuse or breaker controlling the circuit. As with all work in this section, shut off power to the circuit you're working on and test to be sure before proceeding.

Because you'll need to know which incoming cables are *line* wires (from the power source) and which are *load* wires (running on to the next outlet), disconnect the old receptacle while the power is off and separate wires from each other. Turn the power back on and use your voltage tester (p. 235) to determine which pair of wires are ''line.'' That done, turn the power off again.

Most GFCI receptacles have wire leaders, although some have screw terminals. Attach the wires running from the power source to the leaders marked ''line''; attach wires continuing to the next outlet to the leaders marked ''load''; and attach ground wires to the leader marked ''ground,'' and to the pigtail that grounds the box. If there are no outlets downstream, use wire nuts to cap the two load leaders.

When connections are completed, mount the receptacle in its outlet box, turn the power back on, and test the GFCI by pressing its ''on'' or test button, per instructions. If the device won't stay on or devices downstream don't work, you have either a short circuit or a defective GFCI which should be returned. Most makers recommend testing the devices once a month. All GFCI receptacles used outdoors should be housed in gasketed, weatherproof boxes with covers.

Attaching to ungrounded wiring. GFCIs can add protection to presently ungrounded circuits if there is a cold-water pipe nearby. The pipe must be bare metal (not painted). To the pipe, clamp a ground wire of the same diameter as

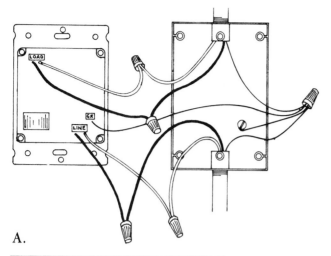

A.

B.

Figure 11.35 GFCI receptacles, (A) GFCI (ground-fault circuit interrupter) receptacles are required in high-moisture areas. Since such devices have lead wires rather than screw terminals, use the wire nuts provided to make mechanical connections to the receptacle. Wires coming from the power source connect to leads marked "line" on the back of the GFCI; wires running to the next outlet connect to lead wires marked "load"; there is a separate lead for ground wires, coded green. (B) An outdoor GFCI receptacle with a gasketed cover.

the individual circuit wires; if there is a valve on the cold-water line, you must also clamp a jumper wire across the valve to ensure the continuity of the ground. (Grounding clamps and jumpers are shown in Figure 11.4.)

This ground wire attaches to the "ground" lead from the GFCI device, to the pigtail grounding the device to the box, and to ground wires running on to outlets downstream. *Important:* Since this is an ungrounded system, you will have to add ground wires to outlets down the line—otherwise, they won't be adequately protected. If there are several outlets downstream that you want to protect, it may make sense to gut the walls; in which case, consider running a new cable protected by a GFCI breaker in the entrance panel.

Final note: Some old cable sheathing gets so frayed that it leaks current, which will continually trigger GFCIs, rendering them useless. Replace such wiring.

Attaching Switches

On the following pages are numerous variations on switch wiring, some of which are complex. The underlying principle of any switch, however, is that it interrupts the flow of current through a hot wire or hot wires and through hot wires only, for neutral wires are always continuous; they are never interrupted. Whether the switch controls a receptacle, fixture, or appliance, hot wires only are interrupted by attachment to the terminals of a switch.

The simplest switching situation involves a single-pole switch. Two cables run into a switch box and are stripped and clamped, as described above. Twist ground wires together and attach them to the box with a grounding pigtail. If the switch has a green grounding screw, run a jumper from the screw to the ground-wire bunch. Join white wires together with a wire nut. Finally, strip individual black wires and attach them to the switch's screws. Although it makes little difference which black wire is attached to which screw, install the switch with the manufacturer's name at the top; that way, the toggle will be in the correct position.

A.

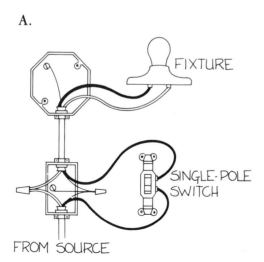

B.

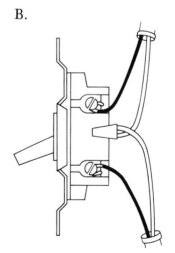

Figure 11.36 Fixture at the end of a circuit. (A) Power from the source enters the switch box and is controlled by a single-pole switch. (B) The neutral is continuous, as is the ground wire.

A slight variation on this setup sometimes occurs when the switch is physically beyond the outlet, that is, when the outlet box is closer to the power source than to the switch box. Figure 11.37 shows a fixture thus situated. In this case, the neutral (white) wire from the power source is connected directly to the fixture, and the ground wires are clustered and wire-nutted. The hot wire from the source, however, the one that should be "interrupted" by the switch, is nutted (without being attached to the fixture) to a wire leading to the switch.

Here, for convenience, we break our rule of using the white wire only as a neutral wire, and instead tape each end of the white wire black, to show that is hot. At the switch, attach the black wire and the white wire taped black to the switch screws. We run the cable in this manner purely for our own convenience, to serve as a *switch loop*. Thus, painting the white wire black is a breach of the rule

in letter only, because both wires are hot. We still have not mixed actual hot and neutral wires.

Note: In the schematics shown for switch wiring, there are not always ground wires running to fixture bases or to switches, for the simple reason that not all such devices have grounding screws on their bodies. If there are such screw terminals for grounding, attach to them via a pigtail from the ground-wire bunch. You should, however, ground to *every* box, with a pigtail from the ground-wire bunch.

A.

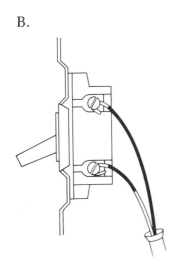

B.

Figure 11.37 Fixture at the end of a circuit. (A) Here, the power enters through the fixture box. The neutral wire connects directly to the fixture, but the hot wire is routed to a switch beyond. (B) For convenience, use the white wire of a two-wire cable as one of the hot wires running to the switch. *Tape the ends of the white wire black* to show that it's being used as a hot wire.

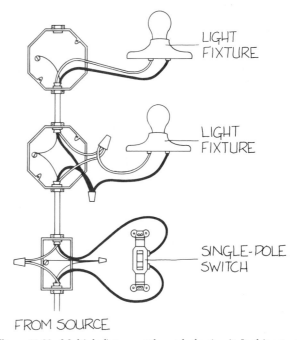

Figure 11.38 Multiple fixtures at the end of a circuit. In this setup, the switch controls all the lights beyond it.

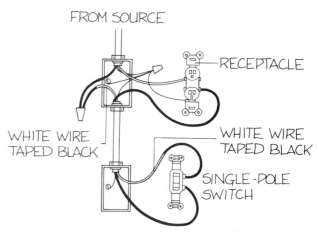

Figure 11.39 Receptacle at the end of a circuit. This receptacle is controlled by a switch beyond it. The incoming neutral wire attaches directly to the receptacle, but the hot wire is routed to the switch. Note that the white wire used as a hot wire is taped black.

As you will note in the largely pictorial section that follows, switch wiring becomes more complex, especially when three- and four-way switches require cable with three and four wires. If you become confused, redraw the setups yourself, clearly identifying hot wires with an "H," neutral wires with an "N," and so on. Tell yourself at each junction, "The neutral wires are continuous: the hot wires are interrupted by switches."

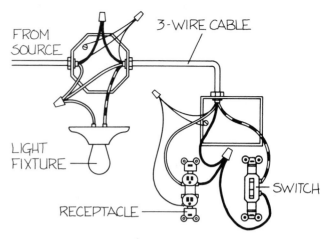

Figure 11.42 Fixture and receptacle at the end of a circuit. For convenience, use a three-wire cable between the fixture box and the other two devices. The switch controls the fixture; the receptacle is always hot.

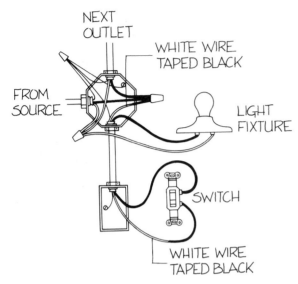

Figure 11.40 Fixture in the middle of a circuit. The switch controls the light fixture only; outlets beyond are always hot.

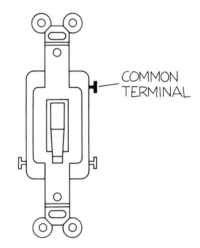

Figure 11.43 Three-way switch. Three-way switches control power from two locations. The switch has two brass screws and a black screw called the "common terminal." The hot wire from the source attaches to the common terminal, and the wire running from the second (three-way) switch to the fixture attaches to the common terminal of the second switch.

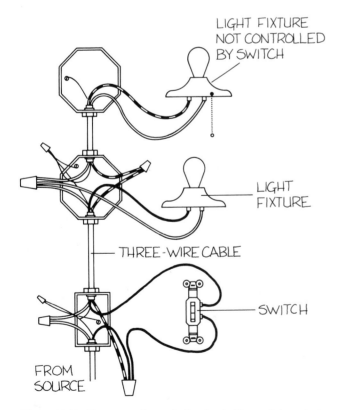

Figure 11.41 Fixtures at the end of a circuit. The switch controls the nearest fixture, but not the one beyond.

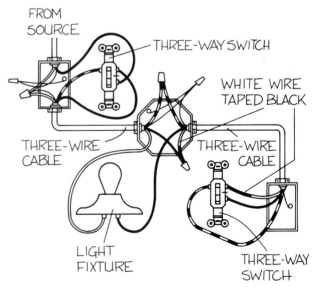

Figure 11.44 Three-way switching. This fixture is controlled by two three-way switches. Use two lengths of three-wire cable here.

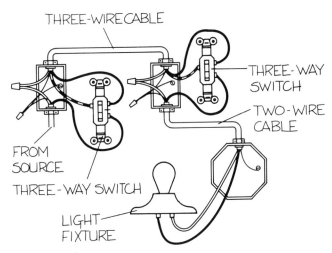

Figure 11.45 Three-way switching. Again, a fixture at the end of a circuit.

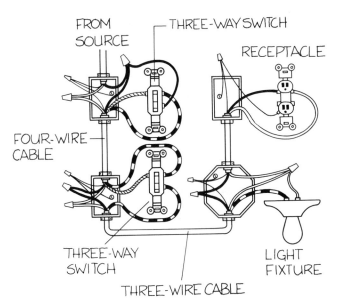

Figure 11.47 Three-way switching. In this example, the two switches control the light fixture while the receptacle is always hot. Although three-wire cable is convenient between the second switch and the fixture, the run between the two switches can be handled best by four-wire cable (which may be hard to obtain), or by two lengths of two-wire cable.

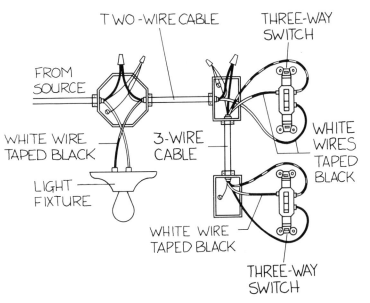

Figure 11.46 Three-way switching. Here, both three-way switches are beyond the light fixture.

Rigid Conduit and Armored Cable (BX)

Where wire is susceptible to damage, Code specifies rigid conduit or armored BX cable. Run it through metal studs, for example, where the wires might gall and short out, where wire runs above the surface and could get tugged or crushed, or where moisture might be hazardous (conduit only). Wiring to devices is largely the same as it is for Romex, except that the metal sheathing of conduit or cable acts as its own ground.

Metal conduit. The two major types of rigid metal conduit are EMT, or thin-walled conduit, and IMC, which is sturdier. The fittings are essentially the same for both, although IMC is intended for industrial use. Both are approved for exterior wiring, when installed with a weatherproof compression fitting, a metal split-ring compression bushing that tightens when you turn down the outermost nut onto the EMT pipe itself. All boxes must also be gasketed to keep moisture out.

Because conduit comes without wires inside, you must pull wire through it. Although wire can usually be pushed easily through straight lengths of conduit 10 ft or less, fish tape is necessary to run wire around bends or through longer lengths.

First, use conduit big enough for the number of wires you need to pull: $\frac{1}{2}$-in. conduit will suffice for most runs of No. 12 wire; $\frac{3}{4}$-in. will do for heavier wires, such as No. 8 or No. 6, needed for stoves and such. Check your local code. Using *pulling compound*, also called pulling lube, will make the task easier, as will having one person to feed wire and one to pull. THHN wire, whose coating is especially slick, is often specified when pulling is necessary. To prevent wires from pulling off, bend them tightly over the end of the fish tape, and wrap well with plastic electrical tape.

In general, thread wire after you've attached conduit to boxes. If conduit bends more than 180 degrees between two boxes, you'll need a *pull box* in the middle of the run, through which wires can be pulled. (These pull boxes are not junction boxes, however, because the wire remains uncut; such boxes just give you access to the middle of the run.) Other than the usual insulated screwdrivers and pliers, only a few special tools are needed to work conduit. The first is a *conduit bender*, which slides over the conduit; rock the bender gently until the desired curve is attained. For $\frac{1}{2}$-in. EMT conduit, a radius of about $5\frac{1}{2}$ in. is usual for a 90-degree bend. The bender will have arrows, which indicate turning radiuses. The other tool is a hacksaw for cutting pipe. For EMT conduit, however, a plumber's pipe cutter leaves a much smoother, squarer cut. Any burrs that result from the cutting must be reamed with a pipe reamer or a *deburring tool*; otherwise, the burrs can puncture the insulation of the wires.

For conduit that is routed over finish surfaces, attach it every 5 ft or so, and within 1 ft of box connections. Connections within boxes are essentially the same as those for Romex cable, the principal difference being that the conduit itself, because it is metal, provides the grounding. To

A.

C.

B.

D.

Figure 11.48 EMT (thinwall) rigid conduit is a complete system, with matched connectors to boxes (A) and couplings (B) to join straight lengths. Because the conduit itself acts as the ground, it is imperative that all mechanical connections be sound. To bend conduit, use a hickey (C). Surface-mounted conduit should be attached every 4 ft with straps, and within 1 ft of boxes (D).

ground individual outlets, run a grounding pigtail from the grounding screw on the device to the box itself.

Armored cable (BX). BX cable is commonly used in old work, and it satisfies most code requirements. In addition to its use in branch circuits, BX is used to protect short sections of exposed appliance wire. Don't use BX in moist or wet areas, however, because its metal armor can rust.

There are three ways to cut BX cable, and two of them take some practice. Method one requires looping and bunch-

ing the cable so the metal sheathing puckers; snip through the pucker with metal shears or diagonal-nosed pliers, being careful not to nick the insulated wires inside. Method two takes a hacksaw cut diagonally across the sheathing: cut, twist the cable and finish the cut with metal shears. Method three uses a Roto-Split, which cuts through sheathing with a hand-cranked cutting wheel; it's a great tool (p. 241).

You should rough-cut lengths of BX about 2 ft longer than the distance from box to box. Then, using one of the

Figure 11.49 It's much easier to pull cable if you have drilled holes at the same height.

methods above, carefully remove the metal sheathing from each end to expose about 8 in. of the insulated wire within.

When you have snipped through the sheathing, rip free the kraft paper surrounding the wires. To keep the severed sheath from cutting into the plastic insulation of individual wires, slide a small plastic (or fiber) bushing between the wires and the metal sheath. Use bushings at all cuts.

Because BX is flexible, support it every 4 ft along its run and within 1 ft of box connections. Staples should be snug, but should not crimp the armor. The most common method of attaching the cable is to staple it to the underside or to the sides of joists, where it runs parallel. Where the cable runs perpendicular, drill $\frac{5}{8}$-in. holes through the center of studs or joists.

Note: Although the sheathing of the cable is metal, it can still be punctured by finish nails when the cable is closer than $1\frac{1}{4}$ in. to the edge of the stud. For that reason, cables near the edge of the studs should be protected with $\frac{1}{16}$-in.-thick nail guards (which are also used to protect Romex cable).

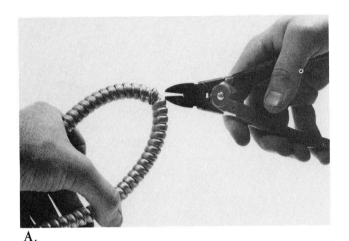

A.

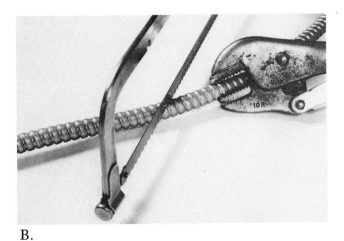

B.

Figure 11.50 The easiest way to cut through BX cable is with a Roto-Split tool (Figure 11.11). Lacking that tool, you can bunch the cable and carefully snip through the puckered cable (A) with diagonal-nose pliers. Or you can hold the cable fast and saw diagonally through it with a hacksaw (B).

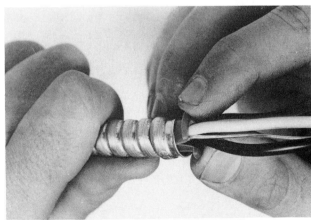

Figure 11.51 Once you have cut through the BX metallic sheathing, slide a plastic or fiber bushing over individual wires so that they won't be galled by metal spurs.

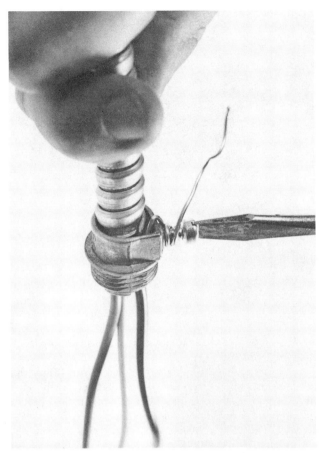

Figure 11.52 Because the metallic sheathing of BX is its own ground, it carries only a small bonding strip—instead of a copper ground wire. Because the real bond to a box comes when a locknut scores its surface, you can wrap the bonding strip once around the connector screw as shown, or simply wrap the strip back around the outside of the cable.

The cable's entry into a box is particularly important when working with BX. As noted above, the end of the cable must be protected by a plastic bushing. After you slip the plastic sheathing over the cut end of the BX, pull back the thin *bonding strip* inside the cable, wrap it loosely around the outside of the cable, then tighten down a BX connector over the end. This bonding strip is not a true ground wire, but by wrapping it around the outside of the cable, you enhance grounding. The bonding strip may also be wrapped one turn around the BX connector screw. The real grounding of cable to box comes, however, when you tighten the lock nut of the connector, scoring the metal.

EXTENDING CIRCUITS

Extending an existing circuit can be an effective way to add outlets, but it requires three important preparatory steps. (1) Check with local code authorities: some codes, for example, do not allow extensions to circuits that are insufficiently grounded. (2) Review the load calculations on page 239 to make sure that you don't exceed the ampacity of the circuit—or the panel. (3) **Shut off the power** to the circuit and test all the outlets—including switches—with a voltage tester (p. 235) before you begin.

Locating New Outlets

Begin with a few questions: Where do you want new outlets? What's the closest live outlet from which you could draw power? What studs, joists, or other framing might be in the way enroute?

To locate the nearest live outlet you could tap into, think spatially, for that outlet may be out of sight, on the other side of a partition, or in the ceiling. Here, circuit maps (p. 240) are helpful. Any outlet is a likely candidate as long as it is live all the time, that is, not controlled by a switch upstream (toward the service panel).

Next, figure out how you'll run new cable from that outlet. The best way is the least disruptive. Routing wires between studs and joists is the most common method, but consider also voids around stairwells, along ducts, or behind door casing.

Another good place to hide cable is behind baseboards. To accommodate the thickness of the cable, you can chisel a shallow slot along the face of studs, dado the back of the baseboard if it's thick enough, or build up the baseboard so that it sticks farther out from the wall. But whatever method you choose, be careful not to nail through cable when you reattach the trim: many codes require nail-protection plates.

For most extensions, however, you'll have to disturb finish surfaces, as in Figure 11.53. Cut out small squares of plaster or drywall; fish cables; and then patch, as shown in Chapter 15. The key to success is knowing where studs and joists are, so you disturb existing surfaces as little as possible. The trickiest part is drilling through top plates of walls: use a $\frac{3}{4}$-in. bit, held as flat to the wall as possible.

Fishing Wire

To run a cable from an existing outlet to a new one, first shut off the power at the service panel. Then remove both the device and the outlet box. This will mean disturbing the

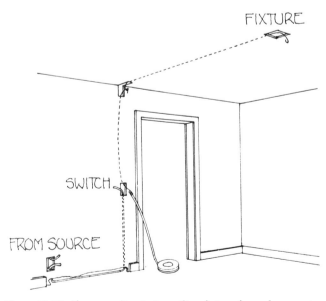

Figure 11.53 If you can't get at a ceiling fixture from above, cut into finish surfaces where the wall meets the ceiling. This will likely mean chiseling into the top plate.

finish surface a bit, because the box will likely be nailed to a stud. To control damage, use a reciprocating saw to cut around the box, being careful not to cut cable wires. Patch-repair this hole before replacing the work box. (It's theoretically possible to fish wires without removing the box, but it's a waste of time. Besides, you can't add cable connectors to a box hidden in a wall.) Cut out a hole where the new outlet will go, as shown in Figure 11.54.

Then drill through obstructions (subflooring, sole plates, etc.) between the two locations, using a $\frac{7}{8}$- to 1-in. bit at least 8 in. long: a hole this width is necessary because the wrapped end of the cable is bulkier than cable alone.

Fishing wires is easiest with a helper. As one person feeds metal *fish tape* down into an outlet cutout, the second person, with another fish tape, tries to catch the first. That accomplished, the first tape is pulled through, to have electrical cable attached to it. Fold cable wires tightly over the fish tape, and wrap well with electrical tape. For each obstruction you encounter, you must again catch fish tapes and reattach the cable until, finally, you reach the cutout for the new outlet.

A.

B.

Figure 11.54 Adding a box. (A) To position a box on an existing surface, trace around the box or a template of one. Receptacles are usually centered 12 in. above floors, switches, 48 in. high. (B) The sharp point of a keyhole saw allows cutting without first drilling starter holes.

Because it's difficult to know exactly how long the cable must be, run a generous amount: there should be at least 1 ft of free wire protruding from each box. Where cable is exposed, staple it every 4 ft along its run, and within 12 in. of outlets, if possible.

Mounting Boxes in Existing Surfaces

Remodel boxes have special mounting devices that hold boxes fast to finish surfaces; the most common is shown in Figure 11.56. Keep in mind that boxes must be big enough to accommodate the number of conductors entering, per Table 11.4.

Wall boxes. Note the height of other outlets, and place new ones at the same, or a similar, height. Trace the outline of the box on a stiff piece of cardboard to make a template; otherwise, trace around the box itself. In the outline, include any ears that stick out from the box.

If the surface is drywall, there are several tools that can cut through it easily. A utility knife takes numerous passes but will do the job. A keyhole saw also works well; jab its sharp tip through the drywall to start the hole. By tilting a saber saw or a reciprocating saw blade gradually into the wall, you do not need to drill starter holes first. For power saws, use a plaster-cutting blade (usually coded white).

To cut through plaster, it is advisable to start cuts at the box's corners, using a drill. Then ease a plaster-cutting blade into the holes. Because plaster is somewhat delicate, you should take it slow when drilling and cutting, so as not to crack the finish around the opening. Some renovators bind the outline with masking tape to further deter cracking while cutting. If you find that the lath behind the plaster is metal, use a fine-toothed metal-cutting blade, and proceed slowly.

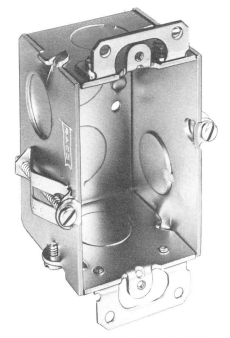

Figure 11.55 A Griptite box works in any hollow wall. Hold the box's ears (at top and bottom) flat against the wall while you turn the screws on either side, thus expanding its anchors. (RACO, Inc.)

Before putting the new box in the hole you should remove the knockout slugs, strip the sheathing off the cable ends, feed cable into the box, and secure it with Romex connectors or the clamps provided in the box.

Attachment varies among box types. *Spring-clip* types are the simplest: to draw Griptite boxes to the finish surface, tighten screws to extend the ears on either side. *Mounting tabs* slip into the space between the box and the edge of the hole; pull them tight against the wall and bend

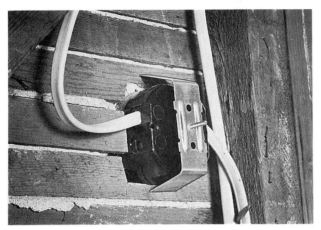

Figure 11.56 Seen from behind: a spring-metal support holds this switch box fast to the back of a plaster wall.

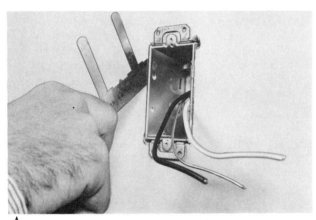

.A.

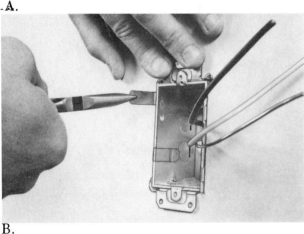

B.

Figure 11.57 (A) Slip mounting tabs into the space between a box and the edge of an opening. (B) Holding the ears of the box flush to the wall, pull the tabs forward and fold them flat into the box.

the tabs into the box, using pliers. Flatten the tabs so that they cannot touch any terminal screw of the outlet. For good measure, wrap the body of the outlet with electrical tape, as shown in Figure 11.30.

Ceiling fixtures. Mounting ceiling fixtures is more complex than mounting wall boxes, primarily because the weight of most fixtures precludes surface mounting the outlet box as you might with a switch box. Instead, you must hang the fixture box from a hanger bar, bracket, or blocking securely attached to structural members. The details of attachment thus depend on (1) access to structural members, (2) the weight of the fixture, and (3) the composition of the finish surface, whether it is plaster, drywall, or another material.

Safety note: Where ceilings are insulated, insulation must be physically held back 3 to 6 in. from recessed electrical cans or outlet boxes, to prevent heat buildup and breakdown of the insulation of the incoming cable wires. This is important because wires feeding the can are not as well insulated against heat as wires within the can.

Unfinished Floor Above. If the floor above a proposed ceiling fixture is not a finished one, your task is relatively easy: remove a section of the flooring and mount a hanger bar between the joists. Begin by drilling a small exploratory hole up from underneath, roughly indicating where you would like to mount the fixture. Insert a bent coat hanger in the hole and twirl it, to locate the joists. By using a long exploratory bit (Figure 3.13), you can drill up through the unfinished floor above and quickly locate the best board to remove. If you can do so easily, pry up the entire floorboard above, using a utility bar and a cat's paw. If that isn't practicable, cut back the board to the nearest joist-centers.

An adjustable hanger bar is a versatile mounting device: it extends to fit the space between joists. If your proposed outlet is near a joist, consider nailing a side-mounting box directly to the joist. That mount, however, is much less strong than a bar which nails to two joists.

Ideally, the box should be centered between two joists, but an approximation will do. Mount the box to the hanger bar and slide it along the bar until you are satisfied with the placement. Hold the assembly in place between the joists and trace around the box onto the backside of the finish ceiling. Drill tiny pilot holes in the corners of the outline, then go below and cut out the outline from the finish side. (If you cut from above, you will get a ragged cut on the finish side.) That done, fish wire, remove knockouts from the box, insert cable connectors, and nail the hanger bar to the sides of the joists. The lip of the outlet box should be roughly flush to the finish ceiling below.

Thread cable into the box, tighten clamps, strip and connect wires to the fixtures, and patch around the fixture if the ceiling needs it. Replace the floorboard by nailing cleats along the upper edge of each joist; nail the floorboard to the cleats.

Where you can't install an outlet box by removing a chunk of flooring above, you will have to make all cuts and attachments from below. This means removing and replacing a much larger section of finish material. The procedures for working from below vary, however, from drywall to plaster ceilings.

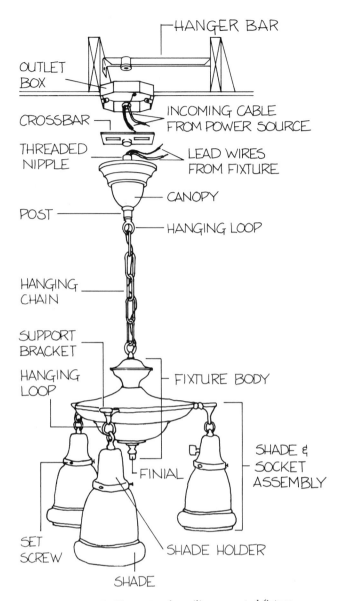

Figure 11.58 Elements of a ceiling-mounted fixture.

Labels in figure:
- HANGER BAR
- OUTLET BOX
- CROSSBAR
- INCOMING CABLE FROM POWER SOURCE
- THREADED NIPPLE
- LEAD WIRES FROM FIXTURE
- CANOPY
- POST
- HANGING LOOP
- HANGING CHAIN
- SUPPORT BRACKET
- HANGING LOOP
- FIXTURE BODY
- SHADE & SOCKET ASSEMBLY
- FINIAL
- SET SCREW
- SHADE HOLDER
- SHADE

the bar between joists and tack it in place. Hold the replacement drywall in place, to see how well the box aligns with the hole you cut for it. Slide the box along the bar until the box aligns with its hole. After putting aside the replacement drywall once more, firmly attach the bar to the sides of the joists with nails or type W drywall screws. Tighten the nut that holds the box to the bar; feed cables into the box, and tighten connector clamps. Then strip wires. Finally, affix the new section of drywall to the joist centers, using type W drywall screws. Patch around the edges of the replacement piece using joint compound. (See Chapter 15 for a discussion of similar repairs to finish surfaces—you may need to add backing for the drywall.)

Plaster Ceilings. In plaster ceilings, you need only cut a strip slightly larger than the box and the offset mounting bar that supports it. Begin by drilling an exploratory hole and locating adjacent joists. Wearing goggles, use a reciprocating saw to cut away an area of plaster about the size of the proposed fixture box. Keep chipping until you uncover the width (and hence, the direction) of at least one piece of lath.

Lath is nailed onto joists; therefore, it runs perpendicular to them. Keep chipping along a length of lath until you have exposed a joist crossing at each end. Compare the length of the mounting bar with the area you've chipped away; their lengths should be about the same. Trace the outline of the bar and box onto the ceiling, and use a saber saw (or a reciprocating saw) with a metal-cutting blade, to cut the lath along the bar-and-box outline. Pull out any lath nails that are in the way.

Fish wire to this new outlet. Remove knockouts from the box, insert cable connectors, feed cable into the connectors and tighten them down, and strip wire in anticipation of final attachments. Set the bar-and-box assembly in the slot you have cut and fasten the bar securely to the underside of the joists, using $1\frac{1}{2}$-in. wood screws or type W drywall screws. Patch the area around the assembly with plaster of paris, applying it in two coats if necessary.

A word of advice: Before patching any finish walls or ceilings, it is advisable though not crucial to test the circuits

Drywall Ceilings. Looking at drywall ceilings first, drill an exploratory hole, as you did above, to locate joists. Cut out a first-sized hole in the middle of the opening; then take exact readings, using a tape measure, to the sides of the joists. Carefully cut back a section of drywall to the centers of adjacent joists.

Because you will be working over your head, wear goggles. Clean up the edges of the cutout area with a utility knife. Remove any nails that would interfere with the replacement piece.

Next, cut out a replacement piece of drywall. Center and trace the outline of the fixture box on the finish side of the drywall and cut out that shape. Determine whether the replacement piece fits easily to the hole in the ceiling, with about $\frac{1}{8}$ in. clearance on all sides. Then set the replacement piece aside.

Fish cable into the newly opened bay between joists. Remove knockouts from the box, attach cable connectors, and fasten (loosely) the box to the mounting bar. Extend

Figure 11.59 A recessed can in the ceiling. If you insulate your ceiling, you must block off insulation so that it is held 3 to 6 in. away from cans. Otherwise, heat could build up and melt wire insulation.

serving the new outlet or outlets. If, when you turn on the electricity to the outlet, you find a short circuit, at least you won't have to patch finish surfaces twice.

Surface Wiring

The earliest kind of residential wiring was surface wiring, which was replaced by the concealed-wiring varieties used today. Present-day surface wiring is useful for extending a circuit or replacing hazardous extension cords, where subsurface wiring would be a problem. Note, however, that surface wiring is not being touted as a way to wire an entire house; neither is it acceptable where using it would overload an existing circuit.

Since there are numerous, distinct types of surface wiring, check with your electrical supplier for details. There are semipermanent, nonmetal types whose use is limited to dry, finished areas; and sturdy metal raceway types, fully grounded, which can be used in basement shops and similar areas. Avoid using any surface wiring in damp areas. The more permanent types feature type TW wire.

Most surface-wire systems get their power from existing outlets, although, of course, the power is shut off before connections are made. An adapter plate fits over the outlets and similarly colored wires are wire-nutted together. There are also adapter plates that connect directly to a service panel; but they are less common. As with all circuits, there must be strong mechanical and electrical connections; but this is especially true with surface wiring, for there may not be a continuous ground if all base pieces are not snapped together securely.

The main element of such systems is a U-shaped channel base which, when screwed in place, houses individual, insulated wires (not sheathed in a cable). Various elements, such as receptacles, switches, and the like, snap into the U-shaped channel base after wiring connections have been made. That done, the base is covered. Connections to various elements are much like those to regular outlets: switches interrupt only hot wires, neutral and ground (here, green insulated wires) are continuous, and so on. The key to success is to keep wires from being pinched by the various snap-in elements. Restrain wire every foot or so, using special clips that hold wire flat against the bottom of the U-channel.

Track lighting. Track lighting is a special form of surface wiring in which lighting fixtures clip into tracks at virtually any point along a track's length. Once attached, the units can be easily removed and placed somewhere else, usually by depressing a small spring at the base of the unit's track adapter.

Tracks for track lighting get their power from existing outlets, usually a fixture outlet in the ceiling. After power is shut off and the wires inside the outlet box are exposed, a universal strap is fixed over the box to facilitate attachment of the track. Wire leads from the track are wire-nutted to the wires in the outlet box. Then an end piece, often called a canopy, attaches to the end of the track, holding it fast and covering the contents of the outlet box. While temporarily holding the track in place, the installer marks its mounting holes on the ceiling. Because tracks and their lights are not heavy, the track may attach to the finish ceil-

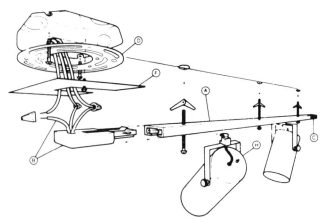

Figure 11.60 Installing a track light to an existing outlet. (TrakLiting)

ing with toggle bolts. To install the track, drill bolt holes in the ceiling; then assemble toggle bolts in the track and gently push toggles into the holes. Finally, tighten the bolts until the track is snug against the ceiling.

Track lighting is quite different from surface wiring, in that all wiring is an integral part of the base and is embedded so it is almost impossible to touch a hot wire with either a finger or a screwdriver that slips. Furthermore, most tracks are polarized; that is, a circuit is complete only when the matched plug of a compatible lamp is inserted. Multicircuit tracks are somewhat more difficult to install and may require professional help.

When positioning track lights, consider their use and the height of the ceiling. If the ceiling is 7 to 9 ft high, tracks are usually installed 2 to 3 ft from the wall they are designed to illuminate. If ceilings are 9 to 11 ft, install tracks 3 to 4 ft from the wall.

CONNECTIONS IN THE SERVICE PANEL

Before working in the entrance panel, see the safety information on pages 233–236. In brief, don't work in the panel at all if the system isn't grounded or if the area around the panel isn't dry (for example, if it's drizzling, don't work on a panel outdoors). To maximize safety, wear rubber-soled shoes and rubber gloves, and use only tools with insulated handles. All electrical devices must be UL-approved.

If you are at all uncertain about safe wiring procedures, have a licensed electrician make all connections to the service panel.

Circuits added to the service panel must not exceed the capacity of that panel. And the wire sizes of all circuits must be matched, as set forth in Table 11.3—matched to the energy load of devices on the new circuit, and to the amperage rating of the fuse or breaker controlling it.

Working Safely

Cut power inside the panel by flipping the main breaker off (or by removing the main fuse in a fuse box). With the main off, power will be live only at the large lug terminals above the main breaker. Unscrew the panel cover and set

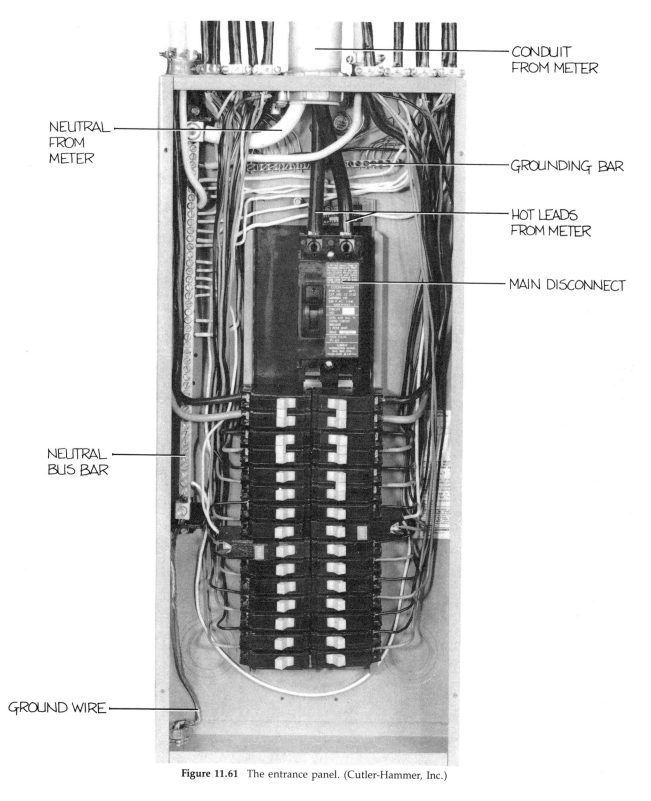

CONDUIT FROM METER

NEUTRAL FROM METER

GROUNDING BAR

HOT LEADS FROM METER

MAIN DISCONNECT

NEUTRAL BUS BAR

GROUND WIRE

Figure 11.61 The entrance panel. (Cutler-Hammer, Inc.)

it aside. The rest of the box should now be safe, but *test with a voltage tester to be sure.* Touch one probe of the tester to a hot bus bar and one probe to the metal panel of the box. The tester should not light up; if it does, flip the breaker again and test once more. If you are still getting power below the main (an extremely rare situation), the main is defective and should be replaced by a professional before you proceed.

Connecting Branch Circuits

Adding or extending a circuit is just a matter of running cable safely, and making sound mechanical connections to boxes, devices, and terminals in the service panel.

To run cable into the panel, knock the appropriate knockout into the panel, using an old screwdriver to start them and lineman's pliers to remove the metal slug. Fit a

A.

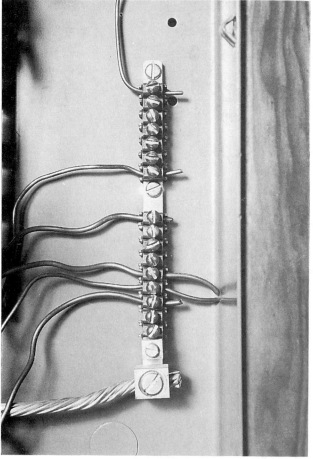

B.

C.

Figure 11.62 Attaching a branch circuit: **TURN THE MAIN DISCONNECT OFF AND TEST WITH A VOLTAGE TESTER BEFORE PROCEEDING.** (A) Strip the sheathing from the incoming cable, feed it through a cable connector, and tighten the connector locknut as shown. (B) Attach the ground wire of the branch circuit to the ground bar in the panel; the large wire at the bottom of the bar is the main ground. Attach the neutral wire to the neutral bus bar. *Note:* In some panels, there is but one neutral/ground bar. (C) Hot wires attach to lug screws on the back of circuit breakers. While the connection should be solid, do not overtighten lug screws or they may strip. Here, two wires attach to a double-pole breaker. (Thanks to Ed Bussa of Bussa Electric, Oakland, CA.)

Romex connector (or a BX or conduit clamp, if that's what you're running); then strip the sheathing from the cable, exposing individual wires. Depending on the size of the box, you should have about 2 ft of unsheathed wire; that way, you can wire to the farthest breaker in the panel if need be. Tighten the Romex connector around the last section of still-sheathed cable. Never clamp down on individual wires; if you do, they could become galled and short-circuit.

Attach ground and neutral wires first. In many panels, there is a single ground/neutral bar that is bonded to the metal box and that has several small lug screws for holding individual wires in place. (In other setups, there are separate ground and neutral bars.) Run the wires around the inside of the box (Figure 11.61), strip about $\frac{1}{2}$ in. of insulation from the ends of the neutral wire, feed the stripped end beneath a lug screw, and tighten it down. Attach the ground wire to a lug screw as well, although, of course, you do not have to strip insulation off bare ground wires. Make sure that the neutral and ground wires are routed away from the hot bus bars and from any hot lugs. Once the panel has been wired completely, many professionals tape together the bundles of wires running around the inside perimeter of the box, to give a tidier appearance.

Finally, attach hot wire(s) to circuit breakers. Again, route the wire around the box, allowing as much slack as possible. Strip $\frac{1}{2}$ in. of insulation from the end of the wire. Snap a breaker in place, as shown in Figure 11.62C, and feed the wire into the lug screw at the back of the breaker. Tighten down this screw, which fastens the wire. If the circuit is 120/240 volt or 240-volt, there will be two hot wires serving the circuit and two breaker lug-screws on the back of the breaker.

Before switching the main breaker back on, flip off each of the circuits you just wired. By doing this, you can pinpoint short circuits immediately when you flip on individual circuit breakers.

When the main breaker and all new branch-circuit breakers are flipped on and they stay on, there are no short circuits; carefully replace the cover of the panel.

Wiring a fuse box is essentially the same as wiring a breaker panel. Each fuse socket has a lug terminal, to which individual hot wires are attached, and there is a ground/neutral bar to which all neutral and ground wires are attached. Analogous to breaker panels, 240-volt circuit fuses have two terminals for hot wires.

Attaching a GFCI Breaker

Ground-fault circuit interrupters (GFCIs) are discussed at length on page 253. Note that in some cases, a GFCI *receptacle* may offer better protection to given outlets than a GFCI circuit breaker would offer. Because GFCIs are extremely sensitive, circuit breakers can be plagued by nuisance tripping, in response to the normal resistance of current along a long cable run.

Hooking up a GFCI breaker is somewhat different from other circuit breakers. Shut off the main disconnect and test with a voltage tester, as before; then strip, run, and clamp cable as it enters the panel.

A 120-volt GFCI breaker, however, has *two* terminals: one for a hot wire and one for a neutral wire. Attach the

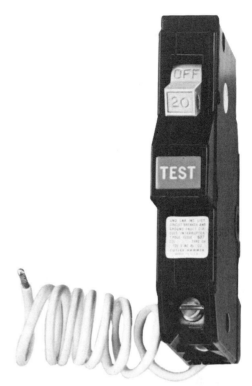

Figure 11.63 A ground-fault circuit interrupter (GFCI) breaker. Because the GFCI breaker responds to a difference in flow between hot and neutral wires, attach the hot and neutral wires of a branch circuit directly to lugs on the GFCI breaker. A white pigtail runs from the breaker to the neutral (or ground/neutral) bar. Test GFCIs after installing them, and once a month thereafter. (Cutler-Hammer, Inc.)

branch-circuit hot wire to the *load* terminal on the breaker; attach the branch-circuit neutral wire to the breaker terminal marked *load neutral*. (In other words, the neutral wire of a circuit so protected does *not* attach directly to the ground/neutral bus bar as most incoming neutral wires do.) A white pigtail from the GFCI breaker then attaches to the ground/neutral bus bar. Note, however, that the ground wire of the circuit *does* attach directly to the ground/neutral bus bar.

Once connections are complete, snap the breaker into place and restore power. Test the GFCI breaker by pressing its test button. The breaker should kick itself off. Reset it by flipping the toggle back to the ON position. Important: Test GFCI circuit breakers occasionally—say, once a month—to make sure that they're working properly.

SPECIAL-PURPOSE CIRCUITS: HEAVY USE

As required by Code, all critical-use stationary appliances must be served by separate, *dedicated* circuits. In addition to appliances such as water heaters, ranges, stoves, washers, dryers, dishwashers, and garbage disposals, ''critical use'' extends to any permanently installed user rated at 12 amperes or more, including motors, oil pumps, burners, fans, and so on.

If a user is a permanent appliance, it should be *hard wired:* that is, the BX cable or conduit emerging from the

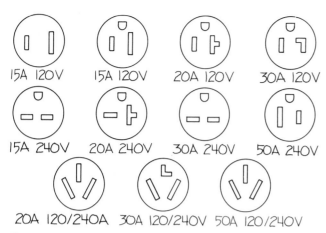

Figure 11.64 Plugs and receptacles are configured so that they can't be mismatched.

wall runs to a connector box on the appliance, wherein service wires attach to wire leads from the appliance. If, on the other hand, the appliance is free-standing and can be moved, it will have a heavy-duty plug specially matched to the cable and receptacle serving it.

Plugs and receptacles for appliances are rated and configured to prevent mismatching. Never use a device too light for the amperage (e.g., do not use a 120-volt-rated plug for 120/240 service). Similarly, shutoff switches must be matched to the amperage rating of the circuits they control (e.g., a 20-ampere switch on No. 12 appliance cable). Still other appliances require connections to be made in covered junction boxes, as in Figure 11.27.

When sizing wire and circuit breakers, read the appliance nameplate and installation instructions. Reviewing manufacturer's literature will also alert you to special connectors necessary to join larger wire sizes. Also consult the *National Electrical Code®*, as it is quite specific about wire size, amperage, and distance. In brief, the size of the wires depends on the amperes drawn and the distance of the outlet from the service panel.

About 240-Volt Wiring

One item may prove confusing to the reader. Although neutral wires are attached to terminals on 120-volt and 120/240-volt plugs and receptacles, neutral wires are not attached to terminals on 240-volt devices. How can a circuit be complete without a neutral wire? In brief, alternating current (AC) alternates electrical pulses between the two hot wires in such a hookup. The hot wires alternate for each other, providing a kind of return for ''spent'' energy, at a given pulse. The pulses are extremely fast, of course.

Furnace

Furnace motors must be protected by an SSU *fused switch*. Should the motor overheat, the fuse on the switch blows and disconnects power—thereby limiting damage to the short section of cable from the switch to the motor, and making repairs a lot easier than replacing a cable all the way back to the panel.

Water Heaters

After the furnace, the water heater is the biggest energy user in the house. For most families, a 40-gallon capacity is more than adequate; a larger tank means that you must keep continuously on hand that much extra hot water. Ratings of water heaters vary greatly. While most can be served by No. 12 wire on a 20-ampere circuit, electrical codes may require No. 10 wire.

Water-heater wire leads are routinely connected to incoming cable in a covered outlet box. The outgoing cable running from that box to the body of the heater is usually BX. The cable from the power source to the outlet box is covered with finish-wall surface. It is particularly important that the metal body of the heater be grounded.

Electric Stoves and Cooktops

Electric stoves, or ranges, are usually attached to power by a 240-volt plug on the end of the appliance's lead cable. That cable should be No. 8 or No. 6, depending on the distance from the service panel. If the stove is a permanent, drop-in type, it should be hard-wired.

Here, the plug mates to a flush-mounted or surface-mounted 240-volt receptacle, usually rated at 50 amperes. The latter arrangement gives the user immediate access to the connection. Where the cable from the source to the receptacle is exposed, the cable should be sheathed in BX or it should be enclosed in a conduit as it runs along the surface. Also, it should terminate in a covered junction box where it turns to run behind finish-wall surfaces. Receptacles themselves vary; flush-mounted models screw into an outlet box; surface-mounted models have a base that screws into a stud behind the finish surface.

Cooktops are usually connected in a covered junction box. Since there is no need to move a cooktop for cleaning around it, this fixed hookup is sufficient.

Air Conditioners

When buying an air conditioner, consider both its cooling capacity (expressed in BTUs removed per hour) and its EER (energy efficiency ratio), which divides the cooling capacity by the wattage of the unit. To estimate the unit's cooling capacity, consider that 18 BTUs removed per square foot per hour is about right. In the South, the figure will be 20 BTUs removed per square foot per hour, or higher. The EER ranges from about 5 to 12. The higher the number, the greater the efficiency; 7 or 8 is fairly good, above 10 is exceptional. Sizing air conditioning systems is discussed further in Chapter 14.

Both 120- and 240-volt air conditioners may be connected by a plug-and-receptacle setup, because it's sometimes important that the unit be disconnected immediately. If the unit runs on 240-volt service, the cord should be no longer than 6 ft; if on 120-volt service, no longer than 10 ft. An air conditioner can be connected within a closed outlet box, but that limits the user's access to the unit. Furthermore, the switch that controls the power of the air conditioner should be within sight of the unit, as close as possible. Large-capacity, whole-house air conditioners routinely require separate panels and slow-burning fuses that accommodate the heavy start-up load of such systems.

Clothes Dryers

Clothes dryers are often wired for 120/240-volt service, since the heating elements require 240 volts and the appliance motor that runs the drum requires 120 volts. This type of circuit is usually rated at 30 amperes, with No. 10 wire or larger recommended. A dryer is routinely connected via plugs and flush-mounting receptacles.

Dishwashers, Garbage Disposals, and Ventilator Fans

Such items as dishwashers, garbage disposals, and ventilator fans are relative lightweights. They are put on separate circuits because their continuous operation is important. Usually, the hot lead to the disposal is interrupted by a switch. A 20-ampere breaker is sufficient for such setups. If the dishwasher and disposal are farther than 4 ft apart,

however, it usually makes more sense to add another duplex receptacle.

Dishwashers are commonly wired to a three-pronged plug, to ensure correct grounding. The cord is 3 to 4 ft long and is routed so that the wheels of the dishwasher, if any, cannot run over the cord. Garbage disposals formerly required an in-box connection; but three-pronged plugs are now accepted by most codes, provided the cords are 18 to 36 in. long and are situated so they cannot be disturbed.

Ventilator fans may be plug- or box-connected; No. 12 wire and a 20-ampere circuit are adequate. Small exhaust fans over cooking areas may be $\frac{1}{4}$ hp or less, but fans ventilating attics and similar areas should be chosen on the basis of the attic's area. To determine the capacity of an attic fan, multiply the square footage of the attic by 0.7 cu ft per minute (CFM, the unit used in rating fan capacity). If your house is in the Deep South, or your roof is dark, multiply the area by 0.9 CFM and use a ventilator fan at each end of the attic. Insulate the roof and increase the natural ventilation up from the eaves by adding ventilator plugs or soffit vents. Chapters 7 and 14 give additional information on fans and vents.

·12·

PLUMBING

The amateur builder has benefited greatly from the standardization of building materials, and nowhere is this more true than in plumbing. Whereas a plumber once had to fashion waste systems from cast iron, oakum, and melted lead, today one needs little more than plastic pipe and a special cement. Such improved technology enables more people to repair, install, and understand plumbing.

The would-be plumber must do three things:

1. Learn the vocabulary. Many novices are overwhelmed by the plethora of plumbing terms, especially the names of fittings. The more you consider what each part does and why it is shaped as it is, the sooner will the confusion abate. No matter how complex an assembly of pipes and parts, what has been put together can be taken apart.

2. Consult local plumbing code regulations, which are designed to protect your health and that of your neighbors. Codes are usually quite explicit about the assemblies that are acceptable, the materials you may use, and at what stages the work must be inspected. Before purchasing a property, have the water tested.

3. Have a plumber familiar with antiquated plumbing make the initial inspection. To quote one professional: ''To the inexperienced eye, all cast iron looks the same. It is not. If you try to cut the old 'light iron' with a conventional cutter, it will probably crush and collapse. I have seen whole drainage systems lost because a decent cut could not be made.''

OVERVIEW

A plumbing system is a loop of sorts, created by *supply* (or delivery) pipes that carry potable water to the house and its fixtures; and by *drainage–waste–venting* (DWV) pipes which carry waste water, effluvia, and septic gases away from the *fixtures*. (By fixtures, we mean sinks, toilets, lavatories, washing machines, and the like.)

These two systems-within-a-system are markedly different. The wastes in DWV pipes fall freely; the water in supply pipes is delivered under pressure. Supply pipes can run almost anywhere, making as many jogs as need be. DWV pipes are more difficult to lay out because, being much larger, they are more likely to encounter obstacles en route; and their ''horizontal'' runs must be pitched so that wastes can fall and gases rise.

Despite their disparities, however, all plumbing parts have one thing in common: they must be tightly joined, and securely supported so they stay that way.

Supply Pipes

The pipe that delivers water to a house (from the city water main or an individual well) is called the *service pipe*. So that the pipe won't freeze, it runs 1 to 2 ft below the frost line and enters the building through the foundation. Typically, the service pipe is controlled by a gate valve (the main shut-off valve) shortly after it enters the building; but municipal hookups may enter a water meter first.

From the shutoff valve, the pipe continues as the *main supply pipe,* also called the cold-water *trunk line.* At some point, a pipe branches off this main and feeds into the water heater. Emerging from the heater, it becomes the hot-water main. From this main run the various *branch pipes* that serve individual fixtures. In general, as pipe runs approach fixtures, they step down in diameter.

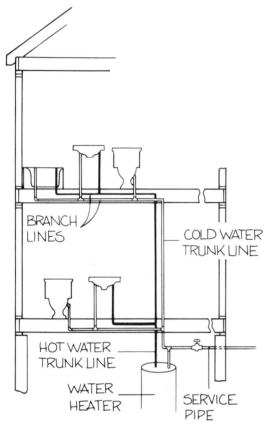

Figure 12.1 The supply system. Originating at a service pipe from the street, the cold-water trunk line supplies all branches; a pipe departing that line enters the water heater and emerges as the hot-water trunk line.

Figure 12.2 The main vein of a leaf is a naturally occurring trunk line, ensuring water to the most distant parts.

The DWV System

The drainage–waste–vent system is a complex of pipes which carry away wastes, vent septic gases, and admit air so that waste materials can fall freely. Every fixture has a *trap* filled with water to keep sewer gases away from living spaces. As *trap arms* leave individual fixtures, they empty into *branch drains* or directly into the *soil stack,* which, in turn, empties into the house's *building drain* (or *main drain*). At the lowest point in this system, the building drain discharges into a city sewer main or a septic tank.

Drain pipes may also be differentiated according to the wastes they carry: *soil pipes* and *soil stacks* carry fecal matter and urine; whereas *waste pipes* carry waste water but not soil. *Stacks* are vertical pipes, although they may jog slightly (*offset stacks*) to avoid obstacles.

Which brings us to venting, the V of DWV. Without venting, wastes would either not fall at all or, in falling, would suck the water out of fixture traps. This principle is easily shown by the grade-school experiment of holding your finger over the end of a drinking straw filled with water. Only when you remove your finger can air enter and water fall.

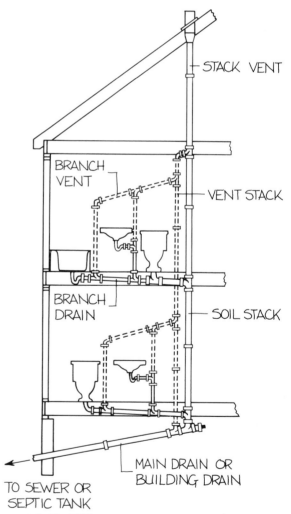

Figure 12.3 The DWV system. Drain pipe must maintain a downward pitch of at least $\frac{1}{4}$ in. per foot; vent pipe, an upward pitch of at least $\frac{1}{8}$ in. per foot. Note that "stack vent" is but another name for the soil stack above the connection from the highest fixture.

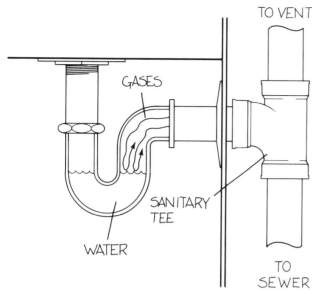

Figure 12.4 Traps hold septic gases at bay, but they rely on vents to operate properly. Without incoming air from the vent, falling wastes would suck water out of traps and allow these unhealthful gases to enter living spaces.

Every fixture must be vented in some manner. In most cases, the trap arm exits into a tee fitting whose bottom leg is a branch drain, discussed above, and whose upper leg is a *branch vent*. Branch vents continue on, often picking up other fixture vents, until they join a *vent stack*, which exits through the roof. (Where that stack is actually the upper portion of the soil stack, it may also be called the *stack vent*.) In any event, the fewer stacks sticking out of the roof, the better.

Finally, an important point: all drain pipes must slope downward at least $\frac{1}{4}$ in. per ft. Where vent pipes run horizontally toward stacks, however, they must maintain a minimum *upward* grade of at least $\frac{1}{8}$ in. per ft.

BASIC TOOLS

With the modest tool collection below, you'll be ready for most plumbing tasks.

Pipe wrench. These days, pipe wrenches are used primarily for disconnecting old metal traps and galvanized steel supply pipes. Position wrenches so that their serrated jaws grip—that is, turn wrenches so that the lower jaw leads. Have two in your toolbox.

Crescent wrench. This tool is also adjustable, but because its jaws are smooth, the wrench will grip only parallel surfaces, not pipe itself.

Slip-nut pliers. A good utility tool for holding nuts, whatever.

Locking pliers. Jaws adjust and clamp down on fittings or whatever—so you have both hands free to hold a torch and apply solder.

Basin wrench. About the only tool for adjusting water nuts on the undersides of sinks and lavs, where supply pipes join.

Strainer wrench. Tightens the strainer and tailpiece assembly, thereby compressing the intervening gaskets.

Pipe cutter. The easiest way, bar none, to get a clean, square cut on pipe. Tighten the cutter so that its cutting wheel barely scores the pipe; then rotate the tool around the pipe, gradually tightening until the cut is complete. Far superior to hacksaw cuts. There are several types. In Figure 12.5 the standard *tubing cutter* has a deburring attachment to take off burrs; use a *close-quarters* cutter where there's no room for a full-sized one. There's also an *ABS cutter*, shown in Figure 12.16A.

Torches. Propane units, long the mainstay of weekend plumbers, are being supplanted by smaller, more convenient mapp-gas torches. They're also hotter, perfect for heating the $\frac{1}{2}$- or $\frac{3}{4}$-in. fittings encountered most often.

Other tools. Rent a *power auger* when plungers and hand

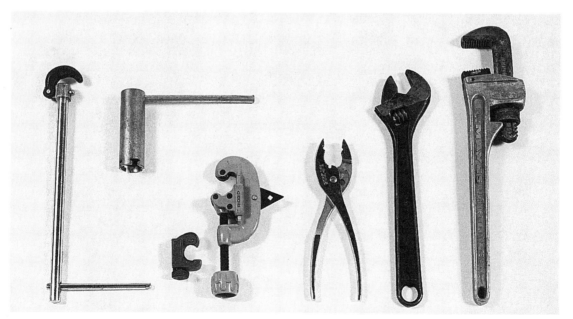

Figure 12.5 Basic plumbing tools. *From left:* basin wrench, strainer wrench, close-quarters pipe cutter, pipe cutter, slip-joint pliers, adjustable crescent wrench, pipe wrench.

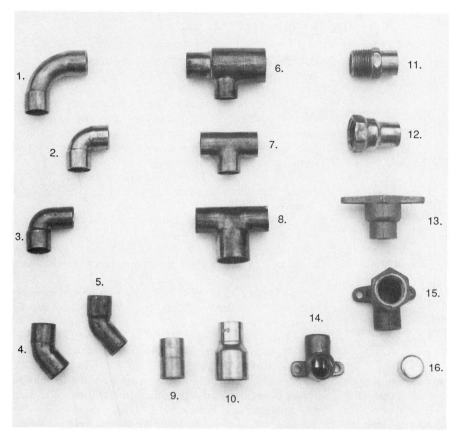

Figure 12.6 Copper supply fittings. 1, Long ell; 2, short ell; 3, street ell; 4, 45° ell; 5, street 45° ell; 6, reducing tee: $\frac{1}{2} \times \frac{3}{4} \times \frac{1}{2}$; 7, $\frac{1}{2}$-in. tee; 8, reducing tee. $\frac{1}{2} \times \frac{1}{2} \times \frac{3}{4}$; 9, coupling; 10, reducing coupling: $\frac{1}{2} \times \frac{3}{4}$; 11, male pipe to copper adapter; 12, female pipe to copper adapter; 13, $\frac{1}{2}$-in. wing; 14, $\frac{1}{2}$-in. female wing 90°; 15, $\frac{1}{2}$-in. wing 90°; 16, cap.

augers can't do the job. An inexpensive handsaw will cut ABS if you haven't got an ABS cutter. Rent a *snap cutter* (Figure 12.18) if you need to extend from cast-iron pipe. See Chapter 3 for others: a $\frac{1}{2}$-in. drill with a right-angle drive is a must if you're running pipe, as is a reciprocating saw.

Plumbing Safety

1. *Get a tetanus shot before you start.*

2. Use only *hand tools* when cutting into supply pipes; a power tool shorting out could be fatal in that situation.

3. Make sure that there's good ventilation when joining pipes: melting solder and plastic pipe solvents give off noxious fumes.

4. When soldering joints in place, be particularly careful of molten flux dripping down from above. *Wear goggles.*

5. Be careful not to start fires when soldering close to studs or joists. Wetting the area beforehand is a good idea; use a plant spritzer. For more on reducing fire hazards, see page 276.

6. When cutting into or connecting to existing DWV pipes, be careful:

    a. Plan the task carefully and have parts ready so that you can close things up as soon as possible. Flush the pipe as best you can beforehand. Support pipes before cutting into them.

    b. Wear heavy gloves when handling drain pipe; a respirator mask is a good idea, too.

    c. Clean up immediately when the job is done.

MATERIALS

Strong, easily worked, and almost universally approved by codes, rigid copper is the preferred material for supply systems. For the same reasons, ABS plastic has supplanted most other DWV types. Thus we'll concentrate on those two materials in the section that follows. But first, a few observations true to all types.

Fittings

Fittings are necessary to join pipe sections, change direction, or receive fixtures. There exist a bewildering number of fittings, but with common sense you can figure which one a job requires.

1. Fittings join pipes. The simplest fitting is a *coupling*, which joins two straight lengths of pipe. A *union* is a coupling you can disconnect.

2. Fittings may change the direction of a pipe run. A *90-degree ell* is a good example of this type, as is a *tee*.

3. Fittings accommodate changes in diameter. A *reducer* accepts, say, $\frac{3}{4}$-in. copper in one side and $\frac{1}{2}$-in. in the other.

4. Some fittings do several things at once. To name just one, a *3 × 2 low-heel inlet* is somewhere between a tee, an elbow, and a reducer.

5. *Adapters* are fittings that join disparate materials. The *dielectric union* shown in Figure 12.7 joins galvanized steel and copper—without electrolytic corrosion. With the *band-*

Figure 12.7 Supply adapters. *Clockwise, from lower left:* angle stop (90-degree shutoff valve) with compression fittings; dielectric union; double angle stop with two valves, which enables you to take two fixtures off a single stub.

seal couplings widely used in DWV systems, you can join both different materials and different sizes, say, 2 in. copper and $1\frac{1}{2}$ in. cast iron.

6. There seems no limit to the specialization possible: *diverter valves* mix water before it goes to a showerhead, *antisyphoning devices* prevent water lines from being sucked backward and tainting the water supply, *sanitary crosses* allow you to install toilets back to back.

Measuring Pipe

When measuring lengths of pipe during installation, keep in mind that most pipe ends slide into fitting *hubs* (sockets). Thus you must add the depth of those hubs to the face-to-face measurement between fittings. The depth of the hub is called the *seating distance* or *seating depth*. Rigid $\frac{1}{2}$-in. copper has seating depths of $\frac{1}{2}$ in., so you'd add 1 in. to a pipe measurement running between two $\frac{1}{2}$-in. fittings. Rigid $\frac{3}{4}$-in. copper has a $\frac{3}{4}$-in. seating depth.

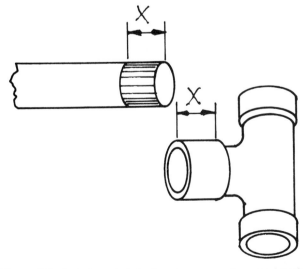

Figure 12.8 Include socket depths when measuring pipe length.

TABLE 12.1

Fitting ABS pipes

Diameter of Pipe (in.)	Distance into Fitting (in.)
$1\frac{1}{2}$	$\frac{3}{4}$
2	$\frac{7}{8}$
3	$1\frac{1}{2}$

Seating depths for ABS plastic are shown in Table 12.1.

Note: Some fittings, *hubless connectors*, have no hubs and hence no seating depths. Hubless connectors are used primarily to join lengths of DWV pipe or to provide a take-off for a branch extension, as shown in Figure 12.51.

Working with Supply Pipe

Rigid copper. Type L rigid copper is the most commonly used inside houses; you should use type M, which has thicker walls, for outdoor installations such as the service pipe from the water meter to the house. Whatever the type, copper is easy to work—with a little practice.

To cut rigid copper, place the tubing cutter on the pipe and gradually tighten its jaws until the cutting wheel just grabs the pipe. Make a complete revolution with the tool, tighten the cutting jaw a quarter turn, and so on, until you cut through the pipe. If you tighten the tool too fast, you will flatten the pipe or score erratically, thus creating a weak joint.

When the cut is complete, clean the end of the pipe with the deburring attachment on the cutter, so that you get a good, solid joint. Burrs also increase turbulence and thus decrease flow through the pipe. Polish the end of the pipe and the inside of the fitting with a fitting brush or with emery paper. Fine sandpaper will do, also, but it leaves particles of grit behind. Once you have cleaned the ends of the pipe, don't touch them or the insides of fittings with your fingers; solder may not stick to a material that has been touched.

Using a flux brush, apply self-tinning flux (soldering paste) to the outside of the pipe and the inside of the fitting. Slide the fitting over the pipe and give a quarter turn to distribute the flux evenly. If the fitting is a directional fitting, such as a tee or an elbow, make sure that the fitting points in the direction you want.

Heat the fitting (*not* the pipe), moving the soldering torch so that all sides of the fitting receive heat directly. The flux will bubble. From time to time, remove the torch and touch solder to the fitting seam. When the fitting is hot enough, the solder will liquefy when touched to it. After a few trials, you'll know if the fitting is hot enough to solder. When the fitting is hot, some fluxes change color, from milky brown to a dull silver.

Two passes with the solder, completely around the joint seam, will make a tight seal; more than two passes is a waste. The solder is drawn into the seam, so don't be apprehensive if you do not see a thick fillet of solder around the joint. Let solder cool before putting pressure on a joint. After a soldered joint has cooled for a minute or so, you can immerse it in water to cool it completely; but be careful when handling metal that is still hot.

Materials **275**

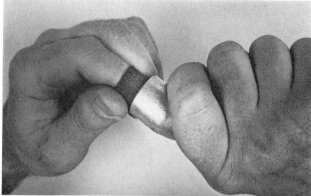

B.

C.

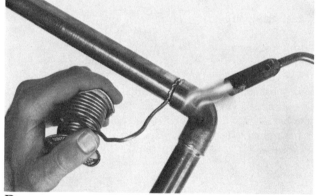

D.

A.

Figure 12.9 Working with rigid copper. (A) Revolve the pipe cutter around the pipe, gradually tightening its jaw until the cut is complete. (B) To ensure a perfect sweat joint, polish the outside of pipe ends and the inside of fittings beforehand. Either a cleaning brush or emery paper will do. Do not touch cleaned surfaces with your fingers. (C) Apply flux evenly around the outside of the pipe and to the inside of the fitting. (D) Apply heat to the fitting, not to the pipe; a heated fitting will draw solder into a joint.

The operation just described is also called *sweat fitting.* Here are additional tips for joining copper:

1. Because some lead in solder does leach into drinking water, most codes allow only the new no-lead solder. Actually, "no-lead" is a misnomer: such solder is 95:5 or 90:10 (tin to lead)—but old solder types were 50:50.

2. Where practicable, sweat-fit (in one operation) all pipes that enter a fitting. If you must reheat a fitting to add a pipe later, wrap the already soldered joint in wet rags to keep its solder intact.

3. Scribe alignment lines on fittings and pipes when their alignment is critical to other assemblies down the line.

4. When space is tight, presolder sections in a vise before-

hand. Then, when placing the section in its final position, you'll have only a joint or two to solder.

5. If a contiguous material might be damaged by heat, solder copper parts first and then make mechanical connections. An example that comes to mind is the threaded outtake on a pump whose body is plastic. Solder the male or female adapter to the copper pipe, then screw it in (or on) the outtake.

6. When soldering close to wood, wet it first with a plant spritzer. There are also asbestos-free flame guards which are particularly appropriate if finish surfaces are nearby. **Be careful** soldering around acoustic tiles or electrical cables.

7. When soldering pipe to a valve, open the valve fully before applying heat. Gate valves are entirely of metal and

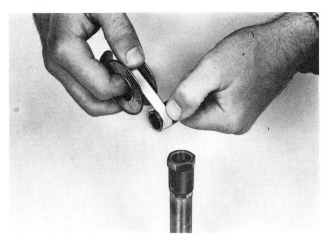

Figure 12.10 When joining threaded parts, apply joint compound to male adapters, or wrap their threads twice around with plastic joint tape. Sweat fittings to pipes before wrapping with plastic tape.

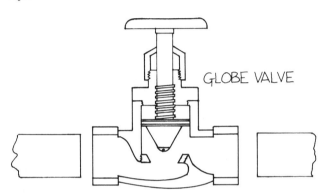

GLOBE VALVE

Figure 12.11 To prevent a globe valve's gasket from seizing, fully open the valve before sweating pipe to it.

will not be affected adversely; but globe valves have neoprene gaskets that can melt and seize up. Incidentally, it is helpful to have unions near most valves so that sections can be disconnected without your having to reheat joints already soldered.

8. If you must disconnect a sweat fitting, apply heat until the solder melts, and gently tap the fitting off the pipe. When the metal is cool, clean the pipe end, reflux, reheat, and resolder. Unless the fitting is an expensive one, such as a gate valve, don't reuse fittings that have already been soldered.

9. When disconnecting a sweat fitting on an existing supply line, always drain the pipe first; otherwise, the solder will not melt. Draining and reconnecting will be much easier if that section can be isolated with a shutoff valve, but it sometimes happens that old shutoffs don't seat perfectly. If that's the case, you can block the resultant dribble of water by balling up a piece of bread in the line to act as a temporary dam while you solder. The bread will dissolve shortly and can be flushed out easily.

Flexible copper tubing. Flexible copper tubing allows you to run pipe through an intricate maze behind cabinets, without needing a lot of fittings. For this reason, small-diameter tubing is used primarily for short supply runs to

dishwashers ($\frac{1}{2}$ in.), icemakers ($\frac{1}{4}$ or $\frac{5}{16}$ in.), and the like. Although larger-dimension ($\frac{3}{4}$ in.) tubing is sometimes used underground, Code does *not* allow its use as general supply pipe indoors, for it is easily damaged. *Nor should it be used for gas supply!*

Flexible tubing is softer than type L rigid copper pipe, so take pains not to collapse the walls of tubing by turning a pipe cutter too rapidly. Flexible tubing comes on rolls and can be fed into some spots where it would be difficult to solder fittings.

Flexible copper is sweat-fitted in the same manner as rigid pipe; but there is also a choice of mechanical fittings: *compression* or *flared.* A compression fitting features a *ferrule* of soft metal that is compressed between a set of matched nuts. A flared fitting requires flaring the ends of the tubing with a special tool. For either type of mechanical connector, remember to slide nuts onto the tubing before attaching a ferrule or flaring an end. Both types of connection are easily

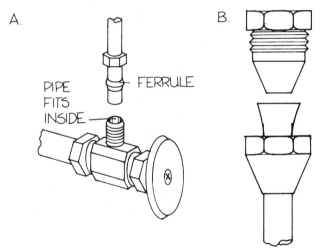

A.

PIPE FITS INSIDE

FERRULE

B.

Figure 12.12 Flexible copper fittings. (A) Compression; (B) flared.

Figure 12.13 Flaring tool. (Ridgid Tool Co.)

disconnected and are used where repairs may be common, such as the supply line to a toilet. Don't reuse ferrules, however; replace them if a connection has been disturbed.

Bend flexible tubing carefully so that you won't crimp it; a tubing bender is available for this purpose. If you do crimp the tubing, straighten it, using an adjustable crescent wrench. Set the distance between the jaws of the wrench on a good (i.e., uncollapsed) section of tubing and slide the wrench up to the crimped section. Revolve the wrench to straighten the crimp.

Galvanized steel pipe. Because decades of use have shown that galvanized pipe will corrode and constrict, reducing flow and water pressure, galvanized is no longer installed as water supply pipe. If your existing system is galvanized, replace it as soon as possible. Should you not wish the additional expense of ripping and replacing all walls, you can replace newly exposed sections of galvanized with copper, but you must use a *dielectric union* (Figure 12.7) when joining copper to steel. Otherwise, electrolysis will take place, and corrosion will accelerate.

Today, galvanized pipe is largely limited to gas-supply service. In this use, the pipe must be threaded—an arduous process without a power threader and, because of safety factors, a very exacting task. For the latter reason, *have a licensed plumber install gas-supply service pipes.* A professional will end each pipe stub with a stopcock valve, to which you can attach a short length of *flexible gas supply.*

Flexible plastic tubing. Flexible plastic tubing (polyethylene) is used outdoors, primarily as underground delivery pipe from a well to a house. It must be isolated from the house water supply by an antisyphon device. Of all types of supply pipe, it is the most resistant to splits caused by freezing, because its walls yield somewhat to the expansion of ice. (You should, of course, drain pipes that are vulnerable to freezing.)

Flexible plastic tubing is easily cut with a pocketknife; such cuts should be square across the pipe, but close will do. Lengths of tubing are joined with ringed plastic couplings inserted into the tubing, and held fast with stainless steel ring clamps. Do not overtighten clamps. If a coupling is difficult to insert, soak the end of the tubing in hot water to soften it. A soap solution also helps.

Where flexible plastic joins metal pipe, use adapters such as those shown in Figure 12.14. Apply plastic joint tape to threaded male parts, and screw metal and plastic together until the joint is snug. An overtightened plastic joint that has split is a common cause of air leaks in supply lines; often manifested by a noisy pump, a pump that runs too long, or by faucets that cough and sputter when turned on.

PVC plastic. Code does *not* allow PVC to be used as supply pipe, because medical research increasingly suggests that PVC releases several known carcinogens—including chloroform, carbon tetrachloride, and DEHP—into water carried by such pipe. PVC may be used for nonpotable exterior uses such as watering a garden, but such runs must be isolated with antisyphon devices to prevent mixing with the house water supply proper. Check your local plumbing code before purchasing PVC parts: it may be banned altogether in your area.

A

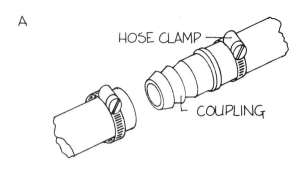

B

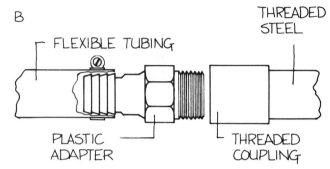

Figure 12.14 Connecting flexible plastic tubing. (A) Simple coupling; (B) to threaded metal.

That noted, working with PVC is much like cutting and joining ABS, explained at some length below. Cut pipe ends square, using a hacksaw or, better, a pipe cutter. Clean the ends of cut pipes, as well as the inside of fittings, with emery paper, and apply special solvent cement to each pipe end and fitting, to join them. Turn fittings a quarter-turn *in one direction only* to spread the cement. Finally, allow glued joints to set adequately before putting pressure on the line.

To use PVC successfully, make sure that you have all the necessary adapters to join the new plastic lines to existing metal lines or to fixtures. Not infrequently, old fixtures have odd-sized delivery or drainage leads, and you can spend days chasing around for that one odd adapter that will let you turn your water back on.

Working with DWV Materials

By far the most common DWV material is *ABS plastic:* it's strong, easy to cut and join, light enough for one person to handle, reasonably priced, and extremely slick inside—which ensures a good flow of wastes. About the only bad thing to be said about it is that it will melt and give off toxic gases in a fire.

PVC waste pipe is much less common, and is usually specified for industrial setups, darkroom sinks, and other situations where wastes are caustic and/or chemical.

Copper waste pipe is corrosion-resistant, strong, relatively lightweight, and in its larger dimensions, very expensive. For that reason, it is often used in tandem with cast iron.

Cast iron is a durable, time-tested material that is preferred by many professionals but not well suited to amateur installation. Ever since band clamps replaced lead and oakum, cast iron has certainly been easier to connect, but it's still tricky to cut. And though its mass effectively deadens the sound of running water—where this is a concern—that mass translates to weight when you're installing it. It also costs 30 to 50 percent more than an ABS job.

Figure 12.15 DWV fittings. The fittings shown are ABS plastic, but with slight variations, could as easily be copper, cast iron, or no-hub. Found here are the more common fittings, there are many more configurations available. A few important distinctions among fittings: (1) Drain fittings have sweeps built into them to hasten the flow of wastes, such as in the long-sweep ell, the Y, the combo, the sanitary tee. Code requires such fittings on drain lines. (2) Vent pipes, on the other hand, can have smaller turning radii because they carry only air. A vent tee, as you can see, is more compact than a sanitary tee, and a vent ell takes less space than a regular ell. (3) Street fittings are hybrids whose male end fits directly into the female hub of another fitting, useful when space is limited. A, Ell; B, long-sweep ell; C, vent ell; D, street ell; E, closet bend, also called a Herkel fitting or a 4×3; F, 45-degree ell; G, $22\frac{1}{2}$-degree ell; H, sanitary tee; I, vent tee; J, double tee; K, reducing tee; L, Y, or wye; M, double-Y; N, combo, or T-Y; O, coupling; P, clean-out adapter; Q, clean-out plug; R, closet flange, which fits over a closet bend; S, P-trap (required by all fixtures except a toilet); T, trap adapter has a slip-nut joint with a plastic washer.

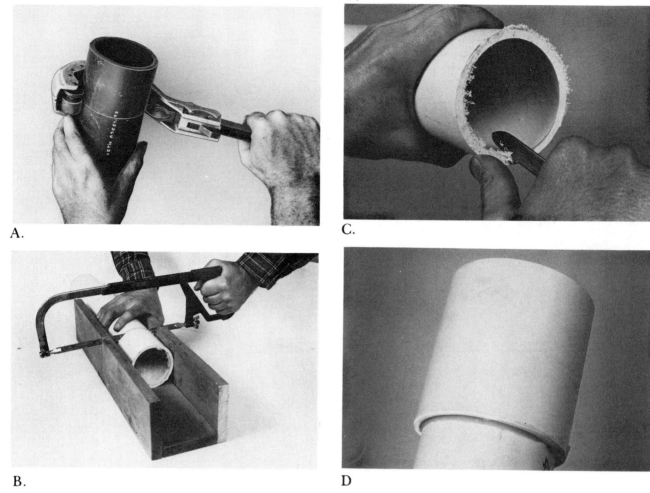

A.

B.

C.

D

Figure 12.16 Plastic waste pipe. (A) A pipe cutter is the easiest, most accurate way to cut ABS pipe. (B) If you saw pipe, build a jig so that your cuts will be square. An old crosscut saw is best because its blade is wide, but a hacksaw (shown here) is also okay in a pinch. (C) After cutting, pare away burrs with a pen knife. (D) Apply cement to the outside of the pipe and the inside of the fitting. Insert the pipe and give a quarter-turn to spread the cement evenly. Allow the joint to dry thoroughly before putting any pressure on the joint. The cement should form an even bead above the shoulder of the fitting.

Most residences will be served adequately by 3-in. building drains, with $1\frac{1}{2}$- and 2-in. branch drains. (Sizing DWV systems is discussed at greater length below.) By all means, consult your local plumbing code, but it's rare that you'd need 4-in. pipe. Vent pipes, as a rule of thumb, are the same size as the drains they serve. DWV fittings, shown in Figure 12.15, have the same names, whatever the material they're made of.

ABS waste pipe. Have a friend help set ABS pipe. The material is lightweight and easy to handle, but it is cumbersome. Once the cement has been applied, you have only a few seconds in which to position the fittings. Another person at the other end of a pipe can push when you do, thus enabling you to seat pieces properly.

Cut ABS with a pipe cutter, gradually tightening the cutting wheel after each revolution. It's possible to cut ABS with a hacksaw, but that method is less likely to produce a cut that is square across. If either method of cutting leaves burrs, clean them off with a pocketknife, then sand with emery paper. Finally, remove all grit with a clean rag.

ABS cement is applied like flux—to the outside of the pipe and to the inside of the fitting. Using the cement appli-

cator, lay on a heavy, even bead all around both surfaces. Fit the pieces immediately so that the pipe will go all the way into the fitting; also, turn the fitting a quarter-turn *in one direction only.* When you are finished, the joint should have an even bead of cement all around. Allow the joint to set completely before putting pressure on it: follow manufacturer's specs.

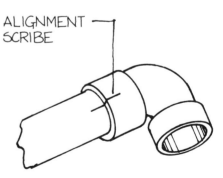

Figure 12.17 Because you should not adjust a cemented fitting once you've given it a quarter-turn, scribe alignment marks beforehand so that you can position it exactly when turning it.

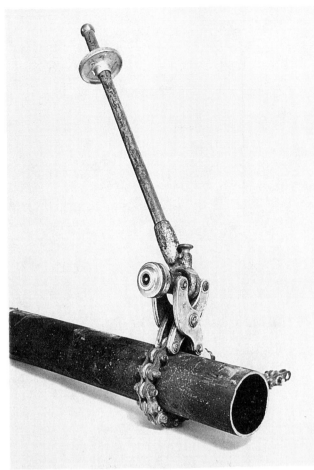

Figure 12.18 Cast-iron cutter.

Figure 12.19 Three band-seal couplings join cast-iron pipe to a no-hub Y fitting; inside each band clamp is a neoprene gasket to ensure a tight fit.

A.

B.

C.

Figure 12.20 Joining dissimilar DWV materials. (A) The traditional way to join hubbed cast iron is with oakum and lead, shown to the side of the sanitary tee. Also depicted is 3-in. copper sweated to a 3 in. × 4 in. enlarger, which can fit into the hubbed piece. (B) A ribbed insert bushing allows you to insert an ABS stack into a hubbed fitting, with no need for oakum or lead. (C) Here a specialized hubless connector, a transition fitting, joins materials of unequal outer dimensions: 3-in. copper and 3-in. plastic. (Thanks to C&D Plumbing, Cheshire, CT.)

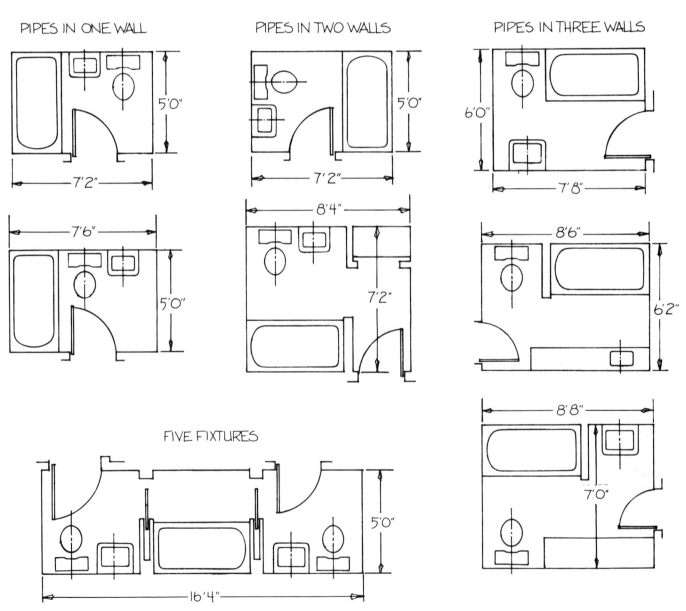

MINIMUM DISTANCES

PIPES IN ONE WALL

PIPES IN TWO WALLS

PIPES IN THREE WALLS

FIVE FIXTURES

Figure 12.21 Minimum fixture and bathroom dimensions. (Adapted from *Architectural Graphic Standards.*)

Because setting times are so short, you must know beforehand exactly in what direction you want the fitting to point, as well as the depth of the pipe's seat in the fitting (see Table 12.1).

It's possible to dry-fit a DWV system before gluing it, but that operation is frustrating and not very productive. Dry runs of pipe are difficult to pull apart; or if you use a lubricant such as petroleum jelly, you must clean the jelly off thoroughly before gluing the pieces together.

Cast iron. If you must cut into cast iron to extend a DWV system, rent a cutter; some types of cast-iron cutters have ratchet heads for working in confined places. Before making cuts, however, carefully support the pipe on both sides of the proposed cut, to prevent movement when a section is removed. It's possible to cut cast iron by scoring around it with a cold chisel, but nonprofessional renovators should not even consider such a tedious and exacting operation.

Once cuts are complete, place a *hubless connector* in the cutout section of cast iron. This fitting simply abuts the newly cut pipe ends, and is held in place by two hubless connectors consisting of neoprene gaskets and steel-band clamps.

When joining DWV pipes of different materials, there are specialized *transition couplings* whose neoprene gaskets are appropriately sized for the different outer diameters (O.D.). There are, for example, copper-to-ABS adapters, cast iron-to-ABS adapters, and so on. These couplings are a real boon to the renovator. Keep in mind, however, that such DWV joints must be supported on both sides of the junction.

Note: Both transition couplings and hubless connectors are drawn tight by band-seal clamps. For this reason, both are sometimes generally referred to as *band-seal couplings.*

In rare instances it is possible to extend the DWV system without cutting into it. Sometimes you can extend outward from an existing clean-out by using a combination of fittings, as shown in Figure 12.36.

ASSESSMENT

If you're upgrading or extending existing supply and DWV systems, begin with the examination of bathrooms and plumbing described in Chapter 1 (pp. 9 and 12). The answers to those questions will tell you if your present pipes are safe and can be extended, or if they must be replaced.

Next, determine if there's enough room for the fixtures you'd like to add. Here, Figure 12.21 will be helpful, for it gives minimum distances required for various fixture groupings. From there go to Figure 12.22, which shows rough-in distances for tub, lav, and toilet. Having tentatively located fixtures, now expose the framing to see if there's room for the pipes to service them—here, we're concerned mostly with DWV pipes because they're bigger.

First, is there room to rough in the pipes or must you cut into framing and, say, double up floor joists so that a drain pipe can descend? The fewer joists you cut into, the better, so run pipe parallel to joists whenever possible. In fact, if waste pipes run perpendicular to joists, try to choose another fixture layout. Next, is there enough height to

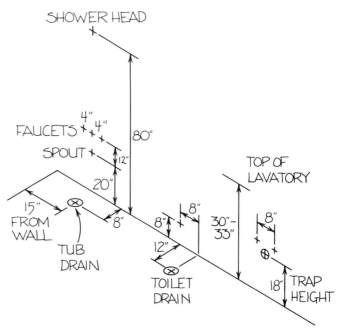

Figure 12.22 Approximate rough-in dimensions.

slope branch drains to the nearest stack? For drain pipes in walls this shouldn't be a problem, but attaining the necessary grade within a floor platform can be a squeaker: *drain pipes must slope downhill at least $\frac{1}{4}$ in. per foot.*

Last, are present pipes big enough to accommodate the increased flow of water to and wastes from additional fixtures? Usually, the answer is yes: most house supply systems are adequately served by 1-in. supply mains, $\frac{3}{4}$-in. trunk lines, and $\frac{1}{2}$-in. branch lines. Extending those lines is straightforward unless pipes are corroded and the water flow is already constricted, in which case you must replace pipes first. DWV pipes in good condition should be large enough to accommodate the wastes of a few additional fixtures, but to be safe, see page 284. Which brings us to layout and two tools—isometric drawings and flow calculations—which help you figure out exactly what parts to order.

LAYOUT

In this section we'll focus on DWV systems. Supply pipe is so much smaller than waste pipe that laying out and installing supply pipe is rarely a problem: in fact, we can cover it in a few paragraphs.

Supply Lines

Using graph or tissue paper, sketch a plan for each floor, including the basement. On the plan(s), note where the service lead enters the house, the position of the water heater, and every fixture or appliance that will use water. Don't forget outdoor spigots.

The most economical layout for supply pipe is a trunk line of $\frac{3}{4}$-in. copper running roughly down the middle of the house, more or less equidistant from fixture groupings on either side. From that $\frac{3}{4}$-in. cold-water trunk, run a $\frac{3}{4}$-in.

takeoff to the water heater, which will emerge as the $\frac{3}{4}$-in. hot-water trunk. From those two trunk lines, draw $\frac{1}{2}$-in. branch lines to individual fixtures. There's no rule which says that those branch lines must come off trunk lines at 90-degree angles, but your drawing—and your installation—will generally look better if they do.

In any event, the layout will be more economical if you run larger pipes down the middle of the house and smaller pipes to fixtures. Another way to conserve materials and space is to cluster fixtures from floor to floor, around the DWV and supply pipes that serve them. By stacking your floor sketches atop each other, you can see how closely fixtures cluster and can see roughly where to route pipes as they rise to the floors above. Or if you're adding fixtures to an existing system, you can see what pipes to extend out from.

Sizing DWV Lines

Sizing drains for individual fixtures is straightforward: just look up the fixture in Table 12.2. A shower, for example, takes a 2-in. pipe; a toilet, 3 in. Vents for individual fixtures are usually a pipe size smaller, because air flows easier than liquids. A 2-in. drain can be vented by a $1\frac{1}{2}$-in. vent; a 3-in. drain by a 2-in. vent pipe.

Sizing a house DWV system is much the same process, but requires some simple calculations to make sure that the cumulative flow of all the branches is not too great for the main drain (and vent) to handle. In most residences, a 3-in. building drain and a 3-in. vent stack are more than adequate, but let's calculate flows anyhow—it's also a good

TABLE 12.2

Sizing drain for individual fixtures[a]

Fixture	Trap/Drain Size (in.)	Flow Units
Bathtub	$1\frac{1}{2}$	2
Shower stall	2	2
Lavatory	$1\frac{1}{4}$	1
Paired lavatories	$1\frac{1}{2}$	2
Kitchen sink and/or dishwasher	2	2
Clothes washer	2	2 or 3
Laundry tub	2	2
Bidet	$1\frac{1}{2}$	2
Toilet	3	4

[a]Figures adapted from Table 4.1 of the *Uniform Plumbing Code.*

way to determine which fittings you need. Every time you change direction, you need a fitting.

Drawing the system. Although plumbers use isometric paper to lay out their pipes, any graph paper will give you a sense of scale. If you're renovating, start by drawing what's there now, beginning with the main drain and the vent stack, and noting their sizes (probably 3 in.). Next draw in fixtures and branch drains, noting their sizes too, and marking where they join the main drain and vent stack—if that juncture is visible—with a heavy black dot. These dots represent fittings.

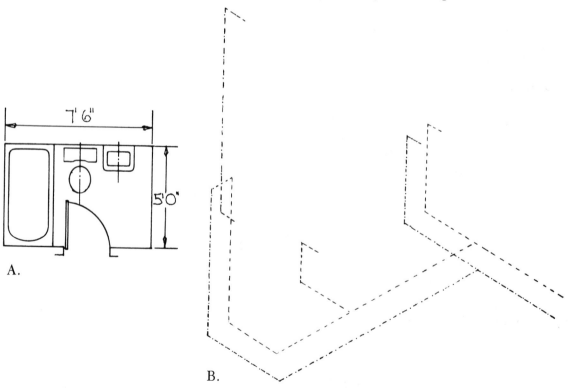

Figure 12.23 Plumbing schematics. Let's envision the setup roughed out in Figure 12.22. (A) The floor plan is a typical three-fixture bathroom with a toilet in the middle. (B) Using plumber's isometric paper to draw the delivery system, we get a three-dimensional profile of the pipes needed—and a first sense of the fittings necessary. Every time a line changes direction, you need a fitting.

C.

D.

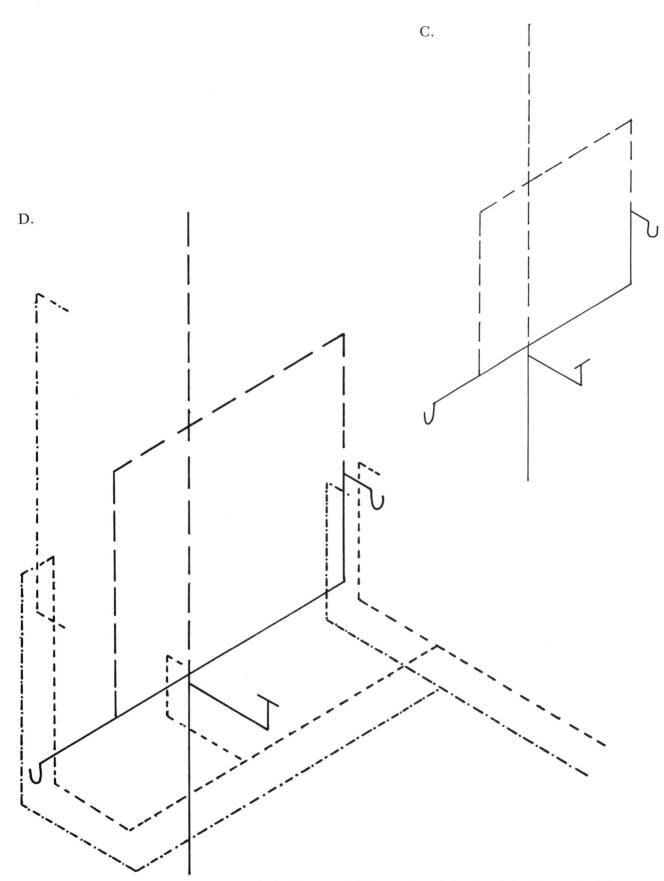

Figure 12.23 Cont. (C) An isometric of the DWV system. Solid lines indicate drain pipes, dashed lines, vents. (D) Combined, the isometrics look like this. The only detail not included is air chambers on supply pipes. With a schematic this detailed, you could go to a plumbing supply store and spec out a job. For a realistic depiction of this setup, see Figure 12.24.

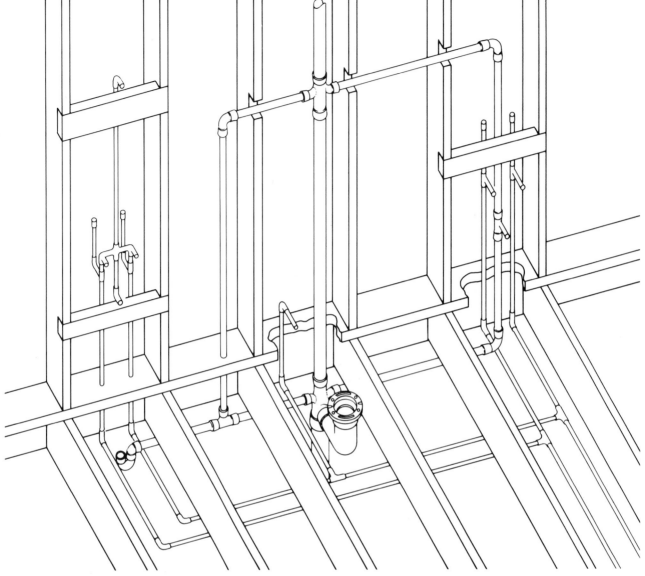

Figure 12.24 What Figure 12.23D would look like assembled. There are many ways to rough in a bathroom, this is one solution.

Now sketch in the fixtures you propose to add, and the branch pipes necessary to tie them into the main drain. Don't forget branch vents, which run to the vent stack. Fittings are discussed in greater detail in Figure 12.15, but some of the more common ones include: *traps* coming off each fixture (toilet traps are internal), *sanitary tees* where trap arms join stacks, *vent tees* and *90-degree ells* where branch vents connect, *T-Y combos* where waste or soil pipes change directions, and so on.

Calculating the flow. Once you've sketched all fixtures, present and future, calculate their cumulative flow, as shown in Figure 12.25, which is based on Table 4-1 of the *Uniform Plumbing Code.* To understand this illustration, imagine water flowing downhill to the main drain: as you pass each fixture, the total flow increases. [Table 12.2 lists flow units (F.U.) for most residential fixtures.] So, looking at the sink at the top of Figure 12.25 (point A), we see that

the sink has 2 F.U., served by 2-in. pipe; further along, at point D, we've picked up the flow of the washer, so we now have 4 F.U.; and at point K, having picked up all the fixtures in the house, 18 F.U., served by a 3-in. drain. If your house's cumulative total is 35 flow units or less, a 3-in. main drain is fine; a horizontal section of 4-in. drain can handle 216 F.U. For branch drains, a horizontal run of 2-in. drain can carry 8 F.U.; vertical 2-in. pipe, 16 units. *Please note:* Although a toilet's unit rating (4) is less than the allowable total for a 2-in. pipe, individual toilets require 3-in. drains.

Local codes vary, but vent stacks should have the same area (in cross section) as the main drain. If it's not possible or desirable to have a single 3-in. vent stack for a house with a 3-in. main drain, the cumulative area of 2-in. and $1\frac{1}{2}$-in. vent stacks must at least equal that of the 3 in. main drain, 28.26 sq in. [Using the formula $A = \pi \times$ radius squared, $3.14 \times (3 \text{ in.})^2 = 28.26$ sq in.]

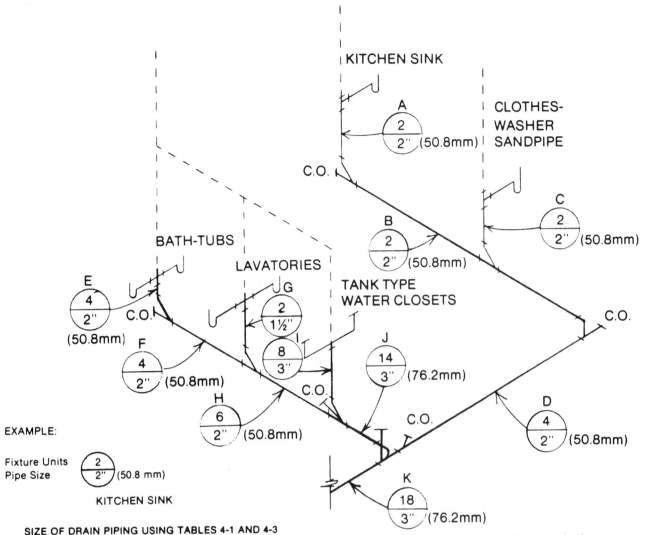

SIZE OF DRAIN PIPING USING TABLES 4-1 AND 4-3
- Obtain fixture unit load from Table 4-1 for each fixture and enter in the upper half of the sizing circle. See example above.
- Using Table 4-3, start from the remote fixture and work back toward the building sewer: adding fixture loads and assigning starting at A and ending at K.

Figure 12.25 Sizing the drainage system. Note the divided circles in the schematic: in the top half, the cumulative fixture unit loads at that point, based on Table 12.2; in the bottom of each circle, the size of drain pipe needed to handle that load. Just before the main drain attaches to the building sewer, there is a cumulative unit load of 18 flow units served by a 3-in. main drain. The system is vented by three 2-in. vent stacks. (This illustration comes from *Uniform Plumbing Code Illustrated Training Manual* and is based upon Tables 4–1 and 4–3 in the 1985 edition, here reprinted courtesy the International Association of Plumbing Officials.)

Venting Options

We've noted several times that renovating plumbing is a trade-off between what you'd like to do and what you can do. The calculations above are important because they ensure that your pipes will be big enough to carry off wastes. But until you expose framing and actually run pipe, it's difficult to know *exactly* how things will fit together. Herewith, a number of configurations that might work for you.

Dry and wet venting. As we noted early in the chapter, vents allow septic gases to escape and, by admitting air, allow wastes to fall. Most of the venting options shown below are examples of *dry venting*, in which a vent stack never serves as a drain for another fixture. If a vent stack is occasionally used as a drain for fixtures above it, it is a *wet vent*.

Important: Wet venting is prohibited by many codes, and the stack should *never* be used to carry soil wastes. But when the vent stack is sized one pipe size larger than normal to ensure a good flow, using it as a wet vent can be safe and will save you money by using fewer fittings and less pipe. Don't defy local codes on wet venting, however; where such prohibitions exist, they are usually enforced. But in practice, many venting hookups are hybrids, as in the stack venting shown in Figure 12.30, where fixtures use the soil stack as both vent and soil stack.

Venting toilets. We'll look at venting toilets first; requiring the largest drains (3 in.) of any fixture, they are the trickiest to route.

Where space beneath a toilet is not a problem, use a setup such as that shown in Figure 12.26A, in which a 2-

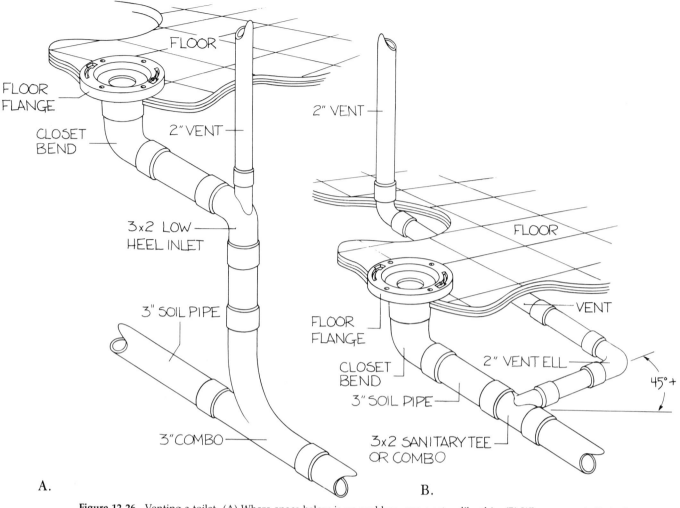

Figure 12.26 Venting a toilet. (A) Where space below is no problem, use a setup like this. (B) Where space is limited, drain and vent pipes must exit less abruptly. Here the critical detail is the angle at which the vent arm departs the soil line—that angle must not be less than 45 degrees, as depicted further in Figure 12.29.

in. vent pipe rises vertically from a 3 × 2 combo, while the 3-in. drain continues on to the house main. Because of the large diameter of this drain, this vent can be as far as 6 ft from the fixture, as noted in Table 12.3.

Where space is tight, say, on a second-floor bathroom with finished ceilings below, the drain and vent pipes will exit less abruptly, as shown in Figure 12.26B. Here, the critical detail is the angle at which the vent leaves the 3 × 2 sanitary tee: as shown in Figure 12.29, that vent takeoff must be 45° degrees above a horizontal cross section of the drain. If it is less than that, the outlet might clog with waste and no longer function as a vent.

TABLE 12.3

Stack-vented fixtures

Diameter of Waste Pipe (in.)	Maximum Distance to Soil Stack (ft)
$1\frac{1}{2}$	$3\frac{1}{2}$
2	5
3	6
4	10

When you've got two toilets back to back, you can save some space by picking up both with a single *figure-four* fitting, also called a *double combo*. From the top of the fitting, send up a 2-in. or 3-in. vent; from the two side sockets, the two 3-in. soil pipes serving the toilets; and use a *long-sweep ell* (or a combo) on the bottom, to send wastes on to the main drain. This detail is about the only way to situate back-to-back water closets, and quite handy for anyone adding a half-bath.

Back venting. *Back venting,* or *continuous venting,* is the dry-venting method shown in Figure 12.27, and it is acceptable to even the strictest codes. (Check anyway, to make sure.) All the fixtures in the illustration have a branch vent—except, arguably, the toilet on the second floor, which vents directly to the soil stack. Routing this maze of vent pipes can be tricky in a renovation.

In a typical installation, the trap arm of, say, a lavatory empties into the middle leg of a sanitary tee. The branch drain descends from the lower leg, the branch vent from the upper.

When a branch vent takes off from a relatively horizontal section of drainpipe, the angle at which it departs is crucial. It may go straight up, or it may leave at a 45-degree

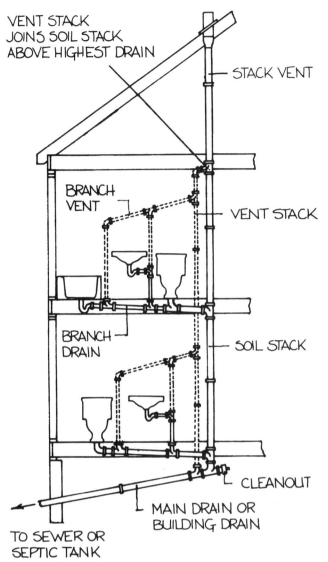

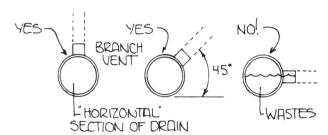

Figure 12.29 Cross section of a branch vent. The angle at which a vent leaves a horizontal drain is critical: it must be at least 45 degrees. If the angle is less than that, wastes may clog the vent.

Figure 12.27 Back-venting: all fixtures have branch vents.

angle, to work around an obstruction. But it must never exit from the side of a drainpipe: if it did, it could become clogged with waste.

Branch vents must rise to a height of at least 42 in. above the floor before beginning their horizontal run to the vent stack. This measurement adds a safety margin of 6 in. above the height of the highest fixture (e.g., a sink set at 36 in.), so there is no danger of waste flowing into the vent. Since branch vents run to a vent stack, they must maintain an upward pitch of at least $\frac{1}{8}$ in. per foot.

Stack venting. Clustering plumbing fixtures around a soil stack is probably the oldest method of venting. In the early days of indoor plumbing, users observed that fixtures that were near the stack retained the water in their traps, whereas those (unvented) that were at a distance did not. This method, known as *stack venting*, employs the soil stack both as a waste drain and as a vent pipe. Although this wet-venting method allows less flexibility in the arrangement of plumbing fixtures, the savings in plumbing supplies are considerable, and cuts through joists and studs are minimized.

When stack venting, don't place a toilet above other fixtures on the stack; its greater discharge could break the water seals in the traps of small-dimension pipes. If you must add fixtures below those already stack-vented, add (or extend) vent stacks and branch vents. The maximum allowable distance from stack-vented fixtures to the soil

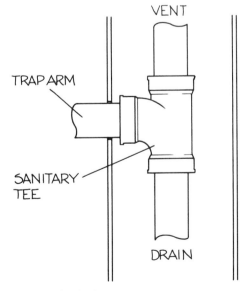

Figure 12.28 Individual trap arms empty into sanitary tees.

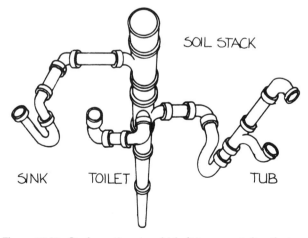

Figure 12.30 Stack venting, in which fixtures vent directly to a soil stack, is effective if the fixtures are close enough. Because of the mass of wastes from a toilet, however, it must always be the lowest fixture on a stack. Some local authorities do not allow stack venting.

stack depends on the size of the pipe serving a particular fixture (Table 12.3).

In theory, you can increase the diameter of the waste pipe of a fixture so that you can stack-vent it; but, in reality, this is impractical. Although Table 12.3 indicates a maximum distance of 6 ft for a 3-in. waste pipe, stack-vented toilets are more commonly located 3 to 5 ft from the stack. Furthermore, the difficulty of routing a 4-in. pipe 10 ft. (through joists) makes back venting much more feasible.

Other venting options. When fixtures are too far away for vent-stack connection—as when a laundry room or a bathroom is on the other end of the house—run a separate vent, or stack vent, from the fixture, up through the roof. This solution, also called *individual venting*, obviates the need for

a long run of branch-vent pipe; it does, however, mean another pipe through the roof.

Common Vents. A common vent is appropriate where fixtures are side by side or back to back. This type of vent is installed with little more than a double tee fitting, or a double combo for back-to-back toilets. An example is shown in Figure 12.32.

Loop Vents. If you plan an island counter in the middle of a room, venting can be problematic. The sink drain is concealed easily enough in the floor platform, but the branch vent, lacking a nearby wall through which it can exit, requires some ingenuity. This problem is solved by the loop shown in Figure 12.33.

In addition to the fittings shown, note these details as well: the loop must go as high under the counter as possible, and at least 6 in. above the juncture of the trap arm and the sanitary tee, to preclude any siphoning of wastewater from the sink; whereas the vent portions may be $1\frac{1}{2}$-in. pipe, drain sections must be 2 in.; and drain sections must have the *minimal* downward pitch of $\frac{1}{4}$ in. per foot.

Mechanical Vents. These devices, also known as *pop vents*, allow you to use a fixture before vent runs are complete (e.g., before you run a vent stack up through the roof). Here's how they work. As water drains from a sink, it creates a partial vacuum within the pipes, depressing a spring inside the vent, and sucking air in. When the water is almost gone and the vacuum equalized, the spring extends and pushes its diaphragm up, sealing off outside air once again.

Mechanical vents are *temporary* vents only. Because their mechanisms can wear out and allow septic gases into living space, they must never be used as permanent vents, nor used in enclosed spaces where they cannot draw air easily.

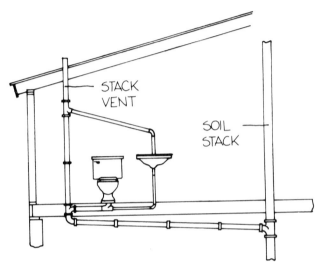

Figure 12.31 Individual venting, favored when fixtures are not near enough to vent to the main soil stack, employs a separate stack up through the roof.

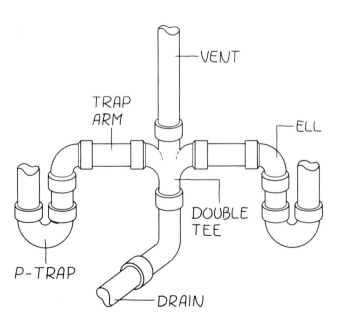

Figure 12.32 A double tee (or T-Y) fitting is the simplest way to create a common vent shared by back-to-back fixtures.

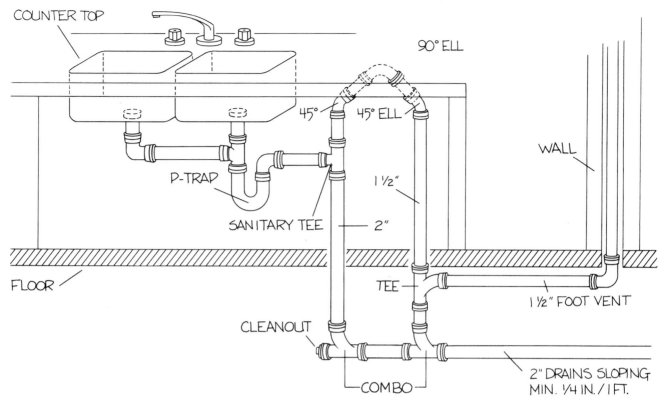

Figure 12.33 Venting an island counter is problematic because there is no wall nearby for a branch vent: the looped vent above is one solution approved by most codes. Critical to its success is the foot vent, which connects to the loop via a Y-fitting; run the foot vent to the nearest wall and up through the roof or, if it's necessary to connect it to another vent, that connection must be at least 6 in. higher than the top of the lav or sink rim served by the looped vent. The looped vent itself should extend as high as possible under the countertop; preassemble the loop to make construction easier.

Additional Details

Drainage fittings. Use a *long-sweep ell* or a *combo* (combination T-Y) when making a 90-degree bend on "horizontal" runs of waste and soil pipes, and where vertical pipes empty into horizontal ones. Use a standard ell when going from horizontal to vertical. Where trap arms join vent stacks, use *sanitary tees*. (Long-sweep fittings are *not* required on turns in vent pipe: regular tees and ells may be used there.)

Clean-outs. Clean-outs are *required* where a building main joins a lead pipe from sewer or septic tank; at the upper ends of waste pipes below the first floor (e.g., where the soil stack joins the building drain); and wherever waste pipes change direction more than 135 degrees. They are advisable whenever heavy flow increases the possibility of clogging, such as in back-to-back toilets. There must be enough room around the clean-out to operate a power auger or other equipment, should that be necessary.

Vent termination. Vent stacks through the roof should be flashed with a suitable watertight base. Stack tops must be at least 6 in. above the roof, along the upper side of the flashing, and at least 3 ft above any part of a skylight or window that can be opened. Considering horizontal distances, a vent stack must not be closer than 12 in. to a parapet wall.

Ordering materials. Take your floor sketches and calcula-

tions to a plumbing supplier. Having sized your DWV pipes according to the flow they'll carry, you will also have determined the sizes of the fittings necessary for every change in direction and fixture takeoff. For each size of pipe, order 20 percent more than you think you'll need. Get extra fittings, too: at least one extra for each type (and size) you think you'll need, plus an extra half-dozen each of the more common fittings such as tees, combos, ells, long-sweep ells, 45-degree ells, couplings, and so on.

These same rules of thumb hold true for supply fittings. Returning extra fittings later should be no problem, but check with your supplier to be sure. Finally, don't forget solder, flux, cement, plastic plumber's strap, propane, emery cloth, and other consumables—plus enough pipe hangers to support pipe every 4 ft.

ROUGHING-IN THE PLUMBING

In this section we will again focus on the DWV system: larger and more difficult to position, it must be roughed out first. (Assume that we're talking about ABS plastic pipe unless noted otherwise.) You can tie into existing supply pipe almost anywhere, and route it with impunity. Routing a DWV system, however, is an accommodation of two givens: the location of the fixtures, as described under "layout" above, and the point at which you tie into the building drain.

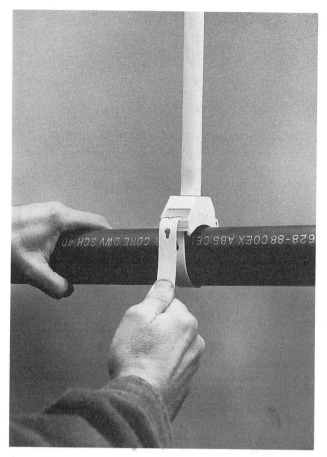

A.

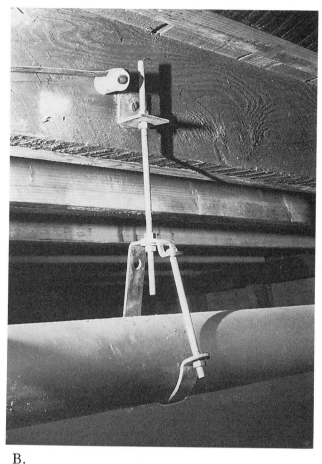

B.

C.

Figure 12.34 All plumbing parts must be tightly joined and securely supported so that they stay tight. (A) Pipe hanger for ABS pipe; (B) hanger for cast iron; (C) stack clamp, or floor clamp.

Roughing-in the Building Drain

It would be impossible to depict all the ways you might connect to a building drain when renovating, so we'll concentrate on three: (1) building out from the sewer lead, where you would start if you were gutting an existing DWV system or installing one for the first time; (2) doing an "end run," or building out from the end of the house drain, where it meets the soil stack; and (3) joining the building drain in mid run (i.e, cutting into a straight section of pipe).

Building out from the sewer pipe. Floor sketches in hand, begin in the basement by marking fixture drains on the underside of the subflooring. You can also mark them on the floor above and drill pilot holes down through the flooring—whatever works. One of those marks will represent the soil stack, which will rise to serve bathrooms on the upper floor(s) and eventually exit through the roof. The building drain—the main drain into which all lesser drains flow—will run from the base of that soil stack to the sewer pipe sticking out of the foundation.

Hanging the Building Drain. Some people stretch string to simulate the layout, but our favorite way to envision the building drain and the points at which branch drains will enter it is to temporarily hang a piece of 3-in. ABS pipe, which comes in 20-ft lengths. Although the drain will be supported every 4 ft when the installation is complete, just tack it in place now with a pipe hanger every 8 ft or so. Do take pains, however, to align the ends of the 3-in. main to the end of the sewer pipe and to the base of the soil stack. Also, using a level and a tape measure, make sure that the drain has a *minimal* downward slope of $\frac{1}{4}$ in. per foot. You'll take this 20-ft length down later to cut it, but if you've set the pipe hangers to the correct height, drain sections will be correctly positioned as you glue them up.

That done, set out the drain pipe and fittings you'll need to run branch lines from fixtures to the building main. Make sure that each of these lines also has the minimal downward slope to the building drain.

Cementing Drain Sections. There are many sequences in which you might connect drain pipe. It seems easiest to start at the lowest point: build out from the sewer pipe, and add fittings for branch drains as you progress toward the soil stack.

Using a hubless connector, join the first section of building drain to the sewer pipe. Just above that connection, add a tee or a T-Y as shown in Figure 12.35, which

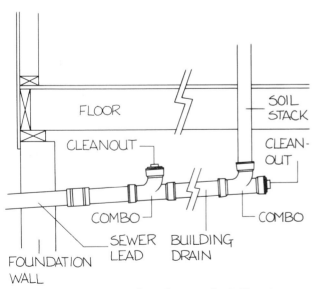

Note that there must be a clean-out at the long sweep where the main drain joins the soil stack. Drains must maintain a minimal downward pitch of $\frac{1}{4}$ in. to 1 ft. Not shown are pipe hangers, which should occur every 4 ft, and on both sides of band-seal couplings.

Figure 12.35 Building out from the sewer lead. There is no one right way to assemble pipes; your solution may vary. Insert a combo (T-Y) fitting near the beginning of the drain and you'll be able to block the new DWV system when you test it for leaks later; it's also a convenient place for a clean-out.

will enable you to block the lowest end of the new DWV system when you test it later for leaks (p. 297).

As you add fittings to serve branch drains, make sure that their takeoffs are properly angled toward the fixture(s) they will serve. Before gluing, dry-fit the pieces and scribe alignment marks on both the pipe and the fitting, as shown in Figure 12.17. Then, when you turn the fitting a quarter-turn to spread the cement, you'll know when to stop.

Where the drain will turn up into the soil stack, attach a long-sweep ell or a combo; in either case, there must be a cleanout above the highest point of this "horizontal" run of building drain. For now, the soil stack itself need only stub out 3 to 4 ft above the first floor, so you can add fittings to extend it later. But take pains to secure the bottom of the soil stack so that it won't slip down later: wrap plastic plumber's strap around the base of the stack, and nail it securely to joists.

Once the main body of the building drain is connected, you can drill individual drain holes through the floor and work up from the main drain to them. Before doing so, however, add pipe hangers so that there is now one every 4 ft along the main drain, and at each hubless connector joint.

An "end run" out from the main drain. Extending the DWV system out from the end of the building drain—where it joins the soil stack—can be the least disruptive way to go. Before any cutting or assembly, however, flush the main drain well with water; shut off all supply pipes so that no one can use fixtures while you've got pipes apart; and support both sides of the section you'll be cutting out. This last point is particularly important so that pipes don't slip down, putting stress on existing connections and possibly misaligning pipes you're tying into. Particularly note the base of the soil stack: if your cuts make it impossible to run pipe strap under the stack, use a stack clamp as shown in Figure 12.34C.

The exact configuration of the end run will depend on the size of the main drain, the fitting currently at the base of the stack, the fixtures you propose to add and the size of the drain needed to serve them, and the room available in which to work. If you are not adding a toilet, the drain extension can be 2-in. pipe, which increases the options you have. If you're adding a toilet, however, you must build out with a 3-in. drain, which precludes using adapters such as *ribbed bushings* (Figure 12.20B) or *male-threaded adapters* (Figure 12.36C), for they would constrict the opening of the receiving fitting too much. If you must extend out with 3-in. pipe, therefore, you may have to cut out the existing T-Y and start over.

If the soil stack currently ends in a long-sweep ell, support the stack and then cut out that fitting, replacing it with a new T-Y. You can then add a new section of drain out from the end of that fitting. (Where the original setup employs a long-sweep ell, there is usually a combo with a clean-out above it, so there is no need to add a clean-out.)

The end-run approach is relatively uncomplicated if there's room to work and enough clear pipe to attach to. (Whether gluing or using hubless connectors, you generally attach them to a length of pipe, rather than attaching to another fitting.) Thus you may have to cut out a longer section, then preassemble a new configuration of fittings (and pipe) and pop it into place.

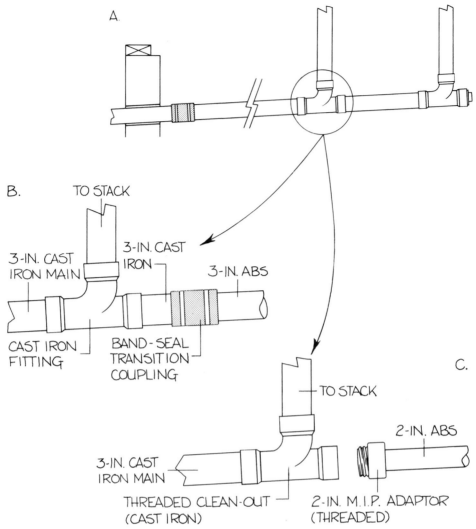

Figure 12.36 When adding fixtures to an existing DWV system, it's common to build out from the end of the main drain. (A) If you build out from a clean-out, you must replace it with a new one at the end of the extension. (B) If the present clean-out is a cast-iron inset caulked with oakum, remove the oakum and the inset and caulk in a new section of 3-in. cast-iron pipe. From there, use a transition coupling to continue with 3-in. plastic. (C) When building out from a threaded cast-iron clean-out, use a plastic M.I.P. (male iron pipe) adapter. Note, however, that this transition reduces the opening, so you can build out only with 2-in. ABS pipe.

Joining the main drain in mid run. Note the above comments about flushing the drain and supporting both sides of the section you remove. (This includes side-to-side support so that pipe sections won't sway when you cut into them.) Before you cut, make sure the branch drain you'll be adding has the minimal downward pitch. Preassemble the replacement section before you cut into the building main, the section being a T-Y combo with short (1 ft) stubs of 3-in. pipe glued in each end. Holding the replacement section in one hand, make crayon marks onto the main drain with the other, to indicate cut marks. But before cutting, one useful tip:

Use hubless connectors with neoprene gaskets to attach the new section to the main drain. Once you've cut into the drain, you'll slide a hubless connector onto each end, insert the replacement section, and then slide the connectors back onto the 3-in. stubs. Trouble is, the neoprene

gasket within won't slide easily because it has a small stop-lip inside, a sort of depth gauge to stop incoming pipe in the middle of the gasket. (Look inside a hubless connector and all of this will be apparent.) Using a utility knife, pare out this lip. Finally, center a hubless connector over each crayon mark you made earlier and make a second mark to indicate the outer end—the end away from the fitting—of each connector. These new marks show where to stop when you slide the connectors on.

Drilling and Cutting into Framing

In many installations it's possible to extend or tie into the main drain without altering the framing. To run branch lines and vents, however, it's almost always necessary to notch or drill into joists and studs. So pipe won't bind as it's routed, pipe holes should be $\frac{1}{4}$ in. larger than the diame-

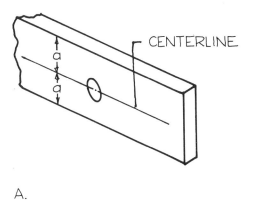

A.

B.

Figure 12.37 Cutting into a structure. (A) Drilled holes must be centered in joists and no larger than one-fourth of the depth of the joist or 2 in.—whichever is less. (B) Notches must be one-sixth of the depth of a joist or less; reinforce any cut which exceeds that size.

ter of the pipe and perpendicular to the surface of the wood. Using a right-angle drill—which fits easily between joists or studs—ensures perpendicularity.

Note: Cutting into framing weakens it. If you can avoid cutting or drilling by rerouting pipes, do so.

Joists. You may *not* cut or drill into joists smaller than 2×6s. If they are 2×6 or greater, you may do so if you observe the following rules:

1. Notch a joist no deeper than one-sixth of its total depth (e.g., 1 in. deep for a 2×6); never notch a joist in the middle one-third of its span, however.

2. You may drill holes along the entire span of a joist, provided that:

    a. Those holes are centered (top to bottom) in the joist.

    b. Holes are no larger than one-fourth of the depth of the joist, or 2 in.—whichever is less.

    c. Hole centers are no closer than the joist is deep (e.g., in 2 × 6 joists, you should space holes at least 6 in. apart).

3. According to the rules above, it's almost impossible to run a 3-in. drain through a joist; instead, create a rough opening with doubled headers (p. 306) for that pipe to pass through.

4. Where holes slightly exceed the allowances above, bolster the weakened area by nailing on $\frac{3}{4}$-in. plywood "sisters" to the joist. Check with local code, though.

Figure 12.38 Protect pipe with a steel nail guard (nail-protection plate).

Studs. Drilling into studs is largely the same.

1. Holes should be centered in studs, and should be no larger than one-third of the stud width.

2. Where pipe would exceed that limit, it's preferable to frame up with oversized studs (e.g., 2×6s) or to increase the stud width by furring out with additional material (e.g., nailing 2×2s onto existing 2×4s).

3. To prevent finish nails from puncturing pipes, affix steel nail-protection plates to the edge of the stud.

4. It is usually against code to notch the edges of studs, but where that is unavoidable, protect the pipe and bolster the stud with a *steel shoe* (Figure 4.11).

Connecting Branch Drains and Vents

Having located fixtures, exposed framing behind, and cut holes through which to route drains and such, now continue assembling pipe. Again, there is no absolute sequence. If it's more convenient to run branch drains into sanitary tees on the stack, build up the stack next; if it's less work to have branch drains empty directly into sanitary tees on the main drain, do that. There are too many possibilities for rigid rules, but in general start with the larger pipes.

Running the 3-in. soil pipe to the toilet is a bit exacting. First center the *closet ell* beneath the hole drilled for the toilet drain, flush to the underside of the floor. Beneath the ell add 2 × 4 blocking end-nailed through adjacent joists, or plastic plumber's strap nailed to joists. Then add pipe sections back to the fitting on the main drain. Apart from aligning pipe, your biggest concern will be positioning the venting takeoff correctly, especially if you use the limited-space configuration shown in Figure 12.26B. Once you're satisfied with the assembly from the main drain to the closet ell, glue all the pieces together. Then go upstairs, apply cement to the *floor flange*, slide the flange over the closet ell, give a quarter-turn to spread the cement, and screw the flange down to the floor. (If the finish floor is not down yet, position the flange atop a few pieces of scrap.)

Next run the smaller fixture drains up from the main drain to the first floor. As you attach fittings to the main, align their takeoffs towards the pipe holes you roughed out in the floor. Remember, too, that drains must maintain a

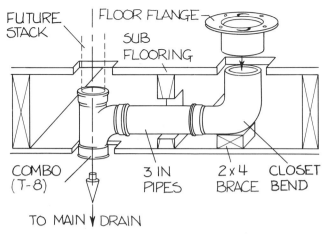

Figure 12.39 Because soil pipes are large, position them first in relation to the soil stack to come. Use plastic plumber's strap to hold closet bends to a 2×4 brace beneath. The floor flange fits over the top of the closet bend.

Figure 12.40 It's wise to block off all horizontal runs. Here, a length of 2-in. ABS that ends in a P-trap and a shower-drain assembly. The ribbed rubber bushing will compress when the top of the assembly is bolted down. Note also the white glue-on cap sealing the pipe for testing. (For this and the two on-site shots immediately following, thanks to Leigh Marymor Plumbing, Oakland, CA.)

pitch of at least $\frac{1}{4}$ in. per ft, and all pipe must be supported every 4 ft. Run tub drainpipe to just beneath the floor, where the tub trap arm will descend, and stub up pipes for lavs and sinks at least 6 in. above the floor. You can extend these pipes later. In any event, all branch drains end in a sanitary tee: the horizontal leg of the tee receives the trap arm from the fixture (discussed in ''Installing Fixtures'' below), and the upper leg of the tee is the beginning of the branch vent.

Next assemble vent lines, starting with the largest vent—often the 2-in. or 3-in. pipe rising from the sanitary tee (or T-Y combo) below the closet ell. Individual branch vents then run to that stack, usually joining it in an *inverted* tee. Because ''horizontal'' runs of $1\frac{1}{2}$-in. branch vents must be at least 42 in. above the floor—or 6 in. above the flood rim of the highest fixture—and those runs must slope upward slightly, the inverted tee in the vent stack will typically be 4 to 5 ft above the floor. But again, these are just

observations, not rules. So, continue to build up the vent stack, with as few jogs as possible, until it eventually passes through a flashing unit (neoprene and metal) set in the roof. Tops of vents must be well above operable windows, as specified in Figure 12.44.

Miscellany: support all pipe—whether vent, drain, horizontal, or vertical—every 4 ft. Also, use plastic plumber's strap to secure the sanitary tees where trap arms, branch vents, and branch drains intersect. Should you use sanitary tees or T-Ys to join branch vents to stacks, invert those fittings so that rainwater will run freely down the stack. Finally, where you must run a length of pipe between two impossibly complicated and already glued-down fittings to complete an assembly, fret not: cut *two* pieces of pipe that just fit, smear their free ends with plastic cement, and slide on a *slip fitting* to join them in the middle.

Figure 12.41 Individual fixture vents rise at least 6 in. above fixtures and join a branch vent that gently ascends to the vent stack at right.

Figure 12.42 A second-story detail: 2-in. vent stubs about to join in a horizontal run to the large stack in the foreground.

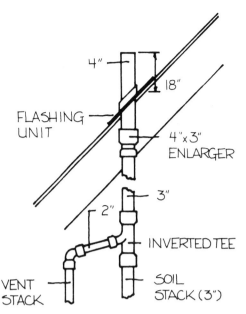

Figure 12.43 The top of a DWV system. Where a vent stack joins a soil stack, invert the tee so that gases rise without impediment and rain runs easily down the pipe. Enlargers are used mostly in cold climates, to offset the constriction of the stack by frost; in temperate areas they're not necessary.

Testing the DWV System

Once the DWV system is roughed out—but before hooking up fixtures—you must test for leaks. The most common test is filling the pipes with water, so start by sealing all pipes except the highest stack, where you'll insert your garden hose. Although that stack need not extend through the roof

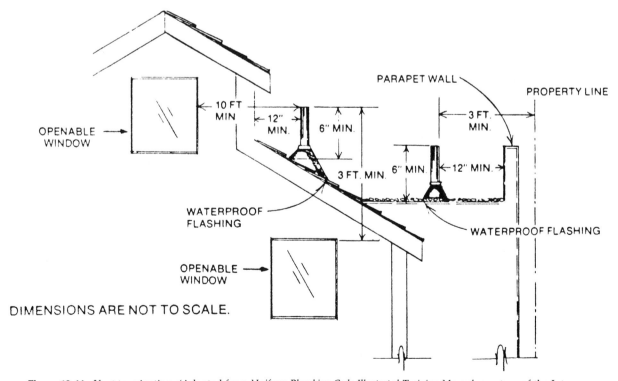

Figure 12.44 Vent termination. (Adapted from *Uniform Plumbing Code Illustrated Training Manual,* courtesy of the International Association of Plumbing Officials.)

yet, it should be at least 10 ft above the highest fitting in the system. Pipe glue should dry at least a day before this test.

There are several types of seals. The most common and least expensive is a *glue-on cap,* typically a lightweight plastic cap that glues inside the pipe stub. When the test is completed, cut off the small section of pipe in which the cap is glued. Where the stack is particularly high, say, several stories, this is the only cap type guaranteed not to dislodge.

The other devices are rubber devices which can be reused. The *jim cap* fits over the end of a pipe and tightens with a ring clamp. *Test plugs* fit into pipe ends and are expanded by a wing-nut assembly. The last plug, known as a *double-dynamiter* out west, is a spring-loaded device which you can rent to close off the lowest point in the DWV system: the T-Y combo at the foot of the building drain. As you'll note in Figure 12.46, this tool has two rubber balls which can be expanded or contracted by turn screws on the shaft. Insert the balls so that the forward one lodges in drain pipe, and expand it; the second ball should block the open leg of the T-Y combo.

Should you see any leaks, drain the system and fix them, then refill. Once there are no more leaks, allow the water to stand at least overnight, or until the inspector signs off on your system. To release the water, contract the balls of the double-dynamiter in the order in which you expanded them. Loosened, the forward ball will allow the test water to run down the drain; releasing the second ball allows you to remove the tool. You might want to label the

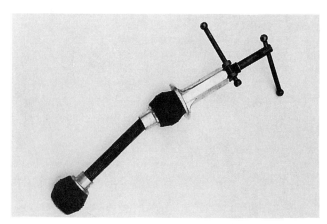

Figure 12.46 When filling the DWV system for testing, use a double dynamiter to block the T-Y fitting at the base of the main drain.

respective turn-screws: release the second ball first and you may get a faceful of very unpleasant water.

If there are finish ceilings in place below second-story pipes and you don't want to risk wetting them with a failed connection, there is an air-pressure test in which all openings are sealed and the system pumped up with air. When a pressure gauge shows no pressure loss for a prescribed period of time, the inspector signs off.

Roughing-in Supply Pipes

The supply system begins with a service lead pipe which runs to the house from the city main or a private well. Connect the house's main trunk line to the service lead with an appropriate fitting. When those two pipes are different materials, they must be joined with a brass nipple or a *dielectric union* to forestall corrosion. *Note:* The dielectric union has an insulator inside which will not conduct electricity. If your electrical system is grounded to the water main, put a jumper across that union.

As noted earlier, a branch off the cold-water trunk becomes the hot-water trunk line. When connecting the water heater (Figure 12.69), put unions and shutoff valves on both the pipe running into the heater and the pipe coming out; this will make periodic drainage and repairs easier. The hot-water main coming out of the water heater should be the same diameter as the pipe feeding into it, or slightly smaller; it should never be larger than the infeed. Finally, be sure to equip the water heater with a pressure-and-temperature relief valve, and aim that valve's drainpipe at the floor.

With hot and cold trunk lines connected, you're set to run water to all fixtures. In general, as pipe runs get closer to fixtures, they step down in diameter. Service pipes are usually 1 or $1\frac{1}{4}$ in. in interior diameter (I.D.); trunk lines are $\frac{3}{4}$ in. I.D.; branch pipes, $\frac{1}{2}$ in. I.D.; and supply risers to toilets and lavatories, often $\frac{3}{8}$ in. I.D. You're saving a little money by using smaller-diameter pipes, but the major reason for stepping down sizes is to ensure an adequate supply of water—with no drop in pressure—when several fixtures are used at the same time.

Where pipes run parallel to joists, support pipes every 4 ft so that they won't belly. Where they run perpendicular, nail support straps to the underside of every other joist.

Figure 12.45 Testing cap (top) and testing plug.

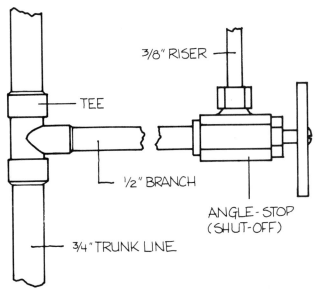

Figure 12.47 Trunk, branch, and riser lines.

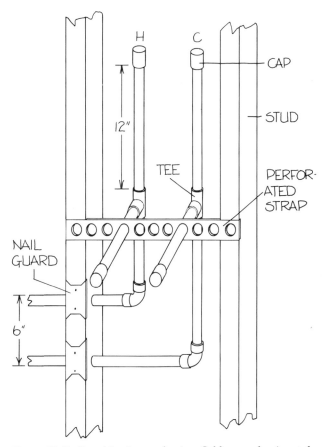

Figure 12.48 Roughing in supply pipe. Solder supply-pipe stubs directly to perforated strap (also called Hold-Rites) nailed to studs. Air chambers should rise 12 in. above the tees from which stubs emerge.

You can also drill holes and run pipe through joists, as spelled out on page 295. Because the water supply system is under pressure, pipe slope is irrelevant, although supply pipes in cold climates should have a slightly downward pitch toward drainage points.

As you route hot- and cold-water pipes, keep them 6 in. apart; they should never touch. To save money, insulate hot-water pipes. At fixtures, always hook up hot-water lines on the left side, cold on the right. When your eyes are shut tight against soap suds and you're groping for a spigot, you'll want to know which is hot.

So that you can service fixtures later, install shutoff valves on each branch pipe feeding in. In addition, the supply pipes to outdoor spigots or to cold rooms should have shutoffs and unions within the main basement. To prevent turbulence and noise, be sure to open all valves completely once the system is hooked up.

While on the subject of noise, you can reduce it greatly by adding *air chambers* as shown in Figure 12.48. The cham-ber, a dead-air space above the tee, cushions the impact of the rushing water, which is stopped dead when a faucet is suddenly shut. (Air compresses, water does not.) And when attaching pipes to joists, use plastic straps and insula-tors (Figure 12.49) to keep pipe from vibrating against fram-ing members.

Figure 12.49 When attaching supply pipes, use plastic straps and insulators to keep pipe from vibrating against framing members.

Figure 12.50 A typical rough-in for a lavatory: perforated strap, stubs, nail plates, DWV pipe. The vertical pipe at the left serves a lavatory on the other side of the wall.

At the tee fittings where supply pipes end in air chambers, and pipe stubs enter living space, it's important to support pipes adequately. Supply-pipe stubs should stick into living space at least 6 in. so that they can be extended later. To keep them from moving, solder stubs to perforated copper strap or heavy-gauge steel straps, nailed or screwed to studs. These straps, also called *Hold-Rites,* are great time-savers. So you don't have a bulge in the finish surface, chisel straps into the studs.

Shower stubs should be 72 to 80 in. high; the diverter valve assembly about 48 in. high; water closet stubs about 8 in. above the finish floor; lavatory stubs, no more than 18 in. above the floor.

The water supply system is its own test. To check pipes before you close up walls, solder caps onto all pipe stubs and open all valves. If there are no leaks, install nail-protection plates over pipes running in studs, and put up finish surfaces.

Extending Pipes to Fixtures: A Brief Review

The preceding sections about installing DWV and supply pipe are lengthy, so here's an encapsulation:

1. Locate DWV and supply runs convenient to tie into, and cut back finish walls to the nearest stud center on either side.

2. Establish the point at which you'll cut into the DWV pipe. Drain stubs for lavatories are usually 18 in. above the floor, for example; stubs for kitchen sinks, 15 in. high. If the fixture is distant from the takeoff point, remember that

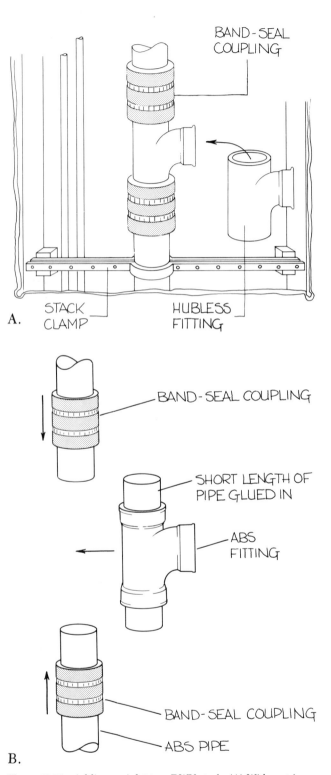

Figure 12.51 Adding an inlet to a DWV stack. (A) With cast iron, use a no-hub tee and hubless connectors. (B) With ABS, glue short lengths of pipe to a sanitary tee, then use hubless connectors to join them to stack sections. There are also ABS slip–couplings (not shown), but cementing them in is messy.

its trap arm must have a minimal downward pitch of $\frac{1}{4}$ in. per foot.

3. Support pipe to be cut into, on both sides of the cut, using strap hangers.

4. Flush DWV pipe, if possible; close gate valves controlling supply pipe, open faucets on line to drain pipe. *Important:* leave faucets open thereafter so you can safely solder on new fittings.

5. Cut existing pipes and debur them. *Important:* Use only hand tools to cut supply pipe; using power tools here is unsafe.

6. Preassemble fitting assemblies for both DWV and supply pipes.

7. Attach DWV fittings.

a. Use a hubless connector to tie the new DWV fitting assembly into the existing DWV line.

b. Slide connectors onto existing drainpipe, insert fitting, point takeoff leg toward fixture, slide connectors onto fitting leads, tighten band-seal clamps on connectors.

8. Join supply fittings.

a. *Important:* If connecting copper to galvanized steel, you must use a dielectric union (Figure 12.7).

b. To join copper to copper, slide slip connectors onto existing supply lines, flux supply pipe and fitting leads, insert fitting, position takeoff legs toward fixtures, slide slip connectors onto fitting leads, heat fittings, apply solder.

9. Stub outs.

a. Initially, supply pipe stubs should extend at least 6 in. into living space and be soldered to a perforated strap nailed across studs.

b. DWV pipe should also stub out at least 6 in., bolstered with plastic plumber's strap wrapped around and nailed to studs. Do *not* use metal strap on plastic pipe.

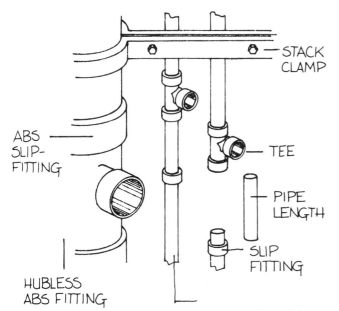

Figure 12.52 To add supply takeoffs, use tees and slip–fittings. Drain the pipe before cutting and soldering.

10. Cap stubs and test the systems.

11. Install finish surfaces, leaving (capped) pipe stubs sticking 6 in. into living spaces.

12. Remove caps and extend pipe to fixtures, as described below.

INSTALLING FIXTURES

This section begins with disconnecting old fixtures, proceeds to a brief review of the steps necessary to extend pipe to new fixtures, and concludes with attaching pipes and mounting fixtures.

Disconnecting Old Fixtures

Note: Use only hand tools on or near water lines, because electrical service is often grounded to the water main. At the very least, cutting into a water line with a metal-cutting blade in a reciprocating saw could destroy the saw; at worst, a short circuit while using a power tool to cut supply pipe could be fatal to you.

Before disconnecting the delivery lines, find the shutoff valves that serve these lines. In most recent installations, shutoffs will be at the base of the pipe; older setups may have only a main valve that shuts off water to large areas of the house. Such main valves are usually in the basement or, in an apartment, embedded in a nearby wall, the floor, or in a closet.

After shutting off the controlling valve, open faucets to drain water. Near the sink there may be unions on each supply pipe, which can be disconnected, using two pipe wrenches. Otherwise, the supply pipe is attached to threaded faucet stems on the underside of the basin. For these, you will need a basin wrench to loosen the nuts.

Disconnecting the drainpipe is similar. Use two pipe wrenches to loosen the slip coupling of the P-trap. Because older galvanized couplings may have seized up, heat the couplings with a propane torch, tapping them lightly with a hammer to free the seizure. Then try again with the wrenches.

When drain and supply pipes have been disconnected, lift the sink off its wall hanger and set it aside. Old, cast-iron lavatories can be quite heavy, so you may want help lifting the fixture. Immediately wad an old rag or a plastic bag stuffed with wadded newspapers in the drainpipe, to keep sewer gases at bay. If you want to reuse old fittings or pipes, uncouple them carefully, or use a pipe cutter or hacksaw to cut through.

To remove a toilet, shut off the water to the unit by turning the supply valve near the base (or back) of the unit. Flush the toilet and remove any remaining water with a cup or with rags. Keep a plastic trash bag handy. Disconnect the tank from the toilet base by loosening the bolts that hold the sections together. If the tank is hung on the wall, you will need a spud wrench (Figure 12.62) to loosen the nuts holding the pipe between the tank and the base. The toilet base is fastened to the floor by two bolts which rise from the floor flange; unscrew the nuts capping the bolts on both sides of the base. Rock the toilet base slightly, to break the wax seal on the bottom; then lift up the base and immediately block the drainpipe, as above.

The connections for a tub may be hidden in the end wall, at the head of the tub. Remove finish surfaces from the back of this wall. The drain-overflow assembly is held together with slip couplings; use a pipe wrench to loosen them. Supply pipes may be joined with unions, or they may be sweat-joined—it's easiest just to cut through the supply risers. Those pipes disconnected, you can move the tub. If a tub isn't a freestanding model, however, you'll have to cut into the finish surfaces around the perimeter at least 1 in. above the tub. Look closely at the top of the tub flange; it's sometimes nailed to studs. Removing these nails without chipping the enamel can be challenging. If the tub will not slide out of its present position, remove an end wall and ''walk'' the tub out. Get help to do this, and be especially careful that the tub does not drop suddenly when you pull its flange away from the supporting blocks underneath.

If, when shutting off water to the fixture or fixtures, you shut off service to other sections of the house as well, cap the disconnected pipes so you can turn the water back on.

Mounting and Connecting Fixtures

The solid mechanical connections necessary along DWV and supply runs are important to fixtures, too: securely mount fixtures to walls, floors, and cabinets.

Lavatories and sinks. Basins and sinks are supported by pedestals, surrounding counters, legs, and brackets mounted to walls—or a combination of the above. Wall-hung sinks are common in older houses, but they require a mounting board ''let in'' flush to stud edges. This is a bit of work, so cabinet-mounted units are far more popular

these days—plus, the cabinet base is good for storage. Whatever support you choose, mount sinks and lavatories at a comfortable height.

Preassemble the Hardware. Before mounting a unit, however, attach its hardware, including faucets and the drain assembly; such connections are far easier before the unit is in place. Typically, the faucet stems—which are threaded—fit through predrilled holes in the sink or lav body, to be drawn tight with a washered nut on the underside. Many makers supply a rubber gasket, but where that's lacking, spread a generous layer of plumber's putty between metal and porcelain. Don't overtighten. Once the faucets are tightened, loosely connect a pair of *risers* to the faucet stems.

Set the Sink. Once you've attached the hardware, apply a bead of silicone caulk to the underside of the sink lip, turn the unit over, and press it down into the flat finish surface of the counter. Most modern units need nothing more to secure them, although some have clip slots on the bottom, which are held down by a lug-and-clip combination similar to that shown in Figure 12.55C. Wall-mounted models slip down into a bracket.

Connect the Drain. With the lav in place, now connect the drain pipe. To the DWV stub sticking out of the walls, glue a threaded male adapter, which will receive a slip coupling. Slide the trap arm into that coupling and tighten (later). The other end of the trap arm turns down 90 degrees and, being threaded, couples to an adjustable P-trap, which you can swivel so that it aligns to the tailpiece coming down from the lav. The other end of the P-trap has another slip coupling, into which the sink tailpiece fits. All pieces in place, tighten the slip couplings and you're hooked up.

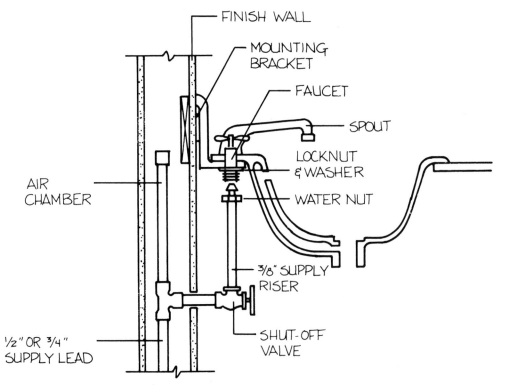

Figure 12.53 Lavatory supply connections.

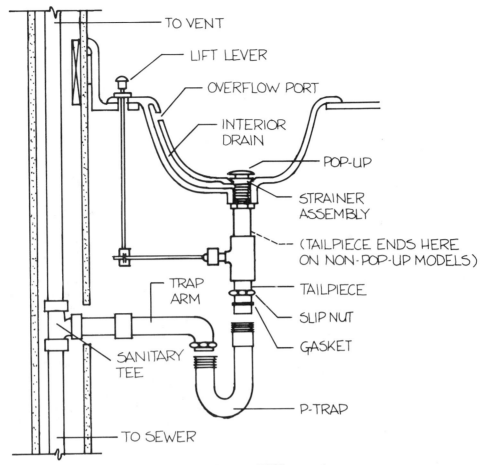

Figure 12.54 Lavatory DWV connections.

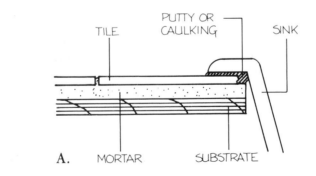

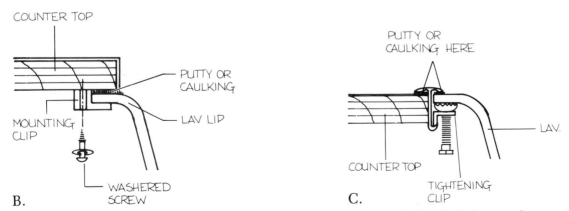

Figure 12.55 Sink lip details. (A) Surface-mounted; (B) under-mounted, with clip; (C) flush-mounted.

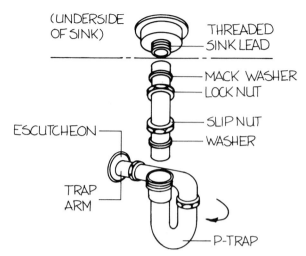

Figure 12.56 Drainage details beneath a sink.

Kitchen sinks are much the same, except that the upper part of a sink tailpiece is threaded to tighten to the bottom of a strainer body. For side-by-side lavs or double sinks, use the double drain connection shown in Figure 12.57. Back-to-back lavs or sinks can tie to a common drain, by using a double-tee similar to that shown in Figure 12.32.

Connect Supply Pipes. To each supply pipe stub, attach a shutoff valve, preferably an *angle stop* with a compression fitting (Figure 12.7). Slide the angle stop's $\frac{1}{2}$-in. socket over the stub and tighten the fitting so that the ferrule inside compresses and forms a positive seal. The riser then feeds into the $\frac{3}{8}$-in. socket on the angle stop. Tighten the second socket, then tighten the upper end of each riser to a faucet stem, using a basin wrench to tighten the water nuts.

An alternative way to attach to supply stubs is to sweat $\frac{1}{2}$-in. male threaded adapters onto the stubs, wrapping Teflon tape on threads, and screwing on a shutoff valve with a $\frac{1}{2}$-in. (threaded) female opening. This method, however, is a lot more work and may strain other sweat fittings when you tighten the shutoff onto the stub. Stick with compression fittings.

Toilets. The horn of a toilet—the integral porcelain bell protruding from the bottom—centers in the floor flange. The flange, and the closet bend to which it is attached, should be centered 12 in. from the finish wall for most toilets.

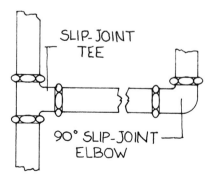

Figure 12.57 For double sink setups, use double-drain connections.

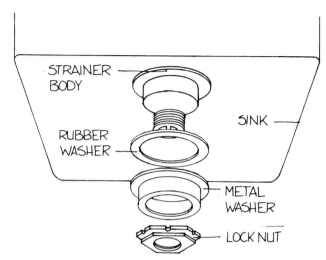

Figure 12.58 Sink strainer assembly. Tighten the locknut onto the threaded tailpiece by gently hammering a screwdriver against it or by using a spud wrench. Put a layer of plumber's putty on the underside of the strainer lip.

If your old toilet was wall hung, its closet bend will probably be centered 14 in. from the wall. Thus if you replace a wall-hung toilet with a standard (close-coupled) unit, there will be an unsightly 2-in. gap between the toilet and the finish wall. Avoid this problem by asking your supplier for a *14-in. rough toilet* which, being 2 in. deeper than standard toilets, enables you to use the existing floor flange.

Ideally, the floor flange sits atop the finish floor, but it's common to see it set on the underlayment—say, particleboard beneath linoleum flooring. Where the flooring is so thin, that's acceptable, but for flooring thicker than $\frac{1}{4}$ in., the flange should sit atop it so that the wax ring will seal the juncture well. Something to keep in mind when setting the floor flange: the flange bolts which hold the toilet down must be parallel to the wall behind, hence the slots receiving those bolts must be more or less parallel to the wall.

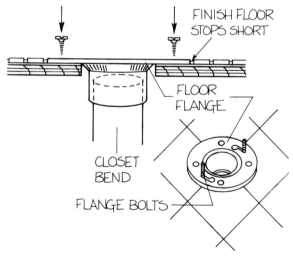

Figure 12.59 Floor flanges fit over the top of closet bends. Set flanges atop subflooring and run flooring flush to it or, where the flooring is thicker than $\frac{1}{4}$ in., set the flange atop the finish flooring so that the wax ring will seal well.

Until you're ready to set the toilet in place, keep the bend opening blocked with a ball of newspaper, to prevent debris from falling down the drain. Just before setting the toilet base, fit a wax ring over the horn of the base and spread plumber's putty along the underside of the lip of the base. The base must be clean and dry if the putty is to stick; knead the putty until it is warm and pliable.

When all is ready, unblock the closet bend, turn the bowl right side up and ease it over the flange bolts. Press down on the bowl to seat the putty evenly. Check the level of the bowl's top, using a level. The wax ring spreads, forming an airtight seal between bowl and flange. If you can still rock the bowl at this point, build up low spots with shims. An alternative method to shimming and puttying is to position the toilet's base and grout around it with plaster of paris.

When you are satisfied that the base is solid and its top level, tighten the nuts on the flange bolts. Because it's very easy to crack porcelain, turn the nuts until they are just snug. Place a wad of plumber's putty in the porcelain nut caps and press them over the ends of the bolts.

Next, mount the tank. If it is a wall-hung model, you must frame a support board into the studs while they are still exposed. Attach the spud pipe to the back of the toilet base, using a *spud wrench* on the nuts provided. Make sure the free end of the pipe is perfectly vertical. With help from a friend, lower the tank over the pipe; then level the top of the tank and mark its bolt holes onto the wall. Remove the tank, drill two pilot holes, and, after sliding the appropriate washers and nuts on the spud pipe, mount the tank and tighten it to the spud pipe.

If the tank is freestanding, and it rests on the back of the toilet base, place its cushion as shown in Figure 12.61. Be sure all bolts that go through the tank have rubber washers; this will prevent leakage. Again, do not overtighten tank nuts.

Attach a new toilet supply much like a sink or lav. But most existing stubs are $\frac{1}{2}$-in. copper supply pipe with a $\frac{1}{2}$-in. male threaded adapter sweat-soldered on. Wrap Teflon plumber's tape around the threads of that adapter and screw on the $\frac{1}{2}$-in. female end of the chrome shutoff valve. The riser from the shutoff to the tank usually is $\frac{3}{8}$-in. chrome and is attached to the shutoff valve in a compression fitting. (If you must loosen the riser fitting after it has been tightened, replace the compression ferrule, to avoid leaks.) The top of the chrome riser has a preflared end that is drawn tight against the threaded stem of the ball-cock assembly which sticks out the bottom of the tank. But remember to thread the riser pipe through the coupling nut and ferrule before tightening the connections at either end.

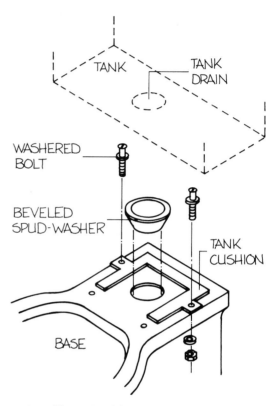

Figure 12.61 The tanks of freestanding models rest directly on their bases; tank cushions accommodate any irregularities.

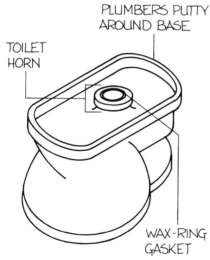

Figure 12.60 Turn the base of the toilet upside-down to apply the wax ring to its horn, and to spread plumber's putty around the base.

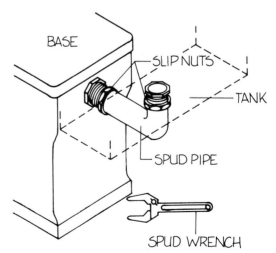

Figure 12.62 A wall-hung toilet has its tank bolted to studs; water flows to the base via a spud pipe.

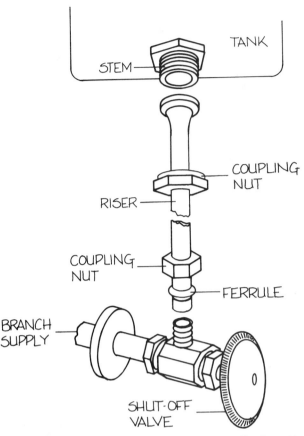

Figure 12.63 Toilet supply detail. Slide a shut-off valve with a compression fitting onto a cold water stub; or, as shown here, sweat a male adapter to the cold-water stub, wrap the threads with plastic plumber's tape, then screw on a shutoff valve. Out of a compression fitting in the top ascends the riser; where the riser joins the toilet tank, it couples to the threaded stem of the ballcock assembly (see Figure 12.75).

Bidets. A bidet is easier to install than a toilet. Although it requires hot- and cold-water connections, the waste is all liquid; therefore, the drain for a bidet is a 2-in. drainpipe. The base should be mounted securely, like that of a toilet, but it doesn't need closet bends or wax rings. The drain takeoff is similar to that of a tub, which is described below.

Bathtubs. Bathtubs come in many shapes, sizes, and materials. When you go to the expense of installing a new tub, visit several suppliers and consider all the design options. The most common materials used in tubs are fiberglass, enameled steel, and enameled cast iron. The first two are lighter and easier to handle, but the last holds heat (and cold) longer and is more durable. (You can add mass beneath a lightweight tub by setting it in a bed of mortar, but be sure to cover the subfloor with 30-lb felt paper so that the moisture won't leach into the plywood.)

Cast-iron tubs are heavy and stable, but steel and fiberglass tubs will flex. To minimize flexion, nail around (or through) the tub flanges with galvanized roofing nails (one per stud) or with nails provided for the purpose. Shooting expandable foam between studs and the backside of a fiberglass shower stall will also reduce flexion. Be careful not to hit enameled surfaces, and cover the tub with a drop cloth. Fiberglass looks terrible once it has been abraded or banged, so consider using aluminum-coated screws instead of nails to secure the unit.

Removing an old tub or installing a new one is usually a major undertaking. At the very least, you'll need several helpers, especially if the tub is an old model of cast iron or a freestanding model that isn't walled in. If the tub (or shower–tub unit) *is* walled in, you'll need to frame and finish accordingly.

First of all, you should double the joists beneath the two long sides of a tub. When the tub's drain-overflow as-

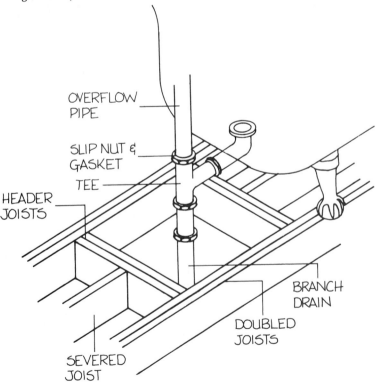

Figure 12.64 Where a tub drain is directly over a joist, cut through that joist and reinforce it as shown.

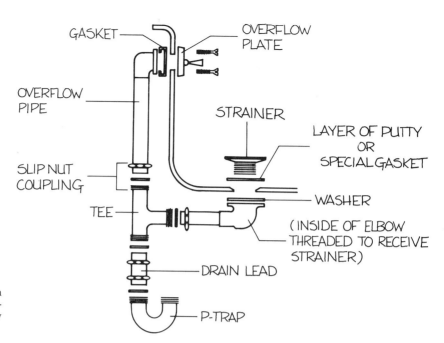

GASKET

OVERFLOW
PLATE

OVERFLOW
PIPE

STRAINER

LAYER OF PUTTY
OR
SPECIAL GASKET

SLIP NUT
COUPLING

TEE

WASHER

(INSIDE OF ELBOW
THREADED TO RECEIVE
STRAINER)

DRAIN LEAD

P-TRAP

Figure 12.65 The overflow-and-drain assembly. Not shown is the plunger assembly that fits down into the overflow pipe.

sembly coincides with a joist, cut through the joist, and box out an opening for the drain. The three walls around a tub must be framed to the dimensions of the tub, and at least one—usually the one at the head of the tub—will be the wet wall which contains the supply pipes. Those three walls must contain whatever supports the tub unit needs, from grabrail blocking to ledgers for the tub's flanges, if any.

A common way to frame out the tub walls is to erect the foot wall and the long side wall first. Take care to level the 2×4 ledgers that will support the tub's flanges. Slide the tub in place and erect the third wall. Use 16d nails to secure the ledgers to the studs.

With the walls up, assemble the tub's overflow unit, being careful to install the gaskets in the proper order and to put a layer of plumber's putty between any metal–enamel joint that isn't gasketed. The overflow plate is held in place by two screws that pass through the tub's body; the drain strainer screws into a threaded elbow underneath. After assembling the parts loosely so that you can fit pipe lengths into the tee, tighten all parts securely. Close the tub stopper, fill the tub above the overflow, and check for leaks.

The last drain connection to be made is a P-trap, which slides onto the tub tailpiece descending from the tee. Adjust the trap so that it aligns with the section of branch drain roughed in earlier. Note, however, that if this drain will be in an enclosed finish space (e.g., you have a finished ceiling below), code requires a glued-together drain. The only compression-fitting allowed in that assembly is a slip-joint where the tub tailpiece joins the p–trap.

Next, attach the tub's supply. Level and set the *diverter valve* to the board set flush to the studs of the wet wall. (Since the body of the diverter is probably cast brass, use brass screws.) The diverter is actually several valves in one, allowing the user to mix hot and cold water and direct the water flow to the shower head and tub spout.

Supply pipes are usually joined to the diverter body by threaded male adapters. The best way to make this connection is to sweat the threaded adapters to the supply pipe first, then wrap the cooled adapters with plastic joint tape. Tighten those adapters into the diverter body, and then solder the free ends of the supply pipes to tees 6 in. below. The middle leg of each tee, aimed away from the tub, accommodates an air chamber that rises behind the diverter valve.

Figure 12.66 Diverter valve and shower/tub rough-in.

Installing Fixtures **307**

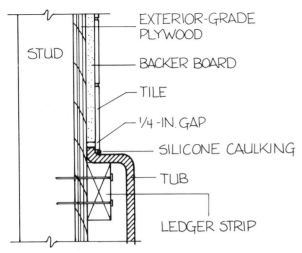

Figure 12.67 Most modern tubs are supported by 2×4 ledgers nailed to the walls that enclose it.

Note: Whatever sequence you follow in attaching supply pipe, make sure all valves are opened fully before heat is applied. Heating closed pipe can cause an explosion or, at the least, destroy the gaskets inside valves.

From the top of the diverter, run a single pipe up to service the shower head. This pipe ends in an elbow, usually a threaded one with mounting ears; when all connections have been made, screw the elbow to its backing board. A threaded nipple screws into the other leg of the threaded elbow, facing the tub. (There is also a spout nipple screwed into the diverter below.) Turn the water on and test for leaks.

Now you are ready to close in the walls around the tub. The walls are flush except for stubs which stick out from the wet wall—the nipples for tub spout and shower head, and the faucet stems which control the flow of hot and cold water. To keep from damaging these parts when applying sheet materials, wrap the parts with duct tape. How far these parts should protrude beyond the wall depends on the manufacturer's specifications.

CONSERVATION AND MAINTENANCE

Because renovation is so broad a topic, this book, for the most part, avoids maintenance tasks and equipment repair. A few tasks in both areas are so ubiquitous, however, that they cannot be avoided, primarily because they affect the use of water and energy or are otherwise important to the health of people living in a house.

When you buy your house, and periodically thereafter, have the water tested to make sure it remains free of contamination and that its mineral content does not exceed certain limits. If the water should be softer, and you lack water-softening apparatus, you may be shortening the useful life of both the water heater and the pipes. Keep complete records of cleaning and maintenance of the septic tank; have the tank checked immediately if you detect wetness or odor around it.

Water Heaters

Because the water heater is the second largest user of energy (after the furnace), it must be maintained if it is to perform at peak efficiency. Drain the water heater at least once a year, to remove sediment that has accumulated. Insulating the unit will also save money. If the water in the heater is too hot, or if its supply of hot water is inadequate for your needs, adjust the thermostat (a small screw setting or dial near the service panel on the side). Usually, units are preset at 150°F, but 120°F is adequate for most use, and the lower setting will save energy.

If the water heater isn't supplying enough hot water, or if it takes too long to recover between uses, raise the thermostat setting; or it may be simply that the valves controlling the supply pipes going in and out are not fully open. It could be, however, that the water heater is too small or too old to perform adequately: note the size and recovery rate (on the metal nameplate on the heater housing), and go shopping.

Figure 12.68 Inset laundry supply.

Electric water heaters have the lowest installation cost, because they do not need to be vented and because there's no need to run a fuel line. The recovery rate of these heaters is the slowest, however, and their operating cost is by far the highest. Gas-fired and oil-fired water heaters cost roughly the same to install and operate, with natural gas being slightly cheaper, at this writing. Solar-heated setups are very attractive because their operating costs are extremely low; installation costs considerably more than that of conventional heaters, although the payback period is 8 to 10 years. (Those who think solar is a passing fancy should note that solar water heaters have been used in Florida for more than 50 years.)

Choose a size of water heater on the basis of need. Do you or your family take showers at the same time? People who prefer baths to showers use more hot water, and hence require larger water heaters. For most families, 40 gallons is plenty. Keep in mind that the type of fuel and the recovery rate are important factors; for example, a 30-gallon gas heater may be the match of a 50-gallon electric unit.

Note: All water heaters must have a pressure-and-temperature relief valve. If, for any reason, the water heater's temperature or pressure goes beyond its design limits, the relief valve will open automatically, releasing hot water and alleviating the condition. Water heaters without a relief valve are exceedingly dangerous, and some have exploded.

Water Conservation

Your use of water, particularly hot water, is an operating cost you should consider, for there are great savings to be achieved with comparatively little effort. Furthermore, many regions of the United States face long-term shortages of potable water due primarily to the deterioration of municipal facilities, depletion of subterranean aquifers, drought, and so on.

Hot-water savings. Here are a number of ways to save hot water:

1. Turn down the water heater's thermostat to 120°F, a temperature adequate for most use. The unit will burn less fuel while keeping water at a lower constant temperature. The only exception to this rule is the automatic dishwasher, which needs water at 140°F to clean dishes properly. Consider installing a small point-of-use water heater near the dishwasher. Some of the better dishwashers (e.g., Kitchen-Aid) have their own built-in water heaters, so you can keep your house water heater at a lower temperature.

2. Insulate the body of the water heater and the hot-water pipes, to prevent heat loss. If the unit is gas- or oil-fired, however, don't cover the vent on the top of the tank or the air intake at the bottom. Stop insulation 2 in. shy of the vent; don't cover the bottom of the unit at all. Never wrap insulation so that it will interfere with the pressure-and-temperature relief valve, whose functioning is crucial to your safety. Heater and pipe insulation are available in kits, or you can fashion your own wrapping. At present, new water heaters have R values of R-3 to R-6, which results in an average heat loss of 10 to 15° F per hour. With insulation, you can cut that loss rate to 2 to 4°F per hour.

3. Locate the water heater as close as possible to the greatest number of users. A lot of heat is lost in transmission to distant points. A point-of-use water heater loses almost no heat in transmission.

4. A holding tank for water from a well allows water to approach room temperature before it is heated in the water heater.

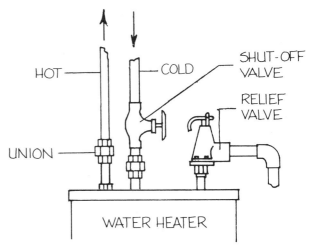

Figure 12.69 All water heaters must have a pressure-and-temperature relief valve, with a takeoff aimed at the floor. For ease in draining or repairing the unit, install unions and shutoff valves on both incoming (cold) and outgoing (hot) pipes. Whenever you work on the heater or its connections, first disconnect the power (or fuel) to it. Be sure that the tank is filled and that all shutoff valves are open before reconnecting power and once again heating the water.

Figure 12.70 Insulate water heaters and pipes to reduce heat loss and save energy.

5. A timer on an electric water heater will prevent energy draw during expensive peak hours.

6. If you live in a warm region, consider putting the water heater in the attic, where heat collects. Make sure the attic joists can support the load, however.

7. Flow-controlled shower heads save up to two-thirds of the total cost of water without affecting the performance of the spray.

8. Solar-heated hot water is viable *now;* the technology available today is cost-effective, and will likely become more so in the future. Although modular setups are more expensive (collectors and heating elements grouped in modules), they allow people with modest plumbing skills to install a solar water heater.

Cutting water use. How much water do you use? A standard toilet flushes 6 gal each time you use it. A shower uses 5 to 6 gal a minute; a bath, 30 to 40 gal; running a tap while brushing your teeth, 6 to 8 gal; an automatic dishwasher, 16 gal for one cycle; a clothes washer, 30 to 50 gal per load.

To reduce consumption without affecting your lifestyle, begin by repairing leaks. Old toilet mechanisms are common offenders. Compare the complex of parts (and hence, difficulty of repair) of an old float-ball setup (Figure 12.75) with such devices as the Fluidmaster (Figure 12.76), which can be adjusted to use less water. Some toilets use only a gallon or two per flushing, and still others use no water at all, for example, the Clivus Multrum, or the Biolet, both composting toilets. Perhaps the ultimate in conservation is the Pure-Cycle system, a high-tech, on-site treatment unit that uses microprocessors to control the recycling of domestic wastewater into pure drinking water. After an

Figure 12.71 A point-of-use water heater boosts water temperature near those appliances that need very hot (140°F) water, such as dishwashers. With this booster in place, you can set the temperature of the main water heater lower to save energy.

initial filling of the 1500-gal tank, you add virtually no additional water.

The most important factor in conservation, however, is one's personal habits (Table 12.4).

Repairs

By examining a mechanism closely, you can usually figure out what has loosened, worn out, or come undone. Start

---

TABLE 12.4

How to save water

Activity	Normal Water Use	Conservation	How to Do It
Shower	Water running, 25 gal	7 gal	Wet down, soap up, rinse off; install shower flow restricter.
Brush teeth	Tap running, 3 gal	1 pt	Use a glass, wet brush; rinse briefly
Tub bath	Full 35 gal	partial—15–20 gal	Minimal water level
Shaving	Tap running, 10 gal	1 gal	Half fill basin and use stopper
Dishwashing	Tap running, 30 gal	5 gal	Wash and rinse in dishpans or sink
Automatic dishwasher	2 cycles per day: 14–30 gal	1 cycle per day 7–15 gal	Fully loaded once per day and use short cycle
Washing hands	Tap running, 2 gal	1 qt	Wet hands, shut water off, massage, then rinse or use basin
Toilet flushing	Depending on tank size, 4–7 gal	1 to 6 gal	Use tank displacement bottles or dams, or convert to manual flush
Washing machine	Full cycle, top water level 50 gal	25 gal	Short cycle, minimal water level, full loads only
Outdoor watering	Average hose 8 gal per minute	Lower priority	Eliminate or maintain plants in stress condition only
Shampoo	12 gal	8 gal	Soap only once and shampoo in the shower
Car wash	6 gal per minute	3–10 gal per wash	Wash car using a bucket; rinse only using hose
Clean sidewalks and driveways	50–100 gal	0	Sweep only

Source: Water Conservation in California, State of California Resources Agency, Department of Water Resources, Bulletin No. 198, Sacramento, 1976; seen in *The Integral Urban House,* The Farallones Institute, Sierra Club Books.

Figure 12.72 Water-saver showerheads. *Left:* Nova; *right:* Con-Serv.

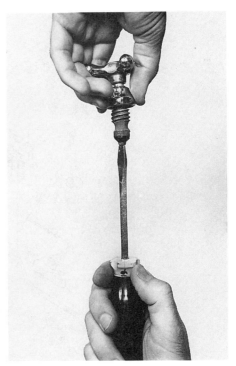

Figure 12.74 The faucet washer is at the end of the faucet stem and can be replaced by removing the small screw at the end.

by looking for the obvious seams between parts, or some ribbed, slotted, or nutted surface that is designed to be turned with a screwdriver or wrench.

Leaky faucets. Leaky faucets are usually caused by worn packing around the stem or a washer at the bottom. If the faucet drips, it's the washer; if it leaks around the handle, it's probably the packing.

To get at worn-out parts, you must first remove a cap (usually embossed with a ''C'' or an ''H''). Older porcelain caps sometimes screw out; modern metal stamped ones can

be pried out. Beneath the cap is a screw, which holds the handle to its splined stem. Remove the handle to get at the packing nut; when the nut is turned counterclockwise, you can lift out the entire faucet assembly. Replace worn-out parts and reinsert the faucet. If it still leaks, have the valve seat (down in the body of the faucet) reground.

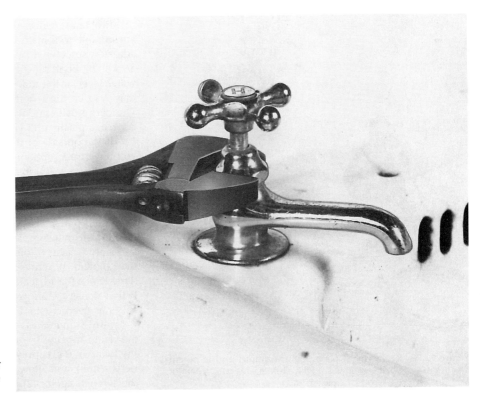

Figure 12.73 To get at the washer most responsible for faucet leaks, first loosen the packing nut.

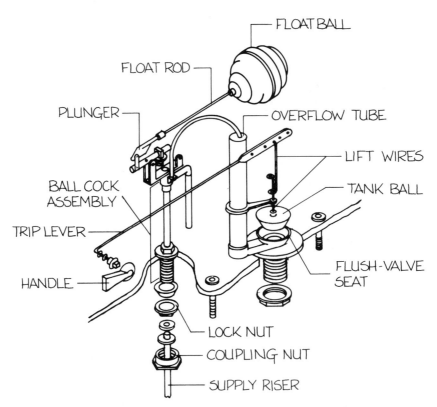

Figure 12.75 Cutaway view of a toilet tank: float-ball mechanism.

When replacing the washer screw, be sure to tighten it well; otherwise, the washer may loosen and moan loudly.

Toilet mechanisms. A float-ball mechanism is so complex, it's surprising it doesn't malfunction all the time. Repair, however, isn't difficult.

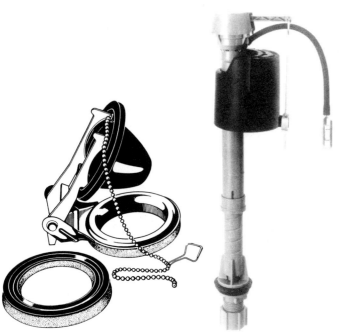

Figure 12.76 Replacement parts that are simpler and more efficient than float-ball assemblies. *Right:* Fluidmaster tank repair kit; *left:* Flusher Fixer kit. (Fluidmaster, Inc.)

The most common problem with these devices is that once the trip wires become slightly coated with mineral deposits, they no longer glide smoothly, and jam up. Jiggling the flush handle will reposition the wires when the corrosion is minimal; but if the problem persists, it's best to replace the wire-and-tank ball assembly with a chain-and-flapper assembly (Figure 12.76, *left*).

Problems concerning water level are almost always attributable to a malfunctioning float ball. The ball can be adjusted somewhat by turning it along the threaded float arm or by bending the arm slightly, to raise or lower the water level. If the toilet flushes incompletely, the problem may also be the length of the upper lift wire; shorten it. The entire ball-and-lever setup can be replaced by a noncorrosive plastic unit (Figure 12.76, *right*).

If the outside of the tank sweats during hot weather, you have three options: (1) cover the tank with an absorbent cloth jacket; (2) install a tempering valve, which mixes hot and cold water flowing into the tank; or (3) line the inside of the tank with closed-cell insulation.

General repairs. Leaks not caused by condensation often result from an incomplete seal between metal and porcelain surfaces. A layer of plumber's putty or a gasket will solve the problem. Where a drain tailpiece running from the underside of a fixture leaks, tighten its slip nut with a wrench. If that doesn't work, replace its gasket; the old one probably has been crushed by the slip nut.

Corrosion makes repair of old plumbing parts tricky. If moderate tugging on a wrench doesn't loosen things, try the following: (1) apply penetrating oil (the automotive variety is fine), and allow it to set for a half-hour before trying the wrench again; (2) if that doesn't work, tap all seized surfaces with a hammer; (3) apply heat to corroded pieces, moving a low flame back and forth, then tap with the hammer again. At this point, with the combination of penetrating oil and heat, exotic smells develop. If the piece still does not yield, look around for a replacement part; some old parts are so corroded that they can't be disassembled without destroying them.

Clogged fixtures. The best cure for clogs is prevention. Sinks should have basket strainers, to limit the amount of food that gets into pipes. Tubs and lavatories should have pop-ups or plugs that fit tightly. Each time you clean a tub, you should check for hair that has accumulated in the top of the drain. Toilets are commonly blocked by wads of paper or nondisposable sanitary napkins.

Most clogs occur in the first fitting within the wall, the tee at which the vent and drainpipes diverge. Your choices for clearing the clogs include:

1. Smear petroleum jelly around the lip of a plunger, to form a better seal; plunge vigorously for a minute or two.

2. Use a plumber's auger. Work it down inside, from the top of the drain. A plumber's snake up through a trap cleanout may also work.

3. Use commercial drain cleaners as a last resort. Once they are in a line, and have not cleared the stoppage, you have to deal with a caustic chemical, which can only make your task more difficult. Follow the manufacturer's instruction to the letter; never mix drain cleaners and bleach (the mixture releases chlorine gas, which is potentially fatal).

4. If the methods in numbers 1 to 3, especially the auger, don't work on a toilet, remove the fixture after draining it. To free a clogged toilet, use a snake from the underside; that will sometimes do the trick. (Not infrequently, the block is a cute little knickknack—formerly displayed atop the tank—that fell in.) Replace the wax ring when reinstalling the toilet.

5. If all fixtures are draining poorly or not at all, call a professional. A vent stack is blocked, or the septic system is full or damaged. If a city sewer system is involved, the problem is usually only the house trap, which can be cleaned easily.

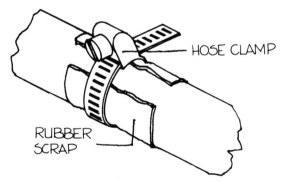

Figure 12.77 This quick repair will stop a leak until the plumbing stores open on Monday morning.

Pipe repairs. The best way to repair a damaged pipe is to turn the water off, drain the lines, cut out the defective spot, and replace it. If you lack the necessary tools, materials, or time to do the job, there are a few quick repairs that should suffice until you can do it right.

If the hole is small, a rubber patch held fast with a ring clamp may work; a screw-and-washer fitting also works. Epoxy patches are rarely worth the trouble because you must drain the line first, and in that event, you may as well repair the pipe correctly; the same goes for "liquid metal repair compounds."

If you fear freezing damage to pipes, take the following precautions:

1. Drain the pipes and pump, making sure that all horizontal runs of pipe are empty. When installing supply pipes, pitch them downward toward drainage spots. Open spigots to hasten drainage.

2. Put antifreeze in toilet tanks and bowls, in all fixture traps (or remove clean-outs), and in the washing machine pump (flush it before using).

3. Leave the water running slowly. This method is not foolproof, nor is it advisable for a long period.

4. Insulate the pipes, both hot and cold, where they traverse cold spots. Heating tape will prevent freezing, but it uses electricity to do this. Heating tape is also useful to prevent oil lines above ground from freezing; better still, bury the lines below the frost line.

5. Thawing frozen pipes is best done by wrapping pipes in cloth and pouring hot water over frozen sections. The cloth retains the hot water. A low flame applied to the pipe also works on metal pipes, but keep the flame moving; hair dryers also work very well. Open faucets during thawing operations. If the pump is straining because lines are frozen, disconnect the electricity.

6. Lines running through parts of the house that are used seasonally should have disconnecting points (unions are best) and drain valves at the lowest points.

Noisy pumps. Get a copy of the manufacturer's manual for your pump. In addition to listing parts, its specifications will suggest procedures for correcting pump problems. A number of adjustments (if not all) are easy for nonprofessionals.

Two of the more obnoxious maladies that afflict pumps are noise and running too long after each use: suspect an air leak. Tighten the clamps around flexible plastic pipe and add plastic joint tape to threaded male parts. The junctions of disparate materials are particularly fertile spots for air leaks, especially if one part is plastic and has cracked. Underground supply pipes (plastic) are notorious for leaking where they join pump leads.

If the pump in question is noisy during normal operation, soundproof it. Use rigid polystyrene or rigid polyurethane sheets. Never use fiberglass batts, which are poor sound insulators, and worse when wet.

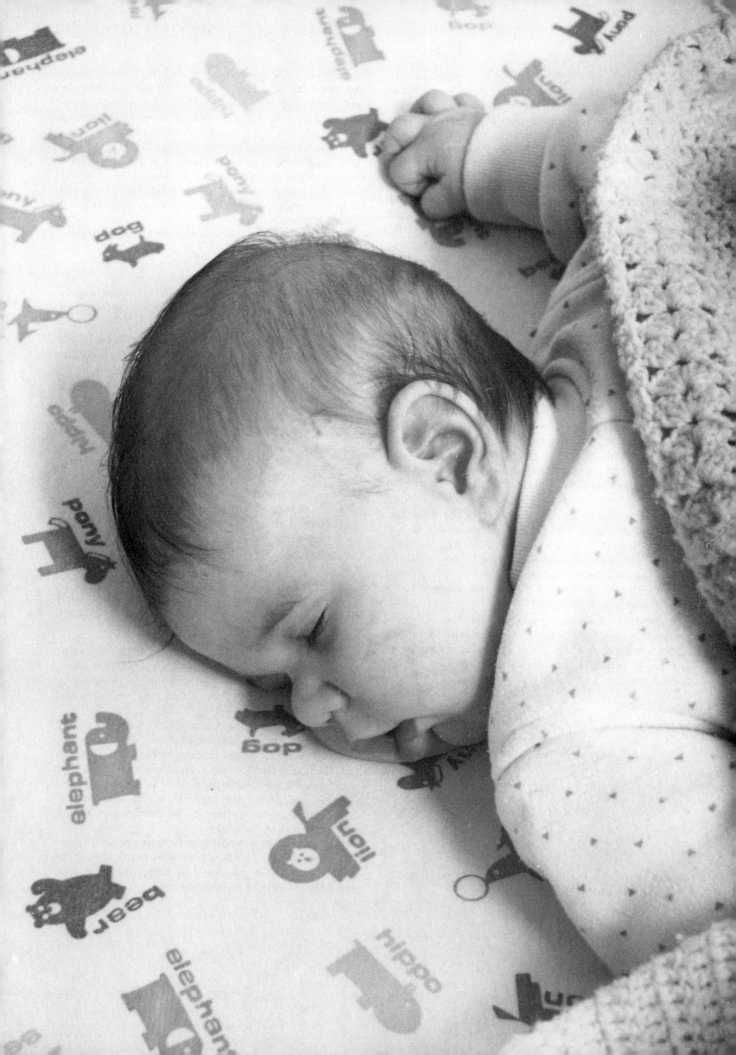

·13·

CONSERVING ENERGY

In the days before cheap energy, architecture was much more varied, more suited to regional climates. Siting was important, as was landscaping, so that a house received the prevailing winds in summer and avoided them in winter. Deciduous trees to the south screened sun in the summer and admitted it in the winter when it was needed. Windows, being expensive, were used more thoughtfully than they are today; in cold areas, they were seldom placed on the north side, and rarely on the west side (afternoon sun) in the Deep South. Overhanging roofs and high ceilings helped keep Alabama plantations cool, while low ceilings and small rooms accomplished the opposite for Vermont farmers. Awnings, shades, and shutters controlled heat, both incoming and outgoing. The habits of the inhabitants were important, too; people stayed warm by keeping busy. They put on sweaters, sat close to stoves and open fires, closed doors to rooms not in use, drank and ate hot foods, soaked in tubs; and kept cool by shedding clothes, wearing loose garments, wetting shirts to increase evaporation, swam, and sat in the shade or against something cool. Nor are these methods merely quaint. Now that the hour of cheap energy is passing, the homogeneity of centrally heated architecture will wane and regionally attuned methods of heating and cooling will return.

This chapter discusses *passive* ways of conserving heat or of cooling; Chapter 14 surveys *active* environmental control, mechanical heating and cooling systems.

The Soft Machine

Because we humans are poorly equipped to withstand extremes of temperature (body temperature varies safely only a few degrees) we modify our environment by wearing clothes and building suitable houses. We have become so successful at this that most of us—at least, in the developed nations—have little sense of how precarious life is without such amenities.

To appreciate how finely tuned our bodies are in relation to our environment, consider the body as a heat engine. Of the food we consume, about 20 percent is converted into energy used for applied work; the other 80 percent is given off (radiated) as excess heat. The more strenuous the activity, the more heat radiated. The heat is released—and the body is cooled—by radiation and perspiration through the skin, and by exhalation of heated air and water vapor from the lungs. Perspiration, or sweating, is a highly effective way of discharging heat, especially when the humidity of the surrounding air is low and there's a breeze to hasten evaporation. When these mechanisms are insufficient, however, heat stroke and death can occur.

When the air is too cool, on the other hand, we lose heat rapidly, especially from the head and limbs. We shiver, get goose bumps (hair follicles become erect, to trap air near the skin), and clasp our arms to our bodies. When the loss rate becomes excessive, our internal temperature drops, and a condition called hypothermia develops which, like heat stroke, can be fatal. But whether it's cold or warm outside, our bodies, being heat engines, constantly lose heat.

Houses extend the habitable environment by allowing us to confine and modify our interior environment so the *rate* at which we lose heat will be comfortable. Asked how we keep warm or cool, most of us would speak of the

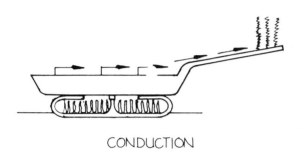

CONDUCTION

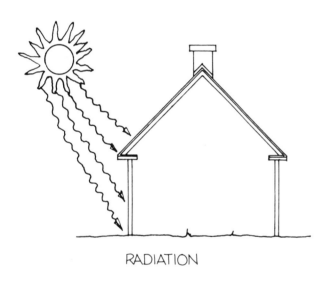

RADIATION

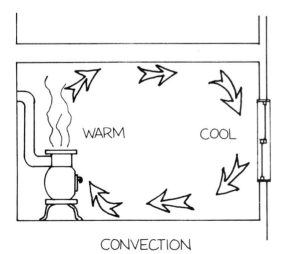

CONVECTION

Figure 13.1 Heat transfer.

warming effect of a furnace or the cooling effect of an air conditioner. This comparison is simplistic; furnaces and air conditioners are designed to heat or cool *air around us* and thus affect the rate of bodily heat loss; the notion is also simplistic because it ignores relative humidity and the movement of air.

Heat Transfer

Heat is transferred by one of three basic mechanisms—*radiation*, *conduction*, or *convection*. Radiation is the movement of heat through space, in the form of electromagnetic waves; heat and light waves radiate in all directions from a central source, such as the sun, a hot stove, or the body. Conduction is the passing of energy from particle to particle, implying the direct contact of two or more objects. Convection is the transfer of heat or cold by the movement of air—heated air rising or cool air descending.

Heat transfer in houses is usually a combination of the three. Sunlight radiates into a room and heats a dark tile floor. The cat lying on the floor receives radiant heat from the sun and conductive heat from the floor. If there's a breeze or a fan blowing, warm air from other heat sources provides convective heat. Heat constantly flows from a warm object to a cool object.

Radiation. There are a number of physical factors that affect the way in which an object receives radiant heat and emits it. If a material *reflects* heat, radiant heat waves bounce off the material and its temperature is affected only slightly. If the heat is *absorbed*, it raises the temperature of the material, and the heat energy is later radiated. Light-colored, smooth objects tend to be more reflective, for example, highly polished metal or white paint. For this reason, foil paper behind an air space is an effective thermal insulator; radiant waves from, say, a space heater are reflected back into the living space. Conversely, dark, rough-textured objects absorb radiant energy. An object that is also dense is an excellent thermal storage mass, for it retains heat (or remains cool) for long periods, emitting energy slowly. At ordinary temperatures, water has the highest thermal capacity of any material; but concrete and most other masonry materials are also good.

Conduction. Building materials conduct heat at different rates. The more resistance a material offers to heat transference by conduction, the higher its resistivity value, or R value. The better the material conducts heat, the lower its thermal resistivity and the poorer insulation it makes. In general, the less dense the material, the better insulant it is and the higher its R value. As you can see in Table 13.1, masonry materials tend to be poor insulators; wood is better, and glass fiber (more commonly called fiberglass) is very good.

It's important to consider the relative conduction (or resistance) of various materials when considering heat loss. Glass, being very dense, is an excellent conductor and an extremely poor insulator; a building's heat loss through its windows can be as great as 60 to 70 percent of the total loss. Double-pane glass is an improvement over single-pane; but even with triple-pane glass the loss is considerable. The improved R value of multipane windows results from the trapped layers of air (1 in. thick or less), which serve as

TABLE 13.1

Some representative R values[a]

8-in. concrete (solid)	0.90
8-in. concrete block (hollow)	1.20
4-in. common brick	0.80
$3\frac{1}{2}$-in. wood stud (on edge)	4.50
$\frac{3}{4}$-in. softwood sheathing	0.75
$\frac{1}{2}$-in. plywood sheathing	0.63
1-in. fiberboard	2.00
Clapboard or shingle siding	0.80
Insulation	
Fiberglass batts, $3\frac{1}{2}$ in.	11.00
Cellulose, 3 in.	10.50
Isocyanurate, 2 in.	15.00
Plaster ($\frac{3}{4}$-in.) or drywall ($\frac{1}{2}$-in.)	0.40
Glass	
Single-pane	0.89
Double-pane	1.91
Triple-pane	2.80
Air films	
Interior wall surfaces	0.70
Exterior surface (winter)	0.15
Exterior surface (summer)	0.25

Source: "Minimum Design Standards for Heat Loss Calculations," U.S. Department of Housing and Urban Development, Publication No. 4940.6. The composite R values for building sections shown in Figure 13.3 are derived from the same source.

[a]The resistance of a material to heat flow is indicated in terms of R values or sometimes in terms of U values (which represent the *transmission* of heat). Thus the two values, R and U, are the inverse of each other: that is, U = 1/R and R = 1/U. In either case, we are discussing BTUs per square foot per hour per degree-difference (between indoors and outdoors).

insulators. Therefore, dollar for dollar, hanging insulated shutters is far more cost-effective than adding layers of glass.

Insulation is effective because, in the case of fiberglass and cellulose, air is trapped in tiny pockets. The R values of isocyanurate and polyurethane are high because they trap Freon which freezes and thaws at room temperature.

Convection. Air that is still is an insulator. In layers thicker than 1 in., however, it beings to circulate in convective loops, thus transferring heat. Air above a heat source rises; near cool objects, it falls; the falling of air in front of a cold window is called "sheeting." In the summer, since the air outside is often warmer than air inside, and because sunlight enters the house, air will rise as it approaches a window.

Because heated air flows from a living space to the surrounding air outside, a considerable amount of heat is lost by convection through gaps and cracks around doors and windows, through the seams of building materials. This convective loss, called "infiltration," can account for 20 to 30 percent of the total heat loss of an insulated house. Because infiltration is easily remedied by adding weather-stripping and caulk, it should be your first priority among heat-conservation techniques.

CALCULATING HEAT LOSS

The calculations in this section will help you determine the heat flow, hence the heat *loss* from heated areas for any and all parts of your house. Once you calculate this loss (in

BTUs), you can convert that number to units of fuel and then to money it's costing you. These calculations are useful, for a number of reasons: to choose the size of a heating system, to calculate the payback period for an improvement, to anticipate operating costs, and to compare heat-saving methods so you can use money wisely. Because heat loss is intangible, we often don't realize how serious it is. Consider that *one* average-sized window, single-paned and with no storm window, represents a fuel cost from lost heat of more than $1,000 over 30 years.

The thermal resistance, or R value, of a building cross-section is a composite of individual elements, including air spaces and air films. To determine how much heat flows through a section, we can use the following simple formula:

$$f = \frac{A \times T_d}{R_c}$$

where

f = flow of heat, in BTUs per hr
A = area of section, in square feet
T_d = temperature difference, in degrees Fahrenheit, between inside and outside
R_c = composite R value of building section

Looking at the typical stud-wall construction in Figure 13.2, we can compute the total R value (R):

$3\frac{1}{2}$-in. fiberglass	11.00
$\frac{1}{2}$-in. drywall	0.40
$\frac{1}{2}$-in. sheathing	0.63
clapboard siding	0.80
air film inside	0.70
air film outside	0.25
$R_c =$	13.78

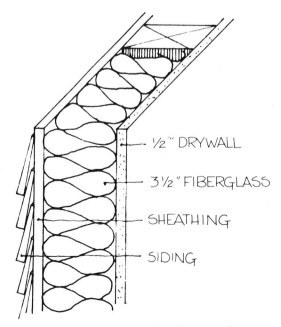

Figure 13.2 Typical stud-wall construction.

What's the rate of flow (f) through 1 sq ft of such a section? Let's suppose that it's 65°F inside and 85°F outside; T_d would then be 20°F:

$$f = \frac{1 \times 20}{13.8} \text{ BTU/hr}$$

$$= \frac{20}{13.8} \text{ BTU/hr}$$

$$= 1.45 \text{ BTU/hr}$$

If it is 70°F inside and 35°F outside, and you want to know the hourly flow of heat through an 8-ft-by-30-ft wall of the same construction, the numbers would be

$$f = \frac{(8 \times 30) \times (70 - 35)}{13.8} \text{ BTU/hr}$$

$$= \frac{240 \times 35}{13.8} \text{ BTU/hr}$$

$$= \frac{8400}{13.8} \text{ BTU/hr}$$

$$= 608.7 \text{ BTU/hr}$$

To calculate the loss through the area over a heating season, you'll need the degree-day total for your area; this figure can be obtained from a local utility or from the U.S. Weather Service (also see Figure 13.18). Modify the formula by using the degree-day total (DD) and the number of hours in a day, 24, in place of T_d

$$F = \frac{DD \times 24 \times A}{R_c}$$

where

F = flow of heat for heating year
DD = degree-day total for your area
24 = hours in a day
A = area of section (square feet)
R_c = composite R value

Let's say that our DD is 6000 and that the total area of the wall is still 8 × 30, or 240 sq ft:

$$F = \frac{DD \times 24 \times A}{R_c}$$

$$= \frac{6000 \times 24 \times 240}{13.8}$$

$$= \frac{34,560,000}{13.8}$$

$$= 2,504,350 \text{ BTU/yr}$$

Look at Table 13.2 to find the number of units of fuel. If you burn oil (140,000 BTU/gal) and your furnace is 60 percent efficient, your next equation looks like this:

$$\frac{2,504,350}{0.60 \times 140,000} = 30 \text{ gal}$$

That's not much of a loss for year; but we're considering a relatively well-insulated wall with an R value of 13.8. Consider one of the walls in Figure 13.3—say, the uninsulated frame wall with an R_c value of 4. Inserting this number in the equation above, and using its R_c, we get

$$F = \frac{DD \times 24 \times A}{R_c}$$

$$= \frac{34,560,000}{4}$$

$$= 8,640,000 \text{ BTU/year}$$

Again using the efficiency rating in Table 13.2, note that the loss is 103 gal for the uninsulated wall; a difference of 73 gal from R-13.8 wall previously considered. Since there are few one-walled houses, the cumulative difference between losses in four such walls would be 4 × 73, or 292 gal. If oil is $1.25 per gallon, we are enriching oil company coffers by $365 a year. The payback time for an insulation retrofit that costs $1500 would thus be less than 5 years. (For more accurate, long-term calculations, see Table 13.3.)

The figures above are, of course, oversimplified, for they don't reflect heat lost through ceilings and roofs, floors over unheated space, or windows. The cross-sections of buildings (Figure 13.3) provide composite R values for

TABLE 13.2

Fuel conversion

	Fuel value	Assumed efficiency (%)	Available heat	Equiv. to 1. gal oil
oil	140,000 BTU/gal.	60	84,000 BTU/gal.	—
natural gas	1,000 BTU/cu ft	65	650 BTU/cu ft	129 cu ft
bottled gas	2,500 BTU/cu ft	65	1625 BTU/cu ft	52 cu ft
electricity (resistance heating)	3,410 BTU/kwh	100	3,410 BTU/kwh	25 kwh
electricity (heat pump)	3,410 BTU/kwh	200	6820 BTU/kwh	12 kwh
hardwood	28 million BTU/cord	55	15.4 million BTU/cord	0.0055 cord

Source: Larry Gay, *The Complete Book of Insulating.* Stephen Greene Press, Brattleboro, VT, 1980.

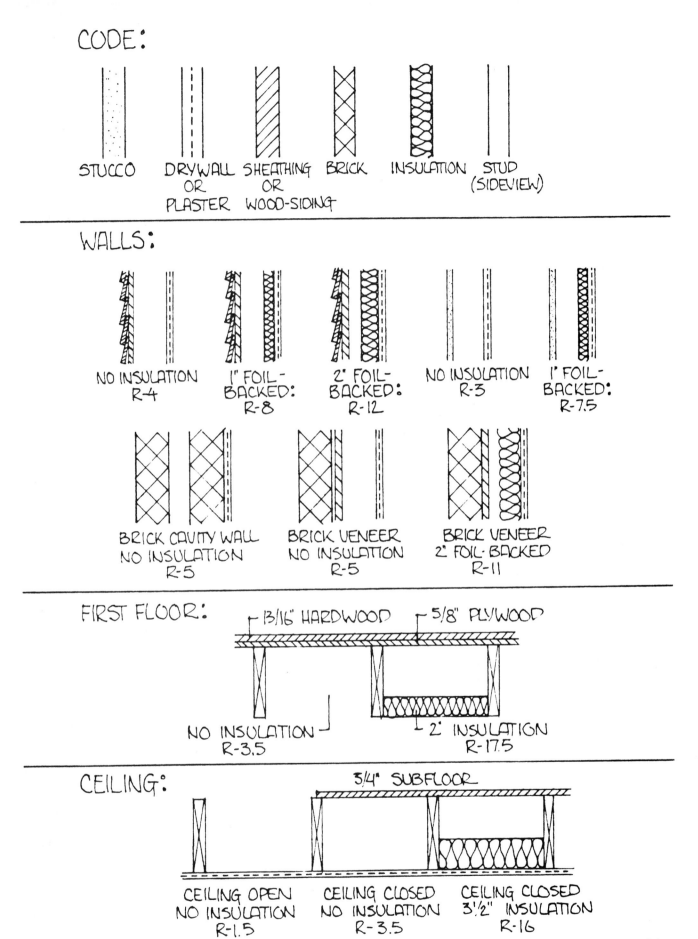

Figure 13.3 R-values for different constructions. The total resistance to heat flow (R-value) is equal to the sum of the resistance of the various components, including air films, air spaces, and the materials themselves. (Adapted from U.S. Department of Housing and Development Publication No. 4940.6.)

TABLE 13.3

Multiplier for taking real energy (energy price increase into account)

Years	Annual Increase in Cost of Energy (%)									
	1	2	3	4	5	6	7	8	9	10
5	1.02	1.04	1.06	1.08	1.10	1.13	1.15	1.17	1.19	1.22
10	1.05	1.09	1.15	1.20	1.26	1.31	1.38	1.44	1.51	1.58
20	1.10	1.21	1.34	1.49	1.65	1.83	2.04	2.27	2.53	2.83
30	1.16	1.35	1.58	1.86	2.20	2.61	3.12	3.73	4.47	5.38
40	1.22	1.51	1.88	2.37	3.00	3.83	4.92	6.37	8.28	10.80

Source: Larry Gay, *The Complete Book of Insulating*, Stephen Greene Press, Brattleboro, VT, 1980.

further calculations. To determine the square footage of each type of building section, subtract the number of square feet of windows from the total wall space and then enter the various sections' R values in the formulas discussed above.

The figures for heat loss through walls, and the savings to be derived by insulating them, are impressive. When it's time to pay for such retrofitting, however, most of us will do the job a bit at a time, as money allows. What, then, are the priorities?

1. Go after an uninsulated ceiling first; while a wall merely of plaster and siding has an R value of about 4, R values for ceilings may be as low as 1.5 (Figure 13.3). Because heated air rises, it will exit rapidly through such low resistance. Furthermore, although access to attics is rarely a problem, ripping into existing walls can be expensive.

2. If you're insulating a wall at a time, start with the north one; then do the west or east ones, depending on the prevailing winds. Do the south wall last, since it is the most likely to be warmed by the sun. (This sequence may be reversed in the Deep South, where you're insulating primarily for cooling).

3. Before spending a dollar on insulation, though, take care of the windows; heat loss through them can be truly staggering.

Glass: The Great Heat Loser

A pane of glass is dense and not very thick ($\frac{1}{8}$ in.); its R value would be less than 0.10 were it not for the air films on both sides. The combination of glass and air has an R value of about 0.89.

Looking at a single-pane window 3 ft by 5 ft, in a 6000-degree-day climate, we get

$$F = \frac{DD \times 24 \times A}{R_c}$$

$$= \frac{6000 \times 24 \times 15}{0.89}$$

$$= 2,427,000 \text{ BTU/year}$$

The loss for just this one window is almost equal to that of the entire insulated wall (R = 13.8) we looked at above. Since the amount of fuel lost is also about the same, this window loses 30 gal. of oil a year! Assuming a modest increase in fuel prices each year (Table 13.3), we see that the

cost of the window's heat loss over 30 years would be well over $1000. (Larry Gay, from whose book Table 13.3 is taken, suggests that if oil is $1 per gallon, and the price increases 3 percent a year, the loss through a window of this size would be $1 × 1.58 × 900, or $1422 in current dollars.)

What, then, are we to do? Opinions vary. For years, double-pane windows were touted as the answer, that is, until triple-pane construction came along. Storm windows over single-pane windows have about the same R value as double-pane windows. Despite the indisputably improved heat resistance of multipane units, however, the cost-effectiveness of these windows is still debatable. The R values are: single pane, 0.89; double pane, 1.90; triple pane, 2.70.

Insert these values in our degree-day formula for the same 3-ft-by-5-ft window, and we get

$$\text{double-pane } F = \frac{6000 \times 24 \times 15}{1.90}$$

$$= 1,137,000 \text{ BTU/year}$$

$$\text{triple-pane } F = \frac{6000 \times 24 \times 25}{2.70}$$

$$= 800,000 \text{ BTU/year}$$

Although these savings are considerable, they still represent a loss of 13.6 gal and 9.5 gals, respectively, per year. Remember, we're talking about loss through only one window, and not an unusually large window, at that.

A much more effective way to reduce heat loss through windows is to use a thermal covering on the inside. In its most rudimentary form, this covering is a sheet of polyethylene plastic or a pull-down paper shade, which does little. At the other end of the spectrum is the InsulShutter, the top of the line. The choices are presented in the section "Window and Door Treatments." A brief look at the performance of a rigid shutter will suffice.

The composite R value (R_c) for a thermal shutter and a single-pane window is:

1-in. rigid urethane	6.50
2 thicknesses $\frac{1}{4}$-in. plywood	0.60
2 in. air between shutter and window	1.00
glass and its air films (approx.)	0.90
$R_c =$	9.00

Using the same area and degree-day figures as above, we can compare the effectiveness of the thermal shutter, as follows:

$$F = \frac{DD \times 24 \times A}{R_c}$$

$$= \frac{6000 \times 24 \times 14}{9.00}$$

$$= 240,000 \text{ BTU/year}$$

Expressed in gallons, the annual loss is only about 2.8 gal, compared with 13.6 for double-pane glass and 9.5 for triple-pane. Considering the cost of triple-pane glass (very high), thermal shutters are a much better buy. If the homeowner had both storm windows and thermal shutters, the annual loss through the window would be approximately 2 gal.

Loss through Infiltration

Another aspect of heat loss that you should consider is infiltration—loss of heat by convection—which occurs at the edges of windows and other building "seams." The money spent on thermal shutters and double-paned glass will be largely wasted if there is massive air leakage around windows. Infiltration can add 20 to 40 percent to a window's total heat loss.

Heat loss by infiltration is commonly calculated by adding the distance represented by cracks and gaps between sashes and frames. For example, around a 3×5 window there would be 3 ft + 3 ft + 5 ft + 5 ft, or 16 linear feet of possible infiltration. The loss per degree difference (between inside and outside) varies according to how tightly the sashes fit:

Window painted shut: $\frac{1}{2}$ BTU per linear foot per degree difference

Medium sash rattle: 1 BTU per linear foot per degree difference

Severe sash rattle: 3 BTU per linear foot per degree difference

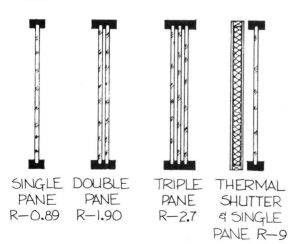

SINGLE PANE R—0.89 DOUBLE PANE R—1.90 TRIPLE PANE R—2.7 THERMAL SHUTTER & SINGLE PANE R—9

Figure 13.4 No matter what its thickness, glass is a poor insulator; thermal shutters dramatically improve the composite R-value of a window.

A storm window will cut infiltration losses in half, but installing weatherstripping and caulk is cheap, effective, and easily within the skills of amateur builders. Therefore, cut infiltration first, as discussed below.

Spending Priorities

How, then, should the renovator spend money to improve heat retention? Consider getting a loan to take care of the windows, insulation, and so on; interest on the money will probably be less than increases in fuel costs. If you want to make improvements as you have the money, though, here are our recommendations for allocating funds:

1. Stop infiltration (by weatherstripping and caulking).
2. Upgrade windows and doors (including thermal shutters).
3. Insulate the roof and attic.
4. Upgrade the heating plant.
5. Insulate the walls.

This list may surprise some people, especially giving insulating walls such a low priority. But to insulate most walls, you must first gut existing surfaces and add a vapor barrier; the operation becomes very costly. Insulating the attic, on the other hand, is rarely an access problem, and adjusting and upgrading the heating plant can curb an additional 30 to 35 percent of current heat losses.

Use Table 13.3 to calculate the payback periods of such improvement. Any payback period of 5 years is money well spent; paybacks of 6 to 10 years are good bets; but depend more on your personal plans and on prevailing interest rates. Paybacks of more than 10 years can be worthwhile if energy costs rise dramatically.

CUTTING INFILTRATION

Saving money is an obvious incentive to cut loss through infiltration; comfort is another. Recall that air movement speeds the rate at which heat leaves your body. While bodily cooling is desirable in the summer, it's uncomfortable to sit near a draft in the winter. This discomfort is particularly apparent around your head and neck, if your favorite chair is near a window.

Assessing Infiltration

Some infiltration is necessary to dissipate cooking odors and moisture from cooking and bathing; it keeps the air from getting stuffy. (You must also have mechanical ventilation to carry off excessive amounts of odors.) The air in a tight house should change completely, in summer and in winter, every 2 to 3 hours. The maximum air change should be once an hour.

Here are a few rules of thumb for assessing infiltration:

1. Walk around the house with a lit cigarette (or a burning incense stick), holding it next to walls where they meet floors, around windows, doors and electrical outlet boxes.

Although your skin will detect cold air flowing in, the smoke will detect warmed air departing.

2. Test the air lock of doors by opening and shutting them. A tight-fitting door will resist closing somewhat because trapped air compresses rather than merely escapes. Size the gaps around the door with a matchbook or a coin.

3. Try to rattle windows (the preceding section tells you how much heat you're losing). Size gaps around sashes with a matchbook or a coin.

4. Walk around the outside of the house, looking closely where disparate materials meet, especially at the top of the mudsill and at building corners. Is there caulking? What is the condition of the paint? If the house is built on piers, examine the construction of the floor closely.

What is the rate of air loss? You are losing about one house change per hour (acceptable) if (1) there are few obvious leaks around walls and doors; (2) storm doors and storm windows fit tightly, with gaps on the exterior caulked and no apparent holes or cracks around the foundation; and (3) there are plywood subfloors beneath floors over unheated areas. If the following conditions exist, you're losing two house changes or air per hour: (1) windows and doors fairly tight but no storms or, best, loose ones; (2) small cracks on the exterior have not been caulked; (3) the building's paint is in poor condition. This rate of loss, while ordinarily tolerable in terms of comfort, is a drain financially. Finally, if there are three changes of house air per hour, you are most probably cold and, soon, poor. The probable conditions are: (1) no storms on windows and doors (you can fit a matchbook between units and their frames); (2) obvious drafts around windows and walls; (3) daylight between sill and foundation; (4) uncaulked cracks on exterior; (5) paint in poor condition; (6) no evidence of building paper beneath the siding; (7) oversized pipe holes through floors over unheated areas.

Infiltration is a defect that is easily corrected. It requires modest skills, little special equipment, and a modest cash outlay. The inside of the house is tightened by *weatherstripping*, the outside by caulking. If you're gutting the interior, also add a vapor barrier, which is extremely effective in stopping infiltration and is crucial to the structural health of an old house newly insulated.

Weatherstripping

Weatherstripping is placed (usually by nailing) around window sashes and doors to prevent air leakage. Although numerous brands of weatherstripping are available most are variations of soft materials that can be compressed in place. Some factors that could affect your choice of materials are: cost, durability, visibility, effectiveness, and ease of installation. Most weatherstripping materials are easy to install. Several types of metal-channel weatherstripping require special tools to install, typically a slip-drive tool with an offset foot that positions fasteners under the channel lip without damaging the metal.

Temporary weatherstripping is the cheapest short-term material. Caulking cord is a soft puttylike cord which is pressed into the seams around window sashes. It's very effective and is so narrow that it's not visually obtrusive. Some drawbacks are that sashes cannot be opened while the cord is in place, and it's not reusable. Poly tape and duct tape are sometimes used to seal windows, but they are not recommended; although they do seal air leaks, they are ugly (even transparent types are visible) and will remove paint when removed in the spring.

Felt and foam strips are the least expensive types of weatherstripping that allow you to operate your windows and doors, as opposed to sealing them shut. These materials are usually attached with small nails, although foam strips are often backed with an adhesive and can be stuck in place. Neither material, however, is worth much. When placed beneath sash rails or between a door and its frame, they compress and lose what resiliency they had when new; when placed along the stiles (vertical parts) of double-hung sashes, they quickly abrade. Because felt becomes sodden quickly, foam is better; but neither material will last much longer than one heating season.

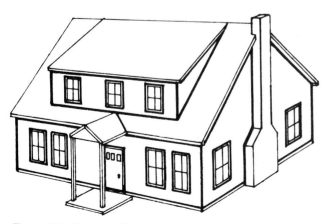

Figure 13.5 Heat loss through infiltration is common where disparate materials meet.

Figure 13.6 Nail weatherstripping around the edges of window sashes and doors.

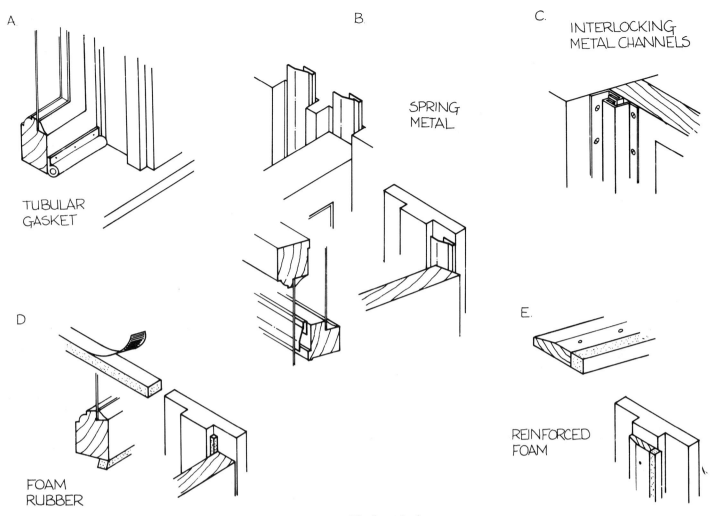

Figure 13.7 Weatherstripping.

A — TUBULAR GASKET

B — SPRING METAL

C — INTERLOCKING METAL CHANNELS

D — FOAM RUBBER

E — REINFORCED FOAM

Reinforced foam and felt strips are bonded to thin wood strips and are thus more durable. To attach them, shut the window or door, cut the strips to length, and slide the strip next to the unit. Press the strip slightly against the door or window until the resilient material compresses, and tack the wooden part to the unit's frame with the small nails provided. Beneath the sash rails (the horizontal parts), however, use unreinforced foam, as shown in Figure 13.7D. Reinforced strips should last several seasons, although they gradually wear out.

Rolled-vinyl or tubular gaskets are effective, easy to install, and probably the least expensive types of permanent weatherstripping. The reinforced part of the strips is usually metal, with slots for attaching screws, or vinyl wire mesh through which nails are driven. These strips are extremely durable and should be compressed adequately along the edges of a window or door, to ensure a tight fit. Because they are an inch or more wide, they are commonly installed on the exterior of the frame and then painted to blend in. Tubular foam strips are also available, but they are not as durable; don't buy them.

Metal tension strips are made of aluminum, brass, or bronze and fit between the edges of a unit and its frame. (Plastic tension strips aren't worth the money). Metal tension strips are quite durable and, because they fit between

the door or window and its frame, are virtually invisible when the unit is shut. Simply tack one side of the strip along the frame and allow the other side to extend (Figure 13.7B); the untacked side is compressed when the door or window is shut. Easy to install, these strips are ideal for doors, providing a tight seal. Attaching them to windows is another matter, for there you must remove the sashes to tack tension strips to the frame. If the sashes fit the frame tightly before this operation, you are probably better off using tubular gaskets. Otherwise, you must plane the sides of sashes to make room for the metal strips. If the sashes fit loosely, tension strips may be a good way to stop rattle and reduce infiltration. They are particularly effective where upper and lower sashes meet, at the "meeting rails." Finally, if the gaps around the doors and windows aren't uniform, tension strips may not be effective, for they extend a uniform width.

Interlocking metal channels are two-piece strips that attach to the frame and the exterior face of a door or window. Double-hung window channels slide in each other as the unit is raised and lowered. Of the types of weatherstripping discussed here, metal channels are probably the most durable, because they aren't under compression—they are also quite expensive. Install the channels on the outside of the unit and paint them so they blend in.

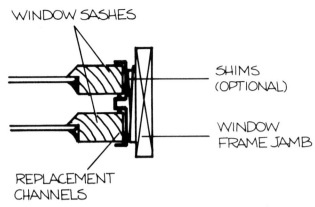

WINDOW SASHES

SHIMS
(OPTIONAL)

WINDOW
FRAME JAMB

REPLACEMENT
CHANNELS

Figure 13.8 Replacement channels require removing and squaring-up the old sashes. An expandable center-strip in the channel fits snug to the sashes and cuts heat loss.

Replacement channels (Figure 13.8) require some work, probably two or three hours per window, and a fair expenditure. These channels—fashioned from stainless steel, zinc, or aluminum—replace existing wood stops and guides. To install them, remove the sashes and pry or chisel out any stops in the jamb frame, creating a perfectly flat surface on both sides of the frame. If the sashes are not exactly square, they must be made so by planing. Any sash weights, cords, or spring lifts must of course, be removed. Refurbished sashes are then fit in replacement channels—a spring loaded center strip accommodates sashes of varying thickness—and the package is fit in the window frame. After shimming the channels to the frame, screw the channels in place and replace interior trim. Where it's needed, pack insulation into gaps and caulk the back side of the trim. Use a hacksaw to cut channels to the proper length. For more about these channels, see p. 116.

Weatherstripping beneath doors must be both weathertight and very durable, because of the heavy traffic it

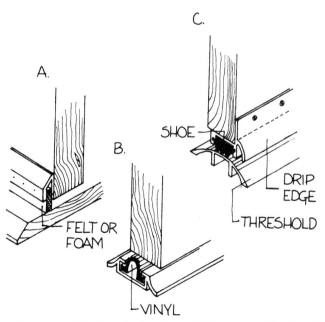

Figure 13.9 Weatherstripping doors. (A) Door sweep (B) gasketed threshold; (C) shoe and threshold.

must bear in normal use. Elements that attach to the underside of the door are called ''shoes'' or ''sweeps''; those that attach to the floor, ''thresholds'' or ''saddles.'' For the best results, use a shoe-and-threshold combination, although that will be the most expensive weatherstripping. To attach the shoe, pull the door's hinge pins and lift the door out so you can get at its bottom. Sweeps that can be attached to the inside face of a door without first removing the door usually are not durable. Shoes and thresholds are commonly a metal channel with a replaceable vinyl insert. Both parts screw into place rather than being nailed—the better to resist friction. Although doors should fit tightly, you may have to plane some off the bottom to accommodate the thickness of the weatherstripping.

Infiltration guards such as outlet gaskets are specialty items that fit behind the cover plate of an electrical outlet. They look exactly like the plates, the only difference being that they include foam gaskets, complete with holes for receptacles and a mounting screw.

Caulking

Caulking is an effective way to stop infiltration: apply an elastomeric (expandable) caulk along the seams of a building's exterior. Caulk is best applied during construction, before trim and siding are installed; but it's also effective when applied afterward, although such application is more visible and subject to weathering. Caulk is intended primarily for exterior use, but by caulking on the back side of trim (as trim is installed) on interior walls you greatly reduce infiltration.

It's best to caulk where building seams occur, disparate materials join, and house planes converge. Caulk around window trim on all sides of the house, for there are often gaps between the trim and the siding. Similarly, caulk:

—around door trim
—at all corners where siding abuts trim
—around all eave and gable-end trim
—where the wood frame of the building meets the foundation
—where siding has been breached by wires, pipes, vents
—where porches join the main house
—along gaps between the chimney mass and the siding

Caulking is easy. Scrape with a paint scraper or a wire brush to remove any loose debris present. The surface (and the weather) should be dry; most caulks set up in 1 to 2 hours. If the temperature is much below 50°F, though, caulk will flow poorly and adhere worse. To start the flow, cut the nozzle of the cartridge at an oblique angle, puncture the inner seal by sticking a nail into the nozzle, and squeeze the trigger of the caulking gun. It's best to cut a small opening first, to gauge the rate of flow; you can enlarge it later if necessary.

For the best adherence, *push* the caulk along. In this manner, the nozzle packs the caulk into the joint as the nozzle rides over it. Applied in this way, caulk rarely needs touching up. Caulk that is pulled along won't seat as deeply, and it may meander. If you have to touch up a

Figure 13.10 Better-quality thresholds have replaceable vinyl inserts.

Figure 13.11 For best results as you caulk, push the tube away from you; pushing packs the caulking into the seam.

sloppy stretch, use a spoon or pointing tool dipped in a suitable solvent.

Caulking does have limits, though. It won't adhere to rotten wood, and it can't fill gaps more than $\frac{1}{2}$ in. wide. Pack gaps that are larger, first, with specially designed packing rods made of sponge rubber, neoprene, butyl, fiberglass, polyurethane foam, or cotton cord. Oil- or tar-based oakum isn't suitable, because the oil from either type will leach into surrounding surfaces and stain them, and because both types of oakum are extremely flammable. Where the gap is more than 1 in. wide, consider patching or replacing the section with a similar material.

Your choice of caulk should be based on several factors (see Table 13.4). Perhaps the most important factor—after durability in weather—is elasticity. Where building joints are subjected to movement or expansion, you must use a flexible caulk that will remain flexible—for example, silicone, polysulfide, polyethylene, polyurethane, butyl, or neoprene. Latex and oil-based caulks won't do in such circumstances. Neither will pressurized spray-foam types of insulation, which are not elastic (they shrink as they cure) and which may start a fire if an electrical outlet is nearby.

Of the caulking represented, the most elastomeric and durable are also the most expensive: silicone, polyurethane, and polysulfide. You can save money by buying a case of caulking or by pooling your efforts with neighbors and buying caulk in bulk (usually in 5-gal drums), and packing your own cartridges. Because its shelf life is limited, never buy more than you can use in one season. How much caulk do you need? Based on cartridges of 11 oz each, you probably need a half-tube for each door and window, five or six tubes to caulk the top of a foundation and two tubes to close the gaps along a two-story chimney.

Consult the manufacturer's literature on the side of the cartridges before buying them, because some of the cleanup solvents are not common. Paint thinner will do for most types of oil- or rosin-based caulk, such as butyl rubber and silicone; toluene will clean up polyethylene, neoprene, and polysulfide. Use methyl ethyl ketone (MEK) or acetone on polyurethane. Nonacrylic latex caulks will clean up with soapy water. Be sure to wear rubber gloves, a respirator mask and goggles when working with these solvents, many of which are highly toxic.

TABLE 13.4

Caulking compounds

Name	Cost	Durability	Elastomeric?	Paintable?	Intended Use
Silicone	Expensive	20+ years	Yes	No	Anywhere
Polysulfide	Expensive	20 years	Yes	No	Anywhere
Polyethylene	Moderate	15–20 years	Yes	Yes	General purpose
Polyurethane	Expensive	20 years	Yes	Yes	Anywhere
Butyl rubber	Moderate	15 years	Yes	Yes	Masonry or metal
Neoprene (also known as nitrile rubber)	Moderate	10–15 years	Yes	Yes	Masonry or metal
Latex	Low	5 years if painted	No	Yes	Not recommended for high exposure; best for interior use
Oil-base	Low	5 years if painted	No	Yes	Same as latex

WINDOW AND DOOR TREATMENTS

Because glass is a poor insulator, most of the heat loss of an insulated house is through its windows. Heat loss through doors is also considerable, although the loss is greater via infiltration around their perimeters than by conduction through them.

You can combat this heat loss in a number of ways. Traditionally, the most common treatment has been on the exterior: adding storm windows or storm doors, repairing or replacing glass and glazing compounds that aren't doing the job. Recently, interior window treatments are in vogue, especially insulated shutters, which increase the R value of windows four to ninefold. Doors with insulated cores are gaining adherents, too.

Storm Windows

Wood storm windows have superior R values to metal ones, but they are heavy and unwieldy: for that reason, more than three-quarters of the storm windows sold today are aluminum triple-track units that can be left in place year-round.

Aluminum windows. Aluminum windows come in three finishes—*mill, anodized,* and *baked enamel.* Mill finish, which is untreated metal, is the least expensive; it turns soft gray with age. Anodized windows are treated against corrosion and coated with an oxide film. Baked enamel finishes are available in a variety of colors and are virtually maintenance-free. Baked enamel windows are the most expensive, but possible color matches enable the renovator to blend windows with house colors rather than settle for conspicuous gray metal.

Inspect storm-window units carefully; even the least expensive ones represent a considerable purchase. Metal should be at least 0.040 in. thick; thicker is preferable. Corners are particularly telling: joints, whether butted or mitered, must fit flush, without separation or sloppy welds. Although some builders hold that butted corners prevent rain from getting behind the frame, mitered corners are adequate if corners are reinforced with right-angle keys, which hold stile and rail together. The meeting rail, in the middle of the unit, is also important; it should be sturdy enough to prevent windows from twisting or warping. Lay the unit flat on a tabletop and ascertain that it is perfectly flat. Units that twist or that have daylight between joints are inferior.

The spring-loaded catches that hold windows in position should catch a sash when it is dropped from a higher catch setting. Generally, metal catches are more durable than plastic ones. Better-quality windows have more catch settings, but three settings—full up, full closed, and half up—will suffice.

Panes themselves should be seated securely in vinyl or rubber strips, which, in turn, are set into the frames. Strips are crucial to the ability of a storm window to reduce infiltration. Strips on one side of the glass only won't do; they must grip the entire pane. The deeper the tracks in which sashes glide, the better the seal. Take time to examine the meeting rail where sashes come together; if they are to keep out wind and rain, they must fit tightly. At the bottom of the frame, there should be two or three small ($\frac{1}{4}$-in.) holes, to allow condensation to escape; water trapped inside a frame will cause the window to rot.

Installing your own storm windows can save you 10 to 15 percent; you must check several things, however, when hanging units. First, determine the plumb, level, and flatness of the original window. If the old window is somewhat out of square, consider building up the storm frame at low spots, so the storm will be as flat as possible. Caulk behind a storm frame before attaching it; this bed of caulk will even out irregularities and form a weathertight seal. (An inexpensive caulk is okay here.) Center the storm over the window; then plumb the sides and sink a few screws so that it will stay in place. Have someone inside raise and lower sashes. If a sash binds, the unit is probably not flat. Locate and correct the twisting before fastening the storm completely.

Settling of the house is *the* problem when installing aluminum storms, for relatively slight settling can cause units to bind. This problem can be relieved by removing and resetting the frame when you first notice binding. Most people continue to operate sashes even when they stick, applying a little more muscle with each season, until the assembly is decrepit.

Wooden storm windows. Good-quality wooden storms are fashioned from straight clear stock free of splits, checks, twists, or other imperfections. (Small, tight knots are acceptable.) The woods most commonly used in construction are Douglas fir, ponderosa pine, southern yellow pine, sugar pine, and various types of white pine. The wood should be kiln-dried to a moisture content of 12 to 15 percent and treated to prevent mildew and insects. Many brands of frame are Wolmanized before painting.

Mortise-and-tenon joints are preferred for corner joints; they successfully resist twisting from normal handling and use. Butted-and-dowled joints are a somewhat distant second choice; surface plates over butted or mitered joints will *not* keep sections from separating.

If the sashes you buy are unprimed, prime them at once to prevent the absorption of moisture. Windows are available clad with PVC, which seals them against rot and bugs; this is the most expensive and most durable coating. Although baked-enamel finishes offer a greater range of colors, they require more maintenance.

Most wooden storms have fixed sashes. Individual sheets of glass should be securely glazed with a full bed of glazing compound or—less desirable—a vinyl gasket set into a wood slot. Triple-track wood storms are available, usually with plastic tracks; but they are very expensive and have a greater tendency to stick than do their metal counterparts.

Homemade storm windows. Inexpensive storms can be made from $\frac{5}{4}$ stock ($1\frac{1}{4}$-in.) ripped into strips 2 in. wide on a table saw. Dado a $\frac{3}{8}$-in.-by-$\frac{3}{8}$-in. slot in the strips as a channel for the glass. A mortise-and-tenon joint is the strongest, but the amateur renovator will be adequately served by half-lap joints where rails and stiles meet. Apply waterproof glue, and clamp joints well. The stock, of course, should be straight and clear, and preferably one of the varieties mentioned above.

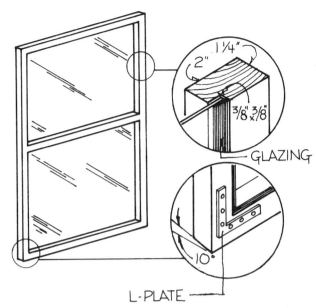

Figure 13.12 Homemade storm windows. Construct your own storms from 5/4 stock, routing out a $\frac{3}{8}$ in. × $\frac{3}{8}$ in. channel to hold the glass. Although corners are best half-lapped, mortise-and-tenoned, or doweled, you can make serviceable joints by butting pieces and reinforcing them on both sides with L-plates. The 10-degree angle on the bottom of the storm matches that of the sill.

When measuring and laying out storm windows, note the position of the meeting rails of the original window (where the top and bottom sashes meet.) The center rail of the storm should coincide with those meeting rails so the view from inside reveals a minimum of wood at the middle of the window. For the best fit to the window sill, bevel the bottom rail 10 degrees, the angle at which most exterior sills are set. Prime well, and glaze the glass. For a good fit to the window frame, apply flexible foam weatherstripping to the back of the storm frame.

Windows That Sweat

Sweating, or condensation, on windows occurs when warm, moist air comes in contact with a cold window pane. This phenomenon commonly occurs where there are only single-pane windows in place; it should not occur on storm windows. In storms that continue to sweat, the point at which the moisture collects is the trouble spot.

If the condensation occurs on the inside of the storm sash, the window is leaking warmed air from living areas. Weatherstrip the sashes of the windows, especially where upper and lower sashes meet. If the condensation occurs on the window panes, the storm is admitting cold air; the best solution is to refit the storm and add permanent weatherstripping to the back or sides of the storm frame. If you can't correct the problem during winter, simply caulk around the storm to reduce the air flow.

There are two exceptions to the rule above, neither of which you can do much about but which, happily, are short-lived. If you have totally gutted your house recently or kept your windows wide open during the warm months, there will be some condensation as the cold months begin; the condition should stabilize in a few weeks. Also, if it's extremely cold—say, 20 to 30°F below—the air outside will

chill the air space between the storms and the sashes. In that event, pray for warmer weather.

Glazing and Glazing Sealants

The term *glazing* refers to glass or plastic used as windows, storm windows, greenhouse panels, and so on. *Glazing sealants* include materials used to seat, or fit, glazing into a frame. To most of us, glazing is synonymous with glass and glazing sealants with window putty; but consider all the possibilities if you are reconditioning or replacing windows or storms. Actual removal and replacement is discussed in Chapter 6; here we're concerned with the materials available.

Glazing. Glass is by far the superior glazing. It is durable, clear, scratch-resistant, and relatively inexpensive. It is also heavy and will break, but that's about the extent of its shortcomings. Most glass sold today is "float glass," a glass produced in a specific manufacturing process that yields a brilliant surface with little optical distortion. Glass is available in many tints and in reflective coatings and temperings. Annealed glass and tempered glass are strengthened by repeated heatings and are thus specified where safety is crucial. Of the two types of glass, tempered is the stronger, shattering into tiny, blunt particles on impact. Tempered glass cannot be cut or drilled, however; so you must specify dimensions exactly when ordering. Where security is a concern, wire glass will resist intruders. Laminated glass, in which two layers of glass are glued to a plastic core, is also specified for safety and security purposes. Patterned glass diffuses light so that privacy is possible without losing incoming light. Insulated glass is comprised of two or more panes, with a layer of air between each pair; although the inner panes are always clear, outer panes may be tinted, coated, or patterned.

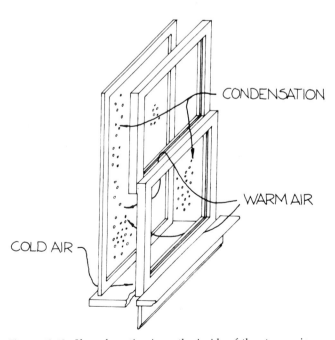

Figure 13.13 If condensation is on the inside of the storm window, weatherstrip the window sashes on the inside. If condensation is on the outside of the window pane, the storm window is leaking air.

Among the types of plastic glazing, the acrylic group is the oldest and most frequently used; some brands are Plexiglas, Lucite, and Acrylite. Acrylics are lightweight, easily worked with drills or fine-toothed saws, and relatively resistant to impact. Although acrylics are clear and free from distortion, they scratch; unlike other plastics, however, they will not yellow. Sheets of acrylic are easily attached to the inside of windows to make an interior storm; special vinyl strips aid fastening and allow removal of the plastic in warm weather.

Polycarbonate plastics (e.g., Lexan) are virtually unbreakable and are less expensive than acrylics; but they yellow with age. Fiber-reinforced polyester (Kalwall, Glassteel, Filon) and fiber-glass plastics generally are not clear; though suitable for use on solar panels or greenhouses, they are not advisable for windows. These plastics yellow in time and will scratch, but most are impact-resistant. Polyethylene sheets serve as interior storms in a pinch, but they are unacceptable in the long run because, while admitting light, they blur everything beyond.

Glazing sealants. Window putty, also called glazing compound, will do for most uses. It's cheap and can be easily applied with a putty knife. Glazing compounds adhere well to surfaces (they should be primed first, however) and resist tearing or puncturing. Glazing compounds harden, though, and should be painted to resist ultraviolet deterioration; their average life varies from 3 to 10 years. Gunnable polymers cost more and last longer (up to 20 or 30 years); included in this category are silicone, polysulfide, and the other high-performance materials shown in Table 13.4. Because high temperatures between the panes can degrade normal glazing compounds, gunnable polymers are an excellent choice for construction with insulated glass. Preformed glazing tapes adhere poorly and puncture easily; don't bother with them. Glazing gaskets, such as PVC, neoprene, and EPDM rubber, are used in conjunction with preformed metal glazing tracks; such gaskets require liquid adhesives.

Interior Windows

There are several ways to insulate windows from the inside—thermal shutters, pocket shutters, removable panels, and thermal shades and curtains. Several factors are involved in determining the best treatment: ease of installation and daily operation, R value of the unit, and tightness of fit for stopping infiltration. In our opinion, thermal shutters are by far the most effective and, in the Snow Belt, well worth the cost.

Thermal shutters. Thermal shutters feature a piece of rigid insulation such as polyurethane, isocyanurate, or polystyrene sandwiched between plywood veneer. The panels are stiffened with ribs of solid wood, to which hinges can be screwed. Where individual panels meet, there should be weatherstripping (usually foam rubber), to prevent infiltration. Although construction details vary, rigid insulation has the highest R value. Plywood veneer protects insulation and provides a pleasing exterior; also, hinges allow the user to swing the shutters out of the way when not in use. The operation of the window is not affected.

InsulShutters are the state of the art of thermal shutters: their stated R value of R-8 is far better than anything of comparable cost, and the weatherstripping probably exceeds its manufacturer's claims. A window-and-shutter combination for a single-pane window has an R value of R-9. Units are available prehung and come in a choice of three mounting arrangements. The finish is good, and the polyurethane panels are backed with foil to increase reflection back into living areas.

If you make your own thermal shutters, start by measuring windows carefully and checking for plumb and level. Never assume that window casings are square. When you are ready to hang the shutters, plumb the sides of the panels; merely matching them to the edges of existing casings will probably result in misalignment. Although you can assemble panels in one of several ways, the method

A.

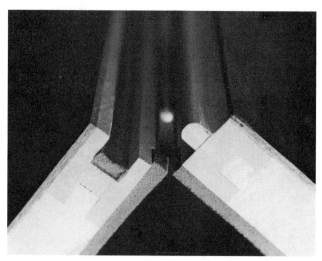

B.

Figure 13.14 (A) Thermal shutters fold flat against the wall when not in use, making them the most convenient interior window treatment. (B) A well-constructed thermal shutter must have a solid-wood frame to be durable; and be weatherstripped where shutter sections join each other, and where they meet window trim. (InsulShutter)

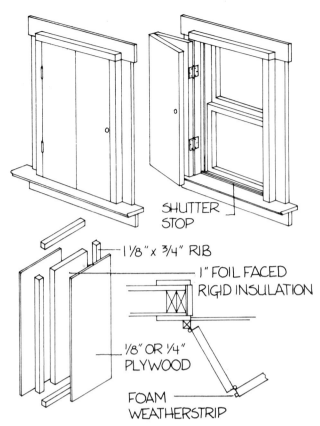

Figure 13.15 Making your own thermal shutters. It's imperative that thermal shutters be made from clear dry stock; otherwise, they'll warp and won't fit tightly to window trim. Butt-joining the ribs of panels may not look elegant, but the joint is strong because the ribs are glued to plywood faces. Be sure to weatherstrip between panels and where the shutters stop against trim.

that requires the least amount of cutting is to butt-join the frame and glue it to plywood facings $\frac{1}{8}$-in. or $\frac{1}{4}$-in. thick. By carefully cutting the plywood so its corners are perfectly square, you can align the ribs of the frame to the edges of the plywood. Any lightweight wood will do for the ribs, as long as it is dry and straight, but No. 2 pine or basswood is preferred. By using $\frac{3}{4}$-in. stock, you can rip down ribs $\frac{3}{4}$ in. by $1\frac{1}{8}$ in. (the latter measurement is wide enough to receive 1-in. butt hinges). Glue the ribs on edge to a piece of plywood and allow joints to dry; then insert (within the ribs) a piece of rigid insulation, 1 in. thick and glue on another piece of plywood. For the best-looking results, cover the edges with a matching veneer tape. Hinges between shutter sections should be chiseled into panel ribs, but surface-mounted hinges will do if the foam strips between sections are thick enough. For the tightest fit, apply adhesive-backed foam strips only after you've hung the shutters.

Pocket shutters. In colonial times, pocket shutters were wood panels that slid into a wall cavity; today, they're made of rigid insulation. Of all the treatments discussed here, pocket shutters are the most difficult to install (especially when retrofitting); you must frame out a new rough opening to accommodate the window and its pocket. Once the shutters have slid into their pockets, however, they are completely out of sight, making them visually the least obtrusive devices of any discussed here.

Installing a window-and-pocket frame is no more difficult than putting in a regular window, but fabricating the unit is best left to a commercial manufacturer. The track is particularly difficult to align so that the panel does not bind, and it must be tight enough to stop infiltration but loose enough so the panel doesn't abrade. One manufacturer, Starflake Windows (Durango, CO.), covers its insulation panel with textured steel, uses PVC tracks, and insu-

Figure 13.16 Pocket shutters are an updated version of a colonial detail, with shutters now insulated and weatherstripped. The unit shown has an insulated pocket as well, so that the wall cavity will retain heat even when the shutter is drawn out in front of the glass. (Starflake Windows)

Window and Door Treatments **329**

lates the pocket, so that the panel won't lose heat when the shutter is drawn across the window. Interestingly, Starflake features only single-pane windows. The company reasons—accurately, I think—that glass is such a poor insulator that little thermal resistance is to be gained by adding layers of glass. With the insulated panel drawn shut across the window, the composite value claimed for Starflake Windows is R-16. This is an expensive route to go; but if your renovation is an ambitious one, of gutting interiors and replacing windows, consider pocket shutters.

Removable panels. Removable panels are little more than sheets of rigid insulation carefully cut so they will fit inside window frames. They are put into place at night and removed in the daytime. The trick to making these panels work is to cut them very carefully and to devise a simple way to hold them in place within the frame. A metal clip, or a nail bent over at the top of the window casing, will hold in the top of a panel, while the bottom simply rests on the windowsill.

For a modest investment (little more than the cost of the sheet insulation), you can achieve a fairly high R value—say, R-6 or R-7. As simple as this approach is, though, it has drawbacks. One drawback is infiltration around the edges of the panels. The more closely you fit the rigid insulation within the frame, the harder the panel is to remove. It's almost imperative that the panels—especially the edges (which abrade on the frame and disintegrate little particles of polyurethane or polystyrene beads onto the floor)—be covered with fabric or a similar material. Finally, you must have room to store the panels during the day.

Thermal shades and curtains. Thermal shades and curtains are usually insulated fabric whose effectiveness depends on how tightly the shade or curtain fits to the window casing. Units that live up to their claimed R value (R-3 to R-5) invariably have side seals in which the edges of shades slide.

Of the fabric shades available commercially, Window Quilt has been in business longest. This shade has five layers, including a reflective plastic center sandwiched between $\frac{1}{4}$-in. polyester fibers; the outer layers are textured. The total effect is pleasant and unobtrusive, and its R value is about 3.5.

Doors

Doors lose heat by conduction and infiltration around the perimeter. Some strategies for preventing either type of heat loss are adding storm doors, replacing old units with insulated-core doors and building on an entryway to reduce wintry gusts.

Storm doors. The following statistics, from the Department of Housing and Urban Development, give a quick idea of the value of storm doors:

Wood Doors	R Value	R Value with Storm Doors
1 in. nominal	1.56	2.70
$1\frac{1}{4}$ nominal	1.81	2.94
$1\frac{1}{2}$ in. nominal	1.04	3.13

The criteria for selecting storm doors are similar to those for buying storm windows. Mill finish is the least expensive and will corrode the fastest. Anodized finish lasts longer and is of intermediate cost. Baked enamel looks best, weathers well, comes in several colors, and is most expensive. Storm doors of wood are somewhat more expensive but offer thermal resistance one-third to one-half greater than that of aluminum ones; also, wood storms look better on old houses.

Whether a storm door is metal or wood, the corners reveal the most about the quality of construction. Regardless of butting or mitering, metal corners should have clean welds and no gaps through which air can leak. Wooden sections should join in mortise-and-tenon joints, finger joints, and so on.

Because so much heat is lost around a door, weatherstripping is crucial; do the detailing carefully. Have the supplier install the storm door; then check it closely for gaps and similar details. A good test is the lit-cigarette method already mentioned; another is to stand outside the door at night and look for light leaks around seams. Airtight storms should open and shut with some resistance, but you should never feel air leaks when both doors are closed.

Doors with insulated cores. Insulated doors are usually hollow steel shells containing insulation foam. Because polyurethane and isocyanurate foams have R values of 6 to 8 per inch, it's not uncommon for doors with insulated cores to have R values of 7 to 15 for a door 2 in. thick.

Because 80 percent of the heat loss around an entrance is at a door's perimeter, however, weatherstripping the unit is perhaps more important than the R value of its core. A two-piece sealing system, such as that shown in Figure 13.9, is preferable. This system should allow an air-infiltration rate of no more than 1.25 cu ft per linear foot of

Figure 13.17 Window-Quilt.

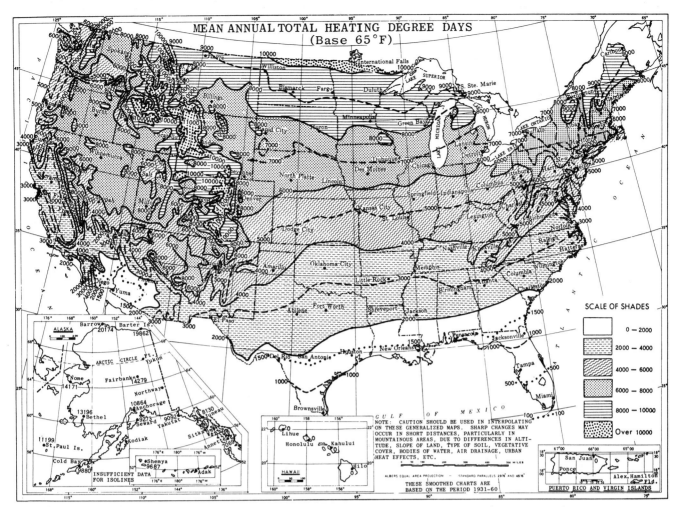

Figure 13.18 (From John L. Baldwin, *Climates of the United States*, U.S. Department of Commerce, Washington, DC, 1973. Reprinted in *Designing and Building Your Own House Your Own Way*, listed in the bibliography in Appendix G.)

perimeter; some door systems have rates as low as 0.05 to 0.10 cu ft per linear foot. When you add glass to an insulated core unit, the R value of the total unit plummets, of course.

Traditionally, the main objections to insulated-core doors have been aesthetic—that doors stained as wood, or those with simulated wood grain or built-up molding, look unrealistic. Happily, steel-door design has improved of late. Because adding a dead-bolt lock or making other modifications may not be easy to accomplish with a steel door, ask your supplier what modifications are allowed. And because most metal doors come precased in a metal frame, be sure to read manufacturer's literature on installing and finishing with trim.

INSULATION

Insulation reduces the flow of heat from living areas to the outside; in the summer, it slows heat gain from the opposite direction. Except for some cellular plastics, most types of insulation trap air in thousands of tiny pockets, preventing convectional heat loss and employing air (which has a good R value) as an insulator.

The term *R value,* explained at the beginning of this chapter, refers to the thermal resistivity of a material—that is, how well it resists the flow of heat. R values of different types of insulation vary greatly, as do other characteristics such as moisture transmission, durability, and fire resistance. These characteristics, and the physical form of the insulation determine the type and placement of insulation.

Note: Moisture flows from high concentration to low, just as heat does. When adding insulation to prevent heat loss, you also affect the flow of moisture from inside to outside. Moisture from cooking and bathing—which easily migrates through an uninsulated wall—may condense inside the wall. This is especially true in a cold climate. Condensation, which can cause the frame of a house to rot in a relatively short time, usually is prevented by adding a vapor barrier (most often a barrier of impermeable plastic, such as polyethylene) to the living-space side of the insulation. There are exceptions to the rule, however; if the subject of vapor barriers still perplexes you, consult the Index. Problems with moisture can also be mitigated by installing kitchen and bathroom fans and by adding soffit vents and ridge vents—both of which are crucial to the condition of a house, especially an old one.

How Much Insulation Do You Need?

The amount of insulation you need depends on the heating requirements of your area, as presented in the degree-day map in Figure 13.18, and the type of heating system you have, as specified in Tables 13.5 and 13.6.

TABLE 13.5

Minimum insulation requirements for oil, gas, and wood, and heat pump—and recommended levels[a]

Location				Degree-Day Range		
		0 to 1000	1000 to 3000	3000 to 5000	5000 to 7000	7000 and up
Ceilings	min.	R-3[b]	R-3[b]	R-6[b]	R-9	R-9
	rec.	R-19	R-19	R-19	R-30	R-38
Frame walls	min.	None	None	None	None	None
	rec.	None	Fill cavity	Fill cavity	Fill cavity	Fill cavity
Walls of heated basements crawl spaces	min.	None	None	None	None	None
	rec.	None	None	R-3	R-11	R-11
Floors over unheated spaces	min.	None	None	R-6	R-6	R-6
	rec.	None	None	R-11	R-11	R-19

[a]Information taken from "In the Bank . . . or Up the Chimney?" It was developed by Technology + Economics. Cambridge, MA for the Department of Housing and Urban Development, it also appeared in *The Old-House Journal*, Sept. 1980, p. 109.

[b]R-9 if the house has central air conditioning.

TABLE 13.6

Minimum insulation requirements for electric resistance heat—and recommended levels[a]

Location				Degree-Day Range		
		0 to 1000	1000 to 3000	3000 to 5000	5000 to 7000	7000 and up
Ceilings	min.	R-6[a]	R-6[a]	R-9	R-9	R-11
	rec.	R-19	R-22	R-30	R-30	R-38
Frame walls	min.	None	None	None	R-3	R-3
	rec.	None	Fill cavity	Fill cavity	Fill cavity	Fill cavity
Walls of unheated basements crawl spaces	min.	None	None	None	None	None
	rec.	None	None	R-6	R-11	R-11
Floors over unheated spaces	min.	None	R-6	R-6	R-6	R-6
	rec.	None	R-11	R-19	R-19	R-19

[a]Information taken from "In the Bank . . . or Up the Chimney?" It was developed by Technology + Economics, Cambridge, MA for the Department of Housing and Urban Development, it also appeared in *The Old-House Journal*, Sept. 1980, p. 109.

[b]R-9 if the house has central air conditioning.

Once you've determined how much insulation you need, consider the R value per inch of each type listed in Table 13.7. Although most people find that batt-type insulation is the easiest to work with, limited space may force you to use more compact, higher-R types. It's permissible to add new insulation over old, provided the old material is dry and in good condition.

What Type of Insulation Is Right?

The type of insulation you install will depend on your heating requirements; the condition of your house, as explained below; and, to a degree, the characteristics of the insulation, as explained in the section below, "Insulation Materials: A Closer Look." The condition of the house, and the relative ease of installing each type of insulation are the most important determinants, though. Look closely at the interior and exterior surfaces. Are they in good repair? Which side of the wall would be easier to insulate?

The preferred method: Gutting interior walls. The best way to insulate a wall is to gut its interior finish surfaces, install foil-backed fiberglass batts, cover the insulation with a polyethylene vapor barrier, and replace the finish surfaces. Most other insulating methods described below will adequately insulate a wall, but they won't put a vapor barrier on the living-space side of the insulation. Without such a barrier, condensation can develop in an insulated wall. If you do not or cannot add a vapor barrier when you insulate, you must find another way to allow water vapor to leave the house.

My advice is to bite the bullet—take out a loan to cover the cost of insulating and replacing interior surfaces, and do the job right. If the interior walls are in poor condition and need repairing anyway, there's no extra cost.

If the exterior needs repair. If the interior is in good shape, and you can't bear the thought of tearing it out, leave the interior alone and insulate through the exterior

TABLE 13.7
Overview of R values

Type of Insulation	R per Inch
Batts and blankets	
Fiberglass	3.2
Mineral wool (rock wool)	3.4
Loose fill	
Fiberglass	2.3–3.2
Mineral wool	2.2–3.3
Cellulose	3.7
Vermiculite	2.2
Perlite	2.6–3.6
Spray-on	
Mineral wool	3.4
Cellulose	4.0–4.8
Polyurethane	6.3–7.2
Isocyanurate	6.8–8.0
Urea-formaldehyde[a]	4.2
Rigid boards	
Polystyrene beadboard	4.2
Extruded polystyrene	5.0
Polyurethane	7.1
Isocyanurate	7.8
Perlite	2.8
Fiberglass	4.0
Reflective	2.0 per inch
aluminum foil (with air space)	of air

[a]Banned by National Consumer Protection Agency.

instead. The method of adding insulation from the outside used most frequently is to pry up siding selectively, drill through the sheathing, and blow insulation into the bays between the studs. You will have to replace the siding you remove. This method has its problems, however. In brief, you still don't have a vapor barrier, and the material blown in can become sodden and ineffective as insulation. If this is the method you choose, add plug ventilators to the siding to allow excess water to escape from the bays.

Another exterior method is to remove existing siding and attach rigid board insulation over the sheathing; then re-side over the insulation. To nail on the new siding, you

may have to add 1-by-2-in. nailing strips between sheets of insulation; but that's not problem. What should you do about water vapor? First of all, use beadboard polystyrene; it's fairly permeable (see Table 13.8), is unaffected by moisture, and an inch-thickness has an R value of 4.2. The cumulative R value of such a wall, including air spaces, is about R-8. Urethane, though it has a better R value, will be much less permeable. Second, don't paint the exterior; stain it. Oil-base paints are relatively impermeable and will trap moisture.

Some authorities on renovation suggest adding rigid insulation right over existing siding, and new siding on top of that: it's done, but rarely well. For one thing, the air-infiltration rate will be high because of the old siding's irregular surface. For another, you'll have to build up the exterior trim so it won't be buried by the additional layers. It thus becomes an unnecessarily complicated procedure; you would be better off ripping out the old siding.

Interior and the exterior in good condition. If the inside and the outside are in good condition, you've got a dilemma. If you live in a region of less than, say, 4000 degree-days, probably the easiest things to do is forego insulation in the walls. Remember, an uninsulated wall has an R value of about R-4. Instead, spend your money reducing infiltration, upgrading windows and doors, and insulating the ceiling. If you live in a climate that's too cold for this strategy, your most sensible choice is probably blown-in insulation and ventilator plugs.

Solid-wall construction. If your house is masonry or solid wood—for instance, a log cabin—you don't have many options. Probably the best thing to do if you really need upgraded insulation is to add a sheet of rigid insulation over present interior surfaces. If that doesn't work, add insulation to the exterior—again rigid board is the best choice. This approach will change the character of the building's exterior drastically; thus, avoid it if possible. Ersatz siding over brick is ghastly, and the same over logs is too silly to consider.

In rare circumstances, the cavity between wythes of brick can be filled; but that should be done by profession-

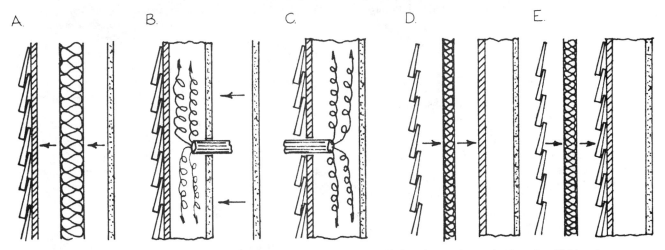

Figure 13.19 A quick look at insulating options. (A) Gut interior, add fiberglass and new finish walls; (B) blow in inslation from interior, add finish wall over old; (C) blow in insulation from the outside; (D) strip old siding, add rigid insulation, re-side; (E) add insulation and new siding over old.

als, and it should feature an insulation that will be unaffected by water.

Summing up. Use batts and blankets of insulation wherever you can, and in cold regions, put a vapor barrier on the living-space side of the insulation to prevent moisture from condensing in the walls. Note, however, that only the walls need a vapor barrier—never ceilings.

Where the area to be insulated is easily exposed—for example attics, beneath floors, and in gutted walls—batts and blankets are again the best choice; rigid boards require too much cutting, and they may not fit well. Where access is limited, fill cavities with loose-fill materials blown in. Rigid boards are suitable for covering existing finish surfaces, exterior sheathing, or subflooring in place already.

Insulation Materials: A Closer Look

Insulation materials vary in physical form, degree of flammability, moisture resistance, durability, methods of installation, R value, and cost.

Fiberglass: Fiberglass batts and blankets are by far the most popular form of insulation. Blankets are available in thicknesses of $3\frac{1}{2}$ to 12 in. and in widths of 11, 15, and 23 in.—to fit between framing 12, 16, and 24 in. on-center, respectively. Depending upon the thickness of the insulation, blanket rolls are 40 to 100 ft long; the total square footage will be marked on a roll's wrapping. Although insulation is usually attached by stapling through paper backing, friction-fit varieties are gaining popularity. Fiberglass is backed with draft paper or foil paper: when allowed an air space in front, foil paper reflects radiant energy back into living spaces. Whatever the backing on the insulation, it should always *face* living spaces.

Fiberglass is fire-resistant, melting at a temperature of about 1600°F. Its backing, however, may be flammable; check the fire rating on the wrapping. This material is durable and will not rot or mildew from dampness, but because the R value of fiberglass decreases when it becomes damp, it's important to install a vapor barrier.

Although fiberglass is proffered as a loose-fill material, it is too light to fill the far corners of a space properly. Wear gloves, goggles, and a respirator mask when handling fiberglass.

Mineral wool. Mineral wool is similar to fiberglass; it has a slightly higher R value, though. The material is available in batts and blankets in the sizes listed above. As loose fill, it is somewhat heavier than fiberglass and is available in 25-lb bags. Use it with a vapor barrier and observe the safety precautions mentioned above for handling fiberglass.

Cellulose. Cellulose is available primarily as loose fill, which can be poured or blown into frame-wall spaces. It's an organic material made, usually, from recycled newspapers, whose effectiveness as an insulation depends on the chemicals used in its treatment, whether it is resistant to rot, mildew, or vermin, or a combination of these. Cellulose is treated with a fire retardant, but it should be regarded as flammable.

Cellulose is the best material to blow into frame-wall cavities. It's heavy enough to settle into distant corners,

maintains its loft, and isn't likely to settle appreciably. It does, however, settle some, creating cold spots at the tops of walls. In reality, however, the qualities of application and of the material itself vary greatly. Cellulose should be used with a vapor barrier, although that is often not possible when you're blowing it into a closed space such as a wall.

It's imperative that you investigate insulation contractors in your area before contracting to have cellulose blown in. If the contractor is sloppy, you could have cold spots, and if he uses improperly treated material, you could have a sodden mess in your walls, rotting out the structure. Cellulose treated with borax or boric acid is a good product with a high R value. Cellulose treated with aluminum sulfate, calcium sulfate, ammonium sulfate, or sodium sulfate, however, can absorb water, rot wood, and corrode electrical boxes. Additional information about treatment chemicals may be obtained from the Underwriters' Laboratory.

Loose-fill cellulose comes in bags containing 4 cu ft and is priced reasonably. Spray-on cellulose, which requires special machinery, is mixed with adhesives and has a higher R value than cellulose poured or blown.

Vermiculite and perlite. Vermiculite (chemically related to mica) and perlite are lightweight granules of expanded minerals. Often combined with masonry materials, they are mixed with cement, forming a lightweight insulating surface coat or as filling for the cells of concrete blocks.

Because both vermiculite and perlite are inorganic, they resist rot, mildew, and vermin and are fire resistant (melting at a temperature of about 2000°F). They resist moisture but should not be subjected to extreme dampness; in high-porosity materials, water can replace air and substantially reduce the material's R value. Use a vapor barrier; without one, moisture can collect, with the same ill effects as those for cellulose.

Perlite sheets have been used with mixed results as an insulation for exterior roofs. In granular form, either material can be poured easily and blown into cavities. Due to the risk of asbestos-like contamination from either material, wear goggles and a respirator mask when handling. Both materials are relatively expensive.

Polystyrene. Polystyrene comes in two forms, beadboard (also called expanded, or molded, polystyrene) and extruded polystyrene (one brand is Styrofoam). Like all cellular plastics, polystyrenes have high R values; however, they can give off toxic smoke at temperatures as low as 600 to 700°F. Check your local codes to determine acceptable fireproofing over such insulation; two layers of $\frac{1}{2}$-in. type X drywall are usually adequate.

Sheets are available in widths of 12, 16, 24, and 48 in.; lengths in multiples of 2 ft, up to 12; and thicknesses from $\frac{1}{2}$-in. to 4 in. Foil-backed types are available, though more for reflecting heat than serving as a vapor barrier. It is not necessary to use vapor barriers with either material; if you are concerned about moisture migration, beadboard is about twice as permeable when extruded.

Because both beaded and extruded polystyrene deteriorate when exposed to ultraviolet rays, they must be covered as soon as possible. Both are used as a base for stucco or plaster, although details vary according to the finish material used and the manufacturer's specifications. Extruded polystyrene's resistance to water makes it a favorite for exterior application, including insulating the foundation above and below grade and as a base for Dryvit, a stucco-like exterior insulation.

Polystyrene is easily cut with a utility knife and can be attached with mastic paste, washered or large-head nails, self-tapping screws (to metal studs), and so on. It is an expensive material but durable and versatile.

Polyurethane and isocyanurate. Polyurethane and isocyanurate are cellular plastic available in rigid sheets and as foam sprayed in place. They have excellent R values per inch. Like polystyrene, both are flammable and give off toxic fumes when they burn. Either material must be fireproofed according to a local code. They also come in sizes similar to polystyrene's and in foil-backed and paper-backed sheets.

Both polyurethane and isocyanurate are even more vulnerable to ultraviolet rays, and both are subject to shrinking, especially varieties that are foamed in place. Because the permeability of either is less than that of polystyrene, neither material should be used for exterior applications or where damp conditions prevail.

Because polyurethane and isocyanurate are similar chemically (isocyanurate has the higher R value), their foam applications are almost exactly the same. In both cases, the quality of a job depends greatly on the contractor; if the foams are to be stable, the mix of component parts must be exact. Foams adhere to almost any material, although they are not used to fill in cavities as is done with blown-in insulation. If you choose to retrofit with this insulation, strip a wall's surface (inner or outer) entirely. Rigid sheets can be cut and attached as with polystyrene sheets. Both materials are expensive.

Urea-formaldehyde. Urea-formaldehyde is another cellular plastic. Relatively inflammable, it is fairly permeable and must be used with a vapor barrier. It travels before setting and can be blown into cavities with some success. However, urea-formaldehyde has been identified as a health hazard by the National Consumer Protection Agency and is banned by many states. Therefore, do not use it your home.

Reflective insulation. Because it reflects radiant heat back into living areas, aluminum foil is classed as an insulant. It is available as backing for most types of rigid board and blanket insulation or by itself, backed with kraft paper. In either application, for the insulation to work correctly, there must be an air space between the back of the finish wall and the face of the foil. This air space can be formed by stapling the foil (or foil-backed insulation) to the inside of the studs $\frac{3}{4}$ in. to 1 in. from the edge of the stud.

If you install only foil paper, for the best results staple three sheets between framing members, spacing each sheet about 1 in. apart. Although foil is an excellent vapor barrier, foil set back from the edge of studs allows heat and moisture to escape through the studs themselves. (This loss is called "thermal bridging.") For this reason, it's advisable to use a polyethylene vapor barrier over foil, to cut air infiltration.

Insulating merely with foil is a relatively inexpensive way to insulate, although installing several layers can be time-consuming.

Installing Insulation

Insulating your house makes good economic sense, and the skills required for the job are modest ones. In general, it's easier to retrofit insulation from the inside. Before discussing specific how-to techniques, though, consider two aspects of insulation that affect your safety and the structural integrity of your house—potential fire hazards and vapor barriers and condensation.

Avoiding fire hazards: The space between a masonry chimney and wooden structural members should be hand-packed with a noncombustible material such as unbacked fiberglass. Structural members in frame houses should be 2 in. from a masonry chimney.

When filling in an attic floor, stop insulation 3 in. short of recessed light fixtures and frame off the fixtures to keep insulation from drifting closer. To prevent sparking when blowing or spraying insulation into wall cavities, turn off the electricity to the areas affected until the job is done.

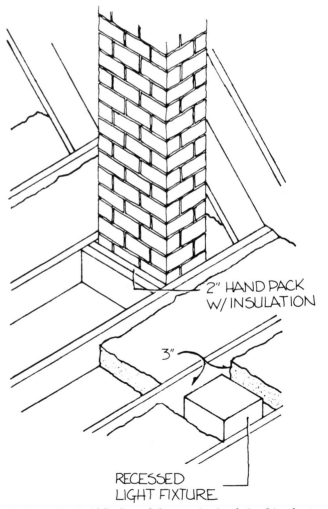

Figure 13.20 Avoid fire hazards by stopping insulation 3 in. short of recessed electrical fixtures. Framing around the chimney should be 2 in. away from the chimney itself.

TABLE 13.8

Permeability to moisture of various building materials

aluminum foil, 1-mil	0 perm
polyethylene, 6-mil	0.05
polyethylene, 4-mil	0.08
kraft paper, foil-faced	0.5
exterior plywood, ½-in.	0.5
kraft paper, asphalt-impregnated	1.0
vinyl wallpaper	1.0
exterior oil-base paint	1.0
urethane, 1-in.	0.4–1.6 perms
extruded polystyrene, 1-in.	1.2–3.0
beadboard polystyrene, 1-in.	2.0–5.8
building paper, 15-lb asphalt-treated	4.0
urea-formaldehyde, 1-in.	26.0
gypsum board, ¾-in.	50.0

Source: Larry Gay, *The Complete Book of Insulating*, Stephen Greene Press, Brattleboro, VT; 1980.

Vapor barriers and condensation. The warmer air is, the more moisture it can hold. Thus, during the heating season, the air inside a house is usually more moist than that outside. When the vapor pressures between inside and outside are out of balance, as they usually are, water vapor migrates through the materials in the building that are, to a degree, permeable. Water vapor migrates until it reaches its dew point, at which time it condenses and changes to liquid.

In most uninsulated houses, vapor migrates harmlessly and condenses on the outside of the house. When a wall is insulated, however, water vapor from living areas often condenses inside the wall, wetting the insulation and potentially rotting the building's frame. Therefore, to prevent water vapor from migrating into the walls, a vapor barrier is usually placed over the insulation just before finish surfaces are applied. Note, however, that vapor barriers should *not* be used on ceilings. Rather, vapor should be allowed to migrate out through the attic.

Relatively impermeable materials such as aluminum foil and sheet polyethylene are used as vapor barriers. They are attached between a living area and the insulation. When insulation is backed by a vapor barrier such as foil-backed paper, the barrier is always placed facing a living space, whether it is in walls, ceilings, or floors. The only exception to this rule is the retrofitting of rigid insulation to a masonry floor or wall, through which moisture can seep by capillary action, or "wick," into living areas. In this situation, apply the polyethylene sheet directly to the concrete block; then affix furring strips (if necessary) and add rigid insulation—*over* the vapor barrier. Wherever it is applied, the barrier must be intact and whole, without tears or gaps.

What happens to the moisture that cannot escape through the walls? It must be vented by mechanical means, such as fans in bathrooms and kitchens, and by dehumidifiers. In the winter months, the moisture within may be a pleasant antidote to the dry air produced by a central heating system. In addition, the attic itself should be vented adequately at soffit and ridge, so heated (and hence, more moist air) can exit of its own accord.

Dissenting opinions. Some respected authorities denounce the use of vapor barriers, arguing that rot is almost

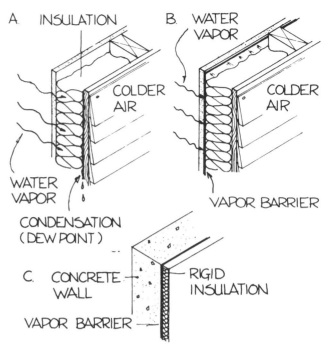

Figure 13.21 Vapor barriers prevent water vapor from condensing inside walls and rotting them. Such barriers are placed on the living-space side of insulation. Exception: Place the vapor barrier between rigid insulation and concrete, where moisture from the soil is a greater threat.

inevitable within the walls of old houses with barriers. It seems to me that they overstate their case, but here are some things to think about:

1. If you live in a warm region, as depicted in Figure 13.22, you *do not* need a vapor barrier; during most of the year, because air temperatures and relative humidity are often as high, and sometimes higher, outside than inside. Further, there are no arctic winds to keep out; thus a barrier to prevent infiltration is less important.

2. What is the permeability of the other materials in the wall cross section? If the outside of the building is covered with oil-based paint, I would agree with the dissenters and not use a vapor barrier on the inside. Oil-based paint on the outside and polyethylene on the inside give vapor little

Figure 13.22 No vapor barrier is needed below the dividing line, which indicates a mean January temperature of 35°F or greater.

chance to escape, making rot probable if moisture was already present when you closed in the walls. If you have both oil exterior paint and a vapor barrier, chances are, the paint on the outside is peeling—the vapor has found its own escape route. As soon as possible, add two plug vents to each bay (the space between the studs and fire stops, if any); that should correct the problem. An exterior painted with latex or stain is fairly permeable, however, so adding a vapor barrier should be no problem.

3. If you are blowing insulation into walls, and hence not adding a vapor barrier to the inside, add plug vents at once. The need for vents is even more urgent in cases where moisture is migrating from the living space and is being stopped by a relatively impervious exterior finish such as an oil-based paint. Painting interior walls with oil-based paint will form a barrier of sorts.

4. If the basement or the crawl space has a dirt floor, a lot of moisture is probably being added to the living space. Cover the dirt with a polyethylene sheet and pour a concrete floor soon. Also, add ventilation.

One person's solution. My method for reducing condensation without rotting a structure is as follows: stain (not paint) the exterior walls, insulate between studs with *foil-backed* fiberglass, and cover the insulation with a 6-mil polyethylene vapor barrier toward the living space. Add soffit and ridge vents to the roof, as well as ventilator fans in the kitchen and bathrooms, and insulate the ceiling (or roof) with *kraft-paper-backed* insulation, using *no* plastic barrier.

While I agree that water vapor should be kept from migrating through walls, it seems unwise to count on fans to remove all moisture. Since the warmest (hence, the wettest) air rises anyhow, moisture collects near ceilings where, unvented, mildew might result. Why not let the moisture permeate out, up through the ceiling, to be evaporated and carried off by the flow of air beneath the roof? A well-vented roof is crucial, for several reasons, and even on cold days the air beneath the roof is warmed and circulating, quickly carrying off all water vapor.

Installing Fiberglass Insulation

Wear the appropriate safety gear when installing fiberglass or mineral wool: respirator mask, gloves, goggles, long-sleeved clothing. Fiberglass is extremely irritating to the skin as well as the lungs (if inhaled) and the eyes. When you're done handling fiberglass batts, wash up with *cold* water. I'm not sure why it works—some builders claim it shrinks pores—but cold water markedly reduces itching.

To cut fiberglass blankets, roll the blankets out with the backed side up. Using a framing square or a piece of scrap wood *to guide your cut,* cut through the insulation with a utility knife; it will take several passes. Cut the insulation slightly longer—say, 2 in.—than the bay in which it will be placed. By pulling the backing up 1 in. at each end of the piece, you can form stapling tabs. If you're cutting several pieces of the same length, put strips of masking tape on the floor; that way, you can quickly roll out insulation to an exact length. Where two pieces of insulation must be used to fill a bay, add length so you can overlap pieces by at least 1 in.

Walls. How the insulation is stapled depends on its backing. Insulation backed with kraft paper can be stapled flat to the edge of the studs, with the stapling tabs meeting at the center of the studs to minimize infiltration. If the insulation is backed with foil, however, the insulation should be recessed 1 in. from the edge of the studs, so there will be an air space between the foil and the back side of the finish wall. In that case, staple insulation tabs to the inside of the studs.

Fit the insulation as tightly as possible in the stud bays; that will reduce infiltration to a minimum. Friction-fit batts should fit tightly between studs, with no slumping; stapling is not necessary there. Because the framing of older houses is sometimes irregular, however, friction-fit batts may not work.

Where more than one piece of insulation is used in a bay, overlap ends by at least 1 in.; for the best results, tape ends together with duct tape. Where there is an obstruction

Figure 13.23 Insulation is easily cut with a utility knife or a sharp pocketknife, proceeding from the backed side as shown.

Figure 13.24 Foil-backed insulation should be stapled to the inside of studs rather than to their edges, to create an air space between foil and the back side of the finish surface. This air space allows the foil to reflect heat back into the living space. (Owens-Corning)

within a bay—such as pipes, bridging, fire stops, or outlet boxes—try to fit the insulation between the obstruction and the exterior sheathing. If that isn't possible, cut separate pieces of insulation to pack behind the obstructions. Before working around electrical boxes, of course, turn off the power. Finally, use a putty knife to pack insulation in the gaps between rough openings and window or door frames. This packing, while somewhat tedious, is well worth the trouble. Caulk gaps that are too narrow to receive insulation.

As already noted, the side of the insulation with backing should always face the living space of a room. When insulation of the walls is complete, get help unrolling sheet polyethylene (4- or 6-mil) and staple it to the face of the framing members, including top and bottom plates. The poly should be slightly longer and higher than walls so that it completely covers them and overlaps adjacent surfaces slightly. Staple every foot or so. Then go back and carefully cut out the openings for windows, outlet boxes, and the like, again overlapping openings slightly. (Power should be off during this operation.) Leave any extra poly along the base or top of a wall; it will be covered later by the finish floor and ceiling, forming a tight seam against the flow of air. Whether the wall insulation is foil- or paper-backed, use a vapor barrier.

Attics. It is relatively inexpensive to insulate the floor of an unused attic. If the attic is finished off, or will be, insulate between the rafters. Where there is only partial access to the space beneath the roof—that is, if parts of it are already covered with finish surfaces—insulate in floors, knee walls, and above collar ties. Where framing members are exposed, use batts, blankets, or loose fill between joists; blankets between rafters; and blown-in insulation where access is limited.

A number of important preparatory steps should be taken before insulating an attic. First, rig a light if there's none; a drop light works well. Second, if there's no subfloor—if the tops of the joists aren't covered—you'll need some planks to walk on. Don't try to scamper from joist to joist; you wouldn't be the first to put a leg through a ceiling. Third, move your materials upstairs and leave them wrapped until you're ready to use them. Fourth, block off the ends of joists with baffles if you're insulating between joists (Figure 13.26); it's imperative that the air flow through an attic be unimpaired.

In an attic with a simple layer of 1-in. boards for a floor, it may be easier to pry up the boards and insulate between joists. Starting at one side, pull up half the flooring; stack the boards out of the way, insulate, and renail the boards. Then do the other side. The easiest way to pull up flooring is with a flat bar or a utility bar. Otherwise, pull up just enough boards so you can blow insulation between joists.

If you're adding insulation to insulation in place, use unfaced insulation; otherwise, you could trap moisture in the original layer. When insulating for the first time, use paper-backed insulation, with the barrier pointed toward

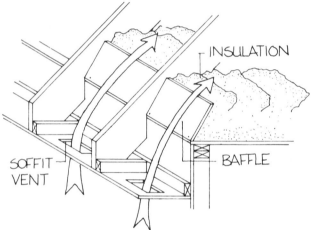

Figure 13.26 When placing insulation in attic space, do *not* block the flow of air up from the eaves. Baffles toe-nailed to top plates and rafters, with 8d nails, should suffice. There should be at least 1 in. of air between the top of the baffle and the underside of the roof sheathing.

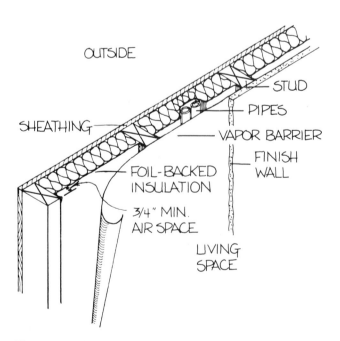

Figure 13.25 Because the foil is not a continuous membrane, moisture could migrate through the exposed stud edges. For this reason, attach a polyethylene vapor barrier after the insulation is in place.

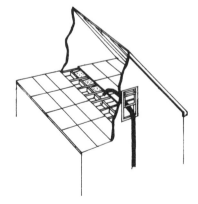

Figure 13.27 The easiest way to insulate under an attic subfloor is to pry up boards running down the middle, perpendicular to the joists. Insert the nozzle into each joist-bay and blow in insulation.

the living space—that is, facing downward. (Don't use foil-backed insulation or plastic vapor barriers in the attic.)

The operation is straightforward; cut batts or blankets to length and fit them in place between joists. Where you encounter bridging, slit the insulation down the middle, 4 to 6 in. from the end, and thread the slit ends around the bridging. If possible, feed insulation under any wiring. Remember to stop short of recessed light fixtures at least 3 in., to prevent overheating. Pack loose, noncombustible insulation between framing and chimney masses. When adding a layer of insulation to an existing one, run the second layer at a right angle to the first.

When pouring loose insulation, simply empty the insulation from the bag into the joist bays and level it with a board or a garden rake. Insulation must stop 3 in. short of recessed light fixtures, as noted above. *Do not cover* this loose-fill with a vapor barrier, or condensation will collect beneath it, causing the R value of the insulation to decrease.

Between rafters and collar ties. Unless you're planning a cathedral ceiling (one that goes up to the peak of the roof),

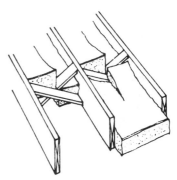

Figure 13.29 Where batts or blankets meet bridging, slit insulation as shown.

collar ties should be in place now, and all vents in soffits, gable ends, or ridge must be installed.

Use insulation backed with kraft paper between the rafters and collar ties; for the reasons stated above, do not cover the insulation with a vapor barrier. Ventilation will carry away any moisture that migrates through finish materials. Because air travels *over* insulation on its way out, the insulation must not be as deep as the rafters themselves. If there is less than 1 in. of free space between the roof sheathing and the insulation, either build up the rafters by nailing 2×2s to the edges (a tedious operation), or insulate with a rigid sheet insulation such as isocyanurate, which has a high-R rating.

Staple fiberglass between the rafters as described in the ''Walls'' section; attach the paper-backed blankets (or batts) to the edge of the rafters. Where rafters meet the collar ties, cut a new piece; trying to run one piece for rafters and ties will create gaps.

Don't forget to insulate the trap door in the attic; gluing a piece of rigid insulation to the back is easy. Similarly, wrap duct work or pipes in unheated spaces.

Insulating first floors. Goggles, gloves and a mask are particularly important here. Insulate first floors from beneath, placing the insulation's backing so that it points up,

A.

B.

Figure 13.28 Insulating between attic joists. (A) Where there is no existing insulation, install paper-backed fiberglass with its backing down, toward living space. (B) Where there is existing insulation, install unfaced batts over the old. Note the board on which the worker is kneeling; use such a board to work on rather than stepping from joist to joist.

Figure 13.30 Whether you install insulation to collar ties as shown, or to rafters (or some combination thereof), there must be at least 1 in. of air space between the top of the insulation and the bottom of the roof sheathing so that the roof will be well ventilated. Goggles are necessary when working with insulation overhead; a respirator mask is advisable, too. (Owens-Corning)

toward living space; here, foil-backed insulation is best. Use unfaced insulation in floors between occupied rooms, though.

Because such positioning of the backing makes it impossible to staple through tabs, you must support the insulation from beneath. There are several ways to support insulation underneath, perhaps the easiest way is to cut lightweight banding steel or thin wood in strips $14\frac{3}{4}$ in. long. Since strips of that length will be slightly longer than the space between the joists is wide, the strips will bow up and hold the insulation in place. This method is quick, and it doesn't require three hands. Another method is to staple chicken wire or a similar screening to the underside of joists. This method works well enough; mesh or screen is expensive, however, and is forever falling down in your face as you try to attach it.

Pay particular attention to the ponywall—below the floor and above the foundation—because much heat is lost there. If you see any daylight, caulk the area well. As you install fiberglass between joists, leave some extra to fold at the ends and thus cover the mudsill and header joist, as shown in Figure 13.31C.

Note: When using foil-backed insulation, you must leave an air space of at least $\frac{3}{4}$ in. between the foil and the underside of the subfloor; that will allow heat to be reflected properly.

Do *not* put a vapor barrier *beneath* insulation in the first floor; that will trap moisture, which could rot the joists. If you're concerned about moisture in the basement, cover exposed dirt with a polyethylene vapor barrier laid right on the ground. If there's a full basement, pour a floor over the plastic as soon as you can; plastic won't last long when walked on. In a crawl space that is seldom entered, however, plastic alone is sufficient.

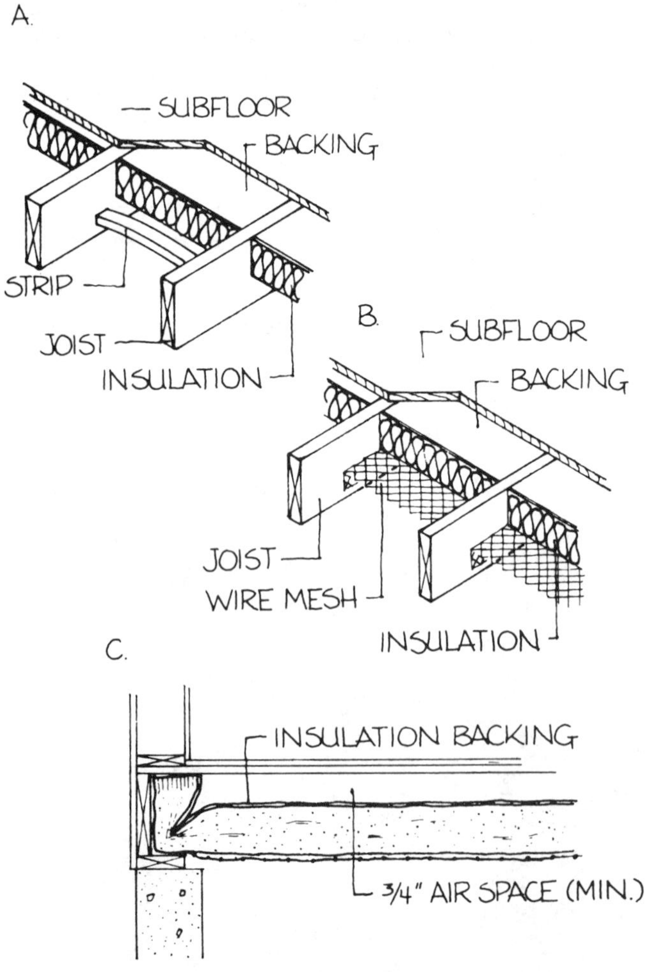

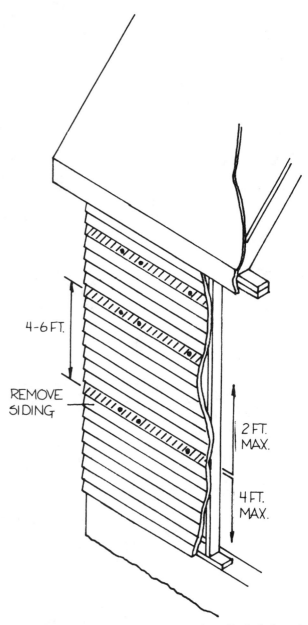

A.

SUBFLOOR
BACKING
STRIP
JOIST
INSULATION

B.
SUBFLOOR
BACKING
JOIST
WIRE MESH
INSULATION

C.
INSULATION BACKING
3/4" AIR SPACE (MIN.)

Figure 13.31 Insulating first floors. The vapor barrier of insulation between the first floor and an unheated basement (or crawl space) must face up toward the living space. The insulation can be supported beneath with strips as in (A), or wire mesh, as in (B). Where the joists meet the sill area, fold the insulation and staple it to the rim joist (C). To weatherseal and insulate this area completely, run rigid insulation up the basement wall until it meets with the folded-over fiberglass.

4-6 FT.
REMOVE SIDING
2 FT. MAX.
4 FT. MAX.

Figure 13.32 Blown-in insulation. To insulate effectively from the outside, drill holes into each bay between studs and fire stops, if any. In the detail shown, there are two holes in each bay to facilitate pumping. Place such holes at least every 4 to 6 ft vertically, because 2 ft is a maximal "upward blow" and 4 ft a maximal "downward blow."

Basement walls. Because fiberglass and mineral wool are adversely affected by moisture, it's best to insulate masonry basement walls with rigid insulation. If you decide to use fiberglass anyhow, first attend to any serious moisture problems (see Chapter 9). Then spot-tack a polyethylene vapor barrier to the basement walls, using mastic paste or construction adhesive. Build a stud wall within the masonry walls and insulate it as you would any other stud wall. A third option (in addition to rigid insulation and fiberglass) is to power-nail furring strips to masonry instead of using full studs. The trouble with this method is, it gives you little depth for the insulation to follow.

Blowing-in Insulation

First, review the comments above, about blown-in insulation. There are advantages and limitations to its use, including possible condensation problems after installation, and cold spots because of settlement.

To blow in insulation, you need special blower equipment, which can often be rented, from the store that sells the insulation. The unit isn't difficult to use. It consists primarily of a large fan and a hopper into which the loose-fill material is poured. A flexible hose runs from the blower to the area being insulated.

Insulating walls. The first step in the operation is to locate the studs. This is usually a matter of looking for siding nails, which are nailed to studs. In most cases, studs will be on 16-in. centers. There are two principal methods of getting access to the bay between studs. The first involves drilling directly through siding and sheathing and prying off siding, then drilling through the sheathing. The second method is the one more commonly used by contractors and hence the one we'll examine.

The removal of siding is discussed at length in Chapter 8. If siding is in good condition, it's worth taking the time to remove it carefully. Using a cold chisel or a shingle bar, sever the shanks of the nails holding the siding in place. There may also be nails from the course above that must be removed. Drill through the sheathing with a 1-in. drill bit or a size recommended by the insulation supplier.

Note: Cut all electrical power to the wall before drilling.

Once you've drilled, make sure there are no fire stops between studs; if there are any, locate them. To do that, feed an electrician's fish tape through the hole, or use an instrument flexible yet rigid enough not to bend when it

A.

B.

C.

D.

Figure 13.33 A sequence of blowing–in insulation. (A) Remove siding by carefully cutting through nail shanks with a cold chisel or shingle hood. Nails from siding courses above may also have to be severed, try not to break siding. (B) Disconnect electricity through the area, drill through the exposed sheathing. Drill into each bay and insert a fish tape or similar device to see where the bay ends. (C) Insert the blower nozzle and fill each bay. (D) Plug holes and replace the siding, caulking any seams and nailing siding into studs where possible. (Work sequence courtesy of Hutchins Insulation.)

encounters an obstacle. There must be one hole per bay—the area bounded by stops and studs. If you find fire stops, drill above and below them and repeat the procedure with the fish tape; otherwise, there will be sections of wall not insulated.

Beginning with the bottom of the house, blow insulation in and plug the holes in the sheath with corks. For good measure, smear a small amount of white glue on each cork; but that isn't really necessary, since the cork will be held in place by the reapplied siding. When each section is full, the motor of the blower will whine because the blown-in insulation will become harder to pump in. Remove the nozzle and plug the hole. Even if there seem to be no fire stops, drill holes every 4 to 6 ft (vertical distance) in a bay, to make sure the insulation falls correctly and fills the space completely. Some contractors drill side-by-side holes in each bay, to minimize air resistance. This procedure involves plugging twice as many holes, but the space is filled more uniformly. Depending on the pressure of the blower, the optimal distance for blowing up insulation is 2 ft, and blowing down, 4 ft.

As you work with the equipment, note how long it takes to fill a space. If a section fills too quickly, suspect that the insulation is hung up on an obstacle such as a nail or a fire stop that you overlooked.

Every job has its quirks. Some houses, especially those in warm climates, have siding that was applied directly to the studs, with no sheathing. You might just pull off lengths of siding, but such big openings offer no resistance to blown-in insulation. Another quirk is that some installers, in their haste, break off sections of siding, then caulk along the broken edge and renail those ruined sections back in place after plugging the holes. Don't let your contractor reuse siding in this manner, for the weathertightness of the exterior is then only as tight as the caulking; it's a shoddy, unacceptable practice.

Insulating attics. To blow insulation into floors beneath attics, pull up boards, preferably down the center of the attic, and expose the joists. Insulation is then blown in parallel to the joists. Because it's difficult to shoot the insulation much more than 6 ft, remove boards at intervals of no more than 12 ft. When applying the insulation, feed about 6 ft of flexible hose under the floorboards, gradually withdrawing the hose as the bay fills.

It is important that blown-in insulation not block the

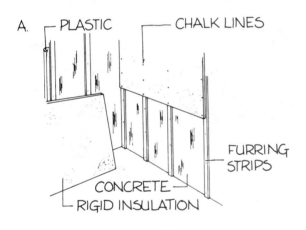

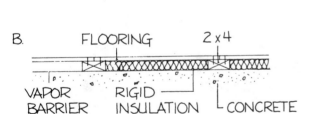

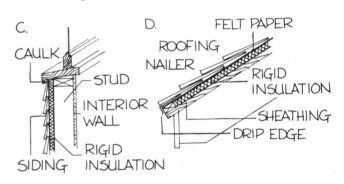

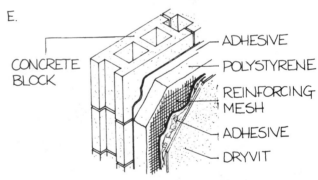

Figure 13.34 Using rigid insulation. (A) Rigid insulation can be affixed to basement walls in a number of ways. Here, the board is nailed to furring strips, themselves power-nailed to the concrete. First, however, a layer of polyethylene has been tacked in place with mastic. (B) Lay a vapor barrier first, next to the concrete, when laying a floor, to prevent the masonry from wicking moisture up to the wood. Power-nail furring strips or 2 × 4's to provide an adequate base for the subflooring and flooring that follow. Use spiral or ringed flooring nails. (C) Rigid insulation is most effectively installed on the outside of a building by first removing the existing siding and then re-siding. You may need to build up exterior trim so that it will sit above the newly raised siding. (D) When the roofing needs replacement, you can easily insulate the roof at the same time without disturbing finish surfaces inside the attic. To prevent rot underneath the roofing, put a layer of felt paper over the rigid insulation; the paper also protects the insulation from ultraviolet degradation. Be sure that roofing nails are long enough to reach into the sheathing. (E) The Dryvit system is an exterior insulation that can be installed over most unpainted masonry surfaces, but not over metal or wood. With this system, rigid insulation is attached to the substratum with special adhesive, a reinforcing mesh is adhered to the insulation, and Dryvit stucco is troweled on the mesh.

space where rafters rest on a top plate. If it does, air can not flow upward from the eaves. To prevent this problem, build baffles at the ends of joists before insulating (Figure 13.26). Note also that insulation must be restrained 3 in. from any recessed light fixtures in the ceiling.

If finish walls and floors are in place in the attic, make several cuts in the surfaces, to gain access to the floor joists. Again, 6 ft is the maximum distance for blowing in insulation; therefore, make access openings accordingly. Kneewalls themselves aren't worth the trouble to fill with blown-in insulation; fill them with batt or blanket insulation instead.

Applying Rigid Insulation Board

Rigid insulation is best used when insulating over existing sheathing, finish materials, or masonry. Closed-cell insulations, such as polystyrene, are nearly impervious to moisture; nevertheless, there should be a vapor barrier between any insulation and a potential source of moisture such as a concrete foundation (see Table 13.8).

Interior applications. Rigid insulation can be installed anywhere inside a house, in any location mentioned for fiberglass or loose-fill insulation. In practice, though, rigid insulation is seldom used inside (basements are one exception), because such insulation is flammable and very expensive, and it makes subsequent finish materials hard to attach. You must use long screws or nails to get through to the studs. Furthermore, rigid sheets are cumbersome and difficult to fit tightly between studs or joists, so infiltration can be a problem. Fitting the sheets around windows and doors is time–consuming because you must build up the casings; the same difficulty is encountered around electrical outlets.

In the basement. Rigid-board insulation can be used in the basement after you have corrected moisture problems (see Chapter 9). Whether you're insulating the floor or the walls, first attach a polyethylene vapor barrier by spot-tacking it to the masonry (concrete wall, etc.) with mastic paste or a construction adhesive. Attach the rigid insulation by first power-nailing furring strips to the masonry and then nailing or gluing the insulation to the furring. Large-head box nails will hold rigid insulation to the strapping; otherwise, use washered nails. Another method of application is to put insulation between furring strips and spot-tack it to the polyethylene barrier. The finish material (paneling or drywall) is nailed to the furring, thus holding the rigid insulation firmly in place.

If you insulate the basement floor, power-nail furring strips to the concrete and put the insulation between them, so the flooring that follows will run perpendicular to—and rest on—the furring. Flooring that rests directly on the insulation will compress, causing the flooring to loosen. For better results, you can also cover furring with subflooring *and* flooring.

Exterior applications. In new construction, rigid insulation over sheathing is becoming a favored method because it eliminates thermal bridging. Briefly, the term *thermal bridging* refers to the considerable loss of heat through studs and other framing members where there is no insulation. Thus, while a wall might have a rating of R-11 between studs, the R rating of the studs themselves—some 20 to 30 percent of the building's surface—is relatively low, about R-5. Continuous exterior sheathing of rigid insulation, with the edges sealed by duct tape, obviates thermal bridging because it covers studs and plates as well.

If you wish to retrofit sheet insulation to the exterior of a building—perhaps because you don't want to disturb interior surfaces—remove the present siding first. Build up casings to accommodate the added thickness of the new rigid insulation, either by prying loose the trim and shimming it from behind, or by leaving the trim on and building up its edges with additional molding. The latter choice is probably the easier of the two, since old trim can be fairly fragile. Attach insulation to the sheathing by nailing it on with washered box nails every foot or so, or by using an adhesive approved by a manufacturer of insulation. Cover all insulation-board seams with duct tape; caulk well where boards meet trim. Do *not* add a plastic vapor barrier additionally because it will trap inside the wall moisture migrating from living areas. Apply new siding.

Note: Because of the building up of the trim and the time necessary to remove and reapply siding, retrofitting sheet insulation to a building's exterior is a formidable undertaking; if there's a cheaper alternative, take it.

More ways to conserve energy. There is now a reliable source for low-voltage power systems, photovoltaic panels, wind generation, hydro turbines and all the accessories needed to install and operate them. The Real Goods Trading Company started by providing power to people in wilderness areas and has now grown to a viable alternative to anyone who wants to rely less on the mammoth electrical grids that most of us are hooked up to.

Their catalogue is a cornucopia of conservation, including low-voltage appliances, recycled paper goods, low-flow showerheads, water purifiers, radon detectors, composting toilets, propane refrigerators, and whole-house systems—even a generator to hook up to your exercise bicycle, so your kids can generate enough electricity to run a TV! To learn more, contact Real Goods at (800) 762-7325, or write:

Real Goods Trading Co.
966 Mazzoni St.
Ukiah, CA 95482

·14·

COOLING AND HEATING

The focus of the preceding chapter—understanding how heat is transferred and how it may be conserved—is equally pertinent to this chapter, although it is about equipment. Were machines wholly automatic and infallible, we could afford to ignore them. But, like humans they overheat and overeat, digest their fuel imperfectly, get run-down and, in general, need a kindly touch. Most of the remedies discussed below cost little and take no great mechanical skills.

VENTILATION AND COOLING

Ventilation is as crucial to the structural health of the house as it is to the comfort of its inhabitants. Hot, humid air trapped in attics and crawl spaces is a summer sauna for lumber, promoting insect infestation and rot; and the problem is as bad in winter in cold climates, for warm air trapped beneath the roof melts snow and leads to ice buildup and water damage. The lack of ventilation is particularly acute in older homes, whose eaves are often sealed off to keep bugs and drafts out, thus creating dead air spaces. So, there being no way to prevent hot, humid air from building up, our concern becomes the most effective way to get it out.

If your attic lacks ventilation, you have essentially two options: (1) install a thermostatically controlled fan in an upper-story window or wall, or in the roof; or (2) encourage the convectional flow of air by increasing soffit vents so that

air can enter, and gable-end louvers or ridge vents so that it can exit. If possible, do both: the more ventilation, the better. Fans are especially effective where summer heat is excessive; put one in each end of the house to increase flow. Time them so that they remove air before heat buildup becomes excessive. The second option—more vents—is appropriate to all houses, for vents consume no energy, aren't subject to mechanical failure as fans are, and all but eliminate the buildup of heat (and ice) around eaves.

In an unventilated roof, temperatures near the peak can rise to 170°F on a hot day, while temperatures near the attic floor might hit 110 to 120°F. So hot a mass of air means a much greater load to overcome when cooling living space in the floors below.

Ventilating the Eaves

There are a number of commercially available ventilation products, including perforated soffit boards and ventilator plugs; you can also fashion your own. The product you choose depends on the amount of air you need to circulate and the manner in which the rafter ends are presently closed off. The rule of thumb for ventilation is 1 sq ft of intake and outflow of ventilation per 150 sq ft of roof. According to a wag in Florida, though, "There are two things you can't have too much of—attic ventilation and fun." Provide for extra ventilation capacity whenever possible.

In Figure 14.2A, the rafter ends are not exposed; here, it is easiest to use ventilator plugs. Where rafters are ex-

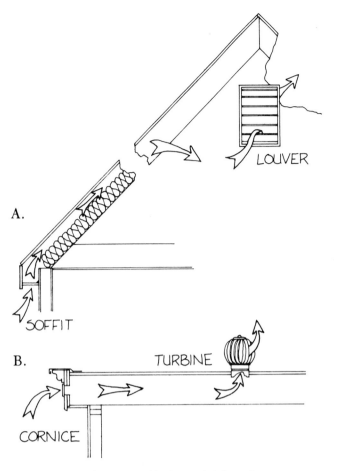

A.

B.

Figure 14.1 Air rises as it is heated.

A.

B.

Figure 14.2 Improving ventilation. (A) Ventilator plugs; (B) perforated soffit-strip vents.

posed, you have a choice of plugs or perforated soffit vent (Figure 14.2B).

Ventilator plugs are easy to install. Just drill into the trim with a hole-cutting saw and insert the plug. Caulk around the edge of the plug for a tighter fit, but that's really not necessary. In any case, seal the edge of the hole, to forestall rot. For the best-looking results, space the vent plugs evenly. Good-quality plug vents are backed with screens, to keep out pests.

In general, perforated soffits allow more air to enter. There are soffit strips which, like plugs, snap into a hole cut in existing soffits. Chalk-line the slot; then start the hole with a drill and cut out the slot with a saber saw or a reciprocating saw. Be careful not to cut into rafter ends.

To install the other type of perforated board, pull off the existing soffit board. Pry the fascia forward just enough to expose the edge of the soffit board, and insert a utility bar between the soffit and the lookout. (A lookout is a board that runs from the end of the rafter to the ledger strip nailed into the sheathing, but not all houses have them.) Pry the soffit loose, trying to keep it in one piece so you can trace it onto new stock. If a frieze board covers the inside edge of the soffit board, your task will be more difficult. If your trim splinters when you try to pry it up (to get at the soffit), reconsider: ventilator plugs may be a better solution.

Finally, you can make your own perforated soffit boards from $\frac{1}{4}$-in. or $\frac{3}{8}$-in. exterior plywood. Cut the pieces

of plywood to size—each board joint should be centered on a rafter end—and drill 1-in. holes (or larger) spaced evenly along the soffit board. Treat the edges of the holes with a preservative and cover the back side of the holes with a strip of fine-mesh screen. Then nail the new soffit in place with 4d galvanized nails, and caulk the edges.

Other Vents

Because air that enters through the eaves will rise in the bays between rafters, you have a choice of venting it at the ridge or at high points in the gable ends. If the attic is finished off with a cathedral ceiling, a ridge vent is probably best.

Ridge vents. Ridge vents require no special framing, only the disruption of the top course of roofing and the removal of strips of sheathing. Snap chalk lines running parallel to

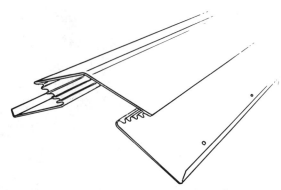

Figure 14.3 Installing a ridge vent. To retrofit a ridge vent, transfer its width to the roof and snap chalk lines along either side of the ridge. Then, using a carborundum blade in a circular saw—wear goggles—cut back the cap shingles on both sides; pry them up with a flat bar. Whereas it is possible to cut through both shingles and the sheathing in one pass, it's preferable to cut the sheathing after the shingles are removed. In any event, do not cut into rafters. Nail the ridge vent directly to rafters and flash as indicated by the manufacturer.

the ridge, down at least 2 in. from the peak. Using a carborundum blade in a circular saw, cut through the roofing along that line. Set your power saw to cut through just the sheathing (not into the rafters).

Over the slot you've created, nail down the ridge vent, using gasketed roofing nails. Because the ridge vent also covers the top of the roofing, be sure the nails are long enough to sink into the rafter; 8d nails should suffice. Caulk the underside of the vent before nailing it on.

Gable-end louvers. The openings for louvers and for in-the-wall fans are quite similar; in fact, fans are usually covered with louvers. Louver slats should have a downward pitch of 45 degrees to minimize water blowing in. As is true of soffit vents, a backing of screen is needed to keep insects out. You can make your own louvers out of clear, 1-in.-thick stock, but bevel cuts can be complex. Buying a manufactured louver makes sense.

Disturb the siding, sheathing, and framing as little as possible. Locate the opening by drilling small holes through the wall; each hole should represent a corner of the opening. Snap chalk lines to establish the cuts made with a reciprocating saw. Cut back the siding to the width of the trim housing the louver (or the louver-with-fan), but cut back the sheathing only to the dimensions of the louvre housing. Box in the rough opening itself with 2×4s and nail or screw the sheathing to them. Flash and caulk a gable-end louver as you would a door or a window.

Ventilating Crawl Spaces and Walls

The same ''more is better'' rule applies to ventilating crawl spaces. The only considerations are: getting vents up as high as possible above grade so that water can't splash into openings and add to the problem; and covering openings with screens so that animals can't get under the house. The most convenient place for vents is in the pony wall atop the foundation. In cold climates, you'll also want shutters to close the openings so that your floors won't become cold.

Where you have the symptom of paint persistently peeling from exterior walls even when the paint manufac-

turer's recommendations have been followed carefully, moisture may be trapped inside. This situation is serious: the structure itself could rot. Some renovators discover this problem after they have added a plastic vapor barrier to the inside of the walls.

To cure this problem, add ventilator plugs similar to those used to ventilate eaves. Each bay between studs should have a ventilator at the top and bottom so that air can rise and carry off the moisture trapped within. (If a fire blocking exists between studs, you will need two plugs for each blocked-off space.) The lower plugs should be at least 3 to 4 ft above the ground. You can also alleviate the moisture problem by cutting back shrubs near the house and by using permeable stains rather than paints (which seal moisture within).

Whole-House Fans

As the name implies, *whole-house fans* can change the air in an entire house, usually within 2 minutes. A whole-house fan is adequate for cooling a house in temperate climates; in warm or hot regions, it is often used with an air conditioner. Such fans are increasingly popular because they cost about a fifth what central air conditioning does, and operating costs are one-fifth to one-tenth those of air conditioning.

Whole-house fans are available in the following widths: 24, 30, 36, and 42 in. They are rated in cubic feet per minute (CFM)—the amount of air they can change—and are sized according to a number of variables. The Hunter Company sizes fans as follows:

Fan size (in.)	House size (sq ft)
24	1,400
30	1,850
36	2,450

In this table, the manufacturer assumes:

1. The square footages cited already have 25 percent of the house's floor space deducted for areas not vented, or which have separate ventilators, such as bathrooms and closets. To determine fan size based on gross square feet, add back the deducted 25 percent; you get 1850, 2450, and 3300 sq ft, respectively.

2. 8-ft ceilings in the house.

3. $\frac{1}{10}$-in. static pressure on the fan.

4. One change of the house's air every 2 minutes. This is an average figure. In Minnesota and Maine, one change every 3 minutes might be adequate; whereas, in Florida, one change per minute might be more appropriate. Choose a slightly oversized fan if you are unsure.

Whole-house fans are commonly placed in the attic, where the buildup of heat is greatest. If a fan cannot be located conveniently near the attic stairwell, it may be necessary to cut a hole in the attic floor joists, as well as the ceiling below, and box out a rough opening. Attaching the fan to the top of the rough opening is straightforward: after placing the unit's gasket on the top of the frame, screw through the holes provided in the housing flange. For the

A.

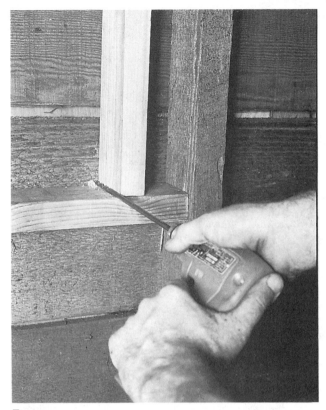

B.

C.

D.

Figure 14.4 Installing gable-end vents. (A) Construct and nail in a rough opening between gable-end studs; make sure that the R.O. is square. (B) Using a long bit, drill pilot holes through the gable end wall, to locate the corners of the R.O. on the outside. (C) Go outside and snap chalk lines through the holes and cut out the rough opening. (D) Wrap the sides of the R.O. with felt paper, flash the top of the vent, nail it up, and caulk. Replace shingles as necessary.

Figure 14.5 Whole-house fan. (Hunter Fans)

best appearance and for safety, get a fan whose face is louvered with slats that close when the fan is off.

To cut fan noise appreciably, put a layer of resilient material—the thicker the better—between the perimeter flange of the fan and the rough opening. One readily available, reasonably priced material is $1\frac{1}{2}$-in.-O.D. high-density water pipe insulation, which you can glue to the R.O. with contact cement.

In warm regions, a whole-house fan is used mostly at night to remove heat that built up during the day, to draw in cool air from outside, and to cool the house's inhabitants by the movement of air. The usual practice is to open windows on the first floor after sundown, when exterior temperatures have dropped, turn off the air conditioner, and turn the fan on. In the morning, before the outside temperature climbs, turn off the fan, turn on the air conditioner, shut the windows, and lower the shades to retain cooler air from inside. The temperature of a well-insulated house rises about 1 degree per hour, so you may be able to do without air conditioning altogether. The fan may be controlled thermostatically or switched on and off manually.

There are limitations to whole-house fans, particularly if temperatures at night stay too high or if the outside air is polluted and you don't want to draw it inside. By and large, though, a fan is an economical way to cool off. To hasten cooling by evaporation, also consider smaller fans in individual rooms.

Air Conditioning

Because of the number and variety of air conditioners, with various features, consult recent issues of *Consumer Reports* or a similar publication before purchasing. The most important consideration is the unit's energy efficiency ratio

(EER), which, in brief, divides the unit's cooling capacity by its wattage. The EER ranges from 5 to 12: the higher the number, the better; a unit with an EER of 9 costs about one-third less to run than one with a rating of 6, even though both machines have the same cooling capacity. Although machines with higher EER ratings are more expensive, you can probably recoup the difference in price within two cooling seasons.

In addition to inquiring about an air conditioner's EER rating, you should ask:

1. Does the unit have directional controls that enable you to aim cooled air where you want? This is particularly important when a unit must be positioned in a corner window. Adjustable louvers are best.

2. How well does its thermostat work? How many degrees must the temperature rise before the unit resumes cooling?

A.

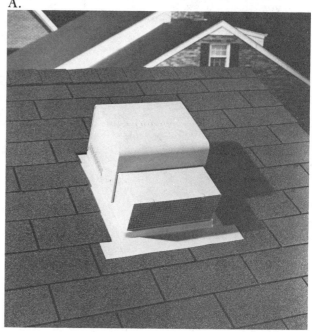

B.

Figure 14.6 Other ventilating choices. (A) Ceiling fan; (B) rooftop fan.

TABLE 14.1

COOLING LOAD ESTIMATE FORM

Customer _____ Estimate by _____ Date _____

HEAT GAIN FROM	QUANTITY	FACTORS					Btu/Hr (Quantity x Factor)
		NIGHT	**DAY**				
			No Shades*	Inside Shades*	Outside Awnings*	(Area x Factor)	
1. WINDOWS: Heat gain from sun.							
Northeast	____ sq ft	0	60	25	20	_____	_____
East	____ sq ft	0	80	40	25	_____ Use	_____
Southeast	____ sq ft	0	75	30	20	_____ only	_____
South	____ sq ft	0	75	35	20	_____ the	_____
Southwest	____ sq ft	0	110	45	30	_____ largest	_____
West	____ sq ft	0	150	65	45	_____ load	_____
Northwest	____ sq ft	0	120	50	35	_____	_____
North	____ sq ft	0	0	0	0	_____	_____

*These factors are for single glass only. For glass block, multiply the above factors by 0.5; for double-glass or storm windows, multiply the above factors by 0.8.

2. WINDOWS: Heat gain by conduction. (Total of all windows.)						
Single glass	____ sq ft	14	.... 14			_____
Double glass or glass block ..	____ sq ft	7	.... 7			_____
3. WALLS: (Based on linear feet of wall.)			Light Construction		Heavy Construction	
a. Outside walls						
North exposure..........	____ ft	30	..... 30		20	_____
Other than North exposure. ...	____ ft	30	..... 60		30	_____
b. Inside Walls (between conditioned and unconditioned spaces only)	____ ft	30	.... 30			_____
4. ROOF OR CEILING: (Use one only.)						
a. Roof, uninsulated	____ sq ft	5	.... 19			_____
b. Roof, 1 inch or more insulation.	____ sq ft	3	.... 8			_____
c. Ceiling, occupied space above.	____ sq ft	3	.... 3			_____
d. Ceiling, insulated with attic space above	____ sq ft	4	.... 5			_____
e. Ceiling, uninsulated, with attic space above	____ sq ft	7	.... 12			_____
5. FLOOR: (Disregard if floor is directly on ground or over basement.)	____ sq ft	3	.... 3			_____
6. NUMBER OF PEOPLE:	____	600	.... 600			_____
7. LIGHTS AND ELECTRICAL EQUIPMENT IN USE	____ watts	3	.... 3			_____
8. DOORS AND ARCHES CONTINUOUSLY OPEN TO UNCONDITIONED SPACE: (Linear feet of width.)	____ ft	200	.... 300			_____
9. SUB-TOTAL	x x x x x	x x x x x	x x x x x			_____

10. TOTAL COOLING LOAD: (Btu per hour to be used for selection of room air-conditioner(s).) _____ (Item 9) X _____ (Factor from Map) = _____

Table 14.1

Published and distributed by the

Association of Home Appliance Manufacturers
20 North Wacker Drive   Chicago, Illinois 60606

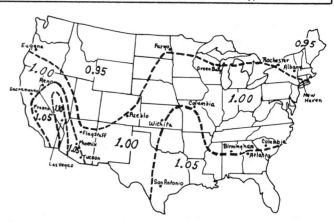

3. How well does the unit remove and disperse moisture from the living space? Will the unit drip inside or out?

4. Is it noisy when running?—this is important if the unit will be placed in a bedroom.

5. Can the unit's air filter be removed and replaced easily?

6. Can the air conditioner be mounted and removed easily? Because a unit should be removed in winter in many parts of the country (to prevent heat loss), how easily can it be handled? Although some units must be balanced on the window sill while side panels are adjusted, other machines have a casing that is mounted independently of the cooling core.

7. If you live in a region with high temperatures or high humidity, what brands seem most durable and/or most effective? Ask your neighbors what kind they bought. Table 14.1 enables you to size an air conditioner; choose a model with 10 or 15 percent of your BTU calculations.

Calculating the cooling load (Table 14.1). If your air conditioner is to be used at night only, use the factors in the shaded column, multiplying those factors by the number of square feet. If you operate the unit day and night, do *not* use the shaded column at all. The instructions that follow are adapted from those on the back of the estimate form furnished by the Association of Home Appliance Manufacturers (AHAM) and are based on an outside temperature of 95°F dry bulb and 75°F wet bulb.

1. Fill in square-footage areas for all windows, from all directions given. If, for example, a window is on a south wall, it will also appear in the southeast and southwest categories. Multiply each window's square footage by the appropriate factor according to whether the window has shades, no shades, or outside awnings. From the totals thus derived select *only the largest load* and enter it in a blank on the extreme right-hand side of the block.

2. Calculate the square footage of each window; total the figures for all the windows. (Here, each window is added only once.)

3. Add the lengths of the walls—south, east, and west and separately, north (the length of the north wall is separate because it is multiplied by a different factor). ''Heavy construction'' indicates insulated frame walls or masonry walls thicker than 8 in.

4. Select only one roof type and enter its square footage.

5–7. These items are self-explanatory; do not include the wattage of any air conditioner, however. (Here, Chapter 11 may be useful to help determine the wattage of typical appliances.)

8. Include only doors that are open continuously. If an arch is wider than 5 ft, add the dimensions of the second room to the dimensions under consideration.

9–10. Add the entries for each item and multiply the subtotal by the correction factor for your area, as shown on the AHAM map. The grand total is the size of the air conditioner you need, in BTUs per hour. In general, it's better to undersize than to oversize the unit, for a smaller unit will run more nearly continuously.

HEATING: IMPROVING THE SOURCE

Our discussion of heating is in three parts: (1) improving the heat source, which examines changes in present equipment that can increase energy savings dramatically with very little work; (2) improving heat distribution, which tells how to extend a heating system or otherwise increase the user's comfort; and (3) alternative systems, a cursory look at several cost-effective but less common heating devices.

First, a few definitions. A *furnace* usually is a warm-air system, a *boiler* a hot-water or a steam system, and a *burner* the firing unit in either the furnace or the boiler, which generates the heat. In each of the many parts of a heating system, there's usually some inefficiency, so that, cumulatively, a system may be wasting up to half your fuel dollars. This is especially true of older systems, which probably were not all that efficient when new. Your assessment should begin with a thorough assessment by an established, local heating contractor who keeps up with the latest technology. There are, for example, *pulse units* which pulse fuel to the burner so that it burns cleaner, sending less up the chimney as waste. Some of the new baseboard radiators and wall convection panels can deliver more usable heat from 120°F water than old cast-iron units could with water 40°F hotter.

Thermostats

A thermostat is a heat-sensitive switch that controls the flow of electricity to a source of heat. Because thermostats are easily installed and operated, they are first on the list of do-it-yourself money-savers. *Note:* Make all adjustments with electricity to the system turned off.

Set-back savings. You can save 8 to 10 percent of your heating bill by setting back the temperature of your thermostat from 65 to 55°F during the night or when you're not home. Although this task is easily done by hand, it requires regular habits and the first person up in the morning finds a chilly house. An energy-saving thermostat with automatic setback control will do the job for you; it will even

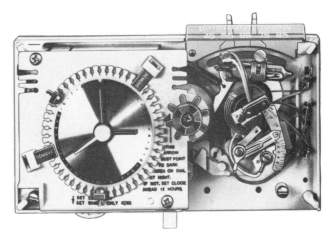

Figure 14.7 Time-controlled thermostats can save almost 10 percent of present heating costs. The model shown has removable pins for several setback settings. (Honeywell)

turn up the temperature an hour or so before your rising time so the house will be warm. The best models have removable pins or adjustable levers for setting the times of temperature raising and lowering. When placing a thermostat, remember that a thermostat located on an outside wall or near cold parts of the house will cause a burner to run more than it should, thus overheating the rest of the house.

Oil Burners

The efficiency of a heating plant that is more than 10 years old can often be improved 25 to 40 percent by replacing the burner with a model of greater efficiency. These newer models feature smaller nozzles and motors with a higher rpm (e.g., 3400) that generate greater pressure and thus more turbulence in the combustion chamber. These burners are usually called "high-speed, flame-retention head." Such units are much more efficient because the flame is kept close to the end of the gun, thus ensuring a better mix of fuel and oil and less soot and waste. Another type of burner, Blueray, increases efficiency by preheating the fuel, thus producing a hot, clean flame.

A heating unit that is 10 years or more old probably has a gun that was oversized when the unit was new—another fuel-wasting situation. In the old days, of course, there was less incentive to use fuel wisely; by oversizing the unit, the contractor had fewer call-backs for maintenance problems. And by using fuel in great bursts, the burner could heat up the house and shut off more quickly. The trouble is, such heating units are most wasteful when starting up, shutting down, or not running at all.

Burner guns with smaller nozzles heat an area less quickly, but because they have a long heating cycle, they burn fuel efficiently over a longer period. If you have a heating system that was converted from coal to oil or gas, you probably have a very inefficient system, because the chamber size very likely is poorly matched to the burner.

An oil burner should be serviced twice a year—at the start of the heating season and at the end. You can perform some maintenance tasks, though, without special equipment and without removing the burner from the furnace. Shut off electricity and the fuel line before starting. Then:

1. Lubricate the motor every 2 to 3 months, using nondetergent 10-weight (10W) oil. Most motors have small cup reservoirs.

2. Change the filter on the oil-supply line. Put a catch pan under the filter and loosen the bolt that holds the bowl to the cover. Take out the soiled cartridge filter, rinse the bowl with solvent (such as gasoline) and put in a new filter. If the gasket between the cover and the bowl is cracked or dried out, replace it.

3. If there's a strainer inside the pump cover, pull off the gasket and strainer basket and soak the strainer in solvent. After any solid matter has softened, scrub the strainer with an old toothbrush, being careful not to misshape the strainer or poke holes in it. Replace all worn parts, especially gaskets, and bolt the cover back on.

Note: Not all fuel pumps have a strainer basket; some have a filter with rotary blades.

4. Clean the dust from the fan's blades at least once a year.

You can get at the blades by unscrewing the transformer and swinging it out of the way (you needn't disconnect the transformer). Dampen brush bristles with light solvent and twirl the brush gently between the blades. The grease should come off easily. Do not use cotton swabs for this operation, as they will lint and contribute to the problem.

Gas Burners

Gas burns much more cleanly than oil, and gas burners—because they have few moving parts—have less down time. You should still have the unit serviced regularly, however; it may also be worthwhile to replace aging burners with new, small-orifice models. Since gas is clean, there should be little soot buildup in the combustion chamber. Nevertheless, at intervals of two to three years, burner assemblies should be removed and cleaned with a wire brush. At the same time, wire-brush the walls of the chamber, afterwards vacuuming soot loosened in the process.

Note: If you smell gas, open windows. *Do not* touch an electrical switch. Extinguish all open flames, and call your gas utility immediately. Although removing a burner isn't difficult, it's best to have someone experienced guide you through the operation the first time. A professional can recommend solvents for cleaning clogged burner pores, as well as suggest ways to clean pores without enlarging them. You should also keep a set of manufacturer's instructions nearby, so you can locate the manual shutoff valve and will be familiar with the procedure for relighting the pilot light.

Automatic Flue Dampers

During standby periods, when the furnace or boiler is not running, most heating plants lose from 10 to 20 percent of total heat produced. Because the combustion chamber remains hot, it draws the cooler air of the basement in and up, out the chimney; experts call this air movement a "stack effect." Automatic flue dampers (AFDs), long popular in Europe, cut down stack effect loss by closing the flue after the burner has been off for a few minutes. Thermostatically controlled, AFDs open immediately when the burner reignites, allowing exhaust gasses to exit.

Automatic flue dampers are installed in the flue and work in tandem with atmospheric, or barometric, dampers which, mounted to the side of the flue, allow additional air to enter, thus improving the draft. (Atmospheric dampers, which are counterweighted, never obstruct flow *within* a flue.) There is no absolute rule-of-thumb on placing the two damper types along the flue; it depends on the recommendation of the Underwriter's Laboratory and those of the manufacturer. Flare AFDs, for example, are placed on the chimney side of an atmospheric damper; Sentinel brand is advisedly placed on the heating-unit side of an atmospheric damper. This pairing of atmospheric and automatic dampers is effective for both oil- and gas-fired systems. There are several types of AFDs, the bimetal strip type generally favored for the flues of gas furnaces; whereas a blade-type (which must be installed by a manufacturer-approved service person) works well in the flues of oil systems—but, again, consult the manufacturer's literature for correct installation procedures.

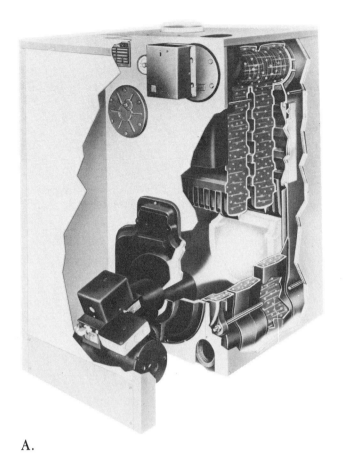

A.

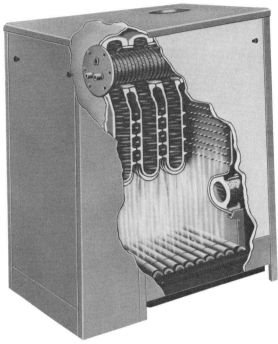

Figure 14.9 Because gas burners are less complex than oil burners, they require less frequent maintenance. Depicted is a hot-water system, with water jackets above the burners. (Burnham Corp.)

B.

Figure 14.8 Oil burners. (A) Oil burners fire into a combustion chamber, here surrounded by boiler jackets filled with water. A plenum, a sheet metal cover, usually surrounds the boiler or furnace. (Burnham Corp.) (B) High-speed flame-retention burners are more fuel efficient because they retain a very hot, controlled flame closer to the end of the nozzle. In this cutaway photo the motor is on the left, the fuel pump on the right, and the air tube and gun assembly in the middle. (Wayne Home Equipment Division)

Other Measures

The fans on hot-air systems are turned on and off by a thermostat near the top of the furnace. By lowering the shutoff temperature slightly, you can make the fan run less.

Hot-water and steam systems benefit from indoor-outdoor thermometers, which cause the boiler aquastat to raise the water temperature in response to the temperature outside, so that on cold days the house heats more quickly. In spring and fall, there's much less short-cycling.

Zoned heating features thermostats in several locations. That way, living areas have higher temperatures while bedrooms remain relatively cool. Improved distribution is also important, as discussed in the next section. By adding ducts, insulating pipes and ducts, adding convectors and balancing valves, releasing air blockage, and so on, you save on fuel costs.

Servicing Your System

It is imperative that you have a good relationship with the outfit that services your heating system. Because service usually comes from suppliers of oil and gas, customers traditionally have been timid about insisting on good service—afraid, possibly, that they would jeopardize their fuel delivery. To be blunt, fuel companies have an interest in heating systems that run reliably, but not efficiently. Don't be intimidated; insist on seeing the results of tests for draft, smoke, CO_2, and stack temperature before and after servicing.

If you have a maintenance contract, call the service outfit whenever burner performance isn't satisfactory. Particularly common and annoying are fuel or exhaust smells, which should not occur in living spaces. Exhaust fumes indicate a leak around the combustion chamber. While a friend activates the burner by turning on the thermostat, observe the plenum for obvious puffs of smoke. Some parts that commonly leak can be sealed with refractory cement (also called furnace cement); never put cement on the burner itself, or you'll impair its functioning. If you smell unburned fuel, inspect the fuel pump and line for wetness.

HEATING: IMPROVING DISTRIBUTION

In early houses, the source of heat was a fire or, later, a fireplace or a stove. The farther one was from the heat source, the colder he was. With central heating, on the other hand, it's possible to regulate the flow of heat in a house and thus equalize the temperature. In forced hot-air systems, flow regulators are fans, ducts, dampers, and registers. In hot-water and steam heating systems, regulators are circulation pumps, pipes, valves, and air vents. All heating systems must be cleaned and, in most cases, lubricated if they are to work properly.

Forced Hot Air

Most forced hot-air systems emanate from a sheet-metal enclosure, or plenum, that surrounds a furnace. From the plenum of newer systems runs a rectangular main duct and round branch ducts (a diameter of 6 in. is common). Older systems may feature an octopus plenum, in which all ducts proceed directly from the plenum; this setup is less versa-

A.

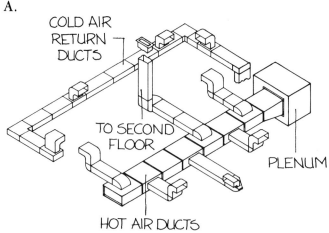

COLD AIR RETURN DUCTS

TO SECOND FLOOR

PLENUM

HOT AIR DUCTS

B.

OCTOPUS PLENUM

Figure 14.10 Forced hot-air systems. (A) Rectangular plenum and ducts; (B) octopus plenum.

tile, though, and requires placing the furnace in the middle of a basement.

Heat loss through transmission is considerable. Seal leaks where ducts join, with duct tape or caulk. Insulate ducts with fiberglass held in place by duct tape, or use special 1-in. foam duct insulation.

To regulate air flow to rooms, open or close dampers and registers. Because the pressure from a blower fan is constant, air flows to distant registers only if they are less restricted (by dampers) than nearer registers. To balance the flow among outlets, partially close the dampers nearest the furnace and open fully those farther away. After changing damper positions, allow 4 to 5 hours for room temperatures to equalize.

Adding dampers. Buy dampers ready-made at most hardware stores. To insert a damper, disconnect the duct affected and drill two holes directly opposite each other. (If the duct is round, wrap a piece of string round it and snip the string to the exact length of one circumference; then fold the string in half to determine an exact half-circumference.) Pull the damper clips back, slide the device into place, and release the bolts into the holes. Rejoin the duct patiently, so you won't crimp or bend it. There can be significant heat loss where damper pins pierce ducts, so cover all punctures with duct tape, and match damper clips with *seal washers* specially slotted to receive them.

Adding registers. Most heating systems can support another register or two; if you aren't sure whether yours can, get advice from a heating specialist. That person can also suggest a configuration that ensures a uniform flow rate to all registers. In general, cut into the main duct if the run to the new register is short—say, 6 to 8 ft; it may make sense to extend the trunk duct, or split it with a "Y" so that both branches get equal flow. If a new register is distant, generally "neck down" the extension duct (i.e., run duct smaller than the trunk line). By keeping blower pressure constant, you increase flow rate when you decrease the size of the pipe. The volume of the new duct must, of course, be big enough to service the room.

Registers are usually placed along outside walls, beneath windows. To get heat to upper floors, run ductwork up inside a wall or through a closet; or frame a special box, as shown in Figure 14.11. Duct sections are available in depths of 3 to $3\frac{1}{2}$ in. that fit nicely between studs; they must be insulated, however, if run up an exterior wall. Where ducts turn up, support them with perforated steel straps beneath the elbow.

When installing horizontal runs, put ducts between joists if possible. There should, of course, be no obstructions, such as wires or pipes between joists. To make sure that the duct will have a clear run, turn off electrical power to the area affected and drill an exploratory hole through the floor at the proposed register location. From this hole, run a taut string to the main duct, keeping in mind the depth of the duct.

The parts needed for installing a run of duct are (1) a takeoff collar, which mounts to the main duct; (2) lengths of duct pipe, with a damper; (3) perforated strap hangers for hanging the duct; (4) a boot, which mounts to the floor; and (5) a register.

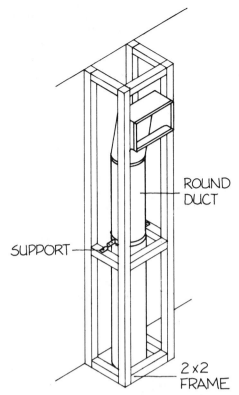

Figure 14.11 Where it's not possible to run ducts up through closets or exterior walls, box out the duct run with light framing. Insulate the duct and support it with tie wire.

Begin by tracing, with a crayon or grease pencil, the shape of the takeoff onto the side or top of the main duct. Perhaps the easiest way to cut out the takeoff opening is to drill holes at each corner and insert a saw blade. A saber saw with a metal-cutting blade works well, but remember to wear goggles and go slowly in order not to snap the blade. Some people swear by snips, arguing that ducts are

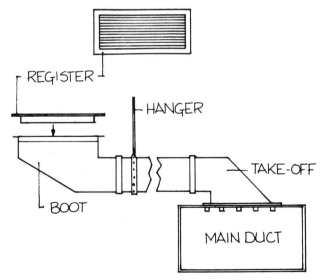

Figure 14.12 From main duct to register. The takeoff collar attaches to the main duct with foldover tabs, shown here, or by self-tapping sheet-metal screws; the boot screws to the flooring; the register sits inside the boot. Support horizontal duct runs every 4 ft.

too flimsy to cut with a power tool: that the cut will be ragged and that broken blades are inevitable. They favor drilling and using *tin snips*: straight jaws for cutting lines, and right- or left-curving for cutting circles in flat sheet stock. Wear heavy gloves when using snips.

When installing a takeoff that has mounting tabs, simply fold the tabs inside the hole just made. Wear heavy gloves to protect your hands. If the takeoff collar is flanged, caulk the opening and attach the flange with self-tapping metal screws.

Next, cut the hole for the register boot, after tracing its body—not its flange, on which it rests—onto the floor. Drill small exploratory holes in each corner of the proposed opening to make sure the boot is between joists. An opening can be cut in one of two ways. If you use a reciprocating saw, first drill holes at each corner so you can insert the saw blade. A circular saw offers somewhat more power, but the cut—called a pocket cut—can be dangerous. Fix the saw blade to the depth of the floor and subfloor; put the heel of the saw plate onto the floor; and, with the blade guard held back and the saw running, ease the blade down onto the line marked. It's not terribly dangerous, but the blade will kick slightly as it encounters the wood flooring. Proceed slowly. Regardless of the tool used, wear goggles, and be sure there are no wires or pipes underneath. Finish off corners with a keyhole saw if you use a circular saw.

If floorboards around the hole are loose, toe-nail them in place or screw them down; predrill nail or screw holes if the floor is hardwood. Put the boot into the hole, but don't secure it yet; you'll need to move the boot when attaching the last section of duct.

Slide round sections of duct together, straight female ends over crimped male ends. You shouldn't have to do additional crimping to make things fit. Temporarily support ducts with pipe straps as you go. If the length of the duct run isn't a multiple of 2 ft—the length of a section of duct—cut the last piece to make it fit. Cut the female end if possible, so it can slide over the last male end. If you need to butt two female ends, join them with a drawband, which looks something like the hubless connector shown in Chapter 12.

When all pieces are connected, hang the ducts permanently with perforated strap, leaving a clearance of 1 to 2 in. beneath subflooring or joists. Screw sections of duct together at each joint with two or three self-tapping screws. Fasten the boot with a screw at each corner of its flange. The register simply drops in place—unless it's a wall register, in which case it screws into the boot.

Blower fan. The blower fan is the *force* in ''forced hot air.'' A motor drives the fan—directly by sharing a splined drive shaft, or indirectly through a pulley-and-belt drive. **Before working on either type, shut off power to the furnace and check terminals with a voltage tester.** For the best performance, clean fans twice a year by vacuuming, and by changing the air filter between the fan and living areas once a month during the heating season. A clogged screen reduces the flow of heat considerably. Oil the fan motor twice a year as well, unless it is permanently lubricated.

Most fan motors have three pins (terminals) on the feed side, the speed of the motor determined by which pin the incoming hot wire is attached to. Thus you can adjust

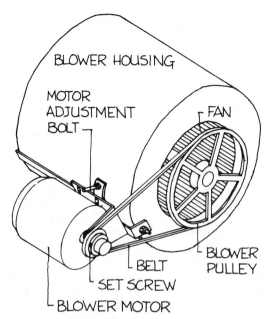

Figure 14.13 Blower-motor terminology.

the speed of the fan and hence the rate of flow. You may, for example, wish to increase the speed (and the flow) to push heat to distant rooms which are presently cool, or to make the house heat up sooner. If, on the other hand, the furnace fan is cycling too often, reducing the speed of the fan will produce a slower, more even—and less noisy—flow of heated air.

Change the rate of flow and you'll soon appreciate the subtlety of heat distribution. Reduce the speed of the fan and you'll usually have to open dampers so that flow is not impeded. It seems paradoxical, but slowing the fan can actually improve heat flow to distant registers.

Before turning power back on, be sure to replace the cover on the fan's junction box.

Several adjustments can be made to improve the performance of a belt-drive blower:

1. Check the belt's condition; if the belt is old or frayed, replace it. By taking the old one to a hardware store, you'll be assured of a new belt that fits well. Check belt tightness after the new one runs for a week or two.

2. A properly adjusted belt should deflect about $\frac{3}{4}$ in. when pressed gently. If it moves less than that, the belt will wear prematurely; more, and it will slip. By turning the adjustment bolt, you can vary the distance between the motor and the blower drum, and hence, the belt's tension.

3. Check all bolts that hold the motor to its mount; they should be tight. Are the pulleys aligned? Using a framing square, put one leg across the motor body and the other across the pulleys. Both pulleys should touch the blade; if they don't, loosen the motor-mounting bolts and slide the motor over until the pulleys are aligned properly.

4. To increase motor speed, tighten (with an allen wrench) the set screw holding the outer pulley face to the motor shaft. Turn the screw clockwise to tighten it, going a half-turn at a time; to loosen the belt and thus slow the fan, turn the screw counterclockwise. By turning the screw clockwise,

you draw the faces of the pulley together, thus constricting the width of the belt channel and forcing the belt out somewhat. Overtightening can cause the belt to wear faster, in addition to putting a greater load on the motor. If, after making these adjustments, the motor seems hot, loosen the screw.

Hot-Water Systems

Hot-water systems are self-contained heating loops which, while filled with water from the house main, do not mingle with the supply of potable water. Except for periodic flushing of the system and the replacement of lost water, the same water is recirculated over and over. The water in these hookups is heated as it moves through a boiler jacket, which is itself heated by a conventional gas or oil-fueled burner. Although it is the room thermostat that calls for heat, an *aquastat* by the boiler determines the temperature of the water. Heated water travels away from the boiler in a main supply pipe to branch pipes and thence to individual convectors, where it gives up heat by a combination of radiation and convection. Its heat spent, the water heads back

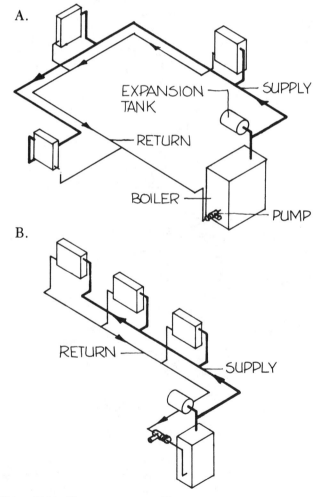

Figure 14.14 Hot-water systems. Shown are a two-pipe reverse-return system (A); and a two-pipe, direct-return setup (B). There are also one-pipe layouts, although their convectors farthest from the boiler tend to be heat starved.

the boiler via return pipes. Because water expands when heated, an expansion tank is used to accommodate changes in pressure. Like domestic water heaters hot-water heating systems must have relief valves for temperature and pressure to prevent explosions. These valves should be tripped once a month to make sure they're in good working order.

Hot-water systems vary in the way water is circulated and in the layout of pipes. Most systems are *hydronic* (forced hot water), in which circulation is aided by a pump near the boiler; there may also be separate pumps for each of several zones. Gravity-feed systems, through which water circulates by hot-water expansion alone, are becoming increasingly rare; the pipes in these systems are much larger. Because an hydronic system circulates water more quickly, water temperature can be lower and convectors smaller. Hydronic setups also have the capacity to heat houses' domestic hot water via a second boiler jacket or a coil in the boiler.

Fine-tuning hot-water systems. As is true of hot-air systems, heat loss during transmission can be considerable. The pipe insulation described in Chapter 12 can save you a lot of money. Another easy saving is achieved by lowering the temperature of the aquastat 30 to 40°F from its factory setting: adjust the aquastat temperature by turning the phillips-head screw on the face of the aquastat console. If the boiler also heats your domestic hot water, and the reduced setting is insufficient for your washing needs, consider adding point-of-use water heaters. Zoned heating is also a big saver; each zone is controlled by a circulating pump or by a central pump with separate automatic zone valves for each zone. (Separate zone valves are the better buy.)

Hot-water systems should be balanced so more or less the same temperature occurs at each convector. Balancing is effected in one of two ways: (1) discharging air that may have collected in the convector, thereby blocking water flow; and (2) adjusting the valve or valves that control the flow of water between boiler and convector.

If a convector fails to heat up although its branch pipe is warm, suspect trapped air. Because water does not compress, a small amount of pressure is enough to cause water to circulate throughout the house. Air, however, compresses; incoming water that encounters an air bubble merely compresses the bubble. Instead of heated, incoming water pushing cooler water out the return pipe, nothing moves, and the convector branch becomes a tiny backwater, unheated and uncirculated. All convectors have a small air-bleed valve at a high point. While holding a cup underneath, loosen the bleed valve until you get a steady trickle of hot water.

Whatever pipe layout you use, the flow to individual convectors can be balanced by adjusting valves. There are four types of valve: gate, balancing, inlet, and thermostatic. Gate valves usually control the flow along a main line and are usually opened full. Balancing valves are placed just off main supply lines, at the beginning of individual branches. Inlet valves are often the convector unit itself. Thermostatic valves are expensive, special inlet valves that respond to temperature. It's a good idea to have an inlet or a balancing valve for each convector; more than one valve per convector is superfluous. Except for the shutoff valve near the furnace, return lines are usually not valved.

Adjusting a valve is a deductive experiment. The cool convector needs more water: you must open valves supplying it and/or restrict water that another, hotter, convector is receiving. Adjust valves in small increments, and wait a day or two for results.

Maintenance. Hot-water systems require little maintenance other than vacuuming convectors and lubricating periodically. Flushing the system (described below), as an annual practice, is seldom recommended by specialists. They argue that introducing air and new water hastens corrosion.

To flush a system, turn off the furnace and close the shutoff valve on the cold water line to the boiler. Screw a garden hose on the boiler draincock and run the other end of the hose to a drain. (If there is no drain, you can buy a small pump that attaches to the chuck of a power drill and pumps the water out of the basement.) To drain the system, open the boiler draincock and all air bleeder valves in the system. When the system is empty, close bleeder valves and flush out any sediment that may have collected in the boiler. That done, close the draincock and refill the system. To get a complete fill, open the bleeder valves until water gurgles in the pipes. Close the valves, light the boiler, and vent air from the system (which takes 3 to 4 hours).

When you drain the system, be sure to open the draincock of the expansion tank at the same time. If the tank has no draincock of its own, the tank can be emptied by disconnecting the union nearest it or by waiting for the rest of the system to empty. When refilling an expansion tank with an inflatable vinyl diaphragm, test its pressure with a standard tire gauge to make sure the pressure is that specified by the tank's manufacturer.

If the furnace is producing sufficient heat, there are no impediments in the lines, the convectors are adequately

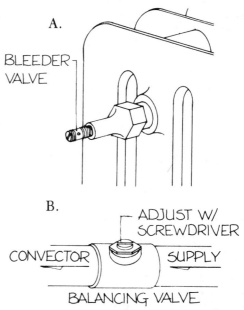

Figure 14.15 Improving heat distribution. Convectors that seem cool or that heat unevenly may have an air block, which can be released by opening a bleeder valve (A) at the highest point, until hot water trickles out in a steady stream. A balancing valve (B) restricts water flow to individual convectors.

sized, and the expansion tank pressure is correct—and you still have cold spots—have a heating specialist check the circulating pump. If there is water oozing from the pump's body, a main gasket is probably worn-out, a relatively inexpensive repair. If the pump itself is inadequate, upgrading it is simply a matter of removing the old one and sliding a new one onto the splined drive shaft.

Adding or upgrading convectors. A number of attractive new convector panels are available to replace the ugly cast-iron radiators most often found (and replaced) in older houses. Some convectors fit along the bases of walls (remove baseboard trim first), whereas other vertical models have larger radiating surfaces. Look at a supplier's catalog.

Because most heating systems are slightly oversized when new, you should have no problem adding a convector or two. If you're adding more than two, if a new convector is more than 20 ft from an existing one, or if you're converting from steam to hot water, have a professional size and lay out the system. Because most new convectors have sweat-copper leads or adapters from threaded nipples, you should review the basic pipe-working techniques discussed in Chapter 12.

To replace an old convector (old cast-iron radiators are, in truth, primarily *convectors;* so we'll use that term throughout), drain it first. Turn off the thermostat and all power to the boiler; then close the intake valve on the supply line. Open the bleeder valve and drain the unit into a bucket. Once the convector is drained, heat its couplings (if they are sweat joints) until the old solder melts. Wear a respirator mask. It's more likely, however, that the couplings are threaded steel unions between the supply shut-off and the convector itself. Covered by layers of paint and not a little corroded, such unions can be difficult to free. Try, in the following order, (1) using a pipe wrench; (2) tapping the joint with a ball peen hammer, then the wrench again; (3) applying penetrating oil to the union, allowing it to work, then hammering and wrenching again; (4) increasing the wrench's torque with a length of galvanized pipe over the handle—but don't strain, because the wrench handle could break; (5) applying heat with a propane torch, then penetrating oil, hammer, and wrench again. Try step 5 only with the windows open and a fire extinguisher nearby: fumes from lead-based paint are toxic.

Once you've disconnected the old unit, plug the openings with rags and drag the convector from the room on an old rug. Rent a dolly if you are removing several; a friend is also helpful. If the new convector is the same length as the old one, you can attach the new unit to existing supply and return leads after adding adapters to the old pipes. Realistically, old pipes with their huge, crusty old valves, can be ungainly: if it's at all possible, remove old pipes below floor level (either by unthreading the pipe or by cutting through it) and make adaptations from old to new materials there.

Adding a convector where there was none before may be simpler; after shutting and draining the lines affected, the principal adapters to be added are tees, which enable you to add branches.

Convector styles and dimensions vary, but most have cores (heat-dispersing elements) which can be separated from back panels. The back panels attach to studs in the

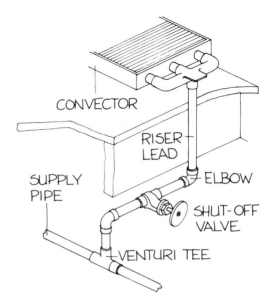

Figure 14.16 Hooking up convectors. Although the transition from old to new pipes will vary, most often a tee on the main supply feeds a branch, with a shutoff valve between the tee and the convector. Or you can use a flexible connector and forgo all the fittings above. Venturi tees allow water to flow in one direction only.

wall behind, and the cores clip to the back panels. Temporarily position both, noting where riser pipes to the convector will exit through the floor. If the new holes differ from the old ones, fill the old holes and drill new ones. For ease of installation, sweat elbows and riser leads to the stem at each end of the convector; there's more room to make final connections from below. Slide the risers into the holes you drilled, snap the core to the now-mounted back panel, and go below to make final attachments from riser leads to supply and return pipes.

Note: When sweat-fitting valves, make sure they are fully open so that gaskets within, if any, won't melt and seize. When spaces are so tight that you can't slide fittings over pipe ends, use slip fittings (see Figure 12.52). Finally, snap end and front panels over the core.

Steam Heat

Steam heating evolved from earlier gravity-fed hot-water systems: when there were no circulating pumps (nor electricity), steam could travel farther and heat faster than water. Many old steam systems are one-pipe systems in which the main steam pipe is also the return pipe for condensed water. For that reason (return of the water), all one-pipe systems must be pitched downward toward the wet-return section.

Most operational maladies encountered with steam systems are a result of water blocking incoming steam. Knocking and hammering occur when very hot steam meets condensed water at a much lower temperature; the noise is from metal expanding and contracting. To reduce hammering or uneven heating in one-pipe radiators, block or shim up the far end so water can run out freely. Knocking can usually be eliminated by raising a low spot where water has collected.

It's important that air be vented from the system so steam will not be blocked. The mechanisms for venting air

A.

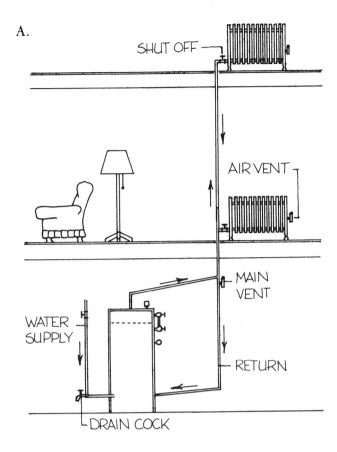

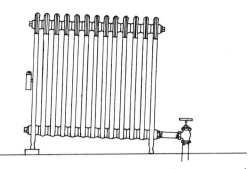

Figure 14.18 An easy and effective way to stop hammering and improve circulation. By elevating the end of the radiator farthest from the intake pipe, you allow condensed steam to run out freely.

are quick-release valves, located on each radiator at the highest point in the pipe layout and where the water return turns downward from the steam-main. Quick-release valves (also called air vents) are usually open, with air being expelled as steam advances. As the steam approaches, metal in the valve expands and the mechanism closes so steam can't escape. When the steam has condensed and the temperature drops, the valves open again. When adding a quick-release valve, observe the following: (1) they are *not* placed at the highest point on the radiator, as they are on hot-water systems; (2) valves along the water-return pipe should be on the upper part of the pipe so they can't fill with water; (3) the self-tapping nipples added for the valves (after drilling into existing pipes) should be of galvanized or black iron capable of withstanding pressures within a steam system. Most modern quick-release valves have settings that can be varied to regulate the amount of heat.

Change valves every three or four years, or sooner if radiators aren't heating adequately. Boiler gauges should be tested at least once a year, when the unit is serviced. The water gauge must show accurately the amount of water in the system, or there could be insufficient heat; the steam gauge should not stick; and the pressure-relief, or safety, valve *must* operate, venting at the prescribed safety limit (usually 15 psi) to prevent an explosion.

HEATING: ALTERNATIVE SYSTEMS

This section is a potpourri of heating devices somewhat less common than the conventional systems just described, although *alternative* is a risky adjective. In 1988, more than a quarter of the homes in California were heated and cooled with heat pumps, and the number is rising rapidly. In cold areas, especially rural ones, woodstoves are the dominant source of heat.

Heat Pumps

Heat pumps work essentially the same way that air conditioners do, except that a heat pump also has a thermostatically controlled reversing valve for changing the direction of the heat flow. In winter, heat is absorbed from outside air by the outside coil and delivered to a house's heat system by the inside coil. In summer, the inside coil soaks up heat from inside the house, and the heat is transferred to the outside coil, where it is dispersed in the outside air.

B.

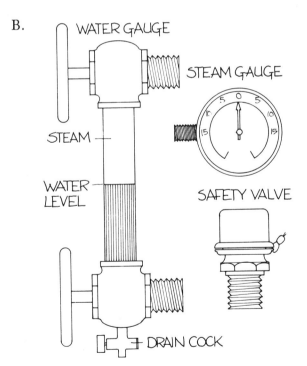

Figure 14.17 Steam heat. (A) In one-pipe systems, steam rises to individual radiators, there giving off heat; steam condenses and runs back down the same pipe until it branches off as the *main return*. Operable quick-release valves are the key to proper steam circulation. (B) Boiler details. The water gauge reflects the water level within the boiler jacket; the steam gauge shows steam pressure; the safety valve opens—usually at 15 psi—to prevent a buildup of pressure that could rupture the boiler.

Figure 14.19 Cutaway of a heat pump. (Lennox)

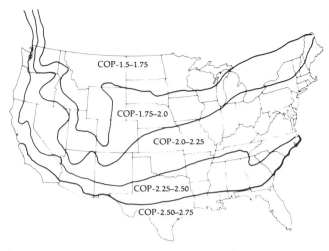

Figure 14.20 Approximate annual range of heat-pump COP. (From Dan Browne, *Alternate Home Heating,* Holt, Rinehart and Winston, New York, 1980.)

The agent of this heat exchange is more often than not Freon 22, a refrigerant that circulates through a heat pump's coils. When Freon circulates as a gas in the outside coil, it is so much colder than the surrounding air—even winter air—that it extracts heat from that air. The Freon, with the heat it picked up outside, is then compressed into a liquid (Freon becomes hot when compressed). Circulating through the inside coil, Freon now gives off heat into living areas, in the process turning back into a gas. Inside and out, powerful fans draw large quantities of air across the pump coils and thus speed the exchange of temperatures.

Obviously, it takes electricity to run the compressors and fans. The ratio of BTU output to input is known as the coefficient of performance (COP). The higher the COP, the more efficient the heat pump. Heat pumps are far more efficient than electrical-resistance heat, and the cooling phase of the heat pump is only slightly less efficient than that of an air conditioner. Thus, although the cost of installing and operating a heat pump is roughly comparable to that of operating a conventional heating system, the heat pump's ability to air-condition a house as well is a considerable gain at no additional cost.

Because heat pumps extract heat from the air, the temperature of that air partly determines the COP. Warm air has more latent heat in it than cooler air; thus heat pumps exhibit greater efficiency in regions with mild winters. Where outside temperatures are near or below the freezing mark, the pump must reverse itself (automatically) from time to time to melt ice that forms on its outside coils; otherwise, the coil would become coated with ice. Deicing, once a problem for heat pumps, no longer is; yet this reverse-cycling does add to the operating cost of a heat pump. In regions with severe winter, it may not be economical to run a heat pump, because an auxiliary heating source must supply up to one-third of the heat needed.

It is possible to design a heat pump large enough to handle all heating needs; however, such a unit would be very large, expensive, and idle much of the time during mild months. Units vary, of course; for example, water-to-air heat exchangers are slightly more efficient than the air-to-air models discussed above. Some single-piece package units can be installed outdoors; some are split-run installations that are installed part inside and part outside; and some remote units are available that have coils which can be fed into the ductwork of existing heating systems. While some units defrost exterior coils at set chronological intervals (whether there is frost or not), others use solid-state devices to monitor the actual temperature of the coils (a much more efficient method). Ask about these different features when gathering information. Perhaps the most important thing to consider, however, is whether to size the unit according to the heating or the cooling load which it must provide. Here again, the average temperatures in your region will be the determining factor.

Most heat pumps are sized according to cooling capacity, thus they are often too small for heating. If you live in a region with 3000 or more degree-days your heat pump should be sized according to heating needs; in areas below the 3000-degree-day line, size the unit according to cooling needs. (Most heat pumps have two speeds, with the cooling cycle requiring the higher speed.)

The map shown in Figure 14.20 shows the approximate, average COP of heat pumps in several regions. As you can see, the efficiency of the heating cycle diminishes the farther north you go. According to builder-author Dan Browne, from whose book the map is taken, "in order for the pump to become competitive with oil, its COP must rise to 2.8 . . . the use of a two-speed heat pump will remain too expensive until manufacturers develop models whose COP is at least 2.8 when the outdoor temperature is below freezing." Because the technology of heat pumps has improved so dramatically in the last decade, however, that level of operating efficiency may soon be met. For people now living in regions with 3000 degree-days or less, the two-speed heat pump is a good buy.

Heatstick

Heatstick is the brand name of a device that recovers heat from an air conditioner or a heat pump; heat that would otherwise be given off as excess into the air outside. According to the manufacturer, the device improves the oper-

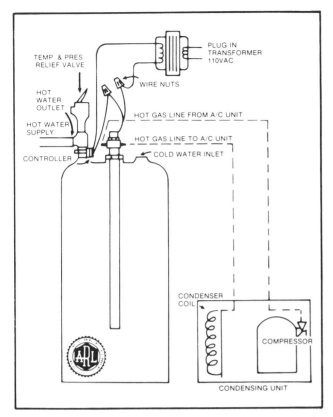

Figure 14.21 The Heatstick heat-recovery device transfers excess heat from air conditioning or heat pumps to the domestic hot-water tank via hot-gas lines and a heat-exchanger stick in the water tank. (Sun Harvester, Inc.)

ating efficiency of the heat pump or A/C unit while recovering approximately five gallons of hot water per hour for each ton of A/C or heat-pump capacity. The Heatstick transfers heat, without a pump, via two gas lines to the unit. Heat thus gained is transferred to a domestic hot-water tank by immersing the Heatstick in the tank.

Wood Heat

Wood heat is a relatively low-cost alternative system. In some parts of the United States where wood is cheap, it is the dominant means of heating. Although wood heat is safe if a few commonsense rules are observed, you should consult local codes as well as your insurance company, before hooking up. Chimneys *must* be cleaned before a wood-burning system is installed; unburned residue on the walls of the chimney can ignite and cause a flash fire. Chimneys must also be lined with a flue tile to be safe.

About wood. Dry hardwood is the best wood to burn; it's denser and gives off more heat than softwood. Old-timers feel that wood must dry for a year after cutting; some claim that 1 year per inch of thickness is best. That may be ideal, but my feeling is that if you cut wood in the spring and get it under cover immediately, it should dry enough by fall. Still, if you can let wood dry longer, do. The thinner the pieces you split, the more surface area there will be and the sooner it will dry. Wood should be covered from rain, but air must circulate freely around the woodpile; if you cover

the pile with sheet plastic, cover just the top, leaving the sides open. When knocked together, dry wood will ring; wet wood will make a thud.

Long-standing country wisdom has it that, because both softwood and green hardwood exude creosote when burned, they should not be used in a wood stove. In actuality, some softwoods contain less creosote than some types of hardwood. What causes chimney fires and rots ungalvanized stovepipe is more than creosote; incomplete combustion also produces tar, ammonia, methane, carbon monoxide, toluene, phenol, benzene, and eventually, turpentine, acetone, and methyl alcohol. But, in any event, avoid burning softwoods or green wood of any kind. For one thing, a lot of heat is wasted by boiling the water out of wet wood; for another, a smoky smoldering fire produces more unburned particulate matter, which will stick to the chimney and eventually cause trouble. It's important, therefore, that each time you start a fire, you open dampers and air controls until the fire is burning well. By doing so, you make a good bed of coals and burn up some of the unburned residue from the previous fire.

Finally, this ditty:

> Beechwood fires are bright and clear
> If the logs are kept a year.
> Chestnut only good, they say,
> If for long 'tis laid away.
> But ash new or ash old
> Is fit for queen with crown of gold.
>
> Birch and fir logs burn too fast,
> Blaze up bright and do not last.
> It is by the Irish said,
> Hawthorn bakes the sweetest bread.
> Elm burns like the churchyard mold,
> E'en the very flames are cold.
> But ash green or ash brown
> Is fit for queen with golden crown.
>
> Poplar gives a bitter smoke,
> Fills your eyes and makes you choke.
> Apple wood will scent your room
> With an incense like perfume.
> Oaken logs, if dry and old,
> Keep away the winter's cold.
> But ash wet and ash dry
> A king shall warm his stockings by.
>
> —Anonymous

What wood stove is best? A good wood stove must be airtight. It must have enough mass to radiate heat and withstand the intense heat of the wood fire (don't burn coal in a wood stove unless the manufacturer specifies it). It must have doors large enough to admit good-sized logs. And finally, it must be easy to operate and to clean. Cast iron is far sturdier than rolled steel; steel can warp and its seams admit air. A thermostatic control is fine if it works; but that's a relatively unimportant factor to consider in choosing a stove. Much more important is a baffle inside the stove, to delay the loss of heat and promote burning.

Buy a stove that fits your needs. If it's your primary source of heat, the firebox should be large (firewood is usually cut in 18- or 24-in. lengths); otherwise, a small stove will heat one or two rooms adequately.

Safety. Fires from wood stoves occur primarily because of leaks and cracks in the stovepipe where it approaches or passes through combustible surfaces, because of direct radiation from stove or stovepipe onto unprotected combustible surfaces, and because of sparks from chimney or stove. Your first line of defense is to inspect and clean the chimney often, especially noting (on metal pipe) any sections that are rusted or leaking creosote. Horizontal runs of pipe are particularly susceptible.

A wood stove should be no closer than 36 in. to an unprotected combustible surface, including stud walls covered with plaster or drywall. Putting a sheet of reflective metal and/or asbestos millboard between a stove and a combustible surface reduces the critical distance to 18 in. The correct way to do things is to affix the metal out 1 in. from the combustible surface; ceramic fence-post insulators do the job nicely; then you can get as close as 12 in., as shown in Figure 14.23. Uninsulated stove pipe should be placed at least 18 in. from combustible materials; manufacturers of *insulated* pipe usually advise going no closer than 2 in. (Actually, "insulated" is a misnomer: dual-wall and triple-wall pipes rely not on insulation but on air movement within pipe walls to keep surfaces cooler.) Also, pipes must be positively located (i.e., held fast by supports, stop collars, and such), so that they cannot move toward combustible surfaces.

Don't forget the bottom of the stove. Never use a stove that has no legs, for good circulation of air beneath the stove is critical. The best treatment there is a layer of bricks bedded in 2 to 4 in. of sand. The entire area should be boxed in with a light, furring-strip frame, to keep the sand from migrating. Before setting up your wood stove, check the joists underneath; double them if you have any doubts about their capacity.

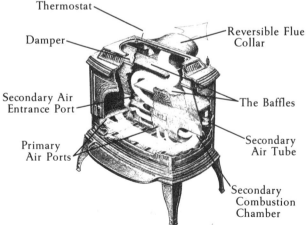

Thermostat

Damper

Reversible Flue Collar

Secondary Air Entrance Port

The Baffles

Primary Air Ports

Secondary Air Tube

Secondary Combustion Chamber

Figure 14.22 A good-quality wood stove must be sturdy, preferably cast iron, and airtight. The models shown are among the finest made in the United States. Although both open like Franklin stoves, they are extremely airtight. Further, they feature internal baffles which retain heat and promote more complete burning. (Vermont Castings, Inc.)

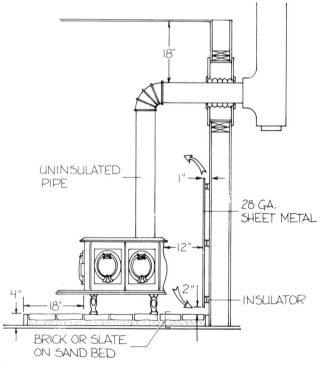

18"

UNINSULATED PIPE

1"

28 GA. SHEET METAL

12"

4"

18"

2"

INSULATOR

BRICK OR SLATE ON SAND BED

Figure 14.23 A safe hookup. The distances shown are from combustible surfaces. Although all distances are critical, especially note the 1-in. distance behind the sheet-metal reflector and the 2-in. gap at the bottom: without air flowing behind the metal, heat will be conducted to combustibles behind. Cementitious Wonderboard (p. 388) is another good sheet material to put behind wood stoves, but again, it too must be held out from the wall with insulators or resilient metal channels.

Figure 14.24 Short runs of uninsulated stovepipe are acceptable, but chimneys must be masonry or class A metal flue pipe. The most reliable are dual-wall or triple-wall metal chimneys whose air movement within the pipe keeps outer walls relatively cool. The Metalbestos unti shown may be as close as 2 in. to a combustible surface when the unit is correctly installed.

More about stovepipes. Most uninsulated stovepipe has a crimped male end and an uncrimped female end which slides over the male end. There is some controversy over whether the crimped end should go up or down. If you're burning wood, put the crimped end down so creosote will run back down into the stove, where it will be burned completely. If you're burning coal (which has little or no creosote), put the crimped end up; smoke escape is the more critical aspect of operation.

With regard to the type of stovepipe used, a short run of uninsulated pipe to the chimney is adequate, and cheap. The chimney itself, however, must be of masonry or insulated metal, and should run up inside the house to retain heat and reduce condensation. Metal chimneys should be insulated (see the Metalbestos section in Figure 14.24). Triple-wall, uninsulated metal chimneys are available that purport to be safe, proponents reasoning that the flow of air between the three layers of metal keeps the assembly cool. The theory is fine; but should any pipe joint clog or corrode, air would be blocked, essentially leaving you with an uninsulated pipe too close to a combustible surface.

A final word

Keep smoke detectors and fire extinguishers nearby.

Pitch stovepipe up at least $\frac{1}{2}$ in. per foot; horizontal runs collect residue.

Don't use chemical chimney cleaners; they shorten a pipe's life.

Use a minimum of three sheet-metal screws to hold the joints of uninsulated pipe.

If your fireplace is smoky, improve its draft by changing its proportions as proposed by Count Rumford, a contemporary of Benjamin Franklin (see Appendix G.)

Figure 14.25 A window greenhouse. (Lord & Burnham)

Solar Systems

Solar systems are classified broadly as *passive*, requiring no additional energy to make the system work; and *active*, requiring additional energy, usually electricity, to circulate heat from panels to storage or from storage to living areas. Most systems are hybrids, with some, for example, circulating heated air to a rock storage and others transmitting a heated fluid to a large holding tank. There are also hookups with photovoltaic cells that convert sunlight directly to electricity; as of this writing, such systems are rudimentary.

The solar industry has left its infancy and has proved itself both reliable and cost-effective. Solar domestic hot-water systems are an excellent buy, with the payback period running about 5 years. Installation costs of space-heating solar systems are so formidable, however, that the payback period averages 20 years or longer. Solar space-heating is a great idea, but no manufacturer has thus far mass-produced units cost-competitive with conventional systems. This type of solar energy simply costs too much for most people to install. Since there is no room here to discuss solar installations in detail, readers should consult *Solar Age* and *Sun World* magazines.

A number of passive, low-cost alterations are available to make your house a more pleasant dwelling. By adding windows on the south side of the house, you admit more radiant solar energy, but be sure to read about reducing heat loss through windows in the preceding chapter. Greenhouses, either as window units or as entire rooms, also admit light. Adding thermal mass to the inside of the house by tiling a floor or building a trombe wall, contributes to heat retention, with the heat slowly radiating back over a period of a hours.

Window greenhouses. Window greenhouses are remarkably easy to install; follow details of installation supplied by the manufacturer. Certain precautions must be taken, however. For example, remove the present sashes, so they won't swell from the increased moisture produced by the plants. Seal window casings with a sealer or clear finish, so they won't absorb water, either. Next, seal around the mounting flange of the greenhouse with a good-quality caulk, such as silicone so that water can't get behind the siding. Finally, be sure to flash the top of the greenhouse where it joins the main house; see Chapter 5.

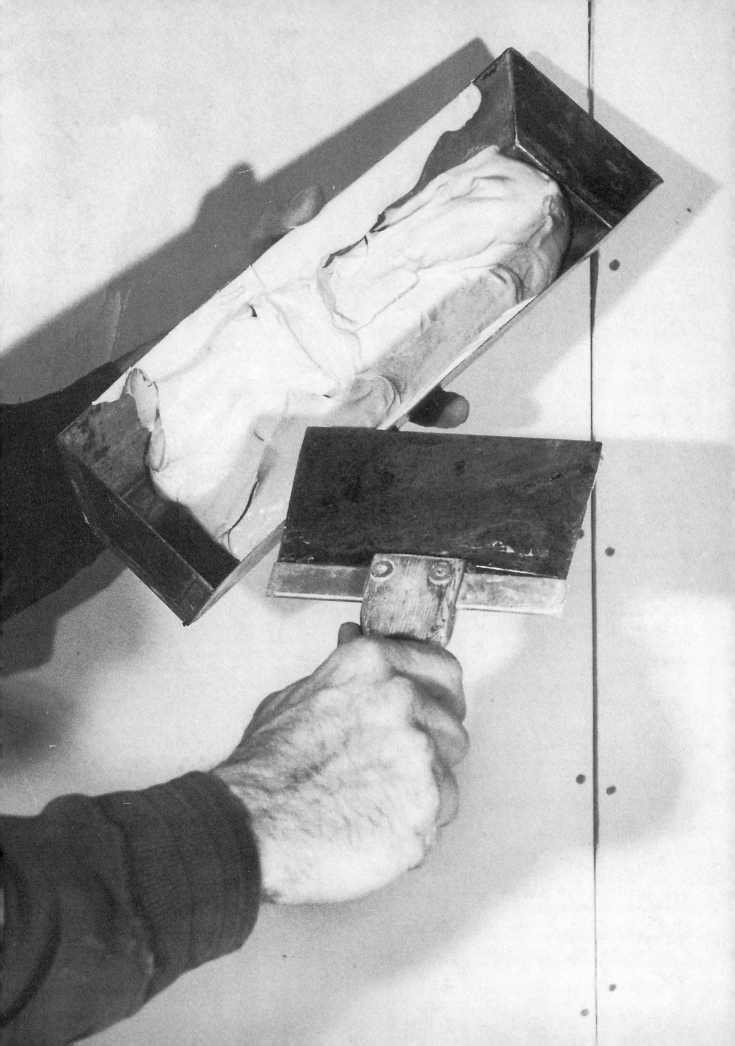

·15·

FINISH SURFACES

The earliest wall and ceiling finishes were probably mud daubs that cut down on the drafts coming through rough walls of sticks and logs. As a structure shifted or rain dissolved the mud, new daub was added. Although present-day interiors are fashioned from more sophisticated materials, they remain vulnerable to some extent, ultimately depending upon the weathertightness and structural integrity of the building.

In this chapter we will look at the most common finish surfaces—drywall, plaster and paneling—and end with a glance at isolating sound. Tile is discussed in the following chapter.

DRYWALL

The most commonly used interior surface is drywall, gypsum panels sheathed in heavy paper. Drywall is also known as wallboard and Sheetrock, the latter being the brand name of the U.S. Gypsum Co. Because gypsum is nonflammable and durable, it is appropriate for most residential uses. Sheets of drywall are screwed or nailed into place, and holes are filled with joint compound. Sheet joints are built up with special tape and several layers (usually three) of joint compound. Drywall is easily installed, though joint work can be tedious.

Tools

Few special tools are required, and of those that are, most are moderately priced:

Tape measure, chalk line, and level. Use these tools for layout.

Utility knife and metal straightedge. Use a utility knife for cutting, a straightedge for guiding a cut; a special T-square is available for guiding drywall, but a framing square will suffice.

Hammer with convex head. Used on drywall nails, the convex head dimples the material without tearing the paper finish.

Screw gun or magnetic screw bit. A power drill with a magnetic bit quickly sinks drywall screws. Drywall screws are perhaps the most versatile connector in renovation; and the screw guns the most useful tool. A *must* for any renovator.

Finish knives. A 6-in. knife is fine for filling nail or screw dimples; it's also used to bed the tape in the first layer of joint compound. A 12-in. finishing knife "feathers out" the second layer of joint compound and is usually adequate for the third, or topping, layer. Knives 16 in. and wider are also available for this last coat.

Two-faced corner knife. This knife is almost indispensable for making clean interior corners. Use a large sponge and

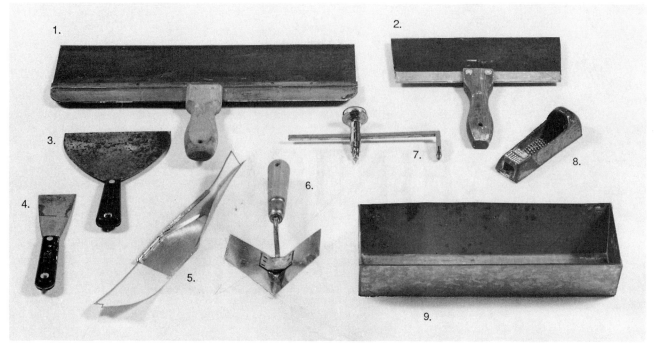

Figure 15.1 Basic drywall tools. 1, 18-in. joint knife; 2, 10-in. joint knife; 3, 6-in. knife; 4, 2-in. knife; 5, tool for pre–bending joint tape; 6, inside corner taping tool; 7, circle cutter; 8, surform for shaving edges; 9, mud tray.

a pail of clean water to keep knives clean (empty joint-compound pails are ideal).

Fine-grit sandpaper (220-grit). Use this grade of sandpaper to smooth dried compound; wrap the sandpaper around a block. Lightweight orbital or hand sanders, such as a Speedblock sand effectively, but they can burr the paper finish if used excessively. Experiment on a small area.

Respirator mask. Essential for sanding, a respirator prevents dust inhalation.

Sheet Materials

Drywall varies according to composition, thickness, and shape of the edge. Drywall's width, 4 ft, is usually constant, but lengths vary; the most common sizes are 4 ft × 12 ft, 4 ft × 9 ft, and 4 ft × 8 ft; the most common type is regular gypsum board with tapered edges. Following are some choices of drywall available.

Composition.
Regular gypsum board. Commonly used on walls and ceilings and available in varying thicknesses, regular board $\frac{1}{2}$ in. and $\frac{5}{8}$ in. thick are most common. Type X gypsum board has special additives that make it fire-resistant.

MR or WR board. Also called "greenboard" and "blueboard," this board is water resistant and is appropriate for bathrooms, laundries, and similar areas. A suitable base for tiles bedded in mastic, it is usually $\frac{1}{2}$ in. thick.

Sound-deadening board. A substrate used with other layers of drywall (usually type X), sound-deadening board is often $\frac{1}{4}$ in. thick.

Foil-backed board. The foil side provides a vapor barrier facing the living sides of room walls; thicknesses vary.

Vinyl-surfaced board. Available in colors, it is attached with special drywall finish nails and left exposed with no joint treatment.

Plasterboard or gypsum lath. A base for plaster, it's available in thicknesses starting at $\frac{3}{8}$ in.; widths 16 in. and 24 in.; length, usually 48 in. Because it comes in manageable sizes, it's widely used as a plaster base instead of metal or wood lath for both new construction and renovation.

Edges. The following types of edging are commonly used:

Tapered. Allows joint tape to be bedded and built up to a flat surface; the most common edge.

Square. Makes an acceptable exposed edge.

Beveled. An edge left untaped, giving a paneled look.

Thickness and length. Drywall comes in various lengths and thicknesses; the longer the sheets you use, the fewer joints you have to cover later. The trade-off is, of course, weight: sheets much longer than 8 ft or thicker than $\frac{1}{2}$ in. become unwieldy, especially if they're covering the ceiling.

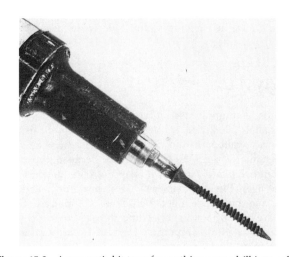

Figure 15.2 A magnetic bit transforms this power drill into a drywall screw-gun.

Although local codes have the final say, use sheets $\frac{5}{8}$-in. thick on ceilings, and on walls whose studs are spaced 24 in. O.C.; that thickness is also specified for all fire wall construction along stairs, between house and garage, and so on; $\frac{5}{8}$-in. drywall is also appropriate where you want extra sound isolation, say, between floors. For all other standard construction, e.g., studs 16 in. O.C., $\frac{1}{2}$-in drywall is fine. Drywall $\frac{1}{4}$- and $\frac{3}{8}$-in. thick are commonly used in renovation to cover existing surfaces that are unsightly but basically sound—cracked plaster, for example. Two plies of $\frac{1}{4}$-in. drywall are also used to wrap curving walls.

Sheets thicker than $\frac{5}{8}$ in. are reserved for special installations such as all-gypsum partitions and shaft linings.

Joint Tapes

Joint tapes vary little one to another, with the major difference being whether they are perforated or not. Perforated types are slightly more expensive and somewhat easier to bed and cover.

Also available are self-sticking joint tapes that obviate the need for a first, bedding layer of compound. According to one restorationist, this type is suitable for repairing holes the size of outlet boxes in plaster and drywall, provided you force the patching material through the holes in the tape.

Joint compounds and textures. Joint compounds come ready-mixed or powdered (requiring water). Ready-mixed compound is much easier to work with, though its shelf life is somewhat shorter than powdered. Joint compounds vary according to the additives they contain.

Premixed, general-purpose compound can be used for all three layers of jointing and is suitable for texturing. It's the best bet for beginners but is slow to dry. Allow a drying time of 24 hours between coats.

Bedding compound maximizes the adhesion of tape to a joint. Particularly good for initial coverings of potential problem spots such as corners and nail holes, it dries more quickly than general-purpose compound.

Topping compound is designed for second and third layers and has less adhesive; shrinkage is minimal. It has a hard surface that is easy to sand.

Quick-setting compound sets in an hour or two. Allows a professional to tape and finish joints the same day. Not recommended for novices.

Wall textures can be trowelled on by hand or sprayed on. Finer, more regular textures require spraying; rougher textures, which can mask irregularities on a wall, should be applied with a trowel. Textured paint is another option.

Some common texturing additives are vermiculite, powdered polystyrene, and fine sand. The first two are excellent for hiding surface defects and for damping sound in a room; of the two, polystyrene yields a rougher finish.

Textures are excellent for hiding surface defects, but they limit your long-term decorating options. If you don't want to spend money on new walls right now, textures may be a good choice. If you're taking pains to hang new drywall, however, think twice—you might prefer a smooth finish later on. Whatever texture you choose, be sure to complete all three coats of joint compound, and cover the wall with an oil-based primer. Always check the manufacturer's specifications; applications can vary.

Nails, Screws, and Adhesives

The connector you choose depends in part upon the material underneath. The substrate usually is wood or metal studs, although gypsum itself is occasionally used as a base. Adhesives are used in tandem with screws or nails, which allows the installer to use fewer screws or nails and thus leaves fewer holes to be filled. For reasons noted below, you'll find the drywall screw the most versatile for attaching to all substrates.

Nails. Drywall nails are galvanized to grip better and resist rusting, and their heads are cupped to hold joint compound. When purchasing drywall nails, consider the thickness of the layer or layers of drywall, and allow additional length for the nail to penetrate the underlying wood $\frac{3}{4}$ in. A longer nail does not fasten more securely than a properly sized one, and it will be subject to the expansion and contraction of a greater depth of wood.

Smooth-shank, diamond-head nails are commonly used to attach two layers of drywall—for example, when fireproofing a wall. Again, the nail length should be selected carefully: smooth-shank nails should penetrate 1 in. Predecorated drywall nails, which may be left exposed, have smaller heads and are color-matched to the drywall.

Screws. Drywall screws are the only way to go: the favorite of professional builders, cabinetmakers, and renovators. Made of high-quality steel, they are superior to conventional wood screws. Use a screw gun or an electric drill with a magnetic screwdriver bit. Because this method of attachment is nonconcussive, there's little danger of jarring loose earlier connections or of disturbing neighbors. The three principal types of drywall screw follow:

Type W. Type W screws hold drywall to wood; they should penetrate studs or joists at least $\frac{5}{8}$ in. If you're applying two layers of drywall, the screws holding the second sheet need penetrate the wood beneath only $\frac{1}{2}$ in.

Type S. Type S screws are designed for metal studs. The screws are self-tapping and very sharp, since metal studs can flex away. At least $\frac{3}{8}$ in. of the threaded part of the screw should pass through a metal stud. Although other lengths are available, 1-in. type S screws are commonly used for single-ply drywall.

Type G. Type G screws fasten to drywall backing boards. At least $\frac{1}{2}$ in. of the threaded part of the screw should penetrate the backing; the most common type G screw used is $1\frac{1}{2}$ in. Other types of drywall screws are used to attach wood trim to metal studs, door frames to metal studs, and so on.

Metal accessories. A number of metal accessories have been developed to finish off and/or protect drywall. *Corner-beads* are used on all exposed corners, to insure a clean finish and to weather the ravages of children. (Interior corners are formed with just tape and compound.) *J-beads* keep exposed ends of drywall from fraying. *L-beads* are used where sheets abut (but are not covered by) door casings. L-beads create a slight reveal (recess) between casing and drywall. J- and L-beads are matched to the thickness of the drywall. Beads are used without tape.

Adhesives. Adhesives are used infrequently, usually where it is impracticable to attach drywall with screws or nails, say, where a lower edge overhangs a foundation jog. Adhesives bond single-ply drywall directly to framing, furring grids, masonry surfaces, insulation, sound-deadening board, and other drywall. Because the adhesive is matched to the substrate, ask your supplier what adhesive is best for the job you have in mind.

Some adhesives are contact cement, which can be rolled on (wear goggles); mastic, applied with a notched trowel; and stud adhesive, which is as thick as conventional caulk. Contact cement and mastic are used to bond sheets of drywall to drywall or to plaster underneath. Note that caulk-consistency adhesive is useful for building up small irregularities between framing members and drywall sheets.

Preparation

For the best results, the drywall should lie flat against the surface you are nailing or screwing to. How flat the nailing surface must be depends upon the desired finish effect. Smooth, painted surfaces with spotlights on them require as nearly flawless a finish as you can attain. Similarly, delicate wall coverings—particularly those with close, regular patterns—will accentuate pocks and lumps underneath; textured surfaces are much more forgiving. In general, if adjacent nailing elements (studs, etc.) vary by more than $\frac{1}{4}$ in., build up low spots. Essentially, there are three ways to create a flat nailing surface:

1. Cover imperfections with a layer of $\frac{3}{8}$-in. drywall, a thickness that is flexible yet strong; $\frac{1}{4}$ in. may suffice. Single-ply cover-up is a common renovation strategy where existing walls are blemished but basically flat. Locate studs beforehand and use screws long enough to penetrate studs and joists at least $\frac{5}{8}$ in.

2. Build up the surface by furring out as described below.

3. Frame out a new wall, as described in Chapter 8, under "Structural Carpentry." If the studs of curtain walls are buckled and warped, it's often easier to rip the walls out and replace them. Where the irregular surface is a load-bearing wall, it may be easier to build a new wall within the old.

Furring Out

Furring out an existing wall usually precedes wood paneling, whose patterns must align exactly. On occasion, though, furring out is a necessary preparation for drywalling—say, when you're covering a masonry wall. Most often, furring strips are 1×2s, although some drywall manufacturers specify 2×2s so drywall screws have plenty to grip. Whatever size your furring, make sure the strips are well anchored to the wall behind. (The composition of the wall will determine what attacher to use: if it's a masonry wall, consult chapters 4 and 9. If it's a stud wall, drywall screws $2\frac{1}{2}$ to 3 in. long will suffice.)

Lay out the furring by first seeing how flat the wall is: stretch strings taut between diagonal corners to get a quick idea of low spots. A straight edge also works. Mark low spots right onto the wall. If the existing wall is a stud wall presently covered with drywall or plaster, test-drill to find studs and mark stud centers clearly so you'll know where to attach furring strips.

Your goal is a flat plane of furring strips over existing studs. Tack the strips in place and add shims (wood shingles are best) at each low spot marked. To make sure the furring strip doesn't skew, use two shims, with their thin ends reversed, at each point. Tack the shims in place and plumb the furring strips again. When you're satisfied, drive the nails or screws all the way in. Actually, it's best to use type W drywall screws here: the points already attached are less likely to be disturbed by screws.

When attaching the finish surface, use screws or nails long enough to attach through furring strips into the studs behind. Strips directly over studs ensure the strongest attachment. Where finish materials are not sheets—for example, single-board vertical paneling—furring should run perpendicular to studs.

Note: Whatever finish material you use, it must be backed firmly at all nailing points, corners, and seams. Where you cover existing finish surfaces or otherwise alter the thickness of walls, it's usually necessary to build up existing trim. Electrical boxes must also be built up with specially designed "extenders"; see Figure 11.19, and consult your electrical supplier.

Furring out over masonry. Masonry surfaces must be smooth, clean, and dry. Where the walls are below grade,

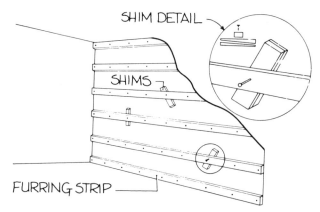

Figure 15.3 Furring strips properly backed with shims create a flat nailing and screwing surface over existing walls. Use two tapered shims at each low spot.

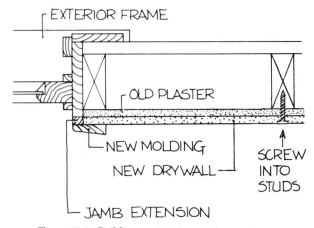

Figure 15.4 Building up interior window casing.

apply a vapor barrier of polyethylene (use mastic to stick it up) and then furring strips. Rent a power-nailer to attach strips to masonry; masonry nails already nailed in can work loose, making a large job tedious. If you decide to hand-nail into masonry, however, drive case-hardened nails into mortar joints; wear goggles, because such nails can fragment.

Laying Out a Drywall Job

When laying out a drywall job, position sheets so you have a minimum of joint work; each joint requires taping and sanding. Choose drywall boards of the maximum practical length.

You can hang drywall with its length either parallel or perpendicular to joists or studs. Although both arrangements work, sheets run perpendicular afford better attachment. In double-ply installation, run base sheets parallel and top ones perpendicular. For walls, the height of the ceiling is an important determinant: where ceilings are 8 ft. 1 in. or less, run wall sheets horizontally; where ceilings are higher, run wall sheets vertically (see Figure 15.5). But these are suggestions, not rules: put up sheets any way that seems easy to you.

As noted above, the edges of most drywall taper, the ends of sheets don't. Thus you should stagger the ends of sheets so you don't have a continuous seam of sheet ends—such seams are monsters to feather out correctly. One other constraint: lay out sheets so tapered edges don't occur within 6 in. of window or door casing. Casing may not lie flat atop a tapered edge. To avoid this concurrence, lay out sheet edges so they meet over a crippled stud above the casing.

Handling Drywall

These tips about drywall should make your job easier:

1. Don't order drywall too far in advance. Drywall must be stored flat, to prevent damage to the edges, and it takes up a lot of space.

2. To cut drywall, you need cut only through the fine-paper surface. Then grasp the smaller section and snap it sharply—the gypsum core will break along the scored line. Cut through the paper on the back. If you're working with a large amount of drywall, lay the stack across sawhorses so that you do not have to stoop as you cut it.

3. Don't be too close with your cuts; measure $\frac{1}{8}$ in. shy on width and length so that you have a little room to fit the sheets. If you cut too closely, you may have to wrestle with the piece to get it into place. Also, where walls aren't square, you may have to trim anyhow.

4. Snap chalk lines on the drywall to indicate joists or stud centers underneath; attachment will be much quicker. If the framing is spaced 16 in. O.C., snap lines at that interval. Remember: drywall edges must be aligned over stud, joist, or rafter centers.

5. Before nailing up drywall, always check to be sure that metal *nail plates* are in place to protect wires and pipes. Few things are as frustrating as discovering a leak or a short after drywall is installed.

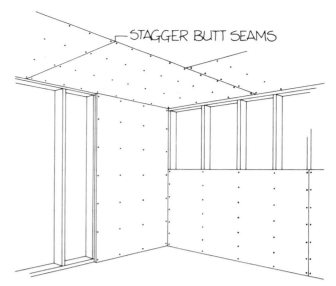

Figure 15.5 Hanging drywall on walls and ceilings. The ceiling height largely determines whether wall sheets are hung horizontally or vertically. Center sheet edges over stud centers.

6. When cutting out holes for outlet boxes, fixtures, and so on, measure from the nearest fixed points—for example, from the floor and/or edge of the next piece of drywall. Take two measurements from each point, so you get the cutout's true height and width.

Locate the cutout on the finish side of the drywall. To start the cut, drill holes at the corners, then finish cuts with a keyhole or a compass saw. (Professionals forgo drilled holes; instead, they start cuts by stabbing the sharp point of the saw through drywall and cutting.) It's more difficult to cut out a hole with just a utility knife, but it can be done.

Attachment

When attaching drywall, it's important that you hold it firmly against the framing behind, to avoid nail pops and other weak spots. Nails or screws must securely lodge in a framing member. If a nail misses framing, pull out the missed nail, dimple the hole, and fill it in with compound; then try again. If you drive nails in too deep, so that the drywall is crushed, drive in another, reinforcing nail within 2 in. of the first. When attaching sheets, nail (or screw) from the center of the sheet outward.

Screws. As noted several times, screws are the premier way to attach drywall; because they grip better, you need fewer of them. In the field, space screws every 12 in., regardless of the thickness of the drywall; along edges, however, sink screws every 6 in. to be safe. Place screws about $\frac{1}{2}$ in. from edges; do the same with nails.

Nails. In the field, space nails every 8 in., and every 6 in. along edges. Maintain those nailing intervals when you're attaching $\frac{5}{8}$-in. sheetrock to the ceiling, but for extra holding strength, use $1\frac{5}{8}$-in. nails—they have a slightly larger head.

Some old-timers swear by double-nailing drywall, though the logic escapes us. In that method, double-nail only in the field, spacing individual nails 2 to $2\frac{1}{2}$ in. apart,

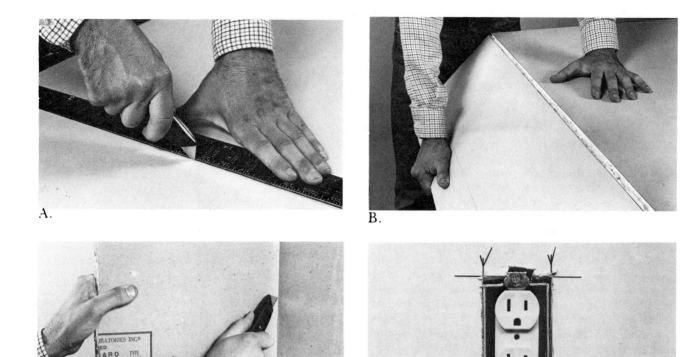

A.

B.

C.

D.

Figure 15.6 Cutting drywall. (A) Chalkline the cut to be made onto the finish-paper side of the drywall; score once along the line with a utility knife. (B) Snap the drywall sharply, as shown: it will break along the scored line. (C) Cut through the back side of the seam. (D) Position cutouts exactly by taking two measurements for each dimension.

and nailing *pairs* a maximum of 12 in. apart. Along sheet edges, however, do not double nails: space single nails every 6-8 in.

Whichever method you choose, remember to dimple each nail head—that is, drive it in slightly below the surface of the drywall—without breaking the surface of the material. Dimpling creates a depression that can be filled with joint compound. Although special convex-headed drywall hammers are available for this operation, a conventional hammer used adroitly will do just fine.

Adhesives. Adhesives are used primarily to affix drywall where nails or screws can't, but it's sometimes used in tandem with those attachers. Adhesive applied to wood studs allows you to bridge minor irregularities along the studs and to use about half the number of nails; space the nails 12 in. apart (without doubling up). Don't alter nail spacing along end seams, however. To attach sheets to studs, use a caulking gun and run a $\frac{3}{8}$-in. bead down the middle of the stud. Where sheets meet over a framing member, run two parallel beads. Don't make serpentine beads; the adhesive could ooze out onto the drywall surface. If you're laminating a second sheet of drywall over a first, roll a liquid contact cement with a short nap roller on the face of the sheet already in place. To keep adhesive out of your eyes, wear goggles. When the adhesive turns dark (usually within 30 minutes), it's ready to receive the second piece of drywall. Screw on the second sheet, as described above.

Hanging Drywall Sheets

Ceilings. Begin attaching sheets on the ceiling, first checking to be sure extra blocking (which will receive nails or screws) is in place above the top plates of the walls. Install ceilings first; that way, you'll have a maximum exposure of blocking to nail or screw into. If there are gaps along the intersection of the ceiling and wall, it is much easier to adjust wall pieces. Also, wall sheets will support the edges of ceiling sheets.

Figure 15.7 Dimpling nails creates a cavity to which joint compound can adhere.

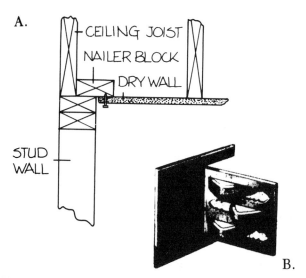

A.

CEILING JOIST
NAILER BLOCK
DRY WALL

STUD
WALL

B.

Figure 15.8 All edges of the drywall must be securely attached. (A) In conventional framing, blocking is nailed into the top plate (and to wall ends) to provide a firm base for drywall attachment. A metal drywall clip (B) can be attached at various points along framing members to achieve the same backing. Use type S drywall screws to attach the drywall to the metal clip. (Panel Clip Co.)

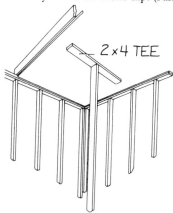

2×4 TEE

Figure 15.9 A homemade tee holds drywall tight to ceiling joists and ensures a sound attachment.

Using two tees made from 2 × 4s, one person can hang a ceiling. Position one tee against a wall, with its top about 1 in. shy of the ceiling joists. Carefully angle a piece of drywall so one end rests on top of that tee. Being careful not to dislodge the sheet-end resting on the first tee, raise the second tee until the entire sheet is snug against the ceiling joists. The tee should be $\frac{1}{2}$ in. to 1 in. taller than the distance of ceiling—with drywall in place—to floor. Gradually shift the tees until the sheet's seams are aligned with joist centers. Or, you can avoid all this trouble by asking a friend to help. A good working platform is a pair of planks stretched across two sawhorses.

Walls. Walls are easier to hang than ceilings, and it's something one person working alone can do effectively, although the job goes faster if two people work together. As you did with ceilings, be sure walls have sufficient blocking in corners before you begin.

When hanging sheets on the wall, always start at the top, butting the first course snug to the drywall on the ceiling. In that way you'll avoid gaps and support ceiling edges better. It's also important that the first sheet on a wall is

plumb—or that you make it so by trimming it. Otherwise, subsequent edges may be cockeyed and may not center over studs.

Because sheetrock is heavy, use jigs whenever possible. The lever shown in Figure 15.11 is handy because it frees your hands to align sheets and sink screws. For tight fits at the bottom, an *edge perforation tool* enables you to mark (and perforate) a cutoff line easily. If friends stop by to help you lift, use them wisely: sink a few screws to secure each sheet and keep moving. You can go back later after they leave and really screw things down.

Figure 15.10 Be sure that sheet edges end over stud centers, as shown, and that the first piece on the wall is snug against the ceiling. (Georgia Pacific)

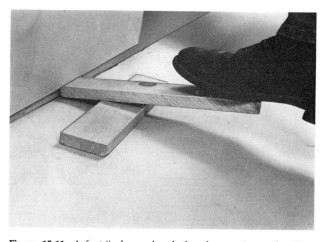

Figure 15.11 A foot-jig leaves hands free for aligning and nailing the sheet. A gap of $\frac{1}{2}$ to 1 in. at the bottom of a sheet is not critical, for it will be covered by the finished floor and baseboard molding.

Finally, accept the fact that you'll waste a lot of drywall. Old houses are rife with non-standard dimensions and odd angles, so don't fight it. You can use larger cutoffs in inconspicuous places like closets, but remember that the more joints, the more taping and sanding. When in doubt, throw it out.

Curved walls. Drywall is quite good for creating or covering curved walls. For the best results, use two layers of $\frac{1}{4}$-in. drywall, hung horizontally. The framing members of the curve should be placed at intervals of no more than 16 in.; 12 in. is better. For an 8-ft sheet applied horizontally, an arc depth of 2 to 3 ft should be no problem, but do check the manufacturer's specifications. Sharper curves may require backcutting (scoring slots into the back so that the sheet can be bent easily) or wetting (wet-sponging the front and back of the sheet to soften the gypsum). Results aren't always predictable, though. When applying the second layer of $\frac{1}{4}$-in. drywall, stagger the layer's vertical butt joints.

Joint work. Where sheets of drywall join, the joints are disguised with joint tape and compound. The procedure is straightforward:

1. Spread a swath of bedding compound about 4 in. wide down the center of the joint. Press the tape into the center of the joint with a 6-in. finish knife. Apply another coat of compound over the first to bury the tape. As you apply the compound over the tape bear down so you take up any excess.

2. When the first coat is dry, sand the edges with fine-grit paper. Wear a respirator mask. Some manufacturers offer products for joints that can be damp-sponged smooth but most professional drywall workers shun this procedure, pointing out that it saves no time and that the dampness can easily raise the finish-paper surface on the drywall. Wipe the dust off. Using a 12-in. knife, apply a topping of compound 2 to 4 in. wider than the first applications.

3. Sand the second coat of compound when it's dry. Apply the third and final coat, feathering it out another 2 to 3 in. on each side of the joint. You should be able to do this with a 12-in. knife; otherwise, use a 16-in. ''feathering trowel.''

Nail holes and screw holes usually can be covered in two passes, though shrinkage sometimes necessitates

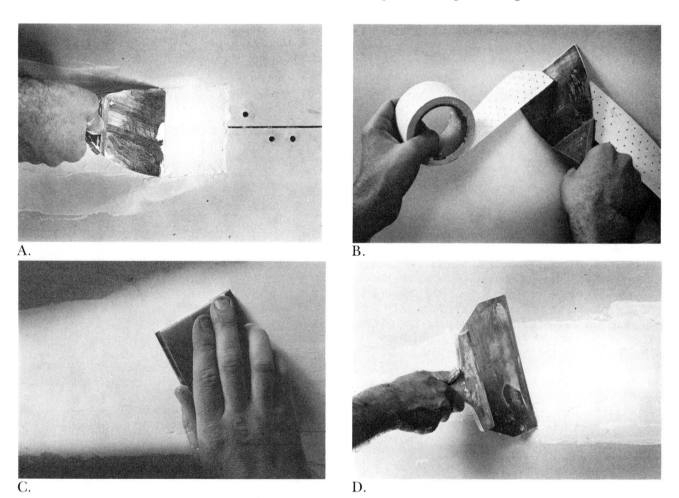

A.

B.

C.

D.

Figure 15.12 Joint treatment. (A) Apply a generous bed of compound for the tape which follows. (B) Use the finish knife to rip joint tape evenly. Center the tape over the joint and press it into place with the knife. Then apply a layer of compound over the tape, burying the tape. As you pull the knife along, bear down to remove excess compound. (C) Once it's dry, sand each application of compound with fine-grade paper. Too much sanding will burr the paper finish. (D) Use a 12-in. finish knife to feather out the second coat of compound; this tool should be wide enough for the third (final) coat as well.

three. Corner beads are no problem if you apply compound with care and scrape excess clean.

Don't be afraid to apply generous layers of compound; without enough, the tape won't stick. Scrape clean any excess, however; sanding it off can be tedious. Use a sanding block on an extension pole for sanding hard-to-reach places; the block has a swivel-head joint. Always wipe after sanding so subsequent layers of compound will stick.

To give yourself the greatest number of decorating options in the future, paint the finished drywall surface with a coat of flat, oil-based primer. Whether you intend to wallpaper or paint with latex, oil-based primer is the best way to seal the paper face of the drywall.

Drywall Repairs

Drywall blemishes are most often caused by structural shifting or water damage. Attend to the underlying cause or causes before attacking the symptoms.

Fix popped-up nails by pulling them out or by dimpling them with a hammer. Test the entire wall for springiness and add nails or screws where needed. Within 2 in. of a popped-up nail, drive in another nail; when the spots are dry, spackle both, sand and prime.

To repair cracks in drywall, cut back the edges of the crack slightly, to remove any crumbly gypsum and to provide a good depression for a new filling of joint compound. Feather the edges of the compound; sand and prime them when dry.

When a piece of drywall tape lifts, pull gently until the piece rips free from the part that's still well stuck. Sand the area affected and apply a new bed of compound for a replacement piece of tape. (The self-sticking tape mentioned above works well here.) Feather all edges.

If a sharp object has dented the drywall, merely sand the concavity and fill it with compound. In cases where the hole goes all the way through, follow the same technique used for repairing holes in plaster walls. A hole larger than, say, your fist should have a piece of backing. Cut the edges of the hole clean with a utility knife. The piece of backing should be slightly larger than the hole itself. Drill a small hole into the middle of the backing piece and thread a piece of wire into the hole; this wire will allow you to hold onto the piece of backing. Spread mastic around the edges of the backing; when the adhesive is tacky, fit the backing diagonally into the hole and, holding onto the wire, pull the masticked piece against the back side of the hole. When the mastic is dry, push the wire back into the wall cavity; the backing will stay in place. Now fill up the hole with plaster or joint compound.

Compound will sag in holes that are too big. If that happens, mastic a replacement piece of drywall to the backing piece. To avoid a bulge around the filled-in hole, feather the compound about 16 in.; or better, if the original drywall is $\frac{1}{2}$ in. thick, use $\frac{3}{8}$-in. plasterboard as a replacement.

Cut holes larger than 8 in. back to the centers of the nearest studs. Although you should have no problem nailing a replacement piece to the studs, the top and the bottom of the new piece must be backed. The best way to install backing is to screw drywall gussets (supports) to the back of the existing drywall. Then put the replacement piece in the hole and screw it to the gussets; use drywall screws, of course.

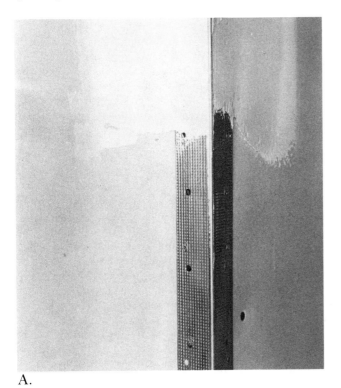

A.

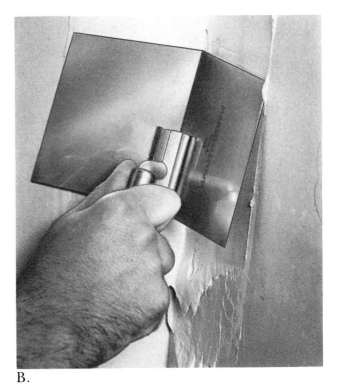

B.

Figure 15.13 Corner treatments. (A) A metal cornerbead protects outer corners from damage. It is nailed or screwed into place and covered with compound; no tape is needed. (B) Inner corners require taping and three coats of compound; a corner knife is almost indispensable for the operation.

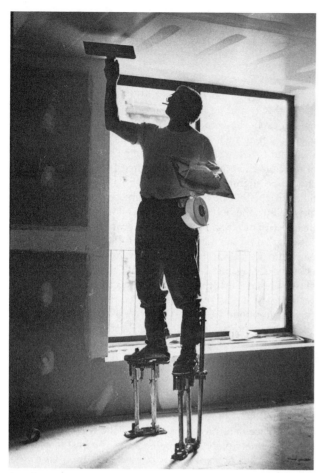

A.

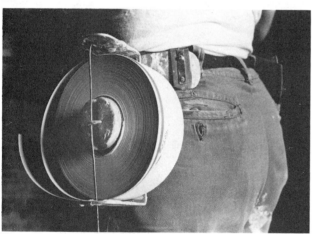

B.

Figure 15.14 After many years in the trade, this man accumulated a few devices (A) to make his job easier. Shoe stilts require practice to use safely; an amateur renovator should lay planks across sawhorses or use scaffolding. The ''hawk'', loaded with compound, is used by both plastering and drywall workers. (B) As the worker needs tape, he reels it off a dispenser on his hip; a workable dispenser can be fashioned from a coat hanger.

WOOD PANELING

There are many types of wood paneling. In contrast to the low-relief, quarter-inch hardboard paneling prevalent in the 1950s, you can now get handsome solid panelings in thicknesses of $\frac{3}{8}$ to $\frac{3}{4}$ in., and in numerous exotic and not-

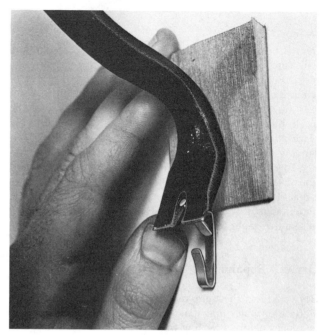

Figure 15.15 To minimize patchwork, protect the wall when removing nails.

so-exotic woods. Hardwoods cost more than softwoods, of course; and prices increase according to the thickness of the paneling. Some veneers are laminated so well to $\frac{1}{2}$- to $\frac{3}{4}$-in. backing that even an experienced woodworker would be deceived. Widths of panels vary greatly, but the length is usually 8 ft. Panels are available unfinished, or prefinished with a stain or other special finish.

You don't need many tools to install paneling: a caulking gun to dispense adhesive; hammers, nails, and a nail set; a screwdriver and screws for panels held with clips; a 4-ft level; and a voltage tester to test electrical outlets before nailing into a wall. If you use a circular saw, cut from the back side of the paneling to get a smooth line on the front; the blade cuts up toward the sole plate of the tool.

Store paneling in the house a few days before using it, so it can adjust to the house's moisture level. To maximize the flow of air around panels, put stickers between boards. Because paneling, particularly prefinished varieties, is easily scratched, leave any protective paper on until it's time to measure and cut.

Preparation

Because of the close joinery at seams, panels require a flat wall surface to attach to. You can shape drywall seams with tape and joint compound; but you don't have that option with paneling. Remove trim and other items that protrude, including picture nails from the existing wall.

With the baseboard trim off, you should be able to see where wallboard had been nailed to studs. If you can't, turn off the electricity to the area and test-drill holes to find the studs, or use a magnetic nail detector. Most framed houses have studs on regular 16- or 24-in. centers; but if your house is old and odd, locate each stud to be sure.

After you have located studs, use a level and a long straightedge to determine high and low spots. Build up uneven walls, as described in ''Furring Out.'' Horizontal paneling that runs perpendicular to studs will not need horizontal furring strips; but most vertical-board paneling

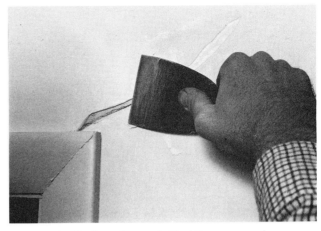

Figure 15.16 Small drywall repairs. Cut back cracks so that the compound will adhere. One coat of bedding compound (which shrinks minimally) should suffice; sand afterwards.

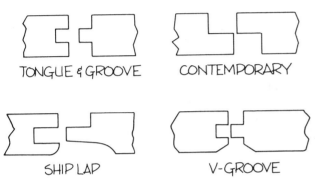

TONGUE & GROOVE   CONTEMPORARY

SHIP LAP   V-GROOVE

Figure 15.17 Panel edges.

(especially paneling that is random width) and 4×8 sheets require horizontal supports beneath. If the existing wall is fairly even and you can attach paneling with mastic, you may not need to furr out the old wall.

If you aren't sure whether moisture is seeping through an existing wall—for example, through an uninsulated plaster wall or a concrete-block basement—apply a vapor barrier of polyethylene before furring out. The poly can be tacked onto masonry with dabs of mastic. It's best to attach furring to masonry with case-hardened nails, or with bolts (Chapter 9).

Installation

Laying out and installing paneling is similar to drywall work. In an old house with surfaces that aren't at right angles make allowances when measuring and cutting. Trim

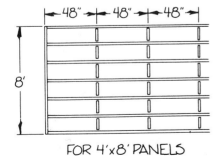

FOR 4'×8' PANELS

Figure 15.18 Furring-strip layout for differing panel types.

for length so you'll have at least $\frac{1}{4}$ in. clearance at the floor, which will be covered by molding.

Start installing panels at a corner, taking pains to get the leading edge of the first panel plumb. Use at least a 4-ft level. If the corner line seems plumb, the leading edge should be too, but don't count on it. More likely, there will be a gap in the corner after you've plumbed the leading edge. To free your hands, tack up the plumbed panel with two small brads. Then set a compass to the widest point of the gap and scribe the profile of the corner line onto the paneling.

Check the fit to the ceiling to see if you must scribe it as well. Because there may not be molding along the top of the panel, it's important that the panel fit tight to the ceiling. Most likely you will not need to trim it. After completing your measurements, pull the brads and trim the panel.

Install the trimmed panel, using colored panel nails or wire brads as necessary to keep the seams from puckering. With the first edge plumbed, you need only butt successive edges up to be sure that they're plumb too. Continue until you must fit the last panel into the far corner: measure carefully from the edge of the next-to-last panel in to the corner, taking several readings to ascertain height and width. Write those measurements right onto the wall. Trim down the last panel and install it.

The first panel on the adjacent wall should also be plumbed and scribed. After trimming along the scribed line you should also back-bevel the edge with a block plane. By forcing that panel into the corner, you'll collapse that bevel slightly, ensuring a tight fit.

When the paneling is installed and finished, use an appropriately colored caulk to fill any imperfections along the seams. Where you used brads or 4d finish nails to hold the edges, set them and fill holes with a color-matched stick filler.

Nailing. To prevent pull-out, angle all nails slightly. The key to successful nailing is to align all nails that show and to be careful not to damage the paneling when driving in those nails. Use $1\frac{1}{4}$-in. finishing nails for panels $\frac{1}{2}$ in. thick or less; for panels $\frac{1}{2}$ to 1 in. thick, use 2-in. nails. Misaligned nails look terrible, so align them exactly 16 in. apart, horizontally and vertically. Many renovators prefer to disguise nails by countersinking and covering them, with putty or by using nails color matched to paneling. To avoid marring the wood, use a nail set to sink nails. A faster method is to

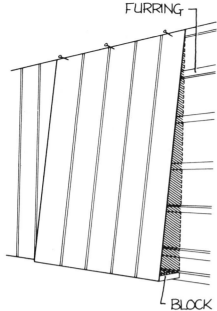

Figure 15.19 Attaching a panel with adhesive. Apply the adhesive to furring strips, tack the panel at top, and press the panel into place so that the adhesive spreads evenly. Then pull out the panel bottom, allowing air to cure the adhesive. When the adhesive is cured (see the manufacturer's specifications), press the panel into final position, and nail it top and bottom; no nails are needed elsewhere.

use a spring-loaded nail gun, which costs about $25. To use it, you squeeze a handle similar to that of a stapler; the machine automatically sets the nail.

Adhesives. Hanging panels with adhesives is not difficult, but removing the panel later will mean destroying it. The first panel on each wall may take time to install because it must be plumbed and its edge may have to be scribed; but subsequent panels are almost effortless by comparison. Using a caulking gun, apply serpentine beads of adhesive to the furring strips or to the surface of the old wall; horizontal beads 12 to 16 in. apart are sufficient. You needn't apply adhesive all the way around the sheet unless it is extremely thin and would curl otherwise (*See* the manufacturer's specifications). Never caulk closer to an edge than $\frac{1}{2}$ in.

Push the panel into place against the adhesive, position the panel, and tack its top with three or four finish nails. Then pull out the bottom of the panel and block it so the adhesive can air cure for 10 to 15 minutes. Remove the blocks, set nails at the top and the bottom, and seat the panel into the adhesive by hammering it with a 2×4 wrapped in a towel. Be careful not to mar the panel.

Miscellany. Solid-board paneling is similar to that manufactured in large sheets. Provide sufficient nailing and gluing surfaces for all joints; plumb and scribe as necessary; and use nails or adhesive to hold the paneling in place. At the ends of boards, use three finish nails on boards wider than 6 in., two nails if less. Nail tongue-and-groove boards through the tongue as you would with flooring; this technique is called "blind nailing." If the last board to fit into a wall is tight, bevel its edges slightly.

Most paneling should be finished with molding. Although miter cuts (cuts at an angle of 45 degrees) look best, coped joints are also appropriate (see Chapter 17).

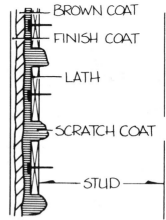

Figure 15.20 Plaster cross–section. The scratch coat of plaster oozes through the lath and hardens to form *keys,* the mechanical connection of plaster to wood.

Repairs

There's little you can do about a panel that's badly damaged; patch-repairing is out. You can try staining wood filler to a basic hue or painting wood grain in with ink, but the flaw will likely show. Replace the piece instead. Salvaging as much as you can, pry off molding and then the panel itself. If you used mastic on the original, you'll recover little. With a chisel, chip out paneling still stuck to studs. Avoid damaging adjacent panels.

For the best color match, take a piece of old material to the lumberyard. When the replacement is in place, gradually stain with a weak mixture of stain. As you approach the color desired, blend in the replacement panel with wax, oil, or varnish—whatever is on adjacent panels.

Scratches can be filled in with successive coats of shoe polish (the dyes and waxes in shoe polish are of high quality) or minimized with an oil-based stain. Always experiment on an inconspicuous section of paneling.

PLASTERING

Plaster is one of the earliest forms of finish wall surfaces, and its longevity is a tribute to its excellence. Application isn't a skill for the layman, however, because plaster sets quickly and the flat surfaces are achieved largely "by eye." *Repairs* to plaster aren't difficult, though.

The tools used to repair plaster are much the same as those needed for drywall: a screwgun or rechargeable screwdriver, 6- and 12-in. taping knives, a mason's hawk, a respirator mask. The last item is particularly important if you'll be using a carborundum blade in a circular saw to cut out old plaster, which is nasty stuff to breathe. There's a lot of grit, so wear goggles, too. For more about plastering technique, see "Stucco" in Chapter 7.

Plastering is a sequential operation: (1) nail lath to studs or joists; (2) trowel a "scratch coat" of plaster onto the lath, with the wet plaster oozing through gaps in the lath (the plaster that oozes through hardens, becoming a mechanical "key"); (3) trowel and rough the "brown" coat; and (4) trowel on a "finish," or "white coat," which becomes the final, smooth surface.

Lath can be a clue to a house's age. The earliest wood lath was split from one board to produce a zigzag effect when stretched and nailed; later wood lath is sawn. Metal

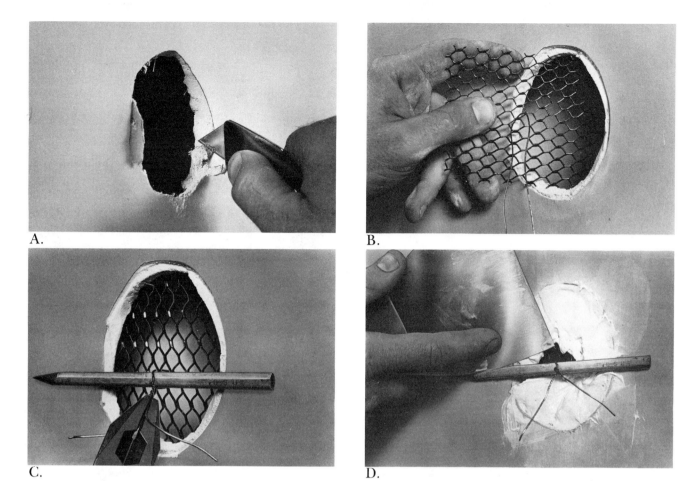

A.

B.

C.

D.

Figure 15.21 Small repairs in plaster. (A) If the plaster has been crushed, clean the hole with a utility knife or a compass saw. Cut back until the plaster is sound or until you reach lath. (B) If the lath is intact, trowel on new plaster. Otherwise, insert a new piece of metal lath, as shown. (C) Tighten the lath by twisting the wire. (D) Fill small holes with two coats of plaster. Fill the hole with the first coat as best you can, then score it horizontally after it has begun to set. (Scoring allows the second coat to adhere better.) When this coat has hardened, snip the wires holding the lath and apply the second coat.

lath is similar to wood lath, in that it allows the scratch coat to ooze through and form keys. Rock lath, a sheet material, has no such holes in it; plaster bonds with fibers in the rock-lath surface. Plaster can also be applied to plasterboard; a single coat over the board finishes the job. Usually $\frac{3}{8}$ or $\frac{1}{4}$ in. thick, plasterboard is a boon to renovators.

Most scratch coats and brown coats were durable because installers mixed animal hair with the plaster. (Old plaster being demolished is vile stuff to breathe, partly because of the hair.) The finish coat usually consisted of gauging plaster and lime; for uniformity, both components were well sifted at the factory. Scratch coats and brown coats were left rough and were often scratched with a plasterer's comb before they set completely, so the next coat would have something to adhere to. Finish coats were always quite thin, to guard against cracking.

Small Repairs

Small cracks or holes in plaster are easily fixed: use either plaster of paris or a special drywall compound, Durabond, to fill such holes. Plaster is favored by professional painters and paperers because it sets up quickly—in 10 to 15 minutes. Do not use joint compound on a hole larger than your fist. Because plaster sets so quickly and so hard, always trowel it on as cleanly as possible. To improve adhesion, add a bonder (p. 139).

Cracks. To repair plaster cracks, clean out loose plaster and undercut the cracks slightly with a penknife or a church key. Such undercutting allows the patching material to harden and form a key that won't fall out. Before patching, apply a bonding agent to bond the new to the old; Plasterweld is one brand. When the patch dries, sand it well with fine sandpaper, wipe it clean and prime the patch with shellac or an oil-based primer before finishing it.

Note: The consistency of the patching materials will vary according to the size of the crack. The larger the crack, generally, the thicker the plaster should be.

Holes. Small holes in plaster walls are not difficult to fix. If the lath is still in place, cut back loose plaster, wet the lath and the surrounding plaster well, and apply new plaster in two coats, leaving the first rough so the second will bond well.

Where lath is *not* solid, cut it out with a utility knife or saber saw, trying not to damage the adjoining lath (or you'll have a larger hole to repair). A quick way to provide backing for the repair patch is to wad newspaper between the wall and the edge of the hole. Although this method works, the patch will fall out eventually if you don't have a mechanical connection.

A better method is shown in Figure 15.21. Scrape the loose plaster from the edge of the hole. Cut a piece of metal lath larger than the hole and thread a piece of wire through the middle of the lath. Then, holding the ends of the wire, slide the lath into the hole. To hold the lath against the back of the hole, twist the wire to a pencil spanning the hole.

After wetting the lath and surrounding plaster, trowel a scratch coat of plaster into the hole; leave the plaster rough. When the coat has set, unwind the wire, remove the pencil, and push the wire into the wall cavity. The metal lath is held firmly in place by the hardened plaster. Trowel on the finish coat.

Large Repairs

A large bulge in a plaster wall or ceiling indicates that the lath has come loose from a framing member, or the plaster has come loose from the lath. Assess the problem by drilling an exploratory hole 1 to 2 in. wide in the bulge.

If the lath has come loose, push the bulge—lath and all—against the framing members. A homemade tee of 2×4s is an excellent tool for pushing a plaster ceiling back

A.

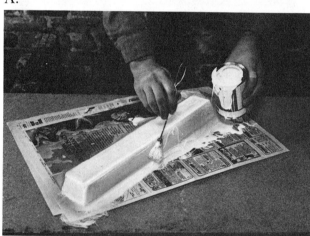

B.

C.

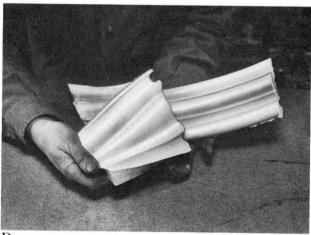

D.

Figure 15.22 Ornamental plaster work. A. When a repetitive plaster pattern is damaged, replace those sections with castings from sections that are intact. Using a 2×4 tee to keep the piece from falling, cut free a good section to serve as a model for casting. Wear a respirator mask and goggles when cutting plaster. (B) Clean any paint off the plaster section and repair any small flaws with plaster of paris or joint compound. Shellac the object so that its surface will be slick; let it dry. To make the mold, paint on a coat of RTV rubber and allow it to dry. Thereafter, alternate strips of cheese-cloth and rubber, allowing each RTV-and-cloth layer to dry before applying the next coat. (C) Peel the RTV mold off the original and pour a new plaster casting into the mold. It may be necessary to support the mold in a bed of sand first, so that the new plaster does not distort the rubber mold. In that case, get a large enough box, fill it with sand, and—before peeling the mold from the original—press the mold into the sand. That accomplished, lift out the mold, and peel the rubber carefully from the original plaster. Then place the empty mold back into the impression made in the sand. Now pour the new plaster, and level it off to the top of the mold. (D) When the plaster is completely dry, lift it and the mold out of the box, and peel off the mold. An RTV-rubber mold should last through many castings. (Photos A–D by Jeff Fox; technical assistance, Joseph Kitchel.) (E,F) When the piece is too big or too intricate to cast yourself, buy period reproductions such as the bracket and medallion depicted. (San Francisco Victoriana)

E.

F.

378 *Chapter 15 / Finish Surfaces*

into place. Chip away plaster where lath strips cross the ceiling joists and screw them to joists with washered drywall or wood screws. Screws should sink into the joist at least $1\frac{1}{2}$ in. Repair walls in a similar fashion. Then apply a bonding agent to the holes you made, and fill them up with plaster.

More often, plaster will have come loose from the lath. There's little you can do about this except chisel away the loose plaster and undercut the sound plaster slightly for a good mechanical key for new plaster. Renail lath that has come loose from framing members.

To fill a hole with plaster, undercut holes larger than a fist and apply at least two coats. Always wet surfaces first. Regular plaster of paris is alright for holes that are $\frac{1}{2}$ ft or less in diameter, but if they are larger, use perlited plaster; it's much lighter than regular plaster.

The easiest way to fill large holes is to screw a piece of plasterboard onto lath. The plasterboard should be slightly thinner than the cumulative coats of plaster, so you can finish the job with one layer of plaster.

Note: Don't nail on the plasterboard; you'll disturb surrounding plaster; use drywall screws instead.

To blend in patches to surrounding plaster walls, first trowel the new patch as smooth as possible and allow it to dry thoroughly. Then scoop drywall joint compound into a paint tray and add water until the compound is thin enough to be rolled—it should not be runny, however. Roll the compound over the patch and onto the original surrounding plaster, using a *stippled roller.* Do not over-roll the compound: you want the stippled texture to blend in with the original texture. Let the compound dry; repeat if the patch is still too smooth. When you repaint the wall, you won't be able to discern patches.

Restoring Plasterwork

To replace a damaged section of figured plaster, cast a new piece from a section that is intact. The casting can be done in one of two ways: leaving the section in place, or removing the section, carefully. In either case, an unlimited number of castings can be made from a mold of the original. Where the mold is large or ornate, support it with a mother mold so the mold won't distort under the weight of the casting material, and so any backcutting can be freed successfully.

To remove the original for casting, cut through the plaster and, in some cases, the lath. When working with plaster crown-molding, for instance, cut a section long enough to enable you to cast a complete pattern repeat. Cut an inch or two above and below the molding, so that you don't damage delicate detail when you remove the piece. The best cutting tool is a circular or a reciprocating saw with a carborundum blade. Have someone support the section as you cut it free.

To replace sections, first cut free damaged lengths, leaving the lath intact, if you can. In most cases you need only apply a generous bed of new plaster to the lath, then insert the replacement section. Wet the replacement piece slightly so it doesn't leach moisture from the bedding plaster, and hold the replacement piece in place for 10 to 15 minutes. If you don't want to strip back to the lath, chisel

and file down the damaged area as flat as possible and use epoxy to attach the new ornament to the base plaster.

About materials. Plaster is a suitable casting material in most cases—it's heavy, though. If your ''original'' object is large—for example, a ceiling medallion—consider using a lightweight polymer instead.

As a *molding* material, plaster has drawbacks. It's fine for simple work with low relief; but if the object is at all ornate, a flexible synthetic such as liquid-rubber latex, RTV silicone rubber, or moulage works much better. The price of these materials varies greatly; therefore, consult your supplier, both to determine the cost and to learn the specific properties of a material. To give the mold longer life, alternate layers of cheesecloth and molding material as you capture the impression from the original.

Preserving ornamentation. Where a plaster ceiling is ornate, and you don't want to lose it, seek out a restoration specialist: a local branch of the National Historic Trust or some other conservancy should have names. Restorationists know some advanced techniques for repairs, such as injecting adhesive behind plaster.

Plastering tips. Plaster mixed in a plastic tub is easily cleaned out. Allow the plaster to dry; then strike or twist the bottom of the tub to make the plaster fall out in chunks.

To mix plaster, pour it into water and mix it by wiggling your fingers in the bottom of the pan. Mixed that way, the plaster will set slowly (10 to 15 minutes) and will be usable longer. If you pour water into plaster, on the other hand, it will set within 5 minutes.

SOUNDPROOFING

Most noise-related problems can be solved inexpensively, without major architectural remedies. Three basic strategies are: (1) deal with the noise at its source; (2) reduce the sound's transmission; and (3) deal with the reception of the sound. If, for example, the den is plagued by a noisy fan in a heating system, you can (1) reduce the noise by re-mounting or replacing the fan, (2) pack insulation where the ductwork passes through a wall, or (3) move the den.

Within a room, use materials that will absorb sound. Such absorbent materials typically are porous or soft, for example, carpet, cork, and cloth. Dense materials, such as masonry partitions, also absorb sound well. On the other hand, hard, highly finished surfaces reflect sound waves and should be avoided if your objective is noise reduction. Think, for example, of the difference between an empty room in a new house and one filled with furniture and books.

Sound-Absorbing Materials

Sound-absorbing materials frequently used for walls and ceilings are cellulose and mineral fibers. Their application, which varies greatly, includes (1) plastic forms, troweled or sprayed on; (2) batts, such as conventional fiberglass; and (3) rigid sheet materials, such as sound-deadening drywall.

Some materials applied in a plastic form are plaster mixed with vermiculite or with perlite and a binder. Such acoustical plaster is applied in a series of successively finer coats up to a depth of 1 in. When the application is over lath, there is also a sound-deadening gain because of the air behind the lath.

Another type of plastic application is mineral, or fiberbase, compounds sprayed on with a special gun. Although multicoat applications are necessary to ensure proper drying, these compounds can be applied in thicknesses up to 3 in. All plastic forms are best left rough, for paint increases sound reflection somewhat.

Most common are fiberglass batts stapled to the studs between drywall finish materials. Two layers of $\frac{5}{8}$-in. drywall, $3\frac{1}{2}$ in. of fiberglass and the air trapped therein muffle sound effectively. You can further reduce the transmission of sound waves by screwing resilient channels to studs or joists before attaching the drywall.

Rigid sound-deadening materials are available as predecorated panels which can be attached to walls or ceilings without subsequent joint treatment. Other sound-deadening sheet materials are covered by regular drywall; still others require elaborate base preparations, as in the case of suspended ceilings.

Suspended Ceilings

Suspended ceilings can deaden sound, conserve energy, and allow the homeowner access to fixtures or pipes above.

Begin by measuring diagonally opposite corners to establish square for the room. Basically, the layout of ceiling tiles is similar to that for ceramic tile, as described at length in Chapter 16. After determining square, then measure the room to see how many tile-units long and wide the room is; if there's less than a full tile on either dimension, split the difference on either end. Determine the height of the new ceiling and run level lines around the room, to which you'll screw L-channel.

Note: The L-channel perimeter may be out of square, but the T-channel grid within is always square. After hanging channels, you will first place the main field of the full tiles in the T-channel grid and the go back later to cut down any irregular tiles around the perimeter.

Chalk-line the new ceiling height and screw or nail L-supports into place. Although attaching the supports to each stud is preferable, the suspended ceiling doesn't weigh much; a nail every 2 to 3 ft along the L-support is

A.

B.

Figure 15.23 Installing an acoustical ceiling. (A) Establish a level line around the perimeter of the room. Within that plane, and perpendicular to existing rafters, lay out parallel lines every 2 ft. These lines locate the main supports of the acoustical ceiling, the T-channels. Attach channels as shown. (B) Crosspieces snap into T-channels. Ceiling tiles merely rest on the suspended channels. (Conwed Corp.)

adequate. Locate the centers of two ceiling joists at opposite ends of the room, and mark off intervals of 2 ft along the length of each joist: panels are 2 ft by 2 ft or 2 ft by 4 ft.

T-channels, the major carrying elements of the system, cross joists at intervals of 2 ft—through the marks you just made. To position main T-channels exactly, stretch a string taut from L-supports on opposite walls. Where T-supports cross beneath 2-ft marks on ceiling joists, they will be suspended from joists (Figure 15.23). T-crosspieces clip into T-supports. As you suspend T-supports, keep checking to be sure they are level.

Flexibility is built into such systems, so you can shift out-of-square layouts slightly. You'll probably have to shorten at least one course of panels; do so in the least conspicuous part of the room.

Isolating Sound

To isolate sound, more ambitious and expensive methods are called for. A common solution is to construct double walls with a cavity of air between them. Wherever sound can be transmitted through the building structure, add resilient materials. Since fans in central heating systems are a common source of noise, attach flexible collars (neoprene or canvas) to isolate vibration along ductwork.

Air trapped in the conventional stud walls (or floors) reduces to some degree the transmission of sound, but ordinary construction can be improved simply by filling parti-

tions with fiberglass insulation. Sound will still be transmitted through studs, however. Improved soundproofing can be achieved by framing, as shown in Figure 15.24.

Metal resilient channels are commonly used to hang ceilings and even walls. The resilient channel allows the ceiling to float from joists above, so it can move imperceptibly as sound waves strike it.

Insulate between ceiling joists with R-19 fiberglass batts, nail up resilient channels, then attach $\frac{5}{8}$-in. drywall to the channels with $1\frac{1}{4}$-in. type S drywall screws. Granted, $\frac{5}{8}$-in. drywall is a bear to handle, but it isolates sound far better than $\frac{1}{2}$-in. drywall.

Double walls effectively isolate sound, but they require a lot of material and take up considerable space. In Figure 15.24C the total width of the wall is 14 in.—two full sets of studs and plates, with 6 in. of insulation between. To further deaden the transmission of sound by structures, one can cut a kerf through the flooring and subflooring between two walls. The kerf should stop short of the joists, however. *Note:* Turn off electricity when cutting such a kerf.

Resilient neoprene or foam-rubber pads above and below plates further deaden transmission, as will metal resilient channels. Any opening in a wall will allow sound to enter. If you need an extremely quiet room, space doors and windows as far apart as possible, and weatherstrip them. You should minimize such breeches in the wall as ducts, back-to-back electrical outlets, and set-in bookshelves, which also transmit sound.

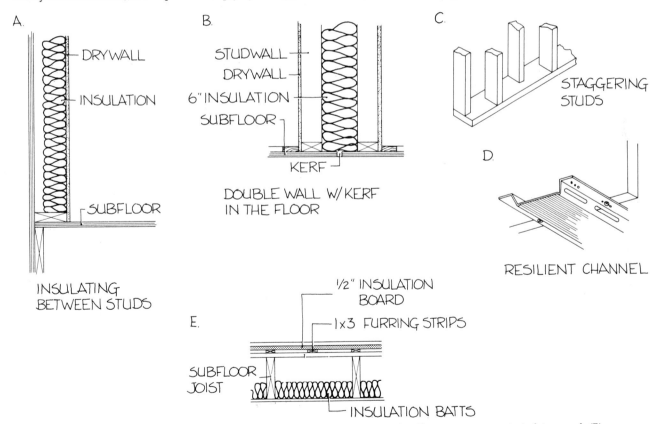

Figure 15.24 Isolating sound. (A) Insulating with fiberglass between stud walls, a common way to isolate sound. (B) A double-wall detail: effective, but expensive to construct. Note the kerf in the flooring. (C) Staggered studs are somewhat more effective than the detail shown in (A) because they increase the dead-air distance that sound must travel. (D) "Hat" channels allow the finish surface to float somewhat, thus flexing as sound waves strike—very effective on ceilings. (E) Another effective way to isolate sound from floors above.

·16·
TILING

Tile surfaces are beautiful, durable, and increasingly easy to install. In this chapter we look at tile types and trim, basic tools and safety, materials, preparations necesary for setting tile, layout, and setting tile on countertops and walls. Readers whose plans are more ambitious should see Michael Byrne's *Setting Ceramic Tile*, beyond question the best book (and video) on the subject: absolutely first-rate.

FACTS ABOUT TILE

It's no news to anyone who's ever visited a tile store that there are a lot of different types to choose from: mosaic tile and quarry tile, ruddy Mexican pavers and elegant marble, brick veneer, stone, cast cement, and so on. There are as many physical distinctions, but the most important to tile users are durability and water resistance. Except for Mexican pavers and quarry tile, most tiles are glazed before firing to make them decorative and durable; firing temperatures, times, and the clay itself determine how durable.

Tile is rated *nonvitreous, semivitreous, vitreous,* and *impervious,* according to how well it absorbs (or resists) water, nonvitreous being most absorptive, and impervious the least so. Because impervious is a commercial grade, and available in a relatively narrow range of colors and sizes, most tile used on residential floors and countertops—where they're likely to see a lot of use—should be vitreous. Wall tiles are usually semivitreous or nonvitreous. There are also solutions to seal tiles and make them more water-resistant; your tile supplier can tell you about them.

Choosing the right tile is a pleasant chore. The first criterion, cost—some tile is breathtakingly expensive—will help you narrow your choices. Availability and suitably for the use you propose are also important; quiz your suppliers. But the final choice is yours. Take home the two or three tiles you favor for a few days. Hold them against cabinets or wallpaper and imagine them multiplied across a surface. The store willing, grind them with your heel and scuff them with pots to see how durable they are; dribble water on the back to see how absorptive. How well do they clean up?

In general, smaller tiles are better suited for small areas such as counters, larger ones more appropriate to, say, patio floors. Light tiles reflect more light and make a room seem larger; dark ones, the contrary. (Lighter tiles also show dirt better.) Very vivid colors or busy designs may be nice as accents, but overpowering in large areas—but again, it depends on your taste.

The grout you choose for tile joints is also something to consider: the closer grout color is to tile color, the more subdued and formal the surface; the more they contrast, the busier, more festive and geometric the tiling will be—and the more your workmanship (or lack of it) will stand out.

Finally, consider the manufacture of the tile. Large tiles of irregular thickness can be handsome but are tricky to align and set properly in mortar beds. For that reason,

Figure 16.1 A custom tile tub and shower by Roberto Zamora, Berkeley, CA.

sheets of uniformly sized tiles attached to a backing are by far the most popular form sold, and the most appropriate for those new to tiling. Prespaced on their sheets, such tile decides the width of grout joints for you. Another very important element is the availability of trim pieces, as shown in Figure 16.2.

Trim tile is specially shaped to trim or finish off surface edges, corners, and the like, and is thus distinguished from the main body of *common,* or *field tile,* installed. (Most handmade tile is available only as field tile, which is easy enough to install on large flat areas, but requires great skill to cut, shape, and fit as trim, where planes converge.) Trim tile is further categorized as *surface,* or *surface bullnose;* and *radius,* or *radius bullnose.* Surface trim is essentially flat tile with edges gently shaped, set in a bed flush to surrounding surfaces; radius trim, on the other hand, curves dramatically and conceals the built-up bed on which it is set. Both types of trim include a range of specialty pieces which finish inside corners, outside corners, wall joints, and so on.

TOOLS AND SAFETY

Because tiling is such deliberate, methodical work it is not inherently dangerous. The few perils that exist can be alleviated by the following measures:

1. There is always water, and frequently power tools, on tiling jobs: power tools should be double-insulated and grounded with a three-prong plug. Further, electrical code requires that all outlets near water be protected with a GFCI device (p. 253). Rubber gloves will make the job safer, as

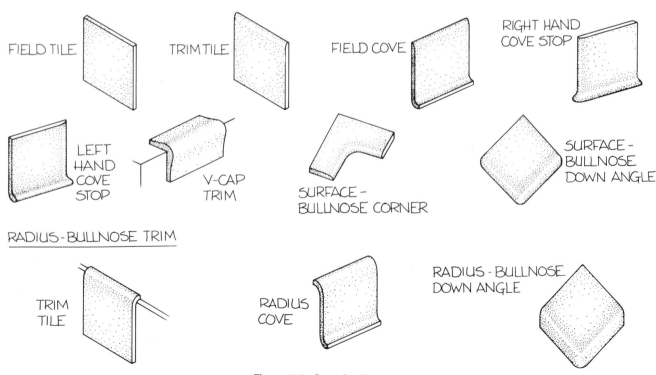

Figure 16.2 Specialty tile pieces.

will rechargeable tools (p. 44) rather than tools plugged into an outlet.

2. Rubber gloves also prevent skin poisoning from prolonged handling of mortar, adhesives, sealers, and the like. Rinse exposed skin at once.

3. Wear goggles when cutting tiles, whether making full cuts with a wet saw or nibbling bites with a tile nipper. All it takes is one tile shard.

4. Wear a good-quality mask with replaceable (charcoal) filters when mixing masonry materials, applying adhesive, cutting through cementitious materials, and so on. Some adhesive ingredients, such as toluene, are known carcinogens. If the mask fits well, you should not be able to smell anything.

5. Take manufacturers' warnings seriously. If they recommend opening windows and turning off the pilot light on a gas stove before applying an adhesive, do it. Read *all* labels before you begin.

Basic Tools

General carpentry tools can be found in pertinent chapters and in the summary on pages 42–44. The tools below are the essentials for tiling; you'll see them in use throughout the chapter.

Safety equipment, as described above: rubber gloves, goggles and a face mask with replaceable filters
Measuring and layout: straightedges, framing square, profile gauge, chalk line, tape measure, story pole
Application: notched trowel, margin trowel, hawk, rubber-faced grout trowel, beater board, rubber mallet
Cutting: snap cutter, tile nippers, utility knife with extra blades
For mortar work: flat trowels, wood floats, float strips, screed boards, a mixing hoe, mortar pans
Cleanup: two plastic buckets, a sponge with rounded corners, clean rags, plastic tarps, steel wool, shop vacuum

Measuring and Layout

Layout for tiling means establishing order and geometry where there is none, for surfaces are never perfectly flat or absolutely plumb. Layout, then, is a series of reasonable approximations. To get the most accurate readings, keep layout tools clean: wipe off mortar or stray adhesive before it dries.

A *spirit level* 3 or 4 ft long is perhaps the first and most necessary layout tool, for it enables you to assess plumb and level before you start, and as you proceed. It is also indispensable when leveling courses of tile on walls. Test its trueness periodically, by reversing its position 180 degrees, or by holding a pair of levels and comparing their readings.

Use a *measuring tape* to determine the size of the room so that you can estimate the tiles you'll need, to triangulate rooms for square, and to help lay out large areas generally. A long *straightedge* is necessary to mark layout lines on the substrate before adhering the tile, and to align tiles once they're down. Professional tile setters have a set of graduated metal straightedges, but wood will do if it is perfectly straight and varnished so that it won't absorb water.

Figure 16.3 Using a storypole to mark tile widths into a mortar bed; the double lines indicate grout joints.

A *framing square* is a quick test for square when you have, say, an ell-shaped counter; extend its use by placing a straightedge along each leg. Snap a *chalk line* to lay out the substrate before tiling.

A *story pole* may not be necessary if your job is modest, but this home-made tool makes complex layouts much easier and is invaluable if your tiles are irregular. A story pole is a long straight board (1×4 or 1×2 is fine) marked off to represent the average width of a tile *plus* one grout joint. With it, you can quickly see how many tiles will fit in a given area, where partial tiles will occur, and so on.

Where tiles abut an irregular surface, transfer its profile to the tile with a *profile gauge;* to fit sheet material such as plywood against, say, a bowed wall, use a *scribe.*

Tools for Setting Tile

Use a *notched trowel* to spread the adhesive that holds tiles to the substrate. Two edges of the tool are flat, to spread the adhesive initially; on subsequent passes, use the notched edges to comb a series of parallel ridges. These ridges allow the adhesive to spread evenly when the tile is pressed into it, thus avoiding spots too thin, or so thick that adhesive would ooze up into tile joints. When spreading adhesive

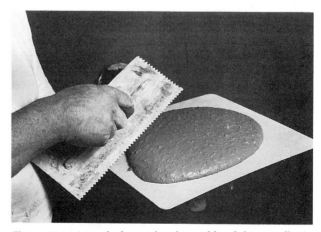

Figure 16.4 A notched trowel and a paddy of thinset adhesive atop a hawk.

with a notched edge, therefore, angle the tool face about 75 degrees to the surface so that adhesive ridges are the full height of the notches. Trowel sizes vary: notch height should be about two-thirds the thickness of the tile.

A *margin trowel* is the workhorse of tilers. It's great for mixing powdered adhesives, cleaning gunk off other tools, buttering individual tiles with adhesive, smoothing mortar, slicing excess, or sprucing up joints.

Tap a *rubber mallet* on a *beater board* (a small board backed with rubber) to seat tiles firmly once they're positioned in adhesive; also, to tap straightedges when aligning wall tiles. A *hawk* is a convenient platform when applying masonry materials to walls.

Use a *rubber-faced grout trowel* to apply grout to tiles. Actually, grouting takes two passes. First spread it generously over the tiled surface, holding the trowel face at a slight angle—say 30 degrees—to the surface. Then, holding the tool at a 60-degree angle and applying a bit more pressure, pack the grout into the joints. At the same time that you pack the grout, you remove excess, so unload the tool periodically into a bucket. To avoid pulling grout from the joints, however, make your passes diagonally across tile joints.

Cutting

Rent a *snap cutter* for making straight cuts. Cutters have a little cutting wheel—make sure that it's not wobbly or chipped when you borrow the tool—that should score the tile in one pull. Then reposition the handle so that the "wings" of the tool rest on the scored tile, and press sharply to snap the tile. For sharp clean breaks, score the tile only once. This tool works reliably until you start trimming less than 1 in.

When exposing cut tile edges (which should be very clean), trimming less than 1 in., or cutting tile that's extremely hard, mark all cuts in advance and make them on a *wet saw*. Mark cuts with a grease pencil so that they won't be erased by the water used to cool the blade; wear goggles; and use the saw's sliding tray to feed the tile into the blade. **DON'T** try to hand-hold tiles when cutting them on this tool.

Use *tile nippers* to cut out sections where tiles encounter faucet stems, toilet flanges, and the like. Nippers take some practice and a lot of patience: using only part of the nipper jaws, nibble away from the sides of a cut into the center, gradually refining the cutout. Especially as you approach your cut lines, go slowly.

If the cutout is entirely landlocked within the tile field, use a *carbide-tipped hole saw* in a rechargeable drill to cut the hole. Michael Bryne makes an excellent suggestion here: To prevent the tile's overheating and cracking as you drill through it, construct a shallow box just larger than the tile, and caulk it so that it holds water; immerse the tile in the water, which will dissipate the heat of the cutting. *Note:* A drill used in this manner should be cordless, to alleviate the chance of serious shocks.

A *utility knife* with extra blades is handy for what-have-you: marking off tile joints in fresh mortar, cleaning stray adhesive out of joints, and so on.

If you use backer board (a cementitious sheet material reinforced with fiberglass) as a substrate, wear goggles and cut it with a *carborundum blade* in a circular saw; it may take several passes, with the blade lowered incrementally. A *diamond blade* in an electric grinder is also purported to work well.

Tiling requires ingenuity. Complex cutouts in tiles, for example, may best be achieved by parallel passes with a wet saw to take out most of an area, and nippers to finish it off. Do whatever works.

Tools for Working Mortar

Setting tiles in a mortar bed requires these additional tools: Rent *mortar pans* and a *mason's hoe* for mixing mortar. Pans come in various sizes—$\frac{1}{4}$ and $\frac{1}{3}$ cu yd are common—and may be plastic or metal. In a pinch, a clean wheelbarrow will do, but make sure that it's free of debris or old cement.

A.

B.

Figure 16.5 Grouting. (A) Use a rubber-faced trowel to apply grout. Do it in two passes: first spread the grout generously, with the tool at a 30-degree angle; then, holding the tool at about a 60-degree angle, press the grout into joints. To keep from pulling grout out, make passes diagonally across tile joints. (B) When the entire surface is grouted and the grout has set about 10 minutes, clean up the excess with a clean, damp sponge. Rinse and wring the sponge often.

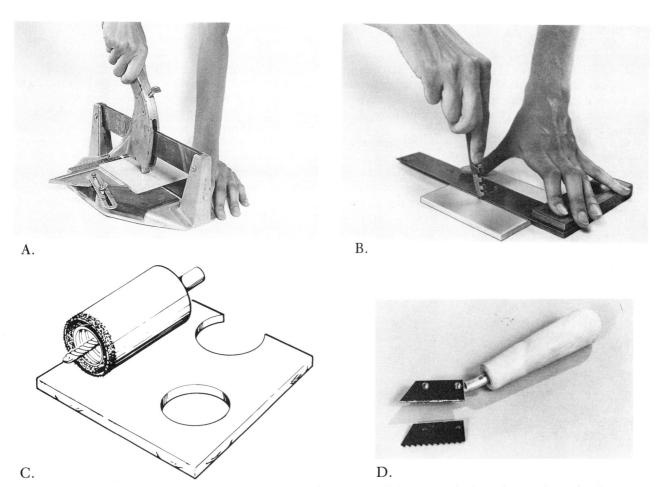

A.

B.

C.

D.

Figure 16.6 Cutting tools. (A) A tile-cutting machine: after scoring with the cutting wheel, simply press the machine's heel down to snap the tile. (B) In a pinch, a glass cutter will also score tile. (C) A carbide-tipped hole saw will create cutouts for faucet stems and the like, but you must keep the tile cool to prevent cracking. See the text. (D) A grout saw is useful to remove old grout.

Apply mortar and level it with *flat trowels;* use a hawk as a hand-held platform when mortaring walls.

When building up with mortar to make walls plumb and floors (or countertops) level, experienced artisans first set pairs of *float strips* (Figure 16.15) in mortar, to the depth of the finished bed. After adjusting those strips to true plumb or level, lay in mortar between those two strips, and then draw a straight *screed board* along the float strips, to bring the mortar to uniform thickness. (A metal straightedge frequently doubles as a screed board.)

Once the mortar is screeded, remove the strips, fill the holes, and smooth the surface with a *wood float* or a *sponge float*. The resultant surface is left a little rough so adhesive will bond well to it.

Figure 16.7 A wet saw.

Figure 16.8 Tile nippers take a little patience: using only part of the jaws, nibble from the sides of a cut into the center.

Clean-Up

Controlling the mess is half the work of setting tile: many of the materials are sticky and all are messy, so keep things clean. Avoid damage to finish floors, cabinet doors, and the like, by covering them with sheet plastic beforehand. Because masonry debris is very abrasive, vacuum it up as it accumulates.

You will also use large sponges with round corners to wipe away excess grout; square corners will lift grout from joints. After you make a pass or two and the sponge pores are full, rinse the sponge at once. The sponge itself, though, should be just damp—never wet—for this operation.

Keep two plastic pails full of clean water for the tasks described above: empty 5-gallon joint-compound pails are very handy. Use clean, dry rags for buffing grout haze off tiles at the end of the job. Have steel wool (the soapless variety) on-hand to remove dried mortar or adhesive from tools.

MATERIALS

A successful tiling job should be good-looking, easy to maintain, and water resistant or waterproof. But above all it must be durable. For as handsome as tile and its gridwork of joints are, they are fragile, wholly dependent upon the strength and stability of the materials beneath.

Anatomy of a Tile Job

A tile job is a sort of layer cake. The bottom layer—or perhaps the table under the cake—is the framing of the house: floor joists, walls studs, or counter rails must be adequately sized and spaced for the loads that follow. Exactly how many layers the cake has depends in part whether you will be tiling over existing surfaces, if the job must be waterproof or water resistant, and what new materials you apply.

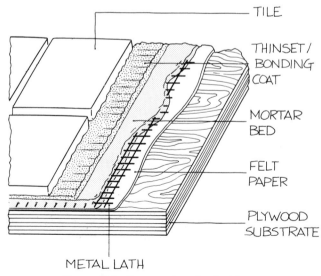

TILE

THINSET / BONDING COAT

MORTAR BED

FELT PAPER

PLYWOOD SUBSTRATE

METAL LATH

Figure 16.9 Cross section of a tile job.

In any event, the lowest layer is called the *substrate,* which, again, may be several layers thick. There may be, for example, two layers of plywood, or mortar over old tile, or backer board over plywood. The substrate is usually covered by a *membrane: a waterproofing membrane* if, say, you're tiling a shower floor; a *curing membrane* if its primary purpose is to help mortar cure slowly. Where the substrate is several layers thick, the upper layer upon which the tile will be set is the *setting bed.* Atop that, a layer of adhesive, sometimes called the *bonding bed,* which bonds the tile to the materials below. The top layer is the tile itself, and the grout that fills tile joints. There may be thin *sealers* applied to the tile later, to make it more water or stain resistant, but don't worry about that now. Moreover, don't let this plethora of terms confuse you; just keep in mind the principle of layering.

Substrate Choices

Before buying any materials, review the discussion of substrates in the next major section, ''Preparation'': in some situations, it just isn't advisable to tile. Here, we'll consider the materials most often installed as substrates.

A substrate must be securely attached to framing members behind; thick and stable enough to support loads without flexing; and when used in wet areas, unaffected by sustained exposure to water.

The premier substrate, we should note from the start, is a *mortar bed.* Plastic when wet, it can disguise surface irregularities and be shaped to a nearly perfect setting bed. Once dry, a mortar bed is strong, substantial and, used in tandem with the right membrane, all but impervious to water.

Backer board, also called *WonderBoard* (one of the more common brands), is a cementitious sheet material reinforced with fiberglass mesh. Extremely sturdy and unaffected by water, it is a good substrate to bond tile to, and especially well suited to countertops. It is usually $\frac{1}{2}$ in. thick, and most commonly available in sheets 2×8 (ft), 3×8, and 4×8, although there are half-lengths (e.g., 3×4).

Plywood is an acceptable substrate in areas that will stay dry most of the time. Because interior-grade plywood may delaminate, use only marine or exterior grades, CDX or better. You may, in fact, have to go to AC exterior, which is expensive, to get sheets free from knotholes or laminate voids, but it's worth it to avoid springy spots.

Drywall, also known as Sheetrock, is an acceptable substrate where walls will remain dry. Water-resistant drywall, also known as *green board,* was long touted for wet areas, but many local authorities, weary of homeowner call-backs and complaints, now prohibit its use in bathrooms. Green board can be waterproofed to a degree, but eventually bumps will compress its gypsum core, and its paper covering will degrade. That's not a problem where it's dry, but unwise in the tight confines of a shower.

In Table 16.1, your choice of materials is greatly simplified. At the top of each category is the preferred substrate, followed by others in descending order. Immediately below each entry are appropriate membranes (if needed) and adhesives.

TABLE 16.1
Substrates, membranes, and adhesives

Wet floors
1. Mortar bed. 30-lb felt paper or rubber membrane; EPDM or CPE rubber recommended for shower pans; latex-, acrylic-, or water-based thinset adhesive
2. Backer board. Rubber membrane; latex-, acrylic-, or water-based thinset adhesive

Wet counters
1. Backer board (preferred by most people because it's easy to install). Rubber membrane or 30-lb felt paper; latex-, acrylic-, or water based thinset adhesive
2. Mortar bed. 30-lb felt paper membrane (mortar is so water-resistant that a rubber membrane is overkill); latex-, acrylic-, or water-based thinset adhesive

Wet walls
1. Mortar bed (able to correct out-of-plumb, out-of-square walls). 30-lb felt paper membrane; latex-, acrylic-, or water-based thinset adhesive
2. Backer board. 30-lb felt paper membrane; latex-, acrylic-, or water-based thinset adhesive

Dry floors
1. Mortar bed. 30-lb felt paper membrane for curing; latex-, acrylic-, or water-based thinset adhesive
2. Backer board. Latex-, acrylic-, or water-based thinset adhesive
3. Plywood. Mastic adhesive

Dry counters
1. Backer board. Latex-, acrylic-, or water-based thinset adhesive
2. Mortar bed. 30-lb felt paper membrane for curing; latex-, acrylic-, or water-based thinset adhesive
3. Plywood. Mastic adhesive

Dry walls
1. Mortar bed (preferred where corners are out of square, out of plumb). 30-lb felt paper membrane for curing; latex-, acrylic-, or water-based thinset adhesive
2. Drywall (fine for walls that are square, plumb). Mastic adhesive
3. Backer board. Latex-, acrylic-, or water-based thinset adhesive

Curing and Waterproofing Membranes

When installing a mortar bed, first install a curing membrane (which goes under the bed's reinforcing mesh) to keep moisture from wicking out of the fresh mortar. By allowing the mortar to dry more slowly, this membrane—usually 30-lb felt paper—ensures a stronger, more durable bed. A layer of felt paper is also recommended for walls above the water line, in wet areas, and on countertops that see water (e.g., in kitchens).

Below the water line, such as in a shower pan, you need a waterproofing membrane to keep water from penetrating and rotting framing members behind. Waterproofing membranes must be impervious (i.e., capable of holding water), so most installed today are sheet rubber, for example, chlorinated polyethylene (CPE), whose seams are sealed with a compatible adhesive.

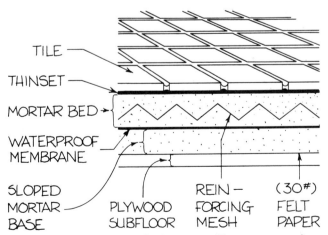

Figure 16.10 Cross section of a shower pan. Here, a waterproofing membrane keeps water at bay, thus protecting the substrate and framing. The felt paper is a curing membrane.

Adhesives

There are three major groups of adhesives (also called *bonding coats*): *mastics*, which come ready-mixed; *thinset adhesives*, cementitious powders that you mix just before setting tile; and *epoxy thinsets*, which, like most epoxies, require mixing a hardener and a resin. Adhesives come in varying quantities; have your supplier recommend the amount needed for the area you're tiling.

Spread all bonding coats with notched trowels, as described in "Tools" above. Because adhesives emit noxious fumes, wear a mask with replaceable filters when working with them. And because most are extremely volatile, observe the safety precautions cited on page 385.

Mastics. Being premixed, mastics are the most convenient of the three, but they are also the weakest. They are fine for attaching tiles to dry counters or walls—say, over plywood or drywall—but they're inappropriate where there's water, heavy use, or heat. Mastics just don't have the strength of thinsets. Moreover, they're inflexible when set, making them unsuitable for bonding floor tiles of any kind.

Mastic also requires a nearly flat substrate, for when it is applied thickly to fill voids, it neither dries well nor bonds thoroughly; thinsets are much more forgiving. Finally, mastic cleans up well with water or thinner if you clean it up right away. Once you've opened a container, however, it does not keep well: throw away leftover mastic after setting tiles.

Thinsets. Thinsets have much greater bonding and compressive strength and, being cement-based, form better chemical bonds with mortar beds or backer board. Thus they are appropriate wherever those materials are the recommended substrates, for both wet and dry areas, and floors.

Despite their common cement ingredients, however, thinsets vary widely, depending on the additives mixed with them. *Water-based* are the weakest of the group, although they are stronger than mastics, all in all. *Latex-* and *acrylic-based* thinsets are mixed with those two liquids, which impart strength, flexibility, and to a limited degree, water resistance. But their greater adhesiveness and faster setting times make these thinsets more difficult to work with. Keep tiles and tools sponged clean, for these adhesives are difficult to remove once they've dried.

Epoxy thinsets. Epoxy thinsets are the most tenacious adhesives available: they have excellent compressive and tensile strength, bond well, yet retain flexibility when dry. Unaffected by moisture once dry, they are suitable for any situation and any substrate. When in doubt, use epoxy.

Of course, there's a catch: epoxies are four or five times more expensive than other thinsets, and temperamental to work with. To their dry ingredients (sand and cement), you must mix liquid resins and hardeners, keeping each in exact proportions. Setting times are similarly exacting: if directions say 20 minutes, set your watch by it. Cleaning up before epoxy sets is imperative; some types sponge clean with water, others with solvents.

Estimating Tile

The most efficient way to estimate tiles is to measure carefully during layout, after you've prepared the substrate. But given the lead times necessary to order many tiles, it's advisable to estimate well in advance, so tiles will be on hand when all the prep work is done.

Several factors affect this estimation: tile size and shape, spacing between tiles, the complexity of the layout, and trim details. Irregular tiles (i.e., those not square or rectangular) and large tiles yield more waste because they cannot be accommodated as easily to layouts. The width of the grout joints is also a consideration, although most tiles smaller than 6 in. come premounted (hence, prespaced) on sheets. Regarding layouts, the more jogs, odd angles, and obstacles in a room, the more waste; very small surfaces to be tiled tend to have porportionately more waste. Finally, calculate the number of trim pieces separate from calculations for field tiles.

Follow this simplified method of estimation:

1. Field Tiles
   a. When determining area, bump all measurements up to the next full foot: for example, a room 13 ft 2 in. × 9 ft 8 in. becomes 14 ft × 10 ft—in other words, 140 sq ft.
   b. When figuring out the dimension of the tile unit—to divide into the area above—include the dimension of the grout joint. If tiles are individual, make a story pole (Figure 16.3) to help visualize the number of tiles plus joints for a given run. If, on the other hand, you're buying sheet-mounted tiles, which are already spaced, use the overall sheet dimension in your calculation: most sheets are nominally 1 ft square. Thus, to cover the room above, 140 sheets.
   c. Add 10% to the number above, for waste, extra tiles for future repairs, and what-have-you: 140 + (10% × 140) = 154 sheets. (If the tile is nonstandard, make this factor 15 percent.)

Figure 16.11 Glazed enamel tiles around the shower and bath, terra-cotta on the floor. (Roberto Zamora)

   d. Don't forget to buy spacers. Tiles mounted on sheets are prespaced, but you must still space between sheets.
2. Trim pieces
   a. For each distinct piece of tile trim (e.g., surface cove, V-cap trim) add 15 percent to the lineal feet of trim indicated by the layout.
   b. Order at least *two* specialty trim pieces for any one-of-a-kind pieces (e.g., radius-bullnose down angle).

Grout

After setting tiles and removing spacers, apply *grout*, a specialized mortar that seals the joints between tiles. Most grouts contain sand, cement, and a coloring agent. There are also additives to increase its water and stain resistance, strength, and flexibility. To be applied properly, grout must be mixed with liquid (water, or water with additives), allowed to stand or *slake* for a brief time, and then final-mixed to the correct consistency. For this reason it is not sold premixed, but rather as a powder; your supplier can recommend the amount you need, based on the area to be covered, the dimensions (including thickness) of the tile, and the width of the grout joint.

Order 10 percent extra grout, for repairs down the line; grout color may be tough to match several years hence.

Speaking of colored grout, it's best bought premixed and of the same lot—there will be a lot number on each sack. It's possible to mix your own colors, but hand-mixing uniform hues is difficult. Besides, there are dozens of colors available from most suppliers. Cement-colored grout is the old standby if you're unsure what color to buy. Whatever color you choose, though, keep in mind that the greater the contrast between grout and tile, the more obvious joints— and workmanship—will be.

Materials Summary

To be sure that you have the necessary ingredients, make a sketch of the layer cake you're making:

Grout
Tile, including trim pieces and spacers
Adhesive (with additives, if needed)
Curing membrane (if mortar bed)
Substrate (may be several layers)
Waterproofing membrane (if needed)

PREPARATION

To prepare for tiling, take a good look at what's presently there; remove fixtures and fittings that interfere with the layout; and build up or otherwise modify the substrate so that it is as solid, level/plumb/square, and flat as you can make it. Preparation is the key to tiling that's good-looking and durable.

Assessing the Area to Be Tiled

How plumb, level, and square present surfaces are will determine which substrate is most suitable for the tiling to follow and if, indeed, you should tile at all. To see how level the surface is, use a long spirit level or a shorter level atop a perfectly straight board.

If your project is a floor or countertop, tiling it should be no problem. Any slope less than $\frac{1}{4}$ in. in 8 ft is acceptable, because you won't notice it. Take several readings, and

Figure 16.12 To prepare for tiling, check all surfaces for flatness, plumb and, in corners, square.

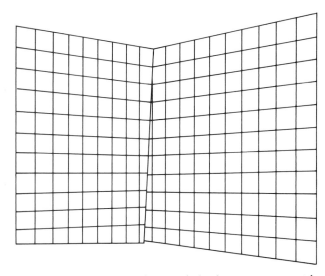

Figure 16.13 Corners too far out of plumb or square cannot be tiled successfully: their shortcomings will be glaringly obvious when tile joints converge.

note not only the overall levelness, but also any bows or dips that might be present: circle them with a pencil. For the best results, the setting bed should be flat and level. If the present surface is wildly irregular, your best bet to level it is a mortar bed. If the irregularities are slight or the floor just needs stiffening, add a substrate of plywood or backer board.

Where two or more tiled planes intersect, be more demanding in your measurements. Where walls meet in a corner, or a tiled floor abuts a tiled wall, level and plumb must be within $\frac{1}{8}$ in. in 8 ft, and the two surfaces must be square. Otherwise, you'll have unsightly tapering cuts and uneven grout lines where planes converge. The only solution here is building up both surfaces with mortar. If, however, discrepancies are much greater than, say, $\frac{1}{2}$ in. in 8 ft, get advice from a professional: walls that far out of whack may need to be reframed. In short, tiling may be prohibitively expensive.

Note that *untiled* walls which are out-of-square or plumb with tiled countertops or floors may be acceptable. You may have to cut tiles at a slight angle along such walls, but those cuts can be covered with trim. If, however, partitions or cabinets are still in the planning stage of your renovation, tell your carpenters which surfaces you're planning to tile, so that they can take special pains to frame walls plumb and set base cabinets level.

An aside: The substrate beneath tile counters or floors should be at least $1\frac{1}{8}$ in. thick, so assess the thickness of present surfaces by drilling a small exploratory hole in an inconspicuous spot. If present surfaces are less thick than that, build them up; otherwise, just tile over. Finally, when building up the floor of an appliance alcove (e.g., where a dishwasher sits under a counter), make sure that the appliance will still have enough clearance when you're done tiling.

Removing Obstructions

One of the most difficult and least satisfying aspects of tiling is fitting tiles around some obstruction in the tile field.

Typically, the thing in the way is a toilet, sink, shower hardware, appliance, or the like. For the best-looking job, remove the object whenever possible, so that tile cuts will be covered by the object when it's replaced. (Set-in tubs, by the way, are not worth moving to tile under.) For the specifics of removing plumbing fixtures, see Chapter 12; here we'll limit our discussion to details that affect tiling.

Whenever you discover deteriorated wood beneath a fixture, that's the time to repair it: cut it back to the centers of the nearest framing members and nail in new plywood as thick as that which you're replacing. Rotten wood left in place will only deteriorate, and eventually ruin the tiling.

Toilets. The chief bugbear of tiling and toilets is the floor flange atop the closet bend. Ideally, it should be flush to or sitting on the finish floor. If, when tiling, you increase the height of the floor only $\frac{1}{4}$ to $\frac{3}{8}$ in., you probably needn't worry about the height of the flange: just tile to within $\frac{1}{2}$ in. of it. When you apply a new wax ring to the bottom of the toilet horn, the wax will compress and seal the joint adequately.

If, however, you add a mortar bed or $\frac{1}{2}$ in. backer board and tile atop that, you'll have to raise the flange or you won't get a good seal. If your closet bend and flange collar are plastic, cut off the old bend-and-flange section and cement on new elements to give you the height you need. If the waste pipes are cast iron, have a plumber make the alterations: there's no place to attach band clamps adequately, and makeshift extender sleeves inside pipe will constrict flow—which is against code.

Sinks. If the sink in question is rimless (i.e., affixed under the counter), just leave it in place and run tiles over the lip (see Figure 12.55 for sink lip details). Where such sinks have metal finish rings, you can tile over those rings if you first rub them with coarse steel wool and wipe them clean with a rag dipped in vinegar. To be sure that tiles adhere to the metal, use epoxy tinset. If faucet handles interfere with tiling, remove them and their escutcheons and tile within $\frac{1}{2}$ in. of faucet stems. The escutcheons will cover the cut tiles later. If building up a new substrate makes the new surfaces too high, buy new valves with longer stems.

Remove self-rimming sinks so that you can tile right up to the rough opening in the counter. When you reinstall the sink later, lay a bead of silicone caulk along the underside of its lip so that it seats well.

Shower hardware. Because mortar and adhesive can discolor chrome, remove all shower hardware before you tile. So the exposed valve stems don't get fouled, cover them with newspaper or plastic. Tile to within $\frac{1}{4}$ in. of stems and pipe leads sticking out of the wall, and caulk the gaps so that water can't get behind the wall. Escutcheons will cover the cut tiles.

Electrical boxes. Turn off the electricity—and test (p. 235)—before working near outlet boxes. To build up an existing box flush to the level of new tiling: remove the faceplate, unscrew the switch or receptacle in the box, and screw in an *extender ring* (p. 244). Run tiles to within $\frac{1}{8}$ in. of the extended box, so cuts will be covered by the faceplate. *Note:* To prevent shorts against the metal extender ring, wrap receptacles with plastic electrical tape (p. 251).

Installing Substrates

The substrate is determined by the presence of water, the amount of use the surface will receive, and whether walls are plumb and square. Floor and counter substrates should be *at least* 1 to $1\frac{1}{8}$ in. thick, i.e., rigid enough to be tiled successfully. They should also have expansion joints and appropriate membranes.

Expansion Joints. All substrates need a $\frac{1}{4}$-in. expansion joint where they abut walls, to prevent grout joints from compressing and cracking when the substrate expands. Typically, these joints are caulked with an elastomeric substance like silicone, although expansion control joints in the middle of large tile floors are often served by foam backer-rod.

Membranes. Felt paper is recommended beneath substrates whenever areas are occasionally wet (e.g., wet walls above the water line, or kitchen countertops). It is also indispensable as a curing membrane beneath mortar beds. For a durable membrane, use 30-lb felt paper, overlapping seams at least 2 in., and bedding it all in a layer of roofing asphalt, which can be flat-troweled on cold.

Where water stands, however—say, in a shower pan—the membrane must be impervious (i.e., capable of holding water). Hence most shower pans installed today are sheet rubber, usually EPDM or CPE, whose seams are sealed with compatible adhesives. Most rubber membranes can be attached to the substrate with latex-based thinsets or other adhesives, but *check the manufacturer's literature for compatibility.*

That noted, on to our list of substrate materials.

Mortar bed. As shown in Table 16.1, a mortar bed is the premier substrate for most situations. Typically, a curing or waterproofing membrane is lain, reinforcing mesh is nailed

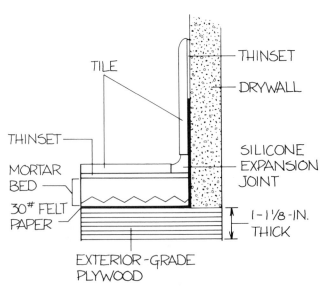

Figure 16.14 Where tiled floors and counters meet walls, they need an elastomeric expansion joint; a grout joint here will crack. In the counter detail shown, this joint is most easily accomplished by grouting the entire counter and then using a utility knife to trim out the grout before it hardens. Note that the felt paper is continuous up the wall.

Figure 16.15 Screeding creates a flat, uniformly thick mortar bed. After setting and plumbing the float strips, move the screed board in a sawing motion from side to side, dumping excess mortar intermittently (see Figure 16.25 for more of the sequence).

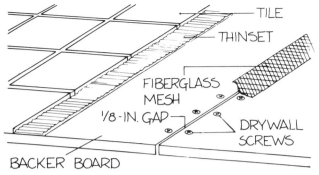

Figure 16.16 Backer board is a stable substrate for tiling, but inclined to crack if it's not adequately supported—or if its edges are butted together. Accordingly, leave a $\frac{1}{8}$-in. gap between sheets and $\frac{1}{4}$ in. around the perimeter. Predrill screws and sink them slightly below the surface. Cover joints with fiberglass mesh, and feather out joints with the thinset before troweling on the thinset bonding coat.

down, and mortar is then applied. (Note, however, that you don't *nail* mesh when there's a rubber membrane beneath it. In that case, press the mesh into an initial mortar bed, then float mortar over that.) To create a bed that is uniformly thick and flat, use the float strips mentioned above under "Tools." After setting strips in parallel columns of mud and tapping in the strips until they are level (or plumb), trowel in generous amounts of mud, and then strike it off level—to the top of the strips—with a screed board. To screed off the excess, move the screed board in a sawing motion from side to side, along the float strips. Dump excess mortar as the screed board fills.

Once the entire surface is more or less level, pull the strips, fill the voids with mortar, then smooth out the surface with a steel trowel. So the thinset coat will adhere later, next rub the surface lightly to roughen it, using a wood float or a sponge float. Allow mortar to set about an hour before squaring any outside edges with a margin trowel. Some professionals set tile the same day, but that takes a touch few novices have. Let mortar set overnight and you'll be safe.

The mortar (or mud) varies: mortar applied to walls has proportionately more cement (1 cement: 5 sand) than the mix applied to floors (1:6) and has lime to help it adhere better; it's also slightly wetter. Avoid a mix too rich in cement because it will be difficult to screed. But to be realistic, mortar is tricky to do right the first time: the right consistency is critical, drying times can be capricious, and getting it perfectly flat before it sets up takes practice. In short, there's a lot to do while the clock is running. For this reason, novices should consider hiring a pro to do a mortar bed and save by doing the tiling themselves.

Backer board. When laminating backer board to another substrate layer, glue and screw it, screwing down into framing whenever possible with drywall screws spaced 6 in. O.C. throughout the field. Construction adhesive is often used, but you'll get a far more rigid substrate sandwich by spreading a thinset latex adhesive with a notched trowel. It's also a good idea to predrill screws, especially along the edges of sheets, to prevent crumbling.

To accommodate expansion, space sheet edges $\frac{1}{8}$ in. apart, and leave a $\frac{1}{4}$-in. gap around the perimeter. Cover gaps between sheets with fiberglass mesh embedded in thinset, taking pains to feather out the adhesive so that the surface is as flat as possible. When using backer board—or any sheet material—cut pieces lengthwise, if possible: if you have 2-ft-wide countertops, for example, cut a single piece of backer board 2 ft × 8 ft rather than two pieces of 2 ft × 4 ft. There will be no waste, and you'll have one less seam to tape and top.

Note: This product is excellent to create a noncombustible surface behind wood stoves: mount it on ceramic insulators so that air can circulate between the backer board and the wall behind.

Plywood. As with backer board above, it's a good idea to laminate plywood to layers below, with construction adhesive or a mastic adhesive notch-troweled on. Check the adhesive label to be sure that it's suitable. Because plywood can expand, leave $\frac{1}{16}$-in. gaps between edges. It may also flex—which could crack tile joints—so take these precautions as well:

1. The total substrate must be at least $1\frac{1}{8}$ in. thick, as in Figure 16.14. Granted, that seems pretty thick for, say, a countertop, but those are ANSI specs and will satisfy local codes most anywhere.

2. Individual pieces of plywood should be at least $\frac{5}{8}$ in. thick.

3. Because you can't be totally sure that existing substrate materials are well nailed, nail or screw new plywood into framing members, whenever possible. If you are nailing new plywood over old, stagger edges so that they don't align.

4. Nail or screw every 6 in., using 16d nails or 3-in. type W drywall screws to reach framing members; use $1\frac{1}{4}$-in. ring nails or screws elsewhere in the field.

Sink all attachers so that they won't snag the notched trowel as you apply the bonding coat. When used as a base for mortar, plywood should be covered with 30-lb felt paper.

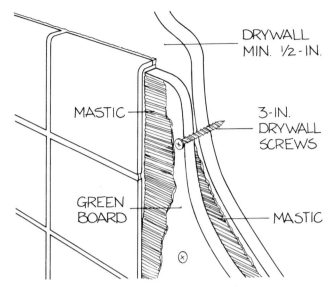

Figure 16.17 Tile over drywall. Sink the screws.

Drywall. Use $\frac{1}{2}$- or $\frac{5}{8}$-in. drywall if you're putting new over old; stagger joints, and be sure that screws sink into framing members. For additional installation tips, see Chapter 15. It's important that you tape, fill, and feather out joints so they're flat, but don't be too fussy—it'll be covered with tile.

Other surfaces. The substrates above are recommended for specific areas, as shown in Table 16.1. But you may consider tiling over surfaces already in place. That's acceptable as long as the substrate is in good repair, won't flex, and is minimally $1\frac{1}{8}$ in. thick, as noted above. Here, in no particular order, are some surfaces you may encounter:

Particleboard. Not advisable: flexes, deteriorates, may not be compatible with chemicals in adhesive.

Painted walls. Okay as long as the wall is sturdy, and not composed of a material prohibited in this list; drill a small exploratory hole in an inconspicuous place to test. Prep painted walls by scuffing with medium–coarse sandpaper and washing them well with TSP (where allowed) or some other agent that aids bonding.

Papered walls. Never an acceptable substrate: strip them.

Paneling. Not advisable, whatever its composition. Being thin, it will flex.

Tongue-and-groove, and other lumber subflooring. Not advisable: flexion problems, particularly along board seams.

Concrete. A good base for tiling, as long as it's free from spalling, flaking, and cracking. (If there are cracks presently, the floor is probably unstable.) After using a straightedge to identify low spots, fill them in with mortar bolstered with a bonding agent (e.g., latex) and screed them level. If surfaces are widely irregular, it makes sense to top it with a mortar bed.

Concrete block, brick. Acceptable substrates as long as they're also free from spalling, cracking, and efflorescence. The problem here is the irregularity of the surface: a mortar bed is the best bet.

Linoleum. Acceptable if there's a single, uncushioned layer. Otherwise, it will flex excessively.

Old tile. Tiling over existing ceramic tile is a good alternative to the mess of ripping it out, as long as the old stuff is not cracking. If it's a countertop, scrutinize the underside for water stains or rot, in which case you should put a waterproofing membrane between old and new. Scuff the tile with a grinder so that the new adhesive will bond, vacuum well, then wipe the entire surface with a rag damp with solvent. Any tile surface is irregular to a degree, however, and for that reason, you should first ''top off'' grout joints with a mortar adhesive—use a flat trowel—then, when that's dry, apply the bonding bed with a notched trowel.

Formica. Tiling over plastic laminates is acceptable as long as they're in good shape. Scuff the surface with coarse sandpaper, wipe with a rag damp with a solvent to remove grit and grease, then use an epoxy-based thinset to bond tiles.

LAYOUT

Layout is the last stage before doing; the last opportunity to take your time and think things through, without the anxiety of racing adhesive as it dries; the last chance to make changes easily.

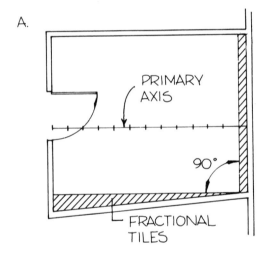

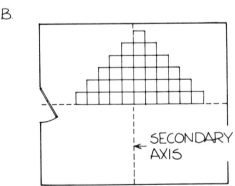

Figure 16.18 When laying out tiles, start with the visual center of the room, the wall, the counter. (A) Here, the primary axis runs from the threshold through the middle of the room, and is marked off in tile widths. Place cut tiles where they'll be least conspicuous. (B) Through a tile roughly centered on the primary axis, run a secondary axis, perpendicular to the first. Tile to these axes.

When tiling, you create a geometric array out of a void, imposing straight lines and right angles on the flat plane(s) of the substrate. The simplest layout requires at least one straight line, hereafter called an *axis*, to align tiles to. Complicated layouts require several *axes* running parallel or perpendicular to each other, to ensure that all tiles in the grid will be aligned. Alignment axes are important because they represent something real: *axes represent the middle of tile joints*, that is, the middle of the grout joints between tiles.

No tile job will be perfectly flat or aligned, of course, but by laying out carefully beforehand, you can make minor adjustments, minimize cuts, and, in general, set up a better-looking job. But most important, you will be able to concentrate wholly on setting tile when the time comes.

Four Rules to Tile By

Just as there are no perfectly flat surfaces, there are no absolute rules. Tiling, like politics, is an art of compromise. If the following rules don't quite fit, bend them:

1. *Use full tiles in focal centers.* A focal center is any area that the eye is drawn to: the edge of a counter, an entryway in a room, a center of activity such as a sink, a large window, a hearth, and so on. This rule is just common sense: full tiles look better than those which are cut down, so cover conspicuous areas with full tiles. Conversely, put cut tiles where they'll be noticed less, away from the viewer; or cover their cut edges with trim.

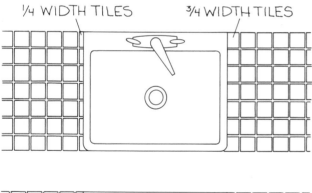

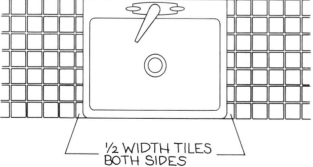

Figure 16.19 Make layouts as symmetrical as possible, especially if both sides of a surface are visible. Here, tiles can be shifted slightly so that (when cut) they will show an equal amount on both sides of the sink.

2. *Cut as few tiles as possible.* Again, common sense. Cut tiles are extra work, and they don't look that good. If you can, lay out the axis a little to the right or left, or vary the width of tile joints a little to gain some space, do so. (If your tiles are sheet-mounted, varying joints is all but impossible.)

3. *Make layouts as symmetric as possible.* This rule is both an extension and, occasionally, a contradiction of the two preceding ones. Consider, if you will, a kitchen sink: certainly a focal center, yet smack dab in the middle of the tile field. Cut tiles are almost a given. Try to adjust the layout (or the sink) so that you'll cut tiles an even amount on both sides of the sink—that will look much better than full tiles on one side and cut tiles on the other.

This is also a good rule for small counters, in which you can see from side to side without turning your head. If you must cut tiles, split the difference on each end.

4. *Don't use tile pieces half-size or smaller.* They look terrible. It's better to fudge tile joints. Or shift the layout so that you have large cut tiles on both ends rather than a row of skinny little slivers on one end alone.

Laying Out Countertops

We'll concentrate on countertops because they vary enough to approximate any situation you're likely to find in layout. In these examples, we'll assume that you've assessed the present surfaces and prepared them so that substrates are ready to tile.

To lay out, you'll need two tools. The first is a framing square, which will tell if the corners of the counter are square; if not, you'll have to cut some perimeter tiles at an angle. Note such conditions on a piece of graph paper.

Next, make a *story pole*, first described on page 385. A story pole is rather like an oversized yardstick divided not into inches, but into units that represent the width of one tile *plus* one grout joint. (If your tiles are irregular, measure several and use the average width.)

Straight counter, without sink. This is the simplest surface to lay out, for it requires only one alignment axis.

Step 1. Using the story pole, get an overall sense of the surface. Will you have to cut tiles? Are walls around the counter square?

Step 2. Choose an edge trim, as detailed in Figure 16.2. Let's assume that you choose V-cap trim, with grout joints $\frac{1}{8}$ in. wide. Place several V-caps along the counter edge, then measure back (away from the edge) $\frac{1}{16}$ in., to indicate the middle of the first grout joint. Snap a chalk line through these marks to get a layout axis. Because the front edge is the focal point of this counter, full tiles will run along this axis.

Step 3. Using your story pole, measure the length of the counter to see if you must cut tiles. If one end of the counter abuts a wall and the other is open, plan a row of full tiles along the open end, thus consigning cut tiles to the corner next to the wall, where they'll be least conspicuous. If both ends of the counter are open, and cut tiles are necessary, move the story pole so that there are symmetrical cuts on both ends. That decided, pencil the tile units along the axis.

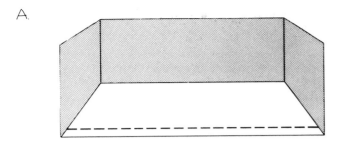

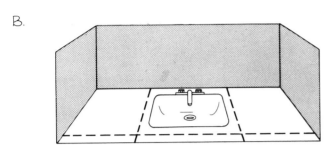

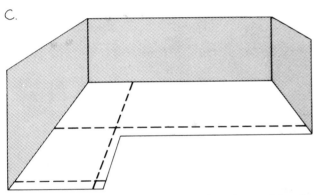

Figure 16.20 Counter layout. (A) A straight counter needs only one alignment axis to indicate the grout joint of the edge trim. (B) When there's a sink or a cooktop in the counter, you should also have a secondary layout axis on either side so that tile cuts will be symmetrical. (C) L-shaped counters will have two major layout axes running perpendicular to each other and any other lines needed for sinks, adjacent walls, and the like.

Step 4. Now hold the story pole perpendicular to the axis and measure to the back of the counter. You can pre–cut tiles, but on a counter this simple it's easier—and your measurements will more accurate—if you measure for cut tiles along the back after all the full tiles are adhered.

Straight counter, with sink. This layout is much the same as the one above, except that in step 3 your main concern is symmetrical tile cuts (if necessary) on either side of the sink. Move the story pole left to right until unit marks are equidistant from each side of the sink's rough opening; then transfer those two marks onto the layout axis running along the front of the counter. Holding your framing square perpendicular to that axis, run lines through those two marks, to the back of the counter.

L-shaped counter. On an L-shaped counter you have, in effect, two counters at right angles to each other, so you will have two major layout axes, perpendicular to each other, running along the front edges. Any other layout considerations are subordinate to these two axes, for these two

lines ensure that the two oncoming tile fields will align. Thus the front edges of the two counter sections *must* be at right angles to each other.

Should walls behind the counters be out of square—as they frequently are in old houses—you'll just have to angle cuts across tiles, at the base of those walls. The position of the sink is secondary. By all means, try to create symmetry around the sink: but that will probably mean moving the rough opening, because the tiles themselves are locked in place by the intersection of the two axes.

Counters with tiled walls behind. Whether the tile on walls behind is only a couple rows high to create a backsplash, or runs up to the ceiling, continue the tile joints established on the countertops. Where walls are square and plumb, this is largely a matter of careful measurement and plumb lines; where they're not, you may have an irregular grout line at the base of the walls.

Laying Out Walls

Never assume a wall to be plumb; always check it with a level. Where there are several walls to be considered, as in walls around a tub, check them all. To reiterate, walls out-of-plumb more than $\frac{1}{8}$ in. in 8 ft cannot be successfully tiled. They must be made plumb: by building up with mortar or by reframing the structure behind.

The layout rules at the beginning of the section also hold true for walls. Decide the focal center of the wall—most likely a window, if there is a focus—and tile to that. A wall also needs layout axes. Don't assume that a corner is a good place to start, for it may not be plumb. Intead, set tiles to *true* plumb and level, as determined by your level.

When tiling a tub alcove, start by laying out the longest wall first. From the lowest point of the tub shoulder, use your story pole to measure up one tiling unit: through that mark, draw a horizontal axis, and extend it to the end walls. (Hopefully, the tub shoulder will be level, but if not, measuring from the lowest point assures that *no more than* a full tile will be required to tile up to that line.)

Next, mark off vertical axes along the horizontal ones. Since the most visible points of the tub alcove are its outer corners, plumb them and measure in toward the inner cor-

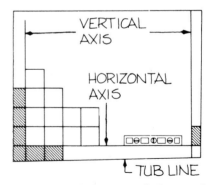

Figure 16.21 Laying out the longest wall along a tub. Start with your level: from the lowest point along the tub, measure up the height of one tile plus $\frac{1}{4}$ in. Draw a level line through that point to create the horizontal axis. Next, marking off tiles along that axis, create a symmetrical layout so that cut tiles (if any) will be equal on each end. Through those last cut-tile marks, mark two vertical axes.

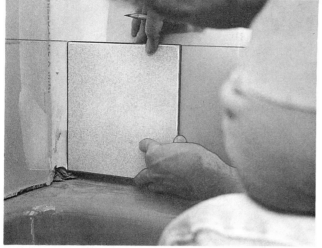

A.

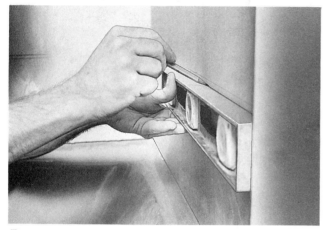

B.

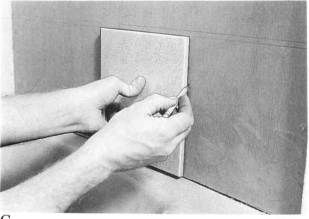

C.

D.

E.

F.

G.

Figure 16.22 Tiling around a tub. (A) Start on the long wall of the tub—it's the most visible part. From the lowest point along that wall, measure up the height of a tile plus $\frac{1}{4}$ in.—the width of a grout joint. (B) Through that measurement, draw a level line, and transfer it to all the walls enclosing the tub. (C) Lay out the long wall so that cuts are symmetrical at each end, as explained in Figure 16.21. On the end walls of the tub—where outer tiles are conspicuous—many tilers start with full tiles on the outside and work in, consigning cut tiles to the corners. (D) Check your measurements again. Here the tiler has nailed up strips above the level lines established in step B, so that he can install the field of tiles quickly. (E) After applying the bonding coat with a notched trowel, set tiles, placing spacers as you go. (F) Every few courses, check for level. (G) With planning and a little luck, even the cuts in the corners look good. After the thinset bonding coat has set, remove the spacers and grout. For more on the process, see the shower sequence in Figure 16.25. (Thanks to Clayton Wilson Construction, Brooklyn, NY.)

ners. If you must cut tiles, put them in the inner corners, as in Figure 16.22G. If you can build up the entire shower area with mud, however, you can dictate the layout and save yourself a lot of work later. Working with a cooperative carpenter, you could, for example, set up the shower dimensions so that each tiled wall begins and ends with full tiles.

SETTING TILE

If tiling seems four-fifths estimation, layout, and preparation, that's not far wrong. Don't begrudge the time it takes to plan, for if you do it right, actually setting tiles will be focused and purposeful.

To briefly reiterate the process:

1. Install the substrate, including membranes and expansion joints.

2. Mark layout axes right on the substrate. Adding layout lines to subdivide large surfaces is not a bad idea if you're new to tiling or your adhesive is fast-drying: a 10-sq ft section is workable for most people.

3. Vacuum the substrate.

4. Have all tools and materials, including cleanup rags and buckets, on hand.

5. Spread adhesive right up to layout lines—but stop just short of them, so they're not obscured with goo.

6. After spreading the adhesive initially with the flat edge of a notched trowel, on subsequent passes use the notched edges to comb a series of parallel ridges. When combing, angle the tool face about 75 degrees to the surface so that adhesive ridges are the full height of the notches.

7. Trowel on a relatively small amount of adhesive, say, 6 to 8 sq ft, until you get the hang of things. Start tiling in the cool of the morning so that the adhesive will set slower.

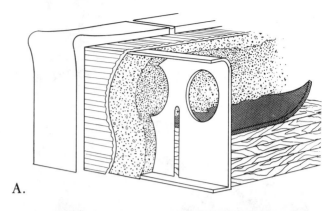

A.

B.

Figure 16.23 Counter edges: getting ready for mortar. (A) When trimming edges with V–cap or radius-bullnose trim tiles, first screw C–metal channel to the edge of the substrate. (B) When trimming with wood, tack up screed strips as shown here; when the mortar has set, replace them with finished wood trim. Note the wire mesh stapled over the curing membrane.

A.

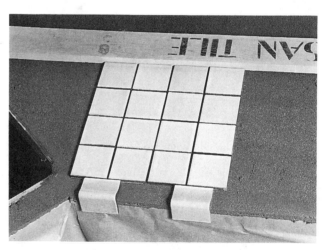

B.

Figure 16.24 A mortar-bed countertop. (A) After the mortar bed has cured overnight, lay it out. This layout is tricky because the sink sits diagonally where two sides of an L-shaped counter converge. The tiler uses two straight boards to establish his layout axes, spaced back from the edge of the counter by (B) a sheet of tiles plus a course of V-cap trim.

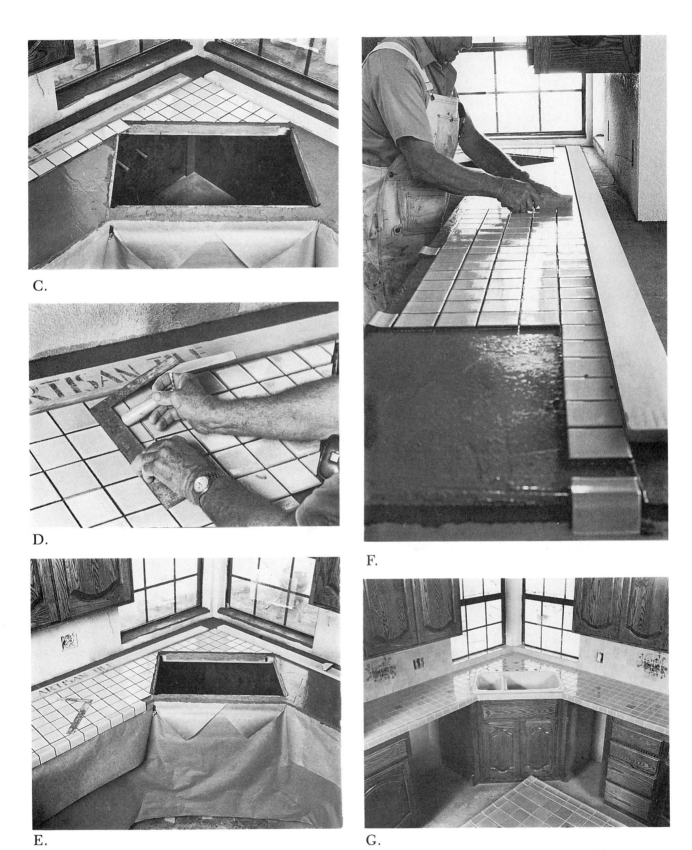

C.

D.

F.

E.

G.

Figure 16.24 (Continued) (C) Once the tiler was happy with the layout he removed the layout sheets—but left the straightedges—applied the thinset with a notched trowel, and started laying up tile in the most problematic spot. (D) To adjust tiles once they're down, tap gently, as shown. (E) One side done, except for the tiles beyond the straight edge, which will be cut and fitted last. (F) Aligning tile to the straightedge. (G) The job complete. (Thanks to Artisan Tile, Walnut Creek, CA, for the work sequence.)

8. Test the consistency of the adhesive by pressing a test tile into it and then lifting it out: its back should be uniformly covered with adhesive. If the adhesive oozes onto the face of the tile when you do this, the bed is too thick; spread the adhesive further.

9. Once you've spread the adhesive, quickly clean the notched trowel.

10. Set the main field of full tiles first, beginning along the main axes and working back. Use spacers. If setting sheet-mounted tiles, position the sheet and then press individual tiles to seat them securely.

11. Set partial tiles and trim pieces next.

12. Clean up excessive adhesive from tile faces, and any that has oozed up betwen tiles—which could prevent grout's gripping. Clean-up takes a light touch so that you don't dislodge tiles.

13. Allow adhesive to cure overnight.

14. Mix powdered grout, starting with about three-quarters the liquid you think you'll need, then gradually adding the rest slowly. Let the grout stand (slake) for 10 minutes. After that, stir again to test its consistency, adding a small amount of liquid, if needed, to make it spread easily. Grout should be a little loose so that it will stick to the unglazed edges of the tile.

15. Using a rubber-faced trowel, spread grout generously over the tiles. Then, holding the tool at a 60-degree angle to the surface, press down a bit to pack the grout into the joints. For best results, make passes diagonally across tile joints.

16. When the grout has begun to set, in 10 to 15 minutes, clean up excess by successive passes of a clean, damp (not wet) sponge. Rinse the sponge often. For best results, use a round–shouldered sponge for this operation.

17. Let the grout cure 15 to 20 minutes, then come back and buff off the haze with a soft, dry rag.

A.

B.

C.

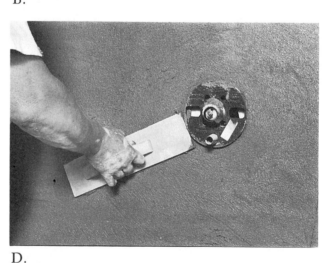

D.

Figure 16.25 A mortar-bed shower. (A) Applying the mud: it will be about $\frac{3}{4}$ in. thick. Note that the wire mesh is overlapped at seams. (B) After the wall is mudded, set and plumb the float strips. This is an important step because it creates walls plumb and square to each other—hence suitable to be tiled. Soak float strips beforehand so that they don't wick moisture from the mortar. (C) When screeding, you create a surface flush to the top of the float strips. As you draw the screed back and forth in a sawing motion, dump the excess mud occasionally. It's important to keep the screed board clean so that it glides smoothly. When the wall is flat, pull the float strips, fill in their channels with mud, and screed the whole surface flat. (D) After the mortar has set somewhat, use a wood float to texture it slightly. This texture helps the bonding coat adhere better.

E.

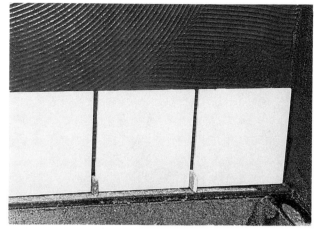

F.

G.

H.

I.

Figure 16.25 (Continued) (E) This unit is to have a mud bed for the shower pan, so it's necessary to build up the lowest course of tiles about 1 in. so that there will be enough "fall" to the drain. Here the tiler creates a sand pack behind a 1-in. lath strip. Once the wall tiles have been set, he'll remove the sand pack and build up the floor of the pan with mortar. (F) Having put the lath strip atop the sand pack (so that the tiles don't sink in), he trowels on the bonding coat and sets the first course of tiles. Note the troweled ridges of the thinset. (G) Leveling the first two courses: the sand pack is a good medium because it gives a little. By tamping down the tiles on the first wall slightly, it will be easier to tamp down (and align) the tiles of the second wall to them. (It's possible to tamp *up* tiles, but very iffy.) (H) After setting tiles in the thinset bonding coat—spread only what you can cover in 15 minutes—go back and tap them in, using a rubber mallet and a rubber-faced beating block. Keep rinsing the block, as thinset will ooze up when you tap the tiles in. Allow the thinset to cure, grout, sponge, and so on, as described in the text. (I) The shower complete, but for two tile soap dishes to come. The outer corners are finished with quarter-rounds. (Thanks to Artisan Tile, Walnut Creek, CA, for the work sequence.)

·17·

FINISH CARPENTRY

After framing walls, running pipes and wires, insulating, and covering walls and ceilings, it's time to put up trim, case doors and windows, and install cabinets. If your renovation has been arduous so far you'll get a second wind here, for finish carpentry makes a house look once again like home.

Trim does much to establish the character of a house, so respect what's there when renovating. Carefully remove (p. 153) and save trim if possible, and use existing profiles to order new. Speaking of which, get bids on custom-milled molding to match what's there. You may pay a setup fee to the mill, but the overall cost of, say, a room's worth of trim should be quite reasonable.

If you will be hanging doors and windows, see Chapter 6; our focus here is *casing* (trimming) those units once installed. Because cabinetmaking could fill many volumes, we'll stick to installation in our discussion; if you want to know more about constructing and finishing cabinets, consult technical sources such as *Fine Woodworking* magazine, listed in Appendix G.

TOOLS AND TIPS

Finish carpentry is work on a fine scale: tolerances are much closer, screws and nails are smaller, materials more fragile. Look closely. Note, for example, the direction of wood grain or delicate details along the edge to avoid splitting them during installation. Similarly, you must be willing to recut trim as many times as it takes to fit it exactly. In short, you must be patient.

Plan ahead, but don't have trim and cabinets delivered until you're ready to install them. They take up a lot of room and are easily damaged. Better wait until lumber has dried and plaster has cured so that finish wood won't wick moisture and warp.

In the sections that follow you'll find a few tools to make finish carpentry easier; for a more complete list, including safety tools, see Chapter 3. Particularly important are goggles or safety glasses, for fine work often means close attention.

Measuring

Accurate measurements require accurate tools. Start by checking your tape measure to be sure that the hook at the end is not bent, which would give false readings; use a pair of pliers to bend it square if necessary. Also important is the little slot in which the hook slides, allowing you to compensate for the thickness of the hook on interior measurements. If the hook has slammed repeatedly against the casing, the slot may be elongated: check for accuracy against another measuring tool.

Where you want the inside dimensions of an object—say, shelves inside a cabinet—use an *extension rule* (a folding rule with a brass slide in its last section). Add the measurement of the extended slide to that of the rule. A retractable tape measure also gives an interior measurement when you

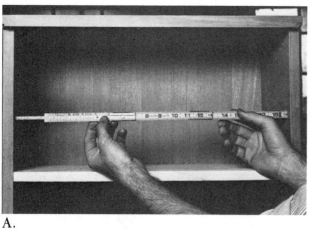

A.

B.

C.

D.

Figure 17.1 Measurement tools. (A) folding rule with extension slide; (B) depth gauge; (C) marking gauge; (D) profile gauge.

add the width of the case, but its reading will not be as accurate.

Use a *depth gauge* to make sure that holes and table-saw cuts are a correct depth. When dadoing drawer parts, for example, cut slots in scrap and take several depth readings to set your dado blades to an exact height. The slide of an extension rule is also an acceptable depth gauge.

A *marking gauge* enables you to scribe a line parallel to the edge of stock, which is important when laying out stock or, say, establishing a $\frac{1}{4}$-in. reveal around a door or window frame (p. 129).

A *profile gauge* is handy when you must duplicate a piece of trim that would otherwise be a nuisance to remove, or when flooring butts an irregular contour.

A *combination square* (Figure 3.6) is both square and (using its 45-degree edge) miter gauge; it is accurate to $\frac{1}{32}$ in.; and with its rule extended $\frac{1}{4}$ in. beyond its body, is an excellent depth gauge with which to "reveal" casing.

When you need exact cuts, use a utility knife to indicate them; granted, pencil marks are easier to see, but knife marks are far more accurate.

Clean Cuts, Close Fits

Above all, be patient. These tips may also help:

1. Keep tools sharp, whether saw, chisel, plane, or utility knife. Whenever the blade becomes fouled with resin or glue, wipe it clean immediately. A sharp tool is easier to push and thus less likely to move the stock you're cutting.

2. When cutting, support one end of the stock securely; if need be, clamp it.

3. When using handsaws, start cuts on pull strokes. As you continue the cut, keep your elbow behind the saw—which makes it much easier to push the saw straight and follow the cut line.

4. Test all power-saw cuts on comparable stock. That is, if you're dadoing plywood drawers, test the depth (and width) of your dado blades on *plywood* scrap.

5. Accept recuts as inevitable. If you're filling and painting trim, "pretty good" is close enough, but if you're doing stain-grade work, cut stock a little long so that you can recut it till it's right.

Cutting Tools

Buy a *power-miter saw* if you've at least one room of trim to do, or several casings; it's well worth the cost. The tool looks like a chop saw (p. 43), but the power miter adjusts to any angle. For best results, buy a 100-tooth carbide-tipped blade for a 10-in. saw; a 200-tooth blade for a 14-in. saw. Save such blades for finish work and they'll last a lifetime.

A *miter box* with a backsaw will also give you excellent results if you're patient; the saw should have 11 to 20 teeth.

A.

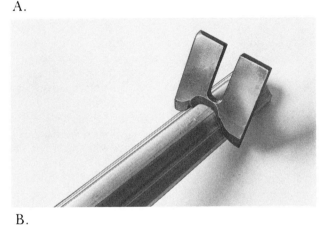

B.

Figure 17.2 Two pieces of molding and the shaper knives that molded them.

Also useful is a *dovetail saw,* a small backsaw with very fine offset teeth; and a *slotting saw,* whose kerf is even finer because its teeth are not offset.

A table saw is handy to have on-site if you don't have a power miter or if you'll be making dado cuts. *Adjustable dado blades* will give you acceptable results if you test-cut scrap first and feed the stock slowly into the blades. Granted, fixed-width dado blades with packing shims and clearing cutters yield cleaner cuts, but the cost is hard to justify for occasional use.

Yet another option is a *miter-trimmer,* also called a miter knife. The blades of a miter trimmer are razor sharp; because they slice rather than saw through wood, their cuts require no sanding, although you may still need to plane the back side of a cut to adjust a miter joint.

Shaving and Shaping

Speaking of planes, *block planes* are well suited to trim work, especially shaving end grain to make miter joints tight. To forestall splitting outer edges, always plane from an outer edge in. Where you plane with the grain, secure the stock and run the plane at a 20-degree angle to the face you're planing, as shown in Figure 17.4. The same is true when filing down an edge; at that angle, tool blades encounter less resistance and clear shavings better. To shave down larger items such as doors, use a *jack plane,* whose longer sole plate spans minor irregularities in the surface.

Figure 17.3 A miter-trimmer produces a cleaner cut than a hand-saw in a miter box; a single stroke severs the trim exactly. The tool adjusts to the desired angle. (Lion Miter-Trimmer)

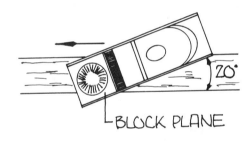

A.

B.

Figure 17.4 Using a block plane. (A) Note the direction of the wood grain before you plane; shave against the grain and the blade is apt to snag. For smoothest planing, hold the plane at a 20-degree angle to the stock. (B) To prevent end grain from splitting as you plane, clamp on scrap as shown. When possible, plane from the outside of the edge inward.

Figure 17.5 Block sander. (Rockwell)

Routers are reasonably priced, but used so infrequently that it makes sense to borrow or rent one; if you're routing something other than edges, get a router fence, too. *Wear safety goggles.*

A *block sander* is useful for shaping contours and sanding in tight places: buy one. *Orbital sanders* are intermediate in cost, weight, and power; better models sand both back-and-forth and orbitally. *Belt sanders* are great for preparing stock and stripping old finishes, but they tend to obliterate details; use them sparingly. Whatever the size of the sander, change the paper often; you shouldn't have to press down on a tool to make it work.

Drilling

Predrilling is the key to attaching trim successfully without splitting it. To predrill for nailing, select a bit whose shank is slightly smaller than the shank of the nail; drill just through the material you're worried about splitting. Where you want to draw two pieces of wood together, use screws and predrill with two bits: one slightly smaller than the shank of the threaded part, one slightly smaller than the

unthreaded part. If you want to sink the head, too, use a *countersink* or *drill-and-counterbore* bit.

Where it's imperative that a drill bit be positioned exactly, there are jigs to help. A *Portaline* will keep a bit perpendicular to the stock, as will a *doweling jig* (Figure 17.6). To position a strike plate exactly in a door edge, use a *center marker* (Figure 6.27). To keep a drill bit from skittering, prepunch the hole with a *hand awl*; if you're screwing down hinges, start holes with a *Vix bit*, available at any good lumberyard.

The workhorse of renovation is the *rechargeable drill* (Figure 3.10), and its worth is never more apparent then when you're holding up an upper cabinet with one hand and screwing it into place with the other.

Other Useful Tips

1. By finishing trim before you install it, you save yourself the bother of keeping stain off paint and paint off stain. Just touch up the finish around joints after you cut them, and wipe saw blades periodically with solvent to keep them clean.

2. If you are working with prefinished trim, do not use wood-dough-type fillers, for their solvent can partially dissolve the finish. Instead, fill nail holes with stick-type fillers.

3. If you'll be finishing trim in place, mask the area around the molding by first stapling 12-in.-wide masking paper to the wall behind. When the finish is dry, yank the paper free.

4. Don't overnail trim. Use 4d finish nails to attach casing to frame edges; 6d to 8d finish nails to attach it to framing behind walls. For baseboard, crown molding, and the like, 8d nails are sufficient.

5. Nail to framing whenever possible. To keep trim from cupping, use two nails at each nailing point; use your square to line up nails for a neat appearance.

6. Don't install casing or baseboard molding until finish floors are down. Floor sanders and carpet knee kickers can bash the dickens out of trim.

Figure 17.6 A doweling jig ensures perpendicular drilling. Here, the edge of a door is drilled so that it can be doweled and splined.

CASING A DOORWAY

Door casing (Figure 6.1) is trim that covers the gaps around a door frame; it thus goes on after a door has been hung. Most often it consists of three pieces—two *side casings* which cover frame jambs, and one piece of *head casing* which goes over the frame head—six pieces if you consider both sides of a doorway.

Three common casing joints are *mitered*, preferred for trim that is molded (shaped), because this joint enables you to match molding profiles as they converge at a corner; *square cut*, in which flat trim simply butts together; and *corner block*, a variation of square-cut that features corner blocks at top and bottom. Installation tips follow shortly, but first a few concerns common to all casings.

Assessing the Frame

Scrutinize the door frame and the finish walls around it. If the frame is not level, plumb, square, or properly *margined* (p. 93), you need to know that from the start.

Frames slightly off level or plumb can be accommodated. It's best if a frame head is level, but if it's not, align casing edges to what's there, using the *reveal* described be-

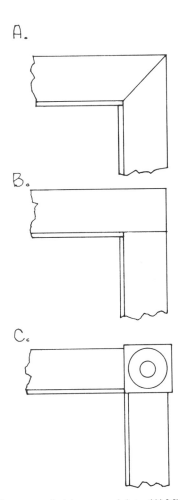

Figure 17.7 Three ways to trim corner joints. (A) Mitered; (B) butted; (C) head block. Note that in each case trim edges are *revealed* (i.e., set back $\frac{1}{4}$ in. from the inside edges of frames).

low. Do the same with side casing along out-of-plumb jambs. Like politics, casing is an art of compromise.

A door frame out of *square* is a bit more work, for that condition affects the casing joints—and the cuts required to make them. Hold your framing square to each corner and note whether it's greater or less than 90 degrees. You'll have to duplicate existing angles when cutting the tops of square-cut casing; for miter joints, you'll have to bisect those angles to match casing profiles exactly. In either case, it means recutting.

The last variable, the *margin*, describes the relation of the frame to the wall in which it's nailed. Ideally, a door frame should be $\frac{1}{8}$ in. wider than the wall is thick, and margined (centered) so that frame edges extend $\frac{1}{16}$ in. beyond finish surfaces. This slight extension permits casing to straddle irregularities around the opening. In reality, however, frames may be sunken or too prominent or, in many older homes, racked.

Prepping the Frame

Short of tearing them out, there's not a lot you can do about frames not level, plumb, or square. But casing will go on a lot easier if you build up or plane down frame edges so that they rise a uniform distance above—or are flush to—surrounding walls.

Frame edges should extend $\frac{1}{16}$ in. beyond finish surfaces, as noted above, and beveled at a slight angle away from the opening. (Newly milled frames arrive prebeveled.) The bevel is desirable but not imperative. If frame edges protrude more than $\frac{1}{16}$ in., first run a depth gauge along the frame to create a cutoff line, sink any nails with a nail set, then plane the frame down to the line.

If frame edges are level or, say, $\frac{1}{16}$ in. below wall surfaces, leave them alone. A slightly recessed edge can be accommodated by the recess milled in the back side of most casing. If edges are sunk more than that, build them up with shim strips ripped from stock the same thickness as the frame. (Most frames are nominally 1 in. thick, $\frac{3}{4}$ in. actual thickness, but measure to be sure.) Scrape the old frame so that it's flat and then glue on the strips, taking pains to match them flush to the inner edges of the frame. Tack strips on with brads if you like, and wipe up excess glue at once.

When you're finished, survey the doorway one last time for anything that might interfere with casing—shims sticking out, globs of joint compound, and so on. Trim them flush.

Marking a "Reveal"

The last preparatory step is arguably the first step of installation. After you're satisfied with the frame edges, mark lines parallel to, and set back $\frac{1}{4}$ in. from, the inside edges of the frame. The edges of the casing align to these lines and are thus recessed $\frac{1}{4}$ in. from frame faces. This detail, a *reveal*, arose from the fact that frames and casings are rarely perfectly straight. So, instead of trying (and failing) to nail such boards flush, fool your eye and delight your disposition by revealing edges $\frac{1}{4}$ in.

Note: Scribed lines all the way around the frame are neither necessary nor desirable. Instead, use the rule of

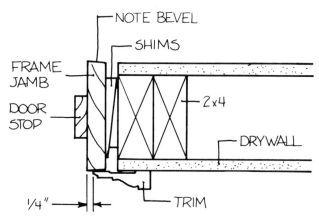

Figure 17.8 Door casing covers the gap between a frame and its rough opening. Reveal casing $\frac{1}{4}$ in. from the face of the frame. Use 6d finish nails to nail interior casing to the wall, 4d finish nails to attach casing to frame edges.

your combination square as a depth gauge: set it to $\frac{1}{4}$ in. and hold it against the face of the frame to make pencil marks or, when it's time to attach casing, simply butt casing to the end of the rule. Where head casing reveals intersect with side casing reveals, mark corners carefully, for they indicate casing joints; otherwise, a light line here and there will do.

Square-Cut Casing

Keep in mind that few frames are perfectly square. Use your framing square to determine whether corners are greater or less than 90 degrees and vary casing cuts accordingly.

1. Rough-cut casing stock a little long: measure down from the reveal marks in the corners to the finish floor and add 1 in. to side casings. (If finish floors aren't installed yet, measure down to a scrap of flooring.) Cut the head casing equal to the width of the frame + the widths of two side casings + 1 in. extra.

2. Cut the bottom of the first piece of side casing square, then align the inside edge of that trim to the reveal marks along the frame jamb.

3. Where the edge of the side casing crosses the reveal line scribed along the frame head, mark the casing with a utility knife.

4. Place the casing in your miter box and cut $\frac{1}{8}$ in. *above* the knife mark you just made on its edge.

5. Once again align the casing to the reveal and tack up the casing, using two small finish nails. Then hold the head casing in place so that you can see the joint clearly: the top of the side casing should butt *squarely* to the underside of the head casing. Note any adjustments to be made.

6. Take down the side casing and make the final cut through the knife mark you made in step 3.

7. Tack the first side casing up and repeat the process for the second.

8. With both side casings final-cut and tacked up, cut one end of the head casing square and align that end flush to the outer edge of the first side casing. Then reach across the doorway and mark the head casing where it crosses the outer edge of the second side casing.

9. Through that mark, cut square the other end of the head casing. *Note:* Some carpenters overhang head casings $\frac{1}{4}$ in. on each end, which looks fine as long as the cuts are square.

10. Now spread white glue atop side casings and tack the head trim in place. Draw the head to the side casings with a single 4d finish nail toe-nailed at each end. To avoid splits, predrill these two nails. Wipe up excess glue with a damp cloth.

11. If there's a slight gap behind the casing, insert a glue-dabbed shim so that it supports both head and side casing. Allow glue to dry, then trim the shim flush to casing. Before painting, caulk any other gaps between casing and wall.

12. Nail all casing securely, spacing nail pairs every 16 in. or so. Nail casing to frame edges with 4d finish nails; use 6d or 8d finish nails to attach casing to framing behind walls.

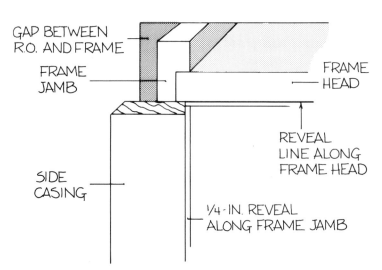

Figure 17.9 The first piece of square-cut casing cut to final length. Note that the top of the casing coincides with the reveal line scribed along the frame head. Square-cut joints are possible only with unmolded trim.

Corner-Block Casing

Installing casings with corner blocks is essentially the same procedure as that described above, except that you now have seven pieces of trim—two base blocks, two cap blocks, two side casings, and one head casing—instead of three to measure, cut, and fit.

1. Start by installing a base block, which is thicker and wider than the longer pieces of casing. Because a side casing rests on it, make sure that the top of each base block is level.

2. Align the inside edge of the block to reveal marks along the frame jamb and tack it into place with predrilled 6d finish nails.

3. Now cut side casing a little long, stand it atop the block, align it to reveal marks along the jamb, mark it with a utility knife, and tack it up as in steps 3–7 above.

4. Do likewise for the base block and side casing on the other side of the doorway, then hold the head casing across both to check their cuts for squareness.

5. Now tack up cap blocks on both sides, aligning their inner edges with those of the side casings—use a straightedge if need be.

6. Measure carefully between the two cap blocks and trim

Figure 17.10 Corner blocks with rosettes. (San Francisco Victoriana)

down the head casing until it butts squarely to the inner edges of both.

7. Nail up all pieces securely, shimming and caulking as necessary.

An explanation. After installing side casing, you might have proceeded directly to cap blocks. By aligning both side casings to a length of head casing, however, you establish a single cutoff line and ensure a visually symmetrical installation.

Mitered Casing

You can install mitered casing by cutting both side pieces first and the head last, as described above. But some carpenters maintain that the only way to match molding profiles closely is to work around the opening: begin with one side casing, cut head casing ends carefully, and end with the second side casing. That's the method we'll consider in the sequence below.

Correctly executed, a miter joint should bisect a corner, so that intersecting casings are cut with exactly the same angle. This exactitude demands persistence. Your framing square will tell at a glance whether the frame is greater or less than 90 degrees, but you'll have to work out the precise angle of the corner by making a lot of practice cuts with the miter saw. In short, use a lot of scrap.

1. Use your combination square to mark a $\frac{1}{4}$-in. reveal around the frame, as described above. Where reveals from head and side casing intersect in each corner, be especially accurate because those points also represent converging miter cuts.

2. Rough-cut the first piece of side casing, keeping in mind that its top cut will shoot up at an angle roughly 45 degrees. Measure up from the finish floor to the reveal mark in the corner and add about 6 in. to be safe.

3. Square the bottom of the side casing, then align the inside edge of that trim to the reveal marks along the frame jamb.

4. Where the edge of the side casing crosses the corner point mentioned in step 1, mark the casing with a utility knife.

5. Place the casing in a miter box and cut $\frac{1}{4}$ in. *above* the knife mark you just made on its edge.

6. On one end of a head casing not yet cut to length, cut an angle matching that atop the side casing. Miter cuts bisect corners, so the two angle cuts should be equal. (*Note:* As suggested above, work out the exact angle—45 degrees *plus* or *minus*—beforehand, using short pieces of scrap.)

7. Align the side casing to jamb reveals, then tack it in place. Hold the head casing in place, parallel to reveal marks in the frame head, and study the miter joint created.

8. If the miter joint is tight, take down the side casing and make a final cut *through* the knife mark made in step 4.

9. Align and tack-nail the side casing, and fit the head casing to it again, aligning head casing to reveal marks along the frame head.

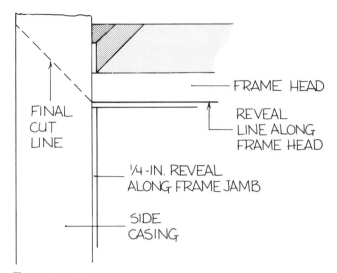

FINISH WALL

FRAME HEAD

FINAL CUT LINE

REVEAL LINE ALONG FRAME HEAD

¼-IN. REVEAL ALONG FRAME JAMB

SIDE CASING

Figure 17.11 Mitered casing is the preferred joint for molded trim. Because it may take several attempts to determine precisely the angle that bisects a corner, start with a piece of molding slightly longer than you need. The final cut line should meet head and jamb reveals where they intersect.

10. Where the edge of the head casing crosses the reveal line scribed along on the second frame jamb, mark the casing with a utility knife. Cut the head casing a little long and trim it to an exact angle.

11. Align the head casing to reveal marks and tack it up; then rough-cut and recut the final piece of side casing until its top corner exactly fits that of the head casing.

12. To prevent gaps later, glue corners and end-nail each joint with one 6d finish nail driven in each direction. The nail needs to be so long because it must pin the two pieces together; prenail to avoid splits. Wipe up excess glue immediately.

Difficult Corners

Building up or planing down the door frame is the best way to avoid joinery problems. But some joints will be problematic no matter what. For those difficult corners, some additional approaches.

If walls are too far below the edge of the frame, casing will tend to fall away and gap along joints. The simplest fix, as noted earlier, is shimming behind the joints: insert shims so that they support both head and side casings. You can also shave down the back edges of joints with a block plane, although this works better on a miter joint than on a square-cut one.

Where walls stick out too far beyond the frame, you can build out the frame with extension strips, or plane down the outer edges of casing to make it lie flat to walls. Scribe a line along the trim beforehand so that you'll know when to stop planing. But you may still have joints that gap at the back and match poorly in front.

If all else fails, use a power-miter saw to cut compound angles in the casing. To create a compound angle, you must shim beneath the casing stock as it lies against the saw fence before cutting. If the door frame is higher than the

wall, shim under the inside edge of the trim an equivalent amount; if the wall is higher than the frame, shim under the outside edge of the casing. We've saved compound-angle cuts until last because they're very exacting work and, considering the small increments you must shave off, difficult to control.

CASING A WINDOW

Casing windows is much the same as casing doors, so read the preceding sections for advice about prepping frames and specifics about installing square-cut or mitered casings. Before you put up casing, however, first install the *window stool*, which covers the sill of the window frame, and the *apron* beneath it. Stools have all but vanished from new construction, replaced by sills with integral stools, which need only be covered with an apron. But replacement stools are still manufactured for renovating windows in older houses—the focus of this section.

The stool rests on the section of the window sill that projects into the living space. Since the sills of most older windows are pitched at an angle of 10 degrees to shed water, the underside of the stool is partially rabbeted at the same angle, so that when the stool is nailed to the sill, the top face of the stool will be level. The rabbet is customarily milled at the factory, into stock $3\frac{1}{2}$ in. wide.

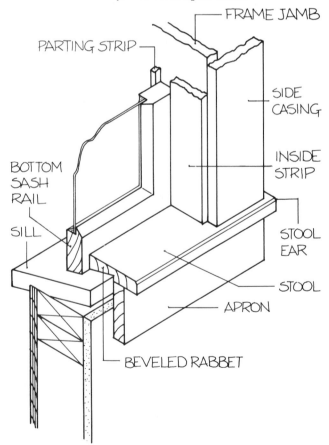

FRAME JAMB

PARTING STRIP

SIDE CASING

INSIDE STRIP

BOTTOM SASH RAIL

SILL

STOOL EAR

STOOL

APRON

BEVELED RABBET

Figure 17.12 Cross section of a double-hung window. Use 6d finish nails to attach interior casing to walls, 4d finish to nail casing to frame edges, and 4d finish nails to tie the stool to the edge of the apron. For better gripping, angle all nails slightly.

Note: If the sill is *not* pitched at a downward angle of 10 degrees, a stool will have to be custom milled with a rabbet that matches the angle of that sill.

Marking

1. Mark $\frac{1}{4}$-in. reveals (p. 407) around the inner edges of the frame except along the sill, which will be covered by the stool.

2. Because side casing sits on stool "ears," mark the width of the casing on both sides of the frame. Align a piece of scrap casing to reveals along both side jambs, then pencil light lines onto the wall to indicate the outer edges of the casing.

3. Measure across the opening, from one pencil line to the other, add 4 in. to the measurement, and rough-cut a piece of stool stock of that length. You'll cut it down later.

4. Next, transfer the inside width of the window to the stool. Have a helper butt the stool to the sill, more or less centered in the frame, while you run a pencil line out from one jamb face, then the other—onto the stool. Use a combination square to make sure that lines run square across the top of the stool.

5. You will cut along each line, stopping when the saw blade reaches the square shoulder in the underside of the stool. So you'll know when you've reached that shoulder, pencil the width of the shoulder onto the *top* of the stool, using a marking gauge or a combination square.

Cutting

6. Now cut across the top of the stool. Use a fine-toothed (11 to 20 teeth per inch) saw held perpendicular to the stock, cutting on the waste side of pencil lines.

7. Now cut in from each end of the stock, to create stool ears. Guide your saw along the shoulder lines, again taking care to stay on the waste side of the line. Clean up cut lines with a chisel.

8. The middle portion of the stool can now fit—albeit tightly—between frame jambs. Your next step is to rip down the rabbeted edge of the stool so that it will be snug against the window sash, and stool ears will be flush to edges of the frame.

So, butt the inner edge of the stool against the sash rail, then pull back $\frac{1}{16}$ in. to allow for the thickness of paint to come. Then measure the distance between stool ears and frame edges: that's the amount to remove. Rip it off on a table saw.

9. Test-fit the stool again. You are now ready to cut each ear to proper length. To do so, transfer the pencil marks on the wall (step 2) onto the stool ears. Because stool ears typically extend $\frac{3}{4}$ in. beyond casing, measure out from each pencil mark $\frac{3}{4}$ in. and mark cutoff lines across the ears. (*Note* $\frac{3}{4}$ in. is a typical extension; copy details found elsewhere in your house.) Cut and shape ears.

Attaching

10. Lightly sand and prime the stool, including its underside, which is subject to a lot of moisture. Let it dry thor-

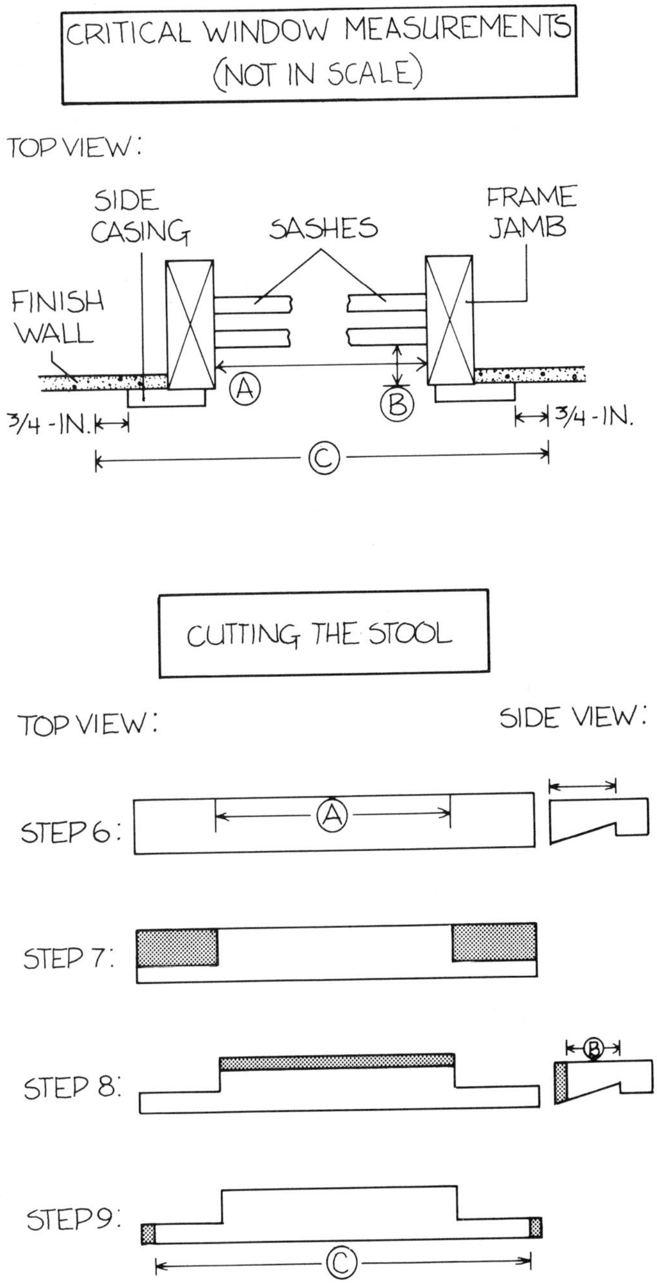

Figure 17.13 Measuring and cutting the stool, as outlined in "Casing a Window." Step 6: After transferring the interior dimensions of the window frame Ⓐ to the stool stock, cut across the stock until the saw blade reaches the stool shoulder. Step 7: Following the shoulder line, cut in from the ends of the stock to create ears. Step 8: Rip down the stock so that its beveled portion is now as wide as Ⓑ in the drawing above (i.e., when the stool is flush to the inner sash, its ears are flush to the wall). Step 9: Trim the ears of the stool so that its overall length is now Ⓒ.

oughly then tack it in place, using three 4d finish nails angled down into the sill.

11. Cut the apron, which is generally the same casing used for sides and head, although here its thicker (outer) edge is butted to the underside of the stool. The apron should be as long as the head casing (i.e., the distance between the marks in step 2). Cope each end of the apron to accentuate its profile.

12. Use your combination square to make sure that the stool is perpendicular to the window sash, then caulk along the underside of the stool to cut drafts. Butt the apron to the underside of the stool and nail up the apron, driving 6d finish nails into the framing beneath the sill. Finally, nail the stool to the apron, using three 4d or 6d finish nails; predrill to prevent splitting.

The procedure for installing jamb and head casing is exactly the same as that for doors, except that here side casing sits on stool ears. Where two windows are separated by a mullion, double-miter the top of the mullion if you're using molded (shaped) trim; with flat trim, just butt it to the underside of the head casing.

INTERIOR TRIM

As noted in the beginning of the chapter, don't have trim delivered until you are almost ready to install it. Prefinished trim will save you a lot of time and frustration; installed over painted walls, such trim need only be touched up at joints. It's also advisable to install baseboard trim after the finish floors are down: such molding will be spared a lot of abuse and it will cover wall–floor joints.

Use the longest, best-looking lengths of trim where they will be most visible. Poor-quality wood and short lengths can be patched together in inconspicuous spots. When a wall requires several lengths of trim, join pieces by mitering their ends rather than just butting them together; they'll look better and shrinkage gaps will be less noticeable. A 60-degree miter joint is less likely to split than a 45-degree miter.

It's important that trim joints occur over stud centers whenever possible. Where that's not possible, say where baseboard butts to door casing, angle at least one nail so that it catches rough framing—say, a sole plate—behind. Solidly nailing trim will keep it in place. For larger pieces of trim, use pairs of nails to keep it from cupping, nailing no closer to the edge than $\frac{1}{2}$ in. It's also wise to predrill trim when there's any question of splitting it; it's always advisable with hardwood trim.

Outside trim corners should always be mitered. (By "outside," we mean corners which project out into a room.) If you miter each piece slightly less than 45 degrees, you'll get a better fit on out-of-square corners. To improve the fit, plane down the miters. Inside corners can be butted or mitered if you're installing flat trim, but molded trim should be *coped*, as described below. Inside corners needn't be nailed, but outside corners can be drawn together with two 4d finish nails end-nailed at a slight angle; definitely predrill to avoid splits. Gluing is also advisable.

Coping a Joint

All trim shrinks somewhat. Where one piece overlaps another, resultant gaps won't be noticeable, but shrinkage on some joints—mitered inside corners, in particular—will be glaringly obvious because you can see right into the joint. For this reason, carpenters cope such joints so that their meshing profiles disguise shrinkage when it occurs later.

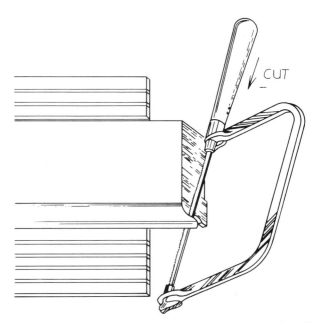

Figure 17.14 Coping a joint. After bevel-cutting a piece of molding 45 degrees, use a coping saw to follow the profile created. Backcut the profile slightly. When butted to molding on an adjacent wall, the coped joint will fit exactly.

Cut the first piece of trim square, butt that end right into the oncoming wall, and tack-nail it up. Coping the second piece of trim is a two-step operation. First cut the end with a 45-degree miter, as if you were making an inside miter joint. Then secure the end of that trim face up and cut along the profile created by the miter; back-cut the face of the trim slightly, as shown in Figure 17.14. When this coped end is fitted in the corner, it will mesh perfectly with the profile of the first piece. If you're not happy with the fit, shave it with a utility knife or recut it from scratch.

Coping requires some inventiveness. If the top of the trim is squared, shift the angle of the blade as you approach the top so that you finish up square rather than back-cut; otherwise, you'll see a gap. If the top of the trim curves like quarter-round molding, back-cutting would create a little spur that will probably break off before you can finish the cut, so don't back-cut the top at all. Instead, leave the rounded top as a 45-degree miter and chisel a corresponding miter into the top of the first, square-cut piece of trim.

Specialty Molding

Some other molding types are chair rails, ceiling or cornice molding, wainscoting, and picture molding. Cutting and installing these types is essentially the same as that already described, except that both inside and outside corners are mitered for very complex profiles, because they are all but impossible to cope.

Some moldings are quite elaborate. In general, cornice moldings are built from the bottom up, with the lowest pieces set to a leveled chalk line. Where the molding is unusually complex, nailing blocks are nailed to the edges of the studs before a finish wall, usually plaster, is troweled flush with the nailers. Not infrequently, an entire cornice molding is preassembled, using glue and nails, before be-

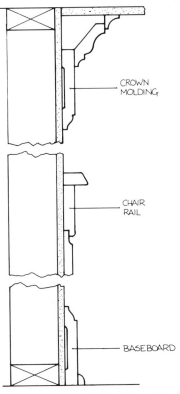

Figure 17.15 Crown molding, chair rail, and baseboard trim. Complex molding is frequently composed of several elements and often built upon blocking to exaggerate the effect.

ing raised. To fit molding to a wall–ceiling junction that may not be square, the combined total of the molding bevels should be slightly more than 90 degrees; otherwise, fill gaps with patching plaster before the molding is painted. Plastic cornice moldings are a reasonable compromise; they are much lighter and easier to install than plaster or wood and are available in numerous styles. This type of molding is usually installed with mastic paste and a few (very few) finish nails driven into studs.

Chair railings were devised to keep the tops of chairs from scraping walls and thus ruining the paint; they should be placed about 30 in. from the floor. Picture molding is usually 10 to 12 in. below the top of the wall.

You can construct a relatively inexpensive wainscoting by capping sheets of wood paneling with 1×6 boards. Cut the paneling in half, making two sections, each 4×4 ft. Paneling with vertical, regularly spaced grooves works well; it gives the illusion of individual boards. Rabbet the back of the 1×6 in about $\frac{1}{2}$ in., so the boards fit easily over the top of the paneling. If you want to ornament the 1×6 top rail slightly, add quarter-round molding above and below. Because this rail holds in the top of the paneling, panels need be nailed only minimally. Stain both rail and paneling. Where the capping rail of the wainscoting meets the jamb casing of a doorway, simply butt the wainscoting if it is thinner than the casing; otherwise, cut a profile into the end of the rail (Figure 17.16).

For wainscoting that is Craftsman-like, use $\frac{1}{8}$- or $\frac{1}{4}$-in. thick redwood plywood; place the grain vertically. Rip

Figure 17.16 Resolving complex intersections depends on the ingenuity of the carpenter. *Left:* The cap of the wainscoting extends onto the side casing, repeating the profile of the head casing over the door. *Right:* Two types of pressed hardwood trim dress up a stair wall.

Interior Trim **413**

Figure 17.17 This window seat has a 2-in. oak top and front panels fashioned from salvaged panel doors. (R. Lear Design)

down redwood lath into strips 3 ft wide, placing the strips vertically every foot or two, and in this manner, cover the edges of adjoining plywood sheets. To cap, use a 1×8 piece of redwood, which is itself capped with a 2×6 board ripped down the middle by a bevel cut. Butt the original edge of the 2×6 against the wall; the bevel cut should project into living space. Attach this beveled cap piece by nailing it down into the top of the 1×8 using 6d nails.

Another handsome, relatively inexpensive wainscoting or panel effect is achieved by using ripped-down panel doors. In Figure 17.17, the molding around the door panels was original; the builder added the quarter-round molding above and below, and a piece of 1×4 as a top rail. The top of the window seat is 2-in.-thick hardwood.

INSTALLING CABINETS

Making cabinets requires a high degree of skill and a shop full of expensive equipment, so most people buy prebuilt units. There is a dizzying array of finishes and configurations to choose from and an equally staggering range of prices, so shop around. Many manufacturers have sales in the beginning of the year, in which they cut list prices 50 percent or more. Sketch the kitchen you think you'd like, survey the space and make a detailed floor plan of existing dimensions so that a salesperson can suggest options. Such consultations are invaluable, and usually free. Cabinets arrive with everything except countertops, although doors and hardware are unattached so they don't get damaged in transport.

Cabinet Quality

Cabinet quality is revealed in the type of joinery used, materials, and general attention to details. Architectural mill cabinets, the common designation for cabinets installed in most houses, are classified as *economy,* the lowest grade; *custom* an intermediate grade; and *premium,* the best grade. The term *showcase* is a designation of fine furniture, better even than premium.

Economy-grade cabinets exhibit several telltale features. Cabinets in this category have no backs, in most cases, using the finish wall surface as backing. The underside of the cabinet, which is not treated, may warp. Although the detail of the doors varies greatly, economy-grade cabinets usually have lipped doors which overlap the face frame of the cabinet body. In effect, lipped doors cover the frame edges, allowing joinery to be somewhat sloppy. End, partition, and shelf edges may not be covered; if plywood or particleboard, edges may be unattractive and may wear.

Custom-grade cabinets are backed, and each section—as, for example, between shelves and drawers—is solid panel rather than mere frame. All edges are covered with veneer or solid-wood edging. Doors may be lipped or flush, requiring much closer tolerances than economy-grade between the edges of the face frame and the doors. Drawers have hardwood guides. Such cabinets always have backing and their undersides are sealed against warpage.

Premium cabinets are made of the best materials. All cabinet corners are mitered; all sections are separated by solid panels; all joints are screwed down and reinforced with blocks in back. Edges are more often than not coverd with hardwood edging. Detailing is left up to the customer, but only in premium cabinets will you see *flush overlay* doors. The edges of such doors are entirely over the face frame, demanding the best possible joinery and alignment.

The thickness of the elements is another indicator of quality. The information given in Table 17.1 was developed by the Woodwork Institute of California and presented in *Manual of Millwork.*

TABLE 17.1

Suggested minimum sizes for cabinet parts (in.)

Face frame	$\frac{3}{4}$
Ends and partitions	
Economy	$\frac{1}{2}$
Custom and premium	$\frac{5}{8}$
Flush overlay (premium)	$\frac{3}{4}$
Shelves	
Economy	
Solid stock or particleboard	$\frac{3}{4}$
Plywood	$\frac{5}{8}$
Custom and premium	$\frac{3}{4}$

Length
    over 3 ft 6 in., and
    adjustable
	1

Tops and bottoms	
Economy	Same as shelves
Custom and premium	$\frac{3}{4}$
Over 4 ft long	1
Backs	
Economy—untempered hardboard	$\frac{1}{8}$
Custom and premium—plywood tempered hardboard	$\frac{1}{4}$
Exposed backing	$\frac{3}{4}$
Drawers	
Sides, subfronts, and backs	$\frac{1}{2}$
Bottoms	$\frac{1}{4}$
Cabinet-door faces, all grades	$\frac{3}{4}$

Source: Adapted from: O. A. Wakita and R. M. Linde, *The Professional Practice of Architectural Detailing,* Wiler, New York, 1977).

Preparation

The key to successful installation is setting cabinets and countertops so they are level, setting cabinet faces so they are plumb, and securing all elements adequately, so they will stay level and plumb. This statement is the cardinal rule of installation; disregarding it can cause doors to misalign or, in extreme cases, cabinet joinery to separate. Because the walls and floors of an old house are frequently out of square, the task becomes one of shimming up (and out) cabinets so they are plumb and square, then covering gaps with molding.

Plumbing and electricity. Wires and pipes must be in place, and finish walls up (though not painted), before cabinets are installed. Chapters 11 and 12 discuss mechanical systems more fully, but some useful details around kitchens and bathrooms are: GFCI receptacles, very sensitive to electrical ''leakage'' and often required by code; vaporproof covers for lights, to forestall shorts or blow-outs where a fixture is located in a high-moisture or high-grease (for example, in a vent bonnet) area; and outlets high enough above countertops to avoid splashing during cleanup.

Note: **Turn off electricity** to the area around the cabinets before test-drilling for studs, sinking screws, or the like. (See p. 151 .) When roughing in systems, protect wires and pipes in surrounding walls by covering them with $\frac{1}{16}$-in.-thick steel plates.

Structural considerations. Surrounding walls and floors must be free of obstructions (except pipe leads) that could interfere with installation of the cabinets. If the slope of the floor is such that new subflooring is necessary, do this before putting up cabinets. Slightly sloping floors are not a problem; you can shim the cabinet base level during installation. It's rare, in fact, that you find conditions so far out of plumb and level that you can't accommodate cabinets by shimming them up or shaving them down.

Remove any baseboard, window, or door trim that might interfere with the cabinets. Locate studs by noting where trim was nailed, or by using a stud detector. Studs should have been installed on 16-in. centers, but test several spots to make sure they were. To make installation easier, chalk-line light lines on the walls, to indicate stud centers.

Upper cabinets are usually attached by screwing through a hanging rail at the top of the cabinet back, through the finish wall, into the studs behind. Sometimes the back of the cabinet is thick enough to support the cabinet's weight without a hanging rail. In either event, the screws—preferably type W drywall—must be long enough to sink at least $\frac{3}{4}$ in. into the studs. Base cabinets are supported primarily by the floor, though some screws go through the backs of the units and lend rigidity.

Metal Studs. There is some disagreement about the ability of metal studs to support the weight of loaded upper cabinets. Since there are numerous gauges of metal studs, use a thicker gauge when possible, for extra support for cabinets. Hedge your bet if you can, though, and don't rely entirely on attachments to metal studs. If cabinets fit in a three-walled alcove such as that shown in Figure 17.18, building

end walls with wood studs will help. If that isn't possible, you might try screwing into the metal studs *and* (an unusual move) into the ceiling joists overhead—make sure that the cabinet joinery of the top won't be pulled apart.

If the walls in back are cement or brick, the backs of the cabinets must be thoroughly sealed to prevent their wicking moisture and warping; attach the units with screws coupled with presunk plastic or lead shields (Figure 4.9). If the wall is hollow masonry—concrete block or structual tiles—use $\frac{1}{4}$-in. toggle bolts or expandable molly bolts. When installing fasteners keep in mind the weight of the *loaded* cabinets.

Cosmetic concerns. Protect the finish of your cabinets at all cost; most prebuilt cabinets come prefinished from the manufacturer, and touching up spots is tedious and rarely satisfactory. When the cabinets arrive, packaged for transport, examine them for signs of abuse or breakage. Don't unwrap them otherwise, leave them in their packing until you're ready to install them.

Once you've installed base units, delay attaching the countertop until the upper cabinets have been permanently attached. Similarly, leave cabinet doors off until all cabinets are set.

It's preferable to put down the finish floor last, to prevent damage; but then you have to cut out the flooring around the base of the cabinets. If you decide to lay the finish floor first, and thus forgo cutting, protect the finish of the floors with at least one coat of sealer; that will keep drywall dust and other debris from scouring the wood. To make moving easier, place cabinets on heavy cloth tarps and drag them. Carpet scraps are also handy to have.

A *few dont's*: (1) Don't use nails to attach anything other than molding; use only *screws* to hang cabinets. (2) Don't use cabinets or countertops as sawhorses; you'll ruin them. (3) Don't leave cabinets uncovered when you leave the site; an unwitting tradesperson might damage them.

Upper Cabinets

If you purchase both upper and base cabinets, install the uppers first; they're much easier to hang if you're not leaning over a base cabinet. Have a small step-stool handy, too: it's helpful to be two feet taller when you screw down upper cabinets.

Getting ready. Use a long straightedge to see how flat walls are, shimming up low spots as necessary. Otherwise, put the backs of upper cabinets flush to the wall.

If you haven't already done so, locate stud centers and pencil them lightly onto the wall. To get a rough idea of how far the bank of cabinets will run, measure the width of each unit and pencil the total onto the wall. Finally, snap a level chalk line onto the wall to indicate the lower edge of the cabinets. Upper cabinets at least 16 in. above finished counters gives you enough height to operate most appliances; you'll find other standard dimensions in Figure 2.10. But suit yourself: consider also your height and reach, the height of upper cabinets, whether they'll run all the way to the ceiling or have open storage above.

To make installation easier, attach a straight 1 × 4 *ledger strip* beneath that chalk line; you can use double-headed nails, or screws for a better grip, but predrill either if you've

A.

C.

B.

D.

Figure 17.18 Hanging upper cabinets. (A) Determine the height of the upper cabinets and draw level lines to indicate the bottom of the units. Screw up a ledger strip below those lines to rest cabinets on, or cut pieces of scrap as shown to support the underside of the cabinets temporarily. Note also the location of studs. (B) Align the bottom cabinet to the line you drew on the wall, and check cabinet sides for plumb. (C) When you're satisfied with the position of the first cabinet, screw the unit to the wall. (D) Once you've temporarily hanged the upper cabinets, go back and align their face frames, shimming behind them until they're flush to a common plane. (Thanks to Larry Mead, Brooklyn, NY.)

got plaster walls which might crack. By setting cabinets on the ledger strip you can install them single-handedly, assured that their bottoms will line up level.

Hanging cabinets. If the bank of cabinets will run to an oncoming wall, start installing in that corner; if both ends are open, begin at either end. If the oncoming wall is plumb, butt the first cabinet to it; otherwise, stop about 2 in. short of the wall and cover the gap later with a piece of trim color-matched to cabinet frames.

After tentatively positioning the first upper cabinet, take it down and predrill screw holes into the mounting rail(s) at the back. Because you want to screw into studs, transfer stud marks from the wall to the backs of all cabinets at this time. If cabinets have both upper and lower mount-

ing rails, predrill both, but screw down only upper rails initially; you may need to shim behind lower ones later. Start a screw in each hole, using Type W drywall screws 2 to $2\frac{1}{2}$ in. long.

Set the first cabinet atop the ledger strip and screw it just tight enough to hold it up. Ideally, you should mount each cabinet section to two studs, but if that's not possible, one stud is adequate. You'll spread the load to other studs when you join adjacent face frames. Don't overtighten screws: you may need to shim behind the top later, and in any event, screwing down too hard can pull loose the back of the cabinet.

Check the fit of this first cabinet. Is its back flush to the wall? Is the face frame plumb? As long as the wall is flat (not bowed) and cabinet faces line up, you don't need to shim.

Figure 17.19 When you've aligned the face frames, clamp them so that you can predrill and screw them together. Use scrap so that you don't mar the frames.

Hang the next cabinet the same way. Predrill its mounting rail, set it on the ledger strip, slide it tight to the first cabinet, screw its top rail to the studs behind, then align the two face frames. This is an important juncture: ideally, the tops and bottoms of frames should line up, and adjacent edges should be flush. If it's necessary to back out a top-rail screw to align the faces, be sure to shim behind it so that it's solidly backed. Repeat this operation for successive upper cabinets until all are aligned; it will take some time.

Joining the face frames. Once frames are correctly positioned, some carpenters now screw together the face frames at the top. We'd recommend that you remove the ledger strip first, because you'll be able to adjust cabinet bottoms better that way. If there's one place where face frames *must* align, it's along the bottom edge, which is right at eye level. So remove the ledger strip and shim as necessary behind the bottoms of the cabinets, taking special pains to shim all joints where cabinets meet, so adjacent face frames will be shimmed to the same height.

When faces are flush and bottom corners aligned, clamp the frames so that they'll stay where you want them and then screw them together. Because face frames are usually constructed from hardwood $1\frac{1}{2}$ to $1\frac{3}{4}$ in. wide, use Type W drywall screws $2\frac{1}{2}$ in. long so you can sink the screw head $\frac{1}{2}$ in. Most upper cabinets are 32 to 36 in. high, so join each frame joint with three or four screws: one 2 in. from the top, one 2 in. from the bottom, the remaining screws spaced evenly between. Use two different drill bits to predrill screw holes: one slightly smaller than the shank of the screw, drilled into both frame edges; the other bit the size of the screw head, drilled $\frac{1}{2}$ in. deep.

When all the face frames are joined, screw the bottom mounting rails to the wall; if there are no bottom rails, just screw through cabinet backs—they're strong enough to take it. Remember to shim behind any part of the back not flush to the wall—but, again, don't overtighten. Later, trim the shims and cover the joint with quarter-round molding, and fill the holes made by the ledger strip.

Base Cabinets

Setting bases takes ingenuity, for you've got to reconcile essentially square cabinets to walls not plumb and floors not level. Happily, there are tricks.

Layout. As you did with upper cabinets, begin by surveying what's there—high spots, low spots, level, and plumb. Then take the cardboard packaging off individual sections and measure them.

The first thing you'll notice is that all base cabinets are not created equal: some may be taller, for starters. The taller ones are end sections, whose sides run the full distance to the floor because they've got an integral *kickspace* on the bottom. The other units have unfinished sides and are not as tall because they're designed to sit on a *plinth*, a simple wood frame which you construct.

(Before we continue with layout, a few words about plinths and kickspaces. Kickspaces are indentations at the bottom of cabinets, which provide room for your toes so that you can belly up to cabinets when preparing food or washing dishes. Otherwise, you'd have to bend over to reach countertops, a sure recipe for backaches. Either the kick-space is built into the base of the unit, as it is with end cabinets, or it is created by supporting units on plinths set back from the face frame.)

Mark base cabinet widths onto your walls to get a sense of where they'll begin and end, and pencil on the floor a line to which you'll align kick plates later. If there is a single straight run of base cabinets, simply start with one end cabinet and work on down the line, much as you did with uppers. If the layout is L-shaped, things are a bit more interesting: you can still start wherever you like, but you may want to set the cabinet in the corner first, for it is there that all cabinets converge, and there their faces and tops must match up.

To simplify explanations, however, we'll assume that the configuration is a straight bank of cabinets and begin with an end section.

Fitting an end cabinet. Draw a plumb line onto the wall to indicate the beginning point, then set an end cabinet in place so that its back is flush against the wall. Have a look. If the end of the cabinet aligns to that line, the back is flush to the wall, and the face frame is plumb, you don't have to do a thing. (It happens!)

More likely, you'll need to shim beneath the cabinet to make it plumb, side to side and front to back. Do so, keeping the back of the unit as close as possible to the wall. Once all faces of the cabinet are plumbed, there will probably be a gap between the cabinet back and the wall. To get rid of this gap so that the cabinet is snug against the wall, you'll need to trim the back edges of the end panels.

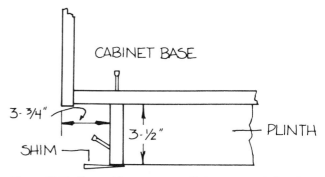

Figure 17.20 To provide toe-room so that you can get close to a counter, extend the overhang of the countertop or, as is more commonly done, recess the plinth beneath base cabinets.

Base cabinets are built to be trimmed. Typically, there's a $\frac{1}{4}$-in. back panel set in a $\frac{3}{8}$-in. rabbet, leaving a $\frac{1}{8}$-in. lip to shave if you need to. So push your cabinet back as close to the wall as you can get it, hold a lumber pencil flat to the wall, and run the pencil point along the end panel, thus transferring the contour of the wall to the back edges of the cabinet. If the widest gap at the back is greater than the $\frac{1}{8}$-in. lip, shave down until you come to the back panels themselves—and stop. You can cover any gaps along the wall later with a piece of quarter-round.

Shave down the bottom of the cabinet, too. You could leave shims in place, but there's no way to hide them beneath an end cabinet sitting directly on a finished floor. Besides, you want this cabinet well supported. Because end cabinets sit on an integral plinth $3\frac{1}{2}$ in. high, you can trim it down as much as you need. Use a block plane or a belt sander to cut down cabinet backs and bottom to "shave lines."

Shave, check for plumb and shave again until it's a good fit. At this point you're ready to secure the cabinet, but delay doing so until you've checked the height of subsequent cabinets.

Setting subsequent cabinets. Next construct the plinth on which subsequent cabinets will sit. Use 1×4 stock set on-edge, because middle cabinets are typically $3\frac{1}{2}$ in. shorter than end cabinets—but measure the height of the cabinet you just set, to be sure. You may save yourself some time later by ripping down 1×4s now and building a shallower plinth. Use 8d common nails to assemble the plinth, end-nailing *spreaders* to the 1×4s running the length of the base; space spreaders every 16 in. or so. It's also desirable to put spreaders beneath every cabinet juncture, but not always possible. From front to back, build the plinth about $\frac{1}{4}$ in. shy to accommodate the thickness of a kick strip and to give yourself a little room for adjustment.

Put the plinth in place, shim it to level, set cabinets atop it, and use a long level to see how heights compare to the top of the end cabinet. Shim up low spots. If the bank of cabinets is too high, disassemble and rip down plinth parts on a table saw, reassembling them again with drywall screws. Shim the new plinth as needed, set the cabinets back on, check height again. If all is well, set the cabinets aside that you can toe-nail the plinth to the subflooring, using 8d common (headed) nails. Here your concern is strength, not appearances, because you'll cover the plinth with a kick strip later. Predrill so you don't split the plinth.

Now secure the end cabinet by screwing through its mounting rails (or back) into studs; use type W drywall screws. Shim minimally behind its back—just enough to keep the panel from flexing when you screw it down. Use 8d finish nails to toe-nail the base of the unit to the subflooring, to keep the cabinet from migrating. As they will be visible, you'll set and fill these nails later.

Now secure the other cabinets one at a time, aligning face frames and screwing them together as you did for upper cabinets. Here, matching the *tops* of frames is the critical juncture, for they are closer to the eye than those at the bottom. There should be only minor adjustments necessary to bring frames in line, say, a shim between a cabinet and the top of the plinth. If any cabinets are high because they

A

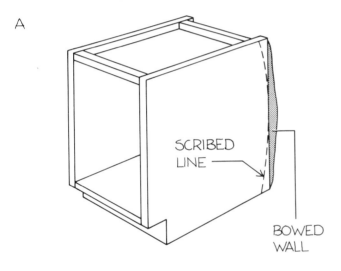

B

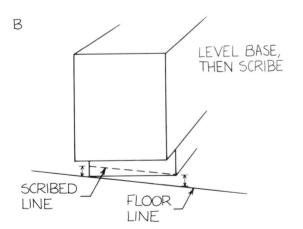

Figure 17.21 Fitting the end cabinet. (A) Level and plumb the cabinet with shims and push the cabinet back as close to the wall as possible. Then, using a scriber or a lumber pencil atop a block of scrap, transfer the contour of the wall to the back edges of the cabinet. Using a saber saw or a block plane, cut down the cabinet along those lines. (B) If the floor slopes, shave the high side and the front as shown.

PLINTH BASE

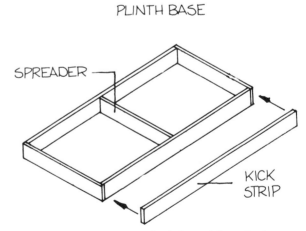

Figure 17.22 Plinths are usually fashioned from 1×4s set on-edge and stiffened every 16 to 24 in. with spreaders. If possible, put spreaders beneath cabinet ends so they'll be well supported; shim beneath the plinth as needed.

have been sloppily constructed, take them down and sand the excess off the bottom.

When all the face frames are aligned to your satisfaction and screwed together, check cabinet backs to be sure that any gaps are shimmed (minimally) so that panels do not pull out when you screw them down. Also, if you shimmed the plinth to level it, center shims beneath each point where cabinets join, to prevent plinth sag and joint separation when the cabinets are loaded. That done, screw cabinet rails to studs and nail cabinet bottoms to plinth edges, using 6d finish nails or $1\frac{1}{2}$-in. square-head trim screws.

Trim shims and attach the kick strip later.

Hanging Cabinet Doors

Doors arrive with hinges preattached; it's your responsibility to align doors to frames and screw those hinges down. It can be tricky to get door tops and bottoms aligned, especially with self-closing hinges mounted to doors, but a simple jig makes the task much easier. First determine exactly where doors should fit over the openings in the face frame: usually, they are centered top to bottom, left to right. Mea-

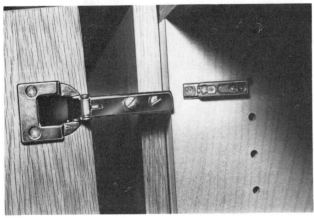

Figure 17.23 Installing ''German hinges.'' (A) After drilling a hole in the back face of the cabinet door, screw down the first section of the hinge so that its arm is perpendicular to the edge of the door. (B) There are two screws on the arm of the hinge: the first holds the arm to the plate fastened inside the cabinet; the second allows you to alter the pitch of the door slightly.

sure up from the bottom of the frames and pencil in a light line to indicate door bottoms.

Align a straight, kiln-dried piece of pine to that line and clamp it to the bottom rail of the face frames. Set doors atop that board, center them left to right over the openings, and screw their hinges to the frames. If the hinges are self-closing, you'll have to hold the hinges flat with one hand while you screw with the other. Predrill to prevent splits, using a Vix bit to center screw holes.

Door pulls and handles often come predrilled for the hardware you selected; generally, holes are centered in the middle of the stiles. If you position the hardware yourself, use a taut string to align all pieces beforehand—it'll look better.

You may want to hold off on hardware, however, until you've installed countertops. Cover the cabinets with masking paper or sheet plastic to protect them from harm, especially if you're installing tile countertops.

Countertops

Tile counters are discussed in Chapter 16; here, you'll find brief descriptions of other materials commonly used for tops. If you've taken pains to align base cabinets, counters will go down with only a modest amount of shimming.

Two materials described below are best installed by professionals. Corian is so expensive that installation is but a small percentage of its total cost, and the supplier eats the loss if he flubs a cut or cracks the counter putting it in. Plastic laminate is another one to field out because it's tough to install even with the right tools—indeed, why bother when laminate specialists can deliver a surface seamlessly wrapped onto an integral splashboard, which they'll then shave to fit your walls? You'll be glad you paid to have it done.

There should be counter space next to all major appliances and work areas. Chapter 2 recommends square footages for counter space, but it's useful here to note that counters are usually 33 in. high and 24 in. deep, to accommodate standard-width sinks and cooktops and to match the width of most appliances. Although thicknesses of countertops vary according to the materials used, $\frac{3}{4}$-in. plywood or particleboard—with edges built up to $1\frac{1}{2}$ in.—is most common. Tile surfaces require a $1\frac{1}{8}$-in. substrate. Edge details vary somewhat, but it's standard for countertops to overhang the front face of a base cabinet $\frac{3}{4}$ to 1 in. If there is a splashboard in the back, it usually rises 4 in. above the counter.

Countertop materials vary greatly, as do the core, or substrate materials beneath and the methods of attachment. Plastic-laminate tops are usually contact-cemented to exterior-grade, $\frac{3}{4}$-in. particleboard or plywood. Cultured marble, Corian, and most natural stones at least $\frac{1}{2}$ in. thick really don't need a substrate; but they are routinely laid over $\frac{3}{4}$-in. plywood, so cutouts for sinks, which are relatively narrow, don't crack. A layer of construction adhesive or silicone fills any irregularities beneath the stone. Counters of solid wood, such as butcher block, should not be mounted to processed-wood boards, though, because they expand and contract at different rates. Instead, screw such wood tops from the underside, through the base-cabinet frames.

The countertop substrate, if there is one, attaches to the frame of the cabinet with screws and several metal plate-braces. L-braces are commonly used to attach the bottom of the countertop to a frame web or to an upright. The simple and effective ''figure-eight brace'' shown in Figure 17.24 must be countersunk in the frame; a $\frac{3}{4}$-in. spade bit with ground-down corners sets the figure-eight perfectly tight and flush. If the countertop is of stone, predrill screw holes in the underside, using a slow-speed, carbide-tipped bit. Get additional advice on mounting from a supplier. In no event should you glue the substrate to the frame underneath. Should you want to change that top sometime in the future, you'd virtually destroy the frame by removing a top so joined.

How sections of substrate join is also crucial to the stability of the finish surface—particulary tile surfaces. Use a single piece of plywood or particleboard whenever you can. Where you must join pieces, use a rabbeted joint, *draw bolts* (washered bolts that fit into T-slots cut in the underside of particleboard), and/or a cleat across the underside. A rabbeted joint works best on plywood. Cut rabbets 1 in by $\frac{3}{8}$ in. for $\frac{3}{4}$-in. plywood; glue and draw the joint together using $\frac{5}{8}$-in. flathead screws. Because particleboard lacks the lamination (and thus the strength) of plywood, tie sections together with draw bolts. Don't overtighten. Use a router to cut T-slots, or have the laminate supplier do it.

Either method of joining is adequate to keep sections from spreading but not likely to control flexion in the sheets themselves. Therefore, support such joints with a wood stretcher glued and screwed to the underside of the joint, or add a web brace to the cabinet frame, immediately beneath the joint. Get help turning the sheets over after you've joined them; to prevent sections from folding, temporarily clamp some wide scrap pieces of plywood across joints.

Attaching a new top over an old one. Most new countertops for old base cabinets are installed after the old top has been removed. Although it's possible to apply one top over another, consider the total counter thickness that will result. If a top is too thick, its edge will look awkward, and the clips that attach the sink might not reach.

Applying another layer of plastic laminate directly over

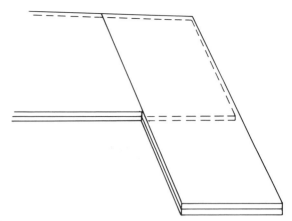

A.

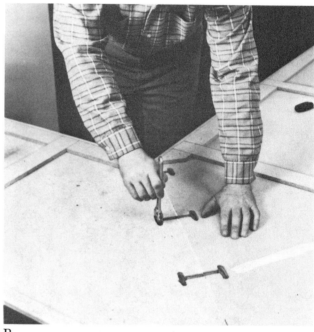

B.

Figure 17.25 Joining sections of countertop. (A) To minimize flexion where pieces of particleboard meet, half-lap pieces as shown and glue them together with contact cement. (B) Less desirable is a single thickness of particleboard mitered and drawn together with draw bolts. It's good for a few years if you support the top well, but in time the particleboard will compress beneath the bolts and the joint will gap.

an existing one will work, if the manufacturer so indicates. Sand the old layer well with 120-grade sandpaper, thoroughly wipe with a tack rag, and apply contact cement. A better method, however, is to attach a thin underlayment over the old surface before adding new laminate. Nail a layer of $\frac{1}{4}$-in. exterior-grade plywood (with all holes plugged and sanded) to the existing counter, with 1-in. spiral underlayment nails spaced every 2 in. Sink nail holes, then glue the new laminate to the surface.

Plastic laminates. You can buy plastic laminates (Formica is one brand) already attached to preformed bases, or you can attach laminate yourself. In the former case, carefully measure the top of the cabinet base, noting all angles and corners. You need only attach the preformed top to the

Figure 17.24 A figure-eight allows you to screw down into the cabinet base and up into the underside of the countertop. Recess the figure-eight so that it is flush.

frame by screwing up from below. Or have a professional do it all.

If you choose to apply the laminate yourself, note that it usually comes in sheets 4 ft by 8 ft by $\frac{1}{16}$ in. Plastic laminates come in a variety of widths, lengths, and thicknesses. In addition to the standard $\frac{1}{16}$-in. stock mentioned above, a $\frac{1}{32}$-in. thickness is available for molded countertops. Another thin laminate is *cabinet liner,* used on the inside walls and shelves of cabinets and sometimes on the bottoms of laminated tables and countertops. In the latter use, the liner seals the unit and virtually eliminates moisture-related warpage. For those few people who are offended by the black edge left by routing laminate edges, there are varieties that carry the surface color through the entire thickness of the material. Store laminate on the job site for 48 hours, so it an acclimatize, before installation, to the temperature and humidity in the house.

Attach plastic laminate to its substrate, usually $\frac{3}{4}$-in. particleboard, with contact cement. The substrate must be solid, clean, and dry; fill any cracks in its face or along the

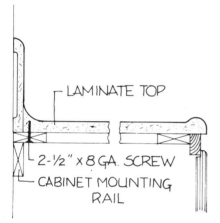

Figure 17.26 When plastic laminate is preformed to a substrate, screw up from the base frame to attach the top.

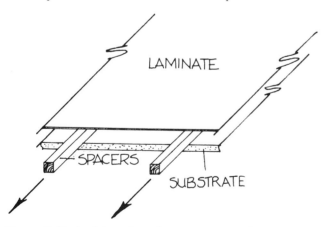

Figure 17.27 Applying plastic laminate is tricky. First turn the laminate over and apply contact cement to it with a short-nap roller; similarly, roll contact cement on to the top of the substrate. Allow the cement on both surfaces to dry until tacky. To position the laminate over the particleboard, turn the laminate over, and rest it on spacer sticks as shown. When the laminate is positioned properly, pull out the sticks from one end to the other, and press the laminate into place. *Note:* Once the laminate touches the cemented substrate, it's there to stay. For this reason, hiring a professional is wise.

edges with wood filler. Sand when dry and wipe with a tack rag. If the substrate is an existing top, it must be attached securely, without bubbles or unsecured edges. Sand it with 120-grade sandpaper, so the new layer will adhere well, and wipe dust off with a tack rag. If the old countertop has metal edging and/or a splash-board, remove either before laminating on the new. Similarly, remove sinks and other appliances set in the counter.

To cut the laminate sheet, score it with a laminate scriber along a straightedge and snap off the edge. Fine-toothed saber-saw blades are also available that will do the trick, but test them on a piece of scrap first. Teeth that are too coarse will chip the ends of the laminate. Fine-toothed plywood blades work pretty well, but they soon dull. Cutting from the back of the laminate can lessen chipping; if you cut from the face of the piece, protect the surface by putting masking tape on the bottom of the saw. Laminate shears work well, but they're hard to find.

Cut the pieces $\frac{1}{4}$ in. longer and wider than the substrate; trim off the excess after the laminate has been bonded. Lay out the laminate so there will be no seams in major working areas, and preferably no seams at all; they can fray and lift up.

Working with adhesive. *Note:* The stronger, quick-drying contact cements are petroleum-based and extremely volatile. Work only in a well-ventilated area and *do not smoke while working.* Also, cut the power to all electric motors and appliances in the room. Extinguish any gas pilot lights by shutting off the gas.

In general, apply contact cement to the back of the laminate and then to the substrate. Because the substrate is more absorptive, it will dry more quickly. Apply cement to counter edges with a $\frac{3}{4}$- or 1-in. brush, to large areas with a 4-in. brush or a short-nap paint roller. The paint roller does a distinctly better job, spreading the adhesive quickly and evenly.

Note: Use only animal-hair brushes to spread cement; nylon and other synthetics might dissolve.

For better adhesion, apply slightly more adhesive toward the edges of both the substrate and the underside of the laminate. The adhesive should not ooze from the edges as you apply pressure; if it does, dab on a solvent approved by the manufacturer and scrape off excess cement *with a scrap piece of laminate.* Solvents frequently used are cement solvent, lacquer thinner, and naptha. Some solvents may dissolve the cement rosin and leave the rubber, but it's easily removed by rubbing with your fingers.

Attaching the laminate. Attach laminate to the edges of the counter first. Spread adhesive on the back side of the edge pieces *and* on the counter edges. When the adhesive is sufficiently dry, press the laminate to the edge of the counter. Immediately apply pressure by tapping a scrap block of wood with a hammer, along the length of the edge. When the edge strip is fully bonded, trim the excess laminate with a straight, carbide-tip router bit; then dress the edges of the strip.

To dress, or clean, the edges of the strip, use a belt sander with medium-fine sandpaper. Make *one* pass with the sander. Some authorities suggest cleaning the edge with a fine-toothed file, but that isn't a good practice where one piece of laminate overlaps another. Invariably, a file creates highs and lows that preclude a clean joint with the top sheet.

If a counter edge is curved, laminate will be easier to apply if you soften it slightly by moving a blow dryer across the surface. Application is also easier if you remove some of the backing of the laminate with a belt sander where a bend is to be made.

To attach the countertop, turn the sheet of laminate upside down and spread contact cement on with a roller. Do the same to the top of the counter substrate. When you can touch a piece of paper (a brown paper bag is good) to either cemented surface without the paper sticking, the two surfaces are ready to bond. Because the two cemented surfaces cannot be shifted once they touch, align the laminate over the substrate *first*. This task is best accomplished by laying $\frac{3}{4}$-in. dowels 1 ft apart, across the width of the counter. With help from a friend, turn the cemented laminate over, onto the dowels. When you're satisfied with the alignment, pull the dowels out one by one, starting at one end of the counter and working toward the other. Apply pressure to the laminate as you pull the dowels out. When all dowels are out, press down the entire surface of the laminate—hammer a flat board or use a rolling pin or J-roller. Although there should be no air trapped beneath the laminate, you can work out any that might be trapped by rolling from the center of the sheet out to the edges. In particular, roll the edges so they bond well.

After laminating the countertop, trim its edges with a router or laminate trimmer. To finish the countertop, bevel the edge joint with a beveled router bit or a smooth file held at a 45-degree angle. Or if you use a flush trimmer bit, use a fine file or fine sandpaper to dull the sharp edge.

Cutouts are best made after the entire counter has been laminated. Then drill pilot holes inside the opening in the substrate; cut around the opening with a fine-toothed saber-saw blade. To prevent moisture from seeping into the particleboard or the plywood, seal the edges with two or three coats of sealant.

Install sinks as shown in Figure 12.55, seating the edges of the mounting lip in plumber's putty or silicone caulk. Don't assume that plastic-laminate tops are indestructible—if water seeps into exposed edges, delamination can occur. If a pot or a pan is extremely hot, it will scorch the surface and possibly cause bubbling and delamination. Finally, the surface can be stained by relatively strong juices such as grape. Try a nonabrasive cleanser.

Stone and synthetic stone.   Marble, granite, and slate are appropriate for use as countertops. Of the three, granite is the most durable—and the most expensive. Although all are heat-resistant, marble stains the easiest; therefore, use a hot plate when setting pots on the countertop. When polished, any stone, but marble especially, is excellent as a bread or pastry counter. Stone that is unpolished, or cleft, is quite handsome; note the cleft-slate counters shown in Figure 2.11.

Have a supplier of the stone make cutouts for such items as sinks. It's possible to make cuts yourself with a carborundum blade lowered $\frac{1}{8}$ in. per pass; but the diamond blade of the supplier's saw will give a more nearly perfect cut. Handle stones gingerly at all stages; they break easily.

So they won't be in the way, have pieces delivered only when you're ready to set them. If the dressed side of the stone has a protective covering, leave it on until the stone is in place.

Methods of attaching stone vary. To even out irregularities between the underside of the stone and the top of the cabinet frame, run generous beads of silicone caulk along the top of the frames; support the stone with a frame beneath, with spreaders at least every 16 in. If the stone is 1 in. or more thick, its weight and the adhesion of the silicone should be sufficient attachment; if you are uneasy, however, have the supplier predrill a few holes into the stone's underside. Use plastic shields and washered screws to anchor it to the frame.

Synthetic stone such as Corian has attachers provided by the supplier. Most synthetic stones are $\frac{3}{4}$ in. thick and can be easily worked with a power saw or a router. For the most part, they don't require a substrate; $\frac{1}{2}$-in. Corian can extend beyond the base of a cabinet up to 6 in. without reinforcement. Most types are heat and moisture-resistant. Cultured marble, on the other hand, must be cut by the supplier; most types of ersatz stone, though not heat-resistant, are stain-resistant.

Wood.   Wood, while beautiful, is poorly suited for countertops. It can be scorched by hot pots and pans and can be swelled by moisture. If you want to use wood, choose the finish with extra care, for it is crucial.

Probably the best finish for wood near sinks is tung oil, which penetrates wood grain, keeps out moisture, and won't chip or crack. It must be reapplied periodically, however. The three grades of tung oil are: pure, tungseed, and polymerized. Although pure tung oil is never quite hard, once the initial coats have stabilized, there is almost no residue; you can handle food on its surface without concern. Pure tung will darken in time. Tungseed oil is half to three-quarters thinner and dries much more quickly; once dry, it is also relatively inert. Polymerized tung oil dries completely in about 24 hours and thus may be the most useful form of tung oil. Apply two or three coats.

If you're looking for a finish that's safe around food, consider lightweight lemon oil, a penetrating oil intended for use on butcher block. Another old favorite is vegetable oil. To apply it, heat the oil until it is hot to the touch; then apply liberally, rubbing it in with a rag. Let the oil set for 10 to 15 minutes, then wipe off the excess. After two or three such applications (with time in between to allow the oil to dry completely), the counter should be ready to use. Peanut or Wesson oil give the best results, though some detractors detect a rancid smell no matter what vegetable oil is used.

Watco oil (linseed oil converted into a rosin) is an excellent finish as well. To apply, merely rub it in with a rag until the wood can't absorb any more. Reapply it occasionally, especially near sinks. Like pure tung oil, Watco darkens wood somewhat. Some users report, however, that Watco will stain from cans left on its surface.

Pure linseed oil dries very slowly. Thin the early coats with half thinner. On the other hand, linseed oil is only half as moisture-resistant as tung oil.

Polyurethane is a tough, durable finish; when repeatedly exposed to moisture, though, it may become cloudy.

Also, it can be nicked, thus reducing its ability to resist liquids. Gloss finish is the hardest; thin the first coat so it soaks into the wood.

Caulk well beneath any sink set in wood, and use a high-grade silicone or a bed of plumber's putty. To clean the counter, use a mild household cleaner or a dish-washing soap; touch up cleaned areas at least once a month with another rubbing of oil. To prolong the life of any wood finish, avoid spills, use hot pads or trivets beneath pots and pans (tile set into a wooden counter can be a handsome spot on which to place hot items), and use a cutting board.

Drawers. Drawers of prebuilt cabinets are usually premounted; thus, there's little for you to do. If the drawer guides are wood, a piece of paraffin or a candle rubbed along their length often alleviates sticking or squeaking. Guides made of metal are, to a degree, adjustable. The screws that hold the guide section to the inside of the cabinet are slotted: loosen the screws slightly and move the sections until they are level, flush with the edge of the drawer spacer (the horizontal rail that separates one drawer from another), and flush with the outside of the cabinet's face frame. Sections of the guides that are attached to the sides of the drawers must be parallel as well; if you suspect they are not parallel, measure from the edges of the drawer, front and back; the measurements should be the same.

A.

B.

C.

Figure 17.28 Drawer glides. (A) Drawer shelf beneath; (B) side guides; (C) adjustable metal.

A.

B.

Figure 17.29 After the cabinet carcasses are plumbed, shimmed, and supported, hang doors, fit drawers, and affix countertops. That done, you're ready to paint; cover the cabinets carefully.

·18·

PAINTING

Painting is probably the most popular renovation task, because its effects are immediate and striking. For not much money, you can get a complete change of scenery and heart. (Nor are humans the only animals that like a change. The bower bird of New Guinea daubs the walls of its nest with crushed berries, and during mating season has been observed to change its rug of orchid petals every day.) If you're painting to boost your spirits, or for whatever reason, keep in mind that painting and papering are *cosmetic* arts, though; they aren't intended to correct underlying structural defects, nor can they.

Preparing surfaces before painting is imperative if the finish is to last. Whether you're painting the interior or the exterior of a building, do the following: (1) attend to all problems of moisture and structure; (2) scrape free all existing paint that is loose or that was applied excessively; (3) fill and sand all surface irregularities; and (4) prime surfaces with a coating that is compatible with the final coat. Always read the instructions on the label of the can, and follow them closely.

TOOLS AND MATERIALS

Buy only good-quality painting materials and tools; they will last longer and give you better results. Cheap brushes shed hairs and otherwise slow you down; cheap paint, which wears poorly and is difficult to keep clean, is a waste of time.

Brushes

The bristles of high-quality brushes are "flagged"; that is the ends of their bristles are split and of varying lengths, enabling them to hold more paint. As you examine brushes, pull lightly on bristles. Are they well attached to the metal ferrule on the handle? Gently press the bristles as though you were painting; they should spread evenly and have a springy, resilient feel.

Types. Don't buy brushes with stiff birstles. Bristles are natural (e.g., hog bristles) or synthetic (usually nylon). Use natural bristles for oil-based paints, varnishes, shellacs, solvent-thinned polyurethanes, and most strippers; nylon bristles dissolve in most of these chemicals. Natural brushes don't work well with water-thinned paints such as latex; their bristles absorb paint in the fiber and become clogged; use synthetic brushes instead. Although some synthetics work with any painting medium, once you've used a brush for a particular type of paint, continue using it for that type.

The size of the brush you use should depend on the amount of paint to be applied. Since rollers are best for covering large surfaces, a 4-in. brush is adequate for edging where walls meet, next to trim, and so on. A 4-in. brush is also adequate for most exterior painting; too large a brush holds too much paint for successful handling.

Brush care. Brush care begins with proper use. Keep bristles compact so they will glide paint on and thus work it in.

Avoid stabbing a tight spot with the tips of bristles. When you put down a brush, don't rest it on the bristle ends; lay it flat. To keep a brush from drying out when not in use temporarily, leave a moderate amount of paint on the bristles.

Clean brushes at once when a painting day is over. Remove excess paint from the bristles by drawing them over a straightedge, *not* the edge of a paint can. Brush out the remaining paint onto a piece of newspaper. Clean the brush in an appropriate solution, for example, turpentine or thinner for oil-based paints, stains, and varnishes; or soap and water for water-based paints. Work the solution into bristles with your fingers; work all the way to the brush's ferrule. (Wear gloves.) After giving the brushes a thorough initial washing, rinse them again in a fresh batch of cleaning solution. When you're satisfied the paint is out, shake and brush out the excess solution. Rinse with warm water, shake out the excess, and comb the bristles. (Solvent-

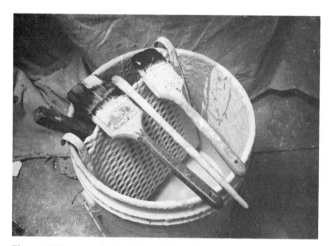

Figure 18.1 A professional's well-used tools. *Left to right:* a 3-in. brush; a small brush for painting in tight spots; a sash brush, whose slant-cut bristles facilitate painting straight lines. The grate in the pail is used to remove excess paint loads.

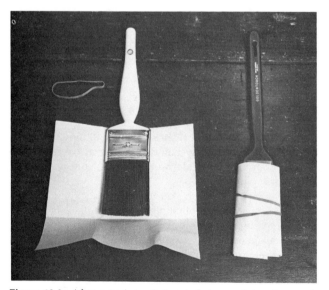

Figure 18.2 After a major painting task is complete, clean and wrap brushes in heavy paper or cardboard to keep their shape.

Figure 18.3 To soak brushes without resting them on their bristles, drill holes through their handles and hang them from short sections of coat hanger.

cleaned brushes require an intermediate cleaning with soap and warm water.) Do not use *hot* water when cleaning brushes; it splits bristles.

If you're putting brushes away for storage, wrap them in heavy paper so they'll keep their shape. Heavy paper is better than foil or plastic bags. Natural bristles that are slightly damp can rot, and any paint thinner left in bristles can dissolve plastic.

To restore an abused paintbrush, drill a hole through its handle and suspend the brush in a can of cleaning solution (Figure 18.3). Alternate soakings and combings with a brush comb until you're satisfied that the brush is clean. Most paint stores have special brush-softener solvents; Brush Wash is one brand. Badly splayed bristles, once cleaned, can be reshaped between two pieces of heavy cardboard held tight by rubber bands.

Rollers and Pads

Rollers enable you to paint large areas quickly and evenly. In addition to the familiar cylinder type, special corner rollers that resemble a pointed wheel are available. There's even a special corner roller that's absorbent on one side only, which is useful for painting the intersection of walls and ceilings. For the best results, however, paint edges, trim, and other tight spots with brushes; use rollers for the rest of the room.

Pads are about the size of a small kitchen sponge and have a short nap; generally, they are used to paint hard-to-reach spots. Both pads and rollers can be attached to extension poles—either sectioned or telescoping—to extend their reach.

Matching rollers with paints. Match the cover of a roller with the paint you intend to use. Synthetic covers are the most versatile and are favored for latex and other water–based paints. Lamb's-wool covers work poorly with water–based paints but well with oil-based ones (except enamels). The short fibers of mohair are well suited to the application of enamels; in fact, mohair is excellent for all jobs requiring a smooth finish and for such clear finishes as varnish and polyurethane.

The nap of the roller is important in achieving the desired effect. Uneven, rough surfaces such as masonry blocks, for example, require a long nap, whereas smooth surfaces require a short nap.

Be choosy when buying roller covers. In general, avoid the cheaper varieties, which are backed with cardboard; they can disintegrate before a job is done. If possible, buy covers on plastic sleeves. As you do with brushes, use a roller cover for only one type of paint (e.g., water-based); don't mix uses.

Roller and pad care. Most of us throw out used rollers, but if you invest in expensive ones, clean them as soon as you have finished a job. Remove excess paint with a putty knife; remove the roller cover from its metal frame and wash in the appropriate cleaner solution, working out paint

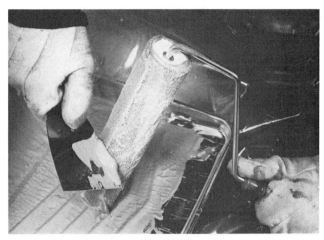

Figure 18.5 Before washing a roller, remove excess paint by rolling it out and by scraping, as shown.

with your fingers. Repeat the procedure with fresh cleaner, then wash with soap and water. Blot excess moisture with a paper towel or a clean rag. Dry the pad with the absorbent side up. Dry the cover by sliding it onto a hanger or a tree branch; it shouldn't lie on its nap while drying. Store the cleaned cover or pad in a paper bag or foil. If a cover or pad wasn't cleaned properly and has become crusty, throw it away.

Spray-Painting Equipment

Spray-painting is most appropriate where surfaces are ornate, multifaceted, textured, or otherwise difficult to cover with a brush or roller. It's also preferred where numerous thin applications of paint are necessary. Although equipment can be cumbersome, spray-painting is well suited to clapboards, shutters, gingerbread trim, fences, and so on.

Equipment typically consists of a compressor, a connecting hose, and a spray gun. The nozzle of the spray gun can be adjusted according to the thickness of the paint and the width of the spray pattern. The gun's trigger controls the flow of paint. Airless paint-sprayers, which are becoming popular, can be rented.

Safety considerations. If the paints used are thinned with solvent or thinner, do not smoke while using a spray gun, and do not use equipment near anyone stripping paint with heat. Keep a fire extinguisher handy. Obtain a compressor with a hose long enough to allow you to hold several loops in your free hand. Wear a respirator mask.

Using a sprayer. Preparation and practice are important. Begin by straining paint through a fine-mesh fabric such as nylon. Follow the manufacturer's recommended ratio of paint to solvent, being sure to test the mixture beforehand on an inconspicuous spot. If you're an inexperienced spray painter, practice. As you spray, (1) keep the gun moving; (2) keep the nozzle parallel to the surface at all times, 8 to 10 in. away; and (3) overlap passes slightly, covering the area completely with half the return pass. Keep in mind that two even coats are preferable to one thick, globby coat.

If the spray gun doesn't work properly, soak the nozzle in solvent and poke the aperture with a broom straw. *Do not* clean the hole with a nail or a similar sharp object;

Figure 18.4 An extension pole enables you to reach high spots without scaffolding, although scaffolding is advisable for a job of any size.

Figure 18.6 A paint-sprayer.

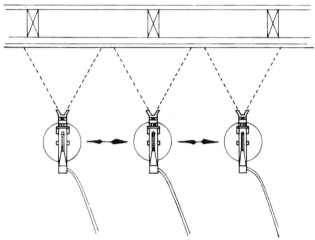

Figure 18.7 When spraying, move with the tool so that paint application will be even. If you remain in one spot and swing the tool in an arc, paint buildup will be uneven.

you could ruin the nozzle. To clean the gun, run solvent *only* through the gun. At the end of each spraying session, clean the gun thoroughly.

Paint

When choosing paint, the first, and most important, consideration is whether the paint is to be used on the house's interior or its exterior. (Here, we are using the word *paint* in its general sense.) Specific choices for a surface are shown in Tables 18.1, 18.2, and 18.3. The grade of paint chosen should depend on the weathering and abuse the surface can take; opt for quality whenever possible. Because paints, stains, and so on change frequently, it's important that you establish a good relationship with a reputable supplier who knows the materials and will advise you well.

In the overview below, paints are divided into five general groups—alkyd, latex, clear finish, stain, and specialty. There are interior and exterior examples of each group and a range of qualities in all groups.

Alkyds. Alkyds are sometimes called oil-based paints. In fact, the alkyd group encompasses several different paint bases, although most alkyds are thinned with petroleum-based solvents. Alkyds are the most durable, washable, tenacious paints; they adhere to almost any surface except those with active alkali, such as "green" plaster and masonry. Paints in the alkyd group level well, dry without brush marks, and cover well. Clean your painting equipment with such solvents as paint thinners and turpentine. Drying time for alkyds is usually 8 to 12 hours.

Latex. Latex paints contain a synthetic base that dries quickly and has little odor; you can usually repaint within an hour or two of completing the first coat. Clean equipment with soap and water. Latex paints are particularly well suited for drywall, for latex does not raise the surface. The covering power of latex is also good, although not quite a match for alkyds. *Note:* Some latex paints contain mercury to retard mildew. Buy only latex paint that specifies "no mercury," for even in small amounts it can cause neurological and kidney damage.

Clear finishes. Included in this group are polyurethanes, varnishes, lacquers, and shellacs. Polyurethane is the most durable of the group and is suitable where there is heavy traffic, such as on stair treads and floors. Spar varnish has similar qualities. Although poly and varnish resist water, they become cloudy with sustained exposure. Shellac is altogether unsuitable near water. Paint thinner cuts and cleans up poly and varnish; refined alcohol works similarly for shellac.

Stains. Stains are a fast-growing group. Although they were originally little more than pigments for coloring wood, they have been combined with other chemical agents to extend their use. Exterior stains are attractive preservatives because they protect wood siding without obscuring its grain. Soaking into wood, they never peel or flake off, and they need reapplication only every 10 years or so. Solid-color exterior stains are now available that cover existing paint and which are cleaned up with soap and water.

Specialty Paints. The category *specialty paints* includes metal sealers, paints used to coat masonry, textured paint; epoxy-base coverings that adhere even to hard, nonporous surfaces such as tile and glass—even paints that do not affect the sound-deadening properties of acoustical tile. These paints are usually paired with special primers and thinners. If you have an unusual painting problem, contact your supplier; there's probably a paint for it.

Other considerations. Select paint on the basis of the surface to be painted and the expected wear. A primer, if necessary, bonds to the surface and keeps the finish coat (topcoat) from being absorbed by the material already there. Primers usually aren't needed when a surface has already been coated with an acceptable coating or when a topcoat can bond directly to a surface.

Topcoats are categorized by degree of gloss. Although manufacturer's names vary, the degrees of gloss are *flat* (also called "dull" or "matte"), *semigloss* (eggshell, velvet, satin), and *gloss* (high gloss, three-quarters gloss).

In most cases, alkyds adhere better than latexes. The smoother and harder the gloss, the better the durability and washability of the alkyd. An alkyd enamel, for example, is among the most durable of interior finishes, being particularly well suited to interior trim around doors and windows. Its high gloss both decorates and protects.

At the paint store. Determine the square footage of the surfaces to be painted, and take the figures to the paint store. Compare your figures with the coverage figures given by manufacturers. Unless a wall is preponderantly glass, don't bother to subtract the square footage of windows and glass doors from your total; you can always use the extra later for touch-ups. In fact, buy extra paint for that purpose. Predicting the coverage of stains is more difficult, especially if the wood in question is untreated. Add 15 percent to 25 percent if the stain is a special order and there is a wait for delivery. That way, you'll be assured of enough stain to finish the job.

Have the supplier mechanically shake the paint for you—unless, of course, it shouldn't be shaken at all; polyurethanes and varnishes, for example, trap air bubbles when shaken.

Tips about Paints and Painting

1. Buy paint in the largest quantities practicable. The savings are considerable between buying paint in 5-gal cans and in 1-gal ones.

2. Primers can be tinted to shades closer to the finish coat, thus saving you money (finish-coat paint is more expensive). Follow the manufacturer's recommendations closely; too much pigment can cause problems.

3. For uniform color throughout, stir paint well. If you anticipate finishing one can in the middle of a wall, mix that can with another so the hue will be consistent.

4. Examine brushes and rollers for loose nap or stray hair before starting. Snip off strays but be moderate.

5. Dampen a brush or roller *slightly* with paint solvent (or water, if that's what the paint is thinned with) before loading it with paint for the first time in a painting session.

6. Before beginning, rub lotion over your hands, arms, and face; cleanup will be easier and any skin irritation that occurs will be reduced. If your skin is especially sensitive, rub Vaseline or a similar substance on exposed areas. Waterless hand cleaner is great for cleaning both hands and arms when the job is done, but it can irritate your eyes. Check the label.

7. "Many hands make work light." If one person paints corners and edges with a brush while another uses the roller on large areas, the job goes quickly.

8. Keep your brush or roller from gunking up. Remove excess with a staightedge.

9. If a bristle comes loose while you're painting, dab it lightly with the tip of the brush to pick up the errant bristle.

10. It's not necessary to lug a paint can around. Paint suppliers sell cheap cardboard pails, or you can use the lid of the can for extremely small amounts.

Safety Considerations

Read the Label. Read the label on the paint can before starting; that way, you'll know what to do before you begin. In addition to information about application, the label contains important safety instructions. Should an emergency arise later—say, a child swallowing paint—the information you need may be covered by drops of paint.

Store Paint Safely. Put paint where children can't reach it. Paint thinner, turpentine, petroleum-based paints, and metal-based paints (especially lead) are extremely hazardous. Paint should be stored where temperatures are moderate; freezing ruins their bonding ability and heat increases their volatility. Close all cans completely. Never store rags or steel wool dirty with solvents, because of the danger of spontaneous combustion. Dispose of such articles.

Provide Adequate Ventilation. Sustained inhalation of some paint fumes can affect the brain, lungs, and kidneys. If you are working on a ladder, and fumes make you dizzy, stop, rest, and get some fresh air. Take label warnings about such hazards seriously. Ventilation is also a problem when stripping paints; lead-based paints are especially dangerous when heated. Wear a respirator mask with a changeable filter when working in an enclosed area, and wear a mask even when you are outside, should the danger warrant.

Avoid Getting Paint in Your Eyes or on Your Skin. Although most latex-based paints are innocuous, solvent-thinned ones can cause extreme irritation. In most cases, flush your eyes with water if you get paint in them, and get to a doctor immediately. To avoid skin irritation, spread Vaseline or Liquid Glove over exposed areas. To minimize the risk of paint getting on your face, (1) avoid working over your head (elevate the work platform instead); (2) don't overload the brush or roller; (3) brush or roll away from your face, especially on the first few strokes after loading up with paint; and (4) wear goggles, especially when using strippers.

Don't Smoke around Paints. This rule is particularly important when using solvent-based paints, thinners, or strippers.

Foot All Ladders and Scaffolding Securely. Never use unstable equipment—elderly aluminum ladders are particularly untrustworthy. Don't be an acrobat to get that last spot; climb down and move the ladder. Scaffolding is not only safer, it will save you time in the long run. Chapter 3 has a lot more on the subject.

PAINTING THE INTERIOR

Planning and preparation are particularly important when painting inside a house. Begin by moving all the furniture out; it could be ruined by splattering paint and, in any event, will impede your work. If it's not possible to move all the furniture out, group what's remaining in the center of the room and cover it with a tarp. Take down drapes and pictures along the walls as well.

If you intend to rearrange the pictures on the wall, now is a good time to pull out all hanging nails; fill holes, so the newly painted surface won't be marred. Put plastic around light fixtures, as well as all hardware you want to leave in place. Ideally, you should remove all hardware, including the cover plates of electrical outlets and switches. Finally, cover the floor with a drop cloth and turn off electric power to outlets.

Preparing Wall and Ceiling Surfaces

Before painting, attend to any imperfections on existing walls or ceilings that paint won't cover. Serious gaps and cracks may indicate a structural problem—for example, a leaking roof and/or some paint on the exterior that is admitting moisture. Chapter 1 can help you figure out just what's happening. If the flaw or flaws seem limited to miscellaneous cracks, bumps, and holes caused by people, see Chapter 15 for information on patching such isolated spots.

Plaster and drywall. Plaster surfaces must be cured thoroughly before painting. Although latex paint can be applied as soon as plaster is dry to the touch, it's best to wait 3 to 4 weeks. Because the alkali in plaster can remain "hot" for up to 3 months, *you must wait* that long before using alkyd paints—unless you prime the surface with an alkali reducer before applying a regular primer. Drywall can be repaired with joint compound, which can receive latex or alkyd paint a day or two after repairs.

Papered surfaces. Generally, it's not a good idea to paint over walls covered with paper, cloth, or a similar material, although vinyl covering in good repair may take painting well. It's best to remove the old wallpaper with a steamer and wash the wall thoroughly with washing soda.

If you decide to paint over paper, examine the paper carefully to be sure there are no bubbles or loose spots. Repaste such bubbles and spots and allow them to dry. If seams are prominent, you should strip the walls; otherwise seams will stick out like sore thumbs.

As a final test, pick an inconspicuous spot behind a door and apply a small amount of undercoat (alkyd enamel primer or shellac). If the paper doesn't lift and the paper's pattern doesn't bleed through, proceed. Be advised, however, that you may be limiting future decorating options, for all subsequent layers of paint or paper depend upon the adhesion of the first layer of wallpaper. The only alternative is to strip down to the bare wall and start over.

Wall covering that is old canvas-backed paper must be removed; it may be held by animal glue, which won't receive primer. Wash the wall thoroughly with washing soda or ammonia (do not mix cleaning solutions). Scrape down any conspicuously high spots and scrub off tenacious spots of glue with steel wool.

Previously painted surfaces. Walls and trim painted earlier require little preparation if they are in good shape. With a paint scraper or a putty knife, remove flaking and loose paint, then sand the spot with a medium to fine grade of sandpaper. If you have only a few spots, wrap paper around a sanding block; otherwise, use an orbital sander with fine paper.

Fill with spackling compound all nail holes or small surface blemishes that paint won't disguise. Where trim has separated or nail holes are evident, fill with spackling compound or wood filler.

Unless it is prohibited by the paint manufacturer, lightly sand all painted surfaces so successive coats will adhere better. After sanding, dry-mop surfaces to remove dust, then wash with a mild detergent solution and rinse with clear water. Allow walls to dry thoroughly before painting. A good test of dryness is to see whether a piece of Scotch tape will stick or not.

Underlying problems. You may need to solve a number of problems before you apply new primer or topcoats. Where existing paint surfaces are cracking, wrinkling, or alligatoring, but are intact, either there are too many layers of paint applied or the underlying layers were misapplied. If there's too much paint, and the surfaces beneath are plaster, strip the paint as described below. Where walls are drywall, the easiest thing to do is simply cover them over with new drywall. If paint is blistered here and there, the cause may be moisture beneath the early coats—this is a common occurrence where plaster was painted prematurely. Where paint has fallen off in large patches or has become discolored, suspect water damage.

Repairing water damage requires some sleuthing. Damage to interior partitions is often caused by plumbing leaks or overflows. For exterior walls, first check the nearest window above the damaged spot; it may have been left open during a rain or the window may need caulking and flashing (see Chapter 7). Deteriorated siding and ailing roofing can also admit water.

Water can collect from within, too, particularly in bathrooms and kitchens. If a dark spot looks like mildew, scrub it with a mild (1:3) bleach solution; wear goggles while scrubbing. Allow the spot to dry thoroughly, then paint it with a mildew-resistant paint. "Kill-stain" applications are also available for use in water-damaged areas; white shellac

Figure 18.8 Preparation is the key to a successful job. Spackle all depressions or cracks, and sand well when the repairs are dry. (Work courtesy of Michael Ross Reitman Co., Brooklyn, NY.)

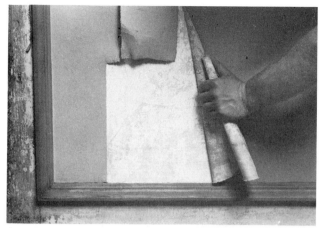

A.

B.

C.

Figure 18.9 Old wall coverings should be stripped before painting. (A) Here the painter removes canvas-backed covering in a front hallway. Since the plaster beneath is in good shape, no patching is needed. After scraping the surface (B) with a Zip-Away tool, which has a removable razor, he washed with washing soda (C), scrubbing it with No. 3 steel wool; afterwards, he sponged the wall with clean water.

Figure 18.10 Remove loose paint spots with a scraper or a putty knife, and then sand well.

can be used to touch up spots, which can then be primed and painted. Prevent recurrence by installing a ventilator fan or a dehumidifier.

Stripping painted walls and ceilings. If there's too much paint on walls and ceilings, or if the paint was misapplied, your preparation for new painting could be extensive. Your choices, basically, are covering over the surface or stripping and scraping. First, determine the type of walls and ceilings involved, by test-drilling in an inconspicuous place. Plaster will be extremely difficult to drill through and its undercoats are light brown; there will also be lath underneath. Plaster can be stripped and scraped. Drywall should be replaced or covered over with a new layer, because its paper backing cannot withstand the scraping and chemicals necessary to remove paint.

Note: We are not discussing stripping wood trim here; that's considered in the section, ''Back to Natural: Stripping and Finishing Wood,'' below.

Stripping the paint off interior surfaces is incredibly tedious and messy; that's why most people just paint over. Good ventilation is an absolute necessity, as are plenty of tarps for the floors. Because of the volume of paint scraps generated, you will need to rent a small dumpster or buy several metal garbage cans. Plastic garbage bags can be dissolved by solvents; use only metal or cardboard to haul scraps away. *Do not* leave flammable debris lying around: get rid of it at once.

The two prinicipal means of removing paint are with liquid (or paste) paint removers and with heat, both requiring scraping. Be extremely careful when applying heat; follow the instructions included with tools. Even a flameless heat gun is hot enough to ignite dust balls in old walls if the tool is used incorrectly. Never use an open flame for removing paint indoors—the danger of fire is too great.

A method that is well suited to paint stripping—whether interior or exterior—involves methylene chloride and a wallpaper steamer. Methylene chloride is a water-based solvent; after applying it to 2 to 4 sq ft of the painted surface, apply steam to the section to hasten the action of the solvent. Then scrape off the paint. Wear gloves and goggles, and work only where ventilation is adequate.

Note: There are indications that methylene chloride, benign as strippers go, can be hazardous to people with heart conditions. Check labels carefully for such warnings.

Scaffolding. Scaffolding is usually associated with outside work, but it's useful inside as well, mainly because it makes surface preparation and painting much easier. Instead of climbing up and down a ladder, you can remain aloft longer and accomplish more. Scaffolding is discussed at length on p. 40.

If your ceilings are high—say, 12 to 14 ft—rent commercial scaffolding. Otherwise, use a combination of sawhorses, stepladders, and planks (Figure 18.11). The primary requisite of any scaffolding is sturdiness; do not use any set-up that is rickety.

Use lumber 2 in. thick for supporting planks, an equivalent thickness of 1-in. stock isn't as strong. A 10-ft. unsupported run is the maximum safe length for scaffold planks. Planks should overhang supports by at least 1 ft, to keep a plank from slipping off its support.

Around stairwells, be very careful; a fall could be serious. Use only the sturdiest ladders and the soundest planks, and be sure that none of the support feet can slip. To protect a wall from ladder marks, wrap ladder ends with sponge or cloth.

Figure 18.11 A simple scaffold can be rigged from two sawhorses and a sturdy 2× plank which overhangs each horse by at least 1 ft.

Applying Paint to Interior Surfaces

Primers. A surface that has aleady been painted may not need priming. For a surface that has not been primed, pick a primer compatible with the topcoat (the label on the paint will tell you). If you need several coats of paint to cover an existing paint job, make one layer a pigmented primer; it's cheaper than a topcoat. To summarize priming:

Alkyd paints adhere best and offer the greatest range of decorating options in the future for drywall and plaster.

TABLE 18.1

Interior painting[a]

Area of application	Flat Alkyd	Semigloss Alkyd	Enamel-Gloss Alkyd	Flat Latex	Semigloss Latex	Polyurethane	Interior Varnish	Shellac	Stains	Sealer Undercoater	Metal Primer	Alkyd Masonry Paint
Drywall (walls and ceilings)	⊗	⊗		⊗	⊗			X		X		
Plaster (walls and ceilings)	⊗	⊗		⊗	⊗			X		X		
Wood paneling	⊗	⊗			⊗	X	X	X	X			
High-moisture areas like kitchens and bathrooms		⊗	⊗		⊗					X		
Wood floors and stair treads						[b]X		X	X			
Wood trim and cabinets	⊗	⊗	⊗		⊗	X	X	X	X			
Concrete floors						X						X
Old brick and block (low alkali)	⊗	⊗	⊗	X	X			[c]X	X			X
New masonry (high alkali)			⊗	⊗	⊗							X
Radiators, convectors, and pipes	⊗	⊗	⊗		⊗						X	
Steel windows	⊗	⊗	⊗		⊗						X	

[a]X paint is appropriate for surface; ⊗ paint is appropriate for surface; prime first.

[b]Polyurethane works best on hardwood; on softwood, it flexes and cracks. Spar vanish (not listed) is good on both softwood and hardwood.

[c]Stains are sometimes used on old masonry to blend in new patchwork with the old; wood stains thinned with solvent (1:3) works fine.

Plaster and drywall can also be sealed with latex primer.

Unpainted wood to be painted should be sealed with an alkyd enamel undercoat

Unpainted wood to be left natural can be primed with the clear finish of your choice: let it dry and sand lightly between coats. All wood should be sealed, however, or it will become grimy and dull.

Wire-brush metal covers, pipes, and trim; wipe with solvent and prime with rust-inhibiting enamel primer.

Prime masonry with cement-based paint, rubber-based primer, or block filler.

Painting the ceiling. Paint the ceiling first, then the walls, trim, and doors, and finally the windows. When your tarp is down, your scaffolding is up, and your hat is on, you are ready to start painting. Paint around the edge of the ceiling with a brush, to a distance of 6 in. from the ceiling–wall joint. This brush-painted edge will allow you to roll out the rest without worrying about getting any on the walls; the job will look better, too. Passes with the roller will disguise the brush marks.

For the best results, paint the entire ceiling at once. Apply paint in small sections of 4 to 6 sq ft, rolling on paint in a zigzag pattern, then spreading it out by rolling across the initial strokes. Work adjacent sections, going across the narrowest dimension of the room. Overlap areas already painted when the roller is almost unloaded. Don't repeatedly overwork an area; once paint is spread evenly, leave it so that the nap marks will level out. Do not go back over an area that has begun to dry.

A.

B.

Figure 18.13 Painting is done best with a brush *and* a roller. While one person edges (A) around electrical outlets, trim, and corners, the other rolls on paint (B). When rolling on paint, start in an upper corner and work down to go over any drips from above. Apply the paint in a zigzag motion, and then spread it out by rolling perpendicular to the first strokes.

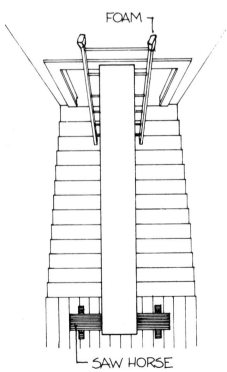

Figure 18.12 Temporary scaffolding on stairs must be well footed to keep its parts from moving. Lodge the lower ends of the ladder into a riser-tread joint. The plank must overhang both the saw-horse and the ladder rung by at least 1 ft, and the ends of the ladder should be cushioned with foam to prevent damage to finish surfaces. If the ladder is rickety, don't use it.

To minimize roller splatter, work out excess paint on the corrugated upper part of the roller tray. Avoid paint buildup toward the ends of the roller, and don't spin the roller when painting, or you'll spray adjoining surfaces.

If the colors of the ceiling and walls are close, prime the ceiling and then the walls, going back later to apply the finish coats.

Painting the walls. Paint the walls with the same combination of brushes used for edging, and rollers for covering broad expanses. Where distances around windows and doors are tight—say, less than $1\frac{1}{2}$ times the width of the roller—it may be more convenient to paint the entire surface with a 4-in. brush. Of course, smaller rollers can be used on restricted spaces. If possible, blend all brush strokes by rolling afterward.

Be very careful when brush edging, or "cutting," along the ceiling. Painting guides are useful for a clean edge, but they become covered with paint and must be cleaned constantly. A steady, patient hand is better. Take care near trim; a crisp line will be difficult to achieve if there is paint buildup. Brush-painted edges should be at least 6 in. wide.

When covering large expanses of wall, work in small, vertical sections of 6 to 8 sq ft, painting from an upper corner of the room down to the baseboard. Working downward, paint over all drips from above. Roll on sections in a zigzag pattern, spreading paint by cross-strokes. The first stroke—when the roller is the most heavily loaded—should always be upward. As you did with ceilings, spread paint from dry areas to the edges of areas already painted, for the best distribution of paint. Take your time and minimize mess.

Painting interior trim. Painting trim requires patience. Even when using masking tape or a paint guide to confine paint lines, don't hurry. For painting trim, you need a 2-in. brush, a sash brush (for close work), and masking tape (or a paint guide).

The sequence in which trim is painted isn't critical, although it's logical to begin with molding near the ceiling, and work down. Where trim is wide, such as baseboards, paint outside edges first, smoothing out your work with broad strokes down the middle. When working with enamel and semigloss paints, it's important to crossbrush whenever possible; that is, you should apply the paint in one direction and smooth it in by painting at a right angle to the first direction. Always paint methodically, work paint in and apply final strokes with the wood grain.

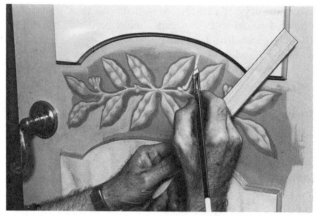

A.

B.

Figure 18.15 When doing detailed work, steady your painting hand by resting it on a stick held beneath (A). A larger brush can serve as a pallet for a smaller one (B). (Courtesy of Artcraft Decorators, New York.)

But first, prep the trim. Fill in all nail holes and cracks with spackling compound or wood filler. Seal the trim with white shellac before painting it, so sap from knotholes, stains, or rust from nails won't bleed through the finish coat. If you aren't sure that paint layers are compatible, test-paint a small patch in an inconspicuous area and observe it for a week or two.

Following are some tips from a pro:

Steady your painting arm by resting it on a stick held underneath (Figure 18.15A). Use a paint-can lid to hold small quantities of paint.

Dip the brush's bristles one-third of the way into the can and remove excess paint by *tapping* the brush against the can. Scraping off the excess against the lip of a can will misshape the brush.

If you are using masking tape to control paint lines, do not put it on newly painted surfaces. Never leave masking tape on for more than 2 days or it will leave adhesive behind and/or lift up paint.

Metal trimmings. Metal trim—whether window casings, radiators, or whatever—must be free from rust and scale, perfectly dry, and at room temperature. Radiators must be off (and be left off) for the period of time recommended

Figure 18.14 A small brush for tight spots.

A.

C.

B.

Figure 18.16 Multipane windows require patience and care to prepare and paint. Masking tape along window muntins (A) keeps large globs of paint off the glass (B); there should, however, be a narrow corridor of paint on the glass to seal out air. A metal painting guard (C) obviates the need for tape, but the guard must be wiped periodically.

by the paint manufacturer (check the label). Because metal window frames conduct outside temperatures, paint the frames at midday, so their temperature will remain at least at 50°F while they dry. Prepare metal by wire-brushing it well; apply naval jelly if you find rust. To remove the jelly, or any grit and grime, wipe the metal with a rag damp with solvent. Prime with a red-lead paint and use just about any topcoat you like. If the metal has already been painted, and the topcoat seems to be holding up well, priming may not be necessary.

Note: Because any coat of paint insulates to some extent, paint only the part of the radiator that is visible; more heat can escape through parts that haven't been painted.

Don't use aluminum paints; they will reflect heat back into the heating unit rather than allowing it to radiate into living areas.

Windows and doors. The easiest way to paint a door is to pull its hinge pins and lay it across a pair of sawhorses. Doors painted in place require stretching and squatting. If you must leave the door in place, wedge it so that it can't move, and work from top to bottom.

If the door surface is flush (perfectly flat), divide it into several imaginary squares, each half the width of the door. Apply paint to an upper corner first, brushing it on cross-grain and working it in with the wood grain. When you apply paint to subsequent sections, overlap strokes slightly onto earlier sections. Then brush both sections vertically and horizontally before going on to other sections.

On paneled doors, again work from top to bottom, painting panels and their edges first, next painting rails (horizontal pieces) top to bottom, and finally, the stiles.

Before painting interior door frames and casing, though, shut the door and note what parts are visible. Paint the door parts to match the trim in each room.

Prepare windows before painting them. If windows are weathered and loose, replace or repair them, as described in Chapter 6.

In multipaned windows, you will find muntins (narrow wood sections between panes of glass); paint horizontal muntins first and vertical muntins next, then the rails of the window sash and finally, the stiles of the sash. For the best air seal, leave a small bit of paint on the window glass, perhaps a border of $\frac{1}{32}$ or $\frac{1}{64}$ in. Avoid excessive paint though; clean globs up immediately. To prevent excess paint from getting on the glass, tape along muntins with masking tape. This taping can be tedious, however; if you're at all steady-handed, you can probably forego the nuisance of taping. Steady your hand by holding a stick underneath.

When painting double-hung windows, lower the outer (upper) sash and raise the inner (lower) one, exposing the meeting, or bottom, rail of the upper sash. Then:

1. Paint the meeting rail, including its bottom edge and as far up the side (stiles) as you can go.

2. Paint the bottom of the bottom sash and the exposed header (top) of the window frame. At this time, you an also paint the exposed jambs (sides or channels) of the window frame, though some experts advise not painting channels, only waxing them, so the sashes will slide freely.

3. Go outside and paint the parts of the window that are accessible, this is, if you are repainting the exterior of the house at the same time.

4. Slide the window sashes back to their original position—drive a light nail into the sashes to prevent finger marks on the fresh paint. Finish painting. To prevent binding, move the sashes as soon as the paint is dry.

5. Paint window casing (trim) last.

Use a razor blade to free sashes that stick. If you decide to paint the channels in which the sashes run, you should probably remove the sashes and scrape down any old paint. Lubricating the sides of the sashes and the channels with tung or linseed oil will aid sliding.

BACK TO NATURAL: STRIPPING AND FINISHING WOOD

Wood is beautiful: the current mania for stripping paint to bare that beauty is wholly understandable. Although stripping paint can be tedious, especially if the woodwork is ornate, it's a labor well rewarded. Before doing a major stripping job, however, test-strip a small patch to determine the type of wood you are dealing with. In the past,

TABLE 18.2

Wood strippers

Stripper	Use	Comments
MILD		
Turpentine	Cuts wax and grease	Wipe on or off with soft rag; use toothbrush or cotton swabs for tight spots
Mineral spirits	Dissolves shellac and varnish	Relatively mild
Denatured alcohol	Dissolves shellac and varnish	Strong; cut with mineral spirits or lacquer thinner for mild mix (15% alcohol)
Baking soda, trisodium phosphates, household cleaners, and ammoniated cleaners	Partially remove shellac and varnish	Act as mild abrasives; vary strength; remove mildew
Prepaint deglosser	Scuffs painted, shellacked or varnished surfaces	Mild abrasives; obviates sanding between coats; partially removes surfaces
STRONG		
Methylene chloride	Good on oil-base paints and all clear finishes	Water-soluble; nonflammable; excellent for indoor use; hold wallpaper steamer over area to speed things up
Methanol, acetone, benzols, and toluol	Dissolve most coatings	Flammable; best for exterior use
Heat gun	Paint removal	Use with nonflammable chemicals; don't use on shellac, varnish, etc., or near window panes
Peel-Away™	Strips ornate trim easily	Wonderful new product. Get info by calling Dumond Chemicals, NYC, NY

builders often used ordinary softwoods because they intended to cover them with paint. Think twice about stripping vast expanses of common pine or spruce.

Using some common sense can save you considerable work. In some out-of-the-way spot, chip off a small area of finish or paint, using a razor scraper. Look at the underlying layers closely. You can also use a heat gun or chemical strippers, but they melt coatings, causing them to fuse. How many layers do you find?

Use the least amount of work and materials to get the job done. If you've discovered that the finish is wax, gently remove it with turpentine applied using a soft rag. Use a cotton swab on ornate areas. If the finish is shellac or lacquer, try a mild mixture of washing soda (sodium bicarbonate) or trisodium phosphate. Denatured alcohol, cut with lacquer thinner or mineral spirits, may also do the trick. Start with a weak solution (15 percent denatured alcohol) on a small spot. Table 18.2 lists strippers appropriate for various coatings, as well as finishes that will enhance and protect wood once it has been exposed.

Safety

As with painting, be sure you have adequate ventilation when stripping or refinishing. Strip woodwork during the warm months so you can leave windows open while you work. Wearing rubber gloves and long-sleeved shirts is a must when using strippers. Wear goggles, too, particularly if you're working at or above eye level. Apply all strippers carefully, brushing them on slowly to minimize splashing clothes or floors. A semipaste stripper is the most manageable form, particularly on vertical surfaces. As you work, lay down newspapers, replacing them as they become splattered. It goes almost without saying that you should strip trim before finishing floors.

Read the labels for all materials. Know how to react when something is ingested or gets on your skin. Keep children and animals away.

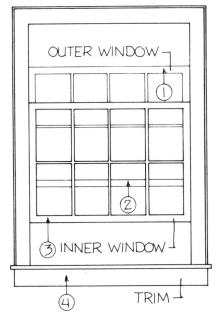

Figure 18.17 The sequence of painting a double-hung window.

The risk of fire is great with many stripping methods. Have a fire extinguisher handy, as well as the phone number of the fire department. In general, it is not wise to use a propane torch or any other flame for stripping mounted wood; there's often no way of knowing what combustibles are hidden in the wall behind. Don't smoke around flammable substances. Further, some strippers (such as those with a benzol base) are so volatile they should never be used inside. Even a tiny spark from steel wool on nail heads or on electrical outlets has been known to cause fires.

Note: Do not mix chlorine bleaches and ammonia: the by-product, chlorine gas, can be lethal.

Equipment for Stripping

A job is much easier if you have the right tools and equipment. Rubber gloves are imperative when working around paint strippers; so are goggles. To minimize mess, have plenty of newspapers to lay down; roll up fouled paper and stuff it in plastic garbage bags. The best brushes for the task are natural bristle and usually, nylon; some of the other synthetic bristles sold for use with latex paint may be dissolved by paint remover. Toothbrushes are good for applying paint remover in tight areas.

Scrapers: Your choice of scrapers is important. Standard paint scrapers and putty knives are fine for removing large areas of paint, but grind down their corners so they don't dig into wood. If you have a lot of woodwork with the same profile, record the profile with a profile gauge and transfer that to a piece of light-gauge (No. 30 or No. 28) metal which you can use as a scraper. Cut out the profile on the sheet steel and sand it lightly to remove burrs.

Dentist's tools work well on ornate work such as pressed wood; also available are molder-scrapers with changeable blades. For final cleaning and rinsing, use steel wool.

Heating apparatus: Heat guns, heating irons, and propane torches are other ways to remove paint. All three should be regarded as dangerous and detrimental to wood if not used properly. Use no flammable solvents around them. Of the three, the propane torch is the most dangerous, because it can start a fire on the surface you're scraping or in the wall behind. If you use a torch, put a flame-spreader on it and keep the flame moving. When the paint bubbles, scrape it.

Place a heating iron right on the wood, lifting it periodically to see whether the paint underneath is bubbling. Because the plate of a heating iron obscures one's view of the painted surface, scorched wood is common; thus the tool is not always effective. If that tool is your choice, however, be sure to scrape off all paint on the heating plate before turning the device off.

The last, and most desirable, implement to be discussed here is a heat gun (similar in appearance to a gun-type hair dryer), which runs on 110- or 220-volt current. Since most heat guns are rated for 14 to 15 amperes, don't use another appliance on the circuit at the same time. A heat gun has its limitations, though: shellac and varnish have low kindling temperatures and tend to burn when heated. Never use a heat gun next to glass—for example, on window muntins—because you could crack the glass.

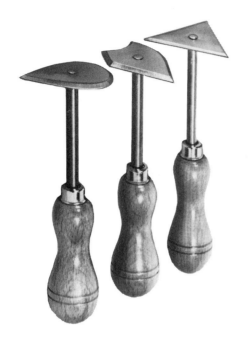

A.

neath. If the wood becomes fibrous and soft, you have applied too much. Rinse the surface and allow it to dry well before continuing.

A sequence of stripping. Here is a standard procedure for stripping:

1. Open windows and spread newspapers or tarps.

2. Wear gloves and goggles, and apply stripper liberally, brushing it on *in one direction only:* away from your eyes. Some strippers erode rubber; cloth-covered rubber gloves will last longer, although they are not as pliable as all-rubber gloves.

3. When the stripper has had time to work, remove the resultant paint sludge with a flat knife or a tool appropriate to the surface. Clean scraping tools periodically.

4. Rub No. 3 steel wool with the wood grain to touch up paint missed by the scraper. Rinse the pad often in household cleaner solution or an appropriate solvent. If you raise wood fiber, either go to a finer steel wool and/or don't scrub as hard. Never use sudsing steel wool pads on woodwork.

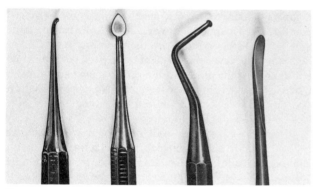

B.

Figure 18.18 Scraping tools. (A) Shave hooks (Brookstone Company); (B) dental tools for ornate woodwork.

Finally, a steamer can be useful for stripping paint. The action of some water-based strippers, such as methylene chloride, is speeded up by heat. The three types of heating apparatus described above dry out the water in strippers, but a wallpaper steamer won't. Don't put the steamer pan right on the surface you're stripping; an inch or two above is better. If you put the steamer on the surface, the stripper could clog steam pores. Never use any heat around solvent-based strippers, though, unless the manufacturer explicitly states that you may.

Stripping with Chemicals

The basic techniques of stripping paint are simple, but the patience and persistence required can be great. Observe the action of the stripping chemical and apply the stripper liberally. Touch up areas where the chemical has dried, then scrape. Give the stripper time to work—15 to 20 minutes if you're stripping several layers of paint. As you work, you'll get a feel for the stripper: apply just enough chemical to strip unwanted finish, without harming the wood under-

A.

B.

Figure 18.19 No-flame heating guns. (A) (Brookstone Company); (B) (HeJet, the Pamran Co.)

A.

B.

C.

D.

E.

F.

Figure 18.20 Stripping woodwork. (A) Wearing rubber gloves to protect your hands, apply paint stripper with a natural-bristle brush. Most synthetic brushes will be dissolved by the stripper. (B) After allowing the stripper to work for 10 or 15 minutes, scrub away loose paint with steel wool. Try No. 1 grade steel wool; if that seems too coarse for the wood, use a finer grade. (C,D) Dental tools are unsurpassed for cleaning fine beading and pressed wood detail. Keep a paper towel handy for cleaning tools frequently. Fine-strip after scrubbing larger expanses with steel wool. (E) Wipe well, and then go back to scrape any spots overlooked. (F) Before staining and refinishing woodwork, rinse it well with clear water to remove all stripper residue. If the stripper contains lye, a vinegar wash will neutralize it. (Work courtesy of Robert Provenzano.)

5. Wipe the scraped woodwork clean with a rinse compatible with the stripper you are using (water with methylene chloride; alcohol for most solvent-based strippers). Use rags or paper towels for the rinse.

6. You should be able to strip missed spots with spot application of the stripper. If, after rinsing, the wood grain is soft or fibrous, allow it to dry overnight before continuing.

7. Before putting a new finish onto the stripped wood,

sand surfaces lightly. If the sandpaper quickly becomes gummed, the wood must be further scraped and/or rinsed. When the wood is dry, sand it again; when the surface is well sanded, wipe it with a tack rag and refinish it.

Dip stripping. Dipping woodwork (or furniture) in a vat of stripping solution is not advisable. If the wood is quite common and you're not worried about the grain being raised, dip stripping will save considerable time. While it is in the tank, however, wood absorbs a lot of the solvent. Wood then swells, often obliterating fine details, and frequently cracks when it dries. Hand–stripping, though tedious, is probably best.

Wood that is dip-stripped may not take a good finish afterward if some of the stripping solvent remains. To neutralize lye, wipe both sides of the piece with full strength vinegar; let it stand for a half-hour, then rinse well with water. Allow the wood to dry thoroughly before finishing.

To remove trim without breaking it, you must be patient and methodical. First, run a stiff putty knife down the edge of the trim to break any paint seal with the wall or with an adjacent piece of trim. (Don't use a razor; it will cut into the wood.) Slide in a putty-knife blade behind the trim, then insert another blade between the wall and the first knife blade; further slide a flathead screwdriver point

between the two blades. Pry up slightly with the screwdriver. Repeat this procedure along the length of the piece.

If the piece doesn't come off easily, try cutting the nails holding it. After prying up the piece in the manner described, slip a metal-cutting reciprocating saw blade behind the wood and saw the nail shanks.

With a flat bar, pry off woodwork that is sturdy enough to be removed in this manner. For optimal results and minimal damage to the wall, first put a wood shingle between the wall and the pry bar. Take your time: if the wood cracks no matter what care you take, try recording its profile and have new molding made.

Before removing trim, map out its entire assemblage. As you remove each piece, label it with a crayon or a piece of plastic punch tape, to guide you when reinstalling that trim. If you're having the trim dip-stripped, consider using a wood-burning stylus to write assembly numbers on the back.

TABLE 18.3 Wood Finishes
(See Table 20.1 for floor finishes.)

Finish	Characteristics	Comments
Butcher's wax	Moderately durable but not a lasting finish; can be applied over hard finishes and rebuffed to increase sheen	Must be reapplied to floors at least 3 to 4 times a year; very nice for old softwood floors and where hard finishes would chip or crack;must be stripped before other finishes can be applied over it
Lemon oil	Brings out rich colors in wood; fair moisture resistance, fair to poor durability	Cannot cover with wax or other finishes, for it remains oily; to take other finishes, must be cut slightly with mild mixture of alcohol and mineral spirits and allowed to dry well
Boiled linseed oil	Neither durable nor water-resistant, yet brings out color and sheen of wood	Good as a conditioner of dry wood; if hard finish desired over it, mix 50-50 with mineral spirits or turpentine, rub in well, let dry 1 to 2 weeks
Antiquing and polishing oil	Can be buffed to a very high sheen; prized for fine furniture finishes; fair to poor water resistance	A finishing coat; not compatible with shellac; use sparingly
Tung oil	Very durable; excellent water resistance	Acceptable to use on wood near water; apply half-dozen coats (including end grain and underside) before setting sink—allow each coat to dry; reapply monthly; good for window sashes where condensation is a problem; good wood conditioner
Shellac	Least durable of hard finishes; poor resistance to water; chips easily; inappropriate for softwoods	Easy to maintain but not durable; sand between coats; will discolor in bright sunlight; becomes milky near moisture
Varnish	Durable, hard finish; can be mixed with tung oil for water resistance; good buffing qualities	For best finish, thin first coat with turpentine, mineral spirits; easy to touch up but won't stick to undercoats of linseed oil or polyurethane; sand between coats
Polyurethane	Durable on hardwoods; good water resistance; available in solvent and water-thinned varieties	Best on hardwoods; when used on softwoods, flexes and dulls; not good where there's standing water; be sure to thin early coats; sand between coats

Refinishing

Once woodwork has been stripped, sand it well, either by hand or by machine. A block sander is the most versatile tool; an orbital sander works well for relatively large, flat pieces; most belt sanders are thoroughly inappropriate. Use No. 90-grit sandpaper, regardless of the sander, and follow that with No. 120-grit. If those grades seem too rough, go to No. 150 or No. 220.

To sand tight areas, fold sandpaper and use the crease; wrap sandpaper around a dowel for concave spots; standard blackboard erasers make excellent sanding blocks. After sanding with a fine-grain sandpaper, wipe the woodwork with a tack rag or a cloth dampened slightly with turpentine. If you intend to stain, now is the time to do so.

First condition wood that is exceptionally dry. A 15 to 25 percent solution of boiled linseed oil or tung oil in a medium of turpentine or alcohol thins the oil. If you want a hard finish, use only one coat of thinned oil. Rub the oil in well with a rag and allow it to dry until there is *no* oiliness to the touch. Before conditioning any wood, however, first check the label of the clear finish you'll eventually use—to make sure it will adhere to wood so conditioned. Usually there will be no problem.

The first coat of any clear finish should also be thinned with alcohol or turpentine (or whatever the manufacturer suggests), which soaks in and bonds well. Brush on the first coat of clear finish and allow it to dry. Sand slightly and wipe with a tack rag before applying another coat. Always paint the outside of trim edges first and then smooth with steady brushstrokes down the middle. Always work from top to bottom.

PAINTING THE EXTERIOR

The photographs in Figure 18.22 emphasize the importance of preparing the surface properly before applying paint. Most of the paint failures depicted are failures of preparation, or the lack of a vapor barrier within.

Common Paint Failures

Blistering usually indicates moisture trapped beneath paint, and is caused by painting over damp wood, green wood, or a preceding coat of paint that isn't completely dry. Such blisters contain water. Air blisters occur when the painter fails to sand between glossy coats of paint or when the surface is too warm to be painted. Lance blisters to find out which problem it is. Scrape all blisters well, allow the wood to dry thoroughly, then spot-prime.

Peeling and flaking, though similar to blistering, suggest a moisture problem that is more widespread. They are a common problem in older houses with no vapor barriers. However, if the house you are renovating has been retrofitted with insulation *and* a vapor barrier, water may have been trapped inside the walls during installation—a decidedly unhealthy condition, since the moisture can rot the structure.

To correct the condition, insert vent plugs in the siding so that moisture can escape. Excess moisture in a house can

Figure 18.21 This chap's ''eczema'' is probably caused by improper priming.

also be removed by ventilator fans. This condition can also be corrected by using a stain rather than a paint; stain is more permeable and will allow water vapor to escape. On rare occasions, flaking occurs because a surface was too warm to paint on.

Wrinkling is caused by paint put on too thick or by painting when the exterior of a house is too cold. This condition is also common where the paint wasn't brushed in well or paint was too thick and should have been thinned slightly. Paint should glide on; the brush should not drag. Sand well before painting again.

Alligatoring is another paint-buildup problem, often occurring after application of paint on a hot, humid day. Either an earlier undercoat did not air completely or the paint above was too thick. Scrape and/or strip.

Crackling resembles alligatoring, but it goes all the way down to the wood siding and is most commonly caused by too many layers of paint. Before painting the surface, strip the cracked paint off; scraping alone is insufficient.

Nail stains can occur where nongalvanized nails were used without being spot-primed with white shellac or a sealer-primer. Sand off the rust marks and prime nail heads.

Bleeding is most common where softwood rosins bleed though the paint, especially around knots. Prime knots with primer-sealer or shellac.

Chalking isn't a problem unless it is excessive. Each time it rains, exterior paint should chalk a little. If chalking is excessive, the painter probably used cheap paint.

Hairline checking indicates a possibly incompatible primer and topcoat. It can also indicate paint that is aging. Scrape and repaint.

Another category of paint failure common to old houses is flaking due to exposure of wood siding to the weather. This form of flaking isn't caused by water, as described above; rather, the wood wasn't primed at all or was allowed to weather too long before it was painted. When paint eventually was applied, it adhered only to a top layer of degraded wood. To remedy this condition, sand the areas affected, apply a water-repellant wood preservative, and prime as soon as the preservative is dry. Again, compare paint labels for compatibility before you begin.

A.

B.

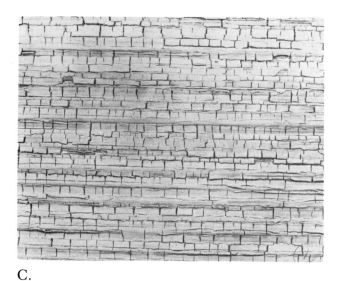

C.

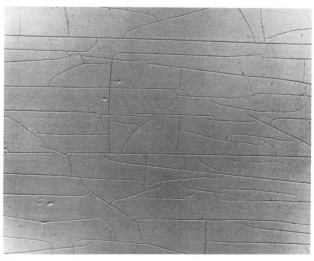

D.

Surface Preparation

Safety review. Please review Chapter 3 about equipment safety before you start. Avoid high work when you're tired. Place a ladder bottom out from a building no more than one-fourth the ladder's height; set firm footing for all ladders and scaffolding. Keep your hips between the sides of the ladder; don't lean out beyond the sides. Wear baggy clothing for freedom of movement. Hang your paint can with an S-hook or a bent coat hanger, so you will have both hands free. Wear hard-soled shoes to fight foot-on-rung fatigue. Moreover, you're well-advised to wear a respirator mask during all phases of prep and painting.

E.

Figure 18.22 Common paint failures. (A) Blistering; (B) peeling and flaking; (C) alligatoring; (D) checking and cracking; (E) excessive chalking.

Also, any surface prep is prodigiously messy, so rent heavy duty tarps to cover your lawn and shrubs. Shake tarps daily to keep up with the debris. An untarped job can mean picking paint scraps out of your grass for years or—even worse—possibly exposing neighborhood kids and pets to old lead-based paint.

Persistent moisture problems. Deal with problems of persistent moisture before painting; causes and remedies are discussed at length in Chapters 5, 6, 7, and 13. Moisture from the atmosphere is rarely a problem unless it gets behind the membranes—the roof and siding—designed to keep it out. Here are some important considerations:

1. A healthy roof should be your first priority. Repair damaged roofing shingles and flashing around chimneys, stack pipes, and similar elements. Maintain gutters and downspouts to prevent water backup.
2. Windows and doors should have cap flashing, and their perimeters should be caulked.
3. Caulk and renail all loose siding, filling holes with wood filler and priming all such spots.
4. If a given face—especially the southern face of a house—has deteriorated, strip it off and replace it rather than repair it piecemeal.
5. Do not use green wood for repairs; it shrinks too much.

Scraping and spot–priming. Before scraping and spot-priming, spread tarps on the ground and over all plants. Scrape back loose paint at least a foot beyond deteriorated areas, using a wire brush, a wide-blade knife, or a scraper. Be sure to scrape the lower edges of clapboards and beneath windowsills. Once loose paint has been removed, sand *all* surfaces to ensure a good bond to the following coat. Lightweight block sanders are the most useful type; orbital or back-and-forth sanders are also appropriate, but heavy-duty commercial belt or rotary sanders sand too deeply and often leave swirl marks. Brush off all sawdust and dirt with a house broom or the air hose of a compressor.

Spot-prime all areas scraped down to the wood, as well as filling in nail holes, caulking or filling cracks, and filling in knotholes.

Spot-prime all areas that need extra attention: wood exposed by scraping, filled nail holes, caulked cracks, siding discolored for any reason. If there are bleeding knots or rusty nail heads, prime them with primer-sealers such as BIN; shellac also works on knotholes. For metal gutters, trim and such, use a metal primer. Fill sunken nail heads and small depressions with exterior spackle. Where wood is badly deteriorated, you should remove it, but if the rot is localized and the trim would be difficult to replace, scrape loose matter away and impregnate the remaining area with one of the epoxy fillers mentioned on page 132.

Finally, if the house is generally grimy, scrub it with a broom or scrub brush dipped in a pail of detergent solution ($\frac{1}{4}$ cup detergent per gallon of warm water). Rinse with a garden hose. Let the scrubbed surface dry completely before painting it.

To thoroughly wash and rinse an exterior, however, rent a *pressure washer*, which has a small boiler and a high-pressure electric pump. (Have the supplier explain its use in detail.) Using a detergent especially designed for such a unit, you can dislodge blistered paint, thus eliminating a lot of scraping. The tool also helps you to identify problem areas, say, incipient rot along the eaves, for you'll see poorly adhered paint falling off in chunks. With the same tool, rinse the surface with hot, clean water. Because the pressure forces water into cracks, allow 2 to 3 days of dry weather for the exterior to dry before painting.

Mildew control. First, determine whether a discolored spot is actually mildew. Wipe it with a rag dipped in bleach; if it's mildew, the spot will disappear, if merely dirt, the spot will remain.

Get rid of mildew by making the surface inhospitable and inedible to organisms that thrive on it. To 1 gal of warm water add $\frac{1}{2}$ cup household detergent, $\frac{1}{2}$ cup trisodium phosphate or 1 qt liquid bleach (the variety containing sodium hypochloride). Do *not* mix chlorine bleach and ammoniated cleaners, however, for that may produce a toxic gas. Wearing gloves and goggles, scrub the mildewed area with this solution. Rinse the spot with a garden hose and allow it to dry. Prime the area with a mildrew-resistant primer—one coat if it's alkyd or oil-based, two coats if latex.

Stripping exterior paints. Do not strip paint unless you must; scraping will suffice for most exteriors. You must strip, however, if existing coats are too thick; how thick that is can usually be determined by checking with your eye and using common sense, especially where paint has cracked down to the wood's surface. Take a penknife or a scraper and dislodge a chunk of paint: anything greater than 15 to 20 mils is too thick to apply more paint on top. (By comparison, most polyethylene sheet plastic is 3 mils thick.) Scaffolding is imperative for such large jobs. Before you start, however, get a bid for *replacing* all the siding: that may make more sense in the long run.

Your choice of paint strippers is similar to that for interior work: sanders; chemicals, water-based or solvent; heat gun or open-flame torch. Sandblasting is another, less plausible possibility.

Sanders. Sanders are not good strippers for most people because they can cut into wood siding too quickly, and you need strong arms to run one all day. Such tools are totally unsuitable for sanding detail woodwork. Smaller sanders (orbital or rotary) are very useful after you've removed most of the paint with another method. Use No. 30 to No. 60 sandpaper (medium coarse) for most exterior finish sanding.

Chemical Strippers. Chemical strippers are an effective but expensive way to strip something as large as a house. Since ventilation is rarely a problem, you can use some of the nastier solvent-based strippers outside; but wear a respirator mask, goggles, and long-sleeved shirt and gloves anyhow. As a stripper, methylene chloride is good; it's water-based and gentle on wood. Use it with a wallpaper steamer, as described for painting interiors. Chemical strippers are particularly appropriate where delicate trim or detail work is involved. Allow the stripper time to work—at least 10 minutes, and possibly 15.

A.

B.

C.

D.

Figure 18.23 Preparing the exterior. (A,B) Where paint flaking is localized, scrape back until you reach well-adhering paint. If flaking is widespread, scrape and sand the entire surface. (C) Exterior trim can be stripped with solvent or, shown here, with heat; use contoured tools for tight spots. (D) Before painting large expanses, spot-paint the underside of siding, around windows and doors, and where siding abuts corners and eaves. (Sweeny Painting; F. J. Manno Co.)

Open-Flame Torch. An open-flame torch is probably the fastest stripper and is a favorite of professionals. Burning, can, however, produce toxic fumes, char wood (adversely affecting the adherence of paint unless the wood is well sanded afterward), and can cause dry materials inside the walls to ignite. Keep the flame moving, scraping as soon as the paint bubbles. Have a fire extinguisher handy.

Note: Avoid inhaling the fumes of lead-based paints; a respirator mask with changeable filters is imperative.

Heat Gun. A heat gun (or heating iron) isn't as effective as an open-flame gun but is much safer. The technique is similar: hold the heat until the paint bubbles, then scrape. Remember that no heat stripper is completely safe; even no-flame models can cause a fire within a wall: always follow operating instructions scrupulously.

Sandblasting. Sandblasting is not advisable for amateur use nor, on most surfaces, by professionals: it removes paint alright, but the method is highly destructive to any surface underneath. It pits and scars wood, destroying its watershedding ability; fine detail is obliterated. Think twice about sandblasting painted brick, too; those walls were

probably painted to begin with because their mortar was fatigued. Sandblast, and you will have to repoint as well.

Whatever stripping method you choose, strip during a dry period. By tacking sheet plastic along the eaves, you will have an emergency tarp to roll down should there be a storm. Avoid exposing old wood to the weather for any period of time. Once the face has been stripped, prime and paint it at once. Before painting, make sure that the surface

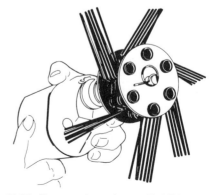

Figure 18.24 Rotary paint-stripper. (Goldblatt Tool Co.)

has been rinsed and is free of chemicals and that is it *dry*. Stripping a house is a big job; you may want to do only one side of the house each summer.

Finally, to reiterate an important point: cover the ground and shrubs with tarps; the debris from stripping paint is messy. It's also voluminous. Therefore, clean tarps at the end of each working day and cart away the debris.

Exterior Paint

The choice of exterior paints is considerable, including specialty ones such as asphalt-based coatings for built-up roofs and metal roofs; deck enamel for porches; paint for canvas awnings; silicone-based preservatives for shake and shingle roofs, mildew-resistant paint and so on. Consult your supplier if you have a special need.

The alkyd family of paints is the workhorse of exterior painting, just as it is for interior painting, because of its superior adhesion. Even when a topcoat is latex, professionals often prime with an alkyd primer.

Stains have become increasingly popular, and some can be applied over paint. The stains mentioned in Table 18.4 though, are the more traditional wood stains.

Painting over preservatives. Generally, it's not advisable to paint over preservatives. If something needs preserving,

it's better to apply preservative and reapply it periodically. In hot, humid regions, though, sills, splashboards, lower courses of siding, and porches may need to be preserved *and* painted, so they will match the rest of the exterior.

Probably the best thing to do is buy Wolmanized lumber, which has preservative pressure-treated into it during manufacture. Such wood can be painted over with fairly good results. Preservatives borne in a metal base such as Cuprinol (copper-based) are somewhat less durable as preservatives but are acceptable as undercoats once they are dry. Creosote and penta are very effective preservatives, but they are too oily to hold a covering of paint.

The final arbiters of the compatibility of a preservative are the paint manufacturers. The labels on paint cans display the information. Most preservatives are highly toxic, so handle them carefully.

Applying Exterior Paint

Optimal conditions. Because the main cause of paint failure or deterioration is moisture, your first requisite for painting is a dry day. Check the label on the can for the recommended drying time, especially if the weather is expected to change soon. Wait several days after a rain, and allow morning mists to evaporate before starting.

TABLE 18.4
Exterior painting[a]

Area of Application	Alkyd, Oil-Based House Paint	Latex House Paint, Stain	Wood Stains, Creosotes, Preservatives	Spar Varnish and Other Clear Finishes[b]	Transparent Sealer	Stain-Blocking Primer	Enamel Trim Paint	Aluminum Paint	Cement-Base Masonry Paint	Latex Masonry Paint
Wood siding (painted)	⊗	⊗				X				
Wood windows and trim (painted)							⊗			
Wood siding and trim (natural)			X	X						
Metal siding	⊗	⊗				X		⊗		
Metal windows and trim	⊗	⊗				X	⊗			
Brick	⊗	X			X				X	X
Concrete block and stucco	⊗	X			X				X	X
Metal roof	⊗					X		⊗		
Galvanized[c] and iron (gutters flashing, etc.)	⊗	⊗				X	⊗	⊗		
Copper				X						

[a]X can be applied directly to surface; ⊗ prime first with compatible primer.

[b]Paints can be applied over lacquers, but not vice versa.

[c]Galvanized surfaces should be left unpainted for at least 6 months, so factory sealant can weather off; or wash surfaces with a mild muriatic acid solution— 1 part acid, 20 parts water. Wear rubber gloves, safety glasses and a respirator mask.

Temperature is another important consideration: paint must set before the temperature drops below 40°F. For that reason, it's best not to paint within 2 hours of sundown if nighttime temperatures could go below that level. Unusually high temperatures are a problem as well, because surfaces that are too hot can cause paint to blister.

The best way to avoid strong sun is to paint in the shade: paint the south face early in the morning; then the west face; the north side at noon; in the afternoon, work the east face and any part of the south face that you didn't finish earlier. Avoid painting in temperatures above 90°F.

Paint the house from top to bottom, working horizontal sections all the way across, until they end at window or door trim, or at the end of a wall. This method minimizes overlap marks. After painting large sections, go back and paint trim, again from top to bottom. Porches and decks should be done last. If you can easily remove any pieces, such as storms or shutters, do so; paint them as they lie across sawhorses or lean against a garage wall.

Priming. Prime all exposed wood. Check the label or the topcoat paint to be sure you get the correct primer. Alkyd or oil-based primers have better adhesion on smooth, dry surfaces; but if the outside is unusually rough, latex may be a better choice. Always sand between primer coats and topcoats.

For bleed-through areas, use sealer-primer; shellac is good for knots and nail holes, but it must also be covered (when dry) with a primer or a topcoat.

Spar varnish is its own primer coat, as are most other clear, exterior finishes. Thin the first coats with a solvent, to permit greater soaking into the surface. Sand lightly between coats. Although some paints (oil and alkyd) may be applied over clear finishes that have dried, the reverse is not true, for the solvents in clear finishes often dissolve paint.

Stains do not need thinning; they should be applied full-strength right to bare wood. Most will not bond, however, to any previous nonstain coats. If you have stripped the house of its original paint, and want to switch to stain, test a small section first.

If you stripped off old paint and now wish to repaint, prime with two coats of oil-based or alkyd primer. Cut the first coat of primer at least 25 percent with solvent, for greater soaking and adhesion. Apply the second coat of primer at full strength. After that, one, or at most two, coats of topcoat is sufficient. It is not necessary to sand between coats of exterior paint.

Where you are working with exposed wood, save some money by using two coats of primer and one of topcoat, rather than one primer and two topcoats. If the paint manufacturer recommends only one coat of each, follow directions. Durable paint jobs depend not upon the number of paint layers but upon the adherence of each layer.

Brushing it on. When possible, mix at the same time all the paint you will need for completing a job, so the house will have uniform color (or colors) throughout. It's also helpful to have extra empty cans, so you can work out of a half-full can; a full can is a nuisance, and a can that is nearly empty means dredging up the thicker paint at the bottom of the can. To maintain consistency, add paint frequently to your work can.

A brush's bristles should be dipped into paint to a depth of about one-third the length of the bristles. Tap—don't scrape—a loaded brush against the rim of the can, to unload excess. Paint the undersides of horizontal siding first; then work paint into the faces. To distribute paint evenly along siding, partially unload the brush by dabbing every foot or so; then spread out the dabs, working them in with cross-diagonals and smoothing them out along the length of the siding.

Work all the way across a horizontal section to avoid lap marks—another excellent reason for scaffolding. Work about six courses of clapboard at a time. Where you encounter nails or butt seams, slap in a little paint and smooth it over, rather than jamming bristle ends into the wood.

Stains apply nicely to natural-wood surfaces with brush pads because a foam pad holds a lot of stain. The only problem is control: load pads with too much stain and it will run. Again, paint the undersides of shingle or clapboard courses first. Most stains contain solvents that are

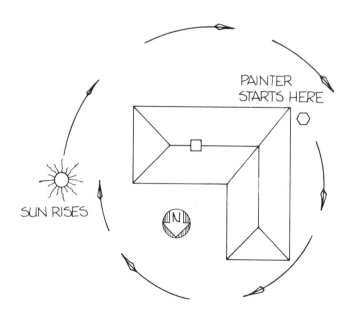

Figure 18.25 Follow the sun around the house as you paint so that you work in the shade. Paint applied in full sunlight may not adhere well.

extremely caustic, so wear a long-sleeved shirt, gloves, a hat with a brim, and safety goggles. Stains are an excellent wood preservative because they are so tough on living things, such as mildew and insects. The same applies to human skin. Use them carefully, therefore. Finally, consider spray-painting the exterior.

Painting masonry. Preparing a masonry surface is important. Use a wire brush to remove loose material. If you find grease or oil on the surfaces, wash it off with a detergent such as trisodium phosphate; then rinse well. Other, more stubborn substances can be handled with a weak solution of muriatic acid; wear goggles and gloves, and rinse well. Fill major cracks and holes before painting, and if there are any moisture problems, deal with them before painting, too (see Chapter 9). Although water-sealer paints are available, none are absolute protection against serious moisture problems.

Use rollers to apply paint to large masonry areas. Where walls meet floors, "cut" edges with a brush; similarly, on steps or in cramped areas, use a brush. For very rough areas, use a 6-in. brush or a roller with a long nap. In either case, apply paint slowly so painting tools won't splatter.

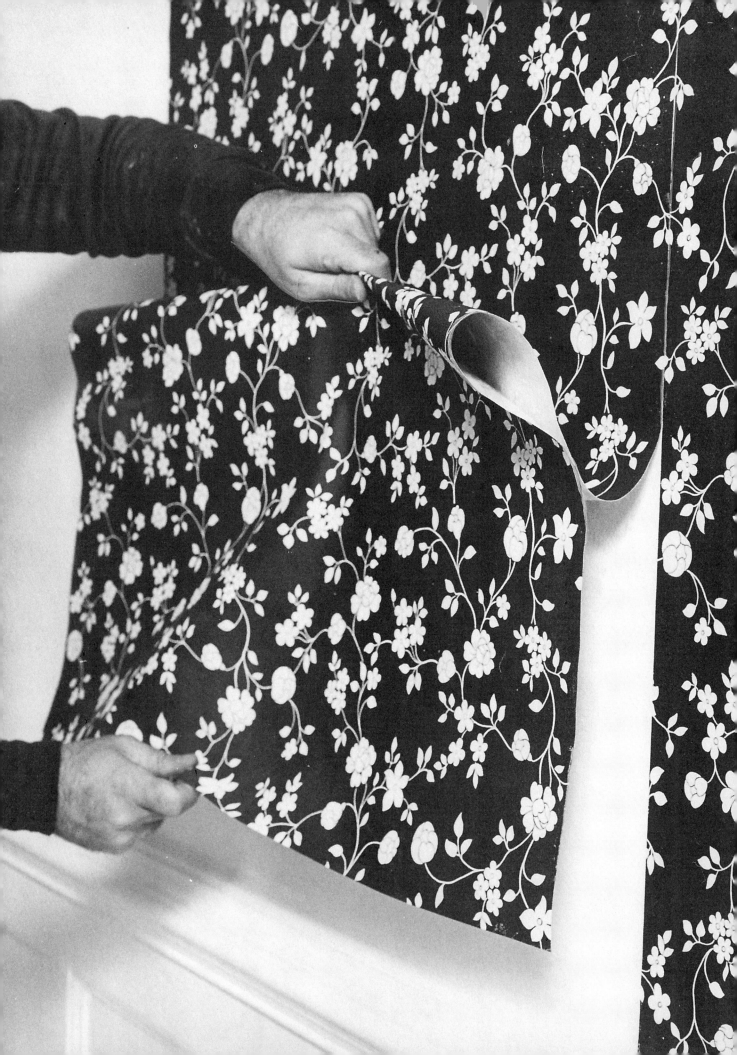

·19·

WALLPAPERING

Wallpaper has long been a popular way to dress up a room, particularly a formal room where there is little danger of the paper getting scuffed or dirty. Paint has been favored for the more lived-in rooms. That's changing. Wallpapers are now available in so many materials that they are more accurately called "wall coverings" and they can be used almost anywhere. Coverings are usually backed with paper or cloth, with cloth-backed wallpaper being stronger and more durable. Facings include vinyl, fabric, rice paper, grasses and bamboo, flocks, foil, cork and wood veneer. Also available are wall coverings that are prepasted, washable, strippable, and grease-resistant.

MATERIALS

Wall Coverings

Wall*paper* is most appropriate where you want fine detail or historically accurate restoration. Although vinyl coverings are increasingly hard to distinguish from those of paper stock, vinyls are still generally glossier than paper. Paper has a much flatter finish but is more vulnerable to grime and abuse; use it in sedate, formal rooms.

Vinyls are the workhorses of wall coverings. They are suitable for areas where there's a lot of traffic and/or moisture. Because vinyl is so durable, it is the most popular

group; the range of designs and finishes has increased greatly. Most types are washable, and cloth-backed ones are usually strippable as well. Although no wall covering is intended to conceal major flaws on the walls behind, heavier vinyls cover minor cracks and irregularities well.

Consider using fabrics as wall coverings to color–coordinate or fabric-match drapes or furniture in a room. You can adapt many fabrics into wall coverings, including bed sheets and expensive off-the-bolt cloth intended for clothing (worsted-wool walls?); or you can buy fabric prebacked with paper, ready for hanging. For the longest life, fabric should be laminated to paper backing; if you choose to adapt a fabric, it should be preshrunk so it won't shrink once paste is applied.

Textures such as rice paper, grasses, burlap, silks, and the like are very expensive ($50 to $200 per roll) and very delicate; thus they aren't advised for novice paperers. The primary difficulty in installing them is that their backing will separate if the paste is too wet or if they are pasted too long before hanging. For that reason, and because such thin coverings reveal even minor blemishes in the walls underneath, you should cover walls with lining paper first.

Foils vary greatly. The better grades are as temperamental as the textured coverings just discussed, although the heavier, vinyl-laminated types are tough, durable, and easier to install. Foils are particularly well suited to small rooms because they reflect light and extend the visual field.

Cork and wood-veneer wall coverings are warm and handsome. Finely milled and manufactured, they make

449

much better use of cork and rare wood than does, say, $\frac{1}{2}$-in.-thick paneling.

You can have wall coverings fabricated from virtually any pattern, although such custom work will cost plenty. Transforming ordinary fabric has already been mentioned; you can also have historical documents or prints fabricated for a study, or wall-sized posters for a family room. Make sure any such custom paper stock is treated with a resistant coating, so it will wear longer.

Finally, there are *borders,* thin strips of wallcovering that run along the edges of walls where the walls meet ceilings, wainscoting, and trim. *Lincrusta,* embossed wallpaper not unlike fine cardboard, is making a comeback; analglypta wall covering, for example, is a modern version of Victorian lincrusta. There are many companies, such as San Francisco Victoriana, that supply such seemingly archaic materials.

Pastes

Like wall coverings, pastes have changed greatly. When buying materials, it's important that you buy a paste compatible with the covering you select; many pastes are closely matched to coverings. Early pastes were merely wheat flour and water; mildew-resistant additives came later. Today, with the introduction of vinyl, many pastes no longer have a wheat-flour medium.

Pastes come premixed or as powders that can be mixed by the user. Premixed varieties are generally stronger adhesives, but they may contain additives that may irritate your skin or eyes. Once opened, premixed pastes also have a relatively short life, drying quickly on the wall and within two hours in the can. Pastes that you mix yourself allow you to vary consistency; they have a longer open-can life, often as long as an entire day.

In general, the thicker the paste, the quicker it dries and the greater the weight it can support. A relatively dry (thick) paste mixture is advisable for delicate coverings such as grass wallpaper, because a paste of such consistency soaks in less and thus is less likely to separate paper backing. Medium consistency—tacky to the touch—is sufficient for most papering tasks.

To reiterate, paste types and consistencies are determined by:

1. The nature of the wall covering. Breathable, or porous, papers or fabrics can be hung with wheat pastes. Use vinyl pastes for nonporous coverings. Some clear pastes (also called ''gels'') are metalling paste and cellulose-based pastes; they're appropriate for porous wall coverings, where the paste seeps through slightly.

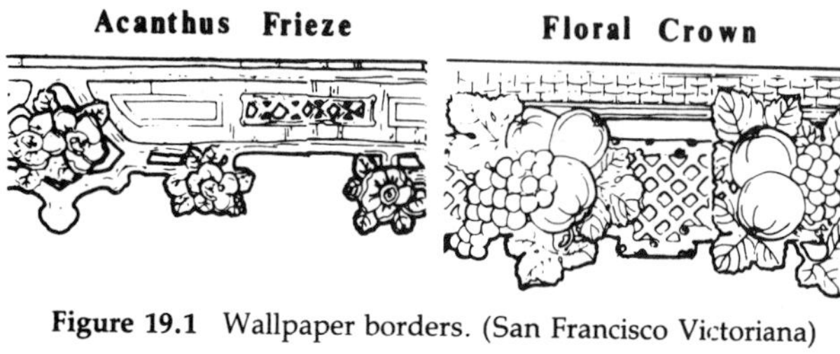

2. The weight of the covering. Vinyl pastes are best for heavy coverings, including weightier paper and cloth backings.

3. Surface factors, especially humidity and the surface finish. Where surfaces are extremely glossy and offer poor bonding, you're limited to lightweight coverings and thin paste. Epoxy pastes are available for extreme papering situations, but they must be specially ordered. Consult your supplier.

Presized pastes: *Sizing* or *size* is a glutinous material that used to be favored for sealing a wall before papering it. Sizing is discussed below, under ''Surface Preparation''; it is mentioned here because most modern pastes are presized (so you won't have to size the wall).

Note: Do not use presized wheat paste with paper-stock wall covering; the paste will shine when dry, especially along the seams. (See Table 19.1 for a reiteration of this point.)

Selecting and Ordering Materials

Most rolls (also called ''bolts'') of wall covering are 27 in. wide, a comfortable working width for most paperers, including amateurs. All the coverings listed in Table 19.1 except wood veneer come in widths of 27 in. and most are available in widths of 18 to 54 in. Wider bolts do yield fewer seams, but they are much more difficult to handle. Whatever the width of the bolt, it contains 36 sq ft of material.

When ordering wall covering, calculate the square footage of walls and ceilings to be papered, taking—in feet—length times height or, in the case of ceilings, length times width. Once you've determined the overall square footage, subtract 12 sq ft for each average-sized door and window. To get the total number of rolls you will need, divide the final total of square feet by 30. You could divide the total by 36 (the number of square feet in a roll), but by using 30 as the divisor, you ensure enough extra for waste.

If the room has numerous jogs or openings, difficult corners, or a lot of trim to cut around, order one or two rolls extra. If the pattern of the covering is bold, there will be greater wastage, because you must match patterns along the seams. Thus, the bolder and larger the pattern, the greater the wastage. Also, an extra roll or two for future repairs is a good idea.

The edges of most wall coverings are pretrimmed: simply butt their edges together after matching patterns. If the edges aren't pretrimmed, trim them now with a razor knife guided along a straightedge; such edges are called ''selvage.''

Choose a wall covering that isn't difficult to hang, that is appropriate to the room's use, and whose pattern and color are right. Textured coverings and foils are difficult and fragile; vinyls are durable and water-resistant; subdued colors are good for quiet areas. Some coverings aren't suitable for old houses that have settled unevenly or that have quirks from previous renovations. Heavy coverings may conceal wall blemishes, but lightweight papers will accentuate such flaws. Furthermore, lightweight papers will not conceal bold paints or vivid patterns underneath. If the walls or trim are out of square, avoid hanging coverings with large patterns; they will draw attention to tilting trim they abut.

Acanthus Frieze   Floral Crown

Figure 19.1 Wallpaper borders. (San Francisco Victoriana)

TABLE 19.1

Choosing and applying wall coverings

Wall Covering	Paste and Application	Comments about Coverings
Wallpapers, including cloth-backed	Standard unsized wheat pastes mixed according to weight of paper: medium texture will do for most papers. Soft-bristled smoothing brushes best; standard hanging procedures; apply paste to paper.	Pleasant, flat finish but susceptible to grime and abrasion.
Vinyls, including those backed to paper, cloth, etc.	Vinyl pastes, whether premixed or powder; premixed pastes offer better adhesion for heavier vinyls; avoid stretching vinyl when smoothing it; use a squeegie to smooth. Otherwise, employ standard hanging methods.	Very durable and abrasion-resistant. Favored for high-humidity areas such as bathrooms. Most types are washable and strippable.
Fabrics (unbacked and paper-backed)	Premixed clear metalling paste or cellulose-base pastes are best for unbacked fabric. Apply paste to wall. For paper-backed types, use vinyl paste and apply it directly to backing. (Wheat pastes don't hold the heavier coatings well.) Avoid stretching fabric; smooth with brush.	Fabrics should be laminated to paper for longer life. Avoid getting paste on fabric; if you do, blot off with a damp sponge.
Textured coverings such as rice paper, grass, and silk	Premixed clear metalling paste or cellulose-base pastes are best here. All coverings are delicate, so hang a lining first to minimize moisture's effects; apply paste to backing, but paste up only one strip at a time. Be careful not to crease; don't roll seams. In general, the drier the paste, the better, since drier mixes are less likely to soak paper backing.	Very expensive and difficult to hang. Invert every other sheet, to minimize uneven coloration or texture. Best used in formal rooms, where abrasion is unlikely.
Flocks (all backings)	Paste depends on backing; use standard hanging procedures, being careful not to get paste on flocking, which all but ruins the piece.	Varieties of vinyl are treated and can be washed (gently).
Foils	Manufacturer will specify whether lining is necessary; if so, apply vinyl paste to backing and get foil on the wall at once. Otherwise, apply paste to the wall first. For metallic wall coverings, add a tablespoon of borax to the paste, to prevent the metal from being oxidized by the wheat paste.	Extremely difficult to hang; separates from backing easily. Turn off electricity to area being papered.
Cork	Vinyl paste is best for adhesion; otherwise, wheat paste is alright. A good mix for cork is thickened wheat paste with a handful or two of vinyl paste mixed in.	Deadens sound somewhat.
Liners (lining paper, foam liner, heavy paper, etc.)	Can be applied to any well-prepared wall surface with most pastes. Vinyl pastes offer the best adhesion. When hanging liner, leave gaps of $\frac{1}{16}$ in. between seams, to avoid overlapped seams, which would show through with top coverings in place.	Not intended for covering major surface defects; used as a base for delicate coverings. Many types of liners available, including some that cover concrete block.
Prepasted coverings	Paste is already on backing; soak according to manufacturer's specifications.	Easy for the novice, generally spurned by professionals. Be sure edges stick.

Note: When you pick up your shipment of wall covering, check the *code number* and the *run-number* on the back of each roll. Code numbers indicate pattern and color, and run numbers tell what batch of code you're getting. The colors of different runs can vary considerably and will be especially noticeable if placed side by side. If you must accept different runs to complete a job, use the smaller quantity in a part of the room that isn't conspicuous. *Also note:* If the edges of pretrimmed coverings are frayed, refuse them. Similarly, refuse vinyls whose edges are crimped, for they cannot be rolled flat. Always store rolls of wall covering flat—not standing on end.

EQUIPMENT

A few special tools are needed for successful papering:

Plumb bob. Use a plumb bob or, for greater versatility, a level, to determine whether walls are plumb and to insure wall-covering edges that are plumb. Snap a plumbed chalk line or rule through plumbed pencil marks to determine the edge of the first piece of wall covering that you hang.

Pasting table. A pasting table should be about 3 ft. by 6 ft. Its top must be washable. A sheet of plywood, covered with plastic and laid across sawhorses, will do; but be sure there are no splinters to pierce the materials you're hanging. Do not use newspaper to cover the worktable; newsprint often bleeds. In order not to scar the top of the table, do all cutting over a separate piece of scrap wood or Masonite; professionals use zinc cutting strips to protect their tabletops.

Tape measure. A standard, retractable tape measure is sufficient for laying out and cutting wall covering to length.

Razor knives. Razor knives with replaceable blades give the finest cuts. If you want clean cuts, don't be stingy with blades; a professional may go through 200 or 300 on a big job. Get a pair of shears for rough-cutting paper from a roll.

Paste brush. To spread wheat paste on backing—or on walls, in some cases—use a paste brush. Use a roller and pan to spread vinyl paste (which is too heavy to brush on). Get advice from the supplier on how long the nap of the roller cover should be.

Soft-bristle smoothing brush. Use a soft-bristle smoothing brush to smooth out wall coverings once they are hung and to even out the paste between the backing and the wall. For heavier papers and vinyls, use a rubber squeegie or a special vinyl-smoothing blade.

Seam rollers. Seam rollers spread glue toward the edges of pieces, to ensure seams that stick well. Seam rollers are not generally recommended for delicate or finely textured papers such as flocks or grasses.

Spackling knife (6 in.). Also called a joint knife, a spackling knife is useful for filling low spots and scraping off high ones. Use it to press the wall covering against trim before cutting away excess paper.

Sponge and pail of water. Have a sponge and pail of clean water handy for wiping the pasting table clean and for re-

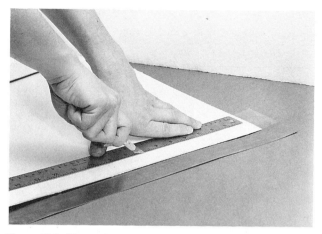

Figure 19.3 Use a zinc cutting-strip to protect the table top and ensure clean cuts. (Brookstone Co.)

moving excess paste. The sponge should be damp only when you are cleaning excess paste off wall coverings already in place. Wipe the entire strip of paper rather than just its edge, so there won't be a sheen along the seams. (We are talking about the more durable coverings; obviously, you should not sponge off a flocked paper, for example.) Also wipe woodwork well, for paste can lift the paint off wood if you try to scrape paste that has dried. Change the water in the pail often.

Other useful equipment is: a sturdy stepladder (wood is best); a long, straight board for detecting irregularities in walls and ceilings; and plenty of clean, soft rags.

If you use prepasted wall coverings, you'll need a water tray in which to soak the strips, thus activating glues; follow the covering manufacturer's advice about how long to soak the pieces. The two methods most often used for soaking the material are cutting pieces to length and rolling them in a loose bolt, and cutting a length of wall covering as you pull it up out of the tray. In the latter case, a sharp

Figure 19.2 Basic papering tools. *Clockwise from left:* level, paste brush, seam roller, sponge, smoothing brush, 6-in. spackling knife, razor knife, shears. (Painting Plus)

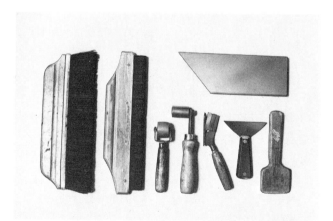

Figure 19.4 Not-so-common papering tools. *From left:* soft-bristled smoothing brush, for delicate materials; stiff-bristled smoothing brush, for vinyl and similar surfaces; curved bone seamroller, an old tool used on delicate coverings; standard seam roller (too wide for delicate coverings); a "zipper" for cutting paper hung on stone or marble; a small scraper for smoothing out heavy vinyl and Flex-wood; a wood paddle for working inside corners of heavy materials such as vinyl; *Top right:* a "Philadelphia plate," for trimming corners to a 45-degree angle. (Tool collection courtesy of Abe Gershbein, Painting Plus.)

blade in your knife is essential; otherwise, the wetted paper will rip easily. After using up each roll, rinse the tray and fill it with clean water for the next batch. A bathtub can be used in lieu of a water tray, but it must be spotlessly clean, and it too should be rinsed between batches of paper.

SURFACE PREPARATION

Preparation of walls and ceilings determines how well the coverings and paste bond to the finish surface beneath, hence the durability and appearance of the papering job.

Walls and ceilings must be clean and dry, and free of cracks, patches, and other flaws that could mar the final appearance. Once you've made such repairs, remove light fixtures and electrical cover plates. Of course, turn off the electricity to all areas to be papered. Move furniture out of the room or into the center of the room, and cover it with a tarp.

Sealing the Surface

In the old days, a wall was *sized*, or brushed with a glutinous mixture to improve the adherence of the wallpaper to follow. Today, the surface is best sealed with a flat, oil-based primer-sealer; many pastes themselves are presized to improve adherence. Old-fashioned sizing is particularly poor if you intend to use vinyl pastes, for it causes the vinyl to crystallize and lump, forming spots where the covering is unattached. Shellac is sometimes used as a sealer, but it is generally inferior to sealer-primer.

Seal surfaces so the wall covering adheres and—just as important—so it can be removed later without destroying the finish surface of the drywall or plaster.

Drywall

Drywall must be sealed before you hang wall coverings; otherwise, the paper face of the drywall will absorb paste; removing the covering at a future date would utterly destroy the drywall itself. To seal the drywall, paint a coat of oil-based primer-sealer, which is an excellent base coat for painting *or* papering.

Do not use a latex primer-sealer beneath wall coverings; if you do, the bonding won't be as good. The latex

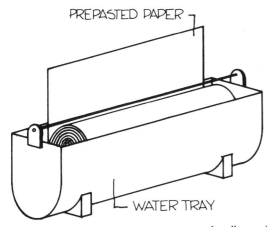

Figure 19.5 A water tray for soaking prepasted wall coverings.

primer can, in effect, pull free from the drywall if the wall covering that follows is too heavy. There are documented cases of walls of vinyl covering slumping and sagging because latex priming was used underneath. The latex stretched and sagged, and so did the material that was bonded to it. You may not encounter this problem if you prime with latex, but you could.

Plaster

Plaster must be well cured before you put anything—paint or wall coverings—over it. The time required for plaster to dry varies, but keeping the house warm will hasten curing time. Uncured plaster contains alkali that is still warm, which will cause paint or paste to bubble. ''Hot plaster'' has a dull appearance; cured, it has a slight sheen.

When the plaster has cured, use an oil-based primer-sealer. Paper when the sealer is dry. If the plaster is old but still has alkali hot spots due to an improper mix, previous painting or papering will have bubbled above such spots. Before proceeding with wall covering, neutralize these spots by rinsing them with a muriatic solution, two parts water to one part mild (10 percent) acid. Allow the acid rinse to set for the prescribed time; then rinse with clean water and allow to dry. Hardware stores usually carry muriatic acid of the correct strength. Wear goggles and gloves during applications and open all the windows to improve ventilation.

Many professional paperers spot-repair drywall and plaster with patching plaster rather than spackling compound because the plaster dries faster.

Surfaces Already Painted

Painted walls must be in good condition, free of holes and cracks. If the old paint is flat, oil-based paint, you are ready to hang wall coverings. All you need is to rinse surfaces first with a mild detergent solution to remove grime, then rinse with clear water and allow to dry. If the paint is aged, another coat of oil-base primer is suggested but not imperative.

If the paint is glossy or semiglossy oil-based paint, sand it lightly with fine sandpaper, using a sanding block or an orbital sander. A sponge mop dampened with water will remove the sanding dust. Commercial deglossers are also available for dulling glossy and semiglossy paint surfaces.

If the old paint might be latex, remove a small patch from an inconspicuous spot and take it to a paint supplier, who will know for sure. Latex paint should be prepared by scraping and sanding. You needn't remove the entire coat of paint, just scuff it enough so that bonding can occur. Work carefully in order to avoid gouging or ripping the wall surface underneath, especially if the surface is drywall. Once you're satisfied with the sanding, wipe the wall clean and paint it with an oil-based primer-sealer.

Surfaces Already Papered

If the wallpaper is in good condition, no more than a layer or two thick and without any prominent texture, you can paper over it. If there are any bubbles, lance them; if any unpasted seams, paste them. Repair any other flaws by stripping back a small section of paper around the flaw and filling the section with patching plaster. Allow the patch to dry thoroughly. Before papering over, however, paint the surface with a flat, oil-based primer. If you don't, the new paste will sink into the paper underneath and there will be bubbles and loose spots galore.

If the existing paper is a vinyl or foil, and your new one is too, use a vinyl-to-vinyl primer in lieu of oil-based priming. Of course, if the old covering is strippable, strip it—unless it was applied incorrectly to an unsealed wall surface. Start stripping the covering in inconspicuous spots, so that if you find the covering was applied incorrectly, and you decide merely to paper over and spare yourself the mess of stripping, you will not have defaced a visually conspicuous area.

Strip existing covering that is in bad shape. Use a wallpaper steamer to loosen the old paste. As you work, try to pull off the old covering in the largest pieces possible. If the paste is especially tenacious, use a spackling knife or scraper; but try not to damage the wall surface underneath. After removing the old paper, wash the wall with washing soda and rinse well with clean water. Patch as needed. If the wallpaper comes off fairly easily, the wall was probably primed correctly; if it isn't, sand, and prime it with an oil-base primer-sealer.

If the bottom layer of wall covering was bonded directly to drywall or unsized plaster, you have a mess on your hands. Remove the old paper as best you can without roughing up its finish; then patch, sand, and prime. Where removing only a small section indicates a tedious, unsuccessful task ahead, cover the old surface with a new layer of $\frac{1}{4}$ or $\frac{3}{8}$ in. drywall. Take your cue from the mistakes of earlier renovators and prime the new drywall.

Other Surfaces

Plaster and drywall are flat and relatively easy to paper. Wood paneling and concrete block have numerous seams and joints, which can show through coverings. Wood filler in panel grooves, or mortar in block joints, is not the answer.

Perhaps the easiest route is to cover the irregular surface with a liner. Liner coverings and pastes vary; your supplier should be able to recommend the best one for your renovation needs. Heavy paper and felt are commonly used over plaster or drywall; foam liners are used over concrete block. Most liners must be specially ordered. Liners will, to some degree, assume the contours of the wall underneath, though; so use a heavy vinyl where the wall is rough. (In making these recommendations, we are assuming that the walls are structurally sound and dry; if they are not, correct *those* problems first.) An alternative is covering the wall with nailing strips and applying a new surface of drywall.

Mildew

If existing surfaces, whether paint or wallpaper, are mildewed, clean them by washing with a solution of 3 qt water, 1 qt bleach, and $\frac{1}{2}$ cup trisodium phosphate. Rinse with clean water and allow the wall to dry for a day or two before

priming the spot with oil-based, mildew-resistant paint. If the surface is wallpaper that has separated, you may be able to wash the backing with the solution and, when it's dry, repaste the piece. Otherwise, patch-repair the covering. Alleviate future moisture problems by venting humid areas properly.

LAYING OUT THE WORK

Before hanging the first piece of wall covering—before ordering materials, in fact—walk the rooms to be prepared, checking walls and woodwork with a level and noting where they are not plumb. Also, use a long, straight board to spot mounds and dips in the surface of the walls. Circle any extreme irregularities. You can hang pretty much any kind and pattern of wall covering you like; but if door or window casing is markedly out of plumb, small patterns will serve better than loud prints.

Always plumb strips of wall covering. Don't assume that casing is plumb and align the edge of the strips to it; if you do, as you continue around the room, you'll find mistakes magnified to grotesque extremes. Plumb the first piece and align successive pieces to it, checking periodically to make sure they are still plumb.

Apart from plumbing all pieces, layout is mostly a matter of disguising where you end the papering. The last piece of wall covering must almost always be cut to fit, thus disrupting its pattern. Thus it is most important to avoid placing this juncture where it will be conspicuous.

Starting and Finishing Points

A usual place to begin papering is at one side of a room's main doorway. You won't notice such a spot when you enter a room, and when you leave it, your eye will likely be distracted by the trim around the doorway. Look around the room; the last piece is usually a small one over a doorway. Another common place to begin and end papering is a corner (Figure 19.6).

To determine exactly where wall-covering seams will occur, mark off intervals 27 in. wide around the room, us-

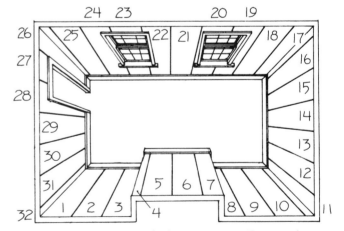

Figure 19.6 One sequence for hanging paper. Always end a papering job in a place where final strips (which must usually be trimmed to fit) are inconspicuous. Here the job begins and ends in a corner.

ing a ruler or a still-wrapped bolt of material as your measure (Figure 19.9A). Because very thin strips of wall covering are difficult to handle and paste correctly, you may want to move your starting point an inch or two, to spare yourself such inconvenience.

If the pattern of the wall covering is conspicuous, you might start layout with a strip *centered* in a conspicuous part of a wall—over a mantle, over a sofa, or in the middle of a large wall. Determine such a visual center and mark off roll-widths from each side of the starting strip, until you have determined where the papering will terminate, again preferably in an inconspicuous spot.

You may want to center the pattern at a window, if that's indisputably where the visual center of the room is. If it's a picture window, the middle of the strip should align to the middle of the window, as shown in Figure 19.7A. If there are two windows, the edges of two strips of paper should meet along a centered, plumbed line between the two windows (Figure 19.7B), unless the distance between windows is less than 27 in., the width of a strip. If the distance is less, center a strip between the windows.

Woodwork and Corners out of Plumb

Strips of wall covering must be plumb, reguardless of tilts in walls or trim. If your first piece of paper, for example, begins next to out-of-plumb jamb (side) casing, overlap the trim by the amount that the casing is off plumb. After brushing out the paper, trim off the overlapping edge of paper. Thus, the leading edge of the paper will be plumb and the next strip, aligned with that edge, will also be plumb (check anyway).

Corners are often out of square; there, you should ascertain what way the walls are leaning, using your level. To rectify this problem, run the edge of the paper on to the adjacent wall—say, $\frac{1}{4}$ or $\frac{1}{2}$ in.—and trim off the rest of the strip. The narrow border on the adjacent wall will itself be overlapped by the first strip on that wall, with the strip being plumbed so that successive strips are plumb. There will be a slight mismatch of patterns where the two pieces overlap; but since it will be in the corner, it won't be obvious. Besides, that strategy will be the best you can do with corners that are out of square.

Three Types of Seam

Before starting installation, it's useful to note that the edges of wall coverings can be joined in one of three ways: butt seam, overlap seam, or double-cut seams.

The *butt seam* is overwhelmingly the most common type used. Strip edges are simply butted next to each other and, where appropriate, rolled with a seam roller. An *over-*

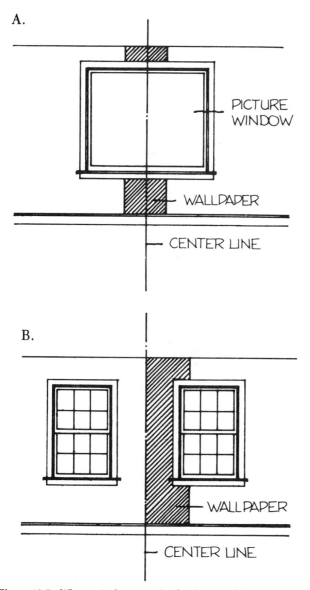

A.

B.

Figure 19.7 Where windows are the focal point of the room, position the wallcovering pattern accordingly. If the window is a large picture window (A), center the middle of the strip on the width of the window. Where there are two windows (B), center the edges of two strips as shown.

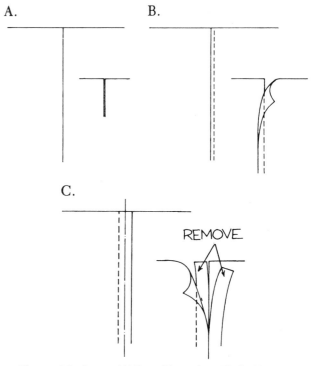

Figure 19.8 Seams. (A) Butt; (B) overlap; (C) double-cut.

lap seam is favored where corners are out of square or when a butt seam might occur in a corner and not cover well. The area of overlap should be as narrow as possible to avoid a large welt that sticks up, or patterns that are mismatched. *Double-cut seams* (also called "through-cut seams") are highly specialized seams and are comparatively difficult for amateurs. They are used primarily on exotic-edged wall coverings or where irregularities in a wall require additional matching of patterns. Double-cutting is shown in Figures 19.8C and 19.20.

HANGING WALL COVERING

Measure out from the door casing, if that's where you begin papering, and draw a plumb line—to which you will align the leading edge of the first strip. The other edge of the strip abuts the casing and is trimmed with a razor knife, as necessary. If the first strip of wall covering is perfectly plumb, successive strips need only be butted edge to edge, and they too will be plumb. Check edges as you progress, however.

Note: If ceilings are to be papered, do them *before* you do the walls. Papering ceilings is discussed after walls because ceilings are more difficult to do and thus are usually painted.

Cutting

Measure the height of the wall and cut several strips to length, keeping in mind that you must leave extra at each end of the strips, for trimming and matching patterns vertically. Cut the first two pieces particularly long. Slide the first strip up and down the wall until its pattern is not cut in half where it meets the ceiling line. The pattern of the paper along the baseboard is less visible, and hence, less important. Match the second strip to the first, and align the patterns along their edges. Thus you'll get a sense of how much waste there must be to match patterns. Depending on the size of the patterns, each strip is usually rough-cut about 3 in. too long and trimmed after it has been pasted to the wall. Do the rough-cutting at the table, using shears, and the trimming on the wall, using a razor knife.

Patterns that run straight across the face of a paper are called *straight match* (Figure 19.9). Patterns that run diagonally are called *drop match*. The latter wastes somewhat more paper during alignment.

Unless you are working with a very delicate covering, cut several strips at a time. Roll the pile of rough-cut strips backward—face in—to counteract the curling of the material, so it will be easier to paste and handle. Be careful not to crease the sheet. Flop the entire pile of strips face down on the table, so the piece cut first will be the first pasted and hung. The table must, of course, be perfectly clean, so the face of the bottom strip will not be soiled.

Pasting

Keep the pasting table clean, quickly sponging up any stray paste so it won't get on the faces of the wall covering. Some

A.

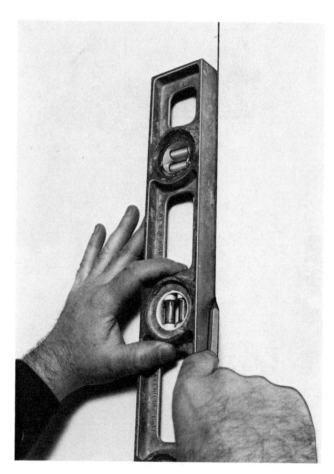

B.

Figure 19.9 Layout and preparation. (A) From the starting point measure the width of the stock, less an overlap onto the jamb (side) casing. (Where the starting point, such as the door casing shown, is not plumb, overlap the piece slightly and trim off the excess paper later.) Have all the necessary tools close at hand (B) Draw a plumb line to align the leading edge of the first strip wallcovering.

C.

D.

E.

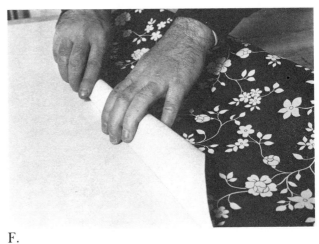

F.

Figure 19.9 (Continued) (C) Measure the height of the wall to be papered, allowing enough extra paper at top and bottom for fitting and trimming. (D) Rough-cut the stock to length with shears. The pasting table shown is a professional's model, light yet strong, easily transported from job to job. (E) When rough-cutting strips to length, remember to allow for pattern repeats. Pictured here is a straight-match pattern. Rolling the cut strips backward—with their backing out—counteracts the tendency of the wallpaper to curl. (Work courtesy of Abe Gershbein, Painting Plus, Easthampton, NY. Mr. Gershbein appears in this and other sequences in this chapter. The author is most grateful to Mr. Gershbein for sharing the mastery of his art.)

materials, such as vinyl, would not be harmed; but many others could be marred.

Mix paste according to the manufacturer's instruction; most pastes will be slightly tacky to the touch. When mixing, go slowly, because even small increments of paste powder or water can change the consistency of the paste radically. Mix thoroughly so there are no lumps. Although the batch of paste you mix—as opposed to premixed pastes—should last a working day, keep an eye on the consistency of the paste. Paste should *glide* on; it should never drag. Rinse the paste brush or roller when you break for lunch and when you quit for the day.

Until you become familiar with papering, apply paste to only one strip at a time. A paste brush offers greater control when spreading paste and is favored when working with wheat paste. If you're working with vinyl paste, use a roller. Apply paste in the middle of the strip, toward the

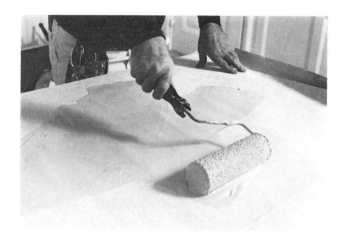

Figure 19.10 Spread paste out from the center toward the edges.

A.

B.

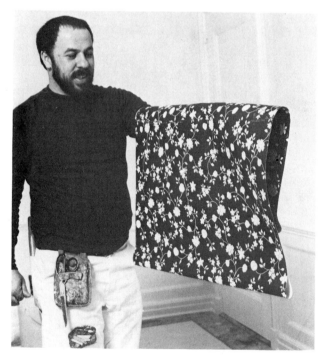

C.

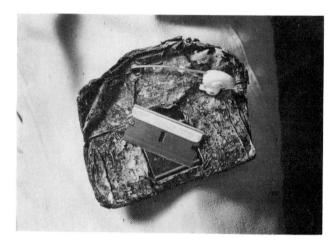

D.

Figure 19.11 Folding the strips. (A) After applying paste to half the strip, fold it over. (B) Finish applying paste and fold the second half over, being careful not to crease the paper. The second fold should stop just short of the first. (C) The folded strip is easily carried. (D) A detail of Figure 19.11C, showing a homemade razorholder, fashioned from a magnetized car-key box swaddled in electrical tape and held to the pants leg by a duck-headed diaper pin given to Mr. Gershbein by a client.

A.

C.

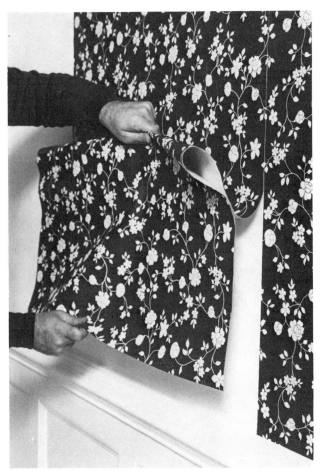

B.

Figure 19.12 Hanging a strip. (A) Unfold the top half of the strip and carefully align it to the plumbed line. Holding one end up, gently slide the strip into place. Subsequent strips align to the edges of strips already hung. (B) After quickly smoothing the upper half of the strip, unfold the lower half. (C) Thoroughly work over the entire strip with a smoothing brush, spreading paste out from the center toward the edges.

again applying paste in the middle and working it toward the edges. Fold over the second half, stopping just short of the first fold. Now you have a pasted strip of wall covering which is easy to carry to the wall, unfold, hang, and smooth. This method of folding is known as "booking."

Be as neat as possible when applying paste; avoid getting paste on the face of the covering. Removing stray paste is always a nuisance and, in the case of some of the more delicate coverings, a disaster. Keep wiping the tabletop clean, as errant paste will quickly get on the covering.

Hanging

To hang wall coverings, unfold the upper fold (leaving the lower fold still folded) and align the edge of the strip to the plumb line you drew earlier. Align subsequent pieces to the leading edge of each preceding piece. Position the upper end of the strip an inch or so above the ceiling line. Smooth the upper end of the strip first, by running a smoothing brush down the middle of the strip and out toward the edges. By working from the center outward, you brush air

top; spread paste to the far edge and then to the near edge. Although the side edges should be covered completely with paste so they will adhere well, the top and bottom of the strip—the extra that will be trimmed—should be left unpasted.

Folding

When you have applied paste to slightly more than half the strip, gently fold over the top half of the strip, being careful not to crease the paper. Paste the second half of the strip,

A.

B.

D.

C.

E.

Figure 19.13 Trimming and finishing. (A) The top of each strip overlaps the ceiling joint (here, crown molding runs along the top of the wall), allowing room to adjust the strip up or down until patterns match. When patterns align, trim excess paper. (B) Fit the wallpaper snugly to woodwork or wall joints with a wide-bladed spackling knife; cut off excess paper with a razor knife. (C,D) Where paper overlaps woodwork, precut it with shears and then trim it exactly with a razor knife. In (C) the paper continues over the door casing; in (D) it approaches an inside corner. (E) After cutting away excess paper and smoothing it down, sponge off any paste on the woodwork.

bubbles, wrinkles, and excess paste from the middle to the edges.

You'll know whether the paste is adhering well. If you have any problems with paste lumps (either from paste that is too thin or paste that is mixed insufficiently) or poor adherence (paste too thin or not spread on thickly enough), pull the strip off the wall, sponge the wall clean, vary your paste mix, and start over. Do not reuse that strip of wall covering.

If the upper half of the strip is adhering well, simply unfold the lower fold and smooth the paper down, again brushing down the center and out toward the edges, with small strokes.

Prepasted wall coverings. Most manufacturers specify that a roll of prepasted covering (or individual strips) be soaked for 30 seconds in lukewarm water; follow this specification. When the soaking period is over, pull the free end of the strip up and, without folding it, put it on the wall. Align and smooth the piece. It's best to precut pieces before putting them in the water tray; otherwise, you will need a helper to cut the roll as you pull up the amount needed.

Trimming

Where wall covering meets woodwork, the ceiling line, the baseboard, and so on, use a wide-bladed spackling knife to press the edges of the piece snug. Cut off the excess of the strip by running a razor knife along the spackling knife (Figure 19.13B). To avoid cutting the paper too short, you may want to take two passes with the razor knife. That is, the paper curls somewhat where it lies over the bulge of the trim. After making an initial cut, tuck the edge of paper flat and cut it again, really close.

Getting on with the Job

Hanging successive strips as just described, match patterns along the edges and slide new strips into place, until the edges barely touch (here, we're talking about butt-joined edges). Smooth with the brush and trim ends with the razor knife. After a pair of seams has set somewhat—in, say, 10 to 15 minutes—go over the seams with a seam roller, thereby evening out paste and bedding the seams securely. Don't use seam rollers on delicate papers, however. Add paste with an artist's brush to edges that haven't quite adhered.

Remove excess paste with a damp sponge, wiping not only the seams but all the strips, to avoid a buildup of diluted paste along the seams. Rinse your sponge often. Obviously, sponge only those wall coverings that can take it; sponging is not something you'd want to do to more delicate specimens. If a covering is delicate, hang it, sweep it out with a soft-bristle smoothing brush, and let it be.

Wipe paste off woodwork immediately. If you haven't pasted the extra paper at each end of the strips, there shouldn't be very much paste on the wood.

Some Small Problems

If you get an air bubble that you can't brush out—particularly a problem with vinyl wall coverings—make a small slit with a razor knife. Then gently force out the air with a smoothing brush. The slit will flatten and be unnoticeable.

If you find a paste lump as you smooth a strip, flatten it as best you can with a spackling knife, being careful not to rip the face of the wall covering. Then smooth with the brush.

If an edge isn't adhering, pull it up slightly and dab on some extra paste with a small brush. Take care not to stretch the wall covering, especially if it's vinyl. Here's another tip when working with vinyl: paper-backed vinyls tend to curl up at the edge, so apply paste generously and allow it to soak into the backing.

If you have not aligned patterns correctly, and you're afraid you will stretch or rip the covering by further effort, pull the strip off the wall. You should be able to rehang the piece; if you can't, quickly sponge clean the wall and hang a new piece.

Papering around Electrical Outlets and Fixtures

Turn off electricity to the outlet or fixture which you are about to paper around—and check with a voltage tester (p. 235), to make sure the power is off. Remove cover plates and other hardware from the outlet, so it sticks out as little as possible.

For an outlet that is relatively flat, simply drape the paper over that section of the wall, as described above. Cut a small "X" in the wall covering, right over the center of the outlet. Gradually extend the legs of the "X" until the wall covering lies completely flat. Smooth the wall covering with a smoothing brush and trim excess paper. If the edges of the cutout aren't adhering well, roll them down with a seam roller. The cover plate of the outlet will cover small cut marks, but cut as close as you can.

Large fixtures require essentially the same procedure, although a bit more preparation in locating the center of the "X". Measure the center of the fixture from two directions—say, up from the baseboard and over from the edge of the nearest strip of wall covering. Transfer those dimensions to the strip of wall covering you are about to hang. If

Figure 19.14 Before hanging paper over an electrical outlet, turn off power to that outlet. Loosely hand the paper, and cut a small X over the center of the outlet. Gradually extend the X until the paper lies flat around the outlet, cut around its outline, and finish smoothing down the paper.

you apply paste after cutting a small "X," be careful not to fray the edges of the cut with brush or roller.

Hang the strip and gradually enlarge the "X" until it fits over the base of the fixture. Smooth down the entire strip, trim around the fixture carefully, and wipe up any paste that may have gotten on the fixture.

Papering Inside Corners

"Inside corners" are what most people call simply "corners." Our aim here is to distinguish them from *outside* corners, which project into living areas. The distinction is necessary because hanging paper on each is different.

If inside corners were perfectly square, papering them would be simply a matter of folding a strip lengthwise, pasting it, and smoothing it in place. Rarely are corners square enough so that you can paper both walls of a corner with one strip of wall covering. The problem is, the second edge of the strip will *not* be plumb if the corner is not square.

To rectify this, you must usually trim the strip about $\frac{1}{2}$ in. after it turns the corner, and then overlap the cut edge with another strip of wall covering. The "second strip" can be the trimming from the first strip. If that is the case, it's easier to match patterns. Your primary concern is, however, plumbing the edge of the second strip. Once the corner is turned, all successive strips must be plumb. You may find it helpful to draw a plumb line on the adjacent wall of the corner, just as you did when hanging the first strip.

Because the disruption of the pattern is in the corner, it won't be very noticeable; match patterns as closely as possible, nevertheless. The overlap seam in the corner should not be wider than $\frac{1}{2}$ in.—less is alright—or the seam will stick out.

Overlap inside corners even when the uncut edge of a strip occurs there coincidentally. Seams merely butted together in corners have a knack for separating.

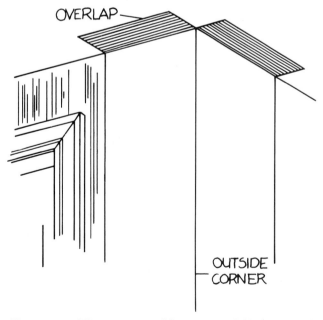

Figure 19.15 Where paper straddles an "outside" corner, notch the top of the strip as shown. Trim off the excess paper and sponge off any paste on the ceiling.

Outside Corners

Outside corners also require care. Never align the edge of a strip to an outside corner; it will look terrible and will likely fray. If the edge of a strip occurs right at a corner, cut it back $\frac{1}{2}$ in. and overlap the corner with the edge of a full strip from the adjacent wall. It's also necessary to cut the top of the wall covering where it turns the corner, as shown in Figure 19.15.

Ceilings

As noted earlier, ceilings are usually painted. But if you must paper them, paper ceilings before walls, for any discrepancies can be more easily covered by strips on the walls than by those on the ceiling. Ceilings are difficult to do be-

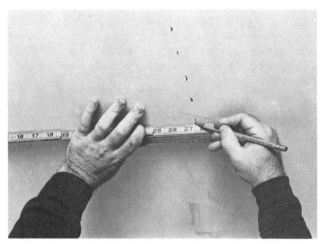

A.

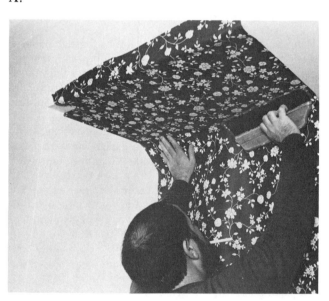

B.

Figure 19.16 Papering the ceiling. (A) Mark the edge of the first strip on the ceiling, measuring from the starting wall. This step is similar to that of aligning a first strip on a wall. (B) The easiest way to apply the paper to the ceiling is to drape it in front of you and smooth it into place as you walk across scaffolding. When the entire strip is up, go back and smooth it thoroughly, working from the center out toward the ends and edges of the strip.

cause you're fighting gravity; therefore, if you are new at papering, get some practice hanging paper on an inconspicuous wall first. At the very least, do not start on a ceiling. Having a helper makes papering a ceiling easier; it may even make it possible.

Hang paper across a room's shortest dimension; the shorter the strips, the easier the paper is to handle. In most cases, begin on an outside, or window, wall, and work inward. It's helpful to mark off the edge of the first strip, using a rule (see Figure 19.16A). If the room isn't rectangular, you will have to trim the edge of the last strip at an angle. Because the last strip should be in an inconspicuous part of the ceiling away from the window, the trimming won't be noticeable.

Cut strips for the ceiling in the same manner as those for walls; match the patterns of successive pieces and leave an inch or two extra at each end, for trimming. Folding up the paper is different, though. The best fold is an "accordion fold"—every $1\frac{1}{2}$ ft or so. Be careful not to crease the wall covering when folding it.

You will need a platform to work from. Ideally, this is a plank across two sawhorses, or across the steps of two sturdy wood stepladders.

As you hang each strip, align it carefully to the edge of the preceding one. Smooth it out and slowly unfold the strip. With your smoothing brush, sweep from the center of the strip outward. Once you have unfolded the entire strip, make any final adjustments to match seams, and smooth well. Roll seams after the strips have been in place for about 10 minutes.

Because papering ceilings is difficult, it will take you longer than walls. Therefore, paste only one strip at a time until you have built up speed and confidence.

Recesses

Papering recessed areas isn't difficult if you allow yourself enough paper for overlapping and trimming, and for making any adjustments in the pattern in the least conspicuous places.

To paper an arch, overcut the paper so that 2 or 3 in. extra hangs down over the opening, roughly following the curve of the arch (Figure 19.18). Wedge-cut the overhanging area and fold it back into the arch, adding a little extra paste to make sure all wedges adhere well to the inside of arch. Then cover the wedge cuts (and the inside of the arch) with a continuous strip $\frac{1}{8}$ in. less wide than the depth of the arch. Be sure all cuts are clean and all edges are secure.

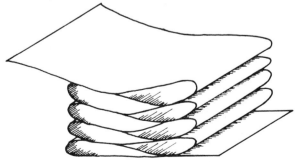

Figure 19.17 An accordion fold.

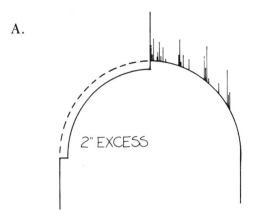

A.

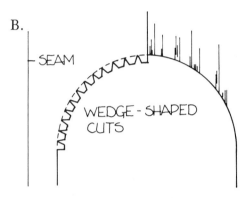

B.

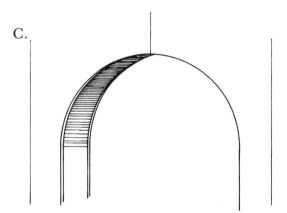

C.

Figure 19.18 Papering an arch. Overlap the edge of the arch slightly; cut the excess into small wedges; smooth the edges back into the arch; and paper the inside of the arch with a single strip.

To paper a window recess, most professionals cover the inside of the recess first. By cutting the strips on the "ceiling" of the recess a little long—say, $\frac{1}{4}$ to $\frac{1}{2}$ in.—you have a flap that can be folded onto the surrounding walls, as shown in Figure 19.19. These flaps are overlapped by strips covering the recess's walls; cut outside strips flush with the edge of the recess. Because there's often moisture around a window, vinyl coverings are best suited for window recesses.

Where many sections of wall covering converge, as around a window recess, it's often necessary to cut down the width of one piece—for example, to wrap a corner—and then resume the pattern with another piece of paper specially cut. The method most often used for resolving this

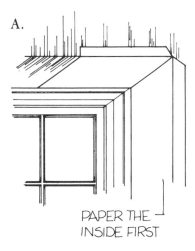

A.

PAPER THE
INSIDE FIRST

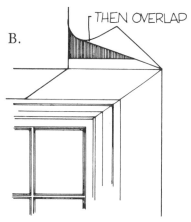

B.

THEN OVERLAP

Figure 19.19 There are several ways to paper a window recess. Here, the inside of the recess is papered first, its strips overlapping slightly onto the main wall. These small flaps are overlapped by strips on the wall surface.

problem is to double-cut a new strip in place, as shown in Figure 19.20.

Cleaning and Repairing Wall Covering

When you're through papering, clean any excess paste from the wall covering immediately; it becomes a mess to remove if you wait until it's dry. Using a clean, damp sponge, wipe away any paste that oozes out when seams are rolled or that sticks to trim. Rinse the sponge often. A terry cloth towel is handy for blotting away moisture after sponging.

Although you can wipe most papers and vinyls, you can only blot excess paste from fragile papers, grasses, and similar materials. If you rub delicate ones while they are wet, the facing will separate from the backing. If a clear gel paste (such as metalling or cellulose-base paste) was used, the excess, being clear, won't catch the eye—leave it alone. Manufacturers of fragile wall coverings may advise other methods of cleaning.

Once paste has dried, you can clean washable wall coverings by gently rubbing them with soap and water. A commercial cleaning dough is available that removes stains when rubbed lightly over a soiled spot. Cleaning dough is much like that used to clean typewriter keys; as the dough gathers grime, fold it over on itself. You can blot (*not* rub) other nonwashable coverings with commercial, stain-removing solvents.

To replace a gash in wall covering, first try to repaste the torn flap. If that doesn't look good, rip—don't cut—a patch from a spare bolt of the same covering. (The ragged edge of a ripped piece will be less obvious than edges cut with shears or a razor knife.) Repair dents and cracks in the wall behind, and gently tear free any unpasted paper around the gash. Paste the back of the ragged-edge replacement, carefully align its pattern with that of the existing covering, and smooth down the patch.

A.

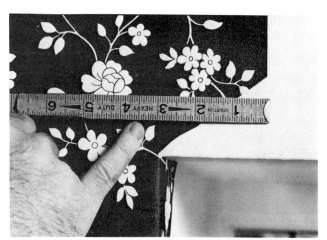

B.

Figure 19.20 Double-cutting. When several wall planes converge, it may be necessary to fold and trim a section of wallcovering and in so doing, disturb or destroy the pattern on some other section. To remedy this problem, double-cut a new strip of wall covering over the damaged section. Use this technique wherever the situation calls for it. (A) In this particular case, the inside walls of a window recess will be papered, while the ceiling of the recess will not be. Cut the paper as shown where the corner of the wall is not square; it's best to cut some extra to tuck into the recess. (B) After trimming the tuck into the recess, measure the width of a replacement patch.

C.

D.

E.

F.

G.

Figure 19.20 (Continued) (C) Paste the back of the replacement patch, and position it over the cutout section of wall covering. Align the pattern of the patch with that of the section beneath, and cut through both pieces with a razor. (D) Peel the excess off the replacement patch. Sponge off paste. (E) Then peel the cutout section of the original wall covering from beneath the replacement patch. (F) Trim the bottom of the patch section to the edge of the recess. (G) Seam-roll the patch section so that it adheres well. Then paper the rest of the wall over the window recess.

·20·

FLOORING

Finish floorings are the last materials to be attached and among the first to wear out. Flooring is crushed a bit by each step, swollen by moisture and abraded by dirt. It also works loose. Correctly selecting and maintaining finishes will extend its life, but equally important to its longevity is the health of the hidden floor beneath—the subflooring and its structural underpinnings.

A flooring grid must be sized and spaced correctly for the loads it will carry and the distances it will span. Joists are discussed at length in Chapters 4 and 8; correctly sizing subflooring for span is mentioned briefly below.

Think of a floor, then, as a grid of interrelated elements. When renovating a floor, think beyond the expanse you can see: be sure the grid is healthy throughout. Somewhat like paint and wallpaper, finish flooring is a relatively thin membrane that cannot long hide serious flaws underneath.

We'll begin the chapter with wood flooring, followed by resilient flooring and carpeting.

FLOOR REPAIRS

Surface problems are caused by (1) a lack of maintenance, (2) excessive moisture, and (3) inappropriate or poorly applied finishes. These maladies may be exacerbated further by flooring which has come loose because of insufficient attachment or structural shifting.

A lack of maintenance is a pervasive cause of flooring ailments, the more lamentable because it's avoidable. Sweeping often is critically important because it removes abrasive grit. Another culprit is water from pipes, fixtures, and house plants—which, allowed to sit directly on flooring, can cause staining, mildew, swelling, warping, and rot within weeks. So be sure to water plants carefully—supporting them on stands, checking beneath them periodically, and wiping up overflow.

Moist wood and damp basements can also be a problem. Most flooring is kiln-dried, but it can pick up moisture and warp if it's improperly stored. Once it's installed there's nothing you can do about it, so be forewarned to buy from a reputable supplier—and bring bundles inside as soon as they're delivered. Moisture under the house can also affect flooring; read the recommendations in Chapter 9 to correct that problem. Cures include installing a dehumidifier, adding vents to improve cross flow, covering crawl spaces with sheet plastic, waterproofing basement walls, and insulating underneath the floor space once it has been dried out.

Stripping and refinishing flooring is discussed at length below, but first let's look at repairs you can make to existing flooring.

Eliminating Squeaks

Squeaks are caused when one piece of wood rubs against another. To stop the squeak, stop the rubbing. Before mak-

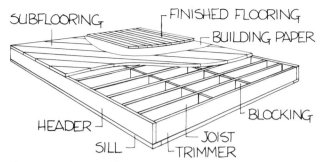

Figure 20.1 A typical floor platform. A floor will be sturdy when its elements are adequately sized for the spans they must traverse and securely attached to create a load-sharing grid. Joists, for example, should be spaced 16 or 24 in. on-center, and all subflooring joints should occur over joists.

ing repairs, first assess the problem by walking the area around the squeak to see how widespread it is. It may be that the installer didn't use enough nails. Consult Table 20.2.

Cures from above. Most squeaks can be stopped by nailing a loose board to its subflooring or, if possible, to a joist. The nails most commonly used to flush-nail hardwood flooring are 4d electro-galvanized finish nails, driven in at a slight angle. If you're nailing down a squeak, nail no more than you must to silence it: a pair of nails every 8 in. is fine. If you have a lot of nailing to do, align nails with a chalk line for neatness. Set nail heads at least $\frac{1}{8}$ in. below the surface. If nails bend, predrill a slightly smaller pilot hole first. Tongue-and-groove flooring is generally blind-nailed with 6d nails.

A bit of powdered graphite (used to free lock mechanisms) sprinkled between two boards may also do the trick. Bounce on the boards to distribute the graphite, then wipe up the excess with a damp sponge. The boards will still move when walked on, but hopefully they will no longer squeak.

Cures from below. If the underside of a floor is exposed, there are several other options to stop squeaks. To locate the spot, have someone upstairs tap the squeak while you mark it below.

A squeak over a joist may indicate subflooring that has worked loose from a joist. For starters, try nailing it down. You can also drive a thin shim—a cedar shingle is fine—between the subfloor and the top of the joist. Put a bit of glue on the shim before driving it in. Don't be overzealous, however; tap the shim in until it's just snug.

An even better method than shimming is adding a piece of blocking between joists, end-nailing it with two or three 16d common nails at each end, then going above and nailing errant flooring down into the blocking.

A squeak may also be caused by flooring separating from subflooring—which you can remedy by adding blocking, as above, or by screwing up from the underside—if the finish floor is at least $\frac{3}{4}$ in. thick. You need at least that depth for the screw to grab onto; $\frac{5}{16}$-in. oak, for example, won't hold a screw.

If the joists seem springy, you may need to bolster the structure, as explained in Chapter 8. There's one intermediate repair, however, that might do the trick: add diagonal bridging or blocking between joists—it may not have been

done when the house was new. If joists are marginally small, this extra stiffening may be all you need. Nail bridging every 6 ft or so.

Replacing Flooring

When replacing sections of damaged flooring, remove no more than you must. And before you start, make sure you can get enough replacement boards of the same stock; otherwise, the patch will be obvious. If the wood is unusual and can not be matched by a lumberyard, consider pulling old stock from closet floors and other inconspicuous areas.

Replacing a single board. When replacing a discolored or damaged board, take pains not to disturb surrounding flooring. The best way to accomplish this is to drill holes across the piece to be replaced and then pry it out in splinters, using a hand chisel.

You can also cut into the damaged board by using a circular saw set to the depth of the finish flooring; then pry it out with a flat bar. Rest the heel of the saw on the floor, pull back the saw guard, and slowly lower the front of the saw sole until the turning blade engages the wood. This is called a *pocket cut*. Be careful: Holding a blade guard back is never advisable if you can avoid it, and the saw may jump when it engages the wood. Let the blade stop before you lift the saw.

Hold the replacement stock next to the hole and mark off the length you need. Cut the end of the stock square across. To make the replacement fit more easily, use a hand plane to bevel its lower edges slightly. If the stock is tongue-and-groove, cut off the lower leg of the groove as shown in Figure 20.2. That done, drive the replacement piece in, using a piece of scrap to cushion the hammer blows.

Tongue-and-groove flooring is usually blind-nailed through its tongue, but that's not possible here: predrill and face-nail two 6d finish nails at either end. Angle the nails slightly so they'll hold better.

Replacing a section. It's sometimes necessary to replace a large section of flooring, usually where the wood has been damaged by water or where a large object, such as a built-in cabinet, has been removed.

Pulling Up Old Flooring. Renovators commonly remove existing flooring when it is damaged, or when they need to run wiring or plumbing between joists. Several tips will make the job more productive. First, turn off electricity running through the area before you start demolishing. Check with a voltage tester (p. 152). Second, do not leave flooring with nails sticking out; either pull the nails or throw away the flooring. Third, rent a dumpster to haul off the debris. Fourth, if you intend to reuse any of the flooring, photograph any unusual patterns, and number parts with a grease pencil (or number tape) as you pull them up.

In truth, reusing flooring is not that common; it's usually ripped up and replaced. The problem is breakage; you can expect to lose at least 20 percent of the boards. To minimize breakage, take up baseboards and start prying along a wall. If you happen to be gutting adjacent walls, the space between studs should allow you to get a wrecking bar be-

A.

B.

C.

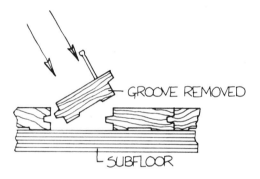

D.

E.

Figure 20.2 Replacing a stained board. (A) First try to bleach out the stain with vinegar or a mild oxalic acid solution. If that fails, remove the old piece by drilling across it and chiseling out remnants. (B) Mark the replacement stock against the hole. (C,D) With a chisel, cut off the bottom leg of the board's groove; fit the piece's tongue into place and nail the replacement down. (E) When the fit is tight, knock the new piece down with a scrap block to prevent hammer marks.

neath the edges of those first boards. If you want to save the flooring, *work very slowly,* prying up each board along its length before trying to pull it up.

Fitting New Flooring to Old. Order replacement stock that's a little thicker than the old stuff, so you can sand it down. In general, avoid replacement stock that's thinner. After vacuuming the subfloor well, spread replacement stock on the floor to match existing pieces in grain and color as closely as possible. Fit pieces tightly to the old, using a heavy screwdriver as a lever.

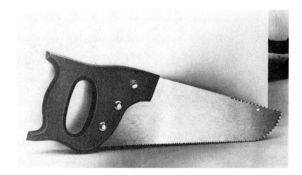

Figure 20.3 The toothed back of the flooring saw enables the user to start a cut without fuss. (Brookstone)

A.

B.

C.

D.

E.

F.

G.

Figure 20.4 Replacing a section of strip flooring. (A) Here, a worker pries up an old section of plywood that had been nailed down decades ago to replace a section of flooring rotted by a leaky radiator. At this stage, replace any subflooring that isn't sound. (B) Intact sections of parquet serve as patterns for sections to be replaced. (C) The main field of flooring meets the parquet border at an angle, traced here on replacement stock. (D) A screwdriver becomes a handy sawhorse. (E) Using a heavy screwdriver as a lever, draw pieces together before nailing. (F) Use light chalk lines on the face of the strip flooring to align nails. To minimize splits and bent nails, predrill nail holes with a smaller-shank drill bit. (G) Where flooring meets a contoured surface, scribe the cut to be made onto the stock. (Thanks to Spagnoli Flooring, Brooklyn, NY)

If you're face-nailing hardwood flooring as shown in Figure 20.4, it's also important to align nail holes. Stretch several taut strings across the section you're replacing, to simulate nail rows. If you predrill your flooring—which is advisable with thin hardwood strips—you can also use the strings as a drilling guide. To size nails and determine spacing, see Table 20.2

The most efficient way to install the flooring, however, is to tack each strip with two or three nails, then go back later and securely nail each one down. Although it's important to set nails at least $\frac{1}{8}$ in., it's not necessary to fill such face-nailing.

Where flooring meets a complex molding or, say, a rounded step, use a compass or a scribe to trace the outline of the surface onto the flooring. To prevent buckling due to expansion, stop wood flooring $\frac{1}{2}$ in. shy of walls and other impediments. Cover such gaps with baseboard molding or a strip of quarter-round shoe molding.

Parquetry Borders. Parquetry borders in older homes are often made of woods now rare or unobtainable. If you need to mimic or replace portions of such borders, test-stain alternative materials in advance of any repairs.

If you're adding a built-in unit to a room with a parquetry border, pull the border and re-lay it in front of the unit, as shown in Figure 20.5. Admittedly, this is a fine point, but borders should run entirely around a room. The border should be equidistant from all walls, as represented by "X" in the illustration.

To match a parquetry pattern exactly, trace the pattern of an intact section, then retrace it (use carbon paper) onto the subfloor where it will be duplicated. Where you must replace individual pieces landlocked by existing flooring, back-bevel them slightly.

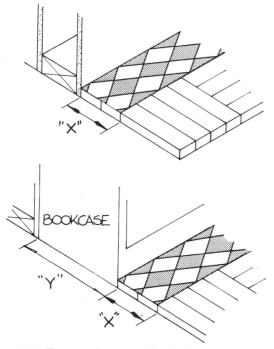

Figure 20.5 To retain the parquet border in a room, remove the border and reset it when adding cabinets. The distance that the border must be moved, represented by Y, is equal to the depth of the built-in.

Subflooring and Underlayment

Subflooring is plywood or 1-in. boards nailed to joists, over which finish flooring is laid. Like any structural material, subflooring has span limits based on thickness. Where subflooring is undersized, there are frequently high spots or flooring separation over joists, as well as sagging and springiness between joists.

Subflooring	Maximum Spans (in.)
1-in. softwood	16
$\frac{1}{2}$-in. plywood[a]	16
$\frac{5}{8}$-in. plywood[a]	20
$\frac{3}{4}$-in. plywood[a]	24

[a]Specs for Douglas fir plywood; western softwood plywood should be $\frac{1}{8}$ in. thicker in each case.

The edges of subflooring should always meet over joist centers or blocking, so there will be adequate backing to which to nail. For maximum holding, use $2\frac{1}{4}$- to $3\frac{1}{2}$-in. annular ring shank or spiral shank nails; you can also use cement-coated or galvanized nails, but they haven't got the same gripping power. For best results, stagger board ends or plywood edges so that not all joints occur along the same joists. To accommodate expansion, leave $\frac{1}{4}$-in. gaps between board ends and $\frac{1}{8}$-in. gaps between plywood edges.

Underlayment is an additional layer—over the subflooring—intended to level out and add rigidity to the subflooring and hence to the flooring that follows. Thus underlayment is appropriate beneath resilient flooring, carpeting and so on—whenever finish flooring is so thin that it would telegraph gaps or irregularities beneath. Particleboard is commonly used for underlayment, but because it lacks the tensile strength of plywood, should not be used as a subflooring material.

STRIPPING AND REFINISHING FLOORS

The point of removing an old finish is to remove old imperfections, scratches, and gouges, as well as caked-on wax and varnish, so the new finish will adhere well and look good. Here again, the conservation of energy—*your* energy—should be your guide. If you don't have to sand off an old finish, don't. Not uncommonly, a floor is merely grimy and dull from numerous coats of wax and scuffing by shoes. A thorough washing may be all it needs.

Before Sanding

Before you sand, determine what's on the floor and what it will take to remove it. You may be able to rejuvenate a floor by scrubbing rather than sanding it down. Scrub a small area of floor with a non-sudsing steel-wool pad dipped in turpentine, denatured alcohol, or mineral spirits. After rubbing in the solvent with a circular motion, wipe up the residue with a sponge. If you've reached clear wood after using a reasonable amount of elbow grease, let the test spot dry; then apply paste wax with a soft rag. Buff by hand.

If you're satisfied with the results of this small test, set all nails that stick up, then scrub the entire floor, using a steel-wool buffer pad in a commercial buffer (readily rented). A screen pad also works. For the best results, remove baseboard molding so you can get close to the edges of walls. Apply solvent by pouring it in small puddles around the floor; work an area 5 ft by 5 ft at a time. As the buffer pad strikes the puddles of solvent, it will spray solvent; therefore, move all furniture out of the room. As an extra precaution, tape newspaper or plastic along the lower 4 ft of the walls; this will protect the paint or wallpaper. Clean up dissolved wax with a damp mop rinsed often. When the cleaned floor is dry, apply a new coat of wax and buff with a lamb's-wool pad.

If the wood flooring has been painted or has built-up layers of clear finish, however, or if it was covered by resilient flooring held down by mastic, sanding is probably your best course.

How thick is the flooring? The crucial test before you actually sand a floor is whether it is thick enough to withstand sanding. If it has been sanded several times before, it may not take it again. The easiest way to determine this is to take off the baseboard molding and have a look; by pulling up a heating register in the floor, you can also judge the thickness of the flooring. If it is, say, $\frac{3}{4}$-in. oak, it can take several sandings. If the flooring is $\frac{5}{16}$ in. thick and has already been sanded, be very careful; use a floor-polishing machine with a screen abrasive rather than a drum sander.

Removing linoleum. There may be a nice wooden floor beneath an unsightly linoleum one. To remove the linoleum, first cut its surface with a linoleum knife. To minimize the mess, try to find the edges of the particleboard underlayment and pry up along them (Figure 20.6). In this manner you should be able to tear out large chunks and minimize the mess. If the linoleum was applied directly to the old flooring, however, you're in for some work. Make

Figure 20.6 If you can locate the seams of the old underlayment and score them with a utility knife, the underlayment will come up in large chunks, making cleanup much easier. After the old flooring and underlayment is up, *pull* all flooring nails or staples; scrape a 6-in. drywall knife across the subflooring to detect any nails you can't see. Then vacuum well. (Mike Mitschang)

a series of parallel cuts, then rip up strips as best you can. The linoleum will break and fragment. The whole business is messy, so have trash cans and boxes ready to haul out the debris. Hook scrapers, broad knives, and flat utility bars are useful in getting under the linoleum and prying it up. The problem is, over the years, the adhesive paste may have become stronger than the linoleum.

Once you've removed as much old flooring as you can, choose among several methods of cleaning up old linoleum scraps and adhesive. Sanding with No. 30 open-coat sandpaper in a drum sander is effective. Sander belts gum up quickly, so buy extra belts. Some old adhesives can be dissolved with hot water. Soak the area with hot water (with, possibly, a handful of trisodium phosphate added); put down several layers of newspaper over the water so it won't dry out too quickly. As you work individual areas, take off the newspaper, rinse again with hot water, and scrape with a hand scraper. Adhesives not affected by water can be dissolved by a petroleum-based solvent. Wear a respirator mask and ventilate rooms well if you use these chemicals, and cut electrical power to the area to minimize sparks. Finally, *do not smoke.*

Stripping with chemicals. Chemical paint removers are seldom used to strip floors. They're noxious, expensive, and easily tracked into other rooms—and you'll generate mountains of scrapings, rags, and newspapers trying to contain the mess. Instead, use a scraper and a *heat gun*; you'll have only minor sanding afterward because you will have raised the grain a bit.

Either of these methods is back-breaking work, but it's sometimes the only recourse you have if the floor has already been drum-sanded several times or is unusually ornate or delicate. It's hands-and-knees work, so get a sturdy pair of knee pads. Equally imperative are good ventilation, goggles, rubber gloves, and a respirator mask which can filter out aromatic chemicals. Should you apply a chemical stripper, always brush *away* from your face and allow it to work 10 to 15 minutes before scraping it up.

Sanding Equipment

Most sanding tools are specialized, but they can easily be rented. Some of these tools are a drum sander, which does most of the heavy work; an edger, a power sander that can get close to edges; and a hand scraper, for going where the edger won't go. A buffer-polisher with a screen abrasive is sometimes used instead of a drum sander to refinish thinner flooring or floors with little finish remaining.

You will also need a respirator mask, sound-protectors, goggles, heavy scissors (to cut sandpaper), and a pencil. If there's an old piece of sandpaper on the machine you rent, save it: old pieces are invaluable templates for tracing new ones.

Drum sander. A drum sander operates on 110-volt or 220-volt power; ascertain which kind you're renting and provide an adequate hookup. A 220-volt machine, for example, may need a 30-ampere circuit, which can be accomplished by running a field receptacle directly from the entrance panel. A 30-ampere, 220-volt circuit has two hot lines, as explained in Chapter 11. Or you can use a heavy extension cord with a 30-ampere plug to run off an electrical dryer outlet.

Have the supplier show you how to change the sandpaper on the drum; amateurs often rip sheets because the sandpaper isn't tight on the drum. Usually, to open the clamp on the face of the drum, turn a nut or keyhole at the end of the drum with a wrench or a special key. On most models, a tracking nut keeps the sandpaper centered on the drum while the machine is operating.

To change sandpaper, unplug the machine and overturn it so the drum faces up. Using the key, open the clamping slot and remove the old paper. Trace the old piece onto the new paper—rolls of sandpaper are cheaper than individual sheets. Feed the ends of the new piece into the drum slot and close it. If the paper flaps as the machine is started, the paper isn't tight enough; refasten the paper.

The drum sander is a powerful machine, and can gouge even the hardest wood if the drum is lowered while the machine is stationary or if the sander is started with the drum down. The position of the drum—up or down—is controlled by a lever on the handle. Keep the drum sander moving when the drum is down; it's sanding whether you're moving forward or backward.

You will need extension cords whose wire is at least as large a gauge as that of the machine's cord. Ask your supplier to recommend a size. On machines that operate on 110 volts, the cord supplied is usually long enough; if the sander uses 220 volts, rent an additional, heavy-duty extension cord.

To prevent sanding over the cord, keep the excess looped around your shoulders, as shown in Figure 20.8. Pull the cord away from the path of the sander.

Sandpaper. The coarser the paper, the more wood it removes. There are two ways of grading the coarseness (or fineness) of sandpaper. The old system of grit-sizing runs from 4 (extra coarse) to 10/0 (very fine). The system commonly used today is based upon the screen mesh that grit can pass through: sizes range from No. 12 (very coarse) to No. 600 (so fine it seems almost smooth). Very coarse papers are also called "open-coat sandpaper" because the grit

particles are farther apart and the paper is thus less likely to gum up. Of the numerous types of grit, silicone carbide is the hardest.

Hardwood floors are usually sanded in two or three passes, the first two with a drum sander and the third with

A.

B.

C.

Figure 20.8 Using an edger. (A) An edger gets right next to the wall; a drum sander cannot. (B) To cut replacement pieces, use an old piece as a template. (C) To soften the sanding edge, leave several used pieces on the machine. (B&D Floors, Brooklyn, NY)

Figure 20.7 Lower the drum of a sander only when it is moving. Walk with the machine as it sands to avoid gouging one spot. For safety, drape extra cord over your shoulders as shown. (B&D Floors, Brooklyn, NY)

Stripping and Refinishing Floors **473**

a polisher-buffer equipped with screen abrasive. Three passes with a drum sander are acceptable, as long as the final sanding is done with fine paper. The first pass is usually with No. 20 sandpaper; the second coat with medium grade, No. 50; and finally, fine, No. 120. When sanding softwood floors, start with 50 to 80-grade paper. Where a lot of old finish must be removed, the first pass is sometimes diagonal to the prevailing wood grain; but all subsequent passes are always *with the grain*.

If you are removing a clear finish that is relatively thin, and the floor is in good shape, two sandings should do it. No. 30 or 60 sandpaper should be followed by No. 120. If the flooring is softwood, refinishing may take three sandings. Begin, however, with No. 80 paper, even if the floors have been painted. If the grit is too fine, the paper will quickly gum up, an indication that you should switch to a coarser paper. Parquet floors are hardwood; because they are thin, however, they should be treated gingerly as well. Start with a medium-coarse paper, switching to a coarser paper if the medium-grade paper doesn't remove enough on the first pass.

Edger and scraper. The edger uses the same sandpaper, at each pass, that the drum sander does. As its name implies, the edger can get to spots that a drum sander can't; the scraper can reach places the edger can't. Get a scraper slightly wider than the strip you're scraping, and sharpen the scraper periodically with a *mill-bastard file*. A sharp scraper is imperative.

The edger's paper is held in place against a rubber disk by a washered nut. Although precut paper disks are available, it's cheaper to trace and cut your own from the same roll you use for the drum sander. To prevent gouging the floor with the edger, many professionals leave three or four used disks beneath the new one, to cushion somewhat the edge's cutting.

Sanding

Final preparations before sanding: remove all furniture; lift out registers from their boots and stuff the boots with newspaper; seal off the room to be sanded with sheet plastic and masking tape; and have plenty of shopping bags on hand so you can unload the sander bag frequently. Protect yourself with a respirator mask and sound protectors. Remove baseboards, as noted above, and sink all nails that might rip the sandpaper. Vacuum the floor well. Finally, survey the floor with a long, straight board to see what high spots might be sanded down.

Routine sanding. The direction of sanding varies somewhat, depending on the type of wood flooring and its condition. The most common way is to sand parallel to the grain of the wood on all three passes. Start along a wall and sand about two-thirds the length of the floor; then pull the machine backward over the strip just sanded. Raise the sander's drum at the end of the backward stroke and wheel the machine over about 6 in.; the next section of flooring you sand should overlap the first slightly (about half the width of the drum). Again, sand down about two-thirds the length of the room and make a backward pass.

Continue sanding until you have reached the opposite wall—you will have sanded two-thirds of the room. Turn the machine 180 degrees and start sanding the other end of the room—the third you haven't yet sanded. Again, sand one pass up and one back. When you reach the area already sanded overlap two or three feet before starting the next pass. In this manner you can blend the sanding of the two sections of the room (see Figure 20.10A)

Note: It is extremely important that you let down and raise the drum only when the machine is moving, that is, when you're walking with it. As you start a forward pass, or as you move over to start a new strip, raise the drum. If you fail to do this, the sander will jerk you, and worse, will gouge the floor unbelievably quickly—so deep the gouge may be all but impossible to sand out.

Other sanding situations. On a floor with minor irregularities that must be leveled, make the first pass with the drum sander at a 45 degree angle to the direction of the floor strips. Successive passes should be parallel to the strips, as mentioned above. This diagonal, first sanding removes more wood than a parallel pass. It also leaves sanding marks which are prominent and which must be removed by subsequent passes. If the floor has been sanded before or is less than $\frac{3}{4}$ in. thick, a diagonal first pass is probably not a good idea.

If the flooring is parquet, block, herringbone, or the like—with wood grain running in several directions—the first pass should be diagonal, the second in the opposite diagonal, and the third parallel to the length of the room (Figure 20.10B). Again, for each pass you sand up and back before moving the machine over. And, of course, raise and lower the drum only when the machine is moving.

Using an edger. After completing each sanding with the drum sander, use the edger with the same-grade sandpaper as you used on the drum. Move the edger constantly to prevent scour marks, going in a back-and-forth motion along the baseboard. You need not press down on the edger to make it work; neither should you press down on the drum sander. If not enough wood is being removed, chances are, the sandpaper is clogged; change it often.

Final touches. For a superb finish (most professional floor-finishers don't go this far), proceed with a screen

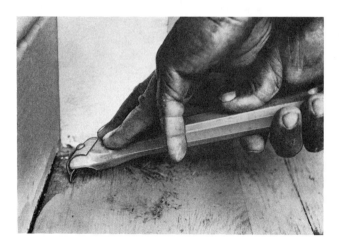

Figure 20.9 A scraper goes where even the edger cannot; there's no need to sand after hand-scraping. Scrape with the grain.

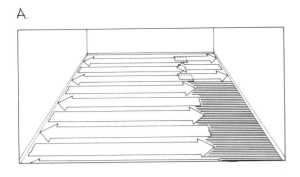

A.

B.

SECOND — FIRST PASS

FINAL

Figure 20.10 Floor sanding schematics. (A) When sanding strip flooring, sand with the courses. Each section gets sanded twice, once as you go forward with the sander and once as you pull the machine back. After sanding about two-thirds of the room, turn the machine around 180-degrees and sand the remaining one-third of the room. Overlap all passes slightly so there are no obvious stopping points. (B) Because parquet or block floors have wood grain going in several directions, make the first two passes diagonally; the last, with the dominant grain pattern of the floor.

abrasive in a polisher-buffer, which operates with a rotary motion. Steel-wool pads are also available for fine work. In any event, when you finish sanding the floor, vacuum it well, then wipe the entire floor (including the nooks and crannies you scraped by hand) with a tack rag. Also wipe all trim on which dust may have settled.

Because atmospheric humidity can raise grain, the final sanding, or screening, should be deferred until just before you're ready to apply finishes to the floor. Do the final sanding in your socks, though sneakers are alright.

Staining and Refinishing

Stain or otherwise alter the color of wood before applying filler materials or finishes. Wear goggles, rubber gloves and a mask for all operations that follow.

If the floor has prominent watermarks, remove them before staining and finishing. Sponge on dilute bleach or a solution of oxalic acid (1 oz acid to 1 qt water) available at most paint stores. After allowing the stain-remover to dry, sand the spot by hand.

Staining. The most widely used stains are oil-based; they soak in well, dry quickly, and are compatible with most fin-

ishes. Apply stain with a rag or a brush. For uniform color throughout the floor, mix all cans of stain (if more than one is required) into one large container. As you use the stain, keep stirring it; the pigment is merely suspended in the oil medium. Wipe off excess stain with clean rags.

Note: Always test-stain a small area first. Make sure you have adequate ventilation while working.

Filler. After staining the floor, apply filler if needed. Obvious places to fill are unsightly gaps between boards, knotholes, splits, and so on. The best way to match color is to mix dust from the sanding with white glue and the stain used on the floor. Mix this to a puttylike consistency and apply it with a putty knife, scraping up any excess and sanding when dry.

Open-grain woods such as oak are sometimes filled, usually with a commercially available filler paste. Again, try the paste on a small area and see if you like its looks; you may decide just to seal open-grained wood without filling.

Finishes. Finishes are roughly divided into *penetrants* (including stains) and *surface finishes*; the former penetrates wood fiber, the latter acts as a surface coat, although members of each group have varying characteristics (see Table 20.1)

In general, penetrants are best for softwood floors, especially where a deep luster is desired. Although penetrants are somewhat less durable, they can be made more so by waxing. You can also touch them up by cleaning the surface and apply new penetrant, or by applying a special reconditioner first.

Penetrating sealers are also used as undercoats for lacquer and varnish, but always check the labels of both finishes before application. There are two classes of penetrating sealers, the slower-drying variety is best for nonprofessionals.

Mop penetrants on with lamb's-wool applicators, wide brushes, or rags. The preferred technique is to apply it generously and wipe up excess. Allow it to dry thoroughly before applying any subsequent coats, some manufacturers recommend buffing with steel wool between sealer coats.

Surface finishes, which always have some sheen, are best for hardwood floors. Since these finishes form a hard membrane over flooring, applying them over softwood may result in cracking and scuffing as the softer wood flexes. Touching up surface finishes requires sanding or a go-over with steel-wool if a new application is to adhere. A word about lacquers—don't use them on floors; they're extremely volatile and noxious. True, you can touch up lacquer, but its drying agents include MEK and acetone, both carcinogens. For that reason, wear a respirator mask with filters capable of blocking the vapors, and be sure that there are *no* open flames—remember pilot lights!—or sparks when applying lacquers.

Brush on a surface finish, applying it across the grain and then smoothing it with the grain, overlapping sections slightly to even out the finish. Work in foot-wide sections across the room. *Note:* Once a finish has started to dry, do *not* go back to touch it up.

Surface finishes should never be shaken; doing so will trap air bubbles. Allow surface finishes to dry fully. Buff

TABLE 20.1

Floor finishes

Finish	Comments
Penetrants	
Stains	Not intended as a finish coat; must be sealed with a compatible surface finish, or waxed.
Oil finishes (linseed and the various tung oils)	Absorbed by wood fiber, they offer fair resistance to moisture, especially tung; easy to touch up; can be rubbed to bring out wood colors; after drying thoroughly must be waxed; not generally compatible with surface finishes.
Stain-sealers (also called "penetrating seals")	The best bet for most residential floors; they soak in and harden somewhat to seal out most stains and dirt; produce matte finish that can be touched up easily; wax to seal or overcoat with compatible surface finish; great range of colors.
Surface finishes	
Shellac	Not particularly good for floors because it chips and has poor resistance to water.
Varnish	Be sure you purchase a variety intended for flooring; glossy and durable, improved by waxing; if you apply it over bare wood, thin first coat 25%; otherwise, apply full strength; takes longer than shellac or polyurethane to dry—at least 8 hours; sand between coats; difficult to touch up.
Lacquer	Characteristics similar to those of varnish, except that worn spots can be touched up with lacquer; new lacquer dissolves and thus blends in; extremely volatile and noxious—you're probably better off using varnish or polyurethane.
Polyurethane	Hard, clear plastic finish, impervious (or nearly so) to water: wears well; probably your best bet for most wood floors; easily brush-applied, with about the same touch-up difficulty as varnish; may *not* be compatible with some other finishes, including other brands of polyurethane; drying slowed somewhat by humidity; air-drying polyurethanes are best for nonprofessional application; moisture-cured types extremely difficult to apply correctly.

with No. 2 steel wool and wipe with a tack rag before applying the next coat.

Whether you are applying penetrants or surface finishes, at least two coats are usually recommended; surface finishes often need three. If you apply a penetrating sealer followed by a compatible surface finish, apply one coat of the former and two of the latter, buffing with steel wool and wiping with tack rags between coats.

Make sure that your floor finish is *not* photochemically reactive, or it may change color when sunlight hits it. This is particularly important with stains and stain-sealers.

Maintenance. Wood finishes will last longest and look best if you vacuum or dust once a week and rewax once or twice a year, or touch-up wax as needed. Never wet-mop or wash wood floors with soapy water, because it can seep down between boards and stain or warp them. In general, paste waxes are more durable but liquid buffing waxes are easier to apply; it's best not to use a liquid wax that has a water base, however. Buff with a 12-in. rotary buffer.

If, after refinishing your floors, you observe that the finish is wearing unevenly, rub down the floor and gently clean old grime with a combination liquid cleaner-wax; use No. 00 steel wool. Wipe up residue with soft rags, let the floor dry for one-half hour, and then buff the floor with a machine, applying a second coat of wax if there are dull spots. If the stain on the floor is dark, use a colored wax.

For random spots, rub with No. 00 steel wool and rewax. If a spot is still noticeable, try again with No. 1 steel wool and a small amount of mineral spirits; touch up the finish when the wood is dry, and wax. If it's a dark spot, use a rag dampened with vinegar instead of mineral spirits; if vinegar doesn't remove the spot, try dilute oxalic acid.

LAYING NEW WOOD FLOORS

Before you lay new flooring, make sure the subflooring is securely nailed to the joists beneath, sufficiently thick to prevent flexion, and swept completely clean. The last point is particularly important if you stripped old flooring: after vacuuming well, scrape the floor with a wide taping knife to detect any nail heads you might have missed. Pull them or drive them down.

If you are nailing over existing flooring, run new flooring perpendicular to the old; if applying flooring over subflooring alone, make sure flooring runs perpendicular to *joists*. Subflooring should be at least $\frac{5}{8}$-in. plywood or 1-in. softwood boards if joists are 16 in. O.C. If you are laying parquet or wood blocks, subflooring should be at least $\frac{3}{4}$-in. plywood. Particleboard of any thickness is not an acceptable subfloor.

Humidity and Wood

Install wood as late as possible in the building sequence—after the windows and doors are fitted and preferably after plastering has been finished. The inside of the house should be 65 to 70°F when the wood is delivered and should stay that temperature thereafter. The bundles of wood should remain inside for three days before use, so wood will lose any incidental moisture it may have picked up in the lumberyard. If the walls of the house are still wet, delay delivery of the wood.

If there is an unheated crawl space beneath the first floor, it must be well ventilated. To prevent moisture from migrating through the subflooring, put a layer of 30-lb felt paper between the subflooring and the finish flooring. All radical changes in heat or humidity adversely affect wood; if flooring is to be applied to an area directly over a heating plant, insulate the basement ceiling. If wood does absorb water after it has been laid, the boards will swell, compressing edges as they do. Subsequently, when the wood dries, you will have noticeable gaps.

Layout and Installation

Wood flooring includes strip flooring, both tongue-and-groove and square-edged; parquet; wood block, and several other variations. Layout varies somewhat between types, with strips generally being parallel to the length of the room (and hence perpendicular to joists) in most cases. Parquet and blocks are set along imaginary *axes* (similar to tile axes, Figure 16.18) that intersect the room. Thickness of wood vary in each group, affecting the nailing schedule as shown in Table 20.2.

It takes few tools to install wood flooring: a chalkline to align nails, a chop saw to cut strips, a scribe if there are any irregular objects to butt flooring to, a screwdriver to hold strips tight against each other, and a tongue nailer which you can rent. Just dump the finish nails—usually cement-coated or galvanized—into the nailer's hopper and go to it. Follow up later with a nail set. A pneumatic nailer is also handy, as you'll see below.

Strip flooring. Strip flooring is, as the name implies, flooring that comes in long strips, usually no more than $3\frac{1}{4}$ in. wide. Most often, it is $\frac{3}{4}$ in. ($\frac{25}{32}$ in.) thick and is tongue-and-grooved; hence, it must be blind-nailed through the tongues of the strips. Wood of this thickness must be nailed; it cannot be installed with adhesive. Neither should it be installed on a floor below grade, that is, below ground level.

Sweep the existing floor or subfloor well, remove baseboard molding, attend to the subflooring, as above, and staple a layer of builder's paper over the existing subfloor (or floor)—after ascertaining the position of the floor joists.

Where there is only a subfloor, run strips perpendicular to the joists; where you're putting a new floor over an existing floor, run new strips perpendicular to old ones. Having made this determination, run the strips parallel to one of the room's long walls, since joists will usually run across its shorter dimensions. If the room is oddly shaped—say, without square corners—run flooring parallel to the main doorway leading into the room.

Once you've decided the general direction of strips, there are two ways to lay out flooring: along a chalk line snapped equidistant from opposite walls, as shown in Figure 20.11; or by starting the first course along one wall, as described below. The first method is preferred for older houses, for it better accommodates rooms out of square. In either method, use a pneumatic nailer to secure the first few courses of strip flooring so they do not get jarred off the starting chalkline. Thereafter, use the tongue nailer.

In the second method, place the first strip $\frac{1}{2}$ to $\frac{3}{4}$ in. from the wall, to allow for expansion—this gap will be covered by the baseboard. It's best to snap a chalk line to position this first course of strips. Put the groove edge of the strips toward the wall, with the tongued edge facing into the room. The first course of strips will be face-nailed, the nails sunk with a nail set; all subsequent courses are blind-nailed according to the schedule given in Table 20.2.

For the best-looking results, stagger the end joints of strips. Perhaps the easiest way to do this is to have a fair amount of flooring stock spread out on the floor so you can quickly choose the pieces you want. Stagger ends at least 6 in., and preferably more, between adjacent courses. At the ends of the courses (where flooring meets walls), again leave $\frac{1}{2}$ in. to $\frac{3}{4}$ in. gaps for expansion.

The last course of flooring must be $\frac{3}{4}$ in. from the opposite wall. You may have to rip down these last pieces of wood to the correct width, on a table saw. Power-nail the pieces in the last course, as you did those in the first course.

As you place each strip, use a piece of scrap flooring and a hammer to drive pieces snug next to preceding strips. Every fourth course (4, 8, and so on) of flooring, measure out from the originating wall to make sure strips are evenly spaced.

Finally, you will need about 5 percent extra strips for wastage. As you break the bands on bundles of flooring, set aside any pieces markedly different in color from others. Lay these pieces in less conspicuous places.

Wide-board flooring. Wide-board flooring is available prefinished from commercial manufacturers and almost green from local sawmills. If you buy from commercial manufacturers, follow their instructions; if you buy from a local sawmill, make sure the flooring has been air-dried for at least a year.

TABLE 20.2

Nailing schedule for hardwood flooring[a]

Size of Flooring	Type and Size of Nail	Spacing
$1 \times 1\frac{1}{2}$, $2\frac{1}{4}$, and $3\frac{1}{4}$	2-in. machine-driven fastener, 7d or 8d spiral or cut nail[b]	10 to 12 in. apart
The following flooring must be laid on wood subfloor:		
$\frac{1}{2} \times 1\frac{1}{2}$ and 2	$1\frac{1}{2}$-in. machine-driven fastener, 5d spiral, cut-steel, or wire casing nail	10 in. apart
$\frac{3}{8} \times 1\frac{1}{2}$ and 2	$1\frac{1}{4}$-in. machine-driven fastener, or 4d bright wire casing nail	8 in. apart
$\frac{5}{16} \times 1\frac{1}{2}$ and 2	1-in., 15-gauge barbed flooring brad	2 nails every 7 in.

Source: Specifications Manual of the National Oak Flooring Manufacturers' Association.

[a]Tongue-and-groove flooring must be blind-nailed; square-edged flooring, face-nailed.

[b]If steel-wire flooring nail is used, it should be 8d and preferably be cement-coated. Barbed brads should also be cement-coated if possible.

A.

B.

C.

D.

Figure 20.11 Installing hardwood, tongue-and-groove flooring. (A) After the old floor is ripped up, flooring nails pulled, and the floor vacuumed well, prepare for the new flooring. Here, an undercut saw held atop a scrap of new flooring cuts trim to the proper height. (B) Cover the subfloor with felt paper or kraft paper. Measure carefully to see what irregularities exist and compensate for them; then snap a chalk line equidistant from—and parallel to—opposite walls. It's imperative that the first boards be nailed down straight: carefully align the first row of flooring to the chalk line. Here, the craftsman power-nails the first strip so that it does not get jarred off the line, as it would by the tongue nailer shown in Fig. 20.11F. (C) Once the first row of flooring is nailed down along the length of the chalk line, gently drive a spline (or ''slip tongue'') into the groove on the other edge of the board; toe-nail the spline with a pneumatic nailer. This first board has two tongues so that you can work out from both sides: remember, T&G flooring is nailed only through the tongues. (D) A pneumatic nailer is also appropriate when there's not room for a tongue nailer, nor room to swing a hammer, such as under the kickspace of a cabinet. Before nailing down this strip, the installer first caulked the underside of the board with construction adhesive. The flat bar keeps the strip from being pushed back too far by the power nailer.

E.

F.

Figure 20.11 (Continued) (E) By staggering board joints and having several boards close at hand, you can nail several at a time. Here, the installer uses the metal head of the mallet to rap in the end of a board. (F) Once you have several rows nailed down and the boards will no longer shift, use a tongue nailer, striking it sharply with the rubber head of the mallet. Leave a gap—to be covered by baseboard trim—when you get to the walls: $\frac{1}{2}$ to $\frac{3}{4}$ in. next to walls parallel to the flooring, $\frac{3}{8}$ in. or so at the ends of the boards. Boards don't shrink as much along their length. (Thanks to Mike Mitschang, Hardwood Floor Craftsman, Oakland, CA, for the sequence.)

Because wide flooring has a greater tendency to warp or curl, the house must be dry when you install the flooring. Ideally, such boards should be nailed or screwed into joists, and all end joints should fall over the centers of joists. Note these centers by chalklining them on the felt paper you place over the subflooring. If you choose old-fashioned, square-head nails, align those nails carefully in straight, parallel lines, for they will be visible.

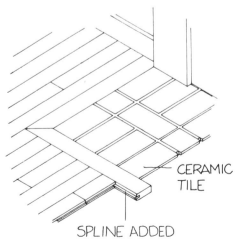

CERAMIC TILE

SPLINE ADDED

Figure 20.12 Adding and toe-nailing a spline is also a good way to secure the ends of T&G boards without face-nailing: here, only the mitered ''cap'' boards will have to be face-nailed. Because tile and wood expand at different rates, it would be wise to caulk this juncture with clear silicone.

Counteracting warpage. If you buy native (locally milled) lumber, it may be warped slightly by the time you're ready to install it. Here are two tips for coaxing the lumber into place so you can nail it down. (1) Nail down one end of the board, then nail a 2×4 block into the subflooring, near the board's unnailed end. Put a wrecking bar between the block and the board edge and pry the board in place. Nail down this end immediately, angling nails slightly so they will hold better. (2) The second method is similar, except that here, use a tapered strip 18 in. long and 2 in. wide (at its widest end). Again, nail a 2×4 block parallel to the board being nailed; drive the tapering piece to force the board over. With either method, be careful not to damage the edge of the board you are prying. Use a scrap block if necessary. Obviously, there are limits to how far you can pry a board before it splits. If a sawyer at the sawmill was consistently off the mark—say, with boards that are uniformly 1 in. wider at one end—you might do better to alternate wide and narrow board ends.

The tendency of wide boards to cup and split can also be countered by screwing them down. Predrill holes for the screws, using a drill-and-counterbore bit; fill the screw holes with plugs cut from the same flooring stock with a plugcutter bit. Put a dab of silicone caulk, instead of glue, beneath each plug, so you can remove it later if necessary.

As is true of other types of flooring, stagger end joints between courses, and align nails, screws, or plugs so there will be a pleasing pattern. Nail boards to each joist that they cross; use at least two nails in at least 1 in. from the edge, for boards up to 6 in. wide; and three nails at each joist for boards up to 12 in. wide.

Laying New Wood Floors **479**

Wood floors over concrete. Some types of thinner flooring, such a parquet and wood block, may be installed over concrete if preparation is correct. Because concrete will transmit moisture, there must be an impervious barrier between wood and concrete; sheet plastic (polyethylene) 4 mils thick is commonly used. It's never wise to bond wood directly to concrete, even when an adhesive purports to be waterproof. Whatever the details of attachment, there must be no serious moisture problems, and the area should be well-ventilated.

The major method of making a concrete floor suitable for wood flooring is nailing 2×4 "sleepers" to the slab. Strip flooring can be nailed directly to the sleepers; block and parquet must be attached to a plywood subfloor over the sleepers. We'd advise a plywood subfloor in either case.

Line the concrete with polyethylene sheets, overlapping edges and taping them to prevent moisture migration. Then lay out a grid of 2×4 sleepers 16 in. O.C. Sleepers should be treated with a chemical that prevents deterioration. *Do not use creosote*, however, because it will soak through the finish flooring and discolor it. Use Wolmanized lumber, Cuprinol, or something similar. Leave $\frac{1}{2}$ in. between the ends of the 2×4s and $\frac{1}{2}$-in. gaps where the 2×4s abut walls. If the sleepers don't run the entire length of the room, overlap them side by side at least 4 in. Power-nail the 2×4s to the concrete; it is possible to do this by hand but difficult to do well. Next, nail the subflooring to the sleepers (see Table 20.2).

Note: In any building task, there are many variations. Some builders feel that there should be a second sheet of polyethylene over the tops of the sleepers. Other builders bed the sleepers in construction adhesive instead of putting a layer of poly underneath, although they do put a layer of poly over the sleepers. If you are installing parquet or block flooring with this method, put a layer of plywood (at least $\frac{5}{8}$ in. thick, and preferably $\frac{3}{4}$ in.) over the sleepers. There are many ways to lay out materials, let common sense be your guide. The important thing is to keep moisture from coming in contact with wood, and to attach materials securely.

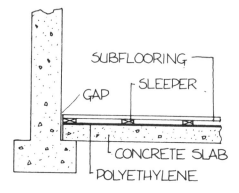

Figure 20.13 Wood floors over concrete are likely to warp if you don't totally control moisture by covering the concrete with sheet plastic. Overlap sheets and seal them with duct tape. After power-nailing sleepers to the concrete, cover them with exterior-grade plywood; leave a gap between the edge of the plywood and any masonry walls.

RESILIENT FLOORING

Resilient floors—linoleum, rubber, vinyl, cork, and asphalt—are, in a word, resilient. Their surfaces bounce back from use that would gouge or crush harder, less flexible flooring materials. Resilient floors do require maintenance, however, and they must be attached securely to a subfloor of sufficient thickness and suitable composition. Correct major subflooring/flooring maladies before making other repairs.

Repairing and Replacing Pieces

Resilient flooring requires little maintenance to keep its surface sheen. Keep the floor free of grit, but don't clean floors unless they need it; a weekly scrubbing with detergent can dull or damage resilient surfaces. Routine sponge-mopping with warm water alone should do the trick; add mild, nonabrasive detergent only if water alone isn't working. If the floor is dull, perk it up with liquid floor polish; strip the polish once or twice a year to prevent yellowing.

Stain removal. The following stains can be removed with ammoniated liquid detergent and fine steel wool: (1) miscellaneous grime, (2) blood, (3) grease and oil, and (4) scuff marks. To remove the stains of red wine, fruit juice, or hard liquor, apply denatured alcohol or a solution of three parts water to one part glycerine. (Glycerine can be obtained at a pharmacy.) Use a damp sponge. Urine stains can be removed with hydrogen peroxide. For cigarette burns, try scouring powder or peroxide; you'll probably want to patch-repair the spot, following the procedures described below. Wear rubber gloves when using any stain remover mentioned above.

Patch repairs. If damage to the tile is slight, mix your own color-matched tile filler by scraping the edge of a spare tile with a utility knife. Pare the edge as finely as you can. To make a paste of the shavings, mix in a small amount of solvent such as nail-polish remover or denatured alcohol. Spread the filler with a putty knife, scraping the mix as flat as possible. When the filler is dry (1 to 2 hours), smooth it further with fine steel wool dipped in a small amount of mineral or linseed oil.

Lancing blisters. Blistered spots in resilient flooring may be due to adhesive that has come loose, or it may be caused by water damage. To make the tile lie flat again, slit the blister with a utility knife; then heat the spot with an electric iron. To keep the iron from scorching the tiles, put a piece of heavy aluminium foil between the iron and the tiles, and keep the iron moving—it will soften the tile enough for you to slip some mastic paste beneath the slit. Rub the area with the heel of your hand, wipe up excess adhesive, and lay a weight over the spot so the adhesive will bond well.

Replacing a tile. To replace a badly damaged tile, warm the tile to loosen its adhesive, using a propane torch or an electric iron held over heavy aluminum foil. To avoid damaging nearby tiles, put foil or damp cloths on them. When the adhesive is soft, pry up the damaged tile with a putty knife or chop it free with an old chisel.

A.

B.

C.

Figure 20.14 Repairing resilient tile. (A) To fill a blemish, scrape the surface of a scrap tile that matches the one to be repaired. (B) Mix the scrapings with a solvent such as nail polish or denatured alcohol until there is a putty-like consistency. (C) Apply the mix to the blemish with a putty knife, and heat the area with an iron to flatten and dry the spot. Protect the iron and the floor with a piece of aluminum foil under the iron.

Scrape off the old adhesive from the underlayment so you can lay a new, level bed. Use a floor scraper if the adhesive resists; avoid damaging tiles nearby or the wood subfloor underneath, however. If the new tile isn't the same thickness as the old, build up the area with alternating layers of felt paper and adhesive until the difference in thickness has been equalized.

The replacement tile should be the same pattern as the original. If it isn't possible to buy a similar replacement tile, try prying up another old one from an inconspicuous spot, such as beneath a refrigerator or in a broom closet. You'll need a lot of patience to get an old one out without ruining it: it's best to soften the tile well with an electric iron and slide a wide-blade knife underneath.

Patch-repairing sheet flooring. To repair a rip or gouge in sheet flooring, get a replacement piece of the same pattern at least 3 in. wider and longer than the damaged spot. Carefully align the replacement to the pattern of the damaged area; tape the edges of the new piece down with masking tape. The flaw should be approximately centered underneath.

Using a straightedge to guide your cut, use a utility knife to cut through both the new piece and the flawed section underneath. With the knife blade, lift out the new section and the damaged section outlined. Much sheet flooring is stapled or glued only around the edges, making it easy to lift out. If the flooring has been glued down all

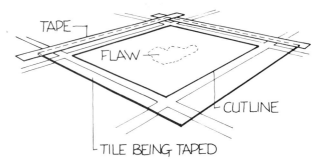

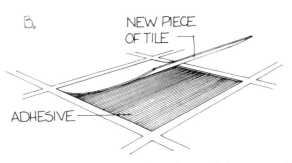

Figure 20.15 Replace a flawed tile with one of the same stock. Carefully align the pattern of the new piece over the old and tape it down as shown (A). Cut through both pieces with a utility knife to create an exact match of old to new. Pull up the tape, set aside the new tile, and pry out the old one. Clean up the subfloor as necessary, apply new adhesive, and press the replacement tile into place (B).

over, however, remove the flawed section carefully by softening the adhesive with a hot iron, as described above. Be careful not to go beyond the limits of the knife cut.

As you prepare to lay in the new piece, first slip some adhesive beneath the flooring still in place. Then apply adhesive to the back of the replacement piece; press it in place, weight it down, and let it stand for a day.

Installing New Resilient Flooring

Although resilient tile wears well and is somewhat flexible, it, too, depends on the integrity of the subflooring underneath. That subfloor must be very regular, or any irregularities such as, say tile patterns or broad gaps will in time become apparent through the new resilient flooring. Resilient materials, after all, aren't very thick, usually between $\frac{1}{16}$ and $\frac{3}{16}$ in.

Underlayment requirements. Subflooring must be sound and—for most types of resilient tiles and sheets—dry. Concrete is an acceptable substratum for some types of resilient flooring and adhesives; check carefully, however, the manufacturer's recommendations. The adhesive itself is crucial, because some types are neutralized by the alkali of concrete. To level minor irregularities, cover the subfloor with a layer of underlayment. Probably the most common underlayment is high-density, exterior-grade particleboard, also known as underlayment-rated hardboard. Whatever the surface, it must be nailed down well with *ring shank underlayment nails* $1\frac{1}{4}$ to $1\frac{1}{2}$ in. long, spaced every 4 in. or so.

Before you do any nailing though, survey the floor for nail heads sticking up even slightly—otherwise they'll telescope through the resilient flooring. Scrape a 6-in. joint knife (used for taping drywall) over the floor to detect heads. If, with light pressure, the blade catches on any nail heads, pound them deeper.

Old resilient flooring may be acceptable as a substratum if well attached; here again, application advice varies from one manufacturer to another. To repeat, the requisites of the underlayment are that it be smooth, that it be attached securely, and that it be free from finishes, including wax, oil, paint, varnish, and so on—that could interfere with the attachment of the new material.

Over Wood. When putting resilient materials over wood, the bugbears are gaps between boards, holes in the surface of the wood, and flexion. No additional underlayment is needed if the present flooring is tongue-and-groove (T&G) less than 3 in. wide, over acceptable subflooring. If the T&G is wider than 3 in., it is advisable to cover it with one of the exterior-grade underlayments mentioned above: $\frac{1}{4}$-in. hardboard or $\frac{1}{4}$-in. PTS (plugged and touch-sanded) plywood. If the existing flooring is single-layered (i.e., without subflooring), cover it with $\frac{1}{2}$-in. particleboard or $\frac{1}{2}$-in. PTS plywood (again, exterior grades). If an existing plywood subfloor is at least $\frac{7}{8}$ in. thick, and is nailed around the edges, it alone (with no additional subfloor) is acceptable for resilient materials. This thickness of plywood is quite expensive, though.

Over Concrete. Follow the manufacturer's instructions scrupulously, especially the advice about adhesives. Types

A.

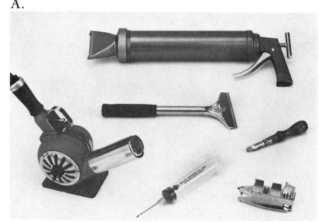

B.

Figure 20.16 Resilient-tile tools. Resilient tiling is popular because it requires few specialized tools; such tools are readily available, however, to make the job easier and more professional. (A) Resilient-tile cutter. (B) *Clockwise from lower right:* hinged scriber, to mark seams in resilient tile; hypo needle, for repairing bubbles and loose spots; heat gun, to soften tile, especially where it must be coved along corners; floor stripper; cove-based gun, to apply adhesive to the back of cove-base molding; utility cutter, for working in tight areas. (Crain Cutter Co.)

of mastic vary further according to whether the concrete is above or below grade (ground level). Some manufacturers specify a layer of adhesive or sheet plastic and then a layer of adhesive before applying tiles or resilient sheets.

Over Old Resilient Materials. If the old material is patterned, the manufacturer may specify new flooring with a foam backing, to blanket the old design. Others may suggest filling the old flooring with a latex floor-patching compound, a tedious job. It's possible to sand old flooring flat but not advisable if one of its ingredients is asbestos.

Important: In all cases, go back over underlayment seams with a *latex compound* (Vitex is one) to feather out edges and fill in cracks. Use a fairly long concrete trowel to apply the compound, allow it to dry, and then sand it lightly.

Installing resilient tiles. Laying out resilient tiles is much like laying wood blocks or ceramic tiles. Beginning at the middle of the doorway, run a primary axis into the room and another, secondary, axis perpendicular to the first. (See Figure 16.18.) Lay tiles a quadrant at a time (a quarter of the room), building up the tiles in a pyramid. Happily, resilient tiles are easy to cut. Using a straightedge as a guide, cut tiles with a utility knife or a linoleum knife and then bend them to complete the cut.

After chalk-lining the two alignment axes onto the floor, carefully spread adhesive in one of the four quadrants, being careful not to obscure axis lines. Apply the adhesive about $\frac{1}{16}$ in. thick; the teeth of your notched trowel will determine the height of the ridges.

After setting tiles along both axes of the quadrant in a rough ''L,'' build up the tiles in a sort of pyramid. As you come to the walls, stop tiles about $\frac{1}{8}$ in. short; that slight gap will be covered with shoe molding. Where tile meets a contoured surface or object, use a profile gauge or a compass to transfer the contour to the face of the tile.

When the tiles are down, they should be rolled. Avoid walking on tiles until the adhesive has set thoroughly; if you must walk on them, though, lay down strips of plywood.

Installing resilient sheets. Follow manufacturer's recommendations closely: whereas some specify setting the entire area of resilient flooring in mastic, others suggest you adhere only edges and seams to allow for expansion and contraction. Adhesives will also vary according to the composition of the material.

These days, resilient flooring is usually vinyl; it is available in sheets 9 to 12 ft. wide. The larger size is somewhat more cumbersome to work with, but it obviates seams in all but the largest rooms. Resilient sheets are available with foam backing or foam interlayers to make a floor even more resilient, hence quieter and warmer. For best results, take the roll of resilient material into the house a day or two before installing it. The warmer the sheet, the easier it is to unroll and cut. For that reason, some installers use a heat gun or a hair dryer to warm up edges when they've got to cove corners. If the material is warm and pliable it will tuck nicely and trim easily; if, on the other hand, it's stiff and unyielding—let it warm up.

Below are two methods for installing resilient flooring. The first should work if the room is fairly square and has few jogs or cutouts. The second method, employing a template, comes from a man with 40 years in the business and it always works.

Method One. Begin by pulling off the baseboard molding, being careful not to damage it. If the existing floor isn't acceptably flat and well secured, attend to that problem immediately. Vacuum the floor well and sponge-mop to pick up any grit that could affect the sheet flooring.

To prepare for layout, measure the room carefully and transfer these measurements to graph paper. This is partic-

ularly important where walls have numerous jogs, or built-ins. If there is one wall in the room that is especially straight, orient your measurements toward it. When unrolling the vinyl flooring, start from that wall. As always, never assume that a factory-cut edge is straight; check the edges of the resilient sheet with a straightedge or a string pulled taut. If the edge isn't straight, snap a chalk-line onto the stock and cut your own straight edge. Note whether all corners are square, as well. When taking up old, resilient sheets, save them and use them as templates for new sheets.

Transfer the room measurements to the new sheet, oversizing all dimensions by 3 in., which you'll cut back as you make your installation. Cut out the new resilient sheet and roll it up backward—with the backing showing—then carry it into the room where you'll install it.

Note: Most applications can be done with one sheet. If you need more than one piece, the *location* of the seams is most important. If possible, put seams in areas of little traffic, at least 6 in. from the joints of any underlayment. Many resilient systems feature special seam-sealing adhesives.

Starting from the straightest, most regular wall in the room, unroll the resilient sheet. Allow the excess to curl up

A.

B.

Figure 20.17 Working with resilient sheets. (A) Never assume that a factory edge is straight: check with a taut string or a straightedge and, if necessary, snap a chalk line to make it so. (B) Cut resilient flooring with snips, a linoleum knife, or a utility knife.

flooring in. The chalk marks will transfer to the backing of the flooring, so you can see where to cut.

Method Two. If the job is a small, complicated room with a lot of cutouts—such as a bathroom—create a felt-paper template first. Roll out a layer of 15-lb felt paper and trim it so that it is 1 inch shy of walls all around. Overlap seams at least 2 in. and join them with *duct tape.* Next, use a utility knife to cut small elliptical "boats" out of the felt paper every 4 to 5 ft. The shape of these "boats" is not crucial—they look more like eyes in Figure 20.19—nor is their size, about 2 in. by 5 in. But these cutouts allow you to fix the felt paper to the underlayment without taping down the edges. So, after you cut out each boat, stretch duct tape across the hole and press it down so that it sticks to the underlayment.

The felt paper secured, now scribe the outline of the room onto the felt paper. Set your scribe to 4 in. and scribe around the room. In corners, profile lines will intersect. Repeat the procedure to double-check the perimeter.

Next, roll up the felt paper template, taking pains to ease it up where it's duct-taped to the floor. Carry the template to the room where you've stretched out the resilient material, face up, to warm and flatten. Position the felt paper on the resilient material and use the duct tape peering through the boats to secure the template to the new flooring. Holding one point of the scribe on the lines you scribed earlier, trace the profile of the room onto the resilient material. *Note:* Keep the scribe points perpendicular to the lines,

A.

B.

Figure 20.18 Installing resilient flooring. (A) Measure the floor and rough-cut those dimensions onto the sheet material; unroll the flooring. Preferably, align one edge to the straightest (fewest jogs) wall in the room. (B) The excess flooring will curl up onto walls; trim it carefully so that it lies flat, running a utility knife along a metal straightedge. Leave a $\frac{1}{8}$-in. gap between the edge of the flooring and the base of the wall—it will be covered by trim. (Armstrong Cork Co.)

where it meets walls. At this point, you'll have to tug and adjust the resilient sheet until it is centered approximately.

Trim the sheet where it meets walls, again, beginning along the straightest wall, which may not require much trimming at all. There should be a gap of $\frac{1}{8}$ in. between the edge of the sheet and the base of the wall, which gap will be covered later by baseboard molding. Guide a utility knife along a straightedge for cuts. It may be necessary to make two cuts along each wall—the first to remove most of the extra 3 in. you allowed, and the second to fine-tune the fit. (It's difficult to see exactly where your cut will fall when the material is curling up onto a wall.) As you cut, press the material into the wall-floor seam as best you can with a wide-blade spackling knife.

Where it is difficult to get a knife in to make cuts—as it is in the kickspace under cabinets—mark the edge of the subfloor with lipstick or blue builder's chalk and roll the

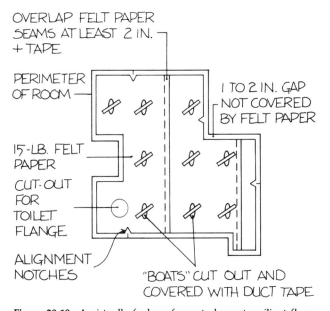

Figure 20.19 A virtually foolproof way to lay out resilient flooring, no matter how complex the room. Start by laying a felt-paper template, about 2 in. shy all of the walls. Overlap felt-paper seams and duct-tape them together. At roughly 4-ft intervals, use a utility knife to cut out roughly elliptical holes in the felt paper; these holes are called "boats" in the drawing. Put duct tape across these holes, so that it sticks to the old flooring beneath. Finally, set a scribe to 4 in. and, drawing lines parallel to walls, transfer the outline of the room to the felt paper. Carefully remove the felt-paper template, next tape it down onto new sheet flooring, and—using the scriber still set at 4 in.—transfer the scribe lines from the felt paper to the new resilient flooring.

as you did when profiling the walls. Take your time transferring and cutting and you'll get an almost perfect fit.

Securing the Sheet. When you've cut the entire perimeter of the resilient sheet, make sure it is lying flat; then secure the edges of the material, as recommended by the manufacturer. Most systems require that you apply mastic around the edges of the sheet, using a notched trowel; other edges can be stapled down. Less common are resilient-flooring systems that require an entire bed of mastic beneath the sheet flooring. (Such a bed is most often specified where there will be heavy traffic or persistent moisture, for example, in bathrooms.) In the latter case, the installer usually rolls up one side of the sheet, applies mastic, rolls the material back down, then rolls up the other half, so the floor beneath it can receive an application of mastic.

Wherever you apply mastic, press the sheet flooring down and roll it to ensure bonding; allow the adhesive to cure fully. For hard-to-reach spots, special adhesive applicators are available. There are also special pieces for finishing off such flooring, for example, matched cove-molding and metal thresholds where sheets end.

Butt seams. Try to avoid seams in the middle of a room, because they are highly visible and subject to wear. After positioning and trim-fitting the larger of the resilient sheets needed, roll out the smaller one so it overlaps the first. Adjust the second sheet to align the patterns of the two pieces. This done, tape the leading edge of the overlapped piece with masking tape, so it can't move.

Holding a metal straightedge to guide your cut, and keeping the blade of the utility knife absolutely perpendicular, cut through both layers of the resilient flooring at the same time. The blade of the knife should be as stiff as possible, because the cut must be clean, and cutting through two layers requires effort. After you make the cut, peel off the tape and remove the excess from the overlapping piece and the larger sheet underneath. The patterns of the two pieces should align perfectly. (Double-cutting wall covering—as shown in Figure 19.20—is similar.)

Next, trim the edges of the second, smaller piece of flooring where it meets walls and other surfaces. To secure the edges of the butt seam, lift one side of the flooring at a

Figure 20.20 Where resilient flooring meets another material, prevent fraying by screwing down a metal edge strip.

time and lightly sand the subfloor underneath to remove any gloss or old finish; wipe up dust with a tack rag. Here again, a heat gun or hair dryer can soften edges and help them lie flat. Do the same to the second edge, then spread a 6-in. swath of mastic down the middle of the subflooring, centered beneath the butt seam. Allow the mastic to become slightly tacky; then press the edges of the sheets down firmly. Wipe up excess mastic and weight the seam until it is totally bonded.

WALL-TO-WALL CARPETING

Carpeting is increasingly popular. It looks good, insulates floors to some extent, and is relatively straightforward to install. Time was, one had to sew together sections 2 ft wide and sink thousands of carpet tacks to hold the carpeting down. Today, however, carpeting comes in widths of 9, 12, and 15 ft; thus seams are less of a problem. Also, hot-melt seam tape allows amateur installers to forego sewing completely. You will need a few special tools, but they can usually be rented from a carpet supplier.

Materials and Tools

Carpet materials include *wool* (handsome and durable but difficult to clean and inclined to build up static electricity; also expensive); *acrylic*, the second choice of many who would buy wool if they could afford it; also durable, easier to clean than wool, less likely to build up static electricity, and good-looking); *nylon*, very durable but less comfortable underfoot, with static electricity a problem; *polyester*, the least expensive but also the least durable; shiny, with less depth of color; and *cotton* and *jute*, used as carpet materials, but not commonly. Carpet is sold by the square yard; installation, should you choose to have it installed, is calculated by the square yard as well.

Types and attachment. There are mainly two types of carpeting, in terms of installation: conventional carpeting, which is laid over a separate padding, and cushion-backed carpeting, which has foam bonded to its back.

To install conventional carpeting, first staple down the padding (whether vinyl, sponge rubber, or latex foams, felts made from animal hair, or jute). Next, nail down tackless strips around the perimeter of the room. Conventional carpeting is then stretched with special tools until its fabric backing catches on the points of tackless strips. Cushion-backed carpeting is routinely bedded in mastic or in double-face tape.

Tackless strips, incidentally, are loaded with tacks. Each point sticks up to grab the backing of the carpet. The strips are so-called because they save the installer the drudgery of hammering each of several thousand tacks. To tack down a carpet without such strips, it's necessary to fold over the edges in a kind of hem and then tack the hem to the floor.

Better-quality carpets are nearly always conventional. Cushion-backed carpeting is generally easier to install; but because it is adhered with mastic, you must destroy the carpeting if you want to take it up. Carpeting usually requires little of the subfloor, since it doesn't mold to the pattern of whatever is underneath, as resilient flooring does. Nor is carpeting brittle, as ceramic tile is. Cushion-backed carpeting is particularly forgiving about the material underneath; that type of carpeting often can be applied directly over concrete, ceramic tile, resilient flooring, and the like, although manufacturers are specific about the adhesive to be used in each type of application.

Tools. Few special tools are required. If you're installing conventional carpeting (with a separate pad), you will need to rent a *knee kicker,* which moves the carpet toward tackless strips, and a *power stretcher,* which stretches carpeting taut across a room, to tackless strips along opposite walls, thereby eliminating sags in the middle. To join seams using hot-melt seam tape, you will need a *seaming iron.* To cut loop-pile carpeting (see the section below, "Carpet Pile and Layout"), get a *row runner.* Otherwise, the tools used are standard ones: utility knife, staple gun, metal straightedge (for guiding cuts), tape measure, hammer, saw or snips (for cutting tackless strips), heavy gloves (for handling strips), screwdriver, and chalk line. A *wall trimmer* is very handy for cleaning up the edges of carpeting; but it may be hard to find one; a utility knife will do, if you can't. If you intend to carpet stairs, also get a *stair tool* (it resembles a brick chisel) and an awl; both allow you to maneuver carpeting into tight places.

If the carpet is cushion-backed, you will need fewer tools—a notched trowel, if the carpet is laid in mastic, a chalk line, a utility knife, tape measure, applicator (for seam adhesive, unless you're using double-face tape), and a metal straightedge.

Measuring and Estimating

To estimate the amount of carpeting you will need, consider: (1) the size of the room, at its widest and longest points; (2) the position of windows and doors; and (3) the direction of the carpet pile. The first two factors are best expressed by sketching the room on graph paper; a scale of $\frac{1}{4}$ in. to 1 ft is a convenient size to work with. The third factor, direction of carpet pile, needs some explanation.

Carpet pile and layout. Most carpeting, especially the better grades, is tufted; its yarn is stitched in a mesh backing. The face of the carpet—which we see—is called the "pile"; the pile is further named according to how the yarns of the carpet are shaped or shorn. Uncut, the pile is called "loop pile"; when the loops of yarn are cut, it is called "cut pile." "Sculpted pile" usually is a mixture of looped and cut, thus creating a pattern.

When carpeting is rolled up after being backed, its pile is pressed down, and it assumes a *direction,* which it retains thereafter. By stroking a carpet's pile, you can determine its "pile direction"; when you face against the direction of the pile, the carpet looks darker, and when you face in the same direction as the pile, the carpet appears lighter. The point is, when you install carpet, the main entryway of the room should "look into" (against) the carpet pile, so that it appears as rich and luxuriant as possible. Also, where it's necessary to join two pieces of carpet, the pile of at least one piece should lean into the seam, thus concealing it to some degree (Figure 20.27). Thus, if you have to

A.

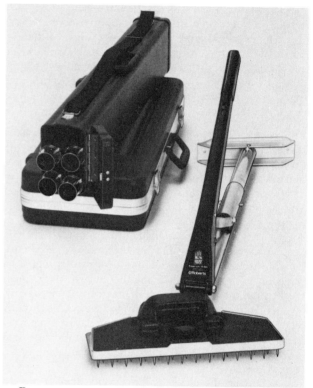

B.

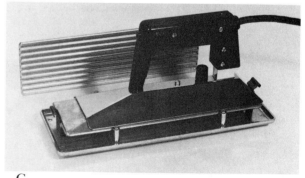

C.

Figure 20.21 Carpeting equipment. (A) *Counterclockwise from top center:* two edge trimmers, which trim carpeting along walls; knee kicker, to stretch carpet onto tackless strips; cutter, which follows the furrows of carpet yarn as you cut; two stair tools, to force carpeting into tight spots before trimming. (Crain Cutter Co.) (B) Power stretcher, which stretches carpet from one side of a room to the other; it comes with extension tubes. (Roberts Consolidated Industries) (C) Hot-melt seaming iron. (Crain)

use more than one piece of carpet in a room, all pile should point in the same direction; otherwise, sections will appear to have different hues.

Measuring. On your scale drawing, measure carefully—wall by wall—the width and depth of all alcoves, doorways, bay windows, built-in cabinet bases, and so on. Take diagonal readings as well, from diagonally opposite corners. Note whether corners are square. Mark doors and windows on your sketch.

After some preliminary discussion with carpet suppliers, you should have an idea of the kind of carpet you'd like, and what its standard width will be (most often, 12 ft). To calculate exactly how much carpet you should buy, reconcile the width of the carpet bolt with the dimensions and traffic flow of the room. Your goal, of course, is to lay out carpet economically and have as few seams as possible. You should also keep in mind the following:

1. Don't run seams into doorways. The heavy traffic through a doorway will eventually loosen seams, and you will have two sections of carpet to trip over. Similarly, try to avoid seams along the traffic between doorways.

2. Try to run seams perpendicular to the major window. The seams should be largely parallel to the incoming light. Seams that run *with* the light—hence, the visual field—are less obvious than those that run *across* it.

3. Orient the pile of the carpet toward the main doorway, so people entering the room will see the deepest color.

4. When carpeting stairs, aim the pile toward the bottom of the stairs; so oriented, it will wear less.

These variables may seem difficult to keep straight; but if you make a scale map of the room on graph paper and cut out some paper to scale, to represent widths of carpeting, the procedure will make sense. Move the paper cutouts around, trimming them where necessary. The length of, say, 12-ft-wide carpeting you must buy is the composite of the pieces you need to cover the room as drawn to scale. If the carpet has a pattern, order extra; that way, you can match up its pattern along seams. Otherwise, just add 3 in. to the length and 3 in. to the width of the room's largest dimensions (the far side of door jambs, alcoves, and so on).

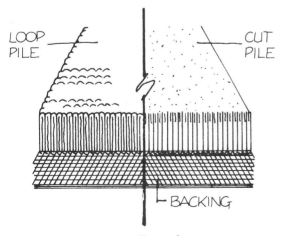

Figure 20.22 Types of carpet.

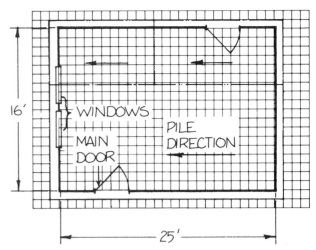

Figure 20.23 Carpeting layout. Estimating the size and layout of carpet means reconciling several variables: having as few seams as possible, placing any seams in out-of-the-way places, wasting the least amount of carpet, placing pile direction so that a person entering the room looks into the pile, and so on. The placement shown is fairly successful. Since carpeting comes in 12-ft.-wide bolts, 41 R.F. (running feet) is about right for this room, allowing about 1 ft extra on all sides, as indicated by the white perimeter.

From these sketches, you can also determine how much backing to buy; it comes in rolls $4\frac{1}{2}$ to 12 ft wide and is laid on the floor in no particular pattern. From the perimeter of the room, you will also know how much tackless stripping to purchase. Strips come in 4-ft lengths; its points' lengths are matched roughly to the type of carpet (type E strip is right for most). Take your sketches to the carpet supplier and have the supplier check your calculations.

Installing Conventional Carpeting

For most floors, carpeting requires little preparation before installation. If the existing floor is wood, it should be sound and relatively flat. Any cracks greater than $\frac{1}{2}$ in. should be filled with wood filler or wood strips; but the gaps of most wood flooring need no treatment, since the padding of the carpet, and the carpet itself, will disguise such gaps. If the floor is ceramic tile or a similar surface that can't be nailed, glue down tackless strips with contact cement or construction adhesive applied to tile and to the underside of the strips. Floors that are highly irregular may best be covered with sheets of plywood or hardboard, as described earlier in this chapter.

Tackless strips. Nail down tackless strips around the perimeter of the room, leaving $\frac{1}{4}$ in. gaps between the strips and the bases of walls; the edges of the carpet tuck into these $\frac{1}{4}$-in. gaps. Since the strips come with nails, you need only hammer each strip down, trying not to hit the points on the strip. Use a finish hammer for this task; it has a smaller head than a framing hammer.

The points of the strip, angled 60 degrees, should always incline toward the wall. Where you must cut short strips, use a saw or snippers; each strip, however short, must be nailed down with at least two nails. Nail down strips *in front of* radiators or built-in cabinets, because it would be difficult to nail down strips or to stretch carpeting behind or under such obstacles. In doorways use special metal edging-strips to secure the edge of the carpet; or you can fold the carpet under 1 in. and nail down that hem.

Padding.   Staple padding down with $\frac{3}{8}$-in. staples every 6 in. around the perimeter of each piece. Padding should overlap slightly the tackless strips, with the excess to be cut off later, using a utility knife. If the padding has a waffled pattern on one side, that side should face up. Where pieces of padding meet, simply butt their edges (don't overlap them) and staple.

If you are applying padding over ceramic tile or something similar, use linoleum paste to hold down felt padding and mastic or a specially prepared adhesive to hold down foam padding. Seal butt-seams with duct tape so the seams can't shift when the carpet is stretched.

When you trim the padding along the tackless strip, be sure to bevel the cut away from the strip, so the padding cannot ride up on the strip when the carpet is stretched.

Rough-cutting carpet.   Cut loop-pile carpet from the pile side, and cut cut-pile carpet from its backing side. Cut the

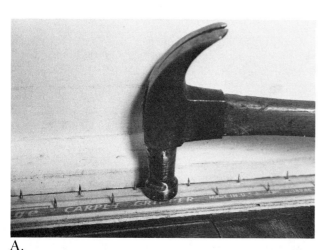

A.

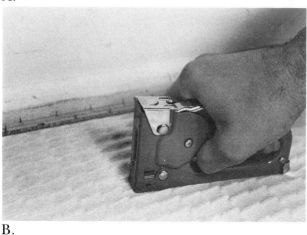

B.

Figure 20.24 Carpet preliminaries. (A) Apply tackless strips around the perimeter of the room; wear heavy gloves to protect your hands. Nail down the strips every 12 in. or so. (B) Staple down the padding beneath the carpet, slightly beveling the edges of the pad so that they won't ride over the tackless strips when the carpet is stretched.

carpet to the general dimensions you measured on your scale map of the room. Delay cutting jogs, odd spots, and final-cutting of seams until the carpet is in place. Unroll the carpet in a spare room, so the fabric can uncurl for 2 to 3 hours.

Note: Before making any cuts, note the direction of the pile if you have more than one piece of carpeting to lay, and hence seams to match.

If the carpeting is loop pile, measure the cutting point on the face of the carpet and make a first pass with the row runner with its blade retracted. This pass separates the rows of pile slightly so you will have a clear view of the cut to follow (Figure 20.25). (Some professionals separate the rows with a screwdriver point first.) Then extend the blade of the row runner and cut with a steady push.

To cut carpeting with cut pile, again, mark the dimensions on the face of the carpet; but notch each end of the proposed cut with a utility knife. Flop the edge of the carpet over so its backing is up, and fit a chalk line in the two notches that you cut in the carpet. Snap the chalk line across the backing and cut along the line with a utility knife guided by a metal straightedge.

Positioning the carpet.   Have someone help you carry the carpet into the room where it will be laid. Roll it out. The edges of the carpet should curl up about 1 in. at the base of the walls. To move a corner of the carpet just a bit once you've unrolled it, pick up the corner and stand with one foot on the carpet and one behind it, toward the corner of the room. Holding the corner of the carpet waist-high with both hands, lift your foot on the carpet and kick the carpet in place. *Note:* Use the *side* of your foot; a heel or toe could stretch or tear the carpet.

If seams are to be made across the carpet, overlap the edges of carpet sections by 1 in.; the edge with its pile leaning into the seam should be on top. That carpet edge should also be perfectly straight: when cutting the seam, use the edge as a guide for the row runner.

Once you have overlapped seams as necessary and otherwise positioned the carpet to your liking (make sure

Figure 20.25 Rough-cut the carpet before placing it in the room where it will be installed. Never assume that a factory-cut edge is straight. Before cutting carpet, run the cutter down the row of pile to be cut, with the blade retracted. This dry run divides the pile and makes the next pass—with the blade down—much more successful. (Crain Cutter Co.)

the pile faces the right way!), go around the room with a utility knife and carefully notch carpet edges where they meet corners, radiators, and the like, making sure the carpet is against the wall all the way around. Don't trim the edges yet, though; that's done after seam-sealing and stretching is finished.

Hot-melt seams. Joining carpet seams with a hot-melt application has all but replaced sewing and is certainly the best way for a nonprofessional to do the job. Join carpet seams before stretching and attaching carpet. A hot-melt seam is strong enough to endure stretching without separating.

First, cut the seam across the carpet. As noted above, overlap carpet edges 1 in.—with the edge whose pile leans into the seam on top. Using the straight edge of the carpet as a guide, run the row runner along, cutting the piece beneath (Figure 20.27). (You may want to make a trial pass with the blade retracted first.) After cutting along the length of the seam with the row runner, use a utility knife to finish the cut where the carpet curls up on the walls. Remove the scrap of carpet you cut free.

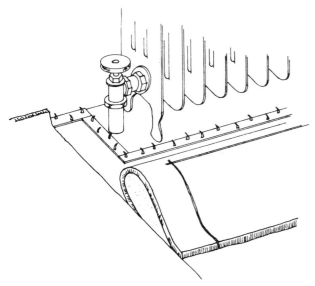

Figure 20.26 Take the carpet to the room where it will be installed; place the carpet (or pieces of carpet) in approximate final position; then carefully cut into the carpet where it must fit around obstructions, such as a radiator.

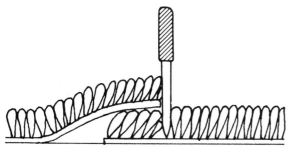

Figure 20.27 Cutting seams is very important and must be done carefully. First, be sure that the pile of both pieces is running in the same direction. Overlap the section by about 1 in., putting the section whose pile points toward the seam on top. Use the straight edge of the overlapping carpet as a guide for the cutting tool (row runner).

Slip a piece of hot-melt seam tape beneath one edge of the carpet and center the tape between the pieces. The face of the seam tape that is adhesive-coated should be up.

Set the seaming iron to the recommended temperature and let it heat up. Center the heated iron over the tape and let the carpet flop down on both sides, covering all but the handle of the iron. Although the speed with which you move the iron will vary, most models take about 30 seconds to heat the tape at a given point. Once the adhesive has melted sufficiently, move the iron farther along the tape, and with your free hand, press down both sides of the carpet over the tape just heated.

This operation isn't difficult, but you must make sure the two carpet edges butt together over the tape, and that one edge does not overlap the other. Bond the seam as

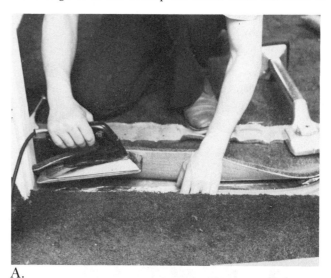

A.

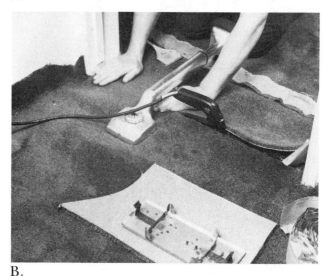

B.

Figure 20.28 Hot-melt seaming. This is the preferred method for joining carpet seams. (A) After cutting carpet sections, center a piece of hot-melt seam tape, adhesive side up, directly beneath the seam. Place the heating iron at the beginning of the seam, as shown, and allow the iron to heat. (B) As the iron melts the adhesive, move the iron along, pressing the carpet down into the melted adhesive of the tape. During this operation, the sections of carpeting rest on the top of the iron: only the handle is exposed. (Roberts Consolidated Industries)

close as you can to the wall; then stop temporarily while the rest of the seam sets. When the seam has bonded completely, pull back the edges abutting the wall and heat up the last length of tape beneath them.

Stretching carpet. Once any seams, are joined, stretch and attach the carpet to the tackless strips around the perimeter of the room. The knee kicker and the power stretcher, both of which can be rented, will help you accomplish this step. Both tools have adjustable knobs on their heads. Adjust the knee kicker so its teeth grab just the backing of the carpet; too deep, and they will dig into the padding. (Adjust the teeth on a piece of carpet scrap.) The teeth adjustment on the power stretcher is similar; and the stretcher's length is also adjustable. The power stretcher, with its sections fully extended, reaches about 25 ft.

Begin in one corner and, with the knee kicker, attach the carpet at two points on adjacent walls (Figure 20.29). Place the kicker about 1 in. from the wall and rap the cushion of the tool quickly with your knee. When done properly, this maneuver carries the carpet forward and onto the points of the tackless strips. The motion takes some practice; but, as more of the carpet is attached, and there is some tension on it, knee-kicking actually becomes easier. As you work along an edge of the carpet, rest your hand

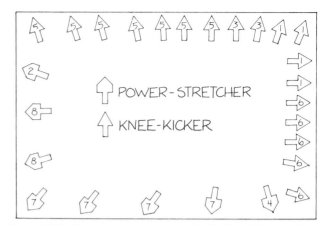

Figure 20.29 To stretch carpeting, apply the knee kicker and the power stretcher alternately, as shown. Either tool should carry the edge of the carpet onto the tackless strip without straining. If you have to strain to get the carpet into place, move the tool or, in the case of the power stretcher, reset its length.

on the section just attached; the extra weight will prevent the section from being dislodged by successive knee kicks.

After securing a corner 2 to 3 ft along each wall, use the power stretcher to stretch the carpet to an adjacent corner (Figure 20.30A). Unlike the knee kicker, which rebounds,

A.

B.

C.

Figure 20.30 Finishing touches. (A) When the power stretcher and knee kicker are used, they fit the carpet into its final position, ready for trimming. (B) Take time to trim carefully around doors and other complex areas. (C) Leave the edges slightly long to tuck in place with the stair tool. (Roberts Consolidated Industries)

the stretcher has a lever that extends the tool and holds it there until the lever is released. Unextended, the head of the power stretcher should be about 6 in. from the wall in question; extended, it should carry the edge of the carpet far enough forward that it catches on the tackless strip. If the carpet does not initially catch on the tackless strips, push down on it with the head of a hammer or with a seam roller. Always push this power stretcher's lever down gently. If the resistance seems too great, reset the length of the tool.

Improperly used, the power stretcher can rip or over-stretch fabric; therefore, proceed cautiously. To avoid punching a hole in the wall, always place a block of scrap wood between the tail end of the stretcher and the wall it rests against. If the stretcher isn't long enough for the room, put a length of 2×8 between the tail end of the stretcher and the wall; but have someone stand on the board so it doesn't kick out when you flip down the lever. Once the second corner is attached, alternate using the knee kicker and the power stretcher in the sequence shown in Figure 20.29.

Trimming. When the carpet is secured, trim it around the perimeter with a wall trimmer, or, that failing, with a utility knife guided along a metal straightedge. Tuck the edge of the trimmed carpet in the $\frac{1}{4}$-in. gap between the tackless strips and the baseboard. If the edge of the carpet bulges up after being tucked, trim it a bit more. The last edges to be fixed are usually those that end in doorways. Where an edge is enclosed in a metal strip, simply tap the strip down with a hammer, with a scrap block in between to prevent

marring. If the carpet is to be folded, turn it under 1 in. and tack down at intervals of 3 in. Brush the pile over tacks.

Carpeting Stairs

Use a high-quality carpet on stairs. Cheap material isn't worth the trouble. Similarly, the padding beneath the carpet should be durable; dense felt or good-quality polyurethane prolongs the life of the carpet, allowing its fibers to bounce back from each footfall. Although carpeting should be the longest length possible, padding may be an individual piece stapled to each step.

Note: Here, again, the direction of the carpet pile is critical. Carpet pile should "aim" toward the bottom of the stairs, the direction of each descending footfall. If pile sticks

A.

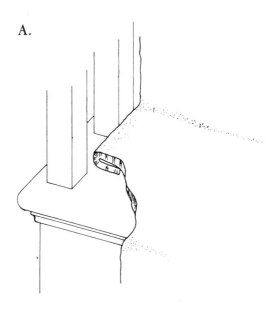

B.

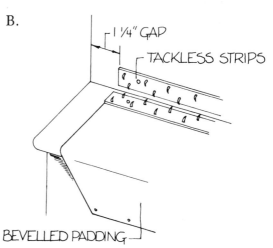

Figure 20.32 Details of carpeting stairs. (A) Along open stairs, allow an extra $1\frac{1}{4}$ in. to tuck under to get a good edge. Secure edges with tacks driven into the riser-tread joint. (B) Tackless strips and padding are also used on stairs, both stopping 1 1/4 in. short of the stair's edge so that they won't interfere with the tucked-under edges of the carpet. Carpeting is best secured by strips pointing into the riser-tread joint, as shown. Bevel padding back from the edge to keep it from being seen from an open side of the stairs.

Figure 20.31 This tucking trimmer cuts and tucks carpet along walls. (Crain Cutter Co.)

up toward the top of the stairs, it will wear out quickly, perhaps in half the time it would if laid correctly.

Estimating. Commercial runner strips are available; but more often, installers cut stairway runners from standard 12-ft- wide bolts of carpet. First, determine the width of the carpet runner. On closed stairs (which have walls on both sides), carpeting runs from wall to wall. On open stairs (with balusters on one or both sides), carpeting runs to the base of the balusters. In either case, each side of the carpet should be tucked under $1\frac{1}{4}$ in., to give a good edge and prevent unravelling. Thus, measure the width of the stairs and add $2\frac{1}{2}$ in. to that width. If the width (including the tuck-unders) is 36 in. or less, you can get at least four pieces from a 12-ft-wide bolt of carpeting.

To determine the length of the stairs, measure from the edge of the nosing to the back of the riser, and from there up the riser to the beginning of the next nosing. Add 1 in. to this measurement and multiply by the number of steps. Add another 2 in. to the total for adjustments at the top and bottom of the stairs.

Sections of carpet should not meet anywhere but in the riser-tread joint. If a section misses, cut it back until it does meet at such a joint. Thus, allow for waste if any lengths of carpeting do not measure out as a multiple of the riser-tread unit.

The above instructions are for straight-run stairs. If yours have bends and turns, it's worth your while to hire a professional. If you are determined to do the job yourself, cut out a paper template for each step that turns. Each template should cover a tread and the riser below. As noted above, add 1 in. for the distance the padding sticks out around the nosing. Old hands at laying carpet, however, feel that stairs should be covered only with continuous pieces, with extra carpet tucked behind riser sections.

Installation. At the joints where risers meet treads, nail on two tackless strips, each $\frac{1}{4}$ in. short of the joint, to allow for tucking in the carpet. The tack points on the riser point down; those on the tread point in, toward the riser. Each tackless strip should be $2\frac{1}{2}$ in. shorter than the width of the tucked-under carpet that will be installed. That is, the $1\frac{1}{4}$ in. of tucked-under edge on each side does *not* attach to the tackless strip; thus strips stop short by that amount. The doubled-under edges of carpet will be secured by one $1\frac{1}{4}$-in. tack on each side, driven into the riser-tread joint.

Padding pieces are as wide as tackless strips are long. They run the full depth of the tread but stop 2 to 3 in. short of the tackless strip on the riser. To keep the pad from being seen from the open side of a stairway, you may want to angle the riser portion of the padding in toward the center of the stairs (Figure 20.32B). Staple the padding every 3 or 4 in. along the top and bottom.

To tuck the edges of the carpet, snap chalk lines on the carpet backing, in $1\frac{1}{4}$ in. from the edge. Score lightly along this line with an awl point (a utility-knife blade is too sharp); then fold over the edge. Weight down the edge for a moment, and the work will go easier.

Secure the bottom of the stair runner first, overlapping the carpet about $\frac{1}{4}$ in. onto the floor; push the carpet into the bottommost tackless strip, at the base of the first riser.

A.

B.

Figure 20.33 Cushion-backed carpeting. (A) Cushion-backed carpeting, already bonded to padding, is bedded in a mastic rather than stretched onto tackless strips. Use a notched trowel to spread the mastic, adhering one-half the carpet at a time. (B) The knee kicker has a reduced role here, although it is used to move edges slightly, as at seams. Carpeting bedded in mastic should have seams rolled and tamped as shown. (Crain Cutter Co.)

Press the carpet onto the strip points with the end of a hammer handle or with a stair tool. Tack the bottom of the rolled edges onto the riser with a $1\frac{1}{4}$-in. tack at each end. Then pack the extra end of carpet into the $\frac{1}{4}$-in. gap between the first tackless strip and the floor.

To cover the first step, stretch the carpet with a knee kicker, starting at the center of the tread. As you push the knee kicker, tamp the carpet into the joint of riser and tread, using a stair tool. Don't overdo the carpet-stretching; if there's too much tension, the carpet will later pull free from the points of the strips. Work out from the center of the step, until the carpet is attached along the entire joint. At the end of each side, secure the rolled-over edge with a $1\frac{1}{4}$-in. tack. Repeat this procedure up the stairs. You don't really need the knee kicker after the first step, however.

If the width of the carpet varies (sometimes a tucked-under hem slips), adjust the width of the section by jabbing an awl point in the hem and jimmy the tool point in and out.

Cushion-Backed Carpeting

Many of the preliminary steps of working with cushion-backed carpeting are the same as those described for conventional carpeting. Here, though, there are no tackless strips and no stretching. Measuring, estimating, layout, and rough-cutting are essentially the same. Because cushion-backed carpeting is fixed in place with a special adhesive, floor preparation is important if the adhesive is to stick. Wash the floor well, and strip it of all wax, paint, and finish. Secure loose boards or tiles. If the floor is below-grade, follow the manufacturer's recommendations about suitable carpeting and adhesives.

Cut cushion-backed carpeting only from the face (pile side), however. When laying the carpet, the direction of the pile is still important, with the main entry into the room looking into the carpet pile.

Decide exactly where the seam between carpet sections will fall, and cut the carpet sections, as described above. Next, pull back the carpet on both sides of the seam. Snap a chalkline down the middle of the seam, and spread adhesive on both sides about 3 ft to either side of the chalkline. Use a notched trowel to spread the adhesive. Carefully roll each edge of the carpet into place, pressing down so there is good adhesion. Just before you roll over the second edge, apply seam adhesive (which joins fabric to fabric) to the primary backing of the first edge and along the floor.

The second edge should abut the first perfectly, with no overlap. If the seam isn't perfect, work it with your fingertips, pushing and pulling until the joint is tight. Jabbing the edges down with a stair tool and rolling them is another technique (Figure 20.33 B). Trim excess fiber with shears, but do it gingerly.

Once you've allowed that 6-ft-wide swath of adhesive (down the middle of the seam) time to set, pull up the unadhered portions of each section, one side at a time. Pull back the carpet until you reach the portion already adhered. Apply mastic as before, and roll the carpet onto it.

To bed the carpet evenly in the adhesive, place a 2×4 on the carpet and hammer along its length, working from the center of the carpet outward. Rollers are also available for this task. Where the carpet bubbles because of air trapped underneath, puncture the center of the bulge with an awl and flatten it by pressing down with your hands.

When all sections have been cemented, work around the perimeter of the room, tamping the carpet in at the bottom of the walls. Trim off excess with a utility knife guided along a straightedge. If any edges of the carpet stick up after trimming, go around again with the stair tool and tamp them down. Finish carpet edges in doorways with metal strips, as described above.

Double-face seam tape or Velco strips around the perimeter of the room, as well as beneath all seams, is another way to secure cushion-backed carpet; but carpeting so attached can wrinkle and shift.

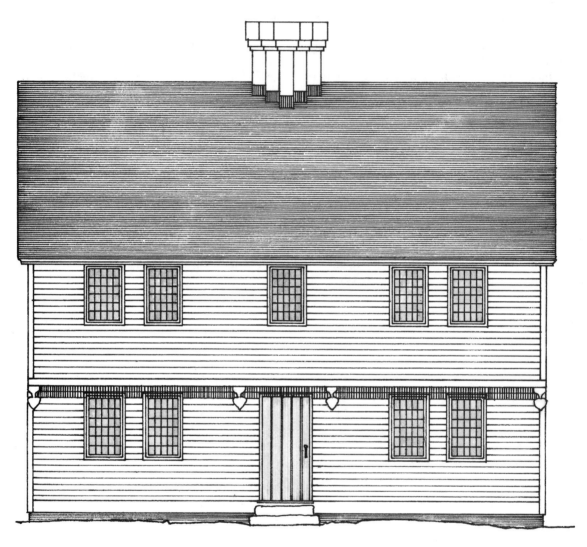

COLONIAL

ORIGINAL ILLUSTRATIONS BY
RICHARD LEAR, RENDERINGS
BY LEONARD DAVIS

·A·
GLOSSARY OF HOUSING TERMS

The glossary in this appendix contains many of the more general building terms. More specialized words are found in their respective chapters and in the Index.

Airway. A space between roof insulation and roof boards, for movement of air.

Anchor bolts. Bolts used to secure a wood sill or plate to concrete or to masonry flooring or walls.

Apron. The inside trim of a window, placed against the wall immediately beneath the stool.

Astragal. Trim (often shaped) that covers the common joint of contiguous windows.

Attic ventilators. Screened openings provided to ventilate attic spaces. They are located in the soffit area as inlet ventilators and in the gable end or along the ridge as outlet ventilators. Attic ventilators can also be power-driven fans used as an exhaust system. *See also* Louver.

Backband. A simple molding sometimes used as a decorative feature around the outer edge of plain rectangular casting.

Backfill. The replacement of excavated earth in a trench around and against a basement foundation.

Balusters. Usually, small vertical members in a railing used between a top rail and stair treads or a bottom rail.

Balustrade. An assembly of balusters, top rail, and sometimes bottom rail; used on the edge of stairs, balconies, and porches.

Barge board. A decorative board covering the projecting rafter (fly rafter) of the gable end. At the cornice, this member is called a fascia board.

Base, baseboard. A board placed at the base of a wall, next to the floor, to finish properly the joint between floor and wall surface.

Base molding. Molding used to trim the upper edge of a baseboard.

Batten. A narrow strip of wood used to cover a joint or as a decorative vertical member over plywood or a wide board.

Batter board. One of a pair of horizontal boards nailed to posts set at the corners of an excavation—used to indicate a desired level; a fastening for stretched strings to indicate outlines of foundation walls.

Bay. The space between any pair of rafters, studs, or joists.

Bay window. Any window space projecting outward from the walls of a building, either rectangular or polygonal in plan.

Beam. A structural member, usually horizontal, that supports a load.

Bearing partition. A partition that supports a vertical load, in addition to its own weight.

Bearing wall. A wall that supports a vertical load in addition to its own weight.

Blind-nailing. Nailing in such a way that the nailheads are not visible on the face of the work; usually through the tongue of matched boards.

Blind stop. A rectangular molding, usually ¾ by 1⅜ in. or more in width, used in assembling a window frame. Serves as a stop for storm and screen or combination windows and to resist air infiltration.

Blocking. Dimension lumber added to bolster a nailing point; also see Bridging.

Board lumber. Yard lumber usually 1 in. thick but always less than 2 in. thick; 2 in. or more wide.

Boiled linseed oil. Linseed oil in which enough lead, manganese, or cobalt salts have been incorporated to make the oil harden more rapidly when spread in thin coats.

Bolster. A short horizontal timber or steel beam on top of a column, that spreads the load of beams or girders.

Boston ridge. Asphalt or wood shingles applied at the ridge or the hips of a roof, as a finish.

Brace. An inclined piece of framing lumber applied to walls or floors to stiffen the structure. Often used on walls as temporary bracing until framing and sheathing are complete.

Brick veneer. A facing of brick laid against and fastened to sheathing of a frame-wall or tile-wall construction.

Bridging, cross-bridging. Small wood or metal members inserted in a diagonal position between the floor joists at midspan to act both as tension and as compression members for the purpose of bracing the joists and spreading the action of loads. Solid bridging, or blocking, uses lengths of dimension lumber for similar effect.

Built-up roof. A roofing composed of three to five layers of asphalt felt laminated with coal tar, pitch, or asphalt. The top is finished with crushed slag or gravel. Generally used on flat or low-pitch roofs.

Butt joint. The junction where the ends of two timbers or other members meet in a square-cut joint.

Cant strip. A triangular piece of lumber used at the junction of a flat deck and a wall to prevent cracking of the roofing applied over it and to aid water runoff.

Cap. The upper member of a column, pilaster, door cornice, molding, and so on.

Carriage. *See* Stair carriage.

Casement frames and sash. Frames of wood or metal enclosing part or all of the sash, which can be opened by means of hinges affixed to the vertical edges.

Casing. Molding of various widths and thicknesses, used to trim door and window openings.

Checking. Fissures that appear with age in many exterior materials and paint coatings.

Collar beam. Members connecting opposite roof rafters; they stiffen the roof structure. Also called "collar ties."

Column. In architecture, a perpendicular supporting member, circular or rectangular in section, usually consisting of a base, shaft, and capital. In engineering, a vertical structural compression member which supports loads acting in the direction of its longitudinal axis.

Combination doors, windows. Combination doors or windows that provide winter insulation and summer protection and often have self-storing or removable glass and screen inserts.

Condensation. In a building, beads, drops of water, or frost that accumulate on the inside of the exterior covering of a building when warm, moisture-laden air from the interior reaches a point where it can no longer hold moisture.

Construction, frame. A type of construction in which the structural parts are wood or a material that is supported by a wood frame.

Coped joint. *See* Scribing.

Corbel out. To build out one or more courses of brick or stone from the face of a wall, to support overhanging elements above.

Corner bead. A strip of formed sheet metal placed on drywall or plaster corners as reinforcement. Also, a strip of wood finish, three-quarters round or angular, placed over a plastered corner for protection.

Corner boards. Trim on the external corners of a house; the ends of the siding often abut the corner boards.

Corner braces. Diagonal braces at the corners of the frame structure, used to stiffen and strengthen a wall.

Cornerite. Metal-mesh lath cut in strips and bent at a right angle. Used in interior corners of walls and ceilings on lath to prevent cracks in plastering.

Cornice. Overhang of a pitched roof at the eave line, usually consisting of a fascia board, a soffit (for a closed cornice), and appropriate molding. On a flat-roofed structure, the cornice is often the uppermost part of the roof, where it overhangs the front of the house.

Counterflashing. Two-piece flashing commonly used on chimneys at the roof line to cover shingle flashing and prevent moisture from entering.

Cove molding. A molding with a concave face, used as trim to finish interior corners.

Crawl space. A shallow space below the living quarters of

a basementless house, normally enclosed by foundations walls.

Cricket. A small drainage-diverting roof structure of single or double slope, placed at the junction of larger surfaces that meet at an angle, such as above a chimney. Sometimes called a "saddle."

Crown molding. A molding used on a cornice or wherever an interior angle is to be covered; also a complex molding at the top of an interior wall.

Curtain wall. A nonbearing wall.

Cut-in-brace. Nominal 2-in.-thick members, usually 2×4s, cut diagonally between studs. *See also* Let-in brace.

d. See Penny.

Dado. A rectangular groove, usually across the width of a board or plank.

Deck paint. An enamel with a high degree of resistance to wear, designed for use on such surfaces as porch floors.

Dew point. The temperature at which a vapor begins to condense as a liquid.

Dimension lumber. Usually lumber 2 in. thick but not thicker than 5 in., and 2 in. or more wide. The term includes joists, rafters, studs, planks, and small timbers.

Doorjamb, interior. The surrounding frame of a door; consists of two upright pieces, called "side jambs," and a horizontal head, or head jamb.

Dormer. An opening in a sloping roof, the framing of which protrudes, forming vertical walls suitable for windows and other openings.

Downspout. A pipe, usually of metal, for carrying rainwater from roof gutters.

Drip cap. A molding placed on the exterior top side of a door or window frame, causing water to drip beyond the frame.

Drip edge. A metal edge projecting over other parts (especially along the edges of roofs), for throwing off water.

Drip kerf. A groove under a sill, which allows water to drip free from a surface rather than cling and run down the face of a house.

Drywall. Interior covering material, usually gypsum board, applied in large sheets or panels. Commonly called "Sheetrock," a major brand.

Ducts. Round or rectangular metal pipes for distributing warm air from a heating plant to rooms, or air from a conditioning device.

Eave. The margin, or lower part of a roof, which projects over a wall.

Face-nailing. Nailing perpendicular to the surface or to the junction of pieces that are joined. Also called "direct nailing."

Fascia or facia. A flat board, band, or face sometimes used

alone, though usually in combination with moldings; most often located at the outer face of a cornice.

Field. Any relatively flat, unobstructed expanse of building material.

Finish, natural. A transparent finish that largely maintains the original color or grain of wood. Natural finishes are usually provided by sealers, oils, varnishes, water-repellant preservatives, and similar materials.

Fire stop. Located in a frame wall, usually consists of 2×4 cross-blocking between studs; impedes spread of fire and smoke.

Flashing. Sheet metal or other material used in roof and wall construction to protect a building from water seepage.

Flat paint. An interior paint that contains a high proportion of pigment; dries to a flat, lusterless finish.

Flue. Fire clay or terra-cotta liners in a chimney through which smoke, gas, and fumes ascend. Each passage is called a "flue." The flues, together with other parts and the surrounding masonry, constitute a chimney.

Fly rafters. End rafters of a gable overhang supported by roof sheathing and lookouts.

Footing. A masonry section, usually concrete, in a rectangular form wider than the bottom of the foundation wall or pier it supports.

Foundation. The supporting portion of a structure below the first-floor construction, or below grade (ground level), including footings.

Frieze. In house construction, a horizontal member connecting the top of the siding with the soffit of the cornice.

Frost line. The depth of frost penetration in soil.

Furring. Strips of wood or metal applied to a wall or another surface to even it and, normally, to serve as a fastening base for finish material.

Gable. In house construction, the portion of the roof above the eave line of a double-sloped roof.

Gable end. An end wall that has a gable.

Girder. A large, or the principal, beam of wood or steel used to support concentrated loads, such as joist ends, along its length.

Gloss. A paint or enamel that contains a relatively low proportion of pigment and dries to a sheen or luster.

Grain. The direction, size, arrangement, appearance, and quality of the fibers in wood.

Grout. Mortar made of such consistency (by adding water) that it will flow into the joints and cavities of masonry work, filling them. In tiling, a specialized mortar that seals the joints between tiles.

Gusset. A flat board, plywood, or similar member used to provide a connection at the intersection of wood members; commonly used at wood-truss joints.

Gutter. A shallow channel of metal or wood set below and along the eaves of a house to catch and carry rainwater away from the roof.

Header. (a) a beam placed perpendicular to joists, to which joists are nailed in framing for chimney, stairway, or some other opening; (b) a beam above a door or window opening; (c) in floor framing, the outermost joists running perpendicular to others in the grid.

Hip. The external angle formed by the meeting of two sloping sides of a roof.

I-beam. A steel beam with a cross section resembling the letter "I."

Insulation, thermal. Any material high in resistance to heat transmission that, when placed in the walls, ceiling, or floors of a structure, reduces the rate of heat flow.

Interior finish. Material used to cover interior framed areas, or materials of walls and ceilings.

Jack rafter. A rafter that spans the distance from the wall plate to a hip, or from a valley to a ridge.

Jamb. The side elements of a door or window frame.

Joint. The space between the adjacent surfaces of two members or components, typically joined and held together by nails, glue, screws, or mortar.

Joist. One of a series of parallel beams, usually 2 in. thick and placed on edge to support floor and ceiling loads and supported, in turn, by larger beams, girders, or bearing walls.

Kerf. A slot; a saw kerf is the thickness of its blade; a drip kerf is cut into the underside of a sill to cause water to drip free.

Laminating. Applying a plastic laminate to a core material. In framing, nailing or bolting two or more pieces of lumber together to increase load-carrying ability.

Landing. A platform between flights of stairs, or where a flight of stairs ends.

Lath. A building material of wood, metal, gypsum, or insulating board fastened to the frame of a building and serving as a plaster base.

Lattice. A framework of crossed wood pieces or metal strips.

Ledger strip. A strip of lumber nailed along the side of a girder, on which joist ends rest. In deck construction, the part of the frame attached to the main house.

Let-in brace. Metal or 1-in.-thick board braces notched into studs. *See also* Cut-in brace.

Light. The space in a window sash for a single pane of glass; also, a pane of glass.

Lintel. A horizontal structural member that supports the load over an opening such as a door or window. Also called a "header."

Lookout. A short, wood bracket or cantilever that supports the overhang portion of a roof or similar structure; usually concealed from view.

Louver. An opening with a series of horizontal slats pitched so as to permit ventilation but exclude rain, sunlight, or vision.

Lumber, dressed size. The dimensions of lumber after it is shrunk from its green dimensions and after machining to size or pattern.

Lumber, matched. Lumber dressed and shaped on one edge in a grooved pattern and in a tongued pattern on the other.

Lumber, shiplap. Lumber edge-dressed to make a close, rabbeted or lapped joint.

Lumber, timber. Yard lumber 5 in. or more in its shortest dimension. The term may include beams, stringers, posts, sills, girders, and purlins.

Lumber, yard. Lumber of a grade, size, and pattern usually intended for ordinary construction, for example, framework and rough coverage of houses.

Mantel. The shelf above a fireplace.

Margin. To center a window or door frame in the thickness of a wall so that frame edges are flush with finish surfaces on both sides, or so frame edges protrude equally.

Masonry. Stone, brick, concrete, hollow tile, concrete block, gypsum block, or a combination of these materials bonded together with mortar to form a wall, pier, buttress, or similar mass.

Mastic. A pasty material used as a cement (as for setting tile) or a protective coating (as for thermal insulation or waterproofing).

Migration. The movement of a jack, or structural member due to the loads upon it; a dangerous situation if a jack is not plumb.

Millwork. Generally, any building material made of finished wood and manufactured in millwork plants and planing mills; term covers such items as doors, window and door frames, blinds, porchwork, mantels, paneling, stairways, molding, and trim, but normally not flooring or siding.

Miter joint. The joint of two pieces set at an angle that bisects the joining angle. For example, the 90° miter joint at the side and head casing at a door opening is made up of two 45° angles.

Molding. A shaped wood strip used for decoration.

Mortise. A slot cut in a board, plank, or timber, usually edgewise, to receive the tenon of another board, plank, or timber.

Mudsill. *See* Sill.

Mullion. A vertical bar or divider in the frame between windows, doors, or other openings.

Muntin. A small member which divides the glass or openings of sash or doors.

Newel. A post to which the end of a stair railing or balustrade is fastened.

Nonbearing wall. A wall supporting no load other than its own weight.

Nosing. Usually, the projecting edge of a stair tread.

On center (O.C.). The measurement of spacing for studs, rafters, joists, and so on in a building, from the center of one member to the center of the next.

Outrigger. The extension of a rafter beyond the wall line; usually a smaller rafter nailed to a larger one, forming a cornice or roof overhang.

Paint. A combination of pigments with suitable thinners or oils; used as a decorative and protective coating.

Paper, building. A general term indicating such sheet materials as rosin papers and felts.

Parting stop or strip. A small wood piece used in the jambs of double-hung window frames to separate upper and lower sashes.

Partition. A wall that subdivides spaces within any story of a house.

Penny. As applied to nails, originally indicated the price per hundred; term is now a measure of nail length and is abbreviated ''d.''

Pier. A column of masonry used to support other structural members.

Pitch. The inclined slope of a roof, or the ratio of the total rise to the total width of a house—that is, a rise of 8 ft. and a width of 24 ft. is a one-third-pitch roof. Roof slope is expressed in inches of rise per 12 in. of run.

Plaster grounds. Strips of wood used as guides or strike-off edges around window and door openings and around the base of walls.

Plate. *Sill plate:* a horizontal member anchored to a masonry wall. *Sole plate or shoe:* the lowest horizontal member of a frame wall. *Top plate:* the highest horizontal member of a frame wall, which supports ceiling joists, rafters, or other members.

Plough. To cut a lengthwise groove in a board or a plank.

Plumb. Exactly perpendicular; vertical.

Preservative. Any substance that prevents the action of wood-destroying fungi or insects.

Primer. The base coat of paint in a paint job; consists of two or more coats.

Quarter-round. A small molding that has the cross section of a quarter-circle.

Rabbet. A rectangular, longitudinal groove cut in the edge of a board or a plank.

Radiant heating. A method of heating, usually consisting of a forced hot water system with pipes placed in the floor, wall, or ceiling; or with electrically heated panels.

Rafter. One of a series of structural members of a roof designed to support roof loads. The rafters of a flat roof are sometimes called ''roof joists.''

Rafter, hip. A rafter that forms the intersection of an external roof angle.

Rafter, valley. A rafter that forms the intersection of an internal roof angle. Valley rafters are usually doubled 2-in.-thick members.

Rail. Horizontal framing members of a panel door, sash, or a cabinet frame. Also the upper and lower members of a balustrade or staircase extending from one vertical support (such as a post) to another.

Rake. Trim members that run parallel to the roof slope and form the finish between the wall and a gable-roof extension.

Reinforcement. Steel rods or metal fabric placed in concrete slabs, beams, or columns to increase their strength.

Ridge. The horizontal line at the junction of the top edges of two sloping roof surfaces.

Ridge board. The board placed on edge at the ridge of the roof, to which the upper ends of rafters are fastened.

Rise. In stairs, the vertical height of a step or flight of stairs.

Riser. Each of several vertical boards used to close spaces between stairway treads.

Roll roofing. Roofing material composed of asphalt-saturated fiber, supplied in 36-in.-wide rolls, with 108 sq ft of material.

Roof sheathing. Boards or sheet material fastened to the roof rafters on which shingles or other roof coverings are laid.

Rough opening (R.O.). A framed opening in a wall, roof, or floor platform.

Run. In stairs, the net width of a step or the horizontal distance covered by a flight of stairs.

Saddle. *See* Cricket.

Sash. A frame containing one or more lights of glass.

Sash balance. A device, usually operated by a spring or a weight, designed to counterbalance the weight of a window sash.

Saturated felt. Felt impregnated with tar or asphalt.

Screed. A small strip of wood, usually the thickness of a plaster coat, used as a guide for plastering. Also a board used to level newly laid concrete.

Scribing. Fitting woodwork to an irregular surface.

Sealer. A finishing material, clear or pigmented, usually

applied directly over uncoated wood to seal the surface.

Semigloss paint or enamel. A paint or enamel that has some luster but which isn't particularly glossy.

Set. To sink below the surface.

Shake. A thick, handsplit shingle.

Shear wall. A wall reinforced to withstand lateral (shear) movement such as that felt during an earthquake.

Sheathing. The structural covering, usually wood boards or plywood, used over studs, joists or rafters of a structure.

Sheet-metal work. All components of a house made of sheet metal, for example, flashing, gutters, and downspouts.

Shoe, base. Molding used next to the floor on interior baseboard. Also the bottom plate of a frame wall.

Shy. To cut something a bit short.

Siding. The finish covering of the outside wall of a frame building, whether made of clapboards, vertical boards with battens, shingles, or some other material.

Sill. In framing (here, also called a ''mudsill''), the lowest member of the frame of a structure; rests on the foundation and supports the floor joists or the uprights of the wall. In door or window construction, the member forming the lower side of the opening, as the window-sill or doorsill.

Sleeper. Usually, a wood member embedded in or placed on concrete, to which subflooring or flooring is attached.

Soffit. Usually the underside of an overhang cornice.

Soil cover. Also called ''ground cover,'' a light covering of plastic film, roll roofing, or similar material used over the soil in crawl spaces of houses to minimize moisture permeation of the area.

Soil stack. A general term used to indicate the vertical main of a system of soil, waste, or vent piping.

Sole or sole plate. See Plate.

Span. The distance between structural supports, such as walls, columns, piers, beams, girders, and trusses.

Splash block. A small masonry block placed beneath a downspout, to carry water away from the building.

Square. A unit of measure—100 sq ft—usually applied to roofing material. In measurement, two adjacent pieces that join in a right angle.

Stair carriage. Supporting member for stair treads. Usually a 2-in. plank notched to receive the treads.

STC (sound transmission class). A measure of the ability of sound insulation to stop noise.

Stile. An upright framing member in a panel door, sash, or cabinet frame.

Stock. The basic materials from which a building element is fashioned. For example, joists may be cut from 2 × 10 stock, or flashing may be cut from 26-gauge aluminum stock.

Stool. A flat molding, usually rabbeted on the underside, that fits over the inside edge of a window sill.

Storm sash or storm window. An extra window usually placed on the outside of an existing one as additional protection against cold air.

Strip flooring. Wood flooring consisting of narrow, matched strips.

String, stringer. In stairs, the supports in which stair ends rest; more or less synonymous with ''carriage.''

Strong. To cut something a bit long.

Stucco. A plaster made with portland cement as its base; used outside.

Stud. One of a series of slender, wood or metal, vertical, structural members placed as supporting elements in walls and partitions. Plural: ''studs'' or ''studding.''

Subfloor. Boards or plywood laid on joists, over which a finish floor is laid.

Suspended ceiling. A ceiling system supported by being hung from overhead structural framing.

Termite shield. A shield, usually of corrosion-resistant metal, placed in or on a foundation wall or other mass of masonry or around pipes, to prevent termite migration.

Terneplate. Sheet iron or steel coated with an alloy of lead and tin.

Threshold. A strip of wood or metal with beveled edges, used over the finish floor and sill of exterior doors.

Toe-nailing. To drive in a nail at an angle, thereby preventing it from pulling free.

Tread. A horizontal board in a stairway, on which one steps.

Trim. The finish materials in a building, such as molding, applied around openings (window trim, door trim), baseboards, and cornices.

Trimmer. Any structural member added to decrease flexion along the length of a rough opening. In floor framing, the outermost joists running parallel to the joist grid.

Truss. A frame or jointed structure of smaller elements designed to span long distances.

Undercoat. A coating applied before a finish or topcoat of paint. It may be the first of two or the second of three coats. Term is synonymous with ''priming coat.''

Underlayment. A material placed under finish coverings, especially thin flooring materials, to provide a smooth, even base.

Valley. The internal angle formed by the junction of two sloping sides of a roof.

Vapor barrier. Material used to retard the movement of water vapor into walls and thus prevent condensation in them. Usually considered as having a permeability value of less than 1.0.

Vent. A pipe or duct that allows air to flow in or out.

Weatherstripping. Narrow, or jamb-width, sections of thin metal or other material designed to prevent infiltration of air and moisture around windows and doors.

Wick. To draw moisture by capillary action.

DUTCH COLONIAL

·B·

CONTRACTORS, ARCHITECTS, AND MONEY

Drawing your own floor plans, ordering building supplies, complying with codes, hiring and overseeing various tradespeople, knocking out walls and hauling out rubble yourself—there are many ways to save money by doing the work. Because renovators' skill and experience vary, there are no easy rules about when you should do the work and when you should hire someone else. There are times, however, when even scarce money should be spent for the talents of a professional, as well as other times when, because of regulations, you *must* hire professionals. In this brief appendix, we consider some of the building specialists who may be able to help you.

It's a good idea to hire a professional when: (1) you're baffled and don't know how or where to start a renovation job; (2) you lack the technical skill to do a job, in which case, learning by the side of a professional makes sense; (3) you're rushed for time and can probably earn more elsewhere (to pay for the work) than you could save by doing it yourself; (4) tasks require special or hard-to-find tools; or (5) the job could be dangerous, for example, installing an electric service panel.

You *must* hire a professional—plumber, electrician, structural engineer, and so on—if a building code or bank agreement so specifies.

If you're new to building, also see Chapter 1, which rates jobs according to difficulty, and Chapter 2, which describes two actual renovations.

RULES OF THE GAME

Building is a difficult business. There's a lot of tension. Jobs rarely go as planned, and the cost of materials seems to rise daily. Locating and managing labor can be frustrating. And so it goes. If you want to be taken seriously by building specialists, follow these rules:

1. *Learn the vocabulary.* This is the first rule of renovation, and you will soon appreciate its importance—for example, when you're buying supplies early in the morning and the guy at the counter is surly, or when you're planning the day's work of a contractor you have hired. Don't be discouraged if it takes a while to learn the terms; but try, you must.

2. *Prepare yourself for discussions; read up the night before.* If, for example, you are working with an electrician, learn enough to ask intelligent questions and understand the answers you get.

3. *Talk money.* Don't be genteel about what you can spend. If, after a discussion of money, you decide you can't afford the services of a professional, postpone the work or ask how the job might be altered so you can stay within your budget. It's fair, as well, to ask how much of an estimate (or bill) is profit and how much represents the cost of materials.

Talking money is also important because it involves discussing options before you sign a contract. By considering different ways to get the job done, you can usually find one way that's affordable. Most contractors with enough personality and time will discuss options in hopes of getting the job, but if your consultations drag on, be prepared to pay for that person's time.

4. *Get it in writing.* A verbal contract is legally binding but difficult to establish as proof in litigations. When someone works for you, set down every specification—time, quality of materials, additional labor, and so on—in a legal document. In many states the business and professions code requires that all contracts over a specified amount, say, $400, must be put in writing to be legally binding on both parties. The local chapter of the American Institute of Architects (AIA) will sell you sample contracts.

5. *Draw details.* Throughout this book you are exhorted to draw the details of projects before you build them. Draw first, and you'll see what special pieces you must buy, what spots will be tricky to assemble, and so on. When it's time to build or refurbish (and the clock is running for people you've hired), you'll know what to do.

6. *Be prepared to work at odd hours.* Many builders can be reached only before 7:00 A.M. and after 9:00 P.M. If you act as your own general contractor, expect calls that go unreturned, materials that don't arrive, and workers that don't show. Be persistent, but always be polite. Intimidation seldom works where harried contractors are involved; exploiting a sense of guilt is far more effective.

IMPORTANT LEGAL CONSIDERATIONS

Before hiring (or not hiring) someone, consult your local building authorities, your bank, and your insurance agency. Be honest about the work you intend to do yourself and the work that will be done by professionals. To some extent, building is risky, and the institution in question may need assurance that you know what you're doing or, failing that, that the tradespeople you hire are competent and are licensed.

Banks

Because it's usually necessary to unbuild part of a house before renovating it, a house is often worth *less* than its purchase price after demolition beings. Discuss thoroughly with your bank payment schedules—the stages of construction at which you can expect money. Most banks allow for "sweat equity," the improvement in the value of a house due to the owner's labor. Find out what standards the bank expects you to adhere to.

Building-Code Authorities

If you hire a licensed contractor, chances are that the person's work will satisfy code requirements. If the work is to be done by you or by an unlicensed contractor, however, the job's correct completion becomes *your* responsibility: if, when the job is inspected by the authorities, some violation

exists, you must pay to have it set right. Similarly, an unlicensed contractor may not have adequate insurance.

Before a contractor can get a license in many states, he must carry *workman's compensation* and *personal liability/personal damage* insurance (PL/PD, for short). In many municipalities, that person must supply proof of workman's comp whenever pulling a permit, or prove that he has no employees. Personal liability protects the contractor (and the homeowner) if a third party gets injured, and personal damage further protects the homeowner should some major structural or mechanical failure arise from work improperly done.

Insurance

As noted above, you may be liable if an unlicensed worker has a mishap, if a friend of yours gets hurt while helping, if there are damages to the public domain (e.g., a water main is crushed), if a tradesperson charges materials to your building-supply account and then fails to complete the job, and so on. Tell your insurance company exactly what your plans are; the company may, for an additional fee, add a "homeowner's risk" clause to protect you. The cost of that added coverage may be sufficient inducement to hire a licensed (and hence, *insured*) contractor to do the work. Do not work or allow others to do so if you are inadequately covered.

Note: In some states (California, for one) construction is *not* covered by homeowners' policies, period. Rather, it is specifically excluded from homeowner's policy coverage. You can get an extension of your coverage to include limited projects, but you must tell your agent what you're going to do, who's going to do it, and how it's going to be done—so they know they're assuming only a limited risk.

Finding and Working with Contractors

Contractors do the actual building; a general contractor is one who oversees all activities of a renovation. Subcontractors are usually specialists in one aspect of construction, such as plumbing or electricity. Because you're entrusting a lot to such individuals, be thorough in selecting the contractor.

Chances are, your friends who have dealt with a contractor will tell you much about the contractor's work, including the negative details. Also, the contractor's aesthetic sense should be close to your own, or at least tolerable, if that person is to have a hand in designing the job.

If you are new to an area and don't know anyone, walk around the neighborhood and note the houses under construction, especially those which look newly renovated. Ask the owners who did the work. Local consumer-affairs agencies oversee contractor-licensing boards, and chambers of commerce may have recommendations; most of them keep files on complaints. Finally, banks and realtors usually know the contractors and their reputations.

Meet with several contractors, and ask to see samples of their work. Ask homeowners who've worked with these contractors if the latter estimated closely, kept to schedules, were easy to work with, were honest. The results of a contractor's work you can judge for yourself. Whatever help

504 *Appendix B / Contractors, Architects, and Money*

you need from a builder—design, ordering supplies, working side by side to learn—explain yourself candidly. Happily, numerous small design and contruction firms have sprung up around the country, which have planning and execution departments under one roof. Often, the chief designer is a former builder with respectable aesthetic judgment. Contractors can suggest reliable subcontractors.

Pricing the Job

Of the several methods of pricing a job, three common ones are straight estimate, cost-plus, and fixed contract.

Straight estimate. Straight estimate can be a simple figure with no cost breakdown. The crudest of the methods mentioned, it allows the contracor some latitude in spending. Because the builder isn't bound to the estimate, however, this method is not recommended for sizable jobs. Always request a cost breakdown.

If you don't know your contractor, a straight estimate is indisputably the best way to go, contractually. If brief, how much is it going to cost? Be aware, however, that there are almost *always* changes once a job is under way: you may want to add or change something, or the contractor may find something unforeseen when he tears out finish surfaces. So you need some provision in the contract for changes, some fair way to figure out who pays for what changes. This fair resolution is equally important to both parties.

If a contractor finds rotten joists, for example, he knows that he can go back and discuss things with you, that he won't be penalized for something you couldn't have anticipated. And the arrangement protects you because you wouldn't want to ignore a problem so serious.

Cost-plus. Cost-plus is a commonly used method in which the contractor estimates the cost of materials and labor (including his costs for taxes, insurance, and so on), then adds a percentage of the total to cover overhead and profit. The final price isn't guaranteed because the cost of materials may fluctuate; but, if a client accepts the bid and agrees to begin within a certain time, the builder has a reasonable chance of getting materials at the projected cost. Cost-plus is usually used for large construction projects.

Fixed contract. A fixed contract establishes a price ceiling for the job and guarantees that the contractor will not exceed that price. This is frequently the way business is done; there are still elements of risk, however. On the whole, the contractor's total must be high enough that he can absorb unforeseen increases. If he goes over the budget, he absorbs the increase; if costs are under, he gets something of a bonus. Even this method is negotiable, though. You might agree to fixed labor costs, with the price of materials allowed to float. In other arrangements, you and the contractor may split money not spent.

THE WORKING SEQUENCE

What follows is a general sequence of hiring and working with contractors. To reiterate two points mentioned above, learn the vocabulary and get everything in writing. Because

a contractor responds to your wishes, you must have a clear idea yourself of what you want to do. Similarly, the builder is bound only by what is stated explicitly in a contract. Most disagreements between contractor and client begin as a failure of communication. Following is an effective procedure:

1. Sit down with your financial records and see how much you have to spend.

2. Define the job as well as you can, gathering photos of similar jobs, clippings from magazines, sketches of your own, and so forth. Note any construction details you know to be nonstandard or unorthodox.

3. Visit several lumberyards and building suppliers for prices, including major items such as appliances. Because these firms want (or should want) the trade, they will sit down with you during off-hours and show you their catalogues. It's important to establish good relations; if a firm seems cooperative and its prices are competitive, try to do most of your shopping there. If you buy in quantity, you can sometimes get a contractor's discount.

4. Sketch floor plans or construction details, as described earlier in this book.

5. Get bids from several contractors. Bids are nonbinding; they are done free and in competition with other contractors. Don't waste people's time; be clear about your needs and wishes, and don't ask for bids from any contractor you aren't serious about.

6. Talk with your bank and determine a final budget. Bankers can suggest several avenues of financing, such as borrowing on the equity in the house to finance at lowest possible rates. The banker will explain how the money will be dispensed, that is, at what stages of construction the bank will advance installments.

7. Select a contractor's bid—but not necessarily the lowest one. Keep in mind that the contractor must also be reliable and, to a degree, congenial. If you are acting as your own general contractor and are lining up several subcontactors, the carpenter may be the kingpin of your project. A carpenter knows, for instance, what structures must be in place before plumbing or electricity can be installed.

8. Develop a work sheet for each room, spelling out materials to be purchased and noting anomalies of construction; your contractor and the lumberyard can help you develop these sheets. Here again, working drawings are crucial. This is the last chance to change details easily, before you sign a contract with the builder.

9. Review the list once more with the contractor, to be sure you are clear about what the contractor will do and what he will charge. Will the contractor, for example, secure the necessary code permits?

10. Return to the bank and get a letter of commitment. This letter guarantees that if you borrow money within a certain period, it will be there, at a predetermined rate of interest.

11. Draw up a contract with the builder, based on the work specifications discussed thus far. It should include, among other points:

    a. The contractor's responsibilities, including, as far as is practicable, work dimensions, specifications, and quality. Describe precisely all major items—for example, appliances and windows—citing catalogue numbers.

b. When the work is to begin and when it should end. It's advisable to have secondary deadlines for different stages of construction (the construction phases suggested by the bank are appropriate).

c. When the contractor gets paid and how much. Don't "front" (pay any of it in advance) the builder money; always keep a 10 to 20 pecent "motivational lag" in your payments.

d. Who cleans up and removes debris. You may, for example, want someone to sweep up at the end of each work day.

e. Establish a termination clause in case things don't work out, as they occasionally do not. Specify how materials ordered up to that point will be paid off, how labor completed will be recompensed and matters of dispute mediated. Binding arbitration is a common way to resolve disagreements and can save you the horrendous expense, aggravation, and delays inherent in the civil legal system. You can find an arbitrator through local branches of the Associated Building Contractors, the AIA, and so on.

f. Have the contractor declare what insurance he carries, and what your liability is. In most states, licensed contractors must carry workman's comprehensive insurance, property damage insurance, and public liability insurance. Bonds limit client liability should the contractor fail to complete a job, a point that is very important, especially if a contractor is unlicensed. Your lawyer should review the contract carefully; in the long run, you have the most to lose. As noted above, show this document to your bank and your insurance agent.

12. Order materials from the supplier. (The contractor may do this for you.)

13. Avoid making changes in the work plans once work has begun. Builders are bothered in varying degrees by changes, which nearly always cost more and invariably disrupt scheduling. All change orders must be in writing and initialed by both you and the contractor. When making changes, deal only with the general contractor or, if so indicated, the job foreman—not with a subcontractor or a worker. By the same token, only one member of your family should negotiate changes; that way, you and your contractor will know exactly who has authorized what.

14. Stick to the payment schedule; don't advance cash at the request of the builder.

15. When the job is done, have pertinent code authorities make inspections before you make final payment to the contractor. At that point, you'll sign a Certificate of Completion signifying that the builder has completed work to your satisfaction. The contractor signs a Waiver of Mechanic's Liens, in which you are absolved of further liability for materials ordered, labor hired, and so on.

16. Return to the bank. With all renovation debts discharged, the property is now clear of encumbrances and the bank can issue a new mortgage which reflects the increased value of the renovated property.

ARCHITECTS AND OTHERS

In recent years more and more architects have been hiring out by the hour rather than by the complete job, enabling owner-builders to use the architect as a part-time consultant. As mentioned above, the advent of designer-builders provides you with another source of planning help, often at a lower cost. Here again, local building codes may have a say in the matter, for example, specifying that the designer be accredited. As you do in choosing a contractor, ask friends and acquaintances about architects you're interested in, and review their work.

Architects

Here's where an architect can be invaluable:

1. *Selecting materials.* Any designer (hereafter, we'll use *designer* to indicate architects as well) worth his or her fee reads reams of manufacturers' literature. For example, there may be a narrow cooktop that fits well into a small countertop. In some cases, a designer who buys often can buy materials cheaper and get them more promptly than you can.

2. *Defining and solving problems involving space.* Imagining walls where there aren't any takes practice, and some people never develop the skill.

3. *Providing work drawings.* It's easier, and in the long run cheaper, to resolve construction details on paper, especially if you're working in tight spaces. If your builder is experienced and resourceful, capable of solving tough problems on the job, you don't need this service. If the job is involved, however—say, one involving several rooms—or it's a particularly complex one, draw accurate, detailed plans or have someone draw them for you.

4. *Satisfying local codes.* If banks and codes demand that work be guaranteed by an accredited person, that's that. You may be able to do the work and have the architect (electrician or plumber, etc.) certify your plans; but many will want to be paid for this certification.

5. *Overseeing job progress.* If you do hire an architect, hire a general contractor too; otherwise, it's you versus the architect, and he knows a good deal more about building than you do. If both designer and contractor are in your employ, however, you have an experienced second opinion, should a conflict arise.

Chronologically, working with an architect looks like this:

1. *Schematics.* Recording what's there, determining what clients' needs are, developing several schematics and selecting one that works best. Roughly 20 percent of architect's services.

2. *Design development.* Further refining one of the schemes, deciding on materials, details, actual dimensions (viz., all the info needed to proceed to working drawings). 20 percent of services.

3. *Construction documents.* Working drawings and written specifications from which to bid and build. 40 percent of basic architect's services.

4. *Bidding.* Answering questions during bidding, helping select builder. 5 percent of services.

5. *Construction consultation.* Weekly visits to sites to solve problems, troubleshoot change orders, supplemental drawings. About 15 percent of services.

(Thanks to Gary Parsons, architect, Berkeley, CA.)

Consultants

Many specialists are available to help people renovating old houses. Structural engineers are imperative if you are thinking about alteration of existing load-bearing walls or otherwise enlarging an area beyond the spanning capacity of the structural members. Many codes require such consultants.

Restoration specialists may be able to help you. They analyze paint and mortar, know how to stabilize deteriorating building materials, are sensitive to problems involving the interaction of new and old materials, know esoteric sources of supply. Quite often, too, they work with local historic preservation groups and are willing to ''moonlight,'' that is, advise you in off-hours. In some parts of the country, university extension services are offered at cost.

Important Sources—Codes and Contracts

Uniform Building Code
International Conference of Building Officials
5360 South Workman Mill Road
Whittier, CA 90601

BOCA Basic Building Code
Building Officials and Code Administrators International, Inc.
4051 West Flossmoor Road
Country Club Hills, IL 60477

Uniform Plumbing Code
International Association of Plumbing Officials
20001 Walnut Drive South
Walnut, CA 91789

National Electrical Code
National Fire Protection Agency
Batterymarch Park
Quincy, MA 02269

Standard Building Code
(Used mostly in the south)
Southern Building Code Conference International
908 Montclair Road
Birmingham, AL 35213

For copies of standard building contracts:
American Institute of Architects
1735 New York Avenue, NW
Washington, DC 20006

MONEY

The first edition of *Renovation* had a section on financing and buying a home, which was outdated before the book left the presses. So if the comments below are brief, hopefully they'll age well.

Getting Information

Start by talking to people who have just bought a home. They will have run the gamut of realtors, banks, builders, and the like and—most important—they have roughly the same perspective you have as a buyer-to-be. Their information will also be current, very useful in winnowing out who's lending and how easy they are to work with.

Realtors. Realtors are the kingpins in most transactions. Obviously, they know where the houses are, but they're also connected to loan brokers, banks, title companies, and so on. The only disadvantage is their point of view: they want to sell the most expensive house they think you can afford. So you must be clear about what you want and convey it emphatically and persistently to the realtor. You must also be a little ruthless initially: if the realtor is just not on your wavelength or doesn't seem to work very hard for you, find another. The hunt is never easy, but a bright, well-connected realtor can get you in houses before they even come on the market.

Bankers. Bankers are the other key players. If you can't find any personal recommendations, start by calling around and asking what rates they're offering. Difficult as it is with a total stranger, be totally open and forthcoming with bankers. If you're thinking of buying an old wreck and doing most of the work yourself, tell them that.

There's a reason for this candor: make sure that your loan will cover not only the purchase price, but also the costs of the renovations. Banks lend on a percentage of the house's value; if extensive demolition precedes rehabilitation, the value of the house actually declines initially. Lenders, therefore, are often reluctant to disburse funds until substantial reconstruction is complete; thus a renovator (you) could be underfinanced during the early stages. Discuss all of this with the bank early on, finding out exactly how money will be disbursed at each stage.

Bankers will also explain escrow, in which the title to the house is held by a third party until certain conditions are met (e.g., termite damage is repaired). Having a lot of work done during escrow may mean you'll do less of it yourself, but it may spare you some major headaches.

By preapplying for a loan before you hunt for houses, you know what your real limits are. This is important because it's easy to get starry-eyed about your future home. When you compare houses, the asking price is actually just the beginning—what will it cost after it's renovated? That is, a $115,000 house with $45,000 worth of renovation to be done is a $160,000 house.

Contractors. Start talking to friends about builders long before you're ready to buy. By having a contractor on tap when you find a house you like, you can get an inspection fast. Having discussed contractors at length above, suffice it to say here that a good contractor can tell you better than anybody what a renovation will cost. And if major structural problems are suspected, he or she can refer you to a qualified engineer. If you want to know what you're getting into, you'll find this information invaluable—especially when it's time to negotiate price.

Buying a House

To find a house and negotiate its purchase, it's best to live in an area awhile and learn of upcoming properties through the local grapevine. When you begin your search in earnest, scrutinize all serious prospects with an assessment list (Chapter 1). If you are diligent in learning about houses in general you will know a true bargain when you see it, and you will be less easily swayed by gimmicks and pressures of the housing market.

The usual sequence in buying a house is assessment; preliminary negotiations with the seller; verbal agreement; buyer's investigation of financing; code, legal, and other matters; and, when financing is secured, closing.

Negotiations. Take negotiations seriously, for they are the basis of the written contract that follows. When you have reached a verbal agreement, the seller will expect you to sign an agreement and put money (called a "binder") in escrow. Here are some tips about negotiating:

Almost anything is negotiable.
Negotiate little items first; save the asking price until last. (You should be able to get an idea of the price range from the price asked by the seller.)
Don't be pressured by competition from other buyers, real or imagined. "There's another couple who is interested" is a realtor's stock-in-trade. Be specific when discussing the outlays which you will have to make to repair the house. Your house-assessment notes will be extremely useful here!
When in doubt, stop talking and think things over.
Keep the discussion personable but not personal. At all costs, be polite.
Don't sign anything until your realtor or lawyer has had a chance to review it.

What to discuss. Virtually all aspects of the house are subject to negotiation. Some important considerations are:

The sales agreement's contingency upon your ability to obtain financing, on the house's being free of serious physical defect, on the title being free and clear.
The sales price.
The seller's willingness to offer a first or second mortgage or otherwise help with financing.
The amount of money to be put down, the date of the formal sales agreement, the date and place of closing.
Appliances and fixtures to be included in the purchase.
What repairs are to be the seller's responsibility.
The house's compliance with existing health, zoning, and building-code regulations.
The date of vacating by the present occupants, if any.

Important Investigations

When you have reached an agreement with the seller, that person's agent (often a realtor) will draw up a sales agreement. Have your lawyer look at it before you sign. At this point, you give a binder to a third party (customarily, a licensed realtor—but *not* to the seller), the property is taken off the market while you investigate financing and matters pertinent to the status of the house itself. The seller may continue to show the property but may not accept another offer until your offer has been terminated. The buyer or the buyer's agent (lawyer) should now:

1. Have the building inspected by a city inspector or a licensed engineer to determine whether code violations have occurred that would interfere with the granting of a Certificate of Occupancy by the municipality. If the building is in violation of a code or codes (there may also be a record of such violations on file at the department that oversees buildings), you may dissolve the agreement with the seller and get your money back or renegotiate the sale. If the city does not offer such inspections hire a structural engineer on your own, to determine whether there are serious building flaws. You will have to assume the cost of such an assessment, but it will be money well spent. If the engineer finds repairs that would be above an amount you and the seller negotiated, renegotiate or void the sale.

2. Inspect zoning regulations for the area. You should have no trouble here if you intend to use the building as is; but if you want to put in an apartment or work out of your home, your intended use may conflict with zoning regulations. In addition, zoning authorities may intend to rezone an area—for example, to make it commercial.

3. Find out whether the bank will give you the money you need to acquire *and* renovate the house. Loan packages are available that allow you to do both. Get a letter of commitment from a bank.

4. Have the title company conduct a title search. This search will ascertain that the property you are purchasing is wholly the seller's to sell, that there are no liens and encumbrances on the title, and that there are no easements (such as special rights of access) that could adversely affect the title. The company will offer a "title search opinion," also, your bank may want title insurance, at closing, in the event that the search overlooked something. Check to see that all property, water, and sewer taxes are paid in full.

Closing Costs

Just before closing, your agent should send you a breakdown-of-costs sheet which tells you just how much money you must come up with at closing. The largest portion of money, of course, is the purchase price of the property, less the deposit made. You will get most of this as a loan from the bank. There may be other costs as well:

1. *"Points."* A small percentage of the total value of the loan may be charged by the bank when mortgage money is hard to get. This is a one-time charge.

2. *Credit check.* A credit check may be required by a bank that doesn't know you. You pay a small fee for the service.

3. *Fire insurance.* Fire insurance is required by the institution lending you the money. As noted above, if you or an unlicensed person is doing the work, tell your agent and have your insurance policy modified accordingly.

4. *Title insurance.* Title insurance is another one-time fee to protect the lender should the title search be flawed in any manner.

5. *Bank charges.* The bank will levy a charge for drafting a mortgage-loan agreement.

6. *Loan installment.* A first monthly loan installment is required in advance by some banks, or the bank may require a pro-rated amount that covers the mortgage between the time of closing and the day of the month when the bank usually bills payments.

7. *Property taxes.* Property taxes are usually paid by the buyer on a pro-rated amount that represents the portion of the tax year in which you own the property. Transfer taxes, percentages of the total purchase price, are, however, one-time arrangements.

8. *Attorney's fee.* Your lawyer will charge a fee for the title search and for preparing documents.

9. *Last-minute adjustments.* Last-minute adjustments must be made with seller, for example, for fuel oil left in the tank.

The Closing

The closing, or settlement, is the formal exchange of documents and the transfer of legal title to the property. Although this transaction often takes place at a title company, the actual location isn't very important nor, in most cases, is the presence of the parties. The one crucial element, however, is scrutiny of the documents by attorneys and bank officials. You will likely pay (with certified checks) all sums required at this stage. The documents listed below are required at closing.

From the seller.

A warranty deed which states that the property is free and clear of encumbrances and that the property is wholly the seller's to sell. (Accept only a *warranty* deed; there are other types.)

Documents showing that any liens and encumbrances found during the title search have been discharged.

Documents from state and/or municipality attesting that all property-related taxes have been paid in full.

A Certificate of Occupancy and zoning approvals or variances. (Who secures the documents is negotiable, but it is often the buyer's responsibility.)

Payment to the realtor; this agent's fee is customarily incorporated in the sales price.

Payment of utility bills up to the date of closing; miscellany.

From the bank.

The loan agreement, which states the terms of the mortgage. This document is usually prepared by the buyer's lawyer and is reviewed by the bank. When you agree to its terms, sign it.

A certified check for the purchase price, less moneys in escrow; you receive this from the bank when you sign the loan agreement.

From the buyer.

The check from the bank, briefly warmed by your hand, is turned over to the seller.

Municipal documents showing payment of transfer and property taxes as prearranged with the seller.

Insurance covering the property from the day of closing.

Checks made out to the bank, as explained in "Closing Costs" above.

Title insurance, as required.

Payment to your attorney (this fee is sometimes paid later).

Other adjustments between buyer and seller.

At closing, the deed usually is sent to the city recorder or town clerk so that the change of ownership can be entered. Shortly thereafter, the deed is mailed back to you. If the fee for recording the deed wasn't included in your attorney's fees, pay the fee now.

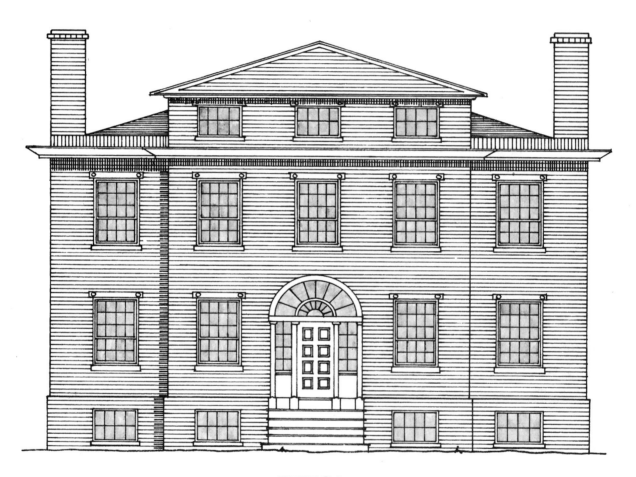

FEDERAL

·C·

SECURITY

The need for security is as much psychological as it is physical: you need not only to keep intruders out but also to keep a sense of well-being within. You can beef up locks and dead bolts after a house has been broken into, but it is far more difficult to reinstill calm and confidence once your home has been violated; truly, an ounce of prevention is better.

In this appendix we'll review some of the physical—and psychological—ways to deter burglars, but actually installing door hardware is covered in Chapter 6.

HOW BURGLARS WORK

Most B&E men look for entry that is quick, easy and quiet. The fewer tools they have to use, the better. If they come upon a house that looks protected, they'll go next door.

1. Kicking a door open is the most common means of illegal entry. With only one or two well-placed kicks, a burglar can tear out the strike plate and dislodge the latch bolt.

2. Inserting a pry bar between the door and the jamb is also effective—and quieter. Where a latch bolt is only $\frac{1}{2}$ in. long, the thief needn't pry much.

3. In populous areas, breaking a window is much less frequent because someone might hear it. Once done, though, it's just a matter of reaching inside and throwing a bolt not locked by a key.

4. Prying out a lock cylinder is fairly quiet but less common because it takes time and some know-how.

5. Cutting and hammering out a lock is rare; it makes too much of a racket.

PUTTING COMMON SENSE TO WORK

Psyching out burglars costs nothing and is as effective as the best hardware you can buy.

1. Lock your doors and windows. Some insurers estimate that Americans could reduce losses a billion dollars a year if they'd lock doors and windows.

2. Don't leave keys under the doormat, under the potted plant, or in other obvious places.

3. Leave a car in the driveway when you're gone, or have a neighbor park there.

4. Post signs of a local security company. This alone can dissuade some would-be culprits.

5. Put your lights on timers.

6. If you'll be out of town for a while, have the post office hold your mail, ask a neighbor to collect your newspaper, and get a neighborhood kid to mow your lawn.

7. Put your telephone on an answering machine, but don't leave a message announcing that you'll be out of town.

511

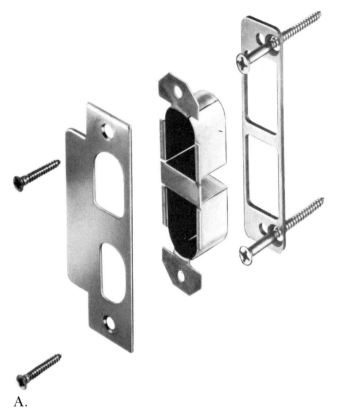

A.

B.

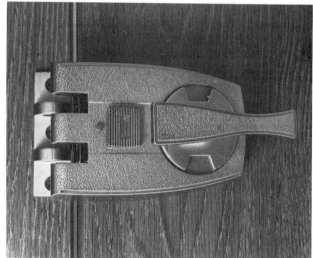

D.

C.

E.

Figure C.1 High-security hardware. (A) Reinforced strike-plate assembly (Schlage Locks); (B) D-11 dead bolt (Medeco Security Locks); (C) interconnected lock set (Schlage); (D) vertical dead bolt (Ideal Security Hardware); (E) replacement cylinder (Medeco).

8. There's nothing like neighbors. Tell them when you're going out of town so that they can watch your house. Return the favor: hang out on the streets with them, and support community crimewatches.

Improving Security

To simplify your choices, let's divide security into three stages of incremental cost and complexity.

Stage one. This first stage is well within the reach of all homeowners and should be considered the minimum you need. You should be able to achieve it in a weekend.

Upgrade Locks and Doorways. Keep in mind that most burglars go in through the back door, so feature it in your upgrade.

1. Upgrade the *strike plates* on your doors. You can have the most formidable locks and dead bolts, but if they slide into a flimsy plate in a $\frac{3}{4}$-in.-thick jamb, they will be ineffective. Strike-frame reinforcers are available, which have 3-in. screws that resist virtually any attempt to dislodge them. (If a door frame is metal, the strike plate probably isn't a problem.) There are also door-reinforcement devices that slide over and screw to the door, thus preventing the door from shattering under impact.

2. A lock of the tubular (key-in-knob) type is weak, in several respects. It can be easily pried or kicked, and its knob, containing the lock mechanism, can be yanked off with little trouble. It's best to replace such units entirely or to add a separate auxiliary *dead bolt.* Replacement units, such as the interconnected lockset shown in Figure C.1, are available; one turn of an inside knob or key opens the latch bolt and the dead bolt.

3. A mortise lock is difficult to replace because of the large mortise in the door stile. A more prudent course might be to add an auxiliary lock. Many such locks are available, including key-operated and knob-operated models. The knob-operated lock doesn't require a key in an emergency; but if there are windows in the door, a burglar can break them and reach in to turn the controlling knob. A *vertical dead bolt* is one very effective auxiliary device because its strike is a sturdy unit that screws to the inside face of the frame so that it is virtually indestructible.

4. A particularly promising innovation is Schlage's Key 'N Keyless electronic lockset. You can open this heavy-duty interconnected lock with a key, or without a key, by turning the door knob to enter a private access code—much as you would a combination lock. (As you turn the knob left and right, digits appear in an LED display mounted in the lock panel.) When you enter the code, the control unit sends an infrared signal so you can open both latch bolt and dead bolt.

5. Replacing only the key cylinder of a lock is another option. The cylinder is relatively easy to install, but this approach is worthwhile only if all other aspects of door safety are first-rate.

6. Buying a new door of solid-panel construction may be advisable if the front door has a lot of glass or a hollow core. You can also bolster existing doors by replacing glass with break-resistant plastic or by reinforcing wood panels with metal bars painted the same color as the rest of the door.

7. If, in the course of your renovation, you expose the studs on the lock side of the frame, nail in horizontal blocking between the studs, about lock-high. This blocking will greatly strengthen the frame area and make it almost impossible to pry apart.

8. Are the hinge pins of exterior doors on the outside of the house? If they are, countersink a small self-tapping screw into each hinge pin so that the pin can't be pulled.

9. Install peepholes at eye level in all doors: they are cheap, easy to install, and invaluable if you want to know who your callers are.

Secure Windows. Make windows harder to force open by drilling through both meeting rails of double-hung windows; insert nails or specialty bolts (Figure C.2) in those holes. Cut a 1-in. dowel to block the tracks of sliding doors or windows. Keeping blinds drawn keeps burglars in the dark about the possessions you've got.

Increase Exposure. Clip back overgrown hedges and bushes that might hide an intruder from the public eye while he's trying to get in. Granted, this reduces your privacy from the street, but hedges can prevent neighbors, police, and security patrols from seeing suspicious behavior. Also cut back trees or branches that might provide access to a second-story window.

Install Lighting. For the front of the house, install floodlights controlled by *photo cells,* which automatically turn on light when it's dark enough: as important for safety as for security. Along the sides and back of the house, install lights activated by infrared sensors; typically, infrared is triggered by body warmth or contact within a given perimeter. This is particularly good feature when no one is home or when the family is sleeping.

Stage two. The second level of security includes all of the above, plus:

Internal Alarm System. Here the idea is to stop a thief before he gets in or, failing that, as he moves from room to room. Again, kudos to Schlage for its ingenious, reasonably priced, and very effective Keepsafer Security System. Basically, it's a wireless system whose sensors and transmitters send signals to a central console which can turn on floodlights, activate sirens, dial an emergency call to a monitoring station, and so on. Because it's wireless, you can install it in an hour or so, with just a screwdriver. Some of

Figure C.2 Special bolt for securing windows. (Brookstone)

Keepsafer's components are shown in Figure C.3; as of this writing, an extended system was under $400.

Window Bars. Bars on basement and first-story windows are a reasonably inexpensive, if obvious, security system. Their biggest shortcoming is that people can get trapped inside during a fire, so specify quick-release latches. If barred units can be unlocked, keep keys out of reach from the outside, but within easy reach—and knowledge—of all family members. Bars are ugly, which you can mitigate somewhat by having a local blacksmith ornament them.

Security Glazing. By replacing window glass with Lexan or other polycarbonate sheet material, you get a window that can't be broken—yet lets in light. Lexan is the material used for bank windows and armored cars. Be advised that the window will only be as strong as the sash in which it's installed.

Such material has some shortcomings, notably the fact that whereas it's tough on one side, it's relatively soft and can be scratched on the other; put the hardened side on the outside. It also can't be cleaned with ammoniated cleaners—in fact, they dissolve it to a degree; instead, use a plastic cleaner. And, over time, the material may cloud up, which is fine if it's in a bathroom window.

Stage three. This level presupposes that you've considered or installed the methods mentioned above. The sophistication and cost of such systems probably isn't warranted unless your manse is in the country, far from neighbors or police.

Hard-Wired System: Here we're talking wires contained within walls, magnetic switches retrofitted to windows and doors, pressure pads to note an intruder's footfall, space or area detectors, and a backup power source in case power is cut accidentally or deliberately. Hard-wired systems with auxiliary sensors secure the perimeter of the house (i.e., they'll go off *before* an intruder gets inside).

Because each window and door must be individually wired, installing a hard-wired system means drilling with extension bits, snaking wires in walls, patching holes, and all that. It's most cost-effective to install as part of a major renovation in which you're gutting walls.

Police/Security Service. A hard-wired system is frequently linked to the police station or a private security service. The biggest problem here is false alarms, serious because local authorities may start charging you for false alarms—or stop coming altogether. Work out some way for police to verify alarms. Any security system also means you'll have to

Figure C.3 Schlage Keepsafer components include: emergency dialer, area detectors, bedside alarm, remote control, central console, backup power supply, window sensors, glass break detectors, smoke alarm, power siren, houselight controllers, lamp modules.

change your behavior (e.g., getting in the habit of turning on the alarm when you leave and turning it off when you return). No system will be effective if used ineffectively.

Fire Safety

Smoke detectors are so inexpensive and easy to install that no house should be without them. Put smoke detectors outside rooms with a higher likelihood of fire (e.g., in the room next to a kitchen); don't put the detector *in* the kitchen or it will be going off every time you burn the bacon. Also put smoke detectors in halls outside bedrooms.

Hard-wired detectors operate on house current and are more expensive; battery-powered units can be easily retrofitted, but their batteries must be replaced periodically (most will alert you in some way when this is necessary).

Additionally, you should have:

A fire plan, particularly important if you live in an apartment or a multistory building
Rope ladders from second-story windows
A fire drill twice a year if you have children
A place where everyone will assemble should you have a fire, important to ascertain that everyone got out okay.

GOTHIC REVIVAL

·D·

A SIMPLE SET OF STAIRS

Although the layout of a set of stairs built from scratch can be complex, actual cutting and assembly is not. The stairs described are, as stairs go, simple, without the elaborate joinery of some types but sturdy and adequate for basement and outside uses. It's assumed that the structure to which the stairs will be attached or on which they will rest is itself sound, as described in Chapter 8; that chapter also defines many of the terms used in this appendix.

CUTTING A ROUGH OPENING FOR STAIRS

Minimum stair widths are commonly 32 in. for secondary staircases, 36 in. for primary residential stairs, and 42 in. for heavy use. Minimal headroom along the entire run of the stairs is 6 ft 8 in. (80 in.). The length of the rough opening depends on the pitch of the stairs (their rate of *rise* relative to horizontal distance traveled, or *run*) and the height of the floor above. Because the widths cited above are *finish* widths—with finish materials and handrail in place—add about 4 in. to establish the width of a rough opening.

To protect the structural integrity of the floor grid, it is necessary to double up the framing around the opening. The doubled joists that bound the long side of the opening are called *trimmers* or *trimmer joists*: those running across the width of the opening are *headers* or *header joists*.

When positioning stairs, try to avoid disturbing such major structural elements as bearing walls and girders. Plumbing, wiring, and heating ductwork are relatively easy to move; do so before cutting into a structure. If you lay out the stairs so their length runs *parallel* to joists, you'll disturb fewer joists. Once you have tentatively located the opening, locate existing joists by test-drilling or by driving a nail upward from an exposed basement ceiling. You'll save labor and lumber by moving the rough opening over slightly so at least one of its trimmers is an existing joist. Snap a chalk line on the flooring to indicate the outline of the rough opening.

Disconnect electrical power to the area. Put on safety goggles, then cut (with a circular saw) on the waste side of the chalkline, with your blade depth set to the thickness of the flooring and subflooring. There may be a lot of hidden nails, so use a carbide-tipped, nail-cutting blade. Where layout corners meet, do not cut beyond the chalkline. Finish the cut with a handsaw and remove the section of flooring and subflooring. If you intend to reuse the flooring, try prying it up around the perimeter of the cut and then work inward; use a utility bar. Remove nails from the flooring as you pry it lose. Where nails resist, go underneath and gently knock up the section, using a length of 2×4 and a wrecking bar. The more patient you are, the more wood you'll salvage. This is definitely hard-hat work.

Before cutting through a joist, shore joists underneath with 2×4 shoring simply constructed and shimmed to fit. Mark the cuts to be made with a framing square so the joist

517

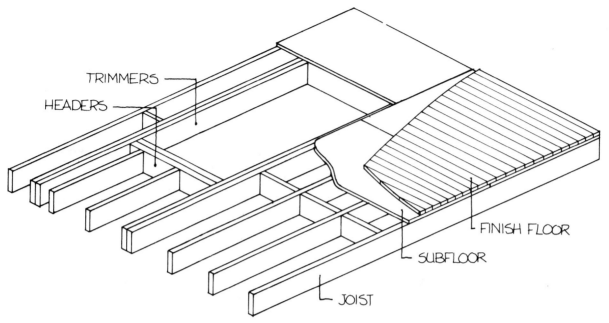

Figure D.1 A rough opening in a floor.

TRIMMERS

HEADERS

FINISH FLOOR

SUBFLOOR

JOIST

ends will squarely abut the headers to come. Since the header joists will be doubled, remember to cut back joists 3 in. on each end of the opening, so the doubled headers will fit flush with the opening's edges. With the subflooring above still in place, you won't have room to finish the cuts with a circular saw; a reciprocating saw or a flooring saw can be used to finish the job. Have someone help you catch the joist sections as you cut through.

Assemble the elements of the rough opening in the following order: inside trimmers; outside headers (nail these headers to cripple joists—remnants of the joists you cut); inside headers; outside trimmers. This sequence allows you to *end-nail* pieces whenever possible; nail the cripples through a header and the headers through a trimmer. As you end-nail pieces, check the juncture with a framing square. For all end-nailing, use three 16d nails; for toenailing, two 12d nails on each side of a board.

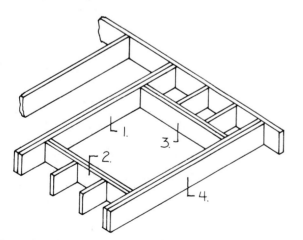

Figure D.2 Framing out a rough opening. To maximize end-nailing (the strongest way to nail a structure together), assemble rough openings in the floor in this order: (1) inside trimmers; (2) outside headers; (3) inside headers; (4) outside trimmers.

The task may be complicated slightly by the present framing. First, it is likely there is blocking between joists, which will have to be pried out before you add trimmers. Second, either your stock may crown or the floor may sag, resulting in gaps between joists and the subflooring above. Overcome this problem by hanging one end of the joist with a joist hanger and jacking the other end snug against the subflooring. Although joist hangers aren't strictly necessary if you can end-nail, they are strongly recommended, since the normal flexion of stair members can loosen nails over a long period.

Finally, should your rough opening run perpendicular to joists (though this should be avoided whenever possible), try to use a girder or carrying timber as one of the sides of the opening. In that circumstance, joist hangers are necessary to support members around the opening.

A BASIC SET OF STAIRS

In this section we look at the construction of a "straight-run" staircase, one that goes up a flight without landings or turns. Construction is simple, as stairs go, and the set is sturdy. If you want a set of L-shaped or U-shaped stairs, consider hiring and assisting an experienced stair-builder; or give your spatial requirements to a mill and have the mill custom-make a set of preassembled stairs. Stair-building is an exacting craft, incorporating as it does a bit of the framing carpenter and a bit of the cabinetmaker.

Our example is "semihoused," meaning that steps are supported beneath by carriages at each end, with each carriage backed by a stringer. If your stairs are 36 in. wide or wider, add a center carriage down the middle to reduce flexion. These stairs are largely free-standing: their upper ends are attached (with metal hangers) to the inside of the rough opening above and, at the lower end, they rest on doubled header-joists. For greater rigidity and durability,

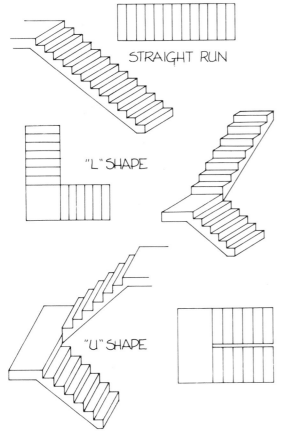

Figure D.3 Types of stairs.

screw or bolt stringers to the studs of surroundings walls, where possible.

The risers and treads of these basic stairs butt together; treads are $\frac{5}{4}$-in. ($1\frac{1}{4}$-in.) oak; risers are $\frac{3}{4}$-in. pine. (If you intend to carpet the stairs, use 2-in. fir stock for both treads and risers.) In high-quality stairs, risers are dadoed into the underside of the treads above and treads are rabbeted into the bottom of the riser (Figure 8.30). In this manner, shrinkage is concealed and dirt kept from working through joints. Admittedly, butt joints are less desirable, but they are much easier to build. If you purchase preassembled stairs, specify dado-and-rabbet details, as well as fully housed stringer construction, so you can tighten treads and risers with wedges.

Determining Dimensions

The vertical distance from finished floor to finished floor is called *total rise*. *Total run* is the horizontal distance that the staircase extends. Although the total rise is fixed by the height of the floor above (and the thickness of its flooring), total run is determined by the size and number of steps chosen. The dimensions of steps, as they are marked on the carriages, are called *unit rise* and *unit run*.

To determine the size and number of steps, let's look at two givens of stair building:

1. *Rise-to-run ratios have certain limits.* Hypothetically, one could make rises and runs of any size; but certain limits

on size have been proved through centuries of use. (The dimensions that follow are for interior steps. To provide for greater safety, outdoor steps should have a minimum tread width, or depth, of 12 in., and a maximum riser height of 6 in.)

    a. Unit rises must be 6 to 9 in.; a comfortable, common height is about 7 in.

    b. Unit runs range from 8 to 12 in.; a comforable width—that is, depth—is 10 to 11 in.

    c. Unit rise plus unit run equals $17\frac{1}{2}$ in.; run *times* rise equals 70 to 75. ($17\frac{1}{2}$ in. is a desirable total, provided you stay within the individual limits of 1a and 1b. The product of run and rise, 70 to 75, is an optimal result also established through long experience.)

2. *The distance between steps must be constant for the entire flight.* Steps that rise uneven distances are extremely unsafe. Our bodies pick up the rhythm of the first few steps and expect subsequent steps to be on the same interval; breaking this rule can cause falls.

Now let's apply these formulas. Measure total rise and convert the resulting measurement to inches. Divide this number by 7 (an average unit rise in inches) to get an approximate number of steps. If we assume a total rise of 108 in. (9 ft), we get $15\frac{3}{7}$ steps, or 15. (If the fraction is more than $\frac{1}{2}$, go to the next highest number.) To determine the unit rise exactly, divide the total rise (108 in.) by 15. This gives 7.2 in., or about $7\frac{3}{16}$ in. as the amount of unit rise. Using formula 1c, subtract $7\frac{3}{16}$ in. from $17\frac{1}{2}$ in. to get the

A.

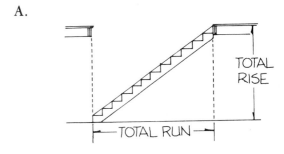

B.

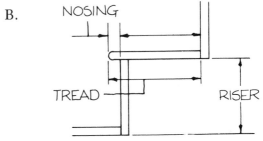

Figure D.4 Determining stair dimensions. (A) Total rise and total run. (B) Unit rise and unit run. "Unit rises" and "unit runs" are more or less the same as "risers"and "treads", but dimensions may vary according to the stock used for risers and treads. In the butt-joined steps pictured, the riser will be the same height as the unit rise marked onto the carriage. But the tread—whose nose protrudes—will be somewhat longer than the unit run. To avoid confusion, we'll use the terms "unit rise" and "unit run" during layout stages.

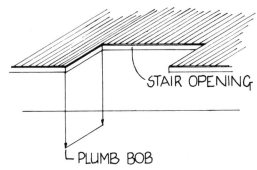

Figure D.5 When determining the total rise, take two readings with a plumb bob as shown, in case the floor below isn't level. If the floor isn't level, use the shorter of the two readings, and shim up the carriage on the lower side of the floor to make sure that the treads will be level.

width (or depth) of the unit run: $10\frac{5}{16}$ in.; actually, $10\frac{1}{4}$ in. is close enough.

Here's a summary of the foregoing computation:

1. **Number of steps:** $\dfrac{108 \text{ in. (total rise)}}{7 \text{ (average unit rise, inches)}} =$

   $15\frac{3}{7}$, or 15 steps.

2. **Unit rise:** $\dfrac{108 \text{ inches (total rise)}}{15 \text{ (steps)}} = 7.2$ in., or $7\frac{3}{16}$ in.

   (to the nearest convenient fraction).

3. **Unit run (in.):** $17\frac{1}{2} - 7\frac{3}{16} = \frac{35}{2} - \frac{115}{16} = \frac{280}{16} - \frac{115}{16} = \frac{165}{16} = 10\frac{5}{16}$, or approx. $10\frac{1}{4}$ in.

4. **Run $\times$ rise** $= 7.2 \times 10.25$

   $= 73.8$, an optimal result (from lc).

5. **Total run:** 15 (steps) $\times$ $10\frac{1}{4}$ (unit run, in inches) $=$

   $15 \times \frac{41}{4} = \frac{615}{4} = 153\frac{3}{4}$ in., or 12 ft $9\frac{3}{4}$ in.

Sizing the Rough Opening

As computation 5 shows, you can figure out the total run by multiplying the number of steps (15) by the unit run ($10\frac{1}{4}$ in.), which gives 12 ft $9\frac{3}{4}$ in. From this total run we can determine the exact size of the rough opening and the length of the stringer and/or the carriage stock needed.

To figure out the length of the rough opening, imagine a man 6 ft 8 in. tall walking upstairs. Assuming the underside of the floor joists to be 98 or 99 in. above the floor, the man could go up two steps ($14\frac{3}{8}$ in.) but not three steps ($21\frac{9}{16}$ in.) before bumping his head. Therefore, the length of the rough opening should be at least $133\frac{1}{4}$ in.—the total run ($153\frac{3}{4}$ in.),minus the width of two steps ($20\frac{1}{2}$ in.).

It is instructive to note how much the size of the total run and the length of the rough opening are affected by minor changes in the unit rise. If we had decided to go with 14 steps instead of 15, the unit rise would have been about $7\frac{3}{4}$ in.; the unit run, $9\frac{3}{4}$ in.; the total run, $136\frac{1}{2}$ in.; and the rough opening (still two step widths subtracted from the total run), 117 in. When you just don't have the room for a stair with a gentler slope, try a different number of stairs; but stay within the limits of the local building code. Keep in mind, too, that at the top and bottom of stairs, you need landings at least 3 ft deep on which to turn around.

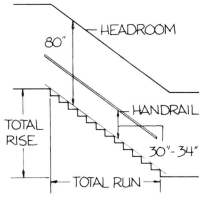

Figure D.6 The stairway must maintain a height of 6 ft 8 in. (80 in.) along its entire run.

Sizing Carriages

To figure the length of the carriage-stringer stock needed, use the Pythagorean theorem, the staple of junior-high math: $C^2 = A^2 + B^2$, where C represents the longest side of a right triangle (in our example, the length of carriage or stringer), and A and B represent the two adjacent sides (total rise and total run). Inserting the numbers from the example above in the formula, we get

$$\begin{aligned} C^2 &= (\text{total rise})^2 + (\text{total run})^2 \\ &= (108)^2 + (154)^2 \\ &= (11,664 + 23,716) \end{aligned}$$

To get C, we take the square root of both sides:

$$\begin{aligned} C &= \sqrt{35,380} \\ &= 188.09 \text{ in.} \\ &= 15 \text{ ft } 8 \text{ in., the length of carriage or stringer required} \end{aligned}$$

Because you'll waste at least 1 ft of stock in laying out and cutting the carriage, and because lumber comes in lengths of 2-ft intervals, you'll need 2 × 12s 18 feet long. Lumber that size is a large, expensive item. This example illustrates why it may be worthwhile to increase the height of the unit rise, thus decreasing the total run, as well as the length of the stock needed for stringers. If we had gone with the $7\frac{3}{4}$-in. unit rise described in the last paragraph, we would need a stringer only 174 in., or 14 ft 6 in. long, easily cut from stock 16 ft long.

Laying Out Carriages

Once you've determined the dimensions of your steps and framed out the rough opening, make a final check of your unit rise with a *storyboard*. A storyboard is a perfectly straight board marked off to the exact length of the total rise—from finish floor to finish floor. Mark off the appropriate number of unit rises; the last mark should coincide exactly with the last mark on the storyboard; if it doesn't, recalculate the unit rise. Marking off a storyboard takes a bit of time, but it's a lot cheaper than miscutting 2×12 stock.

Use a framing square or a plywood triangle of your own making to mark off the steps on the carriage stock.

With the square, mark the unit rise on one leg and the unit run on the other. Customarily, the run is noted on the "tongue" (short leg) and the rise on the "blade" (long leg). To indicate these measurements on the square, use pieces of masking tape or (much better) *square clamps,* which clip in place. Another method favored by carpenters is to construct a plywood triangle with the same dimensions as the step cutout. Carefully measure and cut out this homemade guide; it may be quicker than using a framing square but the triangle must be accurate. Then all you have to do is align the longest side (the hypotenuse) of the triangle against the edge of the stock.

Marking step dimensions on stock is straightforward. The only tricky spots are the ends of the carriages. We'll start with the layout of the upper end of the carriage and assume that the unit rise is 8 in. and the unit run is 10 in.

1. Measure down from the end of the board about 8 in. and make your first mark.

2. Holding the square as shown in Figure D.7A, align riser and run marks to the bottom edge of the board and draw a line from that first mark, across the stock face, along the outside of the blade.

3. Flip the square (Figure D.7B) and in doing so, reverse the riser and run marks temporarily—note that the 10-in. unit run is now on the blade and the 8-in. unit rise on the tongue. Align these marks to the top edge of the board and slide the square until the 10-in mark on the blade is 10 in. from the first line you drew. Draw another line perpendicular to the first, along the outside of the blade.

4. Now flip the square so that it's as it was originally, restoring rise and run marks to blade and tongue, respectively. Align the marks to the top edge of the board and

slide the square along the board edge until the rise mark intersects with the second line you drew. Draw lines on the outside of both blade and tongue. In subsequent steps, continue down the edge of the board.

Following is a brief explanation of what just happened above. The first mark, 8 in. from the end of the board, is somewhat arbitrary; it ensures that you will have enough room at the end of the board for the layout. The first line drawn is a plumb line which, when cut, will abut the inside of the rough opening. The second line is the top tread of the stairs—or will be when you attach tread stock to it. Flip-flopping the square is necessary because one leg is longer than the other and because you need the length of the longer leg to mark diagonal lines across the face of the stock.

Dropping the Carriage

When you've marked off the correct number of steps, finish the bottom of the carriage with a line perpendicular to the last riser line. Flip-flop the square as above. To draw the "first bottom line," measure down 8 in. from the top of the last riser line. Now draw a second line parallel to *but short of the first one*—short by the thickness of the tread stock. This "second line" is the real bottom line, the one that's cut. This slightly redundant operation is called "dropping the carriage"; it ensures that the height of the bottommost tread is the same height as all the others. That is, without subtracting the thickness of the tread from the bottom step, its height would have been 8 in., *plus* $1\frac{1}{8}$ in. ($\frac{5}{4}$ oak tread), while the distance between all other treads would have been 8 in. This notion is confusing to most amateur stair builders. (Figure D.8 should help alleviate confusion.)

At the bottom of the staircase depicted in Figure D.9, there is also a 2×4 ($1\frac{1}{2}\times3\frac{1}{2}$) cutout for a kickplate. This is a good feature for stairs that rest on masonry but quite unnecessary for stairs resting on wood. Wood-to-wood attachment is commonly effected by using two 16d common nails toe-nailed into each face of each carriage, top and bottom. A far superior method, however, is to use metal hangers at top and bottom. If you attach stair bottoms to ma-

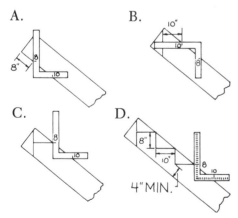

Figure D.7 Marking off the upper end of the carriage. (A) Measure down from the end of the board about 8 in., and align rise and run marks on the framing square to the edge of the board. Mark along the outside edge of the square's blade (long leg). (B) Flip the square over as shown, reversing the rise and run marks. Align the marks on the square with the edge of the board, and slide the square until the run mark (10 in.) is 10 in. from the first line drawn. Along the outside of the blade, draw a second line perpendicular to the first. (C) Flip the square over again, so that the rise and marks are as they were in the first step (A). Align those marks with the edge of the board, and draw lines on the outside of both the blade and the tongue (short leg). (D) To mark successive steps, slide the framing square down the length of the board, keeping the rise and run marks on the square aligned with the edge of the board.

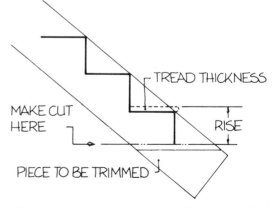

Figure D.8 Dropping the carriage. Mark off the bottom of the carriage similarly to the top end, flip-flopping the square as shown in Figure D.7. To compensate for the thickness of the tread on the bottom step, however, trim off an extra strip of wood equivalent to the thickness of the tread stock.

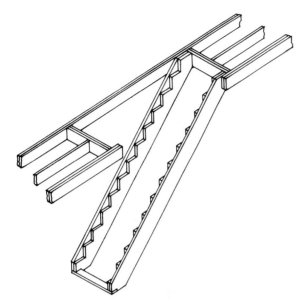

Figure D.9 Before attaching risers and treads to the carriages, tack the carriages (shown here with backing stringers) in place and test them for level, shimming up the low side (if any) of the staircase. Although the kickplate at the bottom of the carriages is not used always, it keeps the carriages equidistant and provides a secure strip through which to nail or bolt, whatever the composition of the floor beneath. (If the floor is concrete, caulk between wood and concrete.)

sonry, use a $\frac{1}{2}$-in. carbide-tipped masonry bit to drill through the kickplate into the concrete; slip expandable lead sleeves in the holes. Tighten the kickplate to the floor with 3-in. lag bolts, which spread the lead sleeves. Put a waterproof layer of felt paper or sheet plastic between the bottom of the stairs and the masonry.

Cutting and Assembly

Carefully cut out the first carriage and use it as a template for the other carriages. If you use a circular saw, finish all cuts with a handsaw. Don't cut any further into the stock than is necessary, because the distance from the inside of the step cutouts to the outside edge of the stock must be *at least* 4 in. Backing stringers as shown in Figure D.9 aren't cut out for steps; only their ends are cut to match the ends of carriages. (Also, don't bother to cut kickplates into stringer bottoms.) Since stringers primarily add rigidity, they needn't be the same width as the carrige stock, although the layout is easier if they are.

Before laminating (nailing together) carriages and stringers, temporarily position the carriages and tack their tops to the inside of the rough opening above. See if the stairs are level by putting boards across several steps and sighting a level. If the two (or three) carriages aren't quite level, shim beneath them temporarily to make them level.

Laminate the stringers and carriages with $2\frac{1}{2}$-in. 10-gauge screws, predrilling them for easier connection. Stagger the screws every 10 to 12 in. Also adequate are 16d common nails at the same interval. Nail the metal hangers to the carriage package before raising the carriages to be attached to the rough opening above. Once the carriages have been positioned and leveled with hardwood shims,

lag-bolt stringers to studs at each crossing. Should there by any gap between a stringer and a wall stud (which could pull a stringer out of line), shim the gap with cedar shingles before lag-bolting the stringer to the stud wall.

Risers are fashioned from 1-in. (nominal) pine and in our butt-joined steps are the same height as the unit rise marked off on the carriages. Tread width is the width of the unit run, plus 1 to $1\frac{1}{2}$ in. for the nosing. Tread stock is available in $9\frac{1}{2}$-in. and $11\frac{1}{2}$-in. width, with the nosing already rounded. Those who wish to make their own treads should use clear oak stock at least $\frac{5}{4}$-in. (actually $1\frac{1}{8}$ in.) thick, create the rounded nose with a shaper blade in a table saw, or a $\frac{3}{4}$-in.-radius router bit.

Attach the bottom riser first. Spread a light bead of construction adhesive on the edge of each carriage edge, then angle-nail the pine risers with two or three 6d finish nails. Oak treads should be glued, then screwed with three

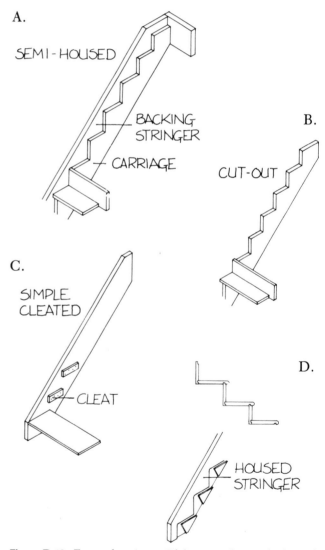

Figure D.10 Types of carriages. Of the types shown, the housed stringer is the most difficult to construct (the stringers are routed out) but the best-looking. Both semihoused and cutouts are strong and useful; the semihoused looks better. Cleated stair treads may pull free and therefore are not recommended.

2-in. 6-gauge wood screws (or 2-in. type W drywall screws) at each carriage. To ease screwing down and to forestall splits, predrill screw holes first. Cut screw-hole plugs from the same stock as the treads for the best color match; use a plug cutter in an electric drill. Finally, if you don't have a center carriage, bolster the steps by screwing and gluing a support block behind the middle (and top) of each riser board; as you apply the tread, put a spot of glue on the top of the support block. Note: Where we use the term "glue" in this passage, assume that we mean construction (sub-flooring) adhesive: its butyl rubber base remains flexible, whereas white glue bonds can break under point-loading.

QUEEN ANNE

·E·

BUILDING A DECK

T The deck described in this appendix is a simple one—sturdy, yet within the skills of a beginner or intermediate builder. If terms or procedures are unfamiliar, consult Chapter 4 or Chapter 8. Because most decks are visible from the street, their construction is often governed by building codes, with the principal concerns being safety, soil stability, and proper setback from property lines.

MATERIALS

When choosing materials, keep in mind that they'll see a lot of weather and of use. If you can afford clear decking, it will last all the longer; accordingly, let your supplier know that you won't accept stock with split ends, which is more likely to rot.

Joists

The type of wood you choose is important, for weathering capacities vary greatly, just as structural strengths do. Yellow (''stinky'') cedar, redwood, tidewater cypress, and white cedar weather well, but their strengths vary greatly. Normally, you can deal with the question of weathering simply by buying pressure-treated wood or applying a preservative yourself. Be sure to apply additional preservative to fresh cuts.

Joist size depends on the distance it must span, with spanning capacity varying considerably among woods. Chapter 4 contains charts showing maximum spanning distances for many species of wood. To be safe, though, use Table E.1, which offers conservative spans for a live load of 40 pounds per square foot, or 40 psf, which should be sufficient to support a good-sized gathering of people on the deck.

Decking

Decking—the floor of the deck—may be fashioned from one of several materials, all of which should be pressure-treated with preservative except redwood and cedar. Theoretically, the thicker the decking, the longer the spanning distance, but common practice favors 2-in. lumber (2×4s, 2×6s, etc) placed in 16 in. O.C., or 24 in. O.C. maximum.

Thus, 2× decking over joists 24 in. O.C. will be able to withstand considerable loads, weather somewhat and still be strong. Space decking so water can drain: an 8d nail between board edges gives a sufficient gap, which will increase somewhat as the wood shrinks. For a bit of visual variety, consider alternating, say, 2×4s and 2×8s. If you choose 1-in. decking, run it diagonally to joists, rather than perpendicular, to give the entire deck greater stability. By planning the dimensions of the deck in multiples of 2 ft, you will save yourself some cutting, since building materials come in lengths of 6, 8, 10, 12, 14, and 16 ft. Do not,

TABLE E.1

Deck joists spaced 24 in. on-center[a]

Group	2 × 6	2 × 8	2 × 10
I—Douglas fir-larch; hemfir; western hemlock; western larch; southern pine; coast sitka spruce	8 ft 4 in.	11 ft 0 in.	14 ft 2 in.
II—Eastern hemlock; tamarack (north); spruce-pine-fir; white and alpine fir; pine (western white, red, eastern white, sugar ponderosa, northern, lodgepole)	7 ft 8 in.	10 ft 0 in.	13 ft 0 in.
III—Northern white cedar	6 ft 8 in.	9 ft 0 in.	11 ft 4 in.

[a]Spanning distances given assume that the lumber grade is Select Structural or No. 1 Appearance; that the load is 40 psf live load, 10 psf dead load; and that the distances given represent relatively conservative figures for each group. Of course, the longer and deeper the lumber, the more expensive it is. Because lumber longer than 16 ft is not usually stocked by lumberyards, it makes more sense to shorten an open span by supporting joists with beams beneath, about midpoint. A 20-ft-long deck, for example, is significantly more rigid and less expensive if constructed with No. 2 western hemlock 2 × 8s. 24 in. O.C., supported midway with a beam underneath; than it would be to use single lengths of No. 1 grade Douglas fir-larch 2 × 12s 16 in. O.C. In general, keep unsupported spans a manageable 10 or 12 ft.

however, assume that the ends of a board are cut square; always check with a framing square.

Posts and Stairs

Posts are routinely 4 × 4s resting on concrete or concrete-block piers, which, in turn, rest on footings (Figure E.8). The methods of attaching posts to concrete vary, but some choices are shown in Figure E.7. It's extremely important that posts be treated with preservative, especially ends that must be cut. Posts should end at least 8 in. above grade (above the soil).

Stairs are constructed as described in Appendix D; the tops of the carriages are attached to a side of the deck, with joist hangers, with nails driven in at an angle, or with bolts. The bottoms of stair carriages rest on a 2 × 6 anchored to the pad or, if you fear that the bottom of the stairs will migrate, build a stair kickplate across the two carriages and bolt the kickplate to the concrete pad with lead sleeves.

Readers who want a more elaborate deck—say, one with railings—should see Appendix G; specifically, the Sunset book, *How to Plan and Build Decks.*

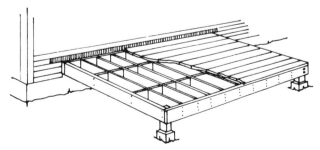

Figure E.1 A simple deck, with two posts, and joists running continuously from the house to the end of the frame.

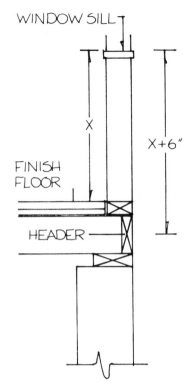

Figure E.2 To locate the deck's ledger (the part of the frame that attaches to the house), measure down to the finish floor from the top of, say, a windowsill. Since most joists will be 2 × 8s or 2 × 10s, add 6 in. to the first measurement, *X,* to locate the center of the header joist. For best attachment, vertically center the ledger.

Note: Wood should never rest directly on concrete; moisture can migrate up through concrete and rot the wood over a period of time. Instead, put an impermeable layer between wood and concrete; a metal termite shield is your best bet, though felt paper or plastic is acceptable. Also, where the deck frame is attached to the house, flash it to prevent water from backing up under the siding.

Attachments

Use connectors that hold well: to secure decking to joists, we suggest 16d galvanzied spiral-shank decking nails—two per joist–crossing. If the decking is 1 in. thick, use 8d or 10d galvanized box or common nails to nail decking to joists—use at least two nails at each joist crossing. Where joists rest on beams, hold the joists in place with 16d nails driven in at an angle. To join framing members 16d commons are adequate, unless you use joist hangers, which come with special case-hardened nails. Use aluminum-coated screws to join handrails, where safety is a consideration. For the best-looking results when nailing down decking, snap light chalk lines on decking so that the nails will be in a straight line.

Use lag bolts to attach the frame of the deck to the house or to supporting posts, or through–bolts with nuts and washers. Use washers beneath the heads of all bolts and, for appearance, predrill to sink the heads of the bolts flush with the face of the frame. Bolts should be as long as the thickness of the lumber, plus 1 in. If you are bolting a 2 × 8 to a 4 × 4 post, the bolts themselves should be at least $2\frac{1}{2}$-in. long, and preferably 3 in. To attach the frame *ledger* to a header of the house, bolts should be at least $3\frac{1}{2}$ in. long, to get through the thickness of the house's sheathing. When attaching a ledger to a header, space two bolts 4 in. apart vertically, every 16 in. along the length of the ledger.

Preservatives

Following is a brief encapsulation for deck-builders. Check with local codes first to see what preservatives are allowed.

Preservative can be applied before or after you build the deck. By applying it beforehand, you ensure a thorough covering of the entire surface of the wood—for example, by soaking it in a bath or preservative. (Soak wood in an old 55-gal drum or a trough made of sheet polyethylene surrounded by cinder blocks.) The trouble with treating the wood first is, you must allow it to dry, it's incredibly messy to handle, and you must retouch any ends you cut.

Perhaps the best method, if you can afford it, is to buy wood that is pressure–treated. Then the preservative will have effectively soaked into the wood fiber and the wood will be dry to the touch. Wolmanized lumber, a process of pressure treating, can even be painted over.

Other preservatives are: penta (pentachlorophenol), very effective except where subjected to continuous wetting and high humidity; metal-based solutions such as Cuprinol, almost as effective as penta but also nontoxic to plants and animals once dry; and waterborne salt preservatives which are effective when applied under pressure. Creosote is the most durable but, to many, the most offensive preservative, smelly and toxic. Limit its use to underpinnings. Some stains also contain preservative.

Wear gloves and a respirator mask when handling treated wood, and goggles if there is a danger of splashing it in your face. For the best results, reapply preservative to the deck periodically.

PREPARATION

When planning a new deck, avoid the most common deck failings:

1. *Rot* can be caused by poor-quality materials, preservatives ineptly applied, insufficient flashing where wood butts wood, a lack of ventilation under the deck, or a foundation that does not extend high enough above the ground.

2. *Springiness* from joists too small or decking spanning too great a distance.

3. *Sagging* due to too small a foundation, or ground settlement.

Another big issue is whether to attach the deck to the house or have it freestanding. A deck tied to a house is somewhat easier to construct because it has an existing wall to make it rigid. But increasingly, professionals favor freestanding decks, primarily because they avoid the problems of flashing, standing water, and rot associated with attached decks.

In regions where winters are mild and there is no snow accumulation, deck surfaces should be at least 1 in. below interior finish floors, to forestall water's being blown in. In the Snow Belt, attached deck surfaces should be at least 8 in. below interior floors to keep melting snow outside. Decks that height invariably bolt to foundations. If you can't meet those minimum clearances, better build a freestanding deck.

Although the deck discussed in the text below is attached to a house, Figure E.11 shows a freestanding one under construction.

Locating the Ledger

When attaching a deck to a frame house, locate the floor platform behind the siding and sheathing. Go into the basement and look at the joist grid, noting the depth of the joists: usually, they are 2×8s or 2×10s. The deck frame bolts through the sheathing into the outermost joist (called the ''header'' hereafter), preferably midway up the header's height, so there will be plenty of wood to bolt to.

To locate the middle of the header, measure down from a windowsill along the wall, down to the finish floor. The middle height of the header hoist should be another 5 to 6 in. below the finish floor. Using this calculation, measure down from the same windowsill—on the *outside* of the house.

Next, position the deck's ledger (the part of the frame attached to the house) so that the height of the ledger is more or less centered on the height of the header, as shown in Figure E.2. Draw a level line across the present siding, to represent the top of the deck. Remember to include the thickness of the decking.

Because line levels do not give accurate readings (the lines sag because of the weight of the level), the best way to draw the line representing the top of the deck is to hold a level atop a straight board or to use a water level. Have a friend hold up one end of the board. Mark along the top of the board or snap a chalk line through leveled points.

Next, cut away the siding; but *first turn off the electricity* to all wires running in the wall behind. Set the powersaw blade to the thickness of the siding only; try not to cut into the sheathing beneath. If the siding has an uneven surface—such as clapboards or shingles—tack a flat board over the siding so the saw will have a flat surface to glide over. (Adjust the depth of the blade accordingly.) Cut the siding, finishing off corners where the blade can't reach with a hand chisel. Pry off the siding with a utility bar.

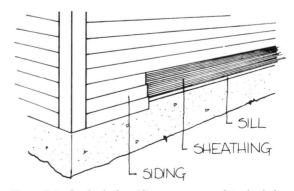

Figure E.3 Cut back the siding to accommodate the ledger plus the thickness of the decking.

Locating the Posts

Where the deck's posts are placed depends on the structural details of the deck, whether there are supporting beams beneath joists (to shorten the distance joists must span) or whether the deck is cantilevered. In our modest example, there are only two posts, one at each outer corner of the deck. In general, there should be a post every 8 ft, whether bolstering beams or supporting the perimeter of the frame.

The outer edge of the deck and its posts can be located in one of several ways. Perhaps the easiest way, if the deck is small and if you have a friend or two to help, is to tack-nail the frame of the deck together, square and brace it, and lift it approximately into position. Tack the ledger piece to the house and support the opposite side on pier blocks. Drop a plumb bob at corners and drive stakes into the ground to represent the center of posts to come. You might also use string and *batter boards* (common in laying out masonry), measuring from diagonal corners to square up the strings. To level the frame, rent a water level, which is easy to use; a transit, which takes more know-how; or a 6-ft. level atop a long, straight board.

Footings

For best results, support posts on a pad or a pier block atop a pad. In cold areas, the pad should set below the frost line, but in temperate climates, a 24-in.-square pad set 12 in. deep should suffice. Note however, that the bottom of the post must be at least 8 in. above grade. After digging a hole slightly larger than the dimensions of your pad, construct a form and place the concrete. A good all-around mixture is 1:2:3 (cement:sand:gravel); reinforce the pad with 3/8 in. rebar.

Two details are common at the base of the post. The first is a post anchor (Figure 4.12) nailed to the base of the post and set in concrete. The other is a precast pier block set into the pad about 10 minutes after it has been placed (i.e., after it has set a little). The base of the post is then toe-nailed to an integral wood block glued to the top of the pier. A continuous concrete pylon (sauna tube) is another way to go, for it is both footing and piers.

Plumb posts and brace them diagonally. Don't worry yet about the height of the posts, you will trim their tops later; but brace any post 4 ft or taller. Finally, three important details. Wood should not rest directly on concrete, so put an impervious layer—preferably a metal termite shield—underneath the post. Also minimize wood-on-wood contact by flashing the tops of beams with 30-lb felt paper or lightweight metal strips. Finally, should any new footings be near the house, grade the dirt around them away from the house.

FRAMING THE DECK

Because all cuts on our example are square, the deck is relatively easy to assemble. Because of the considerable weight of the assembled elements, it's best to raise the frame and secure it to the house and posts, then nail individual joists.

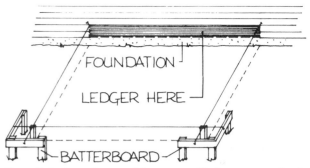

Figure E.4 From the top of the proposed ledger, run two leveled strings out from the house to locate the outer limit of the deck. Drive stakes at the corner points to indicate the position of the footings.

Attaching the Ledger

To keep water from backing up behind the house's siding, first attach a piece of metal flashing to the sheathing. Fold a piece of 26-gauge sheet aluminum or galvanized steel at least 8 in. wide, so that it fits under the siding at least 4 in., over the top of the ledger and down the face of the ledger at least 2 in. When fitting the flashing up behind the siding, you may have to disturb a few siding nails. Using the methods described in Chapter 7, either pry up the nails or cut through them, renailing after the flashing is in place.

To attach the ledger, hold the lumber in place against the section of sheathing you have exposed and level the board with as long a level as you can obtain. Hold the ledger in place by tack-nailing it with 16d nails and/or bracing it with diagonal pieces down to the ground.

When positioning the ledger, remember the thickness of the decking to come. Decking should be slightly below the siding you left intact.

If the ledger is 2-in. stock, use a pair of $3\frac{1}{2}$ in. $\times \frac{3}{8}$ in. lag bolts every 16 in. Each pair of bolts should be 4 in. apart (vertically), so they will be secured solidly to the header joist of the main house, as described above. Drill two test holes and go in the basement to ascertain that the bolts are approximately centered vertically on the header joist. If all is well, proceed with the rest of the bolts along the length of the ledger.

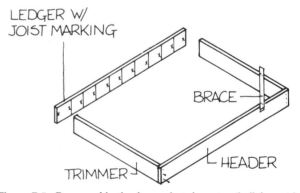

Figure E.5 Preassemble the frame, but do not nail all four sides together just yet. On the ledger and the board opposite it, mark off the position of the joists to come. Square sides and brace as shown.

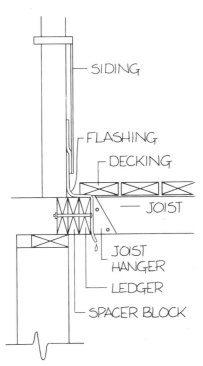

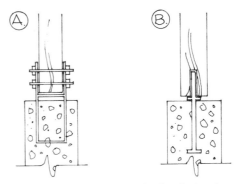

Figure E.7 Pier-top details: (A) steel U-bracket set into the concrete: (B) steel drift pin, on which the post sits.

Figure E.6 The ledger may be attached to the side of the house a number of ways. This is the deluxe way. The spacer block requires using longer bolts, but the assembly prevents water from settling near the house. All ledgers should be slashed as shown, whether there are spacer blocks or not.

also use you eye to determine whether it's bowed slightly. The crown, or high edge, of lumber should always be placed up. Where it isn't possible to end-nail—for example, along a ledger already attached—use joist hangers. For added rigidity, add blocking or bridging between deck joists; place such supports at least every 6 ft along the length of the joists.

Decking, usually laid flat, runs perpendicular or diagonally to the grid of joists. Diagonal decking is recommended if the decking is 1-in. stock, for the triangulation will impart rigidity. As noted earlier, use an 8d nail shank to space decking.

Nail down 1-in. decking with 8d galvanized spiral nails, 2-in. decking with 16d galvanized spirals. For best-looking results, chalk-line rows of nails so that the nails will fall in straight lines. Sink at least two nails at each joist crossing, angling nails slightly for a better grip. Don't fuss too much about the ends of the decking being trimmed exactly right; you can trim the edges of the deck with a power saw after everything has been nailed down. Chalk-line such cuts first, and touch up cuts with a preservative. All ends of decking must, of course, occur over joist centers. End joints that butt to frames should be gapped about $\frac{1}{4}$ in. so that the ends won't rot.

Last, cut perimeter posts to the correct height, using a transit or water level to locate those cuts. Attach handrails and caps with aluminum-coated screws, treat the wood as necessary, and stain.

A variation on the above method is worth mentioning. To provide even better drainage between the ledger and the house, spacer blocks are sometimes placed between the ledger and the house's sheathing. The blocks are also 2-in. stock cut to 8-in. lengths. If you use them, bolt through the spacer blocks when you attach the ledger, using 5 in. × $\frac{1}{2}$ in. bolts to accommodate the additional thickness of the blocks.

Assembling the Deck

With posts plumbed and braced, attach the other pieces of the deck frame to the ledger. The easiest way to do this is to nail together the three remaining sides of the frame, end-nailing lumber with three 20d galvanized nails (or metal connectors) at each corner. Use a framing square to square the corners; then tack-nail a brace across each corner. With the help of a few friends, lift the three sides of the frame in place, making sure the free ends of the frame abut the ledger board.

Because you must take time to level the frame, have temporary supports—spare concrete blocks and scrap wood on which to rest the frame. Adjust the frame until all is level, then end-nail the frame to the ledger with three 20d galvanized common nails at each corner, or use metal plate-connectors. Use bolts to connect the other end of the frame to the posts.

Nail individual joists to the frame, using three 20d galvanized common nails to end-nail each end of the joists. As you handle each joist, check its end to be sure it's square;

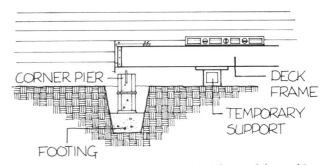

Figure E.8 To temporarily support the deck frame while attaching side boards to the ledger, set concrete blocks some distance from the proposed posts. This arrangement leaves room to set posts later.

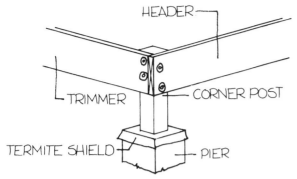

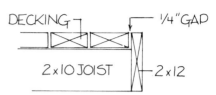

Figure E.9 If the post sits on top of the pier instead of being elevated by a U-bracket, put a piece of metal beneath the bottom of the post. This will prevent moisture from wicking up onto the wood, and it will serve as a termite shield if the metal overhangs the pier as shown.

Figure E.10 This nice detail hides the ends of the decking on all sides. Be sure to leave a $\frac{1}{4}$-in. gap all around for drainage, however.

A.

B.

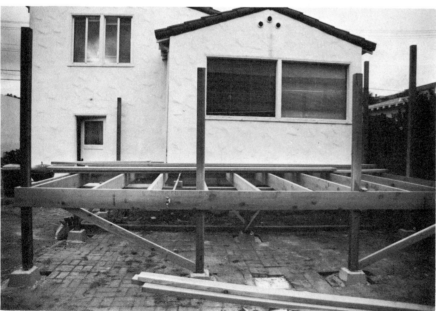

Figure E.11 A freestanding deck. (A) Posts plumbed atop pier blocks, perimeter joists in place, carrying beam up the center. (B) Posts diagonally braced, joists in place.

C.

D.

Figure E.11 (Continued) (C) King post beneath the middle of the carrying beam, diagonally braced in three directions. (D) The finished deck: posts cut and capped, rails attached, decking down, lattice covering the framing beneath. (Thanks to Bolton Construction.)

BROWN SHINGLE

·F·

BUILDING A FENCE

Fences are fun to build. You're out in the fresh air, everybody stops by to visit, once you've set the posts the job is a breeze, and the results are impressive. The fence described below and shown in Figure F–1 is the so-called "Kyle variation," named after a Berkeley artisan whose skills were legendary, if not mythical.

PREPARATION

First clear out whatever's there now and locate the fence line. It's rarely necessary to worry about local codes, setbacks, and all that if you just follow the existing fence line. Do talk with affected neighbors and come to an agreement, however; you don't want to hear about their misgivings after the posts are set in concrete. As Robert Frost noted, "Something there is that doesn't love a wall."

If your old fence is overwhelmed by ivy and blackberry bushes as mine was, you'll need:

A building permit, maybe
A tetanus shot
Leather gloves and goggles
Long-sleeved clothing
An old, dull ax or a brush hook, pickax, branch cutters
    (power tools such as chain saws are ill-advised in undergrowth)
Shovels, rakes, wheelbarrows
A large dumpster (40 ft of ivy filled a 20-cu yd box)
High-school kids to lug debris and cuttings

POST HOLES

Having noted the position of old corner posts before you removed them, first stretch a taut string representing the middle of the fence. Next determine the spacing of the posts: every 6 ft is about right if you're running 2×4 rails between posts; every 8 ft is too far, because rails will start to sag.

Once you've determined the spacing, mark off the posts—I noted their positions with felt-marker dots along the taut string, then plumbed down to the earth. (If you don't have a plumb bob handy, just drop a stone.) If this method seems a little slapdash, it is; you're only trying to locate the center of the holes you must dig, leaving the exact location of the posts for later. Then, to make the next step—digging—much easier, wet the ground well at each point you'll dig.

The best tool to dig with is a *post-hole digger* sharpened periodically with a metal file. If you've got a lot of holes to do, rent a *power auger* and get a beefy friend to hold onto the other end. Power augers are smelly, noisy, and heavy, but not as backbreaking as digging too many holes by hand. Whatever the tool, you'll encounter things in the ground to frustrate your efforts, most notably roots and rocks. Power augers can handle roots and smallish rocks, but periodically you'll have to set the tool aside and go after some intransigent boulder with a shovel and pickax. Goggles, please. Posthole diggers can handle $\frac{1}{2}$-in. roots, but not much beyond that; have a pickax handy.

Figure F.1 A redwood fence in California.

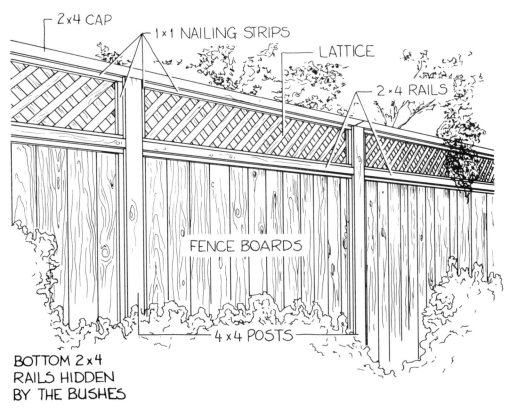

Figure F.2 Fence elements. Set 4×4 posts roughly every 6 ft. The 2×4 rails run atop the posts, as a cap; between posts, about 1 ft below the cap; and between the posts, leveled just above the ground. The lattice and the fence boards are held in place by nails and by the 1×1 strips nailed to posts and rails. Predrill all nails to avoid splits.

Dig down about one-third the height of the posts to come: 3 ft is about right for 10-ft posts. If you put the taut string high enough, you can drop a stone from post marks periodically to make sure that your digging has not wandered off the mark.

Erect the fence the following weekend. Unless you're in terrific shape, you'll need to recover from the postholes. You'll also have the coming week to round up tools and materials.

MATERIALS LIST

For the next stage of the operation you will need:

Two perforated foundation stakes for each post to be set
Small hand sledge
Claw hammer, nail sets
Wheelbarrow and mixing pan
Hoe for mixing
Tarps to cover concrete
4-ft or 6-ft level
Plumb bob, string
Circular saw, chop saw
Drill and bits for predrilling nails
Tape measure, line level
Sawhorses

The materials you order will depend on the design and dimensions of your fence, but mine (36 ft × 7 ft 6 in.) required:

7—4 in. × 4 in. × 10 ft.	posts
9—2 in. × 4 in. × 12 ft.	for caps and rails
72—1 in. × 6 in. × 6 ft.	fenceboards
6—12 in. × 96 in.	rigid trellis
440 lineal ft.	1 × 1 nailing strips
11 sacks	fencepost concrete
2 lb	8d galv. finish nails
2 lb	6d galv. finish nails
1 lb	8d duplex nails

About the list. I had intended to construct the fence of pine, but redwood turned out to be cheaper—plus I didn't have to treat it. If you have stones or masonry rubble to throw into postholes, figure $1\frac{1}{2}$ sacks of fencepost concrete per hole. The 1 × 1 nailing strips held fenceboards in place on both faces of the fence, hence the high total there. Duplex nails are easier to pull out of form stakes when you're done. Other things not noted on the list were 16d galvanized box nails to nail caps and rails to posts, and five $\frac{1}{16}$-in. drill bits I broke predrilling all board ends and nailing strips. Redwood splits easily and I wasn't taking any chances. *Note:* When framing with redwood or pressure-treated lumber, you must use *galvanized* nails.

SETTING POSTS

When you're done digging holes, it's time to set posts. To set posts accurately, you'll need to stretch two new lines. Unlike the line stretched earlier to establish the middle of the fence line, these lines indicate a plane parallel to the fence, yet set back 1 in. from the faces of the fence posts to come. Use a line level to set the first string, for that string represents the cutoff line for the tops of the posts and it must be level. Plumb down from that line to establish the second line, which should be a few inches above the ground. Both lines are set back 1 in. from fence posts so that there is no danger of posts bumping either line and skewing it. Thus when you set posts for plumb, you'll measure 1 in. out from these lines, top and bottom. As a last alignment aid, use a felt-tip pen to mark post positions along the upper string; this time, be exacting.

It's easier to set posts with two people, but a single person with *foundation stakes* can do it. So, two stakes and a handful of duplex nails at hand, set the first corner post. (You can start anywhere, but I started in one corner so I could tie my first post to an existing fence.) Set the post in the hole, tamp it a time or two to compact the soil, then position the post to pen marks along the top line. Next, using your tape measure as a guide, set the post back 1 in. from the two strings so that the post face is roughly plumbed, front to back. Now, holding a carpenter's level, plumb the post side to side. Plumbing is a continual adjustment front to back, side to side.

Figure F.3 Setting a post means plumbing it in two directions at the same time. Use a level to plumb it side to side, while roughly plumbing it front to back—by eyeballing a taut string above. Set the first foundation stake.

Figure F.4 When you've plumbed the post side to side and nailed it to a foundation stake, now use the level to fine-tune the plumb front to back. When you're satisfied with that plumb, drive in the second foundation stake and nail off the post. Use duplex nails for easy removal. Drive stakes into the *top* of the hold.

When the post looks plumb, squat down and pick a foundation stake while steadying the post with your other hand. Gently hold the stake against one face of the plumbed post and, using the face as a guide, angle the stake down into the soft dirt around the hole. Holding the post as steady as you can, pick up the hand sledge and drive the stake in deeper. Check for plumb again, then nail through one of the perforations in the stake, into the base of the post. Check plumb in both directions, hold a second stake against an adjacent face of the post, as shown in Figure F.4, and nail it off. The post is now securely plumbed front to back, side to side. Because the post moves a bit, plumbing takes some patience: keep checking the strings and the level. But foundation stakes make a tricky job so easy that it's hard to imagine why people ever bother with wooden braces.

Continue down the fence line, setting all the posts in like manner. When they're all plumbed and staked, partially fill each hole with stones or clean masonry rubble, being careful not to bump the posts. Then fill the holes with concrete, poking each hole with a stick to distribute the mixture. Mix the concrete and water in a wheelbarrow,

then shovel it in. By filling all the post holes at the same time, you have to clean up the wheelbarrow only once. Some builders shovel dry mix into the hole and add water, but this is a method to avoid. Let the concrete set at least a day, preferably three, before nailing up the other elements.

Setting posts is the hard part, the rest of the fence is a piece of cake. When the concrete has cured, pull out the duplex nails and work the foundation stakes out. At this point you'll be glad you drove stakes into the *top* of the hole, above the level of the pour, so they weren't encased in concrete.

ASSEMBLING THE FENCE

Now trim the tops of the posts. Carefully take down your upper string but leave its nails so you can snap a level chalk line across the posts. Snap the line and cut, using the jig in Figure F.5 to ensure square cuts.

To bolster the posts, now nail up 2×4 rails between each pair of posts, as depicted in Figure F.2. To position the first set of these rails, measure down from the tops of the posts $12\frac{1}{2}$ in.—the height of the trellis, plus $\frac{1}{2}$-in. clearance— and use a combination square to draw lines across the posts. Align rails to the underside of these lines and nail them up, toe-nailing two 16d galvanized box nails through

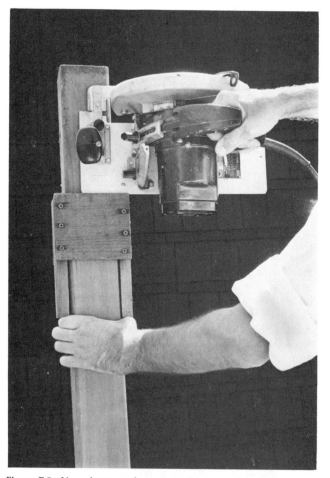

Figure F.5 Use a homemade cutting jig to guarantee a square cut across the top of the post.

Figure F.6 This fence is structurally similar to the example in Figure F.1: 2×4 rails run between 4×4 posts. The 2×4 cap is doubled here, though, with the top 2×4 ripped with a 45-degree bevel on both sides. To create the ''roof'' atop the cap, nail on $\frac{3}{4}$-in. boards; the peak is a full 1×1. To create the rhythm of the fence boards, alternate two 2-in. boards between 6-in. boards; hold in fence boards at top and bottom with 1×1 strips as shown in Figure F.2.

each face of the 2×4. *Note:* When nailing so close to the end of redwood lumber, predrill the nail holes; predrilled wood is also less inclined to migrate when you drive nails. If you're working singlehanded, rails are easier to nail if you clamp stop-blocks to the posts first. Take pains to cut rails accurately, for rails too long will push posts out of plumb.

Next nail on the 2×4s rails that cap the posts. (By putting on caps second, you have room to swing freely when hammering up the first set of rails.) All cap joints should be beveled 30 degrees and centered over posts; use four 16d galvanized box nails per post.

Finish the frame by nailing up the bottom set of 2×4 rails, again predrilling them to facilitate attachment. Where the ground slopes it may be impossible to have all bottom rails aligned to the same height, but take pains to level each board individually.

The frame complete, next nail up the 1×1 nailing strips that restrain the trellis along the top, and the fence boards below. Using your combination square as a depth gauge, set strips in about 1 in. from the edges of the 2×4 rails; use 8d galvanized finish nails, predrilling to prevent splits and to avoid knocking the 2×4s loose. Attach 1×1s along one face of the fence at a time so that you can fit in fence boards (or trellis strips). Having aligned the strips to the 2×4 edges, you can just slap boards to the strips and nail them up. Again, pre-drill to avoid splits.

Have friends on hand when you nail up the 1-in. thick fence boards: one person measuring and cutting boards on a chop saw, one person predrilling the boards with a $\frac{1}{16}$-in. bit and then toe-nailing them up, and one person setting nail heads. It's important to toe-nail the boards so that you nail them to the 2×4s, not to the 1×1 strips; use 6d galvanized finish nails. When all the boards are nailed up and set, then cover nail heads with the second perimeter of 1×1 strips. The fence is somewhat delicate, so if your family breeds mastiffs or plays rugby in the backyard, it's probably not for you. But for a modest amount of time and skill, it's a very handsome piece of work indeed.

CRAFTSMAN BUNGALOW

·G·

ANNOTATED BIBLIOGRAPHY

PERIODICALS

The best sources of information about building and building supplies are periodicals, which can keep track of the latest materials, applications, and trends much better than books can. Try a newsstand; if it doesn't have what you're looking for, go to a public or college library. After sampling several magazines and deciding on those you like, subscribe to them.

Here is a list of magazines that might be of interest.

Consumer Reports. (Mount Vernon, NY) The most aggressive pro-consumer periodical, it goes to great lengths in researching products. Monthly.

Fine Homebuilding. (Newtown, CT) I had a hand in starting this periodical. It's an architectural-building hybrid, a source of ideas and solid information derived directly from practitioners. Bimonthly.

Fine Woodworking. (Newton, CT) For technical information about wood, nothing else comes close. The journal's reviews of shop equipment are similarly without parallel. Fairly technical and scrupulously researched. Bimonthly.

Historic Preservation, National Trust for Historic Preservation. (Washington, DC) The Big One for restorationists; lush color, interesting articles, an invaluable source of preservation materials.

Old-House Journal. (Brooklyn, NY) As the name implies, this periodical is directed at owners of old houses, especially Victorian ones. *OHJ* was one of the pioneers of the urban revival, and it contains tidbits you'll find nowhere else. Monthly.

Whole Earth Review. (Sausalito, CA) This direct descendant of the *Whole Earth Catalogue* of the Aquarian Age continues to celebrate the odd, the euphoric and the useful. Full of excellent reviews on how-to books, sources for exotic tools and materials, and thoughtful essays about what makes life worth living. Bimonthly.

BOOKS

Most of the books below are written by authors with first-hand, on-site knowledge of a topic. Some of the books, self-published or from small houses, have spotty distribution—so if you have trouble finding titles, call or write to:

> Builders Booksource
> Box R
> 1817 Fourth Street
> Berkeley, CA 94710
> (415) 845-6874

I can't think of another bookstore in the country with a broader range of design and construction titles (from popular to *very* technical), a better newsletter, or people more willing to help.

General

Allen, Edward. *How Buildings Work/The Natural Order of Architecture.* New York: Oxford University Press, 1980. A nice place to start if you're new to renovating and/or building; particularly good in describing human-comfort factors; charming art.

Berry, Wendell. *The Unsettling of America.* New York: Avon Books, 1978. Not about building, but filled with thoughtful ideas about American communities and their continuity.

Bullock, Orin M., Jr. *The Restoration Manual.* Norwalk, CT: Silvermine Press, 1966. Much architect's jargon, but with some useful, specific details, and a decent glossary.

Callender, John Hancock, ed. *Time-Saver Standards for Architectural Design Data,* 5th ed. New York: McGraw-Hill, 1974. A big, expensive, professional, well-organized book, most of which will be comprehensible to amateur renovators; although not a how-to book, it does give more information about procedures than *Architectural Graphic Standards.*

Canadian Mortgage and Housing Corporation. *Canadian Wood-Frame House Construction*. Ottawa, Canada: CMHC, 1979. (Reprint of U.S. Agriculture Handbook No. 73.) A succinct paperback with just about everything you need to know; a good back-pocket mentor.

Ching, Francis D. K. *Building Construction Illustrated*. New York: Van Nostrand Reinhold, 1975. At once a source of good details and a precise overview of the elements in all major housing systems. Wonderfully written and illustrated by the author.

Ching, Francis D. K., and Miller, Dale. *Home Renovation*. New York: Van Nostrand Reinhold, 1983. Strong on design and common sense, urging renovators to make the most of what's there.

DiDonno, Lupe, and Sperling, Phyllis. *How to Design and Build Your Own House*. New York: Alfred A Knopf, 1987. A book about new construction, but readable and well illustrated; authors are relaxed and not afraid to offer opinions.

Farallones Institute. *The Integral Urban House*. San Francisco: Sierra Club Books, 1979. A thoughtful approach to renovating more than your urban dwelling, from livestock to disposing wastes and conserving water.

Graf, Don. *Basic Building Data*. New York: Van Nostrand Reinhold, 1985. An oldie but goodie revived. How much does a cubic yard of concrete weigh? You'll find it here.

Harris, Cyril M. *Dictionary of Architecture and Construction*. New York: McGraw-Hill, 1975.

Kaplan, Helaine S., and Prentice, Blair. *Rehab Right* 2nd printing. Oakland, CA: City of Oakland Planning Department, 1979. The best locally or federally funded guide I've seen; remarkably well organized and illustrated; good sections on codes and other legal matters; should be indispensible to California renovators.

Kidder, Tracy. *House*. New York: Avon Books, 1985. A compelling story, wonderfully told, of the inherent conflict between owner, architect, and builder. I wish I'd written it.

Litchfield, Michael. *Salvaged Treasures: Designing and Building with Architectural Salvage*. New York: Van Nostrand Reinhold, 1983. Assessing, removing, reconditioning, and reusing elderly doors, windows, woodwork, hardware, lighting and plumbing fixtures, heavy metal, masonry, and structural members. Design ideas as well.

Locke, Jim. *The Well-Built House*. Boston: Houghton Mifflin, 1988. The author is the contractor in Tracy Kidder's *House*, and his book is an invaluable guide to knowing quality when you see it, coordinating the process, and so on. Nicely done.

Melville, Ian A., and Gordon, Ian A. *The Repair and Maintenance of Houses*. London: Estates Gazette Ltd., 1979 (available in U.S. from Preservation Resource Group, Inc., Springfield, VA). For the professional builder. Oriented toward English houses, especially older ones; virtually nothing on mechanical systems, but a compendium of structural information.

Ramsey, Charles G., and Sleeper, Harold R. *Architectural Graphic Standards*, 7th ed. New York: Wiley, 1980. Since 1932, the most important book on an architect's shelf; a compendium of details, hence, how those tricky spots are handled; sizes and specifications for everything.

Reader's Digest Association. *Reader's Digest Complete Do-It-Yourself Manual*. Pleasantville, NY: Reader's Digest Association, 1977. Lacks an extensive discussion of structures and mechanical systems but is a remarkable book nevertheless; perhaps the single best-selling how-to volume.

Time-Life Books. *The Old House*. Alexandria, VA: Time-Life Books, 1979. For a small book, lots of useful information specific to old houses.

Assessment and Planning

Lifchez, Raymond, and Winslow, Barbara. *Design for Independent Living*. Berkeley, CA: University of California Press, 1982. The best book for designing and modifying homes for disabled people.

Pearman, Donald V. *The Termite Report*. Pear Publishing, 2001 Hoover Ave., Oakland, CA, 1988. How to save money, time, and your home from pests, rot, and earthquakes. One of the only titles on the subject—and it's very good indeed. Solid info from a man with decades in the field, excellent photos.

Rosskind, Robert. *Before Your Build*. Berkeley, CA: Ten-Speed Press, 1983. What questions to ask before you build, by one of the founders of the Owner-Builder Center.

Schmidt, Kathryn. *The Home Remodeling Management Book*. Palo Alto, CA: Egger Publications, 1987. How to plan, organize, and maintain control of your project. Nicely organized.

Syvanen, Bob. *Drafting*. Chester, CT: Globe Pequot Press, 1982. Tips and tricks to thinking spatially and drawing well enough to satisfy most building departments—and builders.

Yuen, Jim J. *Inspecting a Home or Income Property*. Berkeley, CA: Ten-Speed Press, 1987. A nice walk through the process.

Tools

Jackson, Albert, and Day, David. *Tools and How to Use Them*. New York: Alfred A. Knopf, 1978.

Klein Tool Co. *Proper Use and Care of Hand Tools, Pliers, Screwdrivers, Wrenches, Striking and Struck Tools*. Chicago: Klein Tools Co. A handy booklet.

Materials

Vila, Bob. *Guide to Building and Remodeling Materials*. New York: Warner Books, 1986. Comparative shopping for building materials.

Structural Carpentry

Gross, Marshall. *Roof Framing*. Carlsbad, CA: Craftsman Press, 1988. A complicated subject presented clearly.

Koel, Leonard. *Carpentry*. Homewood, IL: American Technical Publishers, 1986. Very good; up-to-date on materials, power tools, and techniques.

Reed, Mortimer P. *Residential Carpentry*. Englewood Cliffs, N.J.: Prentice-Hall, 1985. Good focus on residential aspects, excellent understanding of building sequences.

Syvanen, Bob. *Carpentry,* 2nd Edition. Chester, CT: The Globe Pequot Press, 1988. If he's done a bad book, I haven't seen it.

U.S. Navy Bureau of Naval Personnel. *Basic Construction Techniques for Houses and Small Buildings.* New York: Dover, 1972 (unabridged reprint of 6th rev. ed. of *Builder 3 & 2,* as published in 1970 by the Training Publications Division of the Naval Personnel Support Activity).

Masonry

Koel, Leonard. *Concrete Formwork.* Homewood, Il: American Technical Publshers, 1988. Forms for footings, flatwork, steps, and a lot more.

Kreh, Richard T., Sr. *Masonry Skills,* 3rd Edition. Albany, NY: Delmar Publishers, 1990.

Kreh, Richard T., Sr. *Masonry Projects and Techniques.* New York City: Popular Science Book Club, 1985.

Orton, Vrest. *The Forgotten Art of Building a Good Fireplace.* Peterborough, NH: Yankee Press, 1985. Count Rumford's method for making a fireplace smokeless.

van den Branden, F., and Hartsell, Thomas. *Plastering Skills.* Homewood, Il: American Technical Publishers, 1984. The only coherent book on stucco and plastering.

Electrical Wiring

Mullin, Ray C., and Smith, Robert L. *Electrical Wiring—Residential.* Albany, NY: Delmar Publishers, 1987. A textbook that walks you through planning and doing; very complete.

National Fire Protection Association. *National Electrical Code®* (a new edition each year). Quincy, MA: National Fire Protection Association. *The* last word on wiring safety.

National Fire Protection Association. *National Electrical Code Handbook.* Quincy, MA: National Fire Protection Association. A complete text of the Code, plus an explanation. For professionals.

Richter, Herbert P., and Schwann, W. Creighton. *Practical Electrical Wiring.* New York: McGraw-Hill, 1987. For professionals, very comprehensive.

Richter, Herbert P., and Schwann, W. Creighton. *Wiring Simplified,* 35th ed. St. Paul, MN: Park Publishing. Based on the latest Electrical Code, this modest paperback will suffice for most of us.

Time-Life Books. *Advanced Wiring.* Alexandria, VA: Time-Life Books, 1978. Probably the most thoroughly researched book of T-L's series; excellent on installing service panels.

Whitney, William J. *Electrical Wiring: Residential.* New York: Wiley, 1979. Learning about electricity from a man with decades of experience in the trade.

Plumbing

Hemp, Peter. *Old Plumbing: The Straight Poop.* Berkeley, CA: Ten-Speed Press, 1986. An excellent book on working with old pipe (i.e., how to avoid collapsing it and making more work for yourself).

International Association of Plumbing and Mechanical Officials. *Uniform Plumbing Code.* Walnut, CA. IAOPMO, 1990.

Massey, Howard C. *Basic Plumbing with Illustrations.* Carlsbad, CA: Craftsman Books, 1987. Adequate. There is also a handbook by the same author.

Energy and Related Matters

Earth Works Group. *50 Simple Things You Can Do to Save the Earth.* Berkeley, CA: Earthworks Press, 1990. Saving the world starts at home.

Gay, Larry, ed. *The Complete Book of Insulating.* Brattleboro, VT: Stephen Greene Press, 1980. A nice little book about heat loss and correcting it.

See also, Farallones Institute, *Integral Urban House* (San Francisco: Sierra Club Books, 1979) and book reviews in *Sun World.* Speaking of which, *Sun World* (Sante Fe, NM) is an excellent source of technical information and product reviews. Rodale Books, Emmaus, PA, publishes an ever-expanding list of energy-conservation books.

Tiling

Byrne, Michael. *Setting Ceramic Tile.* Newtown, CT: Taunton Press, 1987. Excellent book, unquestionably the best on the subject; thorough, lucid, beautifully illustrated. Companion video.

Finish Carpentry

Cary, Jere. *Building Your Own Kitchen Cabinets.* Newtown, CT: Taunton Press, 1988. Designing and constructing face-frame cabinets. Excellent book, with a companion video that's just as good.

Levine, Paul. *Making Kitchen Cabinets.* Newtown, CT: Taunton Press, 1988. European, flush-frame cabinets. Subtitled ''A foolproof system for the home workshop,'' this book and video have the clearest explanation of plastic laminates anywhere.

Syvanen, Bob. *Interior Finish Carpentry.* Chester, CT: Globe Pequot Press, 1982.

Paint and Paper

Sandreuter, Gregg E. *The Complete Painter's Handbook.* Emmaus, PA: Rodale Books, 1988.

Time-Life. *Paint and Wallpaper.* Alexandria, VA: Time-Life Books, 1976. Some good tips on papering such difficult areas as stairwells.

Decks

Ortho Books. *Deck Plans.* San Ramon, CA: Chevron, 1985. Complete plans for 12 decks, but little information on how to build them.

Sunset Books. *How to Build and Plan Decks.* Menlo Park, CA: Lane Publishing, 1986. By no means comprehensive, but contains decent building sequences and a span table to help size the underpinnings.

INDEX

X

Y

Z